NATIVE AMERICAN VOICES

third edition

NATIVE AMERICAN VOICES: A READER

Susan Lobo, Steve Talbot, and Traci L. Morris

Prentice Hall

Boston   Columbus   Indianapolis   New York   San Francisco   Upper Saddle River
Amsterdam   Cape Town   Dubai   London   Madrid   Milan   Munich   Paris   Montreal   Toronto
Delhi   Mexico City   Sao Paulo   Sydney   Hong Kong   Seoul   Singapore   Taipei   Tokyo

Editorial Director: Leah Jewell
Editor-in-Chief: Dickson Musslewhite
Publisher: Nancy Roberts
Managing Editor: Maureen Richardson
Editorial Project Manager: Vanessa Gennarelli
Editorial Assistant: Nart Varoqua
Director of Marketing: Brandy Dawson
Senior Marketing Manager: Patrick M. Walsh
Marketing Assistant: Ashley Fallon
Operations Specialist: Cathleen Petersen
Cover Art Director: Jayne Conte
Cover Designer: Bruce Kenselaar and Karen Noferri
Manager, Visual Research: Beth Brenzel

Photo Researcher: Kathy Ringrose
Manager, Rights and Permissions: Zina Arabia
Image Permission Coordinator: Kathy Gavilanes
Manager, Cover Visual Research & Permissions: Karen Sanatar
Cover Art: Gerald Dawavendewa
Full-Service Project Management: Saraswathi Muralidhar, PreMedia Global, Inc.
Project Manager: Cheryl Keenan
Composition: PreMedia Global, Inc.
Printer/Binder: Hamilton Printing Company
Cover: Lehigh-Phoenix Color Corp
Text Font: 10/12 Palatino

Cover Art is of an ancient cloud and bird imagery with a paaho, a prayer bundle rising from it.

Credits and acknowledgments borrowed from other sources and reproduced, with permission, in this textbook appear on appropriate page within text or on page 505.

Library of Congress Cataloging-in-Publication Data
Native American Voices : A reader / [compiled by] Susan Lobo, Steve Talbot, Traci L. Morris. — 3rd ed.
    p. cm.
  Includes bibliographical references and index.
  ISBN-13: 978-0-205-63394-4
  ISBN-10: 0-205-63394-3
  1. Indians of North America.   2. Indians of North America—Government relations.   3. Indians—Social conditions.
4. Indians—Government relations.   I. Lobo, Susan.   II. Talbot, Steve.   III. Morris, Traci L.

E77.N3517 2010
970.004′97—dc22

2009030768

10 9 8 7 6 5 4 3 2

Prentice Hall
is an imprint of

www.pearsonhighered.com

ISBN 13: 978-0-205-63394-4
ISBN 10:   0-205-63394-3

We dedicate this book to Vine Deloria, Jr.—scholar, elder brother, friend.

CONTENTS

PREFACE

We are encouraged by the positive response to the earlier editions of this reader from students, colleagues, and the Native American community in general. The changes and additions to this edition, we believe, will generate an even greater appreciation for the uniquely indigenous-based perspective and hemispheric approach that characterize this volume and that clearly differentiates it from the standard introductory works on Native Americans in the disciplines of anthropology and history.

The idea for this work grew from co-editors Susan Lobo and Steve Talbot teaching an introductory-level college course, The Indian Experience, for several years at the University of California at Davis in the late 1980s and early 1990s. This course and Introduction to Native American Studies were originally developed along with a dozen or so others in the late 1960s by Jack D. Forbes for the then-new Native American Studies program at the University of California at Berkeley and at the University of California at Davis.[1] Talbot was a member of the faculty in the new Native American studies program at the University of California at Berkeley from 1971 to 1974 and consequently helped to develop these introductory courses. The Indian Experience became one of the core courses. Other developing Native American studies or American Indian studies programs in colleges and universities during the 1970s created similar introductory courses.[2] These included the University of Minnesota, Washington State University, Humboldt State University, the University of California at Irvine, the University of California at Los Angeles, Dartmouth College, the University of Wisconsin at Madison, and the University of Arizona. Today, there are well over 100 colleges and universities in the United States and Canada that offer Native American studies programs, and 26 offer graduate degrees.[3]

The 1960s was the time of the "new Indian" movement and renewed activism signaled by the formation of the National Indian Youth Council in 1961, following the Chicago Indian conference, the founding of the American Indian Movement (AIM) in 1968, and the emergence of other protest organizations. They include the continued actions by the Haudenosaunee (Iroquois) and other traditional Indian peoples, such as the Cornwall Bridge blockade on the Canadian border, the occupation of Alcatraz Island in San Francisco Bay in 1969, the 1972 Trail of Broken Treaties to Washington, D.C., and the 72-day Wounded Knee occupation protest in 1973. This was a time when urban-based Indians and their reservation counterparts joined forces under the guidance of traditional elders and religious leaders to press for treaty rights, sovereignty, and self-determination. It was also a time when hundreds of Native young people were able to enter colleges and universities under special admissions programs, receive financial aid, and bring the issues and demands of the larger Native American struggle to university campuses. Like other non-white students on campus

---

[1]We use the terms *Indian, American Indian, Native American,* and *Native* interchangeably throughout this volume, although scholars prefer the term *Native American* because it takes into account the various Aleut and Eskimo groups of Alaska. Sometimes the term *indigenous* is used as an adjective, or capitalized as a noun, when referring to the peoples who are native to the Americas. In this volume we include also the native peoples of the Hawaiian Islands.

[2]In *Studying Native America: Problems and Prospects* (University of Wisconsin Press, 1998, 79–107), Russell Thornton has recorded the historical background and development of Native American studies. Although he writes that "the impetus for the development . . . came from new numbers of Native American students on campus" (p. 87), he understates the Indian student activism and contribution of the traditional Indian community that pressured mainstream institutions of higher learning into establishing the new Native American and American Indian studies programs.

[3]See "A Guide to Native American Studies Programs in the United States and Canada" by Robert M. Nelson, editor (revised February 26, 2009), http://oncampus.richmond.edu/faculty/ASAIL/guide/guide.html.

(African-American, Asian-American, and Mexican-American), Native students encountered very few Indian professors or courses reflecting their cultures and lives. Through extensive meetings and lengthy negotiations and proposals with university officials, including student strikes and other forms of action, Indian programs were founded and relevant courses developed. The idea behind these introductory classes was to bring the "Indian experience" into the classroom and thereby make the college curriculum relevant to the lives of the new population of Native students on campus. The new curriculum was also intended to correct misconceptions and stereotypes about Indian history, religion, and culture among the general student population and the larger society.

The Indian Experience course substituted for the Introduction to American Indians courses traditionally taught in anthropology and also replaced the Eurocentric treatment of Native peoples in the works of mainstream historians. The paradigms for these two disciplines differ substantially from a Native perspective of culture and history, as reflected in the status of Indian nations as colonized peoples. There has been an extensive literature on American Indians in history, and many introductory American Indian books have been produced in anthropology, but very few from an Indigenous perspective, especially in terms of readers suitable for lower-division college students or the general public with an interest in Native Americans. There are, of course, some useful atlases, almanacs, and edited works, including various compilations of Indian literature and poetry, but nothing that approximates an American Indian reader such as we have compiled here. (See the Suggested Readings list in Part I.)

By the early 1990s our ideas had coalesced from our teaching experience in American Indian studies, and the first edition of this reader was published in 1998, and the second edition in 2001. As we introduce the third edition, we are pleased to be joined by co-editor Traci L. Morris (Chickasaw), who has used the earlier editions of the reader extensively in her classes at Arizona State University and elsewhere. She also brings to our joint effort, among other talents, her expertise in the arts and the media.

Unlike history, or even anthropology, the American Indian studies paradigm is multidisciplinary by the very nature of its subject matter—the respective cultures, histories, successes, and experiences of the Indigenous peoples of the Americas. Thus, a major aim of this reader is to provide a representative sampling of the Native American experience. This reader therefore contains not only scholarly articles but also journalistic selections, documents, oral history and testimony, songs and poetry, maps, and art. A related purpose here is to meet the needs of classes at the undergraduate level in the social sciences and related fields, particularly American Indian studies, but also ethnic studies, anthropology, sociology, history, American studies, political science, and even law, education, and social welfare.

This edition of the reader is divided into 10 topical parts that encompass the major concerns and interests of Native Americans. Although we concentrate on the Native peoples of the United States, including Alaska and Hawaii, we have also included representative selections from Canada and Latin America, especially when they illustrate the mutual issues, history, and linkages existing among the Native peoples of the Americas.

The 10 parts are arranged to focus on a series of interrelated themes and have been reformulated for this edition of the reader. Parts I, II, and III lay the foundation, giving an overview of Native perspectives on history and heritage, in addition to basic information on locations and demographics. The objective in Part IV is to facilitate an understanding of the values and stereotypes held by many non-Indians that have created, and in many instances served to maintain, a social context of racism and injustice with which Native people have had to contend. Part V, dealing with the media and the arts, is new to this edition of the reader. It reflects the tremendous response and innovation across the spectrum that is occurring among Native young people in the first decade of the twenty-first century. Part VI focuses on important issues in health, education, welfare, and criminal justice. Part VII deals with spirituality, sacred geography, and the environment. Part VIII focuses on sustainable development, including economic concerns such as casinos, as in the previous edition, but now emphasizing the political/economic/social concept of nation building. Part IX is a new section that deals with the processes of Indian urbanism in the Americas, both ancient and contemporary. The final section, Part X, focuses on the many ways that Native peoples continue to confront, resist, and struggle to survive and flourish as peoples and nations.

At the end of each part are Discussion Questions that will assist in understanding the salient points raised by each selection. These are followed by Key Terms and Suggested Readings. At the beginning of the book are maps of North, Central, and South America, indicating the names and locations of some of the Native peoples and nations discussed in this work. At the end of the volume are appendixes for Native media, Native American/American Indian studies programs in the United States and Canada, and tribal colleges of the American Indian Higher Education Consortium.

Many people have provided inspiration for and contributed to the content of this volume. They include our many colleagues and associates, both Indian and non-Indian, who share our vision. Among them, however, we wish to especially mention Jose Barreiro (Guanjiro/Taino), Victoria Bomberry (Muskogee/Lenape), Duane Champagne (Turtle Mountain Chippewa), Jack D. Forbes (Powhatan-Renape/Delaware), Bruce E. Johansen, Frank Lobo (Acjachemen), Luana Ross (Salish), Susanne Bohmer, Haunani Kay Trask (Hawaiian), Suzan Shown Harjo (Cheyenne/Hodulgee Muskogee), Darryl Wilson (Pit River/Ajuma/Atsuge), Tsianina Lomawaima (Creek), and Barbara A. Babcock.

A most mournful appreciation is given to several colleagues who have passed to the Spirit World since the last edition of this book was published. First is Vine Deloria, Jr. (Standing Rock Dakota), who was the dean of Native American scholarship for half a century. We will miss our good friend Floyd Red Crow Westerman (Sisseton-Wahpeton Dakota), singer, activist, and "camp crier." We will miss the wise counsel of John C. Mohawk (Seneca), who taught in the American Studies Department at SUNY, Buffalo. We also regretfully note the passing of Indian anthropologist Beatrice Medicine (Dakota Sioux).

We express our appreciation to the many readers of the second edition of *Native American Voices*, whose suggestions were helpful as we began work on this third edition. We also wish to express appreciation to our many students who have provided us, the teachers, with valuable feedback from our introductory courses and earlier editions of this reader.

Finally, we acknowledge the assistance and support of the following institutions and professional associations: the Native American Studies Departments at the University of California at Berkeley and at Davis; the American Indian Studies Center at the University of California at Los Angeles; the Department of Anthropology at Oregon State University; the American Indian Studies Program at the University of Arizona; Intertribal Friendship House in Oakland, California; Lane Community College in Florence, Oregon; Arizona State University Department of American Indian Studies; and the Arizona Commission of Indian Affairs.

We especially thank our publisher, Nancy E. Roberts at Pearson/Prentice Hall and her staff. They have been especially helpful during the production process.

ABOUT THE EDITORS

SUSAN LOBO is a consultant, emphasizing research, advocacy, and project design and development. She works primarily for American Indian communities, nonprofits, and nations in the United States and Central and South America. She holds a Ph.D. in anthropology from the University of Arizona and has taught at the University of California at Berkeley, where she was the coordinator of the Center for Latin American Studies. She has also taught in Native American Studies Departments at the University of California, Davis, and at the University of Arizona, and she has taught environmental studies at Merritt College. Between 1978 and 1994 she was the coordinator of the Community History Project archive, housed at Intertribal Friendship House, the Indian Center in Oakland, California. This archive is now at the Bancroft Library, Berkeley. For many years she was also a producer of the KPFA-FM radio series *Living on Indian Time*. She was a co-founder of the South and Central American Indian Information Center and of the American Indian Community History Center.

Her books include *A House of My Own: Social Organization in the Squatter Settlements of Lima, Peru* (1982); *American Indians and the Urban Experience* (co-editor; 2000); *Urban Voices: The Bay Area American Indian Community* (2002); and *The Sweet Smell of Home: The Life and Art of Leonard F. Chana* (2009). She has also written many articles for professional and popular journals. She is currently a distinguished visiting scholar in American Indian Studies at the University of Arizona and a consultant for Tohono O'odham Community Action.

STEVE TALBOT received a master's degree in anthropology and community development in 1967 from the University of Arizona and a Ph.D. in anthropology from the University of California at Berkeley in 1974. In the early 1960s he was an American Friends Service Committee fieldworker in Indian community development on the San Carlos Apache Reservation in Arizona. He served on the board of Oakland's Intertribal Friendship House and was closely associated with Indian student activism, the 1969 Alcatraz occupation, and the founding of the University of California at Berkeley Native American Studies program. He was acting assistant professor of Native American studies there from 1971 to 1974.

He has lectured and taught Native American studies courses in Europe and at several universities in the United States. He chaired the anthropology and sociology departments at the University of the District of Columbia, until 1983, and was a lecturer in Native American Studies at the University of California at Davis from 1988 to 1990. In 1999 Talbot retired from San Joaquin Delta College in Stockton, California. Currently he is adjunct professor of anthropology at Oregon State University and an instructor in sociology and Native American Studies at Lane Community College.

His publications have dealt mainly with Native American sovereignty, religious freedom, and political activism. These include the book *Roots of Oppression: The American Indian Question* (1981); the article "Academic Indianismo: Social Scientific Research in American Indian Studies" in *American Indian Culture and Research Journal* (2002); and the article "Spiritual Genocide: The Denial of American Indian Religious Freedom from Conquest to 1934," *Wicazo Sa Review* (2006). Currently he is completing an introductory text with the working title *Contemporary Native Nations of North America: An Indigenous Perspective*, to be published by Prentice Hall.

TRACI L. MORRIS (Chickasaw/Caucasian) holds a Ph.D. in American Indian Studies. She is the owner of Homahota Consulting and in this capacity serves as the Policy Analyst for Native Public Media. Through Homahota Consulting, Morris provides technical training for Indian country and is a community educator on tribal issues. She has worked with Native urban and tribal communities in the state of Arizona, with state agencies, the Arizona governor's office, the Phoenix Indian Center, the Tucson Indian Center, and tribal leaders in policy analysis, resource development, and training and technical assistance. She has lectured widely over the years to community and government organizations on a wide range of Native issues and topics.

Morris has lectured at universities throughout the country. She has nine years of teaching experience at various colleges and universities in Arizona, including the University of Arizona and Arizona State University. Currently she is adjunct faculty for the American Indian Studies Department at Arizona State University and in the Native American Studies Department at Eastern Central University in Oklahoma.

Morris has also worked in the arts for several museums and galleries, including internships at the Smithsonian Institution's National Museum of the American Indian, at the George Gustav Heye Center in lower Manhattan, and at the Arizona State Museum. She worked as manager and buyer for Tucson's oldest Native American Art Gallery, Bahti Indian Arts.

ABOUT THE ARTISTS

PARRIS K. BUTLER (Mohave), whose art appears at the beginning of a number of the parts of this book, works in a variety of two-dimensional media, including pen and ink, acrylic on canvas, and using various printmaking techniques. In 1985 he received an associate of fine arts degree from the Institute of American Indian Arts, Santa Fe in two-dimensional arts and creative writing.

LEONARD F. CHANA (Tohono O'odham) was born in Burnt Seeds, now Santa Rosa village, on the Tohono O'odham Nation in Arizona. His work is both acrylic and pen and ink stippling, in which images are formed with a multitude of dots. In a recent autobiographical book, *The Sweet Smell of Home: The Life and Art of Leonard F. Chana,* University of Arizona Press, he shows and describes a number of his artworks.

GERALD DAWAVENDEWA (Hopi/Cherokee) grew up in the Hopi village of Munqapi in Arizona. He received a degree in fine arts from the University of Arizona. His work has been shown in a number of museums and galleries throughout the United States. His artwork also includes "Earth bundle," which was sent aboard the Space Shuttle Endeavor launched in 1994. He is a guest lecturer and consultant to various museums, schools, and universities, and he is the author of the book *The Butterfly Dance.*

1

PEOPLES AND NATIONS: FOLLOWING IN THE FOOTSTEPS OF THE ANCESTORS

Hearing the Song
William Stafford

My father said, "Listen," and that subtle song
"Coyote" came to me; we heard it together.
The river slid by, its weight
moving like oil. "It comes at night,"
he said; "some people don't like it." "It sounds
dark," I said, "like midnight, rich. . . ."
His hand pressed my shoulder:
"Just listen." That's how I first heard the song.

Tthis book takes a Native American studies perspective rather than that of mainstream anthropology, history, or sociology. That perspective is what is meant by the subtitle to Part I: "Following in the Footsteps of the Ancestors." Our emphasis and perspective are those of the Indigenous peoples of the Americas as peoples and nations, not as ethnic minorities.

Native American studies (NAS), also known as American Indian studies (AIS), arose as an academic field of study in the late 1960s, during the "new Indian" movement. (We use the term *Native American* to include the Indigenous peoples of the Americas commonly called Indians or American Indians, and also the Alaska Natives, the Inuit of Canada, and the Native peoples of Hawai'i.) As part of this development, 46 undergraduate programs in NAS were founded, 19 programs on college and university campuses in California alone.[1] A 1999 survey by the Association for the Study of American Literatures found 13 programs and departments offering graduate degrees in NAS, at least 4 with Ph.D. programs,[2] and more than 350 professors in more than 100 colleges and universities were identifying themselves as Native American or Alaska Native.[3] The 2008 revised *A Guide to Native American Studies Programs in the United States and Canada* found 130 institutions of higher learning with NAS programs, 26 offering related graduate degrees, 46 with majors, 81 offering minors, and 24 with concentrations.[4]

Russell Thornton (Cherokee), in a recent work (see Suggested Readings), attributes the historical development of Native American studies mainly to the initiative shown by Anglo educational institutions and undervalues the role played by the growing number of Indian students on campus and their mentors, the traditional elders. Thornton's contention may have been the case on some campuses when college administrators responded to Indigenous activism by unilaterally establishing NAS/AIS programs, but at the University of California–Berkeley, the University of California–Davis, and San Francisco State University, the Indian elders and leaders became the "unread libraries" in the late 1960s and early 1970s that were then utilized by student activists and Indian academicians to flesh out the core courses for the new discipline. In short, our perspective on this question finds a different line of development, one that is grounded in traditional Indigenous history, culture, and resistance.

An issue that emerged in the 1960s was the relationship of NAS to the already established academic departments such as anthropology, sociology, art, history, and literature, which are part of the Western scientific and humanities traditions. Some professors in these mainstream departments saw themselves in an adversarial relationship with the new course offerings in Native studies in a kind of "turf war" mentality. Native American studies was not considered an academic discipline in its own right but, instead, was viewed as a nonserious "program" created by Indian ideologues who espoused a cultural nationalism. As NAS has come to maturity as a legitimate field of study, however, this view has all but faded.

Unlike the other disciplines, NAS is multidisciplinary in scope, whereas anthropology, for example, although holistic in context, is not. Native American studies also takes an Indigenous rather than a Eurocentric or Western perspective. Native American studies often asks different theoretical questions than do the other academic disciplines, and it employs a variety of research techniques that are not unique to any single discipline. It is informed by its own paradigm. For example, in *Red Earth, White Lies*,[5] Vine Deloria, Jr. (Standing Rock Sioux), challenged the standard anthropological theories of the Bering Strait land bridge peopling of the Americas and the subsequent megafaunal extinction. A review of that work by John Mohawk (Seneca) in the *American Anthropologist* makes the following insightful comment:

> Deloria's concern is the theory embraced by anthropology that, some 11,000 years ago, ancestors of contemporary American Indians crossed a land bridge which then connected Asia and Alaska and that they found a land with giant creatures who were unafraid of humans and therefore fell prey to skilled hunters. The Indians embarked on a slaughter of these animals, driving them to extinction. . . . Deloria argues the land bridge theory is far more problematic than the anthropology profession generally teaches, there is very little physical evidence and extremely fuzzy logic to support the extinction of the megafauna at the hands of Paleolithic Indians . . . that anthropologists should pay more attention to American Indian stories about what happened in the remote past for clues [i.e., Indian oral history].[6]

In *Native Americans of California and Nevada*,[7] historian Jack D. Forbes (Powhatan-Renape and Delaware-Lenape) examined standard anthropological concepts used by anthropologists in books on American Indians and proposed some conceptual tools from a Native American studies perspective as a better lens with which to view the Indian experience. In a discussion of culture, for example, he criticizes the anthropological "linguistic area" concept as a device for classifying Indian languages. Indians speak a specific language or a dialect of a language, not a language "family" like Algonkian any more than an Englishman speaks Indo-European. Furthermore, Indians are often multilingual, speaking languages or dialects of different language families. Nor do Indians identify themselves by "culture area," a favorite classificatory device employed by anthropology. When a Native person meets another Native, one gives one's name and tribe or nation (sometimes clan affiliation) and not a culture area designation. Yet it is common for anthropology to begin a work on American Indians with a discussion of Indian culture and linguistic areas as if these were the most important things one needs to know to gain an introductory understanding of Native American peoples. This is not an Indian perspective, and even on empirical grounds it can be a faulty concept.

A culture area is defined by anthropologists as a geographic region in which a number of Indian "ethnographic groups" follow a similar way of life that can be identified by a list of similar cultural traits that correspond to the Indians' biotic or physical environment, such as the "Plains Indians" buffalo-hunting culture. Anthropologists identify ten to a dozen culture areas for North America alone. The content of the Smithsonian Institution's multivolume *Handbook of North American Indians*, for example, uses the culture area format as its organizing principle. Today, even some anthropologists criticize the concept for its geographic determinism. "Culture area" ignores more meaningful kinds of classifications, such as recognizing Indian peoples by the similarity of their political organization, military alliances, trade networks, ceremonial practices, and inter-tribal marriage customs. The culture area concept focuses too much on the more esoteric and less politically strategic areas of "pre-Columbian" life rather than on flesh-and-blood peoples striving to retain their cultural traditions and governance in the crucible of Western conquest and neocolonialism.

Another criticism of the culture area concept that should concern even mainstream historians is the time problem, the use of the "ethnographic present" in anthropological works regarding Indians. Ethnographic present is the cultural description of an Indigenous people not as they are living in the contemporary world, but as they were thought to have lived in the past. In the first place, a culture area is a reconstruction, not reality itself, by anthropologists. The aim of anthropologists was to "reconstruct" Indian cultures as they were supposed to have existed in a pure stage or hypothetical Golden Age of their "development" before European colonization rather than to produce a dynamic description of Native Americans as changing yet enduring peoples. Such reconstructions are based on an ahistorical concept, an "outside of time view," since the supposed Golden Age for an Indian people living in one part of the Americas will necessarily be a different time than for those living in another part of the continent. There is necessarily a 100- to 200-year or more time lag in terms of Indian–white contact as Europeans moved from south to north (the Spanish occupation), and east to west (the English, French, and American occupation) across North America in the process of expansion along the Indian frontier. In the Native American studies paradigm, on the other hand, it is important to be "in time," or historical, since one of the essential processes is the dialectics of conquest and resistance.

The discipline of sociology also has limitations when it comes to the Native American experience. It is a common practice to identify Native people as another American ethnic group rather than as many distinct peoples and nations with "a right to the soil" under U.S. Constitutional law. Theirs is not the "immigrant experience" of white ethnics whose ancestors emigrated from Europe to become "hyphenated-Americans" in the process of assimilating into the American "melting pot." Nor does the Indian experience equate to that of oppressed peoples of color, such as African-Americans who were originally brought in chains to the Americas and held down racially and exploited economically thereafter through the "one drop of Black blood" rule. Or take the case of Mexican-Americans as a *mestizo* people of color who became dispossessed victims of the loss of one-third of Mexico's richest lands that became the United States following the 1846 Mexican-American war.

In promoting an Indigenous perspective, Forbes points out that NAS is not a new discipline as is frequently thought.[8] He reminds us that it was a Quechua-speaking Inca scholar who made a scientific study of Spanish colonial society several centuries before most of the contemporary Western academic disciplines such as sociology and anthropology even existed. This scholar was Guaman Poma (Felipe de Ayala), who documented Peruvian customs and life under the seventeenth-century Spanish yoke.[9] (An example of his drawings is included on page 5.) Poma's work was suppressed and remained unpublished for 300 years, but, even so, we might well consider him one of the founders of Native American studies long before the other modern academic disciplines, with the exception of history, came into being.

COREGIMIENTO

COREG.ͦAFRENTAAI,

alcalde hordenario por dos guebos que no le da mitayo.

probincias   como

This drawing by Guaman Poma reflects a scene after the coming of the Spanish in Peru. "The *corregidor* punishes the magistrate for failing to collect a couple of eggs from an Indian laborer."

From Guaman Poma: Writing and Resistance in Colonial Peru *by Roleno Adorno (Austin: University of Texas Press, 1986). Reprinted by permission of Siglo XXI Editores.*

There have been other early Native American scholars, such as Titu Kusi, whose "Relación" in 1570 gave the Inca side of the Spanish conquest, and the Inca Garcilaso de la Vega, who wrote a history of Peru in 1609. Both the Mayan and Aztec cultures were highly literate civilizations before the European invasion burned thousands of their codices, or books. North America, too, had its Native American intellectuals. Pablo Tac, a Luiseño Indian, wrote in 1835 of his experiences and those of his people after the arrival of Spanish missionaries in California. And between 1809 and 1821, Sequoyah (Charles Gist) worked out a syllabary for writing the Cherokee language.

Even earlier, a number of North American Indian peoples made scientific observations and kept records. Many kept "sky charts," which are astronomical observations in connection with the planting cycle and the ceremonial calendar. The traditional Hopi, for example, still maintain this ancient practice through their "sun watchers," or priests, who are able to calculate accurately the lunar and solar calendars. The Tohono O'Odham have their calendar stick, and the Kiowa have their ledger books. The Lakota (Teton Sioux) are known for their "winter counts," which utilize the Lakota concepts of "winters" (years) and generations (about 70 years). These serve as mnemonic devices to recall the event for which each winter was named. The Iroquois wampum belts serve a somewhat similar purpose. Wampum, made from white and purple sea shells, ratified treaties, opened government deliberations, confirmed leaders into office, registered the history of the Iroquois constitution, memorialized the dead, confessed the penitent, and aided prayer. "This belt preserves my words" is the frequent closing remark of Iroquois speeches today. Finally, even Western-trained scholars and ethnohistorians are coming to recognize the value of Indian oral history, the memories of the people, as a valid historical instrument in its own right.

This is what the editors of this current reader mean by "following in the footsteps of the ancestors." It is therefore fitting that we begin our readings in Part I with a dedication to Vine Deloria, Jr. (Standing Rock Sioux). As journalist and writer Bruce Johansen points out, Deloria has been a giant in the field of Native American scholarship and the "godparent" of Native American studies. This new edition of *Native American Voices* is dedicated to this great scholar and memorializes his passing.

Reading 2, "The Rise and Fall of Native American Studies in the United States," presents an analysis of the history and current status of Native American/American Indian Studies. The author, Duane Champagne (Turtle Mountain Chippewa), is an editor and a prolific writer of Native American scholarly works. A professor of sociology at the University of California, Los Angeles, he was formerly director of the university's American Indian Studies Center and editor of its publication, the *American Indian Culture and Research Journal*.

Champagne's thesis is that although there has been a significant development of an Indigenous studies paradigm, the organizational structure of the discipline within colleges and universities has become problematic. The organizational efforts of the field in "U.S. universities have not kept pace with the intellectual developments, and have inhibited the development of American Indian Studies as a fully developed discipline and paradigm" (p. 19). Very few universities have established autonomous NAS/AIS departments, and among those that have there is the difficulty of recruiting Native faculty. The most common form of organization, according to Champagne, is "the interdepartmental model" where faculty are hired into the academic departments of mainstream disciplines and have a tenuous association with a separate NAS/AIS department or program. In some cases an Indian studies program is housed within an ethnic studies department, overlooking the unique history of Native Americans as "first peoples" who have a treaty relationship with the United States government. Champagne details other problems which, when taken together with the organizational problems, constitute "the fall of American Indian Studies." Even so,

Champagne concludes by identifying the steps needed for "Native American Studies going forward."

In Part I we have also sought to lay the groundwork for presenting "Native American voices"—the various names of Native American peoples and nations, their populations, identities and socioeconomic characteristics, as well as some important Indian concepts and issues. Appropriate maps and a table on current demographics are provided to give the student a quick summary overview of these details.

Indigenous identity is a multifaceted and complex issue for Native people in the Americas. In a comprehensive article, Reading 3, "Indigenous Identity: What Is It, and Who *Really* Has It?" Hilary Weaver (Lakota) explores three aspects of this subject: self-identification, community identification, and external identification. She recounts a story told by her father, "the big game," as a metaphor for the identity problem. How one identifies as a Native person "consists of a lifelong process of cultural awareness and understanding" (p. 29). Does one identify as a member of a generalized class of persons by a collective term preferred by Euro-American society, such as Indian, Native American, or Alaska Native? Or a "tribal name," in common usage by the dominant society, such as Iroquois, Navajo, Sioux, or Eskimo? Or as a member of an Indigenous community using the traditional term for ones people, such as Haudenosaunee, Dineh, Lakota, or Yupiaq? Is one's Indian identification a genetic reference or a cultural one in terms of tribal membership and being rooted in a specific Indigenous community? In each case there is a different configuration of self-image, cultural understanding, and values. And given the intermarriage between Native and non-Native persons, with which part or parts of one's genealogy should one identify? A claim of "being Indian" with slight or questionable biological connection or community membership can become a slippery slope that can lead to a charge of identity fraud or misrepresentation.

In terms of Weaver's "external identification" category, there is the question of whether to call an Indigenous society a "tribe" or a "nation." "Tribe" carries the unfortunate characterization of being uncivilized, while "nation" implies a society with a recognized nation state. In a box titled "The Peoplehood Matrix," Tom Holm, professor of American Indian Studies at the University of Arizona, offers the concept of "peoplehood" to define the nature of Native American society in terms of four uniquely interrelated factors—language, sacred history, ceremonial cycle, and place/territory—that differentiate American Indian societies from non-Indigenous nations.

When it comes to external identification, the blood quantum standard used by the U.S. government for determining who is a "legal" Indian and to whom the government is therefore obligated to give treaty-mandated services is especially divisive. The blood quantum device—"full-blood," "half-blood," "quarter-blood," etc.—can define out of existence many bona fide Native people and thereby deprive them of the right to land, resources, and treaty-obligated services mandated under federal Indian law. It also separates federally recognized Native Americans from relatives and neighbors who are unrecognized, or who are not considered Indian because of their blood quantum. There are Native communities that are not recognized by the federal government and therefore do not receive any of the services extended to federally recognized Native nations. Furthermore, as more Indian adults marry inter-tribally, and their percentage of Native or single tribal heritage diminishes over the generations, fewer Native American children can claim enough "blood" of any one tribe or nation to qualify as federally recognized Indians. This trend has been termed *statistical genocide*. Ironically, because U.S. Native Americans are the only racial or ethnic group who must legally prove ethnicity, and because the present policy or custom promotes statistical genocide, Indigenous identity will increasingly become a cultural matter rather than a "pure blood" definition in the twenty-first century.

Mesoamerica and South America are the homelands of more than 40 million Indigenous people, many times the number found in the United States and Canada. The greatest concentrations of Indian people are found in Mexico, Guatemala, Ecuador, Peru, and Bolivia. In Guatemala, 60 to 70 percent of the population are Indian, most of whom speak one of over two dozen Native languages rather than Spanish. All over Latin America, as in the Mayan Indian rebellion in southern Mexico, an upsurge in cultural and ethnic identity and political organizing is testing the limits of established, non-Indian–controlled governments. Evo Morales, an Indian, became the president of Bolivia in 2007, the first Indigenous head of state in South America.

In Latin America "Indianness" is determined largely by cultural rather than racial standards. If one speaks the Spanish language instead of an Indian one and adopts a Ladino or *mestizo* way of life, he or she may no longer be considered an Indian person. Even so, millions of people in Central and South America still speak an Indian language and maintain a Native American identity.

The way statistical genocide works in Canada is somewhat different. As Reading 4, "First Nations: Indigenous Peoples of Canada," by Steve Talbot, points out, Canadian law establishes a "non-status" Indian category, which for decades illogically reduced the number of legal Indians. Until the Canadian Indian Act was changed in 1985, Indians could lose their Indian status if they received "half-breed lands or money scrip" or if an Indian woman married a person who was not an enrolled Indian. Tens of thousands of Indians "vanished" because of this law, and they are only now being reinstated to Indigenous status.

This selection will also acquaint the reader with the three main Indigenous categories of the Native peoples in Canada—Indians, Métis, and Inuit—as well as the peculiarities of Canadian Indigenous policy. Although, for the most part, the Native experience in Canada is similar to that of the United States, there are some important differences in history and policy toward the First Nations of Canada. The Inuit, commonly known as Eskimo in the United States, are a unique case because their population and homeland embrace not only Canada, where they number some thirty-five thousand persons, but also Alaska, Greenland, and Russia—a total of 115,000 persons in all. In Canada, the Inuit in the Northwest Territories have pressed successfully for land claims and political control over their vast aboriginal territory, which they call Nunavut, "Our Land." (A box showing a map of Nunavut and its salient facts follows the reading.) Today, Nunavut is an autonomous province of Canada.

In Reading 5, "Native Peoples of Mexico," David Edmunds makes a similar survey of the Indigenous peoples of Mexico but notes that "unlike the United States and Canada, Mexico attempted to break from the Indian policy of its colonial past" (p. 42) The Mexican constitution of 1821 departed from Spanish policy by making all Indians citizens and launching a program of total assimilation that led to the official origin of a *mestizo* state: overwhelmingly Indigenous racially but Spanish-speaking and Hispanicised culturally. And yet, millions of unassimilated Indian peoples remained. Edmunds sketches a brief historical overview of historical and policy events that have affected Indian policy in Mexico. It is interesting to note that Indians from southern Mexico fought with Emiliano Zapata in the 1910 Mexican revolution over the issue of land redistribution to landless "peasant" farmers. And as recent as the 1960s and 1970s, another Zapatista rebellion took place in Chiapas state by Maya Indians against the federal government. Despite the federal government's attempt to "legislate Indians out of existence" while at the same time embracing the Indian cultural past as Mexico's national heritage, Indian peoples have been left out of the country's political power structure.

A comprehensive overview of the Indigenous peoples of the United States is provided in Table I.1, "Native American Demographics—United States, 2008." Population figures, "tribes" and their relative ranking, reservation vs. non-reservation, respective lands, health, education, and other statistical characteristics give a portrait of the nations and peoples. This demographic overview is mainly for the United States, although some essential statistics are also provided for Latin America.

Following Table I.1 is a box with commentary on one form of "statistical genocide": the way the U.S. Census Bureau undercounts Native people, resulting in their invisibility as a viable Indigenous minority. The Census figures, taken every 10 years, determine, among other things, the level of federal funding for Indian programs in the United States, as well as the political nature of congressional representation in Indian country. Lobo faults the Census Bureau for failing to enumerate [Native Americans] in 'temporary' living spaces such as jails, Halfway houses, hotels, and shelters in the 2000 census. This has led to severe undercounts of Native people, in both urban areas as well as rural regions on and off reservations. Census undercount has been especially serious in large urban areas such as the San Francisco–East Bay of California, since the bulk of the Indian population in the country's most populous state is urban rather than reservation based or rural. In the United States as a whole, more than two-thirds of the Native American population according to U.S. census figures is now considered urban, although the urban versus rural/reservation opposition is in many other respects a false dichotomy, since a high proportion of "urban Indians" continue to relate strongly to their tribal roots in Indian country.

NOTES

1. Charlotte Heth and Susan Gyette, *Issues for the Future of American Indian Studies* (Los Angeles: UCLA American Indian Studies Center, 1984).

2. Robert M. Nelson, ed. *A Guide to Native American Studies Programs in the United States and Canada*, March 1999. http://oncampus.richmond.edu/faculty/ASAIL/guide/guide.html.

3. *Wicazo Sa Review*, 9, no. 1 (Spring 1993): 57.

4. Robert M. Nelson, ed. *A Guide to Native American Studies Programs in the United States and Canada*, revised 21 February 2008. http://oncampus.richmond.edu/faculty/ASAIL/guide/guide.html.

5. Vine Deloria Jr., *Red Earth, White Lies: Native Americans and the Myth of Scientific Fact* (New York: Scribner, 1995).

6. John Mohawk, "Review of Deloria's *Red Earth, White Lies*," *American Anthropologist*, 98, no. 3, 1995: 650–651.

7. Jack D. Forbes, "Basic Concepts for Understanding Native History and Culture," *Native Americans of California and Nevada*. (Happy Camp, Calif.: Naturegraph Publishers, 1982) pp. 156–178.

8. Jack D. Forbes, *Native American Studies Newsletter*, U.C. Davis 1, no. 1 (May 1990): 3, 7.

9. Guaman Poma (Felipe de Ayala), *Guaman Poma: Writing and Resistance in Colonial Peru* (Austin: University of Texas Press, 1986).

DEDICATION

ON THE PASSING OF VINE DELORIA, JR.

Bruce E. Johansen

DEDICATION

Political and intellectual rhetoric in Native America is usually egalitarian. Most Native tradition shies away from the elevation of kings, princes, and popes. No one worthy of such a title would claim it. The passing of Vine Deloria Jr. on November 13, 2005, however, brought forth superlatives. If Native America had a pope—of course, it does not—it would have been Deloria. The grief witnessed upon his passing may be compared to Poland's grief upon the passing of Pope John Paul II, which I witnessed as a lecturer at Lublin Catholic University, where John Paul, as Karol Wojtyla, taught for nearly a quarter-century before he was called to Rome.

University of Colorado Professor Charles Wilkinson, an expert in American Indian law, called Deloria "probably the most influential American Indian of the past century" (Dahl, 2005). "He was also a wonderful human being, brilliant, bitingly funny and profoundly warm and compassionate, always willing to lend a hand or lift a spirit," Wilkinson added (Dahl, 2005).

Deloria died following complications of surgery for a ruptured abdominal aortic aneurysm at Exempla Lutheran Medical Center in Wheat Ridge, Colorado, according to his son Philip, a history professor at the University of Michigan and a noted author in his own right (Williams, 2005). Before the aneurysm surgery complications, Deloria had struggled with recovery problems from colon cancer surgery more than a month earlier.

For many days and weeks after his passing, the news rippled through Deloria's vast extended family in the United States and around the world, by e-mail and personal contact, hand to hand, ear to ear, to "all

Bruce Johansen, ed, from The *Prager Handbook On Contemporary Issues in Native America*, vol. 1, pp. xxi–xxxii.) Article has been excerpted from the original and reference notes appear on page 25.

our relations," in a Native American sense. Even the rocks on which we walk sent their condolences, so it was said. I heard many Native people say that he lives—in his words and in our memories—and that we all go to the other side eventually. Many who knew Deloria drew comfort from the belief that he will be in the other world when they pass over.

University of Minnesota American Indian Studies Professor David Wilkins, who is Lumbee, wrote in *Indian Country Today* that Deloria "was never quite comfortable with the notion that he was, in fact, the principal champion of tribal nations since he wanted—no, demanded—that each Native nation express confidence in its own national identity, develop its own unique talents and together wield their collective sovereignty, that is, their dignity and integrity, in a way that enriches them and the nations around them as well" (Wilkins, 2005). Reacting to his own influence, Deloria tried as best he could to spread his intellectual wealth around. . . .

A SIGNIFICANT VOICE

Deloria, a Standing Rock Sioux, first became nationally known during the late 1960s, following publication of his book *Custer Died for Your Sins*. Deloria also rose to national prominence as a spokesman for Native self-determination movements, becoming a widely respected professor, author, and social critic in several fields, including law, religion, and political science, as well as Native American studies. He was one of the best-known founders of Native American studies as a field of scholarly inquiry in the late twentieth century.

By the late 1990s, Deloria was described by Roger Dunsmore in the *Handbook of Native American Literature* as:

> The most significant voice in this generation regarding the presentation and analysis of contemporary Indian

Vine Deloria, Jr.

affairs, their history, present shape, and meaning. . . . No other voice, Indian or white, has as full a command of the overall data of Indian history or affairs, and no other voice has the moral force, the honesty, to admit mistakes and to redress them, or the edge to bite through the layers of soft tissue, through the stereotypes, myths, and outright lies, to the bone . . . marrow of Indian affairs. (Dunsmore, 1996, 411)

"The great Indigenous visionary, philosopher, author and activist Vine Deloria, Jr. passed over to join his ancestors today, November 13, 2005," said a statement from the Colorado American Indian Movement (2005). "Our thoughts and prayers go to his wife, Barbara, to his children [Philip, Daniel, and Jeanne] and his other relatives [a brother, a sister, and seven grandchildren]." The passing of Vine creates a huge intellectual and analytical void in the native and non-native worlds. . . . It is safe to say that without the example provided by the writing and the thinking of Vine Deloria, Jr., there likely would have been no American Indian Movement, [and] there would be no international Indigenous peoples' movement as it exists today" (Colorado American Indian Movement, 2005).

"He had the courage and the vision," the statement continued, "to challenge the dominating society at its core. He was unapologetic in confronting the racism of United States law and policy, and he was prophetic in challenging young Indigenous activists to hone their strategies. He was our elder statesman and mentor. . . . For many of us, Vine was a contemporary

Crazy Horse" (Colorado American Indian Movement, 2005). A public memorial for Deloria was held on November 18 at the Mount Vernon Event Center, Golden, Colorado, west of Denver, as a scholarship fund was initiated in his name.

An obituary in *The New York Times* recalled that "While his *Custer* book, with its incendiary title, was categorized at the time as an angry young man's anthem, Mr. Deloria's real weapon, critics and admirers said, was his scathing, sardonic humor, which he was able to use on both sides of the Indian-white divide. He once called the Battle of the Little Bighorn, where Lt. Col. George Armstrong Custer and the Seventh Cavalry were defeated by a combined force of Sioux and Northern Cheyenne in 1876 in the Montana territory, 'a sensitivity-training session'" (Johnson, 2005). "'We have brought the white man a long way in 500 years,'" Deloria wrote in a *New York Times* op-ed article during 1976. "'From a childish search for mythical cities of gold and fountains of youth to the simple recognition that lands are essential for human existence'" (Johnson, 2005).

In person, Deloria was known for his sharp onstage wit. Addressing 500 students at Boise State University on February 28, 1998, he jested about nineteenth-century pseudoscientific assumptions that Europeans were the most intelligent race because they had the largest skulls. That was before "the discovery that Apaches had something like 100 cc's more cranial capacity than Harvard professors," Deloria joked (Etlinger, 1998). . . .

Vine Deloria Jr. was born in Martin, South Dakota, on the Pine Ridge Indian Reservation, on March 26, 1933. Educated in reservation schools during his early years, Deloria served in the Marine Corps between 1954 and 1956, before he earned a bachelor of science degree at Iowa State University (granted in 1958) and a bachelor of divinity at the Lutheran School of Theology in 1963. After that, Deloria served as executive director of the National Congress of American Indians. At the same time, Deloria was a member of the U.S. Board of Inquiry on Hunger and Malnutrition. Serving on this hoard, he found black children in the Mississippi Delta eating red clay to deal with hunger (Dunsmore, 1996, 412).

Early in his life as an activist, Deloria channeled his intellectual efforts into legal studies, entering the University of Colorado Law School in 1967. He took up legal studies expressly to advance Native rights. Deloria completed study for his law degree in 1970 and later, in 1990, joined the University of Colorado's faculty, teaching until his retirement in 2000.

While teaching at the University of Colorado, Deloria's home department was history, but he also was affiliated with ethnic studies, religious studies, political science, and the law school, one indication of academic respect he commanded across many disciplines.

COMMON THEMES OF DELORIA'S WRITTEN WORK

Deloria's written work (including twenty books and more than a hundred major articles) stress a common theme, according to Dunsmore: that sin is a major element in U.S. history and that "the sinners are those who have stolen and desecrated the land" (Dunsmore, 1996, 413). On this subject, Deloria quoted Curley, a Crow chief, who is best known to history as one of the scouts for George Armstrong Custer at the Battle of the Little Bighorn in 1876. Curley is not known as a great Native American philosopher, but his words, spoken in 1912, evoke memories of Tecumseh, Sea'th'l, and Black Elk:

> The soil you see is not ordinary soil—it is the dust of the blood, the flesh and the bones of our ancestors. We fought and bled and died to keep other Indians from taking it, and we fought and bled and died helping the whites. You will have to dig down through the surface before you find nature's earth, as the upper portion is Crow. . . . The land is my blood and my dead; it is consecrated; and I do not want to give up any portion of it. (Dunsmore, 1996, 415)

As early as the 1950s, Deloria was engaging in acute criticism of the Indian Claims Commission, arguing that it was a device by which to avoid treaty issues, not address them. He pointed out that laws and regulations announced as so-called help to Indians often perpetuated colonialism. Historically, Deloria argued, the rights of Native Americans have trailed those of other social groups in the United States. For example, slavery of Alaska natives was not outlawed until 1886, two decades after the Civil War.

Deloria has won a broad audience among a wide variety of people for asserting, with a sharp wit, contradictions in the general cant of contemporary U.S. life. For example, in *We Talk, You Listen* (1970), Deloria recalled a conversation with a non-Indian who asked him, "What did you [Native Americans] *do* with the land when you had it?" Deloria said he did not understand the ecological irony of such a question until later, when he discovered that the Cuyahoga River running through Cleveland was flammable. So many combustible pollutants were dumped into the river that the inhabitants had to take special precautions

during summer to avoid accidentally setting it on fire. "After reviewing the argument of my non-Indian friend," wrote Deloria, "I decided that he was probably correct. Whites had made better use of the land. How many Indians could have thought of creating a flammable river?" (Deloria, 1970, 9).

Deloria defined the differences between European and Native American views of the land this way:

> The tribal-communal way of life, devoid of economic competition, views land as the most vital part of man's existence. It is THEIRS. It supports them, tells them where they live, and defines HOW they live. Land does not have the simple sentimentality of purple mountains majesty. . . . Rather it provides a center of the universe for the group that lives *on* it. As such, the people who hold land in this way always have a home to go to. Their identity is secure. They live with it and do not abstract themselves from it and live off it. (Deloria, 1970, 175)

Jousting with missionaries, Deloria in his many speeches sometimes condensed half a millennium of history in North America into one sentence: When the missionaries came, they had the book (the Bible), and Indians had the land. Now, Deloria said, they have the land, and Indians have the book.

Deloria called for adaptation of Native American land ethics to a general non-Indian society that finds itself faced with the environmental damage pursuant to 2,000 years' experience exercising the biblical commandment to multiply and subdue the earth.

> American society could save itself by listening to tribal people. While this would take a radical reorientation of concepts and values, it would be well worth the effort. The land-use philosophy of Indians is so utterly simple that it seems stupid to repeat it: man must live with other forms of life on the land and not destroy it. The implications of this philosophy are very far-reaching for the contemporary political and economic system. Reorientation would mean that public interest, indeed the interest in the survival of humanity as a species, must take precedent over special economic interests. Now the laugh is ours. After four centuries of gleeful rape, the white man stands a mere generation away from extinguishing life on this planet. (Deloria, 1970, 189, 195)

Throughout his life, Deloria continued to write a number of books and articles that often took issue with Eurocentric interpretations of reality. His early books, such as *Custer Died for Your Sins* (1969), *We Talk, You Listen* (1970), and *Of Utmost Good Faith* (1971), continued to spread to new, younger audiences. In all of his works, Deloria has asserted Native American rights of occupancy to the land. Under international law, according to Deloria, Native American nations possess an equitable title of occupancy over lands upon which they lived, "and this occupancy was not to be disturbed except by voluntary and lawful sales of lands to the European country claiming the legal title to the area in question" (Lyons, 1992, 283).

Deloria's writings also compare the metaphysics of Native American and European points of view, especially in legal and religious matters. In *God Is Red* (1973), Deloria argued that American Indian spiritual traditions, far from being out-of-date, are more congruent with the needs of the modern world than is Christianity, which Deloria said fostered imperialism and disregard for the planet's ecology (Johnson, 2005). In *God Is Red* he also contrasts Native American religion's melding of life with a concept of sacred place to the artificial of Old World doctrines.

Deloria compared the nature of sacredness in each perceptual realm. His discussion of sacredness also examines ecological themes in Native American religions. Deloria also compares the ways in which each culture perceives reality: Europeans seeing time as linear and history as a progressive sequence of events; most Native cultures as neither of these. Christianity usually portrays God as a humanlike being, often meddlesome and vengeful, whereas many Native religions place supreme authority in a great mystery symbolizing the life forces of nature.

To Deloria, the great mystery of Sioux theology becomes an ecological metaphor, as he explains ways in which Native American theologies weave a concept of cycles into life, reinforcing reverence for the land and the remains of ancestors buried in it, contrasted to Europeans' ability to move from place to place without regard for location, until the reality of the American land and its often unwritten history begin to absorb them. Deloria's beliefs are not his alone; they may be read in a historical context provided by Luther Standing Bear, Chief Sea'th'l, and other Native American leaders.

Deloria points out that many Native Americans and non-Indians have trouble communicating because, even today, their perceptual realms are different.

> The fundamental factor that keeps Indians and non-Indians from communicating is that they are speaking about two entirely different perceptions of the world. Growing up on an Indian reservation makes one acutely aware of the mysteries of the universe. Medicine men practicing their ancient ceremonies, perform feats that amaze and puzzle the rational mind. The sense of contentment enjoyed by older Indians in the face of a lifetime's experience of betrayal, humiliation and paternalism stuns the outside observer. It often appears that Indians are

immune to the values which foreign institutions have forced them to confront. Their minds remain fixed on other realities. (Deloria, 1979, vii)

Ernest Cassirer, who is cited approvingly by Deloria, wrote that for Native American peoples, "Nature becomes one great society, the society of life. Man is not endowed with an outstanding rank in this society. He is part of it, but he is in no respect higher than any other member" (Cassirer, 1944, 83). Commented Deloria, "All species, all forms of life, have equal status before the presence of the universal power to which they are subject. The religious requirement for all life-forms is thus harmony, and this requirement holds for every species, ours included" (Deloria, 1979, 153–54).

Deloria's work often provides a trenchant critique of progress and civilization, two connotatively loaded words that have propelled the expansion of European lifeways around the earth, two words that are usually invested by European-descended thinkers with connotations of uncontested goodness, or if not goodness—at least of inevitability.

> In recent years, we have come to understand what progress is. It is the total replacement of nature by an artificial technology. Progress is the absolute destruction of the real world in favor of a technology that creates a comfortable way of life for a few fortunately situated people. Within our lifetime the difference between the Indian use of land and the white use of land will become crystal clear. The Indian lived with his land. *The white destroyed his* land. He *destroyed the planet earth.* (Hughes, 1983, 136; emphasis in original)

Entering his late sixties by the year 2000, Deloria often walked with a cane. When people asked him about it, he was prone to say he had "been bitten by a rabid Republican and got a staph infection" (Wilitz, 1997). Complaining about the left-leaning nature of the professoriat, Vincent Carroll, editorial page editor of Denver's *Rocky Mountain News*, pointed out with a straight face that Deloria was the only registered Republican among faculty of the History Department at the University of Colorado at Boulder. Carroll seemed to have missed what most people who knew Deloria knew as obvious: He had signed up as a Republican as a joke.

A consummate observer of academic rituals, Deloria was a critic of research methods often employed by scholars investigating Native American peoples:

> My original complaint against researchers is that they seem to derive all the benefits and bear no responsibility

for the ways in which their findings are used. In making this accusation, I said that scholars should be required to put something back into the Indian community, preferably some form of financial support, so the community can do some things it wants to do. (Deloria, 1991, 457)

Throughout his life, Deloria was a sharp critic of many theories that often had assumed the status of revealed truth among many non-Indian academics. One of these is the assumption that Native Americans populated the Western Hemisphere solely by crossing a land bridge from Siberia, the Bering Strait theory.

Scientists, and I use the word as loosely as possible, are committed to the view that Indians migrated to this country over an imaginary Bering Straits bridge, which comes and goes at the convenience of the scholar requiring it to complete his or her theory. Initially, at least, Indians are [said to be] homogenous. But there are also eight major language families within the Western Hemisphere, indicating to some scholars that if Indians followed the trend that can be identified in other continents, then the migration went from east to west; tourists along the Bering straits were going *to* Asia, not migrating *from* it. (Deloria, 1996)

Although some scholars debate whether Native Americans really had a religious ethic that viewed the earth as mother, contemporary Native American religious and intellectual leaders continue to use the image with a frequency that evokes the rhetoric of Tecumseh and Black Elk. Deloria, who is arguably the father of the late twentieth century's intellectual renaissance in Native America, has been arguing ecological views of history for more than three decades with a rising sense of urgency as environmental crises intensify around the world. The stakes, in Deloria's analysis, include the future of humanity (as well as other animals) as viable species on an increasingly sullied earth.

"It will take a continuing protest from an increasingly large chorus," wrote Deloria, "to reprogram the psychology of American society so that we will not irreversibly destroy the land we live on" (Deloria, 1992, 2). His sense of urgency at the speed of environmental deterioration during the last years of the twentieth century was palatable: "Only a radical reversal of our attitudes toward nature can help us," he said (Deloria, 1992, 2). "Nor do I look Forward to paying the penalties that Mother Earth must now levy against us in order for Her to survive" (Deloria. 1992, 3). He continued:

It remains for us now to learn once again that we are part of nature, not a transcendent species with no responsibilities to the natural world. As we face the twenty-first century, the next decade will be the testing ground for this proposition. We may well become one of the few species in this vast universe that has permanently ruined our home. (Deloria, 1992, 3)

REMEMBERING DELORIA

Inside the Mount Vernon Event Center in Golden, Colorado, Deloria was remembered during the late afternoon of November 18, 2005, by a standing-room-only crowd as an activist who, with biting satire and wit, provided intellectual muscle for the Native American civil rights revolution that began in the late 1960s, propelling Native peoples away from cradle-to-grave government supervision into a new era of self-determination and active pursuit of sovereignty and exercise of treaty-defined economic rights.

Deloria was eulogized not only as an American activist but also as a more general figure who challenged mainstream religious assumptions as well as the industrial state's relationship with the earth. Doug George-Kanentiio, Mohawk activist and close friend of Deloria, recalled his "laser-light ability to zero in on the contradictions, deceptions, and lies which defined so-called 'western civilization'" (George-Kanentiio, 2005, 2).

Floyd Westerman and Joanne Shenandoah sang, after which George Tinker gave a blessing. A slide show provided glimpses of Deloria and his family. He was buried in Golden, Colorado, in the Mount Vernon Cemetery. According to an account provided by Heidi McCann, who attended the service, Philip Deloria said that, in the Lakota way, those who cross over stay here for four days, that he (Vine) visited with everyone he met (McCann, 2005).

Deloria was remembered as a family man and a lover of country music who treasured a note from Gene Audrey, dogs, professional football, and old movies, who fondly recalled his days as a Marine. The program handed out at the service called him "always a warrior, who fought the good fight until the very end [who is] even now exploring the spirit world that captivated his intellect during the course of his life" ("Celebration of the Life," 2005).

At the memorial service, Norbert Hill, a close friend of Deloria's, noted that with his passing "the training wheels had been taken off." It was now time, said Hill, for each of us to continue the struggle that Deloria had led for so long, relying now on our own individual and collective knowledge and talents. It is unquestionably true that over the last four decades we in Indian Country were overly dependent on

Deloria's penetrating knowledge; his exquisite wit; his cunning and hugely effective political, legal, and cultural strategies; and his delicious and biting humor (Wilkins, 2005).

The same day that Deloria was remembered and put to rest, Vincent Carroll, editorial page editor of the *Rocky Mountain News*, still seemed to be seething over Deloria's playful response to his relentless effort to portray the University of Colorado faculty as a hotbed of political liberalism. In a column on the newspaper's editorial page, Carroll coldly recalled Deloria as "wacky" (Carroll, 2005). Carroll condemned Deloria as antiscientific and for maintaining, in *Red Earth, White Lies* (1995), that American Indians "existed here 'at the beginning,' probably as contemporaries of dinosaurs, and this bizarre claim only hints at his contempt for much science" (Carroll, 2005).

The dinosaur quip is Carroll's invention, a gigantic stretch of Deloria's argument in the book. No humans existed *anywhere* for millions of years after the era of the dinosaurs, and Deloria knew that. One can only imagine the letter to the editor Deloria might have written had he been able to reply to Carroll.

Deloria's son Philip did reply:

> Vine Deloria Jr. . . . was open to any number of ideas that might be called "wacky." He was willing to step outside the boundaries of acceptable knowledge. . . . Of course, this isn't the first time the *News* has felt compelled to make light of his intellectual openness and curiosity. Who could forget the complaint a couple of years ago that the Center of the American West's Wallace Stegner Award was being given, not to a legitimate figure of some import, but to a "crank"?
>
> It might interest Mr. Carroll to know that the current thought regarding the peopling of the Americas is trending away from the simplicities of the Bering Straits theory—which, as you know, my father vehemently criticized—to a far more nuanced account, one open to multiple possibilities of multiple migrations. What looked wacky 10 years ago might well look quite plausible 10 years from now. Vine Deloria Jr. took seriously the possibility of an American Indian creationism, a position not so far removed from similar debates unfolding today. I trust that the *News* will be as zealous in patrolling the power and status of "science" when the subject is Christian creationism cloaked as "intelligent design." To do otherwise would be intellectually dishonest, if not also casually racist. . . . Perhaps Carroll might have waited a day? It seems unworthy of the *News*—and egregiously so—to offer such a nasty little comment on the day when Indian people from around the country were arriving *en masse* to grieve his loss and to celebrate his life. Is this the paper's general practice when a complicated thinker and public figure passes on? It seems to me ill-mannered and indecent. (Deloria, 2005)

Beating Indian drums, and demanding a meeting with editors (which was not forthcoming), the Colorado American Indian Movement (AIM) picketed the *Rocky Mountain News* the Monday after Deloria was buried. AIM's spokesman, Glenn Morris, said that Carroll had slurred a man who was "the equivalent of Thurgood Marshall, Frederick Douglass and Martin Luther King rolled into one in the eyes of the Indian world" ("AIM Fire," 2005).

The pickets at "the Rocky" recalled that little seemed to have changed since 1863, when the paper described the Ute people as "a dissolute, vagabondish, brutal and ungrateful race" that "ought to be wiped from the face of the earth" ("AIM Fire," 2005). The protesters also demanded that *Rocky Mountain News* issue an apology (which also was not forthcoming) "for its role in inciting and celebrating the Sand Creek Massacre," an 1864 assault on a peaceful Cheyenne camp in which at least 163 men women and children were murdered and mutilated ("AIM Fire," 2005).

Carroll later apologized by e-mail to Philip Deloria and then complained that he had not known Vine Deloria was being buried the day he published his derogatory column. For a man who postured as an expert news authority and who calls his own opinion column "On Point," it was a rather lame excuse. The date of Deloria's service and burial in a suburb of Denver hardly had been a state secret.

Although editors at the *Rocky Mountain News* recalled Vine Deloria Jr. as a "crank" and a "wacko," *Indian Country Today's* editors described the affection for him that poured from Native America at the same time:

> We remember the beloved teacher for his generosity of spirit. As a professor, Deloria mentored and touched many people across all ethnic and religious persuasions while always managing to teach and guide the work of scores of Native graduate students and young activists, many of whom went on to gain success and prominence on their own. He wrote prefaces and introductions and recommendations by the dozens in careful assessments of the work at hand, but was always ready to add his considerable gravity to the work of newer hands. He would not tolerate fuzzy thinking, however, and could and would hold his students to task. . . . In every generation, to paraphrase the late Creek Medicine Man Phillip Deere, there is one who hits the click-stone just right, and sparks the fire. In his generation, Vine Deloria Jr. sparked the intellectual fire of political, legal, historical and spiritual illumination. He lighted the path to the fountainhead of knowledge, which points the way ahead. ("In Memoriam," 2005)

THE RISE AND FALL OF NATIVE AMERICAN STUDIES IN THE UNITED STATES

Duane Champagne

I believe an argument can he made for decline in American Indian Studies during the 1990s, at least in organizational and resource terms. However, I will argue that there is great promise for American Indian Studies in the twenty-first century as a new and substantial paradigm that will help understand the collective and individual motivations, social and cultural change, and policies for the Indigenous peoples of North America and around the world. Native studies, focusing on the continuity of land, community, self-government, and culture, presents a new and alternative way to understand social groups, mainly Indigenous peoples, and their struggles in the contemporary context with nation-states. The Indigenous paradigm is only now gaining some attention and theoretical articulation, but it is grounded in the experiences, history, and contemporary struggles of Indigenous peoples in the United States and elsewhere. Just as the social movement of Indigenous peoples around the world gained international and national status in many countries, Indigenous studies, or American Indian Studies in the United States, has arisen to reflect, analyze, and support the policies, interests, and aspirations of Indigenous peoples. The Indigenous movement is without great political power, and does not have the favor of nation-states in the international arena, yet it is grounded in the values, cultures, histories, and governments of Indigenous peoples, and is not well explained by the usual studies based on class, race, ethnicity, or cultural studies. In my view, the Indigenous peoples movement, especially since the 1970s, but in principle since the time of first European colonial contact, requires more precise conceptualization on its own grounds as an international social movement of like cases that deserves greater analysis

and policy discussion. The Indigenous movement will not go away, and therefore the Indigenous paradigm, or the need for American Indian Studies, or Indigenous studies, will not recede. The development of an international Indigenous perspective is as strong as any time in history, but the national and international context for the Indigenous viewpoint is not favorable, both in the United States and on the international scene. American Indian Studies, its rise and fall, in many ways mirrors the political struggles of the Indigenous movement, in times when there is less nation-state support from mainstream institutions. Nevertheless, some unique history and circumstances have affected the rise and development of American Indian Studies and continue to inhibit the development of an American Indian Studies discipline.

American Indian Studies, or Native American Studies, I use the terms interchangeably, is a field in formation. American Indian Studies programs and departments first emerged during the later 1960s and early 1970s. Native American Studies is the smallest of the historically American ethnic studies programs, and increasingly the intellectual and policy stepchild of the ethnic studies movement. Nevertheless, practitioners of American Indian Studies are articulating a viewpoint on Indigenous communities that emphasizes central roles of sovereignty, land, cultural preservation, and continuity. Native American Studies is premised on the view that no other discipline studies its areas of interest. Indeed, Native American Studies proposes a perspective that includes institutional, cultural, holistic, and ethnographic understanding of community, but within the context of Indigenous worldviews, and relations to nation-states, the world-system, and cultural globalization. Native American Studies, or perhaps better, American Indian communities, propose that their status and interests require an understanding of their

Duane Champagne in *American Indian Nations*, ed. by George Horse Capture, Duane Champagne, and Chandler C. Jackson. 2007. AltaMira Press. Pages 129–143.

community organization and culture, goals of maintaining self-determination, cultural autonomy and continuity, land, and their own modes of accommodating to nation-states, global markets, and trans-societal information transfers. American Indian communities can be studied from their own points of view, values, and understandings in ways that will give greater analytic power and empowerment to the communities. Native American Studies is working toward an Indigenous paradigm with a focus on the patterns of cultural and community continuity, while at the same time making culturally and institutionally informed decisions and strategies for accommodating to a changing and globalized environment. American Indians are about preserving culture, community, land, and ensuring rights to self-government for figure generations. Native American Studies is developing points of view and conceptualizations drawing on the everyday strategies and conceptions of American Indian communities that require mainstream academics and policymakers to rethink and extend the views of Indigenous groups, as a means to include their views and social-cultural actions outside of the use of class, ethnicity, race, and even nationality. Native American Studies, and more generally Indigenous studies, calls for conceptualizations and strategies that encompass Indigenous issues, rights, and strategies of political, cultural, and territorial survival.

I will develop the argument that a paradigm for Indigenous studies has intellectual and policy promise, although the resource and organizational efforts of U.S. universities have not kept pace with the intellectual developments, and have inhibited the development of American Indian Studies as a fully developed discipline and paradigm.

THE BEGINNINGS OF NATIVE AMERICAN STUDIES

American Indian Studies programs arose within the context of the civil rights movement, and the protest about the Vietnam War, and were accompanied with a demographic shift among Native Americans toward urban life. During the 1950s many American Indians moved to cities, looking for employment and opportunities. Many began to attend colleges in larger numbers, and found that university curricula did not cover American Indian history, culture, and policy in familiar or useful ways. Consequently, American Indian students and communities sought to convince university administrations that American Indian studies needed to include more content about American Indians. The rise of American Indian Studies programs and departments coincided with the rise of ethnic studies programs, usually composed of the major, recognized, historical American minority groups, Afro-American, Asian American, Chicano/Latino, as well as American Indian. Many universities and colleges moved to create ethnic studies departments, and programs, and generally American Indian Studies was included in the movement. The programs reflected the social movement and social change trends of the 1960s and 1970s by efforts to bring more inclusion to members of historically excluded and disadvantaged groups. Minority groups struggled for more inclusion, and ethnic studies programs and departments were a means for introduction of new curricula, research, publications, faculty hiring, and student recruitment. American Indian students entered colleges and universities that heretofore had given them little attention or attention from an outsider's point of view.

Most likely, without the alliance to the larger and more visible ethnic and racial groups, many American Indian Studies programs or departments may not have been established, or at least established in the ways they started, largely as a small ethnic group, with interests of intellectual and social inclusion. The prescribed ethnic studies model, with emphasis on assimilation, inclusion, or perhaps renationalization,[1] proved only a partial model for American Indian points of view. While national trends led toward establishment of ethnic studies, their organization and relations within university administrations varied considerably. The relative success of a program or department often depended on the attention provided by university administrators. Often a successful program needed strong support from well-placed administrators who encouraged new faculty, research, and student recruitment. Administrators, however, come and go, and programs at times had attention and could grow, and at other times, administrations turned attention to other issues, and ethnic studies programs often languished in those contexts.

The trends that led toward contemporary American Indian Studies, however, arose from multiple currents. While the flow of national events toward ethnic studies was critical, there were several undercurrents that help define American Indian Studies and often threw it in intellectual and policy contention with ethnic studies and mainstream intellectual perspectives. Other trends that contributed to the present state of American Indian Studies include the Self-determination Policy (1960s to present), the history and attention of anthropologists, historians, and the rise of ethnohistory, and the American Indian movement toward self-determination and assertion of political and cultural autonomy since the 1960s. While each of the historical American ethnic groups have a unique story and relation with the United States, American Indians fit least into the ethnic group and studies conceptualization. American Indians are composed of hundreds of cultures that have had self-government, territory, and an associated form of community from time immemorial. American Indians do not have an immigrant experience during the past 500 years, as do all other ethnic groups, and American Indian governments, communities, and claims to territory predate establishment of the U.S. Constitution. American Indians are not parties to the Constitution, and most became citizens only in 1924 by an act of Congress, but did not thereby give up rights to membership in an American Indian community. American Indians are more like hundreds of small nationalities rather than an ethnic group. They do not share a common religion, culture, language, territory, or form of government. From the early colonial period in the 1600s to 1871, the European colonial powers and then the United States made government-to-government treaties with American Indian nations.

While American Indians generally have pressed their Indigenous rights to territory and self-government, the most recent policy period of self-determination is related to changing mainstream American views toward minorities, ethnic groups, and poor people's movements, most prevalent during the 1960s and 1970s. Policy and some legal victories encouraged greater assertions of self-government. Tribal governments were encouraged to manage their own affairs, organize tribal government staffs, develop economic market opportunities, and secure wider ranges of federal funding. Increasingly, tribal communities sought restoration of lands, federal recognition of government-to-government relations, legal and political participation and inclusion enough to negotiate their interests and rights. Many American Indian communities that were terminated from federal relations since the 1950s sought congressional acts to restore their rights and status as American Indian communities, and most succeeded. Over 300 federally nonrecognized Indian nations sought federal recognition, while about 560 American Indian communities are currently recognized by the federal government. Native communities sought to control their own schools, established tribally controlled community colleges, and some began to engage in high-stakes casino establishment. After some legal and political

maneuvering, American Indian government rights to manage gaining on tribal lands were upheld, but with negotiated agreements or compacts with their surrounding host states. In the middle 1940s, American Indian leaders and tribal governments formed national organizations like the National Congress of American Indians (NCAI), primarily a Washington lobbying group, all of which is a measure of increased American Indian participation in U.S. civil society. American Indian communities generally are committed to retaining culture, communities, and political processes that are informed by their cultural traditions, but at the same time live in the twenty-first century and want to meet the challenges of globalization and social change on their own cultural terms. Many tribal communities are currently looking for economic opportunities that will give them greater control over resources and support their communities, while many are rethinking their current governing organizations to make them more effective in managing contemporary political challenges, but at the same time responsive to their cultural values and community norms and political processes.[2] This movement toward greater community control and decision-making is one of the primary issues that American Indian Studies has taken up as central to establishing a discipline. Much of American Indian Studies is about contemporary American Indian life, community, and processes of change and cultural continuity. There are hundreds of American Indian communities, and there are many issues confronting the communities, such as education, nation building, contemporary art, the restoration of ceremony, use of traditional art, protection of legal rights, land protection and acquisition, protection of sacred sites and the remains of ancestors, ecological issues, economic development policy, and many more.

American Indian Studies seeks to create a discipline of study about social and cultural change that encompasses the point of view of American Indian people and communities. While the practice of ethnic studies for Afro-Americans, Asian Americans, and Chicano/Latinos generally has risen with the establishment of ethnic studies programs, there is a long historical record and scholarship about American Indians before the 1960s. Jesuit missionaries, traders, colonial officials, trade companies, and colonial governments kept records, wrote reports, and sometimes published their work.[3] In the 1720s, the Jesuit missionary Joseph-François Lafitau wrote about egalitarian and consensual American Indian political processes and cultures, directly contrasting them with the hierarchical, class-based, absolutist monarchies of Europe.[4] His work had some influence on the political theories and Enlightenment viewpoints in France and Europe. Some of the founding fathers, such as Thomas Jefferson, studied American Indian cultures and languages. Benjamin Franklin, among others, had knowledge of American Indian political processes and diplomatic patterns.[5] As early as the 1830s and 1840s, there was considerable speculation about who built the many earthen mounds and remnants of towns found in the eastern United States and Mississippi Valley. Lewis Henry Morgan, who in the 1850s published a book on the Iroquois,[6] did extensive kinship studies among American Indians.[7] Morgan is often considered the father of modern American anthropology and ethnography. Friedrich Engels and Karl Marx used Morgan's work to describe the Iroquois as a classless, precapitalist social organization, where women had political power in a consensual, egalitarian political organization.[8] The egalitarian gender, classless, and consensual political relations became a model for human social organization at the end of history within Marx's evolutionary vision. Franz Boaz and his students formed the School of American Anthropology and practiced salvage anthropology, trying desperately to record language, social organization, and culture before they vanished.[9] The Bureau of American Ethnology within the Smithsonian Institution dedicated a book series and other publications to researchers who were focused on histories and ethnographies of Indian communities.[10] Since the 1960s and 1970s, interest by anthropologists has receded, although there are still many practitioners of American Indian communities. In part because of the Boasian view that American Indian cultures were only significant for research in their pre-European-contact state, most anthropologists started looking for their material in other parts of the world, envisioning that *few* communities of interest remained in North America. Furthermore, Vine Deloria wrote critiques about anthropological methods and humanist interests[11] that led anthropologists to shy away from study of American Indian communities, although Deloria wanted the anthropologists to stay and assist contemporary American Indian communities with their present-day issues, such as poverty, retaining culture and language, political sovereignty, and the legal and legislative issues confronting Indian communities.[12] In more recent years, armed with new theoretical perspectives and viewpoints, many anthropologists have reengaged the study of American Indian societies and are researching contemporary language revival,

cultural and political change,[13] tribal federal recognition, intellectual property rights,[14] repatriation,[15] economic development, urbanization,[16] tribal cultural resource management,[17] and other issues.

There is a long record of colonial history and diplomacy that American historians have taken as their area of study. American Indian history has developed as a subarea within American history. Relations with American Indians are a central part of early U.S. history and colonial relations, and much history is devoted to localities, fur trade, diplomacy, treaties, wars, legislation, U.S. policy, legal case history, and more recently, histories of tribal communities. During the 1970s there was an outpouring of historical works about American Indians, often within the context of military and policy mistreatment.[18] The critiques of U.S. policy toward Indians helped frame the debates about self-determination, and comprised a literature that was indirectly a critique of U.S. policy in Vietnam.[19] While the outburst of historical scholarly attention declined by the 1980s, the subarea of American Indian history within U.S. history changed dramatically. By the 1990s, there was less output but more attention to Native cultures, tribal histories, Indian voices, and a more clearly organized subdiscipline.[20]

Both history and anthropology have their own disciplines, and many anthropologists and historians were not entirely satisfied with the mainstream orientations of the fields. During the 1930s and 1940s, anthropologists and historians began to develop ethnohistory—a synthesis of historical documentary and anthropological ethnographic approaches—and established a society for the study of ethnohistory in 1954. The group established a journal, *Ethnohistory*, and concentrated on the study of the history of American Indians in North America, and in more recent years has expanded its range to include cultures and communities throughout the world. The ethnohistorians focused on detailed histories and cultural studies of social and cultural change. Nevertheless, the ethnohistorians have provided a rich literature that often put Native people and communities at the center of the analysis and described them in continuous and changing social and political contexts that were often missing in the mainstream disciplines.[21] Ethnohistory explores tribal histories,[22] and religious and revitalization movements,[23] and attracts scholars from cultural anthropology, linguistics, archeology, ecology, history, and related fields. In more recent years, American Indian Studies scholars have joined the ranks of ethnohistorians. Ethnohistory seeks to develop a multidisciplinary and inclusive approach to the study of American Indian communities, and in more recent years to Indigenous peoples around the world.

THE RISE OF AMERICAN INDIAN STUDIES

When American Indian Studies programs emerged in the early 1970s, there was already a large amount of literature about American Indians in many fields. History, anthropology, and ethnohistory had dedicated subfields, or primary interests, in the study of American Indians. In addition, many other disciplines also had literatures about American Indian issues. The history of art, ethnomusicology, law, linguistics, increasingly political science, public health, English, and education contained literature or practices that included material about American Indians. Before the 1970s, few American Indians were employed as scholars. While in more recent decades the pipeline has increased, a great many postgraduate degrees for American Indians are in education, law, and professional fields, perhaps reflecting concerns for improving everyday life in Indian communities. In the early 1970s, many Afro-American, Asian American, and Latino/Chicano Studies programs moved to create a literature where there had been relatively little interest from mainstream disciplines. Since then, the ethnic studies programs have made strong arguments, and increasingly their material is entered into the mainstream disciplines. For American Indian Studies, there was already a large and in some ways centuries-old literature, although generally written and conceptualized by several fields, and generally with little intellectual input or vetting by American Indian communities or approaches. Anthropology, U.S. history, and law all had substantial American Indian subfields but nevertheless maintained theories and conceptualizations that were fostered by intellectual and other interests from the mainstream of U.S. society or within the discipline. In many ways, scholars of American Indian culture and history were taught to believe they had the best-informed understanding of American Indians.[24] American Indians were studied because they fit into a theoretical or methodological frame, and the theories and outcomes of studies generally addressed issues in U.S. society or policy. Such orientations are to be expected, and theories and studies often have goals or outcomes that have ramifications beyond the interests of the subjects. Nevertheless, many of the disciplinary academic positions could not be said to constitute American Indian Studies or

an American Indian perspective. The long history of colonial and U.S. relations created images that are part of U.S. culture and identity. While few mainstream American citizens are knowledgeable about the histories, cultures, and legal status of American Indian individuals and communities, they often have formed conceptions from mass media and mythology about American Indians. For better or worse, American Indians are a central part of U.S. past relations and nation building, and a significant part of U.S. history.

American Indian Studies began as interdisciplinary programs. Unlike other historical ethnic groups, there were few American Indian scholars available to immediately take the mantle of a new discipline. Furthermore, there were many academics from several disciplines who were engaged in work about American Indians. American Indian Studies, with a few exceptions, has taken an interdisciplinary approach and, unlike other ethnic studies programs, has been managed by scholars from a variety of disciplines. This approach had the advantage that programs could be constructed from long-standing disciplines, and often seasoned scholars could be called upon to provide guidance and support. This approach, however, did not allow a coherent presentation of a Native Studies voice or perspective, and inhibited discussion and development of American Indians Studies as a coherent disciplinary endeavor.[25] Native Studies needs faculty who are trained in the emerging discipline of American Indian Studies, or scholars who are willing to commit to a Native American Studies point of view. Like all other academic disciplines, American Indian Studies should not be a field of scholars of American Indian descent, that will doom it to a cacophony of multidisciplinary approaches, or the study of American Indians from a variety of points of view, none representing the Native point of view of themselves or their interests either future or past. A scholar of Native descent who works within contemporary mainstream disciplinary worldviews, such as, say, economics or political science, can make contributions to that discipline, and perhaps to Native peoples and issues, but is not taking a Native American Studies approach, and therefore should be supported within a mainstream academic department rather than within Native American Studies. A discipline is an agreed upon way of looking at the world, a generally agreed upon epistemology and methodology, and agreed upon goals and purposes for the knowledge. Native American Studies is not an ethnic diversity program; that view has some advantages of training and integration of scholars, but does not focus on the issues, methodologies, theories, or policies that confront Native communities and peoples in a coherent way. Native American Studies or Indigenous studies has all possibilities for developing a coherent paradigm for powerful scientific, humanistic, and policy analysis that will significantly inform current and future scholarship and serve and promote the issues and values of Indigenous communities and nations.

The effort to define and form American Indian Studies into a discipline with a well-defined method and epistemological view of American Indian histories, cultures, and processes continues into the present. Mainstream disciplines have strong investments in Native historical and cultural material, but not necessarily from the Native point of view. The entry into academia against well-established paradigms and many practitioners of those paradigms constrains the possibility of developing and introducing alternative Native-focused approaches to Indian studies. The control and ownership of American Indian topics of scholarship require that American Indian Studies needs to more clearly define and develop its own paradigm. The Indigenous paradigm must be worked out more clearly by and for scholars, and then Native American scholars need to be produced at the doctoral level to carry on the teaching, research, and policy, and to generate students for the future. There are not enough doctoral programs in American Indian Studies, and we need more, and we need to generate and sustain the scholarly viewpoints and develop an Indigenous paradigm. Gaining control of the intellectual process, training of students, recognition of a viable alternative Indigenous paradigm are necessary for future development of the field. American Indian Studies and Indigenous studies should not be a race-based or even culture-based program, but like all other disciplines is a matter of intellectual and social commitment. Those scholars, Native and non-Native, who can commit to the principles of the discipline, and who are willing to work within paradigms that are meaningful to the cultural, political, policy, and intellectual interests and values of Native communities and nations, should compose the professionals within the discipline.

Since the early 1970s, there have arisen over 100 American Indian Studies programs. The great majority of the programs have not formed departments but are organized as interdisciplinary programs.[26] American Indian Studies departments are rare; most

notable are the University of California, Davis, and the University of Minnesota, Minneapolis, which both have departments, and some of the Canadian universities have departments. Very few U.S. American Indian Studies programs have reached departmental status, and most are formed by interdisciplinary arrangements. In general there are few scholars trained in American Indian Studies at the doctoral level, and so colleges and universities draw upon related fields. Furthermore, while most colleges and universities feel compelled to have ethnic studies or American Indian Studies programs, they are prone not to invest heavily in program development. The typical American Indian Studies program is composed of several faculty who are appointed in outside departments, and whose research or interests lay related to American Indian issues. Departments control the promotions and evaluation of research, and most faculty must conform to the rules, procedures, and expectations of their departments and disciplines to maintain successful careers.

1. The interdepartmental model, where the faculty have different home departments and have only token associations with the American Indian Studies program or departments, is the most common form of organization.[27] Most programs are composed of faculty in non–Indian Studies doctoral degrees who have an expertise in American Indian culture, history, or other fields, and who are willing to teach or cross list their courses in American Indian Studies. This type of organization has the advantage of home departments for the faculty and connections with faculty and organizations outside of American Indian Studies. Faculty gain access to resources and contacts outside American Indian Studies, reducing the possibility of financial and administrative ghettoization. Most Indian Studies programs are organized along the interdepartmental model primarily for economic reasons; it is a way to use existing faculty and not have to invest in more faculty. The major drawback of the interdepartmental model is that there is a weak and underresourced faculty core, and it is difficult to develop a coherent Native perspective in the courses, since the faculty have diverse training and objectives. Faculty can gain tenure in a home department, and that is often considered a strength, but faculty are distracted by departmental demands, and their interests in advancement are usually tied to fulfilling departmental requirements, often leaving less attention for American Indian Studies. Interdepartmental programs are the main way that American Indian Studies

programs are organized around the country, especially among smaller colleges that lack resources for a department. Coherent Indian Studies perspectives are hard to maintain and develop in the interdepartmental programs because of multiple disciplines, departmental demands, and generally short resources.

2. A few universities have adopted departments, and often many Indian faculty see the department as an ideal arrangement for Indian Studies. Departments can hire a core of committed faculty. Although, since few doctorates are awarded in American Indian Studies, it is in practice very hard to identify and hire the scholars who take an Indigenous studies approach. Most prospective Indian Studies faculty are trained in mainstream disciplines and often have little training about American Indian topics, unless they choose to include research about Indians in their dissertation and research. Departments have the advantage of possibly creating a core group of faculty who share common understanding of the methods and goals of research and community relations that constitute the field of American Indian Studies. A disadvantage of the departmental model is that American Indian Studies may become ghettoized financially and administratively.

3. A third model might be called a mixed model, which is a combination of department and associated core faculty. The mixed model works best when it can exploit the strengths of the departmental and interdisciplinary models. Many interdepartmental models may evolve toward departments by creating a mixed model with a small number of core faculty located within a department, while affiliated teaching and research faculty may serve in other departments, cross listing a course within the American Indian Studies program. Mixed models may serve as transitions to departmental status, or as models in their own right. A few faculty can compose the core American Indian Studies faculty which give the program a coherent vision, research, and curriculum about American Indians and congruent with an Indigenous paradigm. Other faculty may choose to remain within the discipline and departments of their graduate training, and associate with the American Indian Studies core faculty. The model has a core faculty, but also has faculty who have ties, interests, and contacts throughout the university that may be of value to the American Indian Studies core faculty and department. One of the most successful Indian Studies programs, at the University of Arizona, uses a mixed model of about a dozen core faculty, and

another ten faculty who have other disciplinary departments but are committed to teaching and participation in the Indian Studies Department.

Another organizational feature of Indian Studies programs is their relation to ethnic studies departments or programs. Many American Indian Studies programs are embedded in ethnic studies programs. While one can make an argument for an association with ethnic studies, often on financial and university political grounds, the theoretical and policy interests and orientations of American Indian Studies are not compatible with the main ethnic studies approaches. Indigenous rights issues concerning sovereignty, land, self-government, and retention of culture are generally not central issues in the ethnic studies paradigms that emphasize diaspora, immigration, and renationalization. Often an Indigenous studies approach has little in common with ethnic studies theory, methods, and policy, and therefore makes substantive research and teaching in common with ethnic studies very difficult, and disorienting for students who want to study Indigenous studies approaches. An Indigenous studies model is a very different theoretical, policy, and methodological path than the diaspora, immigration, and renationalization models of ethnic studies or race relations. Some notable programs, such as those in the three major Arizona universities, have avoided placing American Indian Studies within pan-ethnic organizations for their campuses. Perhaps because Arizona has a relatively large American Indian population and presence, and less of a racial and ethnic minority presence, the pan-ethnic model does not appeal in Arizona. In a large, ethnically diverse state like California, American Indian Studies centers at UCLA and UC Berkeley are associated with ethnic studies, and that arrangement seems natural for university administrators. The disadvantage of ethnic studies organizations is that the perspectives of an Indigenous studies approach can be overwhelmed by the larger presence, resources, and theoretical views of the main ethnic groups.

THE FALL OF AMERICAN INDIAN STUDIES

Unlike other ethnic studies programs, American Indian Studies has been dominated and controlled by a large body of pre-existing scholarship and scholarly disciplines. Elizabeth Cook-Lynn wrote an essay, "Who Stole Native American Studies," that argues that Native American Studies has not been fully developed and has not lived up to its potential for supporting the sovereignty and nation-building interests of U.S. tribal communities.[28] The vision of Native

American Studies is yet to be realized fully, and in many ways has a long way to go in organizational and intellectual development. In some senses, the intellectual control and dominance of several disciplines have inhibited the rival intellectual and social vision of American Indian Studies to emerge and present a full intellectual point of view. American Indian Studies has not been stolen: it has not been allowed to see the light of day. The Native American Studies paradigm has not been fully realized within the present-day intellectual and ethnic competition that characterized the intellectual and resource politics of contemporary American universities. The continued emphasis on race and ethnic identity in mainstream institutions tends to overshadow the less understood perspectives of an Indigenous paradigm grounded in the cultures, sovereignty, identities, land, and nation building of Indigenous peoples.

Native American Studies departments and programs are funded largely through private and state funding. The funding of American Indian Studies puts the administration of American Indian Studies programs directly in the hands of university administrators who for the most part are not well-schooled in the history, culture, or law affecting Native Americans. Natives are generally treated as a racial or ethnic group, since that view fits well in mainstream worldviews and everyday understandings. University administrators are mandated by the state government to provide services, research, and teaching under the direction of state guidance. Since American Indian Studies programs and departments are organized within the traditions, administrations, and funding of American universities, they are generally informed by American forms of organization and criteria for knowledge, teaching, and research. U.S. universities serve the culture and interests of U.S. society, and not those of American Indian communities and nations. There is great pressure to serve university guidelines and values, and unlike most university disciplines, American Indian Studies engages in research, teaching, and community relations that necessarily involve interests, cultural orientations, policies, and legal issues that are not in conformity with the values and interests that inform university purposes, goals, and orientations.

Since universities fund American Indian Studies, they tend to believe that they own them and can administer them in ways that serve the interests of the university and its mainstream non-Indian constituency. As long as Native American communities and nations are not in a position to fund their own universities, they will find it difficult to have their interests and viewpoints expressed in university research, policies, and teaching. Tribally controlled community colleges have gone a significant direction in the way of supporting Native community values and culture within the education pathways for Native students. Nevertheless, much of the tribal community college budget comes from federal government allocations from Congress. Tribally controlled community colleges need to conform to accreditation standards, but many have strong programs in their tribal culture, history, and language. It is unlikely that Native communities will anytime soon support universities, but some tribal communities are in a position to support Native Studies programs, departments, and centers. Contributing tribal communities could specify the purposes and outcomes of gifts to universities so that their contributions serve their values and interests. This is what gift givers generally do when supporting universities; they want to see that certain information is collected, or research, teaching, or policy development is undertaken as a result of the gift. Such gifts will support Native Studies perspectives by giving legitimacy and financial support for the perspectives and research that support tribal goals, values, and policy. Without significant financial support and explicit specification by tribal communities about their needs and interests in higher education, Indigenous perspectives will have a harder time establishing themselves within the university and academic arenas.

In some ways, American Indian Studies has not risen far enough in the direction of stable paradigm to fall very far. The extensive non-Indian intellectual history and scholarship, the administrative dynamics of state universities, and funding constrain the development of American Indian Studies as a discipline and as strong university departments. In recent years these constraints have ameliorated. Many Indigenous scholars are working toward defining an Indigenous paradigm tribally, nationally, and internationally. While I have great faith that an internationally recognized Indigenous studies paradigm will be worked out and gain broad acceptance, the university bureaucratic environment, weak resource support, the emphasis on race and ethnic paradigms over an Indigenous paradigm, and the relegation of Indian Studies to serve general diversity interests for the university will continue to constrain, and often will prevent, full development of Indigenous studies departments and programs at many universities. The struggle to establish Indigenous studies departments, research programs, and full disciplinary status lies before us, and the movement will continue to be long and hard. As George Horse

Capture[29] and Elizabeth Cook-Lynn[30] say that American Indian Studies has not seen the light of day, I think there must be agreement that they are right, and we must look for ways to establish American Indian Studies as a discipline that provides information and supportive policies that will help ensure the continuity of Native cultures and nations many centuries into the future.

NATIVE AMERICAN STUDIES GOING FORWARD

Native American Studies is working toward forming its own discipline. There are several journals now established: *American Indian Quarterly*, *Wicazo Sa Review*, *American Indian Culture and Research Journal*, *Journal of American Indian Education*, and *Red Ink*. Relatively new professional organizations of American Indian scholars and the America Indian Studies Consortium have formed and meet annually. There is an ongoing discussion in the literature about how to define Native American Studies. American Indian communities have significantly different worldviews, social and political orders, and are cast in the position of protecting land, self-government, and generally nondifferentiated cultural forms and institutions. Contemporary scholarly disciplines in American universities reflect the highly organized, social-cultural processes and interests of U.S. society. And that is as it should be. In the same way, Native American Studies needs to reflect the social order, values, and interests of Native American communities. In holistic, institutionally nondifferentiated, Indigenous communities, knowledge is inherently integrated with community, culture, and political and economic relations. Native epistemologies and cultural and institutional interests need to inform the practice and intellectual production of Native American Studies.

The search for a Native American discipline must necessarily look to international Indigenous issues.[31] There are several hundred million people in the world who are living in Indigenous communities. They do not share a common culture, race, or ethnicity, but they share common features, such as culturally holistic, institutionally nondifferentiated, self-governing societies engaged in negotiations for preserving land, self-government, and cultural integrity with a surrounding nation-state. The issues confronting Indigenous peoples are not reducible to race, class, ethnicity, or other common analytical dimensions in use within mainstream disciplines. Races, classes, ethnicities, especially in the United States, do not aspire to the territorial, political, and cultural claims that are at the forefront for American Indian communities. Therefore direct racial, ethnic, and class analyses of American Indian communities do not measure important issues that are front and center for Indigenous communities. The search for Native American Studies is a search for an Indigenous paradigm, which may be defined primarily as a negotiation between Indigenous claims to autonomy and nation-state efforts at incorporation and renationalization. An Indigenous paradigm offers new ways to understand and analyze groups that heretofore have not been central to mainstream scholarship, in part owing to the absence of conceptual and analytical tools. A theory of society or social groups that includes Indigenous perspectives and social processes will be more complete and promises deeper and wider understanding of the human experience.

NOTES

1. Peter A. Kraus, "'Transnationalisim' or 'Renationalism'? The Politics of Cultural Identity in the European Union," in *The Conditions of Diversity in Multicultural Democracies*, ed. Alain-G. Gagnon, Montserrat Guibernau, and François Rocher (Montreal: McGill-Queen's University Press, 2004), 241–264.

2. Charles Wilkinson, *Blood Struggle: The Rise of Modern Indian Nations* (New York: Norton, 2005).

3. See Cadwallader Colden, *The History of the Five Indian Nations of Canada* (New York: Allentown Book, 1904); James Adair, *Adair's History of the American Indians*, ed. Samuel Williams (Johnson City, Tenn.: Wautauga Press, 1930); Edmond Atkins, *The Revolt of the Choctaw Indians*, Landowne Manuscript 809 (London Museum, 1750s); Edmond Atkins, *Indians of the Southern Colonial Frontier*, ed. Wilbur Jacobs (Columbia: University of South Carolina Press, 1954); and Henry Schoolcraft, *Indian Tribes of the United States* (Philadelphia: Lippincott, 1857).

4. Joseph François Lafitau, *Customs of the American Indians Compared with the Customs of Primitive Times*, vol. 1 (Toronto: Champlain Society, 1974), 293.

5. Donald Grinde and Bruce Johansen, *Exemplar of Liberty: Native America and the Evolution Democracy* (Los Angeles: American Indian Studies Center, UCLA, 1991), 141–168.

6. Lewis Henry Morgan, *League of the Iroquois* (North Dighton, Mass.: J.G. Press, 1995).

7. Lewis Henry Morgan, *Ancient Society* (New York: Gorder Press, 1977).

8. See Friedrich Engels, *The Origin of the Family, Private Property, and the State* (Zurich: Hottingen, 1884).

9. As an example, see Thomas Buckley, *Standing Ground: Yurok Indian Spirituality 1850–1990* (Berkeley: University of California Press, 2002).

10. As an example, see James Mooney, *The Ghost Dance Religion and Wounded Knee* (New York: Dover, 1973).

11. Vine Deloria Jr., *Custer Died for Your Sins: An Indian Manifesto* (New York: Macmillan, 1973), 78–100.

12. Steve Pavlik, ed., *A Good Cherokee, a Good Anthropologist: Papers in Honor of Robert K. Thomas* (Los Angeles: American Indian Studies Center, UCLA, 1998).

13. See Thomas Biolsi, *Organizing the Lakota: The Political Economy of the New Deal on the Pine Ridge and Rosebud Reservations* (Tucson: University of Arizona Press, 1992) and Buckley, *Standing Ground.*

14. See Mary Riley, *Indigenous Intellectual Property Rights: Legal Obstacles and Innovative Solutions* (Walnut Creek, Calif.: AltaMira Press, 2004).

15. See David Hurst Thomas, *Skull Wars: Kennewick Man, Archaeology, and the Battle for Native American Identity* (New York: Basic Books, 2000), 209–221.

16. See Susan Lobo and Kurt Peters, eds., *American Indians and the Urban Experience* (Walnut Creek, Calif.: AltaMira Press, 2001).

17. See Darby C. Strapp and Michael S. Burney, *Tribal Cultural Resource Management: The Full Circle in Stewardship* (Walnut Creek, Calif.: AltaMira Press, 2002).

18. See Dee Brown, *Bury My Heart at Wounded Knee: An Indian History of the American West* (New York: Holt, Rinehart and Winston, 1970).

19. As an example, see Ronald N. Satz, *American Indian Policy in the Jacksonian Era* (Lincoln: University of Nebraska Press, 1975).

20. As examples, see William T. Hagan, *Taking Indian Lands: The Cherokee (Jerome) Commission 1889–1893* (Norman: University of Oklahoma Press, 2003); Frederick E. Hoxie, *Parading through History: The Making of the Crow Nation in America, 1805–1935* (New York: Cambridge University Press, 1995); and Richard White, *The Middle Ground: Indians, Empires, and Republics in the Great Lakes Region, 1650–1815* (Cambridge: Cambridge University Press, 1991).

21. Russell Thornton, "Institutions and Intellectual Histories of Native American Studies," in *Studying Native America: Problems and Prospects*, ed. Russell Thornton (Madison: University of Wisconsin Press, 1998), 93–95.

22. As examples, see Georges Sioui, *Huron Wendat: The Heritage of the Circle*, trans. Jane Brierley (East Lansing: Michigan State University Press, 1999); and Bruce G. Trigger, *The Children of Aataentsic: A History of the Huron People to 1660* (Montreal: McGill-Queen's University Press, 1976).

23. As examples, see Anthony F. C. Wallace, *The Death and Rebirth of the Seneca* (New York: Vintage Books, 1972); J. B. Herring, *Kenekuk: The Kickapoo Prophet* (Lawrence: University Press of Kansas, 1988); and Robert H. Ruby and John A. Brown, *John Slocum and the Indian Shaker Church* (Norman: University of Oklahoma Press, 1996).

24. David Hurst Thomas, "The Skull Wars Revisited," presented at American Indian Nations: Yesterday, Today, and Tomorrow: A Symposium, Great Falls, Montana, 2005.

25. Elizabeth Cook-Lynn, "Who Stole Native American Studies," *Wicazo Sa Review* 12, no. 1 (1997): 9–28.

26. Duane Champagne and Jay Stauss, eds., "Defining Indian Studies through Stories and Nation Building" in *Native American Studies in Higher Education* (Walnut Creek, Calif.: AltaMira Press, 2002); and Susan Guyette and Charlotte Heth, *Issues for the Future of American Indians Studies* (Los Angeles: American Indian Studies Center, UCLA, 1985), 1–15.

27. Guyette and Heth, *Issues for the Future*, 74–76.

28. Cook-Lynn, "Who Stole Native American Studies," 9–28.

29. George Horse Capture, personal communication, Great Falls, Montana, 2005.

30. Cook-Lynn, "Who Stole Native American Studies," 24–27.

31. Duane Champagne and Ismael Abu-Saad, eds., *The Future of Indigenous Peoples: Strategies for Survival and Development* (Los Angeles: American Indian Studies Center, UCLA, 2003).

REFERENCES

"AIM Fire: The American Indian Movement Targets the Rocky." *Denver Westwood*, December 15, 2005, n.p. (in Lexis).

Carroll, Vincent. "On Point: Vine Deloria's Other Side." *Rocky Mountain News*, Novermber 18, 2005, n.p.

Cassirer, Ernest. *An Essay on Man*, New Haven, CT: Yale University Press, 1944.

"Celebration of the Life of Vine Deloria, Jr., A" Program distributed at public memorial service, Mount Vernon Event Center, Golden, Co, November 18, 2005.

Cororado American Indian Movement. "In Honor of Vine Deloria, Jr. (1933–2005)." Statement. November 14, 2005.

Dahl, Corey. "Indian Activist and Popular Author Dies; Vine Deloria Jr. Was a retired C.U. Professor." *Boulder* (Colorado) *Daily Camera*, November 15, 2005, n.p.

Deloria, Philip J. "Deloria Reveled in Thinking Outside the Box." Letter. *Rocky Mountain News*, November 23, 2005, n.p.

Deloria, Vine, Jr "Commentary: Research, Redskins, and Reality." *American Indian Quartley* 15, no. 4 (Fall 1991): 457–68.

Deloria, Vine, Jr. *Custer Died for Your Sins: An American Manifesto.* Norman: University of Oklahoma Press, [1969] 1988.

Deloria, Vine, Jr. E-mail to Bruice E. Johansen, May 15, 1996.

Deloria, Vine, Jr. *God is Red: A Native View of Religion.* 2nd ed. Golden, CO: North American Press/Fulcrum, 1992.

Deloria, Vine, Jr. *The Metaphysics of Modern Existence.* San Francisco: Harper and Row, 1979.

Deloria, Vine, Jr. *Of Utmost Good Faith.* San Francisco: Straight Arrow Books, 1971.

Deloria, Vine, Jr. *Red Earth, White Lies: Native Americans and the Myth of Scientific Fact.* New York: Schribner, 1995.

Deloria, Vine, Jr. *We Talk, You Listen, New Turf.* New York: Macmillan, 1970.

Dunesmore, Roger. "Vine Deloria, Jr." *Handbook of Native American Literature.* Ed. Andrew Wiget, New York: Garland, 1996. 411–15.

Etlinger, Charles. "Indian Scholar Blows Holes in Theories: Deloria Says Lazy Scientist Adjust Facts to Fit Ideas." *Idaho Statesman*, February 28, 1998: 1–B.

George-Kanentio, Doug. " Deloria as I Knew Him." *Indian Time* 23, no. 46 (November 17, 2005): 2–3.

Hughes, J. Donald. *American Indian Ecology.* El Paso: University of Texas Press 1983.

"In Memoriam: Deloria, Vine, Jr. *Indian Country Today.* November 17, 2005. <http://www.indiancountry.com/content.cfm?id=1096411939>.

Johnson, Kirk. "Deloria, Vine, Jr., Champion of Indian Rights, Dies at 72." *The New York Times*, November 15, 2005. <http:www.nytimes,com/2005/11/15/national/15deloria.html.

Lyons, Oren, John Mohawk, Vine Deloria Jr., Laurence Hauptman, Howard Berman, Donald A Grinde Jr., Curtis Berkey, and Robert Venbles. *Exiled in the Land of the Free: Democracy, Indian Nations, and the Constitution.* Santa Fe, NM: Clear Light, 1992.

McCann, Heidi. Personal communication with the author. November 19, 2005.

Wilitz, Teresa. "An Anniversary Celebration: Native American Author Exults in Gadfly Role at Newberry Conference." *Chicago Tribune*, September 15, 1997: Tempo 1.

Wilkens, David. "Native Visionary spoke for All Disadvantaged Americans." *Indian Country Today.* December 1, 2005. <http://www.indiancountry.com/content.cfm?d=1096412026>.

Williams, Matt. "Renowned Native American Scholar Dies." *Colorado Daily*, November 14, 2005. <http:www.coloradodaily.com/articles/2005/11/14/news/c_u_and_boulder/news2/txt>.

Baffin Bay

Arctic
Ocean

Ingalik

Koyukon

Yupik

Athabaskan

Aleut

Gwichin

Ahtna

Tlingit

Inuit

Athabaskan

Inuit

Atlantic
Ocean

Haida

Chippewyan

Hudson
Bay

Labrador Inuit

Naskapi

Nuxal

Metis

Metis

Cffia

James
bay
cree

Montagnais

Pacific
Ocean

Sokomish
Quinault

Blackfeet

Okanagan

Dakota

Salish

Dree

Cree

Ojibway

Algonkin

Mi'kmac

Passamoquoddy

Yakima Flathead
Nisqually
Nez Perce

Klamath Bannock
Shoshne

Isstsistas
crow

Hidatsa
Mandan
Arikara

Dakota

Menominee
winnebago

Potawatomi

Mohawk
Oneida

Iroquois

Wampanoag
Narragansett

Karok
Hupa
Pomo

Modoc
wintun
pit river

Lakota

Sioux

Cayuga Seneca
Onondaga
Pamunkies
Delaware

Maidu

Ponca

Kickapoo

Powhatan

Mewuk

Omaha

Shawnee Tuscarora
Chickahominy

Ohlone Yokut

Arapaho

Paiute

UTE

Chumash

Acjachemen
Luiseno
Cahuilla

Havasupa
Hualapai
Mojave
Yavapai

Navajo/dine
Hopi
Zuni
Apache
Pima
Yaqui

Laguna Pueblo

Potawatomi
Seminole
Cheyenne
Cherokee

Osage

Cherokee

Chickasaw

Atlantic
Ocean

Kiowa
Comanche

Creek

Lumbee

Tohono o'odham

Natchez

Choctaw
Yamasee

Cantaba

Yaqui

Kickapoo

Seminole O

Gulf of
Mexico

Arawak

Carib

Native Hawaiians

Hawaiian Islands

pericu

Yucatan
Maya

Caribbean
Sea

Aztec
Mixtec
Trique Zapotec
Chatino

Maya

Mosquito

Cuna

N

Selected
Indigenous Peoples
of North America

0   250   500   750   1000 miles

Pacific
Ocean

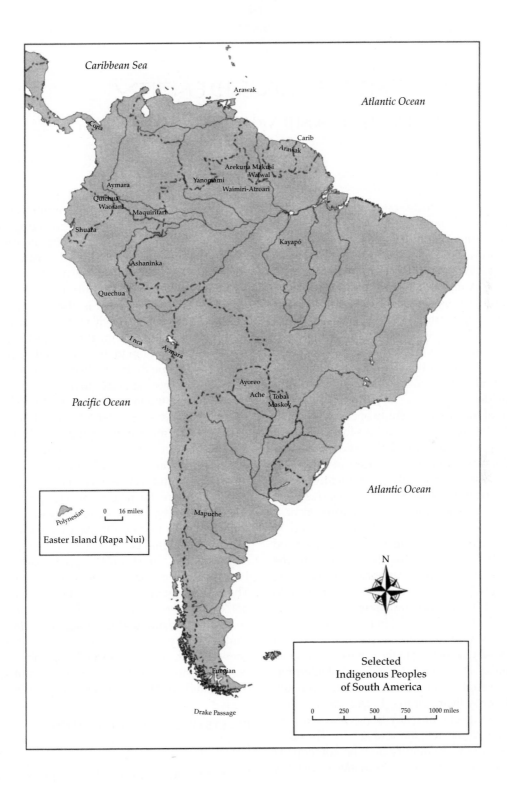

Caribbean Sea

Atlantic Ocean

Arawak

Cona

Carib

Arawak

Aymara

Arekuna Makusi
Wafwal

Yanomami

Waimiri-Atroari

Quichua
Waorani

Maquiritarí

Shuara

Kayapó

Ashaninka

Quechua

Inca

Aymara

Ayoreo

Ache   Toba
Maskoy

Pacific Ocean

Mapuche

Atlantic Ocean

N

Polynesian

0   16 miles

Easter Island (Rapa Nui)

Fuegian

Drake Passage

Selected
Indigenous Peoples
of South America

0   250   500   750   1000 miles

INDIGENOUS IDENTITY
WHAT IS IT, AND WHO *REALLY* HAS IT?

Hilary N. Weaver

Indigenous identity is a truly complex and somewhat controversial topic. There is little agreement on precisely what constitutes an Indigenous identity, how to measure it, and who truly has it. Indeed, there is not even a consensus on appropriate terms. Are we talking about Indians, American Indians, Natives, Native Americans, Indigenous people, or First Nations people? Are we talking about Sioux or Lakota? Navajo or Dine? Chippewa, Ojibway, or Anishnabe? Once we get that sorted out, are we talking about race, ethnicity, cultural identity, tribal identity, acculturation, enculturation, bicultural identity, multicultural identity, or some other form of identity?

The topic of Indigenous identity opens a Pandora's box of possibilities, and to try to address them all would mean doing justice to none. This article provides background information on three facets of identity—self-identification, community identification, and external identification—followed by a brief overview of measurement issues and my reflections on how internalized oppression/colonization is related to identity. The terms *Native* and *Indigenous* are used interchangeably to refer to the descendants of the original inhabitants of North America. These are not, per se, the "right" terms or the only terms that could have been used. They reflect my preferences.

Cultural identity, as reflected in the values, beliefs, and worldviews of Indigenous people, is the focus of the article. Those who belong to the same culture share a broadly similar conceptual map and way of interpreting language. People can identify themselves in many ways other than by their cultures. In fact, identity may actually be a composite of many things such as race, class, education, region, religion, and gender. The influence of these aspects of identity on who someone is as an Indigenous person is likely to change over time.

Hilary N. Weaver, *American Indian Quarterly*, vol. 25, no. 2, (Spring, 2001), pp. 240–255. Notes have been omitted in this section.

Identities are always fragmented, multiply constructed, and intersected in a constantly changing, sometimes conflicting array. Although in reality the various facets of identity are inextricably linked, for the purposes of this essay I will focus on culture as a facet of identity.

While Indigenous identity is a topic that I have done some research on, it is also a topic that I, as a Lakota woman, approach with subjectivity. Rather than solely a limitation, this subjectivity adds an important dimension to the work. Native people must begin to examine their own histories and issues rather than leaving these analyses to nonnatives. My work is influenced by the facts that my mother's parents left Rosebud decades ago after attending boarding school and I live in an urban setting largely made up of Haudenosaunee people. Additionally, my professional affiliation as a social worker leads me to focus on aspects of cultural identity that tend to have practical implications for helping service providers understand their Indigenous clients. As well as drawing on the literature, I draw on my own experiences and bring my personal perspectives to the topic.

My father came from an Appalachian background. He was the one who remembered and told the stories. Thus, I begin with a story about cultural identity. I do not know the original source, but the story rings with an important truth and is a poignant commentary on contemporary Indigenous identity. My appreciation goes out to the original storytellers, whoever they may be. A brief summary of the story is warranted here (See highlighted box 'The Big Game' on page 29.).

FACETS OF CULTURAL IDENTITY

Overview

In recent years there has been a growing literature on identity, accompanied by many deconstructive critiques of this concept. Generally, identification is

"THE BIG GAME"

The day had come for the championship game in the all-Native basketball tournament. Many teams had played valiantly, but on the last day the competition came down to the highly competitive Lakota and Navajo teams. The tension was high as all waited to see which would be the best team.

Prior to the game, some of the Lakota players went to watch the Navajos practice. They were awed and somewhat intimidated by the Navajos' impressive display of skills. One Lakota who was particularly anxious and insecure pointed out to his teammates that some of the Navajo players had facial hair. "Everyone knows that Indians don't have facial hair," he stated. Another Lakota added that some of the Navajos also had suspiciously dark skin. They concluded, disdainfully, that clearly these were not Native people and, in fact, were probably a "bunch of Mexicans." The so-called Navajos should be disqualified from the tournament, leaving the Lakota team the winner by default.

That same afternoon, some Navajo players went to watch the Lakota team practice. The Lakotas had a lot of skillful moves that made the Navajos worry. One Navajo observed, "That guy's skin sure looks awful light." Another added, "Yeah, and most of them have short hair." They concluded, disdainfully, that clearly these were not Native people and, in fact, were probably a "bunch of white guys." The so-called Lakotas should be disqualified from the tournament, leaving the Navajos the winners by default.

The captains from both teams brought their accusations to the referee just before game time. Both teams agreed that Native identity must be established before the game could be played and that whichever team could not establish Native identity to everyone's satisfaction must forfeit. The Lakota captain suggested that everyone show his tribal enrollment card as proof of identity. The Lakotas promptly displayed their "red cards," but some of the Navajos did not have enrollment cards. The Lakotas were ready to celebrate their victory when the Navajo captain protested that carrying an enrollment card was a product of colonization and not an indicator of true identity. He suggested that the real proof would be a display of Indigenous language skills, and each Navajo proceeded to recite his clan affiliations in the traditional way of introducing himself in the Navajo language. Some of the Lakotas were able to speak their language, but others were not. The teams went back and forth proposing standards of proof of identity, but each proposed standard was self-serving and could not be met by the other team. As the sun began to set, the frustrated referees canceled the championship game. Because of the accusations and disagreements that could not be resolved there would be no champion in the Indigenous tournament.

based on recognition of a common origin or shared characteristics with another person, group, or ideal leading to solidarity and allegiance. Beyond this, the discursive approach sees identification as an ongoing process that is never complete. Additionally, identities do not exist before they are constructed.

Most theorists agree that identity exists, not solely within an individual or category of individuals but through difference in relationship with others. Thus, there was no Native American identity prior to contact with Europeans. Likewise, immigrants from various European nations had to learn to define themselves as white rather than according to their national origins or cultural groups. Before contact, Indigenous people identified themselves as distinct from other Indigenous people and constructed their identities in this way. Indeed, this is still the case for many who see themselves as members of their own nations rather than members of a larger group represented by the umbrella term *Native American*.

The constructionist approach to representation states that meaning is constructed through language. Thus, the words we choose to use such as *American Indian*, *Native American*, or *First Nations* not only reflect but shape identity. Likewise, using English translations for Indigenous words shapes meanings. Today, Native people often learn about themselves and their culture in English and therefore adopt some stereotypes and distorted meanings.

The label "Indian" has served to reinforce the image of Indigenous people as linked to a romantic past. "Indians" are the images in old photographs, movies, and museum cases. It is a label for people who are fundamentally unknown and misrecognized by nonIndigenous people. Indeed, an "Indian" is constituted in the act of naming. Those who are relatively powerless to represent themselves as complex human beings against the backdrop of degrading stereotypes become invisible and nameless.

Identity is shaped, in part, by recognition, absence of recognition, or misrecognition by others: "A person or group of people can suffer real damage, real distortion, if the people or society around them mirror back to them a confining or demeaning or contemptible picture of themselves. Nonrecognition or misrecognition can inflict harm, can be a form of oppression, imprisoning someone in a false, distorted, and reduced mode of being." This misrecognition has oppressed Indigenous people and has imprisoned them within a false "Indian" identity.

How an Indigenous cultural identity is defined by Natives and nonnatives has been complex in both contemporary and historical times. It is misleading to assume that all Indigenous people experience a Native cultural identity in the same way just because they were born into a Native community. This glosses over the multifaceted and evolving nature of identity as well as cultural differences among and within Native nations.

Additionally, identity can be multilayered. For some, a subtribal identity such as clan affiliation is primary. For others, identification with a tribe or a region like the Northern Plains is most meaningful. Still others espouse a broader identity as Native or Indigenous people. Different levels of identity are likely to be presented in different contexts: "Thus, an American Indian might be a 'mixed-blood' on the reservation, from 'Pine Ridge' when speaking to someone from another reservation, an 'Oglala Sioux' or 'Lakota' when asked about tribal affiliation, or an 'American Indian' when interacting with non-Indians."

Identity is a combination of self-identification and the perceptions of others. There are widespread disputes about who can assert a Native identity and who has the right to represent Indigenous interests. Such conflicts occur when self-identification and the perceptions of others are at odds. Some people who assert Indigenous identity do not appear phenotypically Native, are not enrolled, and were not born on reservations or in some other Native communities. Some of these individuals indeed have Indigenous heritage, and others do not. Other people are enrolled or have Native heritage but know little about their cultures. This may be because they have no interest or no one to teach them or because of factors such as racism and stereotypes that inhibit their willingness to pursue an Indigenous identity. Some Indigenous communities, such as the Mashpee, have experienced significant racial mixing. Marriage between Europeans and Indigenous people was sanctioned and rewarded by U.S. government officials as a way to assimilate and acculturate Native people. This raises the question, Did the Mashpee and similar Indigenous communities absorb outsiders, or were they absorbed into the American melting pot? These issues of authenticity permeate the story "The Big Game" as players try to exclude others from the competition. Indeed, identity is always based on power and exclusion. Someone must be excluded from a particular identity in order for it to be meaningful.

Self-Identification

Self-perception is a key component of identity. For some, expression of a Native identity may be little more than a personal belief about heritage expressed on a census form. Cultural identity is not static; rather, it progresses through developmental stages during which an individual has a changing sense of who he or she is, perhaps leading to a rediscovered sense of being Native. There is some level of choice involved in accepting a Native identity, although the range of choices is limited by factors such as phenotypical appearances. Choice may also be influenced by social, economic, and political factors. For example, a climate filled with discrimination may lead an individual to reject a Native identity, whereas a climate in which a Native identity is seen as fashionable and perhaps financially profitable may lead an individual to assert an Indigenous identity.

In some instances, asserting an Indigenous cultural identity is related to resisting assimilation. Navajo and Ute youth who grow up off the reservation with limited connections to their cultural past or traditional ceremonies often define their Indigenous identity and cultural pride through resistance to the domination of the white community. For example, attending and doing well in school are defined as important and good by the surrounding white community, yet these youth often drop out, not because they are "bad" or incapable of school success but as a way of defying the dominant society. Resistance of "goodness" as framed by whites and insistence on living their lives as Indigenous people, in the many different ways in which they define it, are at the core of their actions.

Developing a cultural identity consists of a lifelong learning process of cultural awareness and understanding. Because the formation of identity takes place over time, a strong cultural identity may increase with age. In addition to a growing cultural attachment as individuals get older, there seems to be a revitalization in Indigenous cultures and communities across the country. Indeed, individual cultural renewal and collective cultural renewal are intertwined.

In the story "The Big Game," all the players see themselves as Indigenous people, yet the ways in which they define themselves are contested by others. A stalemate occurs when it becomes impossible to reach an agreement between self-definitions and external definitions of identity.

Community Identification

Indigenous identity is connected to a sense of people-hood inseparably linked to sacred traditions, traditional homelands, and a shared history as Indigenous people. A person must be integrated into a society, not simply stand alone as an individual, in order to be fully human. Additionally, identity can only be confirmed by others who share that identity. The sense of membership in a community is so integrally linked to a sense of identity that Native people often identify themselves by their reservations or tribal communities. This stands in striking contrast to the practice of many members of the dominant society who commonly identify themselves by their professional affiliations. Tribal members have an enduring sense of their own unique Indigenous identity. The sense of a traditional homeland is so strong for many Navajos that when outside their traditional territory and away from sacred geography they sometimes experience an extreme imbalance that can only be corrected by returning to their home communities for ceremonies.

Tribal communities, and thus their members, maintain their identities relative to the identities of neighboring communities. In the past, neighboring communities consisted of other Indigenous groups; now they are groups from other cultures. Sometimes identity boundaries are defined by policy and law as well as convention. Tribes have the right to determine criteria for membership. This regulation of membership, in some ways a form of regulating identity, has implications for political access and resource allocation. Likewise, enrollment (or lack thereof) has implications for how a person perceives him- or herself and is perceived by others, both within and outside of the Native community.

Cultural identity not only exists in contrast to surrounding communities; differences are also found among Indigenous people within a community. Csordas describes how the types of healing used by various Navajo people indicate and reinforce their cultural identity. Whether an individual participates in traditional, Native American Church, or Christian forms of healing reflects a sense of identity and self-worth as a Navajo.

For some Indigenous people, a sense of community identity comes increasingly from intertribal or pan-Indian groups. Nagel points to activist developments such as the occupation of Alcatraz; the development of the Red Power movement, the occupation of Wounded Knee, fish-ins, and the Trail of Broken Treaties as turning points in the evolution of Indigenous identity. Through these activist efforts, some Indigenous people began to see Native heritage as a valuable part of personal identity and as a foundation for pan-Indian solidarity. Although a growing climate of activism led to increased cultural renewal, this should not obscure the social and cultural continuity that has been maintained in some communities.

In the story "The Big Game," the players are members of teams. The teams validate and reinforce each member's identity as a basketball player, just as Native communities validate and reinforce the identities of their members. Being part of a larger group is critical to identity in both cases.

External Identification

Native identity has often been defined from a nonnative perspective. This raises critical questions about authenticity: Who decides who is an Indigenous person, Natives or nonnatives? The federal government has asserted a shaping force in Indigenous identity by defining both Native nations and individuals. Federal policy makers have increasingly imposed their own standards of who is considered a Native person in spite of the fact that this is in direct conflict with the rights of tribes/nations.

The role of the federal government in shaping an Indigenous identity can be pervasive but hard to define. The United States declared Indigenous people to be members of domestic dependent nations, wards of the federal government, and even U.S. citizens. This raises interesting questions, such as, What is the influence of social and economic policies on identity? Can someone else's laws define who we are? Do we adopt an identity as farmers because that is what the Allotment Act intended? Deloria sets the stage for many such questions, yet the answers are complex and elusive.

Some Native nations are not acknowledged to exist by the federal government. This lack of recognition has implications for how these tribes/nations are viewed by other people as well as how they view themselves. Issues of authenticity are increasingly debated in the courts as some Native groups seek federal recognition and a return of traditional lands. In the case of the Mash-pee, who sued for a return of land, the primary issue was whether the group calling itself the Mashpee Tribe was in fact an Indian tribe and, if so, whether it was the same tribe that lost land through a series of contested legislative acts in the mid-nineteenth century. A similar issue of authenticity exists for individuals who are not enrolled in their nations for whatever reason: "Although tribal status and Indian identity have long been vague and politically constituted, not just anyone, with some native blood or claim to adoption or shared tradition can be an Indian, and not just any Native American group can decide to be a tribe and sue for lost lands."

Stereotypes have a powerful influence on identity Popular notions of Native identity are stereotypical and locked in the past. In movies and writing, Indigenous people seem permanently associated with notions of the old American frontier. Nonnative people may view Indigenous people as having a harmonious relationship with nature and possessing an unspoiled spirituality. Sometimes Indigenous people are viewed as tourist attractions, victims, and historical artifacts. Vizenor asserts that Indigenous identities have been censored. NonIndigenous people do not want to see aspects of Native people that do not support their own ideas and beliefs, thus leading to a perpetuation of stereotypes. These external perceptions may influence how Indigenous people view themselves.

Historically, Indigenous people knew who they were, and today most continue to trace identity through descent, lineage, and clan, but the federal government's preoccupation with a formal definition has caused many problems. Indeed, there is considerable variation within branches of the federal government as to how Native people are defined, and these definitions are often at odds with state and tribal definitions.

The way we choose to define ourselves is often not the way that others define us. "The Big Game" is an example of how conflicting definitions of identity can lead to hostilities. When the members of one team identify themselves with enrollment cards, this is perceived as a threat to the self-defined identities of those without cards. Likewise, when the other team asserts that identity is grounded in the ability to speak an Indigenous language, this threatens the self-perceptions of those who speak only English. Searching for the "right" criteria is both counterproductive and damaging.

Reflections on the Facets of Identity

The facets of identity interact with and sometimes reinforce or challenge each other. Given the strong emphasis on the collectivity in Indigenous cultures, it is problematic to have an individual who self-identifies as Indigenous yet has no community sanction or validation of that identity. Historical circumstances, however, led to thousands of Native people being taken from their communities and raised without community connections through mechanisms such as interracial adoption, foster care, and boarding schools. Indeed, there are many Indigenous people with tenuous community connections at best, and some of them try to reassert an Indigenous identity and find their way home to their cultures.

Establishing community connections is often an arduous task. Some Indigenous people may offer support and guidance to those who try to find their way home to their tribal communities. This can be a positive experience of reintegration and cultural learning. In other instances, support is not forthcoming, and many roadblocks are raised by other Indigenous people playing a gatekeeping function.

External, nonIndigenous validation of Native identity, unlike community validation, is not grounded in a reasonable foundation. While it makes sense that a community should define its members, it does not make sense for an external entity to define Indigenous people. It is not up to the federal government or any dominant society institution to pass judgment on the validity of any individual's claim to an Indigenous identity. Likewise, it is not up to the Navajos in the story to define who the Lakotas are, nor should the Lakota attempt to define who is truly Navajo.

MEASURING IDENTITY

Although there is no consensus about what Indigenous cultural identity and its various facets are, there is no shortage of attempts to measure this phenomenon. Identity is expressed as a measurable or quantifiable entity far more for Indigenous people than for any other group. The federal government and most tribes use some form of blood quantum measurement. Such measures are commonly used, although biological heritage is clearly not synonymous with any level of cultural connection. When the practice of defining Native identity by blood quantum is combined with the highest rate of inter-marriage of any group (75 percent), Native people seem to be on a course of irreversible absorption into the larger U.S. society. Scholars such as Jaimes and Rose suggest that the federal government has an interest in the statistical extermination of Indigenous people, thereby leading to an end to treaty and trust responsibilities.

Because race is not an adequate indicator of culture, identity is something that should be assessed rather than assumed. Various scales have been developed to assess Indigenous people's cultural identity along a continuum from traditional, to integrated/bicultural, to assimilated. See, for example, the scales developed recently by Young, Lujan, and Dixon and Garrett and Pichette. Such scales are often modeled on scales developed for other cultural groups such as Latinos and tend to have questions that focus on language, ethnic origin of friends and associates, music and food preferences, and place of birth.

Many measures of cultural identity are actually measures of acculturation (into the dominant society). Additionally, some measures, such as the one developed by Zimmerman, Ramirez-Valles, Washienko, Walter, and Dyer, have been developed to assess enculturation, the lifelong learning process of cultural awareness and understanding. Both acculturation and enculturation scales tend to use linear continua. The utility of a linear model in representing such a complex concept has been challenged by scholars such as Oetting and Beauvais, who propose an orthogonal model of cultural identification in which attachment to one culture does not necessarily detract from attachment to another and multiple cultural identifications are not only possible but potentially healthy. Likewise, Deyhle has found that linear and hierarchical models of biculturalism are limited and neglect the context of racism. Theorists and researchers who use linear models often speak of cultural conflict and individuals being caught between two worlds, a circumstance that leads to a variety of social difficulties, but Deyhle believes that this perspective does not accurately depict the realities of Native youth. Rather than determining where someone fits on a continuum between two cultural identities or worlds, it may be more accurate to say that Indigenous people live in one complex, conflictual world.

In the end, although it is clearly inappropriate to make assumptions about an individual's cultural identity based on appearance or blood quantum, most attempts to measure identity are of questionable adequacy and accuracy: "Indianness means different things to different people. And, of course, at the most elementary level, Indianness is something only experienced by people who are Indians. It is how Indians think about themselves and is internal, intangible, and metaphysical. From this perspective, studying Indianness is like trying to study the innermost mysteries of the human mind itself." The conflict in the story "The Big Game" illustrates the difficulty inherent in measuring identity by any one standard.

INTERNALIZED OPPRESSION/COLONIZATION

Perhaps the harshest arbiters of Native identity are Native people themselves. Federal policies that treated Native people of mixed heritage differently than those without mixed heritage effectively attacked unity within Native communities, thereby turning Indigenous people against each other. Some Native people fight others fiercely to prevent them from claiming a Native identity. Sometimes Native people, as well as the federal government, find a financial incentive to prevent others from declaring themselves to be Indigenous. In 1979, the Samish and Snohomish of Puget Sound were declared "legally extinct" by the federal government in part because other Native groups such as the Tulalips did not view them as genuine. Likewise, the Lumbees of North Carolina, one of the largest tribes in the 1990 census, had difficulty gaining social and federal acceptance as constituting legitimate Indigenous communities because of intertribal disputes over timber resources. After a long fight they received only limited federal acknowledgment with the proviso that they receive no federal services.

Internalized oppression, a by-product of colonization, has become common among Indigenous people. We fight among ourselves and often accuse each other of not being "Indian enough" based on differences in politics, religion, or phenotype: "Mixed-heritage members may see traditionals as uncivilized and backwards. Traditionalists may believe that progressives are 'less Indian' because of cultural naivete and that multi-heritage people only claim tribal membership for land and annuity purposes." Such fighting among ourselves only serves to divide communities. In some regions of the country it is common to see the bumper sticker "FBI: Full Blooded Indian." What message does this communicate to people of mixed heritage? Does this mean that they are somehow lesser human beings and cannot have strong cultural connections?

Skin color and phenotype lead to assumptions about identity, suspicion, and lack of acceptance.

A survey of Indigenous helping professionals has found that one of the most prominent challenges of Indigenous people in higher education is struggling with the stereotypes that others hold about them. Sometimes these stereotypes are held by people of other cultural groups, but often they are held by other Native people who make assumptions about cultural identity based solely on physical appearance. These assumptions have led to painful experiences such as ostracism from other Indigenous people and people having their identities contradicted and denied.

Some of the propensity toward exclusivity and denying the cultural identities of mixed-blood people comes from the exploitation experienced by Native people and communities for centuries. There is well-founded suspicion of people who claim a Native heritage but have no apparent connections to an Indigenous community. In today's climate, in which New Age spirituality has become popular and so much cultural appropriation has happened, there is a fear of the ultimate cultural appropriation: the usurpation of Native cultural identity. When people with minimal Native heritage, no cultural knowledge, and no kinship ties attempt to assert an Indigenous identity, it is often hotly contested among Indigenous people, yet this does not appear to be much of an issue for others who are not Indigenous. It is fairly common for the nonnatives I encounter to have difficulty seeing any reason for concern when a person claims to be Native but has no cultural knowledge, community connections, or verifiable ancestry.

Suspicion about the identity of some Native people has been fueled by the recent growth of the Indigenous population according to U.S. census counts. Some people believe that others are inappropriately self-identifying as Indigenous because it may be "fashionable" at this time. Another possible explanation is that now it is safer for people of mixed heritage to publicly proclaim cultural pride in an Indigenous identity. A renaissance in Native cultures has been paralleling dramatic population growth since the 1960s. Political revitalization, linguistic revival, membership growth, and cultural revitalization have all taken place in recent decades. The proliferation of Indigenous organizations and activism has served as a catalyst for the resurgence of individual Native identity as reflected in the census and the renewal of tribal and urban community life.

Although I stated earlier that there is no "correct" terminology for Indigenous people, semantics is certainly an issue that evokes strong feelings. Many people express clear preferences for certain terms (e.g., *Native American* rather than *American Indian* or *First Nations people* rather than more commonly used terms). Indigenous people who attempt to dictate to other Indigenous people what they should call themselves replicate the oppression that has been imposed on them. In recent years many Native nations have begun to return to their traditional names rather than use those imposed by external forces. While many people, myself included, view this as a positive step toward cultural revitalization and pride, it would be inappropriate to impose this requirement on others. As a child I was raised referring to myself as Sioux. As I grew older and the political climate changed, I took pride in calling myself Lakota. It is not unusual, however, for some to continue using the term *Sioux*. This is their right and reflects aspects of their identity. Although the names that Indigenous groups were given by others often have a derogatory origin, we only make this worse when Indigenous people who consider themselves decolonized mock others who continue to use such terms.

While we as Indigenous people were busy guarding against cultural appropriation, we may have missed a much bigger threat to Indigenous continuity. Indeed, there are some nonnatives who pose as Natives and some Natives who sell traditions and spirituality for a profit, but the self-appointed "identity police," those who divide communities and accuse others of not being "Indian" enough because they practice the wrong religion, have the wrong politics, use the wrong label for themselves, or do not have the right skin color, should also be an issue of concern. Some Indigenous people ask, "Are you Indian, or are you Christian?" as if these are mutually exclusive categories. I have seen caring Indigenous people driven to tears at their jobs at a Native community center when they were berated for having some white ancestry. People have been publicly humiliated because someone decided that their tribal affiliations were inappropriate. This harassment and badgering is conducted by Indigenous people, against Indigenous people. The roots for this type of behavior probably lie deep in the accusers' own insecurities about identity and racism learned as part of the colonization process.

Many Indigenous traditions speak of people returning who have been alienated from their communities. I know of no Indigenous people who are not well aware of the generations of Native people that grew up outside their traditions. Although there is no doubt of the existence of these people, there is often suspicion when an unknown individual seeks information on possible community connections. This is one of the factors that mobilizes the "identity police." While, indeed, there probably are some people pretending to have Indigenous heritage along with those who really do, pretenders will ultimately get what they deserve without any intervention from the "identity police."

Through internalized oppression/colonization, we have become our own worst enemy. The hateful accusations that are hurled at some serve to hurt our communities. "The Big Game" illustrates this point. It is a story of the pain we inflict on each other as a result of internalized colonization.

Indigenous identity is a complex and multifaceted topic. I have discussed some of these facets here along with my own reflections on internalized oppression/colonization. Although a variety of literature is cited from people currently writing in this area, the perspective that comes across is a reflection of my own beliefs, sense of self, and identity as a Lakota woman living in a particular time and place. While my views may differ from those of some Indigenous people, others may find something in my words that resonates with their own perspectives.

Sometimes we are our own worst enemies. Our divisions should be reconcilable, but internalized colonization and oppression just lead to deeper divisions. Features of internalized oppression and colonization can be found in many oppressed communities in addition to the Indigenous communities discussed here. Actions and reactions born of internalized oppression and colonization are themselves acts of colonization that mirror the oppressors' acts. Until we are able to put aside our own insecurities that lead us to accuse others, there will be no winners among Indigenous people.

PEOPLEHOOD MATRIX

Tom Holm

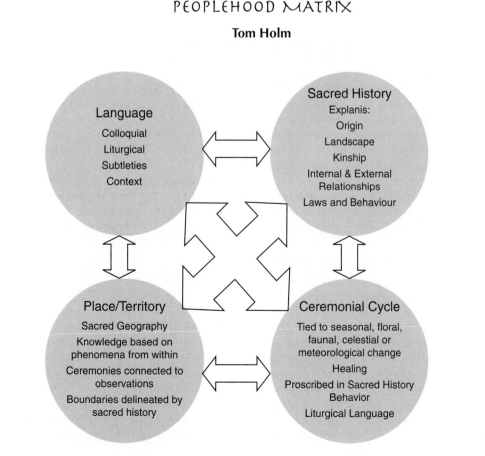

The Peoplehood Matrix demonstrating tribal group identity as delineated byTom Holm.

"Understanding the interrelationship of the four aspects of peoplehood is essential. No single factor is more important than the others and all necessarily support each other as well as a particular group's larger sense of identity. Some of the elements of peoplehood can be symbolic of identity, as in the case of a group's holy land that is no longer its home land. But in the final analysis,the factors of peoplehood make up a complete system that accounts for particular social, cultural, political, economic, and ecological behaviors exhibited by groups of people indigenous to particular territories. The elements of the peoplehood matrix function beyond their use as symbols. The diagram of the peoplehood model shows the four factors as they intertwine, interpenetrate, and interact. Having a distinct language, of course, sets a group apart in and of itself. But a group-particular language, by way of its nuances, references, and grammar, gives a sacred history a meaning of its own, particularly if origin, creation, migration, and other stories are spoken rather than written. Language defines place and vice versa. Place-names, for example, essentially be speak a relationship with the environment or describe an area within the context of a group's sacred history and culture. A particular group's language is, more often than not, liturgical as well as colloquial. Religious ceremonies are usually performed using a language that is familiar within the group. On the other hand, language can be symbolic, and ritual language might not have meaning in any other context than in a particular religious ceremony. The peoplehood model is a holistic matrix and reflects a much more accurate picture of the ways in which Native Americans act, react, pass along knowledge, and connect with the ordinary as well as the supernatural worlds."

Compiled from a lecture and the article "Peoplehood: A Model for the Extension of Sovereignty in Ameican Indian Studies," by Tom Holm, J. Diane Pearson, and Ben Chavis.

FIRST NATIONS
INDIGENOUS PEOPLES OF CANADA

Steve Talbot

CANADA'S FIRST NATIONS: A PROFILE

The 1996 census enumerated almost 800,000 Indigenous people in Canada, constituting 3 percent of the total population of twenty-eight and a half million. Over a half million are legally recognized as Indians. In addition, the Inuit are estimated at 41,000, and the Métis slightly more than 210,000. Before the arrival of Europeans, there were, of course, many thousands more. Some scholars believe that a major decrease in the aboriginal population occurred in the 1500s, as a result of the rapid spread of European-introduced diseases, preceding the actual incursion of Europeans into Native territory.

The imperial designs of two mercantile capitalist nations, France and Great Britain, have left a heavy imprint on the fate of the First Nations of Canada. Beginning in the 1600s, the movement of Europeans across that part of North America that became Canada was initially from east to west, and then, later, from south to north. Conquest took place in several stages: first, exploration along the unorganized frontier; second, trade and Christian missionary activity; third, European settlement with the resulting displacement of the Native peoples; and fourth, administrative control of the subject Indigenous peoples.

In the early historic period, the British created treaties, while the French made few treaties with Indian nations. Both, however, created military alliances with Native peoples to carry out their economic objectives in North America, the French allying with the Mi'kmaq, Malecite, Ojibwa, and Wyandot (Huron), while the British sought support from the Iroquois. The French emphasized the fur trade, intermarried with Indian women, and assimilated the

Native peoples into French culture. The British, who were more interested in farming and settlement, usually came as families, bringing their wives with them. They were convinced of their "racial" superiority over the Native inhabitants.

In contrast to the colonization of the United States, the European invasion of Canada was less populous, slower because of the harsher, northern climate, and tended to impact mainly the more temperate, southern edge of Canadian North America. "Indians in the south were enclaved in small reserves and held as irrelevant to the development of Canadian society" (Price 1979: 214). And in the northern arctic and subarctic, the Native peoples were drawn into the fur trade economy with the Europeans.

Today, there are 600 First Nations bands with an average membership of 500 persons per band. Each band elects a band chief and a representative band council. There are 2,293 separate reserves, with a total area of 10,000 square miles. Less than 30 percent of the total Native population live off the reserves, mainly in the urban areas of Quebec, southern Ontario, southern Alberta, and the Vancouver area of British Columbia. Today these diverse Indian nations are represented by the Assembly of First Nations (AFN), formerly the National Indian Brotherhood.

Language and Cultural Areas

Originally there were approximately 50 different languages spoken, representing eleven language families. Algonkian is the largest, with Cree and Ojibway being the two most representative languages. Algonkian speakers are found in the provinces of eastern Canada, while Cree and Ojibway are spread throughout the south central part of the country. Another large language family is Athabascan whose related languages are spread across northwestern Canada. Siouan languages are found on the Canadian Plains, and Iroquoian languages are situated around the Great Lakes. Many smaller language families are found in British Columbia. Inuktitut is an Eskimoan language of northern Canada. "Only three—Cree, Ojibway, and Inuktitut—are spoken over large areas today and are considered to have excellent chances of survival" (McMillan 1994: 224).

Today, the Algonkian Indians are scattered in small reserves across a large portion of the country. Deep religious respect for the animals hunted is fundamental to Algonkian culture. This spiritual belief is found among the Ojibway of the western Great Lakes, the Cree of northern Ontario and Quebec, the Inu (Naskapi and Montagnais) of Labrador and adjacent Quebec, and the Mi'kmaq and Maliseet of the east coast Maritime Provinces.

The original Iroquoian societies of the Great Lakes, as represented by the Wyandot (Huron) and Haudenosaunee (Iroquois), were hunters and farmers. The Huron and others were largely annihilated in the Beaver Wars during the early contact period, when the Iroquois Confederation eliminated the Wyandot, Tobacco, and Erie in order to dominate the fur trade. Most Iroquoian peoples of the eastern Great Lakes are today represented by the Six Nations Iroquois, who came after the American Revolution. The Iroquoian Mohawk were staunch British loyalists and subsequently fled to Canada under their leader Joseph Brant after the victory by the American revolutionaries. Most settled along the Grand River in southern Ontario. The majority of Canadian Iroquois living today are members of the Haudenosaunee (Six Nations) Confederacy.

The Plains includes homelands of the Blackfoot Confederacy—Blackfoot, Blood, and Peigun—and their former foes, the Plains Cree and Ojibway—who hunted the buffalo. When their numbers were reduced by disease and the buffalo gone, these Indian groups were forced to sign treaties ceding their lands, and then were confined to reserves. Once on the reserves, traditional customs and beliefs, such as the Sun Dance, were suppressed.

The Métis are the product of cohabitation of European (usually French-Canadian) male fur traders with Native women, particularly Cree. They were found mainly in what became the Prairie provinces of Canada. "As the fur trade moved westward, many French-speaking men followed, establishing stable unions with Cree and Ojibway women. Kinship ties from such unions provided alliances that facilitated trade" (McMillan 1994: 235). In the north, English and Scottish employees of the Hudson's Bay Company established similar unions with Cree women. By the end of the 18th century, a large mixed-blood population was living around the Great Lakes. A depleted fur trade led many of them to migrate westward, eventually becoming bison hunters and provisioners for the Hudson's Bay and Northwest fur companies. Despite their cultural and religious differences (the French-speaking Métis were Catholic, and the English-Scottish Métis Protestant), they eventually forged a single, ethnic identity. Today, Canada's "forgotten people" are undergoing a cultural and political awakening.

The Canadian Plateau lies between the Rocky Mountains and the West Coast range. Representative peoples included the Kutenai in the east, and the Salish societies of the interior. Traditional economy involved a seasonal round of hunting, fishing, and gathering. The 1858 gold rush in the Fraser Canyon became a major disruptive force, and small pox and other diseases seriously reduced the Native population of the region. During the 1870s and 1880s, they were confined to small, scattered reserves. Nevertheless, "the Plateau groups never ceded their lands through treaties. Today, land claims are among the most contentious issues, along with such other grievances as legal restrictions on Native fisheries" (McMillan 1994: 231).

The Northwest Coast was the most linguistically diverse and one of the heaviest-populated regions of aboriginal Canada. The Native groups relied on the bounty of the ocean, beach and rivers for economic sustenance, with salmon the main food source. Large dugout canoes plied the waterways between villages built of large, plank houses, virtual monuments in cedar. In the north were the Haida of Queen Charlotte Island, the Tsimshian on the mainland, and the Tlingit in southeastern Alaska and Canada. Further south were the Kwakiutl, Bella Coola (Nuxalk), Squamish and others. Northwest Coast peoples place great emphasis on inherited rank and privileges, a major ceremony being the potlatch. Only a few treaties were signed, and these with the Indian peoples of Vancouver Island in the 1850s. The First Nations of British Columbia today are politically active with land rights being the principal issue. A cultural renewal has marked recent decades.

The Canadian sub-arctic contained Native peoples of the Athapaskan language family, ranging across northern Canada from the west side of Hudson Bay to interior Alaska. The Native peoples were hunters who lived in small, mobile groups, their cultural adaptations differing with the particular environment. They are represented by the Chipewyan in the east, the Beaver in the south, and the Tahltan in northwestern British Columbia. Many Athabascan communities today rely on a combination of trapping, government assistance, and wage labor. "Native political organizations, such as the Dene Nation in the Northwestern Territories, are fighting for recognition of Native land claims and right to self-determination" (McMillan 1994: 234).

North of the tree line are the Inuit, the aboriginal peoples of the Arctic. Inuktitut, the Inuit language, is still widely spoken across the entire region. In earlier times, all groups relied on hunting land and sea mammals, and fishing. Caribou and seals were the primary food source. In the Mackenzie Delta, whaling was an important economic activity. In the central Arctic were the Copper, Netsilik, Iglulik, and Inuit of Baffinland,

with other groups located in northern Quebec and Labrador. Moravian missionaries were active in Labrador and devised an orthography for writing the Inuktitut language. The whaling industry collapsed around 1910, and World War II brought a major military presence in the Arctic. When it became increasingly difficult for the Inuit to continue their subsistence economy, the Canadian government pressured Inuit groups to move into administrative settlements, but these small, urban enclaves soon became known as "ghettos of the North." Land claims have become a major issue in the contemporary political struggle. The Inuit of the Northwest Territories have successfully negotiated a self-governing homeland, Nunavut, with a status similar to a Canadian province.

Indians

Beginning in 1850, Great Britain signed a series of treaties with Indian groups whereby it gained control over most aboriginal territory in southern Canada. In exchange, the Indian bands were guaranteed small reserve lands and perpetual trusteeship under the colonial management of the British Crown. Additional reserves were established until 1923. The Indians also received one-time payments and annuities in cash and goods, and the promise of schools and federal services.

When Canada confederated, the Constitution Act of 1867 made the federal government responsible for "Indians and Lands reserved for Indians." The Indian Acts of 1868 and 1876 defined the relationship between the Native peoples and the federal government by setting up an Indian Department, and creating the legal machinery for colonial management.

> The [1876 Indian] act provided government control over all aspects of Indian life, and served as a vehicle of assimilation by legally suppressing such Native ceremonies as the Sun Dance on the Plains and the potlatch on the Pacific coast. Although the act was extensively rewritten in 1951 and prohibitions on Native traditions were dropped, the act remains essentially a nineteenth-century colonial document. (McMillan 1974: 237)

The Canadian Indian population was legally divided into three categories: status, treaty, and non-status. A status Indian is a person registered or entitled to be registered as an Indian for purposes of the 1876 Indian Act which sets forth a policy of assimilation. Today, "status Indians are members of 633 'bands' across Canada; 'bands' are legal-administrative bodies established under the Indian Act that correspond generally to traditional tribal and kinship group affinities" (Long and Chiste 1994: 335).

"Treaty Indians are those persons who are registered members of, or can prove descent from, a band that signed a treaty. Most status Indians are treaty Indians" (Ibid.).

"Non-status Indians are those persons of Indian ancestry and cultural affiliation who have lost their right to be registered under the Indian Act" (Ibid.). The most common reason was when a status Indian woman married a non-Indian man; she was then considered enfranchised and no longer an Indian. This inequality, reflecting a racist and sexist bias in Canadian law, was reversed in 1985 when the Indian Act was amended to restore registered Indian status to those Indian women and their children. The reinstatement process resulted in approximately 92,000 Indians being added to the registry.

In spite of reform, the colonial nature of the Indian Act remains essentially unchanged. The administration of Indian lands and finances still lie mainly with the federal minister of Indian and Northern Affairs. Indians are also legally subject to all provincially enacted laws, except where such laws conflict with provisions of the Indian Act or treaty rights. "The socio economic conditions on Indian reserves have been described as more typical of Third World countries. . . . Indian life expectancy is ten years below the national average. The suicide rate is double that of the general population, and the rate of violent death is triple" (Long and Chiste 1994: 339).

One feature that distinguishes Canada from the United States is that outside of the Yukon and Northwest Territories, the federal government owns very little Crown land area within its borders. As a consequence, land claims by treaty Indians are directed against the provinces.

Inuit

The Inuit were excluded from the terms of the Indian Act until a 1934 Supreme Court decision, "*Re Eskimos.*" Then they were neglected by the Canadian government until the 1950s, although World War II had already begun to impact their traditional life with the establishment of military bases throughout the North. In short, "The Inuit economy has undergone an enormous change in the last forty years, from a hunting and trapping base to diversification involving tourism, arts and crafts, and development of both renewable and non-renewable resources" (Long and Chiste: 1994: 342).

The Inuit constitute a majority of the population in northern Canada, and they are represented by a strong Indigenous organization, the Inuit Tapirisat of Canada (ITC). The organization was formed in 1971 as the "voice of the north" to press for a land settlement. Today, the Inuit of the eastern Arctic have successfully achieved a self-governing territory, Nunavut, which was created in 1991. The settlement involved a payment of $500 million and 350,000 square kilometers of land, a vast area of the Canadian Arctic. Earlier, in 1975, the Inuit of northern Quebec and the James Bay Cree signed an agreement giving them exclusive hunting and fishing rights, language and education rights in Inuktitut, and a cash and royalties settlement, In return, however, they relinquished any further land claims.

Métis

In 1982, Canada's new constitution included the Métis in its definition of "aboriginal people." The Métis reside mainly in the Prairie provinces and the Northwest Territories. Sometimes called "the children of the fur trade," the mixed-blood Métis revolted when the Hudson's Bay Company sold their homeland to Canada in 1869. The Red River Resistance was led by Louis Riel, Jr., who sought land title for the Métis, and provincial status for the Prairie territories. He attempted to set up a provisional government when Canada refused his demands. He was hanged for "treason" by the government in November, 1985, and is remembered as a national hero to Métis and other contemporary Indigenous peoples.

Despite their recognition by the federal government in 1982, the Métis claim for aboriginal status has so far been unsuccessful. Unlike the Indians and the Inuit, the Métis have always been under jurisdiction of the provinces. They remain impoverished and marginalized in Canadian society.

Recent Events

A 1969 government "White Paper on Indian Policy" called for repeal of the Indian Act, the termination of federal authority and turning services over to mainstream institutions and provincial governments. This assimilationist policy proposal immediately met with widespread opposition from Native peoples who feared further loss of lands, loss of treaty obligations and cultural identity. In the end the White Paper was rejected, and government policy shifted away from blatant assimilation towards limited self-determination for Native peoples.

The 1970s and the decades which followed saw increased political activism among Canadian Natives, leading to the founding of the National Indian

Brotherhood, renamed the Assembly of First Nations in 1981. The Office of Native Claims was established in 1974. It instituted procedures for both "comprehensive claims," based on the idea of aboriginal title to the land, and "specific claims," "based on lawful treaty obligations and the government's mismanagement of band assets" (Waldman 2000: 231). Some 500 specific land claims have yet to be adjudicated.

Confronted by a growing separatist movement in Quebec by French-speaking Canadians, the Liberal government of Prime Minister Pierre Trudeau set out to renovate federalism by adopting a new Constitution and a Charter of Rights, similar to the U.S. Bill of Rights. When the Constitution was revised in 1982, the existing aboriginal and treaty rights of the aboriginal peoples of Canada were recognized and affirmed, with Indian, Inuit, and Métis all identified as aboriginal people, "and a series of First Ministers Conferences were scheduled to work towards a definition of these rights" (Long and Chiste 1994: 347). The Department of Indian Affairs and Northern Development was mandated to carry out measures which would respond to the needs and desires of the Native peoples, and to improve their social, cultural, and economic wellbeing.

The Conferences took place in 1983, 1984, 1985, and 1987 respectively, between the government's First Ministers, the four main aboriginal organizations, and leaders from the Yukon and Northwest Territories. Chief among the issues discussed was that of aboriginal self-government. Unfortunately, the Conferences ended without recognizing additional amendments defining or supporting aboriginal rights. Nevertheless, the Constitution Act of 1982, amended in 1984, had a dramatic affect on Aboriginal legal status in Canada. "During the 1980s and early 1990s, several immense land claim settlements were negotiated by the aboriginal peoples of the western Arctic, the MacKenzie River delta, the eastern Arctic, and the Yukon. . . . The eight Métis settlements in Alberta have also received fee simple title to the 1.28 million acres of land that comprise their communities" (Morse 1994: 515).

A renewed attempt at federalism by the Canadian government took place on August 16, 1992 in what is known as the Charlottetown Accord. The Accord included an attempt to insert the inherent right to aboriginal self-government in the Canadian Constitution by stating that aboriginal peoples "have the right to promote their languages, cultures and traditions and to ensure the integrity of their societies, and their governments constitute one of three orders of government in Canada" (quoted in Long and Chiste 1994: 349). Significantly, the Métis were to be included for programs and funding under the Indian Act. However, in a national referendum, the Charlottetown Accord was rejected by Canadian voters, including a significant number of Native voters. Some Indian voters did not believe that the promised reforms went far enough. Others feared that Constitutional reform would weaken the treaty relationship, and still others opposed the plan to give the Métis a share of government funding.

Irregardless of the significant gains made over the last several decades, Morse (1994: 516) concludes that Canadian Native peoples "are in a significantly weaker legal position than U.S. Indian tribes despite a history of less military conflict, constitutional guarantees, and greater political weight, and the fact that they comprise a five times larger percentage of the Canadian population than do U.S. Indians." Furthermore, overall life expectancy for Canadian Natives is about eight years less than the national average, suicides are six times the national rate, and Natives are incarcerated at more than three times the national rate (Waldman 2000: 231). In recent years, "increased industrial activity and resource development projects in remote wilderness areas has meant new environmental damage, erosion of the Native land base, and disruption of Native ways of life" (Waldman 2000: 232).

REFERENCES

Long, J. Anthony, and Katherine Beaty Chiste. "Aboriginal Peoples in Canada," in *The Native North American Almanac*: 334–354. Edited by Duane Champagne. Detroit, MI: Gale Research, 1994.

McMillan, Alan D. "Canadian Native Distribution, Habitat and Demography," in *The Native North American Almanac*: 223–243. Edited by Duane Champagne. Detroit, MI: Gale Research, 1994.

Morse, Bradford W. "An Overview of Canadian Aboriginal Law," *The Native North American Almanac*: Edited by Duane Champagne. Detroit, MI: Gale Research, 1994.

Price, John. *Indians of Canada: Cultural Dynamics.* Salem, WI: Sheffield Publishing Co., 1979.

Waldman, Carl. *Atlas of The North American Indian.* New York: Checkmark Books. Revised edition. 2000.

FACTS ABOUT NUNAVUT*

Area: 797,600 square miles (one-fifth of Canada), north and west of Hudson Bay.

Population: 29,000 (20,000 Inuit)

Transportation: No roads connect to Nunavut. Flights from Edmonton connect via First Air, Canadian North, Air Inuit, or Calm Air to Yellowknife, where charters are available to Nunavut.

For More Information: Nunavut Tourism: 1-866-Nunavut.
Website: www.NunavutTourism.com Bathurst Inlet Lodge: (867) 873-2595.
Website: www.Bathurstarctic.com

*From AMERICAN INDIAN (winter 2004) p. 52.

(Carl Waldman, Atlas of the North American Indian, Checkmark Books, 2000, p. 232.)

NATIVE PEOPLES OF MEXICO

R. David Edmunds

The Indian policies that have emerged in the United States, Canada, and Mexico are products of their colonial past and reflect the aspirations of European colonial powers and their colonists, moderated by the impact of geography and transformed by historical events since the end of each country's colonial period. . . .

Unlike the United States and Canada, Mexico attempted to break from the Indian policy of its colonial past. Having achieved independence from Spain in 1820, Mexico formulated provisions designed to accelerate the integration of Indian people into the mainstream of Mexican society. Spicer (1960) points out that the new Mexican constitution of 1821 rejected the transitional communities fostered by the Spanish mission system, granted full citizenship to all Indians in the new republic, and theoretically guaranteed to them political rights equal to those of other Mexican citizens. But the government also demanded that Indian communities restructure their political systems so that all adult males would vote for a prescribed set of local officials whose duties and obligations would be established by Mexican law. And in policies similar to those that would emerge half a century later in the United States, Mexican officials decreed that most tribal lands were to be divided among individuals, with sufficient acreage to support their families. Surplus lands (particularly those previously held by missions) were to become the property of the state. Officials argued that such policies would eliminate Mexico's "Indian problem," and that Indians would cease to exist as a separate ethnic group. Federal statutes and policies were forbidden to include the term "Indian," and state constitutions (Sonora, Chihuahua) which were forced to deal specifically with remaining Indian communities were instructed to use the term "indigene" rather than "Indian."

Source: Vine Deloria and Neil Salisbury, "A Companion to American Indian History." Blackwell, 2004, pp. 412-416.

David Weber (1982) indicates that such policies were easier to formulate than to enforce. Mexican control over Native American people in its northern provinces was limited by shortages of manpower and other resources, and nomadic tribes such as the Comanches and Apaches ignored the new mandates. While state and local officials attempted to stop the raids in northern states, even offering bounties on Apache scalps, their efforts proved ineffective.

The kind of central policymaking and implementation found in the United States, and to a lesser degree in Canada, was even more attenuated in Mexico. When officials in Sonora or Chihuahua petitioned the federal government for assistance, bureaucrats in Mexico City generally ignored their pleas; consequently Indian policies formulated in the capital were poorly implemented. Bowen (1983) and Pennington (1983) show how Seri and Tarahumara tribes people refused to accept state attempts to restructure their societies and withdrew into isolated desert or mountainous regions where state officials exercised little authority. The Yaquis, also a sedentary people, resisted the government reforms so staunchly that first the state of Sonora, and finally the federal government conducted a series of military campaigns which reduced their population but failed to break their spirit. Finally, as Evelyn Hu-DeHart (1984) points out, between 1900 and 1910 Mexican officials resettled many Yaquis to Oaxaca and the Yucatan, but most of these exiles returned to Sonora after the fall of the Díaz regime in 1911.

The various regimes that governed Mexico between 1820 and the end of the French Intervention (1867) exercised more control over the administration of Indian affairs in central and southern Mexico, but in these regions they also encountered difficulty implementing policies that reinforced liberal democracy, individual land ownership, and assimilation. As Charles Hale (1968) indicates, much of the difficulty emerged because policymakers in Mexico City were far removed from rural Indian communities. In theory, federal and state policies were designed to redistribute communally held land and assign small farms to former members of the Indian community, but in actuality much of the redistributed land was purchased by large haciendas which then employed the individual Indians (indigenes) as rural laborers. Indian communities managed to retain some communal pasture and woodland as "ejidos," but such ownership was more tolerated than encouraged.

The Ley Lerdo, passed in 1856 and incorporated into the new Constitution of 1857, effectively terminated the ejido landholdings. Designed primarily to limit the power of the Catholic Church, the law forced the church to sell most of its vast landholdings at auction, but it also stipulated that lands held by other corporate bodies, including ejidos, were eligible to be purchased. Jan Bazant S. (1971) argues that policymakers in Mexico City naively assumed that individual Indians would purchase many of these lands, and that the number of small individual landholders would increase. Instead, foreigners and wealthy landowners purchased nearly all the lands and Indians became, as Richard Sinkin (1979) points out, economically and politically dependent upon the haciendas. Unlike in the United States and Canada, where Native American populations were isolated on relatively undesirable lands with little opportunity to participate in the economic life of the nation, many of Mexico's Indians lost control of their lands and were forced to labor for large landowners at subsistence wages.

The administration of Porfirio Díaz (the Porfiriato, 1876–1911) paid little attention to Indian people except as laborers on ranches and haciendas. Intent upon modernizing Mexico, Díaz was heavily influenced by "Cientificos," young Mexican intellectuals who in turn had been swayed by their admiration of the emergent industrial economies in Britain and Germany. Eager to attract foreign capital and present an image of a "modernizing Mexico," the Cientificos denigrated Indian people as obstacles to modernization, either denouncing them in racist terms or arguing that they would have to abandon their cultures and embrace Western civilization before becoming a viable part of the new Mexico (Stabb, 1959; Powell, 1968). Ironically, although the Díaz administration provided funds for the construction of schools and the development of education, most of the funds were spent in urban areas, far from significant Indian populations. Meanwhile, as Nash (1970) illustrates, most Indians resided in small rural villages, continued to speak their native languages, labored for *hacendados,* and subsisted on a scant diet of tortillas, beans, chilies and pulque. As with reservation conditions in the United States, infant mortality rates were high, life expectancy was low (less than thirty years), and modern medical care was non-existent.

Indians participated in the upheavals of the revolutionary period (1910–17), but generally focused their efforts on land reforms rather than ethnic aspirations. Whereas many Native Americans in the United States opposed the Dawes Act and wished to retain their communal land base, Indians from southern Mexico fought with the Zapatistas (the followers of Emilino Zapata), whose primary goal was the seizure of land from large haciendas and its redistribution to the landless (Womack, 1968). Others, influenced by local caciques, supported Diaz or Huerta but their primary purpose also was to regain lost lands, not protect reservation lands from development.

Ironically, as Alan Knight (1986, 1990) argues, many of the reforms later adopted under the Constitution of 1917 were initiated during the brief Huerta dictatorship (1913–14). Rejecting the policies of the Científicos, in 1914 the Huerta regime began the construction of rural schools in Indian villages, sent government agents into the pueblos to assist in organizing community projects, and restored seventy-eight ejidos to the Yaqui and Mayo Indians of Sonora.

Cumberland (1972) and Hall (1981) note that the Constitution of 1917 institutionalized these reforms and added to them. Drawing on policies championed by reformist or revolutionary groups during the preceding decade, Article 27 required that lands taken from Indian communities during the Porfiriato be returned, and authorized legal assistance for communities who charged that their lands had been seized illegally. Private ownership of real estate was no longer promoted as the ultimate form of land tenure, and large landholders who did not use such land or natural resources "in the public interest" could have their lands seized by the government. In theory, some of these confiscated lands would be returned to the remaining Indian communities. Thus during the early twentieth century, while the United States continued to implement the allotment process, Mexico officially returned to a policy of promoting communal lands for indigenes or Indian citizens. Indeed Mexico anticipated the intent, if not the actual practice, of the land consolidation provisions of the Indian New Deal in the United States.

During the 1920s, the federal government's new commitment to its Indian population increased. Knight (1990) argues that the Científicos' disdain for anything Indian was replaced by "indigenismo," the acknowledgement that although Indians' role in the political and social development of Mexico had been minimized since independence, Indians and their cultures were critical to the development of Mexico in the twentieth century. Indigenismo also asserted that the racial and cultural qualities of Indian people were basic hues in the broader spectrum of Mexican identity, and the government would assist the Indian communities in their integration into the formal structure of Mexican society. Unlike the earlier attempts at such integration, which had attempted to eradicate all things Indian, the federal government optimistically planned to proceed "without de-Indianization." Educated, bilingual, and politically mobilized Indian communities would take their place in a modern Mexico, but they would retain their own distinct cultures.

Championed by Manuel Gamio, who served as an Undersecretary of Education, between 1920 and 1940 the Mexican government trained bilingual teachers (many of them Indian) and established schools in many rural Indian villages. Although Spanish did not completely replace Indian languages, most Indians were bilingual by 1940. Ejidos were both encouraged and romanticized as part of the Aztec past. Following the election of Lázaro Cárdenas to the presidency in 1934, the number of ejidos increased. As Knight (1990) shows, Indian traditions in dance, music, and art were co-opted as part of a greater Mexican culture. Similarly, the vivid murals of Diego Rivera and other artists, celebrating Indian valor and suffering in opposition to the "Black Legend" of Spanish colonialism, proliferated in the capital and in other cities. In 1935 Gregorio López y Fuentes was awarded Mexico's first National Prize for Literature for the publication of *El Indio*, which examined the position of Indians in Mexican society. Four years later the Mexican government established the prestigious Instituto Nacional de Antropología e Historia which has devoted much of its focus to the Indian cultures of Mexico. Although federal policies in the United States during the halcyon days of the Indian New Deal also attempted to assist tribal people reassert their identity and cultures during the 1930s, they obviously were far overshadowed by the "indigenismo" in Mexico.

Following World War II the federal government established the Instituto Nacional Indigenista which, as Martin C. Needier (1971) indicates, attempted to promote reform through local Indian communities. Prometores, or "agents of change," were dispatched to the villages where they championed new bilingual programs, health clinics, and cooperative retail stores. Although land reform had languished in the 1940s, during the administration of Adolfo López Mateos (1958–64) almost 30 million acres, much of it in the southern states, was redistributed. Yet Neil Harvey (1990) argues that many Indians believed they did not receive a fair share of this acreage in comparison to the Ladino population. During the late 1960s and 1970s, while the government focused on problems of urbanization and Mexico's international balance of payments deficit, resentment smoldered in some of Mexico's Indian communities. Like reservation residents in the United States, many indígenes remained impoverished and they focused their hostility toward local or state officials whom they accused of corruption.

Nowhere in Mexico were Indians more suspicious of the federal government than in Chiapas. The poorest and most isolated of Mexico's states, Chiapas included regions in which large landowners and local officials had consistently thwarted land and election reforms, and where educational and medical services were minimal. In 1988, following the election of Carlos Salinas de Gortari to the presidency, the federal government again emphasized the role of privatized, individual agriculture. Moreover, as Morris (1992) points out, the Salinas administration charted an economic and political course designed to develop closer ties with the United States, especially through the North American Free Trade Association (NAFTA). Abandoning the agrarian reform of its predecessors, the Salinas regime criticized the communal ejido system as "unproductive" and fostered legislation turning the ejido lands over to individuals, while selling many government-owned public services back to large corporations. George Collier (1994) argues that in Chiapas these activities were interpreted as a further betrayal by the dominant Partido Revolucionario Institutional (PRI) of the Indian communities, and Salinas' policies sparked an armed uprising among the Maya population.

Led by an officer known only as "Sub-Comandante Marcos," in January 1994 an armed contingent of Mayas from Chiapas' eastern lowlands blocked the Pan-American highway and temporarily seized control of municipal buildings in San Cristóbal, the state capital, and in several other cities in Chiapas. Heavily armed Mexican troops eventually recaptured the buildings, but the Ejercito Zapatista Liberatión Nacional (the "Zapatistas"), the rebel army, has continued to conduct a sporadic guerrilla campaign against the federal government since that time.

Although the federal government conducted military campaigns against the Zapatistas, and subsequently concluded an uneasy truce, the Zapatistas remain adamant in their demands. Envisioning a

Mexico in which Indian people retain their political and cultural autonomy, the Zapatistas have demanded that the government honor its commitments to Indian people and permit Indian communities to continue in their communal economic activities. The Zapatista rebellion reminds us that although the Mexican government first attempted to legislate Indians out of existence, then celebrated their historic past without providing a place for them within the political power structure of the ruling party, Indian communities with a strong sense of ethnic identity still persist (Nash, 1995). Like their counterparts in the United States and Canada,

Indian people from Sonora to Chiapas envision themselves as citizens of Mexico, but also as Indians. While recognizing the discrete histories that place them in varying relations to national, state, provincial, and local governments, Indigenous people in the Northern Hemisphere share the common desire to (re)establish control over their lands and cultures. Indeed, the rise of transnational ties among North, Central, and South American Indians may constitute the foundation of the histories to be written during the coming generation, histories that will be both comparative and synthetic.

NATIVE AMERICAN DEMOGRAPHICS—UNITED STATES, 2008

Who Is an Indian

- There is no single federal or tribal criterion that establishes Indian identity.
- Tribal membership is determined by the enrolment criteria of the tribe/nation. Generally, if linkage to an identified tribal member is far removed, one would not qualify for enrolment.
- Tribes/nations determine their own membership criteria. Blood quantum needed varies from tribe to tribe. Some tribes only require proof of descent from an Indian ancestor, while others require as much as one-half blood quantum.
- To be eligible for Bureau of Indian Affairs Services, an Indian must be (1) a member of a federally recognized tribe; (2) of 1/2 or more Indian blood of tribes Indigenous to the United States; or (3) of 1/4 or more Indian ancestry.
- There are many terms used, including American Indian, Indians, Indigenous Peoples, First Nations, Native Americans, and American Indians and Alaska Natives (AI/AN). However, most Indians prefer their tribal name. For example, a Navajo person would prefer to be called Dené, which is the name of the tribe in the Navajo language.

Population

Note: In the 2000 U.S. Census, for the first time, respondents were permitted to select more than one "race." Also for the first time, Indian respondents whose origin was from various Indigenous peoples in South and Central America were recognized, but grouped together as "Latin American Indian." (103,354 Latin American Indian alone; 180,940 Latin American alone or in combination with another "race".)

- 4.5 million American Indian and Alaska Native (one tribe or any combination of Native and other mix)

- 1.5% of the U.S. population
- 2.4 million Native American or Alaska Native and also Native American and Alaska Native in combination with another race.
- Between 1990 and 2002, the Native American population grew significantly: on reservations, it increased by 25%, and in non-reservation areas, it increased by 21%.
- The median age of Native Americans living on reservations is 25 years and 29 years for the total population. (Median age of the United States population is 35 years.)

Tribes and Nations

- 562 federally recognized tribes and nations, including 200 Native villages in Alaska.
- Additionally, there are at least 100 state-recognized tribes.
- Many other groups remain unrecognized.
- 1.9 million AI/AN live on reservations or other trust lands
- A **federally recognized tribe** is a tribe that has a legal relationship with the U.S. government. This is referred to as a **government-to-government relationship**.
- **State-recognized tribe** means that though the Indian tribe is not federally recognized, the state in which it is located recognizes the tribe's status.
- Indians are the only U.S. minority group that must legally prove its minority status (race or ethnicity).

Ten Largest American Indian Tribal Groupings (2000 Census)

1. Cherokee, 729,533 in combination; 281,069 only Cherokee
2. Navajo, 298,197 in combination; 269,202 only Navajo
3. Latin American Indian, 180,940 in combination; 104,354 one tribal group

4. Choctaw, 158,774 in combination; 87,349 only Choctaw
5. Sioux, 153,360 in combination; 108,272 only Sioux
6. Chippewa, 149,669 in combination; 105,907 only Chippewa
7. Apache, 96,833 in combination; 57,060 only Apache
8. Blackfeet, 85,750 in combination; 27,104 only Blackfeet
9. Iroquois, 80,822 in combination; 42,212 only Iroquois
10. Pueblo, 74,085 in combination; 59,533 Pueblo only

Reservation/Non-reservation Distribution:

- In 2000, 34% of Native Americans lived on reservations and 66% lived in urban areas.
- In 2007, Los Angeles County had the highest population of AI/AN, at 146,500.
- Most off-reservation people maintain contact with their home areas and reservations, rancherias, villages, or Native communities.
- There are only two reservations in Alaska, and there are none in Oklahoma, although both states have significantly large Native American populations.
- A reservation is land a tribe reserved for itself or assigned to the tribe when it relinquished other land areas to the United States.
- In 2007, California had the highest population of AI/AN (689,120); followed by Oklahoma (393,500) and Arizona (335,381).
- In 2007, 18% of Alaska's population identified as AI/AN; Oklahoma, 11%; and New Mexico, 10%.
- In 2007, 62% of the U.S. AI/AN population lived in California, Oklahoma, Arizona, Texas, New Mexico, New York, Washington, Florida, North Carolina, Michigan, and Alaska.

Top Ten Cities Where AI/AN Live

1. New York (87,241)
2. Los Angeles (53,092)
3. Phoenix (35,093)
4. Tulsa, OK (30,227)
5. Oklahoma City, OK (29,001)
6. Anchorage (26,995)
7. Albuquerque (22,047)
8. Chicago (20,898)
9. San Diego (16,178)
10. Houston (15,743)

Indian Country

- **Indian country** is a legal concept and is defined as Indian reservations, the Pueblo villages of Arizona and New Mexico, the Native villages of Alaska, and the historical Indian areas of Oklahoma.
- The term is also used to denote everywhere that Indian people live or refer to as their home.

Reservation Resources

- There are 302 forested Indian reservations, which encompass 17.9 million acres of Indian forest lands—7.7 million acres of timberlands and 10.2 million acres of woodlands.
- 199 reservations contain timberlands and 185 reservation contain woodlands.

- Indian land contains an estimated 10% of all energy resources in the United States.

Health

- AI/AN frequently contend with issues that prevent them from receiving quality medical care, including cultural barriers, geographic isolation, inadequate sewage disposal, and low income.
- Some of the leading diseases and causes of death among AI/AN are heart disease, cancer, accidents, diabetes, and stroke.
- AI/AN have increased prevalence of and risk factors for mental health and suicide, obesity, substance abuse, Sudden Infant Death Syndrome (SIDS), teenage pregnancy, liver disease, and hepatitis.
- AI/AN have 30% higher AIDS rates than the non-Indian population.
- AI/AN adults are 1.2 times more likely to have heart disease than the non-Indian population.
- AI/AN adults are 2.3 times more likely to have diabetes as the non-Indian population.
- In 2007, the tuberculosis rate for AI/AN was 5.9% than compared to 1.1% for the non-Indian population in the Pima India of Arizona.
- In 1999–2001, life expectancy for Indians was 2.4 years less than for all other races. This figure represents a 4-year increase over the 1996–1998 rates.
- In 2000–2002, Native infants died at a rate of 8.5 per every 1,000 live births, as compared to 6.8 per 1,000 for the U.S. population in general.
- Native people die at higher rates than other Americans from:
  - Tuberculosis: 600% higher
  - Alcoholism: 510% higher
  - Motor vehicle crashes: 229% higher
  - Diabetes: 189% higher
  - Unintentional injuries: 152% higher
  - Suicide: 62% higher
- Indian youth have the highest rate of suicide among all ethnic groups in the United States, and suicide is the second leading cause of death for Native youth aged 15 to 24 years.

Education

- 76.3% of Indians finish high school.
- About 250 tribal languages are still spoken, but their use is discouraged in the classroom. Native American languages and cultures are undervalued by mainstream institutions.
- 18% of Indians attend college (89,000 are currently enrolled).
- 13% of Indians graduate from college.
- 4.5% of Indians attain graduate degrees

Economic Welfare

- The average household income is $33,300, as compared with $46,200 nationally.
- The poverty rate is 21.2% for Indian families, as compared with 10.2% nationally.
- Unemployment averages 8.6% for Native Americans nationally. Real per capita income of Indians living on reservations is still less than half of the national average,

Percent of American Indian and Alaska Native*
in the Population for States: 2005

Percent of all Residents

- Less than 1.0
- 1.0 to 4.9
- 5.0 to 9.9
- 10.0 or more

United States = 1.0 percent

*Single race.
Source: U.S. Census Bureau, Population Estimates Program, July 1, 2005.

and unemployment is still double that of the rest of the country.
- Between 1990 and 2000, income levels rose by 33%, and the poverty rate dropped by 7%, with little difference between those tribes with gaming and those tribes without gaming.
- Between 1992 and 1997, the number of Native-owned businesses grew by 84%, to a total of 197,000 business, and their receipts increased by 179%.

Other Facts

- Indians do not get payments from the government for being Indian. However, a tribe or an individual may receive payment of income from their lands and resources that the federal government administers for them, such as fees collected from grazing leases.

- Indians do not receive a free college education just for being Indian; however, there are financial aid programs administered through the Bureau of Indian Affairs.
- Indians are U.S. citizens and were extended full citizenship in 1924.
- Indians pay taxes.
- The same laws apply to Indians as to non-Indians.
- Indians do not get casino checks; Indian gaming is strictly regulated by the federal government.
- Indians do not have "special rights"; however, all rights tribes do have are based on treaty agreements and are given in exchange for relinquishing their land to the United States.
- There is not one 'Indian' language. English is the language generally spoken by Native Americans, but nearly 250 tribal languages are still spoken as a first or second language.

THE U.S. CENSUS AS "STATISTICAL GENOCIDE"

Susan Lobo

Students and researchers are urged to take a critical stance when reviewing United States census figures. The methodology employed by the United States census that is carried out every ten years reflects many of the stereotypes and biases of the United States overall. For example, the definition required by the census regarding who is American Indian has varied from census to census and is not necessarily the same criteria used by Native Nations in determining their members. Until recently the census was carried out by enumerators, many of whom arrived at the ethnic or racial identity of those whose doors they knocked on via their own often faulty personal criteria regarding who did or did not "look" Indian. Since the 1990 census "race" has been determined by self-identity which has brought some improvement to this particular aspect of census-taking. Many other concerns remain such as failing to enumerate in "temporary" living spaces such as jails, halfway houses, hotels, and shelters in the 2000 census. This has led to severe undercounts of Native people, in both urban areas as well as rural regions on and off reservations.

This failure to count Native people and others of color has, in a sense, made these uncounted Native people "vanish" for all practical Federal purposes. John Anner, made the comment in 1991, "Statistical genocide" relates to the ways in which figures and statistics are used to determine programs and set policies. Census figures are used to determine, among other things, who gets what in terms of federal funding and congressional representation. If you are not counted by the census, then, in the eyes of government agencies, you don't count. In fact, you don't exist at all." Likewise, Jack Forbes, professor of Native American Studies at the University of California at Davis has said, "Demography for Native Americans, has always pointed towards a struggle against disappearance, or, more precisely, against being forced to vanish!"

As more Native people have come to realize the need to monitor and critique the Census process, some improvements were seen in the 2000 census that found 2,447,989 people self-identifying as "American Indian and Alaska Native" and a total of 4,375,865 self-identifying in the combined categories of "American Indian and Alaska Native" and "American Indian/Alaska Native and another race", which represents approximately 1.53% of the overall United States population that answered the census. However, there is still a long way to go before the U.S. census accurately represents the American Indian population.

References
Anner, John. "To the U.S. Census Bureau, Native Americans are practically invisible." In **Minority Trendsletter,** 4, no.1 (Winter 1990–91): 15–21. Copyright 1991 by the Center for Third World Organizing.

PART REVIEW

DISCUSSION QUESTIONS

Introduction
1. From the information presented in the part introduction, how would you describe Native American studies? How does it differ from the academic disciplines of anthropology and history?
2. Who is Guaman Poma? Why might one conclude that Native American studies is not an entirely new field?

Bruce E. Johansen, *Dedication: On the Passing of Vine Deloria, Jr.*
1. Why is Vine Deloria considered one of the principal founders of American Indian/Native American studies?

2. Describe Deloria's views regarding the environmental crisis.
3. Why was Vine Deloria described at his funeral as "always a warrior"?

Duane Champagne, *The Rise and Fall of Native American Studies in the United States*
1. Explain the "Indigenous paradigm," as defined by Duane Champagne, and why it is important.
2. Describe the founding of AIS/NAS in its social and historical context.
3. What are some of the structural issues in educational institutions that have inhibited the development of AIS/NAS?

NATIVE PEOPLES OF MEXICO

**Hilary N. Weaver, *Indigenous Identity:
What Is It, and Who Really Has It?***
1. What does the story "The Big Game" tell us about Native identity?
2. Explain Weaver's statement "Identity is a combination of self-identity and the perceptions of others."
3. Explain how a reliance on "blood quantum" as the criteria for Native identity will lead to statistical extermination, or genocide.
4. What is meant by "internalized oppression"? Give some examples and discuss.

Steve Talbot, *First Nations: Indigenous Peoples of Canada*
1. What are the three major groups of Native American peoples in Canada? What is the difference between status Indians, treaty Indians, and non-status Indians?
2. In what ways was the colonization of Canada different than that of the United States? What are some of the contemporary results of these contrasting histories?
3. In what ways is language fundamental to Native cultural persistence and identity?

R. David Edmunds, *Native Peoples of Mexico*
1. How has the Mexican government historically dealt with its "Indian problem"?

2. What is an *ejido*, and how is it different from a U.S. Indian reservation?
3. Describe some of the Mexican policies regarding Native communities that fostered assimilation and modernization.
4. What is NAFTA, and how have Indian communities in Chiapas responded to NAFTA?

Table I.1, "Native American Demography—United States 2008"
1. According to the 2000 census statistics, how many people in the United States claim "American Indian or Alaska Native alone" or American Indian or Alaska Native in combination with one or more "other races"? Is this an increase or decrease since the 1990 census?
2. Which are the largest tribes (Indian nations) in the United States, according to the 2000 U.S. census? Which are the major reservations?
3. How would you describe the socioeconomic characteristics of Native peoples in the United States?

S. Lobo, *The U.S. Census as Statistical Genocide*
1. In view of what you read in this selection about the U.S. census count of Indians, how accurate do you think the information is in the box on Native American demographics?

KEY TERMS

assimilation
Bering Strait land bridge theory
blood quantum basis for Indian identity
Charlottetown Accord
culture area
ethnic fraud
ethnographic present
First Nations
Guaman Poma
identity politics
Indian country

Indian Reorganization Act of 1934
Lakota "winter counts"
mestizo
Métis
"new Indian" movement
Nunavut
Quechua
relocation
statistical genocide
urban Indians

SUGGESTED READINGS

CAMPBELL, GREGORY R. "The Politics of Counting: Critical Reflections on the Depopulation Question of Native North America." Pages 67–131 in *The Unheard Voices: American Indian Responses to the Columbian Quincentenary 1492–1992*. Ed. CAROLE M. GENTRY and DONALD A. GRINDE, JR. *Los Angeles:* UCLA American Indian Studies Center, 1994. 67–131.

CHAMPAGNE, DUANE, ed. *Native America: Portrait of the Peoples.* Foreword by DENNIS BANKS. Detroit: Visible Ink Press, 1995. [This is an abbreviated version of *The Native North American Almanac*. Ed. DUANE CHAMPAGNE. Detroit: Gale Research, 1994.]

CROZIER-HOGLE, LOIS, and DARRYL BABE WILSON. *Surviving in Two Worlds: Contemporary Native American Voices.* Austin: University of Texas Press, 1997.

DAVIS, MARY B., ed. *Native America in the Twentieth Century: An Encyclopedia.* New York: Garland Publishing, 1994.

DEJONG, DAVID H. "Choosing the Red Road: Family Legacy, Leadership, and Vine Deloria, Jr.," *Red Ink*, Native Voices, vol. 14, no. 1 (Spring 2008): 86–94.

DELORIA, VINE, JR. *Behind the Trail of Broken Treaties: An American Declaration of Independence.* Austin: University of Texas Press, 1984.

FORBES, JACK D. "Basic Concepts for Understanding Native History and Culture." In *Native Americans of California and Nevada.* Happy Camp, Calif.: Naturegraph Publishers, 1982.

ISMAELILLO and ROBIN WRIGHT, eds. *Native Peoples in Struggle: Cases from the Fourth Russell Tribunal & Other*

International Forums. Bombay, N.Y.: Anthropology Resource Center and E.R.I.N. Publications, 1982.

KROUSE, SUSAN APPLEGATE. "Kinship and Identity: Mixed Bloods in Urban Indian Communities." *American Indian Culture and Research Journal*, 23, no. 1 (1999): 73–89.

MORRISON, BRUCE R., and C. RODERICK WILSON, eds. *Native Peoples: The Canadian Experience*, 2d ed. Toronto: McClelland & Stewart, 1995.

ORTIZ, SIMON. *Woven Stone*. Tucson: University of Arizona Press, 1992.

OSWALT, WENDELL H., and SHARLOTTE NEELY. *This Land Was Theirs*. Mountain View, Calif.: Mayfield Publishing, 1996.

PAVEL, D. MICHAEL, TIMOTHY SANCHEZ, and AMBER MACHAMER. "Ethnic Fraud, Native Peoples, and Higher Education." *Thought Land Action*, 10, no. 1 (Spring 1994): 91–100.

PRICE, JOHN. *Indians of Canada: Cultural Dynamics*. Salem, Wis. Sheffield Publishing, 1970.

PRUCHA, FRANCIS PAUL. *Atlas of American Indian Affairs*. Lincoln: University of Nebraska Press, 1990.

SPICER, EDWARD H. *The American Indians: Dimensions of Ethnicity*. Cambridge, Mass.: Belnap Press, 1980.

STIFFARM, LENORE A., with PHIL LANE, JR. "The Demography of Native North America: A Question of American Indian Survival." Pages 23–53 in *The State of Native North America: Genocide, Colonization, and Resistance*. Ed. M. ANNETTE JAIMES. Boston: South End Press, 1992.

TALBOT, STEVE. "Anthropology versus Native American Studies: Theoretical and Ethical Implications." Pages 133–155 in *The Unheard Voices: American Indian Responses to the Columbian Quincentenary 1492–1992*. Ed. CAROLE M. GENTRY and DONALD A. GRINDE, JR. Los Angeles: UCLA American Indian Studies Center, 1994; "Academic Indianismo: Social Scientific Research in American Indian Studies." Pages 67–96 in the *American Indian Culture and Research Journal*, 26: 4 (2002).

TAYLOR, DREW HAYDEN. *Funny, You Don't Look Like One: Observations from a Blue-Eyed Ojibway*. Penticton B.C., Canada: Theytus Books, 1996.

THORNTON, RUSSELL, ed. "Institutional and Intellectual Histories of Native American Studies," and "The Demography of Colonialism and 'Old' and 'New' Native Americans." In *Studying Native America: Problems and Prospects*. Madison: University of Wisconsin Press, 1998.

WALDMAN, CARL. *Atlas of the North American Indian*. New York: Facts on File, 1985.

II

THE HIDDEN HERITAGE

I don't imagine the turquoise bracelet the dusky wash makes, or the red
hills circling the dreaming eye of this sacred land. I don't imagine
anything but the bracelet around my wrist, the red scarf around my
neck as I urge my pretty horse home.

Joy Harjo, "The Hidden Heritage"*

The Native American heritage is the cultural foundation of the Americas. Whereas the European, African, Asian, and Latino/Chicano heritages are important to a plural society, it is nonetheless the heritage of Indigenous America that is common to us all. It is this heritage, that of the First Americans, which makes all of us uniquely American with respect to the rest of the world, whether we reside in North, Central, or South America. This heritage is made up of two parts. First, there is the biological or genetic legacy of Indigenous America, which forms the major racial ancestry of most Latin American populations. Second, there is the Native American historical and cultural legacy, in which, to an even larger degree, all citizens of the Americas share, regardless of their specific racial, ethnic, or national background.[1]

In Part I we examined the tremendous Native diversity of the Americas. Indigenous peoples today number at least 40 million, most of them living in Central and South America. When European colonists first invaded, there were perhaps as many as 100 million Native people in the Americas. Prior to the arrival of Europeans, the population density was greatest in the highlands of Peru, Colombia, the Yucatan, and the Valley of Mexico. Linguists estimate that there were originally at least 56 language families and many more totally distinct languages. Although many languages were lost in the years following the European invasion, others continue to flourish. For example, today, Runasimi ("language of the people"), or Quechua, is the Indigenous language of a large portion of the populations in the South American Andean highlands, with about 10 million speakers in all. Millions more speak Aymara, and still several million more in southern Mexico and Guatemala speak one of the many Mayan languages. The oral traditions of these many Native American linguistic groups find expression in many contemporary cultural forms, such as music and oratory. Also, several thousand words in Spanish and English derive from languages native to this hemisphere.

In terms of the cultural heritage, there exists today some knowledge and appreciation for the Aztec, Mayan, and Incan civilizations of Central and South America—the monumental architecture, urbanism, astronomy, mathematics, food and mining technology, government, religious ceremonialism, and other cultural contributions. Yet, how many people are aware that a thousand years before the founding of Christianity in the Middle East there was a thriving Mound Builder civilization in what is the present-day eastern United States? The Temple Mound Builders rivaled Egypt in terms of their urban, social complexity and monumental architecture. Yet this impressive cultural development is almost never mentioned in U.S. history and humanities texts and remains a part of the hidden heritage of North America.

Even though a relatively small population in the United States, Native Americans continue to be an indirect but vital factor in the many political, economic, and moral issues of American life, such as fostering gender equality, grassroots democracy and a sense of community, respect for elders, family values, spiritual life, and the struggle to protect the environment. In short, these and other aspects of the hidden heritage of

---

*"The Hidden Heritage," from *Secrets from the Center of the World* by Joy Harjo and Stephen Strom. © 1989 the Arizona Board of Regents. Reprinted with permission of the University of Arizona Press.

[1]Portions of the following discussion are taken from Jack D. Forbes, *Native Americans of the Far West: A Handbook* (Berkeley, Calif.: Far West Laboratory for Research and Educational Development, 1969); and Steve Talbot, "Why the Native American Heritage Should Be Taught in College," *Indian Historian,* 17, no. 1 (January 1974).

Indigenous America make the continuing Indian contribution to the United States an important one, far beyond the number of Native persons in the general population. It is simply impossible on empirical grounds to understand history, government and political science, art, social studies, and the humanities without recognizing that a fundamental part of the contemporary American heritage is Native American.

The way of life of the majority population in the United States is often referred to as "Western" (i.e., a part of Western civilization). In point of fact, however, much that is basic to this way of life originated in the Middle East and North Africa. Consider, for example, the Moorish influence in the Iberian Peninsula, which North African peoples occupied for seven centuries before the Spanish conquest of the Americas. Islamic scholar Ibn-Khaldoun (born in Tunisia in A.D. 1312) studied and taught chemistry, engineering, geography, literature, mathematics, physics, psychology, and sociology. One could contend that the European Renaissance was the result, at least in part, of this North African influence. Thus, the culture of the dominant Spanish and Anglo-American populations of the Americas is, from its European foundation, a very mixed or heterogeneous one.

Once in the Americas, the co-mingling with the Indigenous cultures made the sum total even more of an amalgam. An acknowledgment of these cultural roots is exemplified by *La Plaza de las Trés Culturas* (Plaza of the Three Cultures) found in Mexico City, which celebrates the Spanish heritage, the Indian heritage, and the resulting Mexican "race" with its mestizo culture.

A mixed cultural heritage also became the common legacy of North American people, which derives a significant part of its character from contributions made by Native American groups, although this fact is poorly understood and seldom acknowledged. Even as the seventeenth- and eighteenth-century English way of life was being modified by forest warfare tactics, the fur trade, the Indian slave trade, dressed deerskin clothing (such as that worn by Daniel Boone), the canoe, the toboggan, the political influence of the Iroquois confederation, thousands of Native place names, hundreds of Indian words, mining and food technologies, and numerous other items, Anglo-Americans persisted in obscuring the origin of these cultural changes. Each trait borrowed from the Indians by Euro-Americans was emotionally assimilated and thereby became, in the popular mind, a "frontier" or "American" trait.

From a Native perspective, an understanding of one's heritage comes from knowing about the beginning of time, when the cosmos was taking form and life came into being. Often this understanding is based on Old Stories and the songs that are intimately linked to the land. Pulitzer Prize–winning Kiowa author Scott Momaday in *The Way to Rainy Mountain* referred to his homeland, the western plains of Oklahoma, in this way: "All things in the plain are isolate; there is no confusion of objects in the eye, but one hill or one tree, or one man. To look upon that landscape in the early morning, with the sun at your back is to lose the sense of proportion. Your imagination comes to life and this you think, is where Creation was begun."

The image of the black bear by L. Frank Manriquez and the short poem by William Oandasan that accompanies it (p. 55) underscores the theme for the "hidden heritage."

In Reading 1, "Mis Misa: The Power Within Akoo-Yet That Protects the World," Pit River Nation writer Darryl Babe Wilson explains the deep significance that *Akoo-Yet* (Mount Shasta) in northern California has had for Indian people for countless generations. Yet, how many non-Indian people have heard about Mis Misa, the tiny, yet powerful spirit that lives within the mountain, which "balances the earth with the universe and the universe with the earth"? To mainstream society this mountain appears as real estate, a resource to be developed; a place to stop for food on the way north or south along Interstate 5, or a ski resort for winter holidays. Wilson, however, explains that Akoo-Yet is a sacred mountain and that there is an important message in Mis Misa that everyone in today's world needs to heed. The short poem "The Beginning Was Mist," by Luci Tapahonso (p. 62) continues this theme.

In Reading 2, "Perceptions of America's Native Democracies," Donald Grinde, Jr. (Yamasee), and Bruce Johansen uncover the story of how the U.S. form of government was influenced in major ways by the Six Nations Iroquois Confederacy. This fact can be easily demonstrated by observing the back or green side of a one dollar bill and noting the "American" eagle clutching thirteen arrows in one talon and an olive branch in the other. The olive branch is related to the Greco-Roman heritage. The "American" eagle, on the other hand, was borrowed as a symbol from the powerful Iroquois Confederacy, the ever-vigilant eagle guarding against the Confederacy's enemies, and the arrows originally represented the bunched strength of the Iroquois nations. But, as the two historians explain, the Indian influence was much more significant than just these borrowed symbols; Iroquois traditions significantly influenced U.S. democratic ideals and the U.S. form of government.

John Mohawk continues the story begun by Grinde and Johansen in the box titled "Origins of Iroquois Political Thought." He explains the role of the White Roots of Peace and the Peacemaker in founding the League of the Haudenosaunee and the fundamental contributions to Iroquois political thought. This thought, "the power of righteousness," continues to influence the conduct of Native peoples throughout the Americas and in the larger Indigenous struggle today. In fact, it is a timely message for all the peoples of the world.

Reading 3, "Latin America's Indigenous Peoples: Changing Identities and Forms of Resistance," deals with Latin America's Indigenous peoples as *enduring peoples*. Rather than acculturating to the non-Indian world and disappearing as Indigenous entities, the Indian peoples are now growing in numbers and developing effective political organizations in their struggle for self-government. After providing historical background to explain the differences between the Spanish and English conquests of the Americas, Michael Kearney and Stefano Varese detail the essential forms of "ethnic resilience and opposition" that characterize Latin American Indian peoples for whom rebellion and various forms of resistance are essential parts of the cultural and historical legacy. The nature of political organization for self-government and autonomy, however, is markedly different from political rebellions of the non-Indian society due to the Indigenous concern for the integrity of the land, the traditional Indigenous territories. Of special interest is the authors' discussion of the dramatic growth of Indian refugee populations in California, which are not officially acknowledged by U.S. immigration officials. We are reminded of the following story: Several years ago, before the Zapatista rebellion in Chiapas, Mexico, the governor of Oaxaca visited Santa Rosa, California, where he gave a public address to the local "Mexican" constituents. However, most of the people in the audience identified primarily as Mixteca Indians and were speaking to one another in the Mixtec Indian language, not Spanish!

In Reading 4, "Mexico: The Crisis of Identity," Alexander Ewen (Perepeche) focuses on the various ways that Native ethnic and racial identity has been defined through the centuries and in distinct regions of the hemisphere. In most Latin American countries, including Mexico, the emphasis in externally imposed ethnic identity has historically been on cultural traits such as language and dress. In contrast, the emphasis within the United States has been on biological ancestry, including the concept of blood quantum (full-blood, half-blood, etc.). Ewen points out some of the negative consequences for Native people on political, economic, and cultural levels as a result of these imposed means of determining Indigenous/ethnic identity. For example, in Mexico, the ethos of *mestizaje* becomes a means of assimilation to a national norm, often reducing the political power of Native peoples or even denying their existence altogether. As Ewen emphasizes, there is a long and varied history in Mexico of Indian peoples identifying ways to resist these and other pressures of assimilation or even annihilation. One of the most recent has been the Zapatista movement in Chiapas. This and many other Indigenous forms of resistance and confrontation have deep cultural and historical roots and are linked, as Ewen shows, to events that are widespread throughout the hemisphere.

Gaming and sports are other important components of the Native American heritage. The box "Jim Thorpe: That Championship Season," features the Indian athlete who epitomizes the Indigenous sports hero. This short article by Jim Adams adds new details to the saga of Thorpe and the justly famous Carlisle Indian football team in the early part of the twentieth century.

Some would argue that Thorpe was the greatest American athlete of all time, yet his story is not always known or told. A product of the Carlisle Indian boarding school, he won gold medals in the pentathlon and decathlon at the 1912 Stockholm Olympics, breaking the decathlon world record by an incredible 998 points. Yet he was later stripped of his medals and his records were expunged when it was learned that he had played semiprofessional summer baseball in 1909 for $15 a week. This narrow interpretation of Olympics rules has been widely viewed as unfair and discriminatory by Indians and non-Indians alike. In 1984, after a national campaign, his Olympic medals were finally returned to the Thorpe family.

In Reading 5, "Just Speak Your Language: *Hena'haanehe*," Richard Littlebear explains the importance of knowing and preserving one's Native language, especially in the maintenance of Indigenous culture and identity. Michael Krauss, a well-respected linguist at the University of Alaska, estimates that half of the world's 6,000 languages are moribund because they are no longer learned by children; 90 percent face extinction in the twenty-first century. Bruna Franchetto, a Brazilian linguist, put it this way: "The extinction of a language is the equivalent to the extinction of a species . . . If we lose a different way of linguistically organizing thought, we lose a possible way of seeing reality."

Littlebear presents seven reasons why Native language literacy is important, not the least of which is the maintenance of Indigenous culture and identity. The first reason we save our languages, he writes, is "because it is the spiritual relevance deeply imbedded in our own languages that makes them relevant to us as American Indians today."

BLACK BEARS

long ago black bears
sang around our lodge fires
tonight they dance
alive through our dreams

"Black Bears" from *A Branch of California Redwood* by William Oandasan. Copyright © 1980 by The Regents of the University of California, American Indian Studies Center. Reprinted with permission.

Drawing © 1984, L. Frank Manriquez.

MIS MISA

THE POWER WITHIN AKOO-YET THAT PROTECTS THE WORLD

Darryl Babe Wilson

In the legends of my people there are many events of "our history" that have precise meaning and are completely understandable in our society. Our lessons are from oral "historians." As a people we have been taught, for all seasons, to listen to these stories and to apply the lessons within the stories to everyday life. This is one way to gather spiritual and mental "power" and to maintain emotional as well as physical human strength—to somehow balance our being with the awesome velocity of the churning, continuous universe.

Mis Misa is the tiny, yet powerful spirit that lives within *Akoo-Yet* (Mount Shasta) and balances the earth with the universe and the universe with the earth. Its assigned duty makes Akoo-Yet the most necessary of all of the mountains upon earth, for Mis Misa keeps the earth the proper distance from the sun and keeps everything in its proper place when Wonder and Power stir the universe with a giant yet invisible *ja-pilo-o* (canoe paddle). Mis Misa keeps the earth from wandering away from the rest of the universe. It maintains the proper seasons and the proper atmosphere for life to flourish as earth changes seasons on its journey around the sun.

The lesson establishes that Akoo-Yet was the first mountain created long ago and that it is a seat of power, a spiritual place. It is a mountain that must be worshipped not only for its special beauty and its unique power, but also because it holds Mis Misa deep within it. My old people of wisdom may have identified the mountain as *wiumjoji se-la elam-ji* (living place spirit), or *wiumjoji elam-ji se-la* (living spirit place).

In the "old" lessons and according to the "old" laws, to ascend this mountain with a pure heart and a real purpose, and to communicate with all of the lights and all of the darkness of the universe is to place your spirit in a direct line from the songs of Mis Misa to *hataji* (the heart) of the universe. While in this posture, the spirit of man/woman is in perfect balance and harmony. Few people are able to accomplish this mission. The person must be born for making and maintaining the "connection" between his/her nation and all that there is—and for no other purpose. This is one way nature has of ensuring the health of the whole earth.

In a balanced society that experiences few interruptions, "long range plans" are maintained that will ensure the continuation of the society and the honoring of Mis Misa. The people will continue to live, it is said, for as long as the instructions from the spirit of the universe are honestly obeyed.

When the season approaches that the person who has been assigned this duty prepares to enter the "other" world, a child is dreamed of and born. The planning is intricate since the person "departing" must have sufficient time to train the child to maturity in order that the many lessons and songs are understood as they were created—and are learned with unaltered purity. The most important of all of the lessons, it is said, is to be so quiet in your being that you constantly hear the soft singing of Mis Misa.

To not keep this "appointment" between the society and the powers of the world is to break the delicate umbilical cord between the spirit of the society and the awesome wisdom of the universe. To not listen, intently, to the song coming from Mis Misa is to allow the song to fade. Should the song cease, then Mis Misa will "depart" and the earth and all of the societies upon earth will be out of balance, and the life therein vulnerable to extinction—as the moon was.

It is, therefore, imperative that the practice of communicating with Mis Misa be maintained. Now that "civilization" has entered our Native homeland and permeated our people with half-truths, there are few Original People who think in this manner. The linear thought patterns of "education" have brought some of us to be ashamed of our language, our songs, our traditions.

But, the imposing Euro-American intrusion into this hemisphere will not dominate the Native societies with enough velocity to cause us to forget our songs and to forget to think beautiful thoughts of all of the precious life that surrounds us—or to forget the ceremony that must be maintained in order for that precious life to flourish.

Akoo-Yet and Mis Misa are little known and may never be sacred to "civilization," to which Akoo-Yet is known as Mt. Shasta. There are no songs coming from it. It is a natural resource. It is property of the United States. It is a piece of real estate that contains animals and varmints upon its slopes that must be "harvested" and "controlled" with guns and poisons. The timber is a valuable resource and it must be subject to political gymnastics as individuals within the American government and the corporate society connive to manipulate the income from the sale of the forests to their personal advantage.

Neither the individuals of the American government nor the individuals of the corporate state "see" the thousands of life forms that are a part of that forest. They do not "see" the bacteria necessary to grow the forest, they do not "see" the animals and birds that are displaced or destroyed as the mountains are shaved clean of forests. They do not "see" the insects and the butterflies of the forest as an element in balance with the universe.

However, they do see this mountain as an object that can be "developed" to entertain the skier and the mountaineer. They dream of constructing villages upon its beautiful slopes and of constructing roads around it. In their "land use" plans, civilization intends to create a circus of this majestic mountain of softly singing beauty.

A letter from Grandfather Craven Gibson always arrived with a sense of urgency. He always claimed that he was born on Alcatraz Island in San Francisco Bay around 1860—during the time when the U.S. government was using that rock as a detention center for Original Native People of the west.

While I could barely decipher his broken spelling and the individual letters that he had labored over (as he wrote "in American"), the fact that it came from him demanded immediate attention, as the elders of my Nation are the keepers of truths and treasures, keepers of wisdom and knowledge.

My brother and I arrived at Grandfather Craven's home in *Atwam* (Big Valley, California) in the early evening. After a cup of bitter coffee from his stained mugs, we went outside to study the clear and perfect night sky. Grandfather did not talk about the universe, he talked about the moon. His was a message given in a controlled panic—as one who knows a disaster is about to occur but also understands that it would be more damaging to try to warn the people. The early night was solemn. There was a hush, a quiet. Not even a coyote howled. Wind, still. Wild, silent.

With a gnarled hand, our ninety year old grandfather pointed to the full moon of August, 1973 and said, "Can you see the scars upon the face of the moon, the injured land? That is what my grandmother spoke of long ago. When I was a child long ago, she said there was a war. It was a big war between the people—a war between the thinkings. There was a terrible war. It was between those people who did not care about life and did not care if the moon remained a dwelling place, and those others who wanted the moon to remain a good place to live. That war used up the moon. When the moon caught fire there wasn't even enough water to put it out. It was all used up. The moon burned. It cooked everything. That huge fire cooked everything. Just everything."

We went back into his old and crooked shack and he talked until breaking light about the eroding condition of earth and the eroding condition of the spirit of humanity.

Because Grandfather wanted us to observe the moon, we went outside and stood with him in the early chill. The old people call it *Lok-mhe*, the light just before the silver of dawn. He told us of his fears of how this earth could be *itamji-uw* (all used up) if all of the people of all of the world do not correct their manner of wasting resources and amend their arrogant disregard for all of life.

There was a thickness under the brilliance of a million dancing stars in the moments before first light.

Thirty miles to the north, Akoo-Yet shivered white against the velvet cold black. We were surrounded by the immense silence upon the ancient land of our people of the Pit River Nation, on the flat land of Atwam where the Pit River meanders towards the sea.

(According to legend, the moon bumped earth at Atwam, making a huge circular indentation—as if the surrounding mountains were pushed out by an immense pressure. The mole people, it is said, dug under the moon and with a united thrust, shoved the moon back into its present orbit.)

Our talk turned to Akoo-Yet. "The power that balances the universe, Mis Misa, dwells there," Grandfather said, nodding a white head in the direction of the shining mountain. We knew that we were about to hear another story so old that time could not erode it and so real that only truth and understanding could recognize it.

An old coyote howled in a black canyon somewhere to the south. An owl glided nearby, wings whispering upon the darkness, huge eyes searching for slight movements in the sea of darkness. Over near the mountains there was a soft roaring sound of falling waters as the winds brushed the thousand pines. The perfume of sage moved all around us. A meteor streaked across the night sky, a white arrow—vanished—as if it were but a part of an imagination.

In our custom, one is not supposed to intrude into the silence created while someone who is telling a story hesitates to either search for proper words or to allow the listener time to comprehend. At this moment, however, I thought Grandfather should be aware of some plans for the most precious mountain of all of the mountains of his life. "Grandfather, did you know the white man wants to make buildings upon Akoo-Yet?"

After a deliberate silence Grandfather's frozen posture relaxed. His hands made an outward gesture, showing his worn palms for an instant. Then he said, "Can you say why the white man wants to make buildings there?"

Sometimes I explained things to him like he was a child, but he was a wise, old person. "It is for money and entertainment. They have a ski lift on the mountain now so the people who want to slide down the slopes don't have to climb up there. They ride on a chair. The chairs are pulled to the highest point by huge cables. The cables are held up in the air by towers much like those used by PG&E to move electricity through huge wires from here to San Francisco. Now they want to make a town on the mountain—a city."

There was another silence. Then, with the tired motions of an old grizzly bear, Grandfather said, "It must be time to tell the white people the story of Mis Misa." His story began when the present universe was made:

"When *Quon* (Silver-gray Fox), the power that created all that we know, and *Jamol* (the coyote power that *still* wants to change all that Quon has created) were through with making this land, it is said, Great Power made a law, a rule. It is hard to say. It is a rule or a law or something like that. I will call it a 'law,' but somebody else will call it a 'rule.'

"This 'law,' Great Power placed it within Akoo-Yet. But before, that mountain was just another mountain. By placing the 'law' in there, *Quon* made Akoo-Yet the most powerful of all mountains. He gave the mountain a real job. My Grandmother told me of this 'law.' It is known as Mis Misa by our people. I have never heard it called anything else. It is a small thing. You cannot see it, but you can hear it singing—if you listen carefully."

There was a long pause. We waited. Often much of the meaning of the message that our elders offer is in the quiet between sentences, sometimes it is just a hesitation. But, again, the silence could last for an unbearably long time. It is certain, however, that when you are in the presence of the old ones and they feel it is time for them to continue they simply proceed and you must not forget where they left off—even if the story is continued a year later.

In these long moments of silence I thought of how delicate and intricate the universe really is. Sun shines. Rain falls. Trees grow. Fish swim. Birds fly. Rainbows arch. Earth turns. Seasons change. Grass turns green. But what immense knowledge stirs the universe and yet holds life in a manzanita seed for years before it is heated, dampened, then sprouts?

I reasoned that there probably is not an explanation for the phenomenon of all of existence within the psyche of humanity when there is a "belief" involved because "belief" indicates that the next acceptable argument could replace the present "belief." (I would have to agree with anybody who said that Coyote fashioned "belief" from a "truth" made by Quon but altered, just a little—to make it better).

All of nature seems to be in balance with some completeness, some wholeness that most humans are denied access to.

Breaking the silence Grandfather continued, "We are told to be careful. Be careful while near this mountain. Always come to this mountain with a good heart. Mis Misa knows what you are thinking—always think good thoughts. Listen. If you do not listen you will not hear the singing and this is not respectful. It is like breaking a commandment of the white man's God, they say. You could be punished. Your whole family could be punished—even the children, the babies. That's what they say.

"The purpose of Mis Misa is but one: *To balance the earth with the universe and the universe with the earth.* When Quon created earth and universe long ago, that power understood many things. Also, that power knew that it could not make everything just right. That's a wise power. For this reason power made Mis Misa and put Mis Misa within the mountain. It lives there. You can hear it singing. Remember always this power. It balances the universe. It is a 'law.' It knows what you are thinking."

Grandfather continued to explain how Mis Misa works. It is like a free-swinging pendulum combined with a gyroscope. If the earth wanders slightly off course, Mis Misa adjusts itself to that change. If the stars are slightly off course, Mis Misa adjusts itself to that change also. It is never at rest. It is constantly adjusting. It is forever singing.

Grandfather continued, "My Grandmother was born there (on the moon), so I know. I know because she told me. She told me many things. Many things she told me. That's how I know. My Grandmother was born on the moon. She knew many things and she told me.

"She told how *chool* (the moon) was the last 'earth' but it was *itamji-uw* (all used up). At one time it was pretty. At one time it was cute. There was life everywhere. Just everywhere there was life. There was happiness. Happiness everywhere. But a wrongful power come. I don't know where it come from . . . but it come. From somewhere it come and it denied the people.

"It used *chool*. That wrongful power, it used it up.

"My Grandmother said it, that's how I know the moon was the last earth."

We again studied *chool* glowing full and strong in the silver of dawn.

"Look for signs of war and destruction," Grandfather said. "Do you see there, the ripping as with a flint knife? Over there a bruise. Over there a long scar. There was aches and there was pains. Do you see what my Grandmother said? Can you see the place there where there was war and destruction? Do you now know why *chool* is scarred and bruised and scratched?"

In silence we studied the moon. We wondered about it. I longed to know the exact reason why it is no longer an earth, why there no longer is life dwelling there. My mind raced backwards through an unknown measurement of time until it "saw" the moon, green and blue and covered with life—then my focus returned to the shimmering moon turning around earth and sun in some magnetic loneliness today. Something inside my spirit, a bell or an alarm went off! With a trembling voice, Grandfather's words pierced my thoughts once more as he pursued the story.

"It is said that the power that created earth and the universe made one mistake. It made 'vanty.' 'Vanty' makes a person love himself and nothing else. Nothing else. It is said, we must constantly guard against becoming a part of that wrong, that no good. We must be good to one another. It is easy to be bad to one another. We must not be bad to one another. We must be good to earth. We must be good to life. Do not kill life. We have no choice. This earth is the last place. We call it *atas-p-im mukuya* (to stop, last place). We have no place else to go. We must go back to the stars.

"When *chool* was close to being all used up," Grandfather continued, "the people threw their songs out into the vastness. Out there. It was a long time. Our people were in a big hurry, but it was a long time. Then, earth began to be made by that song. Just by that song! It was prepared. It was green and brown and blue.

"One day during the last war, the war between the thinkings, chool caught on fire. There was fire everywhere. It was flames. People were cooking to death. Everything was cooking to death. Earth was the closest. The people jumped. We landed here in our nation. The other people landed in their nation." *Weet-la* (the demon spirit) landed on an island beyond east salt waters, it is said. "The last to jump was frog. Frog jumped here because he was afraid if he stayed on chool he would have to walk like *weet-la,* so frog came, too."

It was not many seasons later when we found Grandfather. His spirit had proceeded to its rendezvous with destiny. He was looking up into forever with clouded eyes. How I longed to seek more answers from his wisdom, but he could not hear mortal beings, now. There were so many "whys" that I needed answers to. There were so many "whys" the whole earth needed answers to.

Once he showed us where he was going if he died. There was a small spot near the handle of the big dipper that appeared to be unoccupied. That was his destination. There is a glint there now.

"Mt. Shasta," by Frank LaPena, © 1987.

I had a dream. Grandfather had departed. At least his spirit had. He was no longer in his little shack on the flatlands of Atwam.

In that dream I watched Grandfather as he fashioned another "earth" from the "star" that he had created with his power. He labored and labored. He did not see me watching him. He hammered and chiseled. He planted and trimmed. He watered and molded. He stopped a moment to survey his work then smiled and labored again. His old and crooked hands were worn thin with a new employment, a new purpose. He did this and he did that as he prepared a new earth.

Then the light of the "star" hesitated. It glimmered like the light bulb in his ancient lamp. It flickered. It went out. Grandfather yet toiled. "Star" turned green and blue and brown. It turned green with trees and spring. It turned blue with water and with clouds of singing birds. It turned brown with herds of deer and mounds of earth. There were bears and flowers. There was soft drumming and happiness. There was life dancing, dancing in a new sunshine.

From his star, Grandfather turned and pointed his index finger at the top of Akoo-Yet. In my dream I felt Mis Misa shift ever so slightly. Perhaps it wasn't a dream. Maybe Grandfather is, at this moment, laboring to make another "earth" so that we might have a place to go if life is again *itamji-wu* (used up).

I look across the earth seeing so much unnecessary destruction. Forests are being erased throughout this entire hemisphere and around the world. Most rivers are sick and dying. The sky is gray over the huge cities. The air stinks. Pavement covers the meadows where flowers are supposed to grow. Mountains are being moved and removed. Rivers are diverted and the water terribly polluted. Earth is being drilled into and her heart and her guts and her blood are being used as private property for private gain.

There is an immense vacuum where the spiritual connection between human beings and nature is supposed to be—that umbilical cord that we inherited long before our birth and we were instructed to nurture and to protect for all of the existence of our nations. It seems as though too many people think that nature is an element that they are not a part of. They, like the old Coyote, think that nature, life, must be tamed, must be challenged, must be conquered, must be changed in order to make it better.

History has unveiled many battles and many wars. In this era, we can look back through the pages of time like changing channels on the TV. Yes, there have been some terrible wars. Yes, there has been much destruction. Yes, some wars have engaged the entire world.

But those conflicts were over human supremacy—which king or which governing entity would rule the masses and control the bounty of earth. Who would be the master over all of the people and who would control the wealth. Whose gnarled dreams would be unleashed at which time in history to make an indelible mark urged through vanity.

In these conflicts mother earth was treated as a woman slave. She had to yield the materials that were needed to continue the conflagration. She had to yield the waters for the thirsty battalions. She had to yield fruit and food to feed the armies that marched. She had to provide the medicine to heal the wounded. She had to provide the bounty that was the crown for the victor!

These are new times. The whole earth is threatened with extinction. No longer is it acceptable for human beings to contend for the supreme pinnacle of the various societies of earth; from this moment forward there must be a battle, there must be an intense war.

But this time for the salvaging of earth. This time to see whether or not there will be only a "moon" left here one day after all of the products are used up, after the balance of existence has turned for the worse, and after vanity has led us down a time-path that has an absolute expiration date (and, before we discover that my dream of Grandfather was simply that).

Yes, Grandfather's story is *only an Indian story.* But it is a story with evidence—the moon. It is a story that has endured time and maintains its direction and its solemn concern. There is a moon—there is also Mis Misa. Not once have I encountered a reference to that beautiful power within that sacred mountain—while "constructionists" and "progressives" plot the future of development of Akoo-Yet. The "constructionists" see Akoo-Yet as a piece of valuable real estate. They fail to see its sacred value. For how many more seasons can these mistakes find pardon within nature?

My thoughts lead me to walk among the stars every morning during the silver just before dawn, *lok-mhe.* Ringing in my ears the worried words of Grandfather: "When I was a child long ago, my Grandmother said there was a war. It was a big war between the people—a war between thinkings. There was a terrible war. That war used up the moon. When the moon caught fire there wasn't enough water to put it out. It was all used up."

I look upon the moon and worry. I look upon earth and see the corporate entities exercising greed and profit as their reasons for their existence. I see children crying and hungry all around the world. I see the land of my Grandmother and Grandfather being used up.

Yes, there is a callousness in the manner that people have abused the world. Yes, environmentally oriented people must oppose that irresponsibility. Yes, children have a right to live in respect and harmony. Yes, Grandmothers and Grandfathers have an absolute right to peace and protection. Yes, we, the able and capable, have an absolute duty to defend our loved ones in their journey through life.

Yes, there will be a terrible and great war again. There must be, for the silver of dawn, first light, belongs to us all, equally. We must not deny its panorama to anybody—especially those we are, by our spirit, bound to protect forever. We should not fear. Besides the dawn of day and the strength of the power that turns earth around the sun and the sun around a greater wonder, we have, as an ally, Mis Misa.

A RADIANT CURVE

Luci Tapahonso

The beginning was mist.
The first Holy Ones talked and sang as always.
They created light, night, and day.
They sang into place the mountains,
the rivers, plants, and animals.
They sang us into life.

2

PERCEPTIONS OF AMERICA'S NATIVE DEMOCRACIES

Donald A. Grinde, Jr., and Bruce E. Johansen

This is reversing the natural order of things. A tractable people may be governed in large bodies but, in proportion as they depart from this character, the extent of their government must be less. We see into what small divisions the Indians are obliged to reduce their societies.

—Thomas Jefferson, disputing proposals to enlarge
the size of states to be admitted to the Union

All along the Atlantic seaboard, Indian nations had already formed confederacies by the time they first encountered European immigrants—from the "federated republic" of the Creeks in what is now Georgia and Florida; to the Cherokees and Choctaws in the Carolinas; to the Iroquois and their allies, the Hurons, in the Saint Lawrence Valley; to the Penacook federation of New England, among many others. According to Anthony F. C. Wallace, "Ethnic confederacies were common among all the Indian tribes of the Northeast."

Village bands, and tribes speaking similar languages, holding similar customs, and sharing a tradition of similar origin usually combined into a loose union that at least minimized warfare among themselves. The Illinois

From *Exemplar of Liberty: Native America and the Evolution of Democracy,* by Donald A. Grinde, Jr., and Bruce E. Johansen. Copyright 1991 by the Regents of the University of California, American Indian Studies Center, UCLA. Reprinted with permission.

Confederacy, the "Three Fires" of the Chippewa, Ottawa and Pottawatomi, the Wapenaki Confederacy, the Powhatan Confederacies, the tripartite Miami—all the neighbors of the Iroquois—were members of one confederation or another.[1]

By the late eighteenth century, as resentment against England's taxation flared into open rebellion, the colonists' formative ideology displayed widespread knowledge of Native governmental systems. Thomas Jefferson, Benjamin Franklin, James Adair, Father Le Jeune, and others—from framers to farmers along the length of the coast and into the Saint Lawrence Valley—all saw governmental systems that were remarkably similar in broad outline but had their own variations on the common theme of democracy in councils. These systems had evolved to coordinate governance—across geographic distances that must have seemed huge to these transplanted Europeans—and permit maximum freedom to nations within confederations and individuals within nations.

The colonists forming the United States were charged with similar tasks in molding their own emerging nation, so it should not be surprising that early government in the United States (especially under the Articles of Confederation) greatly resembled Native systems in many respects. This is not to say that the founders copied Indian societies—if they had, we would have evolved precincts along family lines, and our senators and representatives would be nominated solely by women—but to say that the Native systems of governance, along with European precedents, were factored into a new ideological equation.

The Iroquois' system was the best known to the colonists (in large part because of their pivotal position in diplomacy, not only between the English and French but also among other Native confederacies); therefore, we begin our examination of how Native confederacies governed themselves with their example. Called the Iroquois by the French and the Five (later Six) Nations by the English, the Haudenosaunee controlled the only relatively level overland passage (the later route of the Erie Canal) between the English colonies on the coast and the French settlements in the Saint Lawrence Valley; their diplomatic influence permeated the entire eastern half of North America.

Cadwallader Colden, who was regarded as "the best-informed man in the New World on the affairs of the British-American colonies," provided the first systematic study of the Haudenosaunee in 1727, which he augmented in 1747. Franklin read Colden's *The History of the Five Indian Nations Depending on the Province of New York in America* before he began his diplomatic

career by representing Pennsylvania in meetings with the Iroquois and their allies. After drawing up his Albany Plan of Union in 1754, which in some respects greatly resembled the Iroquois Confederacy's governmental structure, Franklin's first stop was Colden's estate. Colden held several colonial offices, including lieutenant governor of New York. He also carried on extensive research in various natural sciences and was an anthropologist before the field had a name. Colden was also an adopted Mohawk.

Because of their skills at oratory, warfare, and diplomacy, as well as the republican nature of their government, Colden compared the Iroquois to the Romans. "When Life and Liberty came in competition, indeed, I think our Indians have outdone the Romans in this particular. . . . The Five Nations consisted of men whose courage could not be shaken." Colden's belief that the Indians, particularly the Iroquois, provided the new Americans with a window on their own antiquity was shared by Franklin, Jefferson, and Thomas Paine and, a century later, by Karl Marx and Frederick Engels as well as the founders of modern feminism. For two centuries of revolutionaries and reformers, this belief provided a crucial link between Indian societies and their own as well as a counterpoint by which to judge society's contemporary ills.

Elaborating on his belief, Colden wrote, "We are fond of searching into remote Antiquity to know the manners of our earliest progenitors; if I be not mistaken, the Indians are living images of them," an assumption held in common with many other writers about the New World and its peoples—from Peter Martyr in the sixteenth century to Engels in the late nineteenth century.

> The present state of the Indian Nations exactly shows the most Ancient and Original Condition of almost every Nation; so, I believe that here we may with more certainty see the original form of all government, than in the most curious Speculations of the Learned; and that the Patriarchial and other Schemes in Politicks are no better than Hypotheses in Philosophy, and as prejudicial to real Knowledge.[2]

Colden provided an extensive description of the Iroquois' form of government, which had "continued so long that the Christians know nothing of the original of it."

> Each Nation is an Absolute Republick by its self, governed in all Publick affairs of War and Peace by the Sachems of Old Men, whose Authority and Power is gained by and consists wholly in the opinions of the rest of the Nation in their Wisdom and Integrity. They never

execute their Resolutions by Compulsion or Force Upon any of their People.[3]

The Five Nations have such absolute Notions of Liberty that they allow no Kind of Superiority of one over another, and banish all Servitude from their Territories.[4]

Although some twentieth-century anthropologists maintain that the Iroquois League was only fully formed after Europeans made landfall in North America, the historical records of Europeans such as Colden contained no hint that the Confederacy was in formation at that time. The consensus of seventeenth- and eighteenth-century writers, who saw the Confederacy in its full flower, was that it had formed sometime before colonization. The oral history of the Iroquois indicated a founding date somewhere between A.D. 1000 and 1450. Lewis Henry Morgan and Horatio E. Hale estimated the founding date to be toward the end of that spectrum, although William N. Fenton has placed his estimate even later. What united all these estimates and educated guesses was their agreement that the League was firmly in place before the coming of the Europeans.

According to Iroquois oral history, the Confederacy was formed by the Huron prophet Deganawidah (called "the Peacemaker" in oral discourse), who, because he stuttered so badly he could hardly speak, decided to enlist the aid of Aiowantha (sometimes called Hiawatha) in order to spread his vision of a united Haudenosaunee confederacy. The oral history attributed the Peacemaker's stuttering to a double row of teeth. The Confederacy originally included the Mohawks, Oneidas, Onondagas, Cayugas, and Senecas; the sixth nation, the Tuscaroras, migrated into Iroquois country in the early eighteenth century.

Peace among the formerly antagonistic nations was procured and maintained through the Haudenosaunee's Great Law of Peace [*Kaianerekowa*], which was passed from generation to generation by the use of wampum, a form of written communication that outlined a complex system of checks and balances between nations and sexes. Although a complete oral recitation of the Great Law can take several days, encapsulated versions of it have been translated into English for more than a hundred years and provide one reason why the Iroquois are cited so often today in debates regarding the origins of fundamental law in the United States. While many other Native confederacies existed along the borders of the British colonies, most records of the specific provisions of their governments have been lost.

To understand the provisions of the Great Law, one must first understand some of the symbols it used to represent the Confederacy. The Confederacy itself was likened to an extended, traditional longhouse, with the Mohawks guarding the "eastern door," the Senecas at the "western door," and the Onondagas tending the ceremonial council fire in the middle. The primary national symbol of the Haudenosaunee was the Great White Pine, which served throughout the Great Law as a metaphor for the Confederacy. Its branches sheltered the people of the Five Nations, and its roots spread to the four directions, inviting other peoples, regardless of race or nationality, to take refuge under the tree. The Haudenosaunee recognized no bars to dual citizenship; in fact, many influential figures in the English colonies and early United States, Colden among them, were adopted into Iroquois nations.

Each of the five nations maintained its own council, whose sachems were nominated by the clan mothers of families holding hereditary rights to office titles. The Grand Council at Onondaga was drawn from the individual national councils, but could also nominate sachems outside the local hereditary structures based on merit alone. These sachems, called "pine tree chiefs," were said to have sprung from the body of the people much as the symbolic Great White Pine had grown from the earth.

The rights, duties, and qualifications of sachems were explicitly outlined, and the clan mothers could remove (or impeach) a sachem who was found guilty of any of a number of abuses of office—from missed meetings to murder. An errant chief was summoned to face charges by the war chiefs, who, in peacetime, acted as the peoples' eyes and ears in the council (somewhat as the role of the press was envisioned by Jefferson and other founders of the United States). A sachem was given three warnings, then removed from the council if he did not mend his ways. A sachem found guilty of murder not only lost his title, but his entire family also was deprived of its right to representation. His women relatives who held the rights to office were "buried," and their title was transferred to a sister family. Iroquois law also provided for the removal from office of sachems who could no longer adequately function (a measure remarkably similar to the twenty-fifth amendment to the United States Constitution, adopted in 1967, which detailed procedures for the removal of an incapacitated president). Sachems were not allowed to name their own successors, nor could they carry their titles to the grave—the Great Law even provided a ceremony for removing the title from a dying chief.

The Great Law stipulated that sachems' skins must be seven spans thick, so that they would be able to withstand the criticism of their constituents. The law pointed out that sachems should take pains not to become angry when people scrutinized their conduct in governmental affairs. Such a point of view pervades the writings of Jefferson and Franklin, although it was not fully codified into United States law until the Supreme Court decision *New York Times v. Sullivan* (1964), which made it virtually impossible for public officials to sue for libel.

The Great Law also included provisions guaranteeing freedom of religion and the right of redress before the Grand Council. It even forbade unauthorized entry into homes—measures which sound familiar to United States citizens through the Bill of Rights.

As was mentioned earlier, women played a profound role in Iroquois political life. Although the Iroquois were bound together by a clan and chieftain system, which was buttressed by a similar linguistic base, the League of the Iroquois was much more than simply a kinship state. The basic unit of government was the "hearth," which consisted of a mother and her children. Each hearth was part of a wider group called an *otiianer*, and two or more *otiianers* constituted a clan. The word *otiianer* specifically referred to the female heirs to the chieftainship titles of the League. The *otiianer* women selected one of the males within their group to fill any of the fifty seats in the League.

All the sons and daughters of a particular clan were related through uterine families that often lived far apart. In this system, a husband went to live with his wife's family, and their children became members of the mother's clan by right of birth. Through matrilineal descent, the Iroquois formed cohesive political groups—headed by the "clan mothers"—that had little to do with where people lived or from what village the hearths originated. All authority sprang from the people of the various clans that made up the Iroquois Confederacy. The clan mothers appointed the male delegates and deputies who, after consultation within the clan, spoke for them at tribal meetings where issues and questions were formulated and subsequently debated in council.

Iroquois political philosophy was rooted in the concept that all life was spiritually unified with the natural environment and other forces surrounding people. The Iroquois believed that the spiritual power of one person was limited, but was enhanced when combined with other individuals in a hearth, *otiianer*, or clan. Whenever a person died, whether of natural causes or by force, the "public" power was diminished. To maintain the strength of the group, the dead were replaced either by natural increase or by adopting captives of war. This practice insured the continued power and durability of the matrilineal system as well as the kinship state.

Instead of formal instruments of authority, the Iroquois governed behavior by instilling a sense of pride and belonging to the group through common rituals and the careful rearing of children. Iroquois youth were trained to enter a society that was egalitarian, with power more evenly distributed between male and female, young and old, than was common in Euro-American society. Iroquois culture could be loosely called a "shame culture" because of its emphasis on honor, duty, and collaborative behavior, while European culture was more "guilt-oriented," since it emphasized an authoritarian hierarchy and advancement through the acquisition of property, status, and material possessions. Because the Iroquois prized competence as a protector/provider more than material wealth, their children were trained to think for themselves as well as provide for others. The Iroquois did not respect submissive people who were cowed by authority. With this approach, Iroquois society had no use for the elaborate European mechanisms of control to direct the lives of its citizenry. Ostracism and shame were the primary punishments for transgressors, until they had atoned for their actions and demonstrated that they had undergone a purification process.

The League of the Iroquois arose out of the desire to resolve the problem of the blood feud. Before the tribal councils had the Great Law of Peace to sanctify and buttress their society, blood revenge caused strife. Once a clan was reduced by murder or kidnapping, the victim's kinfolk were bound by clan law to avenge the loss of their relative, resulting in endless recriminations. As long as justice and the monopoly on violence resided in the clans, there was no hope of peace and goodwill.

Visionaries among the Iroquois such as Hiawatha (who lived among the Onondagas) tried to call councils to eliminate the blood feud, but all attempts were thwarted by the evil and twisted wizard Tadodaho, an Onondaga who used magic and spies to rule by fear and intimidation. After having failed to defeat the wizard, Hiawatha traveled to countless Mohawk, Oneida, and Cayuga villages with his message of peace and brotherhood. He found acceptance everywhere he went, with the proviso that he first persuade the formidable Tadodaho and the Onondagas to embrace the covenant of peace. Just as Hiawatha was despairing, the prophet Deganawidah entered his life and changed the nature of things among the Iroquois; together,

"The Peace Tree" from *Migration of the Iroquois*, 2nd ed., by Aren Wkweks. Illustration by John Kahionhes Fadden. Copyright © 1971 by White Roots of Peace, Mohawk Nation at Akwesasne via Rooseveltown, NY 13683. Reprinted with permission.

Deganawidah's tree had four white roots that stretched to the four directions of the earth. A snow-white carpet of thistledown spread out from the base of the tree, covering the surrounding countryside and protecting the peoples who embraced the three life-affirming principles. Deganawidah explained that this tree was humanity, living within the principles governing relations among human beings, and the eagle perched on top of the giant pine was humanity's lookout against enemies who would disturb the peace. He postulated that the white carpet could cover the entire earth and provide a shelter of peace and brotherhood for all mankind. His vision was a message from the Creator, bringing harmony to human existence and uniting all peoples into a single family guided by three principles.

With such a powerful vision, Deganawidah and Hiawatha were able to subdue Tadodaho and transform his mind. Deganawidah removed the evil feelings and thoughts from the head of Tadodaho and commanded him to "strive . . . to make reason and the peaceful mind prevail." The evil wizard was reborn as a humane person, charged with implementing the message of Deganawidah. After Tadodaho's redemption, Onondaga became the central fire of the Haudenosaunee and the Onondagas the "fire keepers" of the new Confederacy. (To this day, the Great Council Fire of the Iroquois Confederacy is kept in the land of the Onondagas.)

Deganawidah then gathered together the clan leaders of the Five Nations (Mohawk, Oneida, Onondaga, Cayuga, and Seneca) around the council fire at Onondaga to hear the laws and government of the Confederacy, which espoused peace, brotherhood, and unity, a balance of power, the natural rights of all people, and sharing of resources, as well as provisions for impeachment or removal of leaders. Moreover, the blood feud was outlawed and replaced by a Condolence Ceremony. Under this new law, when a man was killed, his grieving family could forego the option of exacting clan revenge (the taking of the life of the murderer or a member of the murderer's clan) and, instead, could accept twenty strings of wampum (freshwater shells strung together) from the slayer's family (ten for the dead person and ten for the murderer's own life). In the case of the murder of a woman, the price became thirty wampum strings. Through this ceremony, the monopoly on legally sanctioned violence was enlarged from the clan to the League.

Deganawidah gave strict instructions governing the conduct of the League and its deliberations.

they developed a powerful message of peace. Deganawidah's vision gave substance to Hiawatha's oratory, and so the Constitution of the Iroquois was formulated.

In his vision, Deganawidah saw a giant evergreen (the Great White Pine) reaching to the sky and gaining strength from three counterbalancing principles of life. The first law of nature was that a stable mind and healthy body must be in balance so that peace between individuals and groups could occur. Secondly, Deganawidah believed that humane conduct, thought, and speech were requirements for equity and justice among peoples. Finally, he divined a society in which physical strength and civil authority would reinforce the power of the clan system.

Tadodaho was to maintain the fire and call the Onondaga chiefs together to determine if an issue brought before him was pressing enough to call to the attention of the Council of the Confederacy. If the proposed issue merited council consideration, it would assemble and Tadodaho would kindle a fire and announce the purpose of the meeting. The rising smoke penetrating the sky was a signal to the Iroquois allies that the council was in session. The Onondaga chiefs and Tadodaho were charged with keeping the council area free from distractions.

The Confederacy's legislative process began with a policy debate by the Keepers of the Eastern Door (Mohawks) and the Keepers of the Western Door (Senecas). The question was then thrown across the fire to the Oneida and Cayuga statesmen (the younger brothers) for discussion in much the same manner. Once consensus was achieved among the Oneidas and the Cayugas, the discussion returned to the elder brothers—first to the Senecas and Mohawks for confirmation and finally to the Onondagas for their decision. At this stage, the Onondagas had a power similar to judicial review; that is, they could raise objections to the proposed measure if they believed it was inconsistent with the Great Law. Essentially, the legislators could rewrite the proposed law on the spot so as to be in accord with the Constitution of the Iroquois. Once the Onondaga sachems had reached consensus, Tadodaho gave the decision to Honowireton (an Onondaga chief who presided over debates between the delegations) for confirmation. Finally, Honowireton or Tadodaho returned the legislation to the Mohawks and the Senecas for announcement to the Grand Council.

The overall intent of such a parliamentary procedure was to encourage unity at each step by emphasizing checks and balances, public debate, and consensus. The League's legislative process was similar to the mechanisms of the Albany Plan of Union, the Articles of Confederation, and the United States Constitution.

The rights of the Iroquois citizenry were protected by portions of the Great Law. According to Section 93,

> Whenever an especially important matter . . . is presented before the League Council . . . threatening their utter ruin, then the chiefs of the League must submit the matter to the decision of their people.[5]

Public opinion played an important role. Within the League of the Iroquois, people could have a direct say in the formulation of government policy even if the sachems chose to ignore the will of the people. According to Section 16 of the Great Law of Peace, "If the conditions . . . arise . . . to . . . change . . . this law, the case shall be . . . considered and if the new beam seems . . . beneficial, the . . . change . . . if adopted, shall be called, "Added to the Rafters." This law resembles provisions for popular initiative in several states of the United States, as well as the mechanisms by which the federal and many state constitutions may be amended.

The people of the League could also initiate impeachment proceedings and treason charges as well as alert the council to public opinion on a specific matter. The Iroquois people also had the power to remove the "hereditary" sachems of the League's Council. Upon the death or removal of a Confederacy chief, his title reverted to the women in his clan, who had "inherited the right" to appoint and remove peace chiefs to the Confederacy. After the clan mothers had nominated the next chief (who was always a male), their proposal was put before the men of the clan. The nomination was then forwarded to the council of the League, where the new chief was installed.

The League of the Iroquois was a family-oriented government, which had a constitution with a fixed corpus of laws concerned with mutual defense. Through the elimination of the clan blood feud, the state was given a monopoly on legally sanctioned violence, which brought peace through a fundamental social contract. But the Iroquois were not inclined to give much power to authorities because of their basic psychological and social attitudes. Thus, unity, peace, and brotherhood were balanced against the natural rights of all people and the necessity of sharing resources equitably. Unity for mutual defense was an abiding concept within the League and was represented by a bundle of five arrows tied together to symbolize the complete union of the nations and the unbroken strength that such a unity provides (Section 57 of the Great Law of the Iroquois). With the strength of many came peace for future generations.

The notion of federalism was strictly adhered to by the Iroquois. The hereditary Iroquois sachems were interested only in external matters such as war, peace, and treaty-making. The Grand Council could not interfere in the internal affairs of the tribe. Each tribe had its own sachems, but their role was limited to matters between themselves and other tribes; they had no say in matters that were traditionally the concern of the clan.

Through public opinion and debate, the Great Law gave basic rights to the Iroquois people within a distinctive and representative governmental framework. The Great Law solved disputes by giving all parties an equal hearing. The Grand Council often functioned as a think tank, for thinking was the primary activity that went on underneath the Great Tree. The Iroquois believed that the more thinkers there were beneath the tree, the better. The Iroquois League accorded prestige to the peace chiefs and thus sought to reduce conflict between war and peace chiefs and the generations. The middle-aged peace chiefs were the fire keepers, encircled by warrior/providers, women, and, finally, the public-at-large. Although the tribes had unequal representation, this was irrelevant, since each tribe voted as one. At the level of village, tribe, and Grand Council, consensus devices were used to obtain unanimity and to report up and down the governmental structure. The League was not able to centralize power in matters other than mutual defense, but it was effective in diminishing friction among the Five Nations. The kinship state, with its imagery of a longhouse spread afar, was clearly comprehended by the Iroquois people. Iroquois power rested upon the consent of the governed and was not coercive in areas of military service, taxation, and police powers.

To the colonial Americans chafing under British authority, such a government and attitude toward freedom were powerful examples that could be used in resisting British sovereignty and tyranny. Certainly, the imagery and concepts of the League had a powerful influence on the hearts and minds of the founders and the American people. Likewise, the Iroquois leaders took an active interest in teaching colonial leaders about the tenets of the Iroquois constitution.

The system of the Hurons was remarkably similar to that of their neighbors, the Iroquois. According to Bruce J. Trigger's *Children of the Authentic: A History of the Huron People*, the Hurons' polity, like the Iroquois', was rooted in family structure. Leaders of the various clans used public opinion and consensus to shape decisions, and issues "were usually decided upon by majority vote" and "discussed until a general consensus was reached." No human being would be expected to be bound by a decision to which conscious consent had not been given.

As with the Iroquois, the Huron clans—Porcupine, Snake, Deer, Beaver, Hawk, Turtle, Bear, and Wolf—created familial affinity across the boundaries of their four confederated nations. Members of each clan could trace their ancestry to a common origin through the female line. In each village, clan members elected a civil chief and a war chief. The titles were carried through the female family line, but bestowed on men. While the titles were hereditary in the same sense as in the Iroquois tradition, they did not pass from head to head of a particular family as in most European monarchies. When the time came to choose a leader, members of each clan segment in a particular village had a choice of several candidates, whose personal qualities—"intelligence, oratorical ability, reputation for generosity, and, above all, performance as a warrior"—counted most heavily.

If a village included more than one clan segment (most did, but not all), the elected leaders of each segment formed a village council, which met on purely local issues. The council resolved issues through debate that led to consensus. Each of the four nations, including several villages, held councils that included all the village civil and war chiefs. The four nations—the Attignawantan, Arendarhonon, Attigneenongahac, and Tahontaenrat—also held a central council, which, according to Trigger, probably consisted of all the village chiefs, representing all the clans. Compared to the Iroquois Grand Council, very little documentation exists regarding this council's operations. It is likely that the Huron Confederacy had a looser structure, since its central council met only once a year, usually for several weeks in the spring (although emergency meetings could be called at any time). The meeting of the central council was meant to bind the four nations and served as much as a social occasion as it was a legislative session. Its proceedings were embellished with feasts to install new village headmen, reunions among old friends, singing, dancing, and war feasts. The central council dealt with issues that affected all four nations in common, such as treaty negotiations and trade with Europeans.

When the Huron central council met, the Attignawantan (by far the largest of the four nations) sat on one side of a ceremonial longhouse, across the council fire from the representatives of the other three nations. The speaker, always an Attignawantan, presided over the speeches of welcome and thanksgiving, which were followed by recitation of the agenda. As each item of the agenda was taken up, the representatives stated their opinions in turn, without interruption. Speaking in council called for a special oratorical style, "full of metaphors, circumlocutions, and other rhetorical devices that were uncommon in everyday speech." Members of the council were expected to retain their composure, even during severe disagreement, in order to guide the debate toward eventual consensus. Many procedures, such as those governing debate among the nations on each side of the council fire or those regarding desirable qualities for sachems or grounds for impeachment, probably existed but have been lost to history.

In the early eighteenth century, the Cherokee Nation was composed of sixty villages, averaging three to four hundred persons each, in five regions. Each village controlled its own affairs and sent delegates to a national council only in times of national emergency. The Cherokees took public opinion so seriously that, if a village became too large (about five hundred people) to permit each adult a voice in council, it was usually split in two. It may have been this kind of political organization that Jefferson had in mind when he penned the following comment regarding a proposal to make the states several times larger than the original colonies:

> This is reversing the natural order of things. A tractable people may be governed in large bodies but, in proportion as they depart from this character, the extent of their government must be less. We see into what small divisions the Indians are obliged to reduce their societies.[6]

In Cherokee society, each adult was regarded as an equal in political matters, and leadership titles were few and informal. Therefore, when Europeans sought "kings" or "chiefs" with whom to negotiate treaties, they usually did not understand that the individuals holding these titles could not compel the allegiance or obedience of others. The Cherokees made a conscious effort to keep government to a minimum, in the belief that personal freedom would be enhanced. George Milliken Johnson, a surgeon who lived with the Cherokees during the middle of the eighteenth century, remarked that "subjugation is what they are unacquainted with . . . there being no such thing as coercive Power among them." Another observer commented that it was "by native politeness alone" that Cherokee chiefs were able to "bind the hearts of their subjects, and carry them wherever they will."

As with many other confederacies, a clan system bound the individual Cherokee villages together. A man or woman, traveling outside his or her own village, knew that members of the same clan awaited them to provide hospitality and other support. The clan system cemented the Confederacy, giving it enough strength and endurance to prevent such a high degree of local autonomy from degenerating into anarchy. In village councils, each clan met in caucus before consensus decisions were reached in a general session. In the new United States, the clan system was replaced by the formation of a large number of voluntary organizations that were national in scope. Franklin, for instance, encouraged these kinds of affiliations in order to tie together people in a geographical area that must have seemed vast—not only to immigrants who were accustomed to the smaller scale of Western Europe, but also to their sons and daughters.

The Cherokees also frowned on acquisition of material wealth. Henry Timberlake speculated that the Cherokees buried valuables with the dead to prevent the development of a class structure based on inherited wealth, thereby making "merit the sole means of acquiring power, honor and riches." One cannot help but wonder how this native example affected the ongoing debate in the colonies and early United States over primogeniture—the right of the first-born son to all or most of his father's estate, a European custom bitterly opposed by Jefferson. According to Timberlake's account, the Cherokees maintained a ceremony meant to provide for the poor. During a special war dance, as each warrior was called upon to recount the taking of his first scalp, anyone with something to spare—"a string of wampum" or a piece of silver "plate, wire, paint," or lead—heaped the goods on a blanket or animal skin that had been placed on the ground. The collection was later divided among the poor of the community, with a share reserved for the musicians who had provided entertainment during the ceremony.

The Choctaws, like the Cherokees, elected leaders from each town or village and sent them to a central council. Their system has been characterized as "amazingly efficient," combining "elected officials, unlimited debate, civilian rule, and local self-government."

Some of the similarities among the political systems of the Iroquois, Hurons, and Cherokees probably were not accidental, since all three groups were linked by a common ancestry. Floyd G. Bloomsbury, a linguist, traced the Iroquois and Cherokee linguistic base to a shared language, which split about thirty-five to thirty-eight hundred years ago. There is evidence that the Cherokees migrated southeastward from the Ohio valley and shared the basics of their language with both the Iroquois and the Hurons; this migration continued as late as 1700. In fact, it was about that time that the Tuscaroras moved from an area near Cherokee country to become the sixth nation of the Iroquois.

The similarities in the ways in which colonial observers described Native societies, whether or not the native politics actually operated similarly, may have been due to the purpose of their study. As noted earlier, the observers' perceptions of these societies often were incomplete and profoundly reshaped by their own struggle for liberty; therefore, it is likely that native political reality was much more varied, and differences more pronounced, than many contemporary observers believed. However, their beliefs shaped their perceptions of reality; so, even if this knowledge is deemed incomplete or inaccurate by present-day standards, it does not mean that those who drew an image of liberty from Native societies got nothing from their endeavors. Quite the opposite was true. Views and visions of America also profoundly affected debate and the course of empire in Europe, as knowledge of Native political structures became crucial to the conduct of trade and diplomacy in North America.

NOTES

1. Anthony F. C. Wallace, *The Death and Rebirth of the Seneca* (New York: Vintage Books, 1969), p. 42.

2. Cadwallader Colden, *The History of the Five Indian Nations Depending on the Province of New York in America* [1727 and 1747] (Ithaca, N.Y.: Cornell University Press, 1968), p. xx.

3. Colden, Ibid., p. xx.

4. Colden, Ibid., p. xix.

5. Paul A. W. Wallace, *The White Roots of Peace* (Philadelphia: University of Pennsylvania Press, 1946), sec. 93.

6. Adrienne Koch and William Peden, eds., *The Life and Selected Writings of Thomas Jefferson* (New York: The Modern Library, 1944), p. 408.

ORIGINS OF IROQUOIS POLITICAL THOUGHT

John Mohawk

The story of the White Roots of Peace is the story of the thinking around the events which led to the founding of the League of the Haudenosaunee (as the Six Nations Iroquois call themselves).

This was a time of great sorrow and terror for the Haudenosaunee. All order and safety had broken down completely and the rule of the headhunter dominated the culture.

The Peacemaker sought out the most remarkable survivors of this random and undeclared war and he initiated discussions with them. He offered the idea that all human beings possess the power of rational thought and that in the belief in rational thought is to be found the power to create peace.

The Peacemaker laid forth a promise of a hopeful future, a future in which there would be no wars, a future in which human beings would gather together to use their minds to create peace. He raised the idea of rational thinking to the status of a political principle. He promoted clear thinking as the highest human potential, and he preached it in the spiritual language of his contemporaries.

The Peacemaker spent considerable time moving from individual to individual among the leadership of the peoples who much later would come to be known as the Mohawk, the Oneida, the Onondaga, the Cayuga, and the Seneca nations.

It was not possible to take action to bring about a solution of the blood feuds because people simply could not think clearly in an environment dominated by revenge and death,

fear and hatred. The Peacemaker brought a process of clear thinking to that reality.

He promised them power. Not military power, but the power of righteousness. He defined righteousness as the result of the best thinking of collective minds operating from principles which assume that a sane world requires that we provide a safe environment for our children seven generations into the future.

A people living in fear cannot apply their potentially best thinking to solving their problems. A people living under terror can barely think at all.

The weapons may change, the distinct situations may change, but warfare and human needs remain the same. Human beings, in order to function at their very best, need to believe in a future. To motivate them, they need a vision of that future which they can help to create. They need to believe they have the potential to do what must be done in order to reach that future, and they need to have a collective identity which supports them in doing that.

The White Roots continue to represent a tradition of thinking about ourselves as a species, and the responsibility to use our minds that we will continue to survive and to create a good world for our children seven generations into the future.

Excerpted with permission of the author from *Northeast Indian Quarterly* (Summer 1986). Reprinted by permission of Akwe:kon Press.

LATIN AMERICA'S INDIGENOUS PEOPLES
CHANGING IDENTITIES AND FORMS OF RESISTANCE

Michael Kearney and Stefano Varese

Any attempt to make meaningful and valid generalizations about the contemporary Indigenous peoples of the Americas is a daunting task given their vast geographical extension and wide variation in social forms and living conditions. There are tens of millions of Indigenous peoples, or *indígenas*, in Latin America. Their distribution today generally follows that of pre-Columbian population patterns. Thus, they range from a majority of the population in Bolivia, Peru, and Guatemala to large minorities in Mexico, Colombia, Venezuela, Ecuador, Paraguay, and Chile. A small minority in the vastness of Brazil, *indígenas* nevertheless have acquired unanticipated importance in the politics of their country.

Contemporary Indigenous identities are best understood through historical examination. Several major epochs have shaped the economic and political conditions affecting Indigenous communities. Furthermore, these conditions continue to change, just as anthropological understandings about Indigenous identity have evolved. Therefore, in reviewing the status of the contemporary *indígenas* in Latin America, we must also comment on the development of the concepts that have been used to interpret these identities.

There are various ways to approach the history and identity of Indigenous peoples. Anthropological thinking was dominated until recently by the assimilation model. In this view, the *indígenas* possess traditional social forms and cultures that will eventually give way to modern society, a process that is thought to occur through the acceptance of modern technology and cultural forms whereby *indígenas* are supposed to be acculturated into modern society. This perspective sees contemporary Indigenous identities largely as survivals from earlier periods, especially pre-Columbian times. One implication of this acculturation perspective is that Indigenous communities are destined to disappear as successive generations lose their traditional traits and assimilate into modern society. To be sure, there has been much acculturation and assimilation of *indígenas* who have retained few traits stemming from their original cultures. Hundreds of local Indigenous communities and their languages have completely disappeared over the past five hundred years. But at the same time, many *indígenas* have displayed a remarkable staying power, and in recent years their presence has become ever more notable.

The durability of the *indígenas* called for a different theoretical perspective. The working notion of this theory is that social identity is formed largely in opposition to others in a dialectic of what are called "othering" and "self-attribution." The rest of this chapter explores this twofold phenomenon of leveling and differentiation and assumes that it is inherent not only in local but also in global economic and cultural relations.

FROM PRE-COLUMBIAN TO COLONIAL SOCIETIES

At the end of the fifteenth century, when the first appreciable numbers of Europeans came into their midst, the Native peoples of what is now Latin America were arrayed in numerous and diverse types of societies ranging from nomadic foraging bands to complex state civilizations comparable to those of Asia and Europe. In the two centuries after the arrival of Columbus, the destinies of *indígenas* of the region were overwhelmingly shaped by the devastating impact of this encounter; numerous communities disappeared completely while others suffered population declines of 80 to 100 percent (for an overview of the human tragedy associated with the Conquest, see Galeano 1973). During the ensuing three hundred years the identity of *indígenas* was shaped by their subordinate position as colonized subjects and, later, as subordinated ethnic groups within the postcolonial nation-states dominated by non-*indígenas*.

The Conquest irrevocably incorporated the Indigenous peoples into global relationships with European states in what was becoming a world capitalist system (Wolf 1982). As the logic of that new world order was understood by the political leaders of the time, European nations, to prosper and to be strong vis-à-vis other nations, needed colonies as sources of wealth. According to the theory of mercantilism that gained favor in sixteenth-century Europe and influenced economic thought through the eighteenth, the ideal colonies possessed both natural resources and the Native populations needed to extract them. The resources produced by cheap labor in the colonies could supply industries in the home countries, which in turn would produce merchandise for sale back to the colonies and on the world market in general.

The identity of the *indígenas* during the Conquest and colonial periods was shaped mainly by Spanish, Portuguese, French, and English policies designed, first, to maintain distinctions between the European nations and their colonies in what was called the New World and, second, to maintain, within the colonies, the distinctions between Europeans and the non-Europeans found there. Spanish occupation of the Americas and Spanish colonial policies regarding the *indígenas* contrasted sharply with those of the English in their colonial project in North America, which was effected largely through the migration of prosperous dissident religious communities consisting of entire families. Imbued with notions of religious and economic freedom, they sought worldly and spiritual salvation through industry and commerce in which the Indigenous peoples were seen as having no significant role. Indeed, the English colonists of North America saw the *indígenas* more as obstacles to their projects than as resources.

At the time of its conquest of the Americas, Spain had emerged from several hundred years of military struggle against the (non-European) Moors on the Iberian Peninsula. Indeed, the final episode in that long war, the fall of Grenada in 1492, coincided with Columbus's first voyage to the islands of the Caribbean. To a great extent the subsequent conquest of what became Spanish America was a continuation of Spain's reconquest of the peninsula and was carried out largely as a military and religious crusade. Whereas English settlement in North America sought to clone the communities of England, Spanish America was occupied by battle-hardened military men, for the most part unaccompanied by women and children. Furthermore, whereas the English settlers went to North America to stay, the first waves of Spanish into the Western Hemisphere went to acquire wealth with which to improve their status upon their return to Europe. Unlike the English in North America, who generally viewed the Natives as obstacles to their enterprises, the Spanish regarded Indigenous labor as essential to extract wealth from the gold and silver mines and from plantations that produced commodities such as sugar, silk, indigo, and cochineal for the world market.

In Spanish America, the Indigenous peoples were an essential economic resource that needed to be protected so that it might be perpetually exploited. To this end many existing Indigenous communities were legally recognized and given resources so that they might endure as sources of labor and other forms of wealth for the Spanish crown, the Spanish colonists, the church, and various Catholic religious orders. The catastrophic post-Conquest population declines noted above made labor scarce, however, and necessitated stronger policies for the husbandry of these communities. The subsequent social identities and destinies of the *indígenas* and their communities in Spanish America thus developed under markedly different conditions from the English colonies.

Whereas in North America the Indigenous peoples were not greatly valued as an economic resource and were mostly exterminated outright or forced onto reservations, in Spanish Latin America the larger populations of *indígenas* were concentrated in communities that were in effect internal colonies. By way of contrast, the Portuguese colonists in Brazil regarded the *indígenas* much as the English (and subsequently the Americans) had the *indígenas* in North America. Although many *indígenas* were incorporated into rubber tapping and mining, African slaves assumed a much more important role in the overall economy of Brazil than they did in most of Spanish America.

FROM INDEPENDENCE TO THE MID-TWENTIETH CENTURY

By the early nineteenth century criollos throughout Spanish America had come to think of themselves as more American than Spanish; that is, as residents of the regions in which they were born and with which they identified. When these sentiments culminated in successful independence movements, the independent criollos were faced with the challenge of building nation-states out of the former colonies. Central to the concept of a modern nation-state was the idea of a common national cultural identity. The postcolonial nation-states, striving as they were to create more or less culturally homogeneous citizenries, swept away colonial laws that defined peoples as members of racial castes such as "Indian," "white," "black," and combinations thereof. Although racism did not disappear, it now became imbricated more in a social structure based on class. The main distinctions in this class structure grew out of how one earned a living, and the major divide was between those who did manual labor and those who did not. Of course, the *indígenas* fell almost exclusively into the former category. Thus, although the formal structure of the caste system was dismantled, the position of the *indígenas* on the bottom rung of the social hierarchy was perpetuated.

The architects of the Latin American nation-states assumed that the *indígenas* would disappear from history along with the system of castes. And toward this end some of them enacted reform programs in the mid-eighteenth century aimed at eliminating the colonial laws that protected the Indigenous communities. In Mexico, for example, the liberal pro-capitalist elements that enacted the 1857 constitution dissolved the corporate legal basis of the Indigenous communities that had prevailed during the colonial period. The assumption was that exposure of the communal resources (primarily communal lands) of the *indígenas* to market forces would break down the backwardness of these communities. Thus, they ceased to be regarded as primarily economic resources and were now seen as barriers to the development of the types of modern agriculture and manufacturing taking place to the north in the United States. Indeed, the liberals saw development in the United States as due in large part to the absence of large Indigenous peasant communities such as those in Latin America. In contrast to the colonial period, therefore, in which the *indígenas* were seen as sources of wealth, the Indigenous communities were now regarded as pockets of backwardness that were inhibiting progress.

This situation prevailed for the most part until after World War II, when the United States took a renewed interest in Latin America in the context of the cold war. Concerned to maintain its hegemony in the Western Hemisphere in the face of a presumed communist threat, the United States and various international agencies such as the World Bank sought to promote economic development in Latin America. Indeed, the policies and projects of this period were variations on nineteenth-century developmental goals, except they were now promoted in the cold war context, with the U.S. government and international agencies assuming considerable responsibility for the economic and political development of "backward" communities. In this period the Indians were largely identified as peasants. That is to say, they were seen according to economic and developmental criteria rather than for their identity as Indigenous peoples. The assumption was that "underdeveloped" communities would be transformed into modern developed ones.

During this period the population growth rate in many countries of the hemisphere exceeded the rates of socioeconomic development measured in terms of job creation and improved standards of living. The population growth also affected Indigenous communities, and earlier prognostications about their demise were shown to be inaccurate. Indeed, the simultaneous growth in poverty and numbers of the Indigenous peoples suggested that modern history was taking a turn other than that predicted by the architects of the modern Latin American states and the theorists of development.

THE PERSISTENCE OF THE *"INDÍGENAS"*

After the disastrous biological holocaust caused by the epidemics of the "Columbian exchange" (Crosby 1972), which produced probably the greatest population decline in human history (Denevan 1976; Borah and Cook 1963; Dobyns 1966), the Indigenous peoples of colonial Spanish and Portuguese America began a slow demographic recuperation that by the early 1990s had brought their population to the vicinity of 40 million (Mayer and Masferrer 1979; World Bank 1991). This number, however, is far below the estimates of the hemisphere's original Indigenous population.

There is an intriguing paradox in regard to this obstinate biological and cultural perseverance of the Native American people: How could they

outlast the European military invasion, the resulting biological disaster, the systematic "ecological
imperialism" (Crosby 1986), the meticulous destruction of their institutions, and still undergo a cultural, social, and political recuperation that has
allowed for their continuous and increasing presence in the social and biological history of the continent? The answer to this question has to be sought
in the complex forms of resistance and adaptation
of the various Indigenous peoples over the past five
centuries.

Four fundamental forms of ethnic resilience and
opposition recur in this long history. The first is what
we may call the "moral management" of the cosmos,
a type of environmental ethic and practice found in
the majority of Indigenous societies (Varese 1995).
The second is an economic rationality and a social
philosophy that contrasts with the individualism
and market-based economies of modern societies.
This "moral economy," as Scott (1976, 1985) refers to
it, occurs among some peasant societies and operates with a logic informed by the ecological cosmology noted above. It seeks to preserve the common
resources of the community and minimize internal
economic differentiation. Basic economic resources
are held in common, and access to them is determined by good citizenship, defined by one's willingness to serve the community in ways that often
involve considerable self-sacrifice. Such an economy
is centered more on use-value than exchange-value,
and economic transactions are mediated primarily
by reciprocity rather than by market or profit
considerations.

Related to the specifically indigenous nature of
these two factors is a third: the tendency of *indígenas*
to conceal their ethnobiological knowledge while
maintaining an active exploration, investigation,
experimentation, and conservation of biodiversity.
Finally, Indigenous peoples have been extremely
adaptable in restructuring their political action to
respond to a constantly changing world.

Latin America's Indigenous communities were
able to establish a new, decolonized institutional,
political, and cultural relationship not only among
themselves but also with the nonIndigenous peoples
of the Americas in a number of ways. A reconfigura-
tion of this nature implies a demise of nineteenth-
century nationalistic ideology and practices and the
negotiation of autonomy and sovereignty with
national and international entities (the nation-states,
intergovernmental organisms, the transnational corporations, etc.).

Since the European invasion of the Americas,
Indigenous societies have attempted to conceal their
biotic and biotechnological knowledge, well aware
that such knowledge was among the most contested
cultural domains of the colonial mercantile and evangelical enterprise. For most of the Indigenous peoples, agricultural and food production, as well as
environmental management, were suffused with religious significance. As such, these social practices
were extremely vulnerable to repression by the colonial authorities.

It is well documented that the Spaniards' early
ambiguous attitudes toward the Native American
biotic heritage induced a series of repressive measures against the cultivation and use of certain plants
and resources. The most notorious example is the
Mesoamerican *alegría* (amaranth—called *tzoalli* and
huautli by the Mexicans), whose cultivation, trade,
and consumption were banned throughout New
Spain during the early colonial period with the argument that it was a pagan sacrificial plant. However,
use of medicinal and psychotropic plants and sub-
stances, use of stimulants like coca and of animal and
insect foods, techniques of preparation of food and
fermented beverages, and techniques of food production (e.g., various types of swidden cultivation)
have been contentious areas of cultural and political
control throughout the colonial period and up to the
present.

In Mexico, Bishop Zumarraga, "wished to outlaw pulque [fermented maguey juice] in 1529 because
it smacked of idolatry," and for the missionary "drinking, with its ritual vestiges, was a major obstacle to
evangelical expansion" (Super 1988:75). But similar
aspirations are still at the core of various types of
evangelical fundamentalism practiced, for example,
by the Summer Institute of Linguistics or a number
of Protestant missionaries working with the *indígenas*
(Stoll 1985). In sum, European colonialism brought to
the Americas definite ideas about food and food production that are still very much part of the hegemonic culture and the ideology that informs most
development planning and policy affecting the
indigenous regions.

The Indigenous peoples did not simply react to
colonial impositions. Their responses reflected a variety of strategic accommodations and initiatives. For
example, immediately following the Spanish invasion of Mexico, the Maya people of Yucatan repeatedly resisted the invaders—actions that often turned
into armed insurrections. These rebellions were motivated by a call to reconstitute the precolonial order

and to restore the world's sacredness: to purify a nature contaminated by foreign oppressors. In 1546 the *chilam* (prophet-diviner) Anbal brought together a coalition of the Maya people. On the calendar date of Death and End (November 9), they initiated a war of liberation that sought to kill the invaders, end colonial domination, and purify the earth. The rebels killed Spaniards and their Maya slaves in sacrificial rites and meted out the same fate to all the plants and domesticated animals brought by the Europeans (Barabas 1987; Bartolomé 1984).

In 1786 the Totonacs of Papantla, in southeastern Mexico, rose in rebellion against the Spanish authorities in defense of their threatened trees. A Spanish source observed that "the trees give shade to people and help them to persevere, are useful to tie animals, protect houses from fires, and the branches and leaves are used as fodder for animals" (cited in Taylor 1979:137).

Earlier, in 1742, in the Amazon jungle of Peru, a Quechua messiah, Juan Santos Atahualpa Apu Capac Huayna, fomented a rebellion that mobilized thousands of Ashaninka, Quechua, and a dozen other ethnic groups and kept the Spaniards and Creoles out of the region for a century. Some of the insurgents' revolutionary demands and proposals were informed by an ecologically based morality: the right to live in dispersed villages and households to allow a rational use of the tropical rain forest; the eradication of European pigs considered harmful to farming and human health; the right to freely cultivate and use coca, known as the "the herb of God"; and the right to produce and ceremonially drink *masato,* a fermented manioc beverage of substantial nutritional value (Brown forthcoming; Varese 1973; Zarzar 1989).

Two centuries later, in 1973, among the Chinantecs of Oaxaca, Mexico, an intense messianic movement flared up in opposition to a proposed dam that would flood their territory and force them into exile to distant lands (Barabas and Bartolomé 1973; Barabas 1987). To defend the ecological integrity of their territory, which they considered sacred, the Chinantecs resorted to a diversified strategy that ranged from legal and bureaucratic negotiations with the government and alliance-building with poor mestizo peasants to the mobilization of shamans, the "caretakers of the lines" (the ethnic borders) whose "lightning" or *nahuals* would kill the president of Mexico, Luis Echeverría Alvarez. The Chinantec messianic movement gained cultural and social legitimacy with the sacred appearance of the Virgin of Guadalupe and the "Engineer Great God," who ordered the performance of a series of rituals to strengthen the physical and spiritual integrity of certain ecocultural features such as rivers, mountains, trees, springs, caves, and trails.

On January 1, 1994, Tzeltal, Tzotzil, Chol, Tojolabal, and Zoque Maya *indígenas* organized into the Zapatista National Liberation Army (*Ejército Zapatista de Liberación Nacional,* or EZLN) and declared war on the government, quickly establishing the military occupation of four major municipalities in Chiapas, Mexico. An *indígena* army of eight hundred combatants occupied the city of San Cristobal de las Casas, seized the municipal palace, and proclaimed their opposition to the "undeclared genocidal war against our people by the dictators," and described their "struggle for work, land, shelter, food, health, education, independence, freedom, democracy, justice, and peace" (EZLN 1994).

Of the six points stated in the EZLN's Declaration of War, the first five spelled out their rules of engagement; the sixth stated that the EZLN would "suspend the looting of our natural resources" in the areas the rebels controlled. This armed movement of an estimated two thousand persons was essentially composed of the Mayan ethnic groups noted above. A fundamental objective of the insurrection was the defense of their lands and natural resources. In other public declarations and communiqués, the EZLN also stressed its opposition to the North American Free Trade Agreement (NAFTA), which it considered a "death certificate" for the Indigenous peasants, and to the modification of Article 27 of the Mexican Constitution, which permits the privatization of indigenous and peasant collective and communal lands. "This article 27 of the Constitution, they changed it without asking us, without requesting our input. Now it is time for them to listen to us, because to take our land is to take our life" (IATP 1994). These are but a few examples taken from innumerable historical and contemporary cases illustrating the moral economy that has guided indigenous resistance to economic exploitation and political oppression.

Nevertheless, since at least the mid-seventeenth century, local Indigenous communities have participated in an economic system in which part of the production satisfies subsistence needs while the rest, the surplus, enters circuits of commercial exchange (Varese 1991a). Contemporary Indigenous communities are thus not uncontaminated citadels of precapitalist economy. They are ruled first by the basic principles of moral economy founded on the logic of reciprocity and on the "right to subsistence," and, second, by the necessity of exchange with the surrounding capitalist market. Both principles permeate the social life of prepeasant, peasant, and even some postpeasant *indígenas* who, self-exiled from their communities because of poverty, partially reconstitute this moral economy as urban subproletarian or transnational migrant workers in the agricultural fields of California (Kearney and Nagengast 1989; Zabin et al. 1993).

BUILDING INDIAN SOVEREIGNTY IN THE AMAZON

The creation of the Federation of Shuar Centers in 1964 is a benchmark in the development of new forms of resistance by Indigenous peoples in Latin America. This surprising form of political organization had by 1987 incorporated 240 centers and more than 40,000 Shuar people into a unique social program of economic and cultural self determination. Four years after the Shuar Federation was formed, the Amuesha people (Yanesha) of the Peruvian Upper Amazon convened the first Amuesha Congress, which was later transformed in to a permanent political body called the Amuesha Federation.

Between 1970 and 1974, in an intense series of mobilizations, Colombian *indígenas* organized the Indian Regional Council of Cauca and several other organizations. During the 1970s in Peru, the Indigenous people of the Amazon region formed many local organizations and regional federations—for instance, the Ashaninka Congress of the Central Jungle, the Shipibo Congress and Defense Front, and the Aguaruna Huambisa Council. In the highlands of Bolivia the organized expressions of a strong Aymara and Quechua nationalism were initially shaped by the Katarist movement. To the south in Chile, under the safeguard of Salvador Allende's socialist government, the Mapuches participated in the elaboration and implementation of a *Ley de Indígenas* (Law of the Indígenas). This short-lived taste of multiethnicity ended in 1973 with General Augusto Pinochet's military dictatorship and the death, imprisonment, and exile of the Mapuche leadership.

In March 1984 representatives of five indigenous organizations from the Amazonian countries of Brazil, Bolivia, Colombia, Ecuador, and Peru met in Lima and founded the international organization called the Coordinating Body of Indigenous Peoples' Organizations of the Amazon Basin (*Coordinadora de las Organizaciones Indígenas de la Cuenca Amazónica*, or

COICA). COICA's main political objective was to become a coordinating body that would present a common policy position for all the organized *indígenas* of the Greater Amazon Basin before the region's governments and the international community. COICA's origins can be traced to the three regional, community-based organizations of the early 1960s noted above: the Shuar Federation in Ecuador, the Congress of Amuesha Communities in Peru, and the Regional Indigenous Council of the Cauca in Colombia (Smith 1993). These local organizations, initially unknown to one another, established a model of social mobilization that gave voice to each local community's problems of territorial loss, human rights abuses, and cultural oppression. Throughout the 1970s, numerous other organizations emerged among the Amazonian peoples and began to establish contacts facilitated by the solidarity of various nonindigenous groups, such as sympathetic Catholic missionaries, proindigenous NGOs, and environmentalists.

COICA has primarily been concerned with territorial and environmental rights; human, cultural, and linguistic rights; and rights to economic and political self-determination (Smith 1993; Varese 1991a). Today COICA comprises more than one hundred interethnic confederations of Amazonian groups from Bolivia, Brazil, Colombia, Ecuador, Guyana, French Guyana, Peru, Suriname, and Venezuela, which represent approximately 1.5 million Indigenous people (Chirif et al. 1991; Smith 1993).

COICA's active involvement in the U.N. Working Group on Indigenous Peoples' Rights, in the discussions concerning the ILO's Covenant 169 on Indigenous and Tribal People approved in 1989, and in various committees of the Amazon Treaty Cooperation sponsored by the Inter-American Indigenous Institute brought the members of the organization in contact with an increasing number of international bureaucrats, advocates, indigenous support groups, the leaders of other ethnic minorities, parties, labor organizations, the European Green movement, and funding agencies. In 1986 COICA won an ecological prize, the Right Livelihood award, which gave the organization front-page international coverage and major exposure to official circles. During 1989 COICA was recognized by the World Bank and had established official contact with the European Community (now the European Union). In 1991 COICA gained official advisory status with the Indigenous Commission of the Amazon Cooperation Treaty. Moreover, between 1990 and 1991, it was one of the founding members of the Alliance for Protecting the Forest and Climate, formed with representatives from more than one hundred cities in five European countries (Smith 1993).

This relatively rapid success brought strains to COICA, revealing its structural limitations in representing its constituencies and its lack of means and methods for efficient communications between its community-based units, the regional and national federations, and its central administrative body. And, finally, the central administration had become somewhat autocratic (Smith 1993). By 1992 a general congress of COICA unanimously decided to create a less hierarchical structure and to facilitate communications and accountability by decentralizing decision-making. COICA headquarters were also moved from Lima to Quito.

MESOAMERICAN INDIGENOUS PEOPLES IN THE UNITED STATES

The activities of migrants from Guatemala and southern Mexico to the United States have been one of the most notable developments in the recent history of new Latin American Indigenous movements. Since the outbreak of war in Guatemala during the late 1970s between several indigenous-based guerrilla groups and the government, some tens of thousands of *indígenas* have been killed, and many thousands more have fled the country to seek sanctuary either in Mexico or in the United States. Those who sought refuge in the United States in the past fifteen or so years have settled mainly in Los Angeles. Within the Guatemalan Indigenous community in Los Angeles, many different ethnic groups are represented, each of which is from a distinct community that speaks its own Mayan language. Whereas these refugees were isolated by distance and culture in Guatemala, they have been thrown together in the city's sprawling Latino neighborhoods, where they found common cultural and political bonds. On the basis of this shared heritage, the need to defend themselves as aliens in a strange and often hostile land has motivated them to form several interethnic associations. The largest of these, known as "Ixim," takes its name from the Mayan word for maize, which in cognate forms is found in the languages of all the Guatemalan Indigenous peoples in Los Angeles.

Comparable to the presence of Indigenous Guatemalan refugees in Los Angeles is the presence in California of tens of thousands of *indígenas* from the state of Oaxaca in southern Mexico. At any given time there are some 25,000 to 40,000 Mixtec migrant farm workers in California (Runsten and Kearney 1994). Whereas the Guatemalan *indígenas* are refugees from a horrendous war waged against them, the Mixtecs are mainly economic refugees from a region in which the environment has been steadily deteriorating, undermining the subsistence farming that is their primary livelihood. In the 1980s, Mixtec migrants from various towns formed self-help associations based on their communities of origin, and by the early 1990s these local groups had come together to form a common Mixtec front.

Since the 1960s, uncounted thousands of Zapotecs from Oaxaca have migrated to California to work temporarily or to settle, primarily in the Los Angeles area. As in the Mixtec case, the Zapotecs have formed migrant associations based on their communities of origin, some twenty of which came together in the late 1980s to create a coordinating body, the Oaxacan Regional Organization (ORO).

The objectives of the Zapotec and the Mixtec federations are binational in scope in that they seek to protect and promote the well-being of their members in the United States and also to defend and otherwise support their communities of origin in Oaxaca through financial and symbolic support and by intervening in government policies directed at the Indigenous communities. A major milestone in Oaxacan political evolution in California was the coming together in 1991 of most of the Mixtec and Zapotec groups to form the Mixtec-Zapotec Binational Front, which has since acquired considerable legitimacy with the Mexican government and international agencies. In1994 other Indigenous groups in Oaxaca asked to join the front. These groups represent Mixe, Triques, and Chatinos, thus occasioning another name change, this time to the all-inclusive Frente Indígena Oaxaqueña Binacional (FIOB), which can without terminological inconsistency now accept groups representing any of the sixteen Indigenous peoples of Oaxaca.

The history of the formation of the Guatemalan and Oaxacan Indigenous groups in California is perhaps the most notable example of the transnationalization of Latin American Indigenous politics in that the primary locus of these international groups has been outside not only their home territories but also Latin America. In their organizational forms, as in their personal lives, the members of these groups transcend the boundaries between the United States, Guatemala, and Mexico, and also between the so-called industrial and developing worlds, a distinction that has become largely obsolete as Mesoamerican Indigenous peoples increasingly live transnational lives.

LESSONS FROM EXPERIENCE AND FUTURE PERSPECTIVES

An assessment of the Latin American indigenous movement in the 1990s reveals two crucial concerns of the Indigenous people. The first is the right of self-government and autonomy. These rights are becoming an increasingly prominent part of the democratization process in various Latin American countries. The demands of the Mayan rebels of Chiapas presented to the Mexican government in 1994 are a good example. As mentioned above, the indigenous insurgents demanded communal and regional autonomy, free elections, self-rule, and guarantees of nonintervention on the part of the government in their internal affairs. The second concern is their right to territorial and resource sovereignty. Their demands for ethnic self-determination and autonomy include full control over the lands, water, and resources that fall within their newly defined ethnic boundaries.

The recuperation of ethnic territories and political autonomy is based on three principles, the first of which is the historical depth of the claim. The current territorial fragmentation and reduction in Latin America is the result of centuries of colonial and postcolonial expropriation; therefore, restitution of land and/or reparations are major issues.

The second principle is based on the ethnobiological integrity of territories traditionally occupied by specific Indigenous groups. In other words, bioregions and ethno regions were largely coincident before the territorial disturbances of the Europeans. There is no such thing in the contemporary period as natural, untouched landscape: Rational intervention by *indígenas* over the millennia has shaped and molded the environment and its biotic resources (see Chirif et al. 1991).

The third principle is the repudiation of any solution to territorial and environmental claims that would involve the commoditization of nature. As one Indigenous leader is reported to have stated in objection to the celebrated debt-for-nature swaps promoted by some Northern environmentalists: "It is our nature—and it's not our debt" (Brysk 1992).

Recognition of and respect for these three principles must constitute the ethical framework for any political and economic negotiations between the Indigenous peoples and national and international entities regarding political, territorial, and resource sovereignty. Some of the specific practical aspects of ethno-sovereignty rights that will have to be jointly addressed by *indígenas* and nonIndigenous peoples are briefly mentioned below.

First of all, there is the important question of the social and spatial definition of Indigenous peoples and groups. According to the indigenetic legislation of various national governments, the indigenous ethnic groups are legally defined by their respective constituent communities (e.g., the *regard* in Colombia, the *commanded native* and *commanded capeskin* in Peru, the *commanded indígena* and *elide* in Mexico, etc.). The whole ethnic group, even if legally recognized in some capacity by the state, does not constitute a juridical subject. Nevertheless, the Indigenous organizations of Ecuador have succeeded in obtaining the state's recognition of the term "nationalities" for the various Indigenous ethnic communities, but this is a definitive exception in Latin America.

In view of the disagreement and confusion throughout the continent about ethnosocial definitions and boundaries, indigenous intellectuals and leaders are addressing two levels of sovereignty that are rather complementary: One is "communal sovereignty," which is usually legally recognized by the state. At this level there are local indigenous institutions and authorities and clear social-ethnic boundaries; the rather murky and more complicated biotic boundaries therefore pose a more complex problem of genetic and resource sovereignty.

In contrast, the concept of "ethnic sovereignty" is legally rare or nonexistent from the state's point of view. However, some groups are beginning to define this type of sovereignty (Varese 1988). Total ethnic sovereignty is represented in the numerous Indigenous ethnic organizations that have a legal and fully institutional existence. In this case, negotiated restitutions and formal interinstitutional agreements are required at various organizational levels, including the local community, the ethnic organization, local and central government agencies, and external investors and/or scientific parties. In instances of this type, the issue of biotic, cultural, and resource boundaries is easiest to resolve since there may be an approximate coincidence between ethnopolitical and ethnobiotic boundaries. By "ethnopolitical boundaries," the Indigenous people mean the historically traceable ethnic frontiers, even if they are not actually under ethnic control and are not being reclaimed by the organization as a political objective.

Finally, there is the challenge of further developing organizational and legal forms that recognize and meet the needs of the ever-growing numbers of de-territorialized Indigenous peoples who reside in cities and in nations far removed from their traditional homelands and modes of existence. These issues of boundaries and identities, of sovereignty and self-determination, promise to be increasingly salient issues to the Indigenous peoples of Latin America in the twenty-first century.

REFERENCES

Barabas, Alicia M. *Utopias Indias: Movimientos Socio-religiosos en México.* Mexico City: Grijalbo, 1987.

Barabas, Alicia M., and Miguel A. Bartolomé. *Hydraulic Development and Ethnocide: The Mazatec and Chinantec People of Oaxaca, Mexico,* IWGIA Document No.15. Copenhagen: IWGIA, 1973.

Bartolomé, Miguel A. "La dinámica social de los mayas de Yucatán." Ph.D. diss., Facultad de Ciencias Políticas y Sociales de la UNAM, 1984.

Borah, Woodrow, and S. F. Cook. *The Aboriginal Population of Central Mexico on the Eve of the Spanish Conquest.* Berkeley: University of California Press, 1963.

Brown, Michael F. "Facing the State, Facing the World: Amazonia's Native Leaders and the New Politics of Identity," in Philippe Descola and Anne-Christine Taylor, eds., *L'Homme: Anthopologie et histoire des sociétés amazoníennes.* Forthcoming.

Brysk, Alison. "Acting Globally: International Relations and the Indian Rights in Latin America." Paper presented at the Seventeenth International Congress of the Latin American Studies Association, Los Angeles, September 24–27, 1992.

Chirif Tirado, Alberto, Pedro Garcia Hierro, and Robert C. Smith. *El Indígena y su territorio son uno solo: Estrategia para la defensa de los pueblos y territorios indígenas en lacuenca amazónica.* Lima: Oxfam America, 1991.

Crosby, Alfred W. *The Columbian Exchange: Biological and Cultural Consequences of 1492.* Westport, CT: Greenwood, 1972.

———. *Ecological Imperialism: The Biological Expansion of Europe, 900–1900.* Cambridge: Cambridge University Press, 1986.

Denevan, William M., ed. *The Native Population of the Americas in 1492.* Madison: University of Wisconsin Press, 1976.

Dobyns, Henry F. "Estimating Aboriginal American Populations: An Appraisal of Techniques with a New Hemispheric Estimate." *Current Anthropology,* no. 7 (1966):395–416.

EZLN. *Comunicados del Ejército Zapatista de Liberación Nacional,* January 1, 6, 11, 12, and 13, 1994.

Galeano, Eduardo. *The Open Veins of Latin America.* New York: Monthly Review Press, 1973.

IATP (Institute for Agriculture and Trade Policy). "Chiapas Digest." 1994. Via E-mail.

Kearney, Michael, and Carole Nagengast. "Anthropological Perspective on Transnational Communities in Rural California." Working Paper No. 3 of the Working Group on Farm Labor and Rural Poverty. Davis: California Institute for Rural Studies,1989.

Mayer, Enrique, and E. Masferrer. "La población indígena de América en 1978." *América Indígena,* 39, 2(1979).

Runsten, David, and Michael Kearney. *A Survey of Oaxacan Village Networks in California Agriculture.* Davis: California Institute for Rural Studies, 1994.

Scott, James. *The Moral Economy of the Peasant: Rebellion and Subsistence in Southeast Asia.* New Haven, CT: Yale University Press, 1976.

———. *Weapons of the Weak: Everyday Forms of Peasant Resistance.* New Haven, CT: Yale University Press, 1985.

———. "COICA and the Amazon Basin: The Internationalization of Indigenous Peoples' Demands." Paper presented at the Thirteenth International Congress of Anthropological and Ethnological Sciences, Mexico City, July 29–August 5, 1993.

Stoll, David. *Pescadores de hombres o fundadores de Imperio?* Lima: DESCO, 1985.

Super, John C. *Food, Conquest, and Colonization in Sixteenth-Century Spanish America.* Albuquerque: University of New Mexico Press, 1988.

Taylor, William B. *Drinking, Homicide, and Rebellion in Colonial Mexican Villages.* Stanford, CA: Stanford University Press, 1979.

Varese, Stefano. *La sal de los cerros: Una aproximación al mundo campa.* Lima: Ediciones Retablo de Papel, 1973.

———. "Multi-ethnicity and Hegemonic Construction: Indian Plans and the Future," in Remo Guidieri, Francisco Pellizzi, and Stanley J. Tambiah, eds., *Ethnicities and Nations.* Austin: University of Texas Press, 1988.

———. "The Ethnopolitics of Indian Resistance in Latin America." Working Paper. Cambridge: M.I.T. Center for International Studies, 1991a.

———. "The Ethnopolitics of Indian Resistance in Latin America." *Latin American Perspectives* (1995).

Wolf, Eric R. *Europe and the People without History.* Berkeley: University of California Press, 1982.

World Bank. *Informe sobre el desarrollo mundial.* Washington, DC: World Bank, 1991.

Zabin, Carol, Michael Kearney, Anna Garcia, David Runsten, and Carole Nagengast. *Mixtec Migrants in California Agriculture: A New Cycle of Poverty.* Davis: California Institute for Rural Studies, 1993.

Zarzar, Alonso. *Apo Capac Huayna, Jesús Sacramentado: Mito, utopia y milenarismo en el pensamiento de Juan Santos Atahualpa.* Lima: Ediciones CAAP, 1989.

Latin American motif © Gerald Dawavendewa.

MEXICO

THE CRISIS OF IDENTITY

Alexander Ewen

For many, the proof that what has occurred in Chiapas is not an Indigenous uprising is the high degree of political articulation in the communiqués and social actions of the EZLN. Any action above a childlike and inarticulate level is no longer considered Indigenous. From this point of view, when an Indian ceases to be wretched, he ceases to be Indian.

—Eugenio Bermejillo

The political earthquake that rocked Mexico on the first of January [1994] continues to reverberate across the country's complex social landscape. Powerful national currents have been unleashed, and the status quo, which has held for more than half a century, is clearly shaken. That a few armed Indians in the most remote and impoverished state in the nation could possibly bring down the Mexican house of cards may seem unlikely at first, yet it looms as a foretaste of the displacement and unrest that Mexico could be forced to see before the decade is out.

That it is Indigenous people who have seized the initiative is not surprising, given the lack of choices facing the large Indian populations in Mexico today. Yet the Zapatista movement would have quickly dissipated had it not struck deep chords inside of Mexico and bells of alarm internationally. By blowing out the candles on the NAFTA cake, the uprising was well timed to receive the largest amount of international media coverage and enlist the sympathy of the powerful anti-NAFTA coalition in the United States. It exposed deep divisions among the Mexican elite and marked the Indians and the rural poor as a political force still to be reckoned with. It also tore into the carefully constructed façade of political stability and allowed the world a glimpse of the vast contradictions within Mexican society.

Mexico, a country marked by fatalism and tied to strong traditional roots, living under a glorious and ambiguous ideal called *la Revolución,* has been undergoing as profound a transformation as any in its history. Shifting slowly but surely since the 1940s, this metamorphosis has accelerated at an exponential rate as the last two Mexican administrations cast their lots with the newly emerging global economy. The consequences of this political decision threaten to leave no corner of Mexican life untouched. To this vast transformation have come the Zapatistas and the Indians, raising the stark question. "What is the place of Indian people in this modern Mexico?"—a question the Mexican leadership had hoped it would not have to address.

WHO IS AN INDIAN?

Mexico is home to the largest population of Indigenous people in the Western Hemisphere. Before the European conquest, the Indigenous population reflected in their cultures the vast diversity of the land that would become Mexico. From the authoritarian empires and city-states to the unfettered nomadic hunter-gatherers, virtually every lifestyle and form of government was represented at the time of contact in 1492. The number of Indians was astounding, estimated to be over twenty-five million—a figure that would not be reached again in Mexico until 1950. Today the Mexican Indigenous population is still the most diverse in the hemisphere, with over 230 different languages still spoken.

Unlike the United States, where the question of who is an Indian is largely a matter of ethnicity, in

Alexander Ewen, "Mexico: The Crisis of Identity," from *Akwe:kon Journal,* Vol. XI, no. 2 (Summer 1994). Copyright 1994 by Akwe:kon Press. Reprinted with permission.

Mexico it is much more a question of social class. According to the 1990 Mexican census, seven and a half percent, or approximately seven million of Mexico's ninety-two million people, are Indians. Yet this is only the number of Indians who continue to speak their Indigenous language. Mexicans who speak only Spanish, no matter how pure their Indian blood, are considered *mestizo.* Under the same criterion the number of Indians in the United States would drop from two million to only 350,000. Moreover, this system of identifying Indians excludes small children, who would only become Indians when they learn how to speak. Pure-blooded whites are thus given a greater share of the Mexican population than Indians, a remarkable turn of demographics from the beginning of the century.

Using an ethnic basis, estimates for the number of Indians who belong to a distinct cultural group range as high as forty percent of the total Mexican population. Using the wider criteria of the United States, almost ninety percent of Mexico's population has some Indian blood and might well be considered Indigenous if they desired. The general, non-official consensus is that there are more than twenty-five million Indians in Mexico, making up approximately thirty percent of the total population, who are clearly descended from one of Mexico's 230 distinct Indian tribes.

THE MYTH AND REALITY OF "MESTIZAJE"

The reason for limiting the number of Indians in Mexico is due in part to a Mexican political policy that furthers the Mexican ideal of *mestizaje,* that of the egalitarian mixed-race Mexican nation. Today, Mexico considers almost nine out of ten members of its population to be *mestizo.* Originally, a *mestizo* was a person of mixed Spanish and Indian descent, a category within the complex system of assigning pedigree depending on the mix of Spanish, Indian, African, or Asian blood. This system was necessary during the colonial period of Mexico's history in order to help preserve the rigid racial hierarchy that prevailed at the time. At the top of the hierarchy were the pure-blooded whites, known as the *peninsulares* if they came from Spain and *criollos* if born in Mexico. *Mestizos,* though far from the elite, were considered *gente de razón,* a people of reason. *Indios* were peons, and blacks were slaves.

The slaves are long gone, their descendants largely mixed into the *mestizo* world, and the old system of rigid hierarchy has been replaced by *mestizaje.* This ideal is a uniting force in Mexico, similar to the way the "American Dream" has bound disparate groups of immigrants together in the common quest of finding a new and better life in America. *Mestizaje* combines a tremendous pride in the legendary Indian ancestry with a yearning for white material advantages. The myth dilutes any other ethnic identity and effectively subsumes the citizen to Mexican nationalism. A *mestizo* is one who is neither Indian nor white, but a new race, the prototypical Mexican. Therefore according to Mexico, the definition of who is an Indian depends on whether or not they have succumbed to this myth—whether or not they are acculturated into the Mexican system. If they have, no matter how pure the Indian blood, they are *mestizo.*

After independence, Mexico's colonial heritage of strict racial hierarchy became a structure of racial equality, encouraging all Mexicans to reject their backgrounds and become *mestizo.* All legal distinctions of class and privilege were abolished, and "Indian" as a legal entity disappeared. Any pride in Indian ancestry was tempered by the notion that Indians were backward, primitive, and not fully Mexican. Indeed, by remaining Indian, one was holding back Mexico from its true potential; for Mexico to achieve its glorious destiny, all would have to march through the gate of *mestizaje.* This perspective did little to abate prejudice against Indians, and *indio* remained a pejorative term. Expressions such as "*feo como un indio*" ("ugly as an Indian") are still common throughout much of the country.

Despite the philosophy of egalitarianism, it is white Mexicans that are a model that *mestizos* aspire to. Whites continue to be the elite, and dominate the media, finance, and politics. It is they who are the fashion models and television stars. As a population, whites show a remarkable resistance to the mixing tendencies of the rest of Mexico, and in real terms their population has increased in the past ten years. Though many *mestizos* have now moved into the elite class, they often come to think of themselves as *criollos,* and prefer to be distinguished from the majority of *mestizos.*

Yet to a large extent, *mestizaje* is more than a myth, it is a very real and tangible force, deeply entwined with the heart of Mexico. The *mestizo* class has become the huge middle spectrum of the population, sandwiched between the elite and the Indian and ranging from the upper middle class to the very poor. The pull of *mestizaje* is extremely strong and effective outside of Indian communities. Indians who are relocated or lose their land quickly discard their languages and traditions and embrace the *mestizo* world. They tend to reject the fact that they are Indians, and do not identify as such. To remain Indian would mean repudiating a unifying foundation of the current Mexican identity, an identity that recognizes Indianness, but not Indians. While in the United States it is fashionable to identify oneself as an Indian, in Mexico, one does not do so lightly.

THE CONQUEST

The experience of the Indigenous people of Mexico was, from the inception of Spanish colonial rule, vastly different from that of the United States. The Catholic church, through the encyclicals of Pope Paul III and the advocacy of Bartolomé de Las Casas, established a long lasting Catholic and Spanish policy of assimilating Indians and making them a part of the national culture. The early arrival of the Franciscans, in 1524, and the Jesuits, in 1572, was an acknowledgment by the Spanish Empire that the conquest of New Spain was justified on the grounds of bringing Christianity to the Indigenous populations.

Unlike the Catholics, the early Pilgrims in New England had no illusions of worldwide religious hegemony and concerned themselves more with maintaining their religious and moral purity than proselytizing. English political policy viewed Indians as distinct and separate peoples with which political alliances could be forged, a perspective which would be maintained by the United States until the 19th century.

Except for the most isolated areas, by the time of national independence in 1821. Mexican Indians were overwhelmingly Catholic. In contrast, the United States would wait another sixty years before embarking on a national policy of cultural, religious, and social assimilation. Early Spanish colonists followed the example of Cortés and his Indian mistress, *la Malinche,* and readily settled down with Indian women. The colonial Puritans and their followers were not so inclined, and north of Spanish settlement strict separation of the races was the norm.

The historical demographic profile of both countries was vastly different. The catastrophic declines in Indian populations abated in Mexico by 1650 and by the late 18th century their populations were showing natural rates of increase. There were many restrictions on immigration to New Spain and to Mexico after independence. It would take until 1800, 300 years after the conquest, for the white population of Mexico to exceed one million, assuring an Indian majority well into the 19th century. Indians were always a small minority within the boundaries of the United States. By the time westward expansion began in earnest in 1850, the non-Indian population of the States was twenty-three million, far greater than the Indian population.

The differences between the English and Spanish economies has also played a strong role in shaping the differing Indigenous experiences. Unlike Spain and Mexico, the English and French settlers from the very beginning were practicing a form of free-market enterprise that enlisted Indians as trade partners, suppliers of raw material, and consumers of trade goods. England and France liberally supplied their Indian friends with guns, gunpowder, and horses in return for goods and services. Devastating trade wars that resulted between Indian nations became a significant factor in the expansion of British power into the frontier. On the other hand, the Spanish Empire was interested in incorporation and tribute, not alliance. The fabulous gold and silver treasures taken from the Mexican and Peruvian Indians fueled the world's most powerful military machine, which easily subdued most Native resistance. Still a feudal society, Spain transferred from Europe her system of strictly regulated trading and an economy based on vast landed estates. Indian towns were forced to pay tribute to Spanish lords or gentlemen under the *encomienda* system and the Church under *repartimientos.* In contrast to the Indians north of Spanish settlement, where peonage was virtually unknown, Indians in Mexico were quickly forced to work for the new owners of their lands.

While resistance to Spanish rule continued sporadically through Independence, the subjugation and terrible exploitation of the vast majority of Indians was most characteristic of the colonial period. Subsumed to a dominant Spanish and Catholic culture, Indigenous cultures showed a remarkable ability to retain many of their original features, including religious ceremonies, by subtly blending them with Catholicism. More importantly, as the *encomienda* and *repartimiento* systems did not force them off their lands, Natives managed to keep much of their *ejido* system of land management intact. The Indian wars sparked by the pioneers' insatiable demand for land in America by and large did not find their counterpart in New Spain. Once the conquest was complete. Indians in Mexico found themselves under an oppressive yoke, but at least they could stay on their ancestral lands.

In American history, Indians played a role only to the extent that they engaged the United States in war or were forcibly removed out of the country's way. In Mexico, Indians quickly became an integral part of the social fabric, though starting on the lowest rung of the ladder. The strong interaction between the races began forging a new Mexican society which was to destroy the colonial way of life.

THE INDIAN MASSES

By the time of the Mexican War for Independence in 1810, the Indian majority had become a powerful—and angry—political force, waiting to be unleashed. The war is characterized to a large degree as a struggle for power within the ruling Spanish elite, largely setting the *criollos* against the *peninsulares*, and arising out of the Spanish empire's declining power. Among the dominant factors in organizing the revolt was the political instability arising from Napoleon's overthrow of the Spanish monarchy, disaffection among the *criollos*, and the liberalizing social currents of the Enlightenment. However, once begun, the revolt quickly took on aspects of an Indian war against Spanish and clerical oppression. Both Hidalgo and Morelos were dependent on Indian support for their abortive attempts at independence. Indeed, Hidalgo mobilized almost 50,000 Indians to march on Mexico City, a show of Indian power not seen since the Aztec and Tarascan empires, and the Spanish viceroy was forced to abolish the centuries-old system of Indian tribute in an attempt to keep Indians loyal to the Crown.

Independence for Mexico in 1821 degenerated into a half century of uninterrupted civil war between the reactionary old hierarchy and a new breed of republican reformers. Indians fared badly no matter which ruled. The theft of Mexican lands by Texas and the United States and the punishing wars they began pushed Mexico to the brink of anarchy. Indians took the opportunity to mete out some punishment of their own, such as in the Yucatán, Papantla, and the Sierra Gorda of San Luis Potosí. The liberal administrations of Ignacio Comonfort and Benito Juarez, while abolishing the brutal class system, created as many problems as they solved. The *Ley Lerdo*, enacted in 1856, was intended to dissolve the huge Church estates, which covered almost half of Mexico by mandating the sale of all surplus property. However, the net effect of the law was to transfer these lands to wealthy speculators and ranchers, who quickly expelled the thousands of Indians living on them. In an attempt to create small Indian property holders, the law also forced the sale of *ejidos* next to Indian villages, which were also bought up by speculators. The bitter war over *la Reforma* found Indians divided between those following *caciques* such as Thomás Mejía, who was opposed to the new laws, and Benito Juarez, the first Indian president in the hemisphere. Ultimately, the *Ley Lerdo* set in motion a pattern of economic modernization, culminating with the dictatorship of Porfirio Díaz, that by 1910 had transferred most Indian subsistence lands to wealthy plantation owners and ranchers.

La Revolución, begun once again as a struggle for power between elites, unleashed once more the suppressed anger and bitterness of the Mexican Indians. Conditions among Indians had reached new lows. In 1910 there were more than four million landless Indians in the country, most of them serfs to the 834 *hacendados* who owned ninety percent of Mexico's rural land. Since the Mexican population was still eighty percent rural, they were joined in their plight by an equal number of landless *mestizos*. The feudal order of New Spain had given way to the new feudal world of the *hacienda*.

Unlike the wars for independence, where the non-Indian leadership failed to grasp Indian aspirations and consequently failed to appeal to most of the Indian communities, during *la Revolución* the Indian ideal finally found its voice in the person of Emiliano Zapata. To the universal desire for liberty, Zapata had added the magical word—land!

This hunger for the return of ancestral lands, the simple desire to grow corn on small plots without a crushing tribute, transcended the disintegration of the Revolution and the assassination of Zapata. Despite the lack of participation by Indians and *campesinos* in the drafting of the Mexican Constitution of 1917, the constitutional assembly acquiesced to the seething pressures for agrarian reform. Article 27 became the centerpiece of the new constitution—as remarkable a synthesis of human aspirations as the First Amendment is to the United States. Embodied in the new laws was the belief that the lands in Mexico belonged to the people, for the use of the people. It brought back the ancient Indian landholding system, the *ejido*, as an inalienable part of the national structure and mandated the return of stolen lands. After 400 years, the dreams of Mexico and the dreams of Indians had finally come together.

"INDIGENISMO" AND "INDIANISMO"

The great Mexican champion of Indian rights, Lázaro Cárdenas, who realized many of the unfulfilled promises of the Revolution, was also the great proponent of *indigenismo,* the philosophy of assimilating Indians into the Mexican body politic. In the historic, 1940 Inter-American Indian Conference of Pátzcuaro, Cárdenas acknowledged the political and cultural importance of Mexican Indians, yet urged Indians to subsume themselves to the greater Mexican nationalism, a nationalism evolving into the modern expression of *mestizaje.*

The political philosophy of Indian acculturation had a long history in Mexico, beginning, of course, with the Spanish. Yet in New Spain Indians were acculturated only to the extent that they joined, as a separate and distinct group, the deeply stratified Spanish society. Mixed-breeds would lose their Indian identity, yet simply move up another social layer. The republican period of Mexican independence, dominated by the figure of Benito Juarez, demanded an end to the unjust system of social classes, and as a consequence the end of the distinction between Indians and non-Indians. There was therefore no legal definition in his liberal constitution of 1857 of Indians as a people, nor was one added to the constitution of 1917.

For Cárdenas, *indigenismo* would solve, once and for all, the inherent problems associated with racism and inequality in Mexican society. The means for this gradual, peaceful acculturation would be national organizations such as the Institutor Nacional Indigenes (INI), formed in 1948. The expansion of education, the building of roads and modern infrastructure in the countryside, and the transformation and commercialization of Indian cultures into a folklore were extremely effective in dramatically reducing the sense of Indian identity among Mexican Indians. The tremendous expansion of commercial opportunities as Mexico modernized and restructured its economy created a new urban class with a different conception of Mexico. Mexico, sixty-five percent rural in 1940, had become almost sixty percent urban by 1970.

Most Mexican Indians, moreover, did not have cultures that precluded acculturation. Many of their American counterparts could call on ancient traditions

such as the Two Row Wampum or national heroes such as Crazy Horse to help them resist white culture. In Mexico, however, Indian resistance was frequently led by radical Catholic priests—often Jesuits, until their expulsion in 1768. After Independence the national Indian political position had been almost exclusively represented by large agrarian movements, which by the time of the Revolution, included as many *mestizos* as Indians. After the Revolution Indians continued to put pressure on the government for their rights through large *campesino* organizations such as Confederación Nacional Campesina (CNC). National Indigenous political forces were hamstrung by the lack of pan-Indian identity in Mexico, due to the variety of Indian cultures and their differing situations.

A small break in this long slide to *mestizaje* was organized in Chiapas by the same Samuel Ruíz who today continues to champion Indigenous people. In 1974, in the Native stronghold of San Cristóbal de Las Casas, the seat of the great Bishop Bartolomé de Las Casas, the Indian Congress of San Cristóbal broke from the traditional *campesino* demands and began the process of formulating and pursuing Indian-specific issues. To a large extent the sparks to this movement, known as *indianismo,* ignited during the social upheavals of the late '60s. The formation of the Confederación Nacional de Comunidades Indígenas (CNCI) in 1968 marked a break from Indian organizations in the past, putting forward a platform that for the first time advocated political autonomy for Indian peoples in Mexico. The general anti-authoritarian climate of the late '60s and early '70s, the political liberalization (*apertura democrática*) of the Echeverría regime, and a crisis in the agricultural sector began to shift Indian mobilizing towards the more "radical," Indian-oriented groups. The Congress of San Cristóbal brought many of these new philosophies together, along with a strong turnout of Indians in the region. Many differing organizing currents sprang from this Congress, including the present day Zapatistas, working separately yet united in the spirit of *indianismo,* the Indian way.

The radicalization of Indian movements did not go unnoticed by the Mexican government. Indeed, Echeverría's liberal and nationalistic rhetoric and political actions inspired a wave of land takeovers by *campesinos* tired of waiting for the land reform promises of the Revolution. True to its past behavior, Mexico moved to try to co-opt these radicalizing strains by making them a part of the official platform. The First Congress of Indigenous People, held in

Pátzcuaro in 1975, was presided by Echeverría himself, who called for an *"indigenismo de participación."* The creation from this conference of the Consejo Nacional de Pueblos Indios (CNPI) was designed to take the steam out of a movement that was becoming more assertive about land rights.

Not only did the Indian movement get stronger, the CNPI quickly showed its independence by directly criticizing the policies of Echeverría's successor, José López Portillo. In particular the CNPI denounced the *Ley de Desarrollo Agropecuario*, the centerpiece of Portillo's overhaul of Mexico's faltering agricultural sector, and it repudiated the administration's increasingly anti-Indian development policy. The president responded by dissolving the CNPI and stepping up repression in the countryside.

Under Portillo, corruption in Mexico, always endemic, became a full-scale looting of the country, whipped into a feeding frenzy by the tapping of Mexico's vast off-shore oil riches and the heavy international oil prices. The subsequent collapse of Mexico's economy greeted Portillo's replacement, Miguel de la Madrid Hurtado in 1982. The Mexican peso lost half its value overnight and effectively wiped out any economic gains Indians and *campesinos* may have made after the Revolution. As rural conditions became desperate, militant *campesino* movements such as the national Coordinadora Nacional Plan de Ayala and the Chiapas-based Organización Campesina Emiliano Zapata became the new voices of *indianismo*. As the Mexican infrastructure crumbled, its leaders turned to the global markets in an attempt to stop the free fall.

THE TROUBLED PRESENT

In 1989, Mexico created the Commission of Justice for Indian People in order to draft a proposal to amend Article 4 of the Mexican Constitution. This part of the Constitution, which assures the equality of all Mexicans, was modified to acknowledge "Mexico's multicultural composition based upon Indigenous people" and would "protect and promote the development of their language, cultures, traditional ways, customs, specific means and forms of social organization, and would guarantee to their members true access to the laws of the state." For the first time, Indians were formally recognized by the Mexican government. The new amendment, signed into law in 1990, was immediately attacked by Indigenous organizations as having little practical value and being simply *"indigenismo* with a new set of clothes."

For most observers, changes in Article 4 of the Constitution were simply a way for the Salinas administration to take the sting out of the amendments to Article 27, the symbol of Indian aspirations since the Revolution. Salinas, as economic czar under De la Madrid, had come to the conclusion that "land for the people" was not working and that the Mexican government could no longer afford to subsidize what was an increasingly costly relic of the past. The *ejido* system could not keep up with the tremendous explosion in Mexico's population. Its yield per acre of corn, Mexico's staple grain, was only one-third that of American producers. Yet to protect the *ejidos*, importation of cheaper American corn was allowed only under the most regulated circumstances. Moreover, in lieu of a welfare system, the government had been artificially holding down the national price of Mexico's basic foods, depleting a national treasury that was little more than bankrupt.

While not publicly acknowledged, the real problem was Mexican corruption. It had not only made the state-controlled economic system unviable, it precluded any real solutions without sweeping change in the political order. Yet Carlos Salinas de Gortari was a product of this political order, and had come to power as a result of the backroom machinations of the ruling party, the PRI. For Salinas and his fellow *tecnócratas*, it was therefore easier, and philosophically more desirable, to remove the public sector from its role in running the economy than to directly confront many of the powerfully entrenched PRI interests. Privatization of Mexico's huge apparatus of state-run businesses, co-opting or dismantling the powerful Mexican unions, and increasing foreign investment were to be the underlying principles of his economic policy. NAFTA and GATT [General Agreement on Tariffs and Trade] would provide the investment opportunities and make the country a full-fledged member of the international economic market. Mexican lands and subsoil riches, protected by Article 27, would have to be opened up or sold off to allow more efficient means of exploitation and to fulfill international obligations. Mexico's traditionally closed, state-managed economy was undergoing a sweeping about-face. Nevertheless, mired in a deep economic crisis since 1982, the Mexican people, it seemed, took no notice.

For Indians and *campesinos*, the Revolution, no matter how unfulfilled or poorly applied, was over. The dream of Zapata, and the dream of Indians, was no longer the dream of modern Mexico. The changes to Article 27 effectively inaugurated the breakup of the *ejido* system, which covers nearly half of Mexico's agricultural lands and directly supports more than a quarter of its people. The mechanism for breakup is, in many ways, similar to the American system of allotment of Indian lands in the 1880s, a measure which cost U.S. Indians over two-thirds of their remaining land base before it was repealed. Indian and *campesino* organizations condemned the changes to Article 27, but given the political stranglehold of the Salinas administration, the objections achieved nothing.

Onto this stage have wandered the Zapatistas, upsetting the applecart in a way no one could have predicted. Armed and dangerous, yet charming and reasonable, they called for reform, not revolution, and they rekindled the dying embers of *la Revolución*. For a few months they mesmerized the Mexican public and put the Salinas administration badly on the defensive. It took the assassination of PRI presidential candidate Donaldo Colosio on March 23 to break the Zapatista spell, raising fears among Indians that the deadly act might mean a harder line was taking over.

The Zapatista influence has not been translated into a national political movement largely because the one man who might have the ability to shoulder the aspirations of Indian people has declined to do so. Cuauhtémoc Cárdenas has remained more of a symbol than an alternative, and judging from the unenthusiastic reception he received among the Zapatistas in May, his potential constituents are tired of the lack of charisma, the lack of decisiveness, and most importantly, the lack of a viable platform that takes into account the Indian and *campesino* demands. His traditional urban-leftist perspective has had little in common with the agrarian demands of the Indians and *campesinos*. In the six years since his powerful showing in the presidential elections, he has seen his strength sapped by a never ending series of political miscalculations. His initial coolness to the Zapatistas in an attempt to quell any notion that he supported violence followed by his ill-conceived attempts to curry their support, seems like more of the same. Nor does it appear that he, nor any political alternative, has the strength to buck the new economic order, as voters in Canada found to their chagrin last year. The perennial politician, Cárdenas has now softened his tone and no longer rejects the free trade agreement, his platform more closely resembling [that of] PRI candidate Ernesto Zedillo than that of the Zapatistas.

At this point, in early June, the election is wide open, a scenario unthinkable before January 1st. The conservative PAN has the only candidate with strong personal appeal and is sure to capture the vote of a large share of the growing entrepreneurial class. There is a national sense of dissatisfaction with the PRI and it has become highly unpopular among vast sectors of the electorate, in particular Mexico's ruined middle class. Moreover, there is tremendous pressure from political forces in the United States to keep the election clean, a difficult problem to overcome, given the power of the local party bosses. From the perspective of international finance, it also appears that the PRI is no longer a prerequisite for stable investment and has become dispensable. Indeed, the election of an opposition candidate might be more favorable for releasing the pent-up pressures that the Zapatistas have shown are ever present. Far from monolithic, the PRI has spent a considerable amount of its energy in internal political battles, rather than displaying a unified front.

Yet despite these signs, Zedillo and the PRI are still the favorites to win the election. They certainly have no intention of losing. The PRI has a preponderance of resources and it spends far more on presidential elections than any political party in the United States. If their ability to buy votes falters, they still may try to alter the election results, international pressure notwithstanding.

None of this bodes well for the Zapatistas and for Indian and *campesino* movements in Mexico. Whichever political party takes office in August, it is highly unlikely that they will reverse the current modernization trends that threaten Indian sustainability. The most that Indians can hope for is government aid to soften what will be a very hard landing. With more than twenty million Mexicans dependent on the *ejido* system or living on communal Indian lands, the potential for social upheaval as these lands are lost is frightening. It has the possibility of becoming the largest forced migration of Indian people since the conquest. These people would have no place to go to except to join their impoverished brethren in the crowded Mexican cities and across the American border. However, the policies of the *tecnócratas*, represented by Salinas and Zedillo, seem to have become an irresistible force.

Yet the Zapatistas have clearly tapped into a strong national current. The Indians and the rural poor still remain a powerful bloc and the uprising has given a significant boost to Mexican Indian identity and their will to resist. It helps that the Zapatistas show an intelligence and political savvy rarely seen in a modern Indian movement, or any modern popular movement, for that matter. Subcomandante Marcos has become a celebrity in Mexico, and if he can stay alive, he could well become a national leader. While the Zapatistas have clearly captured the imagination of the Mexican people, whether this will translate into political gains hinges on the strength and unity of the Indians and the *campesinos.*

For Mexico, the future is full of grim possibilities. A quarter of a century of mismanagement and corruption has left a wealthy country bankrupt and unstable. The solutions currently offered by the *tecnócratas* represent a dramatic break from Mexico's traditional past, and yet are based upon purely theoretical economic formulas. The extent to which they can transform

Mexico peacefully and successfully will depend to a large degree on the character and strength of the mass of Mexican people.

It can be argued that the crisis Mexico faces today is a crisis of identity. In many ways Mexico is a tortured transforming soul, not fully ready for the leap into the modern order, not fully rid of its rich past. This deep crisis is represented by Salinas, NAFTA, and a culture of modernity on the one hand, and by Indians, representing *la Revolución,* tradition, and anti-modernity on the other. It is a crisis stripped of its cover by a ragtag Indian army, which raised the question no one had thought to ask, "where is our place, where is the place of Indian people, in this modern Mexico?"

@ 1997 H.J. Tsinhnahjinnie

JIM THORPE: THAT CHAMPIONSHIP SEASON

Jim Adams

This summer's Olympic Games have revived memories of Indian Country's greatest athlete, Jim Thorpe, who stunned the 1912 Olympics in Stockholm, Sweden, with one of the most dominant and versatile performances ever seen. But the Sac and Fox tribesman, who claimed descent from the great Chief Black Hawk, went on that year to other historic victories, built on a literal team effort by Indians of many tribes.

The national college football champion in that pivotal year was neither Harvard nor Yale, but Thorpe's alma mater, the Carlisle Industrial Indian School. Taken together, Carlisle football and Thorpe's exploits at the Olympics have significance beyond sports. Coming at a Native low point, they helped forge pan tribal identity and revive Indian morale.

The Game

Thorpe's gold medals in the decathlon and pentathlon at the Stockholm Olympics established him as the greatest athlete in the world, in spite of the Orwellian rewriting of the record book that would soon follow. But this was only one episode in that championship year. Thorpe was already a star of the famous athletic program of the Carlisle Indian Industrial School in Carlisle, Pa., one of the remarkable successes of that flawed but important social experiment.

Carlisle was founded by Tenth Cavalry Captain Richard H. Pratt. After initially banning football as too brutal, he gave in to lobbying by the students and started a formal program in 1893. Pratt also quickly realized, as many schools have since, that a strong team could compensate for a lack of other resources.

In 1899, Pratt made a major investment, hiring Glenn Scobey "Pop" Warner from Cornell. Warner revolutionized a game then consisting of crushing power plays on the line. With Warner, Carlisle pioneered the forward pass and the spiral throw. Quarterback Frank Mount Pleasant used the newly legal play to devastate Ivy League opponents through the fall of 1907, finally beating arch-rival Harvard.

The team also pioneered coast-to-coast touring. On the way home from an East-West championship game (the first ever), the team gave exhibitions at several Indian schools. At the Haskell Institute in Lawrence, Kan., they caught the imagination of a withdrawn 12-year-old chronic runaway named Jim Thorpe.

Thorpe and Carlisle Football

Thorpe came to Carlisle in 1904, and in 1908 he carried the team to a winning season with his feint-filled running. But in 1909 Thorpe himself 'ran," the notation in his record, leaving school for a try at semipro baseball in North Carolina. Warner lured him back in 1911, with a promise to help him train for the 1912 Olympics.

The 1911 season began the peak years of Carlisle football. After eight straight wins, the team faced Harvard in what has been called one of the greatest football games ever played. Carlisle won 18–15 on Thorpe's last-minute field goal, to a standing ovation from Harvard Stadium.

The post-Olympic 1912 season culminated in a second classic game, an emotional match with Army. Warner gave his team a not very subtle pep talk invoking the Indian Wars. Carlisle went on to give the cadets a major lesson in strategy. Warner had invented a new formation for this game, the double wing. It gave quarterback Gus Welch innumerable openings for runs, passes, and reverses. "Football," said Warner, "began to have the sweep of a prairie fire." The final score was Carlisle 27–Army 6, and it shocked the nation.

Collapse and Resurrection

After this high point, like a classical tragedy, the fall came quickly. Thorpe was a national hero, so it was a national story when the Worcester, Mass., Telegram reported that his two seasons of semipro baseball in North Carolina called his amateur status into question. The Amateur Athletic Union (AAU) refused his apology and demanded the return of his Olympic medals and trophies. The International Olympics Committee (IOC) awarded the gold medals to the runners-up, who initially declined to accept them.

This decision is now seen as an act of "official infamy," serving a hypocritical and elitist (and now repudiated) definition of amateurism and violating the procedural rules of its own day. The campaign to restore Thorpe's medals was kept alive for many years by his daughter, Grace, who passed away on April 1, 2008, at the age of 86. The AAU finally restored Thorpe's amateur status in 1973, 20 years after his death at the age of 65. In 1982, the IOC again recognized him as the gold medalist.

In the immediate aftermath of the controversy, Thorpe withdrew from Carlisle, embarking on an influential career in professional baseball, football, and even basketball. His superstardom helped shape the modern sports economy. His influence was most decisive in football, in which he served as first president of the American Professional Football League, later the National Football League.

The impact on Carlisle was more damaging. Students blamed Warner and Carlisle administrators for not defending Thorpe, and morale plummeted. Financial scandal and Congressional hostility finally closed the school altogether in 1918.

History and Native opinion have not been kind to Carlisle or Superintendent Pratt. But like many social experiments, its most lasting consequences might have been totally unintended. Instead of destroying the Indianness of its students, Carlisle created a new generation of pan-Indian leaders and institutions, dating in part from the 1899 national football tour. Among the leading Indian intellectuals who passed through Carlisle, the school medical director, Carlos Montezuma (Apache), served as football team doctor during its 1899 tour. The Society of American Indians, the first Indian-run pan-tribal national organization, heavily influenced by ex-Carlisle faculty, held its first conference in 1911 during the height of Carlisle's football season.

The football championship coincided with an even broader shift in Indian Country. Somewhere between the massacre at Wounded Knee and the U.S. entry into World War I, the American Indian passed imperceptibly from an enemy of the U.S. Army to its most reliable supporter. It is not a stretch to think that this cementing of loyalty to the United States went hand in hand with the emergence of Jim Thorpe and the Carlisle football team as true American heroes.

Jim Adams, Senior Historian for the Research Unit of the NMAI, has also written about Indian sports news for Indian Country *Today*.

This article draws on two recent first-rate histories of Carlisle football: *The Real All-Americans* by Sally Jenkins (Random House, 2007), and *Carlisle vs. Army* by Lars Anderson (Random House, 2007).

JUST SPEAK YOUR LANGUAGE
HENA'HAANEHE

Richard Littlebear

Why save our languages, since they now seem to have no political, economic, or global relevance? That impression is exactly the reason why we should save our languages, because it is the spiritual relevance deeply embedded in our own languages that makes them relevant to us as American Indians today.

I have challenged myself to come up with different ways to say "just speak your language," because that is really the core of my message, my first idea for preserving our languages. If we all just spoke our languages to our young people, we would have no need for indigenous language curricula or for conferences to save our languages. If we just spoke them, all of our languages would be healthier; but that is not what's happening. We do not speak our languages, and our languages are dying. We are also confronted with a voracious language, English, that gobbles up everything in its way.

Since this is the first and only time we are going to lose our languages, we have to devise new strategies accordingly.

The Cheyenne people began making the change to a different type of culture and to a written language about a century ago. Those of us who speak the Cheyenne language are quite possibly the last generation able to joke in our own language. We are possibly the last ones who can talk in our language about profound physical, psychological, and spiritual topics and do it in the appropriate technical language. We can articulate how we feel in all these regards and know with satisfaction that we have been understood. The generations that succeed us will be unable to articulate those same feelings in Cheyenne, since English is now their first language. And the sad part is that even in their first language,

English, they have trouble talking about the deeper meanings of life, since they are not being taught English very well at school or at home.

A second idea is that language is the basis of sovereignty. We are always talking about sovereignty, and rightfully so, because when we were dealing with the US government during the treaty era, our people were treated as nations equal in stature. It was a government-to-government relationship. We have all the attributes that constitute sovereign nations: a governance structure, law and order, jurisprudence, literature, a land base, spiritual and sacred practices, and that one attribute that holds all of these other attributes together—our languages. So once our languages disappear, each one of these attributes begins to fall apart, until they are all gone.

For instance, land ceases to be sacred and becomes looked on as only a commodity to be bought and sold. Our land base and sacred practices are passed on through our languages, not by English, the language spoken by people who killed our people and oppressed our languages. Think about that. We are still accepting the idea that English is a superior language. The passage of time and the continuing loss of our languages separates us from our sacred references and our sacred sites. We have to refer to them constantly. We need to see that our languages continue to refer to our sacred sites. At Dull Knife Memorial College, where I work, we took a field trip to Bear Butte in South Dakota's Black Hills. Bear Butte is our most sacred site. It surprised me to learn that this field trip was the first time most of the students had ever gone to this sacred area. Many did not know the spiritual significance of Bear Butte.

A third idea is that of protocol in the language used in ceremonies. For instance, there are some rituals that I have never participated in on our reservation.

Littlebear in *Whole Earth,* Spring 2000. 2pp.

Consequently, I am unable to participate in some related activities or to use the language associated with those rituals. The dilemma is that the people who have the right to use that vocabulary and language, and who have done the rituals, are dying. When they die, all of this language will be lost forever. I do not have the years needed to do the rituals, and I don't want to truncate or abbreviate or shortcut them. I keep saying that someone should write these words down on paper and leave them for posterity. The loss of this specialized language will become a major obstacle in retaining the full richness of our languages and cultures. I do not have a solution.

A fourth idea: some of our people go to college and return to us to help preserve our languages and cultures. However they often are not accepted by their own people when they return, or are viewed with suspicion and skepticism. I speak from experience. I have been off my reservation and have earned a doctorate. These factors often lead to my being discounted and dismissed; some of my people assert that I think too much like a white person. The rejection of American Indians by their own people is almost like the rejection of formal education. I just hope that this is not a rejection of learning, because I do not know of any tribal group that ever rejected learning.

Whenever we as American Indian people develop curriculum materials, we tend to immediately confront a faction that opposes their use. Members of our own tribes have produced these materials locally. Yet some faction questions and demolishes our own home-produced materials. What makes this situation even worse is that when we get curriculum materials from outside our geographical and cultural boundaries, we don't utter a word of protest or criticism.

A fifth radical idea is that we must help our own elders and our fluent speakers to be more accepting of those people who are just now learning our languages. We must sensitize our elders and fluent speakers to the needs of potential speakers of our languages. In many of our tribes, the elders are teachers and bearers of wisdom. As a result, when they criticize or make fun of a person trying to speak one of our languages they are taken very seriously, and some people will not even, try to speak the language once they have been criticized by a respected elder of that tribe. When this happens, it hastens the death of that language. Somehow we must turn this negativity around.

I teach the Cheyenne language on my reservation. I tell my students that for this semester they must learn Cheyenne with me using my inferior Cheyenne, and after they are done they can go home and speak the superior Cheyenne that abounds in their families. I say this to preempt needless discussions on what is the correct way of saying things.

A sixth idea concerns our youth, who, even in rural areas, are apparently looking to urban gangs for things that will give them a sense of identity, importance, and belonging. It would be so nice if they would look to our own tribal characteristics. We already have all the things that our youth are apparently looking for and finding in socially destructive gangs. Gangs have distinctive colors, clothes, music, heroes, symbols, rituals, and "turf." We American Indian tribes have these too. We have distinctive colors, clothes, music, heroes, symbols, and rituals, and our "turf" is our reservations.

Another characteristic that really makes a gang distinctive is the language it speaks. If we could transfer the young people's loyalty back to our own tribes and families, we could restore the frayed social fabric of our reservations. We need to make our children see our languages and cultures as viable and just as valuable as anything they see on television in movies, or on videos.

My last idea is that we must remember that our children are not genetically wired for learning and acquiring our tribal languages. Just because our children are born to Cheyenne parents on Cheyenne land and engage in Cheyenne traditional practices does not mean they are automatically predisposed to learning the Cheyenne language. They have to be taught our language. They must learn to speak the Cheyenne language in just the same way they would have to go about acquiring Greek or German or Swahili, especially since for almost all of them English is now their first language. Everybody who works with languages should learn about second-language acquisition and the theories buttressing it, and be able to apply those theories in whatever subject area they are teaching. Teachers of American Indian languages must remember that everybody has to go through some definite stages of acquiring a language. Right now we have children who are mute in our languages, who are migrants to our languages, who are like extraterrestrials to our cultures.

In closing, I want to relate an experience I had in Alaska. I met Marie Smith, the last Native speaker on Earth of the Eyak language. It was truly a profoundly moving experience for me. We talked for about three hours. I felt that I was sitting in the presence of a whole universe of knowledge that could be gone in one last breath. That's how fragile that linguistic universe seemed. It was really difficult for me to stop talking to her, because I wanted to remember every moment of our encounter.

I do not want any more of our languages to have that experience of having one last speaker. I want all of our languages to last forever, to always be around to nurture our children, to bolster their identities, to perpetuate our cultures.

The Cheyenne language is my language. English is also my language. Yet it is Cheyenne I want to use when my time is completed here on this earth and journey on to the spirit world. I want to greet in our Cheyenne language those who've journeyed on before me because I know that Cheyenne is the only language they know, the only language they ever needed to know. And I hope when I meet them on the other side that they will understand me and accept me. Thank you for listening to me.

Hena'haanehe.

PART REVIEW

DISCUSSION QUESTIONS

Introduction
1. Why should the Native American heritage be known to everyone?

Darryl Wilson, *Mis Misa*
1. Who or what is Mis Misa? What is its central purpose or function?
2. How is the Indian's view of Mt. Shasta different from that of many non-Indians?

Donald A. Grinde, Jr., and Bruce E. Johansen,
Perceptions of America's Native Democracies
1. Who are the two founders of the Six Nations Iroquois Confederacy? Name the six nations of the confederacy.
2. How did the Iroquois League function? Briefly describe its legislative process.

John Mohawk, *Origins of Iroquois Political Thought*
1. What was the Peacemaker's message to the Haudenosaunee?
2. What did he mean by "the power of righteousness"?

Michael Kearney and Stefano Varese, *Latin America's Indigenous Peoples*
1. According to the article by Kearney and Varese, how did the Spanish occupation of the Americas and Spanish colonial policies regarding the Indian peoples differ from those of the English?

2. What are the "four fundamental forms of ethnic resilience and opposition" that have occurred in indigenous Latin American history?
3. As demonstrated by the demands of the Mayan rebels of Chiapas, Mexico, in 1994, what are the two central concerns of the Indigenous peoples of Latin America?

Alexander Ewen, *Mexico: The Crisis of Identity*
1. What is the difference between *indigenismo* and *indianismo*, and why is this distinction important to Native peoples?
2. In Mexico, who are *mestizo*?
3. Explain the relationship between NAFTA and the Zapatista movement in Chiapas.

Jim Adams, *Jim Thorpe: That Championship Season*
1. Who was Jim Thorpe, and why is he famous?
2. Why were the gold medals Thorpe's won at the 1912 Olympics revoked? Do you think this was fair?
3. What was Thorpe's role at Carlisle during the famous 1911 and 1912 football seasons?

Richard Littlebear, *Just Speak Your Language*
1. The author enumerates seven ways that knowing one's native language is important to indigenous culture. Explain at least three of them.

KEY TERMS

Aiowantha (Hiawatha)
Anglo-American, Euro-American
Carlisle Industrial Indian School
clan
Cortés, Hernando
Deganawidah, or Peacemaker
ethnic confederacies
Great Law of Peace
Haudenosaunee
indianismo
indígenas

Jim Thorpe
Six Nations Iroquois Confederacy
longhouse
mestizaje
Mis Misa
Mixtec
Mound Builders
NAFTA (North American Free Trade Agreement)
power of righteousness
sachem
White Roots of Peace
Zapatistas

SUGGESTED READINGS

BALLANTINE, BETTY, and IAN BALLANTINE, eds. The *Native Americans: An Illustrated History*. Atlanta: Turner Publishing, 1993.

BARREIRO, JOSE, and TIM JOHNSON, eds. *Opinions and Perspectives from Indian Country*. Golden, Colo.: Fulcrum Publishing. 2005.

BIOLSI, THOMAS. *A Companion to the Anthropology of American Indians*. MA: Malden: Blackwell Publishing, Ltd. 2004.

CHAMPAGNE, DUANE. *American Indian Societies: Strategies and Conditions of Political and Cultural Survival*. Cambridge, Mass.: Cultural Survival,1989.

COUNCIL ON INTERRACIAL BOOKS FOR CHILDREN. *Chronicles of American Indian Protest*. Greenwich, Conn.: Facet-Premier, 1971.

CRUM, STEVEN J. *The Road on Which We Came: A History of the Western Shoshone*. Salt Lake City: University of Utah Press, 1994.

EASTON, ROBERT. "Humor of the American Indian." Pages 177–206 in *The American Indian*. Ed. Raymond Friday Locke. Los Angeles: Mankind Publishing, 1970.

FORBES, JACK D. "Undercounting Native Americans: The 1990 Census and the Manipulation of Racial Identity in the United States." *Wicazo Sa Review*, 6, no. 1 (Spring 1990): 2–26; *The American Discovery of Europe*. city: University of Illinois Press, 2006.

GRINDE, DONALD. *The Iroquois and the Founding of the American Nation*. San Francisco: Indian Historian Press, 1977.

GRINDE, DONALD A., and BRUCE E. JOHANSEN. *Exemplar of Liberty: Native America and the Evolution of Democracy*. Los Angeles: UCLA American Indian Studies Center, 1991.

JOHANSEN, BRUCE. *Forgotten Founders: Benjamin Franklin, the Iroquois and the Rationale for the American Revolution*. Ipswich, Mass.: Gambit,1992.

KATZ, FRIEDRICH. *The Ancient American Civilizations*. London: Phoenix Press, 2000.

LEON-PORTILLA, MIGEL, ed. *The Broken Spears: The Aztec Account of the Conquest of Mexico*. Boston: Beacon Press, 1962.

LEON-PORTILLA, MIGEL. *Pre-Columbian Literature of Mexico*. Norman: University of Oklahoma Press, 1969.

MACLEOD, WILLIAM CHRISTIE. *The American Indian Frontier*. New York: Alfred A. Knopf, 1928.

MOMADAY, N. SCOTT. *The Way to Rainy Mountain*. Albuquerque: University of New Mexico Press, 1969.

SHERIDAN, THOMAS E., and NANCY J. PAREZO, eds. *Paths of Life: American Indians of the Southwest*. Tucson: The University of Arizona Press, 1996.

SILKO, LESLIE MARMON. *Storyteller*. New York: Arcade Publishing, 1981.

SPICER, EDWARD H. *The American Indians*. Cambridge, Mass.: Harvard University Press, 1980.

VLAHOS, OLIVIA. *New World Beginnings: Indian Cultures in the Americas*. New York: Viking Press, 1970.

WEARNE, PHILLIP. *Return of the Indian: Conquest and Revival in the Americas*. Philadelphia: Temple University Press, 1996.

WEATHERFORD, JACK. *Indian Givers: How the Indians of the Americas Transformed the World*. New York: Fawcett Columbine, 1988.

WEATHERFORD, JACK. *Native Roots: How the Indians Enriched America*. New York: Fawcett Columbine, 1991.

WILSON, DARRYL BABE. *The Morning the Sun Went Down*. Berkeley, Calif.: Heyday Books, 1998.

WRIGHT, RONALD. *Stolen Continents*. New York: Houghton Mifflin. 1992.

III
THE AMERICAN INDIAN STORY (HISTORY)

Was He a Fool?

[About Christopher Columbus]

Was he a fool or was he a hero?
The motherf____er was lost, that makes him a zero in
my book! cuz of the lives he took, cuz of the land he
stole, all in the hopes of gold!
trick him, put him down in American mythology as a
hero that never really could be.
You see, his claim to fame was discovering a land
already claimed by 10 million redmen!

he comes to MY land thinking it's India?
I got news for you, you don't have a clue
of where you are, but they still gave you a holiday! the
lie is up, now it's time to pay!
in 1999, whatcha gonna do? people pushed up
so consider yourself through: your name, your fame,
your game, consider it over! when I'm done with you,
you'll be rolling over in your grave, yeah it's just like
that! cuz if you were alive, I'd have to get the gat and
blast your ass outta this atmosphere
a hero to me? You could never be!

I'm not from India, don't call me an Indian!
I'm not American, cuz we got our own land,
or what's left of it,
they took it, stole it, raped it,
and now they're destroying it!
They left my people in poverty, they starve me!
a genocidal catastrophe, how can it be? they say they
got a plan, but they don't understand, they're the damn
reason we're sinking in quicksand!

But those days of sinking are over!
and we know you ain't nothing but a rover.
We had enough of this. We're coming back with fist!
Telling truths about things that are ludicrous.
They take a man like Christopher Columbus, they mold
him, shape him and make him their hero. but the bottom
line is The Facts are simple. you might as well be
honoring a pimple.

"What!?!" A pimple's a thing, disgusting white and
dirty. It's okay to say you heard it from me!
(the comparison) Oh, how embarrassing! To honor a
man who was just on a scam plan!
How the hell did he think this was his land?
"but, that's what they teach us in school?"
it's their plan to fill a land full of fools that think
only whatcha tell'em.
but not me, I won't stop yelling about the truth.
just leave the simple facts to me.
Listen! Open your eyes so you can see

"Was He a Fool?" from WithOut Reservation (WOR), Native Rap Group. Lyrics by Chris LaMarr. Reprinted by permission.

about Columbus and what he did to us
and then you'll see why
we're raising such a damn fuss.

Columbus, The Modern-Day Scenario: unbearable,
incomparable! Suppose some punk
walked straight up in your house, and
yelled out, "Get the Hell Out!"
raped your wife and beat your kids
(that's what he did, God forbid!)
Then to make matters worse, they throw him a party!
a celebration? what a nation, to honor the man who
led to the onslaught! They forgot? I won't let'em.

What is historical truth? Does the story of Indian–white relations taught in our history books accurately reflect the American Indian experience? Or is the history of the Americas actually "his-story"—i.e., white, male, and Eurocentric? These questions came to a head in 1992 in the controversy surrounding the Columbian Quincentennial, the 500-year anniversary of the voyage of Christopher Columbus across the Atlantic Ocean and the "discovery" and conquest of the Americas. How to "celebrate" or observe the quincentennial became a profound question for many Native Americans.

As 1992 approached, the Indigenous peoples of the Americas viewed with alarm the many official declarations and events being planned for the Columbian Quincentennial, which not only excluded them from the planning process but also took on a carnival atmosphere. Spain launched an imitation flotilla of the *Niña*, *Pinta*, and *Santa Maria* for a reinvasion of the Americas, as if the first invasion in 1492 that signaled the beginning of the American holocaust, in which tens of millions of Native people lost their lives, was not tragic enough. In the United States, the city of Columbus, Ohio, enthusiastically organized its AmeriFlora exhibition, which "included everything from an African-American Heritage Consortium to 'Discover Columbus' international soccer tournaments, an air show, a marathon, even a world horseshoe tournament—but no Indians."[1] Enormous sums were earmarked for the quincentennial; Spain alone budgeted US$14 billion, and the U. S. government set aside $28 million.

The quincentennial controversy and Indian reaction to it, however, did have some important positive outcomes. In the first place, Indian people and their supporters all over the Americas organized counter demonstrations and special events to tell the other side of the story. For example, Indian delegates representing 120 Indigenous nations and organizations met in Quito, Ecuador, in July 1990 to organize a hemispheric response. A similar conference took place in Guatemala in October 1992. The many counteractions and Indian protests also nurtured the major "revisionist" movement already under way among anthropologists, historians, and other scholars to produce more complete information and a broader interpretation of the European invasion and colonization of the Americas. For example, the UCLA American Indian Studies Center sponsored a conference of scholars on the American Indian responses to the Columbian Quincentennial and published the conference proceedings as *The Unheard Voices*. (See Gentry and Grinde in Suggested Readings.)

Contributing to this need for a revisionist movement, or truth in history, has been the fact that most scholars who write history are the products of their own particular ethnic past. They have "recorded" and interpreted historical events through the eyes of the "pioneers" and "empire builders," who were almost entirely white males of property and influence. Thus, most general histories of the Americas are not histories of the region, nor are they histories of all of the many peoples who reside there, that is, a people's history. Rather, most such works are essentially chronicles of the European conquest and the subsequent national development of English-, Spanish-, and Portuguese-speaking white people during the succeeding centuries. In the same manner, history courses, because of ethnocentric and racial biases, have all but eliminated the Native American heritage, except negatively, from the scene and therefore fail to explain historical events fully.

An accurate understanding of the history and culture of the entire hemisphere includes a consideration of the role of the Indigenous nations in colonial history and their decisive influence on the course of subsequent historical developments: the fact that the Spaniards based much of their colonial organization on existing Incan, Aztec, and Mayan social organization; the importance of the Indian confederacies in the eastern region of the United States, which were co-equal if not superior in power and influence to the early English colonies; the fact that the U.S. Constitution and governmental structure were modeled, at least in part, on the League of the Iroquois; the fact that Rousseau and other philosophers who inspired Europeans to oppose feudal tyranny and oppression based their views on the personal freedom they found in North American Indian societies; the fact that many outstanding statesmen, generals, and religious leaders throughout the hemisphere were of Native American biological heritage.

Part of the revisionist movement among scholars, especially in history, is the growing interest in ethnohistory. Ethnohistory combines the use of data from several fields, including geography, archival records and reports, diary entries, oral history and biography, archaeology, folklore, and ethnography, in order to construct an integrated picture of the social and ethnic processes taking place among a particular people (in this case, Native Americans) during a particular historical period. The ethnohistorian attempts to get as close to the actual event as possible, for instance through eyewitness accounts and on-the-scene reports. When this approach is taken, for example, the Battle of Wounded Knee, so named by U.S. military historians, becomes the Massacre of Wounded Knee, since eyewitnesses describe the ruthless atrocities of white troops in 1890 against unarmed women and children in which upward of 300 Indians were slaughtered.

A common device used by historians is to divide history into periods differentiated by significant events or historical processes. Mainstream historians, for example, most often divide U.S. history into "colonial," "early years of the republic," "Civil War," and similar historical compartments that perhaps make sense from an Anglo-American perspective. But to call the period in North American Indian–white relations from 1540 to the U.S. Revolution the "colonial period" is misleading and ethnocentric. Although colonialism may have been the situation for the English colonists in North America at the time, the term does not accurately describe the situation of the even more numerous Indian peoples, who were not living as politically subordinated and culturally dominated people. By the 1790s only some of the smaller Indian nations had been eliminated or reduced to colonial dependency. Throughout most of the region between the Atlantic Ocean and the Mississippi River, Indians remained as independent nations. West of the Mississippi River during the same period, Spanish political domination and influence impacted primarily what is now New Mexico, Arizona, and California. From an Indian viewpoint, it was a period of many competing nations (both European and Indian), a period of trade competition, of forced migration of tribes such as the Kickapoo and the Delaware, of shifting alliances, especially among the imperial European powers, of political instability, and of rapid cultural change on the part of both Europeans and the Native peoples.

In Reading 1, "Five Hundred Years of Injustice: The Legacy of Fifteenth Century Religious Prejudice," Steven Newcomb explains the European religious rationale for the invasion of the Americas and the dispossession and genocide of the Indigenous peoples that has led to 500 years of injustice. Newcomb, a leading authority on this question, documents the origins of the Doctrine of Discovery, or Law of the Nations.

His latest work is *Pagans in the Promised Land: Decoding the Doctrine of Christian Discovery* (see Suggested Readings.) When Christopher Columbus landed in the West Indies in 1492 he performed a ceremony to "take possession" of America's "new lands" and peoples. As Newcomb relates, both Spain and Portugal as Christian nations had the official blessing of the Catholic Church to take possession of the new lands for their sovereigns and to "capture, vanquish, and subdue the Saracens, pagans, and other enemies of Christ," to put them "in perpetual slavery," and "to take all their possessions and property." Newcomb goes on to explain how Christian bias became the rationale in the underpinnings of Indigenous policy. This same Christian versus "pagan" bias, which had governed the European powers in the colonization of the Americas, became established after the Revolution in U.S. Indian law with the 1823 Supreme Court decision *Johnson v. McIntosh.*

In a seeming contradiction to the Christian bias in U.S. Indian history, Native peoples in the United States are the only minority group who retain the legal right to territory and whose political status is governed by treaty relations and the concept of sovereignty. Noted legal scholar David Wilkins (Lumbee) traces U.S. Indian legislation through seven policy periods in Reading 2, "A History of Federal Indian Policy." Hank Adams, a 1960s Indian activist, defined sovereignty as "the collective authority of a people to govern themselves." Nevertheless, Indian sovereignty has been steadily chipped away over the last century by the plenary power of the U.S. Congress. The plenary power doctrine gives Congress the power to pass any law it pleases to unilaterally limit the sovereignty of Indian nations. For example, in 1988, Congress passed the Indian Gaming Regulatory Act to promote tribal economic development even though it violates the Interstate Commerce Clause of the U.S. Constitution, which states that only the federal government can "treat with Indian tribes." (See the discussion of Indian gaming by Davis and Feustel in Part VIII.)

Sovereignty issues, especially land claims, and hunting, fishing, and subsistence rights, continue to occupy North American Indian concerns and legal actions. After a 12-year-long quest, Venetie Village (Athabascan) in Alaska received a negative judgment in 1998, when the U.S. Supreme Court reversed a favorable decision by a lower court that had allowed the village to tax and govern its own land. The struggle for sovereign rights that Indian nations in the United States (and the treaty Indians in Canada) continue to pursue gives hope to the Indigenous peoples and nations of Latin America, as well as Hawai'i, in their struggle for self-determination. In Chiapas, Mexico, the Zapatista Indian movement of the 1990s was organized in direct protest to the ending of Mexican national legislation, which formerly protected Indian and peasant land tenure through the *ejido* law, as well as to the deleterious impact of the passage of the North American Free Trade Agreement (NAFTA) on Indigenous economic self-sufficiency. These are the very problems often ignored by mainstream scholars.

Attorney Mario Gonzalez (Oglala Lakota) explains the legal case for the claim by the Lakota (Sioux) and Tsistsistas (Cheyenne) to the Black Hills of western South Dakota in Reading 3, "The Black Hills: The Sacred Land of the Lakota and Tsistsistas." In 1980 the U.S. Supreme Court ruled that the Black Hills, sacred to Indian people, had been illegally taken by the U.S. government in the previous century, when it broke the 1868 Treaty of Fort Laramie. But rather than return the region to its Indian owners, the Court awarded a $102 million monetary compensation. This outcome has been compared to a situation in which a thief (in this case, the United States), who, after confessing to a crime, refuses to return what was stolen and also sets the terms of his own punishment and restitution to the victim. Gonzalez also explains the sacred nature of the Black Hills, with its many holy places, such as Bear Butte, that figure prominently in the Lakota and Tsistsistas religions. Paha Sapa, or the Black Hills, is "the heart of everything that lives," and its sacredness forms the linchpin of the Northern Plains Indian cultures.

In Reading 4, "The Rediscovery Of Hawaiian Sovereignty," Poka Laenui (Native Hawaiian), president of the Pacific-Asia Council of Indigenous Peoples, reexamines Hawaiian history and lays out the historical justification for an independent Native Hawaiian nation. Few Americans realize that Hawai'i was a thriving, internationally recognized nation before Anglo imperialist interests, backed by U.S. Marines, overthrew the constitutional Hawaiian monarchy in 1893. Exploited economically and culturally as a territory for the next 60 years, Hawai'i became a state in 1959. Yet, in that statehood referendum, the question of independence was never raised, and the opinions of Native Hawaiians were never solicited. In past decades, however, there has been a cultural and political revitalization among Native people, with a growing demand for Hawaiian sovereignty. The most recent expression in the quest for justice in the Hawaiian case is the discovery of the 1897–1898 'Aina Anti-Annexation Petitions uncovered recently in the National Archives in Washington, D.C. These contain the signatures of all those Hawaiians opposed to the annexation of the islands by the United States. This petition, combined with the signatories of a second 1897 petition conducted by Hui Kulai'aina, prove that almost 40,000 people, nearly all of the Hawaiians living at the time, opposed the July 7, 1898, annexation. The newly discovered petitions convincingly demonstrate that the Hawaiian people were overwhelmingly opposed to the U.S. takeover and that the treaty of annexation should have been overturned by Congress. Today, the history and true meaning of the petitions are being taught to Native Hawaiian children.

An international issue involving sovereignty for U.S. Native nations is the "border problem." Eileen Luna-Firebaugh gives a riveting account and analysis of this issue in Reading 5, "The Border Crossed Us: Border Crossing Issues of the Indigenous Peoples of the Americas." The author details the devastating problems encountered by more than a half-dozen Native peoples, including the Tohono O'odham, Akwesasne Mohawk, Blackfeet Confederacy, Yaqui, Kickapoo, Cocopah, and Kumeyaay, whose ancient homelands are today bisected by the United States and either the Canadian or Mexican border. The Tohono O'odham Nation in Arizona, whose tribal members reside on both sides of the international border with Mexico, is a case in point. The nation's traditional territory predates the setting of the U.S. border with Mexico. Yet tribal members "who continue to use the traditional border crossing areas are in danger of being shot by U.S. border patrol personnel, U.S. military, or vigilante citizen groups." The official harassment and endangerment of Indian tribal members by U.S. and Canadian border officials violates Indigenous sovereignty, leading to dislocation with non-Indian encroachment, and the "loss of traditional homesteads, inability to control and transverse over traditional lands, colonization, loss of mobility and traditional contacts." Luna-Firebaugh concludes the article with a discussion of the various approaches toward solving the problem—individual, legislative, negotiation, litigation, and international—but concludes that few of these attempts at resolution have so far been wholly successful.

When Rupert Costo (Cahuilla) and Jeannette Henry Costo (Eastern Cherokee) of the American Indian Historical Society rushed their book on California missions into print in 1987 (see Suggested Readings), it was to counteract a worrisome trend on the part of some church scholars to rationalize the genocide of tens of thousands of Indians under the Spanish mission system. There was a serious attempt by some in the Catholic Church hierarchy to canonize the eighteenth-century head of the Franciscan missions in California, Fr. Junipero Serra, in conjunction with the anniversary of the signing of the U.S. Constitution. Rather than "the defender, protector, and father" of Indian people, Serra is viewed by many Indian people as the personification of a barbaric mission system that embodied starvation, enslavement, untold physical abuse and suffering, and that led to the rapid population decline of California Indians. In today's context, the United Nations would define the mission practices as acts of genocide, as illustrated in a box titled "The Crime of Genocide." That is not to say that the Indians put up no resistance. The story of the Tongva Indian leader Toypurina is an example of one of the many rebellions at the missions. If the genocide of the California Indians was indirect during the Spanish mission system, it emerged full force with the 1849 Gold Rush and the ascendancy of Anglo-Americans in California.

Steve Talbot summarizes and contrasts the Spanish, Mexican, and Anglo occupations in Reading 6, "Genocide of California Indians." The Spanish mission system caused incredible harm to Native peoples and led to their rapid depopulation, but it was the gold lust under the Anglo-American occupation of California in 1848–1849, after the Mexican American war that led to the most horrendous instances of Indian genocide. The means by which this genocide was carried out include outright massacres, disease and starvation, treaty fraud ("lost" treaties), indenture and slavery, death marches, and forced relocation.

NOTE

1. C. Patrick Morris, "Who Are These Gentle People?" *American Indian Culture and Research Journal,* 17, no. 1 (1993): 15n.

"I'M OKAY WITH IT AS LONG AS THEY PAY US TAXES, LEARN OUR LANGUAGE AND DO THE JOBS WE AMERICANS DON'T WANT TO DO."

As Long as They Pay Taxes. Jim Borgman. The Register-Guard, *April 12, 2006.*

FIVE HUNDRED YEARS OF INJUSTICE
THE LEGACY OF FIFTEENTH CENTURY RELIGIOUS PREJUDICE

Steven Newcomb

When Christopher Columbus first set foot on the white sands of Guanahani island, he performed a ceremony to "take possession" of the land for the king and queen of Spain, acting under the international laws of Western Christendom. Although the story of Columbus' "discovery" has taken on mythological proportions in most of the Western world, few people are aware that his act of "possession" was based on a religious doctrine now known in history as the Doctrine of Discovery. Even fewer people realize that today—five centuries later—the United States government still uses this archaic Judeo-Christian doctrine to deny the rights of Native American Indians.

ORIGINS OF THE DOCTRINE OF DISCOVERY

To understand the connection between Christendom's principle of discovery and the laws of the United States, we need to begin by examining a papal document issued forty years before Columbus' historic voyage. In 1452, Pope Nicholas V issued to King Alfonso V of Portugal the bull Romanus Pontifex, declaring war against all non-Christians throughout the world, and specifically sanctioning and promoting the conquest, colonization, and exploitation of non-Christian nations and their territories.

Under various theological and legal doctrines formulated during and after the Crusades, non-Christians were considered enemies of the Catholic faith and, as such, less than human. Accordingly, in the bull of 1452, Pope Nicholas directed King Alfonso to "capture, vanquish, and subdue the saracens, pagans, and other enemies of Christ," to "put them into perpetual slavery," and "to take all their

possessions and property." [Davenport:20–26] Acting on this papal privilege, Portugal continued to traffic in African slaves, and expanded its royal dominions by making "discoveries" along the western coast of Africa, claiming those lands as Portuguese territory.

Thus, when Columbus sailed west across the Sea of Darkness in 1492—with the express understanding that he was authorized to "take possession" of any lands he "discovered" that were "not under the dominion of any Christian rulers"—he and the Spanish sovereigns of Aragon and Castile were following an already well-established tradition of "discovery" and conquest. [Thacher:96] Indeed, after Columbus returned to Europe, Pope Alexander VI issued a papal document, the bull *Inter Cetera* of May 3, 1493, "granting" to Spain—at the request of Ferdinand and Isabella—the right to conquer the lands which Columbus had already found, as well as any lands which Spain might "discover" in the future.

In the *Inter Cetera* document, Pope Alexander stated his desire that the "discovered" people be "subjugated and brought to the faith itself." [Davenport:61] By this means, said the pope, the "Christian Empire" would be propagated. [Thacher:127] When Portugal protested this concession to Spain, Pope Alexander stipulated in a subsequent bull—issued May 4, 1493—that Spain must not attempt to establish its dominion over lands which had already "come into the possession of any Christian lords." [Davenport:68] Then, to placate the two rival monarchs, the pope drew a line of demarcation between the two poles, giving Spain rights of conquest and dominion over one side of the globe, and Portugal over the other.

During this quincentennial of Columbus' journey to the Americas, it is important to recognize that the grim acts of genocide and conquest committed by Columbus and his men against the peaceful Native people of the Caribbean were sanctioned by the

Doctrine of Discovery/Christian Nations. Steven Newcomb in *Shaman's Drum*, Fall 1992, pp. 18–20.

abovementioned documents of the Catholic Church. Indeed, these papal documents were frequently used by Christian European conquerors in the Americas to justify an incredibly brutal system of colonization—which dehumanized the Indigenous people by regarding their territories as being "inhabited only by brute animals." [Story:135–6]

The lesson to be learned is that the papal bulls of 1452 and 1493 are but two clear examples of how the "Christian Powers," or "different States of Christendom," viewed Indigenous peoples as "the lawful spoil and prey of their civilized conquerors." [Wheaton:270–1] In fact, the Christian "Law of Nations" asserted that Christian nations had a divine right, based on the Bible, to claim absolute title to and ultimate authority over any newly "discovered" Non-Christian inhabitants and their lands. Over the next several centuries, these beliefs gave rise to the Doctrine of Discovery used by Spain, Portugal, England, France, and Holland—all Christian nations.

THE DOCTRINE OF DISCOVERY IN U.S. LAW

In 1823, the Christian Doctrine of Discovery was quietly adopted into U.S. law by the Supreme Court in the celebrated case, *Johnson v. McIntosh* (8 Wheat., 543). Writing for a unanimous court, Chief Justice John Marshall observed that Christian European nations had assumed "ultimate dominion" over the lands of America during the Age of Discovery, and that—upon "discovery"—the Indians had lost "their rights to complete sovereignty, as independent nations," and only retained a right of "occupancy" in their lands. In other words, Indians nations were subject to the ultimate authority of the first nation of Christendom to claim possession of a given region of Indian lands. [Johnson:574; Wheaton:270–1]

According to Marshall, the United States—upon winning its independence in 1776—became a successor nation to the right of "discovery" and acquired the power of "dominion" from Great Britain. [Johnson:587–9] Of course, when Marshall first defined the principle of "discovery," he used language phrased in such a way that it drew attention away from its religious bias, stating that "discovery gave title to the government, by whose subject, or by whose authority, the discovery was made, against all other European governments." [Johnson:573–4] However, when discussing legal precedent to support the court's findings, Marshall specifically cited the English charter issued to the explorer John Cabot, in order to document England's "complete recognition"

of the Doctrine of Discovery. [Johnson:576] Then, paraphrasing the language of the charter, Marshall noted that Cabot was authorized to take possession of lands, "notwithstanding the occupancy of the natives, who were heathens, and, at the same time, admitting the prior title of any Christian people who may have made a previous discovery." [Johnson:577]

In other words, the Court affirmed that United States law was based on a fundamental rule of the "Law of Nations"—that it was permissible to virtually ignore the most basic rights of Indigenous "heathens," and to claim that the "unoccupied lands" of America rightfully belonged to discovering Christian European nations. Of course, it's important to understand that, as Benjamin Munn Ziegler pointed out in The International Law of John Marshall, the term "unoccupied lands" referred to "the lands in America which, when discovered, were 'occupied by Indians' but 'unoccupied' by Christians." [Ziegler:46]

Ironically, the same year that the *Johnson v. McIntosh* decision was handed down, founding father James Madison wrote: "Religion is not in the purview of human government. Religion is essentially distinct from civil government, and exempt from its cognizance; a connection between them is injurious to both."

Most of us have been brought up to believe that the United States Constitution was designed to keep church and state apart. Unfortunately, with the Johnson decision, the Christian Doctrine of Discovery was not only written into U.S. law but also became the cornerstone of U.S. Indian policy over the next century.

FROM DOCTRINE OF DISCOVERY TO DOMESTIC DEPENDENT NATIONS

Using the principle of "discovery" as its premise, the Supreme Court stated in 1831 that the Cherokee Nation (and, by implication, all Indian nations) was not fully sovereign, but "may, perhaps," be deemed a "domestic dependent nation." [*Cherokee Nation v. Georgia*] The federal government took this to mean that treaties made with Indian nations did not recognize Indian nations as free of U.S. control. According to the U.S. government, Indian nations were "domestic dependent nations" subject to the federal government's absolute legislative authority—known in the law as "plenary power." Thus, the ancient doctrine of Christian discovery and its subjugation of "heathen" Indians were extended by the federal government into a mythical doctrine that the

U.S. Constitution allows for governmental authority over Indian nations and their lands. [Savage:59–60]

The myth of U.S. "plenary power" over Indians—a power, by the way, that was never intended by the authors of the Constitution [Savage:115–17]—has been used by the United States to:

a. Circumvent the terms of solemn treaties that the U.S. entered into with Indian nations, despite the fact that all such treaties are "supreme Law of the Land, anything in the Constitution notwithstanding."
b. Steal the homelands of Indian peoples living east of the Mississippi River, by removing them from their traditional ancestral homelands through the Indian Removal Act of 1835.
c. Use a congressional statute, known as the General Allotment Act of 1887, to divest Indian people of some 90 million acres of their lands. This act, explained John Collier (Commissioner of Indian Affairs) was "an indirect method—peacefully under the forms of law—of taking away the land that we were determined to take away but did not want to take it openly by breaking the treaties."
d. Steal the sacred Black Hills from the Great Sioux nation in violation of the 1868 Treaty of Fort Laramie which recognized the Sioux Nation's exclusive and absolute possession of their lands.
e. Pay the Secretary of the Interior $26 million for 24 million acres of Western Shoshone lands, because the Western Shoshone people have steadfastly refused to sell the land and refused to accept the money. Although the Western Shoshone Nation's sovereignty and territorial boundaries were clearly recognized by the federal government in the 1863 Ruby Valley Treaty, the government now claims that paying itself on behalf of the Western Shoshone has extinguished the Western Shoshone's title to their lands.

The above cases are just a few examples of how the United States government has used the *Johnson v. McIntosh* and *Cherokee Nation v. Georgia* decisions to callously disregard the human rights of Native peoples. Indeed, countless U.S. Indian policies have been based on the underlying, hidden rationale of "Christian discovery"—a rationale which holds that the "heathen" Indigenous peoples of the Americas are "subordinate to the first Christian discoverer," or its successor. [Wheaton:271]

As Thomas Jefferson once observed, when the state uses church doctrine as a coercive tool, the result is "hypocrisy and meanness." Unfortunately,

the United States Supreme Court's use of the ancient Christian Doctrine of Discovery—to circumvent the Constitution as a means of taking Indian lands and placing Indian nations under U.S. control—has proven Madison and Jefferson right.

BRINGING AN END TO FIVE HUNDRED YEARS OF INJUSTICE TO INDIGENOUS PEOPLES

In a country set up to maintain a strict separation of church and state, the Doctrine of Discovery should have long ago been declared unconstitutional because it is based on a prejudicial treatment of Native American people simply because they were not Christians at the time of European arrival. By penalizing Native people on the basis of their non-Christian religious beliefs and ceremonial practices, stripping them of most of their lands and most of their sovereignty, the *Johnson v. McIntosh* ruling stands as a monumental violation of the "natural rights" of humankind, as well as the most fundamental human rights of Indigenous peoples.

As we move beyond the quincentennial of Columbus' invasion of the Americas, it is high time to formally renounce and put an end to the religious prejudice that was written into U.S. law by Chief Justice John Marshall. Whether or not the American people—especially the Christian right—prove willing to assist Native people in getting the Johnson ruling overturned will say a lot to the world community about just how seriously the United States takes its own foundational principles of liberty, justice, and religious freedom.

As we approach the 500th anniversary of the *Inter Cetera* bulls on May 3 and 4 of 1993, it is important to keep in mind that the Doctrine of Discovery is still being used by countries throughout the Americas to deny the rights of Indigenous peoples, and to perpetuate colonization throughout the Western Hemisphere. To begin to bring that system of colonization to an end, and to move away from a cultural and spiritual tradition of subjugation, we must overturn the doctrine at its roots. Therefore, I propose that non-Native people—especially Christians—unite in solidarity with Indigenous peoples of the Western Hemisphere to impress upon Pope John Paul II how important it is for him to revoke, in a formal ceremony with Indigenous people, the *Inter Cetera* bulls of 1493.

Revoking those papal documents and overturning the *Johnson v. McIntosh* decision are two important first steps toward correcting the injustices that have been inflicted on Indigenous peoples over the past five hundred years. They are also spiritually significant steps toward creating a way of life that is no longer based on greed and subjugation. Perhaps

then we will be able to use our newfound solidarity to begin to create a lifestyle based on the first Indigenous principle: "Respect the Earth and have a Sacred Regard for All Living Things."

REFERENCES

Cherokee Nation v. Georgia 30 U.S. (5 Pet.) 1, 8 L.Ed. 25 (1831).

Davenport, Frances Gardiner, 1917, *European Treaties bearing on the History of the United States and its Dependencies to 1648,* Vol. 1, Washington, D.C.: Carnegie Institution of Washington.

Johnson and Graham's Lessee V McIntosh 21 U.S. (8 Wheat.) 543, 5 L.Ed. 681(1823).

Rivera-Pagan, Luis N., 1991, "Cross Preceded Sword in 'Discovery' of the Americas," in *Yakima Nation Review,* 1991, Oct, 4.

Story, Joseph, 1833, *Commentaries on the Constitution of the United States* Vol. 1 Boston: Little, Brown & Co.

Thacher, John Boyd, 1903, *Christopher Columbus* Vol. 11, New York: G.P. Putman's Sons.

Williamson, James A., 1962, *The Cabot Voyages And Bristol Discovery Under Henry VII,* Cambridge: Cambridge University Press.

Wheaton, Henry, 1855, *Elements of International Law,* Sixth Edition, Boston: Little Brown, and Co.

Ziegler, Benjamin Munn, 1939, *The International Law of John Marshall,* Chapel Hill: The University of North Carolina Press.

Steven Newcomb is an American Indian of Shawnee and Lenape ancestry. For over a decade, he has studied the origins of U.S. federal Indian law and international law, dating back to the early days of Christendom. His latest book is *Pagans in the Promised Land: Decoding the Doctrine of Christian Discovery* (Golden, Co: Folcrum, 2008).

A HISTORY OF FEDERAL INDIAN POLICY

David E. Wilkins

A FEDERAL INDIAN POLICY OVERVIEW

The Indigenous nations' struggle to retain and exercise *a* measure of their original political independence in the face of persistent and, at times, oppressive federal policies aimed at the forced Americanization and coercive assimilation of tribal citizens forms the bulk of the story in this book. But there is more to it. The federal government's policies, most of which were aimed at the absorption of Indians, have had a discernible if variable impact on tribal nations, variable in part because these policies themselves were ambivalent—created at different

David Wilkins in American Indian Politics and the American Political System, 2002, Roman & Littlefield Publishers, Inc., pp. 103–118. Notes have not been included in this article. See original.

times, by different individuals and administrations, for different purposes, and for varied tribal nations. And as result of the undulating and unpredictable nature of history, combined with the interaction between the force of federal policies and the responses of Indigenous nations to those policies, Native America is, not surprisingly, vastly different in the year 2000 than it was in 1900, 1800, or 1700.

Table 2.1 provides a general overview of the major policies and laws, and tribal responses to those directives, from the early American period to the present. Of course, such linear charts, as useful as they are, are inherently flawed in that policies do not simply terminate at particular dates. For example, Indian removal, the forced relocation of Indians from their homelands to lands west of the Mississippi, did not

TABLE 2.1: Historical Development of the Federal-Tribal Relationship

Dates	Policy	Major Laws	Relationship	Tribes' Status	Tribal Responses
1770s–1820s	International sovereign to international sovereign	1787 Northwest Ordinance 1790 Trade & Intercourse Act treaties	Protectorate	International sovereigns	Diplomacy, some armed resistance
1830s–1850s	Removal	1830 Indian Removal Act treaties	Government-to-government and trust relationship	Domestic dependent nations	Armed resistance; negotiation under diress
1850s–1890s	Reservation	Reservation treaties	Guardianship	Wards in need of protection	Waning resistance; accommodation
1870s–1930s	Assimilation	1871 End of treaty making 1885 Major crimes act 1887 Allotment Act (Dawes Act)	Guardianship	Wards in need of protection	Accommodation; foot dragging; religious movements
1930s–1950s	Indian self-rule	1934 Indian Reorganization Act (Wheeler-Howard Act)	Renewal of government-to-government and trust relationship	Quasi-sovereigns	Increased political participation; growing intertribal activity
1950–1960s	Termination (assimilation)	1953 Resolution 108 1953 Public Law 280 Urban Relocation Program	Termination of trust relationship	Termination of quasi-sovereign status	Growth of intertribal politics; beginnings of modem resistance
1960s–1988s	Self-determination	1968 Indian Civil Rights Act 1975 Indian Self-Determination Act 1978 Indian Child Welfare Act 1978 Indian Religious Freedom Act	Renewal of govenment-to-government and trust relationship	Domestic dependent nations/quasi-sovereigns	Continued spread of political activity; radical activism until 1970s; Interest-group activity
1988–Present	Self-determination self-governance	1988 Indian Gaming Regulation Act 1988 Tribal Self-Governance Act 1990 Native American Graves Protection and Repatriation Act 1994 Indian Self-Determination Act Amendments 1996 Native American HousingAssistance Act 2000 Indian Tribal EconomicDevelopment and Contract Encouragement Act	Government-to-government and trust relationship	Domestic dependent nations/quasi-sovereigns	Interest-group activity; Increase of international activity

SOURCES: Modified from Sharon O'Brien, American *Indian Tribal Governments* (Norman: University of Oklahoma Press, 1989), 258; Stephen Cornell, *The Return of the Native* (New York: Oxford University Press, 1988), 14.

begin and certainly did not end in the so-called Indian removal period of the 1830s–1850s. Many tribes, in fact, had already been forced out of their homes prior to the 1830 Indian Removal Act, and many thousands of Indians were required to relocate or remove long after the official policy ceased in the 1840s. These later removals were the result of land conflicts (the Navajo-Hopi land dispute from the 1860s to the present) or the construction of dams which required Indians to abandon their homes (e.g., Seneca Indians being forced to relocate because of the construction of the Kinzua Dam in the northeast).

As another example, reservations were still being established after the 1890s, and they may still be established today. The secretary of the interior is authorized under the Indian Reorganization Act of 1934 to create new Indian reservations at his discretion. Nevertheless, table 2.1 provides an accurate, if overgeneralized, way to assess the historical unfolding of the Indigenous–federal relationship.

Students and interested readers seeking details of these policies and tribes' reactions to them can find this information in a number of texts, including Francis Paul Prucha, *The Great Father: The United States Government and the American Indians*, 2 vols. (1984); Angie Debo, *A History of the Indians of the United States*, (1970); Wilcomb E. Washburn, ed., *The American Indian and the United States: A Documentary History*, 4 vols. (1973); Peter Nabokov, ed., *Native American Testimony: A Chronicle of Indian-White Relations from Prophecy to the Present, 1492–1992* (1992); and Colin G. Calloway, *First Peoples: A Documentary Survey of American Indian History* (1999). While it is not possible to provide a detailed policy history here, a synopsis of the major eras will provide some needed historical context.

THE FORMATIVE YEARS (1775–1820s)

Within the first decade of the federal government's existence the fledgling democracy's inexorable need to expand led to increased conflict between Indigenous and nonIndigenous peoples. This expansion was overseen by a Congress and president intent on exerting their authority in Indian affairs by following certain policies: the promotion of civilization and education of Indians, the regulation of trade and commerce with tribes, the establishment of territorial boundaries between the two peoples, the use of treaties to maintain peace with tribes and to purchase Indian lands, and letting states know that they lacked any constitutional authority in the field of Indian policy.

The U.S. Supreme Court during these crucial embryonic years signaled it was a part of the ruling alliance when it handed down an important decision, *Johnson v. McIntosh* (1823), that set a new tone in federal Indian policy. Chief justice John Marshall declared that, based on the doctrine of "discovery," the European states, and the United States as their successor, secured legal title to Indian lands. Indian land rights were not entirely disregarded, but were necessarily reduced even though tribes were not direct parties in this lawsuit and were in fact separate nations.

INDIAN REMOVALS, RELOCATIONS, AND RESERVATIONS (1830s–1880s)

Despite laws like the Trade and Intercourse Acts (1790, 1802, and 1834), which placed severe restrictions on whites who had aspirations of entering Indian lands to trade or settle, and the Civilization Fund Act of 1819, which established the U.S. goal to "civilize" the Indians as an act of humanity, friction continued to mount between the ever-increasing and land hungry non-Indian population and the tribal nations. As result, the eastern tribes, particularly those in Georgia, faced mounting pressure from state and local authorities to surrender their lands and political status. The proposed "solution" to the conflict was the removal of Indians to country west of the Mississippi River, where it was thought the tribes would be able to live in isolation, apart from the corrupting influence of whites.

The idea for Indian removal was first proposed by Thomas Jefferson and was also supported by Presidents Monroe and Adams. However, it was President Andrew Jackson who would see to it that a removal policy was implemented by Congress via a congressional law in 1830. Tribes were compelled to sign a number of removal treaties in which they ceded virtually all their aboriginal territory in the east in exchange for new lands west of the Mississippi.

The 1830s and 1840s witnessed the coerced migration of thousands of Indians from the southeast, to the Ohio and beyond the Mississippi valley, under a program "that was voluntary in name and coerced in fact." The harshness of removal was most vividly seen in the brutal experiences of the Five Civilized Tribes. The Cherokee Nation, who termed their trip to Indian Territory the "Trail of Tears," lost four thousand of their citizens during the march from their homelands in the southeast to present-day Oklahoma.

Federalism was another factor that complicated relations between Indian nations and whites during this period, since there was intense conflict between the federal and state governments over which sovereign was ultimately in charge of Indian policy. The tension peaked in the so-called Cherokee cases: *Cherokee Nation v. Georgia* (1831) and *Worcester v. Georgia* (1832). In *Cherokee Nation,* the Supreme Court declared that Indian peoples constituted "domestic dependent nations" whose citizens were nonetheless "in a state of pupilage and subject to the guardianship protection of the federal government."

In *Worcester,* however, Chief Justice Marshall stated that tribes were distinct political communities, having territorial boundaries, within which their authority is exclusive" Tribal nations, said Marshall, retained enough sovereignty to exclude the states from exercising any power over Indian peoples or their territories. Why the seemingly different conclusions by the same court? In large part because Marshall and the Court had been asked to decide different questions. In *Cherokee Nation,* Marshall provided a definition of the relationship between tribes and the federal government. In *Worcester,* the chief justice and the Court were called on to articulate the tribal-state relationship. Hence, Deloria and Lytle assert that "The *Cherokee Nation Cases* should be considered *as* one fundamental statement having two basic thrusts on the status of Indian tribes," Furthermore, two related aspects of tribal sovereignty emerge from these cases: "Tribes are under the protection of the federal government and in this condition lack sufficient sovereignty to claim political independence; tribes possess, however, sufficient powers of sovereignty to shield themselves from any intrusion by the States and it is the federal government's responsibility to ensure that this sovereignty is preserved."

In the wake of Indian removal, the federal government implemented the reservation policy by the mid-1850s. The new policy was administered by the BIA, which was moved from the War Department, where it had been since its inception in 824, to the newly formed Department of the Interior. From the federal government's perspective, reservations had become necessary because of the discovery of gold in the 1830s, new land acquisitions by the United States (e.g., Texas in 1846 and much of the Southwest in 1848 under the Treaty of Guadalupe Hidalgo), and the construction of railroads that linked both coasts and expedited westward travel.

Gradually, however, expansionist forces largely out of the government's control precluded keeping the Indians and whites apart, and slowly reservations came to be viewed as social laboratories for "civilizing" the Indians. As Commissioner of Indian Affairs Francis A. Walker explained in 1872: "The reservation system affords the place for thus dealing with tribes and bands, without the *access* of influences inimical to peace and virtue. It is only necessary that Federal laws, judiciously framed to meet all the facts of the case, and enacted in season, before the Indians begin to scatter, shall place all the members of this race under strict reformatory control by the agents of the Government. Especially it is essential that the right of the Government to keep the Indians upon the reservations signed to them, and to arrest and return them whenever they wander away, should be placed beyond dispute." Indians on reservations, in other words, were not merely fodder for social experimentation but were also, in effect, prisoners on their own lands.

Indian agents, BIA administrative personnel who historically had served as diplomatic liaisons between tribal nations and the United States, eventually became the key figures in charge of acculturating and fostering the assimilation of Indians. They had virtually unlimited power over the Indians under their care on reservations and often abused that power. As Senator Henry Teller of Colorado, a staunch opponent of Indian allotment and agents' autocratic rule in the 1870s and 1880s, said in testimony before Congress of many Indian agents:

> They are a class of men that, as a general thing, are sent out [to reservations) because they cannot make a living in the East. They are picked up as broken-down politicians, or one-horse preachers that have been unable to supply themselves with a congregation. They go to an Indian agency at a salary that will not employ, in the West in most cases, an ordinary clerk, and hardly a porter. They take these positions; they desire to keep them, whether it is for the salary or whether it is for the perquisites I leave to others to say, but they desire to keep them, and it is their interest that they make these statements that little by little these [Indian] men are progressing; and yet when a new and honest agent goes he frankly says, "these people [Indian tribes] can have made no progress at all."

Christian churches, by the late 1860s, were also assuming a dominant role in Indian lives, a clear indication that the separation of church and state outlined in the First Amendment was irrelevant insofar as tribal nations were concerned. In fact, when President Ulysses S. Grant initiated his peace policy in 1869 as a way to quell the interracial violence on the frontier, involving Christian missionaries directly in the administration of Indians on reservations, this was probably the first explicit example of the federal government crossing the boundaries of constitutional prohibition by seeking to establish a religion among Indian tribes. As part of their authority, church leaders were given the right to nominate Indian agents and to direct Indian educational activities.

Another example of the domestication of Indigenous peoples occurred in 1871, when Congress, by way of an appropriations rider, enacted a provision that no tribe thereafter was to be recognized as an independent nation with whom the United States could make treaties. As mentioned, however, previously ratified treaties were not abrogated, and the Congress continued to negotiate many agreements with tribes. While it is constitutionally problematic whether the Congress had the right to terminate the Indian treaty-making power of the president, the fact is that this action signaled a significant shift in Iindigenous-federal relations, as an emboldened Congress now frequently acted unilaterally to suspend or curtail Indian rights, including treaty rights, when it suited the government's purpose.

ALLOTMENT, AMERICANIZATION, AND ACCULTURATION (1880s–1920s)

By the 1880s the federal government's efforts to assimilate Indians had become quite coercive. Beginning in this era, a U.S. assimilation policy, as Wilmer shows, developed in several stages. These included "replacing the traditional communal economic base with a system of private property; intensified education, primarily through boarding schools; the regulation of every aspect of Indian social life, including marriage, dispute settlement, and religious practice; the granting of citizenship; . . . and finally allowing the Indian tribes to become self-governing by adopting constitutions ultimately subject to the approval of the U.S. government."

Each of these laws and policies played a critical role in undermining the confidence, hopes, and self-respect of Indigenous communities. But most observers suggest that the single most devastating federal policy adopted during this period was the land allotment system, under the General Allotment Act of 1887 and its multiple amendments, and the individual allotting agreements negotiated between various tribal nations and the United States. Most white philanthropists agreed that the Indians' tribal social

structure, generally founded on common stewardship of land, was the major obstacle to their "progress" toward civilization. These individuals, and the organizations they often formed, firmly believed in the need to break up the reservations, distribute small individual plots of land to individual Indians (heads of households received 160 acres, single persons over eighteen received 80 acres, those under eighteen received 40 acres), and then require the allotted Indian to adopt a Euro-American farming existence.

The allotments, however, were to be held in trust—they could not be sold without express permission of the secretary of the interior—for twenty-five years. This was deemed a sufficient period for the individual Indian to learn the art of being a civilized yeoman farmer. U.S. citizenship accompanied receipt of the allotment. Tribal land not allotted to members was declared "surplus," and this "extra" land was sold to non-Indians, whose settlement among the Indians, it was believed, would expedite their acquisition of white attitudes and behavior.

Tribal land estates were diminished very quickly by these policies. For example, the Iowa Tribe's members after their allotment went into effect retained only 8,658 acres; the federal government purchased over 200,000 acres of the tribe's "surplus" land, a loss of over 90 percent of tribal territory. In Oklahoma, the Cheyenne and Arapaho Indians kept 529,682 acres after allotment, but were required to sell over three million acres which had been declared "surplus," a loss of over 80 percent of their lands.

The allotment policy was, in the words of President Theodore Roosevelt, "a mighty pulverizing engine to break up the tribal mass." By 1934, when it was finally stopped, 118 out of 213 reservations had been allotted, resulting in the loss of nearly ninety million acres of tribal lands. The accompanying program that ensued included removal of allotments from trust-protected status by forced fee patent, sale by both Indian landowners and the United States, probate proceedings under state inheritance laws, foreclosure, and surplus sale of tribal lands. This program had disastrous economic and cultural consequences that still adversely affect allotted tribes and individual Indians today.

The Oglala Sioux of the Pine Ridge Reservation in South Dakota, after their military struggles with the United States in the late nineteenth century, slowly began to rebuild their economic life on the basis of a tribal livestock operation. With the able assistance of a committed and honest Indian agent, they built a herd of some forty thousand by 1912. But, required to sign an allotment agreement with the United States, by 1916 their 2.5-million-acre reservation had been completely subdivided. In 1917 a new agent encouraged the Oglala to sell their herd and grow wheat as part of the war effort. Because the tribe had neither the capital nor the experience for arable farming, most of their lands were leased to whites. James Wilson writes,

> By 1930, about 26% of the allotted land had been sold by individual owners, 36% had passed into heirship status and been rented out on a virtually permanent basis to non-Indians, and the reservation had become so fragmented and checker-boarded that the kind of cooperative enterprise for which the tribe's land and traditions fitted them had become almost impossible.

Reservations which were allotted have a number of problems that continue to bedevil the efforts of tribal governments at economic development. The major problem is the fractionation of allotted lands. The sale of surplus land and the loss of many of the fee allotments by Indians left large areas of formerly consolidated lands in a checkerboard pattern, with areas of Indian, non-Indian, state, and federal ownership existing side by side. Efforts to consolidate allotted lands are complicated because allotments, whether held in trust or not, are subject to state inheritance laws if an Indian allottee dies without a will. It is virtually impossible in these circumstances to put together economic grazing or farming units on allotted reservations, because generally there are not enough allotments or fragments of allotments adjacent to one another to form an economically viable block of land for leasing or other forms of economic development. Their highly fractionated ownership has thus left the Indian allotted lands largely undeveloped.

By the 1920s, however, it was clear that coercive assimilation and allotment were not having the desired results, since Indian allottees had experienced fraud and many Indians had actually become landless as a result. This, along with a general mood of progressivism in American political and popular thought, convinced federal policymakers to rethink federal Indian policy.

THE REVIVAL OF LIMITED TRIBAL SELF-RULE (1920s–1940s)

In 1926, Secretary of the Interior Hubert Work authorized Lewis Meriam and the staff of the Institute of Government Research in Washington, D.C., to conduct an investigation of socioeconomic conditions among Indian people. Their two-year study resulted in a major publication, *The Problem of Indian Administration*, the first fairly comprehensive description and analysis of what had happened to Indigenous peoples since the end of the last of the Indian wars. The report's authors detailed the plethora of disastrous conditions affecting Indians at that time: high infant death rates and high mortality rates in general, poverty, horrendous health conditions, inadequate education, poor housing, and the problem of migrated Indians (Indians forced to leave the reservation because of land loss). The policy of forced assimilation, Meriam stated, "has resulted in much loss of land and an enormous increase in the details of administration without a compensating advance in the economic ability of the Indians."

Although most commentators suggest that the Merriam Report was the basis for the Indian Reorganization Act and other reforms instituted during the New Deal era, "there is not much evidence to support this contention." In fact, the underlying tone and direction of the report's many recommendations "continued to assume that Indians had to be led benignly, if not driven, to certain preconceived goals, which were assimilation or a mutually imposed isolation within small Indian enclaves."

In actuality, there were a number of other equally important, if little known, federal studies and a major and long-term congressional investigations conducted during this period that also played key roles in setting the stage for Indian reform. These studies were the Preston-Engle Report on Indian irrigation, a report on "Law and Order on Indian Reservations of the Northwest," a study of Indian agricultural lands, "An Economic Survey of the Range Resources and Grazing Activities on Indian Reservations," and a multiyear investigation conducted by a subcommittee of the Senate Indian Committee, which gave senators personal experience with the depth of Indian poverty caused by their own government's policies and under the BIA's mismanagement.

The combination of evidence from all these reports led to important changes in federal Indian policy, changes that favored restoration of some measure of tribal self-rule. Of course, the federal strategy was to employ tribal culture and institutions as transitional devices for the gradual assimilation of Indians into American society. The vehicle for this transition was the **Indian Reorganization Act** (IRA) of 1934, which represented a legitimate but inadequate effort on the part of Congress to protect, preserve, and support tribal art, culture, and public and social organization.

For those tribes who voted to adopt the measure, the IRA succeeded in ending the infamous allotment policy, provided measures whereby Indian land could be restored or new reservations created, established a $10 million revolving credit fund to promote economic development, permitted tribes to hire attorneys, and authorized tribal governing bodies to negotiate with non-Indian governments. Also included were provisions for the regulation of resources, for establishment of an affirmative action policy for Indians within the BIA, and, importantly, for writing charters of incorporation and chartering and reorganizing tribal governments.

This final provision, the establishment of tribal governing and economic institutions, specifically authorized tribes to organize and adopt constitutions, by-laws, and incorporation charters subject to ratification by vote of tribal members. But problematically, these constitutions and by-laws were also subject to the approval of the secretary of the interior, as were any proposed future amendments to these organic documents. This *is* ironic in a sense, because one of the goals of John Collier, as commissioner of Indian affairs and principal sponsor of this broad measure, was to "minimize the enormous discretion and power exercised by the Department of the Interior and the Office of Indian Affairs."

The act produced a mixed bag of results whose legacy continues today. On one hand, the act was effective in stopping the rapid loss of Indigenous land and provided the institutional groundwork for tribal governments, whose powers have increased considerably since this period. One of the strengths of this act was that while it did not provide tribes with new governing powers, it "did recognize these powers as inherent in their status and resurrected them in a form in which they could be used at the discretion of the tribe."

On the other hand, the act's goal of reestablishing Indian self-rule was less successfully achieved. For example, the tribal constitutions adopted largely followed a constitutional model developed by the BIA that only rarely coincided with tribes' traditional understandings of how political authority should be exercised. Furthermore, for those tribes who had been able to retain some semblance of traditional government, the IRA effectively supplanted those institutions, thus intensifying internal tribal conflicts.

TRIBAL TERMINATION AND RELOCATION (1940s–1960s)

The ending of World War II and the cost-cutting measures that ensued in Washington, D.C., John Collier's resignation in 1945, the Indian Claims Commission Act of 1946 (which allowed Indians to sue for monetary compensation against the United States), a sense among conservatives in Congress and the BIA that the IRA period's policies were "retarding" the Indians' progress as American citizens, and a sense among liberals that Indians were still experiencing racial discrimination in the BIA's still overly colonial relationship with tribes all fueled a drive to abandon tribal reorganization goals and terminate federal benefits and support services for tribes.

The CIA developed criteria to identify those Indigenous groups thought prepared for termination. Federal lawmakers and BIA personnel believed that some tribes—the Menominee of Wisconsin and the Klamath of Oregon—were already sufficiently acculturated and no longer needed the federal government to act as their trustee. These tribes faced immediate termination. Other tribes, those in the Southwest, for example, were to be given more time to acculturate before they too would be legally terminated.

The definitive statement of the termination policy was House Concurrent Resolution 108, adopted by Congress in 1953. This resolution declared that "at the earliest possible time" the Indians should "be freed from all Federal supervision and control and from all disabilities and limitations specially applicable to Indians." Between 1945 and 1960 the government processed 109 cases of termination "affecting a minimum of 1,362,455 acres and 11,466 individuals."

Along with the termination resolution, Congress, just a few days later, also enacted Public Law 280, which conferred upon five states (California, Minnesota, Nebraska, Oregon, and Wisconsin) full criminal and some civil jurisdiction over Indian reservations (with certain reservations being exempted) and consented to the assumption of such jurisdiction by any other state.

The final part of the termination policy trilogy was relocation, a federal policy aimed at the relocation of Indians from rural and reservation areas to designated urban "relocation centers." In 1956 alone, the federal government spent $1 million to relocate more than

12,500 Indians to cities. The relocation policy was a coercive attempt to destroy tribal communalism.

The two largest terminated tribes were the Menominee of Wisconsin and the Klamath of Oregon. Prior to termination, both nations were comparatively well off, with sizable reservations and more than sufficient natural resources. But after termination, several harsh consequences resulted: tribal lands were usually concentrated into private ownership and, in most cases, sold; the trust relationship was ended; federal taxes were imposed; the tribes and their members were subject to state law; programs and services designed for federally recognized tribes were stopped; and the tribes' legal sovereignty was effectively ended.

INDIGENOUS SELF-DETERMINATION (1960s–1980s)

The period from the end of termination in the 1960s to the 1980s was a crucial time in Indigenous-federal relations. It was, according to most knowledgeable commentators, an era when tribal nations and Indians in general—led by concerted Indigenous activism—won a series of important political, legal, and cultural victories in their epic struggle to terminate the termination policy and regain a measure of real self-determination.

Many of these victories arose out of activities and events like the fishing rights struggles of the Pacific Northwest in the 1950s–1970s, the American Indian Chicago Conference in 1961, the birth of the American Indian Movement (AIM) in 1968, the Alcatraz occupation in 1969, the Trail of Broken Treaties in 1973, the 1973 occupation of Wounded Knee in South Dakota, and untold marches, demonstrations, and boycotts.

The federal government responded to this activism by enacting several laws and initiating policies that recognized the distinctive group and individual rights of Indigenous peoples. In some cases the laws supported tribal sovereignty; in other cases they acted to erase or diminish tribal sovereignty. For example, in 1968 Congress enacted the Indian Civil Rights Act (ICRA), the first piece of legislation to impose many of the provisions of the U.S. Bill of Rights on the actions of tribal governments vis-á-vis reservation residents. Until this time, tribes, because of their extra-constitutional status, had not been subject to such constitutional restraints in their governmental actions. The ICRA was a major intrusion of U.S. constitutional law upon the independence of tribes, and it is important to remember that the Indian bill of rights also does not protect tribes or their members from federal plenary power aimed at reducing tribal sovereignty, treaty rights, or aboriginal lands.

Two years later, by contrast, President Nixon explicitly called on Congress to repudiate the termination policy and declared that tribal self-determination would be the goal of his administration. Congress responded by enacting a series of laws designed to improve the lot of tribal nations and Indians generally in virtually every sphere: the return of Blue Lake to the Taos Pueblo people, the Indian Education Act of 1972, the restoration of the Menominee Nation to "recognized" status in 1973, the establishment of the American Indian Policy Review Commission in 1975, the Indian Self-Determination and Education Assistance Act of 1975, the Indian Child Welfare Act of 1978, the American Indian Religious Freedom Act of 1978, and the Maine Land Claims Settlement Act of 1980.

However, by the late 1970s, these Indian political victories (and a number of judicial victories as well) had provoked a backlash among disaffected non-Indians. The backlash was spearheaded by a number of non-Indian organizations, western state officials, and congressional members from states where tribes had gained political and legal victories. Subsequently, bills were introduced that threatened to abrogate Indian treaties, there was renewed discussion of abolishing the B1A, and some lawmakers argued that Indians should be completely subject to state jurisdiction. While tribes and their supporters repelled most of these anti-Indian efforts, they could not prevent the Supreme Court from handing down a series of decisions, beginning in 1978, which dramatically limited the law enforcement powers of tribes over non-Indians (*Oliphant v. Suquarnish*, 1978), weakened tribal jurisdiction over hunting and fishing by non-Indians on non-Indian land within reservations (*Montana v. United States*, 1981), and reduced the water rights of tribes (*Nevada v. United States*, 1983).

The Reagan administrations (1981–1989) were a time of much less certainty for Indigenous self-determination. Although Reagan acknowledged that there existed a "government-to-government" relationship between the United States and recognized tribal nations, his budget cuts devastated the federally dependent tribes. In part to offset these financial losses, Reagan's administration encouraged tribes to consider establishing gaming operations. Indian gaming would have a profound economic impact on a number of tribes and would affect their political relationship with the states and federal government as well.

TRIBAL SELF-GOVERNANCE IN AN ERA OF NEW FEDERALISM (1980s–PRESENT)

By the late 1980s, federal policy was a bizarre and inconsistent blend of actions that, on one hand, affirmed tribal sovereignty and, on the other, aimed at severely reducing tribal sovereign powers, especially in relation to state governments. For example, in 1988, Congress enacted the Indian Gaming Regulatory Act, which affirmed the tribes' right to engage in certain forms of gaming if states engaged in comparable gaming.

Also in 1988, and at the behest of several tribes, Congress adopted an experimental tribal self-governance project aimed at providing self-determined tribes a much greater degree of political and economic autonomy. As leaders of the tribes put it:

> Self-Governance is fundamentally designed to provide Tribal governments with control and decision-making authority *over* the Federal financial resources provided for the benefit of Indian people. More importantly, self-Governance fosters the shaping of a "new partnership" between Indian Tribes and the United States in their government-to-government. relationships. Self-Governance returns decision-making authority and management responsibilities to Tribes. . . . Self-Governance is about change through the transfer of Federal funding available for programs, services, functions, and activities to Tribal control. Tribes are accountable to their own people for resource management, service delivery, and development.

This originally experimental policy, which has been fairly successful for those tribes who chose to enter into a compacting relationship with the federal government (thirty in 1995), was made permanent in 1994 with the passage of Public Law 103–413.

Conversely, the U.S. Supreme Court, also in 1988, handed down two important decisions involving Indian religious rights. In *Lyng v.* Northwest *Indian Cemetery Protective Association*, the Court ruled that the Constitution's *free* exercise clause did not prevent governmental destruction of the most sacred sites of three small tribes in Northern California. And in *Employment Division, Department of Human Resources v. Smith*, the Court granted certiorari and remanded back to the Oregon Supreme Court a case involving whether an Oregon statute criminalizing peyote provided an exception for Indian religious use.

President Clinton issued several executive orders and memorandums during his two terms (1993–2001) that provided Indians a measure of recognition and protected certain Indian rights. "Together," said Clinton, "we can open the greatest era of cooperative understanding and respect among our people ever . . . and when we do, the judgment of history will be that the President of the United States and the leaders of the sovereign Indian nations met . . . and together lifted our great nations to a new and better place." Clinton issued executive orders in the following areas: consultation and coordination with Indian tribal governments, Indian sacred sites, tribal colleges and universities, American Indian and Alaska Native education, and the distribution of eagle feathers for Native American religious purposes.

Although Clinton generally maintained cordial relations with the tribes, Congress, especially after the Republicans gained control of both houses in 1994, and the Supreme Court continued to act in ways that threatened to unravel the political and economic improvements tribal governments had made in the first part of the self-determination era. In particular, a majority of the Supreme Court's decisions involving conflicts between tribes and states have supported state sovereignty over tribal sovereignty, a dramatic departure from historical and constitutional precedent. The issue of Indian gaming seemed to be at the vortex of much of this conflict, which led to a redefinition of federalism that threatened to destabilize tribal status just at a time when the doctrines of tribal self-determination and self-governance were evolving into a permanent presence after a century of direct federal assaults.

CONCLUSION

The policy ambivalence evident in the conflicting goals of sometimes recognizing tribal self-determination and sometimes seeking to terminate that governing status has lessened only slightly over time. Tribal nations and their citizens find that their efforts to exercise inherent sovereignty are rarely unchallenged, despite their treaty relationship with the United States and despite periodic pledges of support in various federal laws, policies, and court cases.

THE BLACK HILLS
THE SACRED LAND OF THE LAKOTA AND TSISTSISTAS

Mario Gonzalez

The Black Hills are the Sacred Land of the Lakota (Sioux) and their friends and allies, the Tsistsistas (Cheyenne). Lakota and Tsistsistas claims to the Black Hills are based on the following legal concepts:

Aboriginal Indian Title: Aboriginal title depends on the law of nations, not upon municipal right. It recognizes the right of tribes as the rightful occupants of the soil, with a legal as well as just claim to retain possession. Exclusive use and occupation "for a long time" prior to the loss of the property by a tribe is sufficient to establish aboriginal title. It entitles the tribes to full use and enjoyment of the surface and mineral estates, and to resources (such as timber) on the land. The right of possession is valid against all but the sovereign and can be terminated only by sovereign act.

"For a long time" can be interpreted as from time immemorial to a given number of years. Both Lakota and Tsistsistas tribes used and occupied the Black Hills for periods sufficient to establish aboriginal title.

Recognized Indian Title: For Indian title to be recognized. Congress, acting through a treaty or statute, must grant legal rights of permanent occupancy within a sufficiently defined territory. There must be an intention to accord or recognize a legal interest in the land.

Only the Lakota claim recognized title to the Black Hills based on land grants under the 1851 and 1868 Ft. Laramie Treaties. (This places Lakota tribes in the anomalous position of having the United States "grant" them title to land they already own under aboriginal title.)

A grant of title under United States law has its advantages, however. The federal courts have ruled that tribal lands held under aboriginal title are not protected by the Fifth Amendment; therefore, Congress can confiscate these lands without payment of compensation. On the other hand, the federal courts have also ruled that confiscation of lands held under recognized title are protected by the Fifth Amendment and require the payment of just compensation.

Religious Liens: Congress recognized religious liens in the American Indian Religious Freedom Act (1978) by acknowledging Native peoples' "right of access" to religious sites on federal lands. Since all land titles in the United States derive from federal grants, it follows that federal grants to states and individuals were made subject to these religious liens.

In *Sequoyah v. Tennessee Valley Authority* (1980), the sixth Circuit Court of Appeals stated that: "while [lack of a property interest in the land] is a factor to be considered, we feel it should not be conclusive in view of the history of the Cherokee expulsion from South Appalachia followed by the 'Trail of Tears' to Oklahoma and the unique nature of [their] religion." This reasoning suggested that religious liens are strongest on lands from which tribes were forcibly removed, such as the Black Hills.

Today, the total Black Hills area remains sacred to the Lakota and Tsistsistas. Although Lakota ownership of the Black Hills is still in dispute, the Lakota and Tsistsistas still possess religious liens to sacred sites located on federal, state and private lands, including: Devil's Tower, Iyan Kara Mountain, Harney Peak, Wind Cave, Hell's Canyon and Craven's Canyon (which contain petroglyphs), Hot Springs (now called Evan's Plunge) and Bear Butte.

THE POWDER RIVER WAR AND 1868 FT. LARAMIE TREATY

The Lakota and Tsistsistas tribes used and occupied vast territories on the northern plains. Some of their territories (such as the Black Hills) overlapped.

The 1851 Ft. Laramie Treaty (Art. 5) recognized Lakota title to 60 million acres of territory, including the Black Hills. The same treaty recognized Tsistsistas title to 51 million acres southwest of Lakota territory.

In 1866–1868, the Lakota fought a war with the United States called the "Powder River War." The War culminated with the signing of the 1868 Ft. Laramie Treaty (and was the first military conflict that the United States ever lost). Under the treaty (Art. 16), the United States agreed to remove its forts along the "Bozeman Trail" which was established to protect hordes of miners and settlers involved in the Montana Gold Rush. The gold rush forced the Lakota tribes to go to war to protect buffalo herds on 1851 Treaty lands from trespassing miners. The very existence of the Lakota people and their way of life depended on the buffalo (which were their source of food, shelter and clothing), and any interference with the tribes' buffalo by U.S. citizens resulted in warfare.

The 1868 Treaty also modified the 1851 Treaty in the following respects:

- Article 2 created a 26 million-acre reservation from the Lakota tribes' 1851 Treaty territory (all of present day South Dakota west of the Missouri River—including the Black Hills) ". . . for the absolute and undisturbed use and occupation . . . " of the Lakota and ". . . other friendly tribes and individuals . . . they may be willing, with the consent of the United States, to admit amongst them." Article 2 also provided that "no persons except those designated and authorized so to do . . . shall ever be permitted to pass over, settle upon, or reside in the territory described. . . . "
- Article 12 provided that no future cession of the permanent reservation (sometimes referred to as the "Great Sioux Reservation") would be valid without the consent of three-fourths (¾) of the adult male Indians, occupying or interested in the permanent reservation.
- Articles 11 and 16 recognized Lakota hunting rights over the remaining 34 million acres of 1851 Treaty territory and an expanded hunting right northwestward to the Bighorn Mountains and

southwestward to the Republican River, ". . . so long as the buffalo may range thereon in such numbers as to justify the chase."

In 1874, Lt. Col. George Armstrong Custer led a military expedition into the Black Hills in violation of the 1868 treaty, and sent out glowing reports of gold deposits. The news resulted in a gold rush and a demand that the Lakota sell the Black Hills.

On June 25, 1876, Lakota and Tsistsistas tribes defeated Custer at the Battle of the Little Bighorn. Congress responded by passing the "sell or starve" act, which provided that no further appropriations would be made for the subsistence of the Lakota (as required by the 1868 treaty) unless they first agreed to cede the Black Hills and Articles 11 and 16 hunting rights.

Thereafter, President Grant appointed the "Many penny Commission" to negotiate the cession of the Black Hills and Articles 11 and 16 hunting rights. When the Commission could not obtain the requisite three-fourths adult male signatures to effectuate a cession, Congress broke the "impasse" by enacting the proposed "agreement" into law on February 28, 1877. (See map showing 1851 and 1868 treaty areas and the 1877 Black Hills confiscated area.)

INDIAN CLAIMS COMMISSION—DOCKET 74-B

In 1946, Congress passed the Indian Claims Commission Act and mandated that tribes file their claims with the Indian Claims Commission (ICC) within five years or lose them. The jurisdiction of the ICC was limited to monetary compensation only, thus, preventing tribes from suing for a return of their ancestral lands.

The Lakota tribes filed their treaty claims with the ICC on August 15, 1950, as "Docket 74." In 1960, the ICC bifurcated Docket 74 and placed all Fifth Amendment claims (i.e., property confiscated by the 1877 Act) in Docket 74-B. The Docket 74-B claims included:

- The Black Hills: On June 30, 1980, the U.S. Supreme Court affirmed a 1974 ICC ruling that the Lakota tribes were entitled to $102 million for the Black Hills. In support of its ruling, the Court found that "a more ripe and rank case of dishonorable dealings will never, in all probability, be found in our history."
- Lakota Hunting Rights: Article 16 hunting rights included two categories—those rights already owned under the 1851 treaty, plus new rights

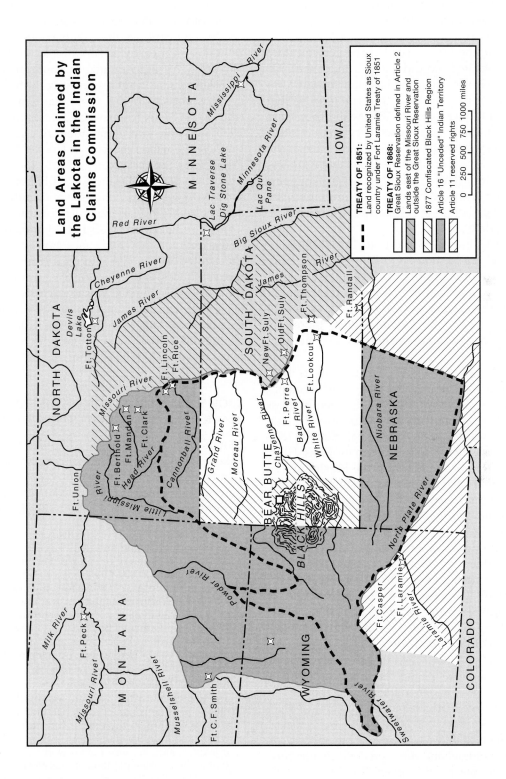

Land Areas Claimed by the Lakota in the Indian Claims Commission

TREATY OF 1851:
Land recognized by United States as Sioux country under Fort Laramie Treaty of 1851

TREATY OF 1868:
Great Sioux Reservation defined in Article 2

Lands east of the Missouri River and outside the Great Sioux Reservation

1877 Confiscated Black Hills Region

Article 16 "Unceded" Indian Territory

Article 11 reserved rights

0   250   500   750 1000 miles

granted west of 1851 treaty lands to the Bighorn mountains. Article 11 hunting rights included new rights granted south of the 1851 treaty lands to the Republican River.

In 1970, the ICC ruled that the new hunting rights constituted "consideration" under the 1868 treaty thereby entitling the Lakota tribes to compensation for these rights if they could prove that they had a higher value in 1877 when they were confiscated than in 1868 when they were created. The U.S. Government, of course, argued that the new rights were worthless because there were less buffalo in 1877 than in 1868 (caused in large part by the Government's policy of eliminating the Lakota tribes' source of subsistence by exterminating the buffalo).

The ICC also ruled that in its final 1974 opinion in Docket 74-B that "[o]n December 29, 1970, [the Lakota tribes through their claims attorneys] notified the Commission that they did not intend to pursue their claims for loss of Article 11 and 16 hunting rights." The Lakota tribes, therefore, ended up with no compensation for their hunting rights.

- Black Hills Gold: The ICC also ruled in its 1974 opinion that the Lakota tribes were entitled to only $450,000 for placer (surface) gold stolen by trespassing miners prior to the passage of the 1877 Act. This ruling was based on the rationale that the 1868 treaty forbade miners to trespass in the Black Hills, and that "[i]n November 1875 the President . . . knowing that such action was in violation of the Government's treaty obligation and that such action would certainly result in thousands of non-Indians entering the Great Sioux Reservation to prospect for minerals, ordered the Army to withdraw from the Black Hills and to cease interfering with miners attempting to enter the reservation. As a direct result . . . thousands of non-Indians entered the Sioux reservation, established towns, organized mining districts, filed and developed mining claims, and mined and removed gold from the reservation." The ICC ruled that this Government action resulted in a "taking" of private property in violation of the Fifth Amendment, even though the beneficiaries were private parties.

No compensation was awarded for the billions of dollars worth of gold and other precious metals contained in the Black Hills even though the U.S. Government was aware of their existence in 1877. Today, the Lakota's sacred lands are commercialized.

Homestake Mine, the largest gold mine in North America, alone has earned more than $14 billion from gold and silver revenues since 1876.

In stark contrast, the Lakota people live in abject poverty on nearby reservations while the U.S. Government and its citizens continue to plunder their land and natural resources year after year.

It is not surprising, then, that one Lakota tribe (the Oglala Sioux tribe) rejected the Supreme Court's 1980 decision and demanded fidelity to Lakota treaties; the tribe filed suit in U.S. District Court at Rapid City, South Dakota, on July 18, 1980, to quit title to the Black Hills and for $11 billion in damages for the denial of the "absolute and undisturbed use and occupation" of the hills for 103 years. U.S. District Judge Albert G. Schatz slammed the courthouse doors in the Tribe's face, however, ruling that the United States was immune from suit in land recovery cases, and that if the tribe wanted to sue for the Black Hills, the ICC was its exclusive remedy.

Other Lakota tribes subsequently joined the Oglala Sioux Tribe in rejecting the $100 million ICC award and getting two bills introduced in Congress to resolve the Black Hills claim.

BROWN HAT'S 1856 VISION OF THE SALE OF THE BLACK HILLS FOR $100 MILLION IN THE YEAR 2000

Brown Hat (also known as Baptiste Good) was a Lakota who kept a traditional calendar known as a "winter count." The Tenth Annual Report of the U.S. Bureau of Ethnology (1888–89) contains the following account of his visit to the southern Black Hills in 1856:

In the year 1856, I went to the Black Hills and cried, and cried, and cried, and suddenly I saw a bird above me, which said: "Stop crying; I am a woman, but I will tell you something: My Great-Father, Father God, who made this place, gave it to me for a home and told me to watch over it. He put a blue sky over my head and gave me a blue flag to have with this beautiful green country. ***My Great-Father, Father God . . . grew, and his flesh was part earth and part stone and part metal and part wood and part water; he took from them all and placed them here for me, and told me to watch over them. I am the Eagle-Woman who tells you this.

The whites know that there are four black flags of God; that is, four divisions of earth. He first made the earth soft by wetting it, then cut it into four parts, one of which, containing the Black Hills, he gave to the [L]akotas, and, because I am a woman, I shall not consent to the pouring of blood on this chief house . . . , the Black Hills. The time will come when you will remember my words; for after many years you shall grow up one with the white people." She then circled round and round and gradually passed out of my sight. I also saw prints of a man's hands and horse's hoofs on the rocks (here he brings in petroglyphs), and two thousand years, and one hundred million dollars ($100,000,000).

Prints of a man's hands and horse's hoofs had significance in 1856. It was a message of death. A dying warrior would leave his bloody hand print on his horse to let his family know that he died in battle.

The message in Brown Hat's vision is a message of death to all the Lakota tribes. It says that the Lakota tribes, and their culture and governments, will cease to exist on earth if they allow the United States Government to force the $100 million ICC award on them in the Year 2000.

What Brown Hat's vision failed to foresee, however, was the determination of the current generation of Lakota to carry on the fight for the Black Hills, not in the battlefields, but through the White men's own legal institutions. It failed to reveal that the Spirit of Crazy Horse would still be alive in1980, when the Lakota people rejected the $100 million award and declared that "the Black Hills are not for sale." The current generation of Lakota will never allow the U.S. Government to force the $100 million ICC award on them in the year 2000.

PETE CATCHES' EXPLANATION OF WHY THE BLACK HILLS ARE SACRED TO THE LAKOTA

The religious significance of the Black Hills to the Lakota tribes was described by medicine man Pete Catches in 1993 as follows:

> To the Indian spiritual way of life, the Black Hills is the center of the Lakota people. There, ages ago, before Columbus came over the sea, seven spirits came to the Black Hills. They selected that area, the beginning of sacredness to the Lakota people. Each spirit brought a gift to the Lakota people.
>
> The first spirit gave the whole of the Black Hills to the Lakota people forever and ever, from this life until the great hereafter life.
>
> The next spirit that came told the Lakota people there is an eternal fire deep in the bowels of the earth, which we know as volcanoes—the fire, the everlasting fire—so the Black Hills belong to the Lakota people, and from it, that eternal fire in the bowels of the Black Hills is the life-giving heat.
>
> The next spirit brought water, commonly known to us now as 'Hot Springs.' We went there ages ago, together healing—which became eventually Evans Plunge, commercialized—where we, Indians, go for our healing in the healing waters of life.
>
> The third spirit brought the air that we breathe. You'll see that—you go to Wind Cave and the Earth breathes

air in and out. That's very sacred. It's needed for life. Without it, we cannot live, nothing can live. The plants need the air, all creation needs air.

> The fourth spirit brought the rock people, which includes the gold, as mentioned here a while ago, and the minerals. That is why the Black Hills [are] sacred to the Oval Office.
>
> The fifth spirit brought medicine. In the area of the Black Hills—that today's pain and disease has to do with AIDS—if we were left alone and if we can go there, we can develop our way of healing—even to the end of time, which is AIDS now, today. We can do that because the Black Hills [are] sacred, because that is life itself.
>
> The next spirit brought animals, the buffalo, the deer, all the small animals from which we get body parts. From the eagle, we get eagle feathers, from many of the smaller animals, we get parts of their body, transform it into our way of life—because all of creation is one unit, one life. We are them and they are us. This is his creation.
>
> The seventh spirit brought the Black Hills as a whole—brought it to give it to the Lakota forever, for all eternity, not only in this life, but in the life hereafter. The two are tied together. Our people that have passed on, their spirits are contained in the Black Hills. This is why it is the center of the universe, and this is why it is sacred to the Oglala Sioux. In this life and the life hereafter, the two are together.
>
> Why should we part with the Black Hills? Land is not for sale.
>
> I'd like a life to look forward to after this life. Generations and generations ago, our people have looked upon the Black Hills as the center of the world, and it's a circle. We began from there and we make a complete circle of life, and we go there after our demise from this world. That is why it is sacred to us.

Today Lakota people are desperately struggling to protect their religious sites in the Black Hills from desecration. Lakota elders recently stopped mountain climbing at Devil's Tower. And the struggle to protect Bear Butte—the most sacred site of all—continues.

BEAR BUTTE: THE SACRED MOUNTAIN OF THE LAKOTA AND TSISTSISTAS

Bear Butte is located on the eastern edge of the Black Hills near Sturgis, South Dakota. It is a place where Lakota and Tsistsistas come each year for vision quests. Traditional leader Larry Red Shirt described the importance of the Sacred Mountain in 1982 as follows:

> [E]ven before the Sacred Pipe was given to us, the vision quest was the oldest ceremony of our people and the original instructions of the Lakota was given by the Creator on a sacred mountain similar to the way the Ten Commandments were given to Moses on a mountain . . . . [T]he Lakota originated in the Black Hills and [the]

sacred instructions given to us by the Creator were given to us on Bear Butte. This makes Bear Butte the central and most sacred mountain to the Lakota people . . . . The sacred calf pipe is the most sacred object with which to pray with in Lakota religion. Bear Butte is the most sacred place to pray with that pipe. Bear Butte and the sacred calf pipe hold the secret to the past, present and future of the Lakota people in this life cycle.

Although similar, Tsistsistas' use of Bear Butte is not identical to that of the Lakota. Elder Walter R. Hamilton described the importance of the Sacred Mountain to the Tsistsistas as follows:

The four sacred arrows of the [Tsistsistas] came from within Bear Butte as a covenant with the Almighty God/Maheo . . . [and the mountain, therefore, is] . . . the holiest place to the [Tsistsistas] people, who use the mountain regularly for pilgrimages, and who think about it every day, and who mention it in their prayers.

Even though Congress confiscated Bear Butte (along with the rest of the Black Hills) in 1877 and granted it to private parties under the Homestead laws, Lakota and Tsistsistas religious practitioners have used the Sacred Mountain for religious ceremonies continuously up to the present time.

In 1962, the State of South Dakota purchased the traditional ceremonial grounds from a private landowner, turned it into "Bear Butte State Park," and began to physically alter the natural topography of the mountain by constructing roads, hiking trails, machine shops, wooden walkways, parking lots, camp grounds and a permanent visitor center for tourists. As a natural and intended consequence, tourist visitation has increased to over 100,000 people per year, while over 4,000 Native Americans participate in religious ceremonies there.

State officials intended some of the construction projects, such as service roads, to benefit Native American worshippers. These officious intermeddlers, however, failed to comprehend that a religious shrine is desecrated by changing its natural features, and that this is the same as destroying it. Desecration denies access by destroying what makes a holy place holy, and renders worship ineffective.

Moreover, the principal ceremony conducted at Bear Butte, the "Vision Quest," takes up to four days to complete and requires solitude and extreme concentration before a worshipper can achieve a vision. It is difficult to concentrate, however, because the growing number of tourists each year has greatly infringed on the ability of Lakota and Tsistsistas people to conduct religious ceremonies. Tourists

have intruded on religious ceremonies by riding up to the visitor center on loud motorcycles; walking up the hiking paths with radios blaring; standing on overlook platforms along hiking trails and photographing worshippers as they pray; taking offerings left by worshippers as souvenirs; taking food and water on the mountain; and allowing non-Native American women on the mountain during their menstrual period in violation of traditional religious practice.

In 1982, the state of South Dakota closed the ceremonial grounds for one month for construction and required worshippers to camp two miles away at Bear Butte Lake. The state even required one worshipper to pay a fee to camp and conduct her ceremonies. This prompted traditional Lakota and Tsistsistas religious practitioners to initiate a lawsuit in federal court (*Fools Crow v. Gullet* 1982) for violations of the Free Exercise Clause of the First Amendment of the U.S. Constitution, the 1978 American Indian Religious Freedom Act and Article 18 of the International Covenant on Civil and Political Rights.

The worshippers asked the court to declare their right to full, unrestricted and uninterrupted religious use of Bear Butte and injunctive relief from construction projects altering the Butte's natural features. U.S. District Judge Andrew Bogue rejected their claims, and suggested that the State might be establishing religion by protecting Native Americans' religious practices at the Butte.

Although permit and registration requirements have often been held per se unconstitutional when applied to exercise of freedom of speech and religion in cases such as *Shuttlesworth v. City of Birmingham* (1969), the state of South Dakota still restricts access to the Butte by requiring worshippers to obtain a permit to conduct religious ceremonies there. This places state officials in a position to arbitrarily approve or deny the exercise of religious freedoms.

Lakota and Tsistsistas religious practitioners ask only that their religious sites and ceremonies be protected to the same degree that mainstream religious sites and ceremonies are protected. If an establishment clause problem exists, it is the failure of the federal courts to provide Native American worshippers the same protection in conducting ceremonies at sacred sites as provided to worshippers at churches and synagogues. This failure to protect Native American worshippers effectively establishes mainstream religions over Native American religions in the United States.

CONCLUSION

The Lakota tribes' rejection of the $100 million ICC award for the Black Hills in 1980 has come to symbolize Native American resistance in North America. The tribes have two primary concerns in rejecting the claim: (1) the protection of the religious sanctity of the Black Hills and (2) the protection of the culture, sovereignty and economic self-sufficiency of the Lakota people.

First, no one would ever expect Christians, Jews and Muslims to accept monetary compensation for their sacred sites and shrines in the Middle East. Yet, these same Christians, Jews and Muslims residing in the United States have no objection to forcing a monetary settlement on the Lakota tribes for their Sacred Black Hills. No amount of money in the world can compensate the Lakota tribes for their religious property.

Secondly, Article 5 of the 1877 Act, in pertinent part, provides as follows:

> In consideration of the foregoing cession of territory and [hunting] rights . . ., the United States does agree to provide all necessary aid to assist the Indians in the work of civilization. ***Also, to provide said Indians with subsistence consisting of a ration for each individual . . ., or in lieu of said articles the equivalent thereof. Such rations, or so much thereof as may be necessary, shall be continued until the Indians are able to support themselves.

The "aid for civilization" and "subsistence rations" received by the Lakota tribes today are part of the quid pro quo for the illegal confiscation of the Black Hills and Lakota hunting rights in 1877. The Lakota tribes currently receive over $300 million annually in Article 5 benefits (although many Lakota feel that this is inadequate consideration when compared to the billions of dollars plundered from their treaty lands each year; a substantial portion of these funds are also used to cover the costs of the federal administrative agencies that oversee Indian affairs). The dollar value of these benefits, multiplied over the next 100 years, would be in excess of $30 billion!

The Lakota tribes are concerned that acceptance of the $100 million ICC award will extinguish not only their title to the Black Hills, but their benefits under Article 5 of the 1877 Act as well. They fear that the United States Government will argue that payment of the award results in a "full discharge of the United States of all claims and demands touching any of the matters involved in the controversy" under Section 22 of the Indian Claims Commission Act.

Thus, the long-term survival of the Lakota people depends on how the Black Hills claim is ultimately resolved. In the meantime, the $100 million ICC award for the Black Hills has grown (with compound interest) to over $380 million since 1980. Still the tribes reject it, insisting that the U.S. Government return the federally held lands to the tribes and settle their claims for the remaining lands held by private parties in a fair and honorable manner, consistent with their religious beliefs.

Should the U.S. Government attempt to force the $100 million ICC award on the Lakota tribes in the year 2000, the Oglala Sioux Tribe is prepared to initiate a new round of litigation in the federal courts to stop payment of the award based on untested legal theories.

REFERENCES

Fletcher v. Peck, 10 U.S. (6 Cranch) 87 (1810).

[Fools] Crow v. Gullet, 541 F.Supp. 785 (D.S.D. 1982); See Affidavits of Larry Red Shirt and Walter R. Hamilton.

Johnson v. M'Intosh, 21 U.S. (8 Wheat.) 543 (1823).

Oglala Sioux Tribe v. United States, 650 F.2d 140 (8th Cir. 1981).

Sac and Fox Tribe v. United States, 315 F.2d 896 (Ct. Cl. 1963).

Sequoyah v. Tennessee Valley Authority, 620 F.2d 1159 (6th Cir. 1980).

Shuttlesworth v. City of Birmingham, 394 U.S. 147 (1969).

Sioux Nation of Indians v. United States, 33 Indian Claims Commission 151 (Feb. 15, 1974).

Tee-Hit-Ton Indians v. United States, 348 U.S. 272 (1958).

United States v. Sioux Nation of Indians, 448 F.2d 371 (1980).

United States Ex Rel Chunie v. Ringrose, 788 F.2d 638 (9th Cir. 1986).

1851 Ft. Laramie Treaty, 10 Stat. 969.

1868 Ft. Laramie Treaty, 15 Stat. 635.

1876 Appropriation Act (Sell or Starve Act), 19 Stat. 176.

1877 Black Hills Act, 19 Stat. 254.

1946 Indian Claims Commission Act, 60 Stat. 1055.

1978 American Indian Religious Freedom Act, 42 U.S.C. 1996.

Hearing before the Committee on Indian Affairs: Oversight Hearing on the Need For Amendments to the Religious Freedom Act, S. Hrg. 103–6, Part 3 (103rd Cong., 1st Sess.); see Testimony of Peter Catches.

International Covenant on Civil and Political Rights, Article 18, General Assembly Resolution No. 2200A (XXI), 16 Dec. 1966, signed by President Carter on Oct. 5, 1977.

Tenth Annual Report of the U.S. Bureau of Ethnology (GPO 1888–1889); See Brown Hat's account of his 1856 visit to the Black Hills.

THE REDISCOVERY OF HAWAIIAN SOVEREIGNTY

Poka Laenui

On January 16, 1893, American marines landed in peaceful Hawai'i armed with Gatling guns, Howitzer cannons, carbines, and other instruments of war, as well as double cartridge belts filled with ammunition. The United States troops marched along the streets of Honolulu, rifles facing Iolani palace, the seat of Hawai'i's sovereignty.

The following day, resident conspirators numbering eighteen, mostly Americans, sneaked to the back steps of a government building a few yards from where the American troops had lodged the night before. There, Henry Cooper, an American lawyer and resident of Hawai'i for less than a year, proclaimed that he and seventeen others were now the government of Hawai'i. Calling themselves the "provisional government" and selecting Sanford Dole president, they were to exist for the explicit purpose of annexing Hawai'i to the United States. American minister plenipotentiary John L. Stevens immediately recognized the "provisional government" as the government of Hawai'i. He then joined in their demand that Queen Lili'uokalani, the constitutional monarch of the Hawaiian nation, surrender under threat of war with the United States. Faced with such a threat, the queen eventually capitulated, but not without protest. These are her words:

> I, Lili'uokalani, by the grace of God and under the constitution of the Hawaiian Kingdom, Queen, do hereby solemnly protest against any and all acts done against myself and the constitutional Government of the Hawaiian Kingdom by certain persons claiming to have established a Provisional Government of and for this Kingdom.
>
> That I yield to the superior force of the United States of America, whose minister plenipotentiary, his excellency John L. Stevens, has caused United States troops to be landed at Honolulu and declared that he would support the Provisional Government.
>
> Now, to avoid any collision of armed forces and perhaps the loss of life, I do, under this protest, and impelled by said force, yield my authority until such time as the Government of the United States shall, upon the facts being presented to it, undo the action of its representative and reinstate me and the authority which I claim as the constitutional sovereign of the Hawaiian Islands.

Rather than undoing its actions, the United States continued in its conspiracy to deprive an independent people of their right to self-determination, forcing Hawai'i to serve as the command headquarters of its Pacific military forces as well as an important finger of the American economic hand reaching into Asia. The United States had "discovered" Hawai'i and extended by force its sovereignty over this once independent Pacific nation.

EARLY HISTORY

Hawai'i's early inhabitants journeyed throughout the vast Pacific, guided by stars, the rising sun, clouds, birds, wave formation, and flashing lights from the water's depth. They touched on many lands, including the most isolated land mass in the world—Hawai'i. As seafarers, they continued commerce with cousins of the South Pacific many years after arriving in Hawai'i. They had occasional contacts with Japan, Great Turtle Island (today North America), and other Pacific Rim places.

Hawai'i remained virtually unknown to Europeans until the arrival, in 1778, of James Cook, captain of the British navy ships *Resolution* and *Discovery*. Cook found a highly developed Hawaiian society and was welcomed in friendship. In an unfortunate misunderstanding, however, Cook initiated violence against the Hawaiian people. The Hawaiian response resulted in his blood flowing into the waters of Kealakekua Bay, Hawai'i, and he journeyed no further.

"The Rediscovery of Hawaiian Sovereignty," by Poka Laenui, in *American Indian Culture and Research Journal*, 17, no. 1 (1993): 79–101. Copyright 1993 by Regents of the University of California, American Indian Studies Center. Reprinted with permission. Portions of the article and the endnotes have been omitted.

Soon after contact with Cook, Hawai'i was cast into world attention and was accepted quickly as a member of the international community. During the reign of Kamehameha I (1779–1819), Hawai'i traded with China, England, the United States, and other nations on a regular basis. On November 28, 1843, Great Britain and France joined in a declaration recognizing Hawaii's independence and pledged never to take it as a possession. When the United States was invited to join this declaration, J. C. Calhoun, secretary of state, replied that the president adhered completely to the spirit of disinterestedness and self-denial that breathed in the declaration. "He had already, for his part taken a similar engagement in the message which he had already addressed to Congress on December 31, 1842."

By 1887, Hawai'i had treaties and conventions with Belgium, Bremen, Denmark, France, the German Empire, Great Britain, Hamburg, Hong Kong, Italy, Japan, the Netherlands, New South Wales, Portugal, Russia, Samoa, Spain, the Swiss Confederation, Sweden, Norway, Tahiti, and the United States. Hawai'i was a member of one of the first international organizations, the Universal Postal Union. Approximately one hundred diplomatic and consular posts around the world were established.

Over the years, many immigrants came to Hawai'i from all parts of the world, many renouncing their former national allegiance and taking up Hawaiian citizenship. The nation of Hawai'i had a literacy rate that was among the highest in the world. It had telephones and electricity built into its governing palace, "Iolani," before the White House had such technology. Multilingual citizens abounded. Hawaiian leaders had excellent comprehension of world and political geography; King Kalakaua was the first head of state to circle the world as part of his plan to weave a tapestry of international economic and political alliances to assure Hawaiian independence. By 1892, Hawai'i was a vibrant, multiracial, multicultural nation engaged in intellectual and economic commerce with the world.

Christian Missionaries Arrive

Early in its exposure to the Western world, Hawai'i became the focus of Christian zeal. The first flock of missionaries arrived from Boston in 1820. Many remained, established homes and families, and were welcomed into Hawaiian society. They became a strong influence over the people.

Over time, many children of missionaries left the pulpits of the church and entered business and politics. After several decades, an alliance arose of missionary offspring and developing business interests. Growing and selling sugar comprised the principal interest of this alliance. Land, labor, and market were its major concerns, and it addressed those concerns through political and social control. The new alliance called itself the "missionary party."

Land Assault

The missionary party drastically changed land relationships in Hawai'i. Formerly land was under the care of the ruling chiefs. They allotted the use of the lands to their subchiefs, who reallotted the remaining lands to their supporters. By 1839, these distributions were revocable only for cause (Bill of Rights of 1839). Land "ownership" in the Western sense did not exist. Land was an integral part of the life of Hawai'i, along with the air, the sunlight, the winds, the waters, and the people. None of these parts was to dominate the others. This was a basic philosophy of existence for Hawai'i's early inhabitants.

Under the influence of the missionary party, however, less than thirty years after missionary arrival, this land relationship was overturned. Land was parceled out in fee simple estates along the traditions of England and the United States. Foreigners could now be permanent landowners in Hawai'i.

Labor Assault

Many of the Indigenous people refused to work at low plantation wages. In response, the missionary party influenced immigration policies, importing laborers to perform the exhausting sugar plantation work on the lands now controlled by them. The sugar industry spread across Hawai'i with easily available lands and cheap imported labor.

Market Assault

With land and labor under control, the missionary party applied itself to the last step in this commercial cycle—securing a market for its sugar. The United States was the logical market, because it was geographically closer to Hawai'i than any other market. Most members of the missionary party were citizens of the United States and had been in constant communication and trade with their mainland. The United States military was hungry for a naval armada in the

Pacific, so it was a willing partner for close relationships with Hawai'i.

To secure the American market, the missionary party saw two alternative solutions: reciprocity agreements or annexation. Reciprocity would permit Hawaiian sugar importation into the United States duty-free. In return, products would be imported into Hawai'i duty free. However, reciprocity agreements were temporary. Annexation offered greater security. Under annexation, Hawaiian sugar would be considered domestic rather than foreign and thus not subject to tariff as it entered the American market.

Initial reciprocity arrangements between Hawai'i and the United States were tried but did not last long. The United States soon wanted more than just an exchange of trade rights. It wanted sovereignty over Pearl Harbor in order to extend its commercial and military arm into the Pacific.

King Kalakaua and Queen Lili'uokalani Under Attack

Kalakaua, previously elected Hawai'i's Mo'i (ruling sovereign 1874–91), refused to cede Pearl Harbor. The missionary party attacked Kalakaua by slander, rumors, and attempts on his life. They accused him of being a drunk and a heathen because he attempted to revitalize the hula and preserve the religious practices of his ancestors. They branded him a womanizer. His character and his activities were continually berated in the press. Yet the people rallied around him and remained loyal in the face of these attacks. The missionary party, so intent on wresting power from Kalakaua, drew lots to decide which of five conspirators would murder him. The one selected was so horrified by his selection that he refused to act.

Following numerous public attacks on Kalakaua's reputation and esteem, the missionary party secretly formed a league, armed themselves, and forced the king at gunpoint to turn the powers of government over to them. In 1887, Kalakaua signed the "bayonet" constitution, the name reflecting the method of adoption. This constitution stripped Kalakaua of power.

Once in power, the missionary party granted the United States exclusive right to use Pearl Harbor. In return, it received an extension of seven years on the existing reciprocity treaty, which would soon have expired. The sugar market was temporarily secure.

Kalakaua died in 1891 in San Francisco, on a trip that was intended to help him recuperate from illness advanced by the activities in Hawai'i. Rumors still abound in Hawai'i that his death was caused by the missionary party's agents in the United States. Lili'uokalani succeeded him.

Quite soon upon her accession, Queen Lili'uokalani received a petition of two-thirds of the registered voters imploring her to do away with the bayonet constitution and return the powers of government to the Hawaiian people. By January 14, 1893, she had completed a draft of a new constitution and had informed her cabinet of her intention to institute it immediately. She was persuaded by the cabinet, which, under the bayonet constitution, was controlled by the missionary party, to put off the constitutional change for a short time, and she acceded to this request. Members of her cabinet rushed to report the queen's intentions to the leaders of the missionary party.

Mr. Thurston, Mr. Dole, and United States Minister Stevens

It is important to identify two men in particular who were at the head of the missionary party. Lorrin Thurston was the grandson of Asa Thurston, one of the first missionaries. Sanford Dole was the son of Daniel Dole, another early missionary. As early as 1882, Lorrin Thurston had already exchanged confidences with leading American officials on the matter of the takeover of Hawai'i. In fact, the United States secretary of the navy assured Thurston that the administration of Chester A. Arthur would look with favor on a takeover. In 1892, in another visit to the United States, Thurston again received the same assurance from the administration of Benjamin Harrison.

When Thurston received word of the queen's intention, he declared that she had no business attempting to institute a new constitution by fiat. Along with twelve others, he formed a "Committee of Public Safety" and arranged an immediate visit to the American minister plenipotentiary in Hawai'i, John L. Stevens, to conspire for the overthrow of Lili'uokalani.

Little convincing was necessary, for Stevens was already one of the foremost advocates for a United States takeover of Hawai'i. Appointed in June 1889 as the United States minister plenipotentiary, he regarded himself as having a mission to bring about the annexation of Hawai'i by the United States. His letters to secretary of state James G. Blaine, beginning less than a month after his arrival, reflect his passion to take Hawai'i for the United States. On March 8, 1892, after three years of promoting the annexation, he writes to ask how far he may *deviate from established international rules and precedents* in the event of an orderly

THE REDISCOVERY OF HAWAIIAN SOVEREIGNTY

and peaceful revolutionary movement and sets forth a step-by-step prediction of future events. In later letters, he argues that those favoring annexation in Hawai'i are qualified to carry on good government, "provided they have the support of the Government of the United States." He continues, "[H]awaii must now take the road which leads to Asia, or the other, which outlets her in America, gives her an American civilization, and binds her to the care of American destiny. . . . To postpone American action many years is only to add to present unfavorable tendencies and to make future possession more difficult." He calls for "bold and vigorous measures for annexation. I cannot refrain from expressing the opinion with emphasis that the golden hour is near at hand. . . . So long as the islands retain their own independent government there remains the possibility that England or the Canadian Dominion might secure one of the Hawaiian harbors for a coaling station. Annexation excludes all dangers of this kind."

Thus, when Thurston met with Stevens on January 15, 1893, the "golden hour" was at hand. It was agreed that the United States marines would land under the guise of protecting American (missionary party) lives. The missionary party then would declare itself the provisional government and immediately would turn Hawai'i over to the United States in an annexation treaty. As a reward, the missionary party would officially be appointed the local rulers of Hawai'i. The United States would obtain the choicest lands and harbors for its Pacific armada.

The landing of the marines is now a matter of history. The queen yielded her authority, trusting to the "enlightened justice" of the United States, expecting a full investigation to be conducted and the United States government to restore the constitutional government of Hawai'i.

On January 18, 1893, the day after Lili'uokalani yielded, the provisional government forbade any of the queen's supporters from boarding the only ship leaving Hawai'i. The new leaders then rushed off to Washington to obtain annexation. By February 16, 1893, a treaty of annexation had been hurriedly negotiated, signed, and presented by President Harrison to the United States Senate for ratification.

President Grover Cleveland

However, Grover Cleveland replaced Harrison before the Senate voted. Meanwhile, traveling as businessmen, the queen's emissaries had managed to sneak to the United States. Upon reaching Washington, they pleaded with Cleveland to withdraw the treaty and conduct the promised investigation. Cleveland agreed and appointed as special investigator the former chairman of the House Foreign Relations Committee, James H. Blount.

After several months of investigation, Blount exposed the conspiracy. Cleveland subsequently addressed Congress, declaring,

> By an act of war, committed with the participation of a diplomatic representative of the United States and without authority of Congress, the Government of a feeble but friendly and confiding people has been overthrown. A substantial wrong has thus been done which a due regard for our national character as well as the rights of the injured people requires we should endeavor to repair. . . .
>
> [Lili'uokalani] knew that she could not withstand the power of the United States, but believed that she might safely trust to its justice. [S]he surrendered not to the provisional government, but to the United States. She surrendered not absolutely and permanently, but temporarily and conditionally until such time as the facts could be considered by the United States [and it could] undo the action of its representative and reinstate her in the authority she claimed as the constitutional sovereign of the Hawaiian Islands.

In summarizing the events, Cleveland concluded:

> The lawful Government of Hawai'i was overthrown without the drawing of a sword or the firing of a shot by a process every step of which, it may be safely asserted, is directly traceable to and dependent for its success upon the agency of the United States acting through its diplomatic and naval representatives.
>
> But for the notorious predilections of the United States Minister for annexation, the Committee of Safety, which should be called the Committee of Annexation, would never have existed.
>
> But for the landing of the United States forces upon false pretexts respecting the danger to life and property the committee would never have exposed themselves to the pains and penalties of treason by undertaking the subversion of the Queen's Government.
>
> But for the presence of the United States forces in the immediate vicinity and in position to afford all needed protection and support the committee would not have proclaimed the provisional government from the steps of the Government building.
>
> And finally, but for the lawless occupation of Honolulu under false pretexts by the United States forces, and but for Minister Stevens' recognition of the provisional government when the United States forces were its sole support and constituted its only military strength, the Queen and her Government would never have yielded to the provisional government, even for a time and for the sole purpose of submitting her case to the enlightened justice of the United States.

The law of nations is founded upon reason and justice, and the rules of conduct governing individual relations between citizens or subjects of a civilized state are equally applicable as between enlightened nations. The considerations that international law is without a court for its enforcement, and that obedience to its commands practically depends upon good faith, instead of upon the mandate of a superior tribunal, only give additional sanction to the law itself and brand any deliberate infraction of it not merely as a wrong but as a disgrace.[1]

As long as he remained president, Cleveland refused to forward the treaty to the Senate. Lili'uokalani was advised of the president's desire to aid in the restoration of the status existing before the lawless landing of the United States forces at Honolulu, if such restoration could be effected in terms providing for clemency as well as justice to all parties. In short, the past should be buried and the restored government should reassume its authority as if its continuity had not been interrupted. The queen first protested that such a promise from her would constitute an unconstitutional act and was therefore beyond her powers to grant, but she later acceded to the demands for general amnesty upon the return of the powers of government.

The provisional government was informed of this decision immediately and was asked to abide by Cleveland's decision, yielding to the queen her constitutional authority. It refused. In doing so, the members protested Cleveland's attempt to "interfere in the internal affairs" of their nation, declaring themselves citizens of the provisional government and thus beyond Cleveland's authority. Only a short time before, they had relied on their American citizenship and thus had justified the landing of United States marines to protect their lives! Cleveland, though filled with principled words, left the United States troops in Hawai'i's harbors to protect American lives.

The Puppet Government Changes Clothes

The provisional government was under international criticism for being a government without the support of its people—existing, in fact, without even a constitution or other fundamental document to afford even the appearance of legitimacy. Faced with an American administration that would not condone the conspiracy yet kept American warships in Honolulu harbor, the conspirators devised a plan to restructure themselves so they would appear to be a permanent rather than a provisional government. When a new American president came to office, the "permanent" government would place the conspiracy back on course.

A constitution giving them permanence and validity had to be drafted. Sanford Dole, acting as president of the provisional government, announced a constitutional convention of thirty-seven delegates: eighteen elected and the remaining nineteen selected by him. The candidates and voters for the eighteen elected positions were first required to renounce Queen Lili'uokalani and swear allegiance to the provisional government. Less than 20 percent of the voting population participated in the election.

The constitutional convention was held, and the document that was adopted was substantially the same as the one submitted by Dole and Thurston. The constitution of the "Republic of Hawai'i" claimed dominion over all lands and waters of Hawai'i and claimed all of Hawai'i's citizens as its own. Foreigners who supported the new regime could vote; citizens loyal to the queen could not. Because the Japanese and especially the Chinese supported Lili'uokalani, they were, as a group, disenfranchised. Further, only those who could speak, read, and write English or Hawaiian and could explain the constitution, *written in English*, to the satisfaction of Dole's supporters could vote.

On July 4, 1894, while Americans were celebrating their independence day by firing the cannons on their warships in Honolulu harbor, Dole proclaimed the constitution and thus the Republic of Hawai'i into existence. Lili'uokalani had lost her throne because she had considered altering the constitution by fiat. Now, circumstances having altered the players, the conspirators invoked the name of liberty and did substantially the same thing.

McKinley: Sleight of Constitutional Hand

When William McKinley replaced Cleveland as president, Dole's group rushed to Washington to complete the conspiracy. With a constitution in hand declaring them the legal government, the new administration of Hawai'i ceded "absolutely and without reserve to the United States of America all rights of sovereignty of whatsoever kind in and over the Hawaiian Islands. . . ." A treaty of annexation was signed.

Realizing the treaty would not get the two-thirds Senate approval required in the United States Constitution, the conspirators circumvented that requirement and settled for only a joint resolution of Congress. The New lands Resolution of July 7, 1898 was passed. Following this congressional resolution, the United

States assumed authority and soon established the government of the "Territory of Hawai'i."

As these events were happening, Lili'uokalani engraved her plea to the American people:

> Oh, honest Americans, as Christians hear me for my downtrodden people! Their form of government is as dear to them as yours is precious to you. Quite as warmly as you love your country, so they love theirs. Do not covet the little vineyards of Jabot's so far from your shores, lest the punishment of Ahab fall upon you, if not in your day in that of your children, for "be not deceived, God is not mocked." The people to whom your fathers told of the living God, and taught to call "Father," and whom the sons now seek to despoil and destroy, are crying aloud to Him in their time of trouble; and He will keep His promise, and will listen to the voices of His Hawaiian children lamenting for their homes.[2]

Her plea fell on deaf congressional ears. And so we close the chapter on Hawai'i as a free and unoccupied nation. Hawai'i was now to undergo years of American brainwashing, colonization, and military occupation. These were to be the payoff years for the conspirators.

THE RECYCLING OF HAWAI'I 1900–1959

Hawai'i now underwent traumatic changes affecting every aspect of life. Sanford Dole, appointed territorial governor, provided government positions and lucrative government contracts for his friends. Monopolies in shipping, finance, and communications developed. The Big Five, a coalition of five business entities with roots in the Missionary Party, controlled every aspect of business, media, and politics in Hawai'i. Beginning with sugar, they took steps to control transportation, hotels, utilities, banks, insurance agencies, and many small wholesale and retail businesses. When they teamed up with McKinley's Republican party and the United States Navy, there was virtually nothing left unexploited.

While the Big Five were taking over Hawai'i, they were propagating the myth of the superiority of the Anglo-Saxon race. In addition, a massive brainwashing program was begun to convince Hawaiians that the United States was the legitimate ruler and that Hawaiians were no longer Hawaiians but Americans. The term Hawaiian was redefined as a racial rather than a national term. Large numbers of citizens were identified no longer as Hawaiians but as Chinese, Japanese, Korean, English, Samoan, and Filipino. The divide-and-conquer tactic was employed even with

the Hawaiian race, when Congress declared that "Native Hawaiians" (at least 50 percent aboriginal blood) were entitled to special land privileges while others of lesser "blood" were not.

Children were forced to attend American schools and were taught to pledge their allegiance to the United States. They were trained in the foreign laws, told to adopt foreign morality, to speak no language but the foreign (English) and to adopt the foreign (American) lifestyle. Official government proceedings were to be conducted in English and not the Hawaiian language. In the schools and colleges, if the language of Hawai'i was taught atoll, it was only in the foreign language departments.

The customs and traditions, and even the cultural names of the people, were suppressed in this recycling effort. The great *makahiki* celebrations honoring Lono, an important god of peace, harvest, agriculture, and medicine, were never observed or mentioned in the schools. Instead, Christmas was celebrated with plays and pageants. People were coaxed into giving children American names that had no ties with their ancestors—names that described no physical substance, spiritual sense, or human mood; names that could not call upon the winds or waters, the soil or the heat; names totally irrelevant to the surroundings.

The arts and sciences of Hawai'i's ancestors were driven to near extinction. The advanced practice of healing through the medicines of plants, water, or massage, or just the uttered words, were driven into the back countryside. The science of predicting the future through animal behaviors, cloud colors, shapes and formations of leaves on trees was discounted as superstition and ridiculed as a collection of old folktales. The Hawaiian culture was being ground to dust.

Massive immigration took place, controlled by the United States. Hawai'i witnessed an influx of Americans, bringing with them a barrage of cultural, moral, religious, and political concepts. Hawaiians were "persuaded" to mimic American ways, to idolize American heroes, and to adopt American lifestyles. As Americans infiltrated, they took choice jobs with government agencies and management positions with business interests. They bought up or stole, through the manipulation of laws applied by them, much of the land and resources of Hawai'i. They gained power in Hawai'i, controlled greater chunks of the economy, controlled the public media, entrenched themselves in politics, and joined in the brainwashing of the Hawaiians to believe they were Americans.

The military turned Hawai'i into its Pacific fortress, converting Pearl Harbor from a coaling and fueling station to a major naval port. It bombed valleys and took a major island (Kaho'olawe) for its exclusive use as a target range. At will, the military tossed families out of their homes and destroyed sacred Hawaiian heirlooms (Lualualei, Oahu), building, in their place, naval communication towers that emitted radiation and ammunition depots that hid nuclear weapons. It declared martial law at will, violating the United States Constitution, and imposed military conscription on Hawaiian citizens. Freedom of trade was stopped. Congress assumed control over foreign relations. Hawaiians could buy only American goods or foreign goods the United States approved. The Big Five controlled all shipping. Every aspect of Hawai'i was Americanized. Military strength was constantly on display. Trade was totally controlled. Education and media were regulated. The secret ballot was a farce.

Hawai'i, that melting pot of cultures, races, languages, and lore, changed from a reality to an advertising slogan for politicians and merchants.

HAWAIIAN STATEHOOD, 1959

Finally, after three generations of brainwashing, Hawaiians were given the opportunity to be equal Americans! The United States placed the following question to the qualified voters in Hawai'i: *Shall Hawai'i immediately be admitted into the Union as a State?* "Qualified" voters were Americans who had been residents of Hawai'i for at least one year. The United States had already assured the vote with the thousands of American citizens brought in through its immigration program and through military assignments, as well as with generations of socialization of Hawaiian citizens. Those who resisted American domination and insisted on their Hawaiian citizenship could not vote.

In posing the statehood question so adeptly, the United States government precluded any real self-determination by limiting the choice to Hawai'i's either remaining a territory of the United States or becoming a state within its Union. The question, Should Hawai'i be free? was never asked. The Americans chose statehood overwhelmingly. . . .

Cultural Rejuvenation

. . . During the 1960s, Hawai'i witnessed the unfolding drama in the United States of the Black struggle for equality, including the riots in Watts, the marches and the bus boycotts, the voter registration drives,

and the massive rallies in Washington, D.C. The American Indian Movement's activities also caught the attention of Hawaiians. The Black and American Indian movements, however, were soon overshadowed by the Vietnam War. Many Hawaiian citizens became directly involved in that war. By the end of the1960s, attitudes toward the United States government had changed; its image had become tarnished.

Many in Hawai'i came out of the 1960s with greater sensitivity toward racial identity and pride in the cultural heritage of Hawai'i. Hawaiians were more willing to challenge governments, either individually or in organizations. Hawaiian music took on new vigor. Hula *halaus* (training schools and repositories of Hawaiian dance) gained wider prestige and membership, canoe clubs became more popular, interest in the Hawaiian language took hold, as well as practice in the natural medicines of Hawai'i and interest in Hawai'i's history. Hawaiian names were used prominently and with greater insistence. People of many different races joined this cultural rejuvenation in Hawai'i.

For Native Hawaiians, land soon became another focus of contention. The eviction of farmers in the Kalama Valley on Oahu sparked a wave of challenges to the system. The movement to protect another island, Kahoolawe, from military bombing expanded the target of protest to the previously "sacred" military establishment. Soon a plethora of new Hawaiian organizations came into being. The issue of Hawaiian sovereignty and self-determination was a natural outgrowth of the disenchantment with Hawaiian social and economic conditions. The combination of all of these factors brought about a new consciousness of injustice—the denial of the Hawaiian nation.

By the second half of the 1970s, the sovereignty challenges were becoming more explicit. In a highly publicized trial of a reputed Hawaiian underworld leader, the defense raised the question of the state court's jurisdiction over a Hawaiian citizen. The Blount Report, President Cleveland's address to Congress, the Newlands Resolution annexing Hawai'i to the United States, and other historical documents and events were made part of the case record. Then the attorney, arguing that he was not a United States citizen but a Hawaiian, challenged the authority of the United States district court to force him to participate as a juror. The case drew wide public attention.

Soon after these events, the evictions of predominantly Native Hawaiians from Sand Island, then from Makua Beach, then from Waimanalo all challenged the jurisdiction of the courts to try Hawaiian citizens. Those eviction cases reflected another direction of growing Hawaiian conscious- ness. The lands in question, originally in the inven- tory of the government of Hawai'i or owned by the Crown and subsequently ceded to the United States by the Republic of Hawai'i, were viewed by Hawaiians not as ceded but stolen lands. However, when asked, before a packed courtroom, to trace the title of those lands, the state's expert witness in the Makua Beach eviction case stated that it was simply state policy that no such tracing was necessary. The court then ruled that the evidence was conclusive that the Republic of Hawai'i had held proper title to cede these lands to the United States.

The Office of Hawaiian Affairs

As part of the awakening consciousness of Native Hawaiians toward the historical injustices perpe- trated against them, they incorporated into the state constitution in 1978 the Office of Hawaiian Affairs. The creation of the OHA marked a first in organiza- tional representation for Native Hawaiians. Indeed, it is a response to Indigenous peoples that appears to be unique in the world.

Unlike the Office of Maori Affairs of Aotearoa (New Zealand) or the Office of Aboriginal Affairs of Australia or the Bureau of Indian Affairs of the United States, the OHA is composed of trustees who are directly elected by the Indigenous people. As a result, in theory at least, they answer to no one but their Hawaiian constituents. However, the OHA is still seen as an organization of limited scope, unable to grasp the full sense of decolonization, since its very existence is dependent on the colonial constitutional regime in Hawai'i. Furthermore, it is based on a race con- stituency and therefore is unable to expand to include all potential Hawaiian citizens. Its current position on Hawaiian sovereignty is that Native Hawaiians should be treated as a tribal nation, as the colonial gov- ernment treats the American Indian nations.

Re-emergence As a Sovereign, Independent Nation

Today, there is a growing vision of Hawai'i becoming an independent nation, rejoining the ranks of other nations of the world. Within this vision, the question of citizenship and residence would be settled not by racial extraction but by one's relationship to Hawai'i—measured by some standard of accultura- tion, vows of loyalty to Hawai'i, ancestry from

Hawaiian citizens prior to the American invasion of 1893, and other similar means. The Native Hawaiians' position in this nation is still being con- sidered. Some possibilities are

1. A weighted voting system for public officials, within an electoral process such that the native vote would not be less than 50 percent of the total votes cast;
2. A bicameral legislature in which the members of one body would be selected exclusively by Native Hawaiian voters;
3. The creation of a council of customs, protocol, and *'aina* (land), within which certain matters would be controlled by Native Hawaiians; and
4. Special provisions for land rights, access and gather- ing rights, and other rights recognized by developing international organizations such as the International Labour Office and the United Nations.

Many more challenges to United States rule in Hawai'i are coming to public notice. In the schools, children are refusing to join in the morning pledge of allegiance to the United States and to stand for the national anthem. Other Hawaiians are refusing to file tax returns or to pay income taxes. More and more people charged with criminal offenses are denying the jurisdiction of American courts over them. A groundswell of protest is being felt in Hawai'i. This groundswell has even affected the Hawai'i State Legislature. The joint houses of the legislature made the following statement:

Recognizing the Year 1993 as the 100th Year Since the Overthrow of the Independent Nation of Hawai'i

Whereas, the year 1993 holds special significance for everyone who has been a part of Hawai'i over the last 100 years for it marks the century point after the United States military committed the first overt act to over- throw the independent nation of Hawai'i; and

Whereas, the Legislature recognizes the increasing dis- cussions and debate here in Hawai'i and at the Congress of the United States of the consequence such an overt act of military aggression against a peaceful and indepen- dent nation has to the citizens and descendants of that nation today; and

Whereas, the Legislature believes that the proper status of Hawai'i's Indigenous people within the political regime of the State of Hawai'i and the United States of America has still not reached its final stage and is still in the process of evolution; and

Whereas, the Legislature recognizes the even broader issue of the proper status of all people, irrespective of race, to exercise the right to self-determination; and

Whereas, the Legislature believes that the full range of consideration of Hawai'i's people's rights and freedoms must be completely explored in order to bring about harmony within Hawai'i's society; . . . now, therefore,

BE IT RESOLVED by the House of Representatives of the Sixteenth Legislature of the State of Hawai'i, Regular Session of 1991, the Senate concurring, that the Legislature determines that the year 1993 should serve Hawai'i as a year of special reflection to the rights and dignities of the Native Hawaiians within the Hawaiian and the American societies; and

BE IT FURTHER RESOLVED that the Hawai'i Legislature determines that the year 1993 be a special time for Hawai'i, not only for special reflection of Native Hawaiians, but for questioning the present and future role of people of every race who today constitute the "Hawai'i society"; and

BE IT FURTHER RESOLVED that the Legislature encourages the promotion of debate revolving around the future of Hawai'i as a Pacific Island society, *within or without the United States of America* [italics added].

NOTES

1. See President Cleveland's address to the U.S. Congress on 18 December 1893: Executive Doc. no. 47, 53d Congress, 2d session, House of Representatives (Washington, DC: U.S. Government Printing Office, 1893).

2. Lili'uokalani, *Hawai'i's Story by Hawai'i's Queen* (Rutland, VT: Charles E. Tuttle Co., 1964).

THE BORDER CROSSED US
BORDER CROSSING ISSUES OF THE INDIGENOUS PEOPLES OF THE AMERICAS

Eileen M. Luna-Firebaugh

For many years, the Tohono O'odham Nation in Arizona has transported tribal members from Mexico to the United States through traditional border crossings for medical treatment. The nation is the only one in the United States that grants full enrollment to its people who are citizens of Mexico. Thus, Mexican citizens who are enrolled members are legally entitled to access health and other services provided by the tribe to all its members.

Since the recent militarization of the U.S.–Mexico border, these routine visits have become more rare and more dangerous. Frequently now, the tribal employees who provide the transportation for Mexican O'odham Nation members have been stopped and harassed by

Eileen Luna-Firebaugh, "The Border Crossed Us: Border Crossing Issues of the Indigenous People of the Americas" from *Wicazo Sa Review*, vol. 17, no. 1, Spring 2002, pp. 159–179. Notes have not been included in this article. See original.

U.S. Border Patrol agents. These agents, operating on the lands of the O'odham Nation, have made the nation's elders and others who suffer from tuberculosis, diabetes, and other life-threatening diseases return to Mexico if they lack U.S. documents. This insistence on official U.S. documentation, rather than recognizing Tohono O'odham Nation membership identification, strikes at the heart of Indian sovereignty and is the focus of this article.

While traditionally it is common for nation-states such as Canada, the United States, and Mexico to protect their borders, the requirement that official documentation be proffered for simple, short-term visits has not been required for most citizens of the North American continent.

This enlightened policy has been replicated in Europe with the European Commonwealth. However, with the hysteria that has resulted from the "Drug War" and the widespread fear of "illegal immigrants," the United States has militarized its northern and southern borders. This militarization has resulted in inconvenience for all border crossers, but has made border crossing by the continent's Indigenous extremely problematic.

Enhanced and restrictive border crossing procedures are an assault on Indigenous sovereignty as well as an assault on the cultural integrity of native societies. The laws of Canada, the United States, and Mexico restrict contacts between the indigenous as citizens of their nations, and as members of families, clans, and religious groups that predate the colonization of the North American continent. The new laws (and regulations) also increase the level of danger for the indigenous. Those who continue to use traditional border crossing areas are in danger of being shot by U.S. Border Patrol personnel, U.S. military, or vigilante citizen groups. For a young Texas shepherd named Ezequiel, U.S. military personnel who opened fire while he tended his goatherd along the Texas-Mexico border cut life short. His death, and the deaths of others, is a result of the increased militarization of the U.S.–Mexico border.

The treaties and agreements that set the international boundaries between the nation-states of the North American continent were negotiated and signed *only* by the colonizers. The indigenous of these border regions, whose lands these borders transect, were not consulted, nor were they signatories to any treaty or agreement. This stands in clear opposition to their rights as nations who were, at that time, fully sovereign, and whose status as sovereign was recognized in later treaties between them and the colonizers. In addition, the fact that some Indigenous nations are mentioned in the colonizers' treaties and some are not, or that some Indigenous nations later negotiated separate treaties or agreements to protect their right to access their traditional lands on either side of the borders, has contributed to a patchwork approach to border crossing rights. While in some cases treaties or agreements have largely resolved the problem for some Indigenous groups, the general failure of the colonizing governments to allow indigenous input into the resolution of border issues has furthered the assault on the sovereignty of Indigenous nations of the North American continent.

The laws that require declaration of citizenship or official documents issued by the colonizing powers are a denigration of the nationhood of Indigenous peoples. A declaration of citizenship in the Tohono

O'odham, Mohawk, Blackfeet, Yaqui, Kickapoo, Cocopah, Kumeyaay, or other Indigenous nations, in response to a question asked by border officials, often results in extended delay and intensive interrogation. Thus all but the most committed Indigenous activist is forced to simply respond "U.S.," "Mexico," or "Canada" to a request for identifying citizenship.

The assertion of the right to cross the international border without undue delay is a long-standing problem. The Indigenous nations of the Americas have attempted to resolve this problem through treaties, legislation, negotiations, and/or direct action. The problem has different parameters on the northern and southern borders of the United States, largely due to historical legacies. The legislative approach has had varying levels of success, with failure often a result of federal action or lack thereof and sometimes attributable to tribal inaction or disagreement. Negotiation and direct action have been effective in some ways, particularly in focusing attention on legal, cultural, and historical inequities, although they result in limited agreements affecting Indigenous nations on a piecemeal basis. These approaches have focused attention on the inequities. The development of a concerted approach by Indigenous nations and peoples is necessary if the problem is to be finally resolved.

The Indigenous nations of the North American continent have been pursuing different avenues. For some, enhanced activism is reaching a boiling point. Other Indigenous peoples are asserting the rights of their citizens and of their nations in a formalized, legalistic manner. The manner in which these assertions of rights may best proceed needs to be considered. The critical question is whether it is proper for nation-states to deny Indigenous peoples access to their traditional sites, regardless of which side of an international border they are on, or to restrict their family contacts or the continuance of their religions and cultures. These issues for the Indigenous of the North American continent must be addressed if indigenous cultures and traditions are to survive.

In this paper I will attempt to describe the scope and dimensions of the problems of border crossing faced by various Indigenous nations through an examination of the patterns of impact and attempted resolution.

THE HISTORY OF THE PROBLEM

Prior to the setting of the U.S. borders with Canada and Mexico, Indigenous peoples had traditional territories with boundaries that were recognized and honored by their neighbors. Villages and other types of settlements existed where water, agricultural possibilities, and trade made the location reasonable. When, however, the international borders were drawn up, little if any regard was given to the separation of native villages, and native nations were not consulted. The lines imposed by the colonizers ignored traditional hunting lands, areas of resource procurement, and religious sites. This complicates political situations throughout the world today. In Uganda and Rwanda, Serbia and Croatia, Jerusalem, and Berlin, lines were drawn and lands awarded without regard for the interest and wishes of the peoples of those lands. Not surprisingly, turmoil has resulted.

The fiction of new boundary lines extended even to the renaming of the Indigenous peoples; for example, the Blackfeet in the United States were named the Blood in Canada. The lines also created division and divisiveness. While the Blackfeet were originally one people, this artificial division began to erode their self-identity, and they have come to see themselves as separate peoples. The colonizing nations afforded their Indigenous groups different rights, which caused further erosion in the continuity of tradition and peoplehood, and also led to factionalism. Indigenous groups have resisted this separation of peoples and have continued their struggle to remain cohesive.

The experiences of some Indigenous peoples split by the borders were very different from the Blackfeet. For some the cultural ties of the people were maintained. For others the ties were severed, the impacts on the culture and traditions were horrific, and there were economic consequences. We will examine these experiences and the ways in which some of these nations have tried to resist the assertions of authority by colonizing powers.

The Northern Border

The United States and England signed over twenty treaties to delineate the northern border. Rights of the Indigenous are mentioned in two, the Treaty of Amity, Commerce, and Navigation of 1794 (otherwise known as the Jay Treaty) and the 1814 Treaty of Peace and Amity (also known as the Treaty of Ghent). The Jay Treaty establishes the right of free passage across the border to Indians dwelling on either side of the border, by either land or inland navigation, into the territories of either Canada or the United States, to navigate all the lakes, rivers, and waters of each country, and to freely engage in trade or commerce with other Indigenous nations. No custom duties are to be assessed against the personal property of any Indian exercising their right to cross. The Treaty of Ghent restored the rights set forth in the Jay Treaty, which had eroded due to the War of 1812.

The United States and Canada treat the Jay Treaty differently; the Canadian government recognizes the rights for Indians per se, and the United States interprets the rights within a political context. The rights and the specific meaning and application of the provisions of the treaty have been addressed and readdressed in the courts of these two nations in a number of legal cases. There has also been legislation that has established restrictions of the rights set forth in the treaty.

Subsequent to the Treaty of Ghent, and prior to 1924, Canadian Indians were allowed free passage into the United States without the production of immigrant visas. However, political winds shifted in the United States during the 1920s, and with the passage of the 1924 Immigration and Naturalization Act, aliens (including Canadian Indians) who were ineligible for citizenship were not permitted as immigrants. This legislation, coupled with the Citizenship Act of 1924, which awarded U.S. citizenship to all Indians born within the boundaries of the United States, was interpreted to mean that Canadian Indians could no longer cross the U.S. border freely, despite the rights guaranteed in the Jay Treaty and the Treaty of Ghent.

The reaffirmation of Jay Treaty rights began again with the U.S. Supreme Court ruling *in U.S. ex rel. Diabo v. McCandless*. In *Diabo*, the plaintiff, a Canadian Mohawk, challenged his deportation under the 1924 Immigration Act, citing the Jay Treaty's guarantees. The court held that the right of free passage in traditional Indigenous homelands is an inherent aboriginal right, even where an international border has been created subsequently. In language that emphasized the Court's holding, the Court stated:

> [T]he rights of Indians [are not] in any way affected by the treaty, whether now existent or not. The reference to them was merely the *recognition* of their right, which was wholly unaffected by the treaty, except that the contracting parties agreed with each other that each would recognize it. . . . From the Indian['s] viewpoint, he crosses no boundary line. For him, this [boundary line] does not exist.

This right of free passage for Indigenous peoples on the northern border was then codified in changes to the Immigration and Nationality Act. However, later amendments to this act further restricted free passage rights. The 1952 act, perhaps reflecting the assimilation and termination era of the time, restricted free passage to those Indians who met a 50 percent blood quantum requirement. This has gradually been changed, perhaps as a result of the era of self-governance, to now allow free passage to any Indian who possesses a tribal membership identification card.

The treaties that exist between Canada and the United States, with regard to the border crossing rights of affected indigenous, have been tested far more often than those treaties that exist between the governments of Mexico and the United States. While the issues for the U.S.–Mexico border may appear to be less complex, that is an illusion. There is only one treaty, with the Kickapoo Tribe of Texas, that deals with the right of passage for the U.S.–Mexico border. The rest of the border area and the Indigenous nations of this region are without any guidelines set forth in treaties or legislation. The result is chaos, a patchwork of executive and administrative agreements, and failed legislation that is difficult to understand or resolve.

The Southern Border

In the southern border area, traditional Indigenous homelands became subject to Spanish colonialism; then in 1821, as a result of Mexico's independence, they came under the authority of the Mexican government. Although the traditional homelands were recognized, the Indigenous peoples were considered citizens of Mexico. No tribal sovereignty was considered or honored. Most of the homelands in Sonora and Chihuahua were then lost, largely through the policy that Mexican citizens were required to apply for land grants. The Indigenous, probably due to their geographic remoteness, inability to speak Spanish, and migratory nature, either failed to receive notice of the land grant process or had no knowledge of it.

The Treaty of Guadalupe-Hidalgo in 1848 split part of the lands off from Mexico. It required that the United States honor the land grants extended by the Mexican government and covered the lands of the Rio Grande, from the Gulf of Mexico to the Pacific. The long-settled Pueblos of New Mexico had received land grant homelands. However, no land grants were created for the Yuman, Apache, O'odham, Kumeyaay, or other Indigenous peoples of the region who did not live in villages. The new border split the traditional homelands of these Indigenous peoples, and they were left without any right of free passage.

MAIN TYPES OF CONFLICT AND ATTEMPTS AT RESOLUTION

While the histories of the northern and southern borders are distinct, Indigenous peoples experienced problems in common: economic, cultural, and demographic. These problems are the result of the impact of colonialism/imperialism on peoples and culture, their historic resettlement patterns, migration patterns, individual lives, and on the individual and cultural responses to colonialism. The Indigenous communities were seriously affected by the creation of international borders. Dislocation, encroachment on the land, loss of traditional homesteads, inability to control and traverse over traditional lands, colonization, loss of mobility and traditional contacts became the norm. Conflict between Indigenous and colonial governments became entrenched. Over time, as many Indian peoples began to think of themselves as Canadian, Mexican, or American first and Indigenous second, the traditional relationships among relatives eroded, and distinctions were perceived.

The individual experiences that some groups of Indigenous peoples faced illuminate the situation for most, if not all, of the peoples of the border regions. The nations chosen for this article are ones that have been politically or legally involved in this issue and have undertaken direct action and/or legal and legislative attempts at resolution.

The Blackfeet, Blood, Sissika, and Piegan Nations

Members of the Blackfeet Confederacy were split by the creation of the U.S.–Canada border. Six bands were on the Canadian side and only one within the boundaries of the United States. While there were few problems with regard to retaining the right to cross the border at will, most obstacles relate to the import and export of certain tariff-free goods, native traditions, and religious ceremonies. Blackfeet ceremonies are commonly conducted with participants from all bands from both sides of the border and require the use of special ritual paraphernalia. According to their tradition, only men are allowed to touch the sacred bundles used in the ceremonies. When ceremonial bundles are carried across the border, this tradition has sometimes been violated by female customs officers.

In order to resolve the problem of import–export regulations and inspection, in the 1980s the Blood Tribe established a border committee, composed of band members, to negotiate for the passage of legislation in Canada. To date, this effort has been unsuccessful. The efforts have also included a call by confederacy leaders from both sides of the border for an Indian-only border crossing between Alberta and Montana. These initiatives are ongoing at this time.

The Akwesasne Mohawk

The land of the Mohawk of the Saint Regis Indian Nation is split between New York State and Quebec. Even though the Mohawk utilized these lands traditionally, the Canadian government has taken the position in court cases that they moved into Canada subsequent to the Jay Treaty. The Canadian government has thus contended that the Mohawk may not avail themselves of the protections granted by the treaty.

The Mohawk Indian Nation has no official U.S. customs crossing. Mohawks have generally taken direct action by crossing their traditional lands at will and disregarding the imposed borderline. They have taken the position that the Mohawk Nation is sovereign and undivided. Since 1815, they have asserted that the border is largely irrelevant, a notion that was not functionally opposed nor directly challenged by the nation-states.

Prior to the militarization of the U.S. border in the 1990s, citizens of the Mohawk Nation had full access to all Mohawk land whether those lands were within the territories of Canada or the United States. The Oka crisis in March 1990 inflamed a situation that was already intense. The U.S. Immigration and Naturalization Service (INS) has repeatedly entered Mohawk lands in pursuit of undocumented aliens and those who smuggle them across the U.S.–Canada border. This intrusion into Mohawk lands continues to date and is as yet unresolved.

The Mohawks have also asserted their rights under the Jay Treaty to take personal goods across the border without payment of customs duties. They have engaged in the transportation of cigarettes for sale, without payment of tax, and in the transportation of immigrants in noncompliance with the immigration laws of the United States. This upping of the economic ante by the Mohawk resulted in the heightened enforcement and legal response by the nation-states in the 1990s. From this case, it appears that the nation-states are unconcerned about Indigenous peoples until economic interests are at stake.

The Tohono O'odham

In 1848, subsequent to the U.S. war with Mexico, the Treaty of Guadalupe-Hidalgo was signed. This treaty ceded the land south of the Gila River to Mexico, thus locating all O'odham land in Mexico. This became a problem for the United States when it decided that a southern rail route to California was needed. As a result, in 1853 the United States purchased almost 30,000 acres in Mexico. The Gadsden Purchase included approximately half of the Tohono O'odham traditional homelands. The rest remained in Sonora, Mexico. This division of the O'odham lands resulted in a border area that is longer than that of the state of New Mexico and Chihuahua.

The effect was devastating for Mexican O'odham people and their culture. Contacts between families were severed and the political history and government structure diverged sharply. The land base of the Mexican O'odham was eroded, and religious and cultural connections to land on both sides of the border were lost to those on the other side.

In order to rectify this situation, the Tohono O'odham adopted and enrolled the Mexican members in the tribe. The Mexican O'odham vote in tribal elections and receive services provided in the U.S. O'odham health clinic. The O'odham maintain an unofficial border crossing on tribal lands that, while known to U.S. Customs, is not regulated by the U.S. government.

The Cocopah

The culture, history, and traditions of the Cocopah are inextricably linked to the Colorado River. They were a seminomadic people who farmed in the floodplain of the river, with villages extending into what are now California, Arizona, Sonora, and Baja California. Those Cocopah who found themselves on the northern side of the U.S.–Mexico border were able to retain their lands, while those on the southern side lost control of their lands and were forced to live within the encomienda system.

Cocopah communities and clans were first split by the Gadsden Purchase, with the majority in Mexico and a small group in the United States. The border originally meant little, and the Cocopah moved freely along the river. However, in the late 1930s, the INS cracked down on this free passage and effectively split the people into two nationalities. After the crackdown, the Cocopah developed an unofficial agreement with the INS that allowed for freedom of passage of Mexican Cocopah into the United States.

The Cocopah were impacted by heightened border crossing controls earlier than other border tribes, possibly because their land is adjacent to a primary river-crossing area. Control of the water of the Colorado was crucial for the United States, particularly during the 1930s when there was rampant agricultural and residential development of Southern California. Thus, due to the accident of geographical location, the Cocopah were seriously affected at a much earlier date than other Indigenous nations along the borders.

The Yaqui

Due to historic migration patterns, some tribes experience border crossing problems even if the border did not split their traditional lands. The Yaqui, or Yoeme, were one such affected people.

The Yaqui were originally centered in the Yaqui River valley near Guaymas in Sonora with a culture that focused on agriculture. The Yaqui were traders and traveled throughout northern Sonora and southern Arizona. After contact the Yaqui entered into an alliance with the Spanish Jesuits and soldiers against the Apache. This alliance did not ease the relationship between the Yaqui and the new state of Mexico, however. During the late 1800s Mexican expansion forced the relocation of many bands of Yaqui and scattered the people across Mexico and into the United States. Others were pushed into the mountains where they waged a guerrilla war against hacienda families and the Mexican military. Some Yaqui relocated to Arizona, settling in and around Tucson and Phoenix. Cultural and religious ties between the villages and bands on both sides of the border continued, however, even in the face of great difficulty.

The ability to conduct ceremonies is essential for the lands to truly become and remain a homeland. For some ceremonies to be held, it is necessary for participants to travel from one nation-state to the other. The increased militarization of the southern border of the United States has resulted in travel restrictions and cultural and religious disruption.

The Kickapoo

The Kickapoo originated in the Great Lakes region and moved from place to place as a result of broken land treaties and a desire to resist the forces of colonization. Some Kickapoo were forced to live in Kansas and Oklahoma, while others fled to Mexico in the 1800s.

In 1832 U.S. Army officials granted tribal members in Mexico the "right of safe conduct" to cross the border into the United States. An 1850 land agreement between the Mexican government and the Kickapoo south of the border granted tribal members the same rights as Mexican citizens and a small reservation in Coahuila. This arrangement has continued to this day. Legislation during the 1990s guaranteed rights of passage for Mexican Kickapoo.

During the 1940s the Mexican Kickapoo were forced to relocate again. Due to a protracted drought and rapid industrialization in the area of their reservation, Mexican Kickapoos began to work in the United States as migrant laborers. Their right to cross the border encouraged their hire through the Bracero program. Many worked in the agricultural fields of the United States during the harvest season and returned home to their reservation during the winter.

The Kumeyaay

The Kumeyaay reside in scattered villages in Baja California and in rancherias and reservations in Southern California. The Kumeyaay traditionally were coastal people, living along the Pacific Ocean. They were ultimately forced inland into eastern San Diego County and further into Mexico.

Until 1993 Kumeyaay routinely crossed from their homes in Baja California into San Diego County, using inexpensive border crossing cards that they obtained from the Instituto Nacional Indigenista (INI), the Mexican counterpart of the Bureau of Indian Affairs (BIA). Unfortunately, the U.S. Border Patrol apprehended non-Kumeyaay using these passes and subsequently refused to accept them, forcing Kumeyaay to obtain Mexican passports for border crossing. The cost of the passports, and the inability of many Kumeyaay to provide the necessary documentation to obtain them, has resulted in a severe restriction of the ability of the Kumeyaay to cross the border.

THE INDIVIDUAL APPROACH TO BORDER CROSSING

In their attempts to continue or reestablish the traditional religious, cultural, and social connections with their relatives across the borders of the nation-states, Indigenous individuals have faced a number of obstacles. In turn, they have established several means to overcome the nation-state-imposed barriers. Over the years, many Indigenous peoples have simply ignored the legalisms of border crossing.

Informal crossing gates were opened on tribal land and were generally used by Indigenous peoples for tribal purposes. However, the recent increased militarization of the border region by the INS, Border Patrol, and U.S. Customs agents cracking down on undocumented aliens and the drug trade has closed many traditional crossing areas. Along the southern border of the United States, many agents are unaware of the inhabitants' ancient migratory ways and customary rights. They have disrupted long-held understandings of the right of mobility throughout traditional Indigenous homelands.

Southwest tribal governments have become concerned about the effects related to this increased border militarization, including stopping, searching, and in some cases the forced return to Mexico of tribal members. In San Diego County, for example, U.S. Border Patrol agents have subjected the Kumeyaay to repeated stops and detentions. This is unacceptable and has resulted in discriminatory behavior. As Mike Connolly, Campo Reservation director of environmental programs stated, "This is our land, and we've been here for thousands of years. It's tough when you're being stopped all the time and asked if you really belong there." Tribes have also been concerned about degradation of tribal land by federal officials, cutting of roads into sensitive and/or sacred lands, and high-speed pursuits over tribal roads, some of which are unpaved, activities that endanger tribal members and livestock.

Indigenous organizations, including the Indian Defense League of America, have taken a confrontational approach to border agents' activities. Members of this organization have, for seventy-one years, organized annual protests along the U.S.–Canada border. Tribal members from the Iroquois Confederacy engage in direct action, making commemorative crossings of the international border at various sites.

Tribal governments have attempted to resolve these issues through meetings and conciliations, which to date have not shown much success. Federal officials have not indicated full support of tribal sovereignty, particularly if it would require seriously addressing tribal concerns. Federal officials have generally responded to the concerns as if they were being communicated by a local government rather than by a sovereign nation. This denies each nation their rights to conduct international relations. Meanwhile Indian peoples on both sides of both U.S. borders have had their routine contacts and social interactions restricted, and border crossing for tribal ceremonies, funerals, and other gatherings have been made much more difficult.

THE LEGISLATIVE APPROACH TO RESOLVING BORDER CROSSING ISSUES

Congressional approaches to resolution of the issues facing the tribes on the southwest border have been spotty at best. The success of the legislative approach depends on the willingness of the federal governments to seriously address the problem, the willingness of the individual tribes to pursue a legislative strategy, and the cooperation of governmental agencies to abide by agreements. For some tribes, the legislative approach has worked well. Legal rights have been established and protected. For others, the approach has been problematic. Legislators have been unwilling to support Indigenous rights, or the tribes have faltered in their attempts to convince their own people or legislators of the wisdom of such a strategy.

Legislation Related to the Texas Band of Kickapoo

The legislative strategy has served the Kickapoo well. During the 1950s the INS granted parole status to the Kickapoo, pursuant to the Immigration and Nationality Act of 1952. Parole status allowed tribal members to cross the border freely with tribal identification cards; however, the cards had to be renewed every year and did not grant them permanent rights to cross the border.

In 1983, the Texas Band of Kickapoo Act was passed, which mandated that tribal membership cards would be sufficient for border passage. It further included that the tribe would be a party to the decision about identification requirements. A tribal roll was established, and members on the roll had five years to apply for U.S. citizenship. Once citizenship was granted, a permanent border crossing card was issued. The Kickapoo who were not U.S. citizens received all citizenship rights other than the right to vote and to hold public office.

The act clarified citizenship for members of the band. However, it did not alter their land status or other rights in Mexico. The act makes band members eligible for Indian services and programs, and provides for consent and cooperation with Mexican officials to ensure the provision of appropriate services for the band. The Texas Band of Kickapoo and a separate Kickapoo tribe are now seeking to expand the rights provided for in the act to tribal members who live in the United States but travel to Mexico each winter for traditional ceremonies.

Legislative Approaches of the Tohono O'odham

The Tohono O'odham Nation has pursued legislation for a number of years. In 1987 a bill was introduced by Morris Udall (D. Arizona) to clarify the right of free passage for members of the Tohono O'odham Nation. The bill provided for the establishment of a tribal roll, and it would have empowered all those on the roll to pass freely across the U.S.–Mexico border and to live and work in the United States. The Reagan administration had serious misgivings about this bill, however. They wanted border crossing privileges extended only to U.S.-residing tribal members and a restriction of the services that would be provided to Mexican O'odham while in the United States. The tribe agreed to compromise on these two clauses. A third clause became the sticking point. The federal government wanted the O'odham to cross only at official border crossings. For the O'odham this was absolutely unacceptable.

While the crossing at official federal crossing points had not been a problem for the Kickapoo, for the O'odham it was an attack on who they were as a people and as a sovereign nation. The Kickapoo had been in the border area for approximately 150 years, a relatively short time for Indigenous inhabitants. The requirement that they pass through at an official crossing was not a cultural or traditional assault. On the other hand, the O'odham had been in the area since time immemorial. They had ancient migratory routes and settlement sites that were still important culturally: The tribe was unwilling to give up these traditional crossing places on tribal land. When this could not be resolved, the tribe requested that the sponsor of the bill pull it from consideration. This assertion of tribal sovereignty and commitment to tradition has become a signpost of the struggle for the O'odham.

In 1998, the Tohono O'odham pursued legislative relief for a second time. The bill, sponsored by Ed Pastor, addressed many of the issues left unresolved in the previous legislative attempt. It included the right of passage at any gate on traditional Indigenous lands, allowed the tribe to monitor these traditional gates; directed that federal officials ensure that their practices do not conflict with religious rights, customs, or traditions of the O'odham; required that federal officials negotiate with the tribe over policies and procedures to be followed on tribal lands; and held federal officials liable for damages under 42 U.S.C. 1983 and 1988 for violation of the right of free passage for the indigenous. This bill also suggested an amendment to Title 8 U.S.C. Sec. 1359, adding Indigenous peoples on the southern border to those on the northern border who have the legal right to free passage subsequent to the Jay Treaty.

This bill did not become law. The Mexican and U.S. governments failed to support it due to concerns regarding the traditional ports of entry. The Tohono O'odham also had misgivings, particularly related to the treatment of nation members as immigrant aliens if their residence was in Mexico. These and other concerns caused interest to lapse, resulting in the decision of Congressman Pastor not to pursue this legislative bill further.

The Tohono O'odham Nation has written and Congress is now considering the proposal of a new piece of legislation that will not raise the same issues of concern as the last. This bill would amend Chapter 2 of Title III of the Immigration and Nationality Act (8 U.S.C. 1421 et seq.) to read:

> To render all enrolled members of the Tohono O'odham Nation citizens of the United States as of the date of their enrollment and to recognize the valid membership credential of the Tohono O'odham Nation as the legal equivalent of a certificate of citizenship or a state-issued birth certificate for all federal purposes.
>
> Sec. 2. Naturalization for Tohono O'odham
>
> Sec. 323(a) Granting of Citizenship. A person who is listed on the official membership roll of the Tohono O'odham Nation, a federally recognized American Indian Nation located in Arizona, is a citizen of the United States as of the date on which such listing occurs.
>
> Sec. 3, treatment of Tribal Membership Credentials. Notwithstanding any other provision of law, the valid membership credential issued to a person who is listed on the official membership roll of the Tohono O'odham Nation pursuant to the laws of the Tohono O'odham Nation shall be considered, for all purposes subject to federal law, equivalent to
>
> (1) A certificate of citizenship issued under Section 341(a) of the Immigration and Nationality Act (8 U.S.C. 1452(a)) to persons who satisfy the requirements of such section; and
>
> (2) A state-issued birth certificate.

The language of this proposed bill explicitly recognizes the inherent sovereignty of the Tohono O'odham and the members of the nation as citizens of the nation. It further establishes that the documents of the nation are all that is necessary for recognition. The bill implicitly pushes back against the incursions of state law into Indian Country, as state-issued documents (such as a birth certificate issued by the state of Arizona) would no longer be required. This would greatly alleviate the problem for many Tohono O'odham, who were born at home during the early years of the twentieth century and do not possess Arizona birth certificates.

THE NEGOTIATION APPROACH

Efforts have been made by Indigenous peoples to resolve border crossing issues through the process of negotiations. Like legislative efforts, these efforts have met with varying levels of success.

Efforts of the Tohono O'odham

In addition to the new legislative proposal, the Tohono O'odham Nation has initiated a different approach, which attempts to avoid the difficulties inherent in the earlier pieces of legislation. The Tohono O'odham is the only Indian nation on the southern border of the United States that has full enrollment for its members in Mexico. Throughout 1999 and 2000, the nation held public meetings and confidential negotiation sessions with the U.S. and Mexican counsels and the U.S. Immigration Service in an attempt to administratively resolve the border crossing issues for its people.

Through negotiations, the U.S. and Mexican government agencies agreed to accept a birth or baptismal certificate or an identification document issued by the Tohono O'odham in lieu of the normally stringent paperwork required to cross the U.S.–Mexico border. Citizens of the nation who should be given priority for border crossing rights due to chronic medical conditions that required them to travel from their homes in Mexico to the nation's health center in the United States were identified, and the necessary paperwork was produced by the nation. Some 104 persons were so identified. By August of 1999, the U.S. Immigration and Naturalization Service had approved 88 of them for American laser visas. The U.S. and Mexican agencies have also agreed to provide visas for the rest of the nation's members residing in Mexico, approximately 1,238 people. One difficulty with this approach is that the nation is forced to shoulder the cost of establishing the identity of these tribal members, projected to be in excess of $100,000.

There is a further issue for many O'odham. Many activists, some of whom are members of the Council of the Nation, reject the idea that citizens of the nation should have to carry tribal identification

papers to cross over their own lands. If this should be approved, the O'odham would become the only people in the United States or Mexico who have to do so.

Efforts of the Yaqui

The Yaqui have made efforts to resolve border crossing issues for their people living in Rio Yaqui, in Sonora, Mexico. The pueblos of the Yaqui Nation of the United States routinely hold religious ceremonies to which ceremonial leaders and participants from Mexico are invited. In many instances, these Yaqui are essential to the ceremonies.

While some ceremonial leaders and participants from Mexico occasionally have been allowed to cross, often they have been refused. The right to cross the border and to carry ceremonial objects has sometimes depended on whether the individual INS officer, or the supervisor on duty, was familiar with the Yaqui and the ceremonial occasion. While the cost for Mexican passports and the inability to produce requisite documents to establish residency and employment are impediments to many Mexican indigenous, the Yaqui face an additional stumbling block, Due to their traditions and their religion, the young men of the Yaqui do not register for the Mexican military. Such registration is required for men under the age of 40 in order to obtain a Mexican passport. These men are thus precluded from crossing the border to participate in ceremonies in the United States.

In 1997 the Yaqui negotiated an agreement with the INS Regional Administration in Arizona. This agreement allowed the Yaqui ceremonial leaders in the United States to identify persons who were invited to the ceremonies and to sponsor their admission into the United States. A letter of sponsorship was sent to INS on a yearly basis, and the right to cross the border was approved.

Although this agreement has been in place for four years, it has not been universally successful. The right of Mexican Yaqui to cross the U.S.–Mexico border still depends on individual INS officials at the regional and border gate level and, unfortunately, the mood that they are in on any particular day.

Efforts of the Kumeyaay

The Kumeyaay have begun to work with Mexican and U.S. officials to provide Mexican passports and U.S. border crossing cards for Mexican Kumeyaay. In this effort the Kumeyaay have followed the approach taken by the Tohono O'odham. The U.S. Kumeyaay began conducting a census in the seven Mexican

Kumeyaay communities. This census will serve as the basis for verifying the status of Mexican Kumeyaay as tribal members of the U.S. Kumeyaay Nation. Once citizenship in the Kumeyaay Nation is established, the nation will provide the requisite formal identification of Kumeyaay who seek travel papers into the United States.

The Litigation Approach

Cases have been brought by Indigenous nations and tribal members to seek to enforce the provisions of the Jay Treaty and the Treaty of Ghent, and to extend those rights to all Indian peoples of the Americas. A recent case sought to clarify that the right of free passage for North American indigenous set forth in the Jay Treaty included the right to purchase and transport goods across the border. Under the treaty, such goods were to be exempt from duty or taxes, so long as they were for personal use. This has changed somewhat, and now the right to transport goods duty-free has been restricted by statute and case law.

In a number of Canadian cases, Canadian Indians were required to pay duty on items for personal use being brought into Canada from the United States, The courts upheld the custom duty since the items being transported (a washing machine, a refrigerator, and an oil heater) were not unusual or unique to Indians. The duty was further upheld since there was no local or municipal ordinance that incorporated the provisions of the Jay Treaty.

In a more recent Canadian case, the former grand chief of the Akwesasne Mohawks challenged the Canadian minister of national revenue over the interpretation of treaties. The plaintiff, Mike Mitchell, asserted that the treaties guaranteed Mohawks duty-free access across the Canada–U.S. border. The Canadian government argued that the Mohawks were immigrants to Canada in 1755 and thus could not claim aboriginal rights in Canada pursuant to the Jay Treaty. The Canadian government also asserted that, as the Iroquoian peoples traditionally charged each other duties to cross their lands, this same right could be asserted by Canada.

The courts of the United States have made similar interpretations of the rights contained in the Jay Treaty. Duties have been attached to Indian-made baskets being brought from Canada into the United States, where the court held that the right to import depends on statutory authority, not the Jay Treaty. In 1977, the U.S. Court confirmed in *Akins v. United States* that a duty applied to goods that were brought into the United States for personal use and not for resale. However, this case let stand a previous ruling by the U.S. District Court of Maine that Indians had the right to pass the border without undue restriction or restraint.

Very recently the right of Canadian Indians to work in the United States was supported by the Arizona courts. In this instance, a Canadian Mohawk had been hired by the Tohono O'odham police department as a police officer. The Arizona Peace Officer Standards and Training (POST) board, which certifies officers, declared that he was not eligible to be a state-certified peace officer because he had not been born in the United States.

The tribe challenged this decision pursuant to the Jay Treaty, which allows natives of the Saint Regis Mohawk Nation to travel between Canada and the United States and to live and work where they choose. While the Jay Treaty was referred to as "old" and "obscure," the Arizona POST board decided to honor its provisions and granted state certification to this officer.

THE INTERNATIONAL APPROACH

The United Nations

Article 27 of the International Covenant on Civil and Political Rights affirms the right of persons belonging to "ethnic, linguistic or religious minorities . . . to enjoy their own culture, to profess and practice their own religion [and] to use their own language." For the indigenous of the North American continent, the rights guaranteed in this covenant are clearly violated by the restrictions to travel across the U.S.–Mexico and U.S.–Canada borders.

To use the Tohono O'odham as an example, there are religious sites on traditional lands that lie on both sides of the U.S.–Mexico border. On an annual basis, many O'odham make a pilgrimage to Magdalena de Kino, Sonora, Mexico, a tradition of Sonoran Desert Catholicism. At other times, O'odham travel to Boboquivari, a sacred mountain on O'odham lands north of the U.S.–Mexico border. Those O'odham without the legal right to travel into Mexico or into the United States are clearly inhibited in their right to practice their own religion, as established by the International Covenant on Civil and Political Rights.

The UN Human Rights Committee and the Inter-American Commission on Human Rights of the Organization of American States have also recognized the need to protect Indigenous rights. These entities have held their "cultural integrity" norm to cover all aspects of an Indigenous group's survival as a distinct culture, understanding culture to include land-use patterns as well as religious practices.

The proposed American Declaration on the Rights of Indigenous Peoples, adopted on June 5, 1997, at the seventh plenary session of the Inter-American Commission on Human Rights of the Organization of American States, specifically sets forth the following:

> Article XVIII. Traditional forms of ownership and cultural survival. Rights to land, territories and resources . . .
>
> 2. Indigenous peoples have the right to the recognition of their property and ownership rights with respect to lands, territories and resources they have historically occupied, as well as to the use of those to which they have historically had access for their traditional activities and livelihood.

International Indigenous Collaboration

The national Indigenous organizations of Canada and the United States have recognized the problem of border passage; however, little has been done politically to try to resolve this issue. In 1988, a regional border rights meeting was held in Idaho, attended by a number of U.S. and Canadian tribes. A policy statement was issued that addressed the right of free border passage of the indigenous, based upon traditional rights of mobility and of the rights guaranteed in the Jay Treaty and the Treaty of Ghent. Certain demands were set forth, including:

1. The right of Indian nations to identify their own nationals
2. The right to be in, travel in, work in, reside in, use the territory of their nations
3. The right to transport their possessions with them and to trade freely with other Indian people
4. The right to receive services in each country on the same basis as other people of their nations

The policy statement contained a number of recommendations that revolved around the creation of a U.S.–Canadian international joint commission, composed of an equal number of representatives from each country and including Native American representation. The commission would have jurisdiction to resolve border disputes or problems, would oversee border stations, and would develop a "cohesive and consistent border crossing policy" for Canada and the United States. While this policy statement was far-reaching and visionary, it unfortunately did not include representation of the indigenous along the U.S.–Mexico border.

One Canadian noted for his criticism of Indian Affairs was quoted as saying in regard to the proposed policy, "This is moving in the wrong direction. I can't for the life of me understand why they would need a special border crossing, unless they're beginning to see themselves as people with no border." This is precisely what began to publicly emerge in the resolve of many cross-border Native peoples.

While nothing came of this policy statement, the issue did not go away. Border issues for the tribes along the U.S.–Mexico border were a continuous problem that received substantial publicity. There were also continued free mobility issues along the U.S.–Canada border. Culminating this decade of continued problems, a joint meeting between Canada's Assembly of First Nations (AFN) and the U.S. National Congress of American Indians (NCAI) was held in July 1999. Indigenous representatives from Mexico (and indeed, throughout the world) attended the meeting, giving new hope for a concerted effort to resolve the issue of indigenous mobility across the imposed borders of their traditional lands.

The Indigenous nations along the U.S.–Mexico border have, since 1997, been active in Alianza Indigina Sin Fronteras (Indigenous Alliance without Borders). This organization, supported by the American Friends Service Committee, includes representatives from the Yaqui, Tohono O'odham, Texas Kickapoo, Kumeyaay, and Gila River Pima/Maricopa peoples from both sides of the border. It emphasizes the development and maintenance of cultural, religious, and, personal ties among Indigenous peoples, as well as organizing and supporting the approaches to resolution undertaken by their members.

Statements made by Indigenous leaders have been striking in their assertion of traditional passage rights. As Tohono O'odham councilman Kenneth Williams stated, "We were here long before other countries were established . . . We are not immigrants. It just so happened that they put the line between us."[4] Chief Ernie Campbell, of the Musqueam Nation, stated, "We did not put any line or border anywhere to separate us. There are no borders among our people." This position was supported by the AFN national chief Phil Fontaine when he declared that the delegates to the joint meeting of NCAI and AFN were "divided by locality but united by common origin and destiny," and further by H. Ron Allen, president of NCAI, when he stated, "We are crossing over this international border that we do not know and do not recognize."

CONCLUSION

The problem of free movement over international borders exists for many of the Indigenous nations of North America. Many of these nations have made repeated attempts to resolve the border crossing issues for their people. Unfortunately, few of these attempts at resolution have been wholly successful.

The traditional approach, while expedient and supportable by many who dislike the necessity of treating with the colonizers, puts those who use it in legal jeopardy. Often, those indigenous seeking to exercise their traditional rights have been apprehended by federal agents. In some instances indigenous have been detained, arrested, or forcibly returned across the international border. Often ceremonial objects have been disrespectfully mishandled, and ceremonial participants have been subjected to questioning and even ridicule.

The litigation approach relies on the decision of the courts of the colonizer, something that is of concern to many indigenous, who contend that the assertion of their traditional rights do not belong in such a forum. Taking cases and issues to court may have favorable results. However, judges or juries who are hostile to the rights and interests of the indigenous may also render decisions that have a negative impact. When this happens, adverse decisions and case law may be set for a significant period of time.

The legislative approach can be highly effective. As Indigenous nations become more active and effective politically, this approach may have a high likelihood of success. However, the development and passage of legislation can be time consuming and, as it depends upon the political will of elected officials, has a high likelihood of compromise, which may result in unsatisfactory results.

Proceeding through international bodies is a compelling approach for Indigenous nations. It strengthens the assertion of nationhood for Indigenous nations and allows for the utilization of covenants already drafted by international bodies such as the United Nations and the Organization of American States. One problem however, is that the United States is not a signatory, to many of these international covenants and thus can contend that it is not bound. In addition, the United States has also refused to recognize the Indigenous nations within the United States as fully sovereign and has resisted their participation in such international organizations as governmental entities.

A further issue is that, given the inherent sovereignty of Indigenous nations, they have tended to proceed independently in their attempts at resolution of border crossing issues. Different approaches have been undertaken, with varying measures of success. Little collaboration has occurred among affected Indigenous nations. However, it is in this area that there is real potential for success.

The joint meeting held by the National Congress of American Indians and the Assembly of First Nations is an initial step toward effective action. The effort made by Alianza Indigena Sin Fronteras to coordinate and support the efforts of U.S.–Mexican Indigenous nations is also worthwhile. However, the efforts are, to date, not coordinated.

Given the imbalance of power held by the federal governments of Canada, the United States, and Mexico, it would be wise for the Indigenous nations of North America, through their respective organizations, to coordinate their efforts to resolve this issue. A unified approach by the Indigenous nations of this continent, through their empowered organizations, could focus the world's attention on the issue of the right to maintain traditional contacts and ceremonies. This approach could force the colonizers to give new consideration to the traditional rights of the indigenous and to the rights guaranteed in laws and treaties. In this way, advancement might be made not only to the resolution of border crossing issues, but also perhaps to the maintenance and protection of other rights long ignored or forgotten.

6

GENOCIDE OF CALIFORNIA INDIANS

Steve Talbot

On January 24, 1848, gold was discovered on the South Fork of the American River in California. One hundred and fifty years later, the state of California observed the sesquicentennial of the 1849 gold rush. The anniversary, however, was no cause for celebration among California Indians. The Spanish mission system, the seizure of California from Mexico by the United States, the influx of thousands of American miners and settlers, and California statehood—all had disastrous consequences for the Indian peoples. Sherburne Cook, an expert on California Indian demography, found that between 1770 and 1900 the Native population experienced a fall from 310,000 to approximately 20,000, a decline of over 90 percent.

GENOCIDE

Given the enormity of the population decline and its rapidity following the gold rush, it is appropriate to examine the concept of genocide as defined in international law. The Convention on the Prevention and Punishment of the Crime of Genocide was unanimously adopted by the United Nations General Assembly on December 9, 1948. It became international law following World War II in recognition of the crimes against humanity committed by Nazi Germany that annihilated millions of people because of their religions or ethnic origins. Ninety-seven nations have ratified the Convention, Most of them within a few years after its passage, but it was not ratified by the United States Senate until 1985 after almost thirty-six years of delay and contentious debate.

The Genocide Convention outlaws the commission of certain acts with intent to destroy, wholly or in part, a national, ethnic, racial, or religious group. What is less known is that the scope of the Convention is much broader than forbidding the actual killing of such groups. The Convention also includes acts of causing serious bodily or mental harm; the deliberate infliction of conditions of life calculated to bring about physical destruction; imposing measures to prevent birth; and forcibly transferring children of one group to another group. Furthermore, the definition includes not only the commission of such acts as punishable, but also the conspiracy to commit genocide, the direct and public incitement, the attempt to commit, and complicity. The Convention specifies that it is genocide whether such acts are committed in a time of peace or in a time of war.

An examination of the California Indian case makes it absolutely clear that the crime of genocide was committed indirectly during the Spanish and Mexican periods of hegemony and directly by the Americans following the 1849 gold rush. The information contained in this essay can provide only a brief outline of the scope of the tragedy.

SPAIN AND THE MISSION SYSTEM

The Spanish period of conquest introduced a system of religious missions that began in 1769 and ended in 1821. Spanish policy was to convert the Indians to Christianity and to use Indian labor to further Spanish economic aims. A chain of twenty-one Franciscan missions were established along a narrow section of the California coast from San Diego in the south to San Francisco in the north. The Spaniards also founded civilian towns (*pueblos*) and military garrisons (*presidios*). In the countryside were *ranchos*, where soldiers and settlers grazed stock using Indian labor.

By 1805 there were twenty thousand neophytes (Indian converts to Christianity) in the Spanish missions. Although Indian persons were recognized as human beings with souls and limited rights, Spanish laws nevertheless permitted armed Spaniards to round up the peaceful coastal Indians and impress

Steve Talbot, "California Indians, Genocide of," in the Encyclopedia of American Indian History, vol. 1, pp. 226–231. © 2008 ABC-CLIO Publishers. Reprinted with permission of ABC-CLIO, LLC.

them into *de facto* slavery. The Indian lands seized were then held in trust by the Spanish crown under the *encomienda* system, by which the Spanish administered their colonies. California became, in effect, a Spanish military colony. Spanish policy was not to annihilate the Native population directly, as occurred later during the gold rush, but rather to absorb it as a labor force for Spanish ranches and the agriculturally based missions. Mission life was brutal and harsh. Indian neophytes were forced to construct the mission buildings, herd the cattle, work the fields, and wait on the mission priests. Men and women were segregated with the men confined to coffin-like rooms with barely enough space in which to lie down, and the women and girls were housed in bare dormitories called "nunneries." Indian marriage and divorce customs were suppressed, along with all aspects of Native religion. Anglo-borne diseases easily ravaged the concentrated mission populations. A measles epidemic in 1806 killed 1,600, and in some missions children under ten years were almost entirely wiped out. Malnutrition was a persistent problem. Labor was unpaid, and the neophytes were punished by the Franciscans for the smallest infractions. Indians who ran away, or who resisted, were severely punished if not killed. Typical punishments included whipping with a barbed lash, solitary confinement, mutilation, use of stocks and hobbles, branding, and even execution.

Although limited in its geographic scope, the harsh conditions of mission life resulted in the disintegration of most coastal Indian societies and a significant decline in the overall Indigenous population of interior California. The total Native population declined by half, from over 300,000 to 150,000 Indians before the end of the mission system.

Missionization often met with Native resistance. Neophytes at times poisoned or murdered the Franciscan fathers. There were also outright revolts. Among the most noteworthy was the 1824 uprising at Missions La Purisima and Santa Barbara. There were also mass escapes, such as the one in 1795 in which over 200 Costanoan Indians fled Mission Dolores. Nonviolent resistance included the practice of abortion and the infanticide of children born out of forced concubinage of Indian women by priests and soldiers.

MEXICO AND SECULARIZATION

After sixty-five years of Spanish rule, the missions were abandoned in 1834 when Mexico achieved its independence from Spain. After the Mexican Revolution, the 1824 Constitution formally secularized the mission system. California's Indians were made citizens of the new republic, and mission property, at least in theory, was turned over to them. Franciscan resistance and the political turmoil of the period, however, forestalled secularization. As late as 1836, the Franciscans continued to mount military campaigns to seize new "recruits" from the interior for labor at the missions. In reality, Mexican policy was essentially the same as that of Spanish rule. Neither Spain nor Mexico acknowledged Indian ownership of the land.

The Mexican period was a time of confusion and disarray for the Indians, and it led to further depopulation. Some of the emancipated neophytes hired themselves out as farm laborers and servants. There were also those who revolted, as in the Santa Ynez Revolt of 1824. Some fled to the interior to join still independent Indian communities. Those employed on the *ranchos* became victims of the hacienda system of peonage bordering on slavery. Yet others were left at the mercy of the *pueblos*, where they were exploited as domestics, plied with alcohol, and left for a life of poverty and debauchery.

These oppressive conditions contributed to the spread of European-introduced diseases that caused most of the deaths during the period of Mexican rule. The Pandemic of 1833 killed an estimated 4,500 Indians, and a smallpox outbreak killed several thousand more. As a result, by the time of the American invasion there were only about 6,000 exmission Indians still residing along the coast, along with 7,000 predominately Indian-Mexicans. There were also about 700 Europeans. More than a 100,000 Natives remained in interior California.

AMERICANS AND THE GOLD RUSH

The American period commenced with the U.S. victory over Mexico and the Bear Flag Revolt by the "Americanos" in between 1846 and1848. The discovery of gold in 1849 and the rush of miners and settlers that followed the discovery completely overwhelmed the Native population. As word of the gold discovery spread, prospectors flocked to the hills to wash the sands and gravels of mother lode streams and rivers. Mining operations destroyed Native fish dams, polluted salmon streams, and frightened away the wild game. A pastoral California, with its Indian population, Spanish missions, and Mexican *ranchos*, was quickly overrun by an invasion of gold seekers from throughout the world, the Forty-Niners. A virulent racism was spawned in the quest for riches, and a holocaust of the California Indians was ensured.

Under the Treaty of Guadalupe Hidalgo, which was signed at the end of the Mexican–American War, the United States was obligated to recognize two kinds of property rights: traditional *rancho* rights of the *Californios* and open land where Indian title was still intact, including Indian villages and the abandoned missions. Yet the American authorities immediately violated the treaty after taking over California.

The discovery of gold at John Sutter's sawmill on the American River in 1848 ushered in a period of extreme abuse of the Indians. To mobilize the dispossessed Indian labor force, the U.S. military government in California decreed that Indians who did not work for ranchers or who did not have an official passport could expect to be tried and punished. Worse, an Indian might be shot on the pretext that he was a horse thief. By the end of that summer, 4,000 miners, half of them Indian, were prospecting for gold. This atmosphere of tolerance toward Indian gold miners lasted no more than a year.

Unlike other Indians in the Far West, Native Californians often lived and worked with non-Indians in the early conquest era. This was especially the case during the Spanish and Mexican periods before 1850. The Gold Rush fundamentally changed this relationship when California became marked by a precipitous Indian population decline, unique in U.S. frontier history. Before the gold discovery, Indians outnumbered whites by nearly ten to one, but by the early 1850s whites had come to outnumber Indians by almost two to one. Gold fever resulted in tens of thousands of immigrants—young single men, flocking to the California gold fields, hoping to strike it rich. Insatiable greed dominated the immigrant population, and unbridled individualism marked the new California society. As a result, the white population steadily rose to more than 200,000 while the Indian population reached its nadir of 23,000 by 1880, about 15 percent of its pre-Gold Rush population.

Most immigrants viewed the Indian people as worthless, and they were appalled by the Mexican custom of sanctioned miscegenation (interracial sexual unions). They were imbued with a frontier mentality that taught them to despise Native peoples as subhuman "diggers." (Many California Indians used digging sticks to harvest roots and other food sources from the soil, hence the name "digger," which became a pejorative.) Before they were driven from the gold fields, some Indian miners were able to enter the trade system by bargaining their gold for trade goods. The traders countered by inventing "the Digger ounce," a lead slug that dishonestly outweighed the legitimate weights used to measure the gold brought in by white miners.

THE MASSACRES

The Forty-Niner Gold Rush initiated a holocaust for California's Native population that scarcely diminished in intensity until the end of the nineteenth century. The Indian people were cheated, debauched by liquor and white demands for sex, starved, rounded up, and herded on brutal forced marches to small reservations (virtual concentration camps), enslaved in debt peonage, brutally murdered and massacred, and denied civil rights and equal justice before California's courts and institutions. The immigrant intruders shot Indians on sight as the Indians were gathering food or fish, or trying to protect their women and daughters from rape and kidnap. Hundreds of Indian homes were burned and the human occupants trapped by surrounding gunfire.

Some Indian peoples, like the Modocs under Kentipoos, also known as Captain Jack, fought back. One hundred and fifty Modoc warriors and their families successfully held off over 3,000 U.S. Army troops for nearly a year. In the end, the resisters were captured and the leaders hanged. After execution, the warriors were decapitated and their heads sent off to Washington for "scientific investigation." Grave robbers later disinterred Kentipoos's body, embalmed it, and displayed it in a carnival in Eastern cities. His skull was not returned to the Modocs by the government until 1984.

Between 1848 and 1860 there were at least 4,267 Indian deaths attributed to the military, or about 12 percent of the Indian population living at the time. Ironically, it was the gold stolen from Indian lands that paid for the ensuing genocide. Towns offered bounties on Indians ranging from $5 for every severed head in Shasta in 1855, to 25 cents for a scalp in Honey Lake in 1863. Some of the worst massacres occurred in northwestern California. Militia groups such as the Klamath Rifles, the Salmon Guard, the Union Volunteers, and the Pitt River Rangers, armed and paid for by the state government, roamed the countryside with the avowed aim to exterminate "the skulking bands of savages."

Possibly the most notorious massacre occurred at Indian Island near Eureka. On February 26, 1860, the peaceful Wiyot people were holding their annual religious ceremonies when they were attacked during the night as they slept by white "volunteers," who slaughtered them with axes. A Major Raines testified to finding one man, seventeen women, and eleven children among the dead. In addition, eighteen women and an unknown number of children had been carried away by their relatives for burial before his arrival. It was later learned that the Indian Island massacre was part of a premeditated plan by some local farmers and stockmen to exterminate the region's resident Indian population. That same night three other massacres took place simultaneously, two at Humboldt Bay and another at the mouth of the Eel River.

DISEASE AND STARVATION

Throughout most of California, the deaths resulting from disease epidemics greatly exceeded those from massacres. In 1853, 500 died in Nevada City of smallpox and typhoid; 800 Maidu died of influenza and tuberculosis in the same year. Venereal disease was contracted mainly from white men who abducted and raped Indian women. Syphilis infected approximately 20 percent of California's Indians, and gonorrhea may have been as high as 100 percent.

Malnutrition paved the way for death from disease. The destruction of Native food sources, either from gold mining or from outright theft, contributed to Indian susceptibility to communicable diseases. Between the years 1848 to 1855, according to Sherburne Cook, Native population declined from approximately 150,000, or about 66 percent, to about 50,000 (Cook, 1978, 93). "This desolation was accomplished by a ruthless flood of miners and farmers who annihilated the Natives without mercy or compensation. The direct causes of death were disease, the bullet, exposure, and acute starvation," he wrote (Cook, 1978, 93).

The mentality that fueled the nineteenth-century genocide continued into the early twentieth century when Ishi, a Yahi Indian, wandered out of the hills of Tehana County in 1911 as the last surviving member of his tribe. Vigilantes had undertaken raids of extermination against the Yahi and other Indian groups of northern California. Alone and emaciated, Ishi finally allowed himself to be taken by those from whom he had hid for so many years. Ishi's story is recounted by Theodora Kroeber in *Ishi in Two Worlds*.

THE "LOST TREATIES"

In 1851 and 1852, President Millard Fillmore sent three Indian commissioners to negotiate eighteen treaties with California Indians. Under the treaty terms, the Indians reluctantly agreed to surrender their land claims, and the federal government agreed in turn to provide some 8.5 million acres of good lands, reservations, and goods and services. It was the era of the gold rush, however, and the greed for gold and California's rich lands motivated the state legislature to pressure the U.S. Senate not to ratify the treaties. The treaties were then conveniently "lost" in the Senate archives and not rediscovered until 1905. Because the treaties were never ratified and then "lost," the Indians were forced to give up virtually all of the promised lands and settle instead for small, temporary *rancherias* and farms, a mere fraction of the original 8.5 million acres that were promised them. The 1887 Dawes (Allotment) Act further reduced California Indian landholdings.

A congressional act of 1928 and a 1946 law creating the U.S. Court of Indian Claims permitted California Indians to sue the government for the lost lands. A 1944 award received under the 1928 act was for $17 million, hardly just compensation considering the billions of dollars in gold and resources realized from the stolen lands. Because of the inadequacy of the 1944 award, a new claims case was entered for other lands illegally taken. Yet the 1964 award paid California Indians only 47 cents an acre for approximately 65 million acres illegally seized.

INDENTURE AND SLAVERY

Until 1867, an estimated 10,000 California Indians, including 4,000 children, were held as chattel. Newspaper accounts of the time noted that while young boys sold for about $60, young women could sell for as much as $200. In some instances, entire tribes were captured, carried into white settlements, and sold. An 1850 state indenture law ordered that any Indian, on the word of a white man, could be declared a legal vagrant, thrown in jail, and have his labor sold at auction for up to four months with no pay.

The indenture law also allowed Indian children to be indentured with the consent of their parents or if they were orphans. The law provided a motive for making Indian children orphans by killing the parents so that the children could then be indentured. Child kidnapping and Indian slavery continued for fifteen years until 1867 when it was finally overturned to comply with the Thirteenth Amendment to the Constitution abolishing slavery and involuntary servitude.

DEATH MARCHES AND FORCED RELOCATION

The so-called humane alternative to extermination was the policy of "domestication." This involved rounding up Indian survivors of the gold rush, or those occupying lands desired by White settlers, and sending them on forced marches to relocation centers, euphemistically called reservations. Brutal atrocities were committed during these death marches. Many hundreds died as a result of the removal operations by the military, because, if they did not die or were killed along the way, they found no provisions, houses, or other facilities once they reached their destinations and consequently became the victims of disease and starvation. Once on the reservations, the relocated Indians faced exploitation at the hands of crooked Indian agents, some of whom sold government-issue cattle intended to feed the Indians and pocketed the proceeds for themselves.

SUMMARY AND CONCLUSION

Sherburne Cook divides the catastrophic population decline of the California Indians into three stages. The first stage took place from 1769 to 1834 during the Spanish period under the mission system. The major cause of the decline was disease. The second stage extends from the end of the mission system in 1834 to the Mexican war with the United States in 1845. The two demographic processes responsible for the decline during this period were disease and the opening up of land to white settlement. The third and worst stage took place between 1845 and 1855, during the American period of the gold rush. This stage witnessed the decline of the remaining Indian population by two-thirds. The causes for this precipitous population decline clearly fall under the definition of genocide: the committing of acts with intent to destroy, wholly or in part, a national, ethnic, racial, or religious group. In California, especially immediately following the Gold Rush, these acts were deliberate and even institutional in scope.

REFERENCES AND FURTHER READING

Cook, Sherburne F. 1976. *The Conflict Between the California Indian and White Civilization*. Berkeley: University of California Press.

Cook, Sherburne F. 1978. "Historical Demography." *Handbook of North American Indians*. Vol. 8: California. Robert F. Heizer, volume editor, 91–98. Washington: Smithsonian Institution.

Costo, Rupert, and Jeannette Henry Costo, eds. 1987. *The Missions of California: A Legacy of Genocide*. San Francisco: Indian Historian Press.

Heizer, Robert F., and Alan E Almquist. 1971. *The Other Californians: Prejudice and Discrimination Under Spain, Mexico,* *and the United States to 1920*. Berkeley: University of California Press.

Kroeber, Theodora. 1976. *Ishi in Two Worlds: A Biography of the Last Wild Indian in North America*. Berkeley: University of California Press.

Moratto, Michael J. 1984. *California Archaeology*. Orlando, Florida: Academic Press.

Norton, Jack. 1979. *Genocide in Northwestern California: When Our Worlds Cried*. San Francisco, CA: The Indian Historian Press.

TOYPURINA: A LEADER OF HER PEOPLE

As the Spanish missions spread throughout California beginning in the 1770s, the Native people were impressed into forced labor to both build the mission buildings and also tend the immense cattle ranches and farming enterprises that were attached to the missions. In spite of the massive number of deaths due to disease and the actions of the Spanish, many Native people resisted the brutality of mission life. This took many forms. Some escaped and returned to their homelands or organizing armed rebellions such as the 1775 revolt at the San Diego mission or later the Chumash revolt at Santa Barbara mission. In 1785 a Tongva woman, Toypurina, who was a powerful and influential religious and political leader from the community of Japchivit organized Native people from six major villages of the region. They carried out an uprising against the San Gabriel Mission in the area where Los Angeles is now. Although the revolt failed and Toypurina and many of the others were captured and punished, her words were recorded at her trial, "I am angry with the padres, and all of those of the mission, for living here on my native soil, for trespassing upon the land of my ancestors and despoiling our tribal domains." She was imprisoned and later exiled to the Carmel Mission in northern California where she stayed until her death twelve years later.

She continues to be revered by the Tongva. There is a painting of what Toypurina may have looked like on the current Tongva tribal website: http://www.tongvatribe.net. See also: http://www.tongva.com.

From Acorn Soup *by L. Frank. Copyright © 1999 by L. Frank. Reprinted by permission of Heyday Books. All rights reserved.*

THE CRIME OF GENOCIDE
A UNITED NATIONS CONVENTION AIMED AT PREVENTING DESTRUCTION OF GROUPS AND AT PUNISHING THOSE RESPONSIBLE

Rupert Costo and Jeannette Henry Costo

Genocide is a modern word for an old crime. It means the deliberate destruction of national, racial, religious or ethnic groups.

History had long been a grim witness to such acts, but it remained for the twentieth century to see those acts carried out on the largest and most inhuman scale known when the Nazi Government of Germany systematically annihilated millions of people because of their religion or ethnic origin. A shocked world then rejected any contention that such crimes were the exclusive concern of the State perpetrating them, and punishment of the guilty became one of the principal war aims of the Allied nations. The charter of the International Military Tribunal at Nuremberg, approved by the Allies in1945, recognized that war criminals were not only those who had committed crimes against peace, and violations of the laws or customs of war, but those who had carried out "crimes against humanity;" whether or not such crimes violated the domestic law of the country in which they took place.

During its first session in 1946, the United Nations General Assembly approved two resolutions. In the first, the Assembly affirmed the principles of the charter of the Nuremberg Tribunal. In the second—the basic resolution on genocide—the Assembly affirmed that genocide was a crime under international law and that those guilty of it, whoever they were and for whatever reason they committed it, were punishable. It asked for international cooperation in preventing and punishing genocide and it invited Member States to enact the necessary national legislation. In a final provision, the Assembly called for studies aimed at creating an international legal instrument to deal with the crime. That was the origin of the Convention on the Prevention and Punishment of the Crime of Genocide unanimously adopted by the Assembly on 9 December 1948.

The term "convention" in international law means an agreement among sovereign nations. It is a legal compact which pledges every Contracting Party to accept certain obligations.

How the Convention Was Prepared

In 1946 the General Assembly requested the Economic and Social Council to undertake the necessary studies for drawing up a draft Convention on the crime of genocide. In 1947 the Secretary-General, at the request of the Economic and Social Council, prepared a first draft of the Convention and circulated it to Member States for comments. At that stage, the Secretary-General was assisted by a group of interna-

tional law experts, among them the late Dr. Raphael Lemkin, who in 1944 had coined the term "genocide." In 1948 the Economic and Social Council appointed an ad hoc Committee of seven members to submit to it a revised draft. That the Committee did, and after a general debate, the Council decided on 26 August to transmit the draft to the General Assembly. At the Paris session of the General Assembly the draft was debated by the legal Committee and adopted by the Assembly on 9 December 1948.

The Definition of Genocide in the Convention

Genocide, the Convention declares, is the committing of certain acts with intent to destroy—wholly or in part—a national, ethnic, racial or religious group as such.

What are the acts? First, actual killing. But it is possible to destroy a group of human beings without direct physical extermination. So the Convention includes in the definition of genocide the acts of causing serious bodily or mental harm; deliberate infliction of conditions of life "calculated to bring about" physical destruction; imposing measures to prevent birth and, finally, forcibly transferring children of one group to another group. Those acts, the Convention states, constitute "genocide." In accordance with the Convention, related acts are also punishable: conspiracy to commit genocide, direct and public incitement to commit genocide, an attempt to commit the crime and complicity in its commission.

To Prevent and to Punish

The Convention first declares that genocide "whether committed in time of peace or in time of war" is a crime under international law which the contracting States "undertake to prevent and to punish."

Main principles established by the Convention are:

1. Contracting States are bound to enact the laws needed to give effect to the provisions of the Convention, in particular to provide effective penalties.
2. States undertake to try persons charged with those offenses in their competent national courts.
3. Parties to the Convention agree that the acts listed shall not be considered as political crimes. Therefore, they pledge to grant extradition in accordance with their laws and treaties.

All those pledges are for national action. The Convention also envisages trial by an international penal tribunal should one be set up and should the Contracting Parties accept its jurisdiction. Furthermore, it provides that any of the contracting States may bring a charge of genocide, or of any of the related acts, before the competent organs of the United Nations and ask for appropriate action under the Charter.

If there is any dispute between one country and another on the interpretation, application or fulfillment of the Convention, the dispute must be submitted to the International Court of Justice at the request of any of the Parties.

Genocide in California

The patterns of genocide in southern California differed from that of the American Gold Rush, and the modern Holocaust of Nazis in Germany.

In southern California the genocide was practiced against the entire race—the Native people of the land. It is not possible to condone the near extinction of this people through the notion that the missionaries believed the Indians were "uncivilized," or that they were children who must be brought to the true religion of Roman Catholicism in the garb of the Spanish monarchy.

The truth is that the evidence of native culture and lifeways, of land use and natural development of a peoples' economy were all about the Franciscans. The land itself, by all appearances, was one in which people, human beings, had cared for, nurtured, and protected its beauty for all to enjoy.

They must have known they were exterminating a race. They did know it. And it was done with utter heartlessness, with utter disregard for the human individual. It was done by trickery, by cajolery, by enticement.

It must not be repeated. Together with the victims of the Nazi genocide, we must say "Never again! Never again!"

"The Crime of Genocide," pp. 126–129 in *The Missions of California: A Legacy of Genocide,* ed. Rupert Costo and Jeannette Henry Costo. Copyright 1987 by the Indian Historian Press for the American Indian Historical Society. Reprinted with permission.

"Obey" by Mike S. Rodriguez, © *1988.*

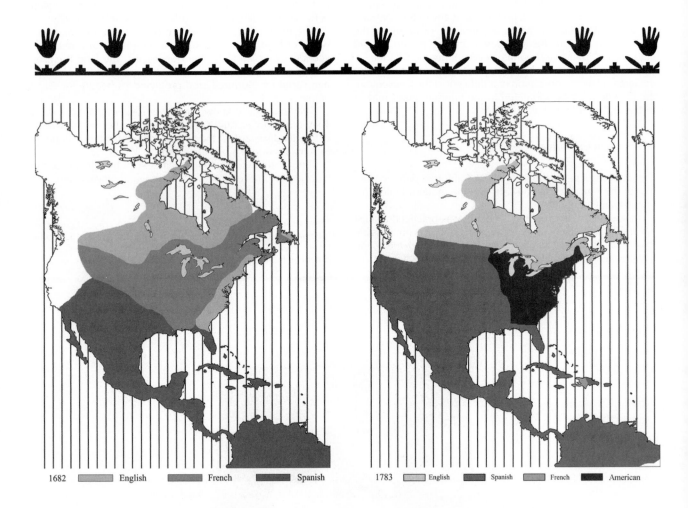

| 1682 | English | French | Spanish |

| 1783 | English | Spanish | French | American |

European Colonial Impact on Native Lands: 1682 and 1783

It is easy to forget how complex and changing the European colonial claims were to Native lands in North America, and what a variety of impacts, not only political but also cultural and economic, that they had on Native peoples and their lands.

The schematic map of 1682 shows the extensive reach of Spanish colonial power that blanketed much of the Americas, extending up from the south through what is now Central America, Mexico, and the United States. The English during this period claimed much of the eastern seaboard and the area in what is now Canada around Hudson Bay. French influence cut a swath between these two other colonial powers.

The second map shows, a 100 years later, in 1783. The French influence was reduced to Haiti, England had maintained its colonial presence around the Hudson Bay, and Spain continued to be a predominating colonial influence throughout much of what is now the United States. Extending westward from the Atlantic seaboard, the new American nation was now being felt by Native nations.

These maps are important to keep in mind when reading about pioneers in their wagon trains moving west of the Mississippi River in the mid-1800s and encountering Native people for the first time. This may have been the first contact with Indian people by these European immigrants traveling west, but for many Indians, it was an old story, and the "White Problem" by the mid-1800s was at least 150 or 200 years old.

@ 1997 H.J. Tsinhnahjinnie.

PART REVIEW

DISCUSSION QUESTIONS

Steven Newcomb, *Five Hundred Years of Injustice*
1. Why does Newcomb also refer to the Doctrine of Discovery as the Christian Doctrine of Discovery?
2. What is the significance of the 1823 *Johnson v. M'Intosh* Supreme Court decision to the Doctrine of Discovery and federal Indian policy?

David E. Wilkins, *A History of Federal Indian Policy*
1. What impact did federalism (the conflict between the federal and state governments over Indian policy) have on Native American sovereignty?
2. What was the government's rationale for passing the General Allotment Act of 1887? What impact did it have on the economic well-being of the affected Indian tribes?
3. In 1953 Congress passed a resolution that authorized the termination of more than 100 Indian tribes. What were the other two parts of this coercive policy? Explain.
4. After reviewing seven Indian policy periods, what does Wilkins conclude?

Mario Gonzalez, *The Black Hills*
1. If the 1851 and 1868 Treaties of Fort Laramie recognized Lakota (Sioux) title to the Black Hills, how did the Lakota come to lose their sacred lands?
2. Explain why the Black Hills are sacred to the Lakota (Sioux) and Tsistsistas (Cheyenne).

3. In 1980 the U.S. Supreme Court affirmed a lower court ruling that the Lakota tribes were entitled to a $102 million compensation for the Black Hills. Why did the Indians refuse it?

Poka Laenui, *The Rediscovery of Hawaiian Sovereignty*
1. What were the circumstances that led the Hawaiian people to lose their sovereignty over the islands to the United States in 1893?
2. What harmful changes took place from 1900 to 1959, during the "recycling of Hawai'i" as a U.S. territory?
3. What are some of the developments that have occurred since the 1960s that have led to cultural rejuvenation and the demand for an independent Hawaiian nation?

Eileen M. Luna-Firebaugh, *The Border Crossed Us*
1. Explain what is meant by "the border problem."
2. List some of the problems encountered by the Tohono O'odham because of the militarization of the border with Mexico.
3. Which of the approaches or solutions to the border problem discussed by the author do you think is the most effective? Why?

Steve Talbot, *Genocide of California Indians*
1. Briefly summarize the Spanish mission system in California. How did it lead to the genocide of the Indians?

2. How or in what ways did the genocide of the Indians in the Anglo-American period differ from that in the Spanish mission period?
3. Why was the depopulation of the Indians greater in the Anlgo-American period than during Spanish and Mexican rule?

Rupert Costo and Jeannette Henry Costo,
The Crime of Genocide
1. How can the UN's definition of genocide be applied to the history of the Franciscan missions in California and that following the Gold Rush in the Anglo-American period, as described in Talbot's article?

KEY TERMS

Anti-Annexation Petitions (1897)
border conflict
Columbian Quincentennial
Doctrine of Discovery (Christian Doctrine of Discovery)
genocide
Hawaiian bayonet constitution
Indian Claims Commission Act of 1946
Johnson v. M'Intosh (1823)
North American Free Trade Agreement (NAFTA)

Paha Sapa
Queen Lili'uokalani
Serra, Fr. Junipero
sovereignty
Spanish California mission system
termination policy
Tohono O'odham
Toypurina

SUGGESTED READINGS

BEBE, ROSE MARIE, and SENKEDWICZ, ROBERT M., eds. *Lands of Promise and Despair: Chronicles of Early California, 1535–1846.* Berkeley, Calif.: Heyday Books, 2001.

CHAPIN, MAC. "The Meaning of Columbus Day," *World Watch* (November/December 208), pp. 8–17.

COSTO, RUPERT, and JEANNETTE HENRY COSTO, ed. *The Missions of California: A Legacy of Genocide.* San Francisco: Indian Historian Press, 1987.

DELORIA, PHILIP J., and NEAL SALISBURY, eds. *A Companion to American Indian History.* MA: Blackwell Publishing, 2002.

DUDLEY, MICHAEL KIONI, and KEONI KEALOHA AGARD. *A Hawaiian Nation II: A Call for Hawaiian Sovereignty.* Honolulu: Naa Kaane O Ka Malo Press, 1990.

GENTRY, CAROLE M., and DONALD A. GRINDE, JR. *The Unheard Voices: American Indian Responses to the Columbian Quincentenary 1492–1992.* Los Angeles: UCLA American Indian Studies Center, 1994.

KIRCH, PATRICK V., and MARSHALL SAHLINS. *Anahulu: The Anthropology of History in the Kingdom of Hawai'i.* Chicago: University of Chicago Press, 1992.

KOHLHOFF, DEAN. *When the Wind Was a River: Aleut Evacuation in World War II.* Seattle: University of Washington Press, 1995.

LYONS, OREN, and JOHN MOHAWK, ed. *Exiled in the Land of the Free: Democracy, Indian Nations, and the U.S. Constitution.* Santa Fe, N.M.: Clear Light Publishers, 1992.

MANN, CHARLES C. *1491: New Revelations of the Americas Before Columbus.* New York: Vintage Books, 2005.

NABOKOV, PETER, ed. *Native American Testimony: A Chronicle of Indian–White Relations from Prophecy to the Present, 1492–1992.* With a foreword by Vine Deloria, Jr. New York: Penguin Books, 1991.

NEWCOMB, STEVEN T. *Pagans in the Promised Land: Decoding the Doctrine of Christian Discovery.* Golden, CO: Fulcrum Publishing, 2008.

Rethinking Columbus. A special edition of *Rethinking Schools,* an urban education journal. Milwaukee: Rethinking Schools, 1991.

SPICER, EDWARD H. *Cycles of Conquest: The Impact of Spain, Mexico, and the United States on the Indians of the Southwest, 1533–1960.* Tucson: University of Arizona Press, 1962.

TALBOT, STEVE. *Roots of Oppression: The American Indian Question.* New York: International Publishers, 1981.

THRUSH, COLL. *Native Seattle: Histories from the Cross-Over Place.* Seattle: University of Washington Press, 2007.

WILKINS, DAVID E. *American Indian Sovereignty and the U.S. Supreme Court: The Masking of Justice.* Austin: University of Texas Press, 1997.

WILKINS, DAVID E., and K. TSIANINA LOMAWAIMA. *Uneven Ground: American Indian Sovereignty and Federal Law.* Norman: University of Oklahoma Press, 2001.

WRIGHT, RONALD. *Stolen Continents: The "New World" Through Indian Eyes.* New York: Houghton Mifflin, 1992.

IV

"THE ONLY GOOD INDIAN . . .": RACISM, STEREOTYPES, AND DISCRIMINATION

Incantation to Dispel New Age Dogma
Parris Butler

don't go cosmic on me baby
i don't wanna be your
native american experience
your five minute sound bite
your oppressed native reality bite
your catharsis
your true life experience a la
all the hollywood stereotypes you ever
absorbed off the silver screen
(this includes all john wayne era renditions
as well as the more recent native
intellectualism/spiritualism varieties)
don't go cosmic on me baby
'cause i don't wanna
indian guide you to, into, or through
a vortex
nor do i wish to provide for you
any form of pan-indian
political dogma
exorcism of karma
or blah blah blah blah
don't go cosmic on me baby
don't recite for me your alleged pedigree
your liberal humanism philosophy
'cause baby i don't wanna be
authentic for your approval
traditional for your perusal
political while you refuse all
actions speaking louder than words
don't go cosmic on me baby
'cause i do not necessarily relate
to your recollection of the native
military vet you once knew
the alcohol addict you once partied with
the traditional native artisan
(probably a jeweler) from whom you
collected whatever
or any other Indigenous tribal person
you may have met known read about
heard about fantasized or otherwise
conjured baby
don't go cosmic on me

One of the means by which Native peoples are colonized and oppressed is by creating and perpetuating the myth of Indigenous cultural inferiority. Pejorative beliefs and sentiments often become so routinized, so deeply entwined with a nation's popular culture, health, welfare, educational, and legal systems that they come to be viewed as "normal," everyday beliefs, which are continually revalidated through thoughts and actions that often operate at an unconscious level in the general psyche of the society and its institutional "gatekeepers." In turn, the racial/ethnic stereotypes of the Native American then become the rationalizations to justify social and economic injustice, and discrimination. In the history of the Americas, extreme ethnocentrism and racism have justified, among other things, murder, assassination, and massacre of Indigenous peoples; the imprisonment of political leaders; the destruction of native food sources; the dispossession of lands and resources and the destruction of Indian economies; the suppression of Indigenous political systems; and forced acculturation through religious missionization and white-run, segregated educational institutions.

At the outset, we need to make a conceptual distinction between the terms *prejudice* and *discrimination*. *Prejudice* is an attitude of mind in which one holds members of another group to be inferior while one's own "race," ethnicity, culture, gender, or class is considered superior. *Discrimination*, on the other hand, is an overt act based on prejudice. Discrimination can be committed by individuals and also by institutions, whether government, church, business, the criminal justice system, or other parts of the society. Discrimination carried out by institutions is termed *institutional*, or *structural, discrimination*. Institutional discrimination is almost always more damaging than individual acts of discrimination, but the eradication of institutional discrimination has an almost immediate democratizing effect on society. Racial segregation in the U.S. South is a case in point. Once racist Jim Crow laws were overturned in 1954, racial segregationists, regardless of their own personal prejudicial views toward African-Americans, were forced to comply with the Supreme Court decision ending the most blatant forms of white privilege based on discriminatory practices. The struggle against anti-Indianism also has an institutional component.

"Redlining" is an example of institutional discrimination. Classic redlining occurs when a bank, loan agency, or financial institution draws a line around a low-income, minority community on a map, or through private understanding, and then denies loans to all the residents within the redlined area, regardless of an applicant's personal credit history. The area redlined is usually a ghetto, barrio, or poor part of town. But it also happens on Indian reservations. In April 1996, the U.S. Justice Department filed a complaint against a Nebraska bank for allegedly charging higher interest rates to American Indian borrowers, predominantly from the Pine Ridge Reservation of South Dakota, than to non-Indian borrowers. Such practices, although illegal, are not uncommon.

Another recent example is the negative ruling by the U.S. Supreme Court that diminishes Native voting rights regarding the Office of Hawaiian Affairs (OHA). The OHA is a Hawaiian state agency that dispenses millions of dollars each year to Native Hawaiians, who constitute at least 20 percent of the state's population. The money is derived from a trust of Native land title that was retained by the Hawaiian people when the United States unilaterally annexed Hawai'i in 1898. At issue is the fact that under the state's constitution, only Native and part-native Hawaiians are permitted to vote for the OHA trustees who manage Native Hawaiian lands. The decision by the Supreme Court reversed this principle when it ruled that allowing only Native Hawaiians to vote for OHA trustees discriminated against non-Natives and is therefore unconstitutional. Allowing non-Natives, who outnumber Native Hawaiians in Hawai'i, to vote on trustees, OHA affairs, and income distribution is an egregious violation of Native sovereignty and an example of institutional discrimination.

In the case of Indigenous peoples, the most extreme form of discrimination has been the legacy of racial murder and wanton killing. Until very recently, South American Indians were being killed by gold miners and other exploiters of the Amazon rain forest. In the United States in earlier years, such killing was condoned by slogans such as "The only good Indian is a dead Indian," coined by General Philip Sheridan in 1868, after celebrating the massacre of Black Kettle's southern Cheyenne on the Washita, and "Nits make lice," as justification for killing Indian children in massacres such as those at Sand Creek in 1864 and at Wounded Knee in 1890. A primary motive for the slaughter to the point of extinction of the great buffalo herds on the Western plains, the Indians' primary food source, was to eradicate the resident Indian populations in order to make room for white settlement and commercial "development." A medal coined at the time pictured a buffalo on one side and an Indian on the other, with the slogan "Every buffalo killed is an Indian gone." Even in the twentieth century, there were racially motivated murders of Indians in the United States that fueled widespread protests in the 1960s and 1970s by the American Indian Movement and other Indian protest groups.

Historically, the two main stereotypes that have victimized North American Indians and have formed the justification for their genocide and ethnocide are the polar terms *Noble Redman* and *Red Savage*. The concept of stereotype connotes the idea of untrue or misleading generalizations about a group. *Noble Redman* is a romanticization of the Indian as a "wild creature" of the forest, akin to the animals, admired but uncivilized and subhuman. Many myths flow from the Noble Redman image, not the least of which is the erroneous belief that all Native peoples were nomadic hunters and gatherers, wandering aimlessly across the land. Following this line of reasoning, if they did not utilize the land, then the European colonists who were agrarian had the God-given right to "go forth and multiply" and "to make the land fruitful." (This was part of the myth of Indians being "dependent nations" in the Doctrine of Discovery/Christian Nations theory discussed by Steven Newcomb in Part III.) As a matter of record, most of the larger Indigenous populations of the Americas, especially those in what is now the Eastern and Southwestern United States, Mesoamerica, and the Andean region, lived in settled communities and were horticulturists. Native Americans had impressive food technology, and over half of the world's foods (including the "Irish" potato) are the result of this horticultural development. Those Native peoples who moved did so within their traditional territories and with an extensive understanding of the seasonal utilization of resources in ways defined appropriate by their cultural and ecological traditions so that no natural food source would become depleted.

The most virulent form of discrimination is terrorism at the hands of vigilante groups, or even by the state itself. As Indian historian Jack Forbes reminds us, the militia movement is nothing new. "Terrorism by bands of armed white men was the primary means used by the United States to harass, weaken, and then to almost wipe out tribe after tribe in the far west. The U.S. Army was usually brought in after irregular armed militias had done the dirty work.[1] Terrorism cannot exist unless the targeted group is dehumanized through negative stereotyping. One need not turn to the 1800s to find an example of vigilante attacks on Indian people. In 1973, during the occupation-protest on the Pine Ridge Reservation at Wounded Knee, the federal government armed and abetted what became known as the "GOON squad" to attack and kill members and sympathizers of the militant American Indian Movement (AIM). The government sent a federal army to quash the 1973 protest at Wounded Knee and later tied up the AIM leadership in long, costly trials in an attempt to destroy the Indian rights organization. Ironically, the courts later judged the government's actions at Wounded Knee illegal, but the damage to AIM and its supporters had already been done.

Likewise, in Central and South America, armed, government-supported vigilante groups often threaten and terrorize Indigenous communities. Guatemala is a case in point; tens of thousands of Indian people have been killed or "disappeared" in the past 40 years of militarist rule and civil strife. In 1999, the Indigenous Alliance without Borders (*Alianza Indigena Sin Fronteras*) called for an investigation of the role of the U.S. military in the torture and killing of Indians by Central American death squads. It is well documented that the U.S. government, in the name of containing a "communist insurgency," has trained paramilitary and military forces to "neutralize" Indigenous peoples who raise a cry for social and economic justice. Training manuals used by the U.S. Army School of the Americas at Fort Benning, Georgia, encouraged the use of extortion, blackmail, beatings, and executions. The alliance charged, also, that Indian women were routinely shocked, burned, starved, exposed, stripped, and sexually molested during torture by U.S.-trained military and paramilitary groups.

In the public mind, genocide connotes the outright killing of a national, religious, or ethnic group, but, as we saw from an examination of the United Nations definition of *genocide* in Part III, it has a much broader meaning under international law. Peonage in the Southern United States under the crop-lien system entrapped not only African Americans but also many Indians as recently as the first quarter of the twentieth century. Involuntary servitude of young Indian women is still widespread in parts of South America. The forcible relocation in the United States of Indian people from their homes under the 1974 Navajo–Hopi Land Settlement Act, in which 12,000 traditional Dineh (Navajo) lost lands, homes, and livestock, and the earlier northward Inuit reloca-tion by the Canadian government in the 1950s, are within the bounds of the United Nations *genocide* definition. So is the removal of Indian children from their homes, which occurred up to the 1990s under the Canadian Indian residential and U.S. federal Indian boarding school systems.

It is within this history of Indian genocide—especially the loss of Indian children to tribal communities—that the sterilization of reservation Indian women by the Indian Health Service physicians and contract doctors became a major concern in the 1970s. In a survey of a half dozen of the largest reservations, the U.S. Census Bureau found that the average number of children per woman for all tribes decreased from 3.19 in 1970 to 1.30 in 1980. The decline in birthrate mirrors a similar decline during the same period for all populations in the United States and is explained by a number of factors. However, regarding Native people, data from some reservation Indian Health Service hospitals and clinics supports the suspicion of medical malpractice resulting in coerced sterilization The reduction in the Indian birth rate was viewed with alarm by Native American activists in the 1970s within the context of the precipitous decline of their populations in earlier centuries. Paradoxically, the lack of family planning that is avail-able to Indian women, whether reservation or urban, continues to be an ongoing issue and also violates a woman's "right to choose."

The concept of cultural genocide, or ethnocide, refers to measures taken by the oppressor group to stamp out Indigenous culture and its social institutions. The assim-ilationist slogan "Kill the Indian but save the man," which was coined by "friends of the Indian" (missionaries and reformers) in the 1880s, epitomizes this concept. The practic-ing of Indian cultural traditions was criminalized on reservations in the United States from 1883 to 1934 under the Courts of Indian Offenses set up by the Indian Office. These Indian "crimes" included not only Indian religious practices but also other customs deemed offensive to Christian missionaries. For example, in 1902 Indian Commissioner W. A. Jones issued his "short-hair" order, which banned not only long hair but also body painting by both sexes, the wearing of Indian clothing, religious dances, and "give-away" ceremonies, which is the custom of giving away goods and possessions on important ritual occasions. These policies were not reversed until 1934, under Roosevelt's New Deal. Nevertheless, some important Indian religious ceremonies and other cus-toms have continued to be banned or subtly discouraged by non-Indian individuals and institutions up to the present.

The Red Savage stereotype, unfortunately, still lingers, but it has been modified to become the "drunken, incompetent" Indian. In Oklahoma, a state containing a large Indian population, the negative stereotype of the "four Ds" ("dark, dumb, drunk, and dirty") still plagued Indian young people as recently as the 1960s. The Noble Redman stereotype nurtured governmental paternalism and its bureaucratic overadministration through the Bureau of Indian Affairs that treated U.S. Indians as "Red children" living under wardship. This treatment foreclosed the possibility of Indian nations' becoming self-governing communities, a status that began to be regained only within the last half of the twentieth century. Derogatory terms such as *squaw* and *redskin* continue to do harm in their denigration of Native Americans. According to the U.S. Geological Survey's Board on Geographic names, the word *squaw* is part of 1,050 geographic names in the United States, most of them in the Midwest and the West, such as Squaw Valley.

The term *redskin* was first used by the captain-general and governor-in-chief of the Province of Massachusetts Bay in a 1755 proclamation promoting the murder of American Indians by placing a bounty on their heads, scalps, and skins. For every male Indian prisoner above age 12 taken captive and brought to the town of Boston, 50 pounds in currency was offered on "Red Skins"; for every male Indian scalp brought in as evidence of his having been killed, 40 pounds was paid. In 1884 the governor of Pennsylvania also offered bounties on male and female Indians. During the Revolutionary War, the British commandant of Detroit became known as the "hair buyer" because he, too, paid bounties for Indian scalps. Signs on the walls of early trading posts announced bounties on "Red Skins," or bounty scalps, along with those on "Otter Skins" and "Beaver Skins." Thus, it is important for non-Indian Americans to know the historical origins of terms that they otherwise might believe to be harmless and inoffensive. Stereotypes such as these do real damage to the self-image of young Indian men and women in today's world.

Fortunately, Native Americans in the United States are beginning to have some success in pressuring states to eliminate derogatory Indian epithets. Maine, Minnesota, and Montana have recently enacted laws to eliminate the word *squaw* from state lands, maps, signs, and markers. Indian sports mascots, which communicate grotesque and negative images, must also be examined in this light. There is an old saying: "Sticks and stones can break my bones, but words can never hurt me." But as the readings in this chapter demonstrate, words *can* hurt. Racial and ethnic stereotypes, through words and images, set a tone and create a context in which prejudice and discrimination are seemingly justified.

In Reading 1, "The Pocahontas Perplex: The Image of Indian Women in American Culture," Cherokee folklorist Rayna Green examines what she terms the "Pocahontas perplex," the national cult and its pre-American origins surrounding the Pocahontas–John Smith legend as celebrated in paintings, poems, plays, movies, and literature. The Indian princess stereotype plays to the notion of the Noble Redman or good Indian who "rescues and helps white men" and becomes Christianized and acculturated. This stereotype, in turn, is counterpoised to its polar opposite, the "savage" Indian, or, in the case of Indian women, the "squaw"—a dull, unattractive beast of burden or whore.

Sociologist Luana Ross (Salish) employs an in-depth interview methodology in Reading 2, "Punishing Institutions: The Story of Catherine (Cedar Woman)," to obtain a better understanding of the causes for the high rate of incarceration of Indian women in the United States. In 1994, for example, Native Americans constituted 2.9 percent of both federal and state prison populations, although Native people were less than 1 percent of the total U.S. population; in Alaska and the northern Plains States, the incarceration ratio was even higher. Ross contends that these findings can be explained by the history of violence, both personal and institutional, that has marked the lives of Indian women. She cites one study that found that 88 percent of imprisoned women had been violently victimized before their incarceration. In fact, the contextualizing of the criminalization process is central to the understanding of female deviance. Furthermore, the violence is institutionalized not only through agencies such as the Indian boarding school and foster home placement but also by the system of incarceration itself. The life history of Catherine (Cedar Woman), fits the typical profile of Indian women prisoners and supports Ross's theory that Indian criminalization is both racialized and genderized.

The box titled "Indian-Named Mascots: An Assault on Self-Esteem" examines the issue of Indian sports mascots, such as the Atlanta Braves and the Cleveland Indians. Tim Giago (Oglala Lakota), the former editor of *Indian Country Today*, demonstrates the ways in which this practice is demeaning.

The box "We're Imitating the Enemy," by Shannon Prince, illustrates the sad fact that even the oppressed can be perpetrators of prejudice and discrimination. A current issue in Indian Country is the attempt by the tribal leadership of the Cherokee Nation of Oklahoma to remove Cherokee "Freedmen" from tribal membership. The Freedmen are the descendants of Cherokee slaves of African heritage who at the close of the Civil War were emancipated and given Cherokee citizenship. Only an affluent elite of Cherokee Indians in Indian Territory held slaves, a legacy of the Southern plantation economy to which they had earlier adapted. A number of the Cherokee slave-owners and their African-descended slaves intermarried to form a class of "Black Cherokees." The controversy highlights the issue of identity politics: blood quantum versus cultural and historical factors as the basis of Indigenous identity. Prince contends that the tribal rights of these Cherokee citizens are threatened and that the unity of the Cherokee nation is at stake.

Reading 3, "Native American Women and Coerced Sterilization," is an edited portion of a longer article by Sally J. Torpy that appeared in the *American Indian Culture and Research Journal* in 2000. The author discusses the reservation health issue involving the alleged abuse of women's reproductive rights by the Indian Health Service in the 1960s and 1970s. Although not IHS policy, there were nevertheless an unusual number of cases of sterilization of Indian women, some as young as 15 years, by public health physicians and contract doctors during this period. The U.S. government's General Accounting Office (GAO) examined only 4 of 12 Indian Health Service regions and found that 3,406 Native American women had been sterilized during the 1970s. The implications for the U.S. Native American population are significant, not only because the overall Indian population is small when compared with other ethnic minorities but also because the population is composed of many different Indigenous mini-nationalities, many with small gene pools. As researcher Sally Torpy states: "A 200 million population could support voluntary sterilization and survive, but for Native Americans it cannot be a preferred method of birth control. While other minorities might have a gene pool in Africa or Asia, Native Americans do not: when we are gone, that's it."

The sterilization debate became a cause célèbre for the Indian Red Power movement that was active in the 1970s and 1980s. It is important to note that the sterilization practice appears to have been reservation based and was not an issue in the urban Indian communities. In fact, urban Indian women were interested in assuring access to family planning. Abortion is no stranger to Indian traditional culture. Most if not all tribes have used traditional means—herbs, teas, natural medicines—to modify procreation. In this sense, Indian women's reproductive rights might be considered a sovereignty issue. Today, the issue is a complicated one because of the growing number of states that are outlawing abortion. South Dakota, which has a stringent anti-abortion law, is a case in point. In May 2006, Cecelia Fire Thunder, the first woman elected to head the Oglala Sioux Tribe of South Dakota, was impeached for proposing to build a woman's wellness center on the Pine Ridge reservation. Her adversaries charged that the health center was a pretext for an abortion clinic. At the time, South Dakota had the country's most stringent anti-abortion law, not allowing an exception in the case of rape, incest, or the health of the mother. It should be pointed out that in both instances, the earlier coerced sterilization controversy and the more recent abortion backlash, the key issue for Indians is the control of women's reproductive rights within the context of each tribe's cultural traditions.

The box "Maze of Injustice: The Failure to Protect Indigenous Women from Sexual Violence in the USA," is a Spring 2008 summary statement of a 16-page report by Amnesty International on the failure to protect Indigenous women from sexual violence in the United States. (See Suggested Readings.)

In Reading 4, "Protecting Native American Human Remains, Burial Grounds, and Sacred Places," a symposium of respected Indian leaders evaluate national legislation and executive orders of the president purported to address Indian religious freedom issues, the most sensitive issue being what Indian people view as the desecration of the bodies and graves of their ancestors. The American Indian Religious Freedom Act (AIRFA) was passed by Congress in 1978 and was later amplified in 1996 by President Clinton's Executive Order 13007 for the preservation of sacred sites. The problems with AIRFA are several: First, its Judeo-Christian assumptions do not adequately address the nature of Indigenous religious beliefs and practices, it has no "teeth," or enforcement provisions, and it is binding on the federal government and its agencies only.

A major issue of concern to the Native American community is the practice by the scientific community of collecting and storing Indian human remains (defined as "specimens") in museums, university anthropology departments, and private collections. Widespread protests by Native organizations led to the passage of National Museum of the American Indian Act in 1989. The act specifically required the Smithsonian Institution to inventory, identify, and return Indigenous human remains to the appropriate Native nation. Then in 1990 Congress enacted the Native American Graves Protection and Repatriation Act (NAGPRA). "NAGPRA sets out the procedures and standards for the repatriation of human remains, funerary objects, sacred items, and objects of cultural patrimony, and provides for the protection and ownership of materials unearthed on federal and tribal lands by institutions that receive federal funding."[2] Discussant Walter Echo-Hawk pinpoints the case of the Kennewick Man to illustrate the difficulty faced by the Native community in the enforcement of NAGPRA. Unearthed in 1996 in the Columbia River gorge, the 9,000-year-old remains of "the Ancient One" (as the Indians call him) has been claimed by both five area tribes and the scientific community who want to do further "study." The legal conflict concerning repatriation is viewed by Native Americans as a backlash from the scientific community that violates intent of NAGPRA, if not the law itself. (These issues are addressed in more detail in Part VII, "The Sacred: Spirituality and Sacred Geography.")

Elizabeth Cook-Lynn is a respected Dakota writer and scholar, and former editor of the *Wicazo Sa Review*. Reading 5, "New Indians, Old Wars," is an excerpt from the concluding chapter of her recent book, *New Indians, Old Wars*, in which she contends that anti-Indianism is a crime against humanity. In making this argument, Cook-Lynn presents the case of the theft of the sacred Black Hills, the broken treaties, and oppression of Native Americans as a metaphor for what is wrong with the United States as a world power. She posits a connection between the U.S. military invasion of Iraq and the earlier conquest and colonization of Indian nations. Anti-Indianism, she writes, is not simply about racism, as is the case for African-Americans. She says, "Anti-Indianism is also about the failure of politics, nationhood and sovereignty, possession of land, indigenousness, and self-determination."[3] Thus the past is prologue to the present.

In the box titled "Free Leonard Peltier," Steve Talbot documents the case of Indian political prisoner Leonard Peltier. Most citizens of the United States are unaware that there are racial and ethnic minority "prisoners of conscience" in the country's jails who were either framed or wrongly convicted because of their ethnicity and political advocacy. Peltier's conviction grew out of Indian protests and the FBI vendetta against the

American Indian Movement in the 1970s. The federal government's controversial imprisonment of Peltier is protested throughout the world and casts an ugly pall on the concept of democracy and the protection of human rights in the United States.

NOTES

1. Jack Forbes, "Irregular Militias Rooted in American History," *Windspeaker*, 13, no. 6 (October 1995), 6.
2. Winona LaDuke, *Recovering the Sacred: The Power of Naming and Claiming*. (Cambridge, MA. South End Press, 2005), p. 79.
3. Elizabeth Cook-Lyon, *New Indians, Old Wars*. (University of Illinois Press, 2007), p. 2008.

THE POCAHONTAS PERPLEX
THE IMAGE OF INDIAN WOMEN IN AMERICAN CULTURE

Rayna Green

In one of the best known old Scottish ballads, "Young Beichan" or "Lord Bateman and the Turkish King's Daughter" as it is often known in America, a young English adventurer travels to a strange, foreign land. The natives are of a darker color than he, and they practice a pagan religion. The man is captured by the King (Pasha, Moor, Sultan) and thrown in a dungeon to await death. Before he is executed, however, the pasha's beautiful daughter—smitten with the elegant and wealthy visitor—rescues him and sends him homeward. But she pines away for love of the now remote stranger who has gone home, apparently forgotten her, and contracted a marriage with a "noble" "lady" of his own kind. In all the versions, she follows him to his own land, and in most, she arrives on his wedding day whereupon he throws over his bride-to-be for the darker but more beautiful Princess. In most versions, she becomes a Christian, and she and Lord Beichan live happily ever after.

In an article called "The Mother of Us All," Philip Young suggests the parallel between the ballad story

and the Pocahontas–John Smith rescue tale.[1] With the exception of Pocahontas' marriage to John Rolfe (still, after all, a Christian stranger), the tale should indeed sound familiar to most Americans nurtured on Smith's salvation by the Indian Princess. Actually, Europeans were familiar with the motif before John Smith offered his particular variant in the *Generall Historie of Virginie* (1624).

Francis James Child, the famous ballad collector, tells us in his *English and Scottish Popular Ballads* that "Young Beichan" (Child #40) matches the tale of Gilbert Beket, St. Thomas Aquinas' father, as well as a legend recounted in the *Gesta Romanorum*, one of the oldest collections of popular tales. So the frame story was printed before 1300 and was, no doubt, well distributed in oral tradition before then. Whether or not our rakish adventurer-hero, John Smith, had heard the stories or the ballad, we cannot say, but we must admire how life mirrors art since his story follows the outlines of the traditional tale most admirably. What we do know is that the elements of the tale appealed to Europeans long before Americans had the opportunity to attach their affection for it onto Pocahontas. Whether or not we believe Smith's tale—and there are many reasons not to—we cannot ignore the impact the story has had on the American imagination.

"The Mother of Us All" became our first aristocrat, and perhaps our first saint, as Young implies. Certainly, the image of her body flung over the endangered head of our hero constitutes a major scene in national myth. Many paintings and drawings of this scene exist, and it appears in popular art on everything from wooden fire engine side panels to calendars. Some renderings betray such ignorance about the Powhatan Indians of Virginia—often portraying them in Plains dress—that one quickly comes to understand that it is the mythical scene, not the accuracy of detail that moved artists. The most famous portrait of Pocahontas, the only one said to be done from life (at John Rolfe's request), shows the Princess in Elizabethan dress, complete with ruff and velvet hat—the Christian, English lady the ballad expects her to become and the lady she indeed became for her English husband and her faithful audience for all time. The earliest literary efforts in America, intended to give us American rather than European topics, featured Pocahontas in plenty. Poems and plays—like James Nelson Barber's *The Indian Princess; or, La Belle Sauvage* (1808) and George Washington Custis' *The Settlers of Virginia* (1827), as well as contemporary American novels, discussed by Leslie Fiedler in *The Return of the Vanishing American*—dealt with her presence, or sang her praises from the pages of literary magazines and from the stages of popular playhouses throughout the east.[2] Traditional American ballads like "Jonathan Smith" retold the thrilling story; schoolbook histories included it in the first pages of every text; nineteenth century commercial products like cigars, perfume and even flour used Pocahontas' name as come-on; and she appeared as the figurehead for American warships and clippers. Whether or not she saved John Smith, her actions as recounted by Smith set up one kind of model for Indian–White relations that persists—long after most Indians and Anglos ceased to have face-to-face relationships. Moreover, as a model for the national understanding of Indian women, her significance is undeniable. With her darker, negatively viewed sister, the Squaw—or, the anti-Pocahontas, as Fiedler calls her—the Princess intrudes on the national consciousness, and a potential cult waits to be resurrected when our anxieties about who we are make us recall her from her woodland retreat.[3]

Americans had a Pocahontas Perplex even before the teenage Princess offered us a real figure to hang the iconography on. The powerfully symbolic Indian woman, as Queen and Princess, has been with us since 1575 when she appeared to stand for the New World. Artists, explorers, writers and political leaders found the Indian as they cast about for some symbol with which to identify this earthly, frightening, and beautiful paradise; E. McClung Fleming has given one of the most complete explications of these images.[4] The misnamed Indian was the native dweller, who fit conveniently into the various traditional folkloric, philosophical and literary patterns characteristic of European thought at the time.[5] Europeans easily adopted the Indian as the iconographic representative of the Americas. At first, Caribbean and Brazilian (Tupinamba) Indians, portrayed amidst exotic flora and fauna, stood for the New World's promises and dangers. The famous and much-reproduced "Four Continents" illustrations (circa, early 16th century) executed by artists who had seen Indians and ones who had not, ordinarily pictured a male and female pair in America's place.[6] But the paired symbol apparently did not satisfy the need for a personified figure, and the Indian Queen began to appear as the sole representation for the Americas in 1575. And until 1765 or thereabouts, the bare-breasted, Amazonian Native American Queen reigned. Draped in leaves, feathers, and animal skins as well as in heavy Caribbean jewelry, she appeared aggressive, militant, and armed with spears and arrows. Often, she rode on an armadillo, and stood with her foot on the slain body of an animal or human enemy. She was the familiar Mother-Goddess figure—full-bodied, powerful, nurturing but dangerous—embodying the opulence and peril of the New World. Her environment was rich and colorful, and that, with the allusions to Classical Europe through the Renaissance portrayal of her large, naked body, attached her to Old World History as well as to New World virtue.

Her daughter, the Princess, enters the scene when the colonies begin to move toward independence, and she becomes more "American" and less Latin than her mother. She seems less barbarous than the Queen; the rattlesnake (Jones' "Don't Tread On Me" sign) defends her, and her enemies are defeated by male warriors rather than by her own armed hand. She is Britannia's daughter as well as that of the Carib Queen, and she wears the triangular Phrygian cap and holds the liberty pole of her later, metamorphosed sister, Miss Liberty (the figure on the Statue of Liberty and the Liberty dime). She is young, leaner in the Romanesque rather than Greek mode, and distinctly Caucasian, though her skin remains slightly tinted in some renderings. She wears the loose, flowing gowns of classical statuary rather than animal skins, and Roman sandals grace her feet. She is armed, usually with a spear, but she also carries a peace pipe, a flag, or the starred and striped shield of Colonial America. She often stands with The Sons of Liberty, or later, with George Washington.

Thus, the Indian woman began her symbolic, many-faceted life as a Mother figure—exotic, powerful, dangerous, and beautiful—and as a representative of American liberty and European classical virtue translated into New World terms. She represented, even defended America. But when real Indian women—Pocahontas and her sisters—intruded into the needs bound up in symbols and the desires inherent in daily life, the responses to the symbol became more complex, and the Pocahontas perplex emerged as a controlling metaphor in the American experience. The Indian woman, along with her male counterparts, continued to stand for the New World and for rude native nobility, but the image of the savage remained as well. The dark side of the Mother-Queen figure is the savage Squaw, and even Pocahontas, as John Barth suggests in *The Sotweed Factor*, is motivated by lust.

Both her nobility as a Princess and her savagery as a Squaw are defined in terms of her relationships with male figures. If she wishes to be called a Princess, she must save or give aid to white men. The only good Indian—male or female, Squanto, Pocahontas, Sacagawea, Cochise, the Little Mohee or the Indian Doctor—rescues and helps white men. But the Indian woman is even more burdened by this narrow definition of a "good Indian," for it is she, not the males, whom white men desire sexually. Because her image is so tied up with abstract virtue—indeed, with America—she must remain the Mother Goddess-Queen. But acting as a real female, she must be a partner and lover of Indian men, a mother to Indian children, and an object of lust for white men. To be Mother, Queen and lover is, as Oedipus' mother, Jocasta, discovered, difficult and perhaps impossible. The paradox so often noted in Latin/Catholic countries where men revere their mothers and sisters, but use prostitutes so that their "good" women can stay pure is to the point here. Both race conflict and national identity, however, make this particular Virgin-Whore paradox more

complicated than others. The Indian woman finds herself burdened with an image that can only be understood as dysfunctional, even though the Pocahontas perplex affects us all. Some examination of the complicated dimensions of that image might help us move toward change.

In songs like "Jonathan Smith," "Chipeta's Ride" and others sung in oral tradition, the Indian woman saves white men.[7] In "Chipeta's Ride," she even saves a white woman from lust-enraged Indian males. Ordinarily, however, she rescues her white lover or an anonymous male captive. Always called a Princess (or Chieftain's Daughter), she, like Pocahontas, has to violate the wishes and customs of her own "barbarous" people to make good the rescue, saving the man out of love and often out of "Christian sympathy." Nearly all the "good" Princess figures are converts, and they cannot bear to see their fellow Christians slain by "savages." The Princess is "civilized"; to illustrate her native nobility, most pictures portray her as white, darker than the Europeans, but more Caucasian than her fellow natives.

If unable to make the grand gesture of saving her captive lover or if thwarted from marrying him by her cruel father, the Chieftain, the Princess is allowed the even grander gesture of committing suicide when her lover is slain or fails to return to her after she rescues him. In the hundreds of "Lover's Leap" legends which abound throughout the country, and in traditional songs like "The Indian Bride's Lament," our heroine leaps over a precipice, unable to live without her loved one. In this movement from political symbolism (where the Indian woman defends America) to psychosexual symbolism (where she defends or dies for white lovers), we can see part of the Indian woman's dilemma. To be "good," she must defy her own people, exile herself from them, become white, and perhaps suffer death.

Those who did not leap for love continued to fall in love with white men by the scores, and here the sacrifices are several. The women in songs like "The Little Mohea," "Little Red Wing," and "Juanita, the Sachem's Daughter" fall in love with white travellers, often inviting them to share their blissful, idyllic, woodland paradise. If their lovers leave them, they often pine away, die of grief, or leap off a cliff, but in a number of songs, the white man remains with the maiden, preferring her life to his own, "civilized" way. "The Little Mohea " is a prime example of such a song.

"Pocahontas Saving Captain John Smith, " steel engraving, mid-nineteenth century.

As I went out walking for pleasure one day,
In the sweet recollection, to dwell time away.
As I sat amusing myself on the grass,
Oh, who should I spy but a fair Indian lass.

She walked up behind me, taking hold of my hand,
She said, "You are a stranger and in a strange land,
But if you will follow, you're welcome to come
And dwell in my cottage that I call my home."

My Mohea was gentle, my Mohea was kind.
She took me when a stranger and clothed me
    when cold.
She learned me the language of the lass of Mohea.
"I'm going to leave you, so farewell my dear.
The ship's sails are spreading and home I must steer."
The last time I saw her she was standing on the strand,
And as my boat passed her she waved me her hand.

Saying "when you have landed and with the one
    you love,
Think of pretty Mohea in the coconut grove."
I am home but no one comes near me nor none do I see,
That would equal compare with the lass of Mohea.

Oh, the girl that I loved proved untrue to me.
I'll turn my course backward far over the sea.
I'll turn my course backward, from this land
    I'll go free,
And go spend my days with the little Mohea.

Such songs add to the exotic and sexual, yet maternal and contradictorily virginal image of the Indian Princess, and are reminiscent of the contemporary white soldier's attachments to "submissive," "sacrificial," "exotic" Asian women.

As long as Indian women keep their exotic distance or die (even occasionally for love of Indian men), they are permitted to remain on the positive side of the image. They can help, stand by, sacrifice for, and aid white men. They can, like their native brothers, heal white men, and the Indian reputation as healer dominated the nineteenth century patent medicine business. In the ads for such medicines, the Indian woman appears either as a helpmate to her "doctor" husband or partner or as a healer herself. In several ads (and the little dime novels often accompanying the patent medicine products), she is the mysterious witch-healer. Thus, she shares in the Caucasian or European female's reputation for potential evil. The references here to power, knowledge, and sexuality remain on the good side of the image. In this incarnation, the Princess offers help in the form of medicine rather than love.

The tobacco industry also capitalized on the Princess' image, and the cigar-store figures and ads associated with the tobacco business replicate the Princess figures to sell its products. Cigar-store Princesses smile and beckon men into tobacco shops. They hold a rose, a bundle of cigars, or some tobacco leaves (a sign of welcome in the colonial days), and they smile invitingly with their Caucasian lips. They also sell the product from tobacco packages, and here, like some of the figures in front of the shops, Diana-like or more militant Minerva (Wonder-Woman)-like heroines offer the comforts of the "Indian weed." They have either the rounded, infantile, semi-naked (indicating innocence) bodies of Renaissance angels or the bodies and clothes of classical heroines. The Mother Goddess and Miss Liberty peddle their more abstract wares, as Indian Princesses, along with those of the manufacturer. Once again, the Princess comforts white men, and while she promises much, she remains aloof.

But who becomes the white man's sexual partner? Who forms liaisons with him? It cannot be the Princess, for she is sacrosanct. Her sexuality can be hinted at but never realized. The Princess' darker twin, the Squaw, must serve this side of the image, and again, relationships with males determine what the image will be. In the case of the Squaw, the presence of overt and realized sexuality converts the image from positive to negative. White men cannot share sex with the Princess, but once they do so with a real Indian woman, she cannot follow the required love-and-rescue pattern. She does what white men want for money or lust. In the traditional songs, stories, obscene jokes, contemporary literary works and popular and pictorializations of the Squaw, no heroines are allowed. Squaws

A cigar-store figure.

An old chewing tobacco advertisement, mid-nineteenth century.

share in the same vices attributed to Indian men—drunkenness, stupidity, thievery, venality of every kind—and they live in shacks on the edge of town rather than in a woodland paradise.

Here, Squaws are shamed for their relationships with white men, and the males who share their beds—the "squaw men"—or "bucks," if they are Indian—share their shame. When they live with Indian males, Squaws work for their lazy bucks and bear large numbers of fat "papooses." In one joke, a white visitor to a reservation sees an over burdened squaw with ten children hanging on her skirts. "Where's your husband?" the visitor demands. "He ought to be hung!" "Ugh," says the squaw, "pretty well-hung!" They too are fat, and unlike their Princess sisters, dark and possessed of cruder, more "Indian" features. When stories and songs describe relationships with white men, Squaws are understood as mere economic and sexual conveniences for the men who—unlike John Smith or a "brave"—are tainted by association with her. Tale after tale describes the Indian whores, their alcoholic and sexual excesses with white trappers and hunters. A parody of the beautiful-maiden song, "Little Red Wing," speaks of her lewd sister who "lays on her back in a cowboy shack, and lets cowboys poke her in the crack." The result of this cowboy-squaw liaison is a "brat in a cowboy hat with his asshole between his eyes." This Squaw is dark, and squat, and even the cigar-store Indians show the changes in conception. No Roman sandals grace their feet, and their features are more "Indian" and "primitive" than even their male counterparts. The cigar-store squaws often had papooses on their backs, and some had corrugated places on their hips to light the store patrons' matches. When realities intrude on mythos, even Princesses can become Squaws as the text of the ragtime song, "On an Indian Reservation," illustrates.

On an Indian reservation, far from home and
   civilization,
Where the foot of White man seldom trod.
Whiteman went to fish one summer,
Met an Indian maid—a hummer,
Daughter of Big-Chief-Spare-the-rod.
Whiteman threw some loving glances, took this
   maid to Indian dances,
Smoked his pipe of peace, took chances living
   in a teepee made of fur.
Rode with her on Indian ponies, bought her
   diamond rings, all phonies,
And he sang these loving words to her:
Chorus:
   You're my pretty little Indian Napanee.
   Won't you take a chance and marry me.
   Your Daddy Chief, 'tis my belief,
   To a very merry wedding will agree.
   True, you're a dark little Indian maid,
   But I'll sunburn to a darker shade,
   I'll wear feathers on my head,
   Paint my skin an Indian red,
   If you will be my Napanee.

With his contact soon he caught her,
Soon he married this big chief's daughter,
Happiest couple that you ever saw.
But his dreams of love soon faded,
Napanee looked old and jaded,
Just about like any other squaw.
Soon there came papoose in numbers, redskin yells
   disturbed his slumbers,
Whiteman wonders at his blunders—now the
   feathers drop upon his head.
Sorry to say it, but he's a-wishing, that he'd never
   gone a-fishing,
Or had met this Indian maid and said:
Chorus:

The Indian woman is between a rock and a hard place. Like that of her male counterpart, her image is freighted with such ambivalence that she has little room to move. He, however, has many more modes in which to participate though he is still severely handicapped by the prevailing stereotypes. They are both tied to definition by relationships with white men, but she is especially burdened by the narrowness of that definition. Obviously, her image is one that is troublesome to all women, but, tied as it is to a national mythos, its complexity has a special piquance. As Vine Deloria points out in *Custer Died For Your Sins*, many whites claim kinship with some distant Indian Princess grandmother, and thus try to resolve their "Indian problem" with such sincere affirmations of relationship.[8]

Such claims make it impossible for the Indian woman to be seen as real. She does not have the power to evoke feeling as a real mother figure, like the black woman, even though *that* image has a burdensome negative side. American children play with no red mammy dolls. She cannot even evoke the terror the "castrating (white) bitch" inspires. Only the male, with upraised tomahawk, does that. The many expressions which treat of her image remove her from consideration as more than an image. As some abstract, noble Princess tied to "America" and to sacrificial zeal, she has power as a symbol. As the Squaw, a depersonalized object of scornful convenience, she is powerless. Like her male relatives she may be easily destroyed without reference to her humanity. (When asked why he killed women and children at Sand Creek, the commanding general of the U.S. Cavalry was said to have replied, "nits make lice.") As the Squaw, her physical removal or destruction can be understood as necessary to the progress of civilization even though her abstracted sister, the Princess, stands for that very civilization. Perhaps the Princess had to be removed from her powerful symbolic place, and replaced with the male Uncle Sam because she confronted America with too many contradictions. As symbol and reality, the Indian woman suffers from our needs, and by both race and sex stands damned.

Since the Indian so much represents America's attachment to a romantic past and to a far distant nobility, it is predictable but horrible that the Indian woman should symbolize the paradoxical entity once embodied for the European in the Princess in the tower and the old crone in the cave. It is time that the Princess herself is rescued and the Squaw relieved of her obligatory service. The Native American woman, like all women, needs a definition that stands apart from that of males, red or white. Certainly, the Native woman needs to be defined as Indian, in Indian terms. Delightful and interesting as Pocahontas' story may be, she offers an intolerable metaphor for the Indian-White experience. She and the Squaw offer unendurable metaphors for the lives of Indian women. Perhaps if we give up the need for John Smith's fantasy and the trappers' harsher realities, we will find, for each of us, an image that does not haunt and perplex us. Perhaps if we explore the meaning of Native American lives outside the boundaries of the stories, songs, and pictures given us in tradition, we will find a more humane truth.

NOTES

1. "The Mother of Us All," *Kenyon Review* 24 (Summer 1962), 391–441.

2. See Jay B. Hubbell, "The Smith-Pocahontas Story in Literature," *The Virginia Magazine of History and Biography* 65 (July 1957), 275–300.

3. The many models, stereotypes and images operative for the Indian in Anglo-American vernacular culture are discussed in my dissertation, "The Only Good Indian: The Image of the Indian in Vernacular American Culture," Indiana University, 1973.

4. E. McClung Fleming, "Symbols of the United States; From Indian Queen to Uncle Sam," in Ray B. Browne et al., eds. *The Frontiers of American Culture* (Lafayette, IN: Purdue University Press, 1967), pp. 1–24; "The American Image As Indian Princess, 1765–1783." *Winterthur Portfolio* 2 (1968), 65–81.

5. For a summary of the philosophical backgrounds of the "Noble Savage" complex of beliefs and ideas, see Roy Harvey Pearce, *Savagism and Civilization: A Study of the Indian and the American Mind* (rpt. 1953, Baltimore: Johns Hopkins University Press, 1967). For references to folk motifs in Indo-European tradition, see Stith Thompson, *The Motif Index of Folk Literature*, 6 vols. (rpt. 1932–36, Bloomington, IN: Indiana University Press, 1955–58).

6. See Clare de Corbellier, "Miss America and Her Sisters: Personification of the Four Parts of the World," *Bulletin of the Metropolitan Museum of Art* 19 (1961), pp. 209–223; James Hazen Hyde, *L'Iconographie des quatre parties du monde dans les tapisseries de Gazette des Beaux Arts* (Paris: Beaux Arts, 1924).

7. Austin Fife and Francesca Redden, "The Pseudo-Indian Folksongs of the Anglo-Americans and French-Canadians," *The Journal of American Folklore* 67, no. 266 (1954): 381; Olive Wooley Burt, *American Murder Ballads and Their Stories* (rpt. 1958, New York: Citadel Press, 1964), pp. 146–49.

8. Vine Deloria, *Custer Died for Your Sins* (New York: Avon Books, 1968), p. 11.

PUNISHING INSTITUTIONS
THE STORY OF CATHERINE (CEDAR WOMAN)

Luana Ross

INTRODUCTION

I met Catherine in 1990, at the Women's Correctional Center in Montana. She is currently serving a forty year sentence and is housed at the women's prison in Billings. When Catherine was first arrested, the local media used a simplistic Adam and Eve theory and presented her as a controlling woman and the driving force behind the crime. In reality, Catherine's "crime" was that she was present when the horrendous murder of a young white man was committed. A plea bargain was arranged and she was charged with a lesser crime, not kidnapping and homicide, with the stipulation that she provide testimony against her male codefendants, who are members of her tribe.

At her sentencing, the judge asked her if she realized why she was sentenced to prison. A bewildered Catherine replied, "No." According to Catherine, the judge responded: "Because you were aware of a crime in progress and did nothing to stop it; therefore, you are just as guilty because you allowed this to happen." Although Catherine did not commit the murder, she lives everyday with the guilt of not halting the crime, as though she could have possibly had the authority to stop two powerfully violent men from killing a young man. To date, Catherine has been in prison for nine years and has been continually denied parole. Because of the seriousness of the crime, in conjunction with the dynamics of racism in the state of Montana, Catherine believes that she is singled out by prison staff and the parole board, and subsequently issued racialized harassment.

Catherine wants her story to be heard because she is committed to breaking the silence of violence and exposing its psychological toll, especially on children. Nevertheless, her identity is disguised in an effort to protect members of her family. Catherine's narrative, only a glimpse into a life filled with turbulence, is based on interviews conducted from 1991 to 1994 and data from legal papers, prison records, newspapers, and personal correspondence.

EURO-AMERICAN CRIMINAL JUSTICE

Native women face overwhelming odds at every stage of the criminal justice system. Rafter (1990) suggests that race and gender influence incarceration rates. Concurring with Dobash, Dobash, and Gutteridge (1986), it is imperative to research the notion of "criminality" by examining the socio-economic conditions in which crimes occur. Some women, Native and non-Native, are imprisoned at the Women's Correctional Center for such "crimes" as killing abusive family members, being at the crime scene, writing "bad checks" to adequately care for their children, and yet others maintain their innocence (Ross 1996, 1997).

Chesney-Lind (1991, 64) submits that the personal lives of imprisoned women and crime-type must be perceived within "the gendered nature of these women's lives, options, and crimes." The contextualizing of the criminalization process is central to the understanding of female "deviance." Personal experiences of imprisoned women reflect the structure of Euro-American society; a structure in which certain subgroups are not only penalized because of their race/ethnicity, gender, and class but controlled as well. This is particularly clear when the violence experienced in prisoners' lives prior to incarceration and their subsequent criminalization is examined. For many imprisoned women the violence began early in their lives, while for others it was not present until they were older (Ross 1997). Chesney-Lind (1991) suggests that 88 percent of imprisoned women in the United States were violently victimized prior to their

incarceration. The lives of prisoners in Montana are comparable to the national data. Their histories are characterized by violence of every form: physical, emotional, poverty, racism, sexism, and classism. Moreover, the violence is institutionalized. These women were violated by family members, boyfriends, jail, reform school, Indian boarding schools, and foster and adoptive care. The oppression, thus, is as complex as it is relentless. Catherine's narrative is typical of the cruelty that many women endured prior to their incarceration and while imprisoned (see Ross 1994, 1997).

One cruelty, and a form of violence, is the fact that Native Americans are over represented in Euro-America's criminal justice system. In 1994, Native people comprised 2.9 percent of both federal and state prisons, although they were only 0.6 percent of the total U.S. population (Camp and Camp 1995). This disparity is more clearly seen at the state level where Natives are 33.2 percent of the total prisoner population in Alaska, 23.6 percent in South Dakota, 16.9 percent in North Dakota, and 17.3 percent in Montana (Camp and Camp 1995). Native Americans in Montana are approximately 6 percent of the total state population. While Native men comprise approximately 20 percent of the total male prisoner population, approximately 25 percent of the total female prisoner population are Native women (Ross 1997). A study on Native women (Ross 1997) suggests that Native women are more likely to be imprisoned than white women or Native and white men, indicating racism and sexism in Montana's criminal justice system.

Catherine fits the typical profile of an incarcerated Native woman (Ross 1993, 1994, 1997): She was thirty-one when she was initially incarcerated, has six children, was beaten by supposed loved ones, and sexually abused as a child and later as an adult. She has a sporadic employment history, quit high school, and was convicted of a violent crime (her first felony). The influence of violence on one's life is readily depicted by Catherine's story and illuminates how personal biography is tied to the larger societal structure.

CEDAR WOMAN

Catherine, Cedar Woman (her Indian name), was born in a log house and grew up on one of Montana's seven Indian reservations. She was raised in a traditional Native American family by members of her extended family. Catherine fluently speaks both her Native language and English, although she is more comfortable conversing in her Native tongue. Of her early life and the wisdom of elders, Catherine comments:

> I grew up on the reservation and lived with extended family members, and attended a Catholic boarding school. My grandmother often shared with me that our Mother Earth is the caretaker for [God]. Also, when other Indian elders talked about visions, I had doubts and wondered if their visions and predictions were true just like any other child would question and wonder. My grandmother, and other elders of neighboring reservations, made predictions during my youth that are now coming true. They raised me to believe in the Native American Church and I learned to maintain my focus on [God] through any situation. We have learned to have faith in [God] through living life and learning to survive. This journey in life helps us to learn; and at some point we have a spiritual awakening that helps us identify that the freedom we are all seeking is within.

Catherine has four sisters and four brothers; one sister and two brothers are deceased. Another brother was adopted by a white family, and the two have never met. She attended a Catholic Indian boarding school, married at a young age, and began having children.

On the surface, it appears that Catherine was raised in a traditional and functional family; however, this is not the case. Catherine never mentions her father and has many negative memories of her mother. Often Catherine's mother was drinking when she would visit her, which greatly displeased other family members. As a child, Catherine rarely saw her mother. What she remembers most about her mother, aside from her drinking, was that she did not appear to like Catherine. She said: "It seemed like she didn't like me. There was no physical contact—like you give your kids a hug and stuff. She never did do that. She would just sit and look at me. She just kind of floated in and out. And the times that she did show up, she was always with white guys. I didn't even know she was my mom. I thought my aunt was my mom."

As Catherine matured she witnessed her uncle physically abuse other family members, including her aunt and her grandmother. She became increasingly angry with her biological mother and, furthermore, reasoned that brutality was an acceptable behavior:

> I was angry at my real mom because she was my mom and she drank all the time. I just didn't want anything from her. And then I just kind of continued in my little

life with that and feeling angry. When I would see my mother, I would let this anger show. Then I started treating her like how I seen my uncle treating my aunt. You know, when my aunt and uncle would go drinking, well when they came back home my uncle would beat her up all the time. There were so many times. I don't know if my brother remembers it, but I always do. We would be the only ones awake and we would watch my uncle. He beat her so many times that sometimes you wouldn't recognize her the next day. And they walked around like nothing happened. . . . I felt funny. I don't know how the other kids felt but I remember feeling real funny. And, I just put my head down and started eating. Then I looked at my grandma and I looked at my aunt. Then my uncle came in and he sat down and started talking. They were all visiting with one another like nothing was going on. You know, like nothing had happened! So then I started thinking that nothing was wrong.

The upheaval and family secrets continued as Catherine grew. She witnessed not only the brutality between her aunt and uncle, she also saw her uncle and biological mother beat her grandmother. Remembering a family thoroughly and painfully immersed in violence, she said: "And he [her uncle] said, 'I'm going to kill your daughter.' And he was just hollering at my grandmother. And they talk about respect for the elders now. And then they wonder why this generation and the ones to come don't have respect for the elders. You learn what you see. I watched my real mother break my grandmother's arm." Despite the turmoil, Catherine's grandmother encouraged her to pray for strength and to leave the reservation. According to Catherine, her grandmother said: "Go somewhere else and learn what's going on out there. Don't be like the rest of them and don't stay around here—it's no good now." To this elder Native woman, the good old days were gone and the reservation grew increasingly violent.

Catherine was eight years old when her uncle began sexually abusing her. Her aunt, rather than stopping the transgression, allowed it to continue. Catherine remembers: "My aunt came and laid down with me one night and she was stroking my hair. I was just a little girl—about eight. She was laying there with me and she was stroking my hair. Then my uncle climbed in bed on the other side and I remember her saying, 'Just lay still and it won't hurt—it'll be OK.' These are the people that loved me; these are the ones I trusted [crying]." Because Catherine's aunt did little to stop the rapes—when her aunt intervened she was abused by her tyrannical husband—she soon became angry with her. As an adult, Catherine discovered that her aunt was taking "sleeping pills" to cope with her own oppression and, subsequently, had little initiative and clearly no power to stop her husband from terrorizing the household.

According to Catherine, her extended family took care of her and her brother, not because of love, but out of a twisted sense of responsibility and family obligation. Catherine watched her family's collapse, which left her feeling insignificant and frustrated:

> You know how you watch the wind blowing? It slowly keeps blowing something apart? Maybe you watch it loosening the dirt and it just keeps blowing away a little bit at a time. That's how I seen our family. My grandmother started drinking. I was just slowly watching everything go and when you're a small child growing up watching all of this, it's scary. I can't think of no other word to make it sound easier, softer. It's just plain scary. And nobody to ever talk to. You see, these adults are people that you come to depend on. They're suppose to know what they're doing; they're the smart ones, you know.

During Catherine's childhood, she was shuffled between various relatives and Indian boarding school. One proposed alternative was to live with her mother, who was drinking heavily and frequently physically abused Catherine and her brother. Catherine's stays with her mother were always short-lived. She preferred to live with her grandmother, but ill health and old age prevented a long-term placement. The family secrets and the silence were unbearable to Catherine, and at age twelve she began skipping school and drinking as a way to numb her pain: "I just felt like I was better off being in my own little drunk world and then I didn't have to think about these things anymore. I knew sooner or later that I would pass out and then I'd forget about it—until I sobered up again."

Witnessing men abuse women provoked a pattern in Catherine's life. Not unexpectedly, Catherine was involved in remarkably abusive relationships with men:

> That's the only thing I knew. Someone would beat me up and I thought they loved me. And this man did both; he beat me up and he used me in a bad way—in a sexual way. And he was telling me he loved me, and I'd listen to him. The way I was raised, I watched my aunts and no matter how bad they got beat up, they still listened to their husbands. You know, this is what I learned. Then all of a sudden my aunt's saying, "Why do you do that? Why do you let these men beat you up and you always go right back to him?" That's what I'm talking about. They're giving that advice away but they're doing it themselves.

One of the men Catherine was involved with was the man who committed the murder that landed her in prison. Not surprisingly, their relationship was extremely abusive and she lived in continual fear of this man: "I started living with him just about a couple of months before we got in trouble [arrested for the murder]. My kids were scared of him and I was really scared of this man. He beat my ex-husband up really bad. . . . He was going to shoot my ex-husband . . . and I begged and pleaded with him and I promised him, 'I'll do anything you ask—just don't do that.'" Describing a remarkably controlling person, she continues: "I couldn't go anywhere by myself—he'd always come with me, even when I went to the bathroom."

Catherine's co-defendants, as well as some tribal members, viewed her testimony against them as "snitching." To Catherine, however, she was merely telling the truth. Remembering prior beatings and intimidation, she was intensely afraid of her boyfriend (her co-defendant) and consequently unable to make a decision regarding her testimony. Family members prayed with her in jail and instructed her on honesty, a virtue in her tribe. According to Catherine, they told her: "We always taught you never to lie; we taught you to be honest. This is how you were raised. You were raised in the Indian way and that's one of the things is when you are Indian, you should not lie. We told you that. If you know something, you'd better say something."

Catherine was still confused about the role of her testimony and the label "snitch." That night she had a dream that aided in her decision to tell the truth:

> I went to bed and I was sleeping. All of a sudden, I felt really cold. And I was in that cell—that little tiny cell. All of a sudden, I just felt like someone was with me. Pretty soon, it got warm. And then I was sitting on a small couch and my grandmother was sitting there. My mother was there and she was holding my hand, but she wasn't saying anything. When I looked over, my other grandmother was sitting kitty-corner from us. Then my two grandfathers were there. One of my grandfathers lost part of his toes due to frost-bite, so he used a cane. When I looked at him, he was doing like I always saw him at home. He was bouncing his cane off the floor and he was singing real low. My other grandfather was sitting behind him. He seemed like he was listening to my other grandfather. Out of my whole family, my grandmother was the one that always did the talking. I mean, when you heard her voice you knew to be quiet. She was talking and leaning over this way. She said, "When we raised you, we told you when times get really hard to pray. This is how we raised you. We told you that but somewhere along the way, I think you forgot. I always talk to you." Then she turned

around and said, "Here, you take this—you're going to need this." And she gave me a piece of cloth. Then she said, "Where you're going, you're going to need this. This is going to help you." Then she turned back around and she said, "We raised you kids right and we always told you to tell the truth. You were raised the hard way, but that was for a reason." She was talking in [Native language]. She said, "We always tell you, don't be crying." I was listening and she turned around and gave me a sandwich. She said, "We told you to pray. Sometimes you have a hard walk. When you get hungry, this is for you." And I turned around and saw my sister [who is deceased]. She was laughing and she said, "Remember we'll always love you." I turned around and put the stuff on a little table behind me. When I turned back around, I was all alone. There was no one there and all of a sudden that warm feeling just started going away and I got really cold again. Then I woke up. I sat there and thought and thought. So that's what helped me make my decision.

Divinely inspired, Catherine made the decision to tell the truth about the crime. That her instructions to do so came in the form of a dream/vision, renders the notion of "snitching" sacrilegious.

MORE PRISONS, MORE VIOLENCE

Because Catherine has been incarcerated for such a lengthy time, she has a keen idea regarding control and punishment. As well, she is cognizant of the racism working within institutional structures. For instance, Catherine was sent to a Catholic Indian boarding school and experienced what she terms a transformation from Indian to Catholic.

> I became aware of disparate treatment years ago when I experienced incarceration after being convicted of an alcohol-related crime, and my experiences in Catholic boarding school. Although some acts of discrimination did not point to race, it suggested indifference toward Indians due to beliefs, traditions, and religions. Addressing issues of discrimination partially refers to Catholic priests and nuns who dictated the attempted conversion of Indians to Christians.

Intensely spiritual, Catherine relies on her Native religion to aid in her survival of the violence in her life prior to her incarceration and the violence of prisonization. She recalls the words of the aunt who raised her: "No matter what they have done, there is always a reason why people do the things they do but there is a solution at the end of every situation and we will all grow from it. And remember to pray before you begin any project because what you put into that project is what you will give to the people."

Similar to many other Native people, Catherine suggests that Native American culture, specifically prayer, gives Native people the strength to endure seemingly insurmountable events. In an effort to analyze discrimination, she questions specifically why Native Americans were subjected to genocidal practices. In an essay she wrote:

> Are Indians targeted in boarding schools and prisons simply because they have their own culture and religion? Does the fact that Indians have strong beliefs, traditions and upbringing make them a challenge for those obsessed to convert them? Perhaps trying to gain control by diverting the Indians attention to a man on the cross and attempting to convince them that their belief in the eagle and Great Grandfather is false or voodoo. Skillfully and manipulatively, authority figures use Indian beliefs in reverse psychology. In this way they gain a false trust, therefore, enabling a slow elimination of Native traditions forcing them to convert to their rules and non-Indian ways.

Catherine recognizes that early efforts to "civilize" and "educate" Native Americans were controlling and punishing. She said: "My memories of Catholic boarding school is one of strict discipline. Military style methods doled out to little Indian children once we were out-of-sight of our parents and grandparents. Little Indian children who could no longer speak Indian nor practice Indian ways were being punished for living their heritage and not allowed to discuss any of the school's disciplinary practices when they went home for visits." Catherine describes the strict regime they encountered as children:

> Disciplinary methods imposed on Indian children by nuns and priests consisted of sitting in the walk-in freezer an hour or more, hitting a brick wall twenty to thirty times with your fists (depending upon the infraction), or kneeling for hours and praying after they made us attend confession. Once four of us little girls would not say the Hail Mary and the Sister Superior marched us into a room and spanked us with a thick wide leather strap until our behinds bled. Then we had to memorize the Hail Mary as part of the sanction, which included attending confession for our disobedience to God. Another occurrence was when some Indian boys stepped out of line and were taken outside to hit the brick building with their fists. They were brought back into class after hitting the brick wall. They were crying and the tops of their hands were cut open and bleeding profusely. They wore bandages on their hands for awhile.

Of course, many Native people resisted such deplorable treatment. It is well known that many escaped by running away from boarding school.

Catherine relays just such an experience and the harsh penalties doled out by supposed servants of the Lord:

> A haunting memory of my cousin and her friend who escaped the boarding school left scars that have helped to develop certain fears which strongly influenced future behaviors. The school, with assistance from the police, organized a manhunt and upon finding them returned them to school for disciplinary action with no notification to the parents. Their sanction, without a hearing, consisted of time-out in a walk-in freezer in the cafeteria and for everyone to view them while we eat our meal. Their sanction lasted approximately two and a half hours. After they were released from the freezer, my friend and I helped them to warm up. My cousin shared with me, while I was rubbing her hands and legs, that they attempted to bring back chokecherries for us. But the cherries were taken away and they were told that this was a bad thing and they would have to be punished because they needed to eat healthier foods. The time-out in the freezer depended upon the infraction, and I witnessed some children held in the freezer longer than two hours.

One of the connections Catherine has made is the incredible similarities in Indian boarding schools and the penal system. An introspective journey enabled Catherine to link her past experiences of abuse to her present experiences in the criminal justice system. As a woman who has been incarcerated for many years, Catherine conclusively understands the prison system as biased against Native people. Additionally, she is well aware of the punishing efforts that exist in a system specifically designed as punitive, although operating under the guise of "rehabilitation."

Regarding the prison's dehumanizing classification process, Catherine said: "The prison system will process individuals by taking all their clothing, jewelry, and any personal items and by conducting a thorough strip search checking all cavity areas for any contraband. Usually the cavity searches are at the discretion of the officers. After the search, they delouse the person with lice shampoo and you are showered and issued your prison attire of a white gown with slippers for your feet. They lock the individual into an intake room for two weeks to a month, depending upon the classification and the conviction. After the classification process, a number is issued and the person is taken to their proper classification unit or allowed in the prison population."

According to Catherine, Indian boarding school had a similar degrading entrance process:

> I recall how we had to line up to be deloused. The awful smells of lice shampoo and the haircuts. Little white T-shirts and cotton panties and later cotton pajamas. Everything was white or dark blue and we marched around like little soldiers. For awhile, we wore dark blue uniforms—blue skirts with vests and white shirts. I do not recall what took place when they allowed us to wear our own clothing, although this came probably after I entered the fourth grade. Standing at attention like little soldiers—very still—not daring to flinch or even blink.

The dehumanizing ritual—whether it was Indian boarding school or prison—started with stripping, delousing, and the wearing of uniforms. The regime in prison, similar to boarding school, is militaristically fashioned. Catherine said that today in the women's prison one stands for the prison count "at 6 A.M., 11 A.M., and 3:30 P.M. and if anyone misses count or is considered disruptive, a disciplinary is issued. I remember in the boarding school days how we had to stand at the foot of our beds for morning and night count."

The oppression of the prison system, particularly for Native women, has been noted (Ross 1993, 1994, 1996, 1997; Sugar and Fox 1990). Prisoners are often left to the discretion of the guards and jailers. Catherine reminisces about being in jail with a relative and the frightful exercise of authority:

> I sat in my cell one night visiting with an uncle who was in the next cell and talking between the wall when we heard keys jingling and doors open. I heard the officers' voices on the other side of the cell block talking to someone—asking questions. The individual said he had nothing to say. Suddenly an officer began raising his voice saying he was going to teach him to do as they told him and never to disagree. Then I heard the sounds of loud slaps—the sounds of someone hitting a person. I heard sounds like someone hitting the wall and then crying. The man asked them to stop—that he had had enough. The slaps didn't stop until only a moan and then dead silence. The only sound was the hum of the air and space in the cell block. The beating lasted for approximately twenty minutes. Sitting quietly, my uncle whispers to me the words of advice from someone more experienced about incarceration. "You act like you never heard nothing and you say nothing. When they [the jailers] come and ask you anything, you smile and tell them it's good to see them and you are doing good."

They relocated Catherine's uncle to another jail. Now she was alone and exceedingly vulnerable as she awaited her trial. Sleepless over the loss of freedom and her family, in addition to the maliciousness of the crime, it was during this time that she was raped by a jailer. And not raped just once, but seven times over a period of three and a half months. In an effort to spare herself emotionally, Catherine methodically reports one rape:

> He [the jailer] took me into the office and told me to be quiet. He told me to lay down on the floor. He said he had something he wanted to try. He had a red condom. He put this on himself and pulled my shorts off. He raped me. When he finished, he stood there laughing at me. Then he went and got a towel and cleaned himself off. He told me to get dressed and then he sat down and told me to do oral sex on him. He told me to get on my knees and then he grabbed me by the face and started pushing his penis into my mouth until he ejaculated. Then he let go of me. He again laughed at me. He took me back to my cell, locked it, and left.

In an intimidating manner, the jailer told Catherine she better not say anything because he had much to lose and no one would believe her anyway. She was, after all, a Native woman and he was a white male with much power and authority. As the rapes continued, Catherine thought she might be pregnant but was afraid to tell anyone. Fortunately, she was not carrying a child. Although Catherine eventually raised the issue of her rape by the jailer to various authorities, nothing was done. In fact, similar to countless other women who are raped while incarcerated, no one believed her.

Because of the brutality in Catherine's life, she is repulsed by violence. She continues to have nightmares about the rapes, beatings, and crime of which she was eventually convicted. She is unable to watch violent movies on television or read about violence because it nauseates her. The sexual intimidation that presently exists in prison (see Ross 1994, 1997), particularly because of her history, repels her. Recognizing the hypocrisy of the criminal justice system, Catherine said: "The part that really bothers me is when I look around the prison. All these workers, you know, we're under their care. We're under their custody. They're the ones that have the lock and key. . . . And they have the nerve to talk about law and order; and they have the audacity to talk about discipline."

Women are particularly vulnerable in the criminal justice system and another issue that is gender specific is the hysterectomies that occurred while Catherine was incarcerated at the Women's Correctional Center (see Ross 1997). Of this form of violence, Catherine said:

> Recalling a personal situation, and as witness to other women experiencing the same, between 1988–1992 there were a great number of hysterectomies within the women's prison. They were referring women for

hysterectomies regularly. Without any information presented and the only solutions for the medical problems pertaining to women's monthly cycle or cervical complications, which could have had a simple remedy other than major surgery. The process of my own surgery developed into a debate with the nurse, which eventually resulted into threats of a disciplinary and strong rebuttal to my Indian upbringing. No other remedy or alternative was ever presented except the surgery. It was discovered later that the uterus was in healthy condition with no scarring or spots when inspected, according to my medical reports.

Before the surgery, Catherine argued with a prison nurse and guard, who escorted her to a room and tried to convince her of the "needed" operation. Additionally, they instructed her to "let go" of her Native beliefs because they would not help her. Catherine reasoned that she needed to see an Indian doctor for severe menstrual cramps and heavy bleeding. According to Catherine, the nurse screamed at her and said: "To hell with your traditions and beliefs. This is a medical issue."

The issue of denial of culture is noteworthy. Although the American Indian Religious Freedom Act was passed in 1978 to ensure that Native cultures could be freely practiced (including while one is incarcerated), there is little or no compliance at the Women's Correctional Center (Ross 1994, 1996, 1997). Catherine sent a memo to the chemical dependency counselor regarding her denial of religion. Because sweet grass and sage were believed by some prison staff to be drugs, she asked the counselor to please offer a cultural-awareness workshop for the staff. White prisoners, as well as prison staff (who are all white), are ignorant of Native culture and frequently refer to Native religion as "voo-doo" (for a thorough analysis see Ross 1996, 1997). In the memo to prison staff it was reported by Catherine that, "One inmate stated to me she has been told by another inmate that Native Americans are fooling staff by telling them we call this sweet grass when what we have is really opium." Catherine finds much solace in her Native culture, although the full practice is denied by prison staff. Evidently, within the prison Native culture is viewed as a liability, not a strength.

CONCLUSION

Catherine's narrative is reflective: By examining personal experiences we gain perspective into societal arrangements. Interrelated systems of oppression render Native women vulnerable to many types of violence found in social institutions. Critical to the understanding of female "deviance" is the contextualizing of the criminalization process. Catherine directly connects her involvement in an inhuman crime to a childhood devoid of love and filled with violence.

The predominant theme in Catherine's narrative is the reality of violence, whether it is individual or institutional. Moreover, Catherine has been imprisoned her entire life. Her prisons—all based on control—took the form of family, boarding school, abusive relationships with men, jail, and the Women's Correctional Center. As such, Catherine's experiences are gendered and racialized. We need to recognize the various ways in which Native women are imprisoned and raped, not only by individuals, but by institutions.

REFERENCES

Camp, Camille, and George Camp. 1995. *The Corrections Yearbook.* South Salem, NY: Criminal Justice Institute.

Chesney-Lind, Meda. 1991. Patriarchy, Prisons, and Jails: A Critical Look at Trends in Women's Incarceration. *The Prison Journal* 71(1):51–67.

Dobash, Russell P., R. Emerson Dobash, and Sue Gutteridge. 1986. *The Imprisonment of Women.* New York: Blackwell.

Rafter, Nicole Hahn. 1990. *Partial Justice: Women, Prisons, and Social Control* (2nd edition). New Brunswick, NJ: Transaction Publishers.

Ross, Luana. 1993. "Major Concerns of Imprisoned American Indian and White Mothers." In *Gender: Multi-Cultural Perspectives*, Judith T. Gonzalez-Calvo (ed.). Dubuque, IA: Kendall-Hunt.

———. 1994. "Race, Gender, and Social Control: Voices of Imprisoned Native American and White Women." *Wicazo Sa Review* 10(2):17–39.

———. 1996. Resistance and Survivance: Cultural Genocide and Imprisoned Native American Women." *Race, Gender, and Class* 3(2):125–41.

———. 1998. *Inventing the Savage: The Social Construction of Native American Criminality.* Austin: University of Texas Press.

Sugar, Fran, and Lana Fox. 1990. "Nistum Peyako Seht'wawin Iskwewak: Breaking Chains." *Canadian Journal of Women and Law.*

INDIAN-NAMED MASCOTS: AN ASSAULT ON SELF-ESTEEM

Tim Giago

It's shaping up to be quite a week. Two baseball teams with American Indian symbols and mascots are into the World Series, and the national media is giving the Indians a chance to respond.

This would not have happened five years ago.

Only in recent years, with the advent of a national forum and a national newspaper have the media doors finally opened to us.

My newspaper, *Indian Country Today,* started the campaign against Indians as mascots more than 13 years ago. My Knight Ridder-Tribune syndicated column opened more windows on the subject.

Out in Indian country some of the more than 20 Indian-operated radio stations have begun to use the airways to get across a point of view.

And yet, with all of this evidence that the majority of Indian people detest being used as mascots, the conservative *Arizona Republic* of Phoenix is still pushing the idea that Indians don't really care one way or the other. By referring to local Indian students—many of whom attend reservation schools with Indian symbols or names—the *Republic* is convinced this is a non-news subject.

Fact is, the Indian people operating or attending reservation schools with team names like Braves, Warriors or Chiefs do not act like your typical non-Indian sports fan.

They do not desecrate sacred Indian objects. They do not perform horrendous portrayals of what they suppose an Indian to be. They do not sing Hollywood war songs or make Hollywood whooping sounds just to prove they are Indian pretenders.

Indian reservation schools with Indian names treat their symbols and subject matter with respect and dignity.

If there is an Indian in America who can watch a Washington Redskin game or an Atlanta Braves game and see the actions of the mostly white, often inebriated sports fan, head adorned with turkey feathers, faces painted with streaks, and not feel insulted, they are not true Indians.

Thom Little Moon. October 26, 1995. © Indian Country Today. Reprinted by permission.

This morning, as I did a talk show for Wisconsin Public Radio, two callers made my day. They tuned in with the idea they were going to give me hell for questioning their right to behave as Indian mascots. After they listened and heard the other side of the story, they called to say they had changed their minds and they now understand why I feel the way I do about mascots.

It all boils down to self-esteem and self-respect.

Everything in life begins or ends with these two emotions. If we cannot respect ourselves or if we have low self-esteem, we turn to things that make us forget. Drugs and alcohol have been the bane of Indian society. What's more, if the white society thinks of us as nothing more than mascots for their fun and games, they will not respect us on matters that are more important to our lives.

A few weeks back several parents watched a "Redskin" football game with their children at a reservation home. Shortly into the game the children became noticeably upset.

"Mom, why are those people acting crazy like that?" asked one child.

"Dad, why are those *wasicus* (white people) making fun of us?" said another.

"Mom, are all Indians bad people?" asked one six-year-old. Sports fans just don't get it.

If even one Indian in America feels insulted by being used as a mascot, that should be enough. We don't have anything to prove, but we certainly have plenty to be angry about.

Sure, there are many important issues we need to address, but self-respect and self-esteem should be near the top of the list because without these two emotions firmly in tow, what else do we have?

So watch the World Series and have a good time. But, just for the moment of one game, put your feet into our moccasins.

Watch the red-painted faces. Watch the fanatics in the stands wearing turkey and chicken feathers in their hair. Watch the fools doing the tomahawk chop and singing that horrible chant.

Then picture that section of fans as people supporting a team called the African Americans. Imagine them doing the same things to black Americans as they are doing to Native Americans.

That's all I ask.

Just watch this spectacle and then put yourselves in our place just this once. If that doesn't register with you, nothing will.

Bigotry against one American is bigotry against all.

Self-respect and self-esteem: Give them back to the American Indian.

Is that so much to ask? After all, you have taken so much from us. Please return these two important things. America will be a better place if you do.

Editorial by Tim Giago, in *Indian Country Today*, October 26, 1995. Copyright 1995 by *Indian Country Today*. Reprinted with permission.

WE'RE IMITATING THE ENEMY

Shannon Prince

Many intelligent American Indian thinkers have already pointed out why the freedmen have a legal right to remain in the Cherokee Nation of Oklahoma.

Cherokee judge Steve Russell has noted in his *Indian Country Today* column that the freedmen have the right, according to Article 9 of the treaty between the United States and the Cherokee Nation of 1866, to be citizens of the Cherokee Nation. He has also reiterated the well-documented fact that many (and one might say nearly all) freedmen have Cherokee Indian blood that the racists who created the Dawes Rolls didn't note simply because of the pseudoscientific belief that "one drop" of black blood negated all others—a fact that shows the nonsense of the claim that the removal of the freedmen from the Cherokee Nation is based on the desire to allow only those with Indian blood to be Indians.

In a ruling with fellow justices on the Cherokee Supreme Court, Cherokee Justice Stacy Leeds powerfully affirmed the legitimacy of the freedmen's claim to Cherokee citizenship, reinstating them in the nation. Furthermore, in her interview with Mike Tosee in "Of Two Spirits: American Indian and African American Oral Histories," Leeds also noted they fought not to be under the jurisdiction of Georgia's laws which would have disenfranchised them. Yet in 1839, the Cherokee passed a law forbidding black and Cherokee marriages. The Cherokee also had violently enforced slave codes that further brutalized black people. We simultaneously fought the ways whites abused us as Native Americans while duplicating the abuses whites used against nonwhites to subjugate black people.

I don't recount these facts out of self-hatred or contempt for our people, but in the interest of accuracy and responsibility. When we discuss history, we have to treat the freedmen with the same respect that we want to receive as Indigenous people. None of us likes rosy imaginings of the Thanksgiving story that romanticize the beginnings of genocide or bleary justifications for the Carlisle Indian Industrial School as a well-intentioned social policy. We Cherokee are a proud and incredible people, which is why we have to be honorable enough to face and apologize for the ugly parts of our history without making excuses or trying to hide the facts.

As Cherokee, we should ask how our ancestors could turn from our teachings of *duyukduh*, which emphasizes balance, interrelatedness and respect for all peoples. We should ask how our leaders and Beloved Women could constitution to include a provision for freedmen citizenship, something another slave-owning Indian nation, the Chickasaw, chose not to do.

Finally, Steve Osburn, Cherokee/Delaware, remarked in a recent piece that while Principal Chief Chad Smith rails against the Congressional Black Caucus' move to deny economic aid to the Cherokee until they honor their treaty (a, move Smith inaccurately refers to as termination), he successfully urged the United States to deny the Delaware federal recognition and funding. The Delaware were forced to remain part of the Cherokee Nation due to the same treaty provisions that are suddenly illegitimate when applied to the freedmen.

While these scholars have brilliantly argued that the removal of the freedmen from the Cherokee Nation of Oklahoma is illegal by the nation's own laws, I argue that beyond being illegal, the removal of the freedmen is also unethical. Those who support freedmen removal are irresponsible heirs of Cherokee history and have internalized colonial expressions of sovereignty.

Cherokee people have historically been both oppressed and oppressors; but so often, that history of oppressing others is ignored or equivocated. It astounds me, as a Cherokee, that our people continued to own slaves after the Trail of Tears. After the Trail of Tears, after suffering and crying under horrendous brutality, the Cherokee knew exactly what dehumanization was: yet we continued to dehumanize others. We didn't have a problem with the unjust hierarchal system that gave some peoples rights at the expense of others; we only had a problem when it was used against us. While we cried on the Trail of Tears, we ignored the cries of blacks and, as a nation, were fine benefiting from the racial hierarchy when it allowed us to enslave others.

In 1831's *Cherokee Nation v. State of Georgia*, the Cherokeeship is a sovereign act, but Indian removal was also a sovereign act. Sovereign acts and moral acts are two very different things. Smith claims that the Congressional Black Caucus is challenging the Cherokee Nation's sovereignty. Actually, what the CBC is doing is showing that sovereignty has consequences, and that when nations make refugees of their people by revoking their citizenship, they risk facing economic sanctions. Back-lash against a nation's sovereign decision is not denial of that nation's sovereignty. Being sovereign means you can make decisions freely—it doesn't mean others have to agree with those decisions.

What Smith wants isn't sovereignty, but sovereignty free of repercussions. It is interesting to me that the Cherokee Nation of Oklahoma is exercising sovereignty in the same way that the U.S. government has often exercised it—by oppressing a darker racial group. Ironically, we're exercising, our sovereign right as Indigenous people to behave just like our imperialist oppressors instead of acting in a way that reflects Indigenous ways of knowing and being. We won't lose face or be less sovereign if we reinstate the freedmen.

Rather, we'll be back on the path of *duyukduh* instead of on the path of imitating our colonizers.

As Cherokee people, we have to decide the right way to handle history, the honorable way to exercise sovereignty, and the correct way to bring forth justice and healing. We have to celebrate the beauty in our culture, soothe our wounds of oppression as well as the oppression we dealt out to others, and practice *gadugi* with all members of the community. We have a long road ahead of us, and recognizing the citizenship of the freedmen is the first step.

Shannon Prince, Cherokee (Aniyunwiya), is a Presidential Scholar, Inaugural Scholar, Mellon Mays Undergraduate Fellow, and junior at Dartmouth College in New Hampshire.

Shannon Prince, "We're Imitating the Enemy," *Indian Country Today*, 27, no. 50 (May 21, 2008): 5.

NATIVE AMERICAN WOMEN AND COERCED STERILIZATION

ON THE TRAILS OF TEARS IN THE 1970S

Sally J. Torpy

During the 1970s, the majority of American protest efforts focused on the feminist, civil rights, and antigovernment movements. On a smaller scale, Native Americans initiated their own campaign. Network television periodically broadcast scenes of confrontation ranging from the Alcatraz Occupation in 1969 through the Wounded Knee Occupation of 1973. The consistent objective was to regain treaty rights that had been violated by the United States government and private corporations.

Little publicity was given to another form of Native American civil rights violations—the abuse of women's reproductive freedom. Thousands of poor women and women of color, including Puerto Ricans, Blacks, and Chicanos, were sterilized in the 1970s, often without full knowledge of the surgical procedure performed on them or its physical and psychological ramifications. Native American women represented a unique class of victims among the larger population that faced sterilization and abuses of reproductive rights. These women were especially accessible victims due to

several unique cultural and societal realities setting them apart from other minorities. Tribal dependence on the federal government through the Indian Health Service (IHS), the Department of Health, Education, and Welfare (HEW), and the Bureau of Indian Affairs (BIA) robbed them of their children and jeopardized their future as sovereign nations. Native women's struggle to obtain control over reproductive rights has provided them with a sense of empowerment consistent with larger Native American efforts to be free of institutional control. The following two situations are examples of the human rights violations committed against Native American women. Both reflect the socioeconomic climate of the 1970s that led to the overt and massive sterilization that irreversibly changed thousands of Native American families' lives forever.

Armstrong County Child Welfare Service agents appeared at Norma Jean Serena's home in Apollo, Pennsylvania in August 1970 and took her three-year-old daughter, Lisa, and four-year-old son, Gary, out of her custody, stating that the children appeared malnourished and needed medical attention. Later that same month, Norma Jean, a Native American of Creek and Shawnee ancestry, underwent a tubal ligation after delivering her son, Shawn, whom workers

From Sally J. Torpy, "Native American Women and Coerced Sterilization," *American Indian Culture and Research Journal*, 21, no. 2 (2008): 1–22. This article has been edited and the references and notes omitted.

immediately removed to a foster home. She signed the consent form for the surgical procedure the following day. Norma Jean's children would not return home for three years, after a jury determined that the social workers had placed her children in foster homes under false pretense.

In November 1970, an unnamed twenty-six-year-old Native American woman entered a Los Angeles physician's office requesting a "womb transplant." Upon examination, the doctor informed her that she previously had been sterilized by means of a hysterectomy, a permanent and irreversible surgical procedure. The young woman, engaged and planning to have a family, was devastated.

These two women are examples of poor women and women of color in the 1970s who found themselves in situations in which physicians determined their reproductive rights.

The eugenics movement, popular throughout the world by the early twentieth century, promoted some American states to introduce compulsory sterilization statutes. Prior to that time, the government sterilized persons only for punitive reasons. In 1907, Indiana enacted America's first compulsory eugenic sterilization (CES) law, with fifteen other states enacting similar laws during the following two decades.

. . .

Even though several states had no statutes to prohibit voluntary sterilization, physicians and hospitals avoided aggressive sterilization practices because of possible malpractice suits. Attitudes changed following the 1969 *Jessin v. County of Shasta* (California) case which determined that no legislative policy existed to prohibit sterilizations. Another liberalization of sterilization practices occurred when the American College of Obstetricians and Gynecologists (ACOG) dropped its "Rule of 120," an age/parity formula for female sterilization. If a woman's number of living children, multiplied by her age, equaled 120, she could undergo sterilization. Though not legally binding, a majority of hospitals observed this formula. In addition the ACOG dismissed its recommendation for two physicians' signature along with the rule that a psychiatric consultation be obtained before scheduling a sterilization procedure. While middle-class libertarians celebrated easier access to and control over their reproductive rights, poor women and women of color became the major targets of coercive sterilization abuse.

Other significant influences in the late 1960s, such as government concern over the growing population, prompted President Richard M. Nixon's appointment of John D. Rockefeller III as chairman of the new Commission on Population and the American Future. President Lyndon B. Johnson's previous War on Poverty reflected fear that world resources would not be able to provide for the future population. Political and social pressures to limit family size and push sterilization helped lead to the new Office of Economic Opportunity, an organization that sought federal funds to provide not only education and training to the poor, but also a less well-known service: contraception. The Family Planning Act of 1970 passed the Senate by an overwhelming vote of 298 to thirty-two.

Statistics reflect the combined impact that this new legislation and medical practices had on minority women. During the 1970s, HEW funded 90 percent of the annual sterilization costs for poor people. Sterilization for women increased 350 percent between 1970 and 1975 and approximately one million American women were sterilized each year.

Physicians and social workers found themselves in a potent situation in which they could use, but in reality abuse, their authority in dealing with poor and minority families and their reproductive rights. The conflicting needs and rights between women of different economic background and color coinciding with new fertility laws, medical advancement, and tenacious eugenic lore, culminated in disaster for many women. Inevitably, examples of blatant and subtle coercion became public.

. . .

Though all the victims suffered great loss, Native American women were easier targets than other minorities due to many unique cultural and societal realities. As a result of these differences and their relatively small population percentages, Native Americans failed to gain much from the broader feminist movement and the liberal attitudes of the late 1960s and 1970s.

In addition to problems of general societal invisibility, Native Americans have been hidden behind an additional curtain of bureaucratic secrecy. Lawyers representing Indian women in court could not, because of the government's request, reveal sealed trial proceedings. In fact, the Federal Freedom of Information Agency refused further release of documents regarding IHS facilities' sterilization policies of the 1970s, claiming that this author did not present adequate justification. Yet years of investigation, government hearings, and court cases finally aided Native American women's efforts to organize and address their needs, their rights, and their futures as the cultural forbears of their race. Oversight hearings, trials, news reports, investigative publications, and interviews with attorneys and Native American women revealed the devastating impact these events had upon the individuals, their families, and their tribal communities.

Norma Jean Serena, the Creek Native American mentioned previously who lost her reproductive rights following the birth of her son in 1970, is one of thousands of Native American women sterilized during the 1970s. The thirty-seven-year-old divorcee also lost custody of her infant son in that same year. Child Welfare and Board of Assistance authorities in Pittsburgh, Pennsylvania convinced Serena that she was too ill and exhausted to care for a baby and they placed her son, Shawn, in a foster home. Months prior to this incident, social workers had come to Serena's home and demanded that she accompany her two-year-old son and her three-year-old daughter to Children's Hospital in Pittsburgh for medical examinations; once there, the caseworkers told the mother that the two children were seriously ill and needed to stay at the hospital. Shortly after, however, they were placed in homes with foster parents who were led to believe they could adopt the children.

When Serena's repeated attempts to visit and regain custody of her three children failed, the distraught mother employed legal assistance from the Council of Three Rivers American Indian Center in Pittsburgh. She eventually filed a civil suit, the first of its kind, to address sterilization abuse as a civil rights issue. She asked for $20,000 in damages from the Department of Public Welfare for the violation of her civil rights.

The all-white jury of six men and two women found the two Welfare Department's social workers "guilty of misrepresenting Serena's case and placing her children in foster homes under false pretenses." Serena received $17,000 in damages in this initial part of her suit, which the Pittsburgh press considered a great victory. However, it would take the threat of contempt of court before Armstrong County Child Welfare authorities released her children in March 1974. By this time, Gary and Lisa had spent three years away from their natural mother, and the baby, Shawn, had been absent from her for two years.

The second part of Serena's case took place in January 1979 and involved the blatant abuse of her reproductive rights. Welfare agents and doctors claimed that Serena agreed to the sterilization and looked forward to having no additional babies. She had no clear recollection of signing the consent form and testimony in court indicated that she had signed a consent form dated the day after the sterilization surgery and childbirth had taken place. Serena's attorney, Richard Levine recalled that the jury had

sympathy for a mother being separated from her children, but they did not experience similar feelings over the loss of her fertility. Instead, Levine believed that the jury did not approve of her living situation—Serena was living, unmarried, with a Black man—even though her civil rights obviously had been denied. The attending physician convinced the jury that he had explained the operation adequately and that she had agreed to it. The jury decided Serena had given consent and its members acquitted the doctors and one male social worker.

Although Serena lost the second part of her suit, many, including Levine, considered the guilty verdict for the illegal removal of her children a victory. Levine stated that the decision, the first of its kind, finally held social workers accountable to the poor. In addition, Serena's case exposed the American public to the reality of epidemic numbers of Native American children being taken from their families, coupled with an equally staggering number of sterilizations of Native American women of childbearing age during the 1970s.

As a result of the publicity generated from this case, along with suspicious sterilizations at the Claremore, Oklahoma IHS hospital, Constance Redbird Pinkerton-Uri, a physician with the IHS in Oklahoma and a law student of Choctaw/Cherokee ancestry, began to call the office of Senator James Abourezk, chairman of the Senate Subcommittee on Indian Affairs, in South Dakota to inform him of this growing problem in Indian Country. She, along with registered nurse Phyllis Jackson and Milo Fat Beaver, an inhalation therapist, had held clinics in a tipi to provide services for patients who either did not want to seek medical attention at IHS facilities or were unable to travel to the closest IHS hospital. It was during these sessions that questionably unethical sterilization practices were revealed to the team. Pinkerton-Uri was not the only concerned person to seek Abourezk's expertise. The senator, also received phone calls from Charlie McCarthy, then an IHS employee in Albuquerque, regarding the same issue. Joan Adams, an intern on Abourezk's staff, handled these calls and subsequently investigated the allegations that Indian women were being sterilized without their consent and under duress. After interviewing tribal leaders and Indian women's groups, as well as examining IHS records, Adams concluded that some of the complaints were legitimate and merited further investigation. Abourezk's intern called for a General Accounting Office (GAO) report in April 1975 to look into both sterilization abuse and the experimental use of drugs on Native American children.

The GAO study, involving Albuquerque, Phoenix, Oklahoma City, and Aberdeen, South Dakota, found that between 1973 and 1976 IHS facilities sterilized 3,406 Native American women. Of these, 3,001 involved women of childbearing age (between fifteen and forty-four). Of these, 1,024 were performed at IHS contract facilities. Since the records of only four of the twelve IHS hospitals were examined over a forty-six-month period, and only 100,000 Native American women of childbearing age remained, the ramifications of these operations were staggering. After studying the report, Senator Abourezk commented that given the fact of the small population of Native Americans, 3,406 Indian sterilizations would be comparable to 452,000 non-Indian women. He noted that the study itself revealed some significant weaknesses in the report. For example, only four of the twelve IHS service areas were examined, and during those three years of investigation, not one woman was ever interviewed to find out whether or not she received adequate counseling and education beforehand or had even consented to the procedure.

The report found that although some kind of informed consent had been, acquired from these women, no one common consent form was used, and the majority of the forms did not adequately satisfy the federal regulations of informed consent. The US District Court defined "informed consent" as the "voluntary, knowing assent from the individual on whom any sterilization is to be performed," and this only after she has been given information pertinent to the operation. In addition, the GAO study discovered that thirty-six females who were either under the age of twenty or were judged mentally incompetent had undergone sterilization procedures. This was in direct violation of moratoriums that HEW had sent to all IHS directors on 2 August 1973. HEW ordered this moratorium primarily to protect these two vulnerable groups. In fact, continued violations forced HEW to reconfirm the moratorium by way of memorandums and a telegram on 16 October 1973, 29 April 1974, and in another memorandum containing copies of revised HEW regulations sent directly to IHS physicians and directors on 12 August 1974.

New requirements for obtaining informed consent applied to an individual when that person was considered "at risk" in regard to her health. Six basic elements comprised HEW's revised consent forms:

(1) A fair explanation of the procedures to be followed, including an identification of those which are experimental. (2) A description of the attendant discomforts and risks. (3) A description of the benefits to be expected. (4) A disclosure of appropriate alternative procedures that would be advantageous for the subject. (5) An offer to answer any inquiries concerning the procedures. (6) An instruction that the subject is free to withdraw his consent and discontinue participation in the project or activity at any time.

The GAO study noted that these HEW regulations did not comply with US District Court Judge Gerhard Gessel's 1974 court order that any individual contemplating sterilization should be advised orally at the outset that at no time could federal benefits be withdrawn because of failure to agree to sterilization. Gessel's rulings were published in the 14 April 1974 *Federal Register* and they specifically addressed this issue to protect individuals from sterilization coercion. The GAO report recommended to the secretary of HEW: (1) the development of a revised and uniform consent form as soon as possible; (2) a program for educating and training physicians regarding sterilization regulations and eligibility; and (3) more frequent monitoring of physicians' compliance with new regulations. GAO investigators called for HEW regulations to be in compliance with the US District Court's ruling that patients be informed orally that they could not lose their welfare benefits. The consent form was also required to have the signature of the person obtaining a patient's permission on the same document.

After reviewing the GAO report and conversing with several IHS health planners, Patty Marks, staff member of Abourezk's Senate Select Committee on Indian Affairs, believed that IHS physicians' attitudes played a significant role in sterilization abuse. She felt they lacked cultural sensitivity, possessed a middle class attitude towards family planning that favored only two children per family, and promoted the belief that unwed mothers and families that were economically deprived should not reproduce. She agreed with the GAO study proposals and strongly advocated consistent and thorough monitoring and enforcement of regulations along with adequate counseling for individuals considering sterilization as a means of birth control. Marks said some tribes, such as the Navajo, already employed counselors; in areas such as Montana, South Dakota, and Oklahoma, however, only the doctor was present to explain to the patient what sterilization involved. This lack of counseling, Marks argued, could result in misunderstandings.

Pinkerton-Uri's reaction to sterilization abuse was not as empathetic as Marks'. She scathingly attacked the Association of American Indian Physicians (AAIP) for ignoring her initial requests for records from the Claremore Indian Hospital. Everett Rhoades, vice-chairman of the Kiowa Tribal Council and a member of AAIP, denied knowledge of the request. Pinkerton-Uri addressed the Indian Health Advisory Board in 1974, expressing the urgent need to improve Indian health care. There would be a real threat to the continuance of Indian tribes' bloodline, she argued, if sterilization procedures went unchecked. The physician commented, "we have a new enemy and the enemy is the knife." Through her own investigations of Claremore Hospital records, she discovered that 132 Native women had been sterilized at Claremore, and of that number one hundred underwent sterilization procedures labeled non-therapeutic, meaning that sterilization was the sole purpose.

The first legal response to the GAO's study came in the form of another class-action suit filed against HEW in 1977 and involved three Northern Cheyenne women from Montana. This case reflects the deep cultural beliefs and attitudes that Native American women possess regarding motherhood. Michael Zavalla, a Tucson attorney, remembered the case's sensitivity and the young women's embarrassment and shame over the loss of their reproductive abilities. He alleged that they were sterilized without their full consent or knowledge of the surgical procedure and its ramifications. Their names were withheld from the media out of their fear of public condemnation within their tribes. Zavalla filed the case in Washington State with the hope that a favorable decision would send a message to hospitals and physicians about the need to obtain proper informed consent and provide full knowledge regarding any operation.

Zavalla directed his suit only against the hospital physicians who allegedly coerced the women into sterilization by implying that they would lose their welfare benefits, that they needed the surgery, or that the surgery could be reversed at a future date. By taking such action, the doctors failed to comply with federal consent regulations. The case, however, never went to trial. Each of the three women was approached by the defendants' lawyers and offered a cash settlement on the condition that the terms of the agreement would remain sealed, along with their names. The women's attorney believed the lawsuit ended this way in order to avoid additional publicity that might encourage further litigation by other victims. Zavalla expressed frustration and disappointment over the outcome of the case, but respected and sympathized with the victims' hesitancy to pursue their suit.

Marie Sanchez, chief tribal judge for the Northern Cheyenne Reservation in Lame Deer, Montana, having heard of these lawsuits and other similar allegations from her tribe, conducted her own investigation on her reservation and found that thirty women were sterilized between 1973 and 1976. Sanchez learned from her interviews that two girls under the age of fifteen were told that they were having their appendix taken out only to discover later that they had been sterilized. Another woman who complained to a physician about migraines was told that her condition was a female problem and was advised that a hysterectomy would alleviate the problem. Her headaches continued, however, until she was diagnosed with a brain tumor.

Sanchez hoped she could motivate these women to file lawsuits against the IHS, but unfortunately the women's traumatized emotions resulting from their sterilizations kept them from coming forward. Sanchez empathized with them and explained that Native American cultures are based on the value of family. For them to publicly admit that they had unknowingly given up their reproductive rights would be devastating for them and their relations. She concluded that "even more discouraging than high legal bills is the risk of losing one's place in the Indian community, where sterilization has particular religious resonance."

What Pinkerton-Uri, Sanchez, Abourezk, and many other Native American advocates attempted to accomplish through government investigations, rallies, and media attention was twofold. They realized the need not only to put an end to further sterilization of a people who could ill afford it, but also to preserve their cultures and traditions. An understanding of these unique cultures and their special relationships with the federal government presents three important factors: (1) how and why Indian women were more vulnerable to sterilization abuse than other minorities; (2) what motivated physicians' abuses of Indian women's reproductive rights; and (3) how social welfare workers' attitudes affected Native American families.

In 1831, Supreme Court Justice John Marshall designated Native American tribes "domestic dependent nations," comparing the relationship to that of a guardian and its ward. Originally the BIA, within the Department of the Interior, held sole responsibility for medical and health-related issues. In 1955, IHS transferred to the Public Health Service (PHS), claiming to provide a "full health program including curative, preventive, rehabilitative, and environmental health services through an integrated system" of hospitals. IHS hospitals were built for Native Americans because most tribes lived in areas where no private medical care or state health services were available.

As of 1977, IHS facilities consisted of fifty-one hospitals, eighty-six health centers (including twenty-six in schools), and several hundred other health stations across the nation. But the health facilities were often located miles from major hospitals and Native American communities. In April 1984 the number of hospitals and health centers had dropped to forty-eight and seventy-nine, respectively. Although it would appear that IHS had an organized, functioning health care package for Native Americans, a 1977 study prepared by the American Indian policy review commission for the United States Congress found the system antiquated and lacking in (1) adequate policy to solve the problems of Indian health; (2) adequate appropriations; (3) adequate mechanism for delivery of services; (4) responsiveness on the part of state and local agencies toward Indians; and (5) oversight and accountability at all levels of Indian Health Service. A 1975 study conducted by the Joint Committee on Accreditation of Hospitals found that over two-thirds of the IHS' fifty-one hospitals were "obsolete and in need of complete replacement." Only twenty-four, less than half, met the committee's standards, and just twelve of the fifty-one hospitals met the fire and safety codes.

Senator Abourezk, longtime advocate for Native Americans, found their health situation disgusting and blamed President Richard Nixon's administration for impounding funds for Indian health care during four out of five years of his term. Abourezk stated that the $15.5 million appropriated and impounded by the Nixon Administration "literally is forcing IHS to play Russian Roulette with the lives of Indian people." By the administration's actions, thousands of people requiring medical attention would have to go without help. Abourezk's office reported that as of June 1974, a waiting list of 20,000, including 13,000 children, existed for corrective surgery. The senator estimated that approximately $40 million more was needed to bring up the level of IHS medical care to that of the national norm, and an additional $10 million was needed to staff hospitals. In 1974 there was only one doctor for every 1,700 reservation Indians. To add to the problem, most of the 492 doctors then assigned to IHS hospitals were recruited from the military draft. When the doctor draft terminated in 1976, IHS lost many physicians, resulting in a severely understaffed medical staff. In addition, the US Senate's decision to exclude PHS personnel from acquiring a bonus of up to $10,000 for every year that military doctors serve past their minimum tour of two years further discouraged recruits.

According to Everett Rhoades, one of only thirty-eight Indian physicians in the United States in the 1970s, the isolation in rural communities, long hours, low pay, and lack of quality housing, schooling, and recreation left physicians disinterested and unenthusiastic about working at an IHS hospital. To compensate for the lack of physicians in the IHS system, to provide supplemental specialty care, and to complement the basic services available to Indian people, the IHS paid for the use of alternative health service facilities. For example, in Claremore, Oklahoma, the IHS hospital had just thirty-five beds to accommodate 33,000 northeastern Oklahoma Indians. Director Thomas Talamini said that because of these figures the hospital must treat the majority of patients on an out-patient basis. As a supplement, the hospital was allotted $373,000 to contract health services with other university medical centers, county hospitals, and private physicians. Unfortunately, Talamini claimed that their quarterly allocation was often spent within six weeks.

Because of inadequate health care, the quality of life on most Indian reservations suffered. Infant mortality was three times the national average and the tuberculosis rate was eight times the national average. The life expectancy for a Native American in 1977 was forty-seven years compared to 70.8 years for the general population. For every seven babies born, one Indian woman was sterilized. With a total Native American population of approximately 800,000 as of 1976, sterilization within many tribes could have a devastating impact on a particular tribe's survival. Pinkerton-Uri made the observation that "there are about only 100,000 women of childbearing age left total. A 200 million population could support voluntary sterilization and survive, but for Native Americans it cannot be a preferred method of birth control. Where other minorities might have a gene pool in Africa or Asia, Native Americans do not; when we are gone, that's it."

This lack of concern for Native Americans' welfare filtered down through the government agencies and directly affected the health and well-being of Indians. An example of this may be found in legislation passed in 1970 that had a direct impact on the economic and sociological attitudes of many eager physicians fresh out of their residencies. President Jimmy

Carter approved the Hyde Amendment, which cut off 98 percent of all federal funding for abortions but maintained reimbursement to hospitals or physicians for 90 percent of sterilization costs. An HEW study reported that if all federal funding for abortions was eliminated, an estimated 250 to 300 deaths could be expected each year and 25,000 serious medical complications would result from self-induced or illegal abortions. With fewer options for Indian and non-Indian women to exercise control over their reproductive rights, physicians took the initiative and pushed the risky surgical sterilization rather than safer alternative means of birth control.

. . .

Lack of staff, quality care, and accessibility to hospitals or clinics, along with the rekindled 1970s interest in eugenics, created an explosive situation for women of color and low income brackets. Family planning workers eagerly introduced Native Americans to sterilization as a form of birth control in the 1960s through HEW pamphlets such as "Plan Your Family". This booklet illustrates a before sterilization picture—a caricature of haggard parents with only one horse and ten children—next to an after sterilization image—a cartoon of happy erect parents surrounded by one child and many horses. This type of paternalistic mindset was widespread throughout the nation.

One of the most common violations of Native American women's right to informed consent was the lack of an interpreter to explain in their own language about the surgical procedure. Frequently, physicians also refrained from explaining its irreversibility or offering optional means of birth control. In many cases, doctors worked in conjunction with a social worker, threatening to withdraw patients' welfare benefits or take their children from them unless they underwent sterilization.

Physicians who claimed they had orally informed Native American women about the surgical procedure and obtained consent were not taking the time or precaution to have a witness present who spoke the woman's language. This led to enormous misinformation and neglect of a woman's right to know and understand in her own language what the operation involved. However, because of the large number of Native languages spoken today, it would almost be impossible for a physician to learn all languages in their serving area. Consequently, considerable confusion occurred in communicating the necessary information on sterilization.

Women interviewed later verified that public and private welfare agencies threatened to cut off their benefits if they bore additional children or to remove the children they already had from their homes. One of the most typical situations in which welfare agents and surgeons would try to convince a mother to agree to sterilization was during labor when she was vulnerable and often medicated. Some women avoided having their babies at IHS facilities for this reason, but unfortunately the majority of women were unaware of the coercion they were often subjected to. The threat of losing one's children to social welfare agencies if the mother did not agree to sterilization, however, proved the most persuasive and coercive technique. Native American women scattered throughout the nation on reservations had little if any access to the pro-choice movement, which might have raised their consciousness, leaving them especially vulnerable to manipulation. Their population—already devastated by disease, inadequate health care and education, wars, removal, cultural genocide through assimilation, broken treaties, and now sterilization—placed a high priority on children as their one hope of survival. Native Americans had and still have a deep sense of family and the importance of extended families.

To appreciate a Native American woman's deep-rooted fear of losing her children to a foster family, boarding school, or adoption, one can look back in history and find ample examples of families losing their children. The phrase *kid catching* in the 1930s on the Navajo reservation will always reverberate through time among Indian families. The phrase referred to the stockmen, police, farmers, and mounted men who came on their reservation to literally round up school-age children to attend faraway government boarding schools. These children, often roped like cattle, were sent to white schools where they were given white names and clothing, forbidden to speak their Native tongue, and often prevented from returning home for three years, sometimes never. Dande Coolidge, a Navajo eyewitness to the yearly roundup of Indian children, recalled that many parents hid their children when they heard the sound of a truck approaching.

Various churches also threatened Native American families through organizations such as the Mormon Church's Placement Program. Joan Rose, a Ute woman from Nevada, remembered the Mormons taking in children from poverty-stricken Indian families. There was great concern for the children's religious education as it was common knowledge that Mormons believed Indians were sinners and Lamenites, one of the lost tribes of Israel, who could become white and immediately be saved if they accepted the Mormon faith. As many as two thousand children per year left their homes to live with a culture that held Native Americans as "dark and loathsome," "cursed by God because of their moral turpitude and ancient wickedness." In fact, they believed that as the children became indoctrinated into the Mormon faith, their skin would lighten.

Statistics reflecting the high number of children placed in boarding schools in a 1971 school census conducted by the BIA were staggering. Approximately 35,000 children lived in such facilities rather than at home. Of the total number of Native American children attending federal schools, over two-thirds—33,672—were in boarding schools. Native Americans expressed grave concerns about the impact that BIA schools had on their children since classes were conducted only in English, and the intent was to assimilate them into the white man's world. Of even larger concern was the distance between the boarding schools and the children's homes. Suicide rates among the teenagers were as high as one-hundred times the national average. Children as young as ten-years-old attempted suicide. In the late 1970s, two BIA-boarding-school boys ran away and froze to death in their attempts to reach their home fifty miles away. Another school on the Northern Cheyenne Reservation reported twelve attempted suicides in an eighteen month period among the two hundred enrolled students.

Thousands of Native American women in the 1970s were faced with either the solicitude of losing their children or the fear of losing their ability to have children. Even if they agreed to sterilization there was no guarantee that they could keep their already-born children. The majority of men and women who exposed sterilization abuse of minority women in the 1970s sought solutions through federal legislation such as monitored enforcement of informed consent forms and more explicit explanation of sterilization procedures. Feminist groups such as the Boston Women's Health Book Collective (BWHBC) and the National Women's Health Network obtained results by appearing at congressional hearings; they also provided certain Native American groups with financial and political support. Native Americans, however, believed that they needed to address their own reproductive rights, to retain their own identity, and to address the specific issues endemic to their cultures. They also saw a connection between

protecting their population growth and guarding their land rights. Consequently, during the turbulent 1960s and 1970s, Native American women and men from different tribes throughout the nation initiated their own method of preventing further loss of reproductive rights. Influenced by other activist groups within society, they assumed the title Red Power following a 1967 meeting of the National Congress of American Indians (NCAI) in Denver. Their goals were to demonstrate a committed and patriotic fight for their own self-determination and freedom from oppressors. Red Power activists took on slogans such as "We shall overcome" and "Custer died for your sins." Pan-Indian movements arose across the country uniting tribes in a common purpose. Although the Red Power movement and the NCAI did not specifically address sterilization abuse, they did influence and inspire Native American women to incorporate some of their policies, such as self-determination over their reproductive rights, into their own organizations.

Several powerful national and international organizations emerged in the 1970s, including United Native Americans, Women of All Red Nations (WARN), and the International Indian Treaty Council (IITC), launching campaigns against the IHS and other government institutions. These organizations attempted to raise the nation's awareness about the oppression of Indian cultures in many areas of their lives. In 1978 Lorelei DeCora Means, a Minneconjou Lakota, met with several other women at the Black Hills to instigate WARN, a militant offshoot of the American Indian Movement (AIM). Loss of women's reproductive rights, loss of Indian children through coercion, the destruction and erosion of the Native land base, and the ultimate loss of cultural continuity were some of their concerns. This organization reflected the abuse that occurred during the 1970s and made concerted efforts to stop unethical sterilizations. Three of the founders, DeCora Means, Madonna Thunderhawk, and Phyllis Young, the latter two both of Hunkpapa Lakota decent, had all been active members of AIM but felt that women needed to have their own voice. At their first meeting women from over thirty Native nations attended this historic occasion where they unanimously recognized that "truth and communication were among our most valuable tools in the liberation of our lands, people, and four-legged and winged relations." The organization published its own newsletter, conducted conferences, and participated in speaking engagements at meetings such as the

International Year of the Child Native Conference and Cultural Festival in Seattle. They worked closely with IITC, at that time headquartered in New York, which assisted the organization in distributing WARN newsletters nationally and internationally.

. . .

In order to preserve their cultural identity, Native Americans realized that their children had to be taught the languages and traditions of their individual tribes. WARN founders Young and Thunderhawk were instrumental in providing Indian children with an alternative educational opportunity to BIA schooling. Launched in the 1970s, these autonomous Indian-taught schools called Survival Schools saved many children from the dreaded boarding schools and gave students an opportunity to be taught by Native Americans who could also provide knowledge of their cultural heritage. By teaching about traditional ways, Indian educators hoped to bolster self-esteem and pride in their race, giving students strength and knowledge to become self-governed Indigenous nations. Survival School supporters hoped this would motivate students to acquire a sense of ethnic identity and stability that might equip them with the tools to better address any future violation of Native American rights.

It must be noted that federal regulation played a significant role in providing protection for children from another major threat: adoption agencies and foster care. In the 1970s, there occurred a heightened awareness about Native American culture and concern over the mass displacement of their children to non-Indian foster and adoptive homes and institutions. To ensure the continuance of their race and the preservation of their families, Senator Abourezk sponsored the Indian Child Welfare Act. It took approximately four years of congressional hearings and investigations before President Jimmy Carter signed the bill in 1978.

The act established the extended family as the primary means by which Native Americans maintain their complex culture. In order to preserve the family, minimum federal standards for the removal of Indian children to foster or adoptive homes must be established. The act also acknowledged that Indian tribes, as sovereign governments, should have a vital voice in any decisions made regarding removal of children from their families. The legislation gave back parental and some tribal authority in regard to Native children's welfare. Although this legislation did abate physicians' and social workers' threats to remove

Indian children if mothers did not agree to sterilization, there remained a powerful opposition group that went unchallenged. The Mormon Church, which was excluded from the act, was allowed to adopt Indian children through its placement program. When Senator Abourezk was questioned about the church's exemption, he claimed that the Mormon law firm of Wilkinson and Barker, Mormon Congressman Gunn McKay, and the Mormon Deputy Commissioner of Indian Affairs, M. E. Seneca, lobbied for and won exemption from the regulations.

Despite some setbacks, Native American women generally feel more secure about their reproductive rights in regard to sterilization procedures. DeCora Means observed that on the Rosebud Reservation, it is a policy now to have Indian midwives or nurse advocates file reports on hysterectomies, which are subject to committee review every three months. Census figures are encouraging, reflecting a steady rise in births from 27,542 in 1975 to 45,871 in 1988.

Native Americans generally believe they have ample reason to fear the extermination of their people through the perceived carelessness of health care and government officials. They feel that their unique relationship with the government lends itself to neglect, lack of quality health care, and land-base threats. As a result of these fears, Native Americans have struggled to gain recognition as sovereign nations through organizations such as IITC. Its current director, Andrea Carmen, continues to actively work on international policies, "protecting human rights, biological diversity, self-determination and traditional cultures." WARN founder, DeCora Means, continues to work on the Rosebud Reservation in South Dakota as a health care advisor, encouraging people to return to traditional foods and food preparation.

In this context Native Americans have survived and continue to challenge the institutions with which they must coexist, especially the IHS and the BIA. It remains to be seen what the future holds for Native Americans. Certainly they have gained greater unity and political stature as a result of IITC and WARN. Self-awareness as a culture has grown and the desire for education and preservation of traditions is evident through their survival schools and efforts to achieve national and international sovereignty.

However, the reality is that Native Americans are a small minority of the nation's population, and they will always struggle to have a voice and be recognized as First Peoples. The impact of Native American efforts not merely to exist but to thrive and multiply as an Indigenous and sovereign people remains to be seen. The Cheyenne Nation has an old saying that states, "A nation is not conquered until the hearts of its women are on the ground. Then, it is done, no matter how brave its warriors nor strong its weapons."

MAZE OF INJUSTICE
THE FAILURE TO PROTECT INDIGENOUS WOMEN FROM SEXUAL VIOLENCE IN THE USA

Amnesty International

More than one in three Native American or Alaska Native women will be raped at some point in their lives. Most do not seek justice because they know they will be met with inaction or indifference.

The report *Maze of Injustice*, released in 2007, unraveled some of the reasons why Indigenous women in the USA are at such risk of sexual violence and why survivors are so frequently denied justice. Chronic under-resourcing of law enforcement and health services, confusion over jurisdiction, erosion of tribal authority, discrimination in law and practice, and indifference—all these factors play a part.

None of this is inevitable or irreversible. The voices of Indigenous women who have come forward to speak about these issues send a message of courage and hope that change can and will happen.

At the one-year mark of the release of *Maze of Injustice*, there is significant, even historical, opportunity for change but there is also real danger that the follow through that is so desperately needed will not happen. It will require working together on all levels to fulfill the promises made.

This update presents the main achievements of the past year in more detail and identifies urgent priorities going forward.

Amnesty International, *Maze of Injustice: The Failure to Protect Indigenous Women from Sexual Violence in the USA: One-Year Update*. Spring 2008.

PROTECTING NATIVE AMERICAN HUMAN REMAINS, BURIAL GROUNDS, AND SACRED PLACES

James Riding In, Cal Seciwa, Suzan Harjo, and Walter Echo-Hawk

INTRODUCTION BY REBECCA TSOSIE

NAGPRA was passed in 1990. It is a very important piece of legislation because it has legally enforceable provisions, and it does many important things and obviously remedied a huge gap in the law prior to that time. Basically, NAGPRA protects Native peoples' rights in several different ways with respect to four categories of cultural items. The first and most important one involves ancestral human remains, which are defined as physical remains of a human body of a person of Native American ancestry. I think when we get into the panel discussion we'll talk about how that is being interpreted today in a contemporary case known in the news media as the Kennewick Man case. It deals with very ancient remains of a Native person that were found in the state of Washington, and whether or not contemporary tribes in that area can claim him as an ancestor under NAGPRA. The statute also applies to funerary objects, both those that are associated with human remains and those that are unassociated. It also applies to sacred objects, which are defined as specific ceremonial objects needed by Native American religious leaders for the practice of their traditional Native American religions. The panelists will discuss how these technical definitions within the statute are being implemented. The final category is objects of cultural patrimony, defined as items having an ongoing historical, traditional, or cultural importance to the Indian tribe or Native Hawaiian organization itself, rather than being property owned by an individual member. Obviously, a key component of this category is the traditional law of the Native nation

James Riding In, Cal Seciwa, Suzan Shown Harjo, Walter Echo-Hawk, "Protecting Native American Human Remains, Burial Grounds, and Sacred Places," *Wicazo Sa Review*, 19, no. 2 (Fall 2004): 169–202

and how it describes the cultural relationship of the people with a particular item.

In addition to outlawing the commercial trafficking of human remains and funerary objects—which was just a horrible, horrible problem, and by the way, still is, despite being illegal—NAGPRA also imposes an obligation on federal agencies or museums to inventory the human remains and the sacred objects in their possession and to disclose the results so that Native people can claim repatriation rights. Those repatriation rights go to culturally affiliated tribes, and there is a technical definition in the statute for that. NAGPRA also applies to excavations that are done after the effective date of that statute on either federal land or tribal land. If they are excavated on tribal land, then they basically belong to the tribe who owns that land. But if they are found on federal land, then you have to go through that whole culturally affiliated process. NAGPRA has two reserve sections, one dealing with what they call "culturally unidentifiable human remains" and one dealing with what they call "unclaimed human remains," in other words, remains in federal repositories that have not yet been claimed. The category of "culturally unidentifiable human remains" was the subject of a grant that we did here at Arizona State University, and many of the people today that are talking to you were members of our working group—Suzan Harjo, Walter Echo-Hawk, James Riding In, Wallace Coffey, and many other people worked very hard to come up with recommendations. We had Native people from all over the country, from Hawaii, from Alaska, from within the states here, who made recommendations on that issue. Professor Riding In will talk to you more about this. The central part of it was that the whole notion of something being "culturally unidentifiable" does not make sense to Native peoples. It just doesn't resonate with Native peoples' traditions. Today it is really troublesome to me. Two days ago I went on the National Park Service Web site. I looked for the report to Congress from the NAGPRA review committee (composed of both Native and non-Native people, which advises on NAGPRA and sort of advises on disputes). They hadn't done an annual report to Congress, as they are supposed to have done, for three years. So they did a three-year report, and their summary of the problems, it seemed to me, did not reflect the reality of what I could see from working on these issues. They said, with respect to culturally unidentifiable human remains, that the review committee had made a recommendation in 2000 and they were just waiting for regulations to be issued. In fact, that isn't the case. It was a very contentious recommendation, and Native people strongly disagreed with the review committee, the whole affair being something of a compromise process between scientists and Native people. The five recommendations that the group came up with were widely adopted in other regions. I am very pleased that the speakers on the panel today will talk to you about these issues and others that we all need to be informed about.

JAMES RIDING IN

Nawa [Hello].

This religious freedom battle has been a long, ongoing struggle, and there is no end in sight. Repatriation is just one part of the struggle. I've been involved in repatriation for a number of years now, and I consider it to be both a spiritual and a sacred journey. Much of our guidance, much of our personal inspiration, involvement, and commitment in this issue comes from spiritual concerns. Spiritual leaders often guide us in our work. It's not archaeologists who tell us what to do, it's not people in academia, it's people who are deeply rooted in the spirituality of our cultures and who are committed to overturning what we consider to be one of the greatest atrocities committed against us: the theft of human remains ancestral to us.

Let me share an incident with you that expresses how sacred this business of repatriation is to many of us. In 1998, the University of Nebraska, Lincoln, faced a situation in which a physical anthropologist was accused of mistreating Native human remains, of using sonic of our ancestors for a puppet show for the amusement of his class, and of committing unethical research. A charge also surfaced indicating that during the late 1960s university employees had incinerated an unknown number of Indian remains simply because they had no scientific value. When that information surfaced, the press did a thorough job of telling the truth about the matter, helping our efforts. Over the years, the press has been a big factor in repatriation; it seems that reporters, editors, and the public can understand repatriation issues. Although the media has oftentimes been an important ally for us in this repatriation struggle, they call also work against us, as in the Kennewick Man case. I want to stress that point.

Facing a public relations nightmare, university officials invited fourteen or fifteen Native nations with a historical connection with Nebraska to send representatives to Lincoln to discuss what should be done to resolve the matter. During the first morning of that two-day meeting, tribal leaders asked all of the non-Indians to leave the room so we could develop a plan of action. During lunch, several of us drafted an agreement on behalf of the Indian leadership that reflected the discussions held earlier that morning. The agreement we wrote called for the university to change the designation of all those human remains in its collections that were listed as "culturally unidentifiable" to be listed as culturally affiliated with the Indian nations in attendance for the purposes of repatriation, to cover the cost of reburying those remains, and to cover the cost of any research that we wanted done so that individual nations could determine if any of the remains in question were affiliated exclusively with them. Another point of the agreement was the erection of a monument on campus to explain what had gone on in terms of the mistreatment and destruction of our ancestors by fire. In the afternoon, we asked the non-Indians to reenter the room, and we presented university officials with the terms of the agreement. To our surprise, the university chancellor accepted them without question.

This meeting resulted in a historical agreement because NAGPRA does not provide for the repatriation of human remains that are classified as culturally unidentifiable. It is a misnomer to say that our ancestors in museums are culturally unidentifiable. Those people who dug up our ancestors claimed ownership of them. In many instances, university anthropologists declared that there was no way to link the human remains in their collections to modern-day Indians, meaning that universities with sets of human remains in that category have no legal obligation to repatriate them under NAGPRA. At the University of Nebraska, there were eight hundred or so human remains classified as culturally unidentifiable, and the agreement provided that the university would recognize a shared group relationship between those human remains and the signatory Indian nations. Repatriation is also a sovereignty issue and that fact gives Indian nations a say in the disposition of human remains.

After that agreement was reached, a working group of tribal representatives began a long process over several meetings to determine what we would do with those remains. What tribal group or groups would rebury them? Where would we put them back into Mother Earth? At one point, we sought spiritual guidance. Sammy Little Owl, a Mandan, Hidatsa, and Arikara from North Dakota, agreed to conduct a ceremony. He has an ability to communicate with our ancestors. Following the ceremony, Sammy said that a number of excited children had run up to him, followed by a leader who said they had lived on a high bluff overlooking the Missouri River and that was where they wanted to be reburied.

Thankfully, the Northern Poncas agreed to share their land for the reburial. Near Niobrara, Nebraska, in 2002, we returned our ancestors to Mother Earth in a site very similar to the one Sammy had described to us. The cemetery sat on a bluff overlooking the Missouri and Niobrara rivers.

A reburial is a very spiritual undertaking. It is done with the greatest reverence, and it brings joy to us because we know that we have removed the spirits of our ancestors from those places where they've been incarcerated, and that we are putting them back into the womb of Mother Earth where they belong. While filling the grave with earth near Niobrara that day, we looked up and saw an eagle flying in circles, going up and up and up until it disappeared. All these things are what I mean when I say this business of repatriation is both a spiritual and a sacred journey. I sometimes refer to my work in repatriation as liberation research. Those of us who participate are trying to liberate the spirits of those ancestors who have been stripped from Mother Earth, from where our ancestors thought would be the final resting place of their loved ones, and put in institutions such as the University of Nebraska where they were treated so terribly. They were placed on public display and studied. Sometimes professors and museum curators used the crania, or skulls, as paperweights. In some situations, Indian students were forced to sit in classrooms that had Indian skulls lined up against the walls. When I was in the service in 1970, I went to Washington, DC, and visited the Smithsonian Institution. What I remember most vividly are the Indian remains,

including skulls, on display. I did not see white skeletal remains on display, only Indians.

The theft of our ancestors happened through a process of colonization done in the names of Manifest Destiny and the rights of discovery. Europeans claimed that they had preemptive rights not only to our lands and resources, but to our dead as well. Repatriation is a struggle for justice, respect, and burial rights. Suzan Harjo and Bunky [Walter] Echo-Hawk were very instrumental in this movement. Along with others, they were leading forces behind the enactment of NAGPRA.

The first trip I took to Washington, DC, for repatriation was in 1989 on behalf of the Pawnee Nation. It was on the eve of passage of the National Museum of the American Indian Act, which provided for a repatriation policy for the Smithsonian. Bunky, his brother Roger, Steve Moore (another Native American Rights Fund attorney), Carole Nuttle (the vice president of the Pawnee Nation at that time), and I went to the Smithsonian to talk to its head official and with Doug Owsley, a physical anthropologist who had a legacy of exploiting the remains of our Pawnee ancestors. In the meeting, I felt that blatant lies were being told to discourage us from seeking information about our relatives. It was an eye-opening experience.

Several months later, Roger and I began research at the Smithsonian on behalf of the Pawnee people. When we entered those places within the Smithsonian where the human remains were kept, we saw row after row of shelves that reached almost to the ceiling. Just walking into those areas gave me such an oppressive feeling. It was a feeling right here [*points to chest*]. It would come and hit me right here, like my chest was caving in. It was a painfully oppressive feeling that conveyed the message that we must do something to liberate the spirits of our ancestors from their state of captivity.

NAGPRA and the National Museum of the American Indian Act provide Indian nations an avenue to repatriate our ancestors. Also, funerary objects are vital, because in our beliefs repatriation cannot be complete unless the funerary objects are placed in the graves along with those remains when they are returned to Mother Earth.

These laws have enabled Indian nations to recover and rebury thousands of ancestral remains. However, there are still tens of thousands of human remains in institutions across the nation, meaning our work is not complete. Many human remains listed as culturally affiliated with Indian nations have not been returned. Sometimes Indian nations reject the repatriation for cultural reasons. Sometimes duly are economic reasons because some Indian nations lack the resources and personnel to do this type of work.

Another important reason for keeping so many of these human remains in institutions is because museum personnel have categorized many of them as culturally unidentifiable. NAGPRA allow the NAGPRA review committee to make recommendations to the secretary of the interior regarding the disposition of the so-called culturally unidentifiable human remains. To date, there have been several sets of recommendations put forward, but none have been adopted. Until a policy is implemented, the fate of those human remains not assigned a cultural affiliation is in doubt. However, as we did at the University of Nebraska, one way to use NAGPRA to rebury these culturally unidentifiable remains is to get the holding institutions to change their designation to that of being culturally affiliated.

In 2001, I participated in another successful repatriation initiative of this nature in Colorado. In that year, the Colorado Historical Society called a meeting to discuss how research should be done to establish cultural affiliation with Indian nations of those human remains in its collections. The position we Indians took was that research was unnecessary to determine cultural affiliation, for we knew that the human remains held by the Colorado Historical Society had a cultural connection with all or some of the Indian representatives at the meeting. I attended that meeting as an observer and was supposed to sit quietly and not say a word. Cal Seciwa, an old friend and colleague at Arizona State University, was selected as one of the session moderators. I talked with him beforehand about what needed to be done. As the meeting commenced, other Native participants reinforced the idea that we must take charge of the agenda by asking the non-Indians to leave and by developing a repatriation agreement. We took these actions. After drafting the agreement, we asked the non-Indians (the people in charge of the Colorado Historical Society and others) to return to the room, presented the proposal to them, and they accepted it Several months later, over three hundred sets of remains covered by the agreement were reburied in Colorado.

There is unfinished business with NAGPRA. The meeting that Rebecca Tsosie referred to took place in this very room in December 2001, when delegates from numerous Indian nations came together and developed a policy statement, or recommendations, calling for the return of culturally unidentified human remains to Indian nations. What we came up with in that meeting was, for one thing, that these remains belong to us, American Indian peoples. Never have we ceded, given up, or surrendered our rights to our dead. This was something that was taken from us through the process of colonization. We have never consented to scientific research on these remains. I want to qualify that point, however. Some Native groups have allowed invasive testing, but by and large I think that most Indian nations oppose that type of research. Another recommendation called for the immediate discontinuation of all scientific research being done on human remains ancestral to Indians. We also asked for the repatriation of funerary objects, and finally we stated that the federal government must absorb the costs of reburials. This solution is a simple matter of justice designed to bring an end to all these past wrongs committed against our ancestors and us in the name of science, in the name of curiosity, and in the name of greed.

Several months after the ASU meeting concluded, the NAGPRA review committee accepted a controversial set of recommendations stipulating that repatriation of these so-called culturally unidentifiable remains would be voluntary and that decisions to do so would be left up to individual institutions. We found that position totally unacceptable because there was no guarantee that we would be able to repatriate any of those human remains and funerary objects affected by the recommendations. In response, some of us went to the review committee meeting at Seattle and challenged those recommendations. As a result of our protests, along with other individuals from throughout Indian Country who saw the recommendations as being pro-science, the review committee changed the language to say that institutions may *offer* to repatriate those human remains, which is significantly different than saying they *may* return them. The interior secretary has not approved those recommendations, however.

Repatriation is an ongoing struggle. It's not over yet. The protection of our sacred sites and the burial sites of our ancestors is a spiritual issue we face everyday. Desecration is an ongoing process. I hope that some of you will take an interest in carrying on this struggle and join the national effort that has been underway for many years.

COMMENT BY REBECCA TSOSIE

The NAGPRA review committee was supposed to hold a meeting on this issue, but they cancelled that meeting and said that they were going to reschedule it. *[James Riding In comments to Rebecca Tsosie.]* Professor Riding In says that it may he held in Washington, DC, so that the federal agencies will have to come and talk about their lack of compliance with the statute, which is another egregious problem, in some ways related and in some ways, obviously, its own problem. There may be 75,000 sets of human remains in that category, but that was a conservative estimate, so it could definitely be well over 100,000. We just don't know. I would encourage all of you to get involved. The review committee is supposed to be a public forum for people to comment and express their views.

CAL SECIWA

Ke'shi *[Hello]*.

I am Shiwi, Zuni. I am one of the founding members of the Zuni Salt Lake Coalition. I want to share the story of the Zuni Salt Lake Coalition and our efforts to protect a sacred site that is a part of the Pueblo of Zuni Reservation. This sacred site, Ma'k'yayanne, Salt Lake, is the home of Ma'l okyattsk'e Salt Woman. Located in west *central New Mexico*, it is also important to many other Southwestern Native people—Acoma, Hopi, Laguna, Navajo, Apache. We all hold this area in reverence, and it is an important part of our spiritual well-being. Not only the lake but also the land surrounding the lake, approximately fifteen miles in radius, is hallowed ground. This area was not included in a congressional act that returned ownership of the lake back to the Zuni Pueblo in 1978. Known as the Sanctuary Zone, it is our Indigenous Geneva, Switzerland. In the times of our ancestors, all warfare was forbidden there and neutrality was observed. All were afforded safe passage, enforced by members of the Zuni Bow Priesthood, to and from the lake and sanctuary area, and allowed to harvest Salt Woman's flesh, salt, which is meant for domestic, ceremonial, and spiritual use.

This long-standing tradition became threatened in the early 1980s when a Phoenix, Arizona, electric utility company, the Salt River Project (SRP), made plans to develop the Fence Lake Coal Mine, eleven miles upstream from the lake. This 18,000-acre coal strip mine would provide five years of coal to be transported by a forty-four-mile rail line, which would cut across ancient pilgrimage trails and destroy shrines and ancestral burial sites, ending at SRP's Coronado generating plant located near St. Johns, Arizona. In turn, electricity would be produced for the customers of SRP, known in the Phoenix area as "our Earth Wise" utility company.

Although I knew of their plans because I served as the tribal administrator with the Pueblo of Zuni during the 1980s, as an SRP customer I was certainly never informed of the plans.

The critical point of contention in opposing the development was the impact on the use of underground aquifers by SRP and the negative effect it would have on the underground springs that feed life-giving water to Salt Woman's home. Observing the efforts of my pueblo's leadership and other tribal leaders' consistent opposition to this development over the last two decades, from a distance, I felt useless to help in any way, except with prayer and hope. However, when I learned in 2001 that New Mexico Mining Permits were approved for development of state lands that SRP had leased and that the federal Life of Mine permits were imminent, I knew some type of action needed to be taken to bring this issue out to the public and to assist my people's efforts to protect Salt Woman's home and surrounding area.

Upon consulting with the Zuni Tribal Council and their staff, I learned that other people and organizations were equally concerned about the issue, and upon contacting some of these folks we all agreed to come together and join forces with the Pueblo of Zuni and other tribes to begin a public, political, and spiritual awareness campaign.

In late September 2001, representatives of the Center for Biological Diversity from Tucson, Arizona, Citizens Coal Council from Denver, Colorado; Water Information Network from Albuquerque, New Mexico; Sierra Club's Environmental Justice Program from Flagstaff, Arizona; Zuni Tribal Council members and "Citizen Cal," all came together at Zuni Pueblo, New Mexico, to discuss and establish principles of understanding, strategies, action plans, and time frames for action. After Presentation and acceptance of our collective plans, the Zuni Tribal Council, through tribal resolution, established the Zuni Salt Lake Coalition (ZSLC) in October 2001. Immediately, the ZSLC issued "A Call to Arms" to different sectors of society in this country and beyond.

We requested assistance from Indigenous, environmental, political, legal, historical, and spiritual communities to bring light to this injustice. Thus, we embarked on a real-life David and Goliath story. We started to implement our actions—postcard mailings, petitions, e-mails—first with the president of SRP, telling him to drop the plans for the mine, and then to the secretary of the interior, Gale Norton, demanding that the federal Life of Mine to SRP not be issued.

Rallies and public presentations were held, letters were issued to the editors, and we conducted two 271-mile spiritual runs: from Phoenix to Zuni in July 2002, then from Zuni to Phoenix in October 2002, concluding with a march on SRP corporate headquarters on Columbus Day. In February 2003, we conducted a twenty-four-hour vigil run around SRP headquarters on the one-hundred-year anniversary of SRP's creation. Through the efforts of our allies from Tonatierra, an Indigenous embassy based in Phoenix, we cultivated the support of Hispanic communities. Our allies in the media produced and aired public service announcements in Spanish, English, Hopi, Navajo, Apache, and Zuni informing the people of our efforts and soliciting their help. The *Shiwi Messenger*, a Zuni community newspaper, produced and published a special edition on the issue. We developed a Web site, www.zunisaltlakecoalition.com, and even had a billboard truck carrying our message of "SRP is targeting our sacred lands/Save Zuni Salt Lake." We sent educational information to various members of Congress, state legislators of New Mexico and Arizona, and other Native and non-Native politicians. The New Mexico Council of Churches and the Arizona Ecumenical Council also supported our efforts with letters of endorsements and testimonials at public events. We gained support resolutions from the All Indian Pueblo Council of New Mexico and the Inter Tribal Council of Arizona, and even got the attention of the UN Indigenous Forum. One of our proudest efforts was to hold a "People's Hearing" at Zuni in July 2003, where over four hundred people participated and gave testimonials in their respective languages and emotions. This was in light of the fact that no official public hearing had been conducted at Zuni by the federal or state agencies.

With all our collective efforts, prayers, and tears, with thousands of voices from all over the world being heard, and contending with growing administrative, legal, and political pressures, on August 4, 2003, the Salt River Project dropped their plans for the Fence Lake Mine. I only wish that they had made this announcement on August 12, the anniversary of the 1680 Pueblo Revolt. This action came as a total surprise, although a pleasant surprise. All enjoyed the taste of victory, but for only a few days.

Within a couple of weeks, the State of New Mexico Minerals and Mining Division issued out the same parcels of land, and more, that SRP had been leasing from the state, soliciting bids for oil, gas, and coal bed methane gas exploration and development, unbeknownst to the Pueblo of Zuni and the ZSLC. We discovered that the federal government, through the Bureau of Land Management (BLM), was going to take similar action. These developments would have similar or even more destructive impacts as the strip mining on the underground aquifers that feed the salt lake. So, with little rest and little knowledge of these extractive industries' methods, we began a new chapter in the struggle to protect our sacred lands. I and other organizational members of the coalition immediately filed administrative protest with the BLM and are now ready to pursue administrative and legal remedies on this matter.

One other disturbing issue still lingering from the battle with SRP is the reburial of eight ancestral remains that were unearthed during the archaeological clearance for the proposed rail line. Although the plans for the mine were dropped, the remains were not returned to their original sites, despite the wishes of the Zuni and Hopi peoples. The application of NAGPRA in this instance did not apply because the remains were on private land. The matter was eventually resolved when the two tribes agreed to have the ancestors reburied on Zuni land in Arizona.

As we all leave here today to continue our inherent rights of exercising our spiritual rights and employ our responsibilities of stewardship over Mother Earth and all that exists, I wish you well with prayers and strength. La: we, that is all, E'la: kwa.

SUZAN SHOWN HARJO

The first time I really appreciated the difference between the way white people thought about death and showed respect for the dead and the way Indians do was when I was about nine years old and I first read Shakespeare's *Hamlet*. I was horrified at the graveyard scene, where the gravediggers are the comic relief—in a play where everyone ends up dead, hence the closing line, "the rest is silent." But in the gravedigger scene you have people yukking it up in a graveyard and Hamlet there with Horatio, his school chum. They're tossing skulls about, and they're visiting with each other and talking about worms crawling through people that were dead, and this was a laugh a minute for the people of England at the time. Hamlet says, while he's holding a skull, "Do you know who this is?" and one of the gravediggers says, "Yay, a horse and madman, it was Yorick, the court jester." It stops the scene cold. Hamlet says, "Alas, poor Yorick. I knew him, Horatio." Then the scene turns serious. I thought, they have to have known the dead people personally. They don't have respect for people and places for the dead unless they knew them, otherwise it's a big joke and about worms crawling around. The stuff of humor for ten-year-olds.

It really taught me that people from European cultures didn't have the same sensibility as we had. The Modocs went to the Smithsonian Institution once, looking for the skull of Captain Jack, one of their revered leaders who had been beheaded. They found it on the desk of a Smithsonian scientist, where it was being used as an ashtray. Well, since that can no longer happen—not because of NAGPRA, just because they don't allow smoking in those institutions anymore. Otherwise, you will still find the skull on the desk, with paper clips and the like. You will find Indian bodies in green boxes, floor to ceiling. It's an extraordinary thing.

One of the most important things that happened in all of our legislative efforts, something that you won't find in any of the legislative history of NAGPRA, was a House hearing about repatriation and about the National Museum of the American Indian. Native Hawaiian men came and stood along three walls of the hearing room. They just stood there. Massive Native Hawaiian men, just standing there. The afternoon before, they had gone to the National Museum of Natural History of the Smithsonian where all these green boxes are, and they had made an appointment and very politely asked to see all their dead relatives. Box after box was brought to them. When the tables were filled with the boxes, they picked up all the boxes and said, "We'll be taking them home now." And they just left. They didn't wait for permission, they didn't wait for a law, they just left. The next day, when they came and stood in that hearing room, there wasn't a Native person in that room who didn't know that we owned the world, and that anything that we were going to do was charmed and blessed and that we would win. It was quite the thing.

I love the stuff that's not in the legislative history. The first repatriation of a Zuni war god on the record was in the late 1970s from the Denver Art Museum. Actually, the first one was a setup, sort of a test to see what people cared about. Maytag, of the Maytag refrigerator fortune, a very nice lady who supported a lot of Native artists in Santa Fe, was incensed that these sacred objects were going up on the block. She called some of us one time about one that was being auctioned from Sotheby's or Christie's, I can't quite remember, one of the large auction houses in New York. She said, "Why don't you just walk in and get it?" And I said, "Because I don't want to be in the slammer." And she said, "How about if I did it?" And I said, "What right would you have to do it?" She

said, "That's why it has to be an Indian." I said, "But I'm not Zuni." She asked some other people, whom I won't implicate by name. Some were willing to do it and some weren't. She said, "Well, I don't think they'll stop me." She thought maybe they would send her a bill, as if it were a shoplifting. If you are very, very rich, and you do some shoplifting, they send a polite note saying, "We notice that you adored the coat that cost $5,000, do send us a check." We thought maybe that would happen. To test it, she went in and said, "I'll take that now. I'm going to return it to the Zuni people." And she walked out. Walked to her apartment. Later flew out to Zuni and returned that war god. No check, no call, no one ever followed up.

That told us a lot. The non-Indians didn't want to litigate this. That was a very important thing. It changed the approach for a lot of us. Not for the litigators among us, but it changed the approach for those of us who were looking for ways to craft policy. Walter Echo-Hawk can tell you how many lawsuits were ready to go when we finally came up with the agreement with the Smithsonian and eleven months later came up with the agreement for NAGPRA. Some things we fell into by accident, some things were calculated. Going after the Smithsonian holdings first was calculated, because they were king of the mountain. We knew that if you beat the king of the mountain, everyone else will come tumbling down. That is what happened. It wasn't automatic, and it was very difficult going those next eleven months and through the NAGPRA negotiations. Nevertheless, once the giant was slain, we did have a much easier time of it. The uncomfortable part was that we were in close proximity to the very people who liked having skulls for ashtrays.

We were part of the process for an Indian dialogue report at the Heard Museum, which was an effort by some in Congress, some in Arizona, and some in museums with large Indian holdings, to slow us down or to obviate the need for national repatriation policy. I chose the Indian side of it, and the Heard Museum's Michael Fox chose the non-Indian side of it, and we ended up with a dialogue report—well, we sort of suspended dealing so that we could get the Smithsonian agreement without their knowledge, without the knowledge of the other side. They were surprised by that and were sort of knocked off their thrones a bit. They were appalled, though, that we were insisting on the term "human remains," for example. In the national dialogue report every physical anthropologist and every archaeologist specifically, by name, disassociated themselves from the term "human remains." They didn't like the term, they wanted to keep saying "bones" and "skeletons" and other scientific terms, "grave goods" instead of funerary objects. They didn't like that we were changing the lexicon. As any good colonist knows, when you change the terminology, you change the terms of the interaction. We knew how to do that because it had been done to us. We insisted on "human remains" and they insisted on having their names withdrawn from that part of the report. They didn't like the implication that human rights attached to our dead relatives, that we had the right to get buried and stay buried, that we weren't the archaeological property of the United States of America or of the museums. It was mighty stuff, just the simple changing of the terms.

One of the terms that is now coming back to haunt us is "unidentifiable human remains." We say, of course, "unidentified." Right now there is a big push to try to categorize a huge number of Native people, dead Native people, as unidentifiable. Some of us suspect that it is in order to conduct DNA testing on them without having anyone able to object. I believe that that is the goal and that the Park Service NAGPRA office is an important part of that effort and maybe even working with people in specific institutions around the country on those tests. I would like to find evidence of that. Maybe some energetic researchers in this audience would like to undertake that effort and help us search. Even the museums, who have now turned in their inventories, for the most part, are saying that the Park Service needs to publish those inventories and let people in Indian Country know what the museums have said, so that we can say, "Oh, in that museum they're saying that they have this many unidentifiable human remains, they've come from such and such a place, we think that they belong to us, and we can claim them." People from very large museums in the meeting that Dr. Tsosie moderated and organized and reported on were saying that 75 percent, 85 percent, maybe a higher percentage, of those people currently classified as unidentifiable human remains can be identified if the Park Service will just release the information, will publish where they were taken from. Just the bare information that the museums have given to the Park Service. Our hope is that everyone will insist on the Park Service doing their job, which they're saying can't be done for "a period of time," meaning until the next ice age. We're saying it needs to be done right now. They want to rush and have a rule that would have the effect of declaring all the human remains now classified as unidentifiable

locked into that definition. We're saying, what's the rush? Why rush now? You've not rushed during any of the implementation of the repatriation laws, and now you want to rush? If you have a vote in any sense or an opinion, let the Park Service and various museums, and Congress in particular, know that the Park Service is not doing a good job, that they may be doing something dastardly, and that the dastards should be investigated.

WALTER ECHO-HAWK

Rebecca Tsosie has asked me to give some quick remarks about the Kennewick Man case. This case is titled *Bounicbsen v. United States*. It was filed in the state of Oregon by some scientists to test the limits of the NAGPRA legislation. Some scientists are unhappy and displeased with the NAGPRA legislation and the social changes brought about by NAGPRA. Before NAGPRA and similar legislation, Native dead were considered property belonging to the U.S. government. These dead were scientific remains and strictly treated as "archaeological resources" of the United States. With the passage of NAGPRA, society acted to change that way of thinking about Native dead and to treat them more like the dead of other races.

NAGPRA is one of the laws that implement the legislative agenda set in motion by the American Indian Religious Freedom Act of 1978. It is a landmark human rights law for Native people. NAGPRA created a backlash in some quarters of the scientific community. I believe that there is a movement among parts of the scientific community to weaken NAGPRA, to slow and impede its implementation. I believe that this lawsuit was brought as part of a strategy to test the actual limits of this statute. The facts of the case are as follows. The Columbia River gorge of Washington State and Oregon is a very ancient tribal area. My wife and her family are from Celilo Falls. The gorge has long been occupied by our Native people. It is the home of many tribal petroglyphs and origin legends that predate the United States. The tribes and bands Indigenous to that area still know their origins and aboriginal ties to the region. In 1996 a person discovered some human remains that were unearthed by erosion on a riverbank along the Columbia River on U.S. Army Corps of Engineers land. The dead man was over nine thousand years old. Five tribes of that area submitted a NAGPRA claim to these remains: the Yakama Nation, the Nez Pe^{r}ce Tribe, the Confederated Tribes of the Colville Reservation, Confederated Tribes of the Umatilla Nation, and the Wanapum Band. My wife and her family are enrolled Yakamas who belong to the Wanapum Band. They filed a joint NAGPRA claim to rebury this man. Based on evidence submitted by the tribes, the Department of the Interior determined that there was enough evidence to culturally affiliate these remains with the five tribes to satisfy the NAGPRA standards and therefore decided to turn the remains over to them for reburial. The evidence consisted largely of oral traditions that these tribes have, and continue to have today, about that region. The scientists were upset because of the very old age of the remains. They wanted to study them, regardless of the feelings of the Native people in the area, as is so often the practice. Some have studied Native American remains throughout their careers without the consent of the next of kin. They brought a lawsuit in the federal district court to enjoin reburial and to get permission to conduct their studies.

This test case is pretty good strategy on their part because from the standpoint of law, our facts for defending the reach of the statute are poor in that these remains are in fact very, very old. It is hard to present ironclad evidence in court of a relationship to remains that are that ancient. Moreover, the location where the remains were discovered is outside of aboriginal tribal areas as determined by the Indian Claims Commission in NAGPRA. So there is a geographic loophole that puts the Ancient One in an area that is not clearly covered by the statute. The scientists did a lot of fund-raising, got a really good attorney, and sued the government. By the luck of the draw, they got a judge who had a burr under his saddle against the government. They took the government "to the cleaners" in the district court. About a year ago, the court ruled in their favor, issuing a ninety-page opinion enjoining the reburial of the remains, overturning the decision of the Department of the Interior to repatriate these remains, and granting access to the scientists to study the remains. This case is now on appeal in the Ninth Circuit. We recently filed a brief in the appeal on behalf of the Morning Star Institute and the Association of American Indian Affairs. We had an amicus brief in the trial court on behalf of the National Congress of American Indians.

The case raises many statutory issues about the proper interpretation of NAGPRA and about the procedures employed for making decisions under the statute. The appeal has been briefed and argued before the Ninth Circuit and is presently on submission. This test case is working its way through the courts. We'll just have to wait and see what the outcome will be and then assess whether any further tinkering with the statute will be necessary. Depending on what the court does, Indian Country may need appropriate congressional action to preserve the intent of the statute. This case illustrates that whenever a historic Native statute is enacted, Native people must be ever vigilant to protect the statute from attacks and uphold the constitutionality of the statute.

NEW INDIANS, OLD WARS

Elizabeth Cook-Lynn

History does repeat itself, and when the Twin Towers in New York and the Pentagon in Washington, D.C., were struck by Al-Qaida in 2001, a defensive and, some say, unnecessary gathering of national power on the part of the United States occurred. War was the result and thousands of young men and women have been sacrificed. There is a connection between this defensive act and the U.S. response to the killing of General G. A. Custer in 1876. In the decade following Custer's defeat and death, Congress passed laws to break treaties, confiscate land, and initiate a genocidal war. Political terror was a strategy used against natives in the same way that military terror is being used in the world today. In 2003, the United States declared war against terror in the Middle East very reminiscent of the war in the northern Plains against the Sioux. That Sioux war lasted from 1876 to 1890, when massacres of innocents occurred everywhere in the northern Plains. At this writing, no one can predict how long the war in Babylon will last, nor who will be buried in the latest mass grave.

The current mission of the United States to become the center of political enlightenment to be taught to the rest of the world began with the Indian wars and has become the dangerous provocation of this nation's historical intent. The historical connection between the Little Big Horn event and the "uprising" in Baghdad must become part of the political dialogue of America if the fiction of decolonization is to happen and the hoped-for deconstruction of the colonial story is to come about. When that historical connection is analyzed, it is possible to understand the consequences of the occupation of the lands of a weak state by a stronger one in the context of modern social and political theory.

Not a lot of the information concerning how the people of the Sioux Nation have felt concerning the Black Hills issue can be read in the documents of

From Elizabeth Cook-Lynn, *New Indians, Old Wars*, Urbana: University of Illinois Press, 2007, pages 204–210.

the so-called business councils that began forming on the Sioux Reservations after the turn of the century, as early as 1915, but some insight can be gleaned not only from what is recorded but also, often, what is not. It seems clear that even the white superintendents of those agencies who had control over what was published in those documents marked the dialogue, but the Sioux speakers portray in the sense of the times they are describing that the federal government had not dealt with them fairly.

In those documents, the question of whether the U.S. government had the right and the authority to take over the Black Hills was only tacitly a part of the discourse. Manifest Destiny was clearly the theory used by the federal government to bolster their authority, which meant that matters concerning the 1851 and 1868 Sioux treaties were largely ignored by the courts and the battery of lawyers who were on the case for decades. There seemed to be no legal way to address that question even after the case went to court (following a quirky authorization by Congress in 1920). The question of authority could not be posed because of restrictions written into the law; it was not posed then nor since. Indeed, compensation has been the only remedy available in law, a remedy rejected by the entire Sioux Nation for many decades. Part of what is revealed in the documents of the past is the fact that when there seems to be no legal redress, victims lose sight of their goals. Groups and individuals who are victims of colonial practice are turned into proxies for colonial intentions and are used by those in power. There is the fear in the resistance movements at the beginning of the twenty-first century that such proxies will be given authority and support by the adversaries.

Prior to and during the court discussion of the case, two world wars intervened and the Indian Citizenship Act was passed in 1924, making Indians citizens of the United States for the first time, a legal process that had been tried and bungled in legislation for many previous decades. One important consequence of this action that made Indians into Americans was to make sure that Indians did not have to renounce their tribal nation citizenship status; this was done because many tribes were opposed to the act. Thus, native tribal Americans to this day hold dual citizenship in the United States and in their tribal nations.

The best that could be done concerning the theft of their sacred lands in the Black Hills, according to their lawyer, a South Dakota politician named Ralph Case, was to file what has become known as Sioux C-$_{531}$, in which the tribe asserted that the United States had taken illegally the treaty-protected Black Hills and failed to fulfill the "trust" responsibility, which was a Fifth Amendment matter. Many unremittingly illegal principles were put into the legislative and legal documents allowing the Sioux to get the case to court. But, most of all, to the Sioux, the entire matter has meant a failure of the "trustee" to protect their treaty lands from seizure, a total of 7.7 million acres, holy and sacred lands essential to their religious interests as a people, and a place of origin.

To the federal government, this has simply meant a failure to pay them for the seizure. The case became a simple claims case (a real estate matter) in which some two dozen petitions were sought, and it was in the courts until 1980 when the Supreme Court called it a "theft" rather than a legal "taking." Because of the limitations placed on how tribal land claims could be brought to the U.S. court system, this matter became only a compensation matter in law. Had the United States paid for it? No. Had it been for sale? No. How, then, could it be a simple real estate matter as the courts have implied? Subsequent discourse has suggested that it was not and is not just a real estate matter. It is a moral, legal, ethical matter of historical significance.

The court actions throughout the litigation process tell us that most of the claims were dismissed by the courts, as was the 1942 *Sioux Tribe of Indians v. United States* case, on the basis that they were, overall, moral claims and outside of the jurisdiction of the Indian land legislation passed in 1920. It was a religious matter, the attorneys deemed, untouchable by the courts, and, according to this interpretation, destined to be dismissed and forgotten. In 1950, the resubmitted claim was dismissed again and during this time, the courts were again assisted by the U.S. Congress in federal efforts to diminish native treaty standings.

In a last-ditch effort to end treaty-protected nationhood for Indigenous peoples all over the country, the disastrous termination and relocation laws were passed by the U.S. Congress in that decade. These termination and relocation laws were meant to end treaty responsibilities (such as health and education and, certainly, land claims) and urbanize large reservation populations to be based in cities such as Seattle, Los Angeles, Cleveland, Minneapolis, Chicago, and Oakland.

In that process, two-thirds of the entire Indian population of the United States was relocated to cities in the West in order to separate them from land, family, Indigenous rights, and religion. It was an enforced assimilation process put into legal terms affirming the federal government's control and weakening tribal governments' authority over Indian citizens.

These are the matters of "old wars" taken up by "new Indians" who know and remember that thousands have died terrible deaths on this unlucky journey described in these pages. The predictable implication of all of this history can be stated in several ways: to honor agreements that threaten no one concerning the lands and rights of native peoples, yet upholding that honor has been the major resistance of White America; to know that land ownership rights are the crux of moral relationships between Indigenous nations and others, yet those rights will not be defended by America; to know that land ownership rights are the key to the survival of tribal peoples everywhere, yet those rights are stolen by America, a powerful nation claiming an honorable place among nations throughout the globe.

The implication of all this history and the reason to write about it is that genocide is a crime against humanity, which means that it is the responsibility of all of us. The facts of this history, stated bluntly, are that the United States has pursued policies throughout the generations that led to the decimation of the first nations on this continent.

America is a new nation. Because of its inexperience and arrogance (as well as its genocidal history toward natives), it is difficult to hold it up as an accomplished beacon of virtue in the world. Because of its intention to be finished with Indians and because of its military and economic power, dangerous contact is still happening to the Indigenous peoples of this continent and around the world.

Inquiring about the intention of one people toward another is the challenge that must be met if we are to unravel colonialism in the future. How can we know the future when we know so little of the past? How can we know what the intentions are for the future of Indians in America when we are told by physicists that 96 percent of matter and energy in the entire universe is completely unknown?

One of the ways is to simply take a look at the experience of the past 500 years of American growth and analyze its connection to Indian lives and Indian survival. If what we find is that anti-Indianism is a concept in American Christian life, just as Islamophobia and anti-Semitism are concepts in Christian Europe, and are all derived from specific occurrences and experiences that have matured over the centuries, that is a place to begin.

Practically speaking, the concept of anti-Indianism in the United States can be best understood if it attempts to take the dialogue between Indigenous peoples and immigrants outside the usual context of "racism" and to put it into the political discussion of "enforced colonialism." This has been the thrust of Indian Studies for the past three decades.

It is one of the unfortunate realities of race dialogue in the United States that the enslavement of Africans for economic reasons and the effort to overthrow that crime against humanity became the essential focus of contemporary dialogue when, in fact, the black–white dialogue is limiting in terms of the broader, more diverse nature of Americanism. The reason that such racial dialogue can be called unfortunate is because it implies that an end to racism is possible, that an end to blackness is possible, and that white America can overcome its early history simply through law. Instead, a broad intellectual endeavor must be undertaken.

Anti-Indianism is not so easily unclaimed as race dialogue because of its Indigenous nature. Anti-Indianism is not only about enslavement, white supremacy, rape, poverty, discrimination, color, busing, whiteness or blackness, guilt, Jim Crow, a piece of the pie, reparations, equality, or even affirmative action. Anti-Indianism is also about the failure of politics, nationhood and sovereignty, possession of land, Indigenousness, and self-determination. Anti-Indianism in America is about the failure of the right to nationhood. Because the First Nations of America (i.e., Indians and their nations) possess all of the traits of nationhood—language, land, military, governing forms, religion, citizenship, and ideology—they are considered unassimilable and, therefore, impervious or even dangerous to American ideals. The crimes against humanity set in motion by this reality are a ubiquitous menace still faced by America and its struggle for justice. Because of the possession of the traits of nationhood by American tribal nations, and because of America's narcissism and arrogance concerning its primacy, there exists a political agenda that cannot be propelled into what America wants to see as its rightful place in the world. To deny the Indigenous peoples their place as sovereigns in this democracy is an unacknowledged crime against humanity. This is one of America's dilemmas as a world power.

Almost all of the knowledge about the traits of Indianism was dismissed during what is called the "discovery period": when Columbus called the natives of this continent simple and good, Cortez said they were savage and cruel (he was military, after all), priests said they were unknown to god, Christians said they were ignorant and deficient, and the military that faced them for a hundred years said they were not human. These descriptions have pervaded all areas of American life—school, church, government, and community— and has resulted in the concept anti-Indianism.

The kind of colonial law applied on Indian lands for at least 200 years may be seen by some observers as the U.S. government's ongoing criminal activity and may even be viewed by some of its victims as the first nationalist politicization of the cultural identity called "Americanism." If that perception is accurate, we are in a very dangerous time. Now, because of U.S. global influence and because of the comparison that can be made to the illegal Indian Reorganization Act (IRA) constitutions written by and for American Indian tribal nations some eighty years ago, the Islamist terror we are witnessing at the beginning of the twenty-first century suggests constant warfare.

For the victims of the colonial power of the United States, both past and present, the roots of terrorism are vivid and may be the direct consequence of nationalistic Americanism as it is being embedded in the recent behavior of the powerful United States, as it writes a new constitution for the entire Iraqi region. Every nation in the Middle East will reject this constitution because it is much like the illegal, colonial IRA constitutions written for and by American Indian tribal nations eighty years ago, charts for democracy that have, unfortunately, failed to meet the needs of the people. Democrat cannot thrive under such heavy-handed colonial power. Unless America begins to understand that its victims will no longer accept the idea begun 1492 that "inferior" races and civilizations can be wiped off the face of the earth, it will face constant war. A necessary corrective to that threshold for the conquest of the world is overdue. The times they are a-changin', we've been told by everyone from Bob Dylan to Bin Laden.

What gives impetus for such events in the modern world? If, as it has been thought by historians like Robert F. Berkhofer and others in their historic analyses, the Indian of the white imagination and ideology concerning civilization and progress has been the result of early contact and experience, how is it that this same ideology comes to bear on the U.S. relationship to those peoples of a modern nation in the Middle East zoo years later? Is the phrase "history repeats itself" just an unreasoned rhetorical device, self-indulges and repetitious, or is it a powerful weapon of ideological work that cannot be thrown off without reactionary strategies?

The answer may be that the ideology of civilizing and Christianizing negatives so deeply embedded in the Euro-American experience is a consistent body of ideas reflecting the continuing social needs and aspirations of Americans. That is the tragedy of history. The people in the Middle East who have been taken over by the United States in a recent war are not uncivilized, and neither were the Indigenous peoples of North America. They are not savages, and neither were the Indigenous peoples of America. Iraqis are not without god, language, or culture. Neither were the peoples of the Americas. Yet they have been characterized as that by Western minds. American Indians and other Indigenous peoples resist the American threat as they would resist any threat that they see invading and settling in their territory. In the case of the Iraqis, they are a modern people: lawyers, surgeons, businesspeople, teachers, religious leaders, international athletes, singers, musicians, pilots, and housewives with houses full of all the modern conveniences. And, indeed, since 1970 they have had a working constitution that might be utilized in the modern world if it is cleansed of its Baathist hegemony. Iraq is not a backward country. It is a Muslim country with thousands of years of history, culture, and civilization that has been the pride of the Arab world.

If an ideology about good and/or bad can continue to be presumed even about modern peoples across the globe by the United States, the most militarily powerful nation known to any era (just as was done with the Indigenous peoples of this continent 500 years ago), what can scholars and thinkers do to find solutions, a balance of power? What is the goal of any nation if it is not self-determination? How is the self-determination of America or Iraq or the First Nations of this country, the right of all peoples, promoted through the events of the past several decades? How is war an answer to fear and ideological power? These are still the questions that plague us all.

Perhaps it is all too simple: the unfortunate people called the "terrorists" of the twenty-first century in Baghdad have become what the "savages" of the northern Plains were thought to be so long ago; thus, powerful and determined colonizers will out. Yet, who controls the stories and who creates the language by which the stories are told is still the ultimate power. To know that is

Copyright 1996, Paul Conrad. Distributed by Los Angeles Times Syndicate. Reprinted with permission.

to know the extent of our loss and to know the possibility of our lives, as indicated by the title of this book: *New Indians, Old Wars*. New Indians must tell the new history about the old wars because they have been witness to savagery and terrorism—and continue to be.

Simply put, the "terrorists" and "savages" (and now "extremists") are called by those names because they resist the colonial effort to seize their lands and resources; make them beggars; convert them to an unknown religion, Christianity; and destroy them economically. Make no mistake: a holocaust happened here in our own lands and it continues here and elsewhere. Long ago, they say, there were bad times. We must tell of them so we can know the future. The Indian wars must be given standing in this ever-growing narrative about America because the terrors the world is now witnessing may be the direct consequence of the events begun in America in the past centuries!

It is essential that educational systems, people of goodwill, writers, and intellectuals of all countries resist the tyranny of failed ideologies and remember to tell our children that, yes, Virginia, history does repeat itself.

FREE LEONARD PELTIER

Steve Talbot

For more than thirty years Leonard Peltier, an Ojibway/Lakota Indian, has been serving two consecutive life sentences in a federal prison for "aiding and abetting" the deaths of two FBI agents in a firefight on the Pine Ridge Reservation in 1975. Yet, there is no credible evidence that Peltier fired the fatal shots, and the case has all the earmarks of a political frame up. Peter Worthington, a former publisher of the *Toronto Sun*, writes that Peltier "was railroaded into prison with the use of fabricated and manipulated and suppressed evidence."

It has been almost fourteen years since former Attorney General Ramsey Clark filed a brief for Executive Clemency, a process that should have taken six to nine months. This request for Executive Clemency was endorsed by 55 members of the U.S. Congress, 60 members of the Parliament of Canada, 202 members of the European Parliament, Archbishop Desmond Tutu, Nobel Prize recipient Rigoberta Menchu Tum, President Nelson Mandela of South Africa, the Reverend Jesse Jackson, and Mother Teresa. His release is now also supported by the Kennedy Memorial Center for Human Rights, the Dalai Lama, and the Archbishop of Canterbury, among many others. Subsequent to his imprisonment, Amnesty International listed Peltier as "a prisoner of conscience" and called for Leonard's immediate and unconditional release.

On a June morning in 1975, in a remote corner of the Pine Ridge Reservation near Wounded Knee, there was a fatal shoot-out in which two FBI agents and an American Indian died. The death of the Indian man went uninvestigated, but the deaths of the agents initiated one of the biggest manhunts in FBI history. More than 150 armed agents in a shoot-first-ask-questions-later search swarmed over the poverty-stricken land of the Oglala Lakota Nation in South Dakota. Eventually, four members of the American Indian Movement (AIM) were indicted on murder charges. One was later released for insufficient evidence, and two others were acquitted after a jury found that they had fired in self-defense. The fourth was Leonard Peltier, who was convicted in 1977. Key witnesses for Peltier were not allowed to testify and unlike the earlier trial of the other two defendants, evidence regarding government violence on the Pine Ridge Reservation was severely restricted. The prosecution claimed that the government had provided the defense with all FBI documents concerning the case, but in actuality more than 140,000 pages had been withheld in their entirety.

Peltier was in charge of an AIM self-defense team of Indian warriors who sought to protect Lakota elders and their families from the assault by federal and tribal vigilante forces that raged out of control following the occupation-protest at Wounded Knee in 1973. In the months following the firefight at Wounded Knee, dozens of AIM members and their supporters were killed or "disappeared," and the FBI, which is federally responsible for investigating homicides on Indian reservations, did nothing. Furthermore, new evidence suggests that the FBI itself was indirectly involved in murders of Oglala citizens.

In March 1996, the U.S. Parole Commission again denied parole to Peltier, even though the presiding parole officer had made a favorable recommendation for a retrial or parole based on the fact that no direct evidence exists against Peltier. He was not eligible for a rehearing until the year 2008, which is 17 years in excess of the commission's applicable guidelines and six years after the date set by Congress for the abolition of the Parole Commission itself. It was hoped that then President William J. Clinton would override the decision of the Parole Commission by granting Leonard

Peltier an executive pardon, but upon leaving office Clinton failed to do so. Currently, his attorneys have filed a new round of Freedom of Information Act requests with the FBI in an attempt to secure the release of the withheld documents relating to the case. Peltier's defense team believes that these documents contain information that would clear Peltier in a new trial.

Peltier, who has spent over 30 years in prison, is in deteriorating health. He suffers from diabetes, high blood pressure, and a heart condition. Time for justice is short. The late U.S. Representative Joe Kennedy summed up the case with the following words: "This government has the moral duty to correct this injustice. Seeing that justice is upheld for Leonard Peltier would amount to a major act of reconciliation for past injustices done to Native American peoples." Noted author Peter Matthiessen, whose book *In the Spirit of Crazy Horse* (1983) is the most authoritative account of the Peltier case, makes this telling comment: "The ruthless persecution of Leonard Peltier had less to do with his own actions than with underlying issues of history, racism, and economics. Leonard Peltier's experience reflects more than most of us wish to know about the realities of Indian existence in America." Perhaps Leonard himself, in his 1999

book *Prison Writings: My Life Is My Sun Dance* (p. 203), says it best:

> This is the twenty-third year [now thirty-third year] of my imprisonment for a crime I did not commit. . . . I can tell you this . . . We seek not revenge but reconciliation and mutual respect among our peoples. We may be of different nations, but we are still of the same society, and we share the same land. We all want justice, equality, fairness . . . the very principles on which America is founded and by its own Constitution supposedly bestows on all within its borders, even Indians. Is that too much to ask?

Compiled from the following sources: Jane Ayers, "Leonard Peltier Should Be Freed," Open Forum, *San Francisco Chronicle*, June 5, 1996; Amnesty International U.S.A., "Prisoner Profile: Leonard Peltier," n.d.; Peter Mathiessen, *In the Spirit of Crazy Horse* (New York: Viking Press, 1983); Jim Messerschmidt, *The Trial of Leonard Peltier* (New York: South End Press, 1983); Leonard Peltier, *Prison Writings: My Life Is My Sun Dance*, ed. Harvey Arden (St. Martin's Press, 1999); "Peltier! International Pressure Mounts for Native America's Mandela," *AIM 4 Awareness* (Double Issue: Spring/Summer 1999): 11; *Quick Facts: Case of Leonard Peltier*, Free Leonard.org, 1893 Clinton St., Buffalo, NY 14206, Email: info@freeleonard.org; *AIM for Freedom for Leonard Peltier, Legal Actions, Free Peltier*, Leonard Peltier Defense Committee, www.whoisleonardpeltier.info.

PART REVIEW

DISCUSSION QUESTIONS

Rayna Green, *The Pocahontas Perplex*
1. Outline the origin and development of the Pocahontas perplex in the national literature and art of the United States.
2. Discuss the meaning and function of the "Indian squaw" image and its relationship to the "Indian princess" stereotype.

Luana Ross, *Punishing Institutions*
1. Catherine (Cedar Woman) grew up in a violent and abusive household. What effect did this fact have on her involvement in the homicide for which she was later convicted and sent to prison?
2. Explain what the author means by the statement that one form of violence that Native American women face is the system of incarceration itself. How is the system of incarceration for Indian women prisoners both racialized and genderized?

Tim Giago, *Indian-Named Mascots*
1. Why does this author find Indian-named sports mascots demeaning?
2. Were you aware that the subject of Indian-named mascots is a volatile issue in Indian country? Having read the material presented in this box, have you changed your opinion?

Shannon Prince, *We're Imitating the Enemy*
1. Who are the Cherokee Freedmen? What is the legal basis for their Cherokee citizenship?
2. On what basis is the Cherokee nation's leadership trying to remove them?

3. Why does the author, a Cherokee, say that "we're imitating the enemy"?

Sally J. Torpy, *Native American Women and Coerced Sterilization*
1. Describe the nature and extent of sterilization of Indian women in the United States during the 1970s.
2. Why was sterilization a source of concern to those in the Red Power movement?
3. What is the significance of the concept of "institutional discrimination" to this issue?

James Riding In, Cal Seciwa, Suzan Harjo, and Walter Echo-Hawk, *Protecting Native American Human Remains, Burial Grounds, and Sacred Places*
1. Congress passed NAGPRA in 1990. What issue in Native America does it address? What, according to the panelists, are its limitations?
2. Who is the Kennewick Man, and why is he especially a concern to the Northwest Indian tribes?
3. What has been the response of the government's Smithsonian Institution to the right of repatriation, as spelled out in NAGPRA?
4. What issue discussed by the panelists concerns the Zuni Salt Lake and the Modoc Indian leader Captain Jack? Explain.

Elizabeth Cook-Lynn, *New Indians, Old Wars*
1. What is the connection between the theft of the Sioux Black Hills and broken treaties of the past, and current

U.S. foreign policy leading to the invasion and occupation of Iraq? Why does the author say that "history repeats itself"?

2. Explain how "anti-Indianism" is different from the "race dialogue" and discrimination experienced by African-Americans.

Steve Talbot, *Free Leonard Peltier*

1. Who is Leonard Peltier, and what is the political significance of his legal case to Native Americans?

KEY TERMS

abortion
American Indian Movement (AIM)
American Indian Religious Freedom Act (AIRFA)
anti-Indianism
Cherokee Freedmen
Courts of Indian Offenses
ethnocide
eugenics
GOON squad
Indian Health Service (IHS)
Indian sports mascots
institutional, or structural, discrimination

Kennewick Man
NAGPRA
Noble Redman stereotype
Peltier, Leonard
Pocahontas perplex
prejudice
prisoner of conscience
Red Savage stereotype
squaw
stereotype
sterilization
Wounded Knee (1973)

SUGGESTED READINGS

AMNESTY INTERNATIONAL. *Maze of Injustice: The Failure to Protect Indigenous Women from Sexual Violence in the USA.* One-Year Update, Spring 2008.

BERKHOFER, ROBERT, JR. *The White Man's Indian: Images of the American Indian from Columbus to the Present.* New York: Vintage Books, 1979.

BRAND, JOHANNA. *The Life and Death of Anna Mae Aquash.* Toronto: James Lorimer & Company, 1978.

BURGOS-DUBRAY, ELISABETH, ed. *I, Rigoberta Menchú: An Indian Woman in Guatemala,* trans. Ann Wright. New York: Verso, 1984.

CHARTRAND, PAUL. "'Terms of Division': Problems of 'Outside Naming' for Aboriginal People of Canada." *Journal of Indigenous Studies,* 2, no. 2 (Summer 1991): 1–22.

HARJO, SUSAN SHOWN. "Chief Offenders." *Native Americas,* 12, no. 4 (Summer 1999): 34–37.

HINTON, LEANNE. "Ishi's Brain." *News from Native California* (Fall 1999): 4–9.

LAWRENCE, JANE. "The Indian Health Service and the Sterilization of Native American Women." *American Indian Quarterly,* 24, no. 3 (Summer 2000): 400–419.

MATTHIESSEN, PETER. *In the Spirit of Crazy Horse.* New York: Viking Press, 1983.

MARCUS, ALAN RUDOLPH. *Relocating Eden: The Image and Politics of Inuit Exile in the Canadian Arctic.* Hanover, N.H.: University Press of New England, 1995.

MOHAWK, JOHN. "Epilogue: Looking for Columbus. Thoughts on the Past, Present and Future of Humanity."

Pages 439–444 in *The State of Native America: Genocide, Colonization, and Resistance,* ed. M. Annette Jaimes. Boston: South End Press, 1992.

NORTON, JACK. *Genocide in Northwestern California: When Our Worlds Cried.* San Francisco: Indian Historian Press, 1979. [Kitty: 1979 is correct]

PELTIER, LEONARD. *Prison Writings: My Life Is My Sun Dance,* ed. Harvey Arden. New York: St. Martin's Press, 1999.

ROSENSTEIN, JAY, ed. *In Whose Honor?* [video documentary on American Indian mascots in sports]. New Day Films, © 1997.

STEDMAN, RAYMOND WILLIAM. *Shadows of the Indian: Stereotypes in American Culture.* Norman: University of Oklahoma Press, 1982.

STILMAN, JANET. "Enough Is Enough." In *Aboriginal Women Speak Out.* Toronto: Women's Press, 1987.

THORNTON, RUSSELL. *American Indian Holocaust and Survival: A Population History Since 1492.* Norman: University of Oklahoma Press, 1987.

WHEELOCK, DAVE, et al. *Without Reservations: Notes on Racism in Montana* [film]. Native Voices Public Television, Montana State University.

WEINBERG, BILL. "Requiem for Big Mountain: The Road to Relocation Is Unrelenting." *Native Americas,* 14, no. 3 (Fall 1997): 30–39.

WRONE, DAVID R., and RUSSELL S. NELSON JR., eds. *Who's the Savage? Documentary History of the Mistreatment of the Native North Americans.* Greenwich, Conn.: Fawcett Publications, 1973.

V

NATIVE REPRESENTATIONS: MEDIA AND THE ARTS

In academics, the term *representations* refers to how meaning is constructed in our minds through language; be it words (e.g., writing, poetry), music (e.g., traditional, modern, or rap lyrics), storytelling (e.g., spoken words, traditional languages), or visual language (all forms of art, filmmaking, and performance). How Native Americans represent themselves or make meaning of their lives and cultures as Native peoples is *very* different from how the dominant culture has represented (mis-represented) them as "Indians" throughout history.

As we have seen in previous parts of this text, Native history is different from American history. However, with the development of the field of American Indian Studies/Native American Studies, history is being revised to include Native voices; this book is a prime example of that process. But, in this day and age, the story is not told only in textbooks. History is conveyed through popular culture in the media—through movies, music, and other arts—where Native stories are being rewritten in Native voices.

Today many people learn about American Indians through school or museums. However, even more people learn about Natives in the media. Historically, people learned about Indians less from school than from folklore, newspapers, novels, images, and serialized stories. In fact, the earliest images and stories of Indians came from the explorers and later the colonists. Columbus was one of the first to write about Indians, and ever since, there have been stories and images of Native Americans permeating the consciousness of American popular culture.

Indian history is the history of America, and it is a part of national folklore in the winning of the West. In fact, by the 1830s most Americans had never seen an Indian. Yet, the image of the Indian fascinated Americans. The "Indian" represented the wild and untamed West, and there were many books about Indians. One example, *The Last of the Mohicans,* is a novel by James Fenimore Cooper from 1826. It was serialized in the mid-1800s, and by the 1900s was made into a movie. In fact, *The Last of the Mohicans* has been made into a movie five times in 80 years! Yet, the author had never seen an Indian! Cooper's romantic portrayal of the "last of his kind" perpetuated the idea that Indians were a dying race, an idea that continued into the mid-twentieth century.

There were other writers in the 1800s who wrote about the "noble savage," and the cannon of work they created became a genre in literature, marking their difference from their literary counterparts in Europe. Their literary territory was the West and the imaginary line between savagery and civilization—that point where white civilization meets the savage West—the perfect ideological location for a literary tragedy. By the 1860s, this literary genre became a full-born Western formula, a formula with which the reader is no doubt familiar—with the outlaw, the Indian, and the hero set in the mythic Old West.

This formula was well honed in graphic novels of the time, called dime novels, and in serialized periodicals or stories in magazines. Also, the Western formula was used in traveling theatrical productions called Wild West shows, modeled after circuses but with a Western theme. Buffalo Bill's Wild West Show and Congress of Rough Riders are among the most famous of these traveling shows, even visiting Europe and playing for the Queen Mother of England in the 1880s. Interestingly, Buffalo Bill saw the new technology of filmmaking as a way to market his Wild West Show, and he made the first movie Western. Even more fascinating, Euro-Disneyland in Paris still presents a live version of *Buffalo Bill's Wild West Show.* And, as we know, the Western is still a popular movie genre in filmmaking today.

For hundreds of years, stories about American Indians have been told in various manners—from illustrations, to paintings, to print and from art to movies. However, the idea and the image of the Indian depicted in these representations is purely a white construction; the Indian is a stereotype that has nothing to do with how present-day

Native Americans perceive or represent themselves.[1] Native Americans were and are real, but the stereotypical Indian is not.

In representing themselves, many Natives take full advantage of all media available today. Native people's ability to counter the stereotypical presentation of "the Indian" is limited only by imagination. Native Americans are extremely visible on the Internet (e.g., in social media), in music, in literature, in academics, in museums, and in the movies. Native American journalists are visible on many sites, including *Indian Country Today*'s Web site. On *Indianz.com* news articles are collected daily and form a working database of sorts on current issues happening in Indian Country. Native American artists, filmmakers, and writers make great use of personal web pages and blogs, social networking sites such as MySpace and Facebook, and YouTube. In addition, many Native American organizations and agencies make use of the Internet. Most of the major museums, such as the National Museum of the American Indian, as well as Native social, political, and business organizations such as the National Congress of American Indians, the Native American Rights Fund, and the American Indian Movement have Facebook pages in order to connect Natives and supporters across the world. Most tribes have "official" Web sites. In terms of social networking, most of the major Indian centers in various cities, including the Chicago Indian Center, have MySpace pages. Artists, authors, musicians, and filmmakers, including filmmaker Chris Eyre, author Sherman Alexie, and artist Steven Yazzie, take full advantage of the Internet, having web pages, blogs, and MySpace and Facebook pages. Native American filmmakers and artists actively use sites such as YouTube to get their movies and short videos out. In fact, the National Museum of the American Indian regularly releases videos through YouTube. The Internet and the social networking community it has created have opened up a new world of connectedness that Native Americans fully participate in. (For more examples, see Appendix A.)

One important fact to remember is that while many Natives are using the Internet, many more are not. Given that upward of 70 percent of Native Americans live in urban areas, it is safe to assume that they at least have access to the Internet through schools, libraries, or their homes. However, just as in other segments of the population, poorer communities have less access to technology than others. Further, on many reservations there is little to no access to the Internet. Reservations are in rural areas and often don't have the infrastructure that other geographic locations have. In 1999, the U.S. government estimated that only 76 percent of households on reservations had telephones, mainly due to lack of infrastructure. For example, there is no telephone service in some rural areas of the Navajo Reservation, making Internet service impossible. Many Navajo people have dial-up access only to the Internet at local community centers or chapter houses, and they may have to drive long distances to reach these locations. Even now, in early 2009, there is only limited cellular service—if any—on the Navajo Reservation! This gap in telecommunications is called the digital divide. There are many entities still working to meet a federal mandate to bridge the gap in access, including National Congress of American Indians and Native Public Media, the federal government, tribal leadership, and telecommunications companies. Despite the digital divide, Native American presence on the web continues to expand, and Native American cultural representations are growing exponentially with the advent of the web and new media.

The first article, Reading 1, "Creating a Visual History: A Question of Ownership," is about creating a visual history or visual culture. Theresa Harlan (Laguna Pueblo) examines how Native photographers depict their own history and concludes that Native people have a very different perspective than do non-Indian observers. Euro-American image making that focuses on the "proud" and the "primitive," she writes, does not "carry messages for survival." Native image makers, on the other hand, depict the everyday world and actions of Indian people in images that "recognize the origin, nature, and direction of their Native existence and communities."

When looking at the visual and literary culture of Native Americans, as well as other oppressed peoples, there is often a very subtle commonality—the use of humor, joking, or teasing. While it may not be obvious or even visible to those not entrenched in the culture or it may look like black humor, peoples who survive oppression survive because they have the ability to laugh. The white stereotype of the "silent, stoic Indian" is a myth; Indian people love to joke and tease. One important function of humor is that it is a social leveler. No one can get too puffed up without some Indian wit cutting him or her down in an easy, teasing but pointed way. Hopi author Emory Sekaquaptewa, in Reading 2, "One More Smile for a Hopi Clown," describes another important function, explaining the world of Hopi clowns. Clowns are an important aspect of many Indian religions: they provide fun and laughter, and they also serve as an ethical and moral compass for the participants in the tribal culture. For example, whether they imitate lewd and mischievous behavior or punish the errant, they are demonstrating the mores of an Indian society.

Another prominent way in which Native Americans represent themselves is through art. The earliest forms of Native art include embellished objects for personal and community use. Often designs were family or clan related or told stories in their depiction. Each tribe in each geographic region had different designs; their uses of materials, color, and objects varied widely. Today, descendents of those peoples create beautiful art using derivatives of many of the same designs, albeit in very different ways and contexts. Contemporary Native American art can be very valuable, for a variety of reasons. In Reading 3, "But Is It American Indian Art?" Traci L. Morris (Chickasaw) discusses the development of contemporary Indian art as an economic system that places monetary value on Indian identity and then looks at young artists who are revising this system or rejecting it all together.

Nowhere can a better collection of Native American art be seen than the Smithsonian Institution's National Museum of the American Indian (NMAI). In Reading 4, "The National Museum of the American Indian," Traci L. Morris presents the history of this museum and the extent of the collections. Be sure to check out the NMAI web page, at http://americanindian.si.edu, for a sampling of art by the artists discussed in Reading 3.

Another way in which Native Americans are challenging the stereotypes and misrepresentations of the past is through filmmaking. Many people say that the newest form of storytelling is filmmaking. Native Americans have taken to filmmaking because of accessibility and the ability to represent themselves and tell their own stories. In Reading 5, "Wiping the Warpaint Off the Lens: Native American Film and Video," Beverly R. Singer (Santa Clara Pueblo/Navajo), a filmmaker and professor at the University of New Mexico, presents an overview of the development of Native American filmmaking. Native American filmmaking began in the 1980s but really gained prominence in the 1990s, with the film *Smoke Signals* (1998), which was a Native written, directed, and acted film that gained box office notoriety. Native filmmaking has plateaued since that time.

Reading 6, "Gone With the Wind: A Decade After *Smoke Signals*, Success Remains Elusive for Native American Filmmakers," is an interview and dialogue with two of the most successful Native American filmmakers, Chris Eyre and Sherman Alexie. They discuss what has and hasn't happened with Native filmmaking in the decade since *Smoke Signals* was released. In order to provide a sampling of the breadth of Native Americans in music and film arts, the box "Native American Media" provides an overview of some of the organizations supporting Natives in music, film, television, and other media.

Part V focuses entirely on Native representations of themselves and combates the stereotypes of Indians that have been and continue to be pervasive in the media. A number of organizations support this endeavor. The box "Native American Media" lists some of the most prominent and active Native media organizations and their Web sites.

A Google search on "American Indians" in late 2008 brought up 6,690,000 sites in 0.17 seconds. To effectively use this volume of sites about American Indians, it is important to be able to determine the difference between factual sites and the nonfactual sites. The box "Web Page Evaluation Checklist" is provided to help the reader determine the validity of Internet sites.

NOTE

1. Robert Berkhofer, Jr. *The White Man's Indian: Images of the American Indian from Columbus to the Present*. New York: Vintage Books, 1979.

CREATING A VISUAL HISTORY
A QUESTION OF OWNERSHIP

Theresa Harlan

In 1992 I guest-curated "Message Carriers: Native Photographic Messages" for the Photographic Resource Center at Boston University.[1] When invited, I could not accept without careful consideration of significant issues such as: ghettoization, opportunism (mine and theirs), and exploitation. Mainstream museums and publications often set apart "artists of color," "multicultural artists," and "ethnic artists," thereby designating us as the "other" or "different." The art and writings of these "other" artists are locked into discussions of "their" art, "their" people, and "their" issues. While there are still few opportunities to exhibit works by Native artists, there are even fewer exhibitions that treat these works in terms of their intellectual and critical contributions. Contemporary Native art is often characterized as angry, created from the voices of the defeated, and confined to the realm of the emotions.

Native people have—but are not perceived as having—diverse histories, cultures, languages, economics, politics, and worldviews. As Native people, we must claim rights to, and ownership of, strategic and intellectual space for our works. We must reject the reduction of Native images to sentimental portraits, such as those depicted by Marcia Keegan in her book *Enduring Culture: A Century of Photography of the Southwest Indians*.[2] Keegan writes, "From the beginning of my acquaintance with them, it was the Indians' confidence and attunement to the eternal verities that inspired my wonder and admiration. Thus it became my enduring commitment to try to experience, imagine, and document that more elusive subject, the traditional Indian way of life."[3] This type of thinking reduces Native survival to a matter

of nostalgia, and precludes discussion of the political strategies that enabled Native survival. The writer bell hooks refers to nostalgia as "that longing for something to be as once it was, a kind of useless act. . . ."[4] and calls for the recognition of the politicized state of memory as ". . . that remembering that serves to illuminate and transform the present."[5]

Native survival was and remains a contest over life, humanity, land, systems of knowledge, memory, and representations. Native memories and representations are persistently pushed aside to make way for constructed Western myths and their representations of Native people. Ownership of Native representations is a critical arena of this contest, for there are those who insist on following the tired, romantic formulas used to depict Native people. Those myths ensure an existence without context, without history, without a reality. An existence that allows for the combing of hair with yucca brushes in the light of a Southwest sunset; competition powwow dancing reborn as a spiritual ceremony; or the drunken Indian asleep on cement city sidewalks unable to cope with the white man's world. These are the representations constantly paraded before us by non-Native photographic publications such as Keegan's *Enduring Culture*, or *National Geographic*'s 1994 issue on American Indians, or Marc Gaede's *Border Towns*. Such constructed myths and representations are given institutional validation in the classroom and are continually supported by popular culture and media.

American classrooms are usually the first site of contest for Native children. In her essay, "Constructing Images, Constructing Reality: American Indian Photography and Representation," Gail Tremblay writes, "When Native children are taught that they are not equal, that their cultures are incapable of surviving in a modern world, they suffer from the pain that has haunted their parents' lives, that haunts their own

From *"Creating a Visual History: A Question of Ownership," by Theresa Harlan as appeared in Strong Heart: Native American Visions and Voices edited by Peggy Roalf. 1995 Aperture Foundation. Reprinted by permission of the author.*

lives. For an Indigenous person, choosing not to vanish, not to feel inferior, not to hate oneself, becomes an intensely political act. A Native photographer coming to image-making in this climate must ask, 'What shall I take pictures of, who shall I take pictures for, what will my images communicate to the world?' "[6]

Photographer and filmmaker Victor Masayesva, Jr., has described the camera as a weapon. "As Hopi photographers, we are indeed in a dangerous time. The camera which is available to us is a weapon that will violate the silences and secrets so essential to our group survival."[7] Writer, curator, and photographer Richard Hill, Jr. of the Tuscarora nation, also named the camera as a weapon, but a weapon for "art confrontation rather than military confrontation. Indians themselves now have taken the power of the image and begun to use it for their own enjoyment as well as for its potential power as a political weapon."[8] Artist Hulleah Tsinhnahjinnie declared, "No longer is the camera held by an outsider looking in; the camera is now held with brown hands opening familiar worlds. We document ourselves with a humanizing eye, we create new visions with ease, and we can turn the camera and show how we see you. The power of the image is not a new concept to the Native photographer—look at petroglyphs and ledger drawings. What has changed is the process."[9]

Masayesva, Hill, and Tsinhnahjinnie speak from the experience of seeing themselves spoken for by outsiders, of seeing the surreal positioned as the real. As Trinh T. Minh-ha says, Native image-makers "understand the dehumanization of forced-removal/relocation/reeducation/redefinition, the humiliation of having to falsify your own reality, your voice—you know. And often cannot say it. You try and keep on trying to unsay it, for if you don't they will not fail to fill in the blanks on your behalf, and you will be said."[10]

When Native people do pick up the camera, often their image-making is greeted with a patronizing welcome. The "Indian" no longer sits passively before the camera, but now operates the camera—a symbol of the white man's technology. The voices and images of Native photographers must be understood as rooted in and informed by Native experiences and knowledge.

Lee Marmon has created, and continues to create, photographic representations of Native people that affirm Native memories, self-knowledge, and presence. Upon his return from World War II, Marmon began taking photographs of the old people in the villages at

*"1491" from the "Feather" series
by Larry McNeil, © 1992.*

Laguna Pueblo—so that there would be something to remember them by. Marmon's photographic remembrances are of a generation of people who had to devise ways to affirm and protect Laguna knowledge despite the pernicious attempts—beginning in the sixteenth century—of the Spanish, Mexican, and later, the United States governments to strip them of land, culture, religion, and the memory of that existence. Thus, these are not merely images of cute old people. The presence of Juana Scott Piño; of Jeff Sousea in *White Man's Moccasins*; or of Bennie at the sheep camp might at first seem ironic or contradictory, as some are dressed in "traditional" clothing and others not. Marmon's photography is not confined to any strict notion of Indianness. It differs vastly from Keegan's inspired commitment to document the "elusive traditional way of life," as these images include the context of Laguna lives and experiences. Marmon did not drive around seeking the best adobe wall to use as a background; he photographed his community while delivering groceries for his family's store.[11] What we see through Marmon's photographs are images of people living and working as they are—and without an implied mystical "elusiveness." Marmon's title, *White Man's Moccasins*, is more than the irony of an old Laguna man wearing high-tops. It is Pueblo objectification of Western society through the appropriation of a popular Western icon.

Marmon's images are of people who do not perceive themselves as confined to any mythic or imagined concepts held by others. They remain fresh because they are not restricted by essentialist notions that Native people must dress as Natives in order to look Native and to be Native. Even some Native documentary photographers fall prey to expressing Native thinking and traditions through what is worn. By doing this, they risk entering into the same trap of only being able to recognize themselves through the eyes of non-Natives.

Zig Jackson provides ethnographic material about non-Native practices in photographing Native people in his series "Indian Photographing Tourist Photographing Indian." The tourists he records are so intent on their subjects and the drama of the moment that they are unaware of Jackson's presence. They exhibit a fascination usually reserved for movie stars, rock stars, scandalized politicians, or famous athletes. For these photographers, the value of Native images is based strictly on appearance. But would they clamor to take pictures of Native people wearing the clothes they wear at school, work, or home? No. Because when Native people wear bright colors, fringe, beads, leather, and feathers, they are "real" Indians. When they are dressed in everyday clothes they are not. Robert Berkhofer, Jr., discussed this in *The White Man's Indian: Images of the American Indian from Columbus to the Present*. "Since Whites primarily understood the Indian as an antithesis to themselves, then civilization and Indianness as they defined them would forever be opposites. Only civilization had history and dynamics in this view, so therefore Indianness must be conceived as ahistorical and static. If the Indian changed through the adoption of civilization as defined by Whites, then he/she was no longer truly Indian according to the image, because the Indian was judged by what Whites were not. Change toward what Whites were made him [her] ipso facto less Indian."[12]

Larry McNeil deliberately avoids representations of the "feathered" Indian and instead chooses a single feather to discuss Native survival. Some critics have described this work as relying on an easily recognized symbol, even a cliché. In fact, to reduce McNeil's use of feathers to a cliché is to accept the dominant thinking that is continually wielded against Native people. (Dominant thinking prevails when Native symbols are reduced to cliché while American colonization continues to be described as Manifest Destiny.) In McNeil's series, Native survival deliberately is not shown through full-color images of powwow dancers. Instead, he keeps to the visceral side of survival through black-and-white depictions of worn and broken feathers set against a dark background. Here, the Native memory of survival is neither romantic nor nostalgic.

James Luna's photo-essay "I've Always Wanted to Be an American Indian," is a satirical jab at those

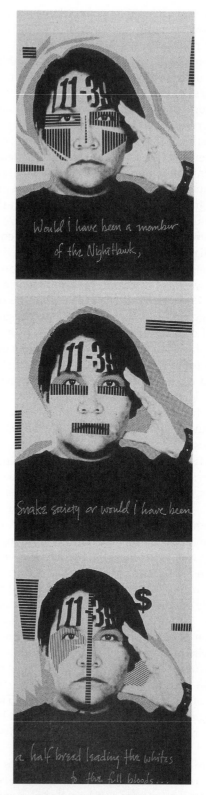

"Would I Have Been a Member of the Nighthawk, Snake Society or Would I Have Been a Half Breed Leading the Whites to the Full-Bloods. . . .?" by Hulleah Tsinhnahjinnie, © 1991.

who at some point discover a thread of Native ancestry in their past and then draw on myths of Indian identity to realize their ancestral inheritance. Luna's wake-up call is for these individuals to realize the reach of racist, political, and economic subordination of Native people, who cannot pick and choose their Native circumstances. Luna escorts the wake-up Indian on a guided tour of his La Jolla reservation, pointing out interesting sites and bits of information. His snapshot photographs of the mission church, schoolchildren, and a disintegrating adobe building are combined with positive and negative snips of information. Statements such as "During the last five years on the Reservation there have been and/or are now: three murders, an average unemployment rate of 47 percent, . . . twenty-one divorces and/or separations . . . thirty-nine births, forty-five government homes built . . . an increase in the percentage of high school graduates."[13] At the end of the tour, Luna asks "Hey, do you still want to be an Indian?"

Hulleah Tsinhnahjinnie reveals the current dispute among Native people over who, in fact, is "Indian." Tsinhnahjinnie's *Would I Have Been a Member of the Nighthawk, Snake Society or Would I Have Been a Half-Breed Leading the Whites to the Full-Bloods*, signed "111–390" (her issued tribal enrollment number) uses self-portraiture to discuss identity politics within a historical context. These graphic, 40-by-30-inch, black-and-white head-and-shoulder shots, which resemble passport or police photographs, support her discussion of the use of photography to identify and control the "other." The reference to the Nighthawk, Snake Societies, and half-breeds comes from a 1920 statement made by Eufala Harjo regarding the practice of the Bureau of Indian Affairs of securing names of Creek, Chickasaw, Choctaw, and Cherokee resistance-group members from "half-breed" informants.[14] Societies were formed to resist tribal leaders' decisions to ignore previous treaty agreements and to accept the 1887 Dawes Allotment Act, which reallocated parcels of lands to individual ownership—thereby overturning tribal practices of land collectively held through the maternal line.

Tsinhnahjinnie is one of the few artists who have taken a public stand on the 1990 Indian Arts and Crafts Act, which requires tribal enrollment numbers, state census roll numbers, or a special "Indian artist" status to be provided by an artist's tribal council in order for Native artists to sell their work as "Indian" art. Tsinhnahjinnie reminds us that we, as Native people, must recognize and understand identity politics as the invention of the United States government.

Jolene Rickard's *Sweka and PCBs* calls our attention to the fact that we may be ignoring or underestimating the dangers that accompany moneyed solicitations of tribal land use for toxic dump sites that contaminate food sources. Rickard draws a connecting line from toxic contamination to the gathering, collecting, fishing, and hunting of foods, and the ritual ceremonies that emanate from those sources. Rickard warns us, "If Indians no longer have a material and spiritual relationship with 'land,' then certain teachings and ceremonies cannot take place. Even when it is possible to transform these teachings into abstract space, without the geographic place of community, experience has shown that the teachings increasingly dissipate."[15]

Sweka and PCBs is not a romantic representation of an Indian man and his relationship to the natural world. It is a warning for all of us to confront our own threatened survival as human beings. We may become our own endangered species along with the salmon and the eagle that feeds on the salmon.

In Pamela Shields Carroll's *Footprints*, family images are printed on cut-out soles of baby moccasins, along with porcupine quills, collected in a small wooden box. *Footprints* evokes family memories that ultimately inform the next generation. The image on the left sole is of Carroll's brother celebrating his third birthday, dressed as a cowboy, sitting on a pony. The right sole depicts Carroll's great-aunt's Sun Dance tipi. *Footprints* is layered with personal memories, but also speaks from historical experience. It is a sister's quiet memory of her brother—and a statement about non-Native influences. The complexity of growing up Native is revealed in a family snapshot, in which her brother, as a child, adopts the

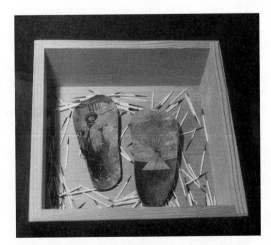

"Footprint" from the "Imprints" series by Pamela Shields, © 1994.

dress of those who were part of the conquest of his larger Blackfoot family. It is also a memory of family participation and responsibility in ceremony, and the health of a community through the Sun Dance. Yet together the moccasin soles represent diverse paths: the left, reflective of outside influences and future generations; the right, inside sources of knowledge and the integrity of Blackfoot culture.

Creating a visual history—and its representations—from Native memories or from Western myths: this is the question before Native image-makers and photographers today. The contest remains over who will image—and own—this history. Before too many assumptions are made, we must define history, define whose history it is, and define its purpose, as well as the tools used for the telling of it. The intent of history is to help us keep our bearings. That is, to know what is significant and, most importantly, to teach us *how* to recognize the significant. What happens when history is skewed, or when we no longer have the same skills of recognition? We as human beings become disabled by the inability to distinguish what is real from what is not. Gerald Vizenor, in his book *Manifest Manners: Postindian Warriors of Survivance*, calls this "Postindian simulations [which] are the absence of shades, shadows, and consciousness; simulations are mere traces of common metaphors in the stories of survivance and the manners of domination." . . . [16]

What Native photographers provide is the possibility of a Native perspective unclouded by White liberal guilt or allegiance to Western heroes. Yet these possibilities are not guaranteed by race or genetics. For if the photographer picks up his or her camera and approaches image-making with the same notions of capturing a "proud/ primitive" moment, then we are not getting a Native perspective. We are seeing Euro-American image-making traditions in action in Native hands. Those images do not carry messages of survival. In fact they are an ominous signal that colonization has been effective, in that the "Indian" can now recognize him- or herself only through the outside, as an outsider.

Native image-makers who contribute to self-knowledge and survival create messages and remembrances that recognize the origin, nature, and direction of their Native existence and communities. They understand that their point of origin began before the formation of the United States and is directly rooted to the land. These Native image-makers understand that the images they create may either subvert or support existing representations of Native people. They understand that they must create the intellectual space for their images to be understood, and free themselves from the contest over visual history and its representations of Native people.

NOTES

1. Gail Tremblay, "Constructing Images, Constructing Reality: American Indian Photography and Representation" in *Views: A Journal of Photography in New England* (Vol. 13–14, Winter 1993), p. 30.

2. "Message Carriers: Native Photographic Messages" was at the Boston Photographic Resource Center at Boston University in October, 1992. The exhibition included the works of Patricia Deadman, Zig Jackson, Carm Little Turtle, James Luna, Larry McNeil, Jolene Rickard, Hulleah Tsinhnahjinnie, and Richard Ray Whitman. Then staff curator Anita Douthat initiated the exhibition. The PRC was instrumental in the success of the exhibition.

3. Marcia K. Keegan, *Enduring Culture: A Century of Photography of the Southwest Indians* (Santa Fe: Clear Light Publishers, 1990), p. 11.

4. bell hooks, *Yearning, Race, Gender, and Cultural Politics* (Boston: South End Press, 1990), p. 147.

5. Ibid.

6. Tremblay, p. 30.

7. Victor Masayesva, Jr., "Kwikwilyaqua: Hopi Photography," in *Hopi Photographers/Hopi Images*, edited by Larry Evers (Tucson: Sun Tracks, University of Arizona Press, 1983), pp. 10–11.

8. Richard Hill, Jr. quoted in Susan R Dixon, "Images of Indians: Controlling the Camera," in *North East Indian Quarterly* (Spring/Summer, 1987), p. 25.

9. Hulleah J. Tsinhnahjinnie, "Compensating Imbalances," in *Exposure* 29 (Fall 1993), p. 30.

10. Trinh T. Minh-ha, *Women Native Other: Writing Postcoloniality and Feminism* (Indianapolis: Indiana University Press, 1989), p. 80.

11. Lee Marmon owns and manages the Blue Eyed Indian Bookshop at Laguana Pueblo.

12. Robert Berkhofer, Jr., *The White Man's Indian: Images of the American Indian from Columbus to the Present* (New York: First Vintage Books Edition, A Division of Random House, 1979), p. 29.

13. James Luna, *Art Journal* (Vol. 51, No. 3, Fall 1992), pp. 23–25.

14. For further discussion see Angie Debo's *A History of the Indians of the United States* (Norman: University of Oklahoma Press, 1990).

15. Jolene Rickard, "Frozen in the White Light," in *Watchful Eyes: Native Women Artists* (Phoenix: Heard Museum, 1994), p. 16.

16. Gerald Vizenor, *Manifest Manners: Postindian Warriors of Survivance* (Hanover, N.H. and London: Wesleyan University Press, University Press of New England, 1994), p. 53.

ONE MORE SMILE FOR A HOPI CLOWN

Emory Sekaquaptewa

The heart of the Hopi concept of clowning is that we are all clowns. This was established at the very beginning when people first emerged from the lower world. In spite of the belief that this was a new world in which no corruption and immorality would be present, the people nevertheless took as their own all things that they saw in the new world. Seeing that the people still carried with them many of the ways of the corrupted underworld, the Spirit Being divided them into groups and laid out a life-pattern for each of them, so that each would follow its own life-way.

Before the Hopi people left from the emergence place, one man chosen by them as their leader went up on a hill. I can just imagine the throng of his people around him who were excited and eager in getting ready to be led out to the adventures of a new world. The leader gets up on this hill and calls out, "yaahahay!" four times. Thus gaining their attention he said. "Now you heard me cry out to you in this way. You will hear me cry in this way when we have reached the end of our life-way. It will be a sign that we have reached the end of the world. We will know then whether we have fulfilled our destiny. If we have not we will see how it is to be done." The leader who was a visionary man chose this way of reminding his people that they have only their worldly ambition and aspirations by which to gain a spiritual world of eternity. He was showing them that we cannot be perfect in this world after all and if we are reminded that we are clowns, maybe we can have, from time to time, introspection as a guide to lead us right. From this beginning when we have been resembled to clowns we know that this is to be a trying life and that we will try to fulfill our destiny by mimicry, by mockery, by copying, by whatever.

This whole idea of clowning is re-enacted at the time of the *katsina* dances. When they are dancing in the plaza the *katsinas* represent the spiritual life toward which Hopi destiny is bent. The *katsinas* dance in the plaza at intervals throughout the day and sometimes for two days. When the clowns come they represent man today who is trying to reach this place of paradise. That is why the clowns always arrive at the plaza from the rooftops of the houses facing the plaza where the *katsinas* are dancing. The rooftops signify that even though we have reached the end, we are not necessarily ready to walk easily into the spiritual world. The difficulties by which clowns gain the place of the *katsinas* make for fun and laughter, but also show that we may not all be able to make it from the rooftop because it is too difficult. We are going to clown our way through life making believe that we know everything and when the time comes, possibly no one will be prepared after all to enter the next world. We will still find the way difficult with obstacles in front of us. Maybe some of us won't make it.

The clowns come to the edge of the housetops around noon and they announce themselves with the cry "yaahahay!" four times. This announces as foretold at emergence the arrival at the end of the life-way journey. And then they make their way into the plaza with all sorts of antics and buffoonery representing the Hopi life quest. In their actions they reveal that we haven't yet fulfilled our destiny after all. By arriving at the late hour, noon, they show that we are lagging behind because we think we have many things to do.

Once in the plaza they act just as people did when they emerged in this world. They presume that they are in a new world, clean and pure. They are where they can finally have eternal life like the *katsinas*; indeed, this is the day all Hopi look forward to. But as they are remarking on the beauty of this place filled with plants and good things they hear the

From "One More Smile for a Hopi Clown," by Emory Sekaquaptewa, as appeared in *The South Corner of Time*, 1980, edited by Larry Ivers. Reprinted with permission of Larry Ivers.

katsina songs. They grope around the plaza looking for someone. They pretend they cannot see them because they are spirits. Finally, one of the clowns touches a *katsina* and upon his discovery of these beautiful beings, the clowns immediately try to take possession of them. "This is mine!" "This is mine!" They even fight each other over the possession of the *katsinas* and over the food and things they find.

The remainder of the afternoon is filled with all sorts of clown performances, many of which are planned in advance. Others just happen. These are satires focused on almost anything whether it be in the Hopi world or in the non-Hopi world. Clowns make fun of life and thereby cause people to look at themselves.

Imagination is important to the clown. There are good clowns and not so good clowns when it comes to being funny and witty. But all clowns perform for the smiles and laughter they hope to inspire in the people. When the clowns leave the kiva on their way to the plaza the last request by each is a prayer something to the effect, "If it be so, may I gain at least one smile."

The clown skits and satiric performances done throughout the afternoon are reminiscent of the corruption that we experienced in the underworld, where we presumably had Conscience as a guide. We chose not to follow the Conscience and it comes into play during the clown performances in the form of *katsinas* that visit the plaza. The Owl *katsina* on his first visit comes with a handful of pebbles, carrying a switch. He appears at each corner of the plaza presumably unseen by the clowns and throws little pebbles at the clowns, occasionally hitting them. These pangs of Conscience are felt but not heeded by the clowns. Owl *katsina* returns to the plaza later accompanied by several threatening *katsinas* carrying whips. And this time, instead of pebbles, he may brush up against one of the clowns. He may even knock him down. Conscience keeps getting stronger and more demanding and insistent. On Owl's third visit, the clowns begin to realize that they may suffer consequences if they don't change their ways. Still, they try to buy their safety by offering Owl a bribe. On the sly, the head clown approaches Owl, presumably unseen by anyone, but, of course, they are in the middle of the plaza and are witnessed by all the spectators. Those two kneel together in an archaic conversation modeled upon an ancient meeting.

Owl finally accepts the bribe of a string of beads and thus leads the clown to believe that he has bought his safety. The head clown asks Owl to discipline the other clowns so as to get them back on the right road, but he thinks he will be safe.

With each of Owl's visits more and more *katsinas* accompany him. They do not come as one big group, but in groups of two or three. Throughout the afternoon the tension builds with the threatening presence of the whip-carrying *katsinas*. All of the spectators begin to identify with the plight of the clowns. You feel like you are the one who is now being judged for all these things.

Owl's fourth visit may not come until the next day. On this visit he brings with him a whole lot of warrior *katsinas*. The atmosphere is one of impending catastrophe. They move closer and closer, finally attacking the clowns, who are stripped and whipped for all they have done. In this way they force the clowns to take responsibility for their actions. After they are whipped, water is poured on them and sprinkled about the audience to signify purification.

When it is all over the threatening *katsinas* come back to the plaza again, but this time they are friendly. They shake hands with the clowns signifying that they have been purified. Then they take each clown the length of the plaza and form a semi-circle around him. At this time the clowns make confessions, but even here they are clowns for their confessions are all made in jest. Having worked up satires for the occasion they jump and sing before the *katsinas*. Their confessions usually are focused on their clan, who, by way of being satirized, are actually honored.

I'll tell you one I heard not long ago. When it was time for this young clown man to make his confession he jumps up and down in front of the *katsina* and says, "Ah ii geology, geology, ah ii." Then he made a beautiful little breakdown of this word so that it has Hopi meaning. "You probably think I am talking about this geology which is a white man's study about something or other. Well, that's not it," he says. "What it really is is that I have a grandmother, and you know she being poor and ugly, nobody would have anything to do with her. She is running around all summer long out in the fields doing a man's job. It breaks her down. She would go out there every day with no shoes and so her feet were not very dainty and not very feminine. If you pick up her foot and look at her sole, it is all cracked and that's what I am talking about when I say geology." Every Hopi can put that together. *Tsiya* means "to crack" and *leetsi* means things placed "in a row," so these cracks are in a row on the bottom of the feet, geology. Things like that are what the confessions are like.

There is a story about the last wish of a Hopi man who died many years ago that shows the character of clowning.

In those days the clown society was very much formalized. It was a practice for men who had great devotion for their ritual society to be buried in the full costume of their office. Of course, this was not seen by the general public since Hopi funerals are rather private affairs.

This story is about a man who had gained great respect for his resourcefulness and performance as a clown. Clowning had become a major part of his life and he was constantly attending to his work as a clown by thinking up new skits and perfecting his performance. As he reached old age he decided that clowning had made his place in this world and he wanted to be remembered as a clown. So he made a special request for what was to be done with him at his death as he realized his time was short. He made his request to his family very firmly.

When he died his nephews and sons began to carry out his request. In preparation for burial the body was dressed in his clown costume. Then the body was carried around to the west side of the plaza and taken up on a roof. While this was being done the town crier's voice rang out through the village calling all the people to the plaza. Everybody was prompt in gathering there. I can just see the women, as with any such occasion, grabbing their best shawl on their way to the plaza. It didn't matter whether they were dressed well underneath the shawl.

When the people arrived they saw this unusual sight on the roof of the house on the west side of the plaza, men standing around a person lying down. When all of the people had gathered, the attendants—pallbearers I guess you could call them—simply, quietly, picked up the body and took it to the edge of the house near the plaza. They picked it up by the hands and legs and swung it out over the plaza as if to throw it and they hollered, "Yaahahay!" And they'd swing it back. Then they'd swing it once more. "Yaahahay!" Four times! On the fourth time they let the body go and it fell down, plop, in the plaza. As they threw the body the pallbearers hollered and laughed as they were supposed to. It took the people by surprise. But then everybody laughed.

© 1997 H.J. Tsinhnahjinnie.

3

BUT IS IT AMERICAN INDIAN ART?

Traci L. Morris

American Indian art, the kind you see in most galleries and that is made for the art market for the last 100 years or so, is actually a conceptual category originating in the early twentieth century, created by well-meaning white supporters of the arts and Indians trying to survive economically. American Indian art and the various systems of instruction, patronage, and economics that perpetuated and propelled it into the industry we see today, continues to be determined primarily by outsiders—by white patronage. As Berkhofer demonstrated in his classic 1979 book, *The White Man's Indian*, images of Indians are a white construction. So, too, is American Indian art, especially what the general public perceives to be Indian art.

This article focuses on the historical development of saleable contemporary American Indian art, beginning in the late 1800s up until the present. American Indian art is an extremely lucrative and market driven field. The sale of Native art is also highly legislated, with the first legislation in the 1930s and the most recent legislation in 2007. Native American art ranges on a continuum and includes anthropological art, historical art, and craft art. Also on the continuum is contemporary art, fine art, and socially critical art. All of these forms may be marketed and saleable. However, some forms are created strictly for the art market and these forms are the subject of this article. It is important though, to keep in mind that all forms are interrelated and may reference other forms of Native art. This graphic demonstrates how all Native art is related; despite mediation and differences in conceptual categorization.

Religious forms of art or sacred items, considered culturally traditional art are often aesthetically embellished, but their use and function prohibit the sale of such pieces. These items are used in ceremonial settings and are therefore considered sacred; one does not sell sacred objects. Examples of culturally

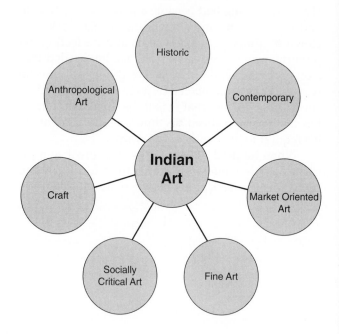

traditional that are aesthetically pleasing include, but are not limited to: textiles, pottery, and beadwork. Traditional art forms are not included on this graphic, nor will they be addressed in this article. Sadly, these items are highly trafficked on the international market today. (See Bomberrry article *Battling for Souls: Organizing the return of sacred textiles to the community of Coroma, Bolivia* in Part VII, Reading 4.)

American Indian art developed for the market in the last one hundred years, the subject of this article, be it historic or contemporary, is expected to be free from political or social comments, ideally demonstrates a cultural heritage directly descended from or connected to a pre-contact past, and is based on stereotypical perceptions and museum misconceptions. Marketability is a major component that drives contemporary Indian art, which is a descendant of styles taught to Native

Americans by white patrons in the early twentieth century. There is no doubt that this is an economic system and one that benefited and continues to benefit both parties. Generations of Native Americans have made their living or supplemented family incomes with the creation of Native art for the marketplace. In many cases, the making of art is a family business and can mean the difference between surviving and living. Economics does not change the fact that Native art is aesthetically pleasing to many, but the stylistic components and aesthetic properties are not being discussed here. The purpose of this article is to focus how this system developed in the Southwest, thus demonstrating how "authentic" Native heritage creates the value.

Although not all agree, derivatives of this mediated and marketable style continue to be taught by Natives to Natives mainly by the Institute of American Indian Art in Santa Fe (IAIA) in New Mexico, or by a family member who attended IAIA or its predecessor the Santa Fe Indian School. This market driven style of Native American art is supported by museums such as the National Museum of the American Indian (NMAI). Santa Fe was historically and continues to be the geographic center of contemporary saleable American Indian Art in the United States. However, in the early twentieth century, Oklahoma had a thriving style of art called the Southern Plains style painting, including the Kiowa Five, which developed at Bacone College, near Muskogee, Oklahoma. Today, Native

American art thrives in Oklahoma and other places throughout the United States, but Santa Fe continues to be the ideological and geographical center of contemporary Native American art.

Historically, the value and authenticity of American Indian art was created by white patrons' intervention in determining subject matter and stylistic elements—patrons who believed that Natives existed in a stereotyped and romantic ethnographic present which was perpetuated by encouraging the artist to look "Indian" by wearing so-called traditional clothing while making and selling art. Indeed, part of the marketing scheme for Native art included selling Indian identity as a means of authenticating the work of art. Through the patronage of white consumers and museums, a cycle of authentication developed. White patrons instructed the Native artist on subject matter, style, and materials, and then they purchased the piece for their museum or personal collection. They then wrote articles about the art for various magazines, thus making the art more valuable. Finally, they and others commissioned more art, which was sold to collectors who eventually donated the works to museums, creating even more value for Native art.

In *The Predicament of Culture*, James Clifford delineates the process for assigning value to American Indian art. He postulates that what he calls the Art/Culture system is a "machine for creating authenticity."[1]

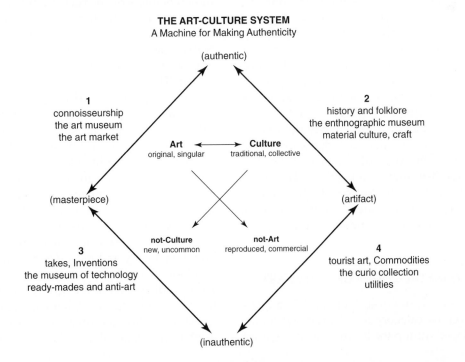

This system classifies and assigns value to appropriated cultural objects, by determining the contexts in which objects belong and circulate. The objects range from art to artifact and their value is determined by their level of cultural authenticity, based on an invented past where western connoisseurship established the parameters of what was or is considered art or aesthetic. As the object moves between various contexts in the cycle of collecting, the final value is determined and assured by the vanishing status of a tribe.[2] Indeed, historic artifacts and contemporary Native art alike establish their authenticity through associations with an unassimilated and unacculturated past.

The Art/Culture system, while historically situated, continues to evolve and to determine authenticity even today. The value of authenticity is monetary and can be observed in Santa Fe, New Mexico on any given summer day as Indian artists sit on the sidewalk under the portal selling art and wearing traditional clothing. Native artists often choose, as a matter of economic necessity, to participate in the art/culture system by wearing traditional clothing while selling art that conforms to the aforementioned stylistic elements. These artists will sell more than a Native artist dressed in average street clothes selling modern Indian art that is not recognizable as such, because the latter artist is not displaying the appropriate signs of being Indian, nor is he/she creating art that has recognizable signs of an authentic Indian past. Indeed, some Native artists make two separate and stylistically distinct kinds of art: the kind of art that conforms to the art/culture system and sells; and art they will make art for themselves or their families. The issue of authenticity as it pertains to Native American art is like a spider web that weaves through everything: issues of Indian identity, stylistic components of art, marketability of the art, the Indian market, the magazines that perpetuate the market, and the academics who study Indian art. Authenticity determines perceptions and representations of Indians and is perpetuated through the Art/Culture system. Legally, tribal enrollment determines authenticity. This disregards cultural definitions by Natives of who is Indian and gives the federal government one more layer of power over the sovereignty of Indian tribes.

HISTORICAL CONSTRUCTIONS OF NATIVE ART

As previously stated American Indian art, is a Euro-American conceptual category and as an art and culture system, developed during the late nineteenth century,

almost as soon as the Indian wars were over. Serious artifact collecting by museums began nearly simultaneously as did the beginnings of American anthropology in the late 1800s. The general public did not start collections until somewhat later. After the turn of the twentieth century, tourism developed, especially in the Southwest, and academics began writing articles about Native American art in popular magazines. The public began collecting Indian artifacts and it quickly became a broadly accepted hobby. The development of a Euro-American mediated American Indian art form was a natural progression beyond the collecting of artifacts. This coupled with the fact that by the 1930s, art was also considered a viable idea for economic stimulus. This is evidenced by the Indian Reorganization Act of 1934 and the Indian Arts and Crafts Act of 1935, both of which advocated the incorporation of art into the curriculum in some of the Indian boarding schools and virtually assured the development of American Indian art into the broad field that it is today.

The most successful and most well documented school that taught American Indians art techniques was the Santa Fe Indian School. The school was established as an Indian Boarding School in 1890. Art classes were offered there as early as 1920. The so-called Studio Style art taught there was intentionally meant to look primitive to appeal to collector's notions of the "Vanishing Indian." To cater to the collector's market, correct subject matter, and methods for painting were determined for American Indian painters by instructors, Indian traders, anthropologists, and museum personnel while the market and the standardization of stylistic components of Native art developed simultaneously. This cycle is now so standardized that it is accepted and not questioned. The Indian art market was conceived of and created by Euro-American patrons, is still going strong and is now self-perpetuated. Many of the so-called traditional stylistic components to which Native art adheres and by which it is judged, were created and determined by Euro-American connoisseurs and patrons for the larger collectors art market. Some stylistic designs in two-dimensional paintings borrow elements from traditional art forms, such as pottery designs or the use of isolated geometric elements used in the creation of a Navajo sand painting. Both historically and now, designs are used in a way that is non-traditional or may have no relationship with traditional Native art. However, American Indian art and Native American art was, or is marketed as traditional, regardless of how designs are used or the relationship of the object to traditional art.

In examining the development of Native art as an art historical conceptual category, Brody and Garmhausen postulate that the earliest white mediated forms occur in the Southwest between 1900 and 1917.[3] This period in Southwest history includes the beginnings of Southwest anthropology, archaeology, and tourism. There was sporadic art production prior to this time when early Southwest Indian traders such as C. J. Wallace commissioned Zuni Indians to create paintings. Anthropologists like Jesse Walter Fewkes who commissioned drawings of Katsinas at Hopi and Edgar Hewett and Kenneth Chapman, both from of the School of American Research (SAR), commissioned Santa Domingo Pueblo artists to create works on paper. Chapman provided materials to tribal members whom he asked to depict tribal images as early as 1901 and then purchased these images for study.[4] Hewett encouraged workers from San Ildefonso, at the Frijoles Canyon Ruins dig from 1904–1914, to draw designs they saw and to produce pictures of tribal ceremonies.[5] Hewett was also responsible for creating the process for authentication and legitimization of Native art forms. He commissioned, collected, and wrote articles about the art he commissioned and collected. Hewett published articles in such magazines as *Ladies Home Journal*, *The Dial*, *El Palacio*, and *Art and Archaeology*. During the summer of 1918, Hewett and SAR employed Native artists Crescencio Martinez, Julian Martinez, Fred Kabotie, Otis Polelonema, Velino Sheje and Alfonso Roybal, also known as Awa Tsireh.[6] In addition to Hewett, there was also a grade school teacher at San Ildefonso day school who, as early as 1910, had urged her students to draw.[7]

Indeed, by the 1920s there were over a dozen Pueblo painters, with no formal art training, who produced two-dimensional easel paintings in and around Santa Fe and Taos, New Mexico. Sometimes referred to as the Santa Fe School of Art, they were largely self-taught and had developed their own small market of white patrons, including local museums, tourists, and white intellectuals and artists such as Mabel Dodge Luhan, John Sloan, and Robert Henri who were living in the area at the time. These artists, authors, and anthropologists contributed much to the early development and dissemination of Native art. In fact, they and others in their social group were intimately involved in the creation of a number of events that were instrumental in creating a market for American Indian Art and events that continue to draw artists and customers today. These events included Gallup Intertribal Indian Ceremonial and Santa Fe Indian Market. Local traders and other white patrons started this "festival and art exhibition" in 1921.[8] In addition to the Gallup Intertribal Ceremonial, the Santa Fe Indian Market, or at least an incarnation of it, began in 1922.[9] Indian Market and Gallup Ceremonial both continue to be the largest venues for Native American art and are the two biggest events of the year in the Native art world.

In addition to creating local and regional markets for Indian art designed for tourists, some of the literati living in and around Santa Fe and Taos organized larger national events, which included the first showings of American Indian Art in New York City. In 1931, the Exposition of Indian Tribal Arts opened in New York City and was the first National Indian Art show of its kind. The show reinforced that Indians were a part of American history, and this show fell right in line with the prevailing view that Indians were vanishing and their culture needed preserving. Because of their prolific collecting and encouragement of quality and authenticity, wealthy collectors actually created a market for Indian art that was self-validating.[10] Ten years later, in 1941, The Museum of Modern Art, in New York City hosted an exhibit of Indian Art of the United States. This show introduced the world to American Indian art at a time of renewed nationalism and was hugely influential on many contemporary artists of the time.

These new markets created consumer demand for Indian art and by the late twenties, this demand was met by training artists at several Indian schools, including the Bureau of Indian Affairs schools such as Haskell Institute, Carlisle, and the Albuquerque Indian School. In partial response to the recommendations of the Merriam Report of 1931 and the artistic environment that had developed in and around Santa Fe, the Santa Fe Indian School implemented an arts program. The school hired Dorothy Dunn to begin teaching in this program in 1932. Dunn was familiar with Indian painting, as she had previously taught at several other BIA schools in the area. She was the instructor at the Santa Fe Indian School from 1932 to 1937. And despite the mythology that she literally created the style that is now considered traditional style or studio style Native American art, it is clear that these styles were already in existence.[11] However, she did standardize the methods for teaching these styles and, further, she taught students how to produce saleable work specifically for the white collectors' market. Students were required to produce suitable subject matter in their art or leave school, and Dunn determined the subject matter. One of her students, renown Apache artist, Allan Houser, later recalled,

> When I got to the studio, it was the old traditional style they wanted from you or not at all. Dorothy Dunn told me that if I was going to do things that are realistic, then you better go on out and take the first bus home. Everyone was encouraged to search their background for traditional things. That's all she permitted us to do. My only objection was this: She trained us all the same way. You either paint like this, Mr. Houser, or it's not Indian art.[12]

For Dunn, it was unacceptable for students to paint any other subject matter or for any other purpose than the Indian market. She was committed to encouraging and facilitating pictures of an unassimilated group heritage, despite the fact that many students wanted quick training in modern non-Indian American art in hopes of competing for commercial success with non-Native artists. As a result, many students left before they were twenty years old, having already done their best work.[13] In effect, Dunn was fulfilling the role that anthropologists, traders, and other educators had filled in the past, only in an officially sanctioned setting.[14] Some of the characteristics of what is called the Studio Style include representations of tribal images in a flat style, with little figure to ground relationship. Also depicted were geometric elements isolated from pottery designs, and figures of birds and animals. The Studio Style is often criticized in academia as white mediated, although similar images were created by Pueblo Indians in kiva mural designs as noted by Hibben.[15] However, what was white mediated was cultural borrowing of design elements. Borrowing designs or crossing tribal motifs would get a student reprimanded as Dunn deemed this "unauthentic," despite the fact that diffusion was and still is prevalent. Indeed, perhaps there was always market mediation. The dynamics changed, however, with the emerging American market dominance: the market was no longer the mediator, but the primary factor. According to Dunn,

> The Santa Fe Indian School, through its art classes, is attempting to recover and develop America's only indigenous art. Much of it has been irretrievably lost, of course, but Indian art students are delving into forgotten places, searching through ethnological papers, studying museum collections, inquiring of their elders, making observations of themselves of what remains of the old cultures, and reconstructing their racial heritage as a basis for building new things which will contribute to America's cultural progress.[16]

The field of Indian Art grew substantially during the years Dunn was instructor. There was already considerable demand for Indian art, but the advent of the Federal Indian Arts and Crafts Board in 1935 and federal policies of creating economic stimulus through the arts, added to the demand. In fact, there were so many requests for showings of Santa Fe Indian School art student's work, that at one point, engagements exceeded 30 shows per year.[17] By 1938, the most successful Native artists were graduates of the Santa Fe Indian School. Dorothy Dunn left her teaching position at the school after only five years. However, the Santa Fe Indian School continued teaching art to Native students according to the principals and styles she created under the direction of former student Santa Clara artist and educator, Geronima Montoya Cruz. Despite continued institutional difficulties and problems with administration, under Cruz, the school continued to teach Dunn's methods through the forties and fifties until the end of the school in 1962.

There were many changes that affected the school during the forties. Many students were lost in World War II and tourism dropped dramatically. Also, many graduates returned to their reservations following training and only produced art to supplement their income. Other problems involved the curriculum; while other schools modified their curricula to meet changing times, the Santa Fe Indian School did not. By the late fifties, the school was considered a dumping ground for problem students, a legacy that would follow the institution until its demise.[18] The same styles of painting that Dorothy Dunn had taught in the 1930's were now institutionalized and being taught on a broader level; if a Native artist's work did not include the stylistic components that were recognized as traditional, their work was not regarded as marketable or authentic. Indeed, this often holds true today.

In 1959, the University of Arizona organized a conference on Indian art, sponsored by the Rockefeller Foundation, and held at the University of Arizona in 1959. The purpose of the Directions in Indian Art conference was,

> To bring into an organized work conference a group of persons qualified through experience and training to explore and set forth the current status of Southwest Indian art. To resolve possible ways and means of preservation and development of Southwestern Indian arts and crafts through: 1) Education of the public in the appreciation of this art, 2) The betterment of the economic conditions of the Indian craftsman and artist, and 3) Opportunities for education of the Indian artist in a period of transition.[19]

The participant list reads like a who's who of Indian art at the time. According to the conference proposal the University sent to the Rockefeller Foundation, potential participants included,

> Indian Craftsmen and artist and other Indians closely connected with these interests; traders who have been and are in direct contact with the Indian; members of the staffs of museums, art galleries, university departments of art and anthropology, Indian arts and crafts guilds, Indian school and other institutions and organizations which have a direct connection with or interest in Indian art.[20]

Some of the actual presenters included Dr. Frederick Dockstader, who at the time was the Assistant Director of the Museum of the American Indian, Heye Foundation; Dorothy Dunn, the former Santa Fe Indian School teacher largely responsible for training an entire generation of Native artists in the Studio Style; Dr. John Adair; Bertha Dutton; Joe Herrera, an Indian artist from Cochiti; Tom Bahti, Indian Trader from Tucson; Pablita Velarde, Santa Clara artist; Fred Kabotie, Hopi artist and educator; Allan Houser, Apache artist and educator at Inter-Mountain Indian School; Charles Loloma, Hopi artist; Clara Lee Tanner, Professor of Anthropology at the University of Arizona and wife of Indian trader John Tanner; and Lloyd Kiva New, Cherokee artist and educator, who would go on to run the Institute of American Indian Art just a few years later.[21]

Dunn is credited with facilitating the larger acceptance of the Studio Style. However, she clung tenaciously to her beliefs that this style was the direct result of an unacculturated past, as is evidenced by her statement at the Directions conference:

> Indian painting is, first of all, art, but in the greater implications of human relationships and history it is something more—something perhaps of a genetic aspect in the riddle of mankind. Unless the legends, songs, ceremonies, and other native customs are recorded by the people themselves, painting must continue to be the principal contributor of Indian thought to the world art and history."[22]

Today, her writing reads at best, as one who romanticizes Indians and at her worst, maternalizing and matronizing.

In contrast to the goals of the conference and to Dunn's remarks, Lloyd New noted,

> Let's admit, sadly if you must, that the hey-dey of Indian life is past, or passing. Let's also admit that art with all peoples has been a manifestation of the lives of those people, reflecting the truth of the times. And if Indian culture is in a state of flux then we must expect a corresponding art. An art whose main concern is recording the past is called history and an art whose main concern is narration of the present is news reporting, and is better done with the pen, not the brush. Effective stylization may be ever so successful as decoration but may not be art.[23]

Dunn's maternalistic attitudes contrast greatly with Kiva New's assimilationist viewpoints, which are well documented. In fact, Dunn and New seemed to be at odds most of their professional lives, as evidenced by numerous papers in the Dunn archives at the Museum of Indian Arts and Culture in Santa Fe, New Mexico. Perhaps these differences were due to generational differences. Or, maybe cultural differences as Dunn was white, on the outside looking in, while New was Indian and trying to get out. Either way, they did not agree on much.

Of the other Indians invited to speak—Pablita Velarde, Fred Kabotie, Charles Loloma, Mrs. Joe Herrera—Allan Houser was the only one to speak of problems with the then current art training of Indians. He suggested more practical art training such as commercial art, stating ". . . commercial art, which pays well, is a competitor to creative art which offers nothing but starvation."[24] Either the other Indian artists/participants said little or their remarks were not recorded. However, what is recorded demonstrates the mixed feelings of Indian participants, some with feelings of gratitude for white patronage, while others were concerned with the general state of Indian education.[25]

The project planners and organizers at the University of Arizona had lofty goals and in October of 1959, just seven months after the Directions in Indian Art Conference, the University of Arizona proposed, sought, and obtained funding from the Rockefeller Foundation for a series of art workshops for young Indian artists. Citing changing economic times and the conflict between traditional and contemporary viewpoints in terms of its effects on younger artists, the proposed workshops sought to bring selected Indian artists between the ages of 17 and 25, to the University for a series of intensive six-week summer workshops, over the course of three years, 1960–1962.

The workshops were designed to expose the young artists to a variety of media, instructors, and hands-on experiences. The students had access to both Indian anthropological resources and historic and contemporary Western art sources. They learned everything from design to marketing principles from both Indian and Anglo instructors. The workshop culminated each year with an exhibit and critique of their work.[26]

The first Southwest Indian Art Project workshop took place on June 6–16th, 1960 with 24 participants.[27] The second workshop was held June 12–22nd, 1961 with 23 students including Fritz Scholder, who went on to become one of the most recognizable and famous Indian artists or artist who happened to be Indian.[28] The Southwest Indian Art Project changed significantly during its final year of 1962 due to unforeseen circumstances. This was the year that the BIA opened the Institute of American Indian Arts (IAIA) in Santa Fe on the old Santa Fe Indian School site. They hired all three Indian instructors away from the Southwest Indian Art Project, including Lloyd Kiva New, and they built on what had been done at the University of Arizona. Further, IAIA accepted 16 students from the Southwest Indian Art Project. In response, the coordinators of the Project changed the summer workshop program, scaling it back to the acceptance and support of "selected students from those returning students"[29] for regular academic study. The University of Arizona eliminated the studio aspect altogether and allowed the remaining eight students to concentrate on whatever area of study they chose. Of this group, Fritz Scholder was awarded a fellowship as a Graduate Assistant plus full scholarship, room and board, travel and materials.[30]

Most people are unaware of the University of Arizona Rockefeller conference or its influence on Native art and artists and, and the fact that IAIA, while influenced by the Rockefeller funded Southwest Indian Art Project summer institutes, was not an outgrowth of them. The BIA and the Indian Arts and Crafts Board created IAIA through a joint effort. George Boyce was the founding director, although at the time the position was superintendent. Lloyd New was hired as the Head of the Art Department and a number of key staff, mostly Indian, were hired, many from the Bureau of Indian Affairs Intermountain Indian School in Utah, including Allan Houser and his wife. In fact, Boyce believed that the success of IAIA was because he hired Native staff and instructors. He deliberately hired Indian artists he considered successful; they were either instructors or they had a national reputation. Those he did hire, Allan Houser, Charles Loloma, and Otellie Loloma significantly influenced the course of the school and the direction of Native art, as they had the most contact with students. The teachers influenced the students and the students then influenced the teachers. IAIA broadened the field of Native arts to include all of the arts, not just painting as the SFIS had embraced.[31]

Boyce was the director/superintendent of IAIA from 1962–1967 and some refer to these years as the "golden period:" a period when much national and international attention was focused on the school and for good reason. During this time a number of students graduated who went on to national acclaim, including T. C. Cannon, Doug Hyde, Kevin Red Star, and Earl Biss.[32] These artists are often referred to as the first generation of the post-studio style as they were the first artists to transcend the Studio Style that Dunn and Cruz taught for so many years at the Santa Fe Indian School.

In 1968, Lloyd New, former Arts Director took over as director of IAIA and he ran the school until 1978. This era was a time of considerable change in IAIA, reflective of the changes in Indian Country and the changing social climate of the United States. While the nation wrestled with Viet Nam, civil rights issues, and political changes, Indian Country was struggling with Indian self-determination, various federal policies, and the American Indian Movement. These social and political changes affected the school and the students attending. New instituted changes: he hired former students, developed a cultural center, and worked to transition IAIA from a high school to a college. In 1968, Russell Means, then an AIM leader, spoke on campus, greatly affecting the student body. During New's tenure, many problems manifested. Inbreeding in staff, due to Indian hiring preferences and hiring of former students, had led to stagnation in style. The school's work had become complacent and the reputation of IAIA declined. The year New retired, 1978, the last high school class graduated. Former graduates of the seventies include Dan Namingha, Roxanne Swentzell, and Grey Cohoe. IAIA had effectively propelled Indian arts to a new height. However, times had changed, and so had policies. The era of the BIA school was over. By this time, in addition to art school and art programs at universities, there were tribal colleges and American Indian Studies programs in universities. Indian artists had numerous choices as to where to get their education.[33]

During the 1980s, as transition and change affected IAIA and as they struggled to compete with other educational institutions in recruitment of students, a new generation of Native artists not affiliated with IAIA garnered national attention. Little is published about IAIA after the 1980s and records have yet to be archived and are currently inaccessible for research.[34]

The 1980s and 1990s generations of non-IAIA trained artists reads like a Who's Who of current Native art. Indeed this time period was the beginning of a period of growth in Native American art. No longer was IAIA the only school that artists received their training from; although, Santa Fe remains the center of the Native Art world, despite developments of art markets in other parts of the country.

Many of today's best recognized Native artists attended various universities and received traditional art school training, including Truman Lowe, Jaune Quick-to-See Smith, Kay Walking Stick, Emmi Whitehorse, Edgar Heap-of-Birds, Diego Romero, Dan Lomahaftewa, Tony Abeyta, Anita Fields, Marcus Amerman, Shelly Nero, James Luna, Nora Naranjo-Morse, and Mateo Romero. However, these artists have transcended the boundaries and limitations of the term Indian artist and some even critique what it means to be Indian in their work. Many, if not most of them do not participate in the art/culture system of marketing their identity to establish value for their art. Perhaps they are reacting to the art that came before them or perhaps the market itself. In any case, there is a divergence between artists who are Indian, producing art for a larger audience and Indian artists, producing art for the Native art buying public.

By the mid-2000s, an entirely new generation of Native artists has taken its place beside the early modernists, the IAIA graduates, and those who worked outside of the art/culture system. Often, these artists create works that are socially critical, self-referential, or overtly humorous. Many of this generation are self-trained or have little formal training. Still others learned the dual system taught at IAIA; create art for the market and art for yourself.

Some IAIA graduates who have transcended the system include Hoka Skenadore or Marla Allison.

Just a few of the other artists of this generation and caliber include, Kade Twist, Virgil Ortiz, Will Wilson, and Sarah Sense. One of the best known artists of this generation is Steve Yazzie. His work, like that of Emmi Whitehorse, transcends the label of American Indian Artist. He is an artist who happens to be Indian and his work is recognized throughout the world, and not for being a Native artist, but for being an artist.

These younger generations have pushed the boundaries of Native American art. While the art/culture system is still firmly in place, new exhibits at museums and galleries have broadened the boundaries of American Indian Art even further. The National Museum of the American Indian works with artists such as Emmi Whitehorse and James Luna, who represent a broad spectrum of variances in Native Art. In recent years, NMAI has become very supportive of socially critical Native art. In 2008, the Heard Museum in Phoenix, AZ, presented the group exhibition *Remix: New Modernities in a Post-Indian World*, which eventually went to the NMAI in New York City. This exhibit addressed issues of identity in American Indian Art. Further, galleries such as the Berlin Gallery at the Heard Museum and its curator, Andrea Hanley, have pushed open new doors for American Indian artists. The art chosen by this curator for the Berlin Gallery, challenges the Art/Culture system and continually breaks down barriers for all Native artists, not just those represented by the gallery.

The new blood from younger generations is exciting. Exhibitions at museums that support these generations is even more exiting. Clearly there are many artists, who are rejecting the art/culture system that is so pervasive in the American Indian Art world, but what the future holds for American Indian Art remains to be seen.

NOTES

1. James Clifford, *The Predicament of Culture: Twentieth-Century Ethnography, Literature, and Art* (Cambridge, Mass.: Harvard University Press, 1988), 224.

2. Ibid., 222.

3. J. J. Brody, *Indian Painters & White Patrons* (Albuquerque: University of New Mexico Press, 1971), 73, J.J. Brody, *Pueblo Indian Painting: Tradition and Modernism in New Mexico, 1900–1930*, ed. J Ann Baldinger (Santa Fe, New Mexico: School of American Research Press, 1997), 29.

4. Winona Garmhausen, *History of Indian Arts Education in Santa Fe: The Institute of American Indian Arts with Historical Background 1890–1962* (Santa Fe: Sunstone Press, 1988), 33.

5. Ibid.

6. Brody, *Indian Painters & White Patrons*, 85, Brody, *Pueblo Indian Painting: Tradition and Modernism in New Mexico, 1900–1930*, W. Jackson Rushing, *Native American Art and the New York Avant-Garde: A History of Cultural Primitivism* (Austin: University of Texas Press, 1995).

7. Garmhausen, *History of Indian Arts Education in Santa Fe: The Institute of American Indian Arts with Historical Background 1890–1962*, 33.

8. Molly H. Mullin, *Culture in the Marketplace: Gender, Art, and Value in the American Southwest* (Durham [N.C.]; London: Duke University Press, 2001), 65.

9. Mullin cites Bruce Bernstein's 1993 UNM Dissertation in saying that Indian Market as it is presently known started in 1971. Despite the Southwest Indian Association for Indian Art's (SWAIA) marketing the event as contiguous since 1922, prior to the 1950s it was not an annual event. In fact, from 1942–1971 the market was held at the annual Santa Fe Fiesta and was not a separate event, in 1971 the event was reorganized under SWAIA who separated it from the Fiesta and located it in the Plaza in Santa Fe.

10. Rushing, *Native American Art and the New York Avant-Garde: A History of Cultural Primitivism*. See especially Chapter Two for an extensive discussion of white patronage and the effects on the market.

11. Mythology reference to Dunn, generally referred to as creating the studio style when in fact she did not, she only taught what was already being taught in the region.

12. Charles Dailey, "Major Influences in the Development of 20th Century Native American Art" (paper presented at the Sharing A Heritage: American Indian Art, Los Angeles, CA, 1984–1982), 43.

13. Brody, *Indian Painters & White Patrons*, 130.

14. Garmhausen, *History of Indian Arts Education in Santa Fe: The Institute of American Indian Arts with Historical Background 1890–1962*, 50.

15. Frank C. Hibben, *Kiva Art of the Anasazi: At Pottery Mound*, ed. Gwen DenDooven, First Edition ed. (Las Vegas: KC Publications, 1975).

16. Jeanne Shutes and Jill Mellick, *The Worlds of P'otsúnú: Geronima Cruz Montoya of San Juan Pueblo*, 1st ed. (Albuquerque: University of New Mexico Press, 1996), 68–9. It is interesting to note the difference between this statement and what Kiva New says in 1962 about tradition being "outmoded."

17. Garmhausen, *History of Indian Arts Education in Santa Fe: The Institute of American Indian Arts with Historical Background 1890–1962*, 54.

18. Ibid., 59.

19. "A Proposal for an Exploratory Workshop in Art for Talented Younger Indians," in *The Arizona State Museum–University of Arizona Southwest Indian Art Project files* (Tucson: Arizona State Museum, 1959).

20. Ibid.

21. "Directions in Indian Art: The Report of a Conference Held at the University of Arizona on March 20–21, 1959" (Tucson, 1959). Note: the participants are listed here as they were listed in the program.

22. Dorothy Dunn, "Training and Evaluation of the Indian Artist" (paper presented at the Directions in Southwest Art, Tucson, Arizona, Fall 1957–1959).

23. Lloyd H. New, "Projections in Indian Art Education," in *Directions in Indian Art* (Tucson, AZ: The Arizona State Museum–University of Arizona Southwest Indian Art Project Files, 1959).

24. "Directions in Indian Art: The Report of a Conference Held at the University of Arizona on March 20–21, 1959".

25. Nathalie F. S. Woodbury, "Comments of Discussants, Notes on Status of Southwest Indian Arts and Crafts," (Arizona State Museum-University of Arizona Southwest Indian Art Project files, 1959).

26. "A Proposal for an Exploratory Workshop in Art for Talented Younger Indians."

27. "Press Release: Ua Exploratory Summer Workshop Set for Young Indian Artists of the Southwest," in *The Arizona State Museum-University of Arizona Southwest Indian Art Project files* (Tucson: 1960).

28. "Southwest Indian Art Workshop Catalogue," in *The Arizona State Museum–University of Arizona Southwest Indian Art Project files* (Tucson: 1961). It is interesting to note, that Scholder until his death in February 2005, insisted that he was not Indian, just of Indian descent. In addition, he ceased creating subject matter that referenced Indians in the early 1970s.

29. "Correspondence between University of Arizona and the Rockefeller Foundation," in *The Arizona State Museum–University of Arizona Southwest Indian Art Project files* (Tucson: 1963).

30. Ibid.

31. Garmhausen, *History of Indian Arts Education in Santa Fe: The Institute of American Indian Arts with Historical Background 1890–1962*.

32. Ibid., 83.

33. Ibid.

34. The inaccessibility of IAIA records is a real shortcoming in American Indian Art history. Not only are they not catalogued, they are stored in boxes and completely unavailable, in any form, to researchers. There is a fairly complete history in Garmhausen's book, but it only goes up to the inception of IAIA. Little is written or published on the subsequent decades.

THE NATIONAL MUSEUM OF THE AMERICAN INDIAN

Traci L. Morris

The National Museum of the American Indian (NMAI), part of the Smithsonian Institution, is the premiere museum of Native American art and culture, containing the largest and most comprehensive collection of Native American art and artifacts in the world. With objects from North, South and Central America, holdings include approximately 800,000 objects, spanning 10,000 years of history through the present, from over 1,000 Native or indigenous cultures.

The National Museum of the American Indian was created by an act of Congress in 1989 and signed into law by President George Bush, Sr.; Public Law 101-185. The acquisition of the vast holdings of the Museum of the American Indian became the foundation of the National Museum of the American Indian. The Museum of the American Indian, which was founded by George Gustav Heye (1874–1957), contained the personal collections of Heye who traveled extensively throughout the western hemisphere. The NMAI collection contains 800,000 objects and a photographic archive of 125,000 images, this collection was assembled over the period of 54 years, beginning at the turn of the twentieth century. Nearly seventy percent of the collections represent cultures in the United States and Canada; the other thirty percent includes objects from Mexico and Central and South America.

NMAI has three facilities including a smaller permanent museum, the George Gustav Heye Center located in lower Manhattan, a Cultural Resources Center which houses and cares for the collections, in Suitland, Maryland, and a large permanent museum on the National Mall in Washington D.C. Additionally, NMAI actively works in collaboration with Native peoples of the Western Hemisphere by facilitating access to the museum's cultural resources and by

A different version of this article appears in the ABC-CLIO Encyclopedia of American Indian History.

cultivating partnerships with communities and organizations through their Community Outreach programming.

The George Gustav Heye Center, located in the Alexander Hamilton U.S. Customs House in New York City, opened in 1994. This branch of NMAI is an exhibition facility for both permanent and temporary exhibitions. It also houses a Resource Center that utilizes computer technology to teach about Native life and links the museum to current Native communities. Also, the Heye Center houses a Film and Video Center that serves the Native filmmakers and community, educators, and the general public.

Built in 1999, the Cultural Resources Center is a research and storage facility for the objects and artifacts in the NMAI collection. It is state-of-the-art in terms of care and storage of the collection and seeks to educate new generations of museum professionals. This facility serves as the center for various museum services, including community outreach, educational outreach, and technological development. It is also a culturally sensitive facility, recognizing that some objects in the collections may have family and community connections, this facility has both public and private areas for use by Native and non-Native researchers and visitors from tribal communities, academics, and artistic and cultural organizations.

In September 2004, NMAI opened a second larger permanent museum on the National Mall in Washington D.C., in front of the United States Capitol. This structure was built by two construction companies including one that is a subsidiary of the Table Mountain Rancheria of Friant, CA, a federally recognized American Indian tribe. The building is 351,263 square feet, 99 feet high and has a dome that rises 120 feet in the rotunda. The creation of the new museum included consultation and collaboration with 500 Natives from 300 communities. In keeping with the consensus of consultants from Indian Country, the building includes round interior spaces, exterior water features, east-facing entrances, and many interior details which reference Native symbols from various cultures. The Grand Opening took place on September 21, 2004 with an elaborate morning procession of Native Americans in full regalia, traditional to each of their distinctive Nations. The procession proceeded from the Smithsonian Institution's Castle along the mall toward the U.S. Capitol for the dedication of the new museum.

NMAI is distinctive in that the institution works collaboratively with Native communities to sustain cultural heritage and to promote living cultures. Through extensive educational programs and community outreach, the museum facilitates communication, education and connections with objects, artifacts, art and between people. NMAI is dedicated to not only preserving and exhibiting cultural artifacts from the past, but giving a voice to contemporary indigenous peoples as its exhibitions are presented from a Native perspective and in a Native voice.

Further Reading: http://americanindian.si.edu

5

WIPING THE WARPAINT OFF THE LENS
NATIVE AMERICAN FILM AND VIDEO

Beverly R. Singer

INTRODUCTION

One of the most important issues facing American Indians concerns the question of identity: What is an Indian? The historical misrepresentations of "Indians" has been outside of tribal control and perpetuated by American cultural, political, academic, and social institutions that promote, produce and communicate information to the public. Indians have been misrepresented in art, history, science, literature, popular films, and by the press in the news, on the radio, and on television. The earliest stereotypes associating Indians with being savage, naked, and heathen were established with the foundation of America and determined by two factors: religious intolerance for cultural and spiritual differences leading to the destruction of Native cultures, and rejection of Indian cultures as relevant subject matter by traditional historians in the writing of U.S. history.

Edited from Beverley R. Singer, *Wiping the Warpaint Off the Lens: Native American Film and Video*. Minneapolis and London: University of Minnesota Press, 2001, pp. 14–23.

The demise of the Indian presence, accompanied by the westward movement of pioneers and viewed as a major American victory, was the result of a struggle among whites for economic, political, social, and religious independence. The ideology of Manifest Destiny was the propaganda used against Indians to justify our extermination. Noted writer D'Arcy McNickle (Métis, enrolled by the Flathead Tribe) recalls that "Until the third decade of the present century, Indian policy was rooted in the assumption that the Indians would disappear." The enduring perception of Indians as an enemy pending extinction cleared the way for anyone to create stereotypes of Indians and to exclude any serious treatment or study of us. Challenged by this inimical history, this book, Wiping the Warpaint Off the Lens, builds on scholarship and interpretation by Native people who have worked to share the totality of the American story in our images.

Over the last twenty years, Native Americans have made some outstanding film and videos. My discussion of these films and videos draws on my experiences as both a Native American and a video maker. As Native American filmmakers, we have faced many struggles in our attempts to make films, competing for limited resources and struggling to overcome popular stereotypes that present us as unintelligent and refer to us in the past tense rather than as people who inhabit the present. What really matters to us is that we be able to tell our own stories in whatever form we choose. This is not to say that whites cannot tell as good Native story, but until very recently whites—to the exclusion of Native people— have been the only people given the necessary support and recognition by society to tell Native stories in the medium of film.

The chance to remedy the lack of literature about telling our own stories is deeply connected to being self-determined as an Indian. It is part of a social movement that I call "cultural sovereignty," which involves trusting the older ways and adapting them to our lives in the present. These rights and traditions include defending our birthrights as agreed to by treaties, speaking our tribal languages, practicing ancestral methods of food harvesting such as spear fishing and whale hunting, gathering medicinal herbs, and using animals and birds for ceremonial purposes.

Our films and videos are helping to reconnect us with very old relationships and traditions. Native American filmmaking transmits beliefs and feelings that help revive storytelling and restore the old foundation . . . The oral tradition is fundamental to understanding Native film and video and how we experience truth, impart knowledge, share information and laugh. Traditional Native American storytelling practices and oral histories are a key source of our recovery of our authentic identity. Leslie Marmon Silko (Laguna) believes that the ability to tell stories is a way of life for Pueblo people. She believes that older stories and newer stories belong to the same creative source that keeps the people together. Furthermore, she states that "the Origin story functions basically as a maker of our identity: with the story, we know who we are." Simon Ortiz (Acoma) writes that in his experience the power of stories—such as the origin stories shared among the Pueblo people—is that words take hold of a storyteller and "go their own way." Story making at this instant becomes the language of experience, sensation, history, and imaginations. Today's storytellers continue the practice of an art that is traced back countless generations and safeguard that the stores are being carried into the future . . .

That the oral tradition is a continually evolving process is apparent in Aboriginal and Native American films and videos, which are extensions of the past in our current lives. Additionally, stories and their telling may also connect us to the universe of medicine—of paranormal and sacred power. Storytellers are highly valued because they have the power to heal the spirit. One of the reasons for making films is to heal the ruptures of the past, recognizing that such healing is up to the viewer.

Poet Luci Tapahonso (Navajo) explains how Navajo stories are viewed as being true by members of her tribe: "A Navajo audience is unlikely to doubt the storyteller's assertion that the events related did indeed occur. It is also understood that the stories or songs do not 'belong' to the teller, but that her or his role is that of a transmitter." Native filmmakers are "transmitters" too! The integrity associated with storytelling or filmmaking in this context remains sincere . . .

DETERMINING OUR SELF-IDENTITY

In 1989, Charlene Teters (Spokane) attended a University of Illinois basket ball game with her son and daughter. After watching a half-time performance by the university mascot named Chief Illiniwek, her life was radically altered. The mascot was a student dressed in Plains Indian regalia wearing an eagle feather headdress and "Indian" warpaint who pranced around the arena to ersatz "Indian tom-tom" music played by the university band. Teters, a graduate student at Illinois at the time recalls seeing her children slump in their seats as the befeathered mascot led a crowd of cheering fans. She was acutely aware that her own and her children's' Indian heritage was violated by the performance of Chief Illiniwek.

Teters questioned the administrators at the University of Illinois about the "Indian" mascot, noting that it was offensive to her American Indian beliefs and practices. University officials were defensive and claimed the mascot was a long-standing tradition meant to honor historical Indians. Teters continued to question the mascot issue and began a personal protest of it, standing on campus with a sign that read "Indians are human beings, not mascots." But instead of receiving support for her efforts to raise student awareness about the unsuitability of having a mascot that misrepresents Indians, she was seen as a threat. The sports fans who upheld the use of the mascot were remarkably hostile in their resistance to eliminate the practice. As news spread of her protest, her criticism produced a backlash of attacks against her and her family from university students, alumni, local businesses, and state officials. Teters's persistence brought national attention to the mascot issue as other universities and high schools with mascots named after Indians began debating their continued use of them. The University of Illinois Regents voted to retain their mascot tradition with support from the state of Illinois. A bill was passed to protect the mascot, although Illinois governor Jim Edgar later vetoed it.

In 1992, Teters graduated with an M.F.A. from the University of Illinois and vowed to continue her opposition to "the Chief." She is a founding member of the National coalition on Racism in Sports and the Media. In 1998, Teters was featured by ABC News with Peter Jennings as the "Person of the Week" for her advocacy against racism in targeting Native Americans.

Teters's history of public challenge to the commercial exploitation of American Indians is the subject of the nationally televised documentary *In Whose Honor?* By Jay Rosenstein, in which she states, "Our people paid with their very lives to keep what we have left. And we have to honor that sacrifice." . . .

The revolutionary artist role with which Teters identifies with is not unique, nor is the Indian mascot tradition the only mis-education that Indians need to recover from and redress. Another form of mis-education about Indians is their negative portrayal by Hollywood. Victor Masayesva Jr., a Hopi filmmaker, responded to a hundred years of Hollywood movie portrayals in *Imagining Indians* (1992). Masayesva features the personal experiences of Native people who have participated in Hollywood productions from the late 1930s to the 1990s and exposes their manipulation by Hollywood filmmakers, comparing their behavior to early Indian agents who took land from Indians for white settlement. Masayesva translates this historical practice and applies it to white filmmakers who take aspects of Indian culture and use their own interpretation of the culture to make their films.

In *Imagining Indians*, Masayesva views the portrayal of "imagined Indians" found in Hollywood movies and the manufacture of Indian art objects as parallel activities that contribute to the commodification and dehumanization of Native people. One scene in the film takes place at the annual event known as the "Santa Fe Indian Market," where the production of Indian art is strictly commercial and driven by collectors who don't care if a set of Indian Kachinas are exactly alike . . . A collector interviewed

at the market admits "We're totally saturated and there's no space to lay these rugs on the floor, and there's no set place to house these dolls (holding up a set of Navajo dolls), but this becomes a disease, one just keeps buying, buying, buying." This replication of popular images of Indians for commercial purposes—whether in films or other forms of culture—contributes to a loss of respect for culture, confused identity, and weakened beliefs about what it means to be a Native American. In a further demonstration of unraveling popular images of Indians, Masayesva turns to his own community of Hopi Indians, who are viewed as a peacefully united people with sacrosanct beliefs. In 1994, a Hollywood film crew sought to film at the Hopi reservation in a place revered by a group of elders who opposed filming there. However the elected Hopi tribal government accepted a payment in exchange for allowing the filming and the matter was dismissed.

While Masayesva relied on historical parallels and real-life events to expose some of the effects on Indians of the years of stereotyping, Sherman Alexie (Spokane/Coeur d'Alene) confronted stereotypes by turning them on their heads and getting people to laugh with Indians rather than at them. His serialized novel *The Lone Ranger* and *Tonto Fist Fight in Heaven* (1993) became the basis for his screenplay for *Smoke Signals* (1998 Miramax), directed by Chris Eyre (Cheyenne/Arapaho). The film is about two young men, Victor and Thomas, who grow up in the shadow of a family tragedy that sets up the undercurrent of their uneven relationship at a reservation in the Northwest. The plot focuses on Victor, the recent death of Victor's father, and the journey the young men take to revisit their past while recovering the father's remains. Alexie's writings creatively explore the range of experiences found in any community that shares values and traditions. Histories are not an exhibition of Native or Indian culture, but a rendering of the feelings of Natives today . . .

The decade of the nineties produced an abundance of Native media about the changes that took place in the 20 years since Deloria called for Indian self-representation. Filmmaking, print journalism, radio programming, and the Internet are compiling our individual stories into the larger story of Native survival and continuance. The result is a growing sense of unity about our place in history and the role we have in helping shape the future . . .

All filmmaking is a risk taking venture, but too often the rationale given by funding organizations for rejecting Native American film proposals is that they are not as good as other proposals and that as filmmakers we lack experience. The underlying attitude is that we as Native filmmakers are unconventional in our approach to filmmaking and too often personally invest to a fault in wanting to make films about our people. But it is only through our participation in filmmaking that we can help to create mutual understanding and respect.

The comprehension of culture as it relates to Native filmmaking comes from the storytelling approach that always pays homage to the past but is not suspended there. The currency of our experience is energized by self expression that validates and comforts our desire to participate in the world of ideas. The process also works to detox our own ingrained stereotypes of Indians that block our creativity. Creating films and other visual art is a dynamic within Native American life that, according to art curator and scholar Rick Hill (Tuscarora), "comes from our ancestors to which we are bound to add our own distinctive (traditional) patterns." Hill's reference to art as a part of life also affirms Masayesva's perspective that filmmaking is not a separate activity but an integral one.

As a general rule Hollywood "Indian" movies are set in the late nineteenth century America. This time frame, according to Navajo filmmaker Arlene Bowman, is a problem when "the average American cannot accept Native Americans' present realities and always look at Indians in the past; I am not putting the past down but we are for real and living today." Bowman, who has a degree in motion pictures and television from the University of California at Los Angeles and has produced two major films, has not been able to access mainstream media in part because the accomplishments of Native American filmmakers are not recognized as valid if they do not conform to expectations of how Indians look and act in movies.

Following the enormous popularity and financial success of *Dances with Wolves* (1990), several new film and television projects were announced, including Kevin Costner's own TIG Productions documentary titled *500 Nations*, which was shown on prime-time CBS-TV in 1995.

Two years before, in 1993, Ted Turner held a press conference to announce his Native American media initiative. This was at the height of the controversy over his ownership of the Atlanta Braves baseball team and his endorsement of the "tomahawk chop" by Braves fans, an arm gesture that is offensive to Native Americans. Turner's project, the Native

American Series, was comprised of TV documentaries, a book, and several historical dramatic films, which were broadcast on Turner Network Television.

Both the Costner and Turner projects were seen by Native filmmakers and writers as hopeful opportunities to be hired as writers, producers, and directors and to promote new images and current views held by Native peoples. I was disappointed, after watching only portions of the Costner and Turner programs, to see that they were merely recycled images of historical photographs of Indians taken by white photographers with emphasis on the social problems facing Indians.

Phil Lucas (Choctaw) was hired to direct one of the documentary programs, and Hanay Geiogmah (Kiowa/Delaware) was listed as cowriter for the Native American Series, but it was obvious that they did not have decision-making power, given the revival of stereotyped images of Indians in many of the programs. Ruth Denny, a journalist for the Circle, an independent Native newspaper published in Minnesota, wrote an editorial about the Costner and Turner projects after she received no response to her request for information from their production companies on how Native Americans could apply for jobs on these productions. In hindsight, her criticism was justified when she wrote, "Native Americans do not need any more Kevin Costner's, Billy Jacks, and John Wayne's . . . The need for the Indian experts is over." Denny is referring to America's history of Indian experts who are white and male.

Directing, producing, and writing for films and television are professional careers not typically associated with Native people, but there have been some refreshing changes in Hollywood of late. A new generation of Aboriginal and Native American actors have appeared in title roles in movies that feature Indians. The nineties have seen a number of Native Americans pursing acting careers in film and television in Canada and in the United States, including Adam Beach (Ojibwe) and Evan Adams (Cree), who were in *Smoke Signals*; Irene Bedard (Inupiat/Cree) who was in the title role of *Lakota Woman* (1994), was the voice of Pocahontas in the Disney production of *Pocahontas* (1995), and was also in *Smoke Signals*. More seasoned performers who also need to be acknowledged include Tantoo Cardinal (Métis/Cree), whose credits began in 1975 with projects in Canada and who was highly acclaimed in the United States after her appearance in *Dances with Wolves*; Gary Farmer (Cayuga), who became a Native cult hero for his role in *Powwow Highway* (1989) and was in *Smoke Signals*; Graham Green (Oneida), who received an Oscar nomination for his performance in *Dances with Wolves*, Steve Reevis (Blackfeet), who had a unique role in *Fargo* (1996) and was featured in the independent film *Follow Me Home* (1997), directed by Peter Bratt; Wes Studi (Cherokee) who portrayed *Geronimo* in the contemporary remake of *Geronimo* (1993), a role he earned after his performances in the most recent rendition of *The Last of the Mohicans* (1992) and *Dances with Wolves*; Sheila Tousey (Menominee), who was cast as a key role in *Thunderheart* (1992) and was featured in the HBO film *Grand Avenue* (1996), written by Greg Sarris (Coastal Miwok).

Although most films and videos produced and directed by Native people document actual life stories, some are narrative films. Native fiction reveals insights familiar to Native people through characters acted by Native people who identify with these roles as belonging to their peoples experiences. An early one of these was *Return of the Country* (1983), written and directed by Bob Hicks (Creek/Seminole) as his graduate thesis film in directing at the American Film Institute in Los Angeles. The film's plot revises all historical assumptions by having Indians discover America and establish a Bureau of Caucasian Affairs, a twist on the actual Bureau of Indian Affairs established by the U.S. federal government. Hicks used his creative license to reverse the dynamics of white and Indian relationships throughout *Return of the Country* by having white children abandon English, shed their European-Style dress, and turn away from Christianity.

Another early narrative film is *Harold of Orange* (1984), written by Gerald Vizenor (Ojibwe). The film is about Harold, an indigenous Indian from the reservation, who applies for a grant to open coffeehouses on the reservation. Harold and his friends, nicknamed "the warriors of Orange," travel to the city in a school bus to present their proposal to a foundation. Their visit, which is an adventure for Harold and his buddies and an education for the whites at the foundation, is very humorous to audiences who know the underlying themes associated with the paternalistic attitudes toward the Indians shown in *Harold of Orange*, such as the myth that all Indians are alcoholics and the insensitive display of ancestral Indian remains in museums. *The Honor of All* (1989), directed by Phil Lucas (Choctaw), is a reenactment of the debilitating effects of alcoholism in an Aboriginal community named Alkali Lake and tells the story of the cultural and spiritual recovery of an entire community. *Tenacity* (1994), directed by Chris Eyre (Cheyenne/Arapahoe), was completed while Eyre was enrolled in the M.F.A. filmmaking program at New York University. The film opens with two young Indian boys about ten years old playing combat on a rural road and their encounter with two white males in a truck who have been partying. *It Starts with a Whisper* (1993), codirected by Shelley Niro (Quinte Bay Mohawk) and Anna Gronau, as about a serious young Aboriginal woman who is unsure of herself and is taken for a joyride by her amusing spirit aunts. *Haircuts Hurt* (1993), directed by Randy Redroad (Cherokee), is a short film about a Native Woman's decision to have her young son's hair cut at a "redneck" (bigoted) barbershop.

As this sample of films shows, Native American filmmakers have many stories to tell about themselves and their culture. If they can be given opportunities to share their work, we just need to sit back, watch and listen.

GONE WITH THE WIND

A DECADE AFTER *SMOKE SIGNALS*, SUCCESS REMAINS ELUSIVE FOR NATIVE AMERICAN FILMMAKERS

Mathew Fleischer

Sherman Alexie stands at the back of a dark, crowded theater at last month's Palm Springs Native American Film Festival, scanning the audience for reactions.

The festival is showing the film made from Alexie's first screenplay, *Smoke Signals*, in honor of its 10th anniversary, and he's keen to see how it has held up over time. "I don't know if I can watch the whole thing," he says, "too many flaws." Onscreen, Alexie's memorable road-trip buddies Victor (Adam Beach) and Thomas-Builds-the-Fire (Evan Adams) sit in a trailer watching old cowboy-and-Indian movies. "The only thing more pathetic than Indians on TV," says Thomas, "is Indians watching Indians on TV." The crowd erupts with laughter and Alexie smiles. It's a great line, and at the time it was written it was certainly true. Despite the dawn of political correctness in the '90s, depictions of Native Americans as either bloodthirsty savages or as the stoic, spiritual antecedents to hippie culture continued to dominate the big screen.

But *Smoke Signals* threatened to change all that. The first major film written, directed and acted by Native Americans, *Smoke Signals* was both a critical and commercial success. Selected for the dramatic competition at Sundance and winner of the festival's Audience Award, it was bought by Miramax and went on to bank $6.8 million at the box office on a budget of less than $2 million. More importantly, it offered Native Americans starved for positive and accurate depictions of themselves something they could watch and be proud of.

The film's success appeared to be a harbinger of a new wave of Native filmmaking. What's happened since? "Absolutely nothing," according to Alexie.

Indeed, a Native film with the cultural impact of *Smoke Signals* has yet to be replicated, and Alexie feels partly to blame. After their film took off, he and director Chris Eyre were bombarded with offers to work together again, but instead of capitalizing on the momentum, the two had a falling-out. Alexie, who was already well known in the literary world as the author of more than 17 books, drew the lion's share of the film's media attention and chose to roll with the praise, leaving Eyre feeling neglected.

"Basically we acted like typical Hollywood assholes," says Alexie.

The two split ways with mixed results. In 2002, Alexie wrote and directed *The Business of Fancydancing*, which despite an interesting, semiautobiographical narrative about a reservation-born poet's struggle to maintain his cultural roots in the white world, was missing Eyre's directorial precision and went straight to DVD. Meanwhile, Eyre directed the thoroughly forgettable *Skins*, as well as several films for television (including 2003's *Edge of America*), all of which lacked Alexie's artistic edge.

If the creative duo who launched the Indian world's first hit has sputtered, the world of Native film has continued to grow, albeit slowly. In 2001, Inuit director Zacharias Kunuk's *The Fast Runner* won the Camera d'Or Prize at Cannes. This year, the Palm Springs Native American Film Festival received more than 360 submissions, up from 180 the year before. Perhaps most notably, *Smoke Signals* star Beach earned strong reviews and serious Oscar buzz for his portrayal of Ira Hayes in Clint Eastwood's *Flags of Our Fathers*.

From Mathew Fleischer, "Gone with the Wind: A Decade After *Smoke Signals*, Success Remains Elusive for Native American Filmmakers," *The Los Angeles Weekly*, April 12, 2007.

Sundance, where *Smoke Signals* first began its amazing run, has also continued to provide a major outlet for Native filmmakers. This year, Creek director Sterlin Harjo's *Four Sheets to the Wind* screened in the dramatic competition and went home with a Special Jury Prize for its leading lady, Tamara Podemski, who plays a reservation girl struggling to cope with city life and the loss of her father.

Yet despite a series of critical successes and the unwavering support of Sundance, which has used the festival as a showcase for Native films dating back to the first edition in 1985, commercial viability has remained elusive.

"Sundance shows around 120 feature films, and only a fraction get picked up and distributed," says Bird Runningwater, associate director of the Sundance Institute's Native American and Indigenous Initiative. "But it does seem that, most often, Native films fall into the category of those not being picked up.

Four Sheets to the Wind might be one of the best films out there that no one has ever seen. Despite drawing favorable comparisons to the box-office dynamo *Garden State*, and despite Podemski's lauded performance, the film has yet to land a theatrical distribution deal. "It's heartbreaking because we saw firsthand how audiences responded to the film," says Podemski. "Someone just needs to get the balls to put it out there."

Ironically, Podemski found out after talks with several high-level executives, the problem with the film is that it isn't "Native enough." "This is a regular film about a family that just happens to have a full Native cast," she explains. "And I was told that the industry just doesn't know what to do with that yet. They only know how to market something that is noticeably 'Native.'"

That people can't yet see the film is especially crushing for Podemski. For a Native actress, positive and challenging modern roles are difficult to come by. "There's definitely a tendency to want to dress us up in buckskin," she says.

Smoke Signals director Eyre agrees. "I don't think a lot of people see value in telling stories about modern Indians," he says. "But I don't see the value in films that show the past. They all end the same way—the Indians die."

The blame doesn't fall entirely on the industry, however. Palm Springs Native American Film Festival programmer Thomas Harris, who screened all 360 of this year's entries, says many Native filmmakers rely too heavily on the tragic realities of reservation life and not enough on substantive storytelling. "Right now, the ratio of documentaries to narratives is about 80/20," he notes. "Which makes sense, because, with digital technology, documentaries can be made very cheaply. But there just aren't enough narrative features out there."

Podemski feels that the desire to inject activism into cinema has hampered the ability of many Native filmmakers to tell compelling stories. "I think our natural instinct is that we have to fight for something or communicate something on a larger level—to change society's consciousness about Native Americans," she says. "But I do think there is a need to focus on story and character and the craft of filmmaking, as opposed to a political or social statement that sometimes gets tied up in the narrative."

Sherman Alexie is more blunt: "If I see one more fishing-rights documentary, I'm going to scream."

Making a narrative film takes money, however—something most Native filmmakers don't have access to. One continuing source of hope is that wealthy casino tribes will begin to invest in Native films. But many casino tribes are cautious about risking their money in the movie business after several tribes were financially burned by 2004's million-dollar debacle *Black Cloud*. Written and directed by Rick Schroder (yes, that Rick Schroder), this story of a Navajo boxer's attempt to make the Olympic team was duly panned by critics, a financial disaster, and replete with virtually every conceivable Native cliché (from the medicine man-like grandfather to characters' conversations with the "spirit world"). Three years later, the film continues to be a source of both humor and embarrassment. That tribes would back a Rick Schroder vehicle instead of supporting one of their own remains one of the greater mysteries of the Native film world.

Still, challenging and thoughtful Native narratives are getting made. Both Alexie and Runningwater cite veteran Sundance filmmakers Blackhorse Lowe (*5th World*) and Cedar Sherbert (*Gesture Down*) as names to watch out for in the future.

"There are more Native Americans working in fiction filmmaking now than ever before," says Runningwater. "While production values are often quite low, they find ways to make their films. The ultimate challenge is telling an original story that audiences can identify with."

Tracy Rector, a Seminole filmmaker who runs the Superfly Filmmaking Seminar for Native youth, sees the next generation of Native filmmakers potentially bridging the gap between the desire to tell truthful indigenous stories and the ability to make movies that resonate with a larger audience. "There's a huge gothic culture on the rez these days," says Rector, "so you're seeing that reflected in the work of young filmmakers. I'm seeing loads of really smart and funny zombie movies from my kids. I actually think it might be the next wave in Native cinema."

Native Zombie movies?

"You know, we did have one zombie submission," notes Harris. "It was about a Native American zombie possessed with the spirit of the white man. A really fantastic idea, but not very well executed."

That may soon change. Blackhorse Lowe is allegedly working with the Sundance Screenwriters Lab to develop a Navajo zombie/horror film, while another experienced Native filmmaker recently contacted Rector about producing a zombie flick.

Alexie, for one, isn't surprised. "Since George Romero turned the zombie movie into one of the more politicized allegorical cinematic forms, it might be natural for the most politicized allegorical ethnic group, us Injuns, to naturally be drawn to the form."

Meanwhile, Alexie's own filmmaking future remains uncertain, zombie or otherwise. "I've dealt with some Custers in my time in this industry," he says, admittedly humbled by his experiences in the film business. Nonetheless, he and Eyre have

reconciled and are hoping to start work on a new project together. The pair recently engaged in serious talks with HBO about shooting Alexie's script about a remote Native Alaskan fishing village, but the project fell through. "They wanted to turn it into Rudy with whales," says Alexie.

Given the industrywide perception that there's no market for culturally authentic Native films, neither Alexie nor Eyre envisions the next *Smoke Signals* breaking through anytime soon.

"We really need that bankable star who can carry a project," says Eyre. "I tell studio executives that all the time and they say, 'You've got that one guy.' I just think to myself, 'Oh, really? That one guy, huh?'"

For now, all eyes will be on Adam Beach, who just landed a recurring role on NBC's popular crime drama *Law and Order: Special Victims Unit*. It's the first major role for a Native actor in which his ethnicity won't be the thrust of his part. "That could really be huge for us," says Eyre.

As for Podemski, she just signed on for a part in a Fox television pilot about the original Dutch colonists of Manhattan. "It's a buckskin role," she laughs, "but it's a really nice one."

And so Indians will still be watching Indians on TV, no longer ashamed of what they see, but hoping for that breakout star who can carry them back to the big screen.

NATIVE AMERICAN MEDIA

Native American Public Telecommunications

Native American Public Telecommunications (NAPT) supports the creation, promotion, and distribution of Native public media. NAPT:

- Produces and develops educational telecommunication programs for all media including public television and public radio;
- Provides training opportunities to encourage increasing numbers of American Indians and Alaska Natives to produce quality public broadcasting programs;
- Promotes increased control and use of information technologies by American Indians and Alaska Natives;

- Provides leadership in creating awareness of and developing telecommunications policies favorable to American Indians and Alaska Natives;
- Builds partnerships to develop and implement telecommunications projects with tribal nations, Indian organizations, and Native communities.

www.nativetelecom.org

Visionmaker Studios

- VisionMaker Video (VMV) is a service of NAPT and functions to promote and distribute Native public media.

- Many films produced by VMV are documentaries are shown on PBS's curated shows, such as *Point of View* (P.O.V.) and *Independent Lens* or become part of public television's schedule.

www.visionmaker.org

Native America Calling

- Native America Calling is a live call-in program linking public radio stations, the Internet, and listeners together in a thought-provoking national conversation about issues specific to Native communities.
- Each program engages noted guests and experts with callers throughout the United States and is designed to improve the quality of life for Native Americans. Native America Calling is heard on 52 stations in the United States and in Canada by approximately 500,000 listeners each week.

www.nativeamericancalling.com

Native American Music Awards

- The Native American Music Awards (NAMA) was created to promote and support Native Music on a national level.
- NAMA is directed toward Native Youth on reservations in order to give them the needed inspiration and opportunities to pursue a professional career in music and to garner greater exposure.
- Organizational objectives are targeted at getting artists up to date on professional industry standards regarding copyrights, publishing, and proper management and booking agent representation as well as touring and getting major record labels to start signing these artists.
- The NAMA ceremony honors indigenous people north and south of the US and Canadian borders.
- NAMA began 10 years ago as a grass roots initiative among industry professionals and record labels such as Canyon, SOAR, Silverwave, Turtle Island, and others.
- The initial NAMA show was launched with 56 annual recordings and has increased to nearly 200 each year. Members from various communities and tribal radio stations serve as the advisory board.
- The NAMA awards ceremony was styled on other national music awards shows. All current Grammy award winners for the Native category have previously won a NAMMY from NAMA.

www.nativeamericanmusicawards.com

Aboriginal Peoples Television Network

- Aboriginal Peoples Television Network (APTN) is a television network that developed originally from Television Northern Canada (TVNC). TVNC was an Aboriginal network with northern and Aboriginal themed programming that broadcast from the Yukon to northern Labrador beginning in 1991.
- APTN is a mandatory service available in over 10 million Canadian households and commercial establishments with cable, direct-to-home satellite (DTH), telco-delivered, and fixed wireless television service providers.
- APTN is aimed at both Aboriginal and non-Aboriginal audiences, with programming to interest all viewers: children's animation, youth, cultural and traditional programming, music, drama, news and current affairs, as well as live coverage of special events and interactive programming, most notably APTN National News: Contact.

www.aptn.ca

American Indian Film Institute

- The American Indian Film Institute (AIFI) is a nonprofit media arts center founded in 1979 to foster understanding of the culture, traditions, and issues of contemporary Native Americans.
- The organization's roots stretch back to 1975, when the first American Indian Film Festival was presented in Seattle. In 1977, the festival was relocated to San Francisco, where it found its permanent home.
- AIFI is the major Native American media and cultural arts presenter in California, and its festival is the world's oldest and most recognized international film exposition dedicated to Native American cinematic accomplishment.
- The goals of AIFI are educational: to encourage Native/non-Native filmmakers to bring to the broader media culture the Native voices, viewpoints, and stories that have been historically excluded from mainstream media; to develop Indian and non-Indian audiences for this work; and to advocate for authentic representations of Indians in the media.

www.aptn.ca

Programs

- The *American Indian Film Festival*, presented at San Francisco's historic Palace of Fine Arts (since 1977) and UA Galaxy Theatres, provides an audience of nearly 5,000 an opportunity to see films by and about American Indians, including many works unavailable in the U.S. through theatres, home video, or television.
- The *Film Library and National Distribution Initiative* uses the research library and catalogue *Films of the American Indian Film Festival 1975–2000* as the basis of a pilot program to promote film works to educational, tribal, and home markets.
- *Tribal Touring Program* includes an outreach festival of select works from the American Indian Film Festival and week-long digital video workshop intensives for youth.

www.aifisf.com

Native Networks/National Museum of the American Indian/Smithsonian Institution

- In 2001 the National Museum of the American Indian (NMAI) launched the Native Networks Web site. The site provides information about new productions and media makers, current areas of special interest, and accomplishments in the field.
- The goal of the Native Networks Web site is to increase interconnectivity and information flow among Native media organizations, media producers, and their audiences.
- Native Networks events at festivals bring together media makers presenting works—in film, video, radio, television, and new media—to discuss ideas, discuss resources, and share concerns and interests.
- Because about 40% of festival participants come from Latin America and 60% from the United States and Canada, festival workshops are presented, through simultaneous translation, in English, Spanish, and Portuguese, and, on occasion, in indigenous languages.

www.nativenetworks.si.edu/nn.htm

American Indian National Center for Television and Film

- The Institute of American Indian and Alaska Native Culture and Development (IAIA) partnered with ABC Disney, CBS, FOX, and NBC/Universal to establishing the American Indian National Center for Television and Film.
- Located in Los Angeles, the National Center's goal is to respond to the need for Native American producers, directors, actors, writers, editors, and others to become actively engaged in the creation of media to more accurately represent contemporary Native American communities.

www.iaia.edu/ainctf/index.html

WEB PAGE EVALUATION CHECKLIST

The web is a great place to do research, but remember that not everything is on the web, especially in American Indian Studies. It is important to remember that putting documents on the web it is easy, cheap, unregulated, and unmonitored. This means that the burden is on you, the user, to establish the validity, authorship, timeliness, and integrity of what you find on the Internet. Unlike with most print publications on the web, there are no editors who verify, edit, and proofread written material so that it meets publishing standards. If you want to use the Internet for research, you will want to carefully evaluate any site you use. When you find it necessary to reference information you find on the Internet, you will want to make sure the sources are credible. Here are some key criteria on which to evaluate web page content:

1. **Is the information accurate?**
   - Can the accuracy of the information be verified by other legitimate sources?
   - Is the information free of spelling and grammatical errors?
   - Is this information available in print as well as online?
2. **Is the author legitimate?**
   - Is the author qualified to write on this topic?
   - Can this information be verified?
   - Is the URL domain preferred? For accuracy and legitimate factual information, stick with sites ending with .edu or .gov.

- Wikipedia warning: This popular Web site is not evaluated or checked for factual accuracy; anyone can create or edit a Wikipedia page—which means it is not necessarily legitimate or accurate! To be on the safe side, do not use Wikipedia as a source.
- Blog warning: These popular web pages are created by anyone who has something to say; they are easy to create and are peoples' opinions and not evaluated or checked for sources.
- Is the page somebody's personal page? Look for a personal name in the address or a commercial web address extension, such as aol.com or geocites.com.
3. **Is the information objective?**
   - Is this public service information?
   - Is the information clearly distinguished from any advertising on the site?
   - Is there a description of the site's sponsor and its purpose?
   - Look for links that say About Us, Philosophy, Background, or Biography.
   - Where did the author get the information? Look for links to scholarly journals or academic books; expect footnotes, links, and/or other documentation to determine the credibility of the writing.
   - Use Google to search for the author's name to see what others are saying about the author.

4. **Is the information current?**
   - When was the data gathered?
   - When was the information written and first published?
   - When was the page last revised?

- For factual information, you want the source to be current; if the information on the page is undated, don't use it!

Wazhazhi-Pod by Ryan Red Corn. *From cover of* Red Ink, *"Pop Culture," Vol. 13, No. 2.* Reprinted by permission.

PART REVIEW

DISCUSSION QUESTIONS

Theresa Harlan, *Creating a Visual History*
1. Why must we reject the reduction of Native images to sentimental portraits and stereotypes?
2. What does the author mean by "ownership of Native representations" from Native memories?

Emory Sekaquaptewa, *One More Smile for a Hopi Clown*
1. Sekaquaptewa states that "the heart of the Hopi concept of clowning is that we are all clowns." Explain what he means by this statement.

Traci L. Morris, *But Is It American Indian Art?*
1. What is the distinction between sacred Native American art and Indian art that is part of the art/culture system, and why is it important for us to recognize this distinction?
2. Explain the role that white patrons of the arts and collectors have had in shaping commercial Indian art. What have been the pros and cons of this mediation, and how does it relate to "authentication" and Indian identity?
3. Do you or does someone in your family create art and if so, what role does the art market (Native or otherwise) play in the economics of the art?

Traci L. Morris, *The National Museum of the American Indian*
1. What aspects of the National Museum of the American Indian make it unique?

Beverly R. Singer, *Wiping the Warpaint Off the Lens: Native American Film and Video*
1. Explain and give examples of how film depictions of stereotypical representations influence the public's view of American Indians.
2. Singer identifies contemporary Native filmmakers as storytellers. Why do you think she says this? What is the role of storytellers in traditional Indian society?

Mathew Fleischer, *Gone with the Wind: A Decade After Smoke Signals,* *Success Remains Elusive for Native American Filmmakers*
1. Have you seen any of the Native films mentioned in this reading or in Reading 5? If so, explain how the film is different than non-Native films and give examples of the ways that it expresses a Native perspective.
2. What does Chris Eyre mean when he says, "I don't think a lot of people see value in telling stories about modern Indians, but I don't see the value in films that show the past"?

Web Page Evaluation Checklist
1. Why is it important to take a critical look at information found on the web? What are the four questions that one should ask when consulting the web?

KEY TERMS

Alexie, Sherman
American Indian Film Institute (AIFI)
Authentic Indian art
Buffalo Bill's Wild West Show
Charlene Teters and Chief Illiniwek
Eyre, Chris
digital divide
Dorothy Dunn
Hopi clowns

Institute of American Indian Arts (IAIA)
Imagining Indians
Indian Country Today
Indian mascots
National Museum of the American Indian (NMAI)
Native history/American history
Native image-making
Smoke Signals

SUGGESTED READINGS

BAKER, JOE, and GERALD MCMASTER. *Remix: New Modernities in a Post-Indian World*. National Museum of the American Indian, 2007.

BATAILLE, GRETCHEN M., ed. *Native American Representations: First Encounters, Distorted Images, and Literary Appropriations*. University of Nebraska Press, 2001.

BERKHOFER, ROBERT, JR. *The White Man's Indian: Images of the American Indian from Columbus to the Present*. New York: Vintage Books, 1978.

BERLO, JANET C., and RUTH B. PHILLIPS. *Native North American Art*. New York, Oxford University Press, 2001.

BERNSTEIN, BRUCE, and W. JACKSON RUSHING. *Modern by Tradition: American Indian Painting in the Studio Style*. Santa Fe, N.M.: Museum of New Mexico Press, 1995.

BIGFEATHER, JOANNA, RAYNA GREEN, et al. *Native Views: Influences of Modern Culture*. Ann Arbor, Mich.: Artrain USA, 2004.

DUBIN, MARGARET, ed. *The Dirt Is Red Here: Art and Poetry from Native California.* Berkeley, Calif.: Heyday Books, 2002.

HALL, STUART, ed. *Representation: Cultural Representations and Signifying Practices.* Thousand Oaks, Sage Publications, 1997.

HARLAN, THERESA, and ANNE GULLY, ed. *Watchful Eyes: Native American Women Artists.* Phoenix, Ariz.: Heard Museum, 1994.

HILL, RICK, NANCY MARIE MITCHELL, and LLOYD NEW. *Creativity Is Our Tradition: Three Decades of Contemporary Indian Art at the Institute of American Indian Arts.* Santa Fe, N.M.: Institute of American Indian and Alaska Native Culture and Arts Development, 1992.

KILPATRICK, JACQUELYN. *Celluloid Indians: Native Americans and Film.* Lincoln: University of Nebraska Press, 1999.

MASAYESVA, VICTOR, JR. *Husk of Time: the Photographs of Victor Masayesva.* Tucson: University of Arizona Press, 2006.

MCMASTER, GERALD, AND LEE-ANN MARTIN. *Indigena: Contemporary Native Perspectives.* Vancouver: Douglas & McIntyre, 1992.

MCMASTER, GERALD, ed. *Reservation X.* Seattle: University of Washington Press, 1998.

ROLLINS, PETER C., and JOHN E. O'CONNOR, eds. *Hollywood's Indian: the Portrayal of the Native American In Film.* Lexington: University of Kentucky Press, 2003.

RUSHING, W. JACKSON, III, ed. *Native American Art in the Twentieth Century: Makers, Meanings, Histories.* New York: Routledge, 1999.

SINGER, BEVERLY R. *Wiping the Warpaint Off the Lens: Native American Film and Video.* Minneapolis, University of Minnesota Press, 2001.

TSINHNAHJINNIE, HULLEAH J., and PASSALACQUA, VERONICA. *Our People, Our Land, Our Images: International Indigenous Photographers.* Davis, Calif.: C.N. Gorman Museum, University of California, 2006.

VI

COMMUNITY WELLNESS: FAMILY, HEALTH, AND EDUCATION

Indian Education Blues
Ed Edmo

I sit in your
crowded classrooms
& learn how to
read about dick,
jane & spot
but

 I remember
 how to get a deer

 I remember
 how to do beadwork

 I remember
how to fish

I remember
the stories told by the old

but

 spot keeps
 showing up
 &

  my report card
  is bad

"Indian Education Blues" by Ed Edmo from *Returning the Gift*, Joseph Bruchac, editor. Reprinted by permission of the author.

Many Indian people throughout the Americas say that a rich person is one who has many relatives. This philosophy epitomizes the Indian world: An Indigenous person always positions himself or herself in a nexus of kin relationships. For the Siouxan Indians of the United States, the ties that bind each one to another are composed of five interlocking social units: *otonwe, ospaye, ti-ospaye, wico-tipi,* and *ti-ognaka*. The Western, or Teton, Sioux are the principal otonwe. They, in turn, are divided into Seven Council Fires, or divisions, the Oglala being the main ospaye of these. The ospaye are further divided into seven tipi-divisions, or bands, and each of these ti-ospaye is composed of one or more camps, or wico-tipi. Finally, each camp is made up of two or more ti-ognakapi (husbanded-tipis).

The Mohawk can always find clan relatives (Deer, Turtle, Snipe, and so on) among any of the other five Iroquoian nations. If a traditional Dineh (Navajo) young man encounters a Dineh woman he fancies, he must find out her clan. If it turns out that they are of the same clan, then they are considered "brother" and "sister," and all thoughts of romantic love must be put aside. In fact, when one Indian meets another Indian, it is traditional that she or he gives a family name and a village or tribal affiliation, or both. These last names, whether from an original Indian language or of European derivation, are well known to other tribal members and even to many Indians of other tribes. The new person can be located spatially in terms of tribal origin and often even genealogically. Indeed, the bonds of consanguinity remain strong in Indian country, whether one resides in a small Indian community or a large metropolitan area.

One is also related to the natural world. Whereas Christianity, which is derived from European peoples, ends prayer with "Amen," Lakota Indians say "All My Relations" to end prayer because all creatures, great and small, are one's brothers and sisters. In fact, as an extension of this kin principle of respect and mutual obligations, an underlying philosophical principle of many Indian cultures is that "the earth is our Mother."

The family and child-bearing roles of women are highly valued in traditional Indian society, and women hold special spiritual power in terms of creating and balancing life in both the human and natural worlds. Author-poet Paula Gunn Allen (Laguna Pueblo/Sioux/Lebanese) contends that most North American Indian societies were originally women centered, or gynocentric (see Suggested Readings). Among some Indigenous nations, such as the traditional Iroquois, clan mothers hold an executive function in which they both choose and remove male clan chiefs and advise them in their decisions. Despite European-imposed laws and policies supporting a patriarchy, women continue to play a central role in the Indian family and often in tribal political life and community affairs as well.

Elders, too, are revered. *Grandmother, grandfather, aunt,* and *uncle* are terms not only of endearment but also of respect. Among most Indian peoples throughout the Western Hemisphere, it is a common practice to address persons of older generations by these kinship terms, even when they are not blood kin. For example, one would respectfully address a non-blood-related person of one's grandparents' generation as "Grandfather," or "*Abuelo*," or "Auntie." Or a non-blood-related person of one's parents' generation might address a younger person as "Nephew" or "Niece." By inference, such non-blood-related persons become as kin.

Many Native peoples practice adoption. The Iroquois Indians in earlier times routinely replaced dead or slain members by adopting enemies taken in battle. The nineteenth-century Apaches raided Spanish settlements to capture women and children whom they then made their own. Ritual adoption, *Hunka*, is still a solemn custom for the Lakota, who regard such "relatives" as even closer than blood kin. One of the emotionally traumatic events for the Lakota was when they were forced by U.S. authorities to give up their white relatives at the close of the nineteenth century, after they were reduced to the status of captured nations under the reservation system.

Because everything in the Indigenous world is interrelated, the integrity of the Native American community and an individual's sense of well-being are based on balance and holism. All forces, both animate and inanimate, must be taken into account in order for the whole person, and by extension, the entire community, to remain in good health—physically, emotionally, socially, and spiritually. This perspective stands in contrast to the highly individualistic, technology-driven, science-for-profit orientation of Western society. In terms of general health and welfare, the Indigenous perspective places value on community as well as individual rights, and it values social capital over economic productive capital. Western individualistic society, on the other hand, measures a nation's greatness through its industrial productivity (gross domestic product) by counting only those things that can be monetarized. This part examines some of the implications surrounding these and related issues.

Today, the Native peoples of the Americas have possibly the worst health problems of any ethnic or minority group. Native Americans in the United States, one of the most affluent countries in the world, have a statistical health profile more in keeping with an undeveloped nation than a modern, industrialized nation. A glance at the health statistics presented in the box titled "Native American Demographics—United States, 2008" in Part I tells part of the story. Tuberculosis and death from accidents are all too common. The rates of heart disease, cancer, and stroke, which used to be lower among Native peoples, than in the general population, are increasing significantly. Type II diabetes is now rampant in Indian Country in the United States. Among some of the Southwestern tribes, more than 60 percent of the adult members are diabetic. Toxic wastes from uranium mining and other harmful activities, which we examine in Part VIII, are causing extremely negative health consequences for Indigenous peoples throughout the Western Hemisphere. For example, stillbirths and spontaneous abortions have increased on the Lakota Sioux reservations, where uranium and other mining have left toxic residues in the soil and groundwater. Allergies and chemical sensitivities are becoming commonplace for many reservation and rural Indian populations in the United States, whereas those conditions were unheard of in the past.

A major cause of poor health is the modern highly processed diet that has replaced the former natural diets of Indian people in the United States. For example, for that one-third of the Indian population that resides on reservations, there are the negative effects of government commodities. "Commods," as they are often termed on reservations, are government surplus food items such as fatty cheese, white flour, and powdered milk (which is indigestible for most Indian people, who lack the enzyme to digest it) that are distributed to the poor. These modern foods are starchy and high in fats and sugar, and they lack the proper vitamins and nutrients for a healthy diet. American Indians have gone from a basically healthy population to one suffering from a variety of serious illnesses and chronic and life-threatening health conditions.

The health situation in Latin America has become increasingly grave as diets have deteriorated because of economic forces associated with "free trade" and global capitalism. The rebellion by the Zapatistas in Chiapas, Mexico, was fueled in part by passage of the North American Free Trade Agreement (NAFTA), which allowed the U.S. corporate grain industry to dominate the Mexican corn market and thereby deprive Mayan Indians and other Native and non-Native farmers of their traditional livelihood.

One of the tragic contradictions in considering these depressing circumstances is the fact that early European observers were nearly unanimous in proclaiming the relative good health of those Indians who had not been in contact with Europeans. From early documents and letters, we learn that "it is verie rare to see a sicke body amongst them. . . . They are never troubled with Scurvey, Dropsy, nor Stone. The Phthisick, Asthma, and Diabetes, they are Wholly Strangers to. Neither do I remember I ever saw one Paralytick amongst them."[1] Much of Native American good health was due to customs of sanitation—clean bodies, clean clothing, and clean homes, to which early Europeans were often unaccustomed—and to diet and exercise.

The original medical contribution of Native America to the world are incalculable. More than 200 medicines used by American Indians have been listed in the *Pharmacopoeia* of the United States since its first edition in 1820, and in the *National Formulary*, first published in 1888. These contributions by Native peoples of the Americas include well-known drugs such as belladonna (used in eye examinations), cascara sagrada (the most widely used cathartic in the world), wintergreen (a precursor of aspirin), cocaine from coca leaves (used for altitude sickness and as a pain reliever), curare (a muscle relaxant), digitalis (for heart disease), quinine (for malaria), and vitamin C from pine bark (to prevent scurvy and as a vitamin supplement).

The original peoples of the Americas are also well acquainted with what contemporary medicine calls psychotherapy. Curing ceremonies and practices by medicine people and Indian doctors are still widely carried out, often with good results. The mind–body (or spiritual) connection that Western medicine is only now beginning to recognize has been part of the curing practices in the Americas for thousands of years.

Ironically, two medicines used by Native Americans for centuries in the generic or natural state without any ill effects now account for millions of injuries and deaths from their overuse: the coca leaf and tobacco. Cocaine is a bitter crystalline alkaloid derived and concentrated from the coca leaf. Although cocaine is useful as a local anesthetic, if taken in large doses, it leads to intoxication and drug dependency. The custom of chewing coca leaves, on the other hand, has been used by Andean Indigenous peoples for centuries to allay thirst, hunger, and the effects of high altitude without harmful side effects. Those Native Americans using tobacco before European contact used it only in ceremonies, where it was (and still is) considered sacred. Most often, Native peoples mixed tobacco with other herbs to form a milder substance, such as *kinnikinnik*, which was smoked ceremonially. European colonists, on the other hand, commercialized and exported tobacco for profit, leading to its non-ceremonial over use and addictive consequences. Today, in the United States, with the re-diffusion of commercial tobacco back into the Native American community, Indians also suffer the detrimental health effects found in the general population; the line between ceremonial and secular use has become blurred.

Social well-being has a story similar to that of community health. Originally, Native Americans lived in self-governing communities, and they managed their justice systems on the basis of norms and mores that were learned through the Indian extended family or clan, as well as from elders in the community. Culture, customary law, and collective sanctions for social control kept the society integrated and deviance in check. There were no police or jails. Under the impact of Western colonialism and oppression, however, the collective rights of Indian tribes and nations became subordinated to—if not completely replaced by—the larger nation-states, which have been governed by non-Native people.

Land alienation, especially, has had a serious effect on Indigenous health and community well-being because of the destruction of Native foods, such as the near extinction of the North American Plains buffalo. Means of the land dispossession include the 1887 Indian Allotment Act in the United States, in which half of the then-remaining tribal land base was lost; the post-World War II "development" of the Amazon Basin that has caused the displacement and deaths of thousands of Indians; the 1971 Alaska Native Claims Settlement Act, which outlawed aboriginal hunting and fishing rights; and the more recent Mexican law privatizing the *ejido* land tenure system of rural farmer and Indian communal lands. In the absence of an effective resistance movement to those external pressures, Native American values and customs break down, the fabric of communal life is torn, and many individuals become alienated, psychologically depressed, and even self-destructive—what Native psychologists refer to as "soul wounds." Rather than "blaming the victim," substance abuse and addiction must be viewed within this context of historically based physical and emotional pain that is perpetuated across many generations.

The Indian extended family was at the center of assimilationist attacks during the worst years of the federal assault on Indian culture, from the 1880s until the 1930s. The Christian mission schools and the federal boarding schools were designed to "kill the Indian but save the man," a form of ethnocide. If the ties to the family, the primary socialization institution for tribal culture, could be broken, so the assimilationists reasoned, then Indian children would grow up culturally "white," and the "Indian problem" would be solved. Following this line of reasoning, in the early years, federal Indian agents in the United States, backed by the reservation police, made raids on Indian communities to force children to attend boarding schools. The Sioux medicine man John (Fire) Lame Deer recalls that the worst threat that his grandparents could say when he was a child to make him behave was "Shh, *wasicun anigni kte*" ("be quiet, or the white man will take you away").[2]

The film *Where the Spirit Lives* vividly portrays the tragic consequences of this system in Canada's residential schools, where Indian children were seized by the Indian agents and parceled out to the various Christian mission schools (see Suggested Readings). (Interestingly, a similar policy is graphically depicted in the film *Rabbit Proof Fence* regarding Australian aboriginal children who were likewise forcibly taken to boarding schools against their parents' wishes.) Throughout Canada, the Anglican Church ran 26 of the church-operated residential schools for Native children, beginning in the 1800s and continuing into the late 1980s. In 1999, Floyd Mowatt, a former resident of one of these schools, won a court case in his suit against the Anglican Church and the Canadian government for sexual abuse that took place as recently as the early 1970s. In a 106-page ruling, British Columbia's highest court found both parties "jointly liable" for violent sexual assaults of Mowatt and several other boys.

The brutal treatment and military discipline in these schools contrasted dramatically with the personal freedom and love that Indian children traditionally received at home. This negative treatment often resulted in severe mental and emotional problems. That sexual abuse was not uncommon in a number of these schools may account for some of the pathology of child abuse (virtually unknown in the past) found in today's generation of some Indian families. For many years, attending boarding school was the only way American Indians could get a high school education, such as it was. They were not allowed in California's public schools until 1935. As recently as 1955, 81 percent of Navajo children were in boarding schools. Boarding schools were the defining experience for generations of Native Americans. One of the unexpected consequences, however, was the thousands of intertribal marriages that produced generations of "mixed-tribal" Indian people. Indian boarding and day school conditions have improved in recent years, and those Indian children going to the few remaining boarding schools do so through their parents' choice. The deleterious effects that the boarding-school system had on Indian individuals and their families are discussed in this part.

Also harmful has been the practice of "out-adoption," which allowed or encouraged non-Indians to adopt or foster Indian children. *Indian Country Today* reports that in both Canada and the United States, from the 1950s to the 1980s, 35 to 40 percent of all Native children were placed in foster care, adoptive homes, or similar non-Indian homes. Many of these children were removed against their parents' will and came from families that were judged by state entities as "unfit." In 1958 the Bureau of Indian Affairs and the Child Welfare League of America made it official policy to promote the adoption of Indian children by white families as a solution to the "Indian problem." Rather than address the underlying structural problems of neocolonialism and resource and labor exploitation that plagued Indian tribes, these agencies saw the Indian family and community as the causes of the general social disorganization of tribal life. Other public and private agencies also began promoting the policy of out-adoption. For example, between 1954 and 1976, the Indian Student Placement Program of the Church of Jesus Christ of Latter-Day Saints placed 38,260 Indian children in Mormon homes. Many of those adopted-out became marginalized, feeling neither Indian nor white, and suffered severe mental and emotional problems.

In 1978, as a result of pressure from Indian and non-Indian lawyers and social workers, the Indian Child Welfare Act (ICWA) was established, giving Native tribes and nations a stronger voice in determining the placement of Indian children whom were fostered or adopted out. This has been one legal step in supporting the sovereignty of Native nations. The intent of this act is to protect the Indian family, community, and tribal integrity from the unwanted removal of children. If a court determines that a child must be removed from his or her parents, it must look to the ICWA, which establishes a series of priorities for placement: first with the child's extended family, and then if this is not possible with other members of the tribe, then next in priority with other Indians who are not members of the tribe, and finally with non-Indians. Armed with this legal tool, Native lawyers, such as those at the Native American Rights Fund (NARF), and social workers, such as those at Indigenous Nations in Oakland, have a means to protect the rights of Indian children, even if removed from their biological family, to be raised in a Native family and frequently in a Native community.

In Reading 1, "*Asgaya-Dihi*," Wilma Mankiller, past principal chief of the Cherokee Nation in Oklahoma, and Michael Wallis explain the deep cultural significance of personal names and Mankiller's own genealogical heritage in Cherokee culture and history. They also recount the evolution of the Sequoyah Training School, which started out as an orphan asylum and then became an asylum for Indian people with severe mental or physical problems, then became a federal boarding school, and finally, today, is a high school. Sequoyah was the famed Cherokee intellectual who is widely credited for devising a writing system that led to Cherokee literacy in the early 1820s.

Deanna Kingston is an Inupiaq Eskimo anthropologist who has been documenting the stories, songs, and dances of her people, the King Island Inupiaq of the Bering Strait in Alaska. In Reading 2, "Traveling Traditions," Kingston describes the ways in which Inupiaq people continue to maintain their traditions and cultural identity, even when they are living and rearing families in the lower 48, away from King Island. Kingston, herself, grew up in Oregon. Nevertheless, one of the mechanisms by which she and her cross-cousins (mother's brother's children, or father's sister's children) continue to claim their identity as Inupiaq people is to engage in the practice of a "teasing" or "joking" relationship. She explains that teasing cousins engage in behavior designed to embarrass one another, but they are not to be offended or to get angry at one another when teased, because "if a person misbehaved or acted inappropriately, it was the teasing cousin's job to tell him to change his behavior." Teasing relationships, which are frequently found among Indigenous peoples as an alternative to the coercive institutions of police forces and prisons, illustrate one of the functions of kinship in the socialization and control of members in the Native community.

The poignancy and strength of family and the loss of those who leave the community, perhaps forever, are found in Frances Washburn's (Lakota) poem "Lakota Warrior."

Reading 3, "American Indian and Alaska Native Health," by Jennie Joe (Navajo) provides an overview of the contemporary and historic situation regarding health issues and concerns, as well as the role the Indian Health Service (IHS) and the Public Health Service (PHS) have played both in health policy and in delivering health care. This reading also focuses on recent changes in health research and the continuing health disparities between Native people and the U.S. population overall. As Joe points out, health services to Native nations are based on treaties created many years ago and then validated through various agreements and structural changes within the Bureau of Indian Affairs and later the PHS. However, as she points out, "How the federally supported health care gets delivered at the community level, however, varies and continues to change." This extreme variation in the quality of health care on reservations and also the uneven availability to Native peoples living off reservations and in urban areas continues to be an ongoing point of concern and often contention. Joe expresses the conclusion that the work toward improving American Indian health and health care is beginning to come about through an emphasis on stronger Native community participation in the management of health care services and in locally designed and implemented health promotion and prevention programs. This is yet another move away from federal control and toward control by sovereign Native nations.

Misconceptions held by non-Indian and Indians alike surround the subject of Indian drinking and alcoholism. Many people believe that Native Americans are genetically predisposed to alcoholism. This stereotypical view is also held by many of the *mestizos* and non-Native people in Latin America regarding Native peoples. These mistaken beliefs provide one of the rationales for inequality in justice found throughout the Americas. In Reading 4, "The Epidemiology of Alcohol Abuse Among American Indians: The Mythical and Real Properties," Philip May, a professor of sociology and psychiatry at the University of new Mexico, sets out to debunk these and related misconceptions. Epidemiology is the branch of medicine that deals with the incidence, distribution, and control of disease in a given population. The first step in any scientific procedure is to define the research problem. The author therefore carefully distinguishes between Indian deaths that are associated with alcohol dependency, or chronic alcoholic drinking, which is only part of the problem, and alcohol-abusive drinking patterns (sporadic binge drinking). He also examines demographic factors, such as geographic, political, and cultural variables, that seem to explain the high rates of alcohol-related problems among the Native American populations of the United States. Ironically, a higher percentage (60 percent) within the total population of non-Indians consume alcohol than do Indians (40 percent). But among Indians who do drink alcohol, alcoholism and alcohol abuse are extremely serious problems.

In the box titled "Delfina Cuero: Her Autobiography," a California Indian elder describes how as a young woman she learned to give birth and to care for her babies "in the real old days." It is through the traditional process of passing knowledge regarding health practices from generation to generation that family and community well-being are maintained. When this process is disrupted, the overall health of a people declines.

Larry Murillo in Reading 5, "Perspectives on Traditional Health Practices," presents a broad view of Native health practices and suggests ways they can be beneficially integrated into existing Western medicine health services for Native peoples. He stresses the value in using a "healthy-community" concept that has implications for health research, for understanding and working with competing cultural values related to health, and for building resource capacity in maintaining good health and in creating appropriate health care.

Many of the health problems plaguing Native Americans today, such as diabetes, cancer, hypertension, and alcoholism, are relatively new among Native Americans and are related to changes in culture, diet, and lifestyle. These problems are increasing at an alarming rate in many Native communities. As a result, there is renewed interest among many tribes in North America in improving nutrition and health through traditional food gathering and preparation, as well as through increased exercise and spiritual ceremonies. The box titled "Restoring Native Foods for Health and Community Well-Being" speaks of one such effort by Tohono O'odham Community Action (TOCA), a Native nonprofit working with Arizona's Tohono O'odham, a tribe that has the dubious distinction of having the highest rate of type II diabetes in the world. Following this box, Ofelia Zepeda (Tohono O'odham) describes in her poem "Squash Under the Bed" the satisfaction and sense of security derived from healthy traditional desert foods. Many people think of Indian fry bread, which is often seen for sale at pow-wows and other Indian events, as a traditional Indian food. In reality, the ingredients—primarily lard and white flour—were first given to Indian people by government non-Indians as a subsistence ration and might be more accurately termed "prisoner-of-war" food or "one-step-from-starvation" food, rather than "traditional." Today, the continued reliance on fry bread as a subsistence food by many Indian people is one contributing factor in the high rates of diabetes and other health problems. Suzan Shown Harjo (Muscogee Creek/Cheyenne) tells of this in the box "My New Year's Resolution: No More Fat "Indian" Food," and Native artist Ryan Huna Smith (Chemehuevi/Navajo) gives us his rendition of "Frybread Man."

Reading 6, "'If We Get the Girls, We Get the Race': Missionary Education of Native American Girls," gives an historical account of what the ordeal of boarding schools was like for Indian children and their families. Author Carol Devens shows how far removed—physically, spiritually, and culturally—from family and tribal community life the schools were and how fiercely the school administrators and teachers were committed to using any means to "civilize" the Indian children. The article also contrasts the teaching approach at the mission schools with that in tribal communities, where each child was surrounded by extended family members instructing and modeling in the knowledge and behavior needed to become a respected adult and an integral part of the family and community. The illustration by Leonard F. Chana (Tohono O'odham) speaks clearly of this philosophy, with the title "Teaching Is Like Culture: It Starts at Home with Parents, Relatives, and Friends."

In the box titled "Reservation Schools Fail to Assimilate All Students," Tim Giago (Oglala Lakota) tells of the multiple and often subtle ways that reservation schools have often not only failed students educationally but also failed their communities by removing the power to control their children's education out of the hands of parents and the local Native authorities. He cites a number of personal experiences in which misguided educational decisions undermined an educational process that could be beneficial for Indian children, their families, and communities.

In Reading 7, "Protagonism Emergent: Indians and Higher Education," Jeffrey Wollock, research director of the Solidarity Foundation, traces the historical development of Indian higher education in the United States. The history of Indian education in the United States includes the founding in 1879 of the Indian boarding-school system under (Colonel) Richard Henry Pratt; the Indian Allotment Act period and the assimilationist phase of the first quarter of the twentieth century led by the Society of American Indians and other "friends"; and the early attempt by Carlos Montezuma to develop an Indian university. This excerpted portion of Wollock's article begins with the New Deal reforms in Indian education under the 1934 Indian Reorganization Act; the impact of the G.I. Bill after World War II; the new attempts to reform Indian education in the 1950s; the heightened struggle that emerged during the 1960s Great Society and the "new Indian" movement, which included the efforts of the National Indian Youth council, among others; the Tribally Controlled Community College Assistance Act, passed in 1978; and the many Native American studies departments and programs in colleges and universities today. (See the map of tribal colleges on page 299.) A major feature of the tribal colleges that distinguishes them from non-Indian institutions of higher learning is the integration of tribal heritage and traditions into the curriculum. The Indian family, kin network, and community are integrated into the programs and operations of these colleges. All the current tribal colleges have adopted this practice, and these colleges are producing some of Indian Country's finest new leadership.

NOTES

1. Quoted in Virgil J. Vogel, *American Indian Medicine* (University of Oklahoma Press, 1970), 151. (Original source: John Lawson, *History of North Carolina* [1714, reprint; Garren and Massie, 1692, 237–238]).

2. John (Fire) Lame Deer and Richard Erdoes, *Lame Deer, Seeker of Visions* (New York: Pocket Books, Simon & Schuster, 1972), 22.

ASGAYA-DIHI

Wilma Mankiller and Michael Wallis

Native Americans regard their names not as mere labels, but as essential parts of their personalities. A native person's name is as vital to his or her identity as the eyes or teeth. There is a common belief that when a person is injured, her name is maligned, just as she might be bruised when in an accident.

Throughout Native American history, there was often a need to conceal one's name. This is probably why Powhatan and Pocahontas are known in history under assumed identities, their true names having been hidden from whites so that their names could not be demeaned, defiled, or destroyed.

If prayers and medicine fail to heal a seriously ill person, the spiritual leader sometimes realizes that the patient's name itself may be diseased. The priest then goes to the water and, with the appropriate ceremony, bestows a new name on the sick person. The healer then begins anew, repeating sacred formulas with the patient's new name, in the hope that these measures will bring about restoration and recovery.

Asgaya-dihi. Mankiller. My Cherokee name in English is Mankiller.

Mankiller has survived in my own family as a surname for four generations before my own. It is an old Cherokee name, although it was originally not a name at all, but a rank or title used only after one had earned the right to it. To call someone Mankiller would have been like calling another person Major or Captain.

There were many titles in the early days of the Cherokees. Each Cherokee town, for example, had its own Water-goer (Ama-edohi) and its own Raven (Golana), and each town had its Asgaya-dihi.

My own people came from near Tellico, from the land now known as eastern Tennessee. My great-great-great-grandfather's name was written down as Ah-nee-ska-yah-di-hi. That translates literally into English as "Menkiller." No record exists of the names of his parents, and the only name recorded for his wife is Sally. The son of Ah-nee-ska-yah-di-hi and Sally was listed as Ka-skun-nee Mankiller. The first name, Ka-skun-nee, cannot be translated, but it is with this man, my great-great-grandfather, that the name Mankiller was established in the family line as a surname.

Jacob Mankiller, born in 1853, was a son of Ka-skun-nee Mankiller and Lucy Matoy. Jacob married Susan Teehee-Bearpaw and, in 1889, they had a son they named John. He was the oldest of eight children. John Mankiller was my grandfather. He married Bettie Bolin Bendabout Canoe. Her Cherokee name was Quatie. Born in 1878, she was nine years older than her husband. My father, Charley Mankiller, was their son.

I know that Lucy Matoy, my great-grandmother and the wife of Ka-skun-nee, came from what we call one of the Old Settler families. Sometime after 1817, these families immigrated of their own free will to what became the Cherokee Nation West, an area west of the Mississippi in the far reaches of Arkansas and beyond, in what would later become Indian Territory. This voluntary immigration occurred two decades before the federal government, anxious to seize Native people's land, evicted Cherokees from their homes in Georgia, Tennessee, North Carolina, and Alabama, forcibly removing them on what was known as "the trail where they cried." As far as the name Matoy is concerned, our history tells us that in 1730, a Chief Moytoy was declared "emperor" of the Cherokees by Sir Alexander Cuming, an unofficial envoy representing the English Crown in America. I can't prove it, but I strongly suspect that the surname Matoy is but another form of the name or title

Amaedohi, which had been corrupted by the English into Moytoy. As far as I can determine, all of my ancestors on my father's side, other than this Matoy line, moved west later on, in the late 1830s, on the Trail of Tears.

At the turn of the century, there was another attempt to ravage our people through several legislative acts which in effect almost destroyed the Cherokee Nation and its ability to function as a sovereign entity. In 1907, Indian Territory was finally devoured and ceased to exist when Oklahoma became a state. Land held in common by the Cherokee Nation was parceled out in individual allotments of 160 acres per family. The land we now call Mankiller Flats in Adair County was assigned to my paternal grandfather, John Mankiller. I never met my grandfather, although I often feel the connection between the two of us. I live on my grandfather's allotment. I have built my house several hundred yards from where his home once stood. Each spring, Easter lilies bloom in what used to be his yard. They remind me of him and of our ancestry.

My father, Charley Mankiller, was born in his father's frame house on November 15, 1914, just seven years after Oklahoma statehood. At the time of his birth, much of the land that had been allotted to the Cherokees was being taken away by unscrupulous business men with the cooperation of Oklahoma's judicial system. Unspeakably greedy people would arrange to be appointed guardians of Cherokee children, and then take control of their individually allotted Cherokee land. As documented in Angie Debo's impressive book, *And Still the Waters Run*, this was practiced most widely in the early 1900s when oil was discovered in Oklahoma and the boom years started.

My father's mother died in 1916 when her son was only two years old. She died in one of the dreaded influenza epidemics that tore through America during World War I. Jensie Hummingbird, my father's older half sister, helped raised him. I remember Aunt Jensie. She spoke no English at all. She did not own a car or get around very much. She tended to stay close to her home. We visited her quite a bit. She was a very kind woman who was sick most of her life. Aunt Jensie had only one son, Charley Hummingbird, who cared for her until she died in 1990.

My grandfather went off to join the army and took part in the Great War that became known as World War I. In fact, a large number of American Indian people served in World War I. This interests me. As a student of Native American history, I realize that the question of United States citizenship for Native people was addressed in the Dawes Act, or the General Allotment Act, of 1887. This was the law that prepared Native people for the eventual termination of tribal ownership of land by granting 160-acre allotments to each Indian family, or eighty acres to an individual. All of the allottees were to become United States citizens, subject to the same criminal and civil laws as other American citizens. Even though Theodore Roosevelt called the Dawes Act "a mighty pulverizing engine to break up the tribal mass," the act failed because Native Americans considered land not as a possession but as a physical and spiritual domain shared by all living things. Many of our people were reluctant to turn away from the traditional view of common ownership of land.

Despite these early measures, Native Americans were not considered official citizens of the United States until 1924. That was the year Congress passed the Indian Citizenship Act, bestowing voting rights and citizenship on all Indians "born within the territorial limits of the United States." Native people, however, were still considered to be outside the protection of the Bill of Rights. Among many Native people, there is a feeling that citizenship was conferred uniformly in 1924 because so many American Indians, like my grandfather, had volunteered for military service during the war.

In 1936, twelve years after the Indian Citizenship Act became law and nine years before I was born, Grandpa Mankiller died. He was only forty-six years old. The official cause of death was pernicious anemia, but we now believe that his death resulted from kidney failure caused by polycystic kidney disease. Severe anemia is a common side effect of kidney failure. My father, in turn, inherited this disease from my grandfather, and it was passed on to several of his children, including me.

There were only two children to mourn their father's death, my father Charley and his only full sibling, his older sister, Sally. She was a beautiful girl who liked to wear fine dresses with her black hair piled on her head. People who knew her as a girl say she was very dainty, always carrying a parasol when she walked in the sun. Sally later married a full-blooded Cherokee named Nelson Leach, and they lived near Rocky Mountain on a portion of the Mankiller family allotment.

Like my dad, Aunt Sally was forced to attend Sequoyah Training School near Tahlequah. This was very customary of the period. Sally began classes there in the 1920s when she was a little girl and stopped attending the school in the early 1930s when she became a young woman.

Sequoyah Training School started as an orphan asylum. The Cherokee National Council passed an act establishing the asylum in 1871 to provide housing for children orphaned by the Civil War. The war was fought partly in the Cherokee Nation, and Cherokees served in both the Union and Confederate armies. Later, the orphan facility became an asylum for Indian people who experienced mental or physical problems of such severity that they could not cope without assistance. Finally, it was turned into a boarding school for Indian children.

In 1914, our people authorized Cherokee Chief W. C. Rogers to sell the school and its forty acres to the United States. It then became a federal institution under the control of the secretary of the interior, and was maintained as an industrial school for "the Indian orphans of Oklahoma of the restricted class," meaning Native people of one-half degree of Indian blood or more. Congress passed an act in 1925 changing the name of the school to Sequoyah Orphan Training School in honor of Sequoyah, the man credited with developing our Cherokee syllabary.

It is still a school for Native people today, but now it is not an orphanage. Known simply as Sequoyah High School, it is one of five Native American educational facilities in Oklahoma. The school, including its residential program, is funded by the Bureau of Indian Affairs and operated by the Cherokee Nation of Oklahoma. Our people not only maintain Sequoyah School, but also oversee the policies that govern it, and the twelve campus buildings. Most of the students are Cherokee, but as many as sixteen other tribes are also represented, coming to Sequoyah from many Indian nations.

Back in the bad old days, the BIA representatives who maintained boarding schools such as Sequoyah would go hundreds of miles and return with Native children. The philosophy, reflecting an errant missionary zeal, was to get Native children away from their families, their elders, their tribes, their language, their heritage. They isolated Native children so they would forget their culture. The boarding-school concept was simply another way for the federal government to deal with what its officials always called "the Indian problem." After first trying to wipe all of us off the face of the earth with violence, they attempted to isolate us on reservations or, in the case of many people such as the Cherokees, place us in an area that the government called Indian Territory. All the while, they systematically conjured up policies to kill our

culture. So the federal government rounded up Indian youngsters and forced them to attend boarding schools whether they wanted to or not. This was true for most tribes, not just the Cherokees.

At Sequoyah School, south of Tahlequah, the capital of the Cherokee Nation, my father and his little sister were forbidden to speak their native language. They could not speak a word of English when they first went there, so they were whipped for speaking Cherokee. The whole idea behind those boarding schools, whether they were government operated like Sequoyah or a religious operation, was to acculturate Native people into the mainstream white society and, at the same time, destroy their sense of self. The boarding-school officials hoped to make the "little Indians" into "ladies and gentlemen." So they cut their hair short and did not allow them to utter one word of their native language. Oftentimes, all visits to family and friends back home were denied. The idea was to "civilize" the children. There was even a popular expression about "killing the Indian and saving the man."

> When I was about seven years old they took me to this damn Indian school of the government's and we had to stand in line and they cut my hair off. They just cut my braids off and threw them into a box with all the other children's braids. My old grandmother went over there and got them and my grand folks stayed at the winter camp all winter to be near me. . . . It was hard being an Indian in them days. Later I learned to be proud.
>
> Archie Blackowl, a Cheyenne,
> *The Indians in Oklahoma*

All his life, my father had mixed emotions about the school named Sequoyah. He spoke of having been punished for only the slightest infractions, and of the many other problems he experienced there. On the other hand, he could get sentimental about the place. It had an orchard, a big garden, and a lot of farm animals. The students provided all the labor necessary to keep the operation going. One Sequoyah superintendent my father spoke well of was Jack Brown, who was part Cherokee and had a great interest in history and literature. Sequoyah was my father's home for twelve years. It was not a perfect home or even a loving place, but it was there that he developed lasting friendships with other Cherokee children and youths from other tribes. At Sequoyah, he also acquired his love of books, a gift he passed on to his children. Most people have mixed emotions about their home. My dad's feelings were perhaps a little more intense because of the acculturation program and what must have been a lonely life in a barren dormitory.

Still, the fact remains that the primary mission of Sequoyah and the other boarding schools was for the children to leave everything behind that related to their native culture, heritage, history, and language. In short, there was a full-scale attempt at deracination—the uprooting or destruction of a race and its culture. Consequently, many young Cherokees and other Native people subjected to the boarding-school experience, including my father, came away from those years of indoctrination more than a little brainwashed.

At many of those schools scattered across this country and Canada, much mental and physical abuse occurred. I have a friend from a Canadian tribe who lived in a traditional community as a girl. It was very isolated. She can recall the young men coming home from religious boarding schools with all sorts of problems. Many of them never married, but stayed to themselves. They turned to alcohol and drank themselves to death before they reached their thirtieth birthdays. My friend and other concerned tribal members were puzzled by this phenomenon. When they examined the problem, they discovered that there had been widespread sexual abuse of the young men in the boarding schools. All of it was documented. And incredibly, some of those problems still exist at some of the boarding schools that remain in operation. In the late 1980s, a Senate select committee investigated sexual-abuse cases at Native American boarding schools. So this is not ancient history.

I am thankful that even though my father was raised in such a boarding-school environment, he did not buy into everything that was being taught. Fortunately, he came from a strong family, and because of his traditional upbringing, the school was not successful in alienating him from his culture. He was a confident man and, to my knowledge, he never felt intimidated in the non-Indian world—a world he came to know even better after he met my mother.

Her name is Clara Irene Sitton. She was born in Adair County on September 18, 1921, to Robert Bailey Sitton and Pearl Halady Sitton. My mother's family was made up primarily of the Sitton and Gillespie families, and their ethnic background was mostly Dutch and Irish. She does not have a drop of Indian blood in her veins, although she sometimes forgets she is white. From the day she married my father, her own life became centered around Cherokee family life.

My mother's ancestry goes back to North Carolina, where her kinfolk from the Sitton side were some of the first iron makers, while the Gillespies

were craftsmen who turned out fine long rifles. It is an intriguing possibility that the Sittons were related somehow to Charles Arthur Floyd, the Dust Bowl–era bandit from rural Oklahoma who was better known as "Pretty Boy" Floyd. They came from the same county in northern Georgia as Floyd and his kinfolk. This family legend has never been proved, but it was always exciting for me to consider, because "Pretty Boy" was a Robin Hood-style bandit, the subject of much myth.

My mother's father was born in 1874. I have been told that Grandpa Sitton was tall and distinguished looking. He was a farmer all of his life. He died, like my father's father, at a relatively young age, in 1932, during the Great Depression when my mother was only eleven years old. A few years before his death, my grandfather had skinned some rabbits and then went to the barn to harness his mules to plow. The mules apparently smelled the rabbits' blood on his hands and became frightened. They wanted to get out of the barn and, in the panic, they pushed my grandfather up against the wall. He suffered serious internal injuries which probably shortened his life.

My mother's mother was born in 1884 and lived until 1973. Her mother died when she was very young, so my grandmother went to live with her half sister, Ida Mae Scism Jordan, in Washington County, Arkansas. In 1903, when she was nineteen years old, Grandma Sitton left her home in Arkansas to visit friends. She came to the Wauhillau community in Indian Territory. That's where she caught the eye of my grandfather. At twenty-nine, Robert Sitton was a confirmed bachelor, but the vivacious, diminutive young woman captured his heart. After a brief courtship, they were married that same year and soon started their family. My grandparents set up housekeeping near Wauhillau, where my grandfather's parents, William and Sarah Sitton, lived. Wauhillau was a thriving new settlement made up of Cherokee people and white pioneers, many of whom had come from Georgia about the same time as the Sittons in 1891.

After a few years, my grandparents packed their belongings in a wagon and a two-seated buggy and moved. They settled on a small farm they bought near the eastern Oklahoma town of Titanic, presumably named after the famous British transatlantic liner that had sunk on her maiden voyage in 1912. They cleared the land to make it suitable for farming. Except for their oldest daughter, Sadie, who stayed with her grandparents in Wauhillau, they sent their children to the one-room Titanic schoolhouse. My grandparents had seven children—three sons and four daughters—born between 1904 and 1921. My mother was their youngest child.

After a couple of other moves, including a stop at the town of Foraker, Oklahoma, in the Osage country, where my grandfather worked for the railroad, they located in Adair County. Grandma Sitton was determined to raise her family in the fresh country air, so she was delighted when they found a farm for sale not far from the community of Rocky Mountain. That was where my mother was born.

I have heard it said that there was not a job on the farm my grandmother would not tackle, including plowing the fields. Folks described her as being spunky. Some years after my grandfather died and her children were raised, she sold her farm and moved into the town of Stilwell to run a boardinghouse.

My parents met when they were young. They had been around each other in the same area most of their lives. They would bump into each other at the general store in Rocky Mountain, a tiny settlement that attracted families from miles around. Mother can recall my dad teasing her when she was a girl. One time she even threw a pie at him. Even though he could make her as angry as a hornet, she was attracted by his good looks and quiet charm. They had a whirlwind courtship.

When they married, my mother was only fifteen years old. Dad was twenty-one. Of course, back in those days in the country, many folks married when they were quite young. My father was earning a rather precarious living by subsistence farming. He raised strawberries and peanuts for cash crops, picked berries and green beans for extra money, and traveled all the way to Colorado during the harvest time to cut broomcorn.

My grandmother was dead set against the marriage. My dad was older and had been raised in an Indian boarding school. He had also worked here and there, and had generally "gotten around." Although her oldest daughter, Sadie, had married a mixed-blood Cherokee, Grandma Sitton did not approve of my father because he was Cherokee. He was different. She objected strenuously to their relationship. But my folks were in love. They simply did not listen. They got married anyway. They went to the Baptist church in the Adair County community of Mulberry, where a Reverend Acorn married them on March 6, 1937. The relationship between my grandmother and parents was strained for the next several years.

By the time I was born in November of 1945, my mother, Irene, had come to learn the culture of the Cherokees. The name Mankiller, which sounds strange to most white people, was not foreign to her because she had lived in Cherokee country all her life and had attended school with many Cherokee people. And even years later, when I grew up, the Cherokee last names were not at all odd sounding to a girl in rural Oklahoma. In fact, Cherokee names in my family were familiar and, quite often, revered. I know family and friends whose surnames are Thirsty, Hummingbird, Wolf, Beaver, Squirrel, Soap, Canoe, Four killer, Six killer, Walking stick, and Gourd. Names such as those just are not unusual.

> The name of honor was received after a person had attained some kind of special distinction in the tribe. This would occur through the performance of an act of great character, or it could be given by a secret society. The second name marked a moment of excellence in a person's life and was not a hereditary position. Hereditary names, such as that of an Iroquois chief, were passed down successively to whoever filled the position for as long as there were people to fill it.
>
> Gerald Hausman, *Turtle Island Alphabet*, 1992

As I matured, I learned that *Mankiller* could be spelled different ways and was a coveted war name. One version is the literal *Asgaya*, meaning "man," combined with the personal name suffix *dish*, or "killer." Another is *Audacity*—an honorary title that also means "Man-killer." Our Cherokee historians and genealogists have always told us that Mankiller was a military title, but we also heard that there was another kind of Mankiller in our past. We know that in the Cherokee medicinal and conjuring style, Man killers were known to attack other people to avenge wrongs that had been perpetrated against themselves or others they served. This Mankiller could change things, often for the worse. This Mankiller was capable of changing minds to a different condition. This kind of Mankiller could make an illness more serious, and even shoot an invisible arrow into the body of an enemy.

Most of what I know about my family's heritage I did not learn until I was a young woman. That is when I discovered that many distinguished leaders from the past held the title of Mankiller throughout the various tribal towns. In the eighteenth century, for example, there was the Mankiller of Tellico, the Mankiller of Estatoe, and the Mankiller of Keowee. One prominent warrior and tribal leader, Outacity, or "Man-killer," apparently joined a delegation of Cherokees visiting London in 1762, during the troubled reign of King George III, fourteen years before the Revolutionary War broke out.

Even though our family name has been honored for many centuries, during the years, I have had to endure occasional derision because of my surname. Some people are startled when I am introduced to them as Wilma Mankiller. They think it's a fierce-sounding name. Many find it amusing and make nervous jokes, and there are still those times when people display their ignorance. For example, I was invited in December of 1992 to attend President-elect Bill Clinton's historic economic summit meeting in Little Rock, Arkansas, just about a month prior to his inauguration. *The Wall Street Journal*, one of America's most respected newspapers, made a rather unfortunate remark about my surname that is best described as a cheap shot.

"Our favorite name on the summit list," stated the *Journal* editorial, "we have to admit, is Chief Wilma Mankiller, representing the Cherokee Nation, though we hope not a feminist economic priority."

Tim Giago, publisher of *Indian Country Today*, a Native American newspaper, quickly fired back at the *Journal:* "The fact that this powerful lady has been featured in several major magazines . . . has appeared on countless television shows, and has been given tons of coverage in major, national newspapers, appears to have escaped the closed minds at the *Journal*. One has to ask if they ever get out into the real world."

Fortunately, most people I come across in my travels, especially members of the media, are more sensitive and generally more aware than that editorial writer. When someone unknowingly or out of ignorance makes a snide comment about my name, I often resort to humor. I look the person in the eye and say with a straight face that Mankiller is actually a well-earned nickname. That usually shuts the person up.

There were times in my childhood when I put up with a lot of teasing about my name. I would want to disappear when roll call was taken in school and everyone would laugh when they heard my name. But my parents told me to be proud of my family name. Most people these days generally like my name, many of them saying that it is only appropriate and perhaps a bit ironic that a woman chief should be named Mankiller. The name Mankiller carries with it a lot of history. It is a strong name. I am proud of my name—very proud. And I am proud of the long line of men and women who have also been called Mankiller. I hope to honor my ancestors by keeping the name alive.

But I have started my story far too early. Especially in the context of a tribal people, no individual's life stands apart and alone from the rest. My own story has meaning only as long as it is a part of the overall story of my people. For above all else, I am a Cherokee woman.

TRAVELING TRADITIONS

Deanna Kingston

Today, after a century of U.S. government policies concerning Alaskan Native people, it is not unusual to find someone like myself who claims a King Island Inupiaq identity without ever having lived on King Island, Alaska. I would like to demonstrate here how I,

"Traveling Traditions" by Deanna Paniatuq Kingston, King Island Inupiaq. Reprinted by permission.

a Native Oregonian, can actively claim this identity even though I currently live in the "Lower 48." My situation is not unique as there are many Native Americans throughout this continent who find themselves in a similar situation, due to various federal government policies that removed Natives from their lands, sent Natives to boarding schools, and strongly encouraged them to move to urban areas. Situations such as mine, which fundamentally change our concepts of identity formation, are common throughout the world. One theorist whose work helps to conceive of these new identities and cultures that are no longer bound by territory is Ulf Hannerz.

Hannerz uses the term *the global ecumene* to mean "the interconnectedness of the world, by way of interactions, exchanges and related developments, affecting not least the organization of culture" (1996:7). Hannerz prefers the term *transnational* over *globalization* because these linkages are not necessarily international as the term *globalization* implies. One aspect of this "transnational global ecumene" is the situation whereby "collectivities" of people who once resided in and were bounded by a particular territory are no longer limited to this territory. In other words, in the past, people's identities were usually defined by where they live. Now, however, because of the ease with which people travel and relocate to other territories, combined with the ability to communicate instantaneously with kin back home, our concept of "culture" must change. Due to this global ecumene, Hannerz now defines "cultures" as "packages of meanings and meaningful forms." Before, it was our assumption that cultures were distinctive to particular "collectivities" and "territories." But because of the ease with which people travel and communicate today, they can bring their traditions and other meaningful forms with them, showing that "culture" cannot be contained within a territory. Thus, the King Islanders, like other Native American peoples, bring their cultures with them as they move from their original territories.

Here, I intend to show the interconnectedness and transnational nature of the King Island Inupiaq community, which still exists although we live as far away from each other as Florida, Connecticut, Oregon, Arizona, and Alaska. The King Islanders are an Eskimoan peoples who used to live on a tiny island in the Bering Strait, 40 miles from the Alaskan mainland. However, due to various reasons, not the least of which is the BIA's (Bureau of Indian Affairs) decision to close the school in 1959, King Islanders are dispersed throughout Alaska and the Lower 48 States. Although the distances are far, we use various technological means to keep in touch with each other. Bear with me as I share an example.

In early fall 1998, on a Thursday evening in my (then) new home in Connecticut, I received an e-mail message from my maternal parallel cousin, Aisana. She told me that her father called her with the news that our mutual cross-cousin, Iilana, had been flown to the Alaska Native Service hospital in Anchorage, where she was in a coma. I was worried because Iilana was only a few years older than I and had always been very supportive of my research. I immediately forwarded Aisana's message to my mother since Iilana was one of my mother's favorite nieces. The next night, my mother called and said that both her brother, Aaluguq, and her step-brother, Aannayak, had called to tell her that Iilana had died. I e-mailed Aisana and then called her to see if she had heard the news, but I was unsuccessful in reaching her. The next day, I received an e-mail message from yet another cross-cousin, Quiruna, who lives in Nome and who is a parallel cousin to Iilana. Quiruna told me that Aisana was on her way to Nome for Iilana's funeral and would be staying with her. (Yes, I have many King Island cousins through my mother). Several days later, I e-mailed the news to yet another cousin, Kukuluk (or as he is known in English, Mark), who is a cross-cousin to me and Aisana and a parallel cousin to both Iilana and Quiruna and who lives in Arizona. He replied that his father had told him about her death over the phone.

Although the situation related here was a sad one, it does show how I, a King Islander in Connecticut, can keep and maintain my connections to my King Island kin, the children of four of my mother's siblings, who live in Oregon, Arizona, and Alaska. Today's telecommunication technology enables these connections and interactions to occur. However, I will note that these connections happened only because of and were facilitated by actual face-to-face interactions. In other words, although technology helps to maintain our connections, it is not a substitute for creating those connections in the first place.

Which brings me to the topic at hand: my interactions with my cross-cousin Mark, who now lives in Arizona. In 1997–1998, we were both living in Corvallis and working at or attending Oregon State University. Mark and I and our siblings were, for the most part, born and raised in Oregon. Thus, we are both King Islanders and Oregonians, which appears to be a contradiction in terms. My cross-cousin Mark and I share a special relationship, one that was traditionally characterized by teasing. The purpose of this "teasing" or "joking" relationship, which is widespread among Eskimoan peoples, is well documented in the ethnographic literature. Specifically, sets of teasing cousins would engage in behavior designed to embarrass one another. Ernest Burch (personal communication) recorded an example from a Kotzebue man: this man and his teasing cousin were hunting for seal on the ice. Just as they spotted a seal near its breathing hole and were crawling quietly toward it, the man farted, startling the seal, who disappeared into the breathing hole. The man's teasing cousin, who was crawling in front, looked back in shock, only to find his teasing cousin laughing at him. Teasing cousins were not to be offended or to get angry at these actions. This is because this relationship served another purpose: if a person misbehaved or acted inappropriately, it was the teasing cousin's job to tell him to change his behavior, an action which is *not* appropriate in any other context. The aspect of this relationship with which I am most familiar has to do with the composition of songs: in the King Island community, there were several sets of teasing cousins who composed humorous songs about each other. Once a teasing cousin song was composed by one person, his or her teasing cousin would "retaliate" with another song and dance (see Kingston 1996).

Mark's father (my uncle) lives in Portland, Oregon. He began teaching me and a few others how to Eskimo dance in 1991 (an aspect of King Island traditions traveling to Oregon). Part of our performance repertoire included several teasing-cousin songs and dances. At the time, I was a master's student at Oregon State, and the experience of this dance group became the basis of my master's thesis (Kingston 1996). In 1997, after a four-year absence, I moved back to Oregon and again became involved in my uncle's dance group. Both of my parents and my brother performed with the group as well as my teasing cousin, Mark. Mark was in his final year of undergraduate study at Oregon State. I was at OSU on a one-year teaching position in anthropology.

Since Mark is my teasing cousin—and since we have several teasing-cousin songs in our repertoire—at our very first performance that year, I teased Mark in order to demonstrate the concept for our mostly non-Native audience. Thus, began the teasing between the two of us. From then on, whenever Mark and I were both able to dance, our performances were characterized by retaliations and counter retaliations, which proved to be as much fun for the audience as they were for us. What follows is a brief description of some of this teasing.

In early November 1997, we performed at a benefit for Indian Art Northwest in Portland, Oregon. To retaliate from the September performance, Mark told a couple of jokes about me. In the first joke, he said that "Dede is so slow! If you want her to laugh at a joke on Monday, you have to tell it to her on Friday!" His second joke was as follows:

> Dede and two friends decided to go to a conference, but instead of driving, they took the train. At the train station, when buying their tickets, they bumped into three other people also going to the same conference. However, these three people bought only *one* ticket. Dede asked why they only got one ticket instead of three and they told her to watch. So, all six got on the train. The other three people crowded into one bathroom and when the conductor yelled for the ticket, one person stuck his arm out holding it. Dede and her friends thought that that was pretty smart, so after the conference was over, they bought only one ticket for the three of them. The other three people did not buy one at all. Dede asked why they didn't and they replied, "Watch and you'll see." So, they all got on the train and the other three crowded into one bathroom and Dede and her two friends crowded into the other. Then, when Dede and her friends weren't looking, one of the other three got out of the bathroom, walked by the door and yelled for the ticket as if he was the conductor. Dede put just her arm out and the other three got their ticket.

I had also planned some teasing for this performance. Several King Island dances involve the use of long gauntlet gloves. They are shoulder-length gloves made of dyed red sealskin with rattles attached to them. Shamans traditionally used them in their dances. I decided that, as a joke, I would make Mark a pair of these gloves. However, sealskin is rather rare in these parts, so I went to a local ladies' boutique and bought a pair of long, tight, white evening gloves that go up to the shoulder. I even bought some brown dye, but since the gloves were polyester, the dye turned the gloves a light lavender in color! Going along with the flow, I then decorated the gloves with bells (in place of rattles) and put some purple felt and fluffy cotton along the opening. I presented these lavender, belled evening gloves to Mark at this particular performance and subsequently made him dance wearing them. I do not know if the audience thought it was funny, but our group laughed so much, I guess the audience had to laugh with us.

Also, in October 1997, Mark was given the Best Undergraduate Oral Presentation award at the national AISES (American Indians in Science and Engineering Society) conference. This award came with laptop, $500, and a trip to Florida to go to the Kennedy Space Center. The OSU AISES chapter asked him to present the same paper at one of their meetings. I asked if I could introduce him, wanting to take advantage of another opportunity for teasing. I was proud of his accomplishments, but I was mindful that the teasing-cousin tradition was also used as a level-ing mechanism, designed to keep people from getting too boastful. So, in my introduction, I alluded to one of Mark's bad habits. That year, Mark asked me to teach him a little bit about the Inupiaq language. We made appointments to meet once a week, and Mark was always late. When I introduced him at the AISES meeting, I said "Mark, as smart as he is, is unable to tell time. So, I am giving him this children's book that will specifically tell him how to do it!" Of course, most of the audience knew about Mark's predilection to be late, and they all got a kick out of it.

Mark retaliated the next month. At a perfor-mance at the Blazer's Boys and Girls Club in Northeast Portland, Mark gave me a shovel, since I was working on my Ph.D. and would need some-thing to dig out of that which was being "piled higher and deeper," and a toy stethoscope, since I was going to become a "doctor." He made me dance wearing the stethoscope.

In January 1998, we performed at the Corvallis Public Library. To help advertise the event, I made up a flier. Mark's father is a big fan of Elvis and had taken to performing an Eskimo Elvis impersonation during our dances. Using that as a point of depar-ture, I designed a flier in which I cut and pasted Mick Jagger's hair onto a picture of Mark dancing. The idea behind it was that just as Mark is the next gener-ation of King Islanders after his father, so too Mick Jagger was the next generation of rock-and-rollers after Elvis. The result was a flier that advertised an Eskimo dance, complete with impersonations of Eskimo Elvis and "Kukuluk" Jagger. In retaliation, Mark asked the audience to sing the following words to the tune of the Oscar Mayer bologna song:

> My teasing cousin has a first name.
> It's D-E-A-N-N-A.
> My teasing cousin has a second name.
> Its K-I-N-G-S-T-O-N
> (make it fit).
> Because Dede Kingston has a way
> Of getting teasing by Mark each day.

In February, we had several performances. Mark was still late or not showing up for his Inupiaq lessons. In one performance, I gave him a calendar for the next five months, highlighting his appointments with me that he needed to keep and future dance per-formances (since he was constantly asking me, "When was that performance again?") and reminding him to show up for his own graduation. He retaliated with a

limerick about me, which I unfortunately (or is that fortunately?) do not remember.

During a performance in May, Mark was still late or not showing up for appointments, so I gave him a pad that could be hung on the refrigerator. The pad had seven sheets, and, on each sheet, I put a reminder or a saying that Mark was to repeat for that day. It was designed to be used over and over again each week. Examples of the reminders and sayings are: "I will remember to check my calendar for upcoming appointments"; "I will wear a watch"; "I will not over commit myself." Mark retaliated with a placard, which I was to hang in my office, that said: "I will get my Ph.D. in 1998 and I will beat Mark to it." At this point, I thought I would be finished, but because of procrastination on my part, it had not quite hap-pened, so this was Mark's dig at me to keep me hum-ble. What's interesting about this poster is that one can tear off the top sheet and the next sheet says "1999" and subsequent sheets say "2000," "2001," and "2002." (I did finish it in 1999.)

Finally, in June 1998, I cannot remember what I did to Mark, but he made me a pair of Eskimo-style boots to dance in. However, these boots consisted of a pair of old blue socks, into which were stuck the soles of an old pair of tennis shoes. He made me wear these makeshift boots just as I had made him wear the makeshift gloves the previous November.

Since we moved to Arizona and Connecticut in the summer of 1998, we have not teased each other as much. But because of what Hannerz calls the global ecumene, or the interconnections that are available to people because of our technological accomplish-ments, Mark and I have managed to continue. The latest two retaliations have occurred via regular mail and via the Internet. I sent him a poster I created in which I tease him for various silly things he has done throughout his life. He recently (March 2000) e-mailed me and said to check his Web site, where he provides a link to my "puny" Web site (which my institution posted before it was ready). Thus, he has retaliated for my poster of him.

The result of these actions and our dancing is that Mark and I and our families have become closer. We have formed our own King Island enclave in Oregon, thus demonstrating how we can be both King Islanders and Oregonians. Within this enclave, we try to practice some King Island customs: singing, drum-ming and dancing, and teasing. In other words, we brought some local King Island traditions into a more global context in Oregon. However, this traveling of traditions is not unusual. For instance, Fogel-Chance

(1993) showed how North Slope Inupiaq women living in Anchorage established and maintained their sharing networks among themselves and their relatives in Barrow in order to continue cultural ideals of food and resource distribution. These women also kept up cultural patterns of communal (rather than nuclear) child rearing and extended (rather than nuclear) family households. Fienup-Riordan (1998) also argued that Anchorage ("the largest Alaskan village") was undergoing a "Yupification" in that the Yupiit in Anchorage are building Yuppie steambaths, practicing and performing Yup'ik songs and dances, and maintaining their sharing networks. She also notes that Athabaskans and Inupiat people living in Anchorage are doing the same thing, showing that global practices are not replacing local ones; rather, these people who are traveling and living elsewhere tend to bring their local practices and identities into a more global setting.

But what has not necessarily been addressed is how the extension of these local practices and identities into a more global context has caused changes in those practices. Of course, folklorists have been aware for some time how different audiences and circumstances give rise to changes in performance, and our dance performances are no different. For instance, in our King Island enclave in Oregon, no matter how true to the local form we have tried to be, this change in context, particularly performing for a non-Native audience, has given rise to changes in the King Island dances we perform. First, we have a narrator or an announcer, usually me, who explains in English what our songs, stories behind the songs, and dances are. I give these long explanations because I find myself unable to appreciate Native American dancing at Pow-wows because I do not know what is going on and because of my earlier experience; when I heard my uncle play tapes of King Island songs in 1985, I found myself bored because I did not know the translation or why my uncle might suddenly laugh. So, I developed a style where I gave in-depth explanations of the movements, the teasing-cousin relationship, translations of the songs, and a narrative about the song's composition, so that the audience could appreciate our performances. However, when the Nome community dances at King Island hall, such explanations are never given because they are not needed. In fact, this sort of behavior on my part may be seen as an act of hubris. In performances for an outside or non-Native audience in Nome, someone may introduce the dance and give a brief statement about it. I have also witnessed King Islanders,

now living in Anchorage, giving a dance performance in New York City, and they also employed someone to explain the dances to the audience, although not to the extent that I did.

Another change we introduced into our performances was the very overt teasing that Mark and I engaged in. In fact, we do this teasing specifically for the audience's benefit. However, we rarely tease each other outside of the public sphere. In private, we generally abstain from this behavior, preferring instead an easygoing friendship. However, as we saw in Burch's example from Kotzebue, teasing between cross-cousins in local communities happened in both the private and the public spheres. Third, in a more local context, community and audience members join in the dances when they feel like it or if they know a particular song and dance. This participation, of course, does not happen with a non-Native audience. Fourth, our performances last anywhere from fifteen minutes to an hour. In the local context, these events often lasted for hours. Fifth, most of the dances we perform are the masked dances or the teasing-cousin songs with humorous stories. However, in the local context in Nome, with just community members present, an hour or more of bench dancing usually occurs. We rarely perform bench dances because non-Native audiences tend to respond more to the sight of exotic people dancing dramatic masked dances and to the humor in the teasing-cousin songs, so we consciously do these songs in order to entertain our audience. Sixth, we often created different dance motions to the King Island songs, so that, even though we use the same songs, our dance motions are different from those of the King Islanders in Nome or in Anchorage. Seventh, for each dance performance, my uncle carefully plans the sequences of songs we perform. In the local Nome community song sequences are not planned, although I believe the Anchorage group did plan their New York City performance. Finally, in recordings of songs from the 1930s and 1940s, Eskimo singers use a high-pitched voice, which is frequently commented on in the ethnographic literature. In contrast, my uncle, who was (and still is) influenced by Elvis and early rock and who has some training in Western music, sings in a voice that is lower-pitched than the tradition singers' voices, so there has been some leaking of global styles into the local form.

Thus, the change in performance context has caused some changes in King Island dance forms. Although we use the same songs as King Islanders in Nome or in Anchorage, and we share some similarities, we have created our own style of dance performance. How we relate to an audience, giving four- to five-minute explanations between dances in a planned sequence, is different from how the Nome community performs—without explanations and without a plan. Our performances are different yet again from the Anchorage King Islanders, who give explanations to their dances but not to the extent that I do. As Hannerz (1996:8) noted, and as Fogel-Chance (1993) and Fienup-Riordan (1998) imply, the general assumption is that cultures are homogeneously distributed within collectivities. In other words, since we are all part of the King Island collectivity, the practices and understandings of teasing-cousin songs and dance performances are thought to be homogeneous. However, Hannerz reminds us (1996:8), this "assumption that [culture] is homogeneously distributed within collectivities becomes problematic, when we see how their members' experiences and biographies differ." I hope I have shown that because our experiences and biographies in Oregon differ from those in Anchorage or in Nome, our performances have also differed. Thus, although local traditions traveled into the global context, when performed in these different settings, they become localized once again. I am reminded of a time when my uncle Aakaagak and his wife, Aapak, visited us from Nome and attended our performance at Oregon State. I asked them later what they thought of our dances, hoping that they enthusiastically approved of our efforts. Instead, they just said they thought they were okay. I was puzzled, but my mom and my uncle both thought that uncle Aakaagak and his wife liked our dance. So, I must assume that our performance really was all right, but they probably were puzzled at the length of my introductions and explanations.

REFERENCES

Fienup-Riordan, Ann. *Yup'ik Community in the 1990s: A Worldwide Web*. Manuscript, 1998.

Fogel-Chance, Nancy. "Living in Both Worlds: 'Modernity' and 'Tradition' among North Slope Inupiaq Women in Anchorage." *Arctic Anthropology*, 1993. 30(1): 94–108.

Hannerz, Ulf. *Transnational Connections: Culture, People, Places*. London: Routledge, 1996.

Kingston, Deanna M. "Illuweet (Teasing Cousin) Songs As an Expression of King Island Inupiaq Identity." *Anthropology Northwest*, no. 9. Corvallis: Oregon State University Department of Anthropology, 1996.

© 1997 H. J. Tsinhnahjinnie

LAKOTA WARRIOR

Frances Washburn

I see you, short and strong, running.
You were six years old, bold and brown,
I hear you, soft and slow, talking.
You were eight years old, quiet and calm.
I feel you, slap and tickle, playing.
You were twelve years old, fool and flirt.
I watched you, learn and leave, seeking.
You were eighteen, student, soldier.

All those years past–*yetsuko he?*
Sometimes I think of you and wonder what might
     have been.
I dream of you, sometimes, and I'm surprised at what is.

Where did you go? Where are you now?
In some remote rice paddy up near the DMZ?
Were your bones gnawed by some dogs
After you died on Tu Do Street where you went only to
Buy one round of Bommity Bom?
They say you were blown up in a fire bombing in Saigon,
S'ke.
They say you're in Cambodia with the montañards,
S'ke.
They say you stepped off a plane in San Francisco
In 1970, a stoned-out heroin addict, disappeared
S'ke.
S'ke.

All these years gone by. *Yetsuko he?*
Your name isn't on the Wall. I looked.
Come home. Just show up at the Sun Dance
Some bright summer day when the people are dancing
And the world is made anew.
Come home. All your relatives are waiting for you,
believing that someday, you'll diddibop home.

Frances Washburn, "Lakota Warrior," *Red Ink*, 14, no. 1 (Spring 2008): 23.

AMERICAN INDIAN AND ALASKA NATIVE HEALTH

Jennie Joe

Reports published by the United States Commission on Civil Rights (2003, 2004) conclude that American Indians and Alaska Natives[1] not only have a high percentage with poor socioeconomic circumstances but also have lower life expectancy than any other racial or ethnic group in the United States and suffers disproportionately from preventable diseases such as diabetes, tuberculosis, cancer, and alcoholism (U.S. Commission on Civil Rights, 2004. vol.3:789–798). Federal studies are meaningful because the federal government has a key role in the delivery and funding of health care resources for American Indians and Alaska Natives. The federal government not only provides direct medical care in some communities but also contracts or awards grants to tribes and urban organizations to provide health care services.

This chapter describes the history and polices that govern health care for American Indians and Alaska Natives. It reviews the contemporary health problems and challenges faced by the health care delivery resources, including the changing picture of health research and the efforts to address health disparities experienced by this population. American Indians and Alaska Natives experience common as well as unique health disparities, including limited access to health-care, and inadequate funding for health.

INDIGENOUS HEALTH RESOURCES

Prior to European contact, most tribal communities were self governing and had well established indigenous health care delivery resources, albeit some were

more complex and highly developed than others. At the core of most, was the belief that all aspects of an individual's life, mental, physical, and spiritual were interrelated. Daily lifestyle and activities placed emphasis on promoting health or the prevention of ill health or misfortune. These beliefs and practices were codified in various tribal taboos, customs, and these practices were taught from early childhood. Thus traditional native health healing practices were holistic as opposed to allopathic medicine which focuses on treating the physical symptoms and it the standard model for health care in the U.S. today. Social and cultural disruptions after contact changed these norms and subsequently had considerable negative impact on the health and life-ways of most tribal communities.

Archaeological evidence indicates the existence of a number of common diseases among Indigenous populations of the Americas before the European contact but warfare and waves of different infectious diseases changed only the demographic of the tribes but severely crippled their ability to maintain their healthy circumstances. The European contact on all the shores of the Americas brought epidemics of unfamiliar and devastating communicable diseases to a population that had no immunity or experience with them (Crosby 1972; Cook 1973). The indigenous healers and their array of treatments modalities were ineffective against these new diseases, and as the epidemics recurred, it resulted in drastic depopulation or extinction of certain tribes ("United States Native Population," this vol.). The rippling effects of the epidemics continued after certain communicable diseases waned. For example, smallpox epidemics often left survivors with unsightly facial and other disfigurement, which drove unknown numbers to commit suicide (E.W. Stearn and A. E. Stearn 1945; Fortuine 1984; Duffy 1951).

American Indian and Alaska Native Health by Dr. Jennie R. Joe. Reprinted by permission of the author.

[1]Native Americans, Indians, and American Indians and Alkaska Natives are used interchangeably in this chapter. Alaska Natives include Inupiat, Yupik, Aleuts, Tlingit, Haida, Tsimshian, Eyak and other Northern Athabaskan tribes.

Understandably, the consequences of communicable diseases also crippled tribes in other ways, especially since these diseases affected the most fragile, namely, the young and the elderly. Infant and childhood mortality slowed population growth while mortality among the aged destroyed a valuable resource for the survivors. In most tribes, elders are the irreplaceable repository of tribal history, language, and cultural knowledge. Because most experienced and knowledgeable healers are elders, the high mortality rates for this group also drastically decreased the tribes' number of skilled healers.

The arrival and settlement of the Europeans over time throughout the Americas also altered indigenous environments through the introduction of imported crops and animals. The importation of some of these unfamiliar domesticated animals and crops also added to the health problems of the Indigenous populations, some directly by the introduction of animal borne diseases through food sources and others indirectly by destroying and replacing indigenous vegetation used as herbal medicines (Head 2001; Boserup 1966; Viola and Margolis 1991).

Most tribes made use of indigenous plants to treat health problems and injuries. The plants were ritually harvested during certain seasons and prepared in a number of different ways. Some were used to treat minor ailments while others were saved for more elaborate healing ceremonies. Skilled herbalists were found in most tribal groups, and they not only treated patients directly but also supplied herbs to the community as well as to other practitioners. As western allopathic medicine evolved, significant numbers of the herbs used by Indigenous groups of the Americas such as digitalis became part of the Pharmacopeia of the United States (Vogel 1970; Shemluck 1982; M. Martin 1981).

Much of the natural world was viewed as sacred and spiritual by Native peoples and this world view was an integral part of daily living. To maintain health, individuals were taught to maintain a balance of the key strands of those elements that made up this state of health: the physical, the mental, the socio-cultural, and the spiritual. Native healers were therefore expected to tend to their patient's needs, which encompassed all of these strands. Dealing with the spiritual aspects of life required healers to be knowledgeable about the use of supernatural sources so that they could call upon these forces to aid them in assisting patients. This special knowledge and access to supernatural resources placed most healers in a uniquely powerful position within their communities. To diminish this powerful

position of healers and the importance of their ceremonies, colonial leaders outlawed some of the more important healing practices such as the Sun Dance in the Northern Plains and the ceremonial pot latches among tribes on the Northwest Coast (L. B. Boyer, R.M. Boyer, and A. E. Hippler, 1974).

The use of Native healers was also undermined in other ways. For example, some physicians (many of whom were missionaries or worked for various religious denominations) refused to provide medical care to Native patients if they exhibited any evidence of having utilized a tribal healer (Joe 2003; Primeaux 1977). The attack on tribal healers and tribal healing ceremonies added to the distrust Native peoples developed for Western medicine. This distrust has lessened over time, but initially many Indian patients did not come to hospitals or to clinics until there were no other alternatives, thus delaying seeking health care until it was too late for successful treatment or cure. The reluctance fueled the popular idea that hospitals were places of death, not places for restoration of health.

The acceptance of allopathic medicine grew gradually, helped by the introduction and use of antibiotics and other scientific medical advances. Today, allopathic medicine is used in all tribal communities, but the use of traditional tribal healing resources (where available) also continues, either alongside allopathic medicine or in combination with other forms of healing, including what is now called integrative or alternative medicine. The increased utilization of allopathic medicine has also been aided by the fact that traditional healing ceremonies are also no longer practiced in a number of tribes, primarily because there are no healers to conduct them.

FEDERAL ROLE IN HEALTH CARE

The new United States initially viewed tribes as sovereign nations and relied on treaties to formalize negotiations, especially in acquiring land. The treaties defined and designated lands ceded by the tribes to the government in exchange for certain benefits, including health care. To maintain these treaty obligations, the federal government placed the welfare of American Indians in the War Department, a unit named the Office of Indian Affairs. In 1836, shortly after it was established, the Office of Indian Affairs initiated the provision of health services to two tribes, the Ottawa and Chippewa (Sorkin 1971).

In 1849, the Indian Office was transferred to the newly established Department of Interior, where it was eventually renamed Bureau of Indian Affairs

(BIA). In 1873, the BIA established a medical and education division within its agency to develop and improve health and education programs for American Indians. At the time of this initiative, mortality rates attributed to infectious diseases were especially high, particularly gastrointestinal diseases which were complicated by severe malnutrition. By 1880, the government was managing four hospitals and had contracts with approximately 77 physicians (Bennett 1958). The health care services delivered during this time were focused primarily on Indian children enrolled in federal boarding schools. Finally in 1911, funding for provision of general but limited health care services for tribes was allocated by Congress.

As the core of the legal basis for the allocation of federal funds for Indian health became codified in the Commerce Clause in the United States, this then gave Congress the right to regulate commerce with Indian tribes and deal with tribes on a government-to-government basis (Bergman AB, Grossman DC, Erdich AM, Todd, JG, and R. Forquera 1999). And because this Constitutional clause distinguished American Indians and Alaska Natives from other minority populations in the United States, it is one of the key policies permitting allocation of federal health care funds for American Indians and Alaska Natives. How the federally supported health care gets delivered at the community level, however, varies and continues to change.

In 1971, the Alaska Native Claims Settlement Act was passed, releasing the remaining unclaimed Native land in Alaska for oil development. In payment for the land claimed by the Alaska Natives, the Act called for the establishment of regional (profit and not for profit) corporations (Mitchell 2001). Thus, while the federal government does provide funding and management of some health resources in Alaska, most regional Alaska Native corporations manage their own village clinics. The Alaska Native Medical Center in Anchorage, the largest hospital serving Alaska Natives, is also operated under a Native community board with representation from all 13 Regional Corporations.

Congressional allocation of funds for health care for American Indians and Alaska Natives is an annual decision, usually requiring lobbying efforts of a number of advocacy groups. The amount allocated varies from year to year because Congress views this allocation as discretionary, not as an entitlement. In other words, federal funding for Indian health is not mandatory or required as is funding for Medicare, which is an entitlement program.

The role of the federal government in the provision of health care services to American Indians and Alaska Natives is based on three major legislative actions: the Snyder Act of 1921; the Transfer Act of 1955; and the passage of the Indian Health Care Improvement Act in 1976. The Snyder Act directed the Indian Affairs Office to ". . . . direct, supervise, and expend such moneys as Congress may from time to time appropriate for the benefit, care, and assistance of the Indians throughout the United States. . . ." The Act included provision for "relief of distress and conservation of health." The Transfer Act allowed for the move of the health care service responsibility from the Bureau of Indian Affairs to the U.S. Public Health Service within the Department of Health, Education, and Welfare (currently named Department of Health and Human Services). The goal of the Indian Health Care Improvement Act has been to improve the health status of American Indians and Alaska Natives so that it becomes comparable to that of the general U.S. population (U.S. Congress. Office of Technology Assessment 1986).

Prior to the passage of the Snyder Act in 1921, a few congressional allocations were made to improve the health of tribes. In 1832, one federal allocation was made to buy and give smallpox vaccinations to selected American Indians. For example, the vaccinations were given to tribes considered "friendly" to the United States (Cohen 1982; J.D. Pearson 2004). The other priority for use of the smallpox vaccination was to administer it to Indians living near military outposts to protect military and non-Indian civilians living on or near the military compounds.

The federal government's self appointed role as guardian for the tribes continues to occur in different ways, sometimes in response to problems encountered. For example, one of the initial responsibilities of the government and the military was the control of trade, making it illegal for non-Indians to sell liquor to natives, though the policy has not always been easy to enforce. Today, the sale or possession of alcohol on many tribal lands is still illegal, but it has not prevented alcoholism or the abuse of alcohol.

Because access to alcohol varied from one tribe to another, the rates of alcohol abuse or alcoholism also differ geographically. A number of other health problems, however, were more common and prevalent across many reservation communities. These public health problems were documented at different time by different groups, one of the most notable included the Meriam Report (Meriam 1928; Cohen 1982; vol.4:309–310). Other disease specific surveys or studies were also conducted by various health organizations (Sievers and Fisher 1981). The results of these studies were mixed but some did pressure the federal government to provide needed resources to address the various health concerns. The piecemeal approach to funding Indian Health program ended with the passage of the Snyder Act. Under the Snyder Act of 1921, the BIA received additional funding to increase the number of health care providers, build new health facilities or to improve existing ones. The improvement of health care to Indian populations, however, was cut short by the advent of World War II. The war effort resulted in the reallocation of the federal resources, resulting in a drastic reduction in federal health resources for health care for tribes. Because of diminished resources, the health status among American Indians continued to deteriorate and mortality rates remained essentially unchanged (Shelton 2004; Sorkin 1971).

In 1954, the responsibility for Indian health held by the BIA was transferred to the U.S. Public Health Services within the Department of Health, Education, and Welfare. At the time of the transfer, some of the leading health problems were still various forms of infectious diseases, malnutrition; and infant and maternal mortality which were the leading causes of death. Public health improvements became a major challenge for the Indian Health Services (IHS). Significant progress was made by IHS in improving the health of American Indians, some of it helped by advances in modern medicine (Brenneman 2000).

URBAN INDIAN HEALTH CARE

Since the 1950s, the number of American Indians and Alaska Native moving to and living in urban communities had greatly increased. In 2000 slightly over 50 percent of American Indians and Alaska Natives lived live in urban or in other off-reservation communities (U.S. Census 2002). Some of this reservation-to-urban migration has been pushed by federal policies while other migrations were forced by lack of employment or educational opportunities on the reservations and in Native villages. Once they relocated, the improved quality of life was not realized; instead most of the relocatees found only meager economic improvement in existing city ghettos, barrios, and other unhealthy industrial sections of the city (Grossman DC, Kreiger JN, Sugarman JR, and RA Forquera 1994).

By the early 1960s, a number of urban-based Indian organizations with the help of advocates began to establish small free storefront clinics to serve Indian families without health resources. Over time, many advocated for the continuation of these clinics by lobbying Congress for a special "add-on" of the federal appropriation for urban Indian clinics as a part of the annual Indian Health Service funding. Fortunately, the passage of the Indian Health Care Improvement Act in 1976 gave the IHS authorization to fund or to support existing urban-based Indian health programs. Initially the "add-on" funded approximately 43 urban-based Indian health programs. In 2006 there were 34.

The types of health care services offered by the urban-based programs vary, depending on the size of their user populations, their proximity to existing Indian Health Service facilities, and their ability to attract and make use of other funding resources. For example, 20 of the existing 34 urban-based Indian health programs offer more direct medical services (Forquera 2001). These clinics face challenges. As the number of uninsured increase, the clinics are finding that the demand for services is rapidly outpacing their ability to provide quality health care. Some of this demand is also due to the increasing number of patients with multiple health problems that require costly care.

EXPERIENCES IN SELF DETERMINATION

For reservation-based tribes, the advent of The War on Poverty in the 1960s ushered in new and successful self-determination experiences for many tribal communities. The federal antipoverty programs allowed tribes to contract or to obtain grants directly from the federal government without going through the BIA. These experiences created a desire by many tribes to build and manage their own governmental infrastructures without permission or oversight by the BIA. The opportunity also helped tribal leaders form national or regional coalitions and began to advocate for ways to increase health resources. The National Indian Health Board became a strong advocate for tribes while the urban health programs also formed their own national organization. Native California tribes also successfully lobbied their state legislature to approve and establish a state Indian health office to help support a network of clinics serving rural and urban Indians.

At the national level, the passage of the Indian Health Care Improvement Act of 1976 (P.L. 94-437) is the most comprehensive legislative health action enacted by Congress. In addition to the provision of health care for urban Indians, the Act also included funding for recruiting and retaining health care professionals serving Native Americans and authorized construction and repair of health care facilities.

In 1975 Congress enacted the Indian Education and Self Determination Act (P.L. 93-638), authorized the BIA and the IHS to allow tribes to take over management of their health care facilities and resources. An amendment to this law now allowed tribes another choice, to reprioritize funds to target health problems they deemed most urgent. In the 1990s, presidential executive order instructed each federal agency to consult with tribal leaders on policies that affect their tribes prior to implementation of new federal programs or implementation of new policies. While the federal government has the majority role in the delivery of health care services to American Indians and Alaska Natives, the funding for these resources has never been sufficient (Joe 2003). For example, in fiscal year 2005, the federal government spent less on Indian patients per capita ($2,133) than it did for the U.S. general population ($5,518) (Indian Health Service 2006).

INDIAN HEALTH SERVICE

The IHS, like its federal counterparts in the armed forces and the Veterans Administration, has specific eligibility requirements that have to be met by those who seek their services. The most basic eligibility criteria used by IHS requires Indian patients to be enrolled members of a federally recognized tribe and to live on or near a tribal reservation or an Alaska Native village (General Accounting Office 2005). Each year, the number of individuals seeking health care from IHS continues to grow, some due to population growth and the addition of tribes who have been successful in getting federal recognition.

In 2006 there were over 560 federally recognized tribes in the United States. According to the 2000 U.S. Census, 2.4 million individuals self identified themselves as American Indians or Alaska Natives while another 1.6 million identified themselves as American Indian or Alaska Native in combination with one or more other ethnicity or race. The IHS serves approximately 1.8 million American Indians and Alaska Natives directly through their own facilities or those delivered by Tribes. In addition, there are approximately 600,000 more served by the 34 urban clinics. Although some medical and health services are provided directly by IHS, an increasing percentage of their budget is funneled to tribal programs through contracts or compact agreements. Today, 68 percent of 488 health facilities serving AI/AN in rural and urban communities are managed by tribes or Indian Organizations (National Indian Health Board 1998; Joe 2003; Roubideaux 2004).

As would be expected, meeting health care costs is a challenge for all health services providers. For example, one major automobile accident can deplete the facility's Contract Health Services dollars (funds set aside annually to cover catastrophic events). The facilities do bill third party payment sources but in many instances the patients may not be enrolled in Medicare or Medicaid (General Accounting Office 2005, M Dixon and Y Roubideaux 2001; Zuckerman et al., 2004).

HEALTH DISPARITIES

Although the health status and longevity of American Indians have improved since the IHS assumed leadership for Indian health, serious health disparities still exist, and health problems are actually increasing for some. Table 1 summarizes health disparities for American Indians and Alaska Natives compared to the national population.

From 1993 to 1997 mortality rates increased among American Indians and Alaska Natives for alcoholism and diabetes but remained constant for accidents, suicides, and pneumonia and influenza. Mortality rates from malignant neoplasms, while less than the mortality rates for the total population, increased significantly at the same time that mortality rates from cancer in the national population decreased slightly. It is worth noting that cancer incidences are low for this population, but cancer mortality rates are high due to late diagnosis and limited access to treatment. Table 1 also illustrates that mortality rates for heart disease continued to increase among American Indians and were slightly higher than the mortality rates for heart disease in the

TABLE 1: Mortality Rates Comparison of the American Indian Population and the U.S. Population all Races

Cause of mortality	1993	1997
Alcoholism	+579%	+638
Tuberculosis	+475%	+400
Diabetes Mellitus	+231	+291
Unintentional Accidents	+212%	+215
Suicide	+70	+67
Pneumonia and Influenza	+61	+67
Heart Disease	+8%	+20%
Malignant neoplasm	−15%	−2%

SOURCE: Trends in Indian Health (1997; 2004)

general population. A majority of the health conditions indicated are preventable.

Life expectancy for American Indians/Alaska Natives is approximately 6 years less than that for the general population, especially among young adults. Unintentional injuries as well as complications association with chronic diseases are two of the main contributors. For example, 13 percent of the mortality occurs among those under the age 25 (US Civil Rights 2003:34). Prolonged poverty, social and cultural disruptions, poor education, limited access to health care, and lack of political presence confound the issue of health disparities for American Indians and Alaska Natives (Trujillo 2000). Poverty rates for American Indians/Alaska Natives between 2003 and 2004 were 24.3 percent, almost similar to 24.4 percent reported for African Americans (Barens, Adams, Powell-Griner 2005). Approximately 27 percent of American Indian/Alaska Natives report they have no health insurance, a percentage that is higher than the 19 percent reported for African-Americans (2000 Census). A majority of American Indians and Alaska Natives without health insurance say they either depend solely on Indian Health Service, urban-based Indian health programs, or go without care (Schneider and Martinez 1997:6).

Data available on health behaviors of American Indians and Alaska Natives also indicate that they are more likely to smoke, abuse alcohol and be overweight, and are less likely to engage in leisure time recreational physical activity. Significant numbers of American Indians and Alaska Natives, especially females also report experiencing psychological distress (Barnes, Adams, and Powell-Griner 2005).

RESEARCH AND ETHICS

In many American Indian and Alaska Native communities, there is a strong resistance to research, including health-related research, and as a result tribes have established various means to exercise greater control over research projects being proposed or conducted in their communities. Most tribal organizations have established research committees, and the Navajo Nation has a federally certified Institutional Review Board. The community members serving on these committees or boards are not only asked by their respective tribes to help oversee studies once underway, but also initially to review the proposed studies to determine if they will benefit the tribe. Understandably, not all applications are

approved. A number of funding agencies have endorsed this practice by requiring investigators to provide documents indicating approval of their project by the tribes as a part of its proposal review process. Tribal research committees also require investigators to get approval from the tribe before publishing or presenting study results. The role ensures that publications of study results do not perpetuate negative stereotypes or other misinformation. Tribal agreements with investigators also ask for reviewing study results.

In many instances, the active role of tribes in research has also increased the demand for certain research methodologies over others. The community-based participatory research model is among those strongly encouraged. It gives tribes an active role in not only determining research priorities, but also in designing the studies as well as assisting with the data collection and analysis. Where tribes have the resources, they have established their own research units to carry out studies requested by the tribe or by governing Indian organizations.

Much of the early research conducted among tribes did not call for community partnerships, and strict protocols for protection of human subjects also did not exist. The consequences of these research activities have been both positive and negative. Some of the early recordings and observations are utilized by tribal members, while others are not acknowledged because they are found to be degrading or replete with misinformation. Other abuses include the lack of respect accorded those tribal members who not only were key informants, but also were not credited for their contributions. Moreover, researchers have not always been motivated to explore questions or problems viewed as important by the tribal communities they studied.

Genetic research proposals are routinely subjected to extra scrutiny by tribes because of their strong resistance to this type of research. In particular, the Human Genome Diversity Project (HGDP) which sought to understand the genetic variation of human species by sampling DNA of various populations worldwide and preserving these cell lines to be studied by future geneticists, has been the subject of some concerns. Indigenous populations are key groups identified as samples for HGDP researchers. Some Indian health advocates and Native researcher believe that future research using these cell lines will be conducted without their permission or patents claimed by researchers who collected the initial samples (Jonathan Marks 1995). Native communities are attractive for genetic research, especially those considered isolated and less contaminated by genetic admixture. One tribe in Arizona, for example, has filed a suit against a genetics researcher and her employers for failing to obtain new consent for conducting research that went far beyond the intent of the original study (Rubin 2004). To avoid breech of research ethics and to foster research partnerships with tribes, some academic institutions have drawn up and implemented special memorandum of agreement.

A branch laboratory of the National Institutes of Health has been operating at the Phoenix Indian Medical Center in Phoenix, Arizona since the 1960s, conducting research on type 2 diabetes, a major health program for the local tribe. While the scientific knowledge gained from these studies are continually welcomed internationally, the relationship between the tribe and NIH has had its share of frustrations, mainly because tribal leaders say they have yet to see a cure developed for diabetes (Sevilla 2000). The problem of diabetes is not only expensive and chronic but poses a serious threat to future survival of the tribe since diabetes is being diagnosed in children as young as age three. Childhood diabetes leads to early onset of costly and disabling diabetic-related complications (Gahagan, Silverstein, and the Committee 2003; Joe and Frishkopf 2006; Tanner 2006). The increase in chronic health problems for children and youth is in fact undoing gains made in improving the health of Indian children through immunization, prenatal care, and childhood nutrition programs.

Not all health-related research being conducted with tribes has been harmful. The participation of the Navajos in one clinical trial in the 1950s that tested the use of Isoniazid for treatment of tuberculosis was a significant contribution (Jones 2002). Another clinical trial conducted with the help of the White Mountain Apache Tribe in the 1980's helped prove that Hemophilus Influenza B vaccine can be useful for children (Dr. J. Justice, personal communication 1999). The Strong Heart Study among tribes from four regions of the United States (a longitudinal study on cardiovascular disease) and the Genetics of Coronary Artery Disease in Alaska Natives have contributed significantly to knowledge about heart disease, the impact of diabetes on heart disease, and the impact of familial or genetic factors on heart disease.

CONCLUSION

The 2000 census figures indicate that American Indians and Alaska Natives comprise a young population, but their health status is a reflection of an older generation, plagued by a growing number of chronic health problems and decreasing life expectancy. Many are eligible for federal health care provided by Indian Health Service or tribal health programs, but many of those living in off-reservation communities do not have health insurance or live in cities where access to health services is not easy. Where health data are collected, researchers find that significant numbers die from avoidable health problems such as diabetes, heart disease, cancer, unintentional accidents, homicide, suicide, some of which are preventable. Retrospective epidemiological data also indicate that major causes of morbidity and mortality for this population have shifted since the second half of the twentieth century from infectious diseases to chronic diseases.

Because the burden of many of these diseases is disproportionate for American Indians and Alaska Natives, intervention and health promotion programs call for community participation and for tribes to have a management role in their health care delivery systems. Increasing numbers now operate some or all of the health programs once managed by the federal government. In addition, tribes and urban groups are active in research, not only in supporting regional Epidemiology Centers, but also in charting their own health-related research priorities. Health researchers are partnering with tribal groups or are hired by them to conduct research that benefits the local communities. Today, health promotion and disease prevention efforts undertaken by tribes also utilize models that emphasize culture and language as an important element in decreasing avoidable deaths and illnesses.

REFERENCES CITED

Barnes, P. M., Adams, P. F. and E. Powell-Griner. 2000 *Health Characteristics of American Indian and Alaska Native Population: United States, 1999–2003. Advance Data from Vital and Health Statistics: No. 356.* Hyattsville, MD: USDDHS, CDC.

Bennett, E. F. 1958 *Federal Indian Law*. Washington, DC: Department of Interior. Government Printing Office.

Bergman, A. B., Grossman, D. C., Erdich, A. M., Todd, J. G., and R. Forquera. 1999 A Political History of the Indian Health Service. *The Milbank Quarterly,* 77(40) 571–604.

Boserup, E. 1966 *The Conditions of Agricultural Growth*. Chicago. Aldine Publishers.

Boyer, L. B., Boyer, R. M. and A. E. Hippler. 1974 The Alaska Athabaskan Potlatch Ceremony: An Ethnopsycho-Analytical Study. *International Journal of Psychoanalytic Therapy*. 3(3) 343–365.

Brenneman, G. R. 2000 Maternal, Child, and Youth Health. Pp.138–150 in *American Indian Health: Innovations in Health Care, Promotion, and Policy*. E.R. Rhoades, ed. Baltimore: The Johns Hopkins University Press.

Cohen, F. S. 1982 *Handbook of Federal Indian Law*. Charlottesville, VA: Michie Co.

Cook, S. F. 1973 The Significance of Disease in the Extinction of the New England Indians. *Human Biology*. 45:485–508.

Crosby, A. W. 1972 *The Columbian Exchange: Biological and Cultural Consequences of 1492*. Westport, Conn: Greenwood Publishing.

Dixon, M. and Y. Roubideaux. 2001 *Promises to Keep: Public Health Policy for American Indians and Alaska Natives in the 21st Century*. Washington, DC: American Public Health Association.

Duffy, J. 1951 Smallpox and the Indians in American Colonies. *Bulletin of the History of Medicine*. 25:324–341.

Forquera, R. A. 2001 *Urban Indian Health, Issue Brief*. Washington, DC: The Henry J. Kaiser Family Foundation.

Fortuine, R. 1984 Traditional Surgery of the Alaska Natives. *Alaska Medicine*. Jan–Mar., 26(1)22–25.

Gahagan, S., J. Silverstein and the Committee on Native American Child Health and the Section on Endocrinology. 2003 Prevention and Treatment of Type 2 Diabetes Mellitus in Children with Special Emphasis on American Indian and Alaska Native Children. *Pediatrics*. 112(4)328–347.

General Accounting Office (GAO). 2005 *Indian Health Service: Health Care Services are Not Always Available to Native Americans*, GAO-05-789. Washington, DC: GAO.

Grossman, D. C., J. W. Krieger, J. R. Sugarman, and R. A. Forquera. 1994 Health Status of Urban American Indians and Alaska Natives: A Population-based Study. *Journal of American Medical Association*. 271:845–850.

Indian Health Care Improvement Act of 1976. U.S. Code, Vol. 25, sec 1601 (1997).

Indian Health Service. 1997 *Trends in Indian Health, 1997*. Rockville, MD: USDHHS, PHS, Indian Health Service.

Indian Health Service 2004 *Trends in Indian Health, 2002–2001*. Rockville, MD: USDHHS, PHS, Indian Health Service.

Indian Health Service Profile. 2006 *Year 2006 Profile, Fact Sheet*. Rockville, MD: USDHHS, PHS Indian Health. Service. January.

Indian Self-Determination and Education Assistance Act, U.S. Code, Vol. 25, sec 450(1975).

Indian Trade and Intercourse Act of 1790, U.S. Code, Vol. 25, sec 177 (1997).

Joe, J. R. 2003 The Rationing of Healthcare and Health Disparity for American Indians and Alaska Natives. Pp. 528–551 in *Unequal Treatment: Confronting Racial and Ethnic Disparities in Healthcare*. B. Smedly, Ed. Washington, DC: National Academy, Institute of Medicine.

Joe, J. R. and S. Frishkopf 2006 "I'm too Young for This!": Diabetes and American Indian Children. pp 435–458 in *Indigenous Peoples and Diabetes: Community Empowerment and Wellness*. M. L. Ferreira and G.C. Lang, Eds. Durham, NC: Carolina Academic Press.

Jones, D. S. 2002 The Health Care Experiment at Many Farms, the Navajos, Tuberculosis and the Limits of Modern Medicine, 1952–1962. *Bulletin of History of Medicine*. 76:749–790.

Marks, J. 1995 Commentary: The Human Genome Diversity Project. *Anthropology Newsletter*.

Arlington, VA: American Anthropological Association. April.

Martin, M. 1981 Native American Medicine: Thoughts for Post Traditional Healers. *Journal of American Medical Association*. Jan. 245(2)141–143.

Meriam, L. 1928 *The Problem of Indian Administration*. Baltimore, MD: Johns Hopkins Press.

Mitchell, D. C. 2001 *Take My Land, Take My Life: The Story of Congress's Settlement of Alaska Native Land Claim, 1960–1974*. Fairbanks: University of Alaska Press.

National Indian Health Board (NIHB). 1999 Tribal Perspective on Indian Self-Determination and Self-Governance in Health Care Management. *National Indian Health Board Health Reporter*, Spring/Summer. Vol. 8, Issue 2.

Pearson, J. D. 2004 Medical Diplomacy and the American Indian. *Wicazo Sa Review*, 19 (1)105–130.

Primeaux, M. H. 1977 American Indian Health Care Practices: A Cross-cultural Perspective. *Nurse Clinicians in North America*. 12(1) 55–65.

Roubideaux, Y. 2004 *A Review of the Quality of Health Care for American Indians and Alaska Natives*. Silver Spring, MD: The Commonwealth Fund.

Rubin, P. 2004 Indian Givers. *Phoenix New Times*. Phoenix, AZ. May 27.

Schneider, A. and J. Martinez. 1997 *Native Americans and Medicaid: Coverage and Financing Issues, Policy Brief*. Washington, DC: Kaiser Family Foundation. December.

Sevilla, G. 2000 20 Years of Research for What? Tribe Ask. Phoenix, AZ: *Arizona Republic*. October 31.

Shemluck, M. 1982 Medicinal and Other Uses of the Composite by Indians in United States and Canada. *Journal of Ethnopharmacology*. May. 5(3) 303–358.

Shelton, B. L. 2004 *Legal and Historical Roots of Health Care for American Indians and Alaska Natives in the United States, Issue Brief*. Washington, DC: The Henry J. Kaiser Family Foundation. February.

Sievers, M. I. and J. R. Fisher. 1981 Diseases of North American Indians. Pp. 191–252 in *Biocultural Aspects of Disease*. H. R. Rothschild, Ed. NY: Academic Press.

Sorkin, A. L. 1971 *American Indians and Federal Aid*. Washington, DC: Brookings Institution.

Stearn, E. W., and A. E. Stearn. 1945 *The Effect of Smallpox in the Destiny of Amerindian*. Boston: Bruce Humphries.

Tanner, L. 2006 Pima Indian Study: Early Diabetes Augurs Early Death. Tucson, AZ: *Arizona Daily Star*. July 26.

Trujillo, M. H. 2000 *One Prescription for Eliminating Health Disparity Legislation*. Unpublished Manuscript. Rockville, MD: DHHS, PHS, Indian Health Service.

U. S. Commission on Civil Rights. 2003 *A Quit Crisis: Federal Funding and Unmet Needs in Indian Country*. Washington, DC: Office of Civil Rights. July.

U. S. Commission on Civil Rights. 2004 *Broken Promises: Evaluating the Native American Health Care System*. Washington, DC: Office of Civil Rights. July 2.

U. S. Census. 2002 *Census 2000 Brief: The American Indian and Alaska Native Population*. Washington, DC: U.S. Department of Commerce, U.S. Census Bureau.

U.S. Congress, Office of Technology Assessment. 1986 *Indian Health Care*, OTA-H-290. Washington, DC: U.S. Government Printing Office. April.

Viola, H. J. and C. Margolis 1991 *Seeds of Change: Five Hundred Years since Columbus*. Washington, DC: Smithsonian Press.

Vogel, V. 1970 *American Indian Medicine*. Norman: University of Oklahoma Press.

Zuckerman, S., J. Haley, Y. Roubideaux and M. Lillie-Blanton. 2004 Service Access, Use and Insurance Coverage among America Indians/Alaska Natives and Whites: What Role Does the Indian Health Service Play? *American Journal of Public Health.* 94:53–59.

A shortened version of this article was published in *Handbook of American Indians, vol. 2, Indians in Contemporary Society*: 97–105. Edited by Garrick A. Bailey. Smithsonian Institution, Washington D.C., 2008.

THE EPIDEMIOLOGY OF ALCOHOL ABUSE AMONG AMERICAN INDIANS
THE MYTHICAL AND REAL PROPERTIES

Philip A. May

Because of the drunken Indian stereotype and other myths often associated with American Indians, it is important to critically examine the detailed evidence that best defines the epidemiology of alcohol abuse among Indians and particular tribal communities. Public health understandings and programs must be based not on myth but on fact. In this paper, twelve major myths, statements, and questions about the nature of the alcohol abuse problem are reviewed. An analysis of current mortality data and an understanding of the extant literature will reveal that many current myths are either false or, at best, half-truths. . . .

IS ALCOHOLISM THE NUMBER ONE HEALTH PROBLEM AMONG AMERICAN INDIANS?

That alcoholism is the leading health problem among Indians is probably the most popular and common statement about alcohol and Indians that one hears from laymen and health professionals alike. It is

Philip A. May, "The Epidemiology of Alcohol Abuse Among American Indians: The Mythical and Real Properties," *American Indian Culture and Research Journal* 18, no. 2 (1994). Copyright © 1994 by Regents of the University of California. Reprinted with permission. A portion of the original article and the endnotes have been omitted.

accepted as gospel by many and is seldom questioned or elaborated on in the planning and implementing of alcohol abuse prevention programs. Yet it is a half-truth at best.

In table 1, an analysis of the most recent Indian Health Service data from 1986 to 1988 indicates that 17.0 percent to 19.0 percent of all Indian deaths are probably alcohol-related. Similar patterns and data are common in other years as well. These data are quite complete in scope, for they include an estimate of the percentage of alcohol-related deaths from motor vehicle and other accidents, suicide, homicide, and alcoholism/alcohol dependence. Therefore, it is true that alcohol is involved in a very high percentage of Indian deaths—substantially greater than the general U.S. average of 4.7 percent. But the term *alcoholism* can be very misleading. Alcoholism generally denotes only alcohol-dependent or chronic drinking behaviors, which are only part of the problem. In table 1 the data are broken down to compare deaths from behaviors that are generally the result of alcohol-abusive drinking patterns (sporadic, binge drinking) with those that result from alcohol-specific/alcohol-dependent drinking styles (chronic, "alcoholic" drinking). In 1986–88, 2,213, or 74.9 percent, of all alcohol-related deaths were from alcohol-abusive

TABLE 1: Estimated Alcohol-Involved Deaths of American Indians in Reservation States, 1986–1988, and the U.S. General Population, 1987

Cause of Death	Total Indian Deaths (N) ×	Estimated % Alcohol Involved =	Indian Alcohol-Involved (N)	Alcohol-Involved U.S. (N)	Alcohol-Involved from Nine IHS Areas* (N)
Alcohol Abusive					
Accidents					
Motor Vehicle	1,687	(.65)	1,097	31,389	847
Other	1,278	(.25)	320	11,683	250
Suicide	534	(.75)	401	23,099	302
Homicide	494	(.85)	395	16,962	279
Subtotal	(3,993)		(2,213)	(83,133)	(1,678)
Alcoholic/Alcohol-Specific**	(742)	(1.00)	(742)	(15,909)	(580)
TOTAL	4,735		2,955	99,042	2,258
Deaths as a percent of total deaths	27.2%		17.0%	4.7%	19.0%

SOURCE: Computed from U.S. Indian Health Service, *Trends in Health and Regional Differences in Indian Health*.

*IHS states that data are more complete in nine of their service areas (Aberdeen, Alaska, Alburquerque, Bermidji, Billings, Nashville, Navajo, Phoenix, and Tucson). The far right column only includes these nine areas.

**Alcoholic-specific deaths include the following causes: alcohol dependence syndrome, alcoholic psychoses, and chronic liver disease and cirrhosis specified as alcoholic.

causes, while 742, or 25.1 percent, were from alcohol-specific/alcohol-dependent causes (alcohol dependence syndrome, alcoholic psychosis, and chronic liver disease specified as alcoholic). Therefore, one would be more accurate in stating that alcoholism per se is not the leading cause of death among Indians. More accurately, alcohol abuse and alcoholism combine to be the leading cause of mortality.

Alcohol-induced morbidity (sickness) is also a great problem among Indians. Again, though, alcohol abuse and alcoholism combine to cause the illness. In fact, alcohol-abuse produces more sickness and injury than do alcohol-specific or alcoholic behaviors. This is also true in mainstream U.S. society.

The importance of these distinctions is great. If public health officials and citizens focus solely on chronic alcoholic behaviors and problems in their planning of intervention and prevention, they will miss the majority (three-fourths) of the problem. Complete alcohol abuse prevention and intervention programs must address the full range of alcohol-abusive and chronic alcoholic behaviors.

DO INDIANS METABOLIZE ALCOHOL DIFFERENTLY OR MORE SLOWLY THAN DO PEOPLE OF OTHER ETHNIC GROUPS?

The most persistent myth about Indians is that they have particular biophysiological reasons for "not being able to hold their alcohol." In fact, not only do non-Indians believe this, but many Indians also believe that their ethnic group has a biological deficit in metabolizing alcohol. One survey among the Navajo asked if Indians have a biological weakness to alcohol that non-Indians do not, and 63 percent of the respondents said yes.

This myth has virtually no basis in fact. Only one study ever reported that Indians metabolize alcohol more slowly than non-Indians, but it was criticized as highly flawed in its use of controls and other methods. All of the remaining studies of alcohol metabolism among Indians have found Indians to metabolize alcohol as rapidly as, or more rapidly than, matched controls who were non-Indian. Furthermore, liver biopsies have shown no discernible difference in liver phenotype between Indians and non-Indians.

Therefore, no basis at all for this myth is found in the scientific literature, and it should not be a consideration in current prevention and intervention programs. Major reviews of alcohol metabolism among all ethnic groups usually conclude that alcohol metabolism and alcohol genetics are traits of individuals and that there is more variation within an ethnic group than there is between ethnic groups. Further, when biophysiologic investigators attempt to explain major alcohol-related behaviors, they generally point to sociocultural variables as the major factors.

ARE INDIAN ALCOHOL-RELATED PROBLEMS UNIQUELY INDIAN?

Certainly some alcohol-related behaviors in which Indians participate seem to be unique in their manifestations. Indeed, this was a major theme of the early literature. But what is often overlooked in practical explanations of Indian drinking behavior is that there are many similarities between Indians and other groups. Further, there may also be common explanations for both Indian drinking and that practiced by other groups.

First, the fact that Indians have high rates of alcohol-related death is influenced by demographic traits. The American Indian population is very young in almost every community. The median age of Indians is in the low twenties overall and is commonly much lower on some reservations. In 1988, the U.S. median age was 32.3. Young populations tend to have much higher rates of death from a number of alcohol-related causes (e.g., motor vehicle and other accidents, suicide, and homicide) than do populations that are elderly or middle aged. Because of the demography of many Indian communities, one would expect to find higher rates of these problems than in the more middle-aged U.S. mainstream. Conversely, one would also expect lower rates of death from chronic diseases such as heart disease, stroke, and cancer among Indians.

Second, geography plays a role in alcohol-related statistics. Because the majority of Indians still live in rural western states, higher death rates are to be expected due to factors such as higher-risk environments, distance from care, time lag to care, and reduced availability of services. Alcohol-related injuries may be more common in rural western environments. Also, serious injuries (from events such as motor vehicle crashes) often become deaths because of the distance to, and timing of, care.

Third, social, political, legal, and local policies may create conditions that exacerbate alcohol-related problems and rates. The low socioeconomic status of many Indians shapes their behavioral patterns. Also, because most reservations are still under prohibition, drinking styles and patterns are such that higher rates of alcohol-related arrest, injury, and mortality are more likely to occur. Changes in policy similar to those enacted in other groups and societies might eventually produce very different alcohol consumption characteristics and patterns of alcohol-related problems. In addition, upward changes in social class and education in the future would change drinking and alcohol-related behavior patterns.

Finally, tribal culture or social practices may contain some of the seeds of both problems and solutions. Elevated rates of alcohol-related death from automobile accidents may arise from dangerous cultural practices such as not wearing seat belts and not

being licensed and well educated in safety and/or defensive driving. The same can be said of many other subgroups of the U.S. population. Even if a person is driving while intoxicated, he might not become an alcohol-related statistic if he is strapped in by a seat belt. Unpublished data from New Mexico surveys show a lower use of seat belts among the youth of some tribes as compared with non-Indian youth in the same schools. But some tribes have higher rates of belt use than others.

In summary, the explanations of high rates of alcohol-related problems and their solutions may well be found in demographic, geographic, political, and cultural variables that are not necessarily uniquely Indian. Researchers, planners, and others must not overlook these relatively simple and conventional explanations in either their studies of etiology or their designs of solutions.

IS THERE A HIGHER PREVALENCE OF DRINKING AMONG INDIANS?

It is often said or implied that a vast majority of Indians drink. Frequently, I have asked audiences at a number of reservations, "What percentage of your adult population drinks?" The response for most sites was frequently "90 percent" or greater. Similar responses about Indians are also common within the mainstream population of the U.S.

The evidence in the published literature is quite different from what most people believe. In fact, there is extreme variation in prevalence of drinking from one tribal group to another. Unfortunately, however, only a handful of extant adult prevalence studies have been published. Nevertheless, from these studies one can conclude that adult prevalence is lower in some tribes than the U.S. general averages; in others, it is about the same as or higher than U.S. averages. Furthermore, drinking prevalence may vary over time in many tribal communities.

Two prevalence studies among the Navajo in 1969 and 1984 indicate that, in both periods, fewer Navajo adults drank at all (31 percent and 52 percent) than adults in the general population of the U.S. (67 percent). But these same studies indicate that Navajo drinking prevalence is increasing.

Two similar studies among the Standing Rock Sioux showed that prevalence was decreasing (69 percent to 58 percent). In 1960, overall drinking prevalence was about the same as in the general population; twenty years later, it was lower than U.S. averages (67 percent).

Studies were also carried out among two other tribes. The Southern Ute and the Broken head Ojibway of Canada demonstrated drinking prevalence rates (80 percent and 84 percent) higher than U.S. averages. The prevalence of adult drinking among Indians, therefore, varies widely from tribe to tribe and over time. Variation over time is also found with Indian youths.

These prevalence studies provided other significant findings as well. Among those who do drink in these tribes, there is a substantially higher prevalence (two to three times) of problem and excessive drinking indicators than among the general U.S. population. Consumption of more than five drinks per situation, as well as experience with delirium tremens (DTs) and blackouts, are much higher in these studies. Therefore, among those Indians who drink, there is a substantial number of problem drinkers who produce a high frequency and variety of problems such as arrests, morbidity, and mortality.

More positive findings are also found in these studies. For example, among Indian males who are in their middle age and older, more have completely quit drinking than among most other groups of U.S. males. Also, in virtually every tribe, a lower proportion of the women drink.

Therefore, the overall prevalence of drinking among Indians is not the most important variable in the epidemiology of drinking. What is more important are the drinking styles, some of which emphasize very problematic behaviors.

DO ALL INDIANS DRINK IN THE SAME MANNER OR STYLE?

Tribal and urban studies have reported various styles of drinking. Most researchers describe two patterns that cause either no or few alcohol-related problems: abstinence and moderated social drinking. But at least two problem drinking patterns are common among subgroups or "peer clusters" in many tribal communities. One is a chronic alcoholic drinking pattern that Frances Ferguson has called "anxiety" drinking. The other is the "recreational" pattern defined by Ferguson and others.

Recreational drinkers are predominantly young (age 15–35) males who are students or relatively new participants in the work world; they drink sporadically for special occasions, at night and on weekends, away from home, and in a celebration or party manner. Some young females also participate in this pattern, but they are less involved and generally for a

shorter period of time. This drinking style is not unlike college fraternity drinkers. Indian recreational drinkers are at very high risk for alcohol-related injury, arrest, and death because of the emphasis on high blood alcohol levels for a "blitzed" experience. Many people mature out of this pattern, but a disproportionate number of Indians die young from recreational drinking.

Anxiety drinkers, on the other hand, are more typical of the chronic alcoholic. They are downwardly mobile, unemployed, and socially marginal to both Indian and non-Indian society. They are predominantly male, but some females fit this pattern. They tend to drink chronically, whether alone or with other drinking buddies. Anxiety drinkers are commonly found spending long periods of time in border towns or in skid row areas of many western cities.

These two types of problem drinkers produce the alcohol-abusive and alcohol-specific problems described earlier. The recreational drinkers produce many of the accident and suicide deaths, while the anxiety drinkers produce the alcoholism deaths (e.g., cirrhosis of the liver) and a preponderance of the pedestrian-vehicle collision deaths.

In summary, there are a number of drinking styles among Indians that affect the epidemiological patterns and create a challenge for prevention and treatment. There is no one Indian drinking pattern.

WHY ARE INDIAN RATES OF DEATH FROM ALCOHOL-RELATED CAUSES SO HIGH?

Many of the answers to this question have already been presented in previous sections. However, the common, stereotypical answer to this question is that "Indians are like that." Just as it is said that the "Irish drink because they are Irish," it is said that "Indians drink because they are Indian." The simple, logical extension of this, then, is that high rates of drinking produce high rates of alcohol-related death and other problems. But we have seen that the prevalence of drinking alone does not explain the high rates of alcohol-related death among Indians.

Recent IHS data (see table 2) indicate that Indians die more frequently than the U.S. averages from motor vehicle accidents (2.95 to 3.89 times higher); other accidents (2.99 to 4.05 times higher); suicide (1.53 to 1.95 times higher); homicide (1.97 to 2.34 times higher); and alcoholism (5.45 to 7.63 times higher). These ratios of Indian to U.S. averages reflect rates, not the actual numbers of deaths. There are three elements of explanation for this different experience. One element can be

TABLE 2: Age-Adjusted Mortality (rates per 100,000) from Alcohol-Abusive and Alcohol-Specific, Causes for American Indians, 1986–1988, and the U.S. General Population, 1987

Cause of Death	Estimated Alcohol-Involved	All IHS Areas	All U.S.	Ratio IHS/U.S.	Nine IHS Areas*	Ratio Nine Areas/U.S.
Alcohol Abusive						
Accidents						
Motor Vehicle	.65	57.5	19.5	2.95	75.2	3.89
Other	.25	45.5	15.2	2.99	61.5	4.05
Suicide	.75	17.9	11.7	1.53	22.8	1.95
Homicide	.80	16.9	8.6	1.97	20.1	2.34
Subtotal		(137.8)	(55.0)	(2.51)	(179.6)	(3.26)
Alcoholic/Alcohol-Specific**	1.00	(32.7)	(6.0)	(5.45)	(45.8)	(7.63)
TOTAL		170.5	61.0	2.79	225.4	3.69

SOURCE: Computed from U.S. Indian Health Service, *Trends in Indian Health and Regional Differences in Indian Health.*

*IHS states that data are more complete in nine of their service areas (Aberdeen, Alaska, Albuquerque, Bermidji, Billings, Nashville, Navajo, Phoenix, and Tucson). The far right column only includes these nine areas.

**Alcoholic-specific deaths include the following causes: alcohol dependence syndrome, alcoholic psychoses, and chronic liver disease and cirrhosis specified as alcoholic.

found in the previous sections, which deal with demographic, social, and political considerations discussed in the literature. The second element of explanation is centered on drinking style. The flamboyant drinking styles that are very common in a number of Indian peer clusters (recreational and anxiety drinkers) emphasize abusive drinking and high blood alcohol levels. Further, heavy drinking peer groups among many tribes encourage, or do not discourage, the frequent mixing of alcohol impairment, risky behavior, and risky environments. Driving while intoxicated, sleeping outside in the winter, aggression, and other unsafe practices are examples of this element.

The mixing of (1) high-risk environments, (2) flamboyant drinking styles, and (3) risky post-drinking behavior combine to elevate Indian rates of alcohol-related death far above those of the general U.S. population. This is true as well with arrest, injury, and other problems for which statistics are recorded.

HOW IS THE DRUNKEN INDIAN STEREOTYPE PERPETUATED BY A NAÏVE AND UNCRITICAL USE OF STATISTICS?

Many authors and speakers on the topic of Indian drinking and alcohol-related problems often cite statistics that do not capture an unduplicated count of the individuals involved in abusive drinking. For example, if one looks at alcohol-related arrest rates, there generally is little opportunity for knowing if the data reflect the experience of a few or a large number of individuals. In Gallup, New Mexico, Ferguson found that 115 alcohol-dependent Navajo males accounted for almost twelve hundred arrests in 1.5 years. A careless or uncritical researcher could report this as twelve

hundred Navajo with a problem, rather than one hundred with a chronic drinking problem and repeated arrests.

When working on my doctoral dissertation in Montana, I stumbled across a situation and calculated an overall arrest rate that further emphasizes this point. On one small Northern Plains reservation (<3,000 people) the arrest rate was 100,103 per 100,000 from 1970 to 1974. In other words, a literal and naive interpretation would be that every man, woman, and child had been arrested at least once during the five-year period. My, what a criminal place one could imagine with these data! Further, 75 percent of these arrests were for alcohol-specific crimes on a dry reservation. Could this mean that three-quarters of all the men, women, and children are such problem drinkers that they are arrested? Certainly not. It was a situation where a small proportion of the population (mainly males) spent time in a "revolving door" situation. They drank excessively in nearby border towns and on the reservation and were in and out of jail, time and time again. How absurd the uncritical use of aggregate and duplicative data such as these arrest statistics can be! But such data frequently are presented uncritically in newspapers, lectures, and even academic and agency program papers.

The same can be said of morbidity data. One person with a drinking problem can generate literally dozens of visits to a clinic, inpatient admissions, and emergency incidents. IHS data showing a large number of patient encounters should not be taken to indicate the prevalence of the problem. Counts of individuals, not visits, should be used for epidemiological purposes, and, even then, one is dealing only with treated prevalence. For example, in a chart review study of IHS records in the Southwest covering ten years, 21.4 percent of the individuals who visited six IHS general clinic facilities were seen at least once for a mental health or alcohol abuse problem. This is not a substantially high percentage based on U.S. estimates. The vast majority of inpatient episodes (83 percent) by these individuals, however, were for alcohol and substance abuse, as were 53 percent of outpatient visits. On average, each episode of mental health and alcohol-related illness presented by these individuals accounted for 3.9 outpatient and inpatient visits before the problem was fully dealt with or was cured. Therefore, just from looking at visits, one might conclude that the problems were much more extensive. Thus, morbidity data, like arrest data, can be highly duplicative in counting or estimating problems, even when estimating treated prevalence.

One should always ask, then, "Are the prevalence data that are being presented representative of true prevalence or treated/clinic prevalence?" Or, more importantly, "Are they nothing more than workload data?" Too often, arrest, morbidity, social welfare caseload, and other statistics are merely workload, contact, or activity counts. Unduplicated data, such as random surveys of individuals in the population to document adult drinking, are best for estimating prevalence. Further, school-based youth surveys tell us little or nothing about adults. Mortality data are much better for estimating prevalence, because people die only once. Indian epidemiological information has suffered greatly over the years, because data used have not often enough been unduplicated counts that provide valid measures of prevalence. In populations with a substantial concentration of high-risk, heavy drinkers, this has led to inaccuracy and distortion of the true extent of the problem. Measuring the repetitive, high-risk, and problematic behavior of a subculture of problem drinkers within a tribe, and using it uncritically, can stigmatize the whole tribe.

WHAT IS THE LEVEL OF SEVERITY OF DRINKING AMONG THE ALCOHOL-ABUSING POPULATION?

Within the drinking populations of most Indian communities, a substantial number of people drink very heavily. These people are found in both the recreational and anxiety drinker populations.

More than 70 percent of Indians who die in traffic accidents in New Mexico have been drinking. A University of New Mexico study of all ethnic groups in the state found that American Indian decedents from crashes had very high blood alcohol concentrations (BAC). The average BACs of those who had

been drinking and were killed in vehicular crashes in New Mexico were Indian .191, Hispanic .189, and Anglo .128. All ethnic groups, therefore, were averaging levels well above the legal intoxication level (.10). Indians killed in alcohol-related crashes had BACs significantly higher than those of the Anglos but not much higher than those of the Hispanics. A full 85.7 percent of the Indian and 82.5 percent of the Hispanic victims who had been drinking were above the legal limit. This compared with 55.4 percent of the Anglos. Thus, the level of drinking among the Indians and Hispanics who drink is very high, probably indicating similar sociocultural patterns of drinking by certain peer clusters among the two groups.

A comparable pattern of blood alcohol levels exists for Indian decedents from suicide. Among those Indians who die from suicide in New Mexico, 69 percent to 74 percent (depending on the year studied) are alcohol-involved, with the alcohol level being quite bimodal. In other words, one-fourth of the victims tend to be completely sober, while three-fourths have very high BACs, as above (work in progress).

Research indicates, then, that those who're members of alcohol-abusing peer clusters in many tribes drink in a manner that produces very high blood alcohol levels. Both suicide and motor vehicle accidents are alcohol-related in a majority of cases. These results also support the notion that there is a connection between heavy drinking and risky behavior.

WHAT IS THE RELATIONSHIP BETWEEN CHILD ABUSE, CHILD NEGLECT, AND ALCOHOL?

The one major study that has examined, in detail, the relationship between child abuse and neglect and alcohol use demonstrates clearly that alcohol often is involved. In northern New Mexico, 85 percent to 93 percent of the Indian child neglect cases and 63 percent of the child abuse cases involve alcohol. Neglect, abuse, and alcohol problems were found to be part of a complex found in a number of multi problem families where intergenerational transmission of pathology was present.

A subsequent paper from the above study compares the abuse/neglect sample to a matched group of Indian control families. Alcohol use and abuse was found to have been present in 58 percent of the control homes at one time or another, as compared to 88 percent in the abuse/neglect target groups. This control study concluded that alcohol seems to be a necessary, but not sufficient, condition for child abuse. This is not unlike the relationship with suicide.

TABLE 3: Estimated Alcohol-Involved Causes of Death for U.S. Indians and Alaska Natives, 1986–1988,** and the U.S. General Population, 1987, by Age, Sex. Rates per 100,000, and Number.

									Rates						
Cause of Death	15–24		Ratio	25–34		Ratio	35–44		Ratio	45–54		Ratio
	Ind.	U.S.		Ind.	U.S.		Ind.	U.S.		Ind.	U.S.	
Male												
MV accident	97.0	55.5	1.7	104.7	36.8	2.8	86.2	25.6	3.4	65.7	21.8	3.0
Other accdt	42.5	18.6	2.3	63.5	23.6	2.7	77.1	23.8	3.2	59.9	23.4	2.6
Suicide	40.7	21.3	1.9	49.6	24.8	2.0	30.3	22.9	1.3	21.7	23.8	0.9
Homicide	32.1	21.9	1.5	44.7	23.3	1.9	38.6	17.1	2.3	19.4	12.1	1.6
Alcoholism*	0.8	0.1	8.0	21.8	3.2	6.8	65.5	12.9	5.1	98.6	24.4	4.0

Total deaths for above causes	4307	2705
% of all Indian deaths	19.6%	12.3%
% of all male Indian deaths	42.1%	26.5%

Female												
MV accident	30.7	19.7	1.6	39.5	11.5	3.4	32.2	9.3	3.5	27.8	9.2	3.0
Other accdt	8.2	3.5	2.3	13.1	4.8	2.7	16.9	5.2	3.3	13.3	6.4	2.1
Suicide	6.5	4.3	1.5	8.3	5.9	1.4	9.3	7.2	1.3	5.0	8.5	0.6
Homicide	10.2	6.0	1.7	10.4	6.9	1.5	9.3	4.8	1.9	4.4	3.6	1.2
Alcoholism*	1.2	0.1	12.0	16.8	1.4	12.0	25.1	4.2	8.4	57.3	7.6	7.5

Total deaths for above causes	1474	951
% of all Indian deaths	6.7%	4.3%
% of all male Indian deaths	20.5%	13.2%

SOURCE: Computed from U.S. Indian Health Service, *Trends in Indian Health.*

*Alcoholism deaths include the following causes: alcohol dependence syndrome, alcoholic psychoses, and chronic liver disease and cirrhosis specified as alcoholic.

**Includes all Indian and Alaska Natives in all parts of the 32 reservation states served by IHS (total deaths in reservation states 1986–1988 = 21,943).

IS ALCOHOL ABUSE ONLY A MALE PROBLEM?

Alcohol abuse, in the form of both alcohol related and alcohol-specific/dependent behavior, takes its greatest toll among Indian males. IHS data from 1986 to 1988 (see table 3) indicate that the number of Indian male deaths from alcohol-related and alcohol-specific causes is much higher (N = 2,705) than for Indian females (N = 951). This is true in every category. Twenty-six percent of male deaths are alcohol involved, whereas 13 percent of female deaths are. Stated another way, in a typical three-year period, 12.3 percent of all Indian deaths are related to alcohol use by males, and 4.3 percent are related to alcohol use by females.

Further, according to the rates in table 3, male Indians fare far worse than U.S. males in general. For example, in a comparison of Indian and U.S. males ages 25–34, the rate for motor vehicle accident deaths among Indians is 2.8 times higher, for other accidents 2.7 times higher, for suicide 1.9 times higher, and for homicide 1.5 times higher; the alcoholism rate is 6.8 times higher.

Indian females, however, do not fare much better in comparison with U.S. female rates. In the same age category (25–34 years), Indian female rates are 3.4, 2.7, 1.4, 1.5, and 12.0 times higher than U.S. females. Thus, Indian females have higher rates of alcohol-involved

death than U.S. females in general, and this is true in most age categories and alcohol-involved causes.

Therefore, although the numbers indicate that alcohol-abusive mortality and alcohol abuse are mainly (in numbers) an Indian male problem, Indian females are also at high risk compared to other U.S. women. This should be kept in mind for alcohol treatment and prevention in Indian Country. Indian women who are in the alcohol abusing categories also have a strong need for attention, especially regarding alcohol-specific causes. The number of female deaths from cirrhosis of the liver (w/alcohol), alcohol dependence, and alcoholic psychosis is one-half the number (46.2 percent) of Indian male deaths from these causes. Chronic alcohol dependence problems are, therefore, more equally shared among Indian females and males than the other alcohol-related causes of death.

IS FETAL ALCOHOL SYNDROME (FAS) A MAJOR PROBLEM FOR INDIANS?

Like many of the problems mentioned above, FAS rates vary greatly from one reservation to the next. Two studies have been carried out on Canadian Indian communities with widespread alcohol abuse, and high rates of FAS have been found. Another study

Rates						Number		
55–64		Ratio	65—74		Ratio	Total Deaths (all ages)	× Est. % alcohol-involved	Total alcohol-involved (all ages)
Ind.	U.S.		Ind.	U.S.				
52.2	21.7	2.4	65.6	24.6	2.7	1452	(65%)	944
82.3	30.3	2.7	113.0	42.6	2.7	1139	(25%)	285
12.2	26.6	0.5	16.7	34.8	0.5	546	(75%)	410
13.0	8.8	1.5	12.6	6.2	2.0	521	(80%)	417
95.4	33.1	2.9	79.5	27.0	2.9	649	(100%)	649
18.3	10.2	1.8	17.7	13.7	1.3	577	(65%)	375
22.8	10.6	2.2	43.7	21.1	2.1	358	(25%)	90
4.6	7.7	0.6	2.4	7.2	0.3	107	(75%)	80
4.6	2.5	1.8	1.2	2.8	0.4	132	(80%)	106
50.2	9.4	5.3	20.1	7.3	2.8	300	(100%)	300

found higher rates of FAS recorded on Indian birth certificates in the U.S. than among any other ethnic group. One other study found both high- and low-risk communities in the same region, with variance based on differing sociocultural and drinking patterns found in the communities. The range of FAS rates in these studies is from a high of 190 per 1,000 children to a low of 1.3 per 1,000 children. However, studies that were based on the largest populations of Indians who were living in relatively stable reservation communities documented rates only slightly higher than the U.S. estimated rate in the 1980s. The overall Southwestern Indian rate in 1978–82 was 4.2 per 1,000, compared to 2.2 for the U.S. overall. Further, the U.S. rate for all races may well be underreported.

Bray and Anderson and Chavez et al. suggest that, among Indians, better surveillance and more complete reporting of FAS occurs. This may be true both in the disrupted Indian communities that were highly alcohol-abusive and therefore were studied by researchers, and also in general birth certificate recording.

Much of the newspaper, popular media, and conference coverage of FAS has been highly dramatic and quite distorted. The figures quoted of "one in three" or "one in four" Indian babies being FAS have no support at all in screening, epidemiologic or scientific studies. This is even true for the small, most highly alcoholic communities such as the one studied by Robinson et al. Furthermore, the more disrupted communities studied are not representative of Indian communities in general. In the studies done among Indian populations where culture and society are more intact, FAS rates are much lower. It is no more accurate to project an FAS rate from one or two disrupted, alcohol-abusing communities onto all Indians than it would be to project the rate from an urban, skid row census tract to all of the U.S. population.

In general, the scientific literature points out that FAS is an "equal opportunity" birth defect and can affect any ethnic group where there are sufficient levels of maternal drinking. FAS, to a great degree, depends on the quantity, frequency, and timing of maternal drinking. In many tribes, there are more alcohol-abstaining women than in the general U.S. population. This obviously protects a substantial portion of Indian children from FAS and lowers levels of prenatal alcohol damage. In almost every population ever studied, a very small number of women produce all of the FAS children. This is very true in Indian epidemiologic studies of other problems as well.

FAS prevention, however, has been cited as an extremely promising area for American Indians. In fact, it is apparent that Indians today are very aware of FAS as a problem, and a large number of established FAS initiatives and prevention programs are underway in Indian communities.

CAN PREVENTION PROGRAMS DESIGNED FOR ONE TRIBE BE ADJUSTED AND APPLIED TO OTHERS?

In spite of the unique social and cultural nature of each tribe, prevention and intervention programs designed for one tribe can be used in others. It has often been implied that each tribal community is so distinctive that programs have limited or no applicability across tribal settings. But a detailed knowledge of the particular history, culture, and current epidemiological features of alcohol abuse in a community will allow for fine tuning and adaptation to other, somewhat similar tribes and communities.

Knowing the demographic and epidemiologic features (age; sex ratio; cultural, social, and economic indicators; mortality; morbidity; fertility; and gender-specific drinking patterns) of a community will facilitate the design and implementation of successful programs of prevention and treatment. The problem with some efforts in the past was that local data were not utilized or available, and relevant studies were not always done. Further, when epidemiological understandings are very general or poor and programs are based on myth, failure is more likely. Facts such as those presented in this paper are the building blocks of prevention and intervention. Improvement in the alcohol-abuse dilemma of Indian communities will require a detailed and specific understanding of the characteristics and epidemiology of the population. Indian health professionals have a responsibility to seek out such data and apply them carefully and sensitively.

CONCLUSION

Many of the myths and common understandings about alcohol use among American Indians are gross oversimplifications. As Benjamin Franklin once stated, "Half the truth is often a great lie." If they are to succeed, programs of prevention and intervention must not be built on common mythical understandings but on empirical fact. Unfortunately, facts and detailed truths are not sought or believed frequently enough.

"The truth is sometimes a poor competitor in the market place of ideas—complicated, unsatisfying, full of dilemmas, [and] always vulnerable to misinterpretation and abuse." As this paper has demonstrated, the truth about Indian drinking is indeed complicated and quite different from the myths. But the insights and explanations that emerge from seeking the facts are those that will help create meaningful improvement.

DELFINA CUERO: HER AUTOBIOGRAPHY

Florence Connolly Shipek

Many stories were told us all the time. The stories used to tell how people are and what to expect from other people in the way of behavior. I only remember a few of the stories now; it is so long since I have heard them.

In the beginning of time lots of wild animals were like people and could talk. There was a coyote and he was a bad man. He was always trying to deceive people and do things that he shouldn't. Then there were these two beautiful girls who were crows and who lived in a tree. An old woman was taking care of the girls and guarding them. But she went to sleep because she was too old. The coyote sneaked up and tried to climb the tree but he couldn't. Then he jumped and jumped but he couldn't reach the girls. The girls couldn't go to sleep because coyote made so much noise jumping. So the girls flew up into the sky and coyote was chasing them and crying and begging them to take him along. The younger girl asked, "Why can't we take him with us?" The older one said, "No, he can't fly." The younger replied, "Why can't we throw something down and pull him up so he can go with us?" But the older one said, "He's too bad; he would eat us." The younger girl must have been falling in love with him because she felt sorry for him. She finally threw down the end of a rope and coyote began climbing up into the sky toward the crow girls. As coyote climbed, he began talking about how he wanted to grab that girl. The older sister got upset and then mad as she heard him talking. She said, "Let's get rid of him. He'll hurt us. He's too different." The older sister cut the rope so that coyote fell and died.

This story explains how we have to watch men—there are some good and some bad men. We knew that these stories were told to teach us how to behave and what to expect. The old people did not have to tell us what the story explained at the end of the story, but I am saying what it meant to us.

Things like that I was told by my grandmother. I still live by the old rules and I've never been sick. I stay away from my daughters when they are pregnant too. When a lady is pregnant, she must not look at anything that is bad, or even see a fox or a snake. You must not look at anything like that or it will mark the baby. You try not to see anything when you are pregnant. The old timers would not let a pregnant woman or a menstruating woman go into a garden. She had to stay by herself and not bother anything. She could not gather wild greens, or was hand do things like that. She could not go near sick persons or garden plants without hurting them.

Grandmothers taught the girls that when they were pregnant they must not eat too much or the baby will be born big or have some kind of trouble. They can eat anything they want unless it makes them sick, except they must stay away from salt. Women are weak nowadays. Long time ago, they just kept on doing regular work, they went out and gathered food and whatever was needed, even heavy things, and it didn't hurt them. They just had to be careful not to see bad things.

In the real old days, grandmothers taught these things about life at the time of a girl's initiation ceremony, when she was about to become a woman. Nobody just talked about these things ever. It was all in the songs and myths that belonged to the ceremony. All that a girl needed to know to be a good wife, and how to have babies and to take care of them was learned at the ceremony, at the time when a girl became a woman. We were taught about food and herbs and how to make things by our mothers and grandmothers all the time. But only at the ceremony for girls was the proper time to teach the special things women had to know. Nobody just talked about those things, it was all in the songs.

But I'm not that old, they had already stopped having the ceremonies before I became a woman, so I didn't know these things until later. Some of the other girls had the same trouble I did after I was married. No one told me anything. I knew something was wrong with me but I didn't know what. Food was becoming hard to find then and we had to go a long way to find enough greens. My husband was away hunting meat. Sometimes the men were gone for several days before they found anything. One day I was a long way from Ha-a looking for greens. I had a terrible pain. I started walking back home but I had to stop and rest when the pain was too much. Then the baby came, I couldn't walk any more, and I didn't know what to do. Finally an uncle came out looking for me when I didn't return. My grandmother had not realized my time was so close or she would not have let me go so far alone. They carried me back but I lost the baby. My grandmother took care of me so I recovered. Then she taught me all these things about what to do and how to take care of babies.

After that, I had my babies by myself. I didn't have any help from anybody. My grandmother lived near us but she knew that now I knew what to do, so she never helped me. I did what I had been taught. I used xa'a· nayul [*Trichostema parishii* Vasey, mint family] or kʷa·s [*Rhus laurina Nutt.,* sumac] to bathe in and I drank a little kʷa·s tea also.

I dug a little place and built a hot fire and got hot ashes. I put something, bark or cloth, over the ashes and put the baby in it to keep the baby warm.

So that the navel will heal quickly and come off in three days, I took two rounds of cord and tied it, and then put a clean rag on it. I burned a hot fire outside our hut to get hot dirt to wrap in a cloth. I put this on the navel and changed it all night and day to keep it warm till the navel healed. To keep the navel from getting infected, I burned cow hide, or any kind of skin, till crisp, then ground it. I put this powder on the navel. I did this and no infection started in my babies. Some women didn't know this and if infection started, I would help them to stop it this way.

When each baby was new born, I bathed it in elderberry blossom or willow bark tea. Then after I had washed the baby's face with elderberry blossom tea, I burned some honey real brown, then put water with it and cleaned the baby's face all over. This takes any stuff [scale?] off the baby's face. The afterbirth is buried in the floor of the house.

Some people are not careful and they eat right away and then the mother nurses the baby and it gets infected. The mother must wait a while to eat, then first eat atole. Next, the mother eats lots of vegetables and drinks lots of herb or mint teas. Never drink water! Never eat beans when nursing a baby, it will ruin the baby.

I did all this myself. When my children were older, if they got sick, I used herbs. That is all I used and my children got well again. There are herbs for stomach pains, colds, tooth aches, and everything that the Indians knew. There is a real good one to stop bleeding right away from a bad cut. There is another good one for bad burns and to stop infection. If a woman drinks lots and lots of xa'a· nayul she can keep from having babies, but there is another herb, even better, that the Indians used to use to keep from having babies every year. They are hard to find now because we can't go everywhere to look for them any more.

I named all of my children myself. I didn't know anything about baptizing them then; I just went ahead like the Indians did and gave them names. When my oldest child was a year or two old, they had a party to welcome him to the group. Everybody got together and they built a big ramada for me and they brought their food together. We had a big fire. I had an uncle that lead the singing and dancing. He led a big xa·tu·p i·mac [fire dance]. They circled around the fire hand in hand and following each other, and jumping with both feet and singing. They were glad because they would have more Indians, another baby added to the group. All the people brought presents for the baby—baskets, ollas, food, mud dolls, or bow and arrows and different things, whatever was right to start the child. Sometimes they also brought tiny things like the real ones, tiny ollas and baskets and bow and arrows. The child was given its name at the party.

By the time my second child who lived was old enough, we didn't have parties for the new children any more. I don't know why, maybe it was too hard to get enough to eat. I'm just telling what happened to me, what I know.

From *Delfina Cuero: Her Autobiography. An Account of Her Last Years and Her Ethnobotanic Contributions*, by Florence Connolly Shipek. Reprinted by permission of the author.

PERSPECTIVES ON TRADITIONAL HEALTH PRACTICES

Larry Murillo

The professional literature related to American Indian/Alaska Native (AI/AN) traditional health practices (THP) is growing. This article uses a broader perspective on THP that includes the practice of medicine people, community ceremonies, and any other sociocultural practices, beliefs, attitudes, and behaviors related to health from an AI/AN perspective. This perspective will broaden the discussion beyond access to sociocultural resources, such as a medicine person or specific practices such as sweat lodges and talking circles, which are noted in professional journals. This broadened perspective will more accurately portray the complexity of health issues in AI/AN communities.

Four issues are presented to illuminate the need for employing and researching THP for AI/AN communities. The first issue identifies support for and barriers to THP in public health research. The second issue describes competing cultural values that have implications for the definition and treatment of illness. The third issue is a brief discussion of broadening community support for THP through building resource capacity using a healthy-community concept. The fourth and last issue will address implications for research and the potential benefits for AI/AN communities.

THP are cited in various professional journals, and their use has been the focus of several studies. Buchwald et al (2000) report that 70 percent of urban AI/AN patients in primary care used traditional health practices. The results of this study suggest that health care providers should anticipate use of THP among urban AI/AN clients. Kim and Kwok (1998) found that 62 percent of Navajo patients had used Native healers, and 39 percent used Native healers on a regular basis. Their study summarized the most common reasons for visits to a medical provider and

the frequency of concomitant use of Native healers. Use of Native healers was highest for arthritis, abdominal pain, depression/anxiety, and chest pain. Gurley et al. (2001) studied service use among AI/AN veterans, comparing use patterns of biomedical care with those of traditional healing options and testing whether utilization varied as a function of need or of availability. Results indicate that traditional options were used more where such options were more readily available. The current service ecology on the Northern Plains and Southwest reservations incorporates both traditional and biomedical forms and has been described aptly as a pluralistic system.

Several researchers have studied such specific traditional practices as the talking circle, storytelling, and sweat lodges. The talking circle produced consistent and significant improvement in levels of knowledge about cancer. Storytelling was combined with the talking circle in one study, and the researchers found that storytelling and talking circles are valuable tools for improving the health of AI/AN people. The sweat lodge ceremony (SLC) has been an integral part of Navajo (and many other tribes') culture for hundreds of years. The role of the SLC has examined in jail-based treatment of alcohol abuse and is a start in providing empirical insight into the traditional ways of Native Americans.

Talking circles, storytelling, and sweat lodge ceremonies comprise a small sample of THP used for individual and community health interventions. Studies are needed of THP utilizing Native healers, herbal medicines, cultural diets, philosophy, traditional ceremonial grounds, healing ceremonies, and traditional forms of living such as hunting, fishing, and shepherding. "Healthy" THP, such as learning an AI/AN language, running, participating in cultural games or powwows or arts and crafts, and recognizing "life passage" events (e.g., birth, death, and marriage), also play a role in the broad sense of healing.

From Larry Murillo, "Perspectives on Traditional Health Practices." Pages 109–115 in *Healing and Mental Health for Native Americans*, ed. Ethan Nebelkopf, New York: AltaMira Press, 2004.

Many indications point to the effectiveness of THP. Native and normative professionals alike are beginning to see the benefit of THP use in AI/AN health agencies. The first landmark support for THP came in 1978, when the American Indian Religious Freedoms Act was passed, signaling the United States government's recognition of traditional medicines and religious ceremonies in health-related matters among AI/AN people. In spite of the repression of Native religions, the ancient art of indigenous healing has survived intact and is still practiced today. Within their communities, indigenous healers continue to provide holistic healing using ancient methods and techniques that have been passed down.

Prior to this recognition by the government, THP had been pushed underground. People in California, for example, remember when their relatives were practicing healing ceremonies but could not even tell their own family of their cultural practices. They could not discuss their beliefs because of the fear of retribution from the Christian church and police. Native practices were generally considered evil and synonymous with witchcraft, devil worshipping, and pagan religion. Even after the Religious Freedoms Act became reality, many Native healers were hesitant to bring their beliefs and practices into the open. This reluctance is beginning to change.

Today a network of indigenous healers acts as a support system lot the AI/AN professionals and community members who ate reviving THP in their personal and professional lives. This informal network exists in both rural and urban settings. Many times a healer from a specific tribe will visit urban settings with a significant population of AI/AN people of the same tribe. Other healers travel to various geographical areas within and between states.

A physician who works in an AI/AN health agency may be aware of this informal network but usually does not have direct access to it. Usually a Native employee, such as an administrator, a clinician, a clerical support worker, or a maintenance or janitorial employee, has contact with individuals or networks of indigenous healers. Each health agency is different in the ways it uses THP activities. The medical, dental, health promotion, and administrative departments of health agencies tend to work less directly with indigenous healers and more with other types of educational activities related to THP. Alcohol and drug abuse programs use sweats and work with Native healers more directly than the medical services do.

Navajo patients in a study (Kim and Kwok 1998) in Crownpoint, New Mexico, commonly sought help from traditional healers for arthritis, abdominal pain, and chest pain. Pain is often difficult to treat and may lead sufferers to explore numerous interventions in hopes of relief. In this situation, AI/AN patients may be more likely to turn to the culturally salient options embodied in then healing traditions than to more recently popularized alternatives (e.g., acupuncture and massage). Traditional health practices often focus on underlying causes, conceptualized as spiritual in nature, rather than on the relief of acute symptoms.

Traditional healing practices are often a significant element of family, community, and spiritual life. In AI/AN communities, traditional healing ceremonies long predate biomedical care. Traditional healing is used to address both the physical and the spiritual needs of AI/AN people. Many people choose alternative or complementary services in keeping with their social networks and belief systems. Increased understanding of this deeply rooted system can improve communication between providers and patients and therefore can help medical providers improve the quality of care provided.

BARRIERS TO TRADITIONAL HEALTH PRACTICES

Research gives some examples of tribal-specific and general ideas concerning barriers. In their research with the Navajo tribe, Kim and Kwok (1998) found that cost was cited by 36 percent of the patients in their study as the reason for not seeking Native healer care and was the most common barrier to Native healer care.

The cost of visiting a Navajo healer includes such customary expenses as transportation, food for all those who participate in a ceremony, and costs of materials needed, such as buckskin or herbs.

It is a common practice for Native healers not to "charge" a fee for their work. A Native healer in modern times must hold a regular job to support a family. In addition to their full time employment, Native healers are expected to serve the community on a twenty-four-hour basis. Native healers are required to travel long distances when they are requested to work with Native patients. The burden of time and travel expense is on the healer. Native people who are aware of this situation typically will help out with healers' travel expenses by finding a place for them to stay, feeding them, and pooling money to pay for gas and for a healer's time. This is done without the healer's requesting a payment. This burden on the Native healer is a major reason so few people will commit to a healer's lifestyle of voluntary community service.

Kim and Kwok found that a lack of trust in Native healers (25 percent), the patient's own religion (23 percent), unsupportive families (12 percent), lack of belief in traditional Navajo medicine (11 percent), lack of knowledge about traditional Navajo medicine (7 percent), good health (4 percent), and lack of local Native healers (3 percent) also acted as deterrents to Native healer care. An important issue surfaced when many patients reported that they did not trust certain individuals claiming to be Native healers. While these patients still believed in traditional Navajo medicine, they could not find a trustworthy practitioner. One patient stated, "There are a lot of quacks out there," applying the term *quacks* to those masquerading as Native healers. In addition, Gurley et al. (2001) include personal time as a barrier: Some ceremonies require a week to perform, and consultations may take hours.

The Indian Health Service (IHS) has a policy that supports access to AI/AN medicine people in order to protect the right of AI/AN people to their traditional beliefs and health practices. However, the IHS does not directly cover payment for traditional health services, and any cost is typically paid "out of pocket" by the patient. There are exceptions, such as when an IHS or tribal program will invite and pay a stipend to a Native healer. Typically the clinic will schedule the healer to work throughout the day and to see a variety of patients.

One final barrier is the unfair expectations of patients who seek treatment from a Native healer. Duran and Duran (1995) state, "our (Native) people place [a] tremendous burden on 'true' spiritual leaders as they pressure them for miracles and quick magical fixes for the pain and suffering that never seems to end."

In pluralistic systems, people pursue hierarchies of resort in selecting particular providers. If the first resort does not produce improvement, other systems will be tried until satisfaction is achieved. Those who are not familiar with traditional Native medicine usually seek it as a last resort. More study is needed in the area of THP and health outcomes.

COMPETING CULTURAL VALUES

Traditional health practices are steeped in the philosophy, language, culture, and ceremonies of AI/AN communities. This "system" of health care was systematically replaced by a medical system provided by the United States government and administered by the IHS. One basic distinction between the AI/AN system and the medical system is the way they each perceive health. The medical approach focuses on physical symptoms, etiology, and interventions. Native medicine uses a holistic approach that includes individual health dimensions: the physical, mental, spiritual, and environmental context of the person.

Waldram (1996) notes there is no concrete evidence concerning whether and how traditional medicine actually works. This is a complex statement mainly because what "works" is based on the medical gold standard of the randomized, double-blind, controlled study. THP are not standardized because there are as many "ways" to practice as there are Native healers. In addition, it does not make sense for Native healers to "treat" everyone the same way when it is perceived that each patient's body chemistry and presenting life situation are different. Research methodology that takes AI/AN epistemology into account must be developed so that THP can be valued within the context of its original culture.

Successful clinical interventions are not possible in an AI/AN setting unless the provider or agency is cognizant of the sociohistorical factors that have had devastating effects on the AI/AN family. This axiom applies not only to those conditions that are in the realm of mental health but also to medical conditions. Diabetes, heart disease, depression, cancer, domestic violence, intentional and unintentional injury, and all public health issues must be understood in the context of individual and community response to historical trauma (Duran and Duran 1995; Brave Heart et al. 1998).

During the process of collecting data for a dissertation project, I have had the opportunity to observe how several AI/AN health agencies are using and developing THP along with providing medical health services. Several sociocultural movements are increasing exposure and access to THP for local AI/AN communities.

Some medicine people and elders have maintained their cultural practices, ceremonies, language, and philosophy. They did so in the face of enormous pressure to assimilate from (a) the mainstream culture, (b) the legal and education systems, (c) Christian religions, and (d) government policy. Mainstream media support a consumer culture whose major value is money and which follows a scientific mantra of the "survival of the fittest." These factors have led to further separation from AI/AN cultural values.

Many AI/AN people attend cultural activities, but the majority of THP are more social and do not provide culturally based health care to Naive people. Powwows and sweats can contribute to the well-being of people. A Native healer with knowledge and experience of healing people is the most direct form of Native health care. One elder recently commented to me that if you have a broken bone, it doesn't matter how many times you go in the sweat; it will not heal the bone. However, there is a need to increase access to a Native healer and to healing-specific ceremonies. There are many AI/AN people who have never been to a healing ceremony or had contact with a Native healer. Many have heard of these things but do not have direct experience.

In California, for example, there are local communities that are restoring songs, ceremonies, and healing practices. This process requires time, patience, and the ability to deal with people who are angry over having lost this knowledge in their family and community. Yosemite National Park, Grinding Rock State Park, and Patrick's Point State Park, all in California, are examples of communities that have rebuilt villages with traditional ceremony structures. This work is usually undertaken by a handful of committed individuals who want to restore (not discover) THP for their community. Many local communities are coming back to a cultural understanding of life.

Native professionals now take advantage of culturally based training from a variety of programs and agencies. The University of Oklahoma sponsors Native Wellness conferences for men and women. The Gathering of Nations (GONA) and Red Road approach have contributed culture-based interventions and curriculum for alcohol and drug abuse programs. No cultural training or support existed when I first began my career in 1984 as an Indian Child Welfare (ICW) worker in Fort Hall, Idaho.

The first training I encountered was by Terry Cross in Portland, Oregon. He received funding to create a training program for ICW workers, and it had a cultural component. The use of THP has grown exponentially since the early 1980s. Efforts to include THP need to be documented and studied to understand its impact on AI/AN communities.

IMPLICATIONS FOR RESEARCH

Documenting THP and its use for health intervention can potentially increase funding from foundations and local, state, and federal agencies. The holistic, cultural approach to health care is very appealing to public health and criminal justice officials everywhere who seek ways to effectively provide treatment, to lower recidivism, and to control costs, The Native American Health Center (NAHC) has implemented a holistic system of care in the San Francisco Bay Area based on a strategic plan that links prevention with treatment in a continuum of care and stresses collaboration with a variety of AI/AN and public agencies. Proof of a THP approach is supported by the NAHC plan, and this plan has resulted in bringing significant resources to the community.

Using a cultural model of health may also open doors to go beyond current thought regarding health of minorities and determinants of health. The determinants-of-health approach can refocus analytical explanations for health outcomes from the immediate biomedical context of health problems to the wider living conditions that interact with individual physiological, psychological, and sociocultural dispositions that give rise to those health problems. This broad approach can eventually lead researchers to explain how THP can be used to improve the health of AI/AN communities. Native researchers will be needed to guide appropriate questions based on culture and to interpret the findings.

NOTES

Brave Heart, M, Yellow Horse, and L. M. DeBroyn. 'The American Indian Holocaust: Healing Historical Unresolved Grief," *American Indian and Alaska Native Mental LIMA Research Journal* 2 (1998): 56–78.

Buchwald, Dedra, Janette Beals, and Spero M. Manson. "Use of Traditional Health Practices among *Native* Americans in a Primary Care Setting," *Medical Care* 38(12) (2000): 1191–99.

Duran, E., and B, Duran. *Native American Postcolonial Psychology.* Albany: State University of New York Press, 1995.

Gurley, Diana, Douglas K. Novins, Monica C. Jones, Janette Beals, James H. Shore, and Spero M. Manson. "Comparative Use of Biomedical Services and Traditional Healing Options by American Indian Veterans," *Psychiatric Services* 52(1) (2001): 68–74.

Kim, Catherine, and Yeong S. Kwok. "Navajo Use of Native Healers," *Archives of Internal Medicine* 158 (1998): 2245–2249.

Waldram, J. B. "Aboriginal Spirituality in Corrections." In *Native Americans, Crime and Justice*, ed. R. A. Silverman and M. O. Neilson. Boulder, Colo.: Westview Press, 1996.

Corn Maiden.
© *Gerald Dawavendewa*. Reprinted by permission.

RESTORING NATIVE FOODS FOR HEALTH AND COMMUNITY WELL-BEING

Susan Lobo

In the early 1960s the O'odham people, known as the Pima and Tohono O'odham, whose homeland is in the hot desert region of Arizona, had almost no recorded cases of diabetes. Today this disease has reached epidemic proportions and over 65% of the adult population suffers from Type II diabetes, the highest incidence in the world. This swift and devastating change has come about through changes to a more sedentary lifestyle and a shift in diet as commodity foods and other non-desert adapted and fast foods have flooded the Tohono O'odham and Pima nations. For thousands of years the O'odham and their ancestors combined a series of well-adapted strategies for producing and gathering foods in the extremely arid lands of the Sonoran desert, and this traditional food system supported the local economy, maintained the people's well-being, and provided the material foundation for O'odham culture.

Tohono O'odham Community Action (TOCA) is one example of a Native community-based non-profit that is pro-actively working to improve health and at the same time strength the cultural and economic foundation. TOCA was founded in 1996 and is dedicated to rebuilding a healthy, culturally vital and sustainable Tohono O'odham nation. This is happening through food system and wellness initiatives, the Tohono O'odham community arts and culture program, the Tohono O'odham basketweavers organization, and the Youth/Elders outreach program. The food system initiative is combating these high rates of diabetes and other health issues and simultaneously creating economic opportunity by reintroducing traditional food production via two farms, community gardens, the marketing of traditional foods, primarily varieties of corn, beans and squash, within the Tohono O'odham community and beyond, and through extensive educational programs. Traditional desert foods are now available throughout the Tohono O'odham nation for sale in stores on the reservation, and available in elderly lunch programs, schools, and hospitals. All of these efforts are consciously stimulating self-sufficiency and cultural vitality, as well as improved health. See www.tocaonline.org.

TOCA's logo by Tohono O'odham artist Leonard F. Chana.

SQUASH UNDER THE BED

Ofelia Zepeda

There was always crooked-neck squash under our beds.
The space under the bed met the criteria of a cool, dark, dry
   place.
These large, hard-skinned squash with speckled, serrated,
green and yellow designs shared space under our beds
with new cowboy boots, lost socks, forgotten toys,
dust, and little spiders.
The squash rested under there with our memory of summer.
Awaiting winter darkness.
With the cold weather, we split the hard skin and expose the
rich yellow meat inside, the bounty of large seeds entangled
in the wetness of their origin.
We saved the seeds for next summer.
We eat the soft, sweet meat of the winter squash.
We swallow the warmth of summer.

Ofelia Zepeda, "Squash Under the Bed." Page 51 in *Where Clouds Are Formed: Poems by Ofelia Zepeda*. Tucson: University of Arizona Press, 2008.

MY NEW YEAR'S RESOLUTION:
NO MORE FAT "INDIAN" FOOD

Suzan Shown Harjo

I promise to give up fat "Indian" food this year and to urge others to do the same. Target number one: the ubiquitous frybread—the junk food that's supposed to be traditional, but isn't, and makes for fat, fatter and fattest Indians.

Frybread is bad for you? Well, let's see. It's made with white flour, salt, sugar and lard. The bonus ingredient is dried cow's milk for the large population of Native people who are both glucose and lactose intolerant.

Usually the size of a tortilla, frybread is an inch thick with a weight approaching a lead Frisbee. It's fried in grease that collects in the dimples of the bread, adding that extra five teaspoons of fat to the lining of the diner's arteries.

If frybread is not eaten at once, it turns into something with the consistency and taste of a deflated football. To make the recipe totally irresistible, it's topped off with margarine, jelly or some other plastic not found in nature.

Frybread was a gift of Western civilization from the days when Native people were removed from buffalo, elk, deer, salmon, turkey, corn, beans, squash, acorns, fruit, wild rice and other real food.

Frybread is emblematic of the long trails from home and freedom to confinement and rations. It's the connecting dot between healthy children and obesity, hypertension, diabetes, dialysis, blindness, amputations and slow death.

If frybread were a movie, it would be hard-core porn. No redeeming qualities. Zero nutrition.

Frybread has replaced "firewater" as the stereotypical Indian staple in movie land. Well-meaning non-Indians take their cues from these portrayals of Indians as simple-minded people who salute the little grease bread and get misty-eyed about it.

"Where's the frybread" is today's social ice-breaker, replacing the decade-long frontrunner, "What did you think of 'Dances with Wolves'?"

But, frybread is so, so Indian. Yes, some people have built their Indian identity around the deadly frybread and will blanch at the very notion of removing it from their menu and conversation.

My heavens, how will the new and deculturalized Indians and wannabes ever relate to the Native people they are paid to consult with if they don't extol the virtues of frybread?

During the opening week of the National Museum of the American Indian's museum on the Mall, a reception for contemporary Native artists ended with a good Indian band's not so great song, "Frybread", whose lyrics consist mainly of the title being repeated ad nauseum. When a non-Indian Smithsonian employee grabbed the microphone and brayed out, "frybread, fryyyyyybread," the dignified artists and patrons ran for the nearest exits.

One Native artist, Steven Deo, is on a campaign to increase awareness about the danger of frybread and other so-called Indian foods. Deo, who is Euchee and Muscogee (Creek) and dances at the Duck Creek Grounds in Oklahoma, has made a poster with the image of the grease bread and the words "Frybread Kills."

"Frybread Kills" is part of a series called "Art for Indians." The series is "specifically aimed at our Native American community," said Deo, "to create a cognitive dialogue about ourselves and our socio-economic class."

Deo's second poster depicts lard and other commodity foods. An equals sign follows the image, so that the message essentially reads: "Commodities = public assistance = welfare."

In economically impoverished Indian communities, the commodities were known initially as "poor food" and morphed into "Indian food." There's even a name for the round, doughy physique that results from the high-starch, high-calorie, high-fat and low-protein food: "Commod bod."

In urban areas and on many reservations, the byproducts of commods have nearly overrun traditional foods. Even week-old bread and berry pies baked in Pueblo ovens are vastly superior to frybread on its best day, but they're running a distant second at pan-Indian events in Pueblo country.

In great cultures, traditional bread stands for health, well-being and wealth, literally and figuratively. Traditional Native breads and foods stack up against any of the world's greatest.

Hopi piki, Muscogee sofkee and everyone's cornbread and tamales remind us why most Native people consider corn one of the highest gifts of creation.

The great Native cooks need only a few ingredients to make bread fit for a feast that is easy enough for daily fare:

Start with any fresh or dried base of pumpkin, wild onions, sage, sunflower seeds, walnuts, beans, green chiles, blueberries, huckleberries, sweet potato, pinon, camas, yucca or anything the cook likes to cook.

Add water and arrowroot, cornmeal, maple sap or any indigenous thickener and stir to the desired consistency. Make into any pleasing shape you want.

Sun dry or boil, smoke, grill or steam over juniper ash, seaweed, mesquite, shucks, peanut or pecan shells, driftwood or anything that's handy and tasty.

Prepare to see some smiles.

While we're at it, let's resolve to throw out all the civilization-era food in our kitchens. You know what to do with any Indian "maidens" or "princesses" or "chiefs" or "braves" on butter, honey, jerky or any products where the profits don't go to Native people. If they are Native-made products with stereotypical, cheesy images, give them a toss and let the Native manufacturers know they can and should do better.

Here's another resolution I urge you to adopt—to consume the "news" with a larger grain of salt than you have in the past. Conservative pundit Armstrong Williams was exposed recently as having been paid by the Bush Administration to promote its "No Child Left Behind" program. And this at a time when education is under funded and the Bushies are loathe to promote history or the arts with federal money.

The Williams' $100,000 understanding should lead us all to investigate who is trying to feed us a line and palm it off as "news." Native people need to resolve to discover the origins of "fair share" and other current anti-Indian propaganda, and find out who gets what money from what source to spread the stories.

The next time you find yourself swallowing some leftover news du jour or get that suicidal urge for frybread, just slather lard all over the magazine or television listing and apply it directly to your midriff and backside. That way, you can have the consequence of the rotten stuff, without having to actually digest it.

Suzan Shown Harjo. First published in *Indian Country Today*, January 20, 2005, p. 3. Updated September 10, 2008. Reprinted by permission.

Frybread man.
© *Ryan Huna Smith*. Reprinted by permission.

6

"IF WE GET THE GIRLS, WE GET THE RACE"
MISSIONARY EDUCATION OF NATIVE AMERICAN GIRLS

Carol Devens

When I saw the lonely figure of my mother vanish in the distance, a sense of regret settled heavily upon me. I felt suddenly weak, as if I might fall limp to the ground. I was in the hands of strangers whom my mother did not fully trust. I no longer felt free to be myself, or to voice my own feelings. The tears trickled down my cheeks, and I buried my face in the folds of my blanket. Now the first step, parting me from my mother, was taken, and all my belated tears availed nothing.

—Zitkala-Sa

Mission school education, with its wrenching separation from family, had a profound impact on Native American girls and on their female kin Zitkala-Sa's description of her departure for boarding school in 1884 characterized the experience of thousands of young girls in the nineteenth century.[1] Most left no written record of their years in school; Zitkala-Sa (Gertrude Bonnin), a Dakota (Sioux) writer and activist on Native American issues, was unusual in that respect. She recorded both her own memories of her school years and her mother's reaction to the Western education of her daughter.

Zitkala-Sa's mother, heartbroken by the child's departure, was convinced that someone had "filled [her daughter's] ears with the white man's lies" to persuade her to leave for school. What else would induce an eight-year-old to quit her mother for the company of strangers? "Stay with me, my little one!" she futilely implored the child, overwhelmed by anxiety about her safety among white people?[2] The woman's fears were not unfounded. Her child's well-being at school was by no means assured, an examination of the experiences of Ojibwa and Dakota girls suggests.[3] A girl's exposure to Anglo-American religious, economic, and gender values often had a permanent effect on her, whether or not she accepted

them. Moreover, the time in school deprived her of the continuing tutelage of her mother and other female relatives—instruction that was key to assuming her place as a woman within her own cultural tradition.

The history of mission schools is a troubling one in which stories of benevolent, self-sacrificing missionaries contend with accounts of relentlessly rigid discipline, ethnocentrism, and desperately unhappy children.[4] Native Americans received their introduction to Anglo-American education at the hands of British missionaries in 1617, following King James's advocacy of schooling Indians to promote "civilization" and Christianity. Dartmouth College soon was established to teach young Indian men, and both Harvard College and William and Mary College incorporated the education of Native youth into their missions. The Church of England's Society for the Propagation of the Gospel in Foreign Parts also regularly instructed Indians until the American Revolution. Following independence, a host of missionary societies was organized with the stated intent of evangelizing Native peoples, among them the American Society for Propagating the Gospel among the Indians and Others in North America (1787) and the New York Missionary Society (1796).[5]

The founding of the interdenominational American Board of Commissioners of Foreign Missions (ABCFM) in 1810 ushered in a new era of missionary endeavor. The combined influences of the religious revival known as the Second Great Awakening and heightened nationalism following the

Carol Devens in American Nations: Encounters in Indian Country, 1850 to the Present, ed. by Hoxie, Mancall, and Merrell. Routledge, 2001, pp. 157–171. (Original source: Journal of World History, vol. 3, n. 2 (1992), pp. 219–237. A portion of the original article and the endnotes have been omitted.

War of 1812 added a further goal to the missionary effort rescuing Indians from destruction by the inexorable march of Anglo-American progress. Numerous denominational organizations were formed, such as the Missionary Society of the American Methodist Episcopal Church in 1820 and the Presbyterian Board of Foreign Missions (BFM) in 1837.[6]

Nineteenth-century missionaries and their sponsors firmly believed in the linear progression of history and in their own elevated place on the ladder of civilization. They clearly understood their charge to be the transformation of Native peoples into Christian citizens. Admittedly, it was a monumental undertaking, "We cannot be too grateful that God did not make us heathens," observed Sherman Hall, of ABCFM's La Pointe mission in Wisconsin, in 1833. "It is an awful calamity to be born in the midst of heathen darkness."[7] Heathenism seemed a surmountable obstacle, however, if children could be brought into the fold at a tender age and raised as Christians. As one missionary put it: "This can only be effectually accomplished by taking them away from the demoralizing & enervating atmosphere of camp life & Res[ervation] surroundings & Concomitants."[8] Although bringing adults to knowledge of gospel truths was important, it was "the rising generation" who provided hope for the salvation of the Native population.

Schooling became the primary means of enticing young Native Americans to reject tradition and seek conversion. To missionaries, the abandonment of native ways for Western ones was a creative rather than destructive process that made new Christian citizens out of savages. School, missionaries hoped, was a way to change Indians from "others" to dusky versions of themselves. Rayna Green, a Native American scholar, has offered this observation of a photograph of pupils at the Hampton Institute, a nineteenth-century boarding school in Virginia for African-American and Native American pupils: "School put them into drawing classes, where young Indian ladies in long dresses made charcoal portraits of a boy dressed his Plains warrior best. These Victorian Indians look toward the camera from painting class, their eyes turned away from their buckskinned model."[9]

Missionaries worked diligently to gather girls and boys of all ages into day and boarding schools near villages and reservations, as well as at distant Indian schools such as the Hampton Institute or the Carlisle School in Pennsylvania (founded in 1879 to prove to the public that Native Americans were educable). Because missionary teachers could not forcibly round up and remove Native American children to schools as their government counterparts often did, it was a real challenge to enroll them. Zitkala-Sa was lured to the Quakers' Indiana Manual Labor Institute in Wabash by tales of lush, rich land bursting with sweet fruits for the child's taking.[10] Charles Hall, a minister at the ABCFM's Fort Berthold mission in North Dakota (which served mostly Mandan, Hidatsa, and Arikara rather than Dakota) in the late nineteenth and early twentieth centuries, reported that "getting the children to go to school was as delicate and cautious work as catching trout. To send a child to school meant, to the Indian, the giving up of all his distinctive tribal life, his ancestral customs, his religious beliefs, and sinking himself into the vast unknown, the way of the white man."[11] After several years, Hall developed a recruitment strategy that he later explained in a section of his memoirs entitled "Capturing Children":

> How to reach the children was a problem. They were told by shrewd parents that owls and bears and white men would harm them, so naturally they ran and hid when we approached. . . . White Shield, the old Rec [Arikara] chief, said in regard to our problem, "If you feed the children, they will come to school like flies to syrup? His advice was taken, and a Friday dinner, in the manner of the white man, was provided. This was as attractive as ice cream and lollipops. The school became a popular institution, especially on Friday.[12]

Other missionaries reported similar use of food and other enticements, such as singing, to get the children into the classroom.[13]

Initially, mission schools concentrated on teaching boys and men, with little emphasis on female schooling. By mid century, however, they had shifted their approach in response to the growing belief among Americans that women, as mothers, must be educated in order to raise virtuous male citizens.[14] According to Isaac Baird, who served at the Presbyterian BFM Odanah mission in Wisconsin, "The girls will need the training more than the boys & they will wield a greater influence in the future. If we get the girls, we get the race."[15] ABCFM's Santee Normal Training School in Nebraska, founded in 1870, exemplified this position in its annual bulletin, which stated that the school's purpose was the "raising up [of] preachers, teachers, interpreters, business men, and model mothers for the Dakota Nation."[16]

Once the commitment to female education had been made, however, missionaries faced low enrollments and high dropout rates. Presbyterian and

COMMUNITY WELLNESS: FAMILY, HEALTH, AND EDUCATION

ABCFM missions to the Ojibwa and Dakota suffered a shortage of schoolgirls and, moreover, were dissatisfied with the performance of the female pupils they did have. William Boutwell, ABCFM missionary at Leech Lake, Minnesota, reported in the 1830s that girls avoided him and refused to come to school; he was uncertain whether fear or shame motivated their response.[17] At the Presbyterian BFM mission in Omena, Michigan, Peter Dougherty thought he could not go wrong with his female school; he had provided women teachers to instruct girls in domesticity arid Christianity as well as same academic subjects. When the school opened in 1848, it had a fine enrollment of twenty-two, but this quickly dwindled, and by 1850 Dougherty was forced to close the school. The boys' school, however, flourished as fathers sent their sons to acquire reading and ciphering skills that allowed them to deal with Anglo-Americans on their own terms.[18] The manual labor boarding school Dougherty opened in 1853 had similar problems, attracting only five girls out of twenty-seven students. The Presbyterians were even more discouraged by the situation at Middle Village, a satellite mission of Omena, where women refused to send any children to school. Their action led to the school's closing in 1858, despite the village men's petition to the BFM to keep it open.[19]

At Sisseton agency in the Dakota Territory, the local U.S. Indian agent, J. G. Hamilton, was shocked by how tenaciously Dakota women clung to their old ways. He urged the Women's Board of Missions (affiliated with the ABCFM) to send a lady to teach the Native women. "I was struck, upon my arrival here some two months ago," he wrote to the Women's Board in 1875, "with the vast difference in the general appearance of the men & women. Contrary to the usual rule, the men of this tribe have made far greater progress & have yielded more readily to civilizing forces than the women have."[20] He hoped that female teachers might be able to reach them. His comment suggests that, like the Ojibwa, Dakota women sought to keep distance between themselves and whites and were reluctant to adapt to Anglo-American customs or values. Susan Webb, a missionary teacher at Santee, reported that "the older women could not read and the younger women would not."[21] The female aversion to interaction included an unwillingness to have their daughters involved in mission schooling. When Captain Richard H. Pratt, founder of the Carlisle School, visited Fort Berthold in 1878 to recruit Dakota children for the Hampton Institute, he had a difficult time securing students, especially girls.

"The people feared to give up their girls," Charles Hall explained, "not trusting the white people."[22]

One teacher contemplating the enrollment problem suggested that the Ojibwa, at least, saw no point in educating girls. Revealing his poor understanding of Ojibwa gender roles and cultural values, he explained that women were destined for a life of servitude. A more likely explanation, however, came from a perceptive missionary who suggested that close ties between mothers and daughters were to blame—that women who maintained a traditional way of life were loath to relinquish control of their daughters' upbringing. It was with tremendous reluctance, for example, that Zitkala-Sa's mother allowed her to go to school. She eventually consented only after concluding that Western education would provide her daughter greater protection against the growing number of Anglo-Americans settling an Dakota lands than traditional training could.[23]

Much like their Ojibwa counterparts, those Dakota girls who did enroll seldom seemed to conform to the missionaries' expectations. Susan Webb commented that her female students always seemed the opposite of what she hoped they would be. She saw her work with them as a lesson in the depths of the human condition: "I think as I work for these girls I am learning the weakness and depravity of our own human natures."[24]

Despite women's traditionalism and their suspicion of missionaries, many girls did end up attending school for at least short periods of time.[25] Once there, they immediately began the physical transformation that missionaries hoped would be a catalyst for their intellectual and spiritual metamorphosis into Christian citizens. A young girl, whether faced with the total immersion of boarding school or the less comprehensive indoctrination attempted by day schools, was presented with an alien world view, behavior code, and language to which she was quickly expected to adhere. It was a confusing and frightening whirlwind of strangers, journeys, haircuts, and loneliness. Zitkala-Sa again provides a window on the experience of starting school: "My long travel and the bewildering sights had exhausted me. I fell asleep, heaving deep, tired sobs. My tears were left to dry themselves in streaks, because neither my aunt nor my mother was near to wipe them away."[26] She recalled how humiliating the mandatory haircuts were for Native American children. "Our mothers had taught us that only unskilled warriors who were captured had their hair shingled by the enemy.

Among our people, short hair was worn by mourners, and shingled hair by cowards!" She had to be dragged out from under a bed before she submitted to having her long braids snipped off. Charles Hall remembered the children's horror of losing their long hair at his school, and the Indian agent, J. C. McGillycuddy, reported that when new Lakota students at Pine Ridge reservation caught a glimpse of teachers giving haircuts, they feared that he intended to disgrace them, and all fled in alarm.[27]

The school world was tough and confusing. Mission schools' programs for girls were intended to indoctrinate them with the ideals of Christian womanhood—piety, domesticity, submissiveness, and purity. By the missionaries' Victorian standards, Native American women were careless, dirty, and unfamiliar with the concept of hard work Indian girls, they complained, were woefully unfamiliar with the lore, paraphernalia, and routines of female domesticity.[28] Schools therefore trained girls in sewing, knitting, cooking, and other domestic skills and tasks, as well as in academic subjects, such as history, natural sciences, arithmetic, and spelling.[29] The content of the curriculum bore no relationship to the intellectual, social, or philosophical constructs in which the girls had been raised. Indeed, the schools' underlying principle was that Anglo-American history, morality, and health were inherently superior to and should replace those of their students' cultures.

This perspective was reinforced by typical textbooks, such as Webb's *Readers*, Webster's *Spelling Book*, Greenleaf's *Intellectual Arithmetic*, and Colbun's *Mental Arithmetic*, used by Ojibwa children in the 1860s at ABCFM's Odanah Manual Labor Boarding School.[30] These books unabashedly proclaimed the Anglo-American vision of progress and morality subscribed to by the missionaries. Even texts written specifically for Native American pupils (ABCFM teachers usually taught in their students' language) tended to be literal translations of standard classroom lessons, that teachers applied to their pupils with little or no regard for context and appropriateness. The sailboats depicted in Stephen Rigg's *Model First Reader* (1873), for example, were a world away from the experiences of the Dakota children learning to read out of this book at the Santee Normal Training School.[31]

The curriculum often placed an even heavier emphasis on vocational instruction for girls than for boys. The thirty-six girls at the Shawnee Quaker School, for example, in 1827 alone produced 400 pieces of student clothing, 50 sets of sheets and

towels, and 80 pairs of socks. They also spun and wove 100 pounds of wool and 40 yards of rag carpet, churned 800 pounds of butter, made 600 pounds of cheese, 2½ barrels of soap, and 100 pounds of candles. In addition, they did daily housekeeping, laundry, cooking, and cleaning. The girls worked in groups, rotating jobs every two weeks in order to learn all aspects of housekeeping.[32] Martha Riggs Morris at ABCFM's Sisseton (Dakota) mission, explained the rationale for this approach, which still held sway in 1881: "The book learning is after all not so important for them, at least after they have learned to read and write fairly well. But to take care of themselves—to learn to keep body and mind pure and clean, to learn to keep house comfortably—these are most important for the advancement of the people."[33]

Ideally, the missions' female teachers were to be role models for appropriate gender activities, values, and work, showing Native American girls through daily example both the techniques of household economy and a womanly demeanor. In reality, however, the teachers were overworked and often ill. Furthermore, rigid schedules and overcrowding often made the situation impersonal and miserable. At the Wesleyan Methodist Missionary Society's Aldersville School in Ontario, Canada, a report of the girls' schedule in 1841 indicated their rigorous life. The children (mostly Ojibwa) arose at 4:30 A.M. in summer, a lazy 5 A.M. in winter. Between rising and 9 A.M., the girls did the milking, prepared the school breakfast, attended prayers and a lecture, made cheese, and did housework. They then spent six hours in the classroom, with a break for lunch, followed by needlework, supper, evening milking, prayers at 8 p.m. and bed at 8:30.[34]

Throughout the 1880s, Martha Riggs Morris complained that her twenty-eight Dakota students were crowded into two tiny buildings measuring 10 × 24 feet and 17 × 24 feet. At the Santee Normal Training School, the Bird's Nest, a boarding home for small girls, was more spacious, having two kitchens, a dining room, teachers' sitting room and bedrooms, sick bay, laundry room, and three dormitories for the girls. Still, both teachers and students felt cramped and hurried.[35] Zitkala-Sa's account of the Wabash school once again personalizes the depressing impact of frantic school regimes on pupils and teachers alike:

A loud-clamoring bell awakened us at half-past six in the cold winter mornings . . . There were too many drowsy children and too numerous orders for the day to waste a moment in any apology to nature for giving her children such a shock in the early morning. . . . A paleface woman, with a yellow-covered roll book open on her arm and a gnawed pencil in her hand, appeared at the door. Her small, tired face was coldly lighted with a pair of large gray eyes. She stood still in a halo of authority . . . It was next to impossible to leave the iron routine after the civilizing machine had once begun its day's buzzing.[36]

Susan Webb's comments about her pupils indicate that the schooling process alienated and confused the girls. "When I look about me," Webb wrote in 1881, "and see how helpless and indifferent apparently are the young women I long to help arouse them to a sense that there is something for them to be doing. I cannot endure the thought that our girls will leave us to settle down with no weight of responsibility."[37] Zitkala-Sa's experience confirmed this: "The melancholy of those black days has left so long a shadow that it darkens the path of years that have since gone by. These sad memories rise above those of smoothly grinding school days."[38]

Stories of her grandmother's experiences in a turn-of-the-century mission school prompted Mary Crow Dog (Lakota Sioux) to write: "It is almost impossible to explain to a sympathetic white person what a typical old Indian boarding school was like; how it affected the Indian child suddenly dumped into it like a small creature from another world, helpless, defenseless, bewildered, trying desperately and instinctively to survive at all."[39] Some young girls at the school killed themselves or attempted suicide to escape an unhappy situation beyond their control.

The demoralizing effect of school programs was often rivaled by their futility. Most of the domestic instruction that girls received was virtually useless when their schooling ended and they returned to the village or reservation. Only if a family had made the transition from tipi or lodge to frame house, as Zitkala-Sa's had, were the girl's Western housekeeping skills applicable—unless she worked as a domestic servant for local Anglo-Americans or at the mission itself Native American girls' servitude filled a perceived need for trained household help; girls at the government's Phoenix Indian School were pressured to become servants, and this may have been the case at mission schools as well.[40]

The conditions that children reported enduring in school led many Native American parents to become firmly entrenched in their opposition to Anglo-American education. Other factors influenced them as well. The loss of the children to school was, in a way, like death in the family and community. "Since you have been here with your writing . . . the place has become full of ghosts," one person told Charles Hall.

In fact, schooling often did end in death, as Hall observed, especially for children at boarding schools, where infectious diseases took a high toll.[41]

The schools' threat to family well-being was heightened for mothers and grandmothers. A girl's participation in mission school undermined the women's ability to oversee her upbringing and to assure that she would take her place as a woman within the tribal tradition. "The grandmothers and many of the parents," reported Eda Ward, a teacher at Fort Berthold, "with their children to be wholly Indian."[42] Female kin were responsible for instructing the child in both the practical and ritual activities that would shape her life as an adult within the community. Schooling removed a girl from the warmth of her kin's care, left her with no one to teach, comfort, or guide her as they would at home. Zitkala-Sa's mother had warned her departing child that "you will cry for me, but they will not even soothe you."[43]

Overworked, ill, and ethnocentric teachers were no substitute for the female network on which a girl's emotional, spiritual, and intellectual development depended. Although many missionary teachers were well intentioned and some really enjoyed their small charges, all were put off by the unfamiliar habits and values of the girls, and by the physical setting of their new environment. After nine years with the Ojibwa around the La Pointe mission, the ABCFM missionary Sherman Hall told his brother that "it is difficult to reach their hearts, or even their understandings with the truth. They seem almost as stupid as blocks. Yet they are far enough from being destitute of natural endowment. Most of them have superior minds by nature but they are minds in ruins."[44] Hall lasted a long time in the missionary field and was seemingly better able to adjust to his surroundings than many of his peers, yet he described his pupils as "ragged, dirty, lousy and disgusting little objects trying to learn to read their own language."[45] His attitude was more positive than that of one of his coworkers, however, who complained bitterly about "the effects of crowding from 40 to 70 dirty vicious Indian children" into a small schoolhouse.[46]

Not all teachers were so intolerant; most of the women at ABCFM's Dakota missions, for example, expressed real fondness for their students and jobs.[47] However, their commitment to "civilizing" their pupils precluded any real understanding of or concession to those pupils' culture or values. Most tried to treat their charges as they would Anglo-American youngsters.[48] By regarding their students simply as children rather than as *Indian* children, teachers essentially denied their very identities. This lack of cultural awareness or empathy contributed to the gulf between student and teacher and to the children's unhappiness and disorientation. Even well-intentioned but uninformed jollity could be a source of alienation and confusion for the newly (dis)located girl Zitkala-Sa vividly remembered an incident at the Quaker school that to the staff must surely have seemed an inappropriate response to an innocuous action. On the night she arrived, "a rosy-cheeked paleface woman caught me in her arms. I was both frightened and insulted by such trifling. I stared into her eyes, wishing her to let me stand on my own feet, but she jumped me up and down with increasing enthusiasm. *My* mother had never made a plaything of her wee daughter. Remembering this I began to cry aloud."[49] Indeed, Native American parents treated their children with respect and reserve. In general, mothers were satisfied to scold a young offender or to threaten that an animal might kidnap her. The rare physical punishment was a light switching with a twig on the hands or knees, and only serious problems warranted it. Mission teachers, however, often were quite free with corporal punishment. Because such punishment was an accepted, even required, part of their own culture, beatings and other methods were frequently used. At ABCFM's Fond du-Lac mission in Minnesota, Edmund Ely, a contemporary of Sherman Hall, moved Ojibwa parents and children to outrage when he pulled children's hair to discipline them.[50] Both the rough play that Zitkala-Sa was subjected to and the strict discipline and corporal punishment that were standard fare in most schools went against Native American child-rearing methods, frightening and humiliating students.

The difference in educational methods between Anglo-American and Native American cultures exacerbated the disorienting impact of the mission schools on girls. Native peoples did not confine either schooling or pupils to classrooms. Children roamed freely, exploring and learning individually and in groups. "I was a wild little girl of seven," Zitkala-Sa recalled. "Loosely clad in a slip of brown buckskin, and light-footed with a pair of soft moccasins on my feet, I was as free as the wind that blew my hair, and no less spirited than a bounding deer. These were my mother's pride—my wild freedom and overflowing spirits. She taught me no fear save that of intruding myself upon others."[51]

A girl's education took place constantly, through listening to and working with elders or in games with peers. Dakota girls engaged in "small play"— impersonating their mothers, and mimicking marital and domestic roles, conversations, and manners. Little girls worked companionably alongside their mothers, cooking, cleaning, and imitating them in beadwork and preparing medicinal plants. Zitkala-Sa's mother attracted her daughter's interest in beadwork by having her assist in designing and working on her own new moccasins. The woman's guidance made the child feel responsible and secure in her skill: "she treated me as a dignified little individual."[52]

Grandmothers also played a critical role in educating girls, enticing them with stories and reminiscences that illustrated tradition and history, drawing them toward an understanding of tribal philosophy and values. In *Waterlily*, Ella Deloria, a Dakota ethnologist, described a girl's relationship with her grandmother. The older woman's role was to make "well-behaved women" of her young charges. She tutored them in how to move, how to interact with elders, where to sit in the tipi. Only with constant and relentless reminding could she be sure that the girls had absorbed the lessons vital to their success in life. Moreover, the grandmother frequently talked with the girls about the children's early years in the camp, furthering their sense of belonging and place.[53] In the evenings, mothers often sent daughters—proudly bearing presents of tobacco or a favorite food—to invite grandmothers to instruct the girls in the myths and lessons that established their own place within the group and their people's place in the world.[54]

Women also guided their daughters and granddaughters through the ritual activities preparing them for womanhood. For example, Ojibwa girls of four or five understood their first vision quests, heading into the forests with their little faces blackened, hoping to establish a relationship with supernaturals. Over the next few years the length of the quests gradually increased; eventually a girl might spend four or more days fasting, sleeping, and dreaming for power. She was ritually greeted and feasted by her mother or a female relative upon her return home, and all listened attentively as she reported on her guardian spirit dreams.[55]

Mothers and grandmothers also presided over a girl's first menstruation. The Ojibwa built a special small wigwam near the main lodge, to isolate the adolescent's newly expanded spiritual powers from men's hunting powers and infants' weak natures. During these days of seclusion and fasting for dreams, the mother instructed the girl in the responsibilities of adult women and oversaw her beadwork and sewing. When a daughter's first menstrual period had ended, her female kin feasted her upon her return to the household and entry into womanhood. Thereafter, she was chaperoned by a grandmother or aunt until marriage.[56] Dakota girls similarly retired to a new tipi set up beyond the circle of the camp, and female relatives cared for them and instructed them in the duties of a wife and mother. When seclusion had ended, the Buffalo Ceremony took place, and female relatives set up a ceremonial tipi. A medicine man then called upon the spirit of the buffalo to infuse the girl with womanly virtue, and he informed the community that her childhood had ended. The mother now attempted to protect her daughter, insisting that she wear a rawhide chastity belt, and her grandmother took it upon herself to constantly accompany the girl.[57]

Clearly, it was difficult if not impossible for a girl at day or boarding school to engage in vision fasts or menstrual seclusion, both for practical reasons of time and distance from women relatives and because of the missionaries' opposition to such practices.[58] Girls who went to school were inevitably less immersed in their cultures and frequently felt less obligated or able to maintain traditional ways. Otter, daughter of Hidatsa shaman Poor Wolf, was only seven years old in 1881 when Charles Hall sent her to the Santee boarding school, 300 miles from her home near Fort Berthold. When she and her sister returned home, her father felt compelled to move because his daughters no longer fit into the old village life. Moreover, Otter, "having found the Christ-road, told her father how to become a child of God" and convinced him to abandon his lifelong beliefs.[59] Similarly, Zitkala-Sa related that after three years at the mission school she felt that she had no place in the world, that she was caught in between two cultures. Four uncomfortable years as a misfit among her people prompted her to return to school and go on to college—without her mother's approval.[60]

Mission education dearly threatened and sometimes eliminated Native American women's ability to supervise their daughters. Its goal was to alienate girls from the cultural values and practices of their mothers and turn them instead to Christianity and the Anglo-American work ethic and material culture. Although missionaries were not overwhelmingly successful in achieving their goal of shaping a new generation of assimilated citizens, their programs did have a long-term and often devastating impact both on girls and on the daughter-mother-grandmother relationship. For Zitkala-Sa, it was a bitter experience. "Like a slender tree," she remembered, "I had been uprooted from my mother, nature, and God."[61]

Teaching Is Like Culture: It Starts at Home with Parents, Relatives, and Friends.
© *Leonard F. Chana.* Reprinted by permission.

RESERVATION SCHOOLS FAIL TO ASSIMILATE ALL STUDENTS

Tim Giago

The attempts to assimilate the Indian people into the great "melting pot" that is the United States through the education process has failed for many reasons.

First of all, in order to convince the young people that an education is beneficial, you must offer a guarantee for the future. When many Indian children discovered that there was no future for them, they reacted by dropping out of school. If getting an education meant being taken from family, friends and home and being isolated in a boarding school under the supervision of strict, often cruel, disciplinarians, then education was a thing to be feared.

Secondly, by isolating the Indian tribes on reservations, far away from the mainstream, the federal government insured solidarity in peer identification.

By including the destruction of a culture into the educational process using a hit-and-run approach, the Indian child became a human guinea pig and, therefore, fair game for every well-intentioned do-gooder and despot willing to give it a try. In order for white educators to create a new kind of Indian, in his own image, he first had to erase the Indian child's culture, religion and identity in order to have a clean blackboard to write his own ideas on.

As each experiment failed, a new one would spring up in its place, and this process was repeated over and over for more than 100 years. Is it any wonder that the Indian people finally said, "Enough is enough!"?

It is as American as apple pie for the average citizen to serve on the PTA or the school board. Do you realize that it wasn't until the 1970s, after the passage of Public Law 93-638, the Indian Education and Self-Determination Act, that Indian parents were allowed the same participation in the education of their children?

One teacher, an Indian woman, became absolutely furious when she was told by a white school administrator that "I'm glad to see that Indian parents are, at last, taking an interest in the education of their children." Her anger was understandable to most Indians. The parents of Indian children were totally excluded, in fact, were discouraged from sharing in the educational processes of their own children. Every aspect of education was in the hands of the BIA or the religious order that ran the mission schools.

The school system was intended to eliminate all ties with the past, not reinforce them.

Entire families were moved to the urban ghettos of this country during the great "relocation" experiment of the 1950s and 1960s. Men and women were encouraged to attend vocational schools and "learn a trade." You will find more unemployed "welders" and "iron workers" on Indian reservations than anywhere else in the United States. After all, what good does it do to teach a person a profession or trade if there are no jobs available in the field when he returns to the reservation?

In discussing the failures of many experiments in the education of Indian children, I am not referring to ancient history. I'm talking about my generation and the generation that followed mine into the reservation school system.

Not long ago I had a reunion with two classmates from an Indian mission school on the Pine Ridge Reservation, and, as usually happens when schoolmates get together, our conversation soon turned to other classmates.

We compared notes on the frequency of tragic incidents that were commonplace among our friends—incidents of tragic death, imprisonment, suicide or alcoholism permeated our conversation. Were these former classmates of ours victims of a misguided experiment in education? To those of us who survived this onslaught on our senses, it was a chilling thought.

Editorial by Tim Giago in *Indian Country Today*, 15, no. 34 (February 15, 1996). Copyright 1996 by *Indian Country Today*. Reprinted with permission.

PROTAGONISM EMERGENT
INDIANS AND HIGHER EDUCATION

Jeffrey Wollock

No facet of 20th century Native life more dramatically illustrates the adaptive, transformative power of Indian cultures than higher education. At the start of this century, the number of Indian college graduates could be counted on one hand. And to the question of the Indian's future in America, only one answer seemed possible: total assimilation. Today, there are thousands of Native college graduates, and more than 30 reservation communities have their own colleges. . . .

TOTAL ASSIMILATION

In 1887, the General Allotment Act, also known as the Dawes Act after its chief sponsor, was enacted specifically to extinguish tribalism and turn Indians into "useful" citizens. Vast tribal lands, held communally, were to be broken up and allotted in severalty to Indian individuals, and all "surplus" land was to be sold off to non-Indians. Although it was not written into the legislation, the supporters of Allotment, notably Sen. Dawes himself, emphasized that success depended on educating Indians in agriculture, ranching, and industrial skills, as well as in English, and the responsibilities of citizenship. When deemed by the government "competent," Indians would become citizens and, hopefully, at some point in the near future, so assimilated as to be indistinguishable from any other Americans.

This mission would be accomplished through a system of federal Indian boarding schools championed by Richard Henry Pratt (1840–1924). It was Pratt's belief that the only way to get Indians into American culture was to separate them at an early

age from all Native cultural influences and place them in the midst of mainstream society. This philosophy was embodied in the federal boarding schools, located far from reservations and run with military discipline, and the "outing system," which temporarily placed Indian students in the homes of white families and schools, and sometimes in jobs working with whites. Under this policy, which would reign until 1934, the characteristic form of Indian education was vocational. . . .

EDUCATION'S NEW DEAL

In 1923, Henry Roe Cloud served on the Committee of One Hundred, a body appointed by Secretary of Interior Hubert Work to report on conditions in Indian country. Also on the Committee were Charles Eastman (Sioux) and the Rev. Philip Gordon (Ojibwa), at that time the only ordained Indian Catholic priest in the country. Though Cloud initially was opposed to government funding, his experience on the committee made him realize that most Indian students simply could not attend college without government help. Thus, the Committee's final report recommended government scholarships for Indians to go to high school and college.

In 1926, Cloud was the only Indian named to the 10-man staff preparing the Meriam report, a successor to the Committee of One Hundred. The section on education was written by W. Carson Ryan, whom Indian Commissioner Charles J. Rhoads would soon appoint head of the Bureau's educational work. The Meriam Report also recommended federal scholarships and loans. Strongly influenced by the Meriam report, Rhoads took a great interest in higher education. He hired Cloud—the youngest of the founding members of the Society of American Indians, now one of the few to make the transition to the post-Meriam BIA—as field representative in September of

From "Protagonism Emergent: Indians and Higher Education," by Jeffrey Wollock, *Native Americas* (Winter 1997). Reprinted by permission of Akwe:kon Press. Portions of the original article have been omitted.

1931. In this position, which he would hold for two years, Cloud started his own education program.

Another important appointment was a young Cherokee educator and community development activist named Ruth Muskrat Bronson (1897–1982), a former eighth-grade teacher at Haskell, educated at the University of Oklahoma, the University of Kansas, and Mount Holyoke College in Massachusetts (B.A., 1925). Like Cloud and Ataloa, Bronson in the 1920s was already campaigning for a kind of education that was not strongly assimilationist, one that would allow the preservation of "what was best" in Native cultures. The Meriam Report had recommended that the Indian Bureau hire a "guidance and placement specialist." In 1930 Bronson took a position with the new Guidance Office in the BIA's Office of Education.

The Meriam Report also emphasized the need for scholarship and loan programs. In 1928, by far the largest share of Indian students in the country (200) were at the University of Oklahoma. In 1930, Congress instituted a loan fund for post-secondary students in nursing, home economics, and forestry, allocating $15,000 annually. In 1932, it authorized $10,000 annually for a tuition fund. In that year, when Bronson took charge of the loan program, there were only 385 American Indian and Alaska Natives in all four-year colleges and only 52 known college graduates. Also in 1932, the University of Michigan inaugurated a scholarship for Indians, becoming one of only five institutions of higher learning to have such a program.

In 1933, President Franklin D. Roosevelt appointed John Collier (1884–1968) commissioner of Indian Affairs. The Collier administration, whatever its shortcomings, represented a momentous change in official Indian policy. Here for the first time was an administration officially committed to the existence and continuity of tribal communities and cultures. The Indian Reorganization Act of 1934 ended Allotment and encouraged tribes to form constitutional governments. Preferential hiring of Indians, a policy inaugurated by the Rhoads administration, was written into law under the IRA. The Indian Bureau now became a magnet for educated Indians who began to transform this notoriously corrupt and ineffective institution and to develop a real Indian intelligentsia and professional corps.

Henry Roe Cloud supported the IRA because he believed in Indian cultural survival and had come to understand the need for federal support of education. The Act set aside $250,000 for post-secondary loans.

Between 1935 and 1944, 1,933 students received them, and of these, 743 graduated, 458 from four-year colleges and universities, 159 from postsecondary vocational schools, 126 from nursing schools. Though the loan program would continue until 1952, time would prove that too many recipients were unable to pay back the loans, and it would be essentially replaced by the nonreimbursable scholarship program of 1948 (HEGP), which continues today.

In August 1933, Cloud was named Superintendent of Haskell, the first full-blood to head a federal Indian boarding school. Though he believed Indians needed to modernize, he greatly respected Native culture. Asserting that under his watch, "Haskell is definitely committed to the preservation of Indian race culture," he instituted new courses on Indian history and art. Yet, consistent with the Meriam Report, he did not favor an Indian college or university, believing that all emphasis should go toward preparing Indians to enter existing universities. When urged by A.A. Exendine of the Bureau (letter, Aug. 23, 1933) to convert Haskell into a college, he respectfully declined.

In 1934–35, there were still only 515 American Indian college students, 181 of whom were receiving federal or tribal assistance. Ruth Bronson, who had been working out of Kansas, moved to Washington in 1935. The following year, Cloud became supervisor of Indian Education, remaining in that position until 1939. Collier also added to his staff a number of young college-educated Indians who would play an important role in the development of higher education, especially D'Arcy McNickle(1904–1977) and Archie Phinney (1904–1949).

McNickle (Flathead), studied history and literature at Montana State University (1921–1925), though he did not graduate. He studied privately at Oxford in the fall of 1925 but, finding himself out of his element and dismayed when he learned it would take two years just to earn a bachelor's degree, soon returned to the United States. In 1929, he enrolled in Columbia University, where he took history courses through 1931.

In 1935, McNickle applied for a job with the BIA. His frustration with the application process illustrates the point that the "Indianization" of the BIA was also a professionalization, with all the good and bad points that implies. For McNickle was a brilliant generalist, a superb writer and historian, but had no "official" qualification in a specialty. His study of anthropology, for example, grew mainly out of a correspondence with anthropological linguist William

Gates of Johns Hopkins. McNickle's application was finally approved in February 1936, and he became administrative assistant in the Indian Organization division, though he often worked with the Tribal Relations division as well.

Archie Phinney, on the other hand, a Nez Perce anthropologist and scholar, was probably the most "qualified" applicant the BIA had ever seen. The first Indian ever to graduate from the University of Kansas, with a bachelor of arts in sociology in 1926, Phinney was hired as a clerk in the BIA in Washington, and took evening graduate courses in ethnology and philosophy at George Washington University. From 1928 to 1932, he did part-time community social work with New York University's Extension Division while continuing graduate research at Columbia University in historical processes in race and cultural contacts under anthropologist Franz Boas, with special emphasis on Indian reservation life.

In January 1944, Phinney served briefly as superintendent of the Fort Totten reservation, North Dakota, but was promoted in November to superintendent of the Northern Idaho agency, his own reservation of Nez Perce, where he tried to set up a viable IRA government and worked to help the tribe preserve their traditions, including the establishment of museum and a library.

Phinney played a central part in developing support for a national Indian organization. The idea actually went back to 1939, when he was one of several Indian delegates sent by Collier to attend a conference on North American Indians in Toronto. Annoyed by lack of opportunity for participation, the Indian delegates, including McNickle, Parker, Louis Bruce, David Owl and Ruth Bronson, staged a walkout on the last day and held a separate meeting. This group kept in touch to discuss the possibility of a national pan-Indian organization that could lobby on Capitol Hill. A few others were brought in. The origin of the National Congress of American Indians, the most important national Indian lobbying organization, lies in this educated Indian bureaucracy of the 1930s.

Most of the NCAI organizers were the college-educated "Young Turks" of Collier's BIA, including Hoover appointees Ben Dwight and Ruth Bronson, and Collier appointees D'Arcy McNickle, Archie Phinney, Ben Reifel (Brule Sioux, 1906–1990—M.S. in biochemistry, South Dakota State, 1932), and Charlie Heacock (Rosebud Sioux—M.S. in biochemistry, South Dakota State, 1933). Some older career BIA men were also involved, such as Peru Farver (b. 1894) who, like fellow-Choctaw Ben Dwight, was an Armstrong Academy graduate, and had also attended Oklahoma A & M College. Bronson's retirement from government service in 1943 left her more time for the project.

Actual legwork among tribes began in 1944. Phinney, by this time superintendent at Nez Perce, was one of the most active organizers. He was elected councilman at the organization's constitutional convention in 1944. Ben Dwight played a key role as chairman of that convention, and Ruth Bronson would run the NCAI's legislative review service in the earliest years of its existence. Bronson was executive director between 1946 and 1949, a period which saw the renewal of pressure on Indians to assimilate and to terminate the existence of tribes, and where it would be up to Indian organizations such as NCAI to protect the gains made under Collier.

THE PROTAGONIST EMERGES

After World War II, Indian veterans began attending college under the G.I. Bill. In 1948, the BIA also replaced the prewar loan program with a new higher education grant program. However, the Eisenhower administration represented a real downturn for Indians. His Indian Commissioner, Dillon S. Myer, fired most of the old Collier staff, replacing them mainly with people who had no direct experience with Indians. McNickle had been acting chief of tribal relations 1949–1950. His classic work, "They Came Here First," probably the first history of Indian-White relations by a Native author, was published in 1949. Though he became chief of tribal relations in 1950, and hung on for another two years as a moderating influence, his position became increasingly difficult, and he finally resigned to pursue Indian affairs outside government.

In 1953, the termination policy, unofficially in place since the end of the war, was made the official "sense of Congress" by House Concurrent Resolution 108. It was a concerted effort to reverse the new philosophy and achievements of the Collier years and a return to the philosophy of allotment, dedicated to the elimination of reservations and dispersal of Indians around the country, especially into urban areas.

A few of the Collier appointees supported termination. Ben Reifel, for example, had joined the Bureau in 1933 advising Indian farmers at Pine Ridge, and had been transferred in 1935 to the Organization Division, and was sent to Plains reservations to help implement the IRA. Reifel now said that Native people should not "cling to the past" and should "adjust to new economic realities." After the war he became superintendent of the Fort Berthold reservation, helping the Bureau of Reclamation force an agreement on the Three Affiliated Tribes for the building of the infamous Garrison Dam. In 1949, he received a scholarship to the Littauer School of Public Administration at Harvard, receiving a master's degree in 1950 and a doctorate in 1952. He then returned to Fort Berthold before becoming superintendent of Pine Ridge in 1954 and area director in 1955. He served in Congress from 1960 to 1971. After his retirement, he would remain active in Indian issues, serving briefly as commissioner under President Gerald Ford.

On the whole, the new NCAI played an extremely important role in the ultimately successful fight against termination. This is not to suggest that college-educated Indians deserve all the credit for this or subsequent advances, but their skills certainly did not hurt and from this point on they would play an increasingly significant leadership role.

Under termination, Indians could not aim for Indian-controlled education. The priority was simply survival. However, termination had effectively mobilized Indians on a national level, and the increased effort would pay off, for of all items on the Indian agenda in the second half of the century, education would make the greatest substantial gains. Eventually true Indian control and content would be achieved.

Some of the important Collier people were already gone—Archie Phinney died in 1949, Henry Roe Cloud in 1950, Ben Dwight in 1953—but at this point two survivors, Ruth Bronson and D'Arcy McNickle, became involved in a project that would soon set a new stage in motion. In March 1957, the Fund for the Republic formed a commission to appraise the status of Indians. Its summary report on education, Brophy & Aberle, 1961, condemned previous policies and recommended enlisting "the support of the Indian community, its neighbors, and tribal and local government officials."

In the mid-1950s, Indian college enrollment continued to increase, but observers were disturbed to find the dropout rate high and apparently unrelated to academic ability. By 1955 there were about 2,000 Natives in post-secondary education, but the ratio of degree graduates remained small: only 66 natives graduated from four-year institutions in 1961. In that year, Ruth Bronson and representatives of support organizations suggested setting up a summer workshop to investigate the problem and plans were

drawn up under the direction of anthropologist Sol Tax (1907–1995). Students would attend these Workshops on American Indian Affairs from 1956 through 1963.

The workshops, most of which were held at the University of Colorado, Boulder, brought to the fore a new figure of the first postwar generation, Cherokee anthropologist Robert K. Thomas (1925–1991). Thomas got his bachelor's and master's (1954) at the University of Arizona and was working toward a doctorate at the University of Chicago under anthropologist Sam Stanley. By the time of the Workshops, he was Professor of Anthropology at Montieth College, Wayne State University, Detroit. From1981 until his death he would direct the American Indian Studies Program at the University of Arizona in Tucson.

Thomas was director of the second summer workshop in 1957, assistant director in 1961, and regular lecturer for 1962 and 1963. Though most of the staff was non-Indian, Thomas played the central role. According to McNickle, who observed the development of the workshops from 1960 through 1963, it was Thomas who "most influenced the shaping of the workshop as a center for discovery and understanding. The teaching faculty looked to him for intellectual challenge, while the students responded by improving academic performances . . . [He was] equally capable of reaching students and encouraging them to stretch their intellectual grasp."

The workshops revealed that most of the students suffered from confused identity and loss of cultural moorings, had internalized white stereotypes of Indians, and knew little of their history and culture. The staff tried to give the students a clearer sense of Indian identity by explaining both Native and white cultures objectively. The response was very positive.

The American Indian Chicago Conference was held in June 1961, at the University of Chicago. It was described as the first comprehensive investigation of the state of the American Indian since the Meriam Report. The method, however, was direct participation. Indians representing hundreds of tribes from every part of the country would come together to draw up a declaration of purpose that would express their common goals. The declaration itself would be a truly representative statement, but the discussions that had to take place in order to arrive at it, and the lasting contacts that would, it was hoped, be made, were no less important.

As the organizers intended, this would already have been a historic gathering, not only for its scope, but for the way it was planned, with local Indian participation in a series of preliminary regional meetings. They had not expected it to become the birthplace of the "Red Power" movement, however.

A group of younger people, led by Clyde M. Warrior (1939–1968)—an active student participant in both the 1961 and 1962 Workshops—felt that the Declaration of Indian Purpose, while correct, was too mild and, in any case, needed to be backed up with organization and activism. Thus, the National Indian Youth Council, in many ways the precursor to the more successful American Indian Movement a decade later, was founded at the conference. Warrior himself seems to have been close to Bob Thomas, and in the 1960s Thomas, though by no means a militant himself, would keep in touch with the NIYC, publishing a number of articles in their newsletter "ABC: America Before Columbus." He coined the term "internal colonization" to describe the situation of American Indians and other Indigenous peoples in the modern world. His writings were important in the development of the militant pro-sovereignty movement of the 1970s. Ward Churchill has called Thomas "the first to openly and coherently apply the concept of colonization to American Indians."

The National Indian Youth Council was made up almost exclusively of young college students who would inaugurate increasingly confrontational tactics, such as "fish-ins," protesting fishing rights violations, to advance Indian causes. As the decade progressed, Indian college students would become further radicalized by the '60s antiwar movement, Black power, and other anti-establishment influences, so much so that the 1969 Alcatraz occupation, though begun by the local Bay Area community, was soon taken over by Indian college students, bringing this kind of protest culture into the Indian movement for the first time.

McNickle's immediate reaction to the Chicago Conference was disappointment. He felt it had not achieved its goals. Only later would its great importance come into perspective. The baton had been passed. To the young radicals of the 1960s and 1970s, the Young Turks of the Collier Era looked like old fogeys. The NCAI, which had itself germinated from a protest walkout in 1939, and was the first national Indian organization formed entirely by and for Indians, was now "the Establishment."

THE GREAT SOCIETY

In the mid-1960s, the United Scholarship Service was the only national Indian organization involved in Indian education. The Economic Opportunity Act, passed in May 1965, made major non-BIA funding available to Indians for the first time. The Higher Education Act (1965) set aside Title III funds for Indian Colleges. Educational opportunities came especially through the Head Start Program.

By 1965, post-secondary Indian enrollment had increased to 7,000 nationwide, but the ratio of graduates from four-year institutions was no larger: in 1968 there were only 181. Enrollment continued to grow rapidly: by 1970, it had reached approximately 15,000. Several thousand received degrees in the 1960s, but Brophy and Aberle, in their final Fund for the Republic report of 1966, still reported a dropout rate of 60 percent.

The stage was now set for a real turning point for Indian higher education. This came during the Johnson and Nixon administrations under two exceptionally important commissioners: Robert L. Bennett and Louis R. Bruce Jr.

Robert LaFollette Bennett was another veteran of the Collier days. A Wisconsin Oneida, he was a graduate of Haskell's short-lived junior college program in 1931 and joined the BIA two years later, serving at the Ute Agency and in Washington. After receiving a law degree from Southeastern University in 1941, and briefly working with the Navajo, he joined the Marines. After the war he worked at the Veterans' Administration, helping Indian veterans get their benefits under the G.I. Bill.

Interior Secretary Stewart Udall, spurred by the rising expectations of Johnson's "Great Society" program, needed to replace outgoing commissioner Philleo Nash with someone who would be respected by tribes and by Congress alike. Bennett, who as area director of the Juneau Area Office in Alaska (1962–1966) had won the respect of Indian leaders around the country for his efforts to protect Native land claims, was appointed Indian Commissioner on Apr. 27, 1966. He was the first Native of the 20th century to hold this position, and the second in history.

In 1969 came the publication of "Indian Education: A National Tragedy," the report of U.S. Senate Special Subcommittee on Indian Education of the Senate Committee on Labor and Public Welfare. Hank Adams, of the National Indian Youth Council, helped Sen. Robert Kennedy draft the report. Now under pressure, Bennett expanded the Bureau's educational efforts, doubling the funding for higher education. Nevertheless, he was criticized both by the Red Power movement and the NCAI for not moving fast enough. The leasing of Indian natural resources that grew out of his promotion of tribal self-determination would also be targeted by the American Indian Movement in the 1970s and 1980s.

After Nixon took office, Bennett resigned on May 31, 1969, in favor of Louis Rook Bruce Jr. (Oglala Sioux/Mohawk, 1906–1989). Bruce had attended Cazenovia Seminary in the 1920s and got a bachelor's degree from Syracuse University in 1930. In the Depression, he developed a program to send Indian youth to teach Indian lore and crafts at summer camps. While not a veteran of the Collier BIA, he had directed the WPA programs for New York Indians in the 1930s and was a founding member of the NCAI. He later taught part-time at Columbia, Penn State and Cornell.

Bruce began to establish programs for off-reservation Indians who had suffered under the relocation policies of termination and to formalize the self-determination policies begun by Bennett. President Nixon officially ended the hated termination policy in 1970, and in May of that year, the Zuñi tribe was given the right to administer all BIA activities in their pueblo, and the Miccosukees of Florida soon followed.

THE TRIBAL COLLEGE

In July 1968, by special federal legislation, the Navajo Community College in Tsaile, Ariz., became the first college founded and controlled by an Indian tribe. Since 1996 it has been known as Diné College.

Part two of the 1969 Senate subcommittee report "Indian Education: A National Tragedy," on higher education, called for more Indian community colleges, advocated Native American Studies programs, suggested improvements in scholarship granting by BIA, and recommended "special recruiting and orienting programs." It also urged that higher education programs for Indians be included in Title III (Developing Institutions) of the Higher Education Act (1965), which would take some power away from the BIA, and that funds from the vocational Education Act (1963) and Higher Education Act be used to support BIA programs.

In 1971, recently retired Indian Commissioner Bennett and John C. Rainer Sr. (Taos Pueblo), founded American Indian Scholarships, Inc. at Albuquerque, N. Mex., to provide grants to Indian graduate students. Since 1989, the organization has been known as the American Indian Graduate Center. Bennett's original motivation was to help more Indians qualify for important positions in the BIA. Fifteen students were funded the first year; in 1994–1995, it would fund nearly 700. As of 1996,

AIGC would be assisting 95 percent of the Indian graduate students in the United States, disbursing about $2 million per annum.

The Indian Education Act (1972) allocated funding for university programs to train Native teachers of tribal students in elementary and high schools. In 1974, by amendment to this act, a special higher education program was set up to provide funds to graduate students, giving priority to the fields of business, education, law, engineering, natural resources, and health. This program was contracted to the American Indian Graduate Center. In 1994, 580 of these grants would be awarded.

At the end of the 1960s, American Indian Studies programs were created at a number of universities. Founded in 1969, the American Indian Studies Program at California State University–Long Beach was the first. Today there are scores of them.[1]

In 1970, on the heels of "Indian Education: A National Tragedy," Will Antell (White Earth Chippewa), Rosemary Christianson and Elgie Raymond founded the National Indian Education Association in Minnesota. In the fall of 1972, Native American Studies programs in a number of universities attempted to form a national organization to secure Title III funding under the Higher Education Act (1965). By this time, however, there were already more than 10 tribally controlled community colleges and one, D-Q University, not under tribal control. Seeing a threat, the colleges, supported by the National Indian Education Association, moved to found the American Indian Higher Education Consortium in January 1973. Its mission was to (1) help Indian-controlled junior colleges get accreditation, possibly to become an accrediting body itself; (2) help find general funds; (3) help develop curriculum, and (4) coordinate communication and contacts among the colleges.

Largely as a result of pressure from AIHEC, the Tribally Controlled Community College Assistance Act was passed in 1978, authorizing funding for all Indian community colleges either chartered or sanctioned by tribal governments. Colleges sanctioned by a tribal government are not under its control—the only leverage being the threat to withdraw the sanction.

In 1970, Haskell Institute, which had long been a high school and was now one of the few surviving federal boarding schools, became Haskell Indian Junior College. It would finally achieve university accreditation in October 1993, offering a bachelor of science degree in elementary teacher education. Since then, it has been known as Haskell Indian Nations University, and is one of three tribal colleges operated directly by the BIA, the others being Southwestern Indian Polytechnic Institute in Albuquerque, and the Institute of American Indian Arts in Santa Fe.

A descendent of the summer Workshops on Indian Affairs, NAES College was opened in 1975 as Native American Educational Services, originally affiliated with Antioch College. Sol Tax and Robert Thomas were active on its board of directors and one of its founders, Robert V. Duncan, was a participant in the 1960 Workshop. As Duncan stated "we have modelled NAES on this notion—the functional role of tribal knowledge and learning for the student and the community." Accredited since 1984 to grant a bachelor of arts in Community Studies, NAES now has branch campuses at Fort Peck, Mont. (1978), Northern Cheyenne (1980), the Twin Cities, Minn. (1988), and Menominee, Wis. (1989).

The American Indian Science and Engineering Society helps American Indians and Alaska Natives pursue studies in science, engineering, business and other academic arenas. It provides financial, academic and cultural support to Native students from middle school through graduate school. It trains teachers to work with Native students and develops culturally appropriate curricula and publications. Based in Boulder, Colo., AISES was founded in 1977 by a number of American Indian scientists, engineers and educators, among them Hopi-Laguna geneticist Frank C. Dukepoo (b.1943), who were concerned about the low enrollment and graduation rates, and the high dropout rates of Indian college students compared with other ethnic groups, as well as the great under representation of American Indians in science and engineering. Since 1983, AISES has been directed by Norbert S. Hill Jr. (Oneida, b. 1946).

In 1993, the Packer Foundation inaugurated a Tribal Colleges Science Program to assist American Indian students with their scientific education so as to be better able to manage the vast land and water resources on their reservations. In 1994, tribal colleges were awarded 11 grants of approximately $50,000 each, to support science programs, renewable for up to three years.

The BIA's Higher Education Grant Program still provides grants to undergraduates. In 1972, 12,438 were awarded, and in 1994, more than 14,800.

On Oct. 20, 1994, the tribal colleges gained land-grant status through passage of a rider to the reauthorization of the Elementary and Secondary Education Act, (108 Stat. 404851), bringing with it a $23 million endowment. As of 1997, there were 30 tribal colleges, 27 of which are two-year institutions. Only Sinte Gleska, D-Q, and Haskell Universities have four-year programs. In 1995–96, these colleges served more than 25,000 students from over 200 tribes. Many entering students are the first in their families ever to attend college.

The American Indian College Fund, in Denver, Colo., raises funds for the member colleges of AIHEC, approximately $800,000 per annum. The Fund contributes an additional $1.5 million to an endowment set up to benefit the tribal colleges. It has a Fund for Cultural Preservation, funded by a National Endowment for the Humanities grant. Its total income in 1994 was $5,238,000.

As Indigenous peoples begin to take their rightful place as peoples of the world, the tribal college is better preparing American Indian youth, if need be, for continuing education in universities anywhere in the world. The fact is that Native people with a sheepskin have greater power to defend and better their community. College as an institution, after all, is simply a tool a society uses to better achieve its goals. In the context of the twentieth century, the borrowing of this institution from Euro-American society, at first regarded as impossible or at least inappropriate, gradually became a necessity.

The tribal colleges and the university Indian programs are still modest institutions with quite limited resources. Yet their existence and growth confirm that from here on, Indians, whether they attend tribal or conventional colleges, will relate to the larger society by developing their communities and cultures, not destroying them. This is a tremendous victory when seen from the perspective of the whole century.

Most uniquely, through its goal of integrating and applying all fields of knowledge to the health and balance of the community, and the larger definition of community which sees the Earth as an interlocking community of communities, the tribal college represents a Native adaptation of the ideal of the university, for in Indian cultures, learning means discovering the principles and the relations of everything. Embodied in a new social form, this return to the university ideal can develop into a great contribution not only to the survival of Native society, but also to the survival of the world through the community of learning.

BIBLIOGRAPHICAL NOTES

In the preparation of this article I am indebted to a number of excellent studies by Western Shoshone historian Steven J. Crum:

"Henry Roe Cloud, a Winnebago Indian Reformer: His Quest for American Indian Higher Education," *Kansas History*, 11 (Autumn 1988), 171–184.

"The Idea of an Indian College or University in Twentieth-century America before the Formation of the Navajo Community College in 1968." *Tribal College*, 1.1 (Summer 1989): 20–23.

"Higher Education," *Native America in the Twentieth Century*, ed. Mary B. Davis. (New York & London: Garland, 1994), 237–239.

And by the late Dr. Bobby Wright, Chippewa-Cree educator and historian from Rocky Boy's Reservation, Mont.

"American Indian and Alaska Native Higher Education: Toward a New Century of Academic Achievement and Cultural Integrity." *Indian Nations at Risk Task Force, Commissioned Papers* (1991, 16 pp.). ERIC Document 343771.

"The Broken Covenant: American Indian Missions in the Colonial Colleges," *Tribal College* 7.1 (Summer 1995): 26–33.

Readers may also wish to consult:

John Williams & Howard L. Meredith, *Bacone Indian University: A History. Oklahoma City* (Western Heritage Books, 1980).

[1]See *A Guide to Native American Studies Programs in the United States and Canada*, Robert M. Nelson, editor, published by the Association for the Study of American Indian Literatures, 28 Westhampton Way, Box 112, University of Richmond, Va. 23173.

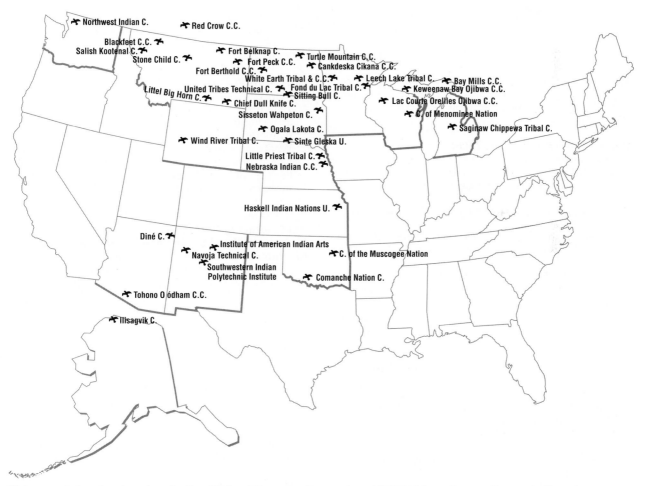

This map is by the *American Indian Higher Education Consortium (AIHEC) http://www.aihec.org/colleges/TCUmap.cfm).* There are 37 tribal colleges and universities *(TCUs)* in the United States, including Alaska, and one in Canada.

Source: The map supplied by AIHEC, © 2004-2009.

© H. J. Tsinhnahjinnie

PART REVIEW

DISCUSSION QUESTIONS

Wilma Mankiller and Michael Wallis, *Asgaya-Dihi*
1. What does *Asgaya-dihi* mean, and why is this name important to the author in terms of her family heritage and Cherokee culture?

Deanna Kingston, *Traveling Traditions*
1. Describe the nature of the "teasing" or "joking" relationship that the author has with her cross-cousin Mark.
2. How do song and dance enter into the teasing cousins custom?
3. What does the author mean by "traveling traditions"?

Jennie Joe, *American Indian and Alaska Native Health*
1. What are the major health issues facing American Indians today?
2. Discuss the role of Indian Health Service and Public Health Service in providing treaty mandated health delivery to American Indians.
3. In what ways are health services effective and how are they lacking? What do you think would be means to improve health prevention and care to American Indians?

Philip A. May, *The Epidemiology of Alcohol Abuse Among American Indians*
1. Are Native Americans genetically predisposed to alcoholism? Do they metabolize alcohol differently or more slowly than do members of other ethnic groups?
2. What is the difference between "anxiety drinkers" and "recreational drinkers?"
3. How does the uncritical use of statistics perpetuate the drunken Indian stereotype?

Florence Connolly Shipek, *Delfina Cuero*
1. According to Delfina Cuero's autobiography, "in the real old days," how did a young woman learn to be a good wife and about childbirth and caring for babies?
2. What things did her grandmother teach her about how to take care of babies?

Larry Murillo, *Perspectives on Traditional Health Practices*
1. Why does Murillo argue for a broader perspective in assessing the role of traditional health practices in contemporary health care?
2. What are some of the ways he suggests that traditional health practices can be integrated into maintaining healthy communities and health care? What are some of the barriers to this integrative approach?

Suzan Shown Harjo, *Restoring Native Foods for Health and Community Well-Being;* **Ofelia Zepeda,** *Squash Under the Bed;* **and Suzan Shown Harjo,** *My New Year's Resolution: No More Fat "Indian" Food*
1. What are some of the Native foods, and why are they healthy foods, compared to the contemporary highly processed diet? What is the link for Native people between changes in diet away from traditional foods and health?
2. Is frybread a traditional Indian food? Why or why not? Historically, what role has it played in Native communities?

Carol Devens, *"If We Get the Girls, We Get the Race"*
1. Compare and contrast the educational experiences of Indian children in boarding schools versus those in their home Native communities.
2. What were the underlying motives for creating the mission boarding schools? Discuss how they relate to religious conversion, to assimilation theory, and to ethnocide.

Tim Giago, *Reservation Schools Fail to Assimilate All Students*
1. According to this editorial by Tim Giago, why has assimilation through the mainstream educational process failed?

Jeffrey Wollock, *Protagonism Emergent*
1. Describe the Indian education policy in the United States since the 1930s New Deal.
2. What role did educated Indians play in the New Deal reforms of the 1934 Indian Reorganization Act?

3. Summarize the emergence and the subsequent development of the Tribal Community Colleges and Native American Studies programs in the 1960s.

KEY TERMS

alcohol abuse vs. alcoholism (addiction)
"all my relations"
Asgaya-dihi
assimilation
boarding schools
corn, beans, and squash
cross-cousin
D-Q University
epidemiology
frybread
healthy-community concept

Indian Child Welfare Act (ICWA)
Indian Health Service (IHS)
Indian Reorganization Act of 1934
Inupiaq
"Kill the Indian but save the man"
Navajo Community (Diné) College
teasing or joking relationship
ti-ospaye
Tohono O'odham Community Action (TOCA)
victim-blaming theory
Zitkala-Sa

SUGGESTED READINGS

ALLEN, PAULA GUNN. *The Sacred Hoop: Recovering the Feminine in American Indian Traditions*. Boston: Beacon Press, 1986.

ARCHULETA, MARGARET L., BRENDA J. CHILD, and K. TSIANINA LOMAWAIMA, eds. *Away from Home: American Indian Boarding School Experiences, 1868–2000*. Phoenix: Heard Museum, 2000.

CHANA, LEONARD L., SUSAN LOBO, and BARBARA CHANA. *The Sweet Smell of Home: The Life and Art of Leonard F. Chana*. Tucson: University of Arizona Press, 2009.

ERDRICH, LOUISE. *Love Medicine: A Novel*. New York: Holt, Rinehart, and Winston, 1984.

JAINE, LINDA. "Industrial and Residential School Administration: The Attempt to Undermine Indigenous Self-Determination." *Journal of Indigenous Studies*, 2, no. 2 (Summer 1991): 37–48.

KAWAGLEY, A. OSCAR. *A Yupiaq Worldview: A Pathway to Ecology and the Spirit*. Prospect Heights, IL: Waveland Press, 1995.

LOBO, SUSAN. *A House of My Own: Social Organization in the Squatter Settlements of Lima, Peru*. Tucson: University of Arizona Press, 1982.

MANKILLER, WILMA, AND MICHAEL WALLIS. *Mankiller: A Chief and Her People*. New York: St. Martin's Press, 1993.

MEDICINE, BEATRICE. "American Indian Family: Cultural Change and Adaptive Strategies." *Journal of Ethnic Studies*, 8, no. 4 (1982): 14–23.

MOMADAY, N. SCOTT. *The Names: A Memoir*. New York: Harper & Row, 1976.

NEBELKOPF, ETHAN, and MARY PHILLIPS, eds. *Healing and Mental Health for Native Americans: Speaking in Red*. Walnut Creek, CA: AltaMira Press, 2004.

SARRIS, GREG. *Grand Avenue*. New York: Hyperion, 1994.

SENESE, GUY B. *Self-determination and the Social Education of Native Americans*. New York: Praeger Publishers, 1991.

PEGO, CHRISTINA M., ROBERT F. HILL, GLENN W. SOLOMON, ROBERT M. CHISHOLM, and SUZANNE E. IVEY. "Tobacco, Culture and Health among American Indians: A Historical Review." *American Indian Culture and Research Journal*, 19, no. 2 (1995): 143–164.

ROSS, LUANA. "Resistance and Survivance: Cultural Genocide and Imprisoned Native American Women." *Race, Gender, and Class*, 3, no. 2 (1996): 125–141.

ROSS, LUANA. *Inventing the Savage: The Social Construction of Native American Criminality*. Austin: University of Texas Press, 1998.

TRAFZER, CLIFFORD E., and DIANE WEINER, eds. "Special Issue: Disease, Health, and Survival Among Native Americans," *American Indian Culture and Research Journal*, vol. 23, no. 3 (1999).

Tribal College: Journal of American Indian Education. A quarterly publication of the American Indian Higher Education Consortium, P.O. Box 720, Mancos, CO 81328.

VOGEL, VIRGIL J. *American Indian Medicine*. Norman: University of Oklahoma Press, 1970.

WEATHERFORD, JACK. *Indian Givers: How the Indians of the Americas Transformed the World*. New York: Fawcett Columbine, 1988.

Where the Spirit Lives. Feature film, filmed in Canada. Beacon Films, 930 Pitner Avenue, Evanston, IL 60202.

WILSON, DARRYL BABE. *The Morning the Sun Went Down*. Berkeley, Calif.: Heyday Books, 1998.

VII

THE SACRED: SPIRITUALITY AND SACRED GEOGRAPHY

Missionaries

Floyd Red Crow Westerman and Jimmy Curtiss

Spread the word of your religions
Convert the whole world if you can
Kill and slaughter those who oppose you
It's worth it if you save one man
Take the land to build your churches
A sin to tax the house of God
Take the child while he is supple
Spoil the mind and spare the rod
Go and tell the savage nation
That he must be Christianized
Tell him, and his heathen worship
And you will make him civilized
Shove your gospel, force your values
Down his throat until it's raw
And after he is crippled
Turn your back and lock the door

Like an ever circling vulture
You descend upon your prey
Then you pick the soul to pieces
And you watch as it decays
'Cause religion is big business
As your bank accounts will show
And Christ died to save all mankind
But that was long ago

Missionaries, missionaries, go and leave us all alone
Take your white God to your white man
We've a God of our own.

Although each Native tribe or nation has its own unique system of spiritual beliefs and practices, there are some commonly held philosophical ideas that are generally shared by Indigenous people throughout the Western Hemisphere. The natural world is the focal point of Indian spirituality. From this foundation spring a number of understandings regarding the nature of the world, and the cosmos in general, as well as the appropriate role of human beings in it. Humans are viewed as intimately linked to one another and morally bound to the natural world in such a way that one's individual, family, and community pasts are intertwined with the Old Stories that teach how things came to be as they are today and right behavior for ensuring that future generations will continue to rely on a balanced relationship with the natural world. All creatures—the two-legged (humans), four-legged, winged, and green things, creatures that swim in the rivers and seas, even the rocks and things that, from a non-Indian philosophical perspective, are considered inanimate—are part of this spirituality or sacred life force. For many Indians living today, this circle of the Sacred to which we human beings are connected, ideally in balance and harmony with nature, also includes the life-giving sun, the many stars of the night sky, and Mother Earth herself. Because this perspective encompasses all time, all places, and all beings, Native Americans generally prefer the term *spirituality* or *the Sacred* rather than *religion*.

Indigenous spirituality has continually come under attack throughout the history of Western conquest of the Americas. In Part IV we examined the deleterious consequences of the early Christian missionaries. Sometimes the imposition of Christianity also had its humorous aspect. Inuit journalist Rachel Attituq Qitsualik reports that "Christianity as brought to Inuit required no small amount of tweaking to make it more palatable." And even then, some things make sense. For example, Sunday, *Naattiinguja*, translates into English something like "waiting for the long day to be over." As she observes: "Long day, indeed, when I was a child, for on Sunday I was not allowed to pick flowers, play, chew gum, read (except the Bible), sing, or do anything else resembling fun. Instead, I had to memorize Old Testament verses."[1]

Spirituality is really the linchpin of traditional Native American culture; it acts as the axis around which all the other components of culture revolve, such as the institutions of government, economy, defense, education, kinship, and the family. In traditional Indian culture there has not been the separation of church from state; Indian political and military leaders were also the spiritual leaders. The great Lakota (Sioux) fighting chief Crazy Horse, for example, was also a holy person. Spirituality thus integrates Indian society and gives it its collective consciousness and social solidarity. It constitutes the "glue," or social cement, of Indian culture: that is, its basic philosophy and values and what it means to be a Native person.

It is worth noting that the early French sociologist Emile Durkheim studied "the elementary forms of the religious life" and concluded that religion embraces more than the anthropomorphized state religions found in the large-scale, class-stratified societies of Europe. Moreover, Durkheim concluded that "the religious life" is universal among all peoples of the world, both Western and non-Western, because the essence of religion is found not in its institutional aspects but, instead, in its sacred community of believers.[2] Religion can therefore be universally defined as *a system of belief and practice relative to sacred things that unite its devotees into a single moral community called a church.* Durkheim's classic definition of religion therefore includes American Indian spirituality in all of its manifestations.

Although "the sacred" underlies everything in the Indian world, some things and places are especially holy. Durkheim was also the first European scholar to understand that all peoples divide the world into two cultural domains—the sacred and the profane, or secular. How cultures make this division, however, can differ considerably. The sacred can include an object, a place, or a ceremony. But which objects, places, or rites are considered sacred and which are considered secular can vary greatly from culture to culture. Christians are accustomed to viewing the crucifix as a sacred object; among many North American Indian nations, an eagle feather holds a similar sacred quality. Also, the Navajo hogan where curing ceremonies are performed is sacred, much as is a Christian church or a Jewish synagogue in Western culture. This difference in the way the sacred and the secular are defined in today's multi-ethnic world is posing a serious point of conflict between Indians and non-Indians, whether in North, Central, or South America.

In a similar vein, sacred places play a major part in Native American spirituality. Among other things, certain mountains, springs, rivers, lakes, caves, and rock formations can be a part of a sacred geography or landscape that is the basis for spiritual belief and practice. The river Jordan holds a sacred significance for Christians, and the Ganges is sacred to the Hindu. In the same way, the Chewana, or Columbia River, is sacred to the fishing Indians of Oregon and Washington. Native American sacred geography has often become a source of conflict between Native peoples and others. In the mainstream culture of the United States, and throughout the Americas, land has come to be defined primarily as real estate, private property that produces profit for its owners. Tourists or hikers entering into areas they consider recreational, but which are sacred to Native Americans, are also a source of conflict. Land is secularized in Western capitalist society, in contrast to traditional Native American thought, in which land is an expression of the sacred.

Indians and other Native peoples also have sacred ceremonies; a Lakota "sweat" purification and an Apache woman's "coming out," or puberty ceremony, are just as sacred in the traditional Indian world as is the Christian communion or baptism in the Judeo-Christian religious tradition. Until 1934, most Indian religious ceremonies in the United States were banned and punished by fine or imprisonment, or both. The First Amendment to the Constitution of the United States begins, "Congress shall make no law respecting an establishment of religion, or prohibiting the free exercise thereof. . . ." Yet, since first contact, Native peoples have had to struggle against laws and actions that prohibited and curtailed this human and constitutional right to religious freedom. The legacy of this abridgment of religious freedom is a continuing source of friction in U.S. Indian–white relations.

Among all peoples in the world, the dead are sanctified after death, although the particular practice or custom varies from culture to culture. American Indians hold an ideal of deeply respecting elders and ancestors. From an Indian perspective, the dead are always buried or cremated in a sacred manner, but from a Western perspective, these Indian dead lay in unmarked graves and therefore become objects for scientific collection and study in what Native critics call "a specimen complex."

These aspects of Native American spirituality and related issues are examined in this chapter.

It is appropriate that we begin our readings for Part VII with the box, "What Is Sacred?" by Anishinaabeg (Ojibwe) writer and activist Winona LaDuke. The excerpt is taken from the introduction to her book *Recovering the Sacred: The Power of Naming and Claiming* (see "Suggested Readings"). LaDuke is a leading Indian environmentalist and two-time Green Party candidate for vice president of the United States. In a series of essays, she expands and deepens our knowledge of the Indian world of the sacred. The sacred is more than beliefs and ceremonies, human remains, and sacred places. It is something shared, a collective experience, and lies at the heart of Indian culture. It includes Native seeds, medicine, and traditional agriculture, such as the Anishinaabeg wild rice, and the Iroquois "three sisters" (corn, beans, and squash). It also includes "relatives," such as the Klamath salmon, the Anishinaabeg sturgeon, and the Nez Pierce Appaloosa horses. "Tate," the wind, is sacred to the Lakota. A special significance is attached to sacred items, such as the "souvenirs" taken by Army soldiers from the killing fields of Wounded Knee, site of the 1890 massacre. LaDuke also includes a section on biopiracy, the Human Genome Diversity Project, and the belief among many Native peoples that the "scientific" collection of indigenous DNA is a violation of the sacred.

Reading 1, "Alone on the Hilltop," by Lakota medicine man John (Fire) Lame Deer and his collaborator, Richard Erdoes, describes the Indian vision quest, which has been widely practiced among the Indian peoples of Western North America. It is a traditional way for young men to seek spiritual power that will guide them on the "good Red Road" of life. For many years, the vision quest and many other spiritual customs were suppressed by the Spanish and later by the United States and Canada, so that they were carried on in secret, if at all. In the United States, Indian religious customs were criminalized under a special Court of Indian Offenses, punished by fines and the withholding of government food rations, until the Indian Reorganization Act reforms of the 1930s. The Indian Act of Canada outlawed participation in ceremonies that were central to many Indians, such as the Plains Sun Dance, or the Northwest Coast potlatch. The vision quest, or "crying for a dream," is now being revived in the United States. Today, the practice includes young women as well as men. Since the Indian movement of the 1960s and 1970s, there has been a strong revitalization or rebirth of American Indian spiritual belief and practice.

Reading 2, "My World Is a Gift of My Teachers," is a selection on Indian art by Frank LaPena, a Nontipom–Wintu Indian artist and professor of Indian studies. He beautifully describes the holistic nature of the Indian spiritual world and how it permeates every facet of traditional Indian culture. The continuity with the past, the place of oral traditions and the role of elders, and the link between the physical and spiritual worlds all figure prominently in Native American culture.

In Reading 3, "Who Owns Our Past? The Repatriation of Native American Human Remains and Cultural Objects," academician Russell Thornton (Cherokee) examines the issue of repatriating the remains of several hundred thousand Native Americans that have come to reside in the U.S. government's Smithsonian Institution and other "scientific" collections. Among the many critical issues that Indians of the United States face, this, without doubt, is one of the most troubling and one about which Native people feel most deeply. How is it, they ask, that only Indigenous people are objects of scientific collection and study? Why not white people? The answer, of course, lies in the history of oppression and racism that characterize Indian–white relations. In 1983 Jan Hammil of American Indians Against Desecration delivered a scathing address to an annual meeting of the American Anthropological Society in which she challenged the scientific community to stop demeaning Indian people by storing the sacred remains of ancestors in the "bags, boxes, and paper sacks" of museums and anthropological laboratories. Thornton details the history of this issue, the contemporary Native American repatriation movement, and the status of the corrective legislation, which is discussed further in the box titled "Indians Are Not Specimens—Indians Are People."

In the United States, the Native American Graves Protection and Repatriation Act (NAGPRA) was passed by Congress in 1990. NAGPRA requires museums to return human remains and funerary objects, as well as other items of cultural patrimony to tribes. The law mandated that by November 1993, museums were to summarize sacred funerary objects and cultural items in their collections and mail the summaries to interested tribes. Then, by 1995, museums were to give "culturally affiliated" Indian tribes, Alaska Native villages or corporations, and Native Hawaiian organizations similar data on all human remains and "associated funerary objects." Adequate funding by Congress to carry out NAGPRA has been slow in coming, however, and the deadlines have been difficult for museums to meet. According to Thornton, however, the once-reticent Smithsonian Institution is now beginning the task of repatriating Indian remains and grave goods. A difficult aspect of the law for many Native groups, however, is how to prove their cultural affiliation to the ancient remains and objects, because they were formerly nonliterate communities relying on oral tradition. They lacked written records that would establish such an affiliation in U.S. courts. Furthermore, many thousands of other Indian people and their tribal communities are currently unrecognized by the federal government and are therefore ineligible under NAGPRA to apply for the repatriation of the remains of their dead relatives and grave goods.

Apart from the repatriation issue itself, another serious issue involving spirituality is the fact that some imprisoned Native people are still being denied protection of their cultural and religious rights. Sweat lodges have been torn down by some prison authorities, and Indian religious ceremonies involving the Pipe religion and the Native American Church have been denied. It is unfortunate that an omnibus bill introduced by Senator Daniel K. Inouye of Hawai'i in 1994, the Native American Cultural Protection and Free Exercise of Religion Act, that would have ended this aspect of religious discrimination, failed to pass Congress.

In Reading 4, "Battling for Souls: Organizing the Return of the Sacred Textiles to the Community of Coroma, Bolivia," Victoria Bomberry, a Muskogee Lenape scholar, examines the issue of the theft of sacred textiles belonging to the Aymara Indians of Bolivia. Once stolen and transported to the United States, these items were viewed by dealers and collectors as commercial art pieces and were sold through the international Indian art market. In this deeply insightful article, Bomberry considers the serious ramifications of the removal of the Coroma textiles from this Indigenous community and explains both the historical and spiritual nature of the textiles, as well as the linkage they provide in integrating the entire fabric of Aymara culture. The repatriation issue (the return of sacred items to Indian societies) has become a key issue throughout the hemisphere and is now an important item on the international Indigenous rights agenda of the United Nations and before the "court" of world opinion. (See a related article by Traci Morris in Part V.)

In Reading 5, "American Indian Religious Freedom Act After Twenty-Five Years," Suzan Shown Harjo (Cheyenne/Hodulgee Muscogee), reevaluates the American Indian Religious Freedom Act (AIRFA) on its 25th anniversary. The occasion was a gathering of Native Americans at Arizona State University's College of Law, who had worked to achieve its passage in 1978.

One must understand that AIRFA was a policy statement of the U.S. government respecting the religious rights of Native peoples. An important element of the legislation was the directive for federal agencies to consult with Native traditional religious leaders. Unfortunately, this consultative policy requirement has been all but ignored. Federal agencies must implement the executive orders "Indian sacred sites" (1996) and "Consultation and Coordination with Indian Tribal Governments" (1998). Harjo writes that it is unfortunate that in AIRFA's evaluation and report back to Congress, the Native American peyote religion became a contentious issue. This was due in part to a 1989 Supreme Court decision that weakened the peyote church as a protected religion. Furthermore, despite reform, religious freedom for Indian inmates of prisons has not yet been fully achieved.

With regard to protecting sacred places, Harjo notes that it was not until 2003 that the Naval bombing of the Hawai'ian sacred island of Kaho'olawe was stopped and the island returned to Native Hawai'ians. She also deplores the "foot dragging" by the Smithsonian Institution to fully comply with the repatriation laws of 1989 National Museum of the American Indian and the 1990 NAGPRA. Some scientists have also sought to defy full repatriation compliance, such as in the issue of the Kennewick Man. (See Reading 4, "Protecting Native American Human Remains, Burial Grounds, and Sacred Places," in Part IV.) The February 2004 decision of the Ninth Circuit Court of Appeals to support "scientific studies" rather than return the Kennewick remains to culturally appropriate tribes also ignores NAGPRA policy. Harjo concludes that protecting sacred places and the repatriation issue are the two most glaring items on AIRFA's unfinished agenda.

NOTES

1. Rachel Attituq Qitsualik, *Indian Country Today*, 9, no. 37 (March 1, 2000): A5.

2. Emile Durkheim, *The Elementary Forms of Religious Life*, trans. Joseph Ward Wain (London: Allen and Unwin, 1915).

RECOVERING THE SACRED
POWER OF NAMING AND CLAIMING
Winona LaDuke

WHAT IS SACRED?

How does a community heal itself from the ravages of the past? That is the question I asked in writing this book. I found an answer in the multifaceted process of recovering that which is "sacred." This complex and intergenerational process is essential to our vitality as Indigenous peoples and ultimately as individuals. This book documents some of our community's work to recover the sacred and to heal.

What qualifies something as sacred? That is a question asked in courtrooms and city council meetings across the country. Under consideration is the preservation or destruction of places like the Valley of the Chiefs in what is now eastern Montana and Medicine Lake in northern California, as well as the fate of skeletons and other artifacts mummified by collectors and held in museums against the will of their rightful inheritors. Debates on how the past is understood and what the future might bring have bearing on genetic research, reclamation of mining sites, reparations for broken treaties, and reconciliation between descendants of murderers and their victims. At stake is nothing less than the ecological integrity of the land base and the physical and social health of Native Americans throughout the continent. In the end there is no absence of irony: the integrity of what is sacred to Native Americans will be determined by the government that has been responsible for doing everything in its power to destroy Native American cultures.

Xenophobia and a deep fear of Native spiritual practices came to the Americas with the first Europeans. Papal law was the foundation, of colonialism; the Church served as hand-maiden to military, economic, and spiritual genocide and domination. Centuries of papal hulls posited the supremacy of Christendom over all other beliefs, sanctified manifest destiny, and authorized even the most brutal practices of colonialism. Some of the most virulent and disgraceful manifestations of Christian dominance found expression in the conquest and colonization of the Americas.

Religious dominance became the centerpiece of early reservation policy as Native religious expression was out-lawed in this country. To practice a traditional form of worship was to risk a death sentence for many peoples. The Wounded Knee Massacre of 1890 occurred in large part because of the fear of the Ghost Dance Religion, which had spread throughout the American West. Hundreds of Native spiritual leaders were sent to the Hiawatha Asylum for Insane Indians for their spiritual beliefs.[1]

The history of religious colonialism, including the geno-cide perpetrated by the Catholic Church (particularly in Latin America), is a wound from which Native communities have not yet healed. The notion that non-Christian spiritual prac-tices could have validity was entirely ignored or actively sup-pressed for centuries. So it was by necessity that Native spiritual practitioners went deep into the woods or into the heartland of their territory to keep up their traditions, always knowing that their job was to keep alive their teachers' instructions, and, hence, their way of life.

Native spiritual practices and Judeo-Christian traditions are based on very different paradigms. Native American ritu-als are frequently based on the reaffirmation of the relation-ship of humans to the Creation. Many of our oral traditions tell of the place of the "little brother" (the humans) in the larger Creation. Our gratitude for our part in Creation and for the gifts given to us by the Creator is continuously reinforced in Midewiwin lodges, Sundance ceremonies, world renewal ceremonies, and many others. Understanding the complexity of these belief systems is central to understanding the soci-eties built on those spiritual foundations—the relationship of peoples to their sacred lands, to relatives with fans or hooves, to the plant and animal foods that anchor a way of life.[2]

Chris Peters, a Pohik-la from northern California and pres-ident of the Seventh Generation Fund, broadly defines Native spiritual practices as affirmation-based and characterizes Judeo-Christian faiths as commemorative.[3] Judeo-Christian teachings and events frequently commemorate a set of histor-ical events: Easter, Christmas, Passover, and Hannukah are examples. Vine Deloria, Jr., echoes this distinction:

> Unlike the Mass or the Passover which both commemorate past historical religious events and which believers understand as also occurring in a timeless setting beyond the reach of the corruption of temporal processes, *Native American religious practitioners are seeking to introduce a sense of order* into the chaotic physical present as a prelude to experiencing the universal moment of complete fulfillment.[4]

The difference in the paradigms of these spiritual practices has, over time, become a source of great conflict in the Americas. Some 200 years after the U. S. Constitution guaran-teed freedom of religion for most Americans, Congress passed the American Indian Religious Freedom Act in 1978 and President Carter signed it into law. Although the act contains worthy language that seems to reflect the founders' concepts of religious liberty, it has but a few teeth. The act states:

> It shall be the policy of the United States to protect and pre-serve for American Indians their inherent right of freedom to believe, express, and exercise the traditional religions of the American Indian, Eskimo, Aleut and native Hawaiians, includ-ing but not limited to access to sites, use and possession of

sacred objects, and the freedom to worship through ceremonial and traditional rites."[5]

While the law ensured that Native people could hold many of their ceremonies, it did not protect the places where many of these rituals take place or the relatives and elements central to these ceremonies, such as salt from the sacred Salt Mother for the Zuni or Salmon for the Nez Perce. The Religious Freedom Act was amplified by President Clinton's 1996 Executive Order 13007 for preservation of sacred sites: "In managing Federal lands, each executive branch agency with statutory or administrative responsibility for the management of Federal lands shall . . . avoid adversely affecting the physical integrity of such sacred sites."[6]

Those protections were applied to lands held by the federal government, not by private interests, although many sacred sites advocates have urged compliance by other landholders to the spirit and intent of the law. The Bush administration, however, has by and large ignored that executive order.[7] Today, increasing numbers of sacred sites and all that embodies the sacred are threatened.

While Judeo-Christian sacred sites such as "the Holy Land" are recognized, the existence of other holy lands has been denied. There is a place on the shore of Lake Superior, or Gichi Gummi, where the Giant laid down to sleep. There is a place in Zuni's alpine prairie to which the Salt Woman moved and hoped to rest. There is a place in the heart of Lakota territory where the people go to vision quest and remember the children who ascended from there to the sky to become the Pleiades. There is a place known as the Falls of a Woman's Hair that is the epicenter of a salmon culture. And there is a mountain upon which the Anishinaabeg rested during their migration and from where they looked back to find their prophesized destination. The concept of "holy land" cannot be exclusive in a multicultural and multi-spiritual society, yet indeed it has been treated as such.

We have a problem of two separate spiritual paradigms and one dominant culture—make that a dominant culture with an immense appetite for natural resources. The animals, the trees and other plants, even the minerals under the ground and the water from the lakes and streams, all have been expropriated from Native American territories. Land taken from Native peoples either by force or the colonists' law was the basis for an industrial infrastructure and now a standard of living that consumes a third of the world's resources.

By the 1930s, Native territories had been reduced to about 4% of our original land base. More than 75% of our sacred sites have been removed from our care and jurisdiction.[8] Native people must now request permission to use their own sacred sites and, more often than not, find that those sites are in danger of being desecrated or obliterated.

The challenge of attempting to maintain your spiritual practice in a new millennium is complicated by the destruction of that which you need for your ceremonial practice. The annihilation of 50 million buffalo in the Great Plains region by the beginning of the 20th century caused immense hardship for traditional spiritual practices of the region, especially since the *Pte Oyate,* the buffalo nation, is considered the older brother of the Lakota nation and of many other indigenous cultures of the region. Similarly, the decimation of the salmon, in northwest rivers like the Columbia and the Klamath, caused by dam projects, over-fishing, and water diversion, has resulted in great emotional, social, and spiritual devastation to the Yakama, Wasco. Umatilla, Nez Perce, and other peoples of the region. New efforts to domesticate, patent, and genetically modify wild rice similarly concern the Anishinaabeg people of the Great Lakes.

It is more than 500 years since the European invasion of North America and more than 200 years since the formation of the United States. Despite these centuries of spiritual challenges, Native people continue, as we have for centuries, to always express our thankfulness to Creation—in our prayers, our songs, and our understanding of the sacredness of the land.

Dr. Henrietta Mann is a Northern Cheyenne woman and chair of the Native American Studies Department at Montana State University. She reiterates the significance of the natural world to Native spiritual teaching:

> Over the time we have been here, we have built cultural ways on and about this land. We have our own respected versions of how we came to be. These *origin stories*—that we emerged or fell from the sky or were brought forth—*connect us to this land* and establish our realities, our belief systems. *We have spiritual responsibilities to renew the Earth and we do this through our ceremonies so that our Mother, the Earth, can continue to support us.* Mutuality and respect are part of our tradition—give and take. Somewhere along the way, I hope people will learn that you can't just take, that you have to give back to the land."[9]

From Winona LaDuke, Recovering the Sacred: The Power of Naming and Claiming. Cambridge, MA: South End Press, 2005, pp. 11–15. The footnotes have been omitted.

PULLING DOWN THE CLOUDS

Ofeliá Zepeda

Ñ-ku'ibadkaj 'ant 'an ols g cewagǐ.
With my harvesting stick I will hook the clouds.
'Ant o'i-wañ̃'io k o'i-hudiñ g cewagǐ.
With my harvesting stick I will pull down the clouds.
Ñ-ku ibadkaj ant o i-siho g cewagǐ.
With my harvesting stick I will stir the clouds.

With dreams of distant noise disturbing his sleep.
the smell of dirt, wet, for the first time in what
  seems like months.
The change in the molecules is sudden,
they enter the nasal cavity.

He contemplates that smell.
What is that smell?
It is rain.

Rain somewhere out in the desert.
Comforted in this knowledge he turns over
and continues his sleep,
dreams of women with harvesting sticks
raised toward the sky.

"Pulling Down the Clouds" from *Ocean Power* by Ofeliá Zepeda.
© 1995 Ofeliá Zepeda. Reprinted with the permission of the
University of Arizona Press.

ALONE ON THE HILLTOP

John (Fire) Lame Deer and Richard Erdoes

I was all alone on the hilltop. I sat there in the vision pit, a hole dug into the hill, my arms hugging my knees as I watched old man Chest, the medicine man who had brought me there, disappear far down in the valley. He was just a moving black dot among the pines, and soon he was gone altogether.

Now I was all by myself, left on the hilltop for four days and nights without food or water until he came back for me. You know, we Indians are not like some white folks—a man and a wife, two children, and one baby sitter who watches the TV set while the parents are out visiting somewhere.

Indian children are never alone. They are always surrounded by grandparents, uncles, cousins, relatives of all kinds, who fondle the kids, sing to them, tell them stories. If the parents go someplace, the kids go along.

But here I was, crouched in my vision pit, left alone by myself for the first time in my life. I was sixteen then, still had my boy's name and, let me tell

you, I was scared. I was shivering and not only from the cold. The nearest human being was many miles away, and four days and nights is a long, long time. Of course, when it was all over, I would no longer be a boy, but a man. I would have had my vision. I would be given a man's name.

Sioux men are not afraid to endure hunger, thirst and loneliness, and I was only ninety-six hours away from being a man. The thought was comforting. Comforting, too, was the warmth of the star blanket which old man Chest had wrapped around me to cover my nakedness. My grandmother had made it especially for this, my first *hanblechia*, my first vision-seeking. It was a beautifully designed quilt, white with a large morning star made of many pieces of brightly colored cloth. That star was so big it covered most of the blanket. If Wakan Tanka, the Great Spirit, would give me the vision and the power, I would become a medicine man and perform many ceremonies wrapped in that quilt. I am an old man now and many times a grandfather, but I still have that star blanket my grandmother made for me. I treasure it; some day I shall be buried in it.

The medicine man had also left a peace pipe with me, together with a bag of *kinnickinnick*—our kind of tobacco made of red willow bark. This pipe was even more of a friend to me than my star blanket. To us the pipe is like an open Bible. White people need a church house, a preacher and a pipe organ to get into a praying mood. There are so many things to distract you: who else is in the church, whether the other people notice that you have come, the pictures on the wall, the sermon, how much money you should give and did you bring it with you. We think you can't have a vision that way.

For us Indians there is just the pipe, the earth we sit on and the open sky. The spirit is everywhere. Sometimes it shows itself through an animal, a bird or some trees and hills. Sometimes it speaks from the Badlands, a stone, or even from the water. That smoke from the peace pipe, it goes straight up to the spirit world. But this is a two-way thing. Power flows down to us through that smoke, through the pipe stem. You feel that power as you hold your pipe; it moves from the pipe right into your body. It makes your hair stand up. That pipe is not just a thing; it is alive. Smoking this pipe would make me feel good and help me to get rid of my fears.

As I ran my fingers along its bowl of smooth red pipestone, red like the blood of my people, I no longer felt scared. That pipe had belonged to my father and to his father before him. It would someday pass to my son and, through him, to my grandchildren. As long as we had the pipe there would be a Sioux nation. As I fingered the pipe, touched it, felt its smoothness that came from long use, I sensed that my forefathers who had once smoked this pipe were with me on the hill, right in the vision pit. I was no longer alone.

Besides the pipe the medicine man had also given me a gourd. In it were forty small squares of flesh which my grandmother had cut from her arm with a razor blade. I had seen her do it. Blood had been streaming down from her shoulder to her elbow as she carefully put down each piece of skin on a handkerchief, anxious not to lose a single one. It would have made those anthropologists mad. Imagine, performing such an ancient ceremony with a razor blade instead of a flint knife! To me it did not matter. Someone dear to me had undergone pain, given me something of herself, part of her body, to help me pray and make me stronghearted. How could I be afraid with so many people—living and dead—helping me?

One thing still worried me. I wanted to become a medicine man, a *yuwipi*, a healer carrying on the ancient ways of the Sioux nation. But you cannot learn to be a medicine man like a white man going to medical school. An old holy man can teach you about herbs and the right ways to perform a ceremony where everything must be in its proper place, where every move, every word has its own, special meaning. These things you can learn—like spelling, like training a horse. But by themselves these things mean nothing. Without the vision and the power this learning will do no good. It would not make me a medicine man.

What if I failed, if I had no vision? Or if I dreamed of the Thunder Beings, or lightning struck the hill? That would make me at once into a *heyoka*, a contrarywise, an upside-down man, a clown. "You'll know it, if you get the power," my Uncle Chest had told me. "If you are not given it, you won't lie about it, you won't pretend. That would kill you, or kill somebody close to you, somebody you love."

Night was coming on. I was still lightheaded and dizzy from my first sweat bath in which I had purified myself before going up the hill. I had never been in a sweat lodge before. I had sat in the little beehive-shaped hut made of bent willow branches and covered with blankets to keep the heat in. Old Chest and three other medicine men had been in the lodge with me. I had my back against the wall, edging as far away as I could from the red-hot stones glowing in the center. As Chest poured water over the rocks, hissing white steam enveloped me and filled my lungs. I thought the heat would kill me, burn the eyelids off my face! But right in the middle of all this swirling steam I heard Chest singing. So it couldn't be all that bad. I did not cry out "All my relatives!"—which would have made him open the flap of the sweat lodge to let in some cool air—and I was proud of this. I heard him praying for me: "Oh, holy rocks, we receive your white breath, the steam. It is the breath of life. Let this young boy inhale it. Make him strong."

The sweat bath had prepared me for my vision-seeking. Even now, an hour later, my skin still tingled. But it seemed to have made my brains empty. Maybe that was good, plenty of room for new insights.

Darkness had fallen upon the hill. I knew that *hanhepiwi* had risen, the night sun, which is what we call the moon. Huddled in my narrow cave, I did not see it. Blackness was wrapped around me like a velvet cloth. It seemed to cut me off from the outside world, even from my own body. It made me listen to the voices within me. I thought of my forefathers who had crouched on this hill before me, because the medicine men in my family had chosen this spot for a place of meditation and vision-seeking ever since the day they had crossed the Missouri to hunt for buffalo in the White River country some two hundred years ago. I thought that I could sense their presence right through the earth I was leaning against. I could feel them entering my body, feel them stirring in my mind and heart.

Sounds came to me through the darkness: the cries of the wind, the whisper of the trees, the voices of nature, animal sounds, the hooting of an owl. Suddenly I felt an overwhelming presence. Down there with me in my cramped hole was a big bird. The pit was only as wide as myself, and I was a skinny boy, but that huge bird was flying around me as if he had the whole sky to himself. I could hear his cries, sometimes near and sometimes far, far away. I felt feathers or a wing touching my back and head. This feeling was so overwhelming that it was just too much for me. I trembled and my bones turned to ice. I grasped the rattle with the forty pieces of my grandmother's flesh. It also had many little stones in it, tiny fossils picked up from an ant heap. Ants collect them. Nobody knows why. These little stones are supposed to have a power in them. I shook the rattle and it made a soothing sound, like rain falling on rock. It was talking to me, but it did not calm my fears. I took the sacred pipe in my other hand and began to sing and pray: "Tunkashila, grandfather spirit, help me." But this did not help. I don't know what got into me, but I was no longer myself. I started to cry. Crying, even my voice was different. I sounded like an older man, I couldn't even recognize this strange voice. I used long-ago words in my prayer, words no longer used nowadays. I tried to wipe away my tears, but they wouldn't stop. In the end I just pulled that quilt over me, rolled myself up in it. Still I felt the bird wings touching me.

Slowly I perceived that a voice was trying to tell me something. It was a bird cry, but I tell you, I began to understand some of it. That happens sometimes. I know a lady who had a butterfly sitting on her shoulder. That butterfly told her things. This made her become a great medicine woman.

I heard a human voice too, strange and high-pitched, a voice which could not come from an ordinary, living being. All at once I was way up there

with the birds. The hill with the vision pit was way above everything. I could look down even on the stars, and the moon was close to my left side. It seemed as though the earth and the stars were moving below me. A voice said, "You are sacrificing yourself here to be a medicine man. In time you will be one. You will teach other medicine men. We are the fowl people, the winged ones, the eagles and the owls. We are a nation and you shall be our brother. You will never kill or harm any one of us. You are going to understand us whenever you come to seek a vision here on this hill. You will learn about herbs and roots, and you will heal people. You will ask them for nothing in return. A man's life is short. Make yours a worthy one."

I felt that these voices were good, and slowly my fear left me. I had lost all sense of time. I did not know whether it was day or night. I was asleep, yet wide awake. Then I saw a shape before me. It rose from the darkness and the swirling fog which penetrated my earth hole. I saw that this was my great-grandfather, Tahca Ushte, Lame Deer, old man chief of the Minneconjou. I could see the blood dripping from my great-grandfather's chest where a white soldier had shot him. I understood that my great-grandfather wished me to take his name. This made me glad beyond words.

We Sioux believe that there is something within us that controls us, something like a second person almost. We call it *nagi*, what other people might call soul, spirit or essence. One can't see it, feel it or taste it, but that time on the hill—and only that once—I knew it was there inside of me. Then I felt the power surge through me like a flood. I cannot describe it, but it filled all of me. Now I knew for sure that I would become a *wicasa wakan*, a medicine man. Again I wept, this time with happiness.

I didn't know how long I had been up there on that hill—one minute or a lifetime. I felt a hand on my shoulder gently shaking me. It was old man Chest, who had come for me. He told me that I had been in the vision pit four days and four nights and that it was time to come down. He would give me something to eat and water to drink and then I was to tell him everything that had happened to me during my *hanblechia*. He would interpret my visions for me. He told me that the vision pit had changed me in a way that I would not be able to understand at that time. He told me also that I was no longer a boy, that I was a man now. I was Lame Deer.

MY WORLD IS A GIFT OF MY TEACHERS

Frank R. LaPena

When singers and holy people were killed, not only was a human bond broken and lives interrupted, but the way to renew the vital connection between the spiritual and the common world was interrupted drastically.

To understand the meaning of contemporary Indian art, it is necessary to consider the bond between the traditional arts and contemporary art as well as several other factors such as the symbiotic relationship between human beings and nature, the function of traditional ceremony and storytelling, and the relationship of vision and dreams to imagery. In Northern California, as in other Indian areas and regions, certain themes flow through the consciousness of the tribal society and its members. The themes are related through creation myths, stories, and songs. These, in turn, relate to understanding and controlling the philosophical and ethical foundation that helps one make a good and meaningful life.

Maintaining the oral tradition of history and stories as part of one's life establishes a relationship between the physical and spiritual realms. In the story of creation, the world is described. Special places such as Mt. Shasta, Doctor Rock, Bag of Bones, Sutter Buttes, Glass Mountain, and other sacred geological features significant to tribal history are identified along with plants, animals, and birds. All things in the physical world—including many spiritual entities connected to the world and certain actions, identified as belonging to the spiritual dimension, that affect this world—are noted.

As one hears different stories, one begins to realize that images of nature and life known and related to by the dominant society are estranged from the Native American view of the world. The Native American sees the world as a "different place" from that seen and described by the dominant society. As a Native American, my world is a gift of my teachers.

These elders, who were wise and gentle people, were singers and medicine people—practitioners of the sacred traditions, customs, and ceremonies. We are taught to respect the earth, for it is a place of mystery, wonder, and power. The earth and the universe are alive, living entities.

Listening to the stories that talk about the sacredness of the world and how it came to be, we also learn how to maintain balance and harmony by adhering to proper rules and restrictions. The magic, wonder, and "commonness" of traditional stories introduce us to a rich source of ideas and concepts useful for the artist. There are also stories of encounters with spiritual entities. Sometimes these circumstantial or accidental encounters are good, sometimes they are bad, sometimes the stories speak of the two kinds of encounters as watershed events that forever affect individuals and history. One important event remembered in oral tradition relates to the "first" contact with the white people. The first time white men were seen by the Wintu, the white men were named "Red Crane" people. The Sandhill Crane was common and loved by the Wintu people, while the red crane was rare and uncommon. We know the world changes; we hear this in our stories, sometimes we can see it change. In today's society, we see such a rapid change that sometimes we wonder how we will be able to maintain tradition.

Despite a dissonance between the traditional and contemporary ways, we confirm the ancient teachings of the earth to have valid lessons for today. Art helps to create order through the use of symbols. These symbols help to maintain the connection between traditional and contemporary cultures by reminding us of our responsibility for the way we choose to live, the way we relate our lives to the universal connection of the sacred circle.

If a person has not seen the dance ceremonies, or if one has not viewed indigenous traditional Indian art, s/he will not know the significance of contemporary Indian art; nor will that person know that the source is traditional and that it has a symbolic meaning. A non-Indian viewer may look at the art and see only artistic designs, forms, and shapes that validate these expressions as art. But they do not explain what the concepts are, where they come from, why they exist as they do, or that they make reference, as this exhibition does, to Indian tribes indigenous to California.

Indian artists work on several artistic levels: conceptual, realistic, and spiritual. Furthermore, there is an acceptance of these three levels of meaning by Native Americans. We are told by our elders how the earth and human beings and other living things came to be. This helps us realize and understand how we can develop our own sense about how we fit into the universe, space, and time and how dreams and visions function to help us maintain the quality of life that is beautiful and powerful. Sometimes our art is done through the instruction that we receive in dreams. We may even be given new symbolic forms in our dreams and visions. The elders' information about the world is a way of understanding the philosophical basis of tradition that teaches us about ethics. When we have an opportunity to have traditional feather basket makers speak of their craft and their art, they tell us that there are certain restrictions, certain kinds of feathers that must be used and why.

California Indians are known the world over for their featherwork. In the "making" of featherwork, each item must be thought of in terms of its eventual use and purpose. Dance headgear and skirts require certain feathers, while feather baskets require another kind. Feathers are not indiscriminately used, but the proper and right kind are used for each object. When the rules are learned and a person has been trained to respect the natural material, then s/he will respect the philosophy that helps the traditional arts to function and be maintained. A fine example of a traditional feather object is the Maidu feather blanket given to John Sutter by the Wilkes expedition in 1841.

In order to connect with other kinds of ideas that help maintain tradition, we need to talk about some of the ideas that are universal to the practice of ceremony. These values and concepts are recognized by other people who wish to maintain a connection to the earth. All things in and of the earth relate one to another and are interrelated in the concept of a sacred circle. This idea, of sacredness, includes all living things; all things in life are living and thus interconnected.

In this relationship, we have the responsibility to maintain and protect all living things, whether flying, crawling, swimming, or human. All of these things are connected, and we recognize the importance of that connection by ceremonies and prayers that speak to that unity. We pray for all things to help maintain harmony and balance in our lives. By uniting spiritual and physical beings in all four directions, with the below and the above, and the spiritual with the natural, we begin each new day as a new beginning.

In renewal ceremonies, such as the Sacred White Deer Dance of the northwestern California people and the Big Head ceremony of the Central Valley, we have an opportunity to think about our place on earth in relationship to the living spirit. The value of maintaining and respecting life is the recognition and importance of helping maintain this ordered symbiotic relationship.

I use the term "art documentation" when a person tries to create a "realistic" presentation of a dance or other subject matter. Whether it is a presentation of the way designs are used specifically or whether it shows overall activity, the art work is primarily to duplicate reality. This art work can be made in a "primitive," naive way or in a super-realistic style. Frank Day, Dal Castro, and Karen Tripp work this way in their paintings. Art done in the spiritual or conceptual way may result in strong design, or it may emphasize certain color connotations, such as intensity in hue—dark or light. The emphasis is on the spiritual in the sense that we have identified the spiritual and the realistic as the duality of life. This is accepted and dealt with in ceremony and traditional thought, and also affects art.

All of the artists in this exhibition have an understanding of these factors, although Frank Tuttle and Brian Tripp are perhaps most abstract and conceptual in the execution of their work. My artwork is more realistic than abstract. When I work in an abstract style, it is usually because I have participated in the ceremony and have had the actual experience, and I feel more comfortable in approaching the subject matter in a more conceptual fashion.

People marketing Indian art are concerned with promoting art to protect the Indian art market. On the other hand, Indian artists are making expressions from their Indianness or traditional training, if they have been lucky enough to receive it. At the same time they are part of today's society and express their art in a contemporary way. Indian societies are not static or dead; they are dynamic and ever-changing. They are still vital and still concerned about what happens around them. They still participate in helping define and determine what the outcome of their life will be. Harry Fonseca's Coyote, on the other hand, has its own flexibility and irreverence for society that allows Coyote's individualism to cope with whatever life throws at him.

In emphasizing the ceremony, ceremonial activities, and the sacred, we acknowledge the major impact of traditional activities on Native Americans today. A person may dress in a cowboy hat, cowboy boots, or in a suit, but when he comes back to the ceremonial grounds and participates in a ceremony, he must dress in traditional gear and immerse himself in a direct, simple, and non-complex relationship. If a person looks at traditional activities and traditional art, there is no separation between everyday life and the traditional way. George Blake works in both the traditional arts and contemporary art forms, which is an expression of his personality. He also has a marvelous sense of humor and social conscience, which are found in some of his art. This concept of unity helps explain why Indian people, and Indian artists in particular, are able to maintain their creativity and their Indianness in their life and in their art. This contrasts with the dominant society, which fractionalizes life, separates avocation and vocation, and makes compartments and separations of the sacred from everyday life.

To maintain the traditional activities, we must also actively pursue traditional art forms. Many of the artists in this show are dancers, singers, or regalia makers; all are active in their communities in other roles.

The traditional way seeks unity in the unitive vision and holistic approach to living. In tradition, we believe that to make a whole and complete person is more desirable than to create a fractionalized person who would be disjointed and nonconnected in body and spirit. Therefore, we use different techniques and styles and are concerned about many things. We can talk about the sacred, we can talk about the spiritual, we can talk about the realistic—we see in the art work exactly that range and variety. If a person were to try to analyze Indian art, s/he would find that Indian art is done in different styles, and that all styles are accepted as valid by the Indian community. Acceptance and recognition of individual effort allows a complete expression to take place.

When we address the universe, we speak to the four directions and to the earth and sky. We include certain powers from each direction and certain significant symbols that we mention which connect ourselves to all of these things. Not only are there specific forms and symbolic imagery associated with different colors from those directions, but in addressing the universe we receive information about the universe and how to live our lives.

The world is alive and all things on her are physical and spiritual in essence. Song is a reflection of this joy and understanding; it is worth reviving and maintaining, for it connects us to our godliness and the spirit that is the power of the universe. In the singing, in the music, and in the words of songs are many dynamic stories and vital types of connections. Song may speak of the physical earth, or it may speak of the spiritual realm. Songs do this by means of symbolic as well as realistic natural imagery. When I think of song as a source of inspiration and imagery, individual singers, fire songs, hand game songs, cry songs, all the places where song is used and the emotions associated with those places come to mind. One of the most important functions of song is in dance.

In analyzing dance as a source for art, we find many paintings relate directly to the ceremony of dance, and reflect the continuity of dance ceremonies as cultural preservers and revival catalysts in Northern California. In the Native American artist, we find a certain sensitivity and relationship to the traditional idea that life is a learning process. We know that as we live our lives, we can learn through experience and come to an understanding of the meaning of our lives. Frank Tuttle speaks of this process when he conceptualizes his art as starting on a journey, beginning with the first step. As he journeys through, his perception and comprehension define his imagery from what he learns. It is somewhat like moving from room to room with new experiences in each room. He keeps moving through these doors and rooms. When he reaches the end and he has an art piece, he will have gone from one door to another, from one dimension and experience to another. Both his thinking and feeling become integrated, which results in a painting that encompasses the full dimension of his journey. I believe that is true of much of the art of Native Americans: the value of the piece is as much a function of the process, beauty, and meaning that goes into creating it as the end result or finished art piece.

A connection to nature is emphasized in much of Jean LaMarr's work. Jean says she likes to use flowers in her paintings, not only because they are beautiful and their shapes and designs are delicate and good to look at, but because there is also a traditional connection that the old people knew and appreciated in the beauty of flowers. When a girl was ready to be named, she was often given the name of a traditional wildflower. The Wintu gathered flowers in the spring and took time to admire and appreciate their beauty. Sometimes a flower was compared to the beauty, delicacy, and transitory life of a human being.

We live our lives by the turning of the seasons and the passage of the Milky Way. We direct our actions by the fullness of the moon and the need to do ceremonies, to put things to rest in winter and awaken them in spring. With our lives and our works we create a metaphor of the universe; all things are one with us. We arrange things according to tradition and pay attention to detail. The essence of color is its power to heal. It is also a spiritual element and represents the four directions.

We carry the best part of humanity here, sharing our dreams in song, dance, and prayer. Dreams have no limits, a desire is once and again human, with all of the weaknesses and strengths. Those whose responsibilities are dreams give us prophecies or answers on ways we should live and think. These dreams direct our actions, give dimension to our symbols, and extend the metaphor of art. What was true once is still meaningful; although it changes as we change, its essence is always the same.

I believe when I pray for the people, the earth, and the universe I am heard. When we begin a ceremony by praying, we give notice of our intentions and our convictions—it is not a frivolous action but a conscious act of will that makes what we do proper and respectful.

It is said a proper place is a sacred place. Fire makes this so. By its warmth and its flame we dedicate our ceremonies and actions. And mountains can be sacred just as Round-houses and dance pits, sacred rocks or ponds, and caves are connected to the holy.

It is no secret that the act of purification is associated with water. It is elemental and by its purpose of being is the basis of life. I extend myself outward and connect to being. I express myself in images to give you dance and art. These actions are limited, the vastness of thought and meaning endless.

If in my mind, I focus on things near to my eyes, my vision is easy; but if I return my vision to the place of origin, I have seen stars move around with anticipation. This has given me excitement and wonder. The "old ones" used to say we are all bound together because time has no boundary and space is only one continuity. We can go to the stars by thinking ourselves there as fast as we think it. There is no separation in the common sense, though certainly we feel distances are real, just as earth is real. It is a living thing—its breath is the wind, its veins the rivers. And if we listen within ourselves we find similar sounds in all living things.

3

WHO OWNS OUR PAST?
THE REPATRIATION OF NATIVE AMERICAN HUMAN REMAINS AND CULTURAL OBJECTS

Russell Thornton

On the morning of Friday, October 9, 1993, a small group of Northern Cheyenne arrived at the Smithsonian Institution's National Museum of Natural History. They had come for their dead. Almost 115 years earlier, on January 9, 1879, at least 83 members of a band of 149 Northern Cheyenne led by Dull Knife (a.k.a. Morning Star) had been massacred by U.S. government soldiers near Fort Robinson, Nebraska, after a final, desperate attempt at freedom. The Northern Cheyenne had fled toward their homelands in Montana, after having been moved to a reservation in Oklahoma to live with the Southern Cheyenne in 1877. They were captured and held in the stockade at Fort Robinson with little food, water, or even heat. They attempted to escape after two weeks. At least 57 Northern Cheyenne were killed during the attempt. Thirty-two others found a brief freedom, until they were trapped on January 22 at the edge of Antelope Creek, where 26 of them were killed during the resulting massacre. Most Cheyenne killed in the escape attempt were buried near the fort; those killed at Antelope Creek were buried nearby in a mass grave. The bones of 17 of the Northern Cheyenne were collected after their brutal deaths for scientific study by the U.S. Army Medical Examiner. Nine of these were obtained from the mass grave at Antelope Creek, which was exhumed in 1880. The bones—mostly crania—were later transferred to the Smithsonian's National Museum of Natural History. The bones were from Cheyenne ranging in age from

forty-nine to a three-year-old child massacred at Antelope Creek. All were now being returned to their people in a joint repatriation with the Peabody Museum of Archaeology and Ethnology at Harvard, which also had some skeletal remains from the Antelope Creek massacre, collected about a month before those of the Army Medical Museum by a Peabody museum curator.

At the repatriation ceremony the human bones were officially turned over to the Northern Cheyenne delegation. The delegation was impressive. The Northern Cheyenne were represented by the tribal chair, the Crazy Dogs society of warriors, the Elk Horn society, Sun Dance priests, four women who were fourth-generation descendants of Dull Knife, and, most important, James Black Wolf, Keeper of the Sacred Buffalo Hat. The remains were carefully arranged on small Pendleton blankets; a pipe ceremony was performed, words and prayers were said, and a drum was played and songs were sung. Each person's bones were then wrapped in a blanket and interred in cedar boxes for the journey home to Montana and final rest. During the ceremony, it was discovered that a shattered lower part of a skull from the Harvard museum matched an upper part of a woman's skull from the Smithsonian. Either at death 115 years earlier or sometime afterward, the woman's head had been broken into two pieces, with each piece ending up at a different location. She was collected as two different people, one part of her going to the Army Medical Museum and eventually the Smithsonian, the other part going to the Peabody. On that day, October 9, 1993, not only was the young Northern Cheyenne woman reunited with her people; her skull itself was reunited.

Russell Thornton, *Studying Native America: Problems and Prospects.*
© 1998. Reprinted by permission of The University of Wisconsin Press. Notes have been omitted.

During the ceremony, a young Native American man from the Smithsonian came up to me and told me about the three-year-old's skull. "The child was a little girl. I saw her. She was dressed in white and had yellow ribbons in her hair. I told the Cheyenne I had seen her, and that she was now happy. They were very pleased. They thanked me for telling them."

After the ceremony in Washington, the remains were taken to Montana for burial. A stop was made on October 12 at Fort Robinson, Nebraska, for ceremonies. The journey then continued to Busby, Montana, where a wake, giveaway, and offerings to the dead took place. A small teddy bear was given to the little girl and placed on the cedar box with her remains. Her remains and those of the other massacred Cheyenne were buried shortly after noon on October 16, 1993, on a hill near Two Moon Monument.

I attended the ceremony in Washington, D.C., as the chair of the Smithsonian Institution's Native American Repatriation Review Committee, which was created by the Congress of the United States to oversee the return of Native American human remains and grave objects held at the Smithsonian Institution. It was an even more meaningful ceremony for me than it would ordinarily have been. My mother had died a few days before; I had stopped in Washington to attend the ceremony while on my way to Vian, Oklahoma, for her funeral the following day. At the ceremony in Washington, I kept thinking that my mother would be laid to rest only a few days after her death, but that these Northern Cheyenne had waited in museums for over a century before they could be buried. My mother had a long, full life and died peacefully. The Northern Cheyenne men, women, and children had short lives, ended by violent, cruel deaths.

REPATRIATION OF HUMAN REMAINS AND CULTURAL OBJECTS

The repatriation of the Native American human remains and also of funerary and other cultural objects is occurring today because of determined efforts by Native Americans to achieve legal changes in American society. It reflects perhaps a new significance for Native Americans in American society, and an important development in the relationship between Native Americans and that society. This legally mandated repatriation is also recognition of tribal sovereignty: remains and objects are repatriated to tribal entities (individuals may make claims if

they can prove direct descent), though the transfer is not from U.S. government to tribal government, but from museum to tribal government. Repatriation certainly should be an important contemporary topic within Native American studies. It has additional significance for the ways Native peoples and the scholarly community relate to each other, including how their respective ethics, values, conceptions, and even bodies of knowledge come together.

Native American Remains As Objects of Study

It has been estimated that skeletal remains of "tens and tens of thousands," possibly "hundreds of thousands," of Native American individuals are held in various universities, museums, historical societies and even private collections in the United States: one number frequently given is 600,000. (Skeletal remains of Native Americans are also held in other countries.) Whatever the actual figure, these estimates show a sizable problem. How many objects belonging to Native American groups these collections hold is pure speculation. In addition to funerary objects (included in burials, made specifically for burials, or designed to contain human remains), there are "objects of patrimony" owned by the entire people, such as wampum belts, and sacred objects, such as medicine bundles. It is also estimated that the skeletons, or more typically pieces of them, of several hundred Native Americans and the countless objects buried with them are uncovered every year in highway, housing, and other types of construction.

Native American remains and grave goods have been objects of study and fascination to non–Native Americans for centuries. In 1620 Pilgrims searching for caches of Indian corn to rob uncovered a grave containing "the bones and head of a little child . . . strings and bracelets of fine white beads . . . and some other odd knacks. . . . We brought sundry of the prettiest things away with us," they wrote, "and covered the corpse up again." Reports of systematic excavation of Native American burial sites and mounds date from the eighteenth century. Thomas Jefferson excavated burial mounds on his property in Virginia, and in so doing became the "father of American archaeology." He wrote of his excavation of a mound, "I first dug superficially in several parts of it, and came to collections of human bones, at different depths, from six inches to three feet below the surface. These were lying in the utmost confusion, some vertical, some oblique, some horizontal, and directed to every point of the compass, entangled, and held together in clusters by the earth. . . . I conjectured that in this barrow might have been a thousand skeletons."

Native American crania became objects of particular scientific interest in the early nineteenth century, and remain so today. Scholars evaluated theories of migration to North America from Asia by comparing Native Americans with Asians. They sought physical evidence to explain physical and cultural differences among Native peoples and between them and other peoples; often cultural differences were seen as a result of racial ones. Various scholars actively collected Native American remains, including Albert Gallatin and Samuel G. Morton. In 1839, Morton published *Crania Americana*, reporting that Caucasians had larger brain capacities and therefore higher intelligence than Native Americans. The "science" of phrenology soon developed, and collecting crania became more widespread as scholars attempted to relate intelligence, personality, and character to skull and brain size.

The Smithsonian Institution opened in 1846 and provided further impetus for the development of American archaeology, physical anthropology, and ethnology. Native American remains and cultural objects were, of course, important. The U.S. Army also became very much involved as its mandate to handle the "Indian problem" expanded after the U.S. Civil War.

On May 21, 1862, Surgeon General of the United States William Hammond suggested that an Army Medical Museum be established in Washington, D.C., to "facilitate the study of methods to diminish mortality and suffering among soldiers." This was during the Civil War, and for the first several years most specimens acquired related to "the injuries and diseases that produce death or disability during war."

After the Civil War, as the former Union Army turned its attention westward to confront Native Americans on the plains, the Army Medical Museum sought to update its collections to reflect this new conflict. On April 4, 1867, Surgeon General J. K. Barnes requested that medical officers also collect:

1. Rare pathological specimens from animals, including monstrosities.
2. Typical crania of Indian tribes; specimens of their arms, dress, implements, rare items of their diet, medicines, etc.
3. Specimens of poisonous insects and reptiles, and their effects on animals.

Nine months later, on January 13, 1868, Surgeon General Madison Mills wrote to army medical directors at the Department of Missouri at Fort Leavenworth (Kansas), the Department of the Platte at Omaha (Nebraska), the Department of New Mexico at Santa Fe, and the Department of Dakota at Fort Snelling (Minnesota), urging them to have their medical officers collect "specimens of Indian crania and of Indian weapons and Utensils." "The Surgeon General," he wrote, "is anxious that our collection of Indian Crania, already quite large, should be made as complete as possible."

By September 1868, the museum had a collection of 143 crania, 47 of which were Native American, representing various tribes. A memorandum issued then said that the museum "chiefly desired to procure sufficiently large series of adult crania of the principal Indian tribes to furnish accurate average measurements. In 1870 Dr. G. A. Otis, then the curator of the museum, reported his conclusions to the National Academy of Sciences during a meeting held there: "Judging from the capacity of the cranium, the American Indians must be assigned a lower position in the human scale than has been believed heretofore."

More than four thousand Native American skulls were eventually collected—from burial scaffolds, graves, and ossuaries, and from battlefields and sites of massacres—and then sent to the Army Medical Museum. Many other museums participated in the collecting of Native American skeletal remains, including the Peabody Museum at Harvard University, the American Museum of Natural History in New York, and the Field Museum of Chicago, which obtained some Native American remains originally sent to Chicago for the 1893 World's Columbian Exposition.

Human ancestors began to bury their dead in some fashion more than 200,000 years ago. Native Americans developed a variety of methods of caring for their dead. These ranged from merely leaving them on the ground, sometimes covering them with stone, to placing them in wooden coffins on the surface of the ground or in caves, to placing them on scaffolds or in a tree, to burial underground, even under the floor of their homes, to cremation. Some tribes kept the remains of their dead in special houses or ossuaries. For example, the Inca Garcilaso de la Vega describes a burial temple in the province of Cofachiqui: "Along all four walls the Indians had set wooden chests. . . . Within the chests . . . , the infidels had entombed the bodies of their dead without any more preservatives against decomposition than if they were giving them burial in the earth."

Most Native American peoples attach an important spiritual quality to the remains of their ancestors. Chief Seattle, for example, explained: "To us the ashes of our ancestors are sacred and their final resting place is hallowed ground, while you wander far from the graves of your ancestors and, seemingly, without regret." During battles, rival tribes would sometimes attempt to destroy the ossuaries, knowing how much pain this would inflict on their enemies. Many Native people think that treating their ancestral remains as objects of curiosity or scientific study is also disrespectful to them and their ancestors. To the Zuni, the removal of human remains from their ancestral lands so desecrated their ancestors that they cannot be returned to Zuni Pueblo for reburial! Many cultural objects are of spiritual significance, sometimes sacred to Native Americans. That skeletons of ancestors and sacred tribal objects are held by museums, scholarly and other institutions, and even private individuals is painful to most contemporary Native peoples.

Collecting Human Remains and Objects

Many human remains and objects subject to legal repatriation were obtained appropriately, with the permission if not actual support of Native Americans at the time. However, many were not; that human remains and objects were obtained by "grave robbing," theft, and fraud adds to Native American discomfort and further legitimizes claims for repatriation, as the four cases briefly described below illustrate.

A major smallpox epidemic among Indian tribes of the central and northwest regions of the United States in the early 1800s killed the great Omaha chief Washinga Sakba ("the Blackbird"). The artist George Catlin, who traveled among Native Americans from the Dakotas to Indian Territory in the 1830s and 1840s, painting the natives he encountered, describes Washinga Sakba's funeral in his journal. Catlin writes that Washinga Sakba was buried on a bluff above the Missouri River, mounted on his favorite white horse, "with his bow in his hand, and his shield and quiver slung—with his pipe and his *medicine-bag*—with his supply of dried meat, and his tobacco-pouch replenished to last him through his journey to the 'beautiful hunting grounds of the shades of his fathers'." When he visited the grave site, Catlin adds, he dug up Washinga Sakba's skull to add it to "others which I have collected on my route."

On December 29, 1890, several hundred Sioux men, women, and children were massacred by troops of the First Squadron of the Seventh Cavalry at Wounded Knee Creek. The Sioux had fled their reservation to practice their new religion—the Ghost Dance. The massacre occurred after the troops had captured them and were attempting to disarm them. The cavalry left with their dead and wounded after the massacre, and sent out a burial detail a few days later. Meanwhile, other Sioux learned of the massacre and collected some of their own dead. When the burial detail arrived on January 1, 1891, a heavy blizzard had covered the remaining bodies with snow. Eighty-four men and boys, 44 women and girls, and 18 children were collected and buried in a mass grave. Some Sioux had been wearing sacred Ghost Dance shirts; they were stripped of these shirts before being dumped into the grave.

Six shirts ended up at the National Museum of Natural History; one was displayed in a museum exhibit with the caption stating that it was taken from the Wounded Knee "Battlefield." In the fall of 1986, I was a fellow at the museum. I remember vividly a trip one afternoon with a curator into the building's attic to examine some of the North American Indian collections. He volunteered to show me these shirts. He pulled out a drawer from a large cabinet, and there they were. Almost a hundred years after it occurred, I was a witness to the legacy of the massacre at Wounded Knee. The shirts have bullet holes and are stained with blood; some still have medicine bags attached.

The Smithsonian officially had twenty-nine "objects" taken from those massacred at Wounded Knee. Besides the six Ghost Dance shirts, they include a blanket from "a dead body," a pair of boys' moccasins, and baby jackets and caps. Their return to the descendants of those slain at Wounded Knee occurred in September of 1998. The Cheyenne River Sioux Tribe represented the descendants in negotiating the request.

Ales Hrdlicka, recognized as a father, if not the father, of physical anthropology, visited Kodiak Island off the coast of Alaska in the 1930s. Representing the Smithsonian Institution, he removed the remains of about a thousand people and 144 associated burial items from an archaeological site called Uyak. The people later said that they resented the intrusion and the removal of the remains, but Hrdlicka was a representative of the government, and they did not know what to do. They never gave him permission. But "he had no regard for the people here. And we had no laws. None that we knew about. We just stood by."

A final, well-known example occurred at the American Museum of Natural History. In 1897, Robert Peary brought to New York City from Greenland six Inuit (Eskimo) and the famous Cape York meteorite, a sacred object to the Inuit. Four of the six soon died of tuberculosis; one, Uisaakassak, eventually returned to Greenland. The sole remaining Eskimo was the well-known Minik, who lived until 1918, after returning to Greenland in 1909, and then coming back to the United States in 1916 to live in New Hampshire. The first of the four to die was Qisuk, father of the then-eight-year-old Minik. After his death, in January 1899, his "bones were preserved, boiled and varnished and mounted as a perfect skeleton." The other three Inuit who died were likewise dissected, and their skeletons added to the museum's collections. Hrdlicka published a paper on Qisuk's brain in 1901, complete with pictures (he called him Kishu or Kissuk). A fake burial had been performed for Qisuk. It was noted by a young anthropologist, Alfred Kroeber, who had studied the six Eskimos in New York and wrote a paper on the Eskimo of Smith Sound without leaving the city. Kroeber indicated that Minik was instructed to "visit the (supposed) grave of his father." Later, Minik discovered that his father's bones were actually on display in the museum. "I can never be happy till I can bury my father in a grave," he lamented. "It makes me cry every time I think of his poor bones up there in the museum in a glass case, where everybody can look at them. Just because I am a poor Esquimau boy why can't I bury my father in a grave the way he would want to be buried?"

The answer, in his case as in the other three described here, was that the bones were being kept in the interest of science.

Important Research

Nearly all of the 4,000 crania at the Army Medical Museum were eventually transferred to the Smithsonian's National Museum of Natural History and added to the remains of approximately 14,500 other Native Americans there (along with non–Native American remains). This supposedly represents the largest single collection of Native American remains in the United States, followed by some 13,500 held by the Tennessee Valley Authority. The University of California also has a very large collection. The Hearst (formerly Lowie) Museum at its Berkeley campus has "the third largest number of catalogued skeletal entries in the United States (more than 11,000)." Most of these remains, "representing more than 8,000 individuals," are from California's northern coast and Sacramento Valley. As for artifacts, there are "roughly 1 million or more pieces" at Berkeley. UCLA and other campuses of the University of California system have smaller numbers of Native American human remains and artifacts.

Research on Native skeletal remains has generated much important knowledge about such diverse topics as population size and composition, cultural patterns of tooth mutilation, diseases present among Native American populations and treatments for those diseases, life expectancies, growth patterns, population affinities, origins and migrations, and diets, including dates at which corn was introduced among various peoples of North America. We now know from studying these remains that tuberculosis was present in this hemisphere before European contact in 1492, as were some infectious diseases, including treponemal infections, that certain Native groups had serious iron deficiencies from a diet heavily dependent on corn, and that among some groups males with more social prestige—as reflected by burial objects—were physically larger than males with less social prestige (perhaps because they had better diets, perhaps because bigger men were simply given more prestige).

Native American skeletal remains have become even more important as objects of study, scholars assert, given recent advances and probable future advances in scientific technology, including the detection of immunoglobulin and DNA sequencing from bone. The study of immunoglobulin could enable scholars to establish explicit disease histories for the skeletons; deciphering their DNA code could enable scholars to establish genetic relationships among historical populations. Moreover, science progresses, and unforeseen and foreseen advances will enable scholars to generate increasingly greater knowledge from the skeletal remains. This is no small issue, and much of the knowledge to be gained could benefit both Native American and other peoples of the world.

Some Views

Native American views that repatriation must occur are typically held despite any scholarly or public good, past or future, derived from the study or display of the remains and objects. Scholars and others assert that the scientific and public value of

322 THE SACRED: SPIRITUALITY AND SACRED GEOGRAPHY

the remains and cultural objects outweigh any claims Native Americans may have. As scholars attempt to reconstruct histories of Native Americans, they argue that the scientific benefits are important not only to the public at large, but also to Native peoples themselves. Some have even sued to be allowed to retain or study remains or objects, as is the case with a recent discovery: Native American remains 9000 years old (or older) and showing some "caucasoid features," an individual dubbed the "Richland" or "Kennewick Man." Other lawsuits have involved the ability to study the remains before actual repatriation.

A related view is that the remains and objects now housed in museums and educational institutions belong not to Native Americans but to all Americans, even to all peoples of the world. They are part of the heritage of all people, not only Native American people. Another view is that the scholars are keeping and studying the remains because Native Americans do not know what they are doing when requesting repatriation. "Someday," they say, "Native Americans will want this knowledge. It is up to us to preserve it for them." (This assertion that scientists are "saving the Indians from themselves" is both patronizing and insulting.)

Native Americans, conversely, assert that other factors out weight science and education, noting that our society places all sorts of restrictions on research. Obviously, research that physically harms humans (and, to a lesser extent, animals) is prohibited. Under conventional ethical standards, one must get "informed consent" from subjects who are aware of the nature and implications of the research, the research must not harm subjects psychologically, and subjects may not be identified without their permission. Yet studying the human remains of their ancestors, for example, causes great psychological pain, Native Americans argue.

Native Americans also point out that skeletons obtained from battlefields and massacres, as many of those in the Army Medical Museum were, are remains of Native Americans who died defending their homelands: all of the United States of America was once Native American land. American society has given much attention to returning to the United States the remains of Americans killed in World War II, the Korean Conflict, the war in Vietnam, and other wars. Do we owe less to those who defended America against the Europeans and the Euro-Americans who took their land? Are Native American warriors killed in battle less deserving of

an honorable burial than American military personnel who died for the United States? (And what about "civilians" killed in battles and massacres?) Most Americans strongly support efforts to repatriate the remains of all fellow Americans who died in Vietnam and elsewhere. What would be the reaction if the Republic of Vietnam refused to return the skeletal remains of American service men and women killed there? What if they said: "We want to keep them and study them. They have much scientific value"?

THE REPATRIATION MOVEMENT

Native Americans have attempted legally to prevent the collection of their human remains and cultural objects for more than a century. During the last few decades, they have increasingly demanded that ancestral remains and sacred objects be returned to them for proper disposal or care. This effort is a social movement: "a concerted and continued effort by a social group aimed at reaching a goal (or goals) common to its members. More specifically, the effort is directed at modifying, maintaining, replacing, or destroying an existing social institution." Thus, social movements are determined and organized group efforts to bring about some objectives, particularly types of social change. Repatriation is an organized effort to return Native American human remains and cultural objects to the communities from which they came.

Social movements are shaped by societies and cultures; goals and objectives are achieved by means available and acceptable at particular times in particular societies and cultures. Social movements in American society today often involve such political processes as obtaining public support and sympathy, lobbying legislators, and getting specific laws passed. This is exactly what occurred in the repatriation movement.

Repatriation is also a pan-Indian movement in two ways: it involves many different Native American peoples, with or without strong tribal affiliations (though, as noted, repatriation is only carried out with tribes or direct descendants); and Native American tribes have joined in it to pursue common, though tribally specific interests. For many Native Americans, with strong tribal ties or otherwise, the repatriation movement ranks in importance with the social movements of other groups in American society—the civil rights movement, the women's movement. The repatriation movement has given Native Americans a new sense of respect—from American society and also for themselves.

Repatriation might also be considered a revitalization movement, a "deliberate, organized, conscious effort by members of a society to construct a more satisfying culture." My own view is that a revitalization movement is a special type of social movement designed "to create a better social and/or cultural system while reviving or reaffirming selected features." Repatriation is truly revitalizing and breathing new life into Native American communities by seeking to recover what has been taken from them.

During past decades, the pan-Indian repatriation movement became successful through the passage of federal and state laws not only calling for the repatriation of human remains and objects to descendants, if known, or, otherwise, appropriate tribes, but also preventing the further disenfranchisement of remains and objects. (Native peoples in Canada have raised similar issues, but similar changes in Canadian law have not yet occurred.) Not only has the success of the repatriation movement revitalized Native America and provided new self-esteem; the task of actually winning repatriations of human remains and cultural objects has also revitalized communities by bringing members together for this struggle as well as reaffirming important knowledge about many cultural and sacred objects.

It is not always an easy undertaking, although the result may be worth it. "As difficult as implementation of the repatriation policy and laws may be in the non-Native world," Suzan Shown Harjo comments, "the truly complex issues are being examined by Native Peoples, who must arrive at a consensus in matters for which most lack specific historical and ceremonial context. Each detail of repatriation, including whether or not to request repatriation, must be worked out within each family, clan, society or nation."

This process can be very important when it comes to sacred objects, sources of much power or "medicine." How does one handle them? Can one handle them? Much of this knowledge was lost by Native Americans, and they may find it difficult to know exactly what to do. One may compare Native American sacred objects with the Ark of the Covenant containing the ten commandments, a source of great power in some religions. What would people do if the Ark was suddenly discovered? Would they open it? Would they touch the stones on

which the ten commandments are carved? The ten commandments are on stone given by a god or creator, and Native American sacred objects also may be of stone, given by a creator.

I attended the 1995 Southeast Alaska Indian Repatriation Conference, sponsored by the Tlingit and Haida Indian Tribes of Alaska in Juneau. During the conference, a TeleVideo hookup with the National Museum of Natural History allowed tribal members to view objects held there. It was gratifying to see a packed room at the University of Alaska Southeast Campus where tribal members ranging from elders to young children had gathered to view important objects. The moderator of the conference, David Katzeek, caretaker (*Hit-s'aati*) of the Shangukeidee clan (Thunderbird of Klukwan, Eagle moiety), and his mother, Anna Katzeek, followed ceremonial protocol and wore regalia as a sign of respect for all involved. Responses by members of other clans also followed the protocol. During the TeleVideo session, elders talked and debated about the masks, hats, and bear knife shown on the video screen, sharing their knowledge with tribal members. It appeared to be a time of real intellectual revitalization for the Tlingit and Haida. One respected participant responded after the conference: "Everything has power, has spirit. The power was strong there this morning, and emotions were strong. . . . One day all the things that have been lost will be returned."

It is important to note, however, that the costs of repatriations, legal or otherwise, may be considerable, straining limited tribal resources.

Much of the early focus of the movement was upon the Smithsonian Institution, since it is the national museum of our country. I was a visiting scholar at the Smithsonian's National Museum of Natural History in 1985–1986. At that time one curator of physical anthropology was Douglas Ubelaker, whose forensic work was popularized in his book *Bones*. Ubelaker has also done extensive scholarly work on the population history of North American Indians, one of my own topics of interest.

At that time, the Smithsonian Institution was being subjected to extreme political pressure from national pan-Indian organizations to return its Native American skeletal collections to Native American tribes. The decision was made by Smithsonian administrators to inform tribes of the skeletal collections and suggest to them that some ancestral tribal members might be among the skeletons of the Smithsonian.

Ubelaker sought my advice. We talked about the draft of a letter informing the tribes of the Smithsonian's holdings along with a computer print-out detailing the geographical origin of the Native American skeletons. I made a suggestion or two, and the revised letter was sent by Adrienne L. Kaeppler, then chair of the Department of Anthropology, to 225 federally recognized tribes. I thought from the beginning that the tribes would show little interest. They were generally focused on local issues; repatriation was not yet an issue of concern to them—at least I had not heard much about it from tribal people. Rather, I told Ubelaker that the demands for repatriation were mainly articulated by "urban" Native Americans. Tribes might very well be supportive of those demands and might eventually become involved, but they had not yet done so to a significant extent. The likely response, I thought, would be no response. My prediction proved correct. Only a handful of responses came in.

National Native American leaders, such as Walter Echo-Hawk of the Native American Rights Fund and Suzan Shown Harjo of the National Congress of American Indians, continued to seek the repatriation of human skeletal remains from the Smithsonian and elsewhere. Native American organizations, such as the American Indians Against Desecration (AIAD), a project of the International Indian Treaty Council, issued a statement calling for repatriation. Native American protests took place at specific museums, such as the Illinois State Museum at Dickson Mounds. Professional associations such as the Council for Museum Anthropology, Society for American Archaeology, American Anthropological Association, and American Association of Museums became involved and issued position papers. A Panel for a National Dialogue on Museum/Native American Relations was established. Various universities also debated the issues, forming committees and panels to develop policies. The University of California system formed a "Joint Academic Senate–Administration Committee on Human Skeletal Remains" in 1990 to develop a policy for the system, and individual campuses formed local committees to implement the policy.

Senator Daniel K. Inouye (Democrat of Hawaii) took up the cause as chair of the Select Committee on Indian Affairs and, as discussed below, linked it to the acquisition of the collection of the Museum of the American Indian in New York City to form the National Museum of the American Indian. One idea considered but discarded was to establish a national mausoleum where Native American remains "'which are not useful for scientific inquiry' would be buried, 'giving due regard to the religious and ceremonial beliefs and practices of those Indians, Aleuts and Eskimos whose ancestors may be included in the Smithsonian collection.'"

The private sector also became involved in the repatriation movement, just as it did in the civil rights movement. Elizabeth Sackler purchased three Hopi and Navajo ceremonial masks for $39,050 at a Sotheby auction in New York City in May 1991. Her intent was to return them to the tribes. She then established the American Indian Ritual Object Repatriation Foundation to help Native groups win the return of important cultural objects in the hands of private individuals and organizations. The foundation continues to be active in repatriation.

State and Federal Laws

Repatriation legislation was enacted on both the state and federal levels.

"All states have laws that address in some manner the disposition of prehistoric aboriginal remains and grave goods," concludes Marcus Price. Although some states "merely apply their criminal laws against grave robbing, trespass, and vandalism, or their general public health and cemetery laws," ever more, he notes, they are establishing "legislation specific to the problem," yet, "there is little consistency in approach." An important example of state legislation was Iowa's reburial statue of the mid-1970s, which protects "prehistoric burial mounds and unmarked cemeteries and presumes ultimate reburial of ancient remains." The landmark state legislation, however, probably was Nebraska's 1989 Unmarked Human Burial Sites and Skeletal Remains Protection Act. In passing the act, Nebraska became the first state with a general repatriation statue. It provides for the protection of unmarked burial sites throughout the state and the repatriation (within one year of a request) to relatives or American Indian tribes of human remains and associated burial goods held in state-sponsored or state-recognized public bodies. In 1991 California, after much effort by Assemblyman Richard Katz, established a new law providing for the repatriation of Native American human remains and funerary objects. The original bill was vetoed by the governor in 1990, but after further amendments was passed again and approved by the governor on September 6, 1991. In large part, Katz's efforts were inspired by the large number of Native American remains held by the University of California system. The University of California had lobbied against the law, preferring instead to develop its own repatriation policy.

The federal government has repeatedly enacted legislation aimed at protecting the rights of Native American groups vis-á-vis ancestral remains and sacred objects. Twentieth-century legislation may be dated from the Antiquities Act of 1906, which granted the federal government jurisdiction over all aboriginal remains and artifacts on federal property. Other important legislation includes the Historical Sites Act of 1935 (supplemented by the Reservoir Salvage Act of 1960), the National Historic Preservation Act of 1966, the Department of Transportation Act of 1966, and the National Environmental Policy Act of 1969.

Recent federal legislation has been sparked by the outspokenness and political sophistication of Native Americans themselves. Native groups have successfully lobbied lawmakers and obtained public support for their repatriation efforts. On August 11, 1978, Senate Joint Resolution 102, the American Indian Religious Freedom Act (AIRFA), made it "the policy of the United States to protect and preserve for American Indians their inherent right of freedom to believe, express, and exercise the traditional religions of the American Indian, Eskimo, Aleut, and Native Hawaiian." Included in this freedom was "use and possession of sacred objects." The Archaeological Resources Protection Act (ARPA) of 1979 soon followed, specifically mandating that the AIRFA be considered in the disposition of archaeological resources, and that "archaeological resources recovered from Indian land are the property of the tribe."

The next important federal legislation on repatriation was Public Law 101-185, the National Museum of the American Indian Act of November 1989, which established the National Museum of the American Indian (NMAI) as part of the Smithsonian Institution. A component of this law mandates that "if any Indian human remains are identified by a preponderance of the evidence as those of a particular individual or as those of an individual culturally affiliated with a particular Indian tribe, the Secretary [of the Smithsonian], upon the request of the descendants of such individual or of the Indian tribe shall expeditiously return such remains (together with any associated funerary objects) to the descendants or tribe, as the case may be."

In October 1990, Public Law 101-601, the Native American Graves Protection and Repatriation Act (NAGPRA), was established. It specifically considers the disposition of Native American human remains and artifacts in federal agencies (other than the Smithsonian), mandating that "any institution or State or local government agency, including any institution of higher learning, that receives Federal funds and has possession of, or control over, Native American human remains or cultural items must comply with NAGPRA." NAGPRA will, therefore, affect most of the approximately eight thousand museums in the United States.

The law increases the protection of Native American graves on federal and tribal land, makes illegal the commercial traffic in Native American remains, requires the inventorying and repatriation to culturally affiliated tribes or descendants of all collections of Native American remains and associated funerary objects held by federal agencies and federally funded museums (and universities), and also requires the repatriation of Native American sacred objects and cultural patrimony. Human remains, funerary objects (either associated or unassociated with currently held remains), sacred objects, and objects of cultural patrimony shall all "be expeditiously returned." ("Cultural affiliation" as defined in NAGPRA means "that there is a relationship of shared group identity which can be reasonably traced historically or prehistorically between a present day Indian tribe or Native Hawaiian organization and an identifiable earlier group.") Under the provisions of NAGPRA, a seven-person review committee monitors and reviews repatriation activities. Three of the members are appointed from a pool nominated by Native American groups and religious leaders; at least two of them must be "traditional Indian religious leaders." Three members are appointed from nominees of museum and scientific organizations, and one member is appointed from a list suggested by the other six members.

The Smithsonian Institution decided to follow Public Law 101-601 as well as Public Law 101-185, thereby extending the mandate of repatriation to include not only human remains and funerary objects but also sacred objects and objects of cultural patrimony. In the fall of 1996, an amendment to the NMAI Act was introduced into the U.S. Senate by Senator McCain (Republican of Arizona), and passed a few months later. It amends the act along the lines of the NAGPRA legislation, setting a strict time schedule and legally requiring the repatriation of objects of cultural patrimony and sacred objects. The Smithsonian is committed to completing its inventory of Native American human remains and funerary objects by June 1, 1998; a summary of ethnographic objects was sent to all tribes shortly after the December 31, 1996 deadline.

The NMAI Act of 1989 contains a provision whereby a Repatriation Review Committee is appointed "to monitor and review the inventory, identification, and return of Indian human remains and Indian funerary objects." This committee is composed of five individuals, at least three of whom are to be selected from individuals nominated by Native American groups. The committee was empaneled in March 1990 and four of the five members were selected from those nominated by Native American groups; two of these are American Indians. The 1996 amendment to the act added two members to the committee, both of whom are to be traditional religious leaders.

The collections of the Smithsonian's newly created National Museum of the American Indian, however, are not under the purview of this committee; rather, the museum's repatriation activities are the responsibility of its own board of trustees, as stated in the act. Consequently, NMAI has its own policies and procedures for repatriation, established in 1991. Recently, the NMAI has been criticized by both Native Americans and museologists for its handling of repatriation. In fact, the Smithsonian Institution as a whole has not been immune to criticism in this regard. Some changes are underway.

International Developments

U.S. federal and state laws for repatriation pertain only to claims made by Native American groups in the United States, and only for remains and objects in the United States. For example, human remains of Native Americans from Mexico or Central or South America are not within the purview of the laws, nor are wampum belts from Iroquois in Canada. Similarly, U.S. law does not apply to remains or objects in any other country. Nevertheless, ever more Native groups in the United States are attempting to recover their ancestors and histories from elsewhere in the world. For example, the Zuni are recovering war gods from other countries, and the Wounded Knee Survivors' Association is attempting to recover from the Kelvingrove Museum in Glasgow, Scotland, a Ghost Dance shirt "reputedly taken from a body at Wounded Knee." The response of the museum in the latter instance was that "it is a very difficult issue for us. It could be seen as a precedent

that could open up our collection to other claims for repatriation."

There are important recent developments concerning international repatriation, however. The Inuit Circumpolar Conference (ICC) is held every four years. This international organization represents around 115,000 Inuit in the Arctic regions of the United States (Alaska), Russia (Chukotka), Canada, and Greenland. Its purposes are to further Inuit unity, rights, and interests, foster policies that safeguard the Arctic environment, and be a full partner in the development of the circumpolar regions. At its 1995 conference, held in Nome, Alaska, the Keepers of the Treasures, Alaska, sponsored a symposium on international repatriation. (The Keepers of the Treasures, a national organization, is dedicated to preserving, affirming, and celebrating Native American cultures.) Speaking at the symposium, I commented that "all repatriation in the United States is international repatriation, given what should be an independent status of Native tribes. Unfortunately, it didn't turn out this way. Native groups are forced to negotiate with museums and institutions rather than with the federal government as equal entities."

Only a month before the ICC, a diplomatic conference was held in Rome to discuss the adoption of the draft UNIDROIT Convention on the International Return of Stolen or Illegally Exported Cultural Objects. Delegates from some seventy countries, with observers from eight, voted to approve the text of the convention, derived after "eleventh hour negotiations following weeks of debate between the art-rich 'source countries' and the so-called 'market countries' where most of the trade in cultural objects takes place." It calls for the return of stolen and illegally exported cultural objects under certain specified conditions. The United States eventually approved the act, a small but important step in international repatriation.

In the international repatriation movement, Native Americans join with other exploited peoples of the world to claim the objects of their history, plundered by thieves as well as colonial or war-occupied governments. The objects at stake include art looted during World War II and the Elgin marbles, Greek works currently in London.

Some Repatriations

According to its own established procedures, some 2,500 of the approximately 18,500 skeletal remains in the collections of the National Museum of Natural

History have been repatriated by the Smithsonian to Native American groups, including some to Hawaiian Islanders. To date, the largest number of repatriated remains were returned to Larsen Bay, Alaska, in October 1991. These were the remains of about a thousand people from the site on Kodiak Island excavated by the Smithsonian physical anthropologist Ales Hrdlicka between 1932 and 1936. In January 1992 the associated funerary objects were returned.

The Smithsonian has also returned human remains to the Cheyenne River Sioux (including the brain of Leon Pretty Voice Eagle), Yankton Sioux, Devil's Lake Sioux, Sisseton-Wahpeton Sioux, Oglala Sioux (the remains of Chief Smoke were returned to a descendant), Two Kettles Sioux (the remains of Chief Puffing Eyes were returned to his family), Southern Arapaho, Shoshone-Bannock, Makah, Pawnee, Southern Cheyenne, Yerington Paiute, Ninilchik, Spokane, the Warm Springs Confederated Tribes, and various Alaskan villages. (Some remains were returned before the federal legislation; in 1984 remains including the skull of the well-known Captain Jack were returned to the Modoc; others were restored to the Blackfeet in 1988.) Funerary objects have been returned to Alaskan groups, and to the Pawnee and the Cheyenne River Sioux. Included in the Warm Springs repatriation were 86,085 objects, mostly beads.

Among the remains repatriated to the Southern Cheyenne were those of Native Americans killed at the infamous massacre at Sand Creek, Colorado Territory, on November 29, 1864. The Colorado militia led by Colonel John Chivington had dismembered and decapitated victims on the spot, sending some to the Army Medical Museum. The remains repatriated to the Pawnee included the crania of six Pawnee, believed by some to have been beheaded after being killed by the U.S. Army only one month after their honorable discharge from the U.S. Army as scouts. A repatriation ceremony for these and other Pawnee remains from the Smithsonian, complete with a military escort, was held at Fort McNair in Washington, D.C., on June 6, 1995. The small wooden boxes containing the remains of the six scouts had folded U.S. flags on top, acknowledging their status as veterans. Senator McCain, the chair of the Select Committee on Indian Affairs, spoke and apologized to the Pawnee on behalf of the U.S. government for what had happened and for the fact that it had taken the government so long to return their dead. The following day, the remains were taken under a military escort to former Pawnee lands at Genoa, Nebraska, for burial. At Genoa, the location from which the Pawnee had earlier been removed to Oklahoma, the remains were buried with other Pawnee remains at the cemetery and covered with a slab of concrete to prevent further disturbance. (Pawnee cemeteries in and around Genoa had been looted for a century by scientists and others seeking bones and artifacts.) A week later, as is the custom of the Pawnee, a final feast for the dead was held by the Pawnee tribe in Pawnee, Oklahoma, where they are now centered.

Other museums, institutions, agencies, and collectors have also returned Native American skeletal remains, both before NAGPRA and as a response to it. California Indian remains have been repatriated to appropriate groups by the Catholic church; the state of Nebraska has returned Pawnee and Omaha skeletons; the University of Minnesota returned 150 sets of remains to the Devils Lake Sioux; Stanford University returned remains of some 550 individuals to the Ohlone; and the University of Tennessee returned 190 sets of remains to the Cherokee.

Cultural and sacred objects have also been returned, by the Smithsonian and other museums, institutions, and private individuals. The Smithsonian repatriated a few cultural objects to the Zia Pueblo (in 1982) and Zuni Pueblo (in 1987) before the legislation, and some others to Native Hawaiians since the legislation. Wampum belts, masks of the False Face Society, a *kano:wa* or ceremonial turtle rattle, and two antler hair combs have been returned to the Iroquois; various ceremonial shields and weapons and altar figurines have been repatriated to the Jemez Pueblo by the NMAI; and medicine bundles and prayer boards have been returned to the Navajo and Hopi. Hopi kachinas have also been repatriated; and several dozen twin War Gods or *Ahayu:da* have been repatriated to the Zuni—nearly all that were missing. Finally, the Omaha's sacred pole was returned to them by the Peabody Museum, as were the skeletal remains and burial offerings of almost one hundred Omaha held by the University of Nebraska.

The NAGPRA legislation of November 16, 1990, gave institutions five years (with a possible extension) to complete inventories of human remains and funerary objects, and three years to provide summaries of unassociated funerary objects, sacred objects, and objects of cultural patrimony. After the inventory, six months are allowed for notifying tribes of affiliated remains and funerary objects. Therefore, only now, at the end of the decade, are full repatriation efforts under NAGPRA commencing, and the Smithsonian is ahead of most other museums and institutions, if not all, in actual repatriations. Nevertheless, many issues remain to be settled in implementing NAGPRA. Two important ones are whether nonfederally recognized tribes are entitled to repatriated remains and objects (as they are by the Smithsonian), and what are institutions to do about remains or objects where cultural affiliation cannot be established? In 1997 an interim rule established penalties for noncompliance with NAGPRA. . . .

INDIANS ARE NOT SPECIMENS—INDIANS ARE PEOPLE

The Smithsonian Institution holds the world's largest collection of Indian skeletal remains. These total more than 18,500, plus an additional 17,000 grave goods. Nationwide, estimates indicate more than 600,000 skeletal remains in universities, research institutions and museums. Indian tribes throughout the United States demand that these skeletal remains and associated grave offerings be returned.

The museums, including the Smithsonian Institution, have been reluctant to release any of their holdings even when the gravesite violations are well documented. But recently there have been exceptions. In 1868, the Army Surgeon General directed medical officers in the west to collect Indian skulls and bones and send them to Washington for study of infection and disease. They collected over 4,000 specimens by plundering Indian gravesites. The Army Medical Museums transferred the "specimens" to the Smithsonian which now owns the looted articles. In 1988, the Smithsonian, when faced with a letter documenting how one army officer in 1892 "collected" the skulls of Blackfeet people, returned the remains of fifteen Blackfeet for proper reburial on the reservation. Last year, Stanford University returned the remains of 550 Indians to the Ohlone-Costanoan Tribe. The University of South Dakota returned 1,200 pounds of remains in August of this year to the Pine Ridge reservation.

As more and more reporters write and broadcast about institutions and their collections of skeletal remains, moral outrage has increased and public sentiment has shifted in favor of the Indians' demands for repatriation. For years, the Smithsonian has taken a hard-line stance that no repatriation will be permitted except when lineal descendants can prove that the museum is holding the skeletons or sacred objects of one of their ancestors. The Smithsonian, however, holds on to the critical documentation. There are some Indian people who feel responsible for all of their ancestors, lineal descendents or not. Consequently, Indian tribes and individuals are calling for the Smithsonian to make available all the skeletal remains taken from certain areas including ancestral and present-day lands. The tribe would decide whether or not to accept the remains.

Faced with mounting pressure from both Indian and non-Indian interests, including members of Congress, the Smithsonian recently agreed to allow the repatriation of skeletal remains to tribes, not just lineal descendants, where "a preponderance of the evidence" indicates that the remains in its collection can be traced to a specific tribe. By limiting the repatriation to cases where it can identify tribal relationship, the Smithsonian has taken a middle of the road stance. A large portion of its collection may ultimately remain in its possession.

The Legislation

At one point, at least six different bills were pending in Congress dealing with the repatriation issue as well as the creation of the new Museum of the American Indian as part of the Smithsonian Institution in Washington, D.C. Disagreement has centered around the Smithsonian's desire to keep its entire collection of Indian bones versus the growing public sentiment calling for the proper respect of the dead. Note: President Bush signed the National Museum of the American Indian Act on November 28. The legislation describes the Smithsonian's policy on repatriation of Indian human remains. If any remains are identified as those of a particular individual or as those of an individual culturally affiliated with a particular Indian tribe, the Smithsonian, upon request of the descendants of the individual or tribe, will return the remains.

From *Indian Affairs*, no. 120 (Fall 1989). Copyright 1989 by Association on American Indian Affairs, Inc. Reprinted with permission.

BATTLING FOR SOULS
ORGANIZING THE RETURN OF THE SACRED TEXTILES
TO THE COMMUNITY OF COROMA, BOLIVIA

Victoria Bomberry

In 1986 the Aymara community of Coroma issued a statement denouncing the theft of their sacred weavings in *Presencia*, the newspaper of record in La Paz, Bolivia. This unprecedented move by an Indigenous community in Bolivia represented an incursion into a medium dominated by a *criollo* elite. The statement that was signed by the *kurakas*, the local traditional authorities of the community launched a sophisticated, long-term struggle to regain the weavings. The *kurakas* demanded that U.S. art dealers and collectors return all photographs and negatives taken during All Saints Day, which is the only day during the entire year when the ancient textiles are displayed. The *kurakas* urged the dealers to stop acquiring the textiles. Letters were sent to U.S. dealers imploring them to return the stolen textiles to Coroma. Unfortunately, no one knew which dealers and collectors had possession of the weavings.

The statement issued by the elders of Coroma raised issues of cultural property and Indigenous rights, as well as important questions of how Indigenous culture is viewed in industrial nations. The people of Coroma provoked an examination of how "art is constructed and perceived in the West," while offering a contextualized vision of the multiple roles the sacred weavings play in their own community. In the case of Coroma, religious beliefs became a powerful driving force for regaining the weavings. The weavings are a necessary part of every aspect of life in Coroma. Weaving is done by the women of Coroma who record and interpret the religious life of the community. Because of this important function

Victoria Bomberry, "Battling for Souls: Organizing the Return of the Sacred Textiles to the Community of Coroma, Bolivia." Copyright 1997 by Victoria Bomberry. Printed with author's permission. An earlier version of this article appeared in *Akwe:kon* (Winter 1993)

the weavings can be considered sacred texts. Additionally, the weavings are the repository of the history of the *ayllus* which make up the community of Coroma.

The case of Coroma illustrates how formal and informal international networks can be successfully activated by local Indigenous groups. The Coromeños were able to mobilize Indigenous groups in Bolivia and the United States, anthropologists, sociologists, archaeologists, communications experts, and attorneys in Bolivia and the United States.

In the following statement (Cruz 1990:1) the Coromeños articulate what the theft of the textiles means to the community.

1. The destruction of the history of the people of Coroma. The textiles are a form of documentation whereby the history of each ethnic group and also the differences between the *ayllus* are written.
2. The dispersion of the different *ayllus* that make up the community of Coroma, as the *q'epis* give identity to the member of each one of the groups.
3. The dismantling of the borders between ethnic groups. In Coroma not only are the *q'epis* guardians for the *J'ilaqatas* and *alcaldes cobradores*, but there are also *q'epis* situated in the corners of the *ayllus* of Coroma demarcating the lands of the *ayllus*. The *q'epis* are also used to mark the boundaries between adjacent groups.
4. The disappearance of the textiles breaks the ties with the ancestors. The textiles are the nexus of communication with the ancestors who are the founding souls of the *ayllus*. Each *awayo*, each *ajxu*, each *unku*, each *llaqota* of the *q'epi* of each *ayllu* has a particular name that is the name of a founding person of the *ayllu*.

5. The loss of the supernatural and religious power that the *q'epis* give to the *J'ilaqatas* during their year of care, conservation and ritual practices. The spirits of the ancestors who reside in the *q'epis* teach the *J'ilaqatas* and give them religious insight.

6. The destruction of the social organization. The *J'ilaqata* of each *ayllu* mediates the naming of the new authorities, the new *J'ilaqatas, alcaldes cobradores, Kurakas, watarunas*. This is done through a rite called *K'anchaku* in which the *J'ilaqatas* consult with the souls of the ancestors.

7. The loss of the documentation of different epochs. They are the documentation of the history of weaving. (Bubba nd:5)

Each of these points involves complex social factors. In the first, for instance, the textiles are represented as text which can be read. Andean scholar Veronica Cereceda (1986:149) writes that a "specific message behind which lies a system that explains the message" is contained in Andean weaving. Cereceda argues that the system is similar to the knots of *quipu* which were used by the Inca to keep historical records and accounts in Pre-Columbian times; her work focused on decoding the system. According to the Coromeños, their weaving expertise was recognized and highly regarded by the Inca.

The history represented in the textiles is specific to the Aymara community of Coroma and reinforces the solidarity of the community. The message and history is read by Coromeños who re-enact, record, and add to the narrative contained in the sacred weavings and *q'epis*. The meaning of the textiles operates in a field of complex systems of knowledge that is integrally tied to the sacred. For the Coromeños, the textiles contain the souls of ancestors who are loved and cared for by the community.

Appropriating the textiles as "art" decontextualizes and reinterprets them as a rarefied aesthetic that can be commodified. In 1983, for example, the Smithsonian Institution collaborated on a traveling exhibition with dealers and collectors of Aymara textiles. A glossy, 159 page catalog, filled with brilliantly colored photographs, accompanied the show. In the introduction William J. Conklin (1983:9) suggests an affinity between Western artists and Bolivian weavers:

> Imagine, then a world in which textiles are the most valued and respected products of the culture—where textiles are the art of the culture—they are movies, the painting, the very color of daily life—where textiles carry meaning and identification—where designer names are your names or perhaps your great-grandmother's.

Conklin equates the sacred weavings of the Aymara with movies and paintings which are accessible and recognizable to Western urbanites. Conklin constructs an individual master artist and links this idea with the world of high fashion and commerce. The reader is invited to see the Aymara equivalent of Calvin Klein come to life on the page.

Conklin's words reveal the enormous gulf between the force of the textiles in their own community and what the words convey to the Western urban dweller. The cultural context of Andean culture falls away. The textiles are not merely the material manifestation of the technical expertise of the individual weavers, but are imbued with a sacred value that is rooted in the creative act. Each thread vibrates between the spiritual realm and everyday lived experience of the community. The threads connect to memory and history in a way that is unrecognizable to the Western audience which voyeuristicly peers at what it imagines to be its own lost past. Conklin (Ibid:9) describes the longing for an unalienated existence that he sees represented by the textiles.

> Something in each of us yearns to see and touch the evidence of time when "things" were not so disposable, when love, and art, and life were conveyed by design—when men, women and children were artists together. The weaving of the aymara, an amazing Bolivian cultural survival from pre-Columbian times, provides just such an opportunity.

In two sentences Conklin evokes a unified past shared by all humanity at some distant time. By juxtaposing the Western artists' affinity to the Indigenous artist with the representation of the Aymara as a survival in anthropological terms, he invites viewers to tour their own unalienated past.

The survival metaphor also signals the rarity of the weavings, which makes them even more attractive in a global marketplace. Aymara culture is commodified and the vehement emphasis on enterprise echoes the project of Columbus, who saw the New World as an exploitative enterprise with gold as the ultimate acquisition. The textiles are the new gold of the Andes that can be excavated in out of the way places, exported and depleted in the space of a generation.

In the same catalog Laurie Adelson (1983:18) remarks on the growing interest in Aymara weaving.

> Not until the late seventies was any serious research directed specifically toward this important textile tradition. The obvious and unfortunate consequence of this lack of interest is that much valuable information has been lost, especially since aymara costume has changed significantly during the last 50–100 years.

Adelson refers to a time period which coincides with the first visits of art dealers into Coroma. This problematizes the relationship of researchers and their institutions and what James Clifford calls "the aesthetic appropriation of non-western others." Incomplete identification of the textiles occurs throughout the catalog. The textiles are identified by the department from which they come, but never by community or *ayllu*. There is no mention of the method of collecting the textiles and most of the "loaned" textiles carry the tag "anonymous lender" which masks the complicated relationships between collectors, dealers and museums.

In another section Laurie Adelson (Ibid.:39) makes a point of accentuating the superior technology of the Aymara before the adoption of European dyes.

> In short the raw materials for making fine high quality fabrics are no longer readily available to the common Aymara. Many of the highly developed arts, including natural dye technology and fine spinning skills that had developed over thousands of years declined rapidly and along with them went the unique fine quality of aymara cloth.

Reversing the more common notion that Indigenous people had inferior technology mystifies the past while it increases the value of antique textiles in the marketplace. The narrative separates the weaving technology from a whole way of life. The category of weaving is the focal point rather than the unique ongoing culture where weaving is still a part of daily activity. Quality is placed in the past, which implies that Aymara culture is in decline. Denying the ongoing Andean weaving tradition where innovation and improvisation constantly occur is necessary in order to keep the myth of vanishing cultures alive. Vanishing, rare, newly discovered textile arts are appealing to collectors as investments and displays of superior sensibilities and taste.

Although countless Indigenous communities have been victimized by the unrestrained greed of Western art dealers and collectors, the Aymara community of Coroma embarked on a multi-layered campaign to recover the stolen textiles. Because of their persistence and dedication to the project of bringing the ancestors home a series of fortuitous events remarkably unfolded. In early 1988, John Murra, Professor Emeritus of Anthropology at Cornell University, sent a postcard to Coroma announcing an ethnic art show in San Francisco. Murra is considered one of the founders of Andean Studies and has repeatedly expressed his concern about the disappearance of ancient textiles from the Andean region. For at least a year, talk of the theft of

ancient textiles from the Andean region and from Coroma in particular had dominated academic circles. Featured on the color postcard was a ceremonial *unku* (a man's tunic made of one piece of cloth) from Coroma. Murra realized that this sale could be a gateway to locating the missing weavings. When the *kurakas* (elders of the community) received the postcard, they were convinced that it was a message sent by the ancestors who were yearning to come home. They immediately decided to send representatives of the community to the United States to locate and retrieve the weavings.

By February 1988, Pio Cruz and Cristina Bubba arrived in San Francisco to locate the textiles and to find the means of bringing them home. They contacted Susan Lobo, a cultural anthropologist who coordinates the Community History Project at Intertribal Friendship House in Oakland. Lobo would play a key role in informing people about the sacred weavings and activating important North American networks of Native Americans, anthropologists, archaeologists, art historians, and textile experts.

Cruz and Bubba pored over documents trying to find legal means to retrieve the textiles. Fortunately, in a meeting with U.S. Customs officials, they learned that if basic customs laws have been violated, cultural property may be recovered. In the case of smuggling, false declaration or false entry, the country of origin must make a claim of ownership in writing for the property to be returned.

From the Bay Area, Cruz and Bubba went to Washington, D.C., where they advised the U.S. Cultural Property Advisory Committee of the theft of the weavings. Cruz and Bubba then returned to Bolivia to organize support from the Bolivian government. By May 6, 1989, the government of Bolivia submitted a formal request for emergency U.S. import restrictions on antique textiles from the community of Coroma.[1]

Within the year the committee recommended unanimously that the United States impose emergency import restrictions on the antique textiles of Coroma for a period of five years. On March 4, 1989, a notice was published in the *Federal Register* which described the textiles that were denied entry. It was only the second emergency action taken by the United States under the UNESCO Cultural Property Convention and the 1983 Convention on Cultural Property Implementation Act. Previously, emergency import restrictions were imposed on pre-Columbian artifacts from the Cara Sucia region of El Salvador in 1987.

By February 1990, the people of Coroma intensified their efforts to bring the sacred weavings back to the community. They sent a delegation once again to the United States to continue the painstaking process of legal negotiations, identification and documentation of the sacred weavings from Coroma, and a new effort to forge cultural and spiritual alliances with Native American groups in California. Pio Cruz, Salustiana de Torrez, Clemente Perez, Cristina Bubba and Benedicto Flores were entrusted with these tasks. The late Salustiana de Torrez was an accomplished weaver who was intimately familiar with the weaving tradition of Coroma. Doña Salustiana was able to identify the weavings confiscated by U.S. Customs by the weave structure and the patterning unique to Coroma textiles. Other members of the delegation who had participated all their lives in the care and maintenance of the sacred weavings could identify them by style and type as well as by marks left by certain ceremonies conducted by the community. It was a heart wrenching time for the delegates because they could view and touch their sacred weavings but they knew that many more obstacles had to be overcome before the souls of the ancestors could be returned to Coroma.

On this occasion the delegates from Coroma and Native people from California pledged mutual support in Indigenous rights efforts. People from the Central Valley representing Tule River Reservation, and the Fresno area participated in the meetings and spiritual ceremonies that followed. For the past twenty years there has been a movement dedicated to cultural revitalization occurring in the Central Valley, as well as other parts of the state which has resulted in tremendous strides in all areas of Native life. The two delegations found common concerns in many aspects of their lives. Joe Carrillo from Tule River remarked during the meeting:

> I have met and discussed this [the Coroma repatriation efforts] with the key spiritual leaders for Central California. Everyone agrees that to be involved to assist in their return would be a spiritual responsibility. A part of this teaching is for some of us to travel and do our share as human beings to allow the spirit to help all Indian people to come together in a spiritual way throughout the world. If in any small way we can contribute to the spiritual process that's happening, then it is good to do. For our people to travel to Bolivia [when the weavings return] is not just a meeting between people, but a coming together of the spirits from our tribes.

During this visit, the delegations forged relationships that were to develop into a strong alliance between diverse groups. Most importantly the meeting created a symbolic space that reenacted the coming together of the people from North and South America. In an exchange of rituals the ancestors from the south were introduced to the ancestors from the north in order that their souls might be comforted during their stay in California. The Coromeños and the representative from California pledged support to one another in their repatriation efforts and religious freedom.

The valiant efforts of the Coromeños to repatriate their sacred weavings back to their community deeply moved diverse sectors of the population. Public sentiment overwhelmingly elevated the Coromeños to the status of the heroic protectors of cultural property. After their first journey North, a Supreme Decree issued by the Bolivian government in May 1988 prohibited exportation of any textile made prior to 1950. The decree, which was signed by Bolivian President Jaime Paz Zamora, also stated that the sacred weavings must be returned to Coroma rather than to a national museum. The victory upheld local customary practice which recognizes the communal ownership of cultural property on the local rather than national level. Clearly, the Coromeños were engaged in multiple negotiations which reaffirmed and at times redefined local and national contracts.

On the local level, the people of Coroma had to deal with the breach of community solidarity that the loss of the textiles engendered. Since the weavings are communally owned, a fact which the Supreme Decree certified, no individual was culturally or legally empowered to sell them. Nevertheless, the men who fell victim to the offers of the dealers felt that they had no choice other than to give up the weavings. One of the men described his anguish over the fact that his family and community were living under conditions of near starvation. In another instance, a man accepted an old tractor in exchange for the textiles. He believed the tractor would make a difference between starvation and survival for the community. It is important to understand the motives of the community members and the unequal power relations between them and the dealers. However, in order to heal the breach within the community the Coromeños chose to see themselves as powerful actors participating in the events leading to the crisis.

The *kurakas* employed traditional methods to determine the factors which were at play throughout the period. The men's failure to protect the *q'epis* from depredation was determined to be a breach in the entire fabric of life of the community. It was paramount for the community to respond appropriately in order to repair the damage. Therefore, one of the immediate responses was to impose jail sentences on those who succumbed to the pressure to give up the textiles. In my view, this is yet another example of how Coromeños began to assert their right to determine the ways in which the community and its ancestors are represented to the outside world. Fortunately, now all but one of the men have been successfully reintegrated into the community. On the other hand none of the art dealers have been imprisoned for the illegal export of the textiles.

Steven Berger, one of the art dealers operating in Bolivia during this time defended his actions in an article appearing in the *San Francisco Chronicle* (Doyle 1992) on September 26, 1992, that reported the return of the textiles: "Believe me, these Indians wanted to sell their textiles. It was the only thing they had of value." His statements revealed his cultural biases, as well as clouded his complicity in destroying the religion and life ways of the Coromeños. He continued: "This was a tradition in the process of breaking down. A well respected anthropologist told me that if the people show you their sacred objects, the tradition is already broken. So at that point I felt free in what I was doing. . . . I love these textiles." Berger's statement reflects not only paternalism, but a dangerous distortion common in Western audiences who read Indigenous cultures as broken and lost. What is left unsaid, but is nevertheless implied, is that loss and destruction is the natural order of things which only reflects deadly defects or lacks in Indigenous people. The Western audience's response to the textiles is to feel what cultural anthropologist Renato Rosaldo calls "imperialist nostalgia," which longs and mourns for what it has destroyed or changed. In the context of the sacred weavings, engaging in "imperialist nostalgia" performs the additional task of erasing the ongoing brutalization of Native peoples. Berger relies on a rescue narrative to create the appearance of altruism and innocence; he obstinately obscures the role he plays in continuing a pattern of abuse and denial. The failure on the part of national and international agencies to adequately respond to the extreme economic crisis brought about by years of drought remains unacknowledged and in fact, hidden from view.

The video produced by the community of Coroma (Council of Authorities of Corona 1988), *El Camino de las Almas*, responds to these glaring omissions. Continuing the strategic trajectory of the

Presencia statement and the jail sentences imposed on the *watarunakuna*, the Coromeños insist on their right to control the representations of their community. The video rigorously exposes the method of "collecting" employed in Coroma[2] by focusing on the events that led to the discovery of the theft. The video ends with the community's elected envoy, Pio Cruz, bicycling across the *altiplano* to begin the search for their sacred textiles. Although the video focuses on the events leading to the pillage of the *q'epis*, it also depicts the daily lives of the people, including ceremonial activities. This courageous act of self-representation straightforwardly asserts their cultural difference from metropolitan audiences that view the video. The video also contradicts the narrative of a defeated people and lost culture. One of the most powerful images of the video is a woman shouting, "Justice!" as she leads people through the street in Coroma. In sharp contrast to the image of pitiful remnants of a lost high culture that Berger most clearly articulates, her presence and attitude mark her and her colleagues as capable social actors who brilliantly delineate the problems facing their community. Against all odds they marshall the resources necessary to get their message to the national and international communities where their struggle to repatriate the textiles will take place.

El Camino de las Almas was awarded the Bolivian Silver Condor for best documentary of 1989. On the international level, the video is used to heighten awareness of the theft of the sacred weavings, as well as to illuminate the problem of international traffic in sacred objects. Its showing in New York in 1990 brought the offer of pro bono legal services by the Center for Constitutional Rights in New York.

Originally, the community envisioned the video as a means to offer testimony in the litigation with the art dealers in the United States. As production began, however, the video emerged as a powerful organizing tool. After each shoot the community gathered to critique the footage which gave them the opportunity to discuss the events and brought more and more Coromeños into the talks and production. A sense of empowerment grew as more people were involved in the project to represent themselves and their point of view to the world.

Young people who had begun to drift away from the community began to show renewed respect and interest in traditional activities and religious rituals since the campaign to regain the weaving began. To some extent the conflicts and tensions between evangelical Christians and traditionalists have been eased through the valorization of Aymara culture by the Bolivian public. On the national level, many urban Aymara and Quechua people re-embraced the common cultural heritage they share with Coromeños. Even though they may reside in the cities of Bolivia, they were summoned by the remembrance and recognition of their own rootedness in Indigenous cultural practices.

After years of struggle forty-two sacred weavings were returned to Coroma on September 24, 1992. Intertribal Friendship House, the oldest urban Indian Center in the United States, sponsored the California delegation that has continued its work with the people of Coroma. Joe Carrillo, Sidney Rubio, and Clarence Yager represent the Central Valley, Susan Lobo and I continue our roles as organizers and cultural mediators. New members of the group include Paiute/Pit River artist Jean La Marr and Hopi videographer Victor Masayesva. We are on our way to meet with the people once again to offer thanks for the safe return of the souls of the ancestors. We are eager to develop new strategies for the safe return of the weavings that are still lost and wandering the world.

The following are excerpts from my journal. I offer them here in an attempt to outline my own reactions as a Native scholar committed to social change. I was stunned by the intense familiarity the people of the Andes and the *altiplano* landscape evoked in me. I was forced to consider our shared and divergent stories as Native subjects living through the postcolonial era, at a time that is described by many Aymara/Quechua political activists in the Andes as *pachacuti*, translated roughly as a time of violent upheaval and reversals. I felt as if we were poised on the verge of a distinct opening that would allow us to see our realities more clearly and passionately. I was forced to confront the reality of Native losses in the United States where you can wander though large cities like San Francisco, New York, Dallas, or Chicago without once encountering another Native person. When I think of loss, I think of the actual annihilation of Native bodies that cannot help but be awakened every time I walk down the street. I found myself experiencing the intense pain of raw grief at the same time that I was exhilarated by the presence of the sheer mass of Native people. The desire for wholeness with which the colonial experience has marked me became almost unbearable in those moments of recognition.

Fredy Yepez, the Bolivian office manager and expert driver from the Inter-American Foundation is at the wheel of the Jeep. He points to one of the many stone *tambos* or Inca inns where messengers and Inca officials spent the night on their journeys through *Tawantinsuyu*, Inca Land. Although the roof of the deserted *tambo* has long ago turned to dust the familiar stairstep-like Andean cross stands in sharp relief against the dark blue evening sky. It reminds me of Northern symbols of the four directions that signal the comfort and intimacy of home. The intricate stonework sends a shiver of longing through me.

The paved road from la Paz ends long before Coroma. Little rain has fallen in the canton of Coroma for six years. The land resembles the long stretches of Nevada desert more than the high plains region of Montana and Wyoming that I expected to see. The whole department of Potosi is stricken with drought. Occasionally, the car crosses railroad tracks and then there is no road at all. The wind has swept all traces of tire tracks from the *altiplano*, and I can hear the tires crunch against the dry earth.

We are still several miles from the village. It is a moonless night and the stone markers where the dry river bed is the easiest to cross are hard to see. A short distance away a bonfire sends crackling sparks into the night sky. We can make out the soft outline of a sheepherder warming himself by the fire. When we approach we see that he is a young boy. As soon as he sees the car he runs away. We stop the car; get out and call to him. He timidly makes his way back toward the car. His shyness passes and he points us toward the gently sloping bank of the river bed where we can safely cross.

Although Coroma is hard hit by drought, the people remain on the land. The population is approximately six thousand in the canton. The township is surrounded by outlying homesteads where the Coromeños make their living as farmers and herders. Crops include the staple items: potatoes, quinoa, and maize, while herders raise the Andean camelids— llama and alpaca as well as sheep. In many places we see dark green potato leaves pushing through the recently sown fields. Cristina Bubba explains that during the school year Coroma is a village of children who come from the outlying areas to attend school. Living in their family homes in Coroma, they keep house and care for one another when school is in session. It is a clear December summer now, and the village is quiet because many children are helping their parents farm and herd.

We arrive early the next morning, a few hours before the sun rises. No one is awake yet so we go to the door of our hosts to get the key. We exchange a few sleep laden words before going to the house where we will stay. The next morning Susan, Jean and I are greeted by Serinina Veles and Valentina Mendita Cruz, the sister of Don Pio. We sit together in the garden between the house and the kitchen as Doña Serinina and Doña Valentina spin the lustrous wool of the llama. We talk about life in Coroma. Later we are to take part in ceremonies for the sacred textiles but now we talk about our lives as Native women from opposites ends of America. Wool filaments stream through the fingers of the women to their drop spindles. The spindles are smaller than those used by Dineh women in the Southwest and a quick spin with the fingers sends the spindles whirring in hand carved wooden bowls. Doña Valentina spins the finest thread I have ever seen done by hand. As the thread lengthens she deftly winds it on the spindle. She says in a matter of fact way: "You should have seen us before the gringos [art dealers] came. We were beautiful then." I feel a fierce pride mixed with rage echo through me.

There are many preparations that have to be attended to before we begin the rituals. The head *Kurakas* and the *J'ilaqatas* consult coca leaves several times to find the most auspicious time for the ceremonies. A ritual specialist is called upon to read the coca leaves. We learn that there are some souls that have yet to make the long journey back to Coroma even though the sacred weavings have returned. There is concern for the safety and well-being of these souls as well as the sacred weavings that are still missing. We are told that the best time for the rituals to begin is in the early afternoon. The *q'epis* will be present during the rituals which will be held in the new community building that was recently completed by the community. It is an open, bright building with newly whitewashed walls. There are several colored posters on the walls announcing meetings and offering health information. It looks very similar to Native American community buildings in the United States.

That afternoon we gather in the community building for the rituals. Sacred objects and gifts are exchanged by the people from the North and South. The spiritual leaders of the Central Valley have sent eagle feathers along with instructions on the care and significance of each feather. Libations are offered to the spirits of the ancestors and offerings are burned at the altar. Coca leaves play a central role in all the ceremonial activities. Coca is offered to the spirits of the ancestors and is passed to everyone attending the

Serinina Veles is an accomplished weaver and leader from Coroma, Bolivia.

rituals. Again the coca leaves are consulted and the religious leaders find that we will continue the rituals for another day. There are things that must be prepared for the following day. A pall of anxiety hangs over the group because we have learned that there are souls desperately trying to make their way to the sacred bundles.

The next day we continue the offerings. The ritual specialist goes outside and we hear the rich full sound of a bell. When he reenters the community building, people are talking excitedly of the return of the ancestors who had been making their way back to the community. Relief and joy are visible on all the faces in the room.

Later we join the secular meeting taking place in the building adjoining the government office. In this context we reaffirm our commitment to support each other on repatriation efforts. The precedent setting example of Coroma is a major victory for Indigenous people. They have been successful in creating a network of allies and heightening international awareness of cultural property issues. The community is in the process of establishing safeguards to protect themselves from loss and theft of cultural property. The tractor sits idly in an old building as the people discuss whether or not they will use it in their community. They debate the impact it will have on community relations, whether it will build community cooperation or impede it. What effects will the introduction of this technology have on the community where traditional farming practices have assured self-sufficiency? What does it mean to have to maintain the machinery and buy the gas? These are some of the questions the people of Coroma have to answer for themselves.

Currently, there are numerous sacred weavings that have yet to be recovered. Although in May 1993 the U.S. ban on imports of Bolivian textiles was extended for another three years, there is no law on the books that stops the exportation of Bolivian textiles. Some of the Coroma weavings may now be in Europe and Japan, where they may be more difficult to recover. Existing international law does not effectively protect cultural property. Attention also needs to be given to situations in which communities believe (rightly so given current levels of assistance) they have no other alternative than to sell their cultural property. In these cases some people will invariably fall prey to unscrupulous dealers or collectors.

National governments and international organizations must support communities as they seek viable alternatives. There are projects operating in Bolivia to ensure the continuation of the weaving tradition, such as the one administered by the Textile Museum in Sucre. People who are interested in Andean textiles should support these efforts. Weaving is a living tradition and there are appropriate ways to acquire works of art, beauty, and fashion that support Indigenous people rather than continue the old patterns of exploitation and violence.

NOTES

1. The request was made under Article 9 of the UNESCO convention of the Means to Prohibiting and Preventing the illicit Import, Export and Transfer of Ownership of Cultural Property. The convention was adopted by UNESCO in 1970 and ratified by the U.S. Senate in 1972.

2. The video was produced in collaboration with UNITAS (National Union of Social Action Institutions) land video producer Eduardo Lopez, and with the cooperation of Katy Degado, Lucha Costa, Sergio Claros, Julio Quispe, Oscar Palacios, Monica and Juan Claudio Lechin.

WORKS CITED

Adelson, Laurie, and Arthur Tracht. *Aymara Weavings* (Washington, DC: Smithsonian Institution Traveling Exhibition Service, 1983.)

Bubba, Cristina, et al. "El propositio de las culturas: Los Textiles de Coroma." *Unitas*. enero, numero 11.

Cereceda, Veronica, "The Semiology of Andean Textiles: The Talegas of Isluga." Anthropological History of Andean Polities, ed. J.V. Murra, et al. (London: Cambridge University Press, 1986.)

Conklin, William J. *Aymara Weavings* (Washington, DC: Smithsonian Institution Traveling Exhibition Service, 1983.)

Council of Authorities of Coroma, Bolivia. *Paths of the Souls.* Video. (Dramatized version of the disappearance of the sacred weavings), 1988.

Cruz, Pio. Personal interview conducted by Susan Lobo. Kensington, California, April 2, 1990.

Doyle, Jim. "S.F. Dealer Defends Trade in Rare Textiles." *San Francisco Chronicle*, September 26, 1992.

5

AMERICAN INDIAN RELIGIOUS FREEDOM ACT AFTER TWENTY-FIVE YEARS

Suzan Shown Harjo

Henceforth it shall be the policy of the United States to protect and preserve for American Indians their inherent right of freedom to believe, express, and exercise the traditional religions of the American Indian, Eskimo, Aleut, and Native Hawaiians, including but not limited to access to sites, use and possession of sacred objects, and the freedom to worship through ceremonials and traditional rites.

—American Indian Religious Freedom Act of 1978, Public Law 95-341

POLICY TO PRESERVE AND PROTECT NATIVE AMERICAN RELIGIOUS FREEDOM

The American Indian Religious Freedom Act turned twenty-five on August 11, 2003. Two months later, Arizona State University's College of Law held a gathering of Native American people who worked to achieve the act's passage and to further its policy promise. Our reflections on the past quarter-century and our calls for future action are contained in the pages of this journal.

Today, there is every reason both to celebrate the American Indian Religious Freedom Act (AIRFA) and to complete its unfinished agenda. In AIRFA, Congress and the president stated plainly that the policy of the United States is to preserve and protect Native American traditional practices and religious freedom. This was necessary in 1978 because Native peoples were still suffering the ill effects of sorry policies of the past intended to ban traditional religions, to neutralize or to eliminate traditional religious leaders, and to force traditional religious practitioners to convert to Christianity, to take up English, and to give up their way of life.

Even though the federal Civilization Regulations that first criminalized traditional religions expressions in the 1880s were withdrawn in the mid-1930s, laws and practices impeding Native Americans' free exercise of traditional religions persisted. Native sacred objects continued to be confiscated and graves

From Suzan Shown Harjo, "American Indian Religious Freedom Act After Twenty-Five Years," *Wicazo Sa Review*, vol. 19, no. 2, fall 2004, pp. 129–136.

looted. Those stolen in earlier times filled federal, state, and private collections, as well as museums and educational institutions in Europe. Native sacred places continued to be desecrated and damaged. Those annexed during the Civilization Regulations period remained in non-Native governmental and private hands, and Native people risked stiff fines and imprisonment for fulfilling religious mandates at those sites.

Native traditional people organized a national coalition in 1967 to gain protections for sacred places and ceremonies, to recover Native human remains and sacred objects, and to promote respect for Native people and rights in general society. As the coalition achieved returns of important sacred places and legal protections for the use of feathers and other sacred objects, it sought a broad policy to remove the federal barriers standing in the way of Native American traditional religious expression. When AIRFA was signed into law, it was greeted with relief, elation, and hope by traditional American Indian, Alaska Native, and Native Hawaiian peoples. After generations of traditional Native religions being driven underground or to extinction, and traditional practitioners being stigmatized as outlaws, AIRFA was lauded as a needed and welcome policy.

POLICY TO CONSULT WITH NATIVE TRADITIONAL RELIGIOUS LEADERS

In sharp contrast to the religious suppression policies, AIRFA established the policy of federal agencies consulting with Native traditional religious leaders on proposed actions regarding Native traditional religious matters. This is an ongoing policy and the context for similar consultative requirements in subsequent federal laws and regulations.

Over the past twenty-five years, many lawyers, both for and against Native traditional interests, have ignored this consultative policy requirement of AIRFA. Governmental agents often overlook it, inadvertently or deliberately, when taking or approving actions affecting traditional religions. Some consult only with tribal government leaders or employees, excluding traditional religious leaders. Some even conduct sham consultations by not seriously considering the information or conclusions of the traditional experts who are being consulted. This occurs most egregiously at present with respect to those developmental decisions that would damage or destroy sacred places. Sadly, some tribal government agents engage in these practices, too, and many Gucci Gulch [the hallways of Congress] lobbyists and federal staffers in Washington, DC, keep a watchful eye on laws and regulations that would interfere with development plans at sacred places.

Part of the continuing religious freedom agenda is to assure that agents at all government levels comply with the consultative policy requirement under AIRFA. It is essential that government agents implement the executive orders "Indian Sacred Sites" (1996) and "Consultation and Coordination with Indian Tribal Governments" (1998), as well as other federal mandates, with the understanding that consultation with traditional religious leaders, not solely with the secular leadership, is a required part of tribal consultation when dealing with those Native peoples with living traditional religions. For those Indian nations that are theocracies, it makes sense for their traditional governments to have sole standing. For the other 99 percent that are not theocracies, it is nonsensical to recognize the secular entities and not recognize the traditional religious entities and practitioners.

AIRFA'S ONE-YEAR REVIEW AND REPORT TO CONGRESS

AIRFA required the president to direct federal "departments, agencies, and other instrumentalities responsible for administering relevant laws to evaluate their policies and procedures in consultation with native traditional religious leaders in order to determine appropriate changes necessary to protect and preserve Native American religious cultural rights and practices."

AIRFA also required the president to "report back to the Congress the results of his evaluation, including any changes that were made in administrative policies and procedures, and any recommendations he may have for legislative action." Over fifty federal agencies participated in the one-year consultation and review process, and the president's report was delivered to Congress in August 1979.

During the review period, numerous federal agents objected to Native American Church peyote ceremonies being characterized in the president's report as a traditional religion, arguing that the use of peyote by American Indians was a relatively new phenomenon and did not constitute a religion. The counterargument prevailed—that its practitioners believed they were practicing a religion, one their ancestors had practiced for a century and more—and ceremonial use of peyote was included as a traditional Native religion. Later litigation over peyote use by one Indian and one non-Indian resulted in a 1989 Supreme Court decision that weakened religious freedom law nationwide and left Native American Church members clinging to an Indian exemption to a regulation prohibiting the use of peyote. At the urging of the Justice Department, Congress amended AIRFA in 1993 to codify the drug regulation and provide for peyote use by Indian members of the Native American Church.

As part of the initial review, Indian inmates were afforded greater access to traditional religious counseling, sweat lodge ceremonies, and use of feathers and other sacred objects, but religious liberty for Native people in prisons has not yet been achieved. During the review year and the following year, federal agencies entered into agreements with Native peoples to provide access to certain sacred places and objects, and to return or jointly manage others. In negotiating these agreements, the agencies accommodated Native traditional religious interests, even in those cases involving national security interests at military facilities.

In some cases, the process began during the review period, but did not conclude until years or decades afterward. One example of this is Kaho'olawe, a former Naval bombing range in Hawaii, where Native Hawaiian people were willing to risk injury and death from unexploded ordnance in order to conduct traditional ceremonies. In mid-1979, the secretary of the navy made the naval stations aware of the requirements of the religious freedom law and pledged to "cooperate with Native traditional religious leaders in an ongoing effort to ensure the free exercise of religious rights while at the same time ensuring the safety of all personnel and the completion of its military mission." A subsequent Island Reserve Commission and required the navy to conduct a munitions cleanup. Kaho'olawe is now safe and, in 2003, was formally transferred to Hawaii.

PROTECTION OF NATIVE AMERICAN SACRED PLACES

Over the quarter-century life of AIRFA, numerous traditional and customary areas have been returned or protected through comanagement agreements. Most of these sacred places are naturally formed churches—lands and waters where people go to pray for the good day, the precious earth, the blessing waters, the sweet air, and peaceful life for all living beings the world over. While some are being protected, others have been damaged or destroyed, and far too many are under attack today.

Each administration and Congress over the past thirty years has returned some Native sacred places, from Taos Blue Lake in the early 1970s to Washoe Rock today. It is equally true that each Congress and administration has opposed lawsuits and a statutory cause of action to protect and defend Native sacred places. Ten years after the passage of AIRFA, the Supreme Court held that neither the Indian religious freedom law nor the First Amendment protected a Native sacred place in California against a Forest Service logging road, and invited Congress to enact a protective cause of action.

Indian traditional and tribal leaders tried from 1989 to 1995 to get a legislative cause of action, but Interior politicos, Justice lawyers, and White House pollsters opposed it. Native leaders then negotiated a substantive agreement on sacred lands, which was changed unilaterally within the administration to a weak restatement of the AIRFA policy. For all its faults, however, the 1996 executive order "Indian Sacred Sites" did remind federal agencies of their continuing obligations to protect sacred placid result in some sites being returned and otherwise protected.

The high court's 1988 ruling started a development rush that has increased in intensity over the past sixteen years, and federal, state, and private developers are ignoring or flaunting laws that could and should be used to protect sacred places. Today, over fifty sacred places are being threatened by development pollution, poisons recreation looting and vandalism.

At the end of 2002, traditional and tribal leaders, practitioners, and advocates who are among the most knowledgeable on these issues developed clear, concise lists of essential elements and objectionable elements for public policy on Native sacred places. Topping the list of objectionable elements is any law that tries to define or limit the sacred. The topmost essential element is a cause of action to defend sacred places in court and to serve as incentive for serious negotiations for the return, comanagement, or protected status of sacred places. Also a high is policy respecting traditional religious tenets and tribal law prohibiting disclosure of confidential and private information about the sacred.

Following those guidelines for essential and objectionable elements would not only keep faith with the people who reached consensus on these matters, but would honor the many people who sacrificed to save sacred places and the legions who were murdered and confined for trying to pray at sacred places.

RETURN OF NATIVE AMERICAN HUMAN REMAINS AND CULTURAL PATRIMONY

AIRFA laid the groundwork for federal museums returning Native human remains and sacred objects and led to the repatriation laws of 1989 and 1990.

The first major gains in the national Native repatriation movement were made during the six months following AIRFA's enactment. The heads of the military museums decided in 1979 that it was in keeping with the new law to return requested Native human remains, sacred objects, and cultural patrimony in their collections. Scientists from the Smithsonian Institution disagreed with that decision and attempted to change it. Failing that, they claimed that the Smithsonian was a private, educational entity, rather than a federal agency with a duty to comply with AIRFA. That notion was overruled by the White House and the Office of Management and Budget, and the Smithsonian became one of the fifty-plus federal agencies reviewing policies under AIRFA.

After the AIRFA review, Smithsonian scientists resisted returning any Native human remains or cultural property. However, bowing to national Native and congressional pressure in the mid-1980s, new institutional leadership directed an inventory of Native human remains in their collections. The accounting—18,500 Native human remains, together with 4,500 Indian skulls from the U.S. Army surgeon general's "Indian Crania Study" in the late 1880s—stunned people in Indian Country and in general society. Native people and members of Congress began developing repatriation law in earnest. At the same time, Native Americans were preparing dozens of lawsuits to recover Native human remains, funerary objects, and cultural property.

In order to slow down the process and gain political leverage, the repositories with large collections of Native human remains and cultural patrimony lobbied Congress for another study, the "National Dialogue on Museum/Native American Relations" (1988–1990). After two meetings, Native people quietly postponed their participation in order to achieve the historic repatriation agreement with the Smithsonian, and returned to the study once the repatriation agreement had been enacted at the end of 1989 as a provision of the National Museum of the American Indian Act. The Smithsonian leadership had opted to go forward with plans to acquire the new museum and to avoid litigation by settling on a repatriation process. Scientists who were opposed to repatriation redoubled their efforts to stop further repatriation law.

The "Dialogue" report was presented to the Senate in January 1990. It reflected the repatriation law that applied to the Smithsonian and recommended new law extending that agreement to all federal and federal-assisted collections. Some of the scientists who participated in the "Dialogue" were so incensed by the report's use of the term "human remains" for what they called "our resources" that they disassociated themselves by name in a footnote from the use of the term. Their objection was that "human remains" implied that international standards of human rights and burial rights applied to dead Native Americans and their relatives. These scientists did not believe that these rights attached to "specimens," "bones," and "grave goods."

The Native American Graves Protection and Repatriation Act of 1990 (NAGPRA) became law eleven months after the 1989 repatriation provision was enacted. As with the 1989 law, Congress enacted NAGPRA as human and civil rights policy for Native Americans and as presettlement of myriad lawsuits Native peoples were on the verge of filing. Congress chose to establish a Native American policy and processes for the return of Native human remains, funerary items, sacred objects, and cultural patrimony rather than to leave it to the courts to decide repatriation policy on a piecemeal basis.

Certain scientists who opposed national repatriation policy have worked to frustrate the repatriation processes and delay repatriations until they can conduct further studies on human remains in their collections. Many are trying to hide the identity of human remains that are the subjects of their studies and to classify them as unidentifiable, in order to avoid repatriating them. Some federal scientists are abetting this effort by attempting to create new regulations to make the unidentified Native human remains the property of the repositories where they now reside.

Others have turned their attention to dismantling repatriation law through the courts. One group has pursued litigation, pitting what they see as a scientific right to conduct destructive studies of the Ancient One, popularly known as Kennewick Man, against the federal government and several related Indian tribes, who want to rebury him. Since the 2003 AIRFA gathering at Arizona State University, the Ninth Circuit Court of Appeals has upheld a district judge's ruling that the scientists can go forward with studies, meaning that they can carve up, drill holes in, and scrape away at the Ancient One.

The February 2004 decision upholds wrongheaded notions that the Ancient One is not Native American within the meaning of NAGPRA and does not have to be repatriated, that NAGPRA is not Native American policy, that a Native American coalition cannot jointly claim him, and that federal-tribal consultation constitutes ex parte communication that somehow violates the scientists' due process. The tribal coalition is seeking a rehearing.

The main policy achievement of the repatriation laws is the recognition that Native Americans are human beings and no longer archaeological resources. Ironically, the Ninth Circuit ruling denies the humanity of the Ancient One, holding that archaeological resources law applies, that he is an archaeological resource, and that archaeologists can have at him. Unless the courts reverse these rulings, this aspect of NAGPRA will become part of AIRFA's unfinished agenda, and Congress will have to revisit and clarify repatriation law.

CONCLUSION

While much progress has been made under AIRFA and its follow-on legislation, there is much to do in order to fulfill AIRFA's promise to preserve and protect Native American religious freedom. AIRFA provided a policy context and incremental process for subsequent action. This has worked well in those areas where Congress has taken specific action—with respect to ceremonial use of peyote, for example. It has not worked well in those areas where Congress has not acted. The failure of Congress and five administrations to create a cause of action for sacred places protection is the most glaring item on AIRFA's unfinished agenda.

The overarching work that needs to be done under AIRFA is to educate Americans who teach and shape public opinion to learn and tell the truth about the history of suppression of Native American religions and religious freedom rights. Judges, policy makers, and those who implement and enforce laws need to be educated about the onslaught of weaponry and laws that denied the religions and the very humanity of Native peoples, and how that onslaught has diminished but not ended. Only when they understand what brought us to this juncture will they appreciate that, because the federal government has used its vast power to do ill, it is necessary for it to take remedial actions in the direction of justice.

That is a fitting way to recognize AIRFA's anniversary and an honorable way to begin its next twenty-five years.

PART REVIEW

DISCUSSION QUESTIONS

Floyd Red Crow Westerman and Jimmy Curtis,
Missionaries
1. What is the Native American view of Christian missionaries in this song?

John (Fire) Lame Deer and Richard Erdoes, *Alone on the Hilltop*
1. What is a vision pit, and what is its significance to traditional Lakota?
2. What does Lame Deer mean by "the spirit is everywhere"?
3. What is the significance of the sweat lodge?

Frank R. LaPena, *My World Is a Gift of My Teachers*
1. How do Native Americans see the world "as a 'different place' from that seen and described by the dominant society"?
2. In what way are songs, dances, and ceremonies inspiration for Indian art?
3. What does the author mean by the title "The World Is a Gift of My Teachers"?

Russell Thornton, *Who Owns Our Past?*
1. What does the author mean by the title "Who Owns Our Past"?
2. Explain how so many Native American human remains came to reside in universities, museums, historical societies, and private collections.

3. What two key laws mandate the protection and repatriation of Native American human remains and sacred objects? What two problems remain?

Indians Are Not Specimens—Indians Are People
1. The U.S. government's Smithsonian Institution holds the largest collection of Indian human remains and associated grave offerings in the nation. How did it come to have such a large collection, and how do Indian people feel about this collection?

Victoria Bomberry, *Battling for Souls*
1. The sacred weavings of the Aymara Indians of Bolivia record and interpret the religious life of the community. What is the cultural and spiritual significance of the theft of these textiles to Indian culture and life?

Suzan Shown Harjo, *American Indian Religious Freedom Act After Twenty-five Years*
1. After reading this article, how would you judge the overall success or failure of the 1978 American Indian Religious Freedom Act?
2. Give an example of how a federal agency has failed to implement or has been slow in implementing the repatriation requirement of NAGPRA.
3. According to Harjo, what "is the most glaring item on AIRFA's unfinished agenda?"

KEY TERMS

American Indian Religious Freedom Act of 1978
Coroma textiles
Durkheim, Emile
elders
First Amendment rights
hanblechia
Indian Crania Study
National Museum of the American Indian (NMAI)
    Act of 1989

Native American Graves Protection and Repatriation
    Act (NAGPRA) of 1990
repatriation
revitalization movement
the sacred
Smithsonian Institution
specimen complex

SUGGESTED READINGS

ALDRED, LISA. "Plastic Shamans and Astroturf Sun Dances: New Age Commercialization of Native American Spirituality," *American Indian Quarterly*, 24, No. 3 (Summer 2000): 329–352.

AMERICAN INDIAN STUDIES CENTER. "Special Edition: Repatriation of American Indian Remains." *American Indian Culture and Research Journal*, 6, no. 2 (1992).

ANYON, ROGER. "Zuni Protection of Cultural Resources and Religious Freedom." *Cultural Survival Quarterly* (Winter 1990): 46–49.

BARSH, RUSSELL LAWRENCE. "The Illusion of Religious Freedom for Indigenous Americans." *Oregon Law Review*, 65 (1986): 363–412.

BECK, PEGGY V., and ANNA L. WALTERS. *The Sacred: Ways of Knowledge, Sources of Life*. Tsaile [Navajo Nation], Ariz.: Navajo Community College Press, 1977.

CHAMPAGNE, DUANE, ed. "Religion." In *The Native North American Almanac*. (Detroit: Gale Research, 1994.)

DELORIA, VINE, JR. *God Is Red*. New York: Grosset and Dunlap, 1973.

DELORIA, VINE, JR. "A Simple Question of Humanity: The Moral Dimensions of the Reburial Issue." *NARF Legal Review*, 14, no. 4 (Fall 1989): 1–12.

DEMALLIE, RAYMOND J. *The Sixth Grandfather: Black Elk's Teachings Given to John Neihardt*. Lincoln, Nebraska: University of Nebraska Press, 1984.

ECHO-HAWK, WALTER. "Native American Religious Liberty: Five Hundred Years After Columbus." *American Indian Culture and Research Journal*, 17, no. 3 (1993): 33–52.

ERDOES, RICHARD. *Crying for a Dream: The World through Native American Eyes*. Santa Fe: Bear and Co., 1989.

GREEN, RAYNA, et al. *American Indian Sacred Objects. Skeletal Remains, Repatriation and Reburial: A Resource Guide*. Washington, D.C.: The American Indian Program, National Museum of American History, Smithsonian Institution, 1994.

HORSE CAPTURE, GEORGE, ed., *The Seven Visions of Bull Lodge*. Ann Arbor, Mich.: Bear Claw Press, 1980.

HULTKRANTZ, AKE. *The Religions of the American Indians*, trans. Monica Setterwall. Berkeley: University of California Press, 1979.

LADUKE, WINONA. *Recovering the Sacred: The Power of Naming and Claiming*. Cambridge, MA: South End Press, 2005.

LIMMERICK, PATRICIA NELSON. "The Repression of Indian Religious Freedom." *NARF Legal Review*, 18, no. 2 (Summer 1993): 9–13.

LOFTIN, JOHN D. "Anglo-American Jurisprudence and the Native American Tribal Quest for Religious Freedom." *American Indian Culture and Research Journal*, 13, no. 3 (1989): 1–52.

MARTIN, KALLEN M. "The Beginning of Respect: The U.S. Repatriation Law." *Native Americas*, 14, no. 3 (Fall 1997): 24–29.

TALBOT, STEVE. "Desecration and American Indian Religious Freedom." *Journal of Ethnic Studies*, 12, no. 1 (1984): 1–18.

TALBOT, STEVE. "Spiritual Genocide: The Denial of American Indian Religious Freedom from Conquest to 1934," *Wicazo Sa Review*, 21, no. 22 (Fall 2006): 7–39.

TROPE, JACK F. "Existing Federal Law and the Protection of Sacred Sites: Possibilities and Limitations." *Cultural Survival Quarterly* (Winter 1996): 30–39.

VIII
NATIVE SOVEREIGNTY: SELF-GOVERNANCE, CULTURE, AND SUSTAINABLE DEVELOPMENT

It Was That Indian
Simon J. Ortiz

Martinez
from over by Bluewater
was the one who discovered uranium
west of Grants.
That's what they said.
He brought that green stone
into town one afternoon in 1953,
said he found it by the railroad tracks
over by Haystack Butte.
Tourist magazines did a couple spreads
on him, photographed him in kodak color,
and the Chamber of Commerce celebrated
that Navajo man,
forgot for the time being
that the brothers
from Aacqu east of Grants
had killed that state patrolman,
and never mind also
that the city had a jail full of Indians.
The city fathers named
a city park after him
and some even wanted to put up a statue
of Martinez but others said
that was going too far for just an Indian
even if he was the one who started that area
into a boom.
Well, later on,
when some folks began to complain
about chemical poisons flowing into the streams
from the processing mills, carwrecks on Highway 53,
lack of housing in Grants,
cave-ins at Section 33,
non-union support,
high cost of living,
and uranium radiation causing cancer,
they—the Chamber of Commerce—pointed out
that it was Martinez
that Navajo Indian from over by Bluewater
who discovered uranium,
it says so in this here brochure,
he found that green stone over by Haystack
out behind his hogan;
it was that Indian who started that boom.

Homelands, culture and tradition, sovereignty and nationhood. What meanings do these terms hold for a people? This part focuses on the interrelationship of these ideas. The readings all provide insights and perspective on the concept of nation building, which is inextricably linked to the concept of sovereignty and the process of sustainable development. Nation building is, arguably, sovereignty in action.

Sovereignty and nation building come in many forms, from the smallest tribal community that asserts sovereignty as a means of protecting fishing or other resource rights that support health and community well-being, to a sovereign nation such as Bolivia with a Native majority population, and now an Indigenous president who is taking steps to create a social revolution based on Indigenous precepts.

Throughout the Western Hemisphere, we see many examples of the ways that Native peoples have asserted ancestral rights and then built on those assertions culturally, politically, and economically to reject or reshape European-based colonial domination and rewrite the future with a Native hand. Assertions of sovereignty are expressions of Indigenous cultural groundings, perspective, and rights in order to protect land and resources and even human life when confronted with comparatively large, dominating nation states that would force change or even obliterate Native peoples and their governing systems.

It is important to understand that the assertion of sovereignty and Native rights is an essential tension of power and control between communities or nations of Native peoples and large nation states. Throughout the hemisphere, the ways in which this tension is dealt with, worked through, or negotiated demonstrates a broad spectrum of expressions. For example, in 1993, in the far north of Canada, in the territory now known as Nunavut, the Nunavut Land Claims Agreement Act was passed through agreement between the Inuit Tapiriit Kanatami and the Canadian government. Nunavut, an Inuit word, means "Our land." By 1999 the transition to a semi-autonomous territory that is 83 percent Native Inuit was completed. The elected premier is guided by a council of 11 elders whose advice is based on *Inuit Qaujimajatuqangit*, or Inuit culture and traditional understandings. There are four official languages—two Native languages in addition to English and French. The emphasis in the educational system is on teaching in the Inuit language, within the appropriate Inuit cultural setting. Although much of the economy of Nunavut is still primarily dependent on Canada, the people of Nunavut play the major role in decision making regarding the shape that this economy takes. Interestingly, a somewhat parallel form of government is found in Greenland, another arctic and predominately Inuit region, which was a former Danish colony. The Greenland government now exercises "home rule" regarding internal affairs and is pushing strongly for full independence from Denmark.

In Central America during the 1980s, tensions reached a fever pitch between the government of Nicaragua and Native peoples along the Atlantic coast, a region known as Mosquitia. There the Miskito, Sumo, and Rama peoples, who are geographically distant and isolated from the Nicaraguan capital of Managua, asserted the need and the right for self-determination amid a struggle for Native control of land and resources in a larger region suffering from government instability, human rights abuses, and outright war. The Nicaraguan government, via a plan termed "autonomy," was anxious to control the territory and integrate or assimilate Native people politically into the larger nation state. On the other hand, the Native people asserted their sovereignty and self-determination. Over time and with extensive negotiation, an agreement of accommodation, while not absolutely desirable to either, was created. Now, in 2009, James Anaya, who is the United Nations Special Rapporteur on the situation of human rights and fundamental freedoms of Indigenous peoples, reports that the Nicaraguan government has formally handed over title to 285 square miles of Indigenous lands in the Atlantic coast region, giving the Native peoples control of their ancestral lands.

Since the mid-1990s in southern Mexico, in the heavily Indigenous state of Chiapas, pressures brought about by the international North American Free Trade Agreement (NAFTA) and long-simmering racism and exploitation of Native people led to the development of the Zapatista Army of National Liberation (EZLN). This Indigenous-based group and its local allies have sought not independence from Mexico but rather the power to have economic and political autonomy and decision-making control so that regional resources could benefit the local Indigenous peoples. This struggle continues, unreconciled, as of 2009.

Another expression of Indigenous sovereignty is seen in Bolivia. Throughout the Andean region—that is, the countries of Bolivia, Peru, and Ecuador—a very large proportion of the population is Indigenous. Since the Spanish invasion and colonial times, Bolivia had been ruled by a small European-derived elite that maintained a strict social hierarchy and control of governmental powers and the economy. The Aymara and Quechua Indian people remained, for the most part, an oppressed majority, while education, health care, and the wealth derived from the resources of the land served and enriched the wealthy elite and international corporations. Slowly, in recent decades, the voice and strength of Indigenous people in Bolivia has been growing. Through a democratic election in 2006, those many Native voices spoke as one not only to transform the government but also to begin the long-term process of social revolution, based on a clear expression of Native rights and philosophical grounding. Part of this process included electing an Indigenous leader, Evo Morales. As Victoria Bomberry explains in the box "¡Evo Presidente!" Bolivian president Morales's speech to the United Nations in 2008 "resonated with Indigenous peoples who have diligently worked for self-determination and sovereignty in all of its manifestations throughout the Americas." (For more discussion of the role of sovereignty and Native rights, including the United Nations Declaration of the Rights of Indigenous Peoples, see Part X.)

Sovereignty is a word we hear a lot today in the news, but what does it mean? The term *sovereignty* means many different things. Generally speaking, it is used to describe the modern nation and its right to self-rule. For example, the United States is a sovereign nation that has the right to govern itself; there is no external ruling power. As contradictory as it sounds, Native American tribes in the United States, all 562 of them, are technically considered sovereign nations in terms of their relationship to the United States. American Indian tribes have a legally defined relationship with the federal government, but their sovereignty is not absolute. According to the *Handbook of Federal Indian Law*, Felix Cohen explains tribal sovereignty as follows[1]:

> As a consequence of the tribe's relationship with the federal government, tribal powers of self-government are limited by federal statutes, by the terms of the treaties with the federal government, and by restraints implicit in the protectorate relationship itself. In all other respects the tribes remain independent and self-governing political communities.
>
> While the U.S. government recognizes American Indian Tribes as sovereign nations, the U.S. congress is recognized by the courts as having the right to limit the sovereign powers of tribes. However, Congress must do so in definite terms and not by implication.

Cohen means that although tribes are sovereign nations and have the right to self-government, they have limited sovereignty in their nation-to-nation relationship with the federal government.

Prior to the existence of the United States, other colonizing countries, such as England, made treaties with Indian tribes. Later, the United States also made treaties with Indian tribes. Treaties are legal international documents that recognize sovereignty. A significant history of treaties and Supreme Court legal decisions defines American Indian tribal sovereignty, and to this day, only Congress has the power to make changes to the relationship between tribes and the federal government. This congressional power is called *plenary power*. States have no inherent jurisdiction over Indian tribes within their boundaries.

In the United States, the nation-building approach to sustainable economic development in Indian Country is the practical application of tribal sovereignty. According to Cornell and Kalt, in various publications, Native nations take different approaches to economic development by asserting their rights to self-governance while simultaneously building the foundation and institutional infrastructure to exercise those rights. The Native nation-building approach to sustainable economic development includes, but is not limited to, strengthening governmental institutions in order to effectively assert sovereignty, diversifying tribal economic ventures, creating innovative social policies for the community, and developing cultural resources of all kinds.[2]

This practice is distinguished from traditional economic development in that nation-building sees development as creating a proactive environment where development can flourish in the long term, as opposed to reactionary development based on funding and shorter-term projects.

Putting sovereignty into practice means that the Native nations assert their sovereign powers, backed up by their respective tribal governmental institutions. The traditional Iroquois, for example, have set legal precedent by using their own nation's passports when traveling to the United Nations European headquarters in Geneva and to other international forums. Other U.S. Indian nations have issued their own license plates. Native governmental institutions work best when they are a cultural match with their respective Indigenous political culture. Also, part of this nation-building approach is making strategic and long-term plans. Finally, tribal leaders head the nation-building efforts and lead by mobilizing the community.

Economic growth is happening throughout Indian Country, but much still needs to be done to overcome the economic disparities that continue to exist. Economic conditions on most reservations lag far behind the general U.S. public economically. It is estimated that tribes will need to continue to grow, but even so, it will still take decades for Natives' incomes to parallel those of the general population. Interestingly, economic growth is occurring equally in both gaming and non-gaming tribes. This is because of diversification of opportunities, with new non-gaming businesses opening.

Arguably, the biggest economic boom in Indian Country in the United States today is Indian gaming, a subject taken up by Sia Davis and Jane Feustel in Reading 2. Nationwide, Indian gambling is a multi-billion-dollar industry. Some tribes have developed large gaming enterprises, with 62 percent of total gaming revenue in 2007 brought in by tribes in just five states: California, Connecticut, Oklahoma, Arizona, and Florida.[3] Congress passed the Indian Gaming Regulatory Act (IGRA) in 1988, with the aim of stimulating tribal economies that did not have adequate resources to support development. This law stipulates that gaming profits must be used in five specific areas: tribal government operations, promotion of welfare of the tribal citizens, economic development, support of charities, and compensation to local non-Indian governments for support services. Contrary to popular belief, the law is very strict in this regard, and while it does not prevent payouts to tribal members, the federal government must approve this sort of action and will do so only after a tribe has met and exceeded the other requirements of the law. In 2007, 230 of the 562 federally recognized tribes operated 425 gaming enterprises in 28 states and generated approximately $26.5 billion in gaming revenue. But in 2008, tribal gaming growth slowed significantly. This is attributed primarily to the precipitous decline in the U.S. economy but may also be due to impending legislation that could negatively affect gaming profits and also the renegotiation of state–tribal compacts or agreements.[4]

It is important to remember that not all tribes have gaming or even want gaming. The Hopi Nation and some traditional Iroquois communities have been opposed to gaming on cultural grounds. Interestingly, some of the tribes with large amounts of earnings going to individual tribal members are tribes with very few members, while some of the largest tribes do not have casinos. This skews the data on average gaming earnings and what the general impact of gaming has been throughout Indian Country. Furthermore, many casinos are quite small or are located in isolated, out-of-the-way locations and therefore cater only to very local and often sparsely populated areas, leading to minimal earnings.

Indian casinos have been called "the new buffalo" because of their economic benefits to depressed reservation economies. Clearly, gaming has been a major economic boom for many tribes, but casino development has critics, both Indian and non-Indian. One of the major issues is the IGRA requirement that in order to have a casino, a tribe must make a compact with its respective state, to be in conformance with state regulations on different classes of gaming and to negotiate compensation in lieu of taxes. Many tribal leaders are greatly concerned with the compacting requirement that forces tribes to deal with states, as this diminishes the tribal sovereignty of Native nations. It is in direct conflict with federal laws which stipulate that only Congress has the power to regulate tribes. One critic of IGRA, Nicholas Peroff,[5] contends that federal Indian policies in the United States have always been about assimilating Indian land and their resources, not about assimilating Indians into the larger U.S. society. He contends that IGRA is part of this legacy; it is only the most recent in a long history of assimilation policies to emerge from the U.S. political system. He concludes that the IGRA revenues both brighten and, paradoxically, threaten the future sovereignty of U.S. Indian tribes.

Gaming has not been without controversy. Communities located near casinos are concerned about the impact on surrounding populations, although the surrounding populations usually see a reduction in unemployment, rising incomes, a reduction of dependence on welfare, and increased tax income. States are often concerned about tax issues because tribal casino profits are not taxed by federal, state, or local governments. Nevertheless, Native nations seek to be good neighbors to their surrounding non-Indian communities. In negotiating agreements with their respective states, tribes compensate for the lack of taxes. For example, in Arizona, tribes pay between 1 and 8 percent of their total gross revenues to the state, depending on their profits.

Gaming has also introduced new identity-related issues to Native American nations and communities; for example, some tribes pay out part of the profits to tribal members in per capita payments. Who is and is not an Indian has become a major question now that money complicates that issue for some tribes. All things considered, gaming has provided positive changes in socioeconomic conditions on many reservations and is an important function of tribal nation building. Nevertheless, gaming cannot meet all the needs of all the Native nations.

Most tribes consider gaming a short-term strategy, using profits to raise the capital to underwrite other forms of economic enterprise. In the meantime, for those tribes that have benefited from gaming, welfare rolls, unemployment, and poverty rates have dropped precipitously. In some tribes, gaming has created full employment for tribal members. Surplus revenues are being used for economic development and diversification, education and scholarships, implementation of tribal community development financial institutions, infrastructure development, elder care, housing developments, social services, and environmental and health programs. These uses of gaming revenue support sovereignty.

Frequently overlooked in discussions of Native sovereignty are the issues of land, economy, and the environment. Native peoples are culturally, ideologically, and spiritually attached to the land. William Brandon reports that during the removal period of the nineteenth century in the expansionist United States, "Whites could not comprehend the Indians' fanatical attachment to a particular part of the earth," and "some watching Whites were moved and some amused when departing Indians went about touching leaves, trees, rocks and streams in farewell."[6] Christopher Vecsey et al., in a book on American Indian religions and the environment, contends that "environmental concerns constitute a foremost dimension of American Indian religions, regardless of specific ecosystem."[7] There is a sacred quality to the relationship between Native peoples and the land, with its resources. Fishing, for example, "is more than a job, more than a right, more than a way to make a living in a money economy. It is a way of life, a relation with the source of life, a means of identity as an Indian."[8] For example, during the first decade of the twenty-first century, when most of us spend our evenings and nights in the enclosure of a house, most often in an urban setting, and frequently surrounded by pollutants in the air and the artificial lights of cities, all of which obscure the night sky, it is easy to become unmindful of the stars and other celestial phenomena that permeated the lives of those living in a more natural environment, as well as the integral role that an awareness of the sky has played in explaining and guiding life.

In the Southwestern United States, in the high desert plateaus of the Eastern Pueblo, Hopi, and Dine Indians, until very recently, coal-mining electrical plants operated strip mines on Indian lands and wasted precious ancient water aquifers to slurry the coal hundreds of miles to the plants, all in the name of supplying electrical power to non-Indian industries and surrounding cities. The Indian peoples of the region have also been left with the resultant pollution, in the form of airborne particulate matter and dangerous residues going into streams and soil as a result of the mining. In the arid environment of the Southwest, the scars from strip mining can never be healed. In one response to this, the Pueblo of Sandia, in 1988, became the first Indian nation to control water quality standards under the Environmental Protection Agency (EPA). Their water quality standards were intended to protect traditional uses of water and are more stringent than the standards in the surrounding state of New Mexico.

From a Native American perspective, the solution to some of these concerns is *sustainable development*, which is defined as development that meets the needs of the present without compromising the ability of future generations to meet their needs. Protection of the environment in harmony with tribal cultural values is one of the defining issues in Indian Country today. As more and more American tribes exert their sovereignty and implement self-determination policies, tribes have greater and greater power over their resources. Tribes are working to create and implement tribal policies, regulations, and administrative capacity in order to protect the environment. Much work still needs to be done, however. Tribes are dealing with a host of environmental problems inherited from decades of mismanagement by the federal government and private industry. A Council of Energy Resource Tribes survey of 25 reservations in the mid-1980s discovered 65 hazardous waste disposal sites within its sample.[9] There are many challenges in addressing the multitude of tribal environmental issues, including funding and jurisdiction. While funding cleanup remains one of the top issues, who has jurisdiction and who doesn't complicate the matter considerably.

Without land and resource rights, Indigenous economic development cannot take place. By the same token, the Native perspective regarding the land as sacred precludes rapacious exploitation of the environment. The poem by Acoma poet and storyteller Simon Ortiz, which begins this part, comments in bitter irony how "that Indian," Martinez, was first lauded for the uranium boom in New Mexico and then blamed for the environmental costs of uranium development when they began to become apparent to the non-Indian community. Today, there are dozens of uranium mines in the Grants Mineral Belt and the San Juan basin. Radioactive pollution throughout this region is now a critical issue, so much so that many of the small Indian nations, such as the

Pueblo Indian communities, are suffering severely from illnesses and even death. Ortiz's poem is therefore a fitting introduction to the articles that follow in this part.

In the United States, the nation-building approach, with sustainable economic development in Indian Country, is the practical application of tribal sovereignty. Some of these issues are addressed in Reading 1, "Remaking the Tools of Governance: Colonial Legacies, Indigenous Solutions," by Stephen Cornell. Native nations take different approaches to economic development by both asserting their rights to self-governance and simultaneously building the foundation and institutional infrastructure to exercise those rights. The Native nation-building approach to sustainable economic development includes, but is not limited to, strengthening governmental institutions in order to effectively assert sovereignty, diversifying tribal economic ventures, creating innovative social policies for the community, and developing cultural resources of all kinds.

Successful tribal economic development depends on the right balance of good tribal government infrastructure and diversification of businesses, tempered with cultural considerations. The box "The Chickasaw Nation: An Example of Nation Building" demonstrates how the Chickasaw tribe has developed economically and culturally since 1987. The box "First Nations Development Institute" is included to highlight Native organizations working in the arena of economic development. This nonprofit Indian organization makes grants to tribal communities to help in economic and asset development. It also supports programs with strongly integrated cultural assets.

Gaming has become a significant means of economic development for some Native nations but far from all. Reading 2, "Indian Gaming in the States: Dispelling Myths and Highlighting Advantages," gives a realistic view of the pros and cons of the gaming industry and just what it means for Indian country. Among the general public, there are a number of misconceptions regarding gaming: just what it is, how it is regulated and utilized within Indian communities, and how widespread the benefits or lack of benefits are. Many people have the idea that all Indians have now become rich because of casinos, but this is definitely not the case. In addition, the complexities of changing economies also bring a number of challenges, as Sia Davis and Jane Feustel discuss in this reading.

The box "¡Evo Presidente!" expresses some of the background and significance of the presidency of Evo Morales in Bolivia, a South American country of approximately 9 million, with a strong majority of Quechua and Aymara Indian people. The social, political, and economic reforms that have taken place in Bolivia in recent years are based squarely on a foundation of Native philosophy and vision.

In Reading 3, "Lovely Hula Hands: Corporate Tourism and the Prostitution of Hawaiian Culture," Haunani-Kay Trask (Native Hawaiian), former director of the Center for Hawaiian Studies at the University of Hawai'i and a leader in the Native Hawaiian sovereignty struggle, documents the commodification of Hawaiian culture and introduces the concept of "cultural prostitution" to describe the harm that is being done to Native Hawaiian traditions and people. She examines the negative impact on four key areas of culture: homeland, which includes the idea of stewardship of the land, seas, and heavens; language and dance; familial relationship; and Hawaiian women. Since World War II, tourism has transformed the Hawaiian Islands and, today, has taken the place of the once-mighty sugar industry. Millions of tourists flood the islands annually, many times outnumbering the local residents and bringing millions of dollars in revenues to the tourist industry. Yet this development has not transferred benefits to Native Hawaiians and most other local residents. Tourist industry jobs for the most part are dead-end, low-paying, and humiliating jobs; land dispossession caused by the development of hotels, resorts, tourist beaches, and golf courses has increased the numbers of homeless or near-homeless Native island residents; and the cost of living is now one of the highest of any place in the United States. Not the least of the negative impacts caused by tourism is the destruction of the once-pristine island environment.

Reading 4, "Indigenous Environmental Perspectives: A North American Primer," is by Winona LaDuke (Anishinaabeg), a recognized international expert on the environment and a spokesperson for American Indian environmental concerns. She is the director of the White Earth Land Recovery Project and also of Honor the Earth. In the 1996 and 2000 presidential elections, she was a Green Party vice presidential candidate on the Ralph Nader ticket. Deep ecology and bioregionalism are key concepts of the Green Party, which make the party a potential ally of American Indian traditionalists. As both an Indian activist and an environmentalist, LaDuke contrasts the Indigenous view of harmony with nature and respect for the environment with the exploitative motivation of colonialism and capitalist development. She also discusses the concept of sustainable development—that is, non-exploitative economic uses of the environment, the land, water, air, and sky. Her article documents in graphic detail the extreme harm that unrestrained capitalist development is causing Native American peoples throughout North America.

The box "Native Environmental Hero: Jesus Leon Santos" highlights the work of Mixteca farmer Jesus Leon Santos, who received the Goldman Environmental Prize in 2008 for sustainable development. Leon Santos leads a community-wide organization of Indigenous farmers who, through a 25-year process, have used traditional Mixteca techniques to plant 2 million native varieties of trees and taken steps to dramatically prevent and even reverse erosion. The Mixteca farmers started this project with a long-term strategy to deal with the erosion that was a major factor in an overall environmental crisis that in turn had led to increasing poverty, malnutrition, and out-migration. In reference to the Spanish invasion that began many years before, Leon Santos says, "the Mixteca region was severely damaged by the exploitation of our natural resources that came with the colonizers." The vision and work of Jesus Leon Santos and many other Indigenous people in the Americas are examples of respecting and caring for the land that nurtures all of us.

The environmental issue or issues that relate to developing an Indigenous sustainable economy differ from tribe to tribe, nation to nation. In Alaska, the over-arching issue is subsistence rights, as explained by Steve Talbot in Reading 5, "Alaska Natives Struggle for Subsistence Rights." Alaska's Native peoples have since time immemorial depended on hunting, fishing, and gathering from their biotic and plant environment. Their economies have been subsistence-based economies, and their cultural practices and spiritual traditions reflect this economic orientation. Today, the majority of Alaska Natives still depend on the land and its bounty for their existence, but this subsistence-based way of life is now threatened. This issue has become extremely contentious since the passage of the Alaska Native Claims Settlement Act in 1971, which "settled" the land ownership question in Alaska and also ended Native hunting and fishing rights. In this reading, Talbot discusses the history and nature of the subsistence rights issue and how it affects the different Native nations of Alaska.

Has the U.S. government been a good trustee of the tribes for revenues received for Indian lands and resources? No. In this respect, the federal government has been terrible beyond belief. In fact, the U. S. government owes both thousands of individual Indians and Indian tribes billions of dollars for mismanaging their trust accounts, accounts set up to receive payments from companies leasing Indian lands and resources. Settlement of these claims has been dragging through the courts for years due chiefly to the recalcitrance of the Department of the Interior and the political administration in Washington. This national disgrace is explained in the box "The Cobell Lawsuit."

NOTES

1. Felix Cohen, *Handbook of Federal Indian Law*, Washington D.C., U.S. Government Printing Office, 1942: 122.

2. Stephen Cornell and Joseph P. Kalt, "Two Approaches to the Development of Native Nations: One Works, the Other Doesn't," in *Rebuilding Native Nations: Strategies for Governance and Development*, ed. Miriam Jorgenson (Tucson: University of Arizona Press, Tucson, 2007), 3–33.

3. Casino City's Indian Gaming Industry Report 2008–2009.

4. Ibid.

5. Nicholas C. Peroff, "Indian Policy as an Emergent Property of the American Policy Making Process," *The Social Science Journal*, 44, no 2 (2007): pp. 319–331.

6. William Brandon, *The American Heritage Book of Indians*. New York: Dell, 1961, 223.

7. Christopher Vecsey and Robert W. Venables, eds., *American Indian Environments: Ecological Issues in Native American History* (Syracuse, N.Y.: Syracuse University Press, 1980), xviii.

8. Ibid., 26.

9. Cornell and Kalt, "Two Approaches."

REMAKING THE TOOLS OF GOVERNANCE
COLONIAL LEGACIES, INDIGENOUS SOLUTIONS

Stephen Cornell

Native nation building is a governance challenge. It is about Native nations enhancing their own capacities for effective self-rule.

It doesn't start out that way. There's a prior step, a necessary condition for Indigenous nation building that has to be established first, and that is the right of self-determination. Obtaining substantial decision-making control over the nation's lands, resources, affairs, and future—this is the first step, the one that leads to the governance challenge. Of course this is a massive task in and of itself. In the United States, despite the successes American Indian nations have had over the last three decades in reclaiming control over some of their affairs, the struggle for self-determination goes on. Indigenous peoples wage that fight against the sometimes contrary actions of Congress, states, and courts, where the fragility of Native rights has been particularly apparent in recent

years. Elsewhere—Canada and Australia, for example—some Indigenous rights of self-determination are relatively secure while others are at grave risk or are simply denied outright. Indigenous self-determination is an ongoing enterprise with enemies to spare and major battles ahead. The fight will not soon be over.[1]

But wherever a significant degree of Indigenous self-determination is in some measure secured, much of the responsibility for the future falls on Native peoples themselves. With genuine decision-making power in hand, they have to take the lead in addressing their problems and rebuilding their nations. Under conditions of genuine self-determination, what does or does not happen increasingly depends on what *they* do, and less on what federal governments or other outsiders do.

The tasks they face are enormous. Colonialism, paternalism, massive resource losses, and cultural suppression have left legacies of poverty, dependency, and bitterness that are difficult to overcome. Some nations in the United States have struck it rich in the gaming industry, but despite the notoriety of gaming and other notable successes, many Native nations in North America remain impoverished. Restoring economic and community health; managing natural resources and environments; revitalizing Indigenous cultures; stemming the tide of language loss; raising educational levels—these are only some of the tasks that face Indigenous communities. And their own ambitions are greater still. Native nations today are wrestling not only with how to improve community life but with *how to preserve a distinctive nationhood*; not simply with how to invent a new program to address a particular problem but with *how to become consistent and effective problem solvers*; not simply with raising living standards on Indigenous lands but with *how to rebuild societies that work*; not only with finding and training leaders but with *how to govern* and *how to implement effective and culturally appropriate systems of governance*. The task, as Chief Oren Lyons of the Onondaga puts it, is nation "rebuilding."[2]

Much of this book is concerned with the last of these tasks: how to govern and govern well. There is a reason for this focus. It is not that self-determination is secure. Far from it. Nor is the focus on governance because the other tasks listed here are unimportant. They are obviously critical to the future of Native nations. But those nations that have most effectively addressed these challenges—including the challenge of practical self-determination in the face of hostility from non-Native governments—have been ones with capable, potent governing tools in hand. They are nations that have been able to mobilize and sustain community energy and ideas in effective pursuit of community goals and to capably exercise the right of self-determination for which they have fought so hard. As Satsan (Herb George), a Wet'suet'en leader from western Canada and head of the National Centre for First Nations Governance, recently put it, "If we have the right to use the land in our own way, we need to get organized to do it. When the [government] has to consult with us, we have to be organized and capable of consulting. We have to know what we want and be able to make our vision effective. . . . This is a governance issue."[3]

THE PECULIAR HISTORY OF CONTEMPORARY TRIBAL GOVERNMENTS

We can think of the institutions of governance as tools, the instruments that Indigenous nations use to address and solve the problems they face—maintaining good relations among themselves, surviving hard times, interacting with other nations, caring for the land, educating the young, and so forth. Prior to the European arrival in North America, Native nations governed and sustained themselves through the skilled use of such tools.

These tools included, on the one hand, agreed-on and often quite specific rules about how rights and powers were distributed and how things should be done. They also included, on the other, specific entities—from councils and chiefs to warrior and medicine societies to clan leaders and town criers—that were charged with carrying out certain governmental tasks, making decisions, enforcing the rules, and getting things done. Such governance tools were hugely diverse. They were not necessarily perfect, but they were often extremely effective, enabling these nations to prosper.[4] And one reason they were effective is that both the rules and the entities or individuals that made or enforced or implemented those rules were chosen by Native societies themselves. They reflected each nation's own sense of what government should be like and its own understanding of the hard realities it faced. The rules were designed both to meet current demands and conditions and to retain the support and allegiance of the people they governed.

Since then, both the conditions facing Native nations and the governing tools they have in hand to address those conditions have changed. First, over time, the economic and social circumstances of Native nations were transformed through catastrophic losses of lands and livelihoods and the development of encompassing and controlling economic and social systems. Second, outside governments forced new institutions on Native societies that reflected outsiders' needs and ideas about how things should be done, and limited Indigenous peoples' freedom to design their own governing institutions and their power to make decisions for themselves. The result is that today, Native nations face a new set of challenges but find themselves burdened, in many cases, by imposed and inadequate governing tools.

The Beginnings of Contemporary Tribal Government in the United States

From the end of the Indian wars and the establishment of the reservation system in the nineteenth century until at least the 1930s—and despite the recognition, in law, of tribal sovereignty—the governance of American Indian nations was largely in non-Indian hands, typically those of the U.S. federal government, first the War Department and later the Bureau of Indian Affairs (BIA) in the Department of the Interior. These federal agencies controlled much of what happened on Indian reservations and, particularly in the latter part of the nineteenth century and early decades of the twentieth, did so largely in the name of assimilation. With few exceptions, Indigenous control over the tools of government was modest, with outsiders not only controlling the financial resources necessary for effective government but also wielding veto power over tribal government actions.

In the 1930s, increasingly aware of the abject poverty of Indian communities and under the influence of visionary reformers, the federal government took several tentative steps toward restoring some form of Indigenous self-government, culminating in passage of the Indian Reorganization Act (IRA) of 1934.[5] This legislation largely ignored the facts that a number of Indian nations had functioning governments, that nearly all still retained some decision-making processes operating within the narrow spaces left to them by federal controls, and that most had elders who had experienced older forms of Indigenous governance prior to federal impositions. It paid little attention to the tools those nations might still have in hand. Nonetheless, the IRA was a departure: the federal government endorsed and encouraged formal structures of tribal government, and following the IRA's passage, there was an intense period of government and constitution making on many reservations, either directly under IRA provisions or indirectly under its influence.

But few of the resulting governments were indigenous creations. On the contrary, not only were they drawn from non-Indigenous models, but they often introduced governing structures that were in direct conflict with the political traditions of the nations they were supposed to govern.[6] Despite commitments among some senior officials in the Interior Department to genuine tribal *self-government*, these governments were shaped by prevailing mainstream legal and political understandings of how Native nations ought to govern— and by the often heavy-handed involvement of BIA field personnel, many of whom did not share the commitment to Indigenous self-government, had little confidence in Indigenous governance practices, and in any case had little intention of relinquishing their authority. As a result, many of the resulting constitutions—intentionally or not— supported the assimilationism that was still at the heart of federal policy. Replicating, for the most part, core American institutions and practices, they were intended to provide Indians with what John Collier, primary architect of the IRA, described as "the experience of responsible democracy"—as if such a thing were alien to North America's peoples.[7]

Until the 1960s, and in some cases longer, most of these governments were small, typically consisting of a popularly elected tribal council or business committee with officers—usually at least a chair and vice chair—chosen either at large by tribal citizens or by the council itself from among its members, and perhaps a skeletal staff of one or two people. They also were designed more for administration than for governance, having only modest law-making powers and lacking such key institutions as independent judiciaries or other dispute-resolution mechanisms (O'Brien 1989). While these governments made some important decisions, the ultimate power in reservation affairs was still the BIA.

Growth in Tribal Government

In the 1960s and 1970s, this gradually changed. The critical event in the 1960s was the establishment of the federal Office of Economic Opportunity (OEO), and the critical event in the following decade was the Indian Self-Determination and Education Assistance Act of 1975. Combined with Indian political activism, including growing tribal political assertions, these developments precipitated both an expansion of tribal governing power and two decades of dramatic organizational growth.

In 1964, Congress passed the Economic Opportunity Act. Among other things, this legislation established the OEO, one of the keystone components of the federal War on Poverty and the Great Society programs of the Lyndon Johnson presidency. OEO, in turn, established a number of programs that affected Indian Country, most importantly the Community Action Program (CAP), designed to attack poverty through the organization and empowerment of poor people themselves (Greenstone and Peterson 1976). American Indians were among OED's target populations and, in a few short years, OEO had organized nearly seventy CAP agencies serving more than 170 Indian reservations (Levitan and Hetrick 1971, 91). Some were established separately from tribal governments and even served multiple reservations; some were established within tribal governments; and some, as at Mississippi Choctaw (Ferrara 1998), began as separate bodies but eventually were folded into tribal government.

These agencies were both new conduits moving federal program monies into tribal hands and new vehicles for tribal assertions of decision-making power. In both cases, they bypassed the BIA and significantly increased tribal control over selected federal programs. As Sam Deloria once pointed out, "the CAP funds were the first discretionary funds that many tribes had had" (P. Deloria 1986, 197).[8] Coupled at last with real resources, tribal decision making began to have some impact.

Nor was OEO alone in developing new relationships with Indian nations. The departments of Commerce, Labor, Housing and Urban Development, and Health, Education, and Welfare (now Health and Human Services) also initiated new Indian programs in the 1960s. Many of these involved tribal governments in program administration or implementation, increasing both funding and administrative employment on reservations.

By the late 1960s, these developments had produced explosive growth in tribal governments. For example:

- The tribal government at Zuni Pueblo had nine employees in the late 1950s; a decade later, largely with the support of federal funds, it had fifty-four. The largest single component of tribal government had become the CAP agency, employing thirty-three people and controlling much of the tribal budget (Ferguson, Hart, and Seciwa 1988).
- Using federal funds, the Navajo Tribe established an Office of Navajo Economic Opportunity in 1965. In short order, according to Iverson (1981, 90), this office "had established a far-flung preschool program, a small business development center, a Neighborhood Youth Corps summer program involving 3,500 Navajo young people, a 'reservation-wide' recreation and physical fitness program, and a local community development program." Soon after came a Head Start program, other educational programs, medical services, a culture center, legal services, job placement, and other services. All had administrative components within a mushrooming tribal government.
- Established in the late 1930s, the Papago (now Tohono O'odham) tribal government remained small for nearly thirty years, consisting of a council and four officers (chair, vice chair, secretary, and treasurer). Starting in 1965, federal funds and program initiatives produced a proliferation of committees, boards, programs, and offices, and a massive tribal administration (Manuel, Ramon, and Fontana 1978).
- Fowler writes that on the Fort Belknap Reservation in Montana, home of the Gros Ventre and Assiniboine peoples, "the War on Poverty programs . . . resulted in hundreds of jobs" (1987, 116) as the tribal government became a major reservation employer.
- On the Fort Yuma–Quechan Reservation in Arizona, according to Bee, "members of approximately 130 of the reservation's 180 families received full or part-time wages from government programs between 1966 and 1969" (1981, 143). Although many of these jobs were temporary training or construction positions, some were longer-term administrative positions in tribal government.[9]

These programs foreshadowed the developments of the 1970s. Castile points out that the CAP agencies demonstrated "the feasibility of self-administration of federally funded programs by Indian tribes" (1998, 41)—indeed, this emerged as a deliberate goal of the CAP initiative. The effort to empower local Native communities received a major boost in 1975 when Congress passed the Indian Self-Determination and Education Assistance Act (P.L. 93-638), the core legislation in the federal government's new policy of self-determination for Indian tribes. This policy encouraged Indian nations to take over direct management of federal programs on Indian reservations, either through contracts with the federal government under P.L. 93-638 or through federal-tribal compacts enabled in subsequent legislation. Faced with urgent social and economic needs within their populations and eager to expand their control of reservation affairs, many Native nations moved quickly to "638" a variety of federal programs (Vinje 1996). Over the next twenty years, these arrangements led to a significant shift not only in program management but in jobs, which rapidly migrated from federal to tribal administrations.

Other factors contributed to the expansion of tribal governments. For example, over the last three decades several Native nations, under internal and external pressure to develop natural resources, rapidly expanded their capacities to monitor and regulate resource extraction, often using proceeds from the sale of resources to do so (see Ambler 1990; also Iverson 1981 and Robbins 1979). Tribal efforts to pursue economic development and to play a larger role in education and health care have contributed to tribal government growth as well.

THE HISTORICAL LEGACY: A MIXED BAG

In the United States, contemporary tribal governments reflect this peculiar history. They are products both of tribal assertions of governing power and of federal policies that, in various ways, have limited that power and often ignored Indigenous political culture. With ambitious goals and complex challenges ahead of them, they are at the same time handicapped by the consequences of this history, including the following: organizational weakness, functional overload, financial dependence on outsiders, a primary focus on program and service delivery, workforce dependence on government employment, a politics of spoils, and an impoverished conception of government.

Organizational Weakness

In the period from the 1930s to the 1960s, few people thought that tribal governments might one day be managing billions of dollars in natural resources, negotiating agreements with states and multinational corporations, or regulating environmental matters or large-scale business activity. Instead, the tribal constitutions that emerged under the IRA and its influence seem designed primarily to administer programs, sign resource-extraction contracts, and "practice" democracy. Most have grown in an *ad hoc* fashion, reflecting not a coherent strategy for building governing capacity but instead the gradual accumulation of offices in response to federal funding opportunities. The result is that most tribal governments from the time are organizationally weak, with few separations of powers, few checks and balances, and unwieldy administrative structures.

Functional Overload

Tribal governments are often the only institutions within Indian nations that have any resources. One result is a community expectation that these governments—and tribal councils in particular—will do every-thing. During executive education sessions in recent years, Native Nations Institute faculty have informally canvassed tribal councilors, asking what they're expected by constituents to do. The range of answers is astonishing: make laws, run businesses, be the ultimate judge in disputes, "fix everything for everybody," protect the nation's future, "be the local ATM machine," protect the land, "give everyone a job," and more. Expected to be involved in everything, both councils and tribal administrations are often overwhelmed.

Financial Dependence on Outsiders

Many tribal governments have become heavily dependent on federal funds for daily operations. As a result, many of their activities are hostage to funding decisions made by non-Indian decision makers who live far away and serve multiple interests, while their operations have to follow guidelines set by outside agencies. This makes it more difficult for tribal governments to pursue tribal priorities, and it is the opposite of self-determination.

A Primary Focus on Program and Service Delivery

Providing services of various kinds is a common and critical governmental function. But in some Native nations, it has become virtually the only governmental function—and the only reliable source of funding. Obtaining grants and developing more social programs can become the primary focus of governmental energy, distracting attention from long-term, strategic goals and from developing solutions that reduce—not increase—dependence on federal dollars and decision makers.

Workforce Dependence on Government Employment

A growing, social service-oriented tribal government, combined with the absence, in many cases, of commercial economic activity, means that on many reservations, the bulk of the jobs are in the public (government) sector.[10] In 1985, out of 1,406 full-time jobs counted in Todd County, South Dakota, which is essentially coextensive with the Rosebud Sioux Reservation, only 214—15 percent—were in productive business. The rest were all in the public sector (Szabo 1985). BIA data from 1997 on public sector employment provide additional illustrations: at Northern Cheyenne, an estimated 82 percent of those employed were in the public sector; at Hualapai, 95 percent; at Pine Ridge, 97 percent (U.S. Bureau of Indian Affairs 1997).[11] Combined with dependence on federal funds, such concentrations leave much of the workforce vulnerable to cutbacks in federal spending. They also concentrate employment in that part of the economy that is least productive of new wealth.

A Politics of Spoils

Where tribal government's primary function has become employment and service delivery, and where most financial resources are controlled by tribal government, control of that government becomes the key to gaining access to economic resources: jobs, money, services. This turns reservation politics into a politics of spoils, having less to do with where the nation is headed or how best to organize tribal operations than with which faction will control the goodies that government can hand out.

An Impoverished Conception of Government

The politics of spoils in turn breeds community cynicism about tribal government, which comes to be viewed by citizens as concerned largely with handing out jobs and services—often to political supporters. Government, in this impoverished conception, is mostly administration. Its task is not to make law or envision the future or shape the nation but simply to run programs and distribute resources. It administers, but it does not *govern*.

Not all Native nations suffer equally from these problems, and some have both confronted and surmounted them. Through sheer determination or exceptional leadership, some American Indian nations have accomplished extraordinary things despite the handicap of inadequate governing tools. But determination and leadership have not been the only keys. Some nations have gone much further, turning tribal government itself into an effective instrument of the national will. They have done so by transforming inadequate governing tools into more effective instruments for rebuilding their communities and nations.

For those nations concerned with overcoming the crippling legacies of colonialism, the critical questions about government are these: *Does the present design of tribal government offer adequate tools for meeting the challenges the nation faces? If not, what steps should the nation take to equip itself with more effective governing tools? Why should any nation settle for governing tools that fail to serve its purposes?*

THE TASK AHEAD: REMAKING THE TOOLS OF GOVERNANCE

Native nations today need governing tools designed to meet the challenges they face: promoting and protecting rights of self-determination, developing and enforcing laws, managing natural resource endowments, revitalizing Indigenous cultures, building sustainable economies, negotiating effectively with corporations and other governments, designing educational and health care systems that reflect Native priorities and knowledge, and so forth. For many

nations, this means the tools of governance need to be remade. The resulting institutions will need both to reflect Indigenous principles and to perform at a high standard.

In practical terms, the new tools will have to be capable of providing a constitutional foundation for self-rule, making laws, making day-to-day decisions, and providing for fair and nonpolitical resolution of disputes.[12]

Providing a Constitutional Foundation for Self-Rule

Effective self-government requires a foundation of basic rules that spell out how the nation will govern itself. This is what a constitution typically does. It specifies the fundamental purposes of the nation's government, how that government is organized, who has what authority and when that authority can be exercised, what the basic rights of citizens are, and how changes in government can be made. Along with a treaty, if the nation has one, a constitution is a foundational agreement—among citizens themselves—establishing the rules by which the society intends to pursue its purposes and the means by which additional rules can be made.

A constitution doesn't have to be written. The old ones certainly weren't. While the Indigenous societies of North America had common rules by which they were organized and functioned long before the Europeans came—in other words, they had constitutions—those rules were not written down anywhere. They were embedded instead in shared cultural understandings in each nation, understandings that indicated how authority was organized and exercised and how things should be done.

While most American Indian nations today have written constitutions, some do not. The key questions about the rules that govern a society are not whether they are written down but whether they are (1) known and understood by the citizens of the nation; (2) viewed by those citizens as appropriate and fair; (3) fairly enforced; and (4) effective at dealing with the issues the community faces. If the rules meet these criteria, then the nation has in hand a set of usable tools for governing. On that basis, it can begin to build a society that works.

Making Laws

Laws specify relationships and rules of behavior for citizens, outsiders, businesses, and even agencies of government. They indicate what things are permissible and what things are not in specific areas of life.

Most nations have a law-making body of some sort, often composed of representatives of the citizens. Such legislative bodies draft, vote on, and enact ordinances and statutes that then become the law of the land and the basis for numerous actions by both citizens and the nation as a whole.[13]

Like a constitution, not all law must be written down. A nation's common or customary law is its often unwritten set of rules derived from culture, history, established practice, tradition, or the gifts of spiritual beings. The canonical example among contemporary American Indian nations is the Navajo Nation, which recognizes Navajo common law as standing beside the Navajo Tribal Code as the law of the land. The tribal council, the president, and the nation's courts all rely extensively on common law in their decisions. Navajo custom and tradition are thus incorporated into the day-to-day governance of the nation (Nielsen and Zion 2005). In many cases, argues Canadian legal scholar John Borrows, "First Nations legal traditions are strong and dynamic" (2002, 27). Whether they're codified or even written down, they address many of the difficult problems that Native nations face, and they can be incorporated directly into contemporary law-making.[14]

As with the constitution, there are some key questions about the laws the nation makes, regardless of their derivation: Are they clear? Are they consistent? Are they fairly and effectively enforced? Can they get the job done?

Making Day-to-Day Decisions

The governments of Native nations typically are confronted with a vast range of decisions, from whether to enter into litigation in a dispute with another government to how to respond to the needs of a family in trouble, from whether to change the management regime in a nation-owned forest to finding the funds to support language revitalization. Much of government's time is spent in making decisions, large and small.

One of the keys to effective government is the ability to make informed decisions in a timely fashion. This requires ways of obtaining the necessary information on which to base decisions and an effective decision-making process that everyone understands and supports.

Implementing Decisions

Once decisions have been made, they have to be implemented. This is typically the task of the administration or bureaucracy. Implementation is a crucial

element of government because it determines how the rules are applied, how policies are carried out, how functions are performed, and how services are delivered. It shapes much of the citizens' experience of their own government, good or bad. An effective government has an administrative system that is capable, predictable, well understood by those dealing with it, and perceived as fair.

Providing for Fair and Nonpolitical Resolution of Disputes

The government also needs to assure the nation's citizens that when they have disputes, either with each other or with the government, they will be dealt with fairly. This requires some sort of mechanism to resolve the disputes—a court, a council of elders, or some other body that can be empowered to evaluate and adjudicate competing claims. The most effective dispute-resolution mechanisms typically are well insulated from other functions of government and from other elected officials such as legislators. This sends a clear message to citizens and outsiders alike that their claims will not be hostage to politics.

That message is critical to the nation's success. As long as people feel their claims will not be fairly addressed or that court decisions or appeals will be politicized, they will tend to mistrust their government and may take their knowledge and their energy and go somewhere else to live their lives, draining crucial assets from the nation.

This same mechanism—a court or other body—also may be charged with interpreting the rules established in the nation's constitution, codes, and common law. Here again, insulation from politics is essential if the nation's citizens are to trust the rules themselves.

POPULATION SIZE AND JOINT INSTITUTIONS

The tasks of governance are demanding, and not only of time and energy. They also demand people. This makes self-government a particular challenge for Native nations with small populations. Such nations face the same tasks that larger nations do, but they approach those tasks with fewer people. For a nation of several hundred citizens or less, only half of whom may be adults, building a governing structure capable of effectively carrying out the nation's business can be extremely difficult. Everyone wears multiple hats; people burn out; it's tough to keep roles and responsibilities clear; there aren't enough people to get it all done; and so forth.

These problems are partly artifacts of history. Particularly in Canada, colonial processes and federal policy broke up language and cultural groups, dispersing single peoples into multiple, postage-stamp–sized reserves with tiny populations. While denying First Nations sufficient land and other resources to sustain their economies, the government of Canada vastly complicated their governance challenges as well. Although this is less of a problem in much of the United States, where reservation-based Native populations are often larger, there are places such as Alaska and southern California where fragmentation and isolation make rebuilding Native nations a particularly difficult task.

One solution is to build governing institutions that link multiple nations, reducing the pressure on individual nations to organize all government functions at the local level. An example is the Northwest Intertribal Court System, created by a consortium of small tribes in western Washington that lacked the resources to form and sustain individual courts of their own. The system provides appellate and other judicial services and support to its member tribes (Harvard Project on American Indian Economic Development 2003). Nine First Nations in Saskatchewan formed the Meadow Lake Tribal Council to manage jointly owned businesses and coordinate service delivery. Several First Nations in southern British Columbia have gone further still, building comprehensive governing institutions under the umbrella of the Ktunaxa Nation Council, reconnecting Ktunaxa communities long dispersed on remnant lands.[15] Other nations have joined forces to manage natural resources, coordinate policing, and deliver health care and other services. Not all government functions have to be carried out at the same level. Some nations may reserve certain functions to themselves while carrying out other functions through joint institutions.

The bases of such joint institution building can be found in shared culture, shared history, or even shared space or ecosystem, as in the case of watersheds shared by several nations. But whatever the bases on which they occur, agreements to join together for certain governance purposes are themselves exercises in self-determination, examples of Native nations finding ways to address the crippling circumstances created by colonialism, including small population sizes. In the process, some nations are restoring older boundaries and bases of identification and action, building new governance tools that reflect much older conceptions of peoplehood.

THE LEGITIMACY CHALLENGE

Governments that lack support from the people being governed—that lack legitimacy in the eyes of their own citizens—are governments on the road to failure. There are at least two sources of legitimacy. One is effectiveness; the other is cultural match.

Effectiveness has to do with the fit between the organization of governance and the real-world circumstances confronting the nation. The issue is stark: Can this form of government accomplish what needs to be done in the circumstances that the nation faces? Is it adequate to contemporary times? A government that is incapable of effectively making and implementing decisions will have difficulty protecting the nation's interests. A government that allows political factionalism to get in the way of needed changes will lose the confidence of its citizens. A government in which the basic rules for how things are done change every time there's a new administration will face lost opportunities and talent as potential partners and skilled citizens decide to invest their energies somewhere else. And so forth.

These are not "Indigenous" problems. They are governance challenges that all human communities face. Can the nation find and retain the expertise it needs to deal with complex issues? Can the nation persuade would-be entrepreneurs to start businesses at home instead of taking their ideas and energy somewhere else? Can the nation resolve its internal conflicts without ripping itself apart? Can it negotiate effectively with another government or with a multinational corporation? Can it get the bills paid? Can it provide justice to its citizens? Can it not only decide what to do but do it well?

If the current form of governance is incapable of solving such problems, then the task before the nation is to develop new tools—or to reinvigorate old ones. Rebuilding Indian nations may require both restoration and innovation, drawing on past principles and practices and, at the same time, on the adaptive skills that Native peoples have long employed as they adjusted to new ecosystems, new trade opportunities, alien cultural influences, and unexpected problems.

But simply being effective is not enough to win legitimacy with the people. A technically proficient government that is at odds with people's beliefs about what governing means and how it should be done will invite abuse. Cultural match, in contrast to effectiveness, is a matter of the fit between the formal organization of governance and people's beliefs about how authority should be organized and exercised.[16] What's fundamentally at issue is political culture: What does the community view as an appropriate way to govern? Does the organization and action of government resonate with the community's ideas about how things should be done? Is it appropriate, for example, to settle disputes this way, or should they be settled some other way? What powers should be in the hands of elected leaders and what powers in the hands of medicine people, or elders, or clans, or others? Do the nation's laws respect Indigenous understandings about appropriate relationships to the land, to sacred spaces, to the animals, to the less fortunate? Are elections the right way to choose leaders in this community? Should decisions be made centrally or locally? And so forth.

Where there is cultural match—a fit between the organization of government and the culture of the people—government is more likely to have legitimacy with the community it governs and to achieve the nation's goals.

But achieving cultural match has become more complicated in recent years than it once was. The legacies of colonialism have been destructive, undermining cultural continuities, rupturing relationships, and belittling—if not outright prohibiting—many Indigenous ideas and practices. The great diversity that has long characterized Indian nations now echoes within them: a typical reservation community today may include not only traditional singers, elders who still speak their own language, and expert craftspeople, but video gamers, graduate-degree-holding professionals, business-minded entrepreneurs, rock-and-roll band members, and computer geeks. In some cases, these may be the same people, individuals who neatly straddle a host of activities and ways of life, old and new. Where is cultural match to be found in such a mix of experiences, views, values, and voices?

The answer, in part, lies in what Diane Smith calls "a process of Indigenous choice" (2004, 27). The process of fashioning new governance tools can itself

be a source of legitimacy as long as that process is Indigenously controlled. The resulting tools may mix traditional and contemporary ideas, Indigenous and imported ones. The source of the ideas is less important than how they come to be part of the nation's life. The solutions that are most likely to find support among the people—the ones with staying power—will be those that are chosen and crafted by the people themselves.

These two sources of legitimacy—effectiveness and cultural match—are related. Governments that resonate with their citizens' ideas of what is appropriate and right are more likely, over the long run, to be effective. The creative challenge for Native nations is to do both: to develop effective tools that build on Indigenous values and principles.

SELF-ADMINISTRATION VERSUS SELF-GOVERNMENT

Through much of the latter part of the twentieth century, tribal governments were mostly administrators and managers, running programs designed by outsiders. This was no accident. It is what, for the most part, the federal government imagined for Indian nations. Even the Indian Self-Determination and Education Assistance Act of 1975 was more about administration than government. Its key theme was the right of Indian nations to take over and manage federal Indian programs previously run by someone else.

There were exceptions to this pattern. The more aggressive Indian nations seized much more authority than the creators of the act envisioned: they *governed*, asserting the rights and capacities not only to manage service delivery but to reshape their nations according to their own designs, to make and enforce laws, to develop and pursue long-term strategies of community development, to negotiate new relationships with other governments, and to exercise meaningful jurisdiction over lands and people within their borders. In doing so, they marked out a path from self-administration to genuine self-government. What's the difference? Table 1.1 offers a summary.[17]

This shift from self-administration to self-government is a fundamental aspect of nation building. At its core, it is about reclaiming governance as an Indigenous right and activity, and then developing the tools to govern well.

TABLE 1.1: Self-Administration versus Self-Government

Self-Administration	Self-Government
Jurisdiction	
is largely limited to management decisions within programs	ranges from decisions about governmental form and resource use to intergovernmental relations, civil affairs, and development strategy
Governmental Form	
is typically shaped or imposed by outsiders, usually federal or state governments	is designed by Native nations
Core governmental Functions	
are to administer social programs and distribute resources, such as jobs, money, and services, to citizens	are to establish constitutional foundations for government and self-determined development; make and enforce laws; make and implement policy decisions; provide for fair and nonpolitical dispute resolution; administer programs
Revenue	
is largely from other governments; efforts to increase revenue focus on lobbying for additional transfers of funds	is from diverse sources (may include transfers); efforts to increase revenues focus on various options under Indigenous control (e.g., tribal enterprises, permits and fees, taxation)
Accountability	
typically goes in one direction, having to do largely with community accountability to funders (usually other governments) for how funds are used and for permission to act	goes both ways, having to do with (1) Native nations' accountability to their own citizens for governing well, (2) their accountability to funders for how funds are spent, and (3) outside governments' accountability to Native nations for policy decisions
Intergovernmental Relations	
require consultation (other governments consult with Indigenous communities, then decide what to do); the assumption is that other governments know what's best for Native nations but should at least talk to them about it	are partnerships (decisions are made jointly where joint interests are involved); the assumption is that Native nations and other governments can work together in a relationship of mutual respect to determine what's best for both

NOTES

1. On recent U.S. court decisions, see Williams (2005). More generally on Indigenous self-determination in European settler societies, see Anaya (1996), Havemann (1999), Ivison, Patton, and Sanders (2000), and Cornell (2005).

2. See the foreword in this volume.

3. In a meeting with visiting Aboriginal and Torres Strait Island leaders from Australia, in Vancouver, British Columbia, May 29, 2006.

4. For a fascinating case examination of just such tools, see Trosper (2002, 2003) on the Indigenous societies of the northwest coast of North America.

5. There are a number of accounts of this development; see, for example, Philp (1977) and Taylor (1980).

6. See, among others, the discussions in Bee (1981), Biolsi (1992), Fowler (1982, 1987), U.S. Department of the Interior (1937), and Rosier (2001).

7. Collier is quoted in Dobyns (1968, 269). On the assimilationism of the IRA, see Collier (1954), Cornell (1988, ch. 6), Ducheneaux (1976), and Spicer (1962, 352, 412–13). On the details of the IRA, see Deloria and Lytle (1984) and Kelly (1975), and on the thinking among senior officials at the time, Rusco (2000, 2006). The IRA did not lead to uniform governance structures. A number of the New Mexico pueblos, for example, and many tribes in Alaska are organized very differently and often with significant continuities with older, largely Indigenous forms, and a significant number of Indian nations operate without written constitutions. However, a substantial portion of Indian nations in the United States are organized under the IRA, and many more have governments of similar structure. Some comparable processes took place in Canada but with even less deference to Indigenous ideas. The Indian Act of 1876, along with other government actions, supported the establishment of First Nation governments but was more restrictive, more widely imposed, and more consciously assimilationist than the IRA. See, for example, Armitage (1995), Borrows (2002), Cairns (2000), H. Foster (1999), and Ladner and Orsini (2005).

8. On CAP in Indian Country, see Levitan and Hetrick (1971), and Castile (1998).

9. All examples in this list draw on Cornell (2000) and Brown et al. (2001).

10. As used here, the public, or government, sector includes all government employment (tribal, state, federal) other than government-operated commercial enterprises.

11. The quality of BIA labor force estimates varies by reservation, and such estimates should be treated with caution. Nonetheless, they have value as indicators of the general situation. See also Antell et al. (1999) on a similar situation on the Wind River Reservation, and Pickering (2000) on the Lakota reservations. Snipp (1991, 239, 240) discusses the high levels of government employment on reservations generally and points out that, given the negligible role of state government on most reservations, the vast bulk of this employment is either tribal or federal.

12. These points are a modified version of the discussion in Cornell, Curtis, and Jorgensen (2004), 6–9.

13. Such rules are often collected in topic areas as codes—for example, a children's code (governing adoption and foster relationships, child protective services, issues surrounding

abuse and neglect, etc.), a criminal code (defining and providing penalties for criminal acts within the Native nation's territory), or a commercial code (specifying what businesses have to do to operate within the nation, what their rights are, and what the obligations are of the nation's government to businesses).

14. Borrows argues further (2002) that First Nations law has relevance not only for First Nations but for non-Native societies as well, and that it deserves recognition in Canadian law. On the incorporation—formal or informal—of Indigenous law in

tribal courts generally, see Cooter and Fikentscher (1998a, 1998b) and the case study in Richland (2005).

15. On the Meadow Lake Tribal Council, see http://www.mltc.net/; on the Ktunaxa Nation Council, see http://www.ktunaxa.org/.

16. According to Lipset (1963, 64), "Legitimacy is evaluative. Groups regard a political system as legitimate or illegitimate according to the way in which its values fit with theirs."

17. This table is a modified version of one in Cornell, Curtis, and Jorgensen (2004, 30–31).

FIRST NATIONS DEVELOPMENT INSTITUTE

Founded in 1980, First Nations Development Institute is a national American Indian-led 501(c)(3) nonprofit organization. Through a three-pronged strategy of educating grassroots practitioners, advocating systemic change, and capitalizing Indian communities, First Nations Development Institute is working to restore Native control and culturally-compatible stewardship of the assets they own—be they land, human potential, cultural heritage, or natural resources—and to establish new assets for ensuring the long-term vitality of Native communities. First Nations was founded with the belief that: "when armed with appropriate resources, Native peoples hold the capacity and ingenuity to ensure the sustainable economic, spiritual, and cultural wellbeing of their communities."

First Nations Development Institute was founded with the belief that Indian Country faces a unique challenge: Unlike

any other impoverished community in the nation, the problem faced by Native communities is not ownership of assets but rather the question of who controls Native assets. First Nations believes that in order to effectively address this challenge, Indian Country needs a multi-faceted approach that uses a wide variety of innovative solutions to assist Native people in controlling the assets they own. At First Nations, those solutions have always been based upon a unique understanding of complex systems and the careful use of traditional knowledge, both of which Indian communities still possess today.

Statement from First Nations Development Institute about its work, 2008.

THE CHICKASAW NATION
AN EXAMPLE OF NATION BUILDING

The Chickasaw Nation of Oklahoma, with more than 38,000 citizens, approximately 21,000 of whom reside in Oklahoma, is an example of contemporary nation building and economic success through the assertion of sovereignty and excellence in self-governance. This Nation has taken control of its own institutions and runs them based on its own vision, and it has developed economic, social, and political systems that are culturally appropriate.

Under the leadership of Governor Bill Anoatubby, who was elected in 1987, the tribe has grown from 250 employees and an $11 million annual budget funded almost entirely by the federal government, to, in 2007, 10,500 employees and a $130 million annual budget coming from federal funding that honors treaty obligations. This is supplemented by revenue from tribal economic development and funds a variety of services. The tribe owns

60 businesses, including motels, restaurants, travel plazas, gaming centers, a chocolate factory, radio stations, a newspaper, and a bank.

Economic Development

- Solara Health Care operates eight hospitals in several states, employing 1,000 people.
- Chickasaw Nation Industries is a family of companies working across multiple fields, including construction, manufacturing, property management, and technology.
- Bank2 is a Native American–owned full-service bank that specializes in Native American home loans. Bank2 has won numerous awards.

Education

- $7 million for education grants, scholarships, and incentive programs
- More than 1,000 Chickasaws from Oklahoma and other states attend Chickasaw Summer Camp/Academy annually
- Child care center
- Internship program

- School-to-work program
- Chickasaw Nation Aviation and Space Academy
- Chickasaw Nation Summer Arts Academy
- Chickasaw Nation Press (the first tribally owned/operated academic press)

Health Care

- New Chickasaw Nation Medical Center facility to opening in 2010, to be the largest Indian health care facility in the United States

Culture

- Chickasaw Cultural Center in Sulphur, Oklahoma, to open in 2009

Housing and Tribal Development

- Chuka Chukmasi ("beautiful home") loan program
- Lighthorse Police Department

Source: Chickasaw Nation Progress Report 2007. See: http://www.chickasaw.net/governor/docs/2007_progress_report.pdf

INDIAN GAMING IN THE STATES
DISPELLING MYTHS AND HIGHLIGHTING ADVANTAGES

Sia Davis and Jane Feustel

INTRODUCTION

During the past decade, nearly 40 percent of Indian tribes have become involved in gaming since their right to do so was confirmed by Congress. Compacts or agreements between tribes, governors and state legislatures are in place, based upon the

From Sia Davis and Jane Feustel, *Indian Gaming in the States: Dispelling Myths and Highlighting Advantages*. Building New Traditions Series. Denver: National Conference of State Legislatures, States and Tribes, 2005, pp. 1–11.

Indian Gaming Regulatory Act (IGRA) of 1988. The huge financial success of a few Indian casinos has created the perception that most Indian tribes across the country are involved in gaming ventures and have achieved significant financial prosperity for their tribes. Such a misconception often brings a negative view that besieges gaming and includes concerns about crowds, traffic congestion, organized crime and potential societal problems such as alcoholism, increased crime and gambling addiction.

ORIGINS OF INDIAN GAMING

After several decades of restrictions, the popularity of gambling began to grow in the 1980s. States began to approve lotteries. At the same time, a few Indian tribes opened bingo halls on their reservations. Legal debates followed between states and gaming tribes over regulation. The Seminole Tribe in Florida was one of the first tribes to open a high-stakes bingo hall. The state sued the tribe, citing that the bingo parlor did not comply with state laws. The resulting 1979 court decision in *Seminole Tribe vs. Butterworth* concluded that this type of gaming fell within the capacity of the Seminole Tribe's inherent self-governing authority. A subsequent court case, *California vs. Cabazon and Morongo Bands of Mission Indians*, was decided by the Supreme Court in 1987. It ruled that California could not impose its bingo laws upon tribal governments. The court recognized that tribes are independent from state governments and, in states where gaming is allowed, the tribes have the right to operate gaming operations.

THE INDIAN GAMING REGULATORY ACT (IGRA)

To mitigate future litigation between states and tribes, to affirm the inherent sovereignty of tribal governments, and to promote an opportunity to generate needed revenue, Congress passed the Indian Gaming Regulatory Act in 1988. Among many major aspects of the act, it created the jurisdictional framework for regulating Indian gaming and affirmed the right of tribes to conduct gaming, but also diminished some aspects of that sovereignty to meet the financial and regulatory concerns of states. Part of IGRA's strategy was to support economic development on reservations, strengthen tribal governments, and provide states a role in the negotiation of gaming compacts.

IGRA categorized gaming into three types—Class I, Class II and Class III. Class I gaming is traditional Indian and social gaming for nominal prizes, such as tribal celebrations or rodeos. Class II gaining covers "games of chance," such as bingo and certain card games where individuals play against each other as opposed to playing against the house. More popular is Class III gaming, and it is under this type of gaming that some tribes have prospered. Usually referred to as "casino-style gaming," this activity includes slot machines, roulette, black jack and other table garner. Tribes have regulatory authority over Class H gaming.

They share regulatory authority over Class II gaming with the National Indian Gaming Commission. To conduct Class III gaming, tribes first must negotiate compacts with states that outline how the tribe's gaming activities will be conducted. Even though such an agreement is negotiated between a tribe and a state, the secretary of the interior must approve the compact.

IGRA also specifies that gaming revenue should be used for five purposes:

- To fund tribal government programs,
- To fund the operation of local government agencies,
- To provide for the welfare of tribal citizens,
- To donate toward charitable contributions, and
- To promote economic development.

These guidelines were developed with the intent that revenue from gaming would be spent to improve local roads and highways, provide health and education services to tribal members, preserve cultural heritage, and provide seed money for the development of new businesses, among other things. Once services are funded and if a revenue allocation plan has been approved by the secretary of interior, a tribe can allocate revenue, in the form of a per capita payments, to members of the tribe.

IGRA also established the National Indian Gaming Commission, the federal agency with oversight over Indian gaming activities. The commission oversees class II and III gaming activities and is charged with ensuring that Indian tribes are the primary beneficiaries of gaming revenue and that gaming is conducted fairly by both casinos and customers. It also is involved in approving gaming compacts and management contracts.

INDIAN GAMING TODAY

How widespread is Indian gaming in the United States? In reality, about 220 of 562 tribes are involved in gaming. Many tribes limit themselves to games of bingo. Fewer than 20 tribes have experienced significant economic success through gaming. The gaming ventures deemed most successful are located near metropolitan areas. Yet, the majority of Indian tribes in the United States are located in rural, remote locations that are too isolated to support a profitable casino on their reservations.

Rarely mentioned are those Indian tribes that oppose gaming altogether; these include the nation's largest tribe, the Navajo Nation, and the smaller Hopi Nation in Arizona. Although the Navajo Nation recently authorized gaming in one small area, these two tribes raise revenue in other ways, despite an unemployment rate of 50 percent on both reservations. Steadfast religious and cultural beliefs have influenced the decision to keep most gaming off their land. Some tribal members, including members of gaming tribes, believe gaming could destroy their culture and traditional ways and lead to future problems.

In many cases, gaming success extends off the reservation into non-Indian communities, and that fact is not always readily noticed. Indian gaming created almost 500,000 jobs nationwide in 2003. For example, Indian gaming is one of the top 10 employers in Minnesota, where more than half the gaming workforce is non-Indian. The Seminole Tribe of Florida, which opened two new casinos in 2004, employs 8,000 people, the majority of whom are non-Indian.

Gaming clearly has offered a successful method to improve economies for some tribal communities in the absence of alternative business endeavors. Where gaming has flourished, it has helped tribes become self-sufficient and has provided revenue that has allowed them to diversify their economic prospects. In addition, the revenue funds many social services that the state or federal government would generally pay for or that would otherwise be unfunded.

GAMING SUCCESS HAS NOT BEEN CONSISTENT

Two tribes that have found gaming to be financially lucrative are the Band of Kumeyaay Indians in California—who operate several casinos, including the Golden Acorn Casino and the Barona Resort and Casino—and the Mashantucket Pequot Tribal Nation in Connecticut, which operates Foxwoods, one of the world's largest casinos. Successful casinos have provided tribes with the resources to diversify their businesses, which remains key to maintaining a sustainable economy.

On the other hand, several tribes attempted gaming on their reservation, but did not reap the benefits they anticipated. The presence of a casino on the Rosebud Reservation in South Dakota has not reduced the Lakota Tribe's 80 percent unemployment rate. Similarly, economic conditions for the Standing Rock Sioux Tribe in North Dakota remained dismal following commencement of its gaming operations in the 1990s. Some casinos have marginal success—not flourishing, but not failing—but do well enough to stay in business and provide a few jobs. For some tribes, the goal is simply to provide this handful of new job opportunities in their community.

CASE STUDIES

THE MASHANTUCKET PEQUOT TRIBAL NATION

CONNECTICUT

Since it opened in 1992, the Foxwoods Resort Casino, operated by the Mashantucket Pequot Tribal Nation, has directly created 13,000 jobs and introduced a total of 41,000 jobs in the state of Connecticut. The gaming operations have had a significant effect on the surrounding communities and the entire state.

- Many believe the resort's presence has helped maintain positive residential property values.
- More than 70 percent of visitors to the resort are from out of state, thereby increasing tourism.

- The tribe pays millions of dollars annually to the state in revenue sharing payments.

After the tribe was named the state's most disadvantaged group in the 1990 census, the Mashantucket Pequots made a drastic rebound as a result of gaming operations. The tribe has been able to diversify its economy and now owns additional businesses, including a pharmaceutical company. Profits from gaming funded the construction of a Native American Museum, which provides both cultural preservation and additional tourism.

THE MOHEGAN TRIBE

CONNECTICUT

The Mohegan Tribe established the Mohegan Sun Casino in 1996. The tribal government receives 46 percent of the total revenue. By 1997, the casino was so successful the tribe was able to return $3 million to the federal Department of Housing and Urban Development to be used for other tribes in need.

Benefits of Mohegan Tribal gaming operations to the state include:

- Along with the Pequot tribe, the Mohegans paid the state more than $400 million from casinos in 2003.
- An additional $500,000 yearly goes to local governments.
- The tribe has contributed to the Connecticut Council on Problem Gambling.

- The tribe developed a workforce readiness policy to help low-income individuals maintain full-time jobs.
- The tribe offers its members a large range of assistance and funding opportunities, including funding for full-time college students and continuing education students, medical care, day care assistance, low-income housing, a public safety department, and cultural and language projects.

Sources: Fred Carstensen et al. *The Economic Impact of the Mashantucket Pequot Tribal Nation Operations on Connecticut.* (Storrs, Conn.: Connecticut Center for Economic Analysis, University of Connecticut, November 2000); Stephen Cornell et al. *American Indian Gaming and Its Socio-Economic Effects: A Report to the National Gambling Impact Study Commission.* (Cambridge Mass.: The Economic Resource Group Inc., July 1998).

GAMING REVENUE AND ALLOCATION

Both state and tribal governments use revenues for similar purposes. State revenue comes from a combination of sources that may include property, income and sales taxes; federal aid; and some forms of gambling (lotteries, bingo, pari-mutuel racing or other approved endeavors). States spend that revenue on public education, social services, road maintenance, law enforcement and a host of other needs of their citizens.

IGRA's provisions maintain that tribes must similarly use the revenue earned from their casinos for services on their reservations such as police and fire departments, medical clinics, housing, child care and education. In addition to providing these services, some Indian tribes also have used gaming proceeds as a major means of promoting economic development and providing employment on reservations.

COEURD D'ALENE, KOOTENAI, NEZ PERCE, AND SHOSHONE-BANNOCK

IDAHO

The Coeurd d'Alene, Kootenai, Nez Perce, and Shoshone-Bannock tribes operate five gaming facilities in Idaho. In all, Idaho Indian gaming operations have directly created 2,196 jobs and indirectly created 2,259 more due to tourists who visit tribal gaming facilities. The gaming facilities alone provided $44.8 million in wages and earnings, and indirectly generated an additional $39 million in wages.

As a result of tribal gaming in Idaho, unemployment levels on reservations have decreased. With more people working, total state and federal subsidies for programs such as welfare and Medicaid have been reduced by approximately $6.2 million

due to gaming employment. Employment boosts self-esteem and the quality of life of many citizens who previously needed public assistance.

In 2002, the state passed Proposition One, the Indian Gaming and Self-Reliance Act, clarifying the definition of tribal video gaming machines and providing tribal contribution of 5 percent of annual net gaming revenue for schools and educational programs on or near reservations.

Source: Steven Peterson and Michael DiNoto, *The Economic Impacts of Indian Gaming and Tribal Operations in Idaho.* (Moscow, Idaho: University of Idaho, August 2002). (Sponsored by the Idaho Coalition for Indian Self-Reliance).

In an effort to mitigate the effects of casinos on nearby communities, a number of tribes share their gaming revenue not only with the state but also with nearby cities and counties. In 2004, the Pechanga Band of Luiseno Indians in California helped fund highway improvements, a new fire station, the hiring of extra county sheriff deputies and a tribal liaison to the district attorney in Temecula. State, local and city governments in Arizona receive revenue from gaming tribes to help support trauma and emergency services, the Arizona Wildlife Conservation Fund and the state's tourism fund. Under a compact with Louisiana, the Coushatta Tribe contributes money to local governments to offset the effects of its casino on the community. Much of the money goes to a local school board and is used to fund building projects, equipment and computers, and bonuses for school employees. Similarly, the Coeur d'Alene Indian tribe in Idaho has been awarding grants to local schools in the northern part of the state since 1994.

National charities also benefit from gaming revenue. Tribes have contributed to popular programs such as Crime Stoppers, the Special Olympics, the Muscular Dystrophy Association, the American Cancer Society and the Juvenile Diabetes Association.

Some tribes also voluntarily contribute to local school districts and local universities and colleges.

LAND ACQUISITION AND GAMING

The Indian Gaining Regulatory Act requires that Indian gaming occur on Indian land. On a reservation, lands might be held in fee by the tribe or held in trust by the United States. Land-into-crust is a policy process where the title of "fee" or private land is converted to federal title. The U.S. Department of Interior owns the property and holds it in trust for the benefit of an Indian tribe. This policy restores portions of land to tribes whose land previously was taken away.

An often misunderstood section of IGRA is section 2719, regarding gaming on lands procured after IGRA's 1988 enactment. Indian gaming is not permitted on lands acquired by tribes after October 17, 1988, unless certain conditions are met.

Since the passage of IGRA, only land located within or adjacent to land that already is part of a reservation or land that was part of a tribe's original reservation (for tribes who currently have no land holdings) can be used for gaming. These conditions can be lifted if it is determined that a gaming establishment on newly-obtained land would be in the

THE UNITED AUBURN INDIAN COMMUNITY

CALIFORNIA

In February 2002, an agreement between California and the United Auburn Indian Community was approved by the U.S. Department of Interior that allowed 49 acres of land to be placed into trust for construction of a gaming facility.

The land, located in Placer County, California, would house a Class III gaming facility that would allow the Indian community a means of earning revenue to become self-sufficient. Components of the compact required that the United Auburn Indian Community agree to:

- Contribute to the state's Revenue Sharing Trust Fund and the California Council on Problem Gambling.
- Pay for public services as compensation for the revenue lost from taking the property off the tax

rolls under a memorandum of understanding with Placer County.
- Employ county welfare-to-work participants in the casino.
- Comply with county zoning and building codes during construction of the facility.
- Construct an on-site wastewater treatment plant.
- Comply with the California Environmental Quality Act.

In reviewing the application, the Bureau of Indian Affairs consulted with state, county and local officials and with the public, and negotiations resulted in approval of the application to the satisfaction of both the Indian community and the state.

best interest of the tribe and its members, but would not be detrimental to the surrounding community. Such a decision can be finalized only if the governor of that state consents and approval is given by the secretary of interior.

Gaming operations also can be established on land recently acquired as part of a land claim settlement, federally recognized as part of an Indian tribe's original reservation, or on land restored to an Indian tribe that is reestablished as federally recognized. In the 16 years since the passage of IGRA, just 23 land-into-trust acquisitions have been granted for gaming purposes and only three of these were off-reservation acquisitions. Trust status can be granted only by an act of Congress, a court decision, or application to the U.S. Department of Interior. Some misconceptions exist regarding the trust land issue because of a perception that Indian tribes want to acquire land specifically for gaming purposes. Most trust land acquisitions involve land for Indian housing, schools, health care facilities and agricultural use.

REGULATION OF INDIAN GAMING

When gaming operations first began, there were inconsistencies in gaming regulation from tribe to tribe. These inconsistencies helped to create the perception that Indian casinos were not adequately regulated. Regulation comes from three sources. An individual tribe's gaming commission has primary regulation over gaming operations. In addition, states hold some regulatory authority; specifically over matters that relate to state-tribal compacts. Federally, the National Indian Gaming Commission is the chief entity that oversees tribal casinos. The commission's role is to monitor and corroborate the work of the tribe's regulation commission, and it is responsible for establishing licensing rules, reviewing yearly audits for gaming operations, approving tribal gaming ordinances and inspecting casinos, among other things. Also at the federal level, the U.S. departments of Interior, Justice and Treasury maintain some regulatory authority.

ECONOMIC DIVERSIFICATION AS A RESULT OF GAMING

Gaming revenues, especially from Class III gaming, frequently provide start-up capital for tribes to initiate other types of business on their reservations. By using gaming revenue as a catalyst to launch or invest in non-gaming businesses, many tribes have experienced the successful growth of diversified economies. Achieving this diversification could ensure future economic stability.

No matter how well a casino flourishes, the establishment of new businesses derived from gaming revenue does not occur overnight and, in most instances, new, non-gaming businesses are small. The creation of certain businesses—such as restaurants or hotels—can directly support a casino. Other businesses—golf courses, RV parks or convenience stores, for example—can cater to reservation visitors or tourists who do not gamble.

Whether large or small, some businesses established with gaming revenue can grow to provide alternative revenue that can help to financially support a tribe. Examples of successful economic diversification include the following.

- The Oneida Nation in New York recently started a charter airline service. Four Directions Air Inc., provides charter service for corporate business travelers.
- The San Manuel Band of Mission Indians in California owns a water bottling plant.
- The White Mountain Apache in Arizona owns and operates a ski resort and hotel.
- The Mescalero Apache in New Mexico owns and manages the Inn of The Mountain Gods, a $20 million luxury resort.
- The Ho-Chunk Nation in Wisconsin owns a construction company, smoke shop, and RV park and campground.
- Perdido River Farms, run by the Poarch Band of Creek Indians in Alabama, leases crop land to area farmers; grows corn, cotton and soybeans, and operates a catfish farm.

Gaming revenue is not always a prerequisite to economic diversity. Well known for the economic diversification they have achieved, The Mississippi Band of Choctaw Indians opened one of its first businesses in 1969—a home construction company. During the next two decades, the tribe expanded its ventures to include a retail shopping center, a printing company, an industrial park, a nursing home and several other companies. Because its other economic development ventures were quite successful, the tribe's first gaming facility did not open until July 1994.

COMMON CONCERNS REGARDING INDIAN GAMING

Gaming, whether in Las Vegas, Atlantic City or on tribal land, conjures up negative images for many. Some view Indian gaming as a concern because of its close proximity to local communities in many states and because of common misperceptions about it, such as nonpayment of taxes, increased crime, and addiction to alcohol and gambling.

Indian casinos do not have to pay taxes on gaming revenues to the state or federal government, just as states do not pay taxes on power ball, scratch or other lottery revenues. Tribal businesses do pay wage, occupational and employment taxes. In terms of federal income taxes, Indian tribes are governments and are not required to pay federal taxes on the income generated by the tribe. Although profits generated by the tribes are not taxed at the state or federal level, per capita payments made to tribal members are taxable. Tribes also pay fees—based on a percentage of net revenue from Class II and Class III operations—to fund the National Indian Gaming Commission.

Gambling in general has a history of criminal involvement, and casinos everywhere deal with the issue. No reports have been officially substantiated that criminal activity increased because of an Indian casino. Moreover, there is no evidence that organized crime has infiltrated Indian gaming. Preventing criminal activity is achieved through tribal, state and federal regulation. One federal law sets the punishment for cheating or embezzling from an Indian casino at a maximum 10-year prison sentence.

Many tribes have implemented programs to mitigate or treat their patrons' gambling addiction or alcoholism problems. The Standing Rock Sioux in North Dakota help fund a hotline for compulsive gamblers, and the Sault Ste. Marie Chippewa in Michigan initiated a gaming rehabilitation program for problem gamblers. In addition, a number of Indian casinos completely ban alcohol.

CONCLUSION

Not all Indian tribes view gaming as their ultimate and only source of revenue. In light of federal shortfalls in funding, however, gaming has provided a basis for economic development for some Indian tribes. The media seldom publicizes—and the public does not always recognize—the fact that most gaming tribes experience only a modest profit from their casinos and that the remote areas, where a majority of tribes live, are a major disincentive to gaming. These locations also make it difficult to establish other types of economic ventures. American Indians have been, and currently are, living in the most poverty-stricken communities in the nation, at a poverty rate of almost 25 percent, compared to the national average of 12.4 percent. To help overcome poverty, tribes—not the federal government—initiated gaming, and this gave them control over their own economies. In those situations where casinos have been successful, the livelihood of both Indians on reservations and non-Indians residing nearby has improved. A tribal government's responsibility to meet its citizen's needs are similar to those of state governments, and gaming has helped some tribes meet these needs.

¡EVO PRESIDENTE!
Victoria Bomberry

In the ancient ruins of Tiwanaku located in the high desert of the Andean cordillera, Evo Morales Ayma was made Mallku on January 21, 2006. Mallku, which means condor, is the highest leadership position in Andean communities. Aymara yatiris who performed the ceremony gave the staff of authority to Evo Morales. Although the official Presidential inauguration would take place on Sunday, January 23, this ceremony expressed the aspirations and revindication of almost two and a half million Indigenous peoples in Bolivia. In Bolivia, the more than thirty-six Indigenous nations hold the majority population, however, they had been virtually locked out of the political process until the early 1990s. On December 18, 2005, in a stunning victory of 53.7 percent of the vote, Evo

Morales became the first Indigenous person in the history of the Republic to be elected president. He is also the first Indigenous person to be President in South America.

On April 22, 2008, President Morales was the first head of state to address the United Nations Forum on Indigenous People, where he presented ten points for saving the planet. This speech resonated with Indigenous peoples who have diligently worked for self-determination and sovereignty in all of its manifestations throughout the Americas. The continuity of an Indigenous worldview represented by Evo Morales was tremendously moving. Thirty-one years earlier the Haudesaunee of North America presented *Basic Call to Consciousness* at the United Nations that outlined an

Evo Presidente!
By Victoria Bomberry. Reprinted by permission of the author.

Indigenous philosophy of based on conviviality and interdependence of human kind and the natural world. President Morales renewing this call said, "We feel that we have the ethical and moral right to talk about these things as Indigenous peoples because we have historically lived in harmony with Mother Earth," he continued, "It is Indigenous peoples who have defended this Mother Earth, Planet Earth."

These concepts have been written into the new constitution of Bolivia that promises a social revolution in Bolivia. The Aymara concept of suma qamaña that means to live together well, is given voice and power in the Preamble and further elaborated in the text. To have an Indigenous President in the Americas at this juncture in human history, who symbolizes these concepts is crucial to the formulation of human organization that makes these concepts real and viable. To Indigenous peoples who are thinking through and enacting self-determination throughout the Americas, Evo Morales is a model of leadership based on these common values.

3

LOVELY HULA HANDS
CORPORATE TOURISM AND THE PROSTITUTION
OF HAWAIIAN CULTURE

Haunani-Kay Trask

This paper was first delivered at a Law and Society conference in Berkeley. The response was astounding since most Americans are simply shocked to learn that even one Native thinks of tourism as a colonial imposition on Hawaiians. Of course, it could be that part of the shock was that this message was delivered by a Hawaiian intellectual, something most American racists consider a contradiction in terms.

I am certain that most, if not all, Americans have heard of Hawai'i and have wished, at some time in their lives, to visit my Native land. But I doubt that the history of how Hawai'i came to be territorially incorporated, and economically, politically, and culturally subordinated to the United States is known to most Americans. Nor is it common knowledge that Hawaiians have been struggling for over twenty years to achieve a land base

Haunani-Kay Trask, from *A Native Daughter*. Copyright 1993 by Haunani-Kay Trask. Published by Common Courage Press, Monroe, Maine. Reprinted with permission. The present version is slightly revised.

and some form of political sovereignty on the same level as American Indians. Finally, I would imagine that most Americans could not place Hawai'i or any other Pacific island on a map of the Pacific. But despite all this appalling ignorance, five million Americans will vacation in my homeland this year *and* the next, and so on into the foreseeable capitalist future. Such are the intended privileges of the so-called American standard of living: ignorance of, and yet power over, one's relations to Native peoples.

Thanks to post-war American imperialism, the ideology that the United States has no overseas colonies and is, in fact, the champion of self-determination the world over holds no greater sway than in the United States itself. To most Americans, then, Hawai'i is *theirs:* to use, to take, and, above all, to fantasize about long after the experience.

Just five hours away by plane from California, Hawai'i is a thousand light years away in fantasy. Mostly a state of mind, Hawai'i is the image of escape from the rawness and violence of daily American life. Hawai'i—the word, the vision, the sound in the mind—is the fragrance and feel of soft kindness. Above all, Hawai'i is "she," the Western image of the Native "female" in her magical allure. And if luck prevails, some of "her" will rub off on you, the visitor.

This fictional Hawai'i comes out of the depths of Western sexual sickness which demands a dark, sin-free Native for instant gratification between imperialist wars. The attraction of Hawai'i is stimulated by slick Hollywood movies, saccharine Andy Williams music, and the constant psychological deprivations of maniacal American life. Tourists flock to my Native land for escape, but they are escaping into a state of mind while participating in the destruction of a host people in a Native place.

To Hawaiians, daily life is neither soft nor kind. In fact, the political, economic, and cultural reality for most Hawaiians is hard, ugly, and cruel.

In Hawai'i, the destruction of our land and the prostitution of our culture are planned and executed by multinational corporations (both foreign-based and Hawai'i-based), by huge landowners (like the missionary-descended Castle and Cook—of Dole Pineapple fame—and others) and by collaborationist state and county governments. The ideological gloss that claims tourism to be our economic savior and the "natural" result of Hawaiian culture is manufactured by ad agencies (like the state supported Hawai'i Visitors' Bureau) and tour companies (many of which are owned by the airlines), and spewed out to the public through complicitous cultural engines like film, television and radio, and the daily newspapers. As for the local labor unions, both rank and file and management clamor for more tourists while the construction industry lobbies incessantly for larger resorts.

The major public educational institution, the University of Hawai'i, funnels millions of taxpayer dollars into a School of Travel Industry Management and a Business School replete with a Real Estate Center and a Chair of Free Enterprise (renamed the Walker Chair to hide the crude reality of capitalism). As the propaganda arm of the tourist industry in Hawai'i, both schools churn out studies that purport to show why Hawai'i needs more golf courses, hotels, and tourist infrastructure and how Hawaiian culture is "naturally" one of giving and entertaining.

Of course, state-encouraged commodification and prostitution of Native cultures through tourism are not unique to Hawai'i. They are suffered by peoples in places as disparate as Goa, Australia, Tahiti, and the Southwestern United States. Indeed, the problem is so commonplace that international organizations—e.g., the Ecumenical Coalition on Third World Tourism out of Bangkok, the Center for Responsible Tourism in California, and the Third World European Network—have banded together to help give voice to Native peoples in daily resistance against corporate tourism. My focus on Hawai'i, although specific to my own culture, would likely transfer well when applied to other Native peoples.[1]

Despite our similarities with other major tourist destinations, the statistical picture of the effects of corporate tourism in Hawai'i is shocking:

Fact: Over thirty years ago, at statehood, Hawai'i residents outnumbered tourists by more than 2 to 1. Today, tourists outnumber residents by 6 to 1; they outnumber Native Hawaiians by 30 to 1.[2]

Fact: According to independent economists and criminologists, "tourism has been the single most powerful factor in O'ahu's crime rate," including crimes against people and property.[3]

Fact: Independent demographers have been pointing out for years that "tourism is the major source of population growth in Hawai'i" and that "rapid growth of the tourist industry ensures the trend toward a rapidly expanded population that receives lower per capita income."[4]

Fact: The Bank of Hawai'i has reported that the average real incomes of Hawai'i residents grew only *one* percent during the period from the early seventies through the early eighties, when tourism was booming. The Census Bureau reports that personal income growth in Hawai'i during the same time was the lowest by far of any of the 50 American states.[5]

Fact: Ground water supplies on O'ahu will be insufficient to meet the needs of residents and tourists by the year 2000.[6]

Fact: According to the *Honolulu Advertiser,* "Japanese investors have spent more than $7.1 billion on their acquisitions" since 1986 in Hawai'i. This kind of volume translates into huge alienations of land and properties. For example, nearly 2,000 acres of land on the Big Island of Hawai'i was purchased for $18.5 million while over 7,000 acres on Moloka'i went for $33 million. In 1989, over $1 billion was spent by the Japanese on land alone.[7]

Fact: More plants and animals from Hawai'i are now extinct or on the endangered species list than in the rest of the United States.[8]

Fact: More than 20,500 families are on the Hawaiian trust lands' list, waiting for housing or pastoral lots.[9]

Fact: The median cost of a home on the most populated island of O'ahu is $450,000.[10]

Fact: Hawai'i has by far the worst ratio of average family income to average housing costs in the country. This explains why families spend nearly 52 percent of their gross income for housing costs.[11]

Fact: Nearly one-fifth of Hawai'i's resident population is classified as *near-homeless,* that is, those for whom any mishap results in immediate on-the-street homelessness.[12]

These kinds of random statistics render a very bleak picture, not at all what the posters and jingoistic tourist promoters would have you believe about Hawai'i.

My use of the word "tourism" in the Hawai'i context refers to a mass-based, corporately controlled industry that is both vertically and horizontally integrated such that one multi-national corporation owns an airline, the tour buses that transport tourists to the corporation-owned hotel where they eat in a corporation-owned restaurant, play golf and "experience" Hawai'i on corporation-owned recreation areas, and eventually consider buying a second home built on corporation land. Profits, in this case, are mostly repatriated back to the home country. In Hawai'i, these "home" countries are Japan, Taiwan, Hong Kong, Canada, Australia, and the United States. In this sense, Hawai'i is very much like a Third World colony where the local elite—the Democratic Party in our state—collaborates in the rape of Native land and people.[13]

The mass nature of this kind of tourism results in mega-resort complexes on thousands of acres with demands for water and services that far surpass the needs of Hawai'i residents. These complexes may boast several hotels, golf courses, restaurants, and other "necessaries" to complete the total tourist experience. Infrastructure is usually built by the developer

in exchange for county approval of more hotel units. In Hawai'i, counties bid against each other to attract larger and larger complexes. "Rich" counties, then, are those with more resorts since they will pay more of the tax base of the county. The richest of these is the County of Honolulu which encompasses the entire island of O'ahu. This island is the site of four major tourist destinations, a major international airport, and 80 percent of the resident population of Hawai'i. The military also controls nearly 30 percent of the island with bases and airports of their own. As you might imagine, the density of certain parts of Honolulu (e.g., Waikīkī) is among the highest in the world. At the present annual visitor count, more than 5 million tourists pour through O'ahu, an island of only 607 square miles. According to a statistician I met at an international tourism conference in Germany in 1986, Hawai'i suffers the greatest number of tourists per square mile of any place on earth.

With this as a background on tourism, I want to move now into the area of cultural prostitution. "Prostitution" in this context refers to the entire institution which defines a woman (and by extension the "female") as an object of degraded and victimized sexual value for use and exchange through the medium of money. The "prostitute" is then a woman who sells her sexual capacities and is seen, thereby, to possess and reproduce them at will, that is, by her very "nature." The prostitute and the institution which creates and maintains her are, of course, of patriarchal origin. The pimp is the conduit of exchange, managing the commodity that is the prostitute while acting as the guard at the entry and exit gates, making sure the prostitute behaves as a prostitute by fulfilling her sexual-economic functions. The victims participate in their victimization with enormous ranges of feeling, including resistance and complicity, but the force and continuity of the institution are shaped by men.

There is much more to prostitution than my sketch reveals but this must suffice for I am interested in using the largest sense of this term as a metaphor in understanding what has happened to Hawaiian culture. My purpose is not to exact detail or fashion a model but to convey the utter degradation of our culture and our people under corporate tourism by employing "prostitution" as an analytic category.

Finally, I have chosen four areas of Hawaiian culture to examine: our homeland, or *one hānau* that is Hawai'i, our lands and fisheries, the outlying seas and the heavens; our language and dance; our familial relationships; and our women.

NĀ MEA HAWAI'I—THINGS HAWAIIAN

The *mo'ōlelo*, or history of Hawaiians, is to be found in our genealogies. From our great cosmogonic genealogy, the *Kumulipo*, derives the Hawaiian identity. The "essential lesson" of this genealogy is "the interrelatedness of the Hawaiian world, and the inseparability of its constituent parts." Thus, "the genealogy of the land, the gods, chiefs, and people intertwine one with the other, and with all aspects of the universe."[14]

In the *mo'ōlelo* of Papa and Wākea, earth-mother and sky-father, our islands are born: Hawai'i, Maui, O'ahu, Kaua'i, and Ni'ihau. From their human offspring came the *taro* plant and from the taro came the Hawaiian people. The lessons of our genealogy are that human beings have a familial relationship to land and to the *taro*, our elder siblings or *kua'ana*.

In Hawai'i, as in all of Polynesia, younger siblings must serve and honor elder siblings who, in turn, must feed and care for their younger siblings. Therefore, Hawaiians must cultivate and husband the land which will feed and provide for the Hawaiian people. This relationship of people to land is called *mā lama 'āina* or *aloha 'āina*, care and love of the land.

When people and land work together harmoniously, the balance that results is called *pono*. In Hawaiian society, the *ali'i* or chiefs were required to maintain order, abundance of food, and good government. The *maka 'āinana* or common people worked the land and fed the chiefs; the *ali'i* organized production and appeased the gods.

Today, *mālama 'āina* is called stewardship by some, although that word does not convey spiritual and genealogical connections. Nevertheless, to love and make the land flourish is a Hawaiian value. *'Āina*, one of the words for land, means *that which feeds*. *Kama'āina*, a term for Native-born people, means *child of the land*. Thus is the Hawaiian relationship to land both familial and reciprocal.

Our deities are also of the land: Pele is our volcano, Kāne and Lono our fertile valleys and plains, Kanaloa our ocean and all that lives within it, and so on with the 40,000 and 400,000 gods of Hawai'i. Our whole universe, physical and metaphysical, is divine.

Within this world, the older people or *kūpuna* are to cherish those who are younger, the *mo'opuna*. Unstinting generosity is a value and of high status. Social connections between our people are through *aloha*, simply translated as love but carrying with it a profoundly Hawaiian sense that is, again, familial and genealogical. Hawaiians feel *aloha* for Hawai'i whence they come and for their Hawaiian kin upon

whom they depend. It is nearly impossible to feel or practice *aloha* for something that is not familial. This is why we extend familial relations to those few non-Natives whom we feel understand and can reciprocate our *aloha*. But *aloha* is freely given and freely returned, it is not and cannot be demanded, or commanded. Above all, *aloha* is a cultural feeling and practice that works among the people and between the people and their land.

The significance and meaning of *aloha* underscores the centrality of the Hawaiian language or *'ōlelo* to the culture. *'Ōlelo* means both language and tongue; *mo'ōlelo*, or history, is that which comes from the tongue, i.e., a story. *Haole* or white people say we have oral history, but what we have are stories passed on through the generations. These are different from the *haole* sense of history. To Hawaiians in traditional society, language had tremendous power, thus the phrase, *i ka 'ōlelo ke ola; i ka 'ōlelo ka make*—in language is life, in language is death.

After nearly 2,000 years of speaking Hawaiian, our people suffered the near extinction of our language through its banning by the American-imposed government in 1896. In 1900, Hawai'i became a territory of the United States. All schools, government operations and official transactions were thereafter conducted in English, despite the fact that most people, including non-Natives, still spoke Hawaiian at the turn of the century.

Since 1970, *'ōlelo Hawai'i*, or the Hawaiian language, has undergone a tremendous revival, including the rise of language immersion schools. The State of Hawai'i now has two official languages, Hawaiian and English, and the call for Hawaiian language speakers and teachers grows louder by the day.[15]

Along with the flowering of Hawaiian language has come a flowering of Hawaiian dance, especially in its ancient form, called *hula kahiko*. Dance academies, known as *hālau*, have proliferated throughout Hawai'i as have *kumu hula*, or dance masters, and formal competitions where all-night presentations continue for three or four days to throngs of appreciative listeners. Indeed, among Pacific Islanders, Hawaiian dance is considered one of the finest Polynesian art forms today.

Of course, the cultural revitalization that Hawaiians are now experiencing and transmitting to their children is as much a *repudiation* of colonization by so-called Western civilization in its American form as it is a *reclamation* of our own past and our own ways of life. This is why cultural revitalization is often resisted and disparaged by anthropologists and others: they see very clearly that its political effect is de-colonization of the mind. Thus our rejection of the nuclear family as the basic unit of society and of individualism as the best form of human expression infuriates social workers, the churches, the legal system, and educators. Hawaiians continue to have allegedly "illegitimate" children, to *hānai* or adopt both children and adults outside of sanctioned Western legal concepts, to hold and use land and water in a collective form rather than a private property form, and to proscribe the notion and the value that one person should strive to surpass and therefore outshine all others.

All these Hawaiian values can be grouped under the idea of *'ohana*, loosely translated as family, but more accurately imagined as a group of both closely and distantly related people who share nearly everything, from land and food to children and status. Sharing is central to this value since it prevents individual decline. Of course, poverty is not thereby avoided, it is only shared with everyone in the unit. The *'ohana* works effectively when the *kua'ana* relationship (elder sibling/younger sibling reciprocity) is practiced.

Finally, within the *'ohana*, our women are considered the life givers of the nation, and are accorded the respect and honor this status conveys. Our young women, like our young people in general, are the *pua*, or flower of our *lāhui*, or our nation. The renowned beauty of our women, especially their sexual beauty, is not considered a commodity to be hoarded by fathers and brothers but an attribute of our people. Culturally, Hawaiians are very open and free about sexual relationships, although Christianity and organized religion have done much to damage these traditional sexual values.

With this understanding of what it means to be Hawaiian, I want to move now to the prostitution of our culture by tourism.

Hawai'i itself is the female object of degraded and victimized sexual value. Our *'āina*, or lands, are not any longer the source of food and shelter, but the source of money. Land is now called real estate; rather than our mother, *Papa*. The American relationship of people to land is that of exploiter to exploited. Beautiful areas, once sacred to my people, are now expensive resorts; shore-lines where net fishing, seaweed gathering and crabbing occurred are more and more the exclusive domain of recreational activities: sunbathing, windsurfing, jet skiing. Now, even access to beaches near hotels is strictly regulated or denied to the local public altogether.

The phrase *mālama 'āina*—to care for the land—is used by government officials to sell new projects and to convince the locals that hotels can be built with a concern for "ecology." Hotel historians, like hotel doctors, are stationed in-house to soothe the visitors' stay with the pablum of invented myths and tales of the "primitive."

High schools and hotels adopt each other and funnel teenagers through major resorts for guided tours from kitchens to gardens to honeymoon suites in preparation for post-secondary jobs in the lowest-paid industry in the State. In the meantime, tourist appreciation kits and movies are distributed through the State Department of Education to all elementary schools. One film, unashamedly titled "What's in it for Me?," was devised to convince locals that tourism is, as the newspapers never tire of saying, "the only game in town."

Of course, all this hype is necessary to hide the truth about tourism, the awful exploitative truth that the industry is the major cause of environmental degradation, low wages, land dispossession, and the highest cost of living in the United States.

While this propaganda is churned out to local residents, the commercialization of Hawaiian culture proceeds with calls for more sensitive marketing of our Native values and practices. After all, a prostitute is only as good as her income-producing talents. These talents, in Hawaiian terms, are the *hula*; the generosity, or *aloha*, of our people; the *u'i* or youthful beauty of our women and men; and the continuing allure of our lands and waters, that is, of our place, Hawai'i.

The selling of these talents must produce income. And the function of tourism and the State of Hawai'i is to convert these attributes into profit.

The first requirement is the transformation of the product, or the cultural attribute, much as a woman must be transformed to look like a prostitute, i.e., someone who is complicitous in her own commodification. Thus *hula* dancers wear clown-like make-up, don costumes from a mix of Polynesian cultures, and behave in a manner that is smutty and salacious rather than powerfully erotic. The distance between the smutty and the erotic is precisely the distance between Western culture and Hawaiian culture. In the hotel version of the *hula*, the sacredness of the dance has completely evaporated while the athleticism and sexual expression have been packaged like ornaments. The purpose is entertainment for profit rather than a joyful and truly Hawaiian celebration of human and divine nature.

The point, of course, is that everything in Hawai'i can be yours, that is, you the tourist, the non-Native, the visitor. The place, the people, the culture, even our identity as a "Native" people is for sale.

Thus, Hawai'i, like a lovely woman, is there for the taking. Those with only a little money get a brief encounter, those with a lot of money, like the Japanese, get more. The State and counties will give tax breaks, build infrastructure, and have the governor personally welcome tourists to ensure they keep coming. Just as the pimp regulates prices and guards the commodity of the prostitute, so the State bargains with developers for access to Hawaiian land and culture. Who builds the biggest resorts to attract the most affluent tourists gets the best deal: more hotel rooms, golf courses, and restaurants approved. Permits are fast-tracked, height and density limits are suspended, new ground water sources are miraculously found.

Hawaiians, meanwhile, have little choice in all this. We can fill up the unemployment lines, enter the military, work in the tourist industry, or leave Hawai'i. Increasingly, Hawaiians are leaving, not by choice but out of economic necessity.

Our people who work in the industry—dancers, waiters, singers, valets, gardeners, housekeepers, bartenders, and even a few managers—make between $10,000 and $25,000 a year, an impossible salary for a family in Hawai'i. Psychologically, our young people have begun to think of tourism as the only employment opportunity, trapped as they are by the lack of alternatives. For our young women, modeling is a "cleaner" job when compared to waiting on tables, or dancing in a weekly revue, but modeling feeds on tourism and the commodification of Hawaiian women. In the end, the entire employment scene is shaped by tourism.

Despite their exploitation, Hawaiians' participation in tourism raises the problem of complicity. Because wages are so low and advancement so rare, whatever complicity exists is secondary to the economic hopelessness that drives Hawaiians into the industry. Refusing to contribute to the commercialization of one's culture becomes a peripheral concern when unemployment looms.

Of course, many Hawaiians do not see tourism as part of their colonization. Thus tourism is viewed as providing jobs, not as a form of cultural prostitution. Even those who have some glimmer of critical consciousness don't generally agree that the tourist industry prostitutes Hawaiian culture. To me, this is a measure of the depth of our mental oppression: we can't understand our own cultural degradation because we are living it. As colonized people, we are colonized to the extent that we are unaware of our oppression. When awareness begins, then so too does de-colonization. Judging by the growing resistance to new hotels, to geothermal energy and manganese nodule mining which would supplement the tourist industry, and to increases in the sheer number of tourists, I would say that de-colonization has begun, but we have many more stages to negotiate on our path to sovereignty.

My brief excursion into the prostitution of Hawaiian culture has done no more than give an overview. Now that you have heard a Native view, let me just leave this thought behind. If you are thinking of visiting my homeland, please don't. We don't want or need any more tourists, and we certainly don't like them. If you want to help our cause, pass this message on to your friends.

NOTES

1. The Center for Responsible Tourism and the Third World European Network were created out of the activism and organizing of the Ecumenical Coalition on Third World Tourism (ECTWT). This umbrella organization is composed of the following member bodies: All Africa Conference of Churches, Caribbean Conference of Churches, Christian Conference of Asia, Consejo Latinoamericano de Iglesias, Federation of Asian Bishops Conference/Office of Human Development, Middle East Council of Churches, Pacific Conference of

Churches. In addition, sister organizations, like the Hawai'i Ecumenical Coalition on Tourism, extend the network worldwide. The ECTWT publishes a quarterly magazine with articles on Third World tourism and its destructive effects from child prostitution to dispossession of Native peoples. The address for ECTWT is P.O. Box 24 Chorakhebua, Bangkok 10230, Thailand.

2. Eleanor C. Nordyke, *The Peopling of Hawai'i* (Honolulu: University of Hawai'i Press, 2 ed., 1989), pp. 134–172.

3. Meda Chesney-Lind, "Salient Factors in Hawai'i's Crime Rate," University of Hawai'i School of Social Work (n.d.).

4. Nordyke, *ibid.*

5. Bank of Hawai'i Annual Economic Report, 1984.

Author's note: *Lovely Hula Hands* is the title of a famous and very saccharine song written by a *haole* who fell in love with Hawaii in the pre-Statehood era. It embodies the worst romanticized views of *hula* dancers and Hawaiian culture in general.

6. Estimate of independent hydrologist Kate Vandemoer to community organizing group, *Kupa'a He'eia*, February 1990. Water quality and ground water depletion are two problems much discussed by State and county officials in Hawai'i but ignored when resort permits are considered.

7. *Honolulu Advertiser*, April 8, 1990.

8. David Stannard, Testimony against West Beach Estates. Land Use Commission, State of Hawai'i, January 10, 1985.

9. Department of Hawaiian Homelands, Annual Report, 1989.

10. *Honolulu Star-Bulletin*, May 8, 1990.

11. Bank of Hawai'i Annual Economic Report, 1984. This figure is outdated. My guess is that now, in 1992, families spend closer to 60% of their gross income for housing costs. Billion-dollar Japanese investments and other speculation since 1984 have caused rental and purchase prices to skyrocket.

12. This is the estimate of a State-contracted firm that surveyed the islands for homeless and near-homeless families. Testimony was delivered to the State legislature, 1990 session.

13. For an analysis of post-statehood Hawai'i and its turn to mass-based corporate tourism, see Noel Kent, *Hawai'i: Islands Under the Influence*, op. cit. For an analysis of foreign investment in Hawai'i, see *A Study of Foreign Investment and Its Impact on the State*, Hawai'i Real Estate Center, University of Hawai'i, 1989.

14. Lilikalā Kame'eleihiwa, *Native Land and Foreign Desires* (Honolulu: Bishop Museum, Press, 1992), p. 2.

15. See Larry Kimura, "Native Hawaiian Culture," in *Native Hawaiians Study Commission Report*, vol. 1, op. cit., pp. 173–197.

INDIGENOUS ENVIRONMENTAL PERSPECTIVES
A NORTH AMERICAN PRIMER

Winona LaDuke

INDIGENOUS NATIONS TODAY

At the outset, it is useful to note that there are over 5,000 nations in the world today, and just over 170 states. "Nations" are defined under international law as those in possession of a common language, landbase, history, culture and territory. North America is similarly comprised of a series of nations, known as "First Nations" in Canada, and, with few exceptions, denigrated in the United States with the term "tribes." Demographically, Indigenous nations represent the majority population north of the 55th parallel in Canada (the 50th parallel in the eastern provinces), and occupy approximately two-thirds of the Canadian landmass.

Although the United States has ten times the population, Indian people do not represent the majority,

Winona LaDuke, "Indigenous Environmental Perspectives: A North American Primer," *Akwe:kon Journal*, 9, no. 2 (Summer 1992). Copyright 1992 by Akwe:kon Press. Reprinted with permission. Portions of the original have been omitted.

except in few cases, particularly the "four corners" region of the United States, or the intersection of Arizona, Utah, New Mexico, and Colorado, where Ute, Apache, Navajo, and Pueblo people reside. Inside our reservations however (approximately four percent of our original land base in the United States), Indian people remain the majority population.

In our territories and our communities, a mix of old and new co-exist, sometimes in relative harmony, and at other times, in a violent disruption of the way of life. In terms of economic and land tenure systems (the material basis for relating to the ecosystem), most Indigenous communities are a melange of colonial and traditional structures and systems. While American or Canadian laws may restrict and allocate resources and land on reservations (or aboriginal territory), Indigenous practice of "usufruct rights" is still maintained, and with it traditional economic and regulatory institutions like the trapline, "rice boss," and family hunting, grazing (for those peoples who have livestock), or harvesting territories.

These subsistence lifestyles continue to provide a significant source of wealth for domestic economies on the reservation—whether for nutritional consumption or for household use, as in the case of firewood. They also, in many cases, provide the essential ingredients of foreign exchange—wild rice, furs, or woven rugs and silverwork. These economic and land tenure systems (specific to each region) are largely "invisible" to American and Canadian government agencies, economic analysts who consistently point to Native "unemployment," with no recognition of the traditional economy.

In many northern communities, over seventy-five percent of local food, and a significant amount of income, is garnered from this traditional economic system. In other cases, for instance, on the Northern Cheyenne reservation in Montana, over ninety percent of the land is held by Cheyenne, and is utilized primarily for ranching. Although not formal "wage work" in the industrial system, these land-based economies are essential to our communities. The lack of recognition for Indigenous economic systems, though long entrenched in the North American colonial view of Native peoples, is particularly frustrating in terms of the present debate over development options.

Resource extraction plans or energy megaprojects proposed for Indigenous lands do not consider the significance of these economic systems, nor their value for the future. A direct consequence is that environmentally destructive development programs ensue, many times foreclosing the opportunity to continue the lower scale, intergenerational economic practices which had been underway in the Native community. For many Indigenous peoples, the reality is that, as sociologist Ivan Illich has noted, "the practice of development is in fact a war on subsistence."

The following segment of this paper includes an overview of North American Indigenous environmental issues, in the format of generalized discussions and case studies. The paper is far from exhaustive, but is presented with the intention of providing information on the environmental crises pending or present in our communities. It is the belief of many Native people that due to our historic and present relations with the United States and Canadian governments, we may be "the miner's canary," or a microcosm of the larger environmental crisis facing the continent. In a final segment of this paper, we return to the discussion of sustainable development, and offer, once again, some present documentation of the practice of "pimaatisiiwin," interpreted as good

life or continuous birth, within the context of our Indigenous economic and value systems.

URANIUM MINING

. . . Uranium mining and milling are the most significant sources of radiation exposure to the public of the entire nuclear fuel cycle far surpassing nuclear reactors and nuclear waste disposal. . . .

Victor Gillinsky,
U.S. Nuclear Regulatory Commission, 1978

. . . Perhaps the solution to the radon emission problem is to zone the land into uranium mining and milling districts so as to forbid human habitation. . .

Los Alamos Scientific Laboratory,
February 1978

The production of uranium or yellowcake from uranium ore usually requires the discharge of significant amounts of water and the disposal of significant portions of radioactive material. Uranium mill tailings, the solid wastes from the uranium milling stage of the cycle, contain eighty-five percent of the original radioactivity in the uranium ore. One of these products, Radium 226, remains radioactive for at least 16,000 years.

In 1975, 100% of all federally produced uranium came from Indian reservations. That same year there were 380 uranium leases on Indian lands, as compared to four on public and acquired lands. In 1979, there were 368 operating uranium mines in the United States. Worldwide, it is estimated that seventy percent of uranium resources are contained on Indigenous lands.

NAVAJO NATION

Spurred by the advice of the Bureau of Indian Affairs and promises of jobs and royalties, the Navajo Tribal Council approved a mineral agreement with the Kerr McGee Corporation. In return for access to uranium deposits and a means to fulfill risk-free contracts with the U.S. Atomic Energy Commission, Kerr McGee employed 100 Navajo men as uranium miners in the underground mines.

Wages for the non-union miners were low—$1.60 per hour, or approximately two thirds of off-reservation wages. In addition, regulation and worker safety enforcement were exceedingly lax. In 1952, the mine inspector found that ventilation units were not in operation. In 1954, the inspector found that the fan was operating only during the first half of the shift. When he returned in 1955, the blower ran out of gas during an inspection. One report from 1959 noted that radiation levels at the operations were ninety times above tolerable levels.

Seventeen years later most of the readily retrievable ore had been exhausted, and the company began to phase out the mines. By 1975, eighteen of the miners who had worked in the Kerr McGee mines had died of lung cancer and twenty-one more were feared to be dying. By 1980, thirty-eight had died and ninety-five more had contracted respiratory ailments and cancers. The incidence of skin and bladder cancer, birth defects, leukemia and other diseases associated with uranium mining also accelerated.

In its departure from the Shiprock area of Navajo, Kerr McGee abandoned approximately seventy-one acres worth of uranium mill tailings on the banks of the San Juan River, the only major waterway in the arid region. As a result, radioactive contamination spread downstream. Southeast of the facility, the Church rock uranium mine discharged 80,000 gallons of radioactive water from the mine shaft (in "dewatering") annually into the local water supply.

In July of 1979, the largest radioactive spill in United States history occurred at the United Nuclear uranium mill near Church rock on the Navajo reservation. The uranium mill tailings dam at the site broke under pressure and 100 million gallons of sludge flooded the Rio Puerco River. Although the company had known of the cracks in the dam for two months prior to the incident, no repairs had been made. The water supply of 1,700 Navajo people was irretrievably contaminated, and subsequently over 1,000 sheep and cattle ingested radioactive water.

By 1980, forty-two operating uranium mines, ten uranium mills, five coal fired power plants and four coal stripmines (spanning 20–40,000 acres each) were in the vicinity of the Navajo reservation. Approximately fifteen new uranium mining operations were under construction on the reservation itself. Although eighty-five percent of Navajo households had no electricity, each year, the Navajo nation exported enough energy resources to fuel the needs of the state of New Mexico for thirty-two years.

The birth defect rate in the Shiprock Indian Health Service area is two to eight times higher than the national average, according to a study supported by the March of Dimes Research Support Grant #15-8, and undertaken by Lora Magnum Shields, a professor at Navajo Community College in Shiprock and Alan B. Goodman, Arizona Department of Health.

LAGUNA PUEBLO

Approximately fifty miles to the east of the Navajo reservation lies Laguna Pueblo, until 1982 the site of the largest uranium strip mine in the world. The Anaconda Jackpile mine comprised 7,000 acres of the reservation, operating from 1952 to 1971, when the economically retrievable ore was exhausted. An "Indian preference" clause in hiring ensured the employment of Laguna workers, and by 1979, 650 persons were employed at the mine, with this reservation reflecting some of the highest per capita income in the region. The significance of this employment, as indicated in other health and economic statistics, had a mixed impact on the local community.

Prior to 1952, the Rio Paguate coursed through an agricultural and ranching valley that provided food for the Pueblo. Rio Paguate now runs through the remnants of the stripmine, emerging on the other side a fluorescent green in color. In 1973, the Environmental Protection Agency discovered that Anaconda had contaminated the Laguna water with radiation.

In 1975, the EPA returned to find widespread groundwater contamination in the Grants Mineral Belt. And in 1978, the EPA came back again, this time to inform Laguna that the water was contaminated and to inform the people that the Tribal Council building, the Paguate Community Center, and the newly constructed housing were all radioactive. In addition, Anaconda was reprimanded for having used low-grade uranium ore to repair the road system on the reservation.

PINE RIDGE RESERVATION

On June 11, 1962, 200 tons of uranium mill tailings from the uranium mill in Edgemont, South Dakota, washed into the Cheyenne River and traveled into the Angostora Reservoir. The Cheyenne River flows from this reservoir down through the hills and across the reservation. The Cheyenne passes within several hundred feet of the Red Shirt Table. These tailings are a part of an estimated seven and a half million tons of radioactive material, abandoned from the uranium mill at the Edgemont mine.

Water samples taken from the Cheyenne River and from a subsurface well on the Redshirt Table revealed a gross alpha radioactivity level of nineteen and fifteen picocuries per liter respectively. Federal safety regulations state that a reading greater than five picocuries per liter is considered dangerous to life. In June of 1980, the Indian Health Service revealed water test results for the Pine Ridge reservation community of Slim Buttes (adjacent to the same area) to indicate gross alpha radiation levels at three times the federal safety maximum. A June 10, 1980 report of the Office of Environmental Health, Bureau of Indian Affairs, Aberdeen indicated that the gross alpha radiation reading for the Slim Buttes water sample was fifty picocuries per liter. A water sample taken from Cherry Creek, on the Cheyenne River Reservation to the north acted as a control sample. It contained 1.9 picocuries per liter, one tenth of that on the Red Shirt Table.

A preliminary study of 1979 reported that fourteen women, or thirty-eight percent of the pregnant women on the Pine Ridge reservation, miscarried, according to records at the Public Health Service Hospital in Pine Ridge. Most miscarriages were before the fifth month of pregnancy, and in many cases there was excessive hemorrhaging. Of the children who were born, some sixty to seventy percent suffered from breathing complications as a result of undeveloped lungs and/or jaundice. Some were born with such birth defects as cleft palate and club foot. Subsequent information secured under Freedom of Information Act requests from the Indian Health Service verified the data. Between 1971 and 1979, 314 babies had been born with birth defects, in a total Indian population of under 20,000.

CANADIAN URANIUM MINING

> We have always been here, and we will stay here. The mines will come and go, they won't have to live with their consequences. We will. . . .
>
> Diné Elder, Wollaston Lake

Previous uranium mining in the north of Canada including Port Hope, has left over 222,000 cubic meters of radioactive waste. Other dumps, including those in the villages of Port Granby and Welcome, contain a further 573,000 cubic meters of toxic radioactive waste. By 1985, over 120 million tons of low level radioactive waste was abandoned near now defunct uranium mines. This amount represents enough material to cover the Trans-Canada Highway two meters deep from Halifax to Vancouver. Present production of uranium waste from the province of Saskatchewan alone occurs at the rate of over one million tons annually.

Uranium mining began at Elliot Lake, Ontario, in 1958, adjacent to and upstream from the Serpent River reserve of Anishinabeg. The uranium mining has continued until recently, but now most of the mine shafts are being closed, as uranium mining investment has shifted to the open pit mines of northern Saskatchewan.

During the mine operations at Elliot Lake, a significant number of miners were exposed to high levels of radiation. According to a report commissioned by Member of Parliament Steven Lewis (and former Ambassador to the United Nations), "in no individual year between 1959 and 1974 inclusive . . . did the average underground dust counts for the uranium mines of Elliot Lake fall below the recommended limits. In another instance, workers at the thorium separation plant operated by Rio Algom (in Serpent River) until the 1970s were exposed to up to forty times the radiation level recommended by the International Commission for Radiological Protection."

Between 1955 and 1977, eighty-one of the 956 deaths of Ontario uranium miners were from lung cancers. This figure is almost twice that anticipated. Another inquiry into the health of uranium miners revealed that there are ninety-three persons suffering from silicosis, ascribed to the Elliot Lake operations by the end of 1974. By early 1975, nearly 500 miners had lung disabilities, wholly or partly ascribed to dust exposure in the mines and mills. Over the next five years, more than 500 new cases had developed.

The Elliot Lake uranium mines produced over 100 million tons of uranium wastes. Most of these were left abandoned by the roadsides and mine sites, where, according to one observer ". . . local residents continue to pick blueberries within a forty foot high wall of uranium tailings. . . ."

In 1978, the Elliot Lake uranium operations continued to spew out 14,000 tons of solid and liquid effluent daily. Most of that effluent was discharged, untreated, into the Serpent River basin. By 1980, dumping of tailings was so extensive that liquid wastes from the mines comprised between one half and two thirds of the total flow. In 1976, the International Joint Commission on the Great Lakes identified the outflow of the Serpent River into Lake Huron as the greatest single source of Radium 226 and thorium isotopes into the freshwater. Perhaps more significant was a 1976 report by the Ontario Ministry of the Environment, which concluded that eighteen lakes in the Serpent River system had been contaminated as a result of uranium mining to the extent that they were unfit for human use and all fish life had been destroyed.

The most significant longterm impact of the Elliot Lake operations will be borne by the Serpent River and other Anishinabeg bands downstream from the operation. A study carried out by the Toronto Jesuit Center for the Environmental Impact Protection Program between 1982–4 documented the following:

- Twice as many young adults (people under the age of thirty-six) reported chronic disease at Serpent River than at two adjacent reserves. The other two reserves had no direct uranium impacts.
- The Serpent River band reported the largest proportion of participants of all ages with chronic disease.
- Pregnancies ending prematurely with fetal death were more prevalent at Serpent River.

In males over 45, "ill health" is reported by more men with exposure to the plant or uranium mine (seventy-five percent) as compared to forty-three percent in men who did not work at the facilities. Additional birth defects were reported in children of men who worked in the uranium related facilities.

By 1986, uranium production in Saskatchewan had doubled, up to over $923 million in exports annually to American utilities. From previous exposure to radiation (resulting from uranium mining over the past twenty years in the north of Saskatchewan), it is estimated that Native people already have eighty times as much radiation in their bodies as residents of the south. The contamination of the north will only become worse with increased uranium mining.

Uranium mining is projected to expand 100% in Canada in the next few years. Five proposed projects are now awaiting environmental impact assessment. (Three of them will be using existing EIS, with two new programs.) The mines include Dominique-Janine Extension (AMOK-a French Company), South McMahon Lake Project (Midwest Joint Venture), McClean Lake Project (Minatco Ltd.), MacArthur River and Cigar Lake mines. Two of the existing three uranium mines, Cluff Lake and Rabbit Lake/Collins Bay are currently expanding, after exhausting original ore bodies. Most of the exploration and test mine work is occurring just west of Wollaston Lake. The Canadian Crown Corporation, Cameco remains the key owner in most of the mining ventures with 20% ownership of Cluff Lake, 66.6% ownership of Key Lake and Rabbit Lake and 48.75% ownership of Cigar Lake.

In November of 1989, a two million liter spill of radioactive water occurred at Rabbit Lake uranium mine. The spill was not reported by the company to the community, but was seen by the community people, who requested to be informed on the contents of the spill from the facility. Almost half of the spill ended up in Wollaston Lake adjacent to a Dene community. The following spring, Cameco pleaded guilty to negligence in the spill, and paid a $50,000 fine.

Evidence of the possible impact on future generations from longterm exposure to low levels of radiation was recently released by a British scientific study. This evidence may have some bearing on uranium mining communities, where longterm health studies have not been undertaken. The study found that exposure of male workers to consistent levels of radiation may cause a mutation in sperm resulting in higher rates of leukemia in their offspring. According to a study by the Medical Research Council of Southampton University (Great Britain), workers exposed to radiation may father children with an increased risk of leukemia. After examining a host of variables, the study team found that children of fathers who worked at the Sellafield Nuclear power plant had a two and one-half times higher risk of contracting leukemia. Fathers who had received the highest dosages over their working life stood six to eight times as high a chance of producing a child with leukemia. Overall, the study found fifty-two cases of childhood leukemia in the health district, with the town of Sellafield exhibiting a ten-fold excess over average figures.

KERR MCGEE SEQUOYAH FUELS FACILITY: CHEROKEE NATION, OKLAHOMA

In 1968, when Kerr McGee began building a uranium processing plant in our community, the people were happy at the thought of employment. Kerr McGee assured the safety of the plant, and now seventeen years later, we have a situation that the majority of us would have never imagined. Most of the waste has been stored in plastic lined ponds, one of which has been leaking since 1974. . . ."

Jessie Deer in Water, Vian, Oklahoma

Sequoyah Fuels Corporation (Kerr McGee) operates a uranium fuels processing plant in Gore, Oklahoma. The plant is within the borders of the Cherokee nation, home to a resident population of over 100,000 Cherokees. The plant converts yellowcake (U 308) into uranium hexaflouride using a "wet process." The products of the plant are trucked onto nearby Interstate 40 for delivery to more than fifty customers, including twenty-five nuclear power plants, seven nations, and the Department of Energy.

The process generates two main streams of liquid wastes, the fluoride stream and the nitrate stream.

The fluoride stream is treated, and then discharged into the Illinois River under a National Pollutant Discharge Elimination System permit issued by the state. The nitrate stream is processed and discharged into a series of sludge ponds, most of which are at their capacity.

Some of the wastes are processed into a "byproduct" known as raffinate. Essentially a toxic sludge, the material contains radioactive elements like radium 26, thorium 230, and uranium as well as a host of other toxic and heavy metals. According to Kerr McGee's own data, the raffinate it sprayed in 1982 contained 178,000 percent more molybdenum than the maximum allowable concentration for irrigation water. Each year, the liquid (now in the form of raffinate) is used as a fertilizer on various portions of the site and other lands owned by the corporation. In total, over 10,000 acres of land are further exposed to radiation by the use of raffinate fertilizer. Over 11.8 million gallons of the fertilizer were used in 1986 alone. One of these sites is the Rabbit Hill Farms, where in 1987, 11,000 bales of hay from the farm were donated to Navajo sheepherders during a hard winter. "Although it hasn't been a banner year for the company, Kerr McGee decided to help because of our longstanding relationship with the Navajos because of mining and oil and gas leases in the area," the company explained.

There have been a number of spills at the site including an overflow of a settling basin in the spring of 1972, 1,450 pounds of uranium hexaflouride spilled into a surface stream in December of 1978, a major spill in December of 1980, and ongoing leaks at the bottom of raffinate pond number two, which has been leaching continuously into the groundwater for ten years. Dr. Richard Hayes Phillips, of the University of Oregon, conducted some research into the effluent discharge of the facility. His findings included the above statistics, and documentation of concentrations of uranium, radium, and thorium in the surface effluent stream which have been measured at 21.3, 2,387 and 5.15 times higher (respectively) than permissible levels.

Within a ten mile radius of the plant, over 200 cancers and birth defects have been recorded. In the town of Vian, population 1,500, 124 persons, or eight percent of the population, had cancer.

COAL STRIPMINING

In 1976, four out of the ten largest coal stripmines in the country were on Indian lands. Today, the circumstances are very much the same, with over one-third of all western low-sulfur strippable coal reserves underlying Indian lands. The majority of the remaining resources are adjacent to the reservations. These statistics are particularly stark in light of a present move to develop low-sulfur coal resources as an alternative to more polluting coal supplies. The North Cheyenne reservation has been at the center of this conflict for almost two decades.

NORTH CHEYENNE COAL

The North Cheyenne reservation lies at the very center of the country's largest deposit of coal. The reservation itself has billions of tons of strippable coal, but the Cheyenne have vigorously opposed this exploitation for over thirty years. Multinational energy corporations working with the approval of the federal and state governments are surrounding the Cheyenne reservation with coal stripmines, railroads, electric generating plants, and transmission lines. Indeed, the largest coal stripmine in the United States is fifteen miles from the reservation, and the four coal generating plants at Colstrip loom just off the reservation border.

The 500,000 acre reservation now sits adjacent to the Powder River coal lease. In 1982, the Secretary of the Interior sold federal public coal for pennies a ton along the entire eastern boundary of the reservation. This was the largest federal coal sale in the history of the United States. It stretches from the Wyoming border, running along the major water source, the Tongue River. Five to seven new coal stripmines are planned proximate to the reservation.

The environmental and social impacts of the coal stripmining are devastating. First of all, the present mining area is included in a vast region known for meager rainfall and limited reclamation potential. According to a 1973 study by the National Academy of Sciences, [in] "those areas receiving less than seven inches of rainfall, reclamation should not be attempted at all, and instead those lands should be designated as a National Sacrifice Area." The stripmining process divests the land of much of the aquifer system, disrupts groundwater systems, and contaminates a good portion of the remaining groundwater.

Centralized electrical generation causes relatively pristine regions, like the North Cheyenne and the adjacent Crow reservation, to bear the burden of reduced air quality, while the end user of electricity is relatively free from the pollution of production. The North Cheyenne, for a number of years, have sought to keep their air quality at a premium by designating their airspace as a "Class One" air quality standard, as recognized by the Environmental Protection Agency. Unfortunately, airborne contaminants from both the mining and the power plant process cause adverse health conditions for the Cheyenne people, including higher incidence of respiratory disease, and lower birth weights.

NAVAJO NATION: BIG MOUNTAIN

> My Mother Earth has been totally hurt. The Peabody Coal mine is going on and also uranium has been mined. We have been badly hurt and she has been hurt. Our ancestor told us that the land has guts just like a human. Heart, liver, lung. All of these things she has inside of her. And now all of these things are in critical condition. . . .
>
> Roberta Blackgoat, Diné Elder—Big Mountain

Similar circumstances occur in the region of the Navajo nation, where at least five coal-fired power plants are located on or adjacent to the reservation. One of those plants, the Four Corners Power Plant was the only manmade object seen by Gemini Two astronauts from outer space. These power plants are fueled by coal from mines such as Black Mesa, where after two decades of stripmining by Peabody Coal and General Electric, the groundwater is contaminated and the water table lowered. This has caused severe hardship to Navajo and Hopi people who live in the area. Perhaps the most significant impact, however, is the forced relocation of over ten thousand Navajo people (an estimated 2,553 families) from the area over the Black Mesa Coal Field. The field contains over twenty-two billion tons of coal, and is presently being mined, with new power plants and a new coal slurry pipeline proposed.

The relocation is legislated under federal law— the Navajo–Hopi Indian Relocation Act, which partitions into two equal parts 1.8 million acres of land formerly held in common by the two peoples. The removal of people from the area makes mining possible, causing their imminent cultural and psychological destruction. There is no word for relocation in Navajo, to move away simply means to disappear.

GWICHIN NATION

Gwichin territory spans the United States–Canadian border in what is known as the Yukon and Alaska. They have continuously inhabited that region for perhaps 30,000 years and retain a way of life based on the land, primarily the porcupine caribou herd,

which numbers around 170,000. The health of the herd is essential to Gwichin survival since every year they may harvest up to 10,000 animals just for domestic consumption.

In light of the Persian Gulf war and insatiable demands for oil, pressure has been building to open up the Arctic National Wildlife Refuge to oil exploitation. The Refuge, presently referred to as America's Serengeti is huge and contains vast concentrations of wildlife. The nineteen million acre refuge hosts perhaps the largest complex Arctic ecosystem, as yet unaltered by industrialization. It is also the only coastline in Alaska still off limits to oil leasing, but it makes up only about 105 miles out of 1,200 miles of coastline.

Prudoe Bay and the Beaufort Sea lie just north of the Refuge, and through the Trans Alaska Pipeline system to Valdez, Alaska, presently supply around two and two tenths million barrels a day. This represents about a quarter of the United States' domestically produced crude oil, and one eighth of total daily consumption. It is estimated that by the year 2000, this oil will be depleted to the point where the pipeline will be operating at twenty-five percent capacity.

Oil in the Gwichin territory of the ANWR represents possibly less than 200 days of American oil needs. If the oil is exploited it will devastate the calving grounds of the porcupine caribou herd, and cause widespread desolation in the animals and the Gwichin. In the fall of 1991, legislation to open the refuge, pending in the American Congress was narrowly defeated.

HOBBEMA: THE IMPACT OF OIL EXPLOITATION

The Cree people near Hobbema, Alberta, have come under great stress as a direct result of oil exploitation in their territory. Fourbands live adjacent to Hobbema—the Samson, Ermineskin, Louis Bull, and Montana bands—with a total population of around 6,500. Oil was discovered in their territory in the 1940s, but it was not until the 1970s that oil royalties began to flood into their coffers. By 1983, at the peak of the oil boom, the four bands were receiving 185 million dollars annually in royalties. Oil royalties gave the average Hobbema family 3,000 or more in monthly payments.

Social upheaval was a direct result of the rapid transition from a land based economy into a cash economy. A century ago, French sociologist Emil Durkheim found a strong connection between suicide and collective crisis. In an 1897 study of suicides in Italy, he charted the relationship between large-scale industrial growth, economic prosperity, and suicides. Incomes skyrocketed by thirty five percent between 1873 and 1889, suicides jumped thirty-six percent between 1871 and 1877 and another eight percent between 1877 and 1889. Similar statistics were reported in other countries undergoing rapid industrialism.

A study of the oil-rich bands of Alberta was commissioned by the Department of Indigenous Affairs in 1984. The study confirmed a similar syndrome—sudden wealth was causing profound social disruption in the bands. The unexpected influx of money led to alcoholism, drug addiction, and suicides. "When we had no money, we had a lot of family unity," recalls Theresa Bull, vice chairman of the Hobbema Health board. "Then we had all this money and people could buy anything they wanted. It replaced the old values. . . . It doesn't bring happiness. It put more value on materialistic possessions. The family and the value of spirituality got lost. . . ."

The town of Hobbema had one of the highest suicide rates in North America from 1980 to 1987. From 1985 to 1987, there was a violent death almost every week in Hobbema, and the suicide rate for young men was eighty-three times the national average. There are as many as three hundred suicide attempts by Hobbema Indians every year. The oil money "stripped them of self respect and dignity," said a social worker. Researchers believe that the true rate for Indian suicides nationally (in Canada) is twelve times the national average.

MERCURY CONTAMINATION AT GRASSY NARROWS

In 1956, the first massive outbreak of mercury poisoning occurred in Minimata Japan. By 1968, the Minimata disaster and the nature of mercury poisoning were well documented. No less than 183 medical papers have been published on the subject. By that year, the number of deaths from the poisoning in Japan had approached 100, with several thousand maimed.

In 1960, four years after the Minimata disaster, Dryden Pulp and Paper began to contaminate the Wabigoon River with suspended solids. In March of 1962, Reed Paper opened its Dryden chlor alkali plant which used mercury to bleach paper products, and then released it into the river to form toxic methyl mercury. An estimated twenty pounds of mercury per day were released into the river. On September 8, 1975, the Ontario Minister of Health publicly admitted that twenty to thirty of the Native people living on the Grassy Narrows reserve had shown symptoms of Minimata disease. He also publicly admitted that they may have underestimated the severity of the problem. Tests were reported where Native people had as high as 358 parts per billion mercury in their blood, but at that time did not show signs of mercury poisoning. Mercury poisoning, however, accumulates in the body over time.

Commercial fishing was closed down, causing a total disruption in the economy. An attempt at getting unpolluted fish from a lake near the White Dog reserve failed when non-Indian lodge owners in the vicinity successfully appropriated the lakes' fish for tourism. With commercial fishing banned since 1970, unemployment on the reserves rose over eighty percent. Between 1969 and 1974 welfare tripled on the White Dog Reserve. At Grassy Narrows, it nearly quadrupled from 29,000 dollars to 122,000 dollars. During that same period of time (between January 1970 and June 1972), 200 Native people in the Kenora area died violent deaths. Since in its early stages mercury poisoning can lead to highly destructive behavior, sometimes falsely associated with alcoholism, this report should have been enough to initiate a fullscale study of mercury poisoning among the Native people.

Mercury discharge continued, virtually unabated until 1970, when more than 20,000 pounds of mercury had been dumped into the English-Wabigoon River system (with 30,000 pounds more unaccounted for). Mercury is in the English River system, and unlike Minimata Japan, which has the advantage of ocean currents, it will take an estimated sixty to one hundred years to clean itself out. There is no evidence that Dryden is even going to clean up the mercury pool below the plant, which is still being flushed into the river system.

ALBERTA TIMBER SALES

The province of Alberta has dealt away timberlands almost the size of Great Britain. This new land rush was completed in December of 1988, with the primary beneficiary being the Japanese multinational Diashowa. Diashowa just completed construction of a pulp mill ten kilometers north of the village of Peace River, and has plans for building two more.

The Alberta government granted Diashowa a twenty year lease to 25,000 square kilometers adjacent to the Peace River, and an additional 15,000 square kilometers plus money for roads, rail lines and a bridge. The company also purchased the rights to log the Wood Buffalo National Park, the last great stand of old-growth spruce in Alberta. The lease expires in 2002, and the mill will pump 5,000 tons of chlorinated organic compounds into the Peace River annually. The land leased to Diashowa overlaps with the traditional lands of the Lubicon Lake First Nation.

The Lubicon Cree have been opposing any development in their territory since they were invaded by oil companies in the late 1970s. By 1982, there were over 400 oil wells in their territory, and traditional hunting and trapping trails were turned into company roads. The ability of the people to sustain themselves from the land decreased significantly. Trapping incomes were devastated, and welfare soared from ten percent in 1980 to ninety-five percent in 1983. While the people suffered, an estimated one million dollars worth of oil was extracted daily from the land.

EMISSIONS DISCHARGE

Formaldehyde is a water soluble gas that is known to irritate the eyes, respiratory tract, and skin. It is also a suspected carcinogen, and has been linked to cancer of the skin, lungs, and nasal passages. Airborne formaldehyde can cause ocular damage and allergic dermatitis. Young children and the elderly are especially vulnerable to the effects of this toxin.

At the rate of between twenty-two and thirty-two pounds per hour, the Potlatch Timber Corporation near Cook, Minnesota is emitting formaldehyde into the air over the Nett Lake reservation. At the conservative rate of twenty-two pounds per hour, this figure represents 164, 208 pounds annually of emissions.

HYDRO-ELECTRIC EXPLORATION

James Bay, at the base of Hudson Bay, is the largest drainage system on the North American continent. Virtually every major river in the heartland ends up there. This makes the bay a rich ecosystem teeming with wildlife, the staging ground for migratory birds, and a feeding area for the largest migratory herd of mammals on the continent—the George's River Caribou herd. Approximately 35,000 Cree, Innu, Inuit, and Ojibway people live within the region and are dependent upon the ecosystem. The way of life is landbased subsistence—hunting, harvesting, and tourism economy in which at least fifty percent of the food and income for the region originates.

The James Bay I project, introduced in 1972, was intended to produce 10,000 megawatts of electricity by putting eleven and one-half square kilometers of land under water and behind dams. The project concentrated along the East Main and Rupert Rivers and ruined the ecology of some 176,000 square kilometers, an area about two-thirds the size of West Germany. The Native people of the area did not hear of the project until planning was well underway.

Following years of futile litigation, 400 kilometers of paved road, three power stations, and five reservoirs were built. Four major rivers were destroyed and five 735 KV power lines cut a swath through the wilderness. The environmental impact is enormous. Mercury levels at the reservoirs are six times safe levels, and some two-thirds of the people downstream from the reservoirs have mercury contamination in their bodies, some at thirty times the allowable level. Vast amounts of hunting and trapping territory have been devastated, causing economic and social dislocation from loss of food and cultural activities.

If the project continues, Phase Two will be even more devastating. The area to be impacted is the size of New England, or 356,000 square miles. These projects, according to Jan Bayea of the National Audubon Society will mean that ". . . in fifty years, this entire ecosystem will be lost."

TOXIC WASTE DUMPS

> When Waste Tech wanted to build an incinerator and dump on our land, they said they would give us thousands of dollars and a nice two-story house. But I thought about the land and how we rely on it—this dump would poison the water and the land. It's not just temporary, my children and grandchildren will have to live on this land forever. Don't listen to these thieves that want our land—we need to protect Mother Earth. . . .
>
> Jane Yazzie, one of the organizers of Citizens Against Ruining Our Environment, which helped defeat a toxic waste dump proposal at Dilcon on the Navajo reservation

Most insidious is the recent set of proposals to dispose of toxic wastes in Native communities. Largely a result of stiff and successful opposition in urban areas, toxic waste operators have increasingly looked to reservations and so-called third world countries as possible disposal sites. The "labor pool" and "underdeveloped economies" of many reservations provide an apparent mandate for development. Additionally, the sovereign status of Indian nations, exempt from state and local laws, in which there is minimal federal regulation of waste dumping, has provided an additional incentive.

In the past few years, over forty-five Indian communities have been approached by waste companies offering multi-million dollar contracts in exchange for the right to dump or incinerate on Indian lands. East of San Diego alone, over eighteen rancherias (small Indian communities) have been approached as possible dumping grounds for garbage and toxic wastes. One community that has already been impacted by a toxic waste dump is the Akwesasne Mohawk reservation.

AKWESASNE

The Akwesasne Mohawk reservation spans the United States/Canadian border, and is home to approximately 8,000 Mohawk people. Through the center of their territory is the St. Lawrence River, the waterway of their people. For generations, the Mohawk have relied upon the river for fish, food, and transportation. Today, the river is full of poison.

In Canada, the Akwesasne reserve has been singled out from sixty-three Native communities located in the Great Lakes basin as the most contaminated. On the American side in 1983, the Environmental Protection Agency designated the area as one of the top "Superfund sites" in the United States.

The General Motors Massena Central Foundry is possibly the most significant PCB dump site in North America. The chemical is known to cause brain, nerve, liver and skin disorders in humans and cancer and reproductive disorders in laboratory animals. Five PCB saturated lagoons, and a number of sludge pits dot GM's 258 acre property, a site adjacent to the reservation. Contaminant Cove, at the conflux of the Grasse and St. Lawrence Rivers, is perhaps the worst. According to the Environmental Protection Agency, fifty parts per million PCBs is classified as hazardous waste. Sludge and vegetation at the bottom of Contaminant Cove have been documented at 3,000 parts per million. A male snapping turtle was located with 3,067 parts per million of PCBs in its body.

At present, a project known as the Akwesasne Mothers Milk Project is undertaking a study of breastmilk, fetal cord, and urine samples of Mohawk mothers on the reservation. A total of 168 women are participating in the study. The primary organizer of the project, Katsi Cook Barreiro, is a practicing midwife who has delivered many children on the reservation. "I've got myself four one hundredths parts

per million of mirex (a flame retardant) and eighty-four one-thousandths parts per million PCBs in my body," she explains. "This means that there may be a potential exposure of our future generations. The analysis of Mohawk mother's milk shows that our bodies are, in fact, a part of the landfill."

NUCLEAR WASTE CONTAMINATION

The Hanford nuclear reservation is well within the treaty area of the Yakima Indian Nation on the Columbia River. The nuclear site contains 570 square miles of land, and a significant portion of it is contaminated with radiation. In August of 1973, over 115,000 gallons of liquid high-level radioactive waste seeped into the ground from a leaking storage tank. The waste contained cesium 137, strontium 90, and plutonium. Other leaks from August of 1958 to June two decades later included over 422,000 gallons reported on the site.

Soil at the site is so contaminated that much has been removed as high-level radioactive waste. The Department of Energy changed concentrations from ten nanocuries per gram of soil permitting a rise to 100 nanocuries per gram of soil allowing for plutonium contamination to rise indefinitely at the site by changing the definition of high-level waste.

Hanford produces a dry fallout of small respirable dust particles that are contaminated with plutonium. This airborne dust is released from smokestacks at the site, and is not contained by the site boundaries.

A significant portion of these wastes are contaminating the air and water in the region of the Hanford reservation, an area in which approximately twenty different Indigenous peoples live.

INUIT BREASTMILK

Studies of Inuit breastmilk in the Hudson Bay region of northern Canada indicate that Inuit women have levels of PCB contamination higher than those recorded anywhere else in the world. The maximum PCB concentration considered "safe" by the Canadian government is one and five tenths parts per million. A Laval University Study, conducted by Dr. Eric Dewailly, in 1988, discovered much higher levels in Inuit women. Dewailly's study of twenty-four samples (one third of all nursing mothers in that year), recorded an average concentration of three and fifty-nine hundredths parts per million of PCBs in breastmilk. Some samples were recorded at fourteen and seven tenths parts per million. The average concentration of PCBs in breastmilk in Quebec is five tenths parts per million.

According to an Inuit spokesperson, Mary Kaye May of the Kativik Regional Health Council, the findings brought "fear and great sadness" to the village. It is assumed that the higher levels are attributed to the Inuit diet of fish and marine mammals (at least nine meals per month) which are known to be concentrating PCBs in the food chain. The PCBs have appeared in the Arctic food chain in recent years, largely attributed to atmospheric distribution of heavy metals, and toxins from southern industries, and from abandoned military, radar, and communications installations utilizing PCBs.

While the toxic contamination of infants is of great concern to the Inuit, there are, for all major purposes, no alternatives. "If the women stop breast-feeding," Mary Kaye May continues, "and with the cost of baby formula at seventeen dollars a can, we will face a frightening number of cases of infant malnutrition."

Related contamination includes radioactive cesium, DDT, toxophene, and other pesticides. Many of them have been banned in North America, but are still used in many developing countries. Dr. Lyle Lockhart (Canadian government Fisheries and Oceans Department, Winnipeg, Manitoba) indicates that "toxins will distill off the warm land and plant surfaces in many of these countries and circulate in the air possibly for years, and gradually condense and accumulate in colder regions like the Arctic and Antarctic, which are becoming the world's dump for these things." As an example, toxophene, a pesticide most commonly used in cotton fields was discovered in a study by Lockhart to be located in the livers of two freshwater fish taken in the Mackenzie River of the Northwest Territories. The severity of the problem is indicated in another study of the polar bear which, because of its high level on the food chain, could be forced into extinction by the year 2006 due to sterility caused by PCB contamination.

ACID RAIN CONTAMINATION

The Anishinabeg treaty areas of northern Michigan, Wisconsin, and Minnesota are impacted by airborne contamination from acid rain at an alarming level. The traditional Anishinabeg diet consists, to a great extent of wild rice, fish, deer, waterfowl, fruits, and herbs. The major protein sources comprising the traditional diet are foods most impacted by acid rain.

Acid pollution is accumulating in the northern lakes, and during spring run-off causes toxic shock to the northern ecosystem, eliminating millions of fish eggs, young fry, molting crayfish, and other animals on the food chain. The secondary impact is the leaching of heavy metals, including mercury into the food system as a result of the acidification process. Presently a number of lakes in the northern area have fish consumption advisories due to mercury contamination. Since 1970, Minnesota has documented a five percent per year increase of mercury in fish tissue. This contamination is attributed to atmospheric deposits originating from coal fired power plants and garbage incinerators. At the present rate of increase, by the year 2015 mercury concentrations in fish tissue will be dangerously high.

MILITARY OCCUPATION

"The militarization, that's what you have to fight," explains Francesca Snow, an Innu woman who has been working actively to stop the siting of a NATO base in her homeland. "They will destroy the land. They will destroy the animals, and they will destroy our life." Father Alexis Jouveneau, a priest who has lived with the Innu for many years, issued a warning to the Canadian government about the NATO base, "You are destroying not only their lifestyle, you are destroying their whole life so that you may proceed with military exercises. At that point, you might as well build a psychiatric clinic right here, and it will soon be overfilled." "If the military goes ahead," says Innu elder Antoine Malec, "You will not see us cry. We will not cry, but our hearts will bleed. . . ."

THE WESTERN SHOSHONE NATION

All nuclear weapon states explode their bombs on unconsenting nations. No nuclear state tests bombs on its own lands and people. The United States doesn't set off nuclear weapons in Santa Barbara or Washington D.C. It bombs the Western Shoshone Nation.

Since 1963, the United States has exploded 651 nuclear weapons and "devices" on Newe Sogobia, the Western Shoshone nation. Because they cause destruction, the 670 nuclear explosions in Newe Sogobia have been classified by the Western Shoshone National Council as bombs rather than tests.

In 1863, the representatives of the United States and Western Shoshone nation signed the Treaty of

Ruby Valley. The United States proposed the treaty in order to end Shoshone armed defense of Sogobia, acquire gold from the territory, and establish safe routes to California. The United States Senate ratified the treaty in 1866 and President Grant confirmed it in 1869. The treaty is still in effect.

The nation of Newe Sogobia has an area of 43,000 square miles, about the size of Honduras, and is bounded by western Nevada, southern Idaho and southeastern California. To maintain control over the area, the United States has usurped almost ninety percent of Shoshone land and resources and placed them under the Departments of Interior, Energy, Defense, Transportation, and other agencies. The Western Shoshone, however continue their occupancy of their traditional lands. They have maintained this, and resisted government efforts to terminate their title through the Court of Claims, by continuing their opposition to a twenty-six million dollar proposal to "settle" their claims and compensate them for their land.

In a recent effort to secure occupancy of the land, the Bureau of Land Management has been attempting to remove the livestock of the Dann family, one of the leading families in challenging the occupation.

HAWAII

Hawaii was the last frontier in an era of United States expansion. It was designated as a state in 1959, eighteen years after Pearl Harbor. Over 180,000 Native Hawaiian people have traditional rights to most of the Islands, and today maintain a precarious land-based existence in the face of increasing tourism and military occupation.

Hawaii is the most militarized state in the country, serving as the center for the Pentagon's Pacific Command. It serves as the headquarters for military activities which purport to control more than half the earth's surface—from the west coast of North America to the east coast of Africa, from the Antarctic to the Arctic.

There are more than 100 military installations in the Hawaiian islands and fully ten percent of the state and twenty-five percent of Oahu are under direct federal control. Hawaii is the loading and reloading base for the Pacific fleet. In 1972, Oahu alone was the storage site for some 32,000 nuclear weapons. One island of the Hawaiian archipelago, Kaho'olawe was a bombing site for almost five decades for Pacific rim countries. . . .

NATIVE ENVIRONMENTAL HERO
JESUS LEON SANTOS

Rick Kearns

NOCHIXTLAN, Oaxaca - In one of the most barren regions in the world, an Indigenous farmer using ancient Mixteca traditions helped to conserve more than 4,000 acres of farmland, prevent massive soil erosion, increase local farm productivity, create more economic growth and, among other things, plant 2 million trees.

For these efforts and others, Jesus Leon Santos of Nochixtlan, Oaxaca, Mexico, was awarded the $150,000 Goldman Environmental Prize for sustainable development for 2008.

The prize, awarded each year in April, was started in 1990 by philanthropists Richard N. and Rhoda H. Goldman to annually honor grass-roots environmental heroes from Africa, Asia, Europe, islands and island nations, North America, and South and Central America. It recognizes individuals for

Rick Kearns, in *Indian Country Today*, July 30, 2008. Pages 1 and continued on 3.

sustained and significant efforts to protect and enhance the natural environment, often at great personal risk. Each winner receives an award of $150,000, the largest award in the world for grassroots environmentalists. Santos was this year's winner for North America.

"Jesus Leon Santos leads an unprecedented land renewal and economic development program that employs ancient Indigenous agricultural practices to transform this barren, highly eroded area into rich, arable land," according to the Goldman Award press statement. "With his organization, the Center for Integral Small Farmer Development in the Mixteca [CEDICAM], Leon has united the area's small farmers. Together, they have planted more than one million native-variety trees, built hundreds of miles of ditches to retain water and prevent soil eroding, and adapted traditional Mixteca Indigenous practices to restore the regional ecosystem."

In a series of presentations he has made in the U.S., Central America and the Caribbean since the award, Santos has recounted the circumstances leading to the environmental disaster of Mixteca—known as one of the most severely eroded areas on the planet, according to the United Nations—and how he and a group of Mixteca neighbors began the process that lead to this achievement.

"It was 25 years ago when we realized we were experiencing a severe ecological crisis that was causing poverty, malnutrition and migration," Santos recalled. "We regret that our ancestors left our lands so deteriorated. The Mixteca region was severely damaged by the exploitation of our natural resources that came with the colonizers."

According to natural history sources, Santos' home region looked very different before the Spaniards arrived.

The Mixteca Alta region of Oaxaca—named for one of the Indigenous peoples who live in that region—had originally been the home of oak forests and shrublands as well as large fields of corn, beans, squash, chiles, tomatoes, potatoes and various fruit trees. By the time Santos was born in 1966, much of the region had been damaged by huge goat farms, first introduced to the area by the Spanish colonizers, and, later, tequila processing plants, among other industries. This area, according to Santos, "was a desert, with no water, nor plants, nor trees, nor anything."

Further damage was done to the area by the adoption of modern farming procedures that required large amounts of chemical fertilizers. The growing of chemical-intensive varieties of corn in the 1980s depleted the soil even more and Mixteca farmers found their yields dropping as well. On top of these difficulties, the farmers suffered even more economic hardships as local maize prices fell as a result of the North American Free Trade Agreement. With cheaper corn coming from the north, their local prices were pushed down and the farmers could no longer afford the new fertilizer and pesticides that the new varieties demanded. The migration out of the area increased as well, along with the amount of land falling into disuse and more erosion. The loss of arable topsoil and other nutrients led, according to the Goldman press release, to erosion of about 83 percent of all the land in Mixteca, with 1.235 million acres considered severely eroded.

Meanwhile, government officials kept pushing the newer techniques. Santos however, knew enough to look back to his Mixteca ancestors for answers to questions about how to prevent the loss of soil and water, as well as how to detoxify the area and the diet of the community. He started with trees that have been grown in the area for centuries.

In the early 1980s, Santos and a group of local Mixtec farmers banded together to form CEDICAM, a democratic organization devoted to reforesting the area and stopping the erosion. They started with the planting of local varieties of trees, mainly the native ocote pines.

"The trees prevent erosion, aid water filtration into the ground, provide carbon capture and green areas, contribute organic material to the soil and provide more sustainable, cleaner-burning wood to residents who cook on open fires," stated the Goldman release.

As more farmers heard about their neighbor's successes with the trees, more orders came in and within a few years CEDICAM started a nursery. Not long afterwards, several community-run nurseries bloomed. A few decades later, by 2007, local farmers were planting up to 200,000 trees a year. CEDICAM is now also teaching communities more sustainable ways of using firewood and wood-saving stoves, helping to protect the local environment as well as reducing the workload of local women who had to travel some distance to collect firewood.

The tree plantings were part of the anti-erosion strategy, but Santos realized they needed to do more. He found ancient terraced agricultural systems in his area and saw another part of the answer. Santos and his allies helped communities rebuild these ancient terraces, which impede erosion and enhance production. Santos pioneered the building of contour ditches, retention walls and terraces to catch rainfall and prevent erosion.

Along with native trees and traditional farming methods, Santos has reintroduced local seed varieties and natural compost fertilizers to his neighbors. He is also involved in promoting local foods and a traditional Indigenous diet.

In a brief phone interview with Indian Country Today, Santos said that with the Goldman Prize money CEDICAM will expand its tree-growing and rainwater retention programs for the 400 families now collaborating with his organization. Santos also explained that CEDICAM had just built a community school to help disseminate the information it has been gathering and will continue with its education outreach to many different regions in Mexico. He also noted that while the Mexican government has not provided any assistance to their projects, now it is sending experts to their region to look at what they are doing. At the end of the phone conversation, Santos wanted to send the following message to ICT's many American Indian readers.

"It gives me great pleasure to talk to you," he said. "The Indigenous people have so much to share with this planet. We are an important part of this earth. We have been the guardians, and it is an important role with which we must continue. . . . We cannot let this responsibility fall into other hands. We must not let the corporations take these resources because this is the legacy for all people, not just a few."

ALASKA NATIVES STRUGGLE FOR SUBSISTENCE RIGHTS

Steve Talbot

Everybody is subsistence here in the village.

Vincent Kvasnikoff, English Bay, Alaska

The 1968 oil discovery and development in Alaska and the passage of the 1971 Alaska Native Claims Settlement Act (ANCSA) brought into focus the immense give-away of Native lands and a corporate model of land ownership imposed on Alaska Native communities by the U.S. Congress. These developments had unforeseen implications for the Alaska Native subsistence rights.

Subsistence in the Indigenous world means more than the minimum necessity to support life. It means living close to nature, growing or gathering one's food, or hunting and fishing, with little reliance on a cash economy. Of course, a Native person must own or have legal access to the land and waters on which subsistence activities take place. But under ANCSA, Alaska Natives ceded title to most of Alaska's 365 million acres, receiving rights to only 44 million acres of land and a money settlement.

Extracting a living from the Arctic and sub-arctic environments in Alaska has always been difficult, but with the colonization of Alaska, and especially the recent penetration by mining, oil, lumber, and land development interests, the ecological balance has become threatened with dire consequences for the Native way of life. Alaska Natives rely on hunting, fishing, and gathering as essential means of subsistence. Since the oil discovery, the traditional land base needed for subsistence activities has been seriously curtailed, and subsistence has been regulated by the state of Alaska without distinction between Native, commercial, and non-Native interests.

Natives who follow a subsistence economy have a very different view of the natural world than do non-Native rural Alaskans:

Alaska Native peoples have traditionally tried to live in harmony with the world around them. This has required the construction of an intricate subsistence-based worldview, a complex way of life with specific cultural mandates regarding the ways in which the human being is to relate to other human relatives and the natural and spiritual worlds. . . . Native peoples developed many rituals and ceremonies with respect to motherhood and child rearing, care of animals, hunting and trapping practices, and related ceremonies for maintaining balance between the human, natural, and spiritual realms (Kawagley 1995: 8).

There are a number of biotic zones in Alaska in terms of its fauna and flora, landscape, and weather. The state has a rich and varied ecology, and the different economic adaptations and subsistence patterns found among its Native peoples correspond to these biotic zones.

THE INDIGENOUS PEOPLES OF ALASKA

The 2000 U.S. Census found 87,205 persons identifying as "Alaska Native only," with a total of 112,942 claiming Alaska Native "and one or more other races." The four "populations" enumerated by the Census were Eskimo, Aleut, Athabascan, Tlingit, and Haida. Within these broad categories there are distinct Indigenous peoples, each living within its own ecological niche and facing serious subsistence issues.

Eskimos

The Eskimo group is the largest, with 45,919 "Eskimo only" and 54,761 claiming Eskimo and one or more other races. The "Eskimo" category actually includes four ethnically related peoples who are distinguished by differences in homeland, language or dialect, traditions, and identity.

The Iñupiat Eskimos inhabit northern and northwest Alaska. The region consists of low-lying coastal tundra, with many streams, rivers, and lakes. Inland, the plain and foothills contain herds of migratory caribou, and the mountains beyond the foothills are home to bears and Dall sheep. The coastal waters are rich in marine life, especially the Bowhead and Beluga whales on which the people have depended for survival for the bulk of their subsistence diet for at least 2,000 years.

A second great Eskimo people are the Yup'ik of southwestern Alaska, whose land extends from Prince William Sound on the Pacific coast to both sides of the Bering Strait, and 6,000 miles east along Canada's Arctic coast into Labrador and Greenland. Nearly 20,000 Yup'ik live in western Alaska, among seventy small communities along the coast and three mighty river systems, the Yukon, Kuskokwim, and Nushagak. The sub-arctic tundra environment along the coast includes seals, walrus, beluga whales, oceangoing and freshwater fish, migratory birds, small animals, berries, and greens. Upriver, the Yup'ik hunt larger animals, including moose, caribou, and bear.

A third Eskimo people are the Siberian Yup'ik, whose traditional lands include Saint Lawrence Island (part of Alaska) and the Russian coast across the Bering Strait.

A fourth group are the Alutiiq, or Pacific, Eskimos. The Alutiiq include several culturally and linguistically related peoples who have inhabited the Alaska Peninsula, Prince William Sound, the lower Kenai Peninsula, and Kodiak Island for at least 7,000 years. The current population of about 5,000 live in scattered villages and towns and are also found in the larger cities of Alaska and other states. They retain a strong Russian influence as a result of Alaska's colonial history in language, religion, and culture. In 1964 a severe Alaska earthquake devastated several of their villages.

Aleuts

The Unangan, or Aleuts, of southwestern Alaska occupy a long and narrow land base, the Aleutian Shumagin and Pribilof Islands, reaching from the Alaskan mainland westward toward the International Date Line. Following the Japanese attack on the Aleutian Islands during World War II, the U.S. government relocated the Unangan islanders to "protect" them from invasion. They were interned in southeast Alaska, most in abandoned canneries without heat, with little food and scant medical care. Disease brought on by unsanitary conditions took many lives, especially among elders and children. After the war, the Unanagan were allowed to go home but found their villages destroyed and their churches and homes ransacked by the U.S. military. Today they strive to maintain their Native island communities, which are threatened by flooding due to global warming.

Indians

Indians is another broad category used to identify the Indigenous peoples of interior and southeastern Alaska, who are different in both physical appearance and culture from Eskimos and Aleuts. They include the many Athapascan-speaking communities of interior Alaska, and the Tlingit, Haida, and other Indians who live in the "panhandle" of southeastern Alaska.

The territory of the Athabascans includes Cook Inlet, Kenai Peninsula, Prince William Sound, and the temperate Matanuska Valley. Their traditional homeland also incorporates the broad plateau of rolling hills and watery tundra located between the Alaska Range north of Anchorage and the Brooks Range above the Arctic Circle. In former times, winters were spent in semi-subterranean homes in small villages along the Yukon and the upper Kuskokwim rivers and their tributaries. During the summer, families moved to fish camps, principally taking varieties of salmon that were dried for preservation, with a sufficient amount stored for winter. Other foods included moose, caribou, black and brown bear, beaver, porcupine, many kinds of fowl, fish and sea mammals, and roots, berries, and other plants. Many contemporary Athabascans follow a modified traditional way of life and rely on these foods to supplement their modern diets, although the rapid growth of the non-Native population in the Greater Anchorage and Kenai Peninsula regions have decreased the plant, fish, and animal habitat. In 1989 the *Exxon Valdez* ran aground in Prince William Sound and spilled nearly 11 million gallons of crude oil, resulting in a tremendous loss of sea life, on which the village people depend for their maritime livelihood and subsistence economy.

Southeastern Alaska is a region of high, rugged mountains, a rainforest terrain, and many large glaciers. The major Indian populations here are the Tlingit and Haida.

Before contact, the Tlingit occupied nearly all of what is today southeastern Alaska, portions of northern British Columbia, and part of the Yukon Territory of Canada. During the summer they lived in temporary wooden houses, and in winter they lived in huge cedar structures, housing up to 50 people of a clan. The staple food was fish, especially salmon, and fishing remains an important subsistence and commercial enterprise today. Approximately 20,000 today consider themselves Tlingit, although at least half of this number reside in the states of Washington and Oregon. The Tlingit are among the most acculturated of Alaska Native peoples, yet they remain proud of their cultural heritage.

The Haida came to Alaska from the Queen Charlotte Islands in Canada. They were under the care of the Presbyterian Church and settled principally at Hydaburg, with the cooperation of the U.S. Bureau of Indian Affairs. Their aboriginal economy was based on fishing, hunting, clamming, and gathering wild berries and dulse. These food-gathering activities continue to reaffirm Haida cultural identity.

Threat to Subsistence

The history of subsistence rights in Alaska is complex. The state is unique for giving subsistence priority in its wildlife management to *rural citizens*, whether Native or non-Native, although the subsistence needs of the two populations are very different:

> The Alaska Statehood Act [of 1959] required that as a condition of entering the federal union, Alaska must disclaim all right and title to any lands or other property (including fishing rights) of Alaska Natives. The State of Alaska ignored this provision . . . and began to enforce its fish and game management laws on all Alaskans, without recognizing any pre-existing rights of Alaska Natives" (Native American Rights Fund 1999: 1).

Then, in 1971, the Alaska Native Claims Settlement Act (ANCSA) officially abolished Indigenous hunting and fishing rights, even though the final House–Senate Conference Committee Report that accompanied ANCSA explained clearly that Congress expected that both the secretary of the interior and the secretary of state "take any action necessary to protect the subsistence needs of the Alaska Natives." In anticipation of federal legislation, the state passed a rural subsistence priority law in 1978, giving priority to "subsistence users," but failed to define *users*. Two years later, in part because the state of Alaska and the secretary of the interior had failed to protect Native subsistence after ANCSA, Congress passed the Alaska National Interest Lands Conservation Act (ANILCA).

Its Title VIII became the federal counterpart to the Alaska subsistence law, as applied to federal lands in Alaska, primarily national parks and wildlife refuges.

Title VIII of ANILCA required that subsistence uses by "rural Alaska residents" be given priority over all other uses of fish and game on federal public lands in Alaska, including sport and commercial. As a compromise, Congress allowed the state to continue managing fish and game uses on federal public lands, but only on the condition that the state legislature adopt a statute making the new Title VIII "rural" subsistence priority applicable on state as well as federal lands. And if the state ever fell out of compliance with Title VIII, Congress required the secretary of the interior to reassume management of fish and game on the federal public lands in Alaska. Congress did not enact "a racial preference" specifying Alaska Native subsistence rights in part because of the state's opposition to doing so. It was assumed that "rural" would work and that Alaska Natives would have to compromise in order to get a preference that the state was willing to enforce.

In 1982 the Alaska Boards of Fisheries and Game adopted the rural residency standard by regulation. Two years later, Athabascan elder Katie John sued in federal court, claiming that the federal government had failed to protect her right to subsistence fishing, as guaranteed under ANILCA. In response, in 1986, the Alaska state legislature amended its subsistence statute to limit the definition of *subsistence uses* to residents of "rural areas," thereby complying with Title VIII. But this statute was reversed in 1989, when the Alaska supreme court struck down the legislature's definition of *subsistence users* because the rural preference clause conflicted with the state constitution. The court ruled that the definition of *rural* in the state subsistence law was out of compliance with ANILCA because the natural bounty of wildlife was for the "common use" of all Alaskans. In 1990, because the state was no longer in compliance with Title VIII, the federal government took over subsistence management of game and the gathering of plant resources on federal areas. Fisheries management remained with the state due to the pending Katie John lawsuit.

The complexity of Alaska's fish and game regulations at this time is illustrated by the fact that four different user groups competed for the salmon runs in south-central Alaska's Copper River: commercial, personal, sport, and subsistence. A reporter for the *New York Times* compared the subsistence debate to affirmative action, "creating similar racial tensions.

The Natives say the issue is their civil rights, while the sportsmen say the Natives are demanding 'special rights' and unfair quotas" (Verhovek 1999: A13). Tlingit leader Rosita Worl summarized the subsistence status of Alaska Natives in the1990s as follows:

> Native subsistence protection had been diminished to rural geographical regions, excluded Native communities engulfed by urban development, and included non-Native rural residents. . . . Subsistence is more than an issue of allocating fish and wildlife resources. Subsistence represents the economic wellbeing of communities which have a minimal cash economy, it embodies their cultural values which recognizes a special and spiritual relationship to their land and animals and unifies them as tribal groups through hunting, gathering, distributing, and sharing their harvests (Worl 1998: 77–78).

Alaska Natives have given overwhelming support for an amendment to ANILCA that would clearly recognize a Native subsistence priority. In 1997, when the governor of Alaska appointed a seven-member Subsistence Task Force that excluded Alaska Natives, 900 Native representatives gathered in Anchorage in a Subsistence Summit. The summit adopted guiding principles and made a dozen policy recommendations. The Native representatives sent a delegation to Washington, D.C., with the summit's recommendations, but their voices were ignored.

The main thrust of ANILCA was to set aside national parks, including the Arctic National Wildlife Refuge (ANWR). The pressure by the energy monopolies and conservative politicians to open ANWR to drilling has become a recurrent issue that not only endangers the pristine tundra environment but also threatens the political unity of Alaska Natives. The Alaska Federation of Natives (AFN) has been at odds with many of the tribal governments with respect to drilling in ANWR, the "Sacred Place Where Life Begins," as the Gwich'in Indians call it. The AFN, with its 207 corporations, passed a resolution in support of drilling for gas and oil, while the Gwich'in and a growing number of Alaska tribal governments, including the Tanana Chiefs Conference, are opposed. Grassroots Natives charge that the Alaska Federation of Natives is run mostly by urban executives who are too reflective of corporate interests.

The Gwich'in are a hunting people, and the 130,000-head Porcupine River caribou herd travels hundreds of miles each year to calve in Gwich'in territory, on the Arctic Refuge coastal plain. Grizzly bears, musk oxen, wolves, golden eagles, and tundra swans all call this unique place home for at least part of the year. A Gwich'in Native from Fort Yukon told an interviewer: "I don't think the word 'subsistence' exists out here. . . . In my language, the closest thing I can come to what you are talking about is—we would say *Tee terra 'in*. It means . . . people working together and sharing to accomplish something, to accomplish common goals" (Anderson 1998: 40–41).

Global Warming and Environmental Pollution

The survival agenda for Alaska Natives not only includes traditional subsistence rights but it also encompasses reversing "rapid global warming, stratospheric ozone depletion, and levels of chemical pollution so noxious that mothers have been warned to avoid breast-feeding their babies" (Johansen 2007: 269).

Climate change has been rapid in the Arctic, detectable within a single human lifetime. It has resulted in the widespread melting of glaciers and sea ice that can mean a serious loss of Native subsistence food. Erosion and flooding affect many Alaska Native villages to some degree. "Six hundred people living in the Alaska Eskimo village of Shishmaref . . . in the far western reaches of Alaska, have been watching their village erode into the sea. . . . In Kotzebue, Alaska, the town hospital was relocated because it was sinking into the ground" (Johansen 2007: 283–284).

Approximately 200 toxic pesticides and industrial chemicals have been found in the bodies of people and animals living in the Arctic. These include mercury, which is released by coal-burning power plants and chemical factories in the temperate zone, but which has migrated northward. The Environmental Programme's Governing Council of the United Nations has officially recognized the arctic as a barometer of the earth's environmental health. "To environmental toxicologists, the Arctic by the 1990s was becoming known as the final destination for a number of manufactured poisons, including, most notably, dioxins and polychlorinated biphenyls (PCBs), which accumulate in the body fat of large aquatic and land mammals (including human beings), sometimes reaching levels that imperil their survival" (Johansen 2007: 272). To compound the problem, the cold temperatures of the arctic slow the natural decomposition of these toxic chemicals. The fear of toxic contamination has led Iñupiat hunters to closely inspect their game animals in the butchering process. Some Alaska Natives are avoiding traditional foods altogether, out of fear that fish and wild game contain pesticides, heavy metals, and other toxins. A study by the University of Alaska, Anchorage, found that pregnant women who eat traditional foods may be exposing their fetuses to dangerous pollutants.

THE STRUGGLE CONTINUES

Alaska Natives do not have the legal protection of hunting and fishing rights that Indian nations of the contiguous states have held under the treaty relationship. When Alaska became a state in 1959, a new fish and game department began enforcing fishing and hunting regulations on White sportsmen and Natives alike on a "first come, first served" basis. The situation came to a head when the oil pipeline boom of the late 1970s created an urban, non-Native population explosion. During the construction of the pipeline, Native communities and their institutions made enormous right-of-way concessions in exchange for promises of Native employment and subsistence protections, neither of which came to fruition. When the Alaska Native Claims Settlement Act was passed by Congress in 1971, Section 4(b) specifically extinguished aboriginal hunting and fishing rights in Alaska:

> Throughout the five-year process of enacting ANCSA, the primary focus was on land ownership, but the issue of subsistence also pervaded the process. Congressional findings in the final Senate bill emphasized protection of "Native subsistence hunting, fishing, trapping, and gathering rights." If enacted, it would have required the Secretary of the Interior to designate public lands around Native villages as "subsistence use areas" . . . and, under certain circumstances, to close them to non-subsistence uses. But both provisions were dropped by the conference committee because the Congress, the oil companies, and the State of Alaska didn't want to delay the land settlement (i.e., the pipeline) in order to deal with subsistence (Alaska Federation of Natives 1998: 1).

The state's fishing and hunting regulations created conditions of hardship for Native subsistence hunters, particularly for Natives living in interior areas of Alaska, where sources of animal protein other than caribou are not available. When a state study found a diminishing of the caribou herd in northern Alaska and attempted to curtail the number hunted, this led to a "caribou crisis" for the Iñupiat Eskimos of the North Slope Borough. The Borough then made its own study and found that the herd was near its normal size.

The North Slope Borough comprises eight small Iñupiat communities in a region of 89,000 square miles, stretching northward from the foothills of the Brooks Range to the Arctic Ocean. The people follow a traditional lifestyle that is heavily dependent on the subsistence harvesting of marine and land mammals, fish, and migratory birds. Caribou are considered their single most important terrestrial subsistence resource. The annual cycle of subsistence activities is a core value of Iñupiat culture. Subsistence hunting puts food on the table in a region where the cost of living is extremely high. In 1998, bread cost up to $6 per loaf, a gallon of milk up to $14, and gasoline as much as $4.50 a gallon. A crisis occurred in 1977 when the International Whaling Commission (IWC) proposed a moratorium on the hunting of bowhead whales. The whale ban deeply affected Iñupiat social and ceremonial life, and it deprived the people of an important food source. The borough swung into action. Supported by the Arctic Slope Regional Corporation, it organized a new Alaska Eskimo Whaling Commission, which questioned the IWC research:

> At a special December meeting of the IWC in Tokyo, attended by a delegation of Iñupiat whalers and state officials, the U. S. succeeded in persuading the IWC to lift the moratorium in exchange for a subsistence quota of twelve whales taken (or eighteen whales struck) for Alaska Eskimos" (McBeath and Morehouse 1980: 90).

The Iñupiat look forward to spring, when the first migratory waterfowl arrive. This is the time when waterfowl are historically hunted in the Delta, but such hunting has been illegal since 1918, under the Migratory Bird Treaty, and swan hunting is illegal in any season in the Delta. In 1961 there was the incident of the "Barrow Duck-In":

> When several Native men including a state legislator were arrested for spring bird hunting, 300 Iñupiat (138 of them holding dead eider ducks which they claimed to have taken illegally), gathered in the community hall. Faced with arresting much of the community, enforcement agents backed down" (Morrow and Hensel 1992: 44).

Approximately 15,000 Yup'ik live in some 50 villages in the Yukon–Kuskokwim Delta of Southwest Alaska. Subsistence hunting, fishing, and gathering is an essential part of local diet and identity. "Subsistence harvests in the Delta are among the highest in the state, in some villages reaching an annual per capita of up to 1100 pounds . . . the generic word for food and for fish is the same" (Morrow and Hensel 1992: 39). Seals, walrus, and beluga whales are also hunted avidly, and sea mammal products are widely shared and traded. Large and small land animals are hunted; berries and both edible and medicinal herbs are gathered. Preserved food stocks see the population through the winter, but by spring they begin to run low, and people hunger for the plentiful waterfowl that come to nest in the watery delta.

There have been other conflicts between Alaska Natives and the state of Alaska involving subsistence practices and Alaska's fish and game regulations. An underlying factor in some of these controversies is the shrinking Native land base. The land allocated to the Native corporations under ANCSA, especially for the villages, is inadequate to sustain subsistence activities on which most village Alaska Natives continue to depend. "Although, as property owners, Natives have the exclusive right to wildlife on their own land, they have no rights as Natives for hunting, trapping, or fishing reserved for them over the ninety percent of Alaska in which their rights were extinguished" (Berger 1985: 92).

In 1984, Katie John and Doris Charles, two Athabascan elders, asked the Alaska State Board of Fisheries to open Batzulnetas, a historic upper Ahtna village and fish camp, to subsistence fishing. Their request was denied, despite the fact that downstream, users were permitted to take hundreds of thousands of salmon for sport and commercial uses. Attorneys for the petitioners from the Native American Rights Fund "filed suit against the State in late 1985 pursuant to Title VIII of ANILCA to compel the State to re-open the historic Batzulnetas fishery" (NARF 2001a: 6). A year later, the state added rural preference to its fish and game statute. However, in 1989, the Alaska supreme court ruled against the state law that limits subsistence uses to Alaska's "rural residents" as violating the "equal access" provisions of the state constitution. Consequently, in 1990, the federal government assumed responsibility for subsistence management of fish and wildlife on federal public lands in Alaska. "A dual management structure commenced with the federal government regulating subsistence on federal lands (60 percent of the state) and the state retaining authority over state (30 percent) and private (10 percent) lands" (Thornton 1998: 30).

Federal authority was later extended to certain navigable waters in Alaska, following the 1995 federal court ruling in *Katie John et al. v. United States of America*. Public lands in Alaska include navigable waters on or adjacent to federal conservation units. The 1995 decision found that Katie John and the other plaintiffs had been illegally denied their right to subsistence fishing by the state of Alaska and the federal government. In 2001 the Ninth U.S. Circuit

Court of Appeals upheld the lower court's decision, ruling that "the federal government has the obligation to provide subsistence fishing priority on all navigable waters in Alaska in which the United States has a federally reserved water right" (NARF 2001b: 2). Following the court's ruling, "with strong pressure from Alaska tribes, the governor of Alaska decided not to seek review of the decision in the U.S. Supreme Court and ended the state's opposition to Native subsistence fishing in navigable waters (NARF 2001a: 5).

On August 27, 2001, Alaska Governor Tony Knowles informed Katie John, the subsistence plaintiff, of the good news. Katie John was an 86-year-old Athabascan Indian. She is the mother of 14 children and adopted children, and she has 150 grandchildren, great-grandchildren, and great-great grandchildren. A few weeks before making his decision, the governor met personally with Katie John at her village home of Mentasta, located at the headwaters of the Copper River in south-central Alaska. He said "I learned more that day than is written in all the boxes of legal briefs in this long lasting court battle. I understand the strength, care and values that subsistence gives to Katie John's family, and to the thousands of similar families from Metlakatla to Bethel, to Norvik to Ft. Yukon to Barrow" (NARF 2001b: 1).

Rural Alaskans, who comprise about 20 percent of the state's residents and 49 percent of the Native population, annually harvest an estimated 43.7 million pounds of usable wild foods, or about 375 pounds per capita. In comparison, urban Alaskans consume only about 22 pounds of wild food per capita. "Although subsistence hunting and fishing accounts for only about 2 percent of the total harvest of fish and wildlife in Alaska (compared to 97 percent for commercial fisheries and 1 percent for recreational hunters and fishers), this harvest provides a significant proportion of the protein consumed in many rural communities" (quoted in Haynes 2003: 280–281).

On April 17, 2002, Rosita Worl (Tlingit) of the Sealaska Heritage Institute testified at a U.S. congressional hearing in support of Alaska Native subsistence hunting and fishing rights. The federal protections under the Alaska National Interest Lands Conservation Act of 1980 must be maintained, she said. "ANILCA has offered the only measure of protection for subsistence against the State of Alaska, which has refused to recognize a rural subsistence hunting and fishing priority" (Worl 2002: 10).

She explained that sharing is a key value of subsistence and the survival of Alaska Native communities. Not only does sharing ensure the survival of the entire community, but it also acknowledges the status of elders by giving them "special shares and parts of an animal." ". . . Sharing with elders functions in many ways like the social security system in which individuals receive retirement benefits. Single women who act as head of households, also receive special shares" (Worl 2002: 4).

In 2006 the AFN set forth its federal priorities. Regarding subsistence rights for Alaska Natives, the AFN candidly stated:

> Today, the only significant protection for our way of life is Title VIII of the Alaska National Interest Lands Conservation Act (ANILCA), which provides a priority for "subsistence" over sport and commercial uses of fish and game to residents of rural Alaska" [but that] "powerful anti-subsistence forces at work in Alaska seek to weaken or even repeal this law" (AFN 2006: 1).

REFERENCES CITED

AFN (Alaska Federation of Natives) 1998 "Subsistence Chronology, A Short History of Subsistence Policy in Alaska Since Statehood," revised edition.

Anderson, David B. 1998 "A View from the Yukon Flats," *Cultural Survival Quarterly*, 22, 3 (Fall): 40–43.

Berger, Thomas R. 1985 *Village Journey: The Report of the Alaska Native Review Commission.* New York: Hill and Wang.

Haynes, Terry L. 2003 "Ethical Issues and Subsistence in Alaska," *Kroeber Anthropological Society Papers*, No. 89/90L: 273–286.

Johansen, Bruce E. 2007 Chapter 6, "The New Inuit," Vol. II, *The Praeger Handbook on Contemporary Issues in Native America.* Westport, Conn.: Praeger.

Kawagley, A. Oscar 1995 A Yupiaq Worldview: A Pathway to Ecology and Spirit. Prospect Heights, Ill.: Waveland Press.

McBeath, Gerald A., and Thomas A. Morehouse 1980 *The Dynamics of Alaska Native Self-government.* University Press of America.

Morrow, Phyllis, and Chase Hensel 1992 "Hidden Dissension: Minority–Majority Relationships and the Use of Contested Terminology," *Arctic Anthropology*, 29, no. 1: 38–53.

NARF (Native American Rights Fund) 1999 "Alaska Native Subsistence," *Justice Newsletter*, pp. 1–6.

www.narf.org/pubs/justice/1999spring.html 2001a "Executive Director's Message," *Native American Rights Fund Annual Report.*

2001b "Katie John Prevails in Subsistence Fight," *NARF Legal Review*, 26, no. 2: 1–6.

Thornton, Thomas F. 1998 "Alaska Native Subsistence: A Matter of Cultural Survival," *Cultural Survival Quarterly*, 22, no. 3 (Fall 1998): 29–34.

Verhovek, Sam Howe 1999 "Alaska Torn Over Rights to Live Off the Land," *New York Times*, July 12: A1, A13–A15.

Worl, Rosita 1998 "Competition, Confrontation, and Compromise: The Politics of Fish and Game Allocations, *Cultural Survival Quarterly*, 22, no. 3 (Fall 1998)3: 77–78.

2002 "Alaska Native Subsistence: Cultures and Economy." Testimony presented to the U.S. Senate Committee on Indian Affairs, Oversight Hearing on Subsistence Hunting and Fishing in the State of Alaska. Washington, D.C., April 17.

THE COBELL LAWSUIT

The U.S. government owes Indians billions of dollars for mismanagement of individual money accounts and tribal trust funds.

In 1996, Elouise Cobell, a Blackfeet Indian and a banker by profession, initiated a class action suit regarding the U.S. government's management of the Individual Indian Monies (IIM) trust account. Cobell became the lead plaintiff for more than 500,000 individual Indian landowners. Since then, *Cobell, et al. v. Kempthorne, et al.* (formerly *Cobell v. Norton)* has grown to become the largest class action lawsuit ever filed against the U.S. federal government. The Indian plaintiffs contend that for more than a century the government sold land held in trust without the Indian owners' consent, without appraisal, and without informing the trust

beneficiaries. It is estimated that the government's liability might reach $40 billion.

The lack of accurate government accounting began with the passage of the 1887 Allotment Act, the absence of an adequate banking system, and sloppy bookkeeping by the Department of the Interior. Unlike banks, the Department of the Interior has no standards or outside oversight; from 1887 on, it has made a hash of Indian fund accounting. "In an average year, $500 million or more was deposited into the Individual Indian Trust accounts from companies leasing Native American land for grazing, oil drilling, timber, coal, and other natural resources" (Johansen 2004: 31). The money collected by the Department of the Interior was supposed to have been sent to the Treasury and placed into the individual

Indian trust accounts. Over the years, however, financial records became garbled, incomplete, or lost. When the extent of mismanagement became obvious, Congress passed the 1994 Trust Reform Act, but the problems did not go away. As recently as 1999, during the course of the litigation, it was discovered that the Departments of the Interior and the Treasury had "inadvertently" destroyed 162 boxes of vital trust records during the course of the trial. "In 2002, the Department had lost track of 22 percent of the IIM account holders" (FCNL 2005: 2).

> In this case the government has not only set the gold standard for mismanagement, it is on the verge of setting the gold standard for arrogance in litigation strategy and tactics.

> Judge Royce C. Lamberth, U.S. District Court for the District of Columbia, February 23, 2005

The U.S. government has been stonewalling a settlement of the lawsuit for a decade. Finally, in March 2007, not wanting the issue to go to court, the government offered to pay $7 billion partly to settle the Cobell lawsuit. That offer was rejected by the plaintiffs, who estimate that the government's liability could exceed $100 billion. A possible breakthrough was reached on January 30, 2008, however, when a federal judge ruled that the Department of the Interior had "unreasonably delayed" its accounting for billions of dollars owed to the individual Indian landholders and that the Department had failed in its accounting responsibilities. Cobell issued a statement, saying "This is a great day for Indian country. . . . We've argued for over 10 years that the government is unable to fulfill its duty to render an adequate historical accounting,

much less redress the historical wrongs heaped upon the individual Indian trust beneficiaries" (Indian Country Today, Feb. 2, 2008).

The Cobell lawsuit involving Indian individuals is only the tip of the iceberg. The mismanagement by the federal government of *tribal* trust fund accounts exceeds that of individual Indian trust funds. U.S. Attorney General Alberto Gonzales has estimated the amount of money involved at $200 billion. "The trusteeship is deeply rooted in treaties, laws and agreements. . . . Tribal trust funds are solely monies of tribes; they are not taxpayer dollars and they are not federal program funding. . . . As a result, the federal government today purports to hold about $3 billion in approximately 1,450 trust fund accounts for over 250 tribes" (NARF 2007: 2). On December 28, 2006, attorneys from the Native American Rights Fund filed a class action lawsuit, *Nez Perce Tribe, et al. v Kempthorne, et al.*, on behalf of potentially more than 225 tribes, "seeking full and complete accountings from the federal government for hundreds of tribal trust fund accounts worth billions of dollars" (NARF 2007: 1).

References
Friends Committee on National Legislation (FCNL) 2005 *Indian Report*, I-75, Second Quarter: pp. 1–5.
Indian Country Today 2008 "Federal Judge Rules United States Botched Trust Accounting," *Indian Country Today*, 27, no. 35 (February 6, 2008).
Johansen, Bruce E. 2004 "The Trust Fund Mess: Where Has All the Money Gone?," *Native Americas*, Fall/Winter 2004: 26, 28–33.
Native American Rights Fund 2007 "Leave No Tribe Behind," *NARF Legal Review*, 32, no. 1 (Winter/Spring 2007): 1–6.

PART REVIEW

DISCUSSION QUESTIONS

Simon J. Ortiz, It Was That Indian
1. The poet is speaking satirically in this poem. What is the underlying message?

Stephen Cornell, Remaking the Tools of Governance: Colonial Legacies, Indigenous Solutions
1. What does Cornell refer to when he speaks of the "colonial legacy"? Discuss in what ways this legacy has curtailed traditional Native economic practices. Give examples.
2. Give examples of three contemporary Native strategies for creating and strengthening governance and tribal economy.

First Nations Development Institute
1. How are Indian people reasserting control of their assets, and how is the nonprofit sector assisting in this?

The Chickasaw Nation: An Example Of Nation Building
1. Locate the Chickasaw Nation on a map, review the website www.chickasaw.net/, and then discuss the

Chickasaw strategy for economic development as a part of nation building.

Sia Davis and Jane Feustel, Indian Gaming in the States
1. What is the link between gaming and broader economic development for Native nations?
2. What are some of the common myths and misunderstandings regarding Indian gaming?
3. What are the benefits of gaming to the Indian community? Give examples. What are some of the problems that have been generated as a result of gaming? Give examples.

Victoria Bomberry, ¡Evo Presidente!
1. What makes the presidency of Evo Morales in Bolivia so extraordinary, and what message does it send to Native peoples throughout the Western Hemisphere?

Haunani-Kay Trask, Lovely Hula Hands: Corporate Tourism and the Prostitution of Hawaiian Culture
1. Discuss the impact of tourism on Native Hawaiian employment opportunities, housing, cost of living, and the environment.

2. How has "cultural prostitution" harmed the Native Hawaiian people in four important areas of traditional Hawaiian culture?

Winona LaDuke, Indigenous Environmental Perspectives: A North American Primer
1. What is the relationship between colonialism and Indigenous underdevelopment?
2. What have been the environmental consequences of uranium mining for Native peoples of the United States and Canada?
3. What other environmental problems does the author document in terms of the impact of resource expropriation on North American Indian lands?

Rick Kearns, Native Environmental Hero: Jesus Leon Santos
1. Locate the Mixteca territory on a map and describe this environmental zone.

2. What actions taken by the Spanish colonization and later large-scale farming enterprises led to the depletion of the land and the poverty of the Mixteca people?

Steve Talbot, Alaska Natives Struggle for Subsistence Rights
1. What have been the effects of the Alaska Native Claims Settlement Act (ANCSA) on the lives of Alaska Natives?
2. What is the relationship between ANCSA and the petroleum industry?
3. Give three specific examples of the ways in which Alaska Native subsistence rights, and therefore ways of life, are being threatened. What actions are Alaska Natives taking to confront these threats.

The Cobell Lawsuit
1. Who is Elouise Cobell, and why do many Indian people consider her a heroine?
2. Why are Indian people suing the U.S. government? What is the legal basis for the Cobell lawsuit?

KEY TERMS

Alaska Native Claims Settlement Act (ANCSA) of 1971
aloha
Aymara
bingo and casinos
Chickasaw
Class III Gaming
cultural prostitution
economic development
environmental degradation
Evo Morales

Indian Gaming Regulatory Act
Mixteca
Native American Rights Fund (NARF)
Native nation building
Quechua
Seven generations
sovereignty
subsistence rights
sustainable development

SUGGESTED READINGS

ANDERSON, TERRY L. *Sovereign Nations or Reservations: An Economic History of American Indians.* San Francisco: Pacific Research Institute for Public Policy, 1995.

BROWN, DENISE FAYE. "Mayas and Tourists in the Maya World," *Human Organization*, 58, no. 3 (1999): 29–35.

"Casino City's Indian Gaming Industry Report 2008–2009."

COHEN, FELIX S., HAROLD LECLAIR ICKES, and NATHAN R. MARGOLD. *Handbook of Federal Indian Law with Reference Tables and Index.* Buffalo, New York: William S. Hein & Co. 1988.

CANBY, WILLIAM C. *American Indian Law in a Nutshell*, 4th ed. St. Paul, Thomson West, 2004.

DELORIA, VINE, JR. *American Indians, American Justice.* Austin: University of Texas Press, 1983.

Drumbeat for Mother Earth. Film produced by the Indigenous Environmental Network and Greenpeace.

GEDICKS, AL. *The New Resource Wars: Native and Environmental Struggles Against Multinational Corporations.* Boston: South End Press, 1993.

GRINDE, DONALD A., and BRUCE E. JOHANSEN. *Ecocide of Native America: Environmental Destruction of Indian Lands and Peoples.* Santa Fe: Clear Light Publishers, 1995.

THE HARVARD PROJECT ON AMERICAN INDIAN ECONOMIC DEVELOPMENT. *The State of Native Nations: Conditions Under U.S. Policies of Self-Determination.* New York: Oxford University Press, 2008.

JORGENSON, MIRIAM, ed. *Rebuilding Native Nations: Strategies for Governance and Development.* Tucson, AZ: University of Arizona Press, 2008.

LADUKE, WINONA. *All Our Relations: Native Struggles for Land and Life.* Cambridge, Mass.: South End Press, 1999.

MULLIS, ANGELA, and DAVID KAMPER. *Indian Gaming: Who Wins?* Los Angeles: UCLA American Indian Studies Center, 2000.

WILKINS, DAVID E. *American Indian Sovereignty and the U.S. Supreme Court.* Austin: University of Texas Press, 1997.

WILKINS, DAVID E., and K. TSISNINA LOMAWAIMA. *Uneven Ground: American Indian Sovereignty and Federal Law.* Norman: University of Oklahoma Press, 2001.

IX

URBANISM: ANCIENT AND CONTEMPORARY

"Indians in cities?! You must be kidding." No, our intention in Part IX is to set the record straight. The stereotype lingers that Native peoples are now and have always been rural folk, frozen in time, and that they have been exclusively wandering hunters and gatherers or farmers. This stereotype is closely linked with the equally fanciful and stereotypical notion of "wilderness," a natural region scarcely touched and even less inhabited by humans, just waiting, vacant and virgin, for wave after wave of Europeans to step ashore or ride up from the south to claim it, name it, and occupy and "civilize" it. Yet the reality is that many Native societies in the Western Hemisphere were also, and are today, characterized by urbanism—that is, city life in all its many forms. In addition, what may have appeared to outside eyes, sensibilities, and limited knowledge as vacant "wilderness" was in times past in reality many cases Native urban hinterlands, complementary to and providing resources for cities or seasonally occupied, high-density ceremonial centers.

When the Spanish came into what is now the United States in the 1600s and 1700s, they found and commented on the many Pueblo towns along the Rio Grande and on the Hopi Mesas. These towns were not very different in size from the many towns and cities throughout Europe at that time. Stories even circulated among the Spanish that these were possibly the fabulous and fabled cities of gold north of Mesoamerica. Also in what is now the United States was the great Mound Builder civilization of the Southeast, including the well-known Cahokia, a 4,000-acre temple mound site in Illinois, near St. Louis. There were also large three-story buildings in the complex Chaco Canyon in the Southwest.

To the south of what is now the United States, there were long-standing urban traditions in Mesoamerica and the Andes, in which some of the urban complexes date back over 3,000 years. Paved highways and intricate communication systems, irrigation systems, monumental architecture, massive public arts, and complex and hierarchical societies characterized these complexes. Jack D. Forbes in Reading 1, "The Urban Tradition Among Native Americans," reminds us that Native people have made and continue to make their homes throughout the entire hemisphere, in urban areas that include not only the modern, European-established cities but also those many ancient urban complexes that are truly indigenous to this hemisphere—Cahokia, Teotihuacan, Tikal, Chaco Canyon, Cholula, Moche, Cuzco, and Tiahuanaco, among many others. Forbes sets the tone of this part, demonstrating that prior to the relatively recent incursion into the Western Hemisphere by peoples from across the seas, this entire hemisphere, in all its urban and more rural forms, was all the Native homelands. Reading 1 takes the broadest geographic approach in this part.

Today, the tradition of Native or Indigenous urbanity continues. According to the 2000 census, approximately two-thirds of all Indian people in the United States live in cities, and large numbers of Native or Indigenous people live in urban areas in Canada, Peru, Chile, Mexico, and Guatemala. Many urban Indian communities exist and flourish as a part of towns and cities throughout the Americas. Likewise, many major cities, such as New York, Chicago, and Los Angeles, have significant and vibrant Indian or Indigenous communities, many of them multitribal and growing. This part conveys something of the spirit, history, context, dynamics, and voice of Indian life in cities.

The small number of publications on Native urban themes and topics is particularly striking when compared to the vast and active interest and literature on other American Indian topics and contexts. This is one example of the continuation of the stereotype that everything Indian is rural and far away in time and place. And yet, the reality and vitality of continuing Indian life is urban, rural, and everything in between. For Indian people, these varied settings are interrelated in multiple ways. The rigid rural/urban dichotomy and accompanying stereotypes are not a true expression of Indian reality, yet they have been one of the molds and barriers that have continued to shape research, writing, and the perceptions of Native life among the general population.

Both the 1990 and 2000 U.S. censuses, despite problems with undercount and bias, reaffirmed that large numbers of Indian people live in urban areas. Also, the process of carrying out these recent censuses demonstrated and underscored the lack of understanding by the U.S. Census Bureau, and, by extension, many other governmental agencies, regarding the very nature of urban Indian populations and communities. These miscounts and problems with the census methodology not only fueled continued misperceptions regarding Indian life in cities, but also justified reduced funding for the many greatly needed social services for Indian people living in cities. If the census does not indicate the existence of Indian people in urban areas, then of course it can be reasoned that no funds are needed, for example, for Indian clinics or culturally based education programs. The word has even been circulated in some circles that this urban miscount was a form of "statistical genocide," yet another burden from the U.S. government for Indian people to deal with.

A prominent, very influential approach during the 1940s and 1950s to urban and urbanization research was that of the sociologist Robert Redfield, who proposed a "folk–urban continuum." Although he proposed a continuum, his work has generally been interpreted as a dichotomous model. Closely associated with urban studies of that period and also very influential in establishing urban research and policy was the reoccurring stereotype that associated urbanization with "social disorganization," the "culture of poverty," and "cultural breakdown," thematic concepts that linger on today in popular thinking and policymaking. These concepts tend to "blame the victim" for poverty and family and community problems rather than realistically acknowledge the effects of ineffective policy, racism, loss of land and culture, and overwhelming pressures to assimilate.

Although some of these negative attitudes and concepts are criticized with good reason, many continue today to influence and shape both research and political and economic policy that affects Indian people living in urban areas. For example, during the 1940s through 1960s, they influenced the development and implementation of government policy affecting Indian lands, resources, and economic and social options. This is seen most prominently in the termination and relocation policies of the 1950s and their aftermath, lasting into the 1970s. Termination policy in essence aimed to end treaty rights and sovereignty of some Native nations. Similarly, relocation has been characterized by some as "a one-way bus ticket into the city." Both of these policies, along with the absence of economic and educational opportunities on reservations, were major catalysts for Indian people in the United States to migrate in large numbers into urban areas beginning in the mid-1950s. Consequently, large urban Indian communities developed and continue today to grow in cities such as Los Angeles, New York, the San Francisco Bay Area, Seattle, Denver, Chicago, Milwaukee, and others. In Reading 2, "Reflections of Alcatraz," Lanada Boyer tells about some of her relocation experiences. In 1950, according to the U.S. census, approximately 13 percent of Indian people lived in urban areas. By 1990, it was 53 percent, and by the 2000 census, over 66 percent; that is, two-thirds of those enumerated by the census were living in urban areas.

Journalists and others writing during the relocation period and after often characterized only the negative aspects of Indian life in cities. Additionally, both the media and the educational system reinforce many of the pervasive stereotypes that situate Indian people primarily in a rural and often romanticized historical past, making it very difficult to reveal these ideas for what they are: stereotypes that are very difficult to discard.

Little by little since the 1970s, the voice and varied Native urban experiences have begun to emerge. As discussed by Carol Miller in Reading 4, "Telling the Indian Urban: Representations in American Indian Fiction," American Indian fiction writers, including Scott Momaday and Leslie Silko, and others such as Joy Harjo and Simon Ortiz took important steps in breaking out of the restrictive rural, past-tense mode. They, and now many other Native writers, have been able to move freely in their writing to creatively reflect on Indian realities, aspirations, and visions, wherever they might be taking shape in both urban and rural contexts. Miller also addresses the more abstract representation of cities and their many connotations by Native people. She provides insights into the ways that contemporary Indian fiction writers utilize their works to counter stereotypes, especially those of invisibility and victimization, that exist in the non-Indian imagination. As Miller asserts, often these stereotypes and images are reversed in the literature that provides an Indian perspective, expressing cultural vitality in settings of positive change and settings that include the many faces of Native urban experiences. Her analysis shows the contrast between European-based and derived notions of place and relationships with those of Native peoples. She considers concepts such as "urban" and "community" from an Indian perspective. Then she raises the questions "How alien is an urban environment?" and "What are the foundations of 'civilized' behavior?"

Artists such as poet Esther Belin ("Ruby's Welfare") and photographers Hulleah Tsinhnahjinnie and Pena Bonita have laid aside the constraining rural stereotypes and have become well known for their depictions and social commentary regarding some of the nuances of urban Indian life. Hulleah Tsinhnahjinnie's images in "Metropolitan Indian Series, #1" demonstrate the longing, the loneliness, and at the same time the hopefulness that coming to the city can represent. The whimsy of Pena Bonita's "The Youngest Trapper on 7th Street" playfully helps us acknowledge the resourcefulness that is all around us. There are other Indian voices, younger voices—such as rap poets W.O.R. (Without Rezervation), and their "Growin' up on the Rez"—that assert city-born and raised Indian pride. Through these varieties of Native voices, it has become evident that there is not one urban experience, but there are many experiences and multiple perspectives. There are many ways of being urban and being Indian.

In Reading 3, "Is Urban a Person or a Place? Characteristics of Urban Indian Country," Susan Lobo emphasizes the overall nature of many urban Indian communities in the United States: their structure, the dynamics within these communities, and some of the ways that linkage and interaction take place with surrounding non-urban areas. Just what is an urban Indian "community," and what are some of the ways it is both defined and conceptualized by its members? This is a tricky question, and the often-used concept of "community" may not be as simple or one-dimensional as it appears. In this reading, the urban Indian community generally is characterized as "a widely scattered and frequently shifting network of relationships with locational nodes found in the Indian organizations and activity sites of special significance." This definition emphasizes the less obvious urban Indian community structure, based on relationships and relationship networks, rather than on the more frequent definitions of urban "ethnic" communities that rely on geographic locations and boundaries often seen when describing a Chinatown or a Hispanic barrio. Thus, in many urban Indian communities, community is not essentially defined as a place but rather as a network of relationships that bond people together. This is ultimately one of the ways that identity is established and maintained in a city. "Tribalness," or Indian identity, is not lost in urban settings but rather has been redefined and augmented.

This part also discusses urban social and political activism, particularly regarding the role of women. Lanada Boyer, in Reading 2, "Reflections on Alcatraz," recounts her experiences during the 1969 Indian occupation of Alcatraz Island in San Francisco Bay and the ripples of social awareness and political activism that changed the lives of many Native people and communities for years to come. In Reading 5, "Women's Class Strategies as Activism in Native Community Building in Toronto, 1950–1975," Heather Howard-Bobiwash describes activism of a different sort—activism that creates ways to strengthen the urban Indian community structural foundation and urban organizational base. It is telling to compare and contrast these two effective, but different, approaches to activism; that described by Boyer and that described by Howard-Babiwash. Victoria Bomberry, in the box "Downtown Oklahoma City, 1952," lets us in on what it was like when she was a little girl, growing up in a racist urban situation and as her increasing awareness gave her not only a sense of herself and her mother, but also a sense of the surrounding society, where racism hovers nearby.

In this part we take note of the hemispheric nature of the urbanization process in which Native people are now engaged. It is taking place not only in the United States but in Canada and throughout Latin America as well. Likewise, it is important to understand the ongoing linkages of support and reciprocity on an individual level and on a community-to-community level that continually take place between urban and rural Native communities. There are multiple ways in which urban Indian communities have reconnected to more rural tribal homelands or nations and, in so doing, have often redefined or enriched what it is to be Indian, both rural and urban. Gerald Dawavendewa's art, "Checking out the Competition," at the beginning of this part is a scene that could take place as easily at an urban powwow or on a rural reservation.

GROWIN' UP ON THE REZ

W.O.R

Growin' up on the rez, just like a ghetto or hood
cuz the man claims my people are always up to
no good. but let me take you for a ride to my side.
check out my people that's filled with red pride!
and I gotta kick it down for them, no reason to pretend.
see, we're in it 'til the end. see I got their back
and they got mine! this just happens to be our way of life.

and it couldn't be any other way see. cuz the man
keeps trying to waste me, and my future, my present,
my past. but you know we're good to go. we'll see
who lasts longer, cuz we're coming much stronger!
they'll have to wonder when they feel our red
thunder! we'll never die, we'll never ever fade away!
and the rez makes damn sure we're here to stay.

(Hook)
we'll never die, we'll never ever fade away
we'll never die, we'll never ever fade away.
cuz that's life on the rez. cuz that's life on the rez!

Take a walk through my hood, looking around
every single face is brown. and you know that it's
damn good to be down. everything is all good it's
all'ight! this here's the hood that made the Hiddesee.
and even though in the O—I'm without, when I hit
the rez I'm back home without a doubt! and they
claim what we got is negative. it's the system dissin'
the way we live. cuz positive is what I see! cuz they
know with the rez they can never get me! so I'll flow
it out to the fools who dis our old ways, this is OUR
old school, and OUR land and OUR ways and OUR
laws! and you know that we'll fight the fight for the
just cause! that's how it is, on the rez as long as we
have it, yo we'll never be dead.

(Hook)
A red child is born, and you know we go on and on.
can't stop until we're strong, like we were way back in

the days. Indian people have me amazed, we'll never
die, simply multiply
and we survived their attempted genocide!
and since we stood the test, my ancestors rest in peace.
and thank you for allowing me to survive with my red
pride. and for that WOR will never ever switch sides!
cuz we got the rez and we got the people and that's
stronger than the white man's evil. so don't fade my
hood, cuz you know what? I think my people are just
too damn good to be played out or fade out.
people like us were simply made to survive any situation
   given.
When you live your life on the rez, that's
how you live it. fool, see it's all good! and all the way
live with our pride in our rez, you know we'll survive!

"Growin' Up on the Rez," from Without Rezervation, Native rap
group. Lyrics by Chris La Marr. Reprinted by permission.

Checking Out the Competition.
© *Gerald Dawavendewa*. Reprinted by permission.

THE URBAN TRADITION AMONG NATIVE AMERICANS

Jack D. Forbes

Urbanization is an extremely important concept because virtually all European writers imagine that "civilization" arises only with cities. Indeed, the very word *civilization* is derived from the Latin *civitat* and *civitas*, citizenship, state, and, in particular, the City of Rome, which is in turn from *civis*, a citizen. The word *city*, as well as the Castilian *ciudad*, is derived similarly.

A people that does not have cities or urban centers will ordinarily not be viewed as being "civilized" by Eurocentric writers and, indeed, the dualistic split between "nature" and "culture" in much of Eurocentric thinking is also a "country" versus "city" split, as I discuss elsewhere.

Most European writers picture Native Americans as peoples living in the countryside, in jungles, forests, on the plains and pampas, or in small villages surrounded by mountains as in the Andes. Naturally, then, it becomes problematic for them when they discover that huge numbers of First Nations people reside today in cities such as Buenos Aires, Lima, La Paz, Quito, Guatemala City, Mexico City, Toronto, Denver, Chicago, Los Angeles, San Francisco—Oakland, and so on. What many non-Native writers do not realize is that the First Americans have, in fact, gone through periods of deurbanization and reurbanization on various occasions in their history and that urban life has been a major aspect of American life from ancient times.

In fact, it may well be that the Americas witnessed a greater process of urban development in pre-1500 C.E. times than did any other continent, with the growth of the most elaborate planned cities found

An earlier version of this reading appeared in the *American Indian Culture and Research Journal*, 22, no. 4, 1998. Reprinted by permission of the American Indian Studies Center, UCLA. Copyright Regents of the University of California. Notes for this reading have been omitted.

anywhere. In fact, the evidence seems to indicate that from about 1600–1700 B.C. until the 1519–1520 C.E. period, the largest cities in the world were often located in the Americas rather than in Asia, Africa, or Europe.

Before discussing ancient urbanization, however, we should say something about what constitutes an *urb* (Lat. for city) or *odena* (Otchipwe for town or city; *olana* in Powhatan). The archaeologist John H. Rowe, in discussing ancient urbanization in Peru, states that

> an urban settlement is an area of human habitation in which dwellings are grouped closely together. The dwellings must be close enough to leave insufficient space between them for subsistence farming, although . . . gardens may be present.

Rowe distinguishes several kinds of urban settlements, including the *pueblo*, where all of the residents are engaged in subsistence activities at least part of the time, and the *city* where some residents are engaged in other activities such as manufacturing, trade, service, administration, defense, crafts, etc. He also differentiates between cities and pueblos where all of the people are gathered in the settlement and the surrounding countryside is basically empty, and cities or pueblos with a scattered rural population around them (somewhat like ceremonial or market centers can exist with rural settlements scattered around them).

Rowe proposes to refer to urban settlements with fewer than two thousand inhabitants as small and to those with more than two thousand as large. (The U.S. census regards any place with 2,500 or more persons as being urban.) Of course, I would add that the density of surrounding areas must be considered also, since one might find a series of hamlets separated by fields or forest that together form a close-knit economic and social unit. In any case, the population of American cities frequently far exceeds two thousand,

and metropolitan areas (such as around Goleta in Santa Barbara County, California) could have many pueblos of a thousand residents each in a rather small area.

We can also analyze *urbs* in other ways. Let us note the following distinctions: (1) multiethnic (multitribal, multilingual, multiracial) *urbs* as opposed to single-ethnic *urbs*; (2) *urbs* organized in *calpulli*-style kinship neighborhoods as opposed to cities with dispersed kinship; (3) metropolitan areas that include areas of countryside and villages or barrios associated intimately with a ceremonial or market center as opposed to distinctly separated urban-rural zones; (4) megacities such as Chan Chan or Tenochtítlan as opposed to smaller cities.

It is very possible that many ancient American cities were organized into *calpulli*-like kinship-based divisions. *Calpulli* is the Nahuatl word for a semi-self-governing neighborhood or unit comprised of related persons—that is, a tribe, band, or other kinship group. It also would appear that many of the greatest *urbs* in America were multilingual. Even in areas where one language family predominated over a wide area, there are clear examples where many different dialects were spoken in the *urbs* as well as occasional unrelated tongues (such as Nahuatl in the Maya area). In the urban traditions of Mexico and Guatemala, groups speaking various Maya, Mixe-Zoque, Nahuan, and other languages are frequently mentioned as living in the same city or region or as migrating together into some other group's territory. Incidentally, it is in the Olmeca-Tulapan region on the coast of the Gulf of Mexico that the oldest date of the Mesoamerican calendar seems to be grounded, a date of 3113 B.C. or 3114 B.C. (August 11, 13, or 20 or September 8 according to the anthropological interpretation of the long count found on Maya monuments, or March 20 as found in the Tepixic Annals). This date is probably related to the process of urbanization in the Olmeca-Tulapan region, perhaps marking the founding of a complex or community there or at the very least marking the period when maize agriculture provided the dietary basis for intensive population concentrations. On the other hand, it might refer to a great astronomical event.

But before discussing the period of year 1 A.C. (American Calendar), let me return for a moment to the classification of urban areas. One of the special characteristics of American life in such diverse regions as Peru, Mesoamerica, and the Mississippi Valley is the very early development of ceremonial centers, usually featuring mounds or pyramid like

structures. I interpret these mounds as being symbolic breasts of Gahesina Haki (Mother Earth), especially when a structure is placed on top of the mound, as was usually the case. Such breasts would serve to link Americans spiritually with the nurturing power of Gahesina Haki.

Many of these mounds become-huge (as at Cahokia, Teotihuacan, Cholula, and Moche), rivaling the largest pyramids of the ancient Kemi (Egyptian) people. In any case, these ceremonial structures are not always surrounded by a dense civilian settlement or city but are often surrounded by farmlands and unpopulated areas, in which small to medium towns or hamlets are located. It would appear that the ceremonial center and the dispersed settlements together form a unit, that is, that they are part of a single social unit that can be seen as being urban without being concentrated. Is that possible? Can we conceive of a large area with many small towns or hamlets working together to support a market center/ceremonial center/educational center as a kind of city? Indeed we must, because otherwise we cannot explain the erection of such centers (with all of the immense amounts of labor involved) or their enlargement and management over hundreds of years.

We also must come up with a new term for this type of urban development, one that resembles some modern "garden cities" but has at its hub a communal center with spiritual as well as secular purposes. I propose that we speak of "heart circle" to describe a region where one finds a long-enduring association between many small communities and a spiritual "heart." Such a circle has many urban characteristics, but the productivity of its landscape is not marred by the intensive and continuous erection of streets and structures. Such heart circles may, indeed, reflect a profound wisdom and a benign socialist democracy. They ensure an adequate protein base for all persons in the region, with so-called wild animals, trees, and plants being preserved and protected from exploitation, while at the same time being harvested on a regular but respectful basis.

One of the problems for all early *urbs* is to insure that large concentrations of people can indeed obtain a balanced diet. Some scholars believe that some American cities collapsed because their populations became too large and concentrated to allow for an adequate food supply, and, in particular, a balanced one with sufficient nonmaize sources of protein.

In any event, not all American *urbs* evolved as heart circles. In fact, there is an immense variety among early American towns, in part because of the great variety of geographical settings. Marine environments sometimes provided sufficient food for population growth without horticulture, as among the Calusa of Florida, the Chumash of the Santa Barbara Channel, and some Pacific Northwest nations. Likewise, the careful management of nondomesticated animals, plants, and trees, as found with the eco-managing peoples of California, sometimes led to substantial population growth. Nonetheless, the evolution of agriculture was a major step toward urbanization in many regions from the Mississippi Valley southward.

Seeds of cultivated squash found in an Oaxaca cave have been dated at 9975 B.P. (before the present). By 8000 B.P. the squash rind had the orange color of modern pumpkins (*cucurbita pepo*). In any case, American horticultural science has been pushed back to almost ten thousand years ago, a date comparable to the origins of domestication in Africa and Asia. In the eastern area of the United States the domestication of cucurbits, sunflowers, and other plants (except maize) goes back to about 4500 B.C. Maize was domesticated in Mexico by about 5000 B.C. and spread into the southwest U.S. by 2000–1500 B.C. By 700–900 C.E. the widespread production of maize began to revolutionize Mississippi Valley lifeways. In coastal Peru the cultivation of cotton and other crops may have begun as early as 3500 B.C., contributing along with marine resources to urban developments after 2000 B.C. when maize culture becomes evident. The continued study of plants by Native people illustrates their intellectual vitality during these many millennia, since at least a hundred and fifty plants were adapted to horticulture in the Americas, in addition to the management and/or regular use of hundreds of unaltered species.

It is interesting that weaving with cotton seems to develop about the same time as ceramic manufacturing, but apparently in different regions. The earliest ceramics found thus far are from the mouth of the Amazon, along the north coast of Colombia, and from Valdivia, Ecuador, dating between 3600 and 3000 B.C. (about the same time as fired clay objects were being produced in Louisiana). In Mexico, bowls and jars of stone appear by 3400–2300 B.C. and ceramics by 2300–1500 B.C. A soapstone bowl industry developed in the southeast U.S. between 3000 and 1000 B.C., preceding ceramic bowls. Specialized manufacturing seems to have existed at Huaca (Waka) Prieta in Peru after 3000 B.C., where thousands of fabrics made of cotton and other fibers have been found.

Since 4000 B.C., America has had many shared developments. For example, recent work has demonstrated that Louisiana is home to the earliest dated human-built mounds in the hemisphere, one complex (Watson Brake) being dated at 5400–5000 years ago, with other sites yielding dates in the 3500–4000 B.C. range. The Monte Sano mounds near Baton Rouge had a permanent structure and charcoal dating to circa 3500 B.C. The Watson Brake complex forms a series of linked mounds, shaped like a doughnut around a central area. The people of these early mounds were fisher-folk as well as eco-managers of game, trees, and plants (or what some writers like to call "hunter-gatherers"). To the east is another complicated series of mounds (Poverty Point) dated to circa 1700 B.C. or 1500 B.C., depending on the source. All of these mounds were preceramic except for the numerous fired clay blocks noted above.

The American determination to construct mounds or raised platforms and other ceremonial structures can also be seen in Mesoamerica and the Andean region, with mounds appearing along the Peruvian coast after 2600 B.C. and especially after 2000 B.C. Callejon de Huaylas near Huaricoto began about 2800 B.C. It has thirteen ceremonial hearths of a type subsequently found elsewhere in the highlands of Peru. Aspero, a huge preceramic center by about 2000 B.C. has seven known mounds and six other structures. Work began there by 2600 B.C. and continued on for several hundred years.

In Mexico earthen constructions appear in the 1200–900 B.C. period in Olmeca-Tulapan (southern Vera Cruz-Tabasco) at San Lorenzo, a major ceremonial center located near the Rio Coatzacoalcos. There a mesa was artificially altered with large amounts of fill and ridges were constructed outward on three sides. But the major feature of this site is its huge basalt heads, eight of them, the largest weighing some twenty tons. The site is also very rich in Olmeca-type art works and figurines whose style has led to wild speculation on the part of European-American scholars. It is thought that San Lorenzo was destroyed in 900 B.C., but the cultural tradition continued on at La Venta. Mounds or pyramids as such seem to appear after 900 B.C., as at Cuicuilco near Mexico City where a circular pyramid was erected, 60 feet high and 370 feet in diameter, with four tiers and four other structures nearby (all buried beneath lava prior to discovery). About the same time the people called the Olmeca erected pyramids of clay in the region of Tollan or Olmeca-Tulapan, as at La Venta. There during the 900–400 B.C. period the

Americans built a giant pyramid that stood some thirty meters high, containing perhaps more than two hundred thousand cubic meters of fill. Estimates indicate that its construction required eight hundred thousand man-days and a supporting population of at least eighteen thousand. In Oaxaca the Zapotec (or Binizá people, meaning People of the Clouds) also began the construction of their great centers of Monte Alban and Mitla (circa 800–500 B.C.). Great Kaminaljuyú, near Guatemala City, evolved after 1700 B.C., with, several hundred great temple mounds and some large clay temple mounds completed by 500 B.C. at the latest. On the Pacific Coast at Izapa large numbers of earthen mounds were also built. This site was occupied from the 2000–1000 B.C. period and reached its peak after 500 B.C. Izapa is interesting because of its Connections with the Olmeca area and also because, located on the Pacific, it could have had connections with South America.

The eagerness of many Americans to devote huge amounts of labor to building "breasts" soon spread. After 800–500 B.C. they appeared northward among the so-called Adena peoples of the Ohio Valley and vicinity. There immense numbers of mounds were constructed which were also used for burial purposes, thus they are often known as burial mounds. (A mound of this kind was excavated in Virginia, incidentally, by Thomas Jefferson.) During this same period the earliest large Maya cities (Nakbe, 600 100 B.C., and Tikal, a bit later) were the sites of platform and higher mounds. And far to the south at Qaluyu, near Pucara in the Lake Titicaca region of Peru-Bolivia, Americans were building a low mound several acres in size in 1000–500 B.C., with a later one, reportedly shaped like a catfish, after 700 B.C.

John Rowe would probably not regard the mound complexes or heart circles as being urban unless they were surrounded by a certain number of dense structures leaving no room for farming in between. But is this structural density really the key to urbanness? I must argue that the key to urbanness is not the presence of closely spaced structures but rather the intimate interaction of substantial numbers of people in a given geographical space. In other words, urbanness is a form of association where communication and networking, as opposed to isolation, are the norm. I will also argue that mounds (as well as the trading of goods, diffusion of art styles, and spread of technical knowledge) are strong evidence for communication and social interaction.

The early period of medium-size or small villages, coupled with common public works projects in the areas mentioned above, such as the mounds, signified the gradual development of greater population densities and the concomitant expansion of agriculture. This led to the development of cities along the lines envisioned by Rowe (but often of much greater size). Many European archaeologists also imagine that this period was accompanied by the development of nondemocratic political systems (command systems) and by hierarchical social structures. They often use terms such as *chiefdom* to refer to political units and they see social hierarchy in every grave with gift offerings, just as every executed person becomes a human sacrifice, and so on. Basically, these are all projections from their own European and Middle Eastern historical experiences, projections that may have no validity at all for Americans.

Knowing something about contemporary Indigenous Americans would lead me to suspect that the mounds and other great works were constructed voluntarily by devoted persons whose spiritual values took precedence over other considerations. I would imagine the republics that constructed these ceremonial (and perhaps educational) centers as being large cooperative systems of together-living persons. But, of course, this is not the perspective of most of my colleagues of European background, who see incipient kingdoms, tribute-states, and empires in the heart circles, and who regard the development of hierarchy and oppression as necessary steps in the long bloody trail of becoming "civilized."

We can turn to the Andes for the earliest large cities in the Americas, and especially to the coast where rich maritime resources coupled with trade led to population concentrations in narrow river valleys. After 3000 B.C. small urban settlements became very common, as at Huaca Prieta in Chicama, where what are assumed to be public buildings have been identified. Rio Seco has two mounds about four meters high to create a raised substructure for an important building. By about 2500 B.C. there were towns with permanent buildings both along the coast and in the highlands, many of which have monumental architecture. The early structures were small, but by the 2000–1500 B.C. period some were enormous.

Rowe describes the site of Aspero as a "huge preceramic center by about 2000 B.C.," with seven mounds, as noted above. No population estimates are given for Aspero, but Las Haldas, north of Lima along the coast, is described as a very large city with perhaps ten thousand or more people. Its area covers a site of two kilometers by one kilometer, and it features a complex and imposing temple structure with sunken circular courts. A date of 1631 B.C. has been obtained for Las Haldas. It was probably the largest city in the Americas at that time (1700–1400 B.C.) and very possibly one of the largest in the world, outside of Kem (Egypt) or Mesopotamia.

Another early *waka* (sacred site) was Chiquitanta (El Paraiso) at the mouth of the Chillon River, Peru. Dating from 1600 B.C., it is considered the largest pre-ceramic complex of monumental architecture yet known in South America, with at least six mounds. The two largest mounds are over three hundred meters long, being built of cut stone, plastered over with clay. In between is a patio with a temple structure at one end. Clearly, such a center required a large population nearby to construct and maintain it. Other urban developments continue to appear thereafter along the Peruvian coast, as at a site in Acarí, dated about 1297–997 B.C. The site may include public buildings and could be a city according to Rowe. By 1000 B.C. the Americans there were cultivating cotton, gourds, lima beans, squash, guava, and peanuts. During this same era, from about 1200–200 B.C., a cultural tradition known as Chavín spread to many centers throughout a great part of Peru. The site after which the culture was named, Chavín de Huantar, is dated from 850–200 B.C., but the tradition itself is worth commenting upon here because of the cat motifs that remind one of similar themes in Olmeca art of the same period. It strongly suggests ideological contact between Mesoamerica and the Andean region, but also contact with Amazonia. Scholars, have suggested that Chavín iconography shows an Amazonian tropical forest influence, which is quite understandable since the city is located on a branch of the far-flung Amazon River system.

At this point, it is wise to note that ancient urbanization along the alluvial plains of the Amazon, as well as on the eastern slopes of the Andes, is very likely, but data seems hard to come by. This may, however, ultimately prove to be a key area for American cultural evolution because of the nature of the environment along the rich rivers. In any case, cities of two thousand persons are quite possible along the Amazon, and one Apinayé village had 1,400 persons as late as 1824, even after the effects of disease and slave raids. Robert L. Carneiro has calculated that tropical forest agriculture, centered on manioc, can be extremely productive in the alluvial areas. He states that the Kuikuru, with whom he studied, have an agriculture that is "more productive than horticulture as practiced by the Inca." The average Kuikuru gardener spends only about two hours per day in manioc cultivation, leaving quite a lot of leisure time, and making possible food surpluses. Thus, there are many areas of the Americas where we cannot, as of yet, make any certain statements about urban experiences in ancient times.

The next place where urban developments seem to begin is in the Tollan region of Mexico, along the Gulf Coast but in reach of the Pacific Coast via the Strait of Tehuantepec. The center of San Lorenzo has already been described (1200–900 B.C.) as a major ceremonial and artistic center. But it also required a large adjacent population to aid in all of the earthwork and artistic productions, which included such architectural innovations as U-shaped basalt storm drains with the individual pieces laid end-to-end. (It is noteworthy that a somewhat analogous drain system existed at Chavín in Peru). About two hundred house mounds at San Lorenzo have been located, which could mean a resident population of some size. If this was one of our early American universities, then, of course, these houses could have been for students and faculty.

The period beginning about 900–800 B.C. is fascinating because urban developments and mound building moved forward in many parts of the Americas, from the Andean region north to the Ohio Valley. Is this because there was regular communication, perhaps by maritime and river routes? To my knowledge, no one has adequately studied the tendency of many Native Americans to travel vast distances both for trade (the *pochteca* of Mesoamerica are well known as traders) and for such purposes as learning about new things, seeing new places, and studying under new teachers. Until such a study is carried out we cannot know much about American ancient travelers, but we do know that navigation, both in the Caribbean Atlantic and the Pacific Coast sectors was extremely well developed before 1492 C.E.

About 850 B.C. Chavín in Peru evolved into a major city and center, with an occupation area of about one kilometer by one-half kilometer. Its ruins include a great temple which is considered by some to be one of the most remarkable surviving monuments of American antiquity. As noted, the city has cat motifs and a great pyramid, a north pyramid, a great plaza, and the temple site. Canals were created to run fresh water through the temple. Chavín seems to have reached its peak in 400–200 B.C. Later it survived as a ceremonial center, with habitation areas abandoned.

Farther north, urban developments also occurred in the regions of Guatemala (at Izapa and Kaminaljuyú, for example) and Tollan or Great Tula on the Gulf. Gordon Brotherston tells us that in ancient Mesoamerican texts Tula "is most often presented as the city with which recorded political history itself begins." It is also described as having four parts with twenty towns, which leads me to believe that Tula, Tollan, or Olmeca-Tulapan was a region and not a single city. This is, I believe, borne out by the introduction of Adrian Recinos to the *Popol Vub*, in which he identifies many cities in Tula including Zuiva and Nonohualco. In any case, Tollan plays a major role in the later history of peoples speaking many different languages (Mayan languages, along with Nahuatl and others) who trace their origins, at least in part, to the many cities of the region. Though the people of the region are called Olmeca they probably were not a single group at all, but rather a cultural tradition. Some archaeologists believe that an Olmeca state or empire existed, but there is no evidence to support any particular theory about social structure. European scholars often interpret the huge basalt heads as being portraits of specific rulers, and other statues are also supposed to be kings or leaders, but numerous other interpretations are possible. For example, if it is true that the American calendar, a writing system, and written mathematics evolved here (which is not certain), then why not imagine that the heads and statues are of great thinkers, inventors of the new tools for recording events and for calculating solar movements?

As noted earlier, La Venta (900–400 B.C.) was one major Olmeca site, among many that have still not been studied or located. A large population was doubtless living the region, judging from the public works constructed. About the time of La Vanta's decline, the *urb* of Tres Zapotes, further north, became significant and maintained cultural connections with Izapa along the Guatemalan Pacific Coast. But also much urbanization was taking place in interior Mexico, as at Cholula where, around 500 B.C., people are said to have arrived from the Olmeca region. The pyramid constructed at Cholula possesses a greater volume than the Cheops pyramid in Kem (Egypt). Its base was 440 meters long and it was formerly higher than 210 feet. This became one of the largest solid single structures in the world. Interestingly, the later great pyramid at Cahokia is 1,080 feet long—compared with 1,440 for Cholula—and at least 100 feet high—about half as high. But both possess a greater mass than the Cheops pyramid.

At about same time as the growth of Cholula, the Binizá (Zapotec) people began to quicken the pace of urbanization at Monte Alban in Oaxaca. The early period saw the construction of a temple platform with drawings of the "dancers," figures thought by some to portray conquered enemies (but which, of course, could represent a great many other things). The most significant aspect, however, is the presence of hieroglyphs das associated with each of the figures. Current knowledge regards this as "the earliest body of writing in Mesoamerica," leading to the idea that "it may be that it was the Zapotec who invented writing and the Mesoamerican calendar?" On the other hand, it is quite arguable that Monte Alban was one of the great centers of learning of its day and that scholars of many nations resided there in order to study calendrics and associated disciplines. Eventually, Monte Alban became "a truly urban civilization" with estimated population of twenty to forty thousand residents. Its ruins cover about nineteen square miles, an area comparable to Thebes in Kern and larger than Rome at its peak.

During this same period, trends towards urbanness accelerated to the south in the Paten region of Guatemala and adjacent areas of Mexico and Belize. The people living in this area are largely Maya-speakers today, but in earlier times there may have been other languages spoken as well. Many smaller towns developed, along with great population density, after about 2000 B.C. Some of these towns may not have ever come to exceed a thousand residents, but people from surrounding hamlets seem to form part of their together-living circles.

On the other hand, large cities and ceremonial centers also appear somewhat later than Izapa and Kaminaljuyú. The latter is considered by some to be one of the greatest of all archaeological sites in the Americas, with a sophisticated culture by 800 B.C. It must have been an extremely large city but, sadly, it has been largely destroyed by the growth of modern Guatemala City.

Further north, cities such as Nakbe and Tikal, to name but two, grow greatly beginning in the 600–500 B.C. period. Some believe that that Nakbe was established first, but Tikal seems to have exceeded it in importance. The latter was built in the midst of a heavily populated countryside covering an area of fifty square miles. In this region "family compounds" are said to be seldom further than five hundred yards apart. Estimates of Tikal's population range from twenty to eighty thousand, making it, without a doubt, one of the world's largest cities prior to its abandonment soon after 889 C.E.

During roughly the same period (600–150 B.C.) the Valley of Mexico was becoming ever more densely populated with many urban settlements such as Cuicuilco. However, it was lacking in major cities in comparison to areas in the south. But another wave of great city-making was soon to begin, preceded slightly by a similar surge in southern Peru and Bolivia.

Rowe tells us that many Andean towns qualify as urban in the period after 700 B.C., but all appear to have been deserted by 3100 A.C. (B.C./A.D. I), with people spreading out in farming communities in fertile river valleys. The one exception was Tiahuanaco (Paypicala) at Lake Titicaca, which may have already been a city in Early Horizon times. Dates indicate its existence from circa 239 B.C. to at least circa 800 C.E.—about eleven hundred years. Tiahuanaco became a great city, with a core area of at least one and one-half by one and one-quarter kilometers. One author states that the Aymara (Colla) people believed that Paypicala (their name for the city) was the middle of the world. In any event, Tiahuanacan cultural influences gradually spread over a vast area.

Another important urban settlement with imposing public buildings was Pucara, located in the Titicaca basin. In the region were several other Pucara-like cities as well. In the Ica Valley along the coast a few "very large urban settlements" also appeared at about the same time (circa 100 B.C.). The Callango (Media Luna) site is one kilometer across with fifteen small adobe mounds (probably public buildings or temples). Later, irrigation canals were built to serve the agricultural needs of the area.

To put things in perspective, we can regard Tiahuanaco, Tikal, Monte Alban, and Cholula as being among the great "new" cities of the post–500 B.C. period. They also were contemporaries of Teotihuacan, Taxim (El Tajin), El Pital, Huari, and other cities that began perhaps slightly later (150 B.C. to 100 C.E.). Interestingly, many of these great cities declined or were abandoned after about 800 C.E. This issue of abandonment is extremely significant, and quite clearly must be examined from a hemispheric perspective. Some scholars focus only upon abandonment in the Valley of Mexico, or in the Peten, or in Peru and Bolivia, when, in fact, the issue is perhaps a continental one.

In any case, from about 3100 A.C. until about 3900 A.C. (800 C.E.) America was home to an incredibly large number of great cities and urban regions, including many that I have not mentioned or that scholars have not even described yet. There is no doubt but that America was far more urbanized than

was Europe in this era, especially since Rome and Athens had become much reduced in size after the German invasions.

Far to the north, population densities were increasing in all of the river valleys of Sinaloa, Sonora, and Arizona. An example of gradual urban development is Skoaquik (Snaketown), a Hohokam town along the Gila River. Skoaquik commenced in about 400 B.C. and lasted until 1100–1200 C.E. It went through many phases, often reflecting influences from Mesoamerica including ball courts, irrigation canals, and the construction of a platform mound in circa 500 C.E. It seems to have had about a hundred houses at any given time, thus yielding an in-town population of a thousand or more. The construction of at least three miles of hand-dug canals by 300 B.C. (or earlier) would indicate a large, supportive population in the area, as well as direct contact with Mesoamerica.

About 150 B.C. major urban development commenced in the Valley of Mexico with carefully planned designs featuring avenues and plazas arranged in a systematic manner totally unknown in most European cities of the time. Teotihuacan, soon to be the largest city in the world, came to possess a ceremonial area of seven square miles. It eventually had a population between 125 and 250 thousand persons. The total urbanized zone covers over twenty square kilometers (five times larger than Rome within its walls), but evidence indicates that the entire valley was utilized as a food-producing area for the city, with highly efficient chinampa horticulture around the great lake in the center.

Teotihuacan commenced cityhood with about seventy-five hundred people, but by 150 C.E. it had become much larger (forty-five thousand or more), and impressive public monuments such as the gigantic Pyramid of the Sun had been completed, along with the complex of major north–south and east–west avenues. The discovery that there are seven caves or caverns under the Pyramid suggests that Teotihuacan was connected with the ancient city of Seven Caves in Tabasco (Olmeca-Tulapan). Recinos mentions Vucub-Pec (Seven Caves in Maya) along with Tulan-Zuiva and Vucub-Zivan (Seven Revines) as being places visited by the Quiché and the Yaqui (a Nahuatl-speaking group) in their migrations. A tradition relating to the origin of the people who established themselves in Anahuac (central Mexico) has them coming from Chicomortoc, when is said to mean seven caves or ravines also. Thus Teotihuacan was perhaps selected as a sacred site from early times.

Clearly, Teotihuacan became a major spiritual and educational center for Mesoamerica, as well as a center for trade and manufacturing. In addition to pilgrims and students who were probably attracted from great distances, large numbers of the local people of the Valley of Mexico came to be housed there in some four thousand apartment like dwellings, perhaps exchanging farming for craft activities as the food production system in the countryside became ever more efficient.

Teotihuacan was a multilingual city, with a barrio of Oaxacan (Zapotec) people, a barrio of people using Early Classic Maya pottery from the Peten, and probably people who spoke Mixtec and Nonohualco languages, the latter from Tabasco. The dominant language of this fantastic City of the Great Spirit (Deity) was perhaps Nahuatl, but this is not certain. Teotihuacan "outposts" existed as far away as Matacapan on the Vera Cruz coast and at Kaminaljuyú in Guatemala. The influence of the city's lifeways reached virtually throughout Mesoamerica.

Some archaeologists speak of a Teotihuacan "empire" but evidence for such a command state is lacking or ambiguous. Europeans seem to love to discover empires, perhaps because Euro-Asian history is so replete with an emphasis on one great command society after another. The fact that cities come to share certain physical similarities is insufficient to establish the existence of a common command state, as one can readily see by comparing Shanghai, Singapore, New York, and Toronto. The appearance of similar features in New York and London, such as subways and tall buildings, does not prove that both belong to the same empire, although they clearly share material traits.

The period from about 3100 A.C. to 3200 A.C. is remarkable for the evolution of several extremely significant cities in both Mesoamerica and South America. It is almost as if the two areas were following the same rhythm of growth. In the coastal region of Vera Cruz the great centers of Taxim (E1 Tajin) and El Pital developed. The latter is located on the Namla River, accessible by small boat from the Gulf of Mexico. It is forty miles south of Taxim and features some two hundred structures, including earthen pyramids more than eighty feet high, most of them covered with stucco. The city center covers almost one mile square but is surrounded by about forty square miles of outlying settlements with raised fields and sophisticated irrigation systems. The population must have been as dense as that of Taxim (which had tens of thousands of residents).

Little is known about El Pital because the area was still unrestored and unstudied as of three years ago.

Taxim may have evolved slightly later, but it certainly became a uniquely beautiful center with a remarkable style of architecture, related to that of Maya country in certain respects. It is located on the Tecolutla River, near sites going back to 2900 B.C. Taxim covers 2,550 acres (about four square miles) and seems to have become a major administrative and religious complex. The city had at least ten ball courts with large-scale irrigation projects and terraced hillside agriculture in the vicinity. Taxim endured until about 1100 C.E.

Along the coast of the Andean region many cities developed or grew during the period after 3200 A.C. (100 C.E.). There were large urban sites in the southern valleys of Peco, Ica, Nasca, and Acarí. Tambo Viejo was the largest urban site in the latter valley, with an area of about one kilometer by one-half kilometer. The greatest city in the southern region was Huari, located twenty-five kilometers to the north of present-day Ayacucho. "The site of Huari is enormous," according to Rowe. The Huari culture included the "construction of very large building complexes consisting of plazas, corridor and . . . rooms laid out according to a formal plan." Rowe believes that Huari was an imperial city. According to Rowe, "It represents the formation of an imperial state with a well organized administration." Regions that came under Huari influence tended to have large part of the population concentrated in large cities. This is similar to what was happening at Teotihuacan at the same time.

After about 800 C.E. both Huari and Tiahuanaco were abandoned, although their cultural influences continued to exist until circa 1100 in northern Peru. In any case, "in a large part of southern Peru and Bolivia the abandonment of cities was general." Virtually no new cities were established in the region and "the entire pattern of settlement in large cities was eliminated." Nonetheless, the Ica Valley continued to have imposing ceremonial centers after 800, but settlements were small. Apparently, heart circles had replaced concentrated urban centers.

Further north, however, cities such as Pachacamac continued to thrive until gradually declining in the period between 1100 and the Inca conquest (the fifteenth century). Pachacamac was "a very large city" in circa 800, with a beginning in the 3200 A.C. era. It and Cajamarquilla were already large *urbs* in the 100–800 C.E. period.

Along the north coast of Peru the early pattern had been heart circles, that is, ceremonial centers rather than concentrated cities. This pattern contin- ued, for the most part, during the Moche or Mochica period (about 100 to 750–800 C.E.). The Moche life- ways (named after a single settlement also known as Early Chimu) involved advanced irrigation systems, heavy use of crops such as maize, beans, avocados, squash, chili peppers, manioc, potatoes, coca and peanuts, heavy reliance on seafood, and the use of tamed llamas, guinea pigs, and muscovy ducks. The people built huge pyramids, including the famous Huaca (*waka*) del Sol, a massive adobe brick structure with 50 to 140 million bricks used in the construction. The mound is 135 feet high and covers about twelve and a half acres (450 feet wide by 1,200 feet long). It is comparable to those at Cholula and Cahokia.

The Mochica peoples were sophisticated metal- workers and wonderful artists, producing unique portraitlike ceramics of the finest possible quality. They traded in all directions. The population was very dense, in spite of the absence of large cities. One place, Pampa Grande in the Lambayeque Valley, had pyramids surrounded by an expansive urban center supporting ten thousand people. Some scholars think that the Mochica were highly warlike, since armed men are often illustrated in their art. Interestingly, the archaeologists seldom comment upon the highly erotic nature of Mochica art.

In any event, the Mochica lifeways were modified in the 750–900 period when influences from the south, called Tiahuanacoid by some and Huari by others, became dominant. The southern ways included the introduction of cities, and Rowe notes that there were many large and imposing cities as a result. But by 1100 C.E. local lifeways began to revive, leading into the Chimu culture.

During this general period, the Calusa people (or their predecessors) in southern Florida were constructing mounds along the coast. One was first inhabited in 50 C.E. while others were built in stages between 600 and 1400. Significantly, these mounds have yielded papaya seeds and chili pepper seeds, the first in the U.S. (dated about 3100 A.C.). This illustrates direct contact with the Caribbean and, via the Caribbean, perhaps with South America as well.

The region of northern Central America and southern Mexico, similar to Peru, Bolivia, and central Mexico, was going through a great period of urban development in the period of 250–900 (3350–4000 A.C.), so much so that this has been referred to for years as the Classic Period. There were numerous great cities in addition to Nakbe and Tikal, such as Copan, Palenque, Becan, and Dzibilchaltun, to name but a few. The latter is said to have had forty thou- sand people at its peak, while Tikal may have had up to 125 thousand. Perhaps some three million persons were living in the lowlands of Peten, Yukal-Peten (Yucatan), and adjacent areas. One might consider the entire region urbanized or, at least, consider all areas urban-linked. Gobá, an important city in Yucatan, with a twelve-tiered pyramid, has a dated monument of November 30, 780, which also counts back 1,422,000 days to the date of August 11I, 3114 B.C., or what I am calling year 1 A.C. In any case, the great cities in much of the area were abandoned around 900 (4000 A.C.) just as in southern Peru and Bolivia. No one knows why such abandonments occurred in either region, although many theories exist including one focused on revolts by the *macewalob* (the *macebuales*, or common people).

Some of the Maya-like people seem to have moved north for a time into central Mexico. The city of Cacaxtla, near Cholula and Tlaxcala, is thought to have been founded by Olmeca-Xicalanca from the Gulf Coast, perhaps being the Xicalanca capital after 650. The city features elaborate murals of a Maya type (but, of course, art knows no ethnic boundaries and always transcends language distinctions). Cacaxtla seems to have been very carefully aban- doned in about 900 (4000 A.C.). Various chronicles of Maya peoples, such as the *Popol Vub*, indicate many migrations during this era, primarily from Olmeca- Tulapan (Tabasco) into Yucatan, Peten, and highland Guatemala, perhaps. Some of the migrants were pos- sibly non-Maya in origin, such as Ah Zuytok Tutul Xiu (987–1007) who took up residence at Uxmal and whose group remained dominant there until the Spanish invasion. The Tutul Xius were said to be from Nonoual (or Nonoualco) in Olmeca-Tulapan by one chronicle.

It would seem that at about this time, a group of Toltecas (people from Tollan or Olmeca-Tulapan) migrated into the Valley of Mexico. There they joined forces with some Chichimec people led by Mixcoatl (Cloud Serpent) and founded the new city of Tula to the north. The spiritual figure of Quetzalcoatl is inti- mately connected with this new Tula and, indeed, with old Tollan as well. One source tells us that Quetzalcoatl was associated with the Nonoalco peo- ple of Tabasco, and, as we shall see, that is where Topiltzin Quetzalcoatl returned after the fall of this new Tula (in 1064 according to the Cuauhtitlan Annals, but perhaps later according to some schol- ars). Tula became a very impressive city, with an art style that later influenced Chichén Itzá. Some scholars believe that Tula was the capital of kingdom or empire and that the Toltecas were quite warlike, but other evidence suggests exactly the opposite type of culture. In any case, Topiltzin Quetzalcoatl was forced eventually to flee to the Gulf coast and from thence to Tabasco and Yucatan.

Significantly, during this period, when the new Tula existed and many cities were being abandoned in Mesoamerica, there was a quickening of the pace of urbanization in the north. In southern Arizona the Hohokam entered into the so-called colonial period from 500 to 900 C.E., during which their area of cultural influence expanded. The prevalence of Mesoamerican ball courts, which were played upon using rubber balls, shows direct trade with the rubber-producing regions of the Mesoamerican Tropical lowlands. Between 900 and 1100 the Hohokam culture reached its peak, with villages concentrated near the Gila and Salt Rivers. More irrigation canals were dug and pottery manufacturing reached the stage where thirty-gallon jars could be produced. Pottery was traded widely, and copper balls from Mexico were obtained. At the same time, the size of towns in northern Arizona, New Mexico, and Sonora was increasing, while a similar process was occurring in the Mississippi Valley and its tributaries. This stage was probably due to increased mastery and/or adoption of maize horticulture, along with resultant population increases and perhaps the acceptance of an urban way of living.

The origins of what is known as Mississippian culture are not entirely clear, but by the period of 700–1000 the major elements of the way of life seem to have emerged. Typically, social units seem to have included a major town and ceremonial center with a number of outlying hamlets, a still larger number of farmsteads, and resource gathering locations, such as quarries and fishing locations. The larger towns had platform mounds around an open plaza, with structures located on top of the mounds in the southern Mesoamerican style. The larger mounds were built over a period of three hundred years or more, thus indicating stability as well as devotion. According to James B. Griffin,

Towns vary in size, but a population of three to five hundred would probably be the norm. A population of over one thousand would have indicated a major town, while sites like Cahokia, Moundville (Alabama), or Angel in southwestern Indiana are unusual with populations of two to five thousand or perhaps even ten thousand for the central Cahokia area at its peak.

In the Ohio Valley region a tradition known as Hopewell preceded Mississippian influence and spread outward between 900 and 1300. This tradition featured large communal projects such as burial mounds and great earthworks. One site has an elevated circular platform five hundred feet in diameter, reached by a graded six-hundred-foot long road. At the other end of the road is an oval area enclosed by a low earthen rampart twenty feet wide. Inside are burial mounds. The Hopewell people are said to have been the finest metalworkers in pre-European North America. They traded very widely, with a network covering all of eastern North America and extending as far west as the Rocky Mountains.

In the Southwest and northwest Mexico, urbanization increased rapidly after about 900 (4000 A.C.), with the construction of large towns that are often in the form of row houses or apartments arranged in an arc or in a rectangle, or in the shape of an E. Generally, most towns at this time were compact masses of contiguous rooms (from twenty to about a thousand). During this period many of the Great Pueblos of Arizona and New Mexico were built including Pueblo Bonito (919–1130), Aztec (1110–1121), Mesa Verde area (1073–1262), White House (1060–1275), Showlow (1174–1393), and Yellowjacket (southwest Colorado, 950–1300). Yellowjacket was the largest city in Colorado and it contained the highest density of ceremonial structures found in the Southwest. Also included in the city were 182 kivas, a great kiva, 17 towers, and a great tower. Some room blocks were three stories high. About thirty thousand persons may have resided at Yellowjacket and in the adjacent fertile Montezuma Valley at its peak in the mid-1200s, whereas about four thousand persons are estimated to have been living in the nearby Mesa Verde cliff dwellings at about the same time.

It is clear that many of the pueblos of the Southwest were ceremonial centers in the same sense as were the centers of the Mississippi, Mesoamerica, and Andean regions. The difference seems to be the use of kivas going down into the earth rather than breasts going up into the sky. But both made use of plazas, apparently for ceremonial activity, even as they do today. One also should not overlook the educational functions of such large centers. Recently scholars have begun to examine the elaborate system of trails leading in virtually all directions from the great Chaco Canyon centers and have also begun to question whether some of these towns were not primarily religious or educational centers.

Pueblo Bonito, built in an arc shape, had at least eight hundred rooms and many stories. Aztec, also related to the Chacoan tradition, had at least three stories with 221 rooms in the lower story, 119 in the second, and 12 in the third, but much has been destroyed over the years. Strangely, Aztec was abandoned about 1130 and then reoccupied in 1220–1260, perhaps in response to environmental factors. In 1276–1299 tree-rings indicate a severe drought in the region, and at about that time most of the large cities were abandoned.

New towns began to be established in the Rio Grande Valley as well as to the south of the Chaco region. An example is San Marcos (1100–1680), south of Santa Fe. Immigrants, perhaps from the Four Corners, swelled its population along with that of other pueblos in the vicinity. San Marcos had two or more stories, with twenty-two room blocks surrounding five large plaza areas. It had about two thousand ground-floor rooms, with perhaps five thousand rooms in all (although not necessarily occupied at the same time). Clearly, the population was very substantial. In 1680, after Spanish oppression and diseases had taken a toll, six hundred persons were still residing there.

Many of the new towns established after 1300 (some went back to 1150 and just grew after 1300) were—and are—quite large. They frequently were multistoried, some going up to four stories in height. These cities had streets and plazas and good-sized populations, with many exceeding a thousand residents. Pecos, a very large pueblo, had perhaps two thousand residents and was four stories high in 1590. In modern times the populations of such survivors as Isleta, Laguna, Santo Domingo, and Zuni have all exceeded a thousand, while many others have been close to that figure. Among these are our oldest continually occupied cities, including such places as Acoma, Oraibi, and Taos.

During the same era, peoples of the Mogollon-Mimbres tradition inhabited many pueblos in Arizona and vicinity, eventually building Casa Grande and Pueblo Grande near Phoenix. Casas Grandes, Chihuahua, and Sahuaripa, Sonora, were large pueblos in north Mexico. Most of the towns were abandoned after 1400–1450, in a trend similar to what happened in many parts of the Mississippi Valley.

Turning to South America, the period of 1200–1400 witnessed the growth of the great city of Chan Chan, whose ruins still cover an area of up to eleven square miles and whose population was estimated at between fifty thousand and two hundred thousand persons (probably making it larger than any other city in the world, outside perhaps of eastern or south Asia, until the rise of Tenochtítlan). Chan Chan had a harbor at its west wall, with docks that could be closed with gates. It had a well-laid-out plan of residential districts with gardens, pyramids, and extensive irrigation canals (one seventy-three miles long). The Chimu culture possessed great engineers, indicating an advanced educational system. They were able, for example, to construct a huge dam in the Nepeña Valley. Chan Chan is said to have been the largest premodern city in South America, but the great metropolis declined before the rise of the Inca State. The latter's culture did not favor large cities, organizing the people instead into smaller cities with granaries and intensive agricultural zones. The major exception was Cuzco, the capital, which was a carefully planned city laid out in the form of a puma. In the early 1500s Cuzco had some four thousand residential buildings, along with neighborhoods serving particular social functions in keeping with the Mean "welfare state" system of production and rational planning.

Further north, large cities continued to exist in Mexico, as at Mayapan in Yucatan (1250–1350) where eleven to twelve thousand people lived, and at Dzibilchalt with even a larger population, as noted. Many cities had disappeared throughout Mexico, but in the central area, Cholula, Atzcapotzalco of the Tepanecas, Culhuacan, Texcoco, and others remained fairly large. In 1325 the people known as the Aztecs or Mexicas founded Tenochtítlan on an island in the Lake of Texcoco and during the 1400s it became, with its close neighbor Tlaltelolco, the greatest city in the world, perhaps the greatest city ever created by human beings anywhere.

Much can be written about Tenochtitlan, but I will be very brief. Its population is variously estimated at from one hundred thousand to two hundred thousand (or much more), but all agree on the incredible beauty and "modernity" of the city—with its geometrical arrangement of both streets and canals, its causeways and freshwater aqueduct to the mainland, and its some two hundred thousand canoes operating on the lake and along the canals. It was a thoroughly planned city with public health concerns of a startlingly advanced nature. The removal of hazardous trash and feces and the provision of fresh water and plentiful food supplies made Tenochtitlan a model city. However, we should note that it was probably patterned in this respect after earlier cities in the Americas. All of this was destroyed by the invading Spaniards.

In many parts of America, large settlements existed. Unfortunately, time and space does not allow for a careful documentation of cities in the Caribbean or in many other areas. One example will suffice to show, however, that many Americans were town-dwellers, even in regions we might normally think of as being rural. Scholars have found that a Mandan town in North Dakota in the 1550–1675 period covered 3.43 hectares and had 103 dwellings, surrounded by a ditch and palisaded earthwork on three sides (with the river on the fourth). Long rectangular houses were aligned in rows, with an open plaza in the center and a large rectangular structure located therein, probably a ceremonial building. Ethnographic data supports a population of some ten to fifteen persons per dwelling, and so the town very much resembles many small cities located in other regions, such as the Mississippi and Ohio Valleys. After European contact the size of northern plains towns declined greatly.

Meanwhile, in the Mississippi Valley and throughout much of the southeastern U.S. the Mississippian tradition reached its peak of development after 1100–1200. Many large and impressive ceremonial centers and associated cities typify the period, represented especially by huge centers in such places as Moundville (Alabama), Angel (Indiana) and Cahokia (Illinois). The largest and probably the greatest was Cahokia, a city that not only featured its own group of impressive mounds, but that also stands at the center of hundreds of other mounds within a radius of seven miles. One of its early visitors compared its population with that of Philadelphia in 1811 (a city of fifty thousand). But it was more than simply a residential, commercial, and ceremonial metropolis. It appears also to have been a

major calendric and astronomical center with many "circles" designed to record solar movements precisely. A beaker found in an offertory pit near a winter solstice sunrise position has on it a cross symbol remarkably like the Maya symbol for sun and time, Cahokia is also thought to have been a political center, controlled by a ranked, hierarchical society, but such opinions simply do not jibe with the political behavior of the people who are descended from the Cahokians, namely many Siouan-speakers (and perhaps others, including Iroquoians and Algonkians).

A decline seems to have occurred after 1300-1400 for many of the large cities, especially north of Memphis. The end is said to be abrupt in southeastern Missouri (c. 1350) but perhaps a bit later elsewhere. To the south, however, some areas showed new growth, and large towns still existed in 1541 when the Spaniards invaded the southeast and caused a massive decline in population. For example, the city of Etowah in Georgia, founded around 1200, reached its peak of about three thousand persons just before 1500. Some mounds and associated villages continued in use until the eighteenth century in the lower Mississippi Valley, as among the Natchez and Choctaw.

Over vast areas of America the Native peoples lived highly urbanized lives for many millennia. Other Americans lived in sizable towns of a permanent character, usually with many other nearby towns in the region. Often ceremonial centers and heart circles were associated with these cities and towns. Much of this was destroyed by the European invasions and by the resulting population declines and dislocations. But we need to be able to study the earlier centuries if we are to fully comprehend our aboriginal American heritage. Our concepts should not be formed wholly by the period of European intrusion.

REFLECTIONS OF ALCATRAZ

Lanada Boyer

It was 5 January 1965 when I left on the Greyhound bus from my home reservation of the Shoshone and Bannock tribes to go to San Francisco. I was a participant in the Bureau of Indian Affairs Relocation Program, which sent tribal members from their reservations into the major cities of the nation to get work or learn a trade.

There were no jobs on the reservation, and the "No Indians or Dogs Allowed" signs had barely been taken down in my home town of Blackfoot, Idaho. Poverty, hardship, and despair had grown to be the way of life on the reservation. As a result of governmental rule, our reservation and people were suffering.

I was raised from childhood in an environment of tribal politics. My father was the tribal chairman for a number of years. His resistance to the government's attempts to steal our water and lands through the Shoshone Nation Land Claims put our whole family in jeopardy. I would help my father write letters to officials to get assistance for our reservation, and it was in this way that I began to understand about the continuing war against our people.

It was a very hard time for us all; the 1960s did not bring change. When the BIA offered relocation to the city, I took the opportunity, along with many others who left their reservations. We were not aware that the federal government's plan to "drop us off" in the cities was another insidious method of depriving us of our reservation lands and membership in our tribes. Some of us knew that non-Indians were exerting intense political pressures to gain more of our lands for their economic benefit.

We began our new lives in the cities, socializing primarily with our own people. On the reservations,

it was easy to divide Indians against Indians; but in a major city, we are so glad to see other Indians, we don't care what tribe they are. They are Natives, and that's all that counts.

The San Francisco Indian Center became a focal point of social life for many relocated tribal members in the Bay Area. The center sponsored both pow-wows and non-Indian dances. It published a newsletter that many Bay Area Indian residents received. Other Indian organizations, such as the Oakland Friendship House and the San Jose Indian Center, grew out of the Bay Area where Indians were living. Our organizations eventually became a part of the city, and we were acknowledged along with other city minority organizations. Whenever Mayor Alioto went to the Mission District where many of us lived, he would meet with the Latino and Spanish groups, the Mission Rebels (Blacks), and the Indians. We were recognized as a political unit, and gradually we became politicized.

I cofounded United Native Americans with Lehman Brightman, who actively led our political efforts in the Bay Area. Lee was a former University of Oklahoma football star whose intelligence, wit, and concern led him to become a strong Native American advocate. We networked with other organizations and the California Indian Education Association. One of our first efforts was to seek reform of Bureau of Indian Affairs policies to allow relocated Indians more than a one-way ticket to the city. We wanted to attend the universities in the Bay Area, but, since a college education was beyond our means, we requested assistance from the BIA, which had put us there. Instead, the BIA ended the relocation program in 1966.

With the support of the San Francisco Mission District organizations, I was accepted by the University of California, Berkeley. In January 1968, I was the very first Native American student to be accepted through special admissions into the Economic Opportunity

Program, on probationary status. I kept up my grades and went off probation. At first, it was lonely being a Native on a campus of fifty thousand students; then I met Patty Silvas, who was a Blackfeet from Salinas, California. She was the only other Native on campus and had entered through regular admissions. We worked together to develop good university support.

It was not long before other Native students were admitted; my program allowed me to recruit for UC Berkeley. After a while, we had enough students to form our own Native student organization, which I chaired. The campus was still simmering from the free speech movement, the civil rights and antiwar protests, and it was natural for us to get caught up in the heat of campus unrest with the Third World Strike.

The Third World Strike at Berkeley in 1969 was the most expensive of the Berkeley campus protests, because the university assembled the largest force of Berkeley police and National Guard ever. They marched in with their bayonets unsheathed and fogged the campus with pepper gas. Every class was interrupted and stopped. All of the Third World Strike leaders were arrested on various charges. After the gas cleared away, I became one of the coalition leaders on the four-person negotiation team for our Third World College. We were victorious in establishing our own Department of Ethnic Studies, consisting of Black, Chicano, Asian, and Native American studies programs within the university. Ours was the very first such department in the nation.

It was during this time that the issue of Alcatraz Island became a target of interest for us. In 1964, after the prison had been abandoned, a group of Lakota, consisting of Russell Means, Hank Means, Belva Cottier, Richard McKenzie, and others, had tried to reclaim the island as federal surplus property. Their efforts had been treated as a joke by the media.

Now the island was being considered for purchase by a wealthy developer who wanted to build a casino there. We were concerned that the developer would be allowed to build his casino and the earlier claim would be ignored. This would mean that the federal government had no intention of honoring either the federal surplus laws giving lands back to Native peoples or the 1868 treaty that was the basis of the Lakota claim in 1964. This failure to uphold another treaty was enough to push our buttons.

The students at UC Berkeley and San Francisco State had already formed a Native student alliance, so when Richard Oakes, chairman of the San Francisco State student organization, contacted me at Berkeley about having the students symbolically take Alcatraz Island for the Indians, I said, "Sounds great. Let's do it." He informed me that Adam Nordwall, a local Bay Area Indian businessman, was going to rent a boat to sail around the island to publicize the Indians' claim. We made arrangements to get the students together on a Sunday afternoon to sail around the island. Four of our students jumped off the boat and attempted to swim to the island. We got very little publicity, but it was a nice boat ride on a Sunday afternoon, compliments of Adam Nordwall.

During this time, the San Francisco Indian Center burned to the ground. The community was devastated. The students got together and decided to take over the island as our new center for Indians in the Bay Area. On 14 November 1969, we met on the San Francisco docks and looked for a boat to rent. Finally, we spotted some fishermen just pulling in, and I approached the first man off the boat, asking him to take us to the island one way. Since the island was closed to the public, I had to convince him that we wanted to go for a special purpose. I told him we wanted to go to the island for a ceremony, which might take us awhile. He asked where our food was, and I told him we were fasting. He agreed to take us and charged us three dollars per person. Earl Livermore paid for those of us who did not have any money.

As we waited for the rest of our group, it began to grow dark. The fishermen were getting impatient, and I was afraid they would back out, so we pulled away from the dock. As we were leaving, I could see outlines of figures and legs running, so I asked the fisherman to go back and pick up our friends. It was Richard Oakes and a few of the San Francisco State students. This gave us a total of fourteen Indian students. The fisherman took us out to the island and dropped us off.

We were on the island and it was beautiful. The view was a "knockout," with lights all over the Bay Area. Earl Livermore was on the mainland and would contact the press to let them know we were on the island. We split into groups and agreed that, if some of us were found, the others would continue to hide out and hold the island. It felt like a game of hide-and-seek, and we were not afraid. At times, a search party would be very close to us, and it was hard to keep from giggling or laughing. All that night, the coast guard looked for us with searchlights in the old buildings, but we eluded them.

In the morning, we got together and decided to splinter off into smaller groups. A few hours later, Rick Evening, Kay Many Horses, and I were hiding out when we heard our names being called. I said to

Rick, "I thought we were going to hold out and not give ourselves up." He said he would go see what was going on. A few minutes later, he came back and said Richard Oakes had identified himself when the press arrived and had made a deal with the coast guard that none of us would be arrested if we all gave ourselves up. I did not want to say anything to Richard in front of everybody for the sake of unity, so, reluctantly, I got into the boat.

When we got back to the mainland, the rest of the students were upset with us for coming back. They had begun mobilizing a statewide effort to get other Native students to join us on the island. They were upset with Richard for making a deal to come back. We decided to continue the mobilization effort and go back to the island.

On 20 November 1969, Native American students from the major California colleges and universities arrived with their families to take the island. My sister, Claudene Boyer, and my son, Deynon Means, arrived with this landing party. My oldest son, Devon, was not with me when we went to Alcatraz. When we arrived on the island and made our way up to the second level, I sensed a wonderful, forbidden excitement among our group. The weather was good and the view spectacular as we set up our lookout points on top of the prison. We camped out in sleeping bags all over the island. It felt great to be there and to direct our energies into a stand for Indian people everywhere.

We took the island because we wanted the federal government to honor our treaties and its own laws. The previous claim had been made back in 1964, so we were the follow-up. We also wanted to focus attention on Indian reservations and communities throughout the nation where our people were living in poverty and suffering great injustice.

The next day, the press and all kinds of people arrived on the island. The international media focus embarrassed the federal government. The United States is always the first to point out human rights violations in other countries, without regard to its own treatment of Native Americans, Blacks, Chicanos, Asians, and poor people. We hoped to expose the atrocities that the federal government has perpetrated and continues to perpetrate against our people. Every day, as news of the island takeover traveled throughout the country, our people kept arriving. We were in full view of the entire world, and the government made no move to take us off the island.

Many people, diverse tribal groups and nonNatives alike, came to visit the island. Some were just now re-identifying as Indians and "wannabe's." We were the tattered remnants of a proud and cultured people—what was left of our once strong and healthy nation. We did not all look or behave like our ancestors, because we were the products of our times. We were finally "civilized Indians," from liars and thieves to genuine Indian chiefs. The government's racist efforts to deny us our heritage and to assimilate us into the American mainstream had backfired with the Alcatraz takeover.

In the weeks to follow, the residents quickly set out to organize the island. Everybody wanted to claim fame and to be included in the formation. I sat back and watched everyone scramble for leadership and for recognition by the media.

We had good leadership. As long as everybody wanted to be involved in the hard work of organization and island logistics, that was great. We had a big job ahead, and everybody was doing what needed to be done. Because I did not intend to drop out of school, I needed to attend to my classes, so I did not want to take on any extra responsibilities unless I had to.

The media identified Richard Oakes as the leader on the island, and he wanted the responsibility, so that was agreeable with us. Richard was smart and aggressive—a handsome Mohawk who always knew what to say. We were proud of Richard. We maintained our student autonomy on the island, recognizing the separate campus organizations and community organizations. The students and their families stayed on the island as long as they could but eventually left to continue their studies.

I continued my residence on the island but kept my apartment on the mainland and commuted to the university to maintain my studies. My sister did not leave the island during most of the occupation. Deynon and I would hitchhike off the docks at Alcatraz and would occasionally catch a sailboat or speedboat to the marina on Sunday afternoon, clean up, and check into my classes.

When the government blocked our water barge and boats from docking on the island, Richard successfully brought in food and provisions on the opposite side of the island, where it was impossible to dock because of the high cliffs. When the government took the water barge away, we brought water over in a boat that Creedence Clearwater Revival bought for us. They bought the boat from "Captain Cliff," whom we hired to take us back and forth from the mainland to the island. We named our boat the *Clearwater*.

Initially, we took up residence in the prison block. It was winter in the Bay Area, and it rained most of the time, but we were able to survive under those conditions, because life was not very different from the poverty on the reservations or in the urban ghettos. It was inconvenient to live on the island without water, electricity, or heat, but most of us became conditioned to the elements. People who were not conditioned to the elements got sick when they stayed.

We formed an island organization called Indians of All Tribes. A lot of rivalry and competition always existed on the island. I sensed that the Indian men did not want to recognize the authority of the women, because they had been assimilated into white society and its male chauvinism.

Everyone had a job on the island—to help on the boats, with the school, or anywhere else they were willing to work. Stella Leach, a registered Indian nurse, and Dr. Tepper had moved out to the island right after the invasion. They operated the first aid unit and provided medical support. Dr. Tepper finally went back to his medical practice in Oakland, but Stella stayed on the island.

Grace Thorpe kept up public relations with the mainland. Sometime later, she bumped heads with the island council and left, but not until after she had helped the Pit River Indians to hold their land in Northern California, which was threatened by Pacific Gas and Electric (PG&E) Company. A group of Alcatraz Indians joined the Pit River Indians to protect their sacred site; in a confrontation with the police, it took nearly a dozen officers to carry Grace Thorpe off the property.

Richard Oakes was hurt on the mainland during a fight in a bar; he was hit over the head numerous times with a pool stick. He made a miraculous recovery in the hospital, thanks to Thomas Banyacya and an attending group of medicine men (including Mad Bear Anderson) from the Iroquois Confederation, only to face great sadness later. Richard and his family left the island when his daughter Yvonne died after falling four stories in an apartment building in the guards' quarters.

During the occupation, a number of Alcatraz Indians left for Washington State to support the Nisqually Indians, who were fighting for fishing rights at Franks Landing. President Nixon signed a bill that returned the sacred Blue Lake to Taos Pueblo. More funding was appropriated by Congress for programs on the reservations. Indians from Alcatraz supported the Pyramid Lake Paiute people in their efforts to keep their sacred lake. Alcatraz provided help to Indian efforts to establish D-Q University in Davis, California. Alcatraz was a "rock"

that hit the water and sent out a thousand ripples: Nearly a thousand documented events resulted from the occupation of Alcatraz.

SPIRITUAL REBIRTH

I took up residence on the second level of a house. My house, which I had painted red, had a beautiful view of the bay, and my room had enough space for my two double beds, like a hotel room. The other bed was for my guests, such as medicine man Pete Mitten and his wife, from New York, who stayed with me during their visit to the island, and Thomas Banyacya and his wife, Fermina.

Thomas Banyacya told me that he had traveled internationally since being appointed as a translator by the chiefs in 1945. After the bombing of Hiroshima, the Hopi had become alarmed at the destructive direction of the United States. According to their rock writings and prophecies, the bomb marked the beginning of a harmful era and had to be stopped somehow by warning as many people as possible of what was to come.

Thomas told me that he and his wife had come to Alcatraz to see for themselves what was happening. In accordance with the Hopi prophecies, the "tree of Indian life" was cut off at the base, but, through the nourishment of the ancient roots, sprouts were growing out of the base of the tree. It was encircled with a design that matched the Bay Area, and the tree growing new sprouts was located where Alcatraz lay in the bay. He said that the young people are the new sprouts growing out of the Indian tree of life. The takeover of Alcatraz symbolized this rebirth.

Thomas told me about the Hopi prophecy. To my understanding, the world had ended three times before this world. It was always the result of misusing modern inventions for destructive purposes instead of for peace. This time, it was not supposed to happen. All people would have the choice of continuing in the destructive direction or coming back to the sacred circle of life and perpetuating the spiritual ways of our forefathers. We need to clean up the earth and the environment now, before the three purifiers come from the east. If the people do not change their ways, the earth will shake to wake up the people. Our ancestors will help us survive through the purification if we maintain our beliefs, practices, and spiritual ways.

My personal experience happened one night while I was asleep in my room. I woke up to see a fire in the curtains. Because I was still half asleep, I did not think; I followed my first instinct, which was to protect my son. I threw myself at the fire and put it out with my hands. There had been two other fires that same night, and the men had just finished battling another blaze on the island. I lived over the dining hall, and the men were downstairs having coffee when I emerged from my room carrying my son, with smoke following behind me.

I handed Deynon over to someone and then fell over. My hands were badly burned, and I had gone into shock. Shock felt good to me, because I felt no pain and it was good to see everyone working together. Several people ran upstairs to see if the fire was out; others rushed to put my hands into cold milk and to carry me to a bed they had assembled in the kitchen. They put my hands into milk because we had no water. There was no boat scheduled until the next day, so they could not take me to the mainland.

They must have suspected arson, because they put me on a cot in the kitchen and guarded me all night. My *eyes* were closed, but my spirit could see everything all around me. It was an experience I'll never forget. I saw Stella sitting by me all night, and I knew when she fell asleep. I knew who looked into the window at me during the night while on guard duty. I remember the first rays of dawn coming over the horizon, and I remember our one rooster crowing. Stella covered me with the Pendleton blanket that my parents had given me. I remembered my mother telling me how to receive spiritual strength from saying her prayers at sunrise. I gathered my blanket around me, slipped out of the kitchen into the yard and over to the edge of the island. I lifted my

Stella Leach, who worked as a nurse on Alcatraz during the occupation, stands in front of the island ten years later, November 1979.

hands to the sun and prayed as it rose over the Bay Bridge in the east. I experienced a deep knowledge inside me that I would be all right.

The boat arrived in a few hours, and Stella took me over to Dr. Tepper's office in Oakland. My hands were charred black, and my fingers were huge and swollen like boiled wieners. I had from first- to third-degree burns on both hands. The doctor said they were burned down to the tendons. His medical diagnosis was that I would never be able to use my fingers again.

I refused Dr. Tepper's advice to go to the hospital. He peeled the charred skin off my hands to reveal raw, pink fingers. Then he applied a burn ointment and covered it with bandage dressing. He said it would take six months to a year before I could use my hands. I went back to the island, and, miraculously, my hands healed within six weeks with hardly any trace of scarring. I recovered full use of all my fingers. This was my very first spiritual experience. I had learned what to say by repeating everything my father taught me; I knew what to do by remembering my mother's words of caution and guidance.

The federal government sent Bob Robertson to negotiate with us on the island. We looked forward to this occasion and were as friendly as possible in order to encourage a good relationship. We did not have much, but we offered him coffee and brownies for this occasion. We did not use sugar, because it attracted insects; instead, we used saccharin in small tablets, which was much more efficient for our living conditions. We asked him if he wanted sugar in his coffee and he said "yes," so we put in saccharin. His report to Washington said that we had put LSD in his coffee and he had refused to drink it. Actually, I never noticed whether he drank his coffee. How paranoid he must have been!

This experience gave me keen insight into how the game of "divide and conquer" is played. Robertson told us he would not work with a "bunch of young militant Indians" who did not have the support of the responsible adult Indian community. We told him we were not militant Indians because we were unarmed.

To further our negotiations to obtain the island for our people, we formed the Bay Area Native American Council (BANAC), composed of all the Bay Area Indian organizations as a support group for Alcatraz. Robertson's first ploy was to fund BANAC, hoping that the Alcatraz residents would resent the government's funding of the off-island organization while the island organization was dependent on contributions. However, this did not cause anyone to blink an eye, because no one knew what it was to be funded in the first place. The money gave BANAC a larger voice in Indian affairs and a more vivid profile.

Next, Allen Miller, a San Francisco State student, and I went to Washington, D.C. to gather more support from the National Congress of American Indians (NCAI). This organization was composed of tribes throughout the country, and we needed their formal support. John Belindo, the NCAI director, was not very receptive. Perhaps Robertson had gotten to him before we did. We were told that it would be up to the delegation. Their national convention was in Alaska, so we had to go to Alaska to seek support.

Bob Robertson was way ahead of us in lobbying against Alcatraz. He knew we had formed BANAC to quash his claim that Alcatraz did not have the support of the responsible adult community. Robertson's propaganda to the tribes was not only that we were young militants but also that we were "urban" Indians. He told the tribes that the urban Indians were after a slice of the "federal economic pie." The reservations were already receiving very little federal funding, and the pie would be sliced even smaller if the tribes supported the militant urban Indians. We could not even get on the agenda, and we were barred from the NCAI convention.

Robertson found adversaries to our cause among various tribal chairmen and established the National Tribal Chairman's Association (NTCA). Thus he created an effective tool to divide Indians against Indians. Tribes fell into the trap. Negotiations on the island disintegrated. The government position was to let us stay, hoping that we eventually would lose support and disappear. To speed the process, they would send out "plants" to observe us and to stir up infighting among the island residents.

The island council appointed me as the island's public relations representative. I started by talking with press people about the island, about our people, and about the reservations. Then I was invited to the mainland to appear on news programs to discuss the island situation.

Several times, the local media reported that the coast guard had seen weapons being loaded on the island. I knew that the federal government was trying to set us up to get killed. When it began to look dangerous for us, I called a press conference on the island to dispel any rumors that we had guns. I had the children line up with their toy guns and throw them away. I said if the coast guard had seen guns, it must have been the children's toys, and now there were none.

I was dead set against guns on the island. My experiences at Berkeley had shown me what happened to the Black Panthers after they were reported to be armed and militant. They were all killed. My mother never allowed guns in our home while I was growing up. She always said that my brothers were

Oohosis, Cree from Canada, and a friend on the mainland dock on the day of their forced removal from Alcatraz Island, June 11, 1971.

too young and hot-headed, so I never had any use for guns. Thomas Banyacya told me that the word *Hopi* meant peace and that our people were the true people of peace. I would not allow the symbolism of Alcatraz to be defiled by violence. Besides, I am a mother, and I would not let anyone endanger my son or the other children on the island.

A San Francisco leftist magazine by the name of *Ramparts* had paid my fine during the Third World Strike at Berkeley. Peter Collier of *Ramparts* asked me if he could take some pictures and do a story about the problems on my reservation. When the story came out, I posed for the cover with a red paintbrush in my hand and the words "Better Red Than Dead." To me, it meant we should be proud of being Native Americans and we should not assimilate and let our culture die. I did not realize I was pushing buttons from the McCarthy era. Since *Ramparts* was not a mainstream magazine, I did not think it would receive wide circulation. I thought speaking out would help create a better understanding, but my words were twisted in the press.

Jane Fonda saw the article and came out to the island. She said she wanted to go to Fort Hall, so I took her to my reservation to meet my parents. After she visited with them and some of my father's friends, she went back to California, inviting me to appear on several local television shows in Los Angeles. My son Deynon and I went to Los Angeles, and then I went to New York for the Dick Cavett Show. Deynon stayed at Henry Fonda's house in California with Jane's husband, Roger Vadim, who remained with their daughter Vanessa and Deynon while Jane and I were in New York.

I had never been on a television show, and it made me feel extremely uncomfortable. During the first commercial break on the Cavett show, I got up and walked off, because I thought I was supposed to leave. I felt awkward, wondering if I was supposed to be witty and funny about the injustices perpetrated against our people.

During this time, after Richard Oakes had left Alcatraz, Stella Leach got fed up with the politics and the constant attacks on her and her family, and she left also. As a member of the Alcatraz council, I had to become more involved, since many of the other members had left.

John Trudell, who ran "Radio Free Alcatraz," became the spokesperson for the island. John had strong leadership qualities and a good speaking voice and always had something meaningful to say. John became the new leader for Alcatraz, and we worked well as a team. I welcomed the opportunity to have John in the spotlight, making the presentations to the media, while I, in the background, prepared the press releases.

It was about this time that I wrote the planning grant proposal for Thunderbird University and Cultural Center, named for a group of Indians in the Bay Area called the "Thunderbirds." The island chose the architectural firm of McDonald and Associates of San Francisco to develop the design and model. We unveiled our plans on our first anniversary on the island, 20 November 1970.

As the executive secretary of the Bay Area Native American Council (BANAC), I was asked to go to Washington, D.C. with the other officers. Before I left the island, we held a meeting, at which John Trudell became very angry with me and made some rude accusations. I did not want to throw more fuel on the fire by having a confrontation; instead, I rushed down to the docks to catch my boat for the mainland. All of the island residents were aware of the rift.

Ethel Kennedy set up an appointment for me to discuss the Alcatraz situation with Edward Bennett Williams. On 21 January 1971, I wrote a letter to the island, with copies to the island attorneys and BANAC, requesting approval to secure Edward Bennett Williams as legal counsel to pursue the litigative end for Alcatraz.

While in D.C., I stayed with Edgar Cahn, author of *My Brother's Keeper*, and his wife, Jean, who were responsible for many of the poverty and advocacy programs for Native Americans and poor people throughout the country. President Nixon had been elected and was now taking office. Edgar's contact in the White House, Bobby Kilberg, was writing Nixon's inauguration address, which was to be titled the "President's White House Address on American Indians." This message set the tone for programs directed to benefit Indians on reservations throughout President Nixon's administration. The very first and last help we ever received was too short-lived.

When I received no response from the island, I went back to see what was going on. John Trudell told me that the island attorneys had advised him and the other residents not to give approval to litigate. I wanted to hear what an Indian attorney would recommend and recruited John Echohawk, director of the Native American Rights Fund. Echohawk went to the island and gave his legal opinion that it would greatly benefit the island and the cause if we initiated litigation.

By this time, Trudell's wife, Lou, had given birth to their son Wovoka on the island. The baby was the only Native American born on liberated territory in five hundred years. John had the respect and awe of both the island residents and the non-Indian public. Under the Alcatraz attorneys' advice, the occupiers voted down the litigation. John Trudell could have changed their minds if he had wanted to, but no one could change John's mind about seeking litigation.

I did not give up the litigation issue and went back to the student organizations to seek their support. Richard Oakes had left San Francisco State by then and was living in Northern California with his wife's family and tribe. He was eventually shot to death by white racists. Allen Miller and several of the original Native American students were still attending San Francisco State.

The students at UC Berkeley and San Francisco State were still very concerned about Alcatraz. I told them that the island population was under the influence of the attorneys who had advised against litigation. The island people were down-to-earth, good people who had sacrificed the modern conveniences of the mainland and sometimes went without food in order to "hold the rock." I felt helpless to try to reach them; the divisive gap was just too wide.

The students were very supportive. They decided to take back the island, outnumbering the antilitigation population and putting the movement back on track. I was greatly encouraged by this unselfish gesture. We set the date and met with our groups to arrange for boats to go out to the island. All of the students would take their families to live on the island. It would soon be summer, school would be out, and our academic survival would not be immediately threatened.

The day before we planned to go, the federal government took the remaining people off the island without a confrontation. We were devastated. We suspected that we had had an informer among us.

After the government took Alcatraz back, we all went our separate ways. I guess that is how a tree grows; it splits into many branches. We were always afraid that, if the government had given us Alcatraz, they would have said, "We gave you Alcatraz; you got what you wanted!" They would have expected us to be satisfied with that. No, we want much more.

We want to live as free people in our own country. We want the government to pass laws to respect our Mother Earth, with real enforcement to protect the land, the water, the environment, and the people. We want freedom of religion—the right to be human. We want our ancestors' remains to be returned to our homelands. We want the federal government to stop contributing to the destruction around the world and to set a good example so we can all be proud to be Americans.

The Alcatraz occupation could have gone much more smoothly. People could have cooperated and supported us more. We could have had all the answers and no arguments. We have a long way to go before we can live in a balanced world and be the best people that we can be. We made many mistakes, but this is how we learn and grow.

We can see today that the tree of Indian life is growing stronger, more mature and complex. Our ancient roots continue to give our spirits strength and guidance. We did not get the island, but we aroused the consciousness of all people, including ourselves, to our plight. Every individual and every nation still has a story to be told. Within these stories are our guidelines for the future.

The island is a reminder of our ongoing relationship with the federal government. It is an infamous prison that carries the burden of the wicked deeds of others, the bondage and captivity of our people, the painful stories of human misery and suffering. The federal government has never recognized our claim and has failed to enforce many treaties and federal laws protecting our rights and those of many others.

Under the Department of the Interior, the Bureau of Indian Affairs manages our lives in the same way that Golden Gate Parks and Recreation manages Alcatraz Island. The island is surrounded by the water of the bay, just as we are surrounded by the ignorant and selfish interests of capitalistic industrialized societies. The structures on the island grow old and weather beaten, treated with dishonor and disrespect, as are our culture and religion, and the sacred laws of our mother earth.

Today, our people continue to live in poverty—the victims of genocide and injustice. We are political prisoners in our own homelands. We have no individual constitutional protections, because we are considered "political entities." If truth and justice were truly practiced by the federal government, our traditional governments, our religious leaders, and our people would be recognized today. Our hardships have made our spirits grow stronger. We give thanks for our many blessings and pray that the sacred circle of life continues forever.

IS URBAN A PERSON OR A PLACE?
CHARACTERISTICS OF URBAN INDIAN COUNTRY
Susan Lobo

Is urban a person or a place? Urban is a place, a setting in which many Indian people at some time in their lives visit, "establish an encampment," or settle, into. Urban doesn't determine self-identity, yet the urban area and urban experiences are the context and some of the factors that contribute to defining identity. The intent of this chapter is to delineate some of the general structural characteristics of urban Indian communities in the United States and to indicate the ways that urban communities interplay with individual and group identity. While most of the focused research for this discussion has been carried out since 1978 in the San Francisco Bay Area, and the principal examples given here are specific to that region, many of the comments also are applicable on a general level to other urban Indian communities such as those found in Seattle, Los Angeles, and Chicago. The works, for example, of Garbarino and Straus in Chicago, Liebow in Phoenix, Shoemaker in Minneapolis, Bramstedt and Weibel-Orlando in Los Angeles, Danziger in Detroit, and Guillemin in Boston indicate parallels and counterpoints to the regional focus of this chapter.[1]

Each Indian community throughout the United States and Canada has its unique character. Yet, traveling from one to another, visiting friends and family, and participating in events around the country; one notices many underlying similarities that characterize urban Indian country, and these fundamental similarities create a setting that is "like home" in the city. Some of the significant factors influencing the parallels among different urban Indian communities, as well as each community's unique qualities, include the historical role played by the relocation program

and other types of policy-driven external influences; the degree of proximity and ease of travel and communication between cities and tribal areas, reservations, and homelands; and the availability of employment, housing, and educational opportunities in urban areas. An in-depth comparative study of various urban Indian communities is long, long overdue.

This chapter is based on long-term applied work, research, and personal engagement in the San Francisco Bay Area American Indian community. I began in 1978, as a co-founder of, and have continued as the coordinator of, the Community History Project located at the Oakland American Indian Center, Intertribal Friendship House (IFH). The center was established in 1955 and, along with the Chicago Indian Center, is one of the oldest urban Indian centers in the United States. It was founded in response to the federal relocation program and to the incipient demographic shift by Indian people from rural to urban areas that was then getting under way.

Intertribal Friendship House, as one of the early urban Indian institutions nationally, and the Bay Area Indian community overall continues to loom large in the Indian country cognitive map. Many Bay Area Indian residents remark that wherever one goes, no matter how remote, how seemingly unlikely, you can bet that whomever you may be talking to will say, "Sure I know Oakland. We used to go to the Wednesday night dinners at IFH all the time," or "We were there for a while when I was young and I remember my Mom took me over to see the buffalos at the San Francisco zoo when I was six, for my birthday. Boy, they were sure in bad shape. I still remember her saying that they didn't know how to really take care of them." IFH is identified by many as the emotional "heart" of the Bay Area Indian community. It is the ideal urban Indian community crossroads, where the Community History Project, a photographic and

An earlier version of this chapter appeared in the *American Indian Culture and Research Journal*, 22, no. 4 (1998) 89–102 and this version appeared in the *American Indian Urban Experience*, edited by Susan Lobo and Kurt Peters (Walnut Creek, CA: Altamira Press), 2001, pp. 73–84.

oral history archive, has developed. This is a collection of contemporary urban-focused historical materials that is referred to as a community resource archive because of the active involvement of "the community" in both formulating and building the archives and in using it for purposes identified by the community itself.

The IFH Community History Project, which started as a narrowly defined oral history project, has grown into an extensive Indian-controlled and community-based research unit and archive of taped oral histories, photographs, videos and films, documents, and ephemera focusing on the Bay Area American Indian community from the 1940s to the present. This is, to my knowledge, one of the very few, and also the most extensive, archive emphasizing Indian history within an urban area. It is also a working archive, open to the Indian community as well as to outside researchers, and it is actively circulated, added to, reformulated, interpreted, and used for a wide array of educational and advocacy purposes. Immersion in this material, participation in the continual flow of community events and activities, and working jointly with Indian community members on an ongoing basis on a variety of community projects are the foundations for the description and analysis that follows.

Methodologically, this kind of deep, long-term, and unabashedly personal involvement in a community allows for an understanding of both those aspects of the community that shift and those aspects that persist over time, sometimes stretching across generations. For example, there are those delicate balances of power, informed by kinship and tribal affiliation, or the routes that leadership and alliance formation take, all unfolding fluidly over long periods of time.

THE COMMUNITY

For American Indians living in the Bay Area and for our definitional purposes here, the Indian community is not a geographic location with clustered residency or neighborhoods, but rather it is fundamentally a widely scattered and frequently shifting network of relationships with locational nodes found in organizations and activity sites of special significance. It is a distinct community that answers needs for affirming and activating identity; it creates contexts for carrying out the necessary activities of community life; and it provides a wide range of circumstances and symbols that encourage "Indian" relationships at the family and community levels.

The American Indian community in the San Francisco Bay Area is characterized here on a general level as a social group in which:

1. Community members recognize a shared identity.
2. There are shared values, symbols and history.
3. Basic institutions have been created and sustained.
4. There have emerged consistent features of social organization such as those related to social control and the definition of distinctive and specialized gender-related and age-related roles.

There are geographic markers around the Bay that set the stage for community activities: the enclosing hills, the Bay, and the bridges that connect the East Bay with San Francisco and San Francisco with Marin County. However, these geographic features only set the stage for the "Indian map" of the area of shared abstract connotations, where people speak of "going to the Healing Center," a residential treatment center for women and their children, or nodding with the head to the north of downtown Oakland and saying, "over by CRC," an American Indian family and child assistance agency. People in the Indian community know where these points of reference are; those not participating in the community would not know. Or, for example, when an Indian person comments, quite possibly totally out of context, "You going to Stanford?" the question is not, "Do you attend Stanford University?" but rather, "Will I see you at the Stanford Pow-wow this May?" Or when someone says "I saw your niece up at Hilltop," the reference is to a high-profile Indian bar, not to be confused with a shopping mall of the same name. Each of these examples illustrates one of the ways that Indian people in the Bay Area talk about or interpret their environment, which is both a setting for community as a place and is also deeply intertwined with the network of relatedness that ties the community members together. Theodoratus and LaPena express this idea well in reference to Wintu sacred geography, "It [this paper] is about topographical features that are the embodiment of Wintu expression of an ordinary and nonordinary world. It is about a concept of land and interpretations of that natural universe that translate into a coherent world."[2] In the case of the Bay Area Indian community vision of community, it is both the topographical features and the built environment that are a part of creating this "coherent world."

This physical environment, while the backdrop and the grounding for much of the community activity, is not "the community," which instead finds its focus in relationship dynamics and in the more abstract realm of shared knowledge that informs and shapes actions. Nor is an urban Indian community situated in an immutable, bounded territory as is a reservation, but rather it exists within a fluidly defined region with niches of resources and boundaries that respond to needs and activities, perhaps reflecting a reality closer to the way Native homelands were before the imposition of reservation borders. For example, with the development and flourishing of D-Q University, an Indian-controlled community college, the conceptualization of the Bay Area Indian community extended sixty miles to the north to include this institution as an outlaying entity.

On tribal homelands, a major source of identity is embodied in the land and, often, the old stories and songs that tie personal reality to time and place. As Basso notes, "Knowledge of place is therefore closely linked to knowledge of the self, to grasping one's position in the larger scheme of things, including one's own community, and to securing a confident sense of who one is as a person."[3] Yet, in an urban community there essentially is no land base, except for a few recently purchased buildings and properties. Or, on the other hand, as someone recently pointed out to me, "All of it is our urban territory." In this urban context, the Indian organizations come to powerfully represent Indian "space" or "a place that is Indian" and are intimately tied to identity. Consequently, the control, the programs, and the guiding values of these organizations are under constant scrutiny, negotiation, and adjustment by core community members who act as community arbitrators.

To many outside the urban Indian community, it is an invisible population, not only because of the abstract and no geographically clustered nature of the community but also because of the continued existence of a series of stereotypes regarding Indian people. A widespread and mistaken assumption held by the general public is that American Indians have "vanished" or live overwhelmingly on reservations in rural areas. In reality, this is an expanding population, and the majority of Indian people now live in urban areas. From the perspective of much of the social science literature, as reflected in federal and state policies, as well as in criteria frequently utilized by funding sources, there is an oft-cited mindset that imposes a dichotomy between urban and rural, based on the lingering stereotype that *Indian* is synonymous with rural and that urban is somehow not genuinely Indian. Although there are certainly

differences in these two types of settings, establishing rural/urban as the defining characteristic of identity is not realistic from an Indian point of view and serves to further officially alienate Indian people from homelands. One of the most notorious recent policies reflecting this attitude was relocation, initiated in the 1950s and based on government assumptions that Indian people, once removed or relocated from tribal homelands, would become urban . . . definitively. Conversely, for many Indian people the urban areas are visualized at one level more as an extension of home territory or, as one person put it, "our urban encampment out here." For those living in the city, even those a few generations removed from tribal homelands, these strong linkages to "back home" are, for the most part, not broken. One simply extends the sense of territory, often keenly aware, for example, that sacred places are found at home and that after death one will very likely be buried there. With third- and fourth-generation urban people, this connection to home may change and take new forms, but it nevertheless continues.

The underlying Native sense of community—if viewed fundamentally as a network of relatedness that has become structured in many tribal homelands into formalized, federally prescribed tribes—reemerges in the city, as the rigid, bounded "tribe" demanded of federally recognized tribalness falls away. The federal government's image of tribes as social entities within a geographically rigid demarcated territory or reservation, governed by a body of elected officials, and with stringently designated criteria for membership is not transferred to urban Indian communities. Here in cities, in contrast, the social entity is reconstituted with a structuring based on a network of relatedness; the fluid territory has changing outer limits; there is no overarching formalized governing body; and membership is defined by a series of strongly situational and to some degree negotiable criteria.

The most striking urban parallel to the tribal political structuring found on rural reservations is the legal not-for-profit status of many urban Indian organizations, in which there are a governing board of directors, by-laws, and possibly membership lists. However, Indian people in the city, in contrast to the situation in a reservation tribal setting, are not governed by these organizations, nor do the organizations establish and enforce criteria for community membership. Also in the city, people may choose whether to become active in any particular organization at any specific time.

Although structured differently, the urban community comes to hold many connotations for Indian people that are similar to those of the tribe. The urban community gives a sense of belonging, a need to look inward to this social entity, and a feeling of responsibility to contribute to the well-being of the members, via support of the continuity and flourishing of urban institutions. In the Bay Area, one occasionally hears joking reference to the Indian community as "The Urban Tribe."

One of the underlying objectives of the federal relocation program initiated in the 1950s was the assimilation of American Indians into an envisioned mainstream. Yet, to many Indian people in the Bay Area, the existence and resiliency of the Indian community are expressions of resistance to pressure and domination by the non-Indian world. One factor in this persistence is the fluid network-based social structure. As Indian people often explain it, the community itself has the potential for regeneration. The community is ephemeral in nature, as the trickster Coyote has taught people to appreciate, with the power to continually take new forms and thus endure. Or it is described as being like the old-time warriors' strategy to disperse, vanish, become invisible, and then regroup to fight again another day. This dynamic is a familiar one to Indian people, who throughout the history of Indian–white relations and before have sought ways to persist as individuals and as Peoples. The institutions in the Indian community are in continual flux, able to disassemble and reassemble. Yet through all of this motion, there is an underlying network structure that allows for persistence.

The urban community in addition to having become the doorway to urban jobs and education also functions as a refuge for those who have unsolvable problems or who are deemed undesirable in their home reservation area. The villain Emo, in Silko's classic novel *Ceremony*, is last mentioned leaving New Mexico: "They told him to never come back around here. The old man said that. I heard he went to California. . . . 'California,' Tayo repeated softly, 'that's a good place for him.'"[4] The urban community is also a gateway for those such as Jackson discusses who have been alienated from their tribal roots and who wish to reidentify as Indian.[5]

There are also those with hazily defined distant Indian ancestry who create a niche for themselves in the urban Indian community and who are generally accepted if they make a substantial contribution to the community well-being. Increasingly, the urban community is a doorway into Indian country for

Indian people who were "adopted out" in infancy or childhood—that is, were raised in foster care or adopted by non-Indian families—and who seek to reestablish their Indianness in adulthood. Some of these mechanisms of reidentification have been discussed by Snipp in regard to the increasing U.S. census count of American Indians.[6]

Also, the American Indian community is characterized by a geographic mobility as people move into and out of the city, make return visits to their rural home territories or reservations, or sometimes return there for good. People speak of circulating through or of establishing a temporary urban living situation as a way of indicating that living in the Bay Area is viewed by some as an extension of their original territory. At the same time, people often speak longingly of "back home," and there are shared in-group and tribally specific understandings of the connotations that "back home" holds. These are expressed in jokes ("You know that one about the Doggy Diner down on East 12th and the two Sioux guys who just come into town?"), in music (WithOut Rezervation—WOR, the name of a rap group whose CD cover speaks of the group's tie to "the mean streets of Oakland"), and in reference to aspects of the natural world. Movement through space, as movement through time, is a part of living.

In addition to increasing dramatically in population over the past fifty years, the Bay Area Indian community, as characteristic of many urban Indian communities, has become increasingly diverse and complex in the following ways:

1. *There has been a proliferation of organizations*, the crucial nodes on the network of community. This array of organizations has become increasingly specialized as community needs become apparent and funding and human resources become available. For example, the generalized multiservice Indian Center has spawned a now-separate preschool and a number of other educational efforts as well as many specialized cultural arts and social activities and social service–focused organizations and projects.

2. *The community is now multigenerational.* Whereas those first to come into the Bay Area through relocation in the 1950s were primarily young single people and young families, the infant fourth generation since relocation is now often seen playing at their mothers' feet during meetings. This generational layering means that experiences, urban personal histories, and orientation toward both urban

and rural contexts have become increasingly varied. The urban angst expressed in the now-classic and still-enjoyed Floyd Red Crow Westerman songs of the 1970s such as "Quiet Desperation" and "Going Home" are contrasted with the more hard hitting contemporary urban Indian music.

3. *The community is multitribal*, and as intertribal marriages continue to occur, the children and grandchildren are themselves often multitribal. Being multitribal has the potential to enrich each child's identity but also to create complexities related to tribal enrollment and tribally based cultural knowledge. Recent research in the Bay Area in which 290 women were interviewed indicated ninety-two tribes represented, thirty-five in-state tribes and fifty-seven from out of state.[7]

4. *The community is linked* in increasingly diverse ways to often geographically distant people and places in Indian homelands. The term *Indian country* has come to include the urban communities. Family members visit from home, and visits to home are made to attend funerals, visit relatives, or take children there for the summer. Many people return home for personal and spiritual renewal. Some return home to avoid problems with the law. Some older people decide to retire back home. Medicine people frequently come out to the city for ceremonies, or people return home for ceremonies. There is the recent and increasing presence in the city of the nearby "Casino Tribes" via their in-town offices and staff. There are also those living on the streets who follow an annual seasonal route between various cities and rural areas.

5. *There is increased economic and class* diversity in the Bay Area Indian community, some resulting from educational opportunities that first became available in the late 1960s and some that are the result of business and professional successes. There are those living hand to mouth on the streets, and there are those arriving in splendor at the gala annual American Indian Film Festival at the Palace of Fine Arts in San Francisco. Those living on the streets are not excluded from the community, nor are those living in the hills of Berkeley. In fact they may all sit at the same long table at the Indian Center during a community feast. There are the many whose education does not include high school graduation, and there are those completing their doctorates in ethnic studies, anthropology, or education at the University of California at Berkeley or Stanford, or those taking advanced computer courses at the community-based United Indian Nations in Oakland.

6. *There is now a recognized urban history*, and a community persona, that is frequently referenced and that creates a framework for shared identity. A series of events and people, tied to dates, is shared in the minds of community members as being symbolically significant. For example, particularly memorable are the occupation of Alcatraz, the Bay Area Princess competitions, the old Intertribal Friendship House Music Festivals, and the annual Stanford Pow-wow. Everyone knows who is being referred to when there is mention of Floyd or Bill within specific contexts. And the old-timers have full recollections of Walter and Mrs. Carnes. Remembrances are filled with shared connotations. "Remember when they drew the ticket for that raffled car, there was standing room only, and it was the director's girlfriend who got it!" Ah, yes. And what about the meeting twenty-three years ago, "And your grandmother stood up and in front of everyone said that about my aunt at that board meeting." Everyone gives "that look," remembering this event well; if they weren't there they certainly heard about it in detail. A well-known activist leader recalled recently to a group, "And we started right here. We started the Longest Walk to Washington, D.C., right at this door." Many nodded in agreement and remembrance. These are parables of life in the city and a means of validating the shared historical content of urban living as a community.

IDENTITY

The defining of "Who is Indian?" and the issue of who does the identifying are emotion-laden topics anywhere in Indian country, with implications of inclusion and exclusion. For example, there is self-identity; there is identity externally imposed; there are the situationally appropriate shifts in identity; and there are the shifts in identity that may occur over a lifetime. In urban areas, although no role exists comparable to tribal roles, there are a number of other ways that one is identified by self and others as a community member and as Indian. The urban Indian community is most frequently invisible to the non-Indian world, both informally in the general public mind that has not discarded the stereotype that everything Indian is rural and in the past, and formally via institutions such as the U.S. Census Bureau, which has yet to adequately count urban

Indian people.[8] Likewise the federal emphasis on ancestry as the outstanding defining criteria, represented in a blood quantum model, is a much narrower and limiting criterion than that found in urban Indian communities.

From within the urban community, there is a very different perspective regarding membership than that found on those tribal homelands that are structured by federally imposed criteria. As is defining the urban "territory," defining membership in the urban Indian community and the link to Indianness, as defined by the community, is fluid. Membership in the Indian community is known and agreed upon through informal consensus. Indian people feel comfortable with this approach. This is the way it is, through consensus, rather than written on a piece of paper, a document. There is a shared understanding by participants of the social boundaries of the American Indian community as well as of membership within the community. These boundaries and the community membership are fluid, however, and always under review and negotiation. Those non-Indians who do not participate, who are external to the community, are not aware of these dynamics that tie the community together and mark who is "in the community," and who is not. Defining Indianness in the city is therefore essentially released from the burden of the formalized documentation imposed on federally recognized tribes. For example, recently, in preparation for the board election at one of the urban organizations in the Bay Area, a board member, as a strategy to channel the election outcome, sent out a letter indicating that, in order to vote, community members should bring documentation proving they were Indian. Many people, those who could bring forward documentation and those who could not, were acutely offended; the strategy backfired, and the board member was roundly criticized for taking an inappropriate stance. Her request was ignored at the polls.

Another example in an urban setting of the rejection and disdain for a federally imposed tribal formula emanating from governmental demands for enrollment numbers was demonstrated by a group of Bay Area Indian artists in protest of laws requiring proof of Indianness in order to exhibit their art as Indian artists. One artist, Hulleah Tsinhnahjinnie, took a series of defiant photographs of herself with numbers painted across her forehead. In essence, these people are asserting, "I am Indian because I say I am." "I am Indian because you know me and my family and see me participate in the community."

"And I am Indian because I know what it is to be Indian: the protocols, the jokes, the knowledge of shared history, the racism and struggle that are part of who we all are." "Trying to identify me as a number is fucked."

Thus, in urban areas Indian identity is defined through:

1. *Ancestry:* Does a person have Indian relatives and ancestors and function as a member of an Indian extended family?
2. *Appearance:* Does a person "look Indian"?
3. *Cultural elements:* Is the person knowledgeable of the culture of his or her People and of those pan-Indian values and social expectations shared within the urban Indian community?
4. *Indian community participation:* Does the person "come out" for Indian events and activities in the Indian community and contribute to the community well-being?

The weight and combination given to these elements vary situationally to determine Indian identity and to some extent are always under community assessment, shifting with the changing times. For example, there are many people well accepted in the Bay Area Indian community who may not "look very Indian" or who may not have verifiable documented Indian ancestry, yet through a long history of active participation in and contribution to the community well-being, as well as by demonstrating a thorough understanding of Indian values and protocols, will be deemed without hesitation to be a member of the Indian community . . . until a conflict arises, then this combination may be critically scrutinized.

Also in an urban area there is an element of choice as each individual determines to what degree and in what circumstances tribal membership and urban Indian community participation are actualized. Thus, situationally, individuals may choose which criteria of Indianness may be activated and when. Some Indian people living in the Bay Area are affiliated with a home tribe but do not choose to participate in or identify with the urban Indian community during a particular time in their life. Others are actively engaged as members of their home tribe and are also participants in, and identify with, the Bay Area American Indian community. Others may not be enrolled and may not be active participants in their home tribe, yet they may be very involved and active in the urban community. There are also some people who, though identifying as Indian, neither participate in nor identify with the urban community or a home tribe. There are some people who have chosen at some point in their life, as a result of racism, assimilation pressures, or out-marrying, to pass as a non-Indian, for example as Mexican, Italian, or white. Increasingly, many of these individuals are choosing to reevaluate their racial self-identity and often to reestablish their American Indian identity by reintegrating into and becoming active in an urban Indian community.[9]

The position of children in the urban community is a telling one. In an urban community as tribally diverse as the Bay Area, there may come to be, after two or three generations, a number of children who, while undeniably Indian genetically may have difficulty becoming enrolled in any one particular tribe because of their mixed tribal ancestry and tribally specific criteria for enrollment. There is also the consideration that some children with a mother from a patrilineal tribe and a father from a matrilineal tribe may not be recognized by, or enrolled in, either tribe. These children of mixed tribal heritage and those of Indian–non-Indian heritage who may have difficulties related to formal tribal enrollment, often, nevertheless are active and accepted participants in the urban Indian community. Indian parents who are involved in the Bay Area community, and whose children for one of the reasons sketched here do not have strong ties to a home tribe, often express concern that their children will lose their identity as American Indians and they agonize over the problems for their children that may be associated with tribal enrollment. A major theme of activities in the Bay Area Indian community is that participation validates and heightens Indian identity, and parents frequently facilitate their children's participation, knowing that this participation will foster a strong sense of Indian identity, as well as acceptance by the community. For example, children may join in special educational efforts such as attending Hintil Kuu Ca's preschool and after-school programs, may participate with the family in pow-wows and other activities, or may come with their families to events such as the Wednesday Night Dinner at Intertribal Friendship House.

CONCLUDING REMARKS

This chapter raises the caution that a much-used concept such as "community" may not be as simple, or as one-dimensional, as it appears. It is important to pay close attention to the ways that people, and communities of people, perceive and define their environment, both the physical and social aspects.

Some of the fundamental ways that the complex urban Indian community in the San Francisco Bay Area has constituted itself and, in turn, how this community structuring is related to identity have been delineated here. Conceptually, the community here is primarily abstract, based as it is on a series of dynamic relationships and shared meanings, history, and symbols rather than on the more commonly assumed clustered residential and commercial neighborhood. Although most Indian people living in the San Francisco Bay Area are by and large adept users of the roads and freeways, take advantage of the recreational opportunities the parks offer, and live in a wide range of apartments and houses, this physical environment, while the backdrop and the physical grounding for much of the community activity, is not "the community," which instead finds its focus in relationship dynamics and the more abstract realm of shared knowledge that informs and shapes actions.

NOTES

1. Merwyn S. Garbarino, "Life in the City: Chicago," in *American Indian in Urban Society*, ed. J. Waddell and R. Watson (Boston: Little, Brown and Co., 1971); Terry Straus, *Retribalization in Urban Indian Communities* (San Francisco, paper presented at the American Anthropological Association Meetings, 1996) and *Native Chicago* (Chicago, University of Chicago Press, 1998); Edward B. Liebow, "Urban Indian Institutions in Phoenix: Transformation from Headquarters City to Community," *Journal of Ethnic Studies*, 18; no. 4 (1991); Nancy Shoemaker, "Urban Indians and Ethnic Choices: American Indian Organizations in Minneapolis, 1920–1950," *Western History Quarterly* (November 1988); Wayne G. Bramstedt, *Corporate Adaptations of Urban Migrants: American Indian Voluntary Associations in the Los Angeles Metropolitan Area* (Ph.D. diss., University of California, 1977); Joan Weibel-Orlando, *Indian Country, L.A.: Maintaining Ethnic Community in Complex Society* (Urbana: University of Illinois Press, 1991); Edmund Jefferson Danziger Jr., *Survival and Regeneration: Detroit's American Indian Community* (Detroit: Wayne State Press, 1991); Jeanne Guillemin, *Urban Renegades: The Cultural Strategy of American Indians* (New York: Columbia University Press, 1975).

2. Dorothea J. Theodoratus and Frank LaPena, "Wintu Sacred Geography," in *California Indian Shamanism*, ed. Lowell Bean (Menlo Park, Calif.: Ballena Press, 1992), 211.

3. Keith H. Basso, *Wisdom Sits in Places: Landscape and Language among the Western Apache* (Albuquerque: University of New Mexico Press, 1996), 34.

4. Leslie Marmon Silko, *Ceremony* (New York: Viking Press, 1977), 260.

5. Deborah Jackson, *Urban Indian Identity and the Violence of Silence* (San Francisco, paper presented at the American Anthropological Association Meetings, 1996). Another version of this paper appeared in the *American Indian Culture and Research Journal*, 22, no. 4 (1998).

6. C. Matthew Snipp, *American Indians: The First of This Land* (New York: Russell Sage Foundation, 1989).

7. Dorie Klein, Elaine Zahnd, Bohdan Kolody, Sue Holtby, and Loraine T. Midanik, *Pregnant and Parenting American Indian Study* (Berkeley: Western Consortium for Public Health and San Diego State University Foundation, 1995).

8. For discussion of the Indian undercount in the Bay Area, see Susan Lobo, *Oakland's American Indian Community: History, Social Organization and Factors That Contribute to Census Undercount* (Washington, D.C.: Center for Survey Methods Research, Bureau of the Census, 1990) and Susan Lobo, *American Indians in the San Francisco Bay Area and the 1990 Census: Ethnographic Exploratory Research Report no. 18* (Washington, D.C.: Center for Survey Methods Research, Bureau of the Census, 1992).

9. Snipp, *American Indians*.

AMERICAN INDIAN COMMUNITY HISTORY COLLECTION

Susan Lobo

Beginning in the 1950s, as more and more Indian people moved from rural reservations and communities, the shift to urban centers was continuous so that by 1990 at least half of all Indian people lived in cities. Today an even larger proportion of the Indian population lives in cities, and many of the urban Native communities have grown to become complex and vibrant. However, the documentation—whether in books, articles, or films—of this dramatic and historic process of migration and the creation of urban Indian communities has been slow in catching up to the events of the past fifty years.

The American Indian Community History Collection is one of the very few archival collections of urban oral histories, photographs, posters, and many other forms of documentation that exists and where Indian people and the general public can go to find in-depth primary materials. This archive focuses on the multi-tribal urban Bay Area American Indian Community and is now found at the Bancroft Library on the campus of the University of California at Berkeley.

The project to collect these materials was started in the mid-1970s by Geraldine Lira, Susan Lobo, and Marilyn St. Germaine, and it was housed for many years at Intertribal Friendship House, the Indian center in Oakland. Starting out as an oral history project to document the lives and experiences of those who migrated to the Bay Area and who created the urban community, it grew and expanded as many people in the Indian community contributed to and participated in what ultimately became a "community resource archive." These materials that had been collected then served for many years in a multitude of practical ways to benefit the Indian community, for example, through exhibits, in the creation of educational materials, and for radio programs.

The book *Urban Voices: The Bay Area American Indian Community* contains a small sampling of the materials in this large collection. (See Recommended Readings.) The Bancroft website is http://bancroft.berkeley.edu/

DOWNTOWN OKLAHOMA CITY, 1952

Victoria Bomberry

One of my earliest memories is like a well-worn black and white snapshot. It is the view from our front yard on what was then the outer southwestern edge of Oklahoma City. I would stand barefoot in the grass in my thin white panties,

Downtown Oklahoma City 1952 by Victoria Bomberry. Reprinted by permission.

gazing at the skyscrapers that rose like fierce monoliths out of the prairie. Mesmerized, I tried to invent words to match their grandeur. It frustrated me to the point of anger that my tongue would not or could not capture what I saw. It seemed that I would make unintelligible word sounds forever. I had no way of knowing that it was just practice that I needed to make the sounds of the words that I wanted to say.

I learned the magical names of the three tallest buildings even though I could not say them correctly: The Hilton and The Biltmore Hotels, and finally the third and grandest, the First National Bank. It was the most exciting because it had a long, thin, needlelike tower that pierced the sky. The gleaming glass, smooth pale concrete, and cool, shimmering steel of the tall buildings fueled my young imagination. To me, the simple skyline was a fairytale city rising out of the dry, dusty landscape. Even during the daylight hours their silhouettes seemed to glow, and at night the red light at the tip of the tower throbbed expectantly. The pulsing light seemed to be a thousand miles away from the working-class neighborhoods that sprang out of sandstone and clay on Oklahoma City's South Side after World War II.

It must have been 1952 and I was three years old. Bob Poole had a grocery store at the corner of 44th and May. A new shopping center catty corner from Bob Poole's had the most modern incarnation of the five- and ten-cent store of the day that we said as if it were one word, *Teegeenwhy* (TG&Y). Lee Roy, the teenage boy next door, worked at the soda fountain that was part of any drugstore worth visiting. Next to the shopping center was a pale red brick church that had what I thought had to be the steepest and whitest wooden steeple in the Bible Belt.

Our neighborhood was racially mixed. There were white Americans like Flossie, her husband, and their sons. Flossie's husband was a phantom of sorts. He seemed to be at work all the time, and his first name was never used around the house. I did see a long row of workpants—neatly fitted on metal frames to evenly crease and stretch them so Flo didn't have to do heavy ironing—hanging on the clothesline in the back of their house. Flo had a husky voice from the Chesterfields she always held in her tobacco-stained fingers. She often invited my mother to her house for coffee. When my mother sat with her at her kitchen table Flossie seemed to have the lowdown on everything. Hers was the graveled voice of city wisdom.

The Villareal and Esquivius families were across the road, while the Muñoz family lived next to Lee Roy's house. They spoke Spanish among themselves but knew English too. All of them had come up from Mexico to work in the slaughterhouses and meat packing companies near the fairgrounds. They looked like us and cooked beans and corn like we did. When I looked at them I just saw Indians, The Ezequiel brothers were hardworking too, but friendly. They always greeted all the children in the neighborhood.

The unmarried brother was the taller of the two. He combed his hair in a high, shiny pompadour and kept his mustache well trimmed. He performed magic tricks and, like all good magicians, never gave away his secrets. There were disappearing nickels, quarters that appeared in surprised ears, pencils that miraculously turned into useless floppy rubber. We were delighted and always asked him to perform magic tricks. With a magician's gleam in his eye, he kept us begging for more.

The Smith kids lived next to the Villareals with their mother and stepfather. He was a mechanic who parked his shiny black, chrome-trimmed motorcycle close to the kitchen door right against the house. Around the corner a family welding business operated out of a makeshift garage. The neighborhood kids loved to go past the garage so we could sneak a dangerous peek at the sparks that rained off the red-hot metal under the welding wand. We liked tempting fate since we had been warned that without a protective mask you could go blind if you looked.

Our family had hard-boiled eggs and toast every Sunday before my mother sent me to Sunday school promptly by eight o'clock. It didn't start until eight-thirty, so there was no chance of being late. She was always conscious of time and what people would say if we edged in the door, even with a minute or two to spare. Although we lived in a neighborhood where brown and white coexisted, she knew how tentative the world really was. The boundaries between people were stretched in new ways, and our place in the city was never really secure because of the muttering complaints of white folks who were always on the look-out for a misstep. Those complaints could interpret and condemn us within the structure of the racial stereotypes of the day. Mama would say, with a laugh that hinted of defiant resignation, "When in Rome, do as Romans do!" Of course, our Romans did not have to get up as early as we did, nor work as hard as Mama and Daddy. Indian time was early at Grandma's country home and at our home in the city.

I really do not recall my first trip downtown, but what I do remember is that my mother would always say don't forget to put on your shoes. I vividly recall when, in the excitement of the moment, I forgot; I did not give my gleaming white sandals a single thought in my hurry to get out of the door. My tough little feet walked easily across concrete and nudged the occasional pebble out of my way. I happily jumped over the cracks in the sidewalks. Each hop caused my hair to pull at my temples, since it was tightly and neatly braided for the occasion. I smiled at strangers and felt sorry for them when they didn't smile back, imagining some deep heartbreak was the cause of their furrowed brows and unsmiling faces.

Just as we were getting ready to go into Montgomery Ward's, my mother noticed. She was so embarrassed and ashamed when she looked down at my sun-browned feet. She must have felt that they gave us away instantly. No matter that her hair was perfectly curled and her flowered skirt draped her slim but shapely hips just so. Or that her white blouse made of cool cotton ironed smooth by her expert hands was fresh with sun, clean air and the slight touch of starch. It didn't matter that her carefully plucked brows looked natural and classy at the same time and that the shape of her lips was accented by luscious red lipstick. It didn't matter that her daughter was dressed to the nines in a pretty little summer dress. Or that she had all the family bills in her purse with the money to pay them. All her care, self-confidence, and competence were stripped away because I had no shoes. No shoes and the brownest of brown feet, and of course, by that time the bottoms were blackened with the dirt and soot of downtown city streets.

I looked in my mother's face and felt her distress and shame. It burned my cheeks deep red. I looked down at my feet and realized that the unsmiling faces of strangers carried a different meaning from what I had thought. I imagined I heard them whisper through clenched teeth—dirty Indians, look at the dirty Indians. Instead of feeling sorry for them, I felt the sting of their rejection and something that I didn't know at the time was their hate. In my young mind, I blamed myself for being a thoughtless disgrace who publicly shamed my mother. I was angry with myself for hurting her. I was angry with her for caring about what strangers thought. Anger was like a small, hard hickory nut stuck in the middle of my throat. I wanted my mama to protect me from their hard stares—maybe stand up even straighter and proclaim her pride in strong brown feet that didn't need shoes to protect their tender bottoms or straps to confine them.

What I did not understand then that I do understand now is that my mother was just as wounded by the looks. It didn't matter that my mother was an educated, intelligent, hardworking woman and looked it. Mother and daughter were judged and found lacking before anyone ever saw my feet. They were just an excuse to treat us with disdain. Maybe Mama wanted to protect me when she laughed, but I heard a different kind of laugh from one that signaled that it was all right. It was a laugh that covered embarrassment turning to shame.

I rode the escalator that day without my usual joy at safely jumping over the teeth at the tops and bottoms of the disappearing stairs. My delight in escaping their bite was gone. I wanted to go home to the sounds of Muscogee, Spanish, and gravelly English.

RUBY'S WELFARE

Esther Belin

Standing in line
after being told
Indians don't stand in line
'cause a Kiowa woman at window #6
helps the skins

Time passes me
still in line

Man at window #1
tells me welfare is a luxury
and how come I don't have a job
check the time
I smile
place my forms in the box marked
LEAVE FORMS HERE
black black and bold
welfare is a luxury
place your form in our box
play by our rules

I laugh
sit
smoke a Virginia Slim
and talk to the spirits

People talk about luxury
but what they mean is obligation
to remain lower class
for food
$5.15 an hour
doesn't feed three

Again
I check the time
light another Virginia Slim
not finished with the spirits

Luxury
the U.S. forgot the definition
forgetting who allowed them to create the U.S.
obligation of treaty
honored through
IHS and a truckload of commods
luxury overextended
obligation 500 years behind

Ready to light Virginia Slim #3
I'm called by window #6

"Ruby's Welfare" by Esther Belin. Reprinted by permission of the author.

Metropolitan Indian Series, #1, 1984. © Hulleah J. Tsinhnahjinnie

TELLING THE INDIAN URBAN

REPRESENTATIONS IN AMERICAN INDIAN FICTION

Carol Miller

End-of-century demographic information reveals that a surprisingly large number of Indian people—almost half of the approximately two million who identified themselves as Native American in the last census—now live away from reservation and trust lands. Except for the fact that the American Indian

From Carol Miller, in *American Indians and the Urban Experience*, eds. Susan Lobo and Kurt Peters (Walnut Creek, CA: AltaMira, 2001), pp. 29–45. Originally appeared in American Indian Culture and Research Journal vol 22, no 4, 1998.

population is significantly younger and growing more rapidly than that of the nation as a whole—a fact that has been true for decades but is confounding to presumptions of doom and vanishing—a descriptive profile reveals information that mostly confirms what Indian people already know: our population is significantly poorer and at greater risk than the nation's at large. The proportion of American Indian families living below the official poverty level is, in fact, almost three times that of all families taken together, and the per capita income of Indians is less than half that of whites. Indians also have higher death rates attributable to accidents, suicides, and homicides; and the second leading cause of death for Native young adults is directly linked to the effects of alcoholism.

Frequently motivated by poverty at home and the promise of greater economic opportunity elsewhere, Indian people, especially since World War II, have congregated in growing numbers in urban areas, where the particularities of their lived experience are either largely unexamined by non-Native American society or understood only within the broad categories of stereotype. In popular culture, images of Indianness are seldom associated with town and city spaces, and yet for many individuals and families, those spaces are where they live out their lives—as they have done for several generations. What does urbanization mean for cultural identities and tribal communities? How do ideas of homeland and ancestral values maintain themselves or shift their Awes when they are transformed within urban environments? To what degree, if at all; may this movement be understood as a "(re)taking place"— a double breaking out—both from federally designated boundaries historically intended to isolate and contain Native people and from an equally pervasive confinement within the anachronistic fantasy-wildernesses of the white imagination?

These questions have been consistently addressed by American Indian writers, who have long grappled with postcontact cultural interactions in all the settings—including towns and cities—where they have been acted out. Exploring some of these fictional representations, especially in their relation to one another, is instructive for several reasons. In addition to providing significant information about a consequential and ongoing Native American diaspora essentially ignored by mainstream white society, narratives about urban America as Indian country also reinforce the link between contemporary and ancestral storytelling traditions. And in doing so, they provide an important medium not only for sustaining culture but for creating a significant illustrative resource about the pragmatic business of "going along" in the world, just as the old stories always have done. Imaginative print-language "tellings" that explore intersections of Indianness and urbanization share the serious functionality of traditional Native storytelling, a functionality made even more important because of five hundred years of cultural disruption. The power of stories to influence actuality is

certainly what Leslie Marmon Silko asserts in the poem that begins her 1977 novel *Ceremony*:

I will tell you something about stories,
[he said]
They aren't just entertainment,
Don't be fooled. They are all we have, you see,
all we have to fight off
illness and death.

This essay argues that American Indian storytellers writing about urban Indian experience participate in specific struggles against illness and death by constructing increasingly diverse and transcendent accounts that counter images of invisibility and victimization. Moreover, in doing so, they frequently reassert a particularly Native, American idea of urbanness that expresses positive change and cultural vitality. And viewed within the context of the broader American literary canon, these storytellers contribute significantly to a function of literature that Elizabeth Cook-Lynn has recently lamented as having been left mostly unaddressed in the twentieth century: the power of narrative to "stir the human community to a moral view which would encompass all of humanity, not just selected parts of it."

Even as Native writers represented them in early manifestations, towns were emblematic of both cultural alienation and physical risk or danger. For example, in *Cogewea the Half Blood*—published in 1927 and credited as one of the earliest novels by an American Indian woman—Mourning Dove (Okanogan) constructs the town as a dehumanizing "othered" space that exposes her Indian characters to degradation and physical threat. Much of the novel, which concerns the conflicted identity and resulting life choices of Mourning Dove's mixed-blood heroine, is set in the already disrupted middle ground of the privately owned ranch belonging to Cogewea's sister and her white husband. Juxtaposed against this culturally mediated space, ancestral home and values are represented by two metonymical sites: the tepee of Stemteema, Cogewea's traditional grandmother, and Buffalo Butte, the girl's favorite haunt—an unspoiled natural space in which spirit voices still have the power to speak. The central problem of the novel is cast in the terms of post-Victorian domestic romance. Will Cogewea be seduced by the urbane but villainous Densmore, her fortune-hunting white suitor, or will she choose Jim, the mixed-blood foreman who loves her? Beneath the surface of melodramatic plotting, the novel's imagined physical spaces take on symbolic significance in their exploration of cultural conflict and integrity.

The town is significant as symbolic space at two narrative moments. In the first, Cogewea visits the town in order to compete in both the "Squaws'" and "Ladies'" horse races, which are part of the white community's annual Fourth of July celebration. Her victory in both races precipitates confrontations that call into question the supposedly civilized behavior of white society while foregrounding the alienating terms of Native and non-Native cultural conflict. Town is the place where, subjected to the sexual insults of the "gentleman whites," Cogewea reflects with regret on "the passing of an epoch, when there were no 'superiors' to 'guide' her simple race to a civilization so manifestly dearth of the primitive law of respect for womanhood" (65). Town is also the place where the breakdown of Native traditions of communality is made evident by the bitterness directed at Cogewea by other Native women because of her mixed-blood status. And town is the place where blatant white racism cheats Cogewea of her deserved recognition as winner of the Ladies' race and threatens Jim with imprisonment and physical violence when he speaks up for fair treatment.

Later, in another suggestion of urban place as symbolic space, the city is the intended destination of Densmore's and Cogewea's disastrous elopement. When the villain's plans are thwarted by the discovery that Cogewea has no wealth of her own, the city is the place to which the exploitative and abusive Densmore flees. It represents an alienated way of living that Cogewea rejects when she ultimately chooses Jim and reinserts herself into the "splendid world" (284) of Buffalo Butte.

In this early representation, therefore—and also in almost every subsequent fictive intersection of Indianness and Euro-American urbanity—town and city spaces are, for Indian people, places of risk, separation, disillusion, and dissolution. Why? Perhaps because Euro-American urban spaces have evolved as sites in which genuinely fundamental differences between Native and non-Native conceptions of place, culture, and relationships of power are brought into sharpest relief. Historian Inga Clendinnen has pointed to the destructive contemporary consequences of centuries of what she identifies as "unassagueable" cultural otherness.' Such worries might seem confirmed by the quite distinct and contending ideas held by colonizers and Native people about nature in relationship to civilization and civilized behavior. Within the

earliest images of the colonizers' appropriation of the American landscape—their earliest into the wilderness to construct an idealized "city upon a hill"—there is an implicit tension between nature and civilization and a resulting projection of the need for transformation and cultural imposition. This tension is written indelibly on both the practical outcomes of colonization and on its resulting intellectual and artistic production. The American wilderness represented, after all, a complicated dichotomy within the white imagination: freedom, renewal, and unlimited possibility at one polarity, and anarchy, error, and disappointment at the other. From the beginning, the European sensibility both romanticized and abhorred the "New World" as at once paradisiacal and primitive—but in either case conceived in opposition to Western ideas of civilization. Among those already in residence in this world, there was apparently no such dichotomy. Inverting the categories of civilized and primitive by means of the hindsight of several centuries of postcontact experience, Luther Standing Bear would write, "Only to the white man was nature a 'wilderness' and only to him was the land 'infested' with 'wild' animals and 'savage' people."

In its most fundamental character, the very act of "westering"—the European and later Euro-American drive toward the western horizon—involved aspects of separation, isolation, and disillusion that reinforced the dichotomous perspective of migrants to the "New World." The Jeremiad tradition of lamentation of unworthiness as accompaniment to exultant conquest, so apparent in the writings of so many early colonizers, is a reflection of this sense of dividedness. It is present as well in the symbolic and actual dysfunction of the colonizers' first attempts at urbanness. Howard Kushner argues that this dysfunction explains the surprisingly high mortality rate among settlers in Jamestown, one of the earliest "urban" settings established by English settlers, many of whom were apparently so disillusioned by a frontier that was supposed to provide effortless wealth that they starved to death unnecessarily. From an Indian point of view, there is an intriguing irony in Kushner's suggestion that the settlers' appropriation of serotonin-inhibiting maize as their undiversified dietary staple contributed to their dysfunction: "When the vision fell short of its promise, they,' became depressed and lethargic. Unable to return to a rejected past, they found in self-destruction a viable alternative."

On the one hand, then, were the physical and psychological separations the colonizers imposed upon themselves in order to bring about their objective of establishing a purer civilization than that they were leaving behind. Even more consequential to tribal people of the time were the separations imposed on those already in possession of the American "wilderness" as they were systematically dispossessed of their precontact homelands. The resulting history of contention between the ideals of democracy and the interests of nationalism translated into a permanent psychological dualism that Dolores Hayden has called a "despair about placelessness . . . as much a part of American experience as pleasure in a sense of place."

Such a history of dividedness and contradiction is summed up by D. H. Lawrence's assertion that "the American landscape has never been at one with the whiteman." It is manifested throughout much of the canon of several centuries "masterwork" American literature predicated upon recursive versions of heroic alienation from place and culture. James Fenimore Cooper's ambivalent idealization of the heroic individualism integral to opening and civilizing the frontier, for example, could never quite be reconciled with his protagonist's elegiac nostalgia for primitive America as an unspoiled natural space. Thoreau, credited as the founder of American nature writing (ironically, from an American Indian perspective), promotes in *Walden* and other journal writing a self-reflexive model of the vision quest derived directly from an appropriated aesthetic authority he establishes at the cost of erasing prior Native presence and possession. Hawthorne's finely drawn tension between the repressiveness of Puritan town life and the liberating lure of the demonic forest creates another field for contradiction, in which the cosmopolitan is set against the "primitive," with characters such as Hester Prynne and Young Good, man Brown paying the price for daring to negotiate a morally and intellectually ambiguous middle ground. Melville's Ishmael survives Ahab's monomaniacal challenge of the natural world perched upon Quequeg's highly metaphorical coffin. And Twain's Huckleberry Finn, navigating the moral currents of the symbolically changed Mississippi, finally rejects his North-South exploration of the border between the frontier and the ethically flawed, "civilized" territory of nineteenth-century America. Carrying on the "westering" fantasy of his progenitors, he strikes out alone toward an imaginary, untrammeled future in California. In the perpetual wilderness of the mythical West, he is the archetypal American cousin of Peter Pan, free from the obligations both of civilization and adulthood.

Moby Dick and *The Adventures of Huckleberry Finn* are both representative American "great books," constructed upon alienated sensibilities and set in action within fragmented landscapes where nature and civilization can never be fully reconciled. Reconciliation, made even less possible by the exacerbated insecurities of twentieth-century modernism and postmodernism, is also largely unattainable within the pantheon of more contemporary "masters"—for example, Faulkner, Fitzgerald, Hemingway, Salinger, and Pynchon—whose most indicative works focus on the failures of individuals to come to terms either with each other or with the corrupted natural, urban, and even entropic galactic landscapes that surround them. Their storytelling offers a vicarious projection of the alienation that results when individualism cannot be integrated into community, or when community is finally imagined but fails to mesh with the actual shortcomings of lives lived within it.

Our Indian ancestors who might have been contemporaries of Ishmael or Huckleberry Finn, and who were engaged in life and death struggles to preserve the integrity if their own particular communities, would surely have considered such contradictory being as pathological—some form of soul sickness. They would not have understood a view that considered individuals unconnected to their societies, or that divided the human world from the natural one or from that of the other sentient beings, human or otherwise, who "peopled" the immediate environment. This is the distinction critic William Bevis introduces in his examination of "homing" as a distinctive structural and thematic feature of many contemporary narratives by American Indian writers. "Native American nature is urban," Bevis writes.

> The connotation to us of 'urban,' suggesting a dense complex of human variety, is closer to Native American 'nature' than is our word 'natural'. The woods, birds, animals, and humans are all 'downtown', meaning at the center of action and power, in complex, unpredictable and various relationships.

If human and natural worlds are unified rather than divided, traditional cultures have no impetus for conceiving nature as wilderness or as in any sense primitive. Within the relational epistemologies of most Native peoples, the earth is almost universally mother; the sun may be father; the moon, grandmother; and human and nonhuman entities are bound together in ancestral kinships and clan connections based, upon interdependence and obligation. Place and person are inextricably bound. The elements constituting place are as much character as setting, participants in complex and unifying systems of kinship that help to define how civilization itself is constructed and maintained. Culture exists within what Keith Basso has called a "place-world," significant because "what people make of their places is closely connected to what they make of themselves as members of society and inhabitants of the earth." It is not illogical then, that traditional Indian communities situated in their natural settings of complex activity and interrelationship would have considered that very quality of culturally determined and specialized urbanness an essential component of their conception of themselves as civilized.

Dakota writer and ethnologist Ella Deloria presents exemplary portraits of the traditional Dakota camp circle as urban in precisely Bevis's sense of dense and varied social constructions in two books, *Speaking of Indians* and *Waterlily*, both apparently drafted in the 1940s but published more than forty years apart. In the former, Deloria describes an ideal community based on a "scheme of life that worked," a community that understood itself to be highly civilized, that prized its civilization as crucial to functional existence, and that had developed sophisticated social codes to maintain, that civilization. "I can safely say," Deloria writes,

> that the ultimate aim of Dakota life, stripped of accessories, was quite simple: One must obey kinship rules; one must be a good relative. . . . Without that aim and the constant struggle to attain it, the people would no longer be Dakotas in truth. They would no longer be even human. To be a good Dakota, then, was to be humanized, civilized. And to be civilized was to keep the rules imposed by kinship for achieving civility, good manners, and a sense of responsibility toward every individual dealt with. Thus only was it possible to live communally with success; that is to say, with a minimum of friction and a maximum of good will (25).

Deloria had been a field worker for Franz Boas, and she uses the skills of both storyteller and ethnographer to show how this ultimate aim of civilized behavior was pragmatically attained in people's everyday interactions. In the extended fictional narrative *Waterlily*, unpublished until 1988, the voice is the teller's. The story centers on the personal, family, and community interrelationships of a young Dakota woman residing in a traditional camp circle seemingly untouched by cultural disruption. As such, it presents a detailed portrait of the complex and indissoluble interdependencies of individual and communal well-being based on an unshakable premise of biological and social kinship relations

and an economic system of distributing wealth by "giving to get." Significantly, in the cosmology of the observing Dakotas, it is whites who are considered primitive because of their inhumane treatment of their own children. And when small pox introduced by whites decimates the tightly bonded social circle that cannot imagine the necessity of isolating those who are ill, the epidemic works as a figure foreshadowing broader philosophical tensions between individualism and communality that distinguish non-Native and Native cosmologies. Deloria's narrative illustrates how the very essence of civilized conduct within traditional Native societies derives from that particularized sense of communal urbanness in which, Bevis argues, identity becomes "for a Native American, . . . not a matter of finding 'one's self,' but of finding a 'self' that is transpersonal and that includes a society, a past, and a place."

What happens, however, when this exemplary idea of Indigenous urbanness grounded in the matrices of communality, tradition, and homeland is exposed to the stresses of Westernized urbanization? Deloria addressed that question in *Speaking of Indians*, published in 1944, toward the end of World War II, which dramatically accelerated the urbanization of Indian people as large numbers of Native men and women entered the armed services or moved to the cities to work in war industries. Speaking of—talking about rather than to—Indians, Deloria attempts to predict the impact of these changes from the perspective of an insider and to speculate about their effects both on those left in traditional communities and those who have "moved into the cities and are meeting problems they have never faced before" (145). Her purpose is not merely to valorize the traditional past but to contextualize that past by referencing it against the present and future of post-war America. She imagines a model of sojourning rather than of permanent migration, since "many Indians cannot yet feel complete with just their little family, their spouse and children" (146). Of those who had become city dwellers, Deloria argues that their traditional backgrounds include virtues that make them excellent workers. Demands non-Natives take for granted, however—paying rent, handling larger amounts of money than have even been available before, securing child care—are foreign and discomfiting. Acknowledging and to some degree even welcoming intensified pressures to assimilate, Deloria also imagines new demands for agency and authority as Native people claim what their recent investment in the preservation of democracy has earned them:

> the right to talk the common language of America, and I don't mean just literally, but figuratively as well. That is to say, they will want to participate in the larger thought and life of the land and not be given special work scaled down to their abilities, as if those abilities were static, or to their needs, as if those needs must always be limited to tribal life (148).

Successful adaptation will depend upon white society's willingness to forego paternalism and to provide genuinely equal opportunity and participation. But it will also depend upon a transposition of the elemental parts of that Dakota scheme of the life that worked—those qualities of civilized and fully human community—into the new locations of contemporary experience. Native people, Deloria asserts, must be allowed the motivation of their own values—especially ancestral allegiances to kinship and to the well-being of future generations. Deloria's representation of movement from tribal to urban communities is important for its perception that the culturally specific urbanness of the traditional past offers an effective foundation to create a coherent and productive urban present. But writing at yet another diasporic moment for Indian people, what she cannot or perhaps chooses not to anticipate in any detail is a future in which that foundation is continually undermined by a materialist environment of sustained racism, poverty, and cultural denigration.

Succeeding generations of American Indian writers would address that future. Two of the most successful, writing from the empowered center of what has been called a renaissance of American Indian narrative, undertake constructions of the city in relation to Indianness that may seem on the surface to reiterate each other but more accurately illustrate an evolution of narrative purpose upon which other writers continue to build. Both Scott Momaday, in *House Made of Dawn*, and Leslie Marmon Silko, in *Ceremony*, present post-World War II America as a critical moment of dislocation. Both tell highly intertextual stories engaging the questions posed at the beginning of this discussion. In their contemporary representations, what happens when Indian people leave their traditional communities for new lives in the city? What does city life mean—for them and for the communities they leave behind or to which they return? Momaday, acknowledging the centrality of oral traditions upon which Silko draws in

Ceremony, has called her book a telling, but he might as correctly have called it a retelling, since, at the surface, the plots and protagonists of Silko's novel and his own seem to echo each other. It may seem, in fact, that in many ways the two stories are actually the same story. The points of plotting and characterization at which they converge, however, suggest older storytelling traditions and employ deliberate recursion to mark the importance of the story both writers choose to tell. Extending from those convergences, Momaday and Silko ultimately draw quite distinct, though complementary, conclusions.

For Momaday, the city represents a site of ultimate exile, the place where his protagonist Abel hits a rock bottom even more destructive than his experience in prison, which Momaday doesn't describe at all. One of Momaday's targets is "relocation"—the federal policy that supposedly attempted to hasten assimilation but resulted instead in the accelerated development of an urban Indian underclass. In Los Angeles, surely among the most alien of alien environments for tribal people, Abel, his friend Benally, and Tosamah, Momaday's urban trickster/Priest of the Sun, each represent aspects of the dysfunction resulting from this dis/relocation. Abel and Benally are assigned dead-end jobs that lead neither up nor out. Tosamah preaches to his displaced "congregation" that they have come to live in the white man's world and on that ground they are "as children, mere babes in the woods." In the reverse-wilderness of the city, they are bombarded by white ways conveyed by the white "Word," which is empty, incomprehensible, and devoid of truth. Benally describes downtown in just those terms—as an alien space where "it's dark . . . all the time, even at noon" (140); where the old men who sell papers are always yelling at you but you don't understand what they're saying. "You know, you have to change," he says. "That's the only way you can live in a place like this. You have to forget about the way it was, how you grew up and all" (148).

Benally has internalized contradiction, separating himself from place and its associations of family and home. He wants—at least he tells himself he does—what the city seems but actually fails to offer—"money and clothes and having plans and going someplace fast" (158). He tries to convince himself that in the tribal place he has left behind, "there's nothing there . . . just the land, and the land is empty and dead. Everything is here. Everything you could ever want. You never have to be alone" (181). Benally seems oblivious of the values Bevis associates with the older Indigenous urbanity, attaching his aspirations instead to the material version he finds in L.A. But his life in the city is actually despairingly lonely and hopeless, forcing escape into alcohol and pipe dreams. Occasionally, however, another sort of escape is possible when he allows himself to call up childhood memories of his grandfather telling stories in the firelight of his family's sheep camp. There, he had been "right there in the center of everything, the sacred mountains, the snow-covered mountains and the hills, the gullies and the flats, the sundown and the night, everything—where you were little, where you were and had to be" (157). For Benally, the city is an infectious and deadening environment of alienation.

Momaday refuses to present, however, an image of urban Indianness in unequivocal or stereotypical terms of victimhood. Abel's experience of urbanization appears potentially even more injurious than Benally's since it accelerates a virulent soul sickness already established by a lifetime of disrupted attachments of both family and traditional community. But Abel, the Longhair, resists the city. His time in the city, in fact, brings on a crisis that can only be resolved through resistance and will lead either to annihilation or to reintegration with his traditional world. Far away from his desert home, beaten almost to death by a sadistic cop, lying in a liminal space where he is reached by the sounds of both the sea and the city, Abel feels, hears, and sees something else as well: a restoring vision of the runners after evil who, within the traditional belief system that he has previously found impenetrable, give design and meaning to the universe. This vision will eventually turn him homeward, away from the city. But it does more, suggesting a transcendent cultural and spiritual agency with the power to link landscapes that are tribal and urban, ancient and contemporary.

Even in the city, Momaday insists, visions are possible, people come together to chant and pray, peyote rituals are conducted and, amidst the cacophony of brassy music and street traffic, the Priest of the Sun serves notice that "something holy was going on in the universe" (114). Tosamah preaches that, within the white world, the word, ubiquitous and unreliable, has "as an instrument of creation . . . diminished nearly to the point of no return" (95). His remembering of his grandmother as storyteller illustrates, however, that for Native people, consummate being may yet be derived from the uses of language. Story is the medium that allows the past and those who lived within it to take hold of the imagination so that the listener may confront that which is sacred, eternal,

and timeless. Momaday's novel is itself just such an instrument of creation and it points the way to other stories that may function similarly to show Native people how to, as Tosamah says with only partial cynicism, "get yours" (98).

If, in Momaday's cosmology, language is potently creative, it may also be an instrument of destruction, an idea Leslie Marmon Silko takes up in her 1977 novel *Ceremony*. Witchery—a human capacity for destruction and violence in dimensions both personal and political—is the name Silko gives to what she sees as an escalating threat to the survival of all living things. The origins of this capacity are unknowable, but it is set in irrevocable motion by Destroyers who imagine it first in a story—the particular story of the European conquest of the New World. Once in play, Silko imagines, witchery is carried forward in an expansive design of accelerating violence deriving from personal, transpersonal, and transnational culpability. The novel's central narrative strand concerns how this design must be countered by a process of ceremonial regeneration that rejects violence and internalized guilt and restores ancestral balance within human and natural worlds.

Silko's story is set mostly in and around the pueblo community to which her protagonist Tayo returns after his service in World War II, but some of the story unfolds in city spaces—this time Gallup and Albuquerque—presented as dehumanizing outlands that pervert and destroy those who are attracted to them. Tayo's mother is one of those who is destroyed, and Tayo's memories of his time with her living in a tin shelter thrown together in a vagrant camp in Gallup are nightmarishly sordid: a toddler's bewildered endurance of neglect, alcoholism, promiscuity, and violence. In the bars of Gallup where his mother leaves him, "He could not remember when he first knew that cigarettes would make him vomit if he ate them. He played for hours under the tables, quiet, watching for someone to drop a potato chip bag or a wad of gum" (108).

The meanness of Gallup is far removed from the civilized society Deloria describes—a society based, at least in the ideal, upon the premise of striving to treat everyone as a relative and motivated by its dedication to future generations. Dakota or Pueblo, the fundamental tenets of civilized behavior have been dependent upon communality. Over thousands of years, Silko explains, Pueblo people had shared the same consciousness. "The people had known, with the simple certainty of the world they saw, how everything should be" (68). But the entanglement of tribal and European values has resulted in many kinds of separation:

> All creation suddenly had two names: an Indian name and a white name. Christianity separated the people from themselves . . . because Jesus Christ would save only the individual soul; Jesus Christ was not like the Mother who loved and cared for them as her children, as her family. (68)

Gallup is a foreign, removed site in which the radical breakdown of traditional communality is acted out. But remnants of that shared ancestral consciousness are still strong enough to engender an individual and collective internalization of guilt. Tayo's mother internalizes what the teachers and missionaries tell her about "deplorable ways of the Indian people" (68) and is ashamed enough to break away and go off with the white men in Albuquerque who smile at her as if she were white. Shame deepens her isolation and seals her destruction, but, significantly, it is a collective guilt that will infect not only her family, but the entire community that wants her back. "For the people," Silko writes, "it was that simple, and when they failed, the humiliation fell on all of them; what happened to the girl did not happen to her alone; it happened to all of them" (69). The novel's narrative movement is about how this internalized guilt and humiliation must be purged by a process of ceremonial reintegration. A detail of significance and irony, however, is that one of the principal agents of this reintegration, the mixed-blood medicine man Betonie, resides tenaciously in the hills directly above Gallup. "It strikes me funny," the medicine man says, "people wondering why I live so close to this filthy town. But see, this hogan was here first. Built long before the white people ever came. It is that town down there which is out of place. Not this old medicine man" (118). Like Momaday, Silko is not willing to surrender place, even urban place, as a domain in which ancestral authority *is* without power and provenance. Like Momaday too, however, her resolution involves her protagonist's necessary return to a contained tribal community. Only the murderous Emo stays outside, migrating to California, which is, we are told, a good place for him. "Westering" for Silko clearly suggests something Mark Twain wouldn't have imagined: a destination of poetic justice for those who perpetuate witchery.

In the more recent *Almanac of the Dead*, Tucson, where Silko herself lives, has become an even more surreal location of perversion and violence, an unredeemable "city of thieves." For Silko, however, the ultimate urban metaphor of postcolonial devastation is real estate developer Leah Blue's dream city: Venice, Arizona. Leah Blue and the capitalist establishment she represents don't care that their faux-Venice, intended for the wealthy and complete with canals and waterways, will require deep-water drilling—the ultimate penetration and despoiling of the Mother for profit. Silko elevates the imagery of urban America to the level of parody—a decadent city of the future imagined as a baldly materialist resuscitation of the European past. In doing so, she undercuts centuries of nationalist exceptionalism and illustrates her largest theme. The compounding destructive synergy of the original theft, which implicated the colonizers' first images of virgin territory made to give way to a city on a hill, can be averted only by a reversal of history and a restoration of tribal land. In *Almanac of the Dead*, Silko's representations of the intersections of Indianness and urban America serve a larger visionary purpose engaged with the preservation of the sacred earth.

Momaday and Silko have created influential representations in which urbanization is essentially figurative: a destructive process culminating in an ultimately universal fatality. Cities in these foundational novels are places to go home from if you can because your own life and those of others depend on it. As the demographics remind us, however, more and more Indian people are living urban lives. Many others have established a pattern of movement between tribal and urban communities. Many do not come from contained tribal communities, do not perceive themselves as sojourners but rather as permanent city dwellers, and may in fact be several generations into complex urban experience in which identity, tribal connections, and notions of culture are shaped anew. Fifty years from the post-war moment of Ella Deloria's gaze, other narrative representations are beginning to emerge that acknowledge that staying within or reintegrating with traditional homeplaces are not the only options for the preservation of viable personal and cultural lives. This discussion concludes by examining two alternative views of how traditional Indian urbanness is transformed within contemporary city spaces.

Ojibway writer Ignatia Broker's little-known narrative *Night Flying Woman* is a genre-stretching blend of fiction and memoir whose central subject is the process of postcontact change and adaptation endured by her several-generations-removed Ojibway ancestors. Broker asserts the ties of the traditional past to a personal/transpersonal urban present by remembering that past but finally returning to the context of the contemporary moment. Her narrative strategy is deceptively simple. She uses a series of sequential flashbacks to slip the reader back in time as she, recalls the stories her grandmother told her, which her grandmother in turn heard from her grandmother. These stories center upon the lives of Oona and her family as they first flee from, but eventually have to negotiate, experiences of cultural disruption that begin with relocation to reservation villages and are then compounded by conversion to Christianity, boarding school experience, and loss of and traditional practice. Broker's strategically important narrative springboard for this story of the past, however, is a prologue—a brief description only a few pages in length—about the quality of post-war urban life for Indian people in Minneapolis and St. Paul. *Night Flying Woman* problematizes stereotypes of vanishing and victimhood, in part by its use of this prologue to counter the essentializing tendencies of previous urban representations.

The prologue's title, "The Forest Cries," appears to point to the woodland pas of Broker's Anishinabe forebears, suggesting familiar themes of dislocation and loss while simultaneously recalling the animate urban complicity of human and natural worlds. But since the prologue is set not in the forest but in the city, when Broker lived for more than forty years, the title actually works to contextualize present time and place by suggesting its connection to the time and place of the ancestral past. Referring to her more recent personal past, Broker acknowledges the power relationships affecting life in the urban neighborhood to which she brought her children in the 1950s:

> That day thirty years ago when we moved here, me and my children, we were the aliens looking for a place to fit in, looking for a chance of a new life, moving in among these people, some of whose "forefathers" had displaced my ancestors for the same reason: looking for a new life.

However alien the city might make Indian newcomers feel, it is potentially a location of opportunity. Over time, their urban neighborhood stops representing contamination or danger for Broker's family. It becomes the place where her children go to school and church and marry. Even though, as adults, they may be "in faraway places, they seem to have their roots here, for they had lived in no other place while growing up" (2).

Broker's initial experience of the city might be viewed as providing a more detailed account of Deloria's suppositions about war-industry migrants. Moving from the reservation in 1941, she writes that she worked in a defense plant by day and took classes to supplement inadequate schooling at night. But if the city offered opportunity, it also subjected Indian people to all sorts of discrimination, especially in housing, where they were often turned down by landlords or forced to share illegal rentals of substandard housing in over-crowded conditions. Broker refuses, however, to emphasize the victimization of urban Indian experience, concentrating instead on traditional values of communal sharing and respect and the economic system of "giving to get" that could still be sustained and nourished.

> I think now that maybe it was a good thing, the migration of our people to the urban areas during the war years, because there, amongst the millions of people, we were brought to a brotherhood. . . . And because we, all, were isolated in this dominant society, we became an island from which a revival of spirit began. (5)

New communities, "vibrant with sharing," (6) began to be formed, and they stimulated activism and agency.

> After that, the tide of Indians moving to Minnesota's urban areas increased, and today there are ten thousand of us. As the number grew, newfangled types of Indian people came into being: those demanding what is in our treaties, those demanding service to our people, those working to provide those services—and all reaching back for identity. (7)

Although Broker does not ignore aspects of alienation and inequity in city life, she, does assert the good of urban migration. Her larger story may be about how her people's present evolved from and maintains relationship with its past. Her book also provides an overview, if not a detailed examination, of the creation of urban pockets of community where political and cultural power can be nurtured and where the meanness of contemporary urbanization may be mitigated by traditional values.

That more detailed examination, although drawn from another geographic and cultural landscape, is what Greg Sarris provides in *Grand Avenue*, a first novel about the tangled lives of Pomo families living in "the Hole," the worst part of Santa Rosa, California, fifty miles from San Francisco. Grand Avenue is far from grand; it's the synecdochic marker of an Indian ghetto, and Indian people would easily be able to substitute other such street names for similar neighborhoods in any city or town in America with a significant Indian population. Like most of those other neighborhoods, Grand Avenue is a racial mix—Indians, African Americans, Mexicans—of those on the lowest rungs of the economic ladder. One feature of the neighborhood is a park frequented mutually by old people, children, and gangs; another is a slaughterhouse whose owner uses it at night as a place of assignation for the neighborhood girls he recruits into prostitution. Work for most of those who live on Grand Avenue is seasonal, low paying, and punishing—picking fruit in the apple fields or packaging in the local cannery. Indian families form and re-form as economic needs demand in overcrowded "apartments" that are actually refurbished army barracks separated by mudtracks. Sarris's portraits of dysfunction—alcohol, drugs, promiscuity, family breakdown—are a realistic representation of the circumstances of many Americans, whatever their ethnicity, race, or economic circumstances. But it is a distinctly Indian—distinctly Pomo—version of contemporary life that Sarris constructs. Within this version, there are new complications attached to the possibilities of separation and reintegration, and new circumstances to factor into equations describing the values of culturally determined concepts of urbanness.

In some of the ways Sarris's stories detail and reinforce the destructive toxicity to which these characters are exposed, they may seem reiterations of already established cultural parameters. Sarris's "poisoners," for example, converge with Silko's notions of destroyers and their witchery. As in Silko, the struggle between the poisoners and those who use their medicines to heal rather than hurt has been carried on from time immemorial. Both writers invest this struggle with an ironic agency, decentering whiteness as neither cause nor effect. Another feature that Sarris's portrayal of contemporary community shares with those previously imagined by Momaday and Silko is the exercise of a hybridized spirituality. In *Grand Avenue's* opening story, "The Magic Pony," for example, the mother paints on her living room wall a mural that appears to conflate traditional and Christian symbolism: a green forest demarcated by fingernail-polish pink crosses to protect her family against the sources of trouble and poison.

In other ways, however, Sarris destabilizes conventional expectations about the features of Indianness. Sarris's Indians are far from universally sharing a sense of reverence for and relation with the natural world. "I'll leave you in the woods, you hear! I'll leave you with the white people" (34), one mother threatens her daughter, indicating the degree to which nature and whiteness have taken on a similar bogeyman alienness. How could such a breakdown have occurred? Significantly, for Sarris's Pomo families there is no ancestral homeplace, no traditional tribal community to return to. Santa Rosa Creek is the home from which, generations ago, these clans were dispersed, split up, driven out; and contemporary Santa Rosa is where they have returned to a present now bewildering in the ways it intermingles with the past. Sarris's interweaving stories of five generations build a composite allowing him to feature complicated contemporary issues—the consequences of mixed-race identity, cross-group racism, internal exploitation, even inadvertent incest resulting from the breakdown of kinship systems in an urban setting. On Grand Avenue, rare are those who do not make hate and insecurity "best friends" (39), who do not open their hearts to poison, the "misuse of power" (21), who overcome loneliness to find even temporary tenderness, who reject the escapes offered by alcohol, sex, violence, or fantasy.

For Sarris no less than for other Native writers, the past impinges on the present, but the intersections of cultural transformation and permanent urbanization he addresses seem to preclude previous outcomes, which involved reintegration in traditional homeplaces or acknowledgment of shared communal consciousness. Particularly in the last three stories in his collection, however, we begin to see how older values reconfigure themselves as the tools that might be used to construct a more hopeful contemporary urban place-world.

The first of these, "The Indian Maid," is told from the point of view of Stella who, in order to make a better life for herself, has to struggle against the grain of her sisters' envy and her mother's failures. Leaving Santa Rosa for a good job in even more urban Tucson is for Stella a sign of possibility rather than betrayal, but a mishap on the eve of her departure helps her to recognize the depth of her connections to family. Stella will be able to leave, but she will take with her a clear understanding of the content of her mother's dream on the night, years before, when she had returned to her own family: "They were all happy, I might have told my mother that night. They didn't fight. It was simple, a lesson an eight-year-old could discern. Appreciate one another. Get along. Share" (183).

In "Secret Letters," the apparent success of Steven, a postal carrier, and his wife Reyna, a teacher, in securing a good life away from Grand Avenue—one that includes acknowledgment of their cultural ties—is threatened by Steven's concern for Tony, an illegitimate son conceived unknowingly years before with his own sister. Contradictory loyalties lead Steven to deceive his wife and children about why he wants to move back to Grand Avenue where the boy lives. A disastrous attempt to shore up the boy's self-esteem by sending him a series of letters in which Steven pretends to be an anonymous admirer precipitates a brush with the law and the revelation of his secret. Sarris offers no easy solutions to the entanglements of Steven's past and present, but the final scene allows a reconciliation of Steven's divided loyalties and an assertion of the power of love over blame and betrayal:

> At the dinner table tonight my two children, Shawn and Raymond, seem unusually calm, given what happened. . . . I must tie up the story for them. But how do I begin? Where?
>
> "What's the lesson in this story?" I ask, unable to think of anything else. But my children are way ahead of me.
>
> "When's Tony coming to dinner?" Shawn asks.
>
> "Tomorrow," my wife says.
>
> "Tomorrow," I say. (208)

And finally, in "The Water Place," the healer Nellie Copaz, ostracized by her family because of her medicine powers and marriage to a white man, is able to form a bond with Alice, her gentle, overburdened young relation, which revitalizes ancestral power and passes it forward in the service of simple happiness and the cessation of recrimination. If the city has been an ultimate site of triumph of the machine over the garden, in this story, Nellie's riotous garden is a reversal of that triumph, a symbolic evocation of the tenaciousness of nature—and the first thing that attracts Alice to Nellie's door. Even—and especially—in the blight of Grand Avenue, Nellie exhorts Alice, "It's important to talk. Us Indians here are all family. That's the trouble, no one talks. Stories, the true stories, that's what we need to hear. We got to get it out. The true stories can help us. Old-time people, they told stories, Alice. They talked. Talk, Alice, don't be like the rest" (219). Alice does talk, but Nellie comes to value something else as more important: Alice's gift for making and creating new designs for the baskets that are one of the traditional sources of Pomo tribal identity and power. In the midst of a dispiriting town/city environment, which breeds anger, self-loathing, and fear among the young and the old, Alice is "as clear as water, as open as the blue sky" (222).

No matter how mean the streets, how deep the wounds of separation, how far removed from their original time and place contending conceptions of wilderness and civilization, these evolving representations converge on the power that remains in relational being, in family, and in the stories by which these are conveyed. In that convergence is a healing functionality that can indeed help to build the resilience that urban Indian people need to challenge the demographics. More universally, these stories of the Indian urban answer Elizabeth Cook-Lynn's call for narratives capable of stirring the human community to an encompassing moral view.

5

WOMEN'S CLASS STRATEGIES AS ACTIVISM IN NATIVE COMMUNITY BUILDING IN TORONTO, 1950–1975

Heather Howard-Bobiwash

Another important decision was to come to Toronto and live with my grand-daughters. I was very concerned for them. They had finished High School and wanted to go to Business College. So I decided to come with them just for a year. That's all I intended. But then I became involved in the Indian community here in Toronto, and realized the bad image Indians have . . . and so I felt I just couldn't leave . . . It never occurred to me that I would run a boarding house for other students. I was only thinking of my relatives.

—Verna Patronella Johnston, quoted in *I Am Nokomis, Too*, 173–74

This was the response Verna Patronella Johnston (Anishinaabekwe, 1910–1995) gave anthropologist Rosamund Vanderburgh who asked why she came to Toronto in the 1960s from her home on the Cape Croker Reserve located about one hundred miles northwest of the city. Vanderburgh documented Johnston's life in the book, *I Am Nokomis, Too*, published in 1977.[1] Her words, "I was only thinking of my relatives," embodies a common transition for Native women in rural-urban migration, from their roles as providers of shelter, food, and cultural knowledge transmission to kin, to new roles as activists and strategists for building community for Native people in the city.

Like Johnston's granddaughters, between the end of World War II and the early 1970s, many Native women in Ontario came to Toronto in the hopes of accessing higher education, jobs, and freedom denied them on reserves under the oppression of federal government tutelage. However, much of the literature on Native rural-urban migration in Canada concentrates on an association between urbanization and social problems, or on Native peoples' "failure" to assimilate into urban society.[2] Conversely, I contend that attention to women's experiences in the

history of Toronto Native community building illustrates diversity and complexity in the socioeconomic life of Native urban migrants. For some, their personal journeys to Toronto positioned them as members of an emergent Native "middle class," itself characterized by the particularities of Native historical and cultural experiences, which I will discuss in the first section of this article.

In particular, many Native women in this position did not equate their relative economic success with assimilation. Rather, they utilized their class mobility to support the structural development of Native community organizations and promote positive pride in Native cultural identity in the city. In the second section, I sketch some of the intersections between Native women's lives and the development of community for thousands of Native people in Toronto between 1950 and 1975. I describe the involvement of Native women in the North American Indian Club (1950–1978), from which emerged the Native Canadian Centre of Toronto (founded 1962), the city's oldest Native community center, and the women's participation in the Native Centre's Ladies' Auxiliary. Their experiences also highlight the specificity of emerging Native "middle-class" identity in Toronto. This is further explored in the third part of this article, examining the engagement of Native women in socioeconomic class mobility, Native image-making, and networking with women members

From Heather Howard-Bobiwash, in *The American Indian Quarterly*, 27, nos. 3 and 4 (Fall 2003): 566–582. Reprinted with permission from University of Nebraska Press, Lincoln, copyright 2004.

of the Toronto white elite. Their work here served as a means to generate positive forms of Native identity grounded in notions of cultural pride and authenticity, while also securing resources to empower Native community self-determination.

"SO, YOU ARE COMING TO TORONTO"

Work in the City and the Emergence of the Urban Native "Middle-class"

"So, you are coming to Toronto," was the title of a pamphlet issued by the Canadian Department of Indian Affairs for Native people who, by the late 1930s, had begun migrating in large numbers to the city. The undated pamphlet (estimated by the Toronto Native Community History Project to have been issued around the end of the World War II) featured on the cover three attractive young Native women in nurse's uniforms. Inside, practical paternalistic suggestions were given, such as "pay your rent, be on time for work, and spend your money wisely." In a further attempt to de-emphasize stereotypical "Indianness," it also warned young Native people that "consumption of alcoholic beverages has led to the ruin of many people," and they should "follow all the rules of personal hygiene, cut your hair, and refrain from questionable entertainment." On the other hand, the pamphlet also advised that Native people should not be "alarmed if many foolish questions are asked of you. Many people have not had the benefit of your experience and who is better prepared to advise them about Indians than yourself? Always be courteous in your reply, even if the question appears silly."[3]

This pamphlet was addressed specifically to young Native people attending a particular technical school in Toronto, but it is a rare concrete example of federal attempts to control the behavior of urbanizing Native people in Canada. Unlike in the United States, Native urban migration in Canada in the last century was in many instances more a form of resistance to the assimilative oppression of government control and surveillance on reserves than it was a strategically implemented plan concocted by federal authorities to assimilate Native people into mainstream.[4] It was responded and reacted to more than it was instigated. In Canada, it was believed that the intense suppression of Native languages, ceremonial life and subsistence practices, along with re-education in the ways of dominant society (the purpose of the residential school system) would be enough to ensure a

smooth transition of Native people into mainstream society. While much damage was accomplished, Native people also utilized and maximized the "tools of the oppressors" to resist assimilation and to organize their struggles to strengthen and assert Native cultural identity, self-determination, and inherent rights within the urban context.[5]

Various pathways led individual Native women to come together as "middle-class" activists. Some found their way to the city and to higher education through work as nannies in the homes of wealthy Toronto families. In interviews I conducted for the Toronto Native Community History Project in connection with my dissertation research, a number of women told how working as nannies opened new doors for them. Many had good domestic skills, but little English language competency. Time spent with a white elite family gave them the chance to improve their English, and some were allowed to attend classes in secretarial school, nursing, or teaching in their time off. Several also strategically engaged the "benevolence" of their wealthy white employers and other new contacts in mobilizing the funds and political will necessary to establish and develop Native-based community organizations and services, beginning with the North American Indian Club in 1950, and the Native Canadian Centre of Toronto, incorporated in 1962.[6]

These Native women, along with men who gained skills in the armed forces, or trained as teachers and in technical trades, began to form a professional middle class in the burgeoning Native community in the city. They actively sought to integrate into the cosmopolitan and consumer lifestyle of mainstream society in the city, while valuing and promoting their Native heritage. They also tended to hold relatively conservative political views, in contrast to their peers who were involved in the Red Power movement, one of whom described the Toronto Native community in 1974 as "the biggest number of middle-class Native people in Canada [who] liked the benefits they were receiving from the system, or were afraid of the system. They wanted to prove they were not the trouble-makers."[7]

This urban Native "middle class" needs to be understood within the parameters of specific historical, cultural, and socioeconomic contexts for Native and non-Native relations in Canada. Wotherspoon and Satzewich note that no serious examination of the complexities of socioeconomic class among Canadian Native people has been undertaken with the exception of discussions of their position as an "underclass" in relation to the larger class structure of Canadian society. This has given rise to an impression of Native people as homogeneously constituent of this underclass and to a silence "on the theoretical and political significance of class and gender divisions within the aboriginal population."[8]

The legacy of imperialism and colonialism, the specific and enduring nature of Native poverty, and practical and symbolic gendered divisions of labor are also contributing factors to understanding how class is conceptualized from a Native perspective. Socioeconomic relations emerging from imperialism and colonialism contributed a particular blend of occupational, ethnic, and gendered characteristics of Native Canadian identity. There is an association between Native identity and particular rural, "bush," and reserve occupations, such as fur-trade, guiding, and lumber work. These "traditional" jobs correspond to the symbolic opposition between Native and urban identities. They likewise contribute to a gender division in urban Native identity. "Traditional" jobs are mostly associated with men, and this has perhaps added to the limitations on the types (general labor) and duration of work (short-term and transient) for Native men during the early days of mass urban migration in the post–World War II period. Native women, on the other hand, had come to occupy jobs in the colonial economy that were relatively transferable to the urban context, such as domestic work. Women also accessed opportunities made available to them through Christian conversion efforts, becoming involved in church activities and organizing.[9] Canadian Indian policy since the mid-1800s also actively instituted a virtually irreversible state of extreme poverty among Native people. Just as "urban" and "Native" have been constructed as impossible contradictions, "poor" and "Native" have correlated as an inseparable basis of Native identity.[10]

In the ethnographic literature, Edgar Dosman's 1972 study of Saskatoon, and Mark Nagler's research in Toronto in the 1960s, offer some further insights on the socioeconomic diversity among Native people in these cities. Dosman describes a Native "aristocracy" or "affluent" group, which is defined not strictly by wealth, but by such factors as living in stable families and comfortable, well-located homes with infrequent address changes. They also tend to have job stability, which is essentially defined as an "absence of dependence on public welfare."[11] Interestingly, Dosman notes that while these characteristics seem to indicate assimilation, in fact the "affluent" Native people are least likely to suffer from Native identity crisis, shame, or disorientation. It is they who advocate

pride in Native identity and promote urban pan-Indian culture.[12]

Nagler's 1970 ethnography of Native urbanization in Toronto did not offer an analysis of occupational differences between the 85 men and 65 women he interviewed. However, scrutiny of the jobs he listed as "Characteristics of Indians Interviewed" reveals that Native women in the study could be categorized in higher numbers in occupations considered professional, middle-class, or "white-collar" as Nagler terms them, and men were statistically more present among working class or blue-collar sectors. Forty-five percent of the women were found to be in "professional" or "middle-class" occupations, such as health professions, office work, and teaching, compared with 19 percent of the men.[13]

What is defined as "middle-class" among Native people may be set at a "lower" bar than in the rest of the Canadian population. That is, it is not merely determined by salary, but by perceived prestige associated with jobs such as secretarial or office work. Sherry Ortner provides a model for how classes are relationally constituted, in that "they define themselves always in implicit reference to the other(s);" she further argues that "it appears overwhelmingly the case in working-class culture that women are symbolically aligned, from both the male point of view and, apparently, their own, with the "respectable," "middle-class" side of those oppositions and choices."[14] When this approach is applied to understanding the urban Native middle-class, it is clear that some Native people moving to the city are not simply becoming assimilated because they "adopt" the wider North American cultural goals of aspiring to "middle class" lifestyles. Rather than a linear movement towards assimilation, there is a production of urban Native culture that is a process relational to "class." For Native people the definitions of lower, middle, working, or professional class categories are constructed through the ongoing interactions within and between Native and non-Native communities.

WOMEN'S LIVES AND ORGANIZATIONAL DEVELOPMENT

North American Indian Club, Native Canadian Centre of Toronto, and Ladies' Auxiliary

I found the pamphlet, "So, you are coming to Toronto," among the personal papers donated to the Toronto Native Community History Project, by a founding member of the Native Canadian Centre of Toronto, Ella Rush (Six Nations). She had attached a note to the back of it that read, "Rules the Indian Affairs gave to all the newcomers (mostly girls) who came down to Toronto." Rush came from the nearby Six Nations of the Grand River reserve in the 1930s to train to be a nurse. Through school and work, she came to meet many other young Native people, who like herself, were in the city to make better lives for themselves than could be had on the increasingly economically and culturally depressed reserves. They formed a social network, which quickly came to include people from a wide diversity of Native tribes. Many pursued higher education (which meant beyond the limit of grade eight available on reserves) through military training and in technical schools, where they became nurses, teachers, and secretaries.

Verna Johnston first came to Toronto in 1945. In 1965, she opened a boarding home for young Native women while they attended technical schools—so they could become "career women" as she put it— more independent and not confined to what she felt was the limited option of marriage. In the environment of "Indian consciousness-raising" of the 1960s and 1970s, Johnston became acutely aware that the younger generations of urbanizing Native people needed the help of "Nokomis," meaning "grandmother" or a knowledgeable respected Elder. Within her home for girls, and eventually at many public venues, she taught crafts and spoke on Native culture and language with the goals of defeating stereotypes and promoting pride among urban Native people. In 1970 she published the book, *Tales of Nokomis*, a collection of stories she learned from her "Grandma Jones."[15] Johnston recalled the sense of "Indian awakening" during these times and articulated how the experience of coming to the city, and the need to establish a sense of Native identity and community, stimulated both collective and her own individual consciousness:

> I grew as a person in those years, and I don't mean just running the house for Indian students. I came into contact with Indians from other parts of Ontario, and other provinces. I found out that there were a lot of Indians working to help their own people. . . . That is Indians helping Indians—it's not the same as white do-gooders! Indians who have lived in the city know what it's all about, they are the best ones to help people. City Indians had really good ideas about how to help their people adjust to city life.[16]

The first known gathering place for the burgeoning Toronto Native community in the twentieth century was at the house of a family named Jamieson who were from the Six Nations of the Grand River

Reserve, approximately fifty miles southwest of the city. As early as the mid-1920s, they welcomed all young Native people into their home, primarily to provide an opportunity for them to meet and socialize with each other. After World War II, Ella Rush and several others (mostly women) who had met regularly at the Jamiesons' felt they should try to form a club. They approached the YMCA and founded the North American Indian Club there in 1950. Under the auspices of the YMCA, a minimum number of members were required to form a new club. Patricia Turner, also of Six Nations, who was a founding member along with her mother, remembered that a few Native men took out several memberships to meet the male numbers requirement.

At that time, it was estimated that only two or three hundred Native people lived in the city. In retrospect, the numbers may have been much higher. In light of the racism Native people faced in the city the tendency of many was to respond with "invisibility," attempting to "pass for white" if possible. Many were made to feel ashamed of their heritage or were cut off from their roots through removal to residential schools like Hettie Sylvester, an Anishnaabekwe from the Beausoleil First Nation who related that, "Being at residential school for twelve years took away a lot of my culture. I thought I was like everyone else. It wasn't until I left that I realized I was Indian. And it wasn't until the last few years that I began to understand what being Indian means."[17]

Sylvester came to Toronto in 1940 when she was nineteen. She got her first job housekeeping and working as a nanny through the YWCA and was an early member of the Indian Club. She was later a founder of the Native Canadian Centre's craft shop, which still provides an important source of income for the Centre, and she was president of the Centre's Ladies' Auxiliary for fifteen years. Her residential school experience highlighted her inequality in racial terms when she came to the city, not "realizing she was Indian until she left." However, the city was also a place where she could meet other Native people and utilize resources to organize a cultural community, in which her own identity as an Aboriginal person could be cultivated.

Another early member of the Club, Lillian McGregor (Anishnaabekwe), came to the city as a teenager during World War II and worked as a nanny. McGregor pursued her education to become a nurse. Born on Whitefish Reserve on Birch Island in 1924, she spent her childhood there. During the summers in 1938 and 1939, she worked at a tourist lodge in her area. In 1939, when she had completed the eighth grade, she worked as a waitress at the lodge. This, she says, helped her to learn more English and to gain more confidence in herself. This was also where McGregor had the Opportunity to become the nanny for a family from Toronto. Not wanting to jeopardize her chance of getting a higher education, she, her family, and the Toronto family worked it out so she could complete high school while looking after the children and doing her housework duties in the evenings and on weekends. McGregor is still very active in the community, serving as Elder in Residence at the University of Toronto, where she received an honorary doctorate in 2002, and on the Native Canadian Centre's Taam Kadinikiijiik (Elders Council). Her opportunities in the city rested upon her own ambitions, but they were fostered also within a context of cross-cultural class negotiations between her own family, who were prominent on the reserve, and the Toronto elite family who had the power to assist her.[18]

The differentiation Verna Johnston made between Native people helping each other and the work of "white do-gooders," underlines a duality carefully managed by Native women involved in community organizing in Toronto in the 1950s and 1960s. In addition to their involvement in establishing the North American Indian Club, and the Native Canadian Centre of Toronto, the women formed the Native Centre's Ladies' Auxiliary in 1963. These women were particularly instrumental in the continuity and development of Native cultural pride, through education, social support, and the institution of an urban market for Native art and crafts, which supplied both financial and cultural support to the Native Centre and the community in Toronto.

Native women who organized community activity also shared the experience of being on the front-line of the immediate social, health, employment, and educational needs of Native people in the city. Therefore, in addition to organizing social events, early North American Indian Club activities also included hospital visiting, as well as clothing and food drives. Later, the Ladies' Auxiliary provided counselling and inmate-visiting at the Kingston Prison for Women. The *Toronto Native Times* reported several times on the Ladies' Auxiliary's trips to Kingston, and the social conditions that put the women in jail in the first place became a central concern for the Auxiliary.[19] The Auxiliary's first president, Millie Redmond, a Potawatomi from Walpole Island First Nation, became interested in trying to help women in penal institutions set up their own clubs, on one occasion saying, "Perhaps a club could be formed to coordinate programs which would

help the women's stay behind bars be a more pleasant and meaningful experience. Perhaps our visit will help create the kind of interest necessary for such a club to be formed."[20]

Redmond, who passed away in the early 1990s, is often credited in the Native community with being the main founder of the North American Indian Club, which she started in her home. She was also behind numerous other Native programs and organizations in the city. In the 1930s, she was a frequent visitor to the Jamiesons' house mentioned earlier. She reflected on how that experience led her to think about forming a community organization for Native people in the city:

> I wanted to do something—meet other Native people. And that's how I got the Native Indian Club started in my home, where I'd start to meet Native people. We wanted to get a club going, just like the Scottish and the Irish, and the German clubs. And we didn't have any so we called the Y and asked them to help—and sure enough they did. I helped form the Ladies' Auxiliary with Ella Rush. . . . Helping to form the Indian Club was one of the real good things because we got to know each other.[21]

Other Ladies' Auxiliary women like Josephine Beaucage (Anishnaabekwe) also made the trips to Kingston penitentiary to demonstrate and teach craft-making. She saw teaching as part of her mission to bring traditional practices and elements of Native culture to spaces where they might re-affirm Native identity and forge links of cultural solidarity, whether they be the city or the penitentiary.[22] Beaucage was born on the Nipissing Reserve in 1904. She worked for Northland Boatlines as well as in tourist camps. These were jobs she held during the summer; in the winter she and her husband worked on their traplines. In 1960, her husband suffered brain damage from nearly drowning in a boating accident, and their daughter, who lived in Toronto, convinced her mother to bring him to the city where he might receive better health care. Unfortunately he never recovered and died in 1970.

Beaucage pursued higher education in secretarial school and then taught herself how to do beadwork, a craft for which she soon learned she had a natural talent. She was responsible for starting beadwork classes at the Native Centre and in a number of other locations, many of them sponsored by the Toronto Board of Education. Eventually, she was busy teaching traditional crafts throughout the province of Ontario. Beaucage's work life and her commitment to sharing her bead-working skills with others illustrate not only the contributions of women to cultural continuity and community, but also to the wider economy. About her career as a bead-worker and Native crafts instructor, she recalled,

> I started to go out teaching in different places. I went to reserves [all] around . . . And when I used to go these reserves, I ordered all my leather through B. B. Smith here in Toronto. I used to order by thousands, hundreds and thousands of square feet of leather for each course that I give. And the same with the bead company. I got my beads from a big bead company here in Toronto and that was the only bead company I would deal with. When [the owner] saw me he would say, "Boy, thank you for your advertisement—for advertising us".[23]

These women were particularly instrumental in the development of the urban market for Native art and crafts, which supplied structural, financial, and cultural support to the Native Canadian Centre and to the wider Native community in Toronto. For example, between 1963 and 1968, Ladies' Auxiliary member Dorothy Jones was responsible for obtaining crafts from local reserves to sell to raise money for the Centre. An outspoken advocate for Native people representing themselves, Jones placed a high emphasis on the authenticity of the crafts. In 1966, in the first edition of Centre's Newsletter (later to be called Beaver Tales) it was reported that,

> Mrs. Dorothy Jones personally selects all the articles in the display in an effort to be sure that the handicraft is a true representation of high quality Indian handicraft, indicative of the ability of the old-time craft workers . . . Here you may find lovely hand-loomed necklaces of beads, (made by Indians long before the Japanese made replicas for the tourist trade), fur-trimmed moccasins, beautiful woven baskets for various purposes, birchbark and horn rattles, drums and quill boxes . . . At the present time, Mrs. Jones could use more birchbark and sweetgrass items, but remember—of careful workmanship![24]

Hettie Sylvester's recollections of how the Native Centre's craft shop was started during her service as president of the Ladies' Auxiliary illustrates how the Ladies' Auxiliary's work combined cultural, social, and economic concerns in their volunteer service to community development. They were not only generating economic development through the organization of craft production and sales, they emphasized and articulated the value of positive Native identity pride and strength within the urban context. They also ensured the availability of some form of traditional social structures, particularly in terms of the roles of women as advisors and cultural transmitters.[25] Sylvester recalled fondly,

> I said, "Let's get Indian Crafts." I always had in my mind that I was an organizer. When I got to be president

I was the busiest person, there was a project going on every month, fundraising or something . . . I enjoy[ed] working there, and not only as a salesperson. A lot of people come in and talk to me as their mother, I think. They come talk to me and tell me their problems. It is really interesting to listen to them and what they go through. I don't know why, there was a counselling room back there, but maybe they see me as motherly, I don't know. I liked it. I enjoy talking to these people.[26]

The variety of experiences of these Native women contradicts the stereotypical molds to which Native people are generally expected to conform, grounded in the deeply entrenched view that there is some fundamental contradiction between Native identity and the cosmopolitanism of the city. Social geographer Evelyn Peters questions the assumption that being urban and Aboriginal necessarily constitutes an impossible and contradictory schism of identity. She describes how, conventionally, city living has been most often presented as the antithesis of Native culture. The imagery of "Aboriginality" in dominant European thought has equated "authentic" Native culture with the natural, mystical, and "non-civilized" world.[27] The conditions of urban living subvert the possibilities of generating and sustaining authentic Native cultural communities in cities. However, Native people in Toronto challenge the urban-Indian "oxymoron," not by assimilating, but by generating a rich and diverse Native community. The achievement of this richness and diversity has been the result of a range of dynamic struggles mediated by race, gender, and class relations with non-Natives and within the Native community.

NATIVE URBAN CLASS MOBILITY, COMMUNITY BUILDING, AND NETWORKING WITH ELITES

As part of the emergent Native middle class, many of the Ladies' Auxiliary women were also key in a strategic collaboration with wealthy white women, which helped to provide much of the funding needed to establish the Centre. In particular, they nurtured relationships between the Native Canadian Centre and the Imperial Order of the Daughters of the Empire (IODE).[28] The IODE is an international organization, founded in 1900, and devoted to Commonwealth citizenship. It was made up primarily of women from the urban industrial upper class, who engaged in a variety of benevolent works. In the 1960s IODE women turned their attention to concerns of Canadian national identity and citizenship. They focused their energies and resources on the integration of immigrants and Native people into

Canadian society. IODE members were mobilized by a combination of ideological, gender, and class motivations that included their sense of duty to act benevolently and charitably towards the less fortunate in society, and to contribute to the project of nation-building, patriotism, and citizenship. In the 1960s, they were instrumental in the establishment of at least five urban Native Friendship Centres across Canada, including the Toronto Centre.

The IODE's relationship with the Toronto Native Centre, and with Native people across the country, manifested itself most in the person of Peggy Jennings (IODE's Citizenship Convenor), who served as the first president of the Native Canadian Centre of Toronto's board of directors. She used her influence with her wealthy acquaintances and vocalized the concerns of urban Native people in the media. For instance, Mrs. John D. Eaton (of the Eaton's Department store chain) was also recruited as a member of the Native Centre's board of directors. She donated $25,000 of the $45,000 price tag for their second building purchased in 1966.

Between 1963 and 1967, Jennings appeared frequently in the print media across the country, reprimanding her fellow non-Native citizens for their lack of sensitivity to Native people, and praising Aboriginal people coming to the cities for their great potential to become good Canadian citizens. She also lauded their emphasis on pride in their national and cultural heritage. Jennings led the IODE pressures on the Federal Minister of Immigration and Citizenship, then overseeing Indian Affairs, for an in-depth study of "all aspects of the life of our Indian citizens to help them achieve equality of opportunity so they may become full participating members of Canadian society."[29]

The middle-class status of some of the Native women involved in the Indian Club and the Ladies' Auxiliary afforded them a degree of "leisure" that allowed them to commit time and effort to community service. They pursued the dual goals of ensuring and maintaining the integrity of Native cultural identity in the city and building financial support for the establishment and delivery of services to Native people. This initially captured the attention of organizations like the IODE. The women of the Native Centre's Ladies' Auxiliary and the IODE held in common a conservative and shared desire to see

improvements in the social conditions and recognition of Native people in Canada. Where they differed were in the underlying culturally-based motivations behind these perspectives. The culture of the dominant class deployed an ideology that constructed gender roles in terms of a "calling" to carry out the bidding of the empire and citizenship. Native women's actions were based in their common experiences of politicized identity, cultural appropriation and devaluation, and the need to affirm Native cultural identity and build strong self-determined communities.

Native women's volunteer work in the early years of community building in Toronto did not represent a uniform platform for action, but rather was composed of diverse perspectives that changed over time, and depended much on the concerns and directions taken by those in leadership positions. Under the guidance of Millie Redmond, for instance, the activities of the North American Indian Club and the Ladies' Auxiliary led to the establishment of social services for Native people in the city. Verna Johnston, Dorothy Jones, and Ella Rush were significant in affirming a positive image for Native people in the urban environment, as well as the development of a discourse around the authenticity of Native identity emergent from the common experiences of people from diverse Native cultural backgrounds. Women like Hettie Sylvester and Josephine Beaucage were instrumental in the development of the urban market for Native art and crafts, but also contributed to the transference and adaptation of traditional Native women's roles of leadership and cultural transmission in the urban context. The type of Native women's activism described in this article highlights the links between gender and class mobility for urban Native people and the shaping of identity and community. They illustrate the dynamics of Native urbanization in the post–World War II era, particularly in terms of the gendered character of volunteer service and of educational and employment opportunities in the city for Native people. Native women's work and volunteer service has impacted the struggle for social equality and community development. Native women have also rejected the restrictions of reserve life, maximized opportunities in the urban context, and cultivated a space for the revitalization and growth of Native culture and identity, while striving for social justice.

NOTES

I am very grateful to the Native Canadian Centre of Toronto and the many people there, including past members of the Ladies' Auxiliary for their confidence in me and their insights into this research. I am also most thankful to my coeditor of this volume, and a tremendous mentor, Dr. Susan Applegate Krouse. I also acknowledge the financial support of the Fonds FCAR (Formation des chercheurs et aide a la recherche—Quebec) doctoral scholarship, the Social Science and Humanities Research Council of Canada, and the Department of Anthropology, University of Toronto.

1. Rosamund Vanderburgh, *I Am Nokomis, Too: The Biography of Verna Patronella Johnston* (Don Mills ON: General Publishing, 1977).

2. For example, Hugh Brody, *Indians On Skid Row* (Ottawa: Northern Science Research Group, Dept. of Indian Affairs and Northern Development, 1971); Trevor Denton, "Strangers in Their Land: A Study of Migration from a Canadian Indian Reserve" (PhD diss., University of Toronto, 1970); Edgar Dosman, *Indians: The Urban Dilemma* (Toronto: McLelland & Stewart,1972); Larry Krotz, *Urban Indians: the Strangers in Canada's Cities* (Edmonton: Hurtig, 1980); Mark Nagler, *Indians in the City: A Study of the Urbanization of Indians in Toronto* (Ottawa: Canadian Research Centre for Anthropology, Saint Paul University, 1970); Joan Ryan, *Wall of Words: The Betrayal of the Urban Indian* (Toronto: PMA Books, 1978); William Stanbury, *Success and Failure: Indians in Urban Society* (Vancouver: University of British Columbia Press, 1975).

3. Pamphlet issued by the Dept. of Indian Affairs "So, you're coming to Toronto (circa 1945–1950). Ella Rush Collection (pamphlets, flyers, and posters), Toronto Native Community History Project, Native Canadian Centre of Toronto.

4. For an overview of U.S. urban relocation policy, see Donald L. Fixico, *Termination and Relocation: Federal Indian Policy 1945–1960* (Albuquerque: University of New Mexico Press, 1986).

5. Heather Howard-Bobiwash, "Dreamcatchers in the City: An Ethnohistory of Social Action, Gender and Class in Native Community Production in Toronto" (PhD diss., University of Toronto, 2004).

6. The Native Canadian Centre of Toronto is the oldest existing Native organization in Toronto and was the third Friendship Centre established in Canada following Winnipeg (1958) and Vancouver (1960). For a detailed history of the Native Canadian Centre of Toronto, see Roger Obonsawin and Heather Howard-Bobiwash, "The Native Canadian Centre of Toronto: The Meeting Place for the Toronto Native Community for 35 Years," in *The Meeting Place: Aboriginal Life in Toronto*, ed. Frances Sanderson and Heather Howard-Bobiwash (Toronto: Native Canadian Centre of Toronto, 1997): 25–59.

7. Vern Harper, *Following the Red Path, the Native People's Caravan, 1974* (Toronto: NC Press, 1974): 44.

8. Terry Wotherspoon and Vic Satzewich, *First Nations Race, Class, and Gender Relations* (Regina: Canadian Plains Research Center, 2000).

9. For more on Native women in imperial/mission/colonial history, see Karen Anderson, *Chain Her By One Foot: The Subjugation of Women in Seventeenth-Century New France* (New York: Routledge, 1991); Carol Devens, *Countering Colonization: Native American Women and Great Lakes Women, 1630–1900* (Berkeley: University of California Press, 1992); Eleanor Leacock, "Montagnais Women and the Jesuit Program for Colonization," in *Myths of Male Dominance: Collected Articles on Women Cross Culturally* (New York: Monthly Review Press, 1981); Nancy Shoemaker, ed., *Negotiators of Change* (New York: Routledge, 1995); Susan Sleeper Smith, *Indian Women and French Men: Rethinking Cultural Encounter in the Western Great Lakes* (Amherst: University of Massachusetts Press, 2001); Sylvia Van Kirk, *Many Tender Ties: Women in Fur Trade Society 1670–1870* (Winnipeg: Watson & Dwyer, 1980).

10. Evelyn Peters, "'Urban and Aboriginal': An Impossible Contradiction?" in City *Lives and City Forms: Critical Research and Canadian Urbanism*, ed. Jon Caulfield and Linda Peake (Toronto: University of Toronto Press, 1996).

11. Dosman, *Indians*, 48.

12. Dosman, *Indians*, 56.

13. Nagler, *Indians in the City*, 95–103.

14. Sherry Ortner, "Reading America: Preliminary Notes on Class and Culture," in *Recapturing Anthropology: Working in the Present*, ed. Richard Fox (Santa Fe NM: School of American Research Press, 1991), 172.

15. Heather Howard-Bobiwash, "'Like Her Lips to My Ear': Reading Anishnaabekweg Lives and Aboriginal Cultural Continuity in the City," in *Feminist Fields: Ethnographic Insights*, ed. Rae Bridgman, Sally Cole, and Heather Howard Bobiwash (Peterborough ON: Broadview Press,1999): 119–20; Patronella Johnson, *Tales of Nokomis* (Don Mills ON: Musson, 1975).

16. Rosamund Vanderburgh, *I Am Nokomis, Too: The Biography of Verna Patronella Johnson* (Don Mills ON: General Publishing, 1977): 122, 141.

17. Edna Manitowabi, "Hedy Sylvester: The Founder of the Centre's Craft Shop," *Boozhoo, Newsmagazine of the Native Canadian Centre of Toronto* 1:4 (1987): 35–37.

18. "'There's So Much To Learn Each Day': A Profile of Lillian McGregor," Native *Canadian Newsletter* (Native Canadian Centre of Toronto) 10:1 (October 1996): 1, 3.

19. The *Toronto Native Times* was a community-based monthly newspaper Published by the Native Canadian Centre of Toronto between 1968 and 1981. Including this publication, The Centre has always produced some form of regularly-appearing serial during its forty-plus year history.

20. Irene Lee. "Ladies' Auxiliary Visits KP", *Toronto Native Times*, (Native Canadian Centre of Toronto) (April 1971): 2(4), 8.

21. Millie Redmond, interviewed by Evelyn Sit. Toronto Public Library Indian History Project, OHT 83030 (1983): 27, 28, 29.

22. Josephine Beaucage, interviewed by Cyndy Baskin. Toronto Public Library Indian History Project, OHT 83037 (1983).

23. Interview with Beaucage, 13.

24. Canadian Indian Centre of Toronto Newsletter, Feb.–Mar. 1966, 4.

25. See Susan Lobo, this volume.

26. Hettie Sylvester, interviewed by Jaime Lee. Toronto Public Library Indian History Project, OHT 82020 (1982): 9–10.

27. Peters, City Lives and City Forms, 48.

28. For a more detailed account of the relationship between the IODE, the Native Canadian Centre of Toronto, and other national action on behalf of urban Aboriginal people in the 1960s, see Heather Howard-Bobiwash, "'For Home and Country': Community, Citizenship, and Native/non-Native Women's Action in the History of the Native Canadian Centre of Toronto.," *Anthropologica: Journal of the Canadian Anthropological Society* (under review).

29. "IODE Asks for Study of Indians," (Ottawa—CP), Unidentified Toronto Native Community History Project News-clipping file, c.1963. The Toronto Native Community History Project has an extensive collection of news clippings, which are believed to have been collected by members of the Native Canadian Centre of Toronto's Ladies' Auxiliary between 1962 and 1968. Many are undated and the sources unidentified. This particular clipping was determined to date during or prior to 1963 as "Minister Bell" is mentioned. His term as Citizenship Minister was from 1957–1963 under Prime Minister John Diefenbaker. It is interesting that IODE women were advocating this in-depth study before the pivotal "Hawthorne Report" was commissioned by the government in 1964 (1966, "A Survey of the Contemporary Indians of Canada Economic, Political, Educational Needs and Policies"). In 1969, Prime Minister Trudeau cited this report to propose the elimination of Indian Status and assimilate Native people completely into Canadian society. This prompted nationwide protest from Native people, often said to mark the official beginning of the Red Power movement in Canada.

Youngest Trapper on 7th Street
© Pena Bonito. Reprinted by permission.

PART REVIEW

DISCUSSION QUESTIONS

Introduction

1. Discuss some of the stereotypes that continue to make Native people living in cities "invisible."
2. What are some of the characteristics of ancient urban centers that have existed in the Western Hemisphere for centuries? What are some of the reasons that the history of these Native cities and civilizations is not included in the curriculum of most secondary schools and at the college level in courses in American history?
3. Why is it important to have an accurate census count? What are some of the ways that national and local governments and nonprofits use census figures?

Jack D. Forbes, *The Urban Tradition Among Native Americans*

1. What, in European-derived perspective, are some of the conceptual links between *cities*, *civilization*, and being a *civilized* person? What were some of the impacts for Native peoples when Europeans with these conceptual perspectives arrived in the Western Hemisphere?
2. Describe the characteristics of one of the ancient Native American cities.

3. Locate the following on a map: Cahokia, Tiahuanaco, Teotihuacan, Nasca, Cholula, Tical, Hohokam, Mississippian culture, and Chaco Canyon.
4. One often reads or hears that the Mayan Indians "vanished" or that there is mystery surrounding "why the Mayas are a vanished race." Do you believe these are true statements? Why or why not?

Lanada Boyer, *Reflections of Alcatraz*

1. Why did the Indian students occupy Alcatraz Island in 1969?
2. Describe the author's spiritual experience on Alcatraz.
3. How did the government negotiator, Bob Robertson, try to divide the Indians and weaken support for the occupation?

Susan Lobo, *Is Urban a Person or a Place?*

1. Explain why the term *urban Indian* inaccurately defines Indian identity.
2. Describe the characteristics of the "Indian community" and explain why it is a more meaningful concept in understanding the urban experience than is geographic location. How has the Indian community in urban areas become increasingly diverse and complex?

Victoria Bomberry, *Downtown Oklahoma City, 1952*
1. Explain the awakening to the existence of racism that this little girl goes through. Why was this new understanding about the society around her a pivotal experience?

Carol Miller, *Telling the Indian Urban: Representations in American Indian Fiction*
1. Who is Scott Momaday, and why is he an important figure in contemporary literature? He was the first American Indian to be presented with what award?
2. What is an "Indian perspective," and how has it been presented and represented in fiction by Native writers? How has an Indian perspective been expressed when discussing relationships and sense of place, both urban and rural?

Heather Howard-Bobiwash, *Women's Class Strategies as Activism in Native Community Building in Toronto, 1950–1975*
1. Describe the class and racial divides that existed in Toronto during the period of time depicted in this article.
2. What is a *strategy*, and what does it take to develop and put a strategy into action?
3. How is *activism* defined in this article? What are some of the other forms that activism takes? Give concrete examples.

Photography and Poetry in This Part
1. Which is your favorite photograph or poem in this part? Why and what does it tell you about Native life in the city?

KEY TERMS

Andean civilizations
"back home"
Cahokia
census undercount
community building
identity crisis
Leslie Marmon Silko
Mesoamerica
mound builder

network of relationships
occupation of Alcatraz
relocation policy
Scott Momaday
Teotihuacan
termination policy
urban Indian centers
urban stereotypes
W.O.R. (WithOut Rezervation)

SUGGESTED READINGS

FAGAN, BRIAN M. *Clash of Cultures*, 2nd ed. Walnut Creek, Calif.: AltaMira Press, 1998.

JACKSON, DEBORAH DAVIS. *Our Elders Lived It: American Indian Identity in the City*. DeKalb: Northern Illinois University Press, 2002.

JOHNSON, TROY R. *We Hold the Rock: The Indian Occupation of Alcatraz, 1969–1971*. San Francisco: Golden Gate National Park Association, 1997.

JOHNSON, TROY, JOANE NAGEL, and DUANE CHAMPAGNE, eds. *American Indian Activism: Alcatraz to the Longest Walk*. Urbana: University of Illinois Press, 1997.

KROUSE, SUSAN APPLEGATE, and HOWARD, HEATHER A., eds. *Keeping the Campfire Going: Native American Women's Activism in Urban Areas*. Lincoln: University of Nebraska Press, 2009.

LAGRAND, JAMES B. *Indian Metropolis: Native Americans in Chicago, 1945–75*. Urbana: University of Illinois Press, 2002.

LOBO, SUSAN. *A House of My Own: the Social Organization in the Squatter Settlements of Lima, Peru."* Tucson, University of Arizona Press, 1982.

LOBO, SUSAN. *Urban Voices: The Bay Area American Indian Community*. Tucson: The University of Arizona Press, 2002.

LOBO, SUSAN, and PETERS, KURT, eds., *American Indians and the Urban Experience*. Walnut Creek, Calif.: AltaMira Press, 2001.

MANN, CHARLES C. *1491: New Revelations of the Americas Before Columbus*. New York: Vintage Books, 2005, Chapters 6 and 7.

NATIONAL URBAN INDIAN FAMILY COALITION. *Urban Indian America: The Status of American Indian and Alaska Native Children and Families Today*. Seattle: The National Urban Indian Family Coalition, 2008.

PAMIREZ, RENYA K. *Native Hubs: Culture, Community and Belonging in Silicon Valley and Beyond*. Durham, N.C.: Duke University Press, 2007.

REYES, LAWNEY L. *Bernie Whitebear: An Urban Indian's Quest for Justice*. Tucson: University of Arizona Press, 2006.

SANDERSON, FRANCES, and HOWARD-BOBIWASH, HEATHER. *The Meeting Place: Aboriginal Life in Toronto*. Toronto: Native Canadian Centre of Toronto, 1997.

WEATHERFORD, JACK. *Indian Givers: How the Indians of the Americas Transformed the World*. New York: Fawcett, Columbine, 1998.

WEIBEL-ORLANDO, JOAN. "Urban Communities," in *Indians in Contemporary Society: The Handbook of North American Indians*, vol. 2. Washington, D.C.: Smithsonian Institution, 2008.

INDIGENOUS RIGHTS: STRUGGLE AND REVITALIZATION

Indianismo!
Tom LaBlanc

Listen! Can you hear the warm southern air flowing
through the bamboo and reeds? Making music out of
this confusing noise. Can you hear the silent heartbeat
of all those massacred? Reach down and touch the
tortured bodies! Touch the tortured bodies hidden
deep within the Peruvian dungeons. Dungeons. . . .
The sacred hoop is whole once again! We are all
related! . . . We will liberate the natural world.
Indianismo! . . . But now, we will reunite the family
of life! We who love life, as a way of living, now we
live. . . .
We will come alive dancing to the same song. We will
liberate the natural world. We who live, as a way of
living, now, we live.

¡Escuchen! ¿Pueden oir el aire tibio del sur, pasando a
través de los junquillos y los bambúes, transformando
este ruido confuso en música? ¿Pueden oir el silencioso
palpitar del corazón de todos los masacrados? ¡Estiren
sus manos y toquen los cuerpos torturados! ¡Toquen
los cuerpos torturados escondidos en los profundos
socavones peruanos, tan profundos! Socavones. . . .
¡El círculo sagrado es completa de nuevo! Somos una
misma familia. . . .
Liberaremos la Madre Tierra. ¡Indianismo! . . .
Pero reuniremos la familia de la vida. Nosotros los
queamamos la vida como manera de vivir. ¡Ahora
vivimos! . . .
Renaceremos danzando la misma música. Liberaremos a la Madre Tierra. Nosotros los que vivimos
como manera de vivir. Ahora vivimos.

This book has addressed a number of issues of critical importance to Native American peoples as oppressed minorities in North America and as oppressed majorities in most Latin American countries. They include the hidden heritage and the distortion of history; genocide, racism, and stereotyping; the violation of religious freedom; the destruction of the environment; health and education problems; structural conditions leading to high incarceration rates; environmental issues; and the struggle for sovereignty and nation building, among others. In this part, we turn to the concept of self-determination.

To a great extent, the long resistance by the Indigenous peoples of the Americas to oppression and neocolonialism has involved reclaiming self-governing status in order to freely determine what the relationship should be between Native nations and the larger nation-state. The solution concept is self-determination, and according to the United Nations, this is a basic right of sovereign nations under international law. *Sovereignty*, as Indian activist Hank Adams (Assiniboine/Sioux) once defined it, is the collective authority of a people to govern itself. It is the collective force that binds a national community together and gives it the right to define its membership, choose its form of government, conduct foreign relations, make its own laws, and regulate its property and resources.

What has been debated in the international arena during the past several decades is whether Indigenous peoples, including those of the Americas, have the necessary attributes to govern themselves as independent entities. If they do, then they should be accorded the right of self-determination. But the recognized nation-states have been reluctant to relinquish privileges and power over Indigenous peoples, their territories, and resources.

It is frequently argued that Native peoples cannot exercise sovereignty as independent nations for a variety of reasons. In *Behind the Trail of Broken Treaties*, in the chapter titled "The Size and Status of Nations," the Indian scholar Vine Deloria, Jr., critiqued the five most common arguments against Native American tribes of the United States attaining self-determination: (1) Indian land areas are too small for nationhood status; (2) Indian reservations are surrounded by the larger U.S. nation (can there be nations within a nation?); (3) the tribal populations are too small; (4) they lack an independent economic base; and (5) they lack sufficient education and technical competence to run their own affairs.[1] Deloria counters each objection by documenting examples of fully recognized, independent states, including those represented at the United Nations, such as Liechtenstein, San Marino, Monaco, and Vatican City, that have one or more of these same characteristics and yet are given status as independent nations.

Self-determination takes different political forms. The *mini-state* has the option of contracting out its need for defense, postal, or educational services, for example, to the larger nation encapsulating it. Indeed, this idea resembles the nation-building movement embraced by a growing number of Indian tribes in the United States (see Part VIII). Why can't the Native peoples throughout the Americas have the same right to self-determination and take their place in the international community of nations? This right would seem especially obvious for those larger, even majority Indian peoples of Latin America, such as Bolivia.

In *The Road: Indian Tribes and Political Liberty* (see Suggested Readings), Russel Barsh and James Youngblood Henderson suggest that *treaty federalism* is a realistic option for Native American tribes in the United States. By this they mean that the federal government would reinstitute the treaty process (which was unilaterally ended by Congress in 1871) to govern all the Indian tribes. Treaties would then govern the relations between the Indian nations and the U.S. government as co-equal powers. Another option is *statehood*, at least for the larger tribes, such as the Navajo Nation. In Canada, the Inuit territory of Nunavut has self-governing status, although the Canadian government retains ownership of its natural resources.

Originally, the U.S. federal government negotiated with the Indian peoples as sovereign nations in nation-to-nation agreements, and this status was made legitimate in more than 300 treaties. Treaties, together with the Constitution and Supreme Court decisions, are the highest law of the land under the U.S. form of government. The problem, of course, arises in the fact that the United States has badly compromised or broken all the treaties, and Indian sovereignty has been steadily eroded over the decades by the unilateral actions of Congress. This history has been particularly galling to the Indian tribes. As the Native American Rights Fund wrote in a recent fund appeal letter:

> Suppose the government of the United States took your land, lost or stole your money, and broke virtually every promise it ever made to you. Suppose your rights, *your constitutionally guaranteed rights* [emphasis added], were being violated every day . . . and you were a member of the poorest, most undeserved, most discriminated against population in the country. In other words, suppose you were a Native American. . . . what would you do to get justice?

What was the legal justification for the breaking of Indian treaties in the United States, and can the process be reversed? The turning point in the history of U.S. Indian relations, according to Indian legal scholars such as Deloria, was the 1823 *Johnson v. M'Intosh* court decision, which gave the right of discovery by European (Christian) nations and by the United States precedence over the aboriginal (land-owning) rights of Native peoples. (This point is discussed in Reading 1 in Part III.) *Johnson v. M'Intosh* was followed by the 1831 Supreme Court decision *Cherokee Nation v. Georgia*, in which Chief Justice John Marshall ruled that rather than completely independent nations, Indian tribes are "domestic dependent nations." Marshall's decision paved the way for the plenary power doctrine of Congress, which means that the U.S. Congress can break any treaty or make any law with regard to Indians when doing so is in the interests of the larger nation. In 1871, Congress unilaterally ended treaty making with the Indian nations altogether.

The 1960s and 1970s saw an upsurge in the Native American struggle in the United States for land, cultural and religious rights, social justice, and the restoration of *sovereignty*. Some of the events of the "new Indian" movement, as it has been termed, are described throughout this book and are summarized by John Mohawk in Reading 1. The highlights include the following: the founding in the United States in 1961 of the National Indian Youth Council by militant Indian college students; a series of Indian "fish-ins" in Washington State in support of the treaty right of Northwestern tribes to fish, beginning in 1964; the founding of the Alaska Federation of Natives in 1966 as a response to threatened land rights and resources under the Alaskan Statehood Act and the Prudhoe Bay oil discovery; the blockade of the international bridge on the Canadian–U.S. border by the Mohawks at St. Regis in 1968, in support of their 1794 Jay Treaty; the founding of the American Indian Movement (AIM) in Minnesota, also in 1968, to combat urban racism; and AIM later leading Indian people across the nation in a range of protests. There were also the occupation of Alcatraz Island in San Francisco Bay in 1969; the 1972 Trail of Broken Treaties caravan to Washington, D.C.; and the Indian rights protest at Wounded Knee on the Pine Ridge Reservation in 1973. After the Wounded Knee protest, the year 1975 saw a firefight on the Pine Ridge Reservation between aggressive federal agents and the AIM warriors in which two FBI agents and a young Indian man were killed. This event led to the unjust conviction and imprisonment of Leonard Peltier, which is documented in Part IV. In the United States, the International Indian Treaty Council was founded in 1974. Indigenous groups throughout the Americas and in Australia, New Zealand, and Scandinavia began organizing and taking their grievances to the United Nations and other international bodies.

By the late 1970s, both the U.S.-based International Indian Treaty Council in the United States and the Canadian-based World Council of Indigenous Peoples had received nongovernmental status with the United Nations in order to place the case of Native American rights before the court of world opinion. In 1977, the first world gathering of Native American peoples convened at the United Nations headquarters in Geneva, Switzerland. This was the international Conference on Discrimination Against the Indigenous Populations in the Americas, organized by a committee of nongovernmental organizations (NGOs) at the United Nations. (See Reading 3.) It was followed by a second United Nations NGO conference in 1981, Indigenous Peoples and the Land. A Working Group on Indigenous Populations under the United Nations Economic and Social Council was established the following year. In 1985 the Working Group began drafting the Declaration on the Rights of Indigenous Peoples. The UN General Assembly declared 1995–2004 an International Decade of the World's Indigenous Peoples. The Working Group was replaced by The Permanent Forum on Indigenous Issues, a 16-member body of independent experts, 8 of whom are nominated by the government states, and

8 nominated by the Indigenous peoples themselves but reflecting the 7 geocultural regions of the world, with 1 rotating seat. The draft was finished in 1993, but it took more than a decade to work its way through the UN procedural channels before being approved by the General Assembly in 2007. (See Reading 2.)

The Indigenous struggle had become internationalized. Other important events have taken place in recent years, but the developments cited above were among the forerunners of the contemporary Indigenous movement at home and in the international arena, a movement that deepened spiritually and broadened politically in the 1980s and 1990s to include the rights of the world's 370 million Indigenous peoples.

At the same time these developments were occurring at the United Nations, Native American groups throughout the Americas were continuing their struggle against oppression at home. The Cree Indians of Canada unsuccessfully fought the flooding of their lands in Quebec by the James Bay hydroelectric project, termed James Bay I. Native villages in Alaska lobbied the U.S. Congress to safeguard their lands and monetary rights by passing the 1991 amendments to the Alaska Native Claims Settlement Act. In the Pacific Northwest, treaty tribes waged an intense struggle to protect their rights "to fish in their accustomed places." Indian groups in the Amazon basin organized to oppose the genocidal actions of mining corporations and land developers intent on destroying the rainforest and the lands and livelihood of the Indian peoples. In fact, Indigenous groups throughout Latin America were organizing into ethnic associations and political coalitions.

By the 1980s, it was clear that a revitalization movement was taking place. The term *revitalization* means that Native American culture and traditions were having a rebirth, a cultural renaissance. Academic books and publications noting this development include *The Return of the Native*, by Stephen Cornell; *American Indian Activism*, edited by Troy Johnson, Joane Nagel, and Duane Champagne; *American Indian Ethnic Renewal*, by Joane Nagel; *Return of the Indian*, by Phillip Wearne; and the journal *Native Americas*, published by the American Indian Program of Cornell University (see Suggested Readings). In Canada and the United States, many Native people who had become alienated by the reservation system, Christian missionization, the boarding school system, and termination and relocation policies were returning to their spiritual and cultural roots. Paradoxically, urbanization and relocation resulted in the growth of vibrant and active urban Indian communities, which became the "seed bed" of much of the new leadership for the growing resistance and revitalization movement in the United States. Resistance, community, and nation building go hand in hand.

In Reading 1, "Directions in People's Movements," it is to the events of these eight and a half decades of struggle that Seneca scholar, John Mohawk, speaks. The names and meanings of U.S. Indian policies and laws, he implies, may be totally foreign to most non-Indian Americans (for example, the 1934 Indian Reorganization Act, which stopped the loss of the Indian land base, or the destructive relocation and termination policies of the 1950s). Yet such laws and policies are household words for most Indians in the United States. The same is true for the First Nations of Canada. Native peoples are also cognizant of important political activities and events in their respective struggles. In the United States, these include the 1969 Alcatraz Island occupation; the Trail of Broken Treaties caravan to Washington, D.C., in 1972; the 1973 protest at Wounded Knee; the worldwide effort to free Indian political prisoner Leonard Peltier; the many efforts to pass and then enforce the 1978 American Indian Religious Freedom Act and related legislation; participation in the international Indigenous conferences and meetings at the United Nations to draft the Declaration on the Rights of Indigenous Peoples; and the many activities aimed at repatriation of ancestral remains from museums and academic archaeological collections, as well as cultural and language restoration projects and programs.

Other important events have taken place in the Indigenous struggle since Mohawk's article was written. In Latin America, Native peoples were resisting the oligarchical governments of their respective nation-states, the impact of global capitalism and free trade neo-liberalism, U.S. interventionist policies in support of corrupt governments and the penetration by multinational corporations (in the name of fighting communism or the drug trade), and even some of the policies and actions of leftist rebel groups that often exclude Indigenous peoples from their reform agendas.

In the countryside and urban squatter settlements of Latin America, but especially in the cities and metropolitan areas of the United States, a new sense of Indianness and "place" was developing. The Intertribal Friendship House in Oakland, California, and the American Indian Community House in New York City are examples of the new urbanism, discussed in Part IX. Since the 1980s there has also been a reaching out to the elders and spiritual leaders, many of whom still reside "back on the rez." A number of urban Indians were returning to the reservations, some to stay and others to relearn or strengthen their knowledge of their Native American language, culture, and spiritual traditions. Some reasserted their Indian identity by returning to their original Indian family names. There has also been a revival throughout Indian Country of spiritual practices and traditions: the sun dance, the sweat lodge, the peyote church, and tribe-specific dances and ceremonies.

The 1990s and the beginning of the new millennium have seen a further expansion of activism, including Indigenous coalitions and Indian-based political parties, in response to continued depredations and oppression. The First Nations in Quebec, Canada, challenged the Quebec separatists, who had threatened to split off from the larger nation. If Canada can be split, they asked, why can't the Cree and the Inuit, who are the only permanent residents of the 175,000-square-mile sub-Arctic region of northern Quebec, have their own independent province?

In Hawai'i, following the regressive decision by the U.S. Supreme Court to invalidate Hawaiians-only voting in Office of Hawaiian Affairs elections, one of several Native rights organizations, Ka Lahui Hawai'i, issued a new call for Native unity. Ka Lahui Hawai'i advocates a nation-within-a-nation relationship to the United States as a way for Hawaiians to govern their own affairs.

Native peoples from North, Central, and South America increased contacts and began organizing politically to oppose their common oppression. The United Nations–sponsored Earth Summit that took place in Rio de Janeiro in June 1992 was attended by Native American representatives from throughout the Americas in the common struggle to protect the environment. Native peoples in Central and South America formed new political organizations and coalitions to press for recognition and their rights as Indigenous peoples before their respective national governments and at the United Nations. In December 2006, Evo Morales became the first Indigenous person in South America to become head of state as president of Bolivia. (See the box "¡Evo Presidente!" in Part VIII.)

Decades of activism reached a milestone of achievement on June 29, 2006, when the Human Rights Council of the United Nations approved the Draft Declaration on the Rights of Indigenous Peoples. Then on September 13, 2007, the United Nations General Assembly, after negotiating some compromises, adopted the declaration. The text of the declaration is presented as Reading 2, "Declaration of the Rights of Indigenous Peoples." One hundred forty-three member states voted "yes," eleven abstained, and four voted against the declaration. Those voting "no" included the United States, joined by Canada, Australia, and New Zealand—nation-states containing millions of Indigenous peoples. Facing international and internal pressure, the Canadian House of Commons later passed a resolution to endorse the declaration and called on its government to "fully implement the standards contained therein." The declaration has the support of many countries with large Indigenous populations, such as Mexico, Peru, Bolivia, Guatemala, and the Nordic nations. Bolivia especially was a strong advocate of the declaration. The box following Reading 2 indicates the unequivocal level of support given the Declaration by Indigenous organizations. At its midyear session in 2007, the National Congress of American Indians (NCAI) adopted a resolution in support of the draft declaration. The NCAI is the oldest and largest national organization of American Indian and Alaska Native tribal governments in the United States.

The declaration, with its 46 articles, is a comprehensive statement addressing the rights of Indigenous peoples the world over. Among its protections are articles stipulating the right of Indigenous peoples not to be forcibly removed from their lands; the right to spiritual and religious freedom; the right to media in Indigenous languages; the attention to the special needs of elders, women, and children; the right to traditional medicine; protection of the Indigenous environment; right to cultural heritage; right to identity and membership; protection from divided international borders; and observance and enforcement of treaties and agreements. Other United Nations bodies—such as the Internal Labor Organization's Convention No. 169 and the Convention on Biological Diversity (Article 8-j)—have also addressed Indigenous rights. The Organization of American States (OAS) is in the process of working on an Indigenous declaration that validates and supports the UN declaration.

A key right accorded by the declaration is the right to self-determination. By this right, an Indigenous people can freely determine its own political status and pursue its economic, social, and cultural development while retaining, if it chooses to do so, the right to participate fully in the political, economic, social, and cultural life of the larger nation-state. For several years, negotiations at the United Nations on the draft declaration were stalled over the issue of whether to use the word *peoples* or *populations* in the title and text of the declaration. In terms of international law, *peoples* have the right to self-determination, whereas *populations* do not. The latter are considered minorities who can be accorded civil rights and labor protection but not the right to self-determination.

It is ironic to note that it was an Iroquois leader, Cayuga chief Deskaheh, who traveled to Geneva in 1923 to address the League of Nations about the right of his people to live independently, according to their own laws and cultural traditions. His courageous attempt was rudely rebuffed, and it was 85 years before the United Nations adopted the Declaration on the Rights of Indigenous Peoples.

Reading 3, "Visions in Geneva: The Dream of the Earth," by Jose Barreiro (Taino Nation), relates the story behind the historic first international meeting by Indigenous delegates in 1978, described earlier. Barreiro attended the gathering as a reporter for *Akwesasne Notes*, a prominent Indian newspaper, and ended up interpreting for the traditional delegates who wanted to discuss spiritual and cultural issues nation to nation, people to people. As a result, he obtained an insider view of the deeply held views and values of the elders in attendance. Many of the delegates wanted to have a deeper "conversation" than was possible under the official protocols of a UN forum, one based instead on sharing spiritual traditions, prophecies, symbols, and values. Barreiro calls the traditional dialogue he witnessed "the dream of the earth."

The box titled "Rigoberta Menchú Tum" contains a photo of this universally recognized Indian woman leader of the Guatemalan Indigenous struggle and recipient of the 1992 Nobel Peace Prize. Traditional Indians of the United States and Canada have a deep affinity for the Native peoples of Mexico and Guatemala. The governments of Canada and the United States have failed to acknowledge these spiritual and cultural connections, but Native peoples of North, Central and South America have been exchanging visits for hundreds of years and have found many commonalties in their cultural traditions, spirituality, and struggles.

In Reading 4, "Hawaiian Language Schools," Leanne Hinton, a professor of linguistics at the University of California at Berkeley and director of the Survey of California and Other Indian Languages, provides a fascinating description of the innovative language schools that are reinvigorating the Native Hawaiian culture. For many years, the Hawaiian language was officially discouraged and even suppressed following the loss of Hawaiian independence in the 1898 takeover by the United States. The establishment in 1983 of the Pūnana Leo preschools and the Kula Kaiapuni Hawai'i elementary and high schools have begun to reverse this particular aspect of ethnocide. The ethnogenesis of the Hawaiian people is told in chants and dance, so knowledge of the Hawaiian language is instrumental in preserving Hawaiian identity and culture. Hinton finds that this experiment in Hawaiian language revitalization is very successful, providing a model for the revitalization of other Native American languages. As an aside, the Hawaiian language schools do not exclude non-Native Hawaiian students from attending, but parents and their children must make a commitment to learning the Native language and culture if they are to be involved.

Native Americans may be North America's most valuable human resource because they give the society a sense of place, a relationship of stewardship to the environment, and a spiritual dimension. Native peoples are often the first to experience the deleterious effects of environmental degradation. We examined several dimensions of this issue in Part VIII. In Reading 5, "Call to Consciousness on the Fate of Mother Earth: Global Warming and Climate Change," Jose Barreiro, assistant director of research at the National Museum of the American Indian (NMAI), reports on the museum's sponsorship of *Mother Earth 7/07/07*, an event organized by Indigenous peoples to increase awareness of global climate change. He also reminds the reader of a historic landmark 30 years earlier, when traditional Iroquois elders presented "A Basic Call to Consciousness" to the 1977 Indigenous conference at the United Nations headquarters in Geneva, Switzerland. (See Suggested Readings.) As Barreiro reports, "it fell to Onondaga Faithkeeper Oren Lyons to present this statement of purpose."

The deleterious impact of global warming on Mother Earth is already being felt in a catastrophic way by the Indigenous peoples of the arctic. The box following the Reading 5 is a report on an increasing number of Alaska Native coastal villages that are facing the imminent threat of flooding due to the rising sea level. The Native American Rights Fund, a Native legal firm, is among the law firms representing the Native village of Kivalina in a suit against oil and energy corporations for contributing to global warming.

It is appropriate to end this part, and the book itself, with Reading 6, "Closing Address," by an outstanding Native American, Phillip Deere (Creek), from the 1980 Fourth Russell Tribunal. The Russell Tribunal on the Rights of the Indians of the Americas, held in Rotterdam, November 1980, provided an international forum for Native peoples and nations to present their cases before an independent panel of jurists, officials, and prominent citizens. Their messages are for all the peoples of the earth, not just for the Indigenous peoples of the Americas. In the final analysis, we all share the planet and, ultimately, the same fate.

The people shall continue!

NOTE

1. Vine Deloria, Jr., *Behind the Trail of Broken Treaties: An Indian Declaration of Independence*. (Austin: University of Texas, 1985), 48–51.

DIRECTIONS IN PEOPLE'S MOVEMENTS

John Mohawk

The Indian plays much the same role in our American society that the Jews played in Germany. Like the miner's canary, the Indian marks the shift from fresh air to poison gas in our political atmosphere. Our treatment of Indians, even more than our treatment of other minorities, reflects the rise and fall in our democratic faith. . . .

—Felix Cohen, father of the study of American Indian Law

Helen Hunt Jackson wrote about injustice to Native peoples a century ago. European writers wrote about it before that, and some have written about it since then. The American Indian people have been abused, disinherited, their nations shamelessly attacked, their rights ignored or abused, their lands taken, their people killed or driven into exile on marginal lands. Jackson called it "A Century of Dishonor" and decried the fact that the United States had been carrying on a policy of deliberate aggression against the Indian peoples—a policy which had led the U.S. to break every treaty ever made with Indian people which contained any recognition of their rights as distinct peoples.

Generations of people, especially in North America and Europe, have known of these horrible injustices. In fact, the injustices have become almost a part of Americana, and are generally presented to school children as the unfortunate results of "cultures in conflict," sometimes which shouldn't have happened but did happen in the past and now it's too late to do anything about it.

The Indian people, of course, are also aware of the nature of these injustices. On many Indian territories, the people have spoken of the day when they will receive justice from the Americans or the Canadians—the day the Black Hills will be returned, the day the fraudulent treaties will be exposed and the people will get their lands back in the Cayuga or Oneida country, the Ojibway or the Cherokee lands. If it has become legendary among European peoples that the

American Indians have been wronged, it has also been a kind of "reservation legend" that those wrongs would somehow be brought right someday, that somebody would find a way to bring the Indian people justice.

For years (perhaps for something nearing two centuries) people have sought legal remedies to these problems. There arose among some of the people the thought that what was needed was an Indian lawyer who really understood the law—someone who could champion the Indian peoples' cause through the courts and bring justice where none was ever found before. That line of thinking was fairly strong in many communities during the first half of this century.

The U.S. policies toward Native peoples have been consistent in one respect—they have moved to destroy the Native peoples. Following the American Revolution, the United States embarked on a series of wars of extermination, and the extermination policy was a dominant theme until after the War of 1812. Then came the removal period—the U.S. policy which attempted to remove all the Native peoples to lands in the "INDIAN TERRITORIES" west of the Mississippi. There were some horrible chapters in that period . . . the Trail of Tears, which removed the Cherokee Nation from their lands in Georgia, was the most widely known, but there were other horrors of that period, many of them, which are less well-known to the public.

The Removal Policy was interspersed with more wars of extermination as the United States enacted its famous (or infamous) Manifest Destiny, and the wars which ensued continued until the 1880s and [were] officially terminated in 1890, a convenient date because of the Wounded Knee massacre of men, women and children at a place which is now known on the maps as the Pine Ridge Reservation.

By that time (1890) the U.S. was in the serious process of taking Indian lands by fair means or foul. Congress passed The Dawes Act in 1887, an act which was said to be in the best interest of the Indians because it provided Indian families with "allotments" but which was argued on the floor of Congress to be the largest land rip-off in history. Land rip-off it was. The Dawes Act caused millions of acres of Indian land to be transferred to the hands of non-Indians, many of whom were speculators. It was another shameful chapter in a history with consistently little but shameful chapters.

But even the Dawes Act, the armies, the wars and other assorted swindles failed to fully exterminate the Indian peoples. As the 20th century dawned, Native peoples still occupied some valuable lands— lands made more valuable as the need for natural resources of a growing industrial society expanded. At the period following World War I, the policy of disinheritance and alienation of Native peoples took a new turn. The new idea was that Indian people would be legally absorbed into the mainstream American society. The hidden agenda of that policy was that Indian peoples' remaining resources would also be absorbed, a fact which made the policy much more attractive to those who had little or no interest in making Native peoples into American citizens.

In 1924, the American Indian Citizenship Act was passed. It was not an act intended to convey benefits to the Indians, but one intended to convey benefits to the people who had interests in Indian lands and resources. It was Step One in the Plot to Take Indian Lands, though the public relations campaign which accompanied the act heralded it as a new step in "righting the wrongs" done to the Indian peoples.

Step Two (in the twentieth century) came in 1934. The federal government was very consistent in its objectives to the extent that, decade by decade, it enacted what it perceived needed to be enacted to disinherit the Indian people of all power over their lives and, not incidentally, their resources. In1934, the Indian Reorganization Act was passed. This was heralded by the propagandists of the day as an act which reorganized Indian government in such a way that it was more "democratic," as though a government set up by Washington under Washington's rules and with the support of Washington's military and with moneys controlled by Washington could somehow be more democratic. Indian people were induced to accept the Indian Reorganization Act by promises that IRA governments would more likely be successful in applying for government funds, an inducement which continues to this day. There was, of course, a catch. To get the government funding, Indian people had to agree to do what the federal government wanted of them. It is a system called neocolonialism.

The next step in this process came to light in 1946 when Congress passed the Indian Claims Commission Act. The idea behind this act, according to the publicists, was to correct the wrongs done to Indian people when their lands were stolen either with the complicity of the federal government or when the federal government failed to act to protect Indian interests. It was not an entirely charitable act. It provided that Indian people could sue for recovery of damages for takings of land, but that they could only recover the value of the land in dollars at the time of the taking, and they could not recover any of the land irregardless of the enormity of the injustice at the time of the taking. As a legal policy, it was unique in the annals of U.S. law. The hidden agenda of that act was that it enabled a small cadre of law firms which specialized in Indian claims work to become very wealthy while at the same time it effectively and forever quieted title to lands which, through the corrupt proceedings, the U.S. had admitted were illegally taken.

The need to quiet titles forever came about because the U.S. was in the process of enacting another policy which came to light in the 1950s— the Termination Policy. During the 1950s (under a Republican Congress) laws were enacted which had the effect of simply declaring that Indian peoples, nations, tribes or whatever, simply no longer existed, and that their lands were, in a word, forfeited. The Termination Policy was intended to achieve the long-held objective of the United States to destroy, once and for all, the Indian peoples.

Those legal policies, which for many Indian peoples were in fact life-threatening policies, were accompanied by social policies which shared the same agenda. The reservations had suffered a two-centuries long assault by social policy agents which intended to destroy the cultures of the peoples and thus, the ability of the Indian people to act as a people. Thus, while the wars of extermination were in full swing, there were intensive missionary penetrations of Indian communities which had the effect of creating divisions and disunities in the Indian Country. The missionaries stayed on through the Removal Policy period and were joined during the 19th century with "educators," whose objective, as one famous educator once said, was to "destroy the tribe." Education has political objectives. The educators moved with a zeal equal to that of the missionaries to destroy the social fabric of the Indian peoples. It has been, sadly, a tremendously effective campaign. One of the things that the education policy set out to do was to acquaint, at least on a rudimentary level, the Indian people with the culture and legal processes of the United States. The idea was to present the United States as a just society with a "system" which, if allowed to work, could set right grievous wrongs. Armed with that ideology, Indian people in this century set out to set right the wrongs done to them through the political and legal processes which their "education" told them existed at the heart of the U.S. system of government and laws.

During the 20th century, the people on the Indian territories talked extensively of legal remedies to regain their lands and their self-government. That approach actually was strengthened and expanded during the period following World War II even though U.S. policy was growing increasingly hostile to Indian peoples everywhere.

The whole process reached a crisis in the 1960s. In 1968, Congress passed an act called the Indian Civil Rights Act. Much can be said about the intent of that act, but in fact many Indian people read the act in such a way that it seemed to them to protect their rights, at least against the neo-colonial governments erected by the Indian Reorganization Act. Within a short time, however, the courts moved to interpret the act in such a way that it did not protect their rights against the Tribal governments (which were and are in major ways controlled by the Bureau of Indian Affairs and the Interior Department) in anything but a habeas corpus provision. The Indian Civil Rights Act was a diversion, a promise without substance. It did not protect Indian rights, but merely individuals' rights in certain situations involving arrests by tribal authorities. By 1972, conditions on some of the Indian reservations were indeed intolerable, especially at Pine Ridge Reservation in South Dakota. On that reservation, the BIA had set up a land tenure system which effectively denied the Lakota people any say in the use of huge parts of their land base. It was a complicated policy of land-use swindle which existed (and exists) there. The plight of the Oglalas is a good place to look for an understanding of the situations under which Native peoples live and the role of the BIA in their everyday lives.

The BIA has set up land tenure (land use) rules on Pine Ridge which are quite complicated but which serve a definite end. According to these rules, there are lands which are "allocated" to certain families. When the heads of those families died, the lands were divided among the heirs. Since a person has two parents, it is seen that one might inherit rights in two parcels of land. By the third generation, one might inherit rights to very small parcels of land from eight landholdings, each parcel of which might be too small to support [a family], especially in situations where people had large families.

The BIA provides rules that amount to a dictum that in cases where the landholdings of an individual are too small and/or too scattered to provide an individual's support, the BIA would step in and manage the allotments (power they seem to derive under their "trust" responsibility). Thus, the BIA steps in and then leases the lands of individuals to large ranchers, paying the proceeds to the individual landowners. That policy, almost without saying, causes large-scale injustices. In some cases, the BIA was leasing the lands of Oglalas to large ranchers for as little as $1 per acre per year. The rental moneys were then deducted from the family allowances of the landowners. Effectively, the "landowners" were dispossessed from their lands, and in effect, received no compensation and had no rights or power over the disposition of those lands. It has been a situation unique in U.S. law, but not unique in "Indian" law.

In 1972, the Oglala people organized an entity they called the Oglala Sioux Landowners' Association. This group tried to effect what amounts to a land reform policy under which they would reacquire control over their own lands. They ran head-on into IRA Tribal Chairman Dick Wilson whose job (and whose interests) lies in maintaining the status quo. His resistance to reform caused the people to organize the Oglala Sioux Civil Rights Organization which soon had as its objective the impeachment of Wilson.

There was much general discontent in the Indian Country by 1972. Indian peoples in the urban areas had begun to respond to the experience of racism during the 1960s. In 1968, Indian people had occupied Alcatraz as a move to demonstrate their general discontent and as a statement of their intent to survive as a people. Alcatraz was the birth of a new movement in the sense that it served as a touch post for Native people who were seeking change and it demonstrated to them that concerted action could have some results, however faltering those efforts may seem to us now. Also in 1968, the American Indian Movement was organized in the St. Paul-Minneapolis area, originally as a kind of citizens action group to protect Indian people from police violence.

That movement gained great popularity among an Indian population which had suffered decades of abuse. Native people who had been victims of the organization policies of the federal government which accompanied the Termination Era joined the movement *en masse*. AIM, meanwhile, reached out to the Indian communities to oppose the injustices suffered by individuals at the hands of police agencies, championing the causes of men and women who had been ravaged by racist court systems. Their efforts, which brought both publicity and the feeling of power which accompanies organization, generated widespread support among the Indian people. As the summer of 1972 wore on, word that AIM was organizing a protest march on Washington and the BIA on the eve of the 1972 Presidential Election spread throughout the Indian communities. When the caravans began arriving in Washington in October of 1972, there were several thousand supporters.

Dubbed the Trail of Broken Treaties, the march on the BIA evolved into an occupation of the BIA building at the very moment that the country was suffering through the national election which reseated Richard Nixon as president of the United States. The country was also going through the agonies of the social disintegration being felt as a result of the Vietnam War. The "BIA Takeover," although it was not a planned event and could hardly have been interpreted as a threat to the United States, apparently set in motion the federal response which declared a domestic war on the American Indian Movement and its supporters.

The situation on the Pine Ridge Reservation coincided with the rise of the American Indian Movement, although the two were hardly of the same roots and in the beginning had somewhat different objectives. The leadership of the opposition to Wilson at Pine Ridge called upon the leadership of the American Indian Movement for help, and in February 1973 the two groups initiated the occupation of Wounded Knee, an event which occupied the front pages of newspapers in the United States and Europe for nearly three months. It is interesting that through all that time, the root causes of the Wounded Knee action were never articulated through the press—i.e., the basic injustices which were the reason that the Oglala Sioux Landowners' Association

and the Oglala Sioux Civil Rights Organization had been formed.

DISCIPLINE—RESPECT—ENDURANCE

The events of Wounded Knee may not have done much to educate the American or the European public about the injustices suffered by the Indian people, but it did much to educate many young Indian people, and it did form at least the appearance of a leadership potential among the Indian people. The "Reign of Terror" conducted by the FBI and other military operations after the Wounded Knee occupation, the emergence of Cable Splicer and Garden Plot (domestic paramilitary counterinsurgency programs), the exposure of spies and infiltrators such as Doug Durham and the political assassinations conducted by the BIA police and other law-and-order factions ended for all time the question of whether or not there could be a peace movement toward justice for Indians in the United States. The "Wounded Knee trials" which followed saw FBI agents perjure themselves on the witness stand, witnesses who were coerced into perjuring themselves, and a federal judge actually publicly denounce the FBI's activities as an outrage to the American concept of justice. The trials also did much to educate the movement leadership to the nature of the system they were facing. There was a lot more resistance to reform than people had been taught. The legal systems consistently failed to protect peoples' rights in court against the abuses of power which were enacted in the name of the United States.

Those years (1973 to the present) have been a wild and tumultuous time for Native people. Movement people challenged the U.S. policies which prescribe the extinction of the Indian peoples through legal strategies designed to disempower and to disinherit and they were met by the paramilitary and military forces of the United States. It became clear that, to the Right Wing, Wounded Knee was used as a training ground for domestic war. Military groups were mobilized from all over the country. Information about secret paramilitary organizations—private police forces which were not under the control of the government—emerged, painting a picture of an underground Right Wing army, similar in character to the "Death Squads" of Argentina, which had access to official police and intelligence agency files [and which] not only existed but was in a position to act. It was a frightening spectre.

Movement leaders were indicted and persecuted relentlessly by the State of South Dakota and by the federal government. People were arrested, assaulted, and forced underground. Many spent time in jail. Murder convictions were obtained against people on the flimsiest of circumstantial evidence, and those convictions resulted in long jail sentences. Those who were present, those who experienced that time, could not fail to understand that the United States and the people in power in the United States intended to suppress all opposition through whatever means necessary. Those who saw the Wounded Knee trials and the aftermath of the occupation of Wounded Knee would not easily be persuaded that there was any hope for justice for the Indian people.

By 1974, the movement leadership was in a position to call a meeting at Wakpala on the Standing Rock Reservation in South Dakota. At that meeting, several thousand people approved a plan to create an organization (called the International Indian Treaty Council) to take the problems of the Indian people to the United Nations and other international forums. The Indian people within the movement had learned a real lesson—there is no justice for the Indian people under the domestic laws of the United States. There never will be.

It was a major stepping stone, a major landmark in the strategy of the people who had set out to struggle for the survival of the Indian peoples and nations. It was a strategy which emerged at a fateful time for the movement. The Indian people were under a concerted attack on all fronts. The following summer, FBI agents attacked the Jumping Bull Ranch on Pine Ridge and a gun battle ensued. Two agents and one Indian man were killed in that incident, and the largest manhunt in history (up to that time) followed as the FBI and U.S. Marshalls invaded Pine Ridge in search of those who were suspected participants in the shootout. Eventually warrants were obtained for four men, three were brought to trial and the other, Leonard Peltier, escaped to Canada. The others were effectively exonerated for their part in the incident, some jurors calling what happened at Jumping Bull an act of self-defense. Peltier was extradicted from Canada on the testimony of Myrtle Poor Bear, testimony which the FBI knew to be false and which Poor Bear later recanted. Peltier was then tried and convicted of complicity in the deaths of the two agents. He remains incarcerated in the federal penitentiary at Marion, Illinois, one of the political prisoners whose history and plight truly sheds light on the American judicial system, and on the U.S. policies toward Indian people.

The Peltier story is particularly enlightening. At about the same time as the shooting FBI assault on the Jumping Bull Ranch, Tribal Chairman Dickie Wilson was signing over to the federal government a large tract of the Pine Ridge Reservation. Later, it was announced that minerals had been discovered on that tract of land. . . . It would stretch the credibility of all concerned to believe that this sequence of events was mere "coincidence." The United States had announced that there was a critical need for "energy" for the future, and reports surfaced which indicated that there were plans at high levels to create "national energy sacrifice areas" as sources of that energy.

In 1977, a large delegation from North America traveled to Geneva and gave testimony to the acts of the United States, charging that the United States was and is committing the crime of genocide against the Native peoples. This event sparked a new round of international outreach by Native peoples, and educated the movement about the global nature of the struggle. Native peoples claiming their rights to land, culture, political sovereignty and survival continue to emerge. It is a movement, as a result, which represents the interests of millions and millions of people.

The Longest Walk in 1978 provided some evidence that the people in the movement had learned a great deal about the nature of the enemy. The Longest Walk attracted the largest gathering of Native people of this century—perhaps, according to one eyewitness estimate, as many as thirty thousand people. The statement which ensued from that event was insightful. The people demanded an end to the most evil of the U.S. policies and specifically cited the Rule of TeeHitTon by which the courts have claimed that the U.S. can take Indian lands not protected by treaty without due process of law or compensation. The Longest Walk manifesto also attacked U.S. colonialism and neo-colonialism, and gave support to Indian political prisoners. The message to the United States from that gathering was clear: The Indian people demanded justice, and an end to exploitation. They supported the Navajo people who faced removal in this century, and denounced the genocidal policies of the United States.

Incredibly, the story of the Indian peoples' struggle for survival is largely a story untold. There can be little doubt that the United States is continuing in pursuit of a policy which has as its goals the destruction of the Indian peoples and communities. They have said as much. There can be little doubt that those plans are motivated by the desire to exploit

Indian people, and to dispossess them of their land and water. The largest dispossession of a people in North America is at this writing taking place on the Navajo country, a dispossession which will destroy a huge part of the Traditional Navajo people just as surely as the persecution of the Jewish people in Europe destroyed their communities four decades ago. There is practically no coverage of this momentous event in the press or other mass media. While the Chairman of the Navajo Nation flies to Washington in his Lear jet, poor Navajos are being driven from their lands in order that the energy companies and a few wealthy Hopi families can use the lands to enrich themselves. Such is the U.S. policy relative to the Navajos and the Hopis. And just as surely as that policy is destroying those people today, just as surely as that policy initiated the Reign of Terror which blanketed the Pine Ridge Reservation in 1973–1977, just as surely as that policy resulted in the near-massacre of a large number of people in the Mohawk Nation in 1980, that policy will come home to each and every one of the Indian communities, one at a time. The Native peoples of this land are under attack. That fact cannot be ignored, and it cannot be resolved in courts, because the courts are one of the instruments of the attack.

The Native peoples are under attack in a number of areas, and the road to survival is a complex path. There is no single solution. Many things need to be organized. Some of these things are economic in nature, some are spiritual, some are political. The clearest lesson of the past is that no one and no single strategy will "save" the Indian people from extinction.

The move toward an access to the international community which might provide some publicity or perhaps even some international action is one of the steps which might lead to a small bit of relief from the worst abuses of the United States. The movement, which has also taken shape in recent years, toward the self-sufficiency of Native communities and peoples is also an important aspect of the overall struggle. But the largest move needs to take place among the Native peoples. There is not enough information reaching the communities to raise the consciousness of the Native people about the nature of the attack which they are under.

DECLARATION ON THE RIGHTS OF INDIGENOUS PEOPLES

ADOPTED BY THE UNITED NATIONS GENERAL ASSEMBLY RESOLUTION 61/295 ON 13 SEPTEMBER 2007

The General Assembly, Guided by the purposes and principles of the Charter of the United Nations, and good faith in the fulfillment of the obligations assumed by States in accordance with the Charter,

Affirming that indigenous peoples are equal to all other peoples, while recognizing the right of all peoples to be different, to consider themselves different, and to be respected as such,

From www.un.org/esa/socdev/unpfii/en/drip.html.

Affirming also that all peoples contribute to the diversity and richness of civilizations and cultures, which constitute the common heritage of humankind,

Affirming further that all doctrines, policies and practices based on or advocating superiority of peoples or individuals on the basis of national origin or racial, religious, ethnic or cultural differences are racist, scientifically false, legally invalid, morally condemnable and socially unjust,

Reaffirming that indigenous peoples, in the exercise of their rights, should be free from discrimination of any kind,

Concerned that indigenous peoples have suffered from historic injustices as a result of, inter alia, their colonization and dispossession of their lands, territories and resources, thus preventing them from exercising, in particular, their right to development in accordance with their own needs and interests,

Recognizing the urgent need to respect and promote the inherent rights of indigenous peoples which derive from their political, economic and social structures and from their cultures, spiritual traditions, histories and philosophies, especially their rights to their lands, territories and resources,

Recognizing also the urgent need to respect and promote the rights of indigenous peoples affirmed in treaties, agreements and other constructive arrangements with States,

Welcoming the fact that indigenous peoples are organizing themselves for political, economic, social and cultural enhancement and in order to bring to an end all forms of discrimination and oppression wherever they occur,

Convinced that control by indigenous peoples over developments affecting them and their lands, territories and resources will enable them to maintain and strengthen their institutions, cultures and traditions, and to promote their development in accordance with their aspirations and needs,

Recognizing that respect for indigenous knowledge, cultures and traditional practices contributes to sustainable and equitable development and proper management of the environment,

Emphasizing the contribution of the demilitarization of the lands and territories of indigenous peoples to peace, economic and social progress and development, understanding and friendly relations among nations and peoples of the world,

Recognizing in particular the right of indigenous families and communities to retain shared responsibility for the upbringing, training, education and well-being of their children, consistent with the rights of the child,

Considering that the rights affirmed in treaties, agreements and other constructive arrangements between States and indigenous peoples are, in some situations, matters of international concern, interest, responsibility and character,

Considering also that treaties, agreements and other constructive arrangements, and the relationship they represent, are the basis for a strengthened partnership between indigenous peoples and States,

Acknowledging that the Charter of the United Nations, the International Covenant on Economic, Social and Cultural Rights (1) and the International Covenant on Civil and Political Rights, (2) as well as the Vienna Declaration and Programme of Action, (3) affirm the fundamental importance of the right to self-determination of all peoples, by virtue of which they freely determine their political status and freely pursue their economic, social and cultural development,

Bearing in mind that nothing in this Declaration may be used to deny any peoples their right to self-determination, exercised in conformity with international law,

Convinced that the recognition of the rights of indigenous peoples in this Declaration will enhance harmonious and cooperative relations between the State and indigenous peoples, based on principles of justice, democracy, respect for human rights, non-discrimination and good faith,

Encouraging States to comply with and effectively implement all their obligations as they apply to indigenous peoples under international instruments, in particular those related to human rights, in consultation and cooperation with the peoples concerned,

Emphasizing that the United Nations has an important and continuing role to play in promoting and protecting the rights of indigenous peoples,

Believing that this Declaration is a further important step forward for the recognition, promotion and protection of the rights and freedoms of indigenous peoples and in the development of relevant activities of the United Nations system in this field,

Recognizing and reaffirming that indigenous individuals are entitled without discrimination to all human rights recognized in international law, and that indigenous peoples possess collective rights which are indispensable for their existence, well-being and integral development as peoples,

Recognizing that the situation of indigenous peoples varies from region to region and from country to country and that the significance of national and regional particularities and various historical and cultural backgrounds should be taken into consideration,

Solemnly proclaims the following United Nations Declaration on the Rights of Indigenous Peoples as a standard of achievement to be pursued in a spirit of partnership and mutual respect:

ARTICLE 1

Indigenous peoples have the right to the full enjoyment, as a collective or as individuals, of all human rights and fundamental freedoms as recognized in the Charter of the United Nations, the Universal Declaration of Human Rights (4) and international human rights law.

ARTICLE 2

Indigenous peoples and individuals are free and equal to all other peoples and individuals and have the right to be free from any kind of discrimination, in the exercise of their rights, in particular that based on their indigenous origin or identity.

ARTICLE 3

Indigenous peoples have the right to self-determination. By virtue of that right they freely determine their political status and freely pursue their economic, social and cultural development.

ARTICLE 4

Indigenous peoples, in exercising their right to self-determination, have the right to autonomy or self-government in matters relating to their internal and local affairs, as well as ways and means for financing their autonomous functions.

ARTICLE 5

Indigenous peoples have the right to maintain and strengthen their distinct political, legal, economic, social and cultural institutions, while retaining their right to participate fully, if they so choose, in the political, economic, social and cultural life of the State.

ARTICLE 6

Every indigenous individual has the right to a nationality.

ARTICLE 7

1. Indigenous individuals have the rights to life, physical and mental integrity, liberty and security of person.
2. Indigenous peoples have the collective right to live in freedom, peace and security as distinct peoples and shall not be subjected to any act of genocide or any other act of violence, including forcibly removing children of the group to another group.

ARTICLE 8

1. Indigenous peoples and individuals have the right not to be subjected to forced assimilation or destruction of their culture.
2. States shall provide effective mechanisms for prevention of, and redress for:
   a. Any action which has the aim or effect of depriving them of their integrity as distinct peoples, or of their cultural values or ethnic identities;
   b. Any action which has the aim or effect of dispossessing them of their lands, territories or resources;
   c. Any form of forced population transfer which has the aim or effect of violating or undermining any of their rights;
   d. Any form of forced assimilation or integration;

Any form of propaganda designed to promote or incite racial or ethnic discrimination directed against them.

ARTICLE 9

Indigenous peoples and individuals have the right to belong to an indigenous community or nation, in accordance with the traditions and customs of the community or nation concerned. No discrimination of any kind may arise from the exercise of such a right.

ARTICLE 10

Indigenous peoples shall not be forcibly removed from their lands or territories. No relocation shall take place without the free, prior and informed consent of the indigenous peoples concerned and after agreement on just and fair compensation and, where possible, with the option of return.

ARTICLE 11

1. Indigenous peoples have the right to practise and revitalize their cultural traditions and customs. This includes the right to maintain, protect and develop the past, present and future manifestations of their cultures, such as archaeological and historical sites, artefacts, designs, ceremonies, technologies and visual and performing arts and literature.
2. States shall provide redress through effective mechanisms, which may include restitution, developed in conjunction with indigenous peoples, with respect to their cultural, intellectual, religious and spiritual property taken without their free, prior and informed consent or in violation of their laws, traditions and customs.

ARTICLE 12

1. Indigenous peoples have the right to manifest, practise, develop and teach their spiritual and religious traditions, customs and ceremonies; the right to maintain, protect, and have access in privacy to their religious and cultural sites; the right to the use and control of their ceremonial objects; and the right to the repatriation of their human remains.
2. States shall seek to enable the access and/or repatriation of ceremonial objects and human remains in their possession through fair, transparent and effective mechanisms developed in conjunction with indigenous peoples concerned.

ARTICLE 13

1. Indigenous peoples have the right to revitalize, use, develop and transmit to future generations their histories, languages, oral traditions, philosophies, writing systems and literatures, and to designate and retain their own names for communities, places and persons.
2. States shall take effective measures to ensure that this right is protected and also to ensure that indigenous peoples can understand and be understood in political, legal and administrative proceedings, where necessary through the provision of interpretation or by other appropriate means.

ARTICLE 14

1. Indigenous peoples have the right to establish and control their educational systems and institutions providing education in their own languages, in a manner appropriate to their cultural methods of teaching and learning.
2. Indigenous individuals, particularly children, have the right to all levels and forms of education of the State without discrimination.
3. States shall, in conjunction with indigenous peoples, take effective measures, in order for indigenous individuals, particularly children, including those living outside their communities, to have access, when possible, to an education in their own culture and provided in their own language.

ARTICLE 15

1. Indigenous peoples have the right to the dignity and diversity of their cultures, traditions, histories and aspirations which shall be appropriately reflected in education and public information.
2. States shall take effective measures, in consultation and cooperation with the indigenous peoples concerned, to combat prejudice and eliminate discrimination and to promote tolerance, understanding and good relations among indigenous peoples and all other segments of society.

ARTICLE 16

1. Indigenous peoples have the right to establish their own media in their own languages and to have access to all forms of non-indigenous media without discrimination.
2. States shall take effective measures to ensure that State-owned media duly reflect indigenous cultural diversity. States, without prejudice to ensuring full freedom of expression, should encourage privately owned media to adequately reflect indigenous cultural diversity.

ARTICLE 17

1. Indigenous individuals and peoples have the right to enjoy fully all rights established under applicable international and domestic labour law.
2. States shall in consultation and cooperation with indigenous peoples take specific measures to protect indigenous children from economic exploitation and from performing any work that is likely to be hazardous or to interfere with the child's education, or to be harmful to the child's health or physical, mental, spiritual, moral or social development, taking into account their special vulnerability and the importance of education for their empowerment.
3. Indigenous individuals have the right not to be subjected to any discriminatory conditions of labour and, inter alia, employment or salary.

ARTICLE 18

1. Indigenous peoples have the right to participate in decision-making in matters which would affect their rights, through representatives chosen by themselves in accordance with their own procedures, as well as to maintain and develop their own indigenous decision-making institutions.

ARTICLE 19

States shall consult and cooperate in good faith with the indigenous peoples concerned through their own representative institutions in order to obtain their free, prior and informed consent before adopting and implementing legislative or administrative measures that may affect them.

ARTICLE 20

1. Indigenous peoples have the right to maintain and develop their political, economic and social systems or institutions, to be secure in the enjoyment of their own means of subsistence and development, and to engage freely in all their traditional and other economic activities.
2. Indigenous peoples deprived of their means of subsistence and development are entitled to just and fair redress.

ARTICLE 21

1. Indigenous peoples have the right, without discrimination, to the improvement of their economic and social conditions, including, inter alia, in the areas of education, employment, vocational training and retraining, housing, sanitation, health and social security.
2. States shall take effective measures and, where appropriate, special measures to ensure continuing improvement of their economic and social conditions. Particular attention shall be paid to the rights and special needs of indigenous elders, women, youth, children and persons with disabilities.

ARTICLE 22

1. Particular attention shall be paid to the rights and special needs of indigenous elders, women, youth, children and persons with disabilities in the implementation of this Declaration.
2. States shall take measures, in conjunction with indigenous peoples, to ensure that indigenous women and children enjoy the full protection and guarantees against all forms of violence and discrimination.

ARTICLE 23

Indigenous peoples have the right to determine and develop priorities and strategies for exercising their right to development. In particular, indigenous peoples have the right to be actively involved in developing and determining health, housing and other economic and social programmes affecting them and, as far as possible, to administer such programmes through their own institutions.

ARTICLE 24

1. Indigenous peoples have the right to their traditional medicines and to maintain their health practices, including the conservation of their vital medicinal plants, animals, and minerals. Indigenous individuals also have the right to access, without any discrimination, to all social and health services.
2. Indigenous individuals have an equal right to the enjoyment of the highest attainable standard of physical and mental health. States shall take the necessary steps with a view to achieving progressively the full realization of this right.

ARTICLE 25

Indigenous peoples have the right to maintain and strengthen their distinctive spiritual relationship with their traditionally owned or otherwise occupied and used lands, territories, waters and coastal seas and other resources and to uphold their responsibilities to future generations in this regard.

ARTICLE 26

1. Indigenous peoples have the right to the lands, territories and resources which they have traditionally owned, occupied or otherwise used or acquired.
2. Indigenous peoples have the right to own, use, develop and control the lands, territories and resources that they possess by reason of traditional ownership or other traditional occupation or use, as well as those which they have otherwise acquired.
3. States shall give legal recognition and protection to these lands, territories and resources. Such recognition shall be conducted with due respect to the customs, traditions and land tenure systems of the indigenous peoples concerned.

ARTICLE 27

States shall establish and implement, in conjunction with indigenous peoples concerned, a fair, independent, impartial, open and transparent process, giving due recognition to indigenous peoples' laws, traditions, customs and land tenure systems, to recognize and adjudicate the rights of indigenous peoples pertaining to their lands, territories and resources, including those which were traditionally owned or otherwise occupied or used. Indigenous peoples shall have the right to participate in this process.

ARTICLE 28

1. Indigenous peoples have the right to redress, by means that can include restitution or, when this is not possible, just, fair and equitable compensation, for the lands, territories and resources which they

have traditionally owned or otherwise occupied or used, and which have been confiscated, taken, occupied, used or damaged without their free, prior and informed consent.

2. Unless otherwise freely agreed upon by the peoples concerned, compensation shall take the form of lands, territories and resources equal in quality, size and legal status or of monetary compensation or other appropriate redress.

ARTICLE 29

1. Indigenous peoples have the right to the conservation and protection of the environment and the productive capacity of their lands or territories and resources. States shall establish and implement assistance programmes for indigenous peoples for such conservation and protection, without discrimination.

2. States shall take effective measures to ensure that no storage or disposal of hazardous materials shall take place in the lands or territories of indigenous peoples without their free, prior and informed consent.

3. States shall also take effective measures to ensure, as needed, that programmes for monitoring, maintaining and restoring the health of indigenous peoples, as developed and implemented by the peoples affected by such materials, are duly implemented.

ARTICLE 30

1. Military activities shall not take place in the lands or territories of indigenous peoples, unless justified by a relevant public interest or otherwise freely agreed with or requested by the indigenous peoples concerned.

2. States shall undertake effective consultations with the indigenous peoples concerned, through appropriate procedures and in particular through their representative institutions, prior to using their lands or territories for military activities.

ARTICLE 31

1. Indigenous peoples have the right to maintain, control, protect and develop their cultural heritage, traditional knowledge and traditional cultural expressions, as well as the manifestations of their sciences, technologies and cultures, including human and genetic resources, seeds, medicines, knowledge of the properties of fauna and flora, oral traditions, literatures, designs, sports and traditional games and visual and performing arts. They also have the right to maintain, control, protect and develop their intellectual property over such cultural heritage, traditional knowledge, and traditional cultural expressions.

2. In conjunction with indigenous peoples, States shall take effective measures to recognize and protect the exercise of these rights.

ARTICLE 32

1. Indigenous peoples have the right to determine and develop priorities and strategies for the development or use of their lands or territories and other resources.

2. States shall consult and cooperate in good faith with the indigenous peoples concerned through their own representative institutions in order to obtain their free and informed consent prior to the approval of any project affecting their lands or territories and other resources, particularly in connection with the development, utilization or exploitation of mineral, water or other resources.

3. States shall provide effective mechanisms for just and fair redress for any such activities, and appropriate measures shall be taken to mitigate adverse environmental, economic, social, cultural or spiritual impact.

ARTICLE 33

1. Indigenous peoples have the right to determine their own identity or membership in accordance with their customs and traditions. This does not impair the right of indigenous individuals to obtain citizenship of the States in which they live.

2. Indigenous peoples have the right to determine the structures and to select the membership of their institutions in accordance with their own procedures.

ARTICLE 34

Indigenous peoples have the right to promote, develop and maintain their institutional structures and their distinctive customs, spirituality, traditions, procedures, practices and, in the cases where they exist, juridical systems or customs, in accordance with international human rights standards.

ARTICLE 35

Indigenous peoples have the right to determine the responsibilities of individuals to their communities.

ARTICLE 36

1. Indigenous peoples, in particular those divided by international borders, have the right to maintain and develop contacts, relations and cooperation, including activities for spiritual, cultural, political, economic and social purposes, with their own members as well as other peoples across borders.
2. States, in consultation and cooperation with indigenous peoples, shall take effective measures to facilitate the exercise and ensure the implementation of this right.

ARTICLE 37

1. Indigenous peoples have the right to the recognition, observance and enforcement of treaties, agreements and other constructive arrangements concluded with States or their successors and to have States honour and respect such treaties, agreements and other constructive arrangements.
2. Nothing in this Declaration may be interpreted as diminishing or eliminating the rights of indigenous peoples contained in treaties, agreements and other constructive arrangements.

ARTICLE 38

States in consultation and cooperation with indigenous peoples, shall take the appropriate measures, including legislative measures, to achieve the ends of this Declaration.

ARTICLE 39

Indigenous peoples have the right to have access to financial and technical assistance from States and through international cooperation, for the enjoyment of the rights contained in this Declaration.

ARTICLE 40

Indigenous peoples have the right to access to and prompt decision through just and fair procedures for the resolution of conflicts and disputes with States or other parties, as well as to effective remedies for all infringements of their individual and collective rights. Such a decision shall give due consideration to the customs, traditions, rules and legal systems of the indigenous peoples concerned and international human rights.

ARTICLE 41

The organs and specialized agencies of the United Nations system and other intergovernmental organizations shall contribute to the full realization of the provisions of this Declaration through the mobilization, inter alia, of financial cooperation and technical assistance. Ways and means of ensuring participation of indigenous peoples on issues affecting them shall be established.

ARTICLE 42

The United Nations, its bodies, including the Permanent Forum on Indigenous Issues, and specialized agencies, including at the country level, and States shall promote respect for and full application of the provisions of this Declaration and follow up the effectiveness of this Declaration.

ARTICLE 43

The rights recognized herein constitute the minimum standards for the survival, dignity and well-being of the indigenous peoples of the world.

ARTICLE 44

All the rights and freedoms recognized herein are equally guaranteed to male and female indigenous individuals.

ARTICLE 45

Nothing in this Declaration may be construed as diminishing or extinguishing the rights indigenous peoples have now or may acquire in the future.

ARTICLE 46

1. Nothing in this Declaration may be interpreted as implying for any State, people, group or person any right to engage in any activity or to perform any act contrary to the Charter of the United Nations or construed as authorizing or encouraging any action which would dismember or impair, totally or in part, the territorial integrity or political unity of sovereign and independent States.
2. In the exercise of the rights enunciated in the present Declaration, human rights and fundamental freedoms of all shall be respected. The exercise of the rights set forth in this Declaration shall be subject only to such limitations as are determined by law and in accordance with international human

rights obligations. Any such limitations shall be non-discriminatory and strictly necessary solely for the purpose of securing due recognition and respect for the rights and freedoms of others and for meeting the just and most compelling requirements of a democratic society.

3. The provisions set forth in this Declaration shall be interpreted in accordance with the principles of

justice, democracy, respect for human rights, equality, non-discrimination, good governance and good faith.

(2) See resolution 2200 A (XXI), annex.
(3) A/CONF.157/24 (Part I), chap. III.
(4) Resolution 217 A (III).

RESOLUTION IN SUPPORT OF THE UN DECLARATION ON THE RIGHTS OF INDIGENOUS PEOPLES

National Congress of American Indians

—WHEREAS, we, the members of the National Congress of American Indians of the United States, invoking the divine blessing of the Creator upon our efforts and purposes, in order to preserve for ourselves and our descendants the inherent sovereign rights of our Indian nations, rights secured under Indian treaties and agreements with the United States, and all other rights and benefits to which we are entitled under the laws and Constitution of the United States, to enlighten the public toward a better understanding of the Indian people, to preserve Indian cultural values, and otherwise promote the health, safety and welfare of the Indian people, do hereby establish and submit the following resolution; and

WHEREAS, the National Congress of American Indians (NCAI) was established in 1944 and is the oldest and largest national organization of American Indian and Alaska Native tribal governments; and

WHEREAS, the member tribes of the NCAI are committed to the protection of the rights of US Tribal Nations under US Law and policies and under International Law, policy and practice and to support for the protection of such rights on behalf of all other indigenous nations; and

WHEREAS, representatives of indigenous nations throughout the world and individual advocates for the rights of indigenous peoples, working through the United Nations Human Rights Council, have developed a Declaration on the Rights of Indigenous Peoples that was adopted on June 29, 2006 by the UN Member Nation delegates to the Council; and

WHEREAS, the Declaration affirmatively supports and articulates the rights of Indigenous Peoples (nations) to full

self-determination, the protection of treaty rights negotiated by Indigenous Nations with various Nation States as a matter of International Law and Policy, the possession use of their ancestral homelands, and the right to free, prior and informed consent before being subjected to the law of various nation states within whose boundaries they may be located; and

WHEREAS, adoption of the Declaration by the United Nation would support and reinforce the respect and protection of full self-determination rights by and on behalf of US Tribal Nations as well as the protection of tribal lands and treaties as a matter of international law and policy and is therefore in the vital interests of all US Tribal Nations; and

WHEREAS, the UN General Assembly having voted to table action on the Declaration during debate in November and December, 2006, has now scheduled further debate and final action on the Declaration at their Fall-2007 session.

NOW THEREFORE BE IT RESOLVED, that the NCAI does hereby express its strong support for the UN Declaration on the Rights of Indigenous Nations and for House Concurrent Resolution 156 that would put the US Congress on record recognizing the importance of the UN Declaration to the vital interests of US Tribal Nations and urging full support and a favorable vote by the US Ambassador to the United Nations for the Declaration as approved June 29, 2006 by the UN Human Rights Council; and

BE IT FURTHER RESOLVED, that this resolution shall be the policy of NCAI until it is withdrawn or modified by subsequent resolution.

VISIONS IN GENEVA
THE DREAM OF THE EARTH

Jose Barreiro

Jose Barreiro (Taino Nation), Ph.D., is assistant director for research at the Smithsonian's National Museum of the American Indian.

It was 30 years in coming when, on September 13, 2007, the United Nations General Assembly adopted the Declaration on the Rights of Indigenous Peoples, which affirms and promotes indigenous self-determination over culture, lands, and intellectual property. The declaration provides "a major foundation and reference . . . a key instrument and tool for raising awareness on and monitoring progress of indigenous people's situations and the protection, respect, and fulfillment of indigenous peoples' rights," stated Victoria Tauli-Corpuz, chairperson of the UN Permanent Forum on Indigenous Peoples. The declaration was first drafted and circulated at a unique historical gathering at Geneva, Switzerland in September 1977. There, Indigenous peoples of the Americas joined together for the first time to address the UN.

I went to the conference as a reporter for the national Native newspaper, *Akwesasne Notes*, but after a session when the elder delegates had grown frustrated with the assigned UN interpreters, an Arawak elder from Venezuela asked me to translate. As it turned out, I interpreted meetings for three days—between Aymara and Hopi, Seneca and

From Jose Barreiro, in *American Indian* (National Museum of the American Indian, Smithsonian), Winter 2007, p 41–44 and 47.

Editor's note: On September 13, 2007, after 30 years of sacrifice and deepening strategy the Indigenous peoples of the world achieved the passage of the United Nations Declaration on the Rights of Indigenous Peoples. Dr. Joe Barreiro, the National Museum of the American Indian's assistant director for research, attended the historic session in 1977 that launched the Indigenous international movements. In the following narrative, Barreiro shares recollections of that profound effort.

Maquiritari, Mapuche and Lakota, and, at the larger gatherings, formally between North and South. It was a privilege to be so conscripted. One could sense an important movement emerging.

One late afternoon, after a day of political presentations and testimonies about military terror, sessions on cases of land theft and cultural destruction replete with compelling testimony from the various delegations, two Mapuche elders requested a deeper conversation. The elders felt their message had not quite been shared. They passed word they wanted to share "dreams," original cultural instructions with other elders at the gathering.

That Geneva elders' meeting, which went on for hours—a translator's potential nightmare—turned into enchantment as elders shared messages and stories that captivated and energized. As I translated at length, many of the words shared have stayed with me over these many years. They are, for me, a sort of preamble to the 30-year movement that culminated this past September with the passage of the UN declaration.

I remember the younger Mapuche man who opened the meeting for the elders. He set up a small altar, a stone on a wooden stool. On it, with a thin sash, he traced the four directions. Then he introduced his "uncle," who had traveled with him.

"I come from a land of mountains and pine forests," the elder said. While his people had not traveled much, they had heard that other Indians lived in the North. And now they were happy to meet and hear directly from these other Indigenous "people who also came from a place."

The Mapuche elder reminded everyone of what Constantino Lima, a Bolivian Aymara leader, had

A group photo of the Indigenous delegates from around the world at the close of the Geneva gathering in 1977.

said during the gathering: "As 'indios' they discriminated against us; then let us now, as indios, unite against those who would discriminate against us." "But," the elder Mapuche said. "There is more. Yes, we are discriminated and persecuted, but more than who we are as 'Indians,' we are also natural peoples of our regions, our valleys, rivers, the places where we belong, our ancient roots. That also unites us."

The Mapuche man referred to a prayer he had heard from Seneca elder Corbett Sundown. Chief Sundown had burned tobacco for the whole delegation on the first day of the conference. He had recited the Haudenosaunee (Iroquois) Thanksgiving Address, about which the Mapuche elder said, "In our ancient tradition, in our language of the star world family, the cosmic family, there, too, they speak about the Mother Earth. The Moon, as they also say, is our Grandmother."

The Aymara and Quechua activists of Bolivia, a young and very political group, also rose to deepen their discourse. "We like that the talk goes this way,"

one said. So he spoke of *Pachamama*, the Mother Earth. He addressed the *Alma Mundo*, the goddess spirit or Soul of the World; he spoke of their peoples' emergence from the waters of Lake Titicaca and of the connection of their people to the four corners of their lands, or the *Tewantinsuyo*.

It went around the circle. A Maquiritari chief addressed the theme of their peoples' origin stories, tracing their way of relating to the natural world of the tropics. From the north, Minnesota Ojibway elder Patricia Bellanger spoke about the many abuses being suffered by the Mother Earth. "Before the problems of human beings, always, we must consider the state of Mother Earth," the Anishinabe matron said. Her words drew beyond immediate consensus, visceral resonance from the group.

A Hopi elder remembered by many, David Monongwe, was in that circle. He also commented on the Four Directions, on the symbol put down by the young Mapuche who stood near him. Wrapped in a blanket, hair tied back in a bun, the old man spoke of avarice as a big problem facing Indians. He spoke of a

Hopi prophecy that tells of an Earth in peril, if human beings did not learn to live as grateful children of the Mother Earth, "to be humble" before nature.

Elder Monongwe's comments gave way to a discussion of the Four Directions traditions that seem to range among many Native peoples. A Quiche leader present remarked also on the widespread symbol of the circled cross. In the Quiche, one of the more than a dozen Mayan languages, it represents "point of origin," he said. "Just like our meeting here. It is a beginning." He also said the Maya altar upon which the copal is burned in ceremony is traced as a quadrated circle aligned with the Four Directions just like the two Mapuche had used in theirs. As the sessions progressed, everyone spoke in their own way, in their own language, to the consciousness inherent in their cultures.

Each delegation at Geneva in 1977 had brought well-prepared documents detailing their political, legal, and economic histories, and many carried verifiable litanies of human rights violations ranging from assassinations of leaders to massive land displacements to wholesale assault and slaughter by both militaries and bands of thugs, in many countries of the Americas. Talented international lawyers carried briefs attesting to these many issues. But in that and other talking circles, I like to remember how the Indian elders decided to speak from their cultural bases and how so much of that talk was about the human relationship with "the Earth."

"The world is alive," I translated for Art Solomon, an Odawa elder from Ontario, who rose up to encapsulate the meaning of the stories. "Everything lives, including the stones and the mountains. What makes us see this as one people, whether it is called 'Indian' or not, is that our elders understood about who the human being is in this world."

Phillip Deere, Muskogee elder and medicine man, was in that circle. He was an unforgettable man, always keen-minded. "People of the Four Directions," he said. "I bring you a message that is also a prophecy. The old people say that the time of the Indian is coming . . . that we the Indian people would find each other."

The elders present nodded assent to Deere's message. Others spoke: Larry Red Shirt of the Lakota brought in his Sacred Pipe and spoke on the meanings of the sacred directions in his tradition; Leon Shenandoah (Tadadaho) spoke on the original instructions of his tradition and pointed to the "main responsibility of the human being to offer thanksgiving."

"These old things all carry messages," Deere acknowledged as he embodied the firm, wise, and certain approach of a deeply cultured Indigenous man. "For a long time it has been impossible for elders to want to share these things. Our peoples have felt many insults about our way of life."

But perhaps now the time was approaching, the Muskogee elder said. Many Christians as well as scientists were more welcoming of indigenous knowledge. "The old Indian prophecies, they must come about; this is the time; everywhere in this world, no matter how small a group they are, every Indigenous people have a right to be who they are."

At Geneva in 1977, a shared protagonism emerged among these Native leaders to formally begin sharing their essential universe of thought. They knew they had found each other, and that encounter would be repeated a hundred, a thousand, ten thousand times over the following three decades. The present endorsement of this representative movement's "declaration" by the vast majority of the nations of the world is an important and useful milestone. The dream of the earth runs deep.

RIGOBERTA MENCHÚ TUM

"Today, throughout the Americas, people are reflecting deeply about the identity of the Indigenous peoples and are starting to take seriously the arguments in favor of pluriethnic and multicultural societies. From our diversity will come the true wealth of the Americas.

Even though another millennium is coming to an end without an end to the grave and systematic violations of the rights of Indigenous peoples, we have not given up hope on our struggle to establish a new basis for social relations, based on justice, equality, and mutual respect between our peoples and cultures. . . .

After so many years of struggle, this period seems to be the end of five hundred years of injustice, five hundred years of night. We are moving into the light of a new era for our peoples. After so many years of waiting for a new dawn, we believe that our voices will make themselves heard, that you will listen to us, and support our legitimate aspirations."

Rigoberta Menchú Tum, recipient of the 1992 Nobel Peace Prize. She is a leader of the Guatemalan Indian struggle.

From the Foreword by Rigoberta Menchú Tum in *Return of the Indian*, by Phillip Wearne (Temple University Press, 1996). (See *I, Rigoberta Menchú*, edited by Burgos-Dubray, in the Suggested Readings.)

HAWAIIAN LANGUAGE SCHOOLS

Leanne Hinton

. . . Last fall I made my first-ever trip to Hawai'i, and spent three fascinating days touring the Hawaiian Pūnana Leo (preschools) and Kula Kaiapuni Hawai'i (the elementary and high schools), where the Hawaiian language is the language of instruction in all grades. This program, creating a new generation of fluent speakers and thus saving the Hawaiian language from extinction, is by far the most ambitious and advanced language revitalization program in the United States, and has much to teach the rest of us.

HISTORY OF HAWAIIAN LANGUAGE LOSS

Hawai'i, our newest state, was an independent monarchy until the end of the 19th century. The loss of Hawaiian independence began in 1887, when a group of businessmen with ties to the United States and the support of American troops established the "Bayonette Constitution." In 1893, Queen Liliuokalani was deposed, again with the support of American marines. In 1898 the "Republic" of Hawai'i was set up, and soon after that it was annexed to the United States. The Hawaiian people thus lost their power and autonomy.

As for the language, until the political events that led to annexation, Hawaiian was not only the primary language of the islands, but also the main language of the schools. Hawai'i created the first high school west of the Rockies (taught in Hawaiian), and the literacy rate (in Hawaiian) was among the highest in the world. The Hawaiian people had long been aware of the advantages that knowing English could give, and strong efforts had been made by the royal family to give Hawaiians the opportunity to learn English. In fact, in the late 19th century, the Hawaiian princess Pauahi founded the Kamehameha schools,

prestigious private schools that can only be attended by children of Hawaiian ancestry. The schools were initiated with English as the language of instruction, so that Hawaiian children would learn to speak that language of such economic importance.

But once the control of Hawai'i was lost to its people, a problem not foreseen by the royal family occurred: it was now the Hawaiian language that children had no opportunity to learn. The story is a variation on a theme well known to Native Californians. The Bayonette Constitution cut out funds for Hawaiian-language education, and finally, English-only legislation in 1896 closed down the Hawaiian-language schools completely. Teachers visited homes to tell the parents not to speak Hawaiian to their children, one of the many factors that soon led to the loss of Hawaiian even as the language of the home. Out of a population of 200,000 people of Hawaiian heritage, the 1990 census lists less than 9,000 speakers, almost all elderly. (There is one exception to this trend: on the tiny island of Ni'ihau, privately owned and closed to the public, Hawaiian is still spoken natively by all age groups and used as the language of daily communication among the two hundred people there.)

LANGUAGE IMMERSION SCHOOLS

The 'Aha Pūnana Leo was established in 1983 by a small group of educators determined to have their own children and those of other interested families educated in the Hawaiian language. A few of these families had also made the decision to use Hawaiian as the language of their home (even though they themselves knew Hawaiian only as a second language). They developed a series of preschools inspired by the Maori "Language Nest" model, where no English would be used in the classroom, and all education would take place in the Hawaiian language. Once the lead-group was old enough,

"Hawaiian Language Schools," by Leanne Hinton, *News from Native California*, 10:4 (Summer 1997). Reprinted with permission of the author. Portions of the original and notes have been omitted.

Hawaiian-language classrooms were established in the public schools. The Pūnana Leo actually began while it was still illegal to use Hawaiian in the schools. It took a three-year campaign at the state legislature by parents and community members to change the laws, thus ending eighty years of outlaw status for the language. From the small beginning of a single preschool, 'Aha Pūnana Leo has grown to have nine preschools scattered among the islands; there are also a public laboratory high school outside of Hilo, thirteen public elementary schools that have Hawaiian-language tracks, and even one K-12 public school that has all-Hawaiian instruction (Ānuenue School near Honolulu).

I had the opportunity to visit several schools on O'ahu and Hawai'i in November 1996. I will try to write about my experiences here more or less in the order that I experienced them.

THE ADVENTURE BEGINS

Hawai'i—my first visit to this state that doesn't seem like part of the United States at all, because it's too far away, too exotic, too fragrant with tropical flowers. It's November, close to Thanksgiving. I have spent a couple of days with my family visiting old friends in Kawaihae, where they have a bamboo farm, and I have become happily accustomed to the pleasant tropical breezes wafting through their beautiful indoor-outdoor house. I have not previously been able to make contact with any of the schools I want to visit, but after speaking with a long chain of friends and friends of friends, the right person is contacted at last. Nāmaka Rawlins, director of the 'Aha Pūnana Leo, gives me permission to visit the schools, and a wonderful adventure begins. I leave my family exploring the beaches and volcanoes of Hawai'i without me, and head off.

WAIMEA PUBLIC SCHOOL

My first visit is to the combined kindergarten/first grade class at Waimea Public School. I come into the spacious, comfortable classroom during lunch break and introduce myself to Kumu Iakona, the head teacher (*Kumu* is a title of address meaning teacher), who makes me feel welcome. The room has a set of low tables with several children's chairs around each. There is also a big rug at the front of the schoolroom, where the class spends most of their time when they are not doing individual projects. Around the walls are numbers, the alphabet, and captioned pictures, all in Hawaiian. Even the screen

on the computer shows all Hawaiian words; when I glance at it, it is showing a Hawaiian-language home page on the Internet.

There are many books around the classroom. The one that captures my attention is out on a table for teacher use: the 1995 edition of *Puke Hua 'Ōlelo' Mānaka Kaiao—New Words*. This bilingual dictionary, with a new edition put out every couple of years, is the most important language reference work for teachers in the schools. In order to teach all the subjects that must be taught, thousands of new words have to be developed that were never uttered in Hawaiian before. A quick look through the dictionary shows new Hawaiian words for such concepts as electric current, bank account, jet stream, interactive (computer), fax, and pogo stick. Kumu Iakona explains to me that there is a Lexicon Committee that gets together every month in Hilo to make up new words or accept new words sent in by teachers from all over the islands. It is important for all of the schools to use the same new words, rather than making up their own, because the new words will be in books and curriculum materials developed centrally in Hilo and sent out to all the schools. Still, sometimes different islands have their own words— for example, a type of edible sea urchin is *hā'uke'uke* on the island of Hawai'i, *hā'ue'ue* on Maui, and *hā'kue'kue* on Ni'ihau. Ni'ihau, the one place where Hawaiian is the medium of communication for all topics, has coined many of the words that are now in the new words dictionary.

Kula Kaiapuni Hawai'i, the name of the Hawaiian language immersion schools, is a new phrase—*Kula* is from English "school" and has been a part of the language since the early 19th century, but *Kaiapuni* is a new word meaning environment.

In a few minutes the kids come in—about fifteen of them—accompanied by another teacher, who turns out to be a parent helper named Pualani Colburn. All the schools I will visit have parent volunteers helping actively; family involvement is one of the keys to success in the Hawaiian language program. The children sit down on the rug at the front of the schoolroom. They talk quietly until everyone has settled in, and then the teachers begin the session with a Hawaiian song accompanied by percussion on an *ipu* (a gourd instrument), and the children get up and dance to it. Hawaiian music and dance are a very important part of the curriculum at all grade levels. The dances often tell stories, with the beautiful hand and arm movements being a kind of sign language.

The song and dance focus the attention of the class and unite them. When the song is over, one girl comes up with objects and coupons in an envelope. From the back of the room, and with no English being spoken, I can't tell what they are—but I know it is show-and-tell time. The teacher describes the objects and starts a discussion. The whole discussion takes place in Hawaiian, even though not all the children are fluent yet. While some of them have a couple of years of Hawaiian language education at preschool, others started learning Hawaiian only about two months ago when the school year began. Some of the kids seem to be thinking about how to say what they want to say, and the teachers encourage them, saying, "And then what?" (in Hawaiian, of course), or providing a word or phrase. At one point, the children get to talking about Rudolf the Red-Nosed Reindeer. Between Rudolf and the subsequent discussion of Thanksgiving, I know I must still be in the United States after all.

The discussion turns to the coming holiday: the English word "Thanksgiving" is uttered by a few students. The teachers tell the class the Hawaiian way to say it: La Ho'omaika'i. Later, No'eau Warner, one of the founders of the movement, tells me that when first starting to set policy, they discussed whether to reprimand children for speaking English, as their grandparents had been reprimanded for speaking Hawaiian. The psychological damage inflicted by that old policy was obvious, and they decided that when a child spoke English, the teachers would just answer in Hawaiian, possibly repeating in Hawaiian what the child had said, for the child's benefit. This policy works well—there are a lot of happy, talkative children here, speaking fluent Hawaiian or on their way to it.

One teacher sets up a table while the other continues the class discussion. A student comes to the teacher who is setting up the table and describes how sore her loose tooth is making her mouth, all in Hawaiian. Pretty soon I understand what the teacher is setting up—she is putting dabs of toothpaste on paper towels for the students to use. Two by two, the students get their toothbrushes and come to brush their teeth while the others watch a Hawaiian-language video about traditional food preparation.

A FEW ABBREVIATIONS IN HAWAIIAN

kk	for *kuaka* "quart"
klk	for *Kelekia* "Celsius"
klkal	for *kilokalame* "kilogram"
kp	for *kapua'i* "foot"

During the video and toothbrushing, Kumu Iakona tells me about how they help parents learn the Hawaiian language, sending them a sheet every week with words and phrases they can use with their kids at home. This week's sheet is based on the word *'ō lelo* "to speak":

> *'ō lelo hou*
> to repeat
> *e 'ō lelo Hawai'i kākou!*
> Let's all speak Hawaiian! (us inclusive, three or more)
> *he aha kāna 'olelo?*
> What did he/she say?
> *hiki iā 'oe ke 'ō lelo hou?*
> Can you say it again?

The feeling in this room—like all the schools I visit—is warm, nurturing, and relaxed. I would love to stay all day, but all too soon it is time to leave, for I have another stop to make—the Waimea Preschool, about eight miles outside of town.

WAIMEA PRESCHOOL

At the preschool, the children are napping—a disappointment to me! But it gives me a chance to look around and talk with the teachers and parent helpers. This preschool opened in 1995. The preschools are private, not part of the public school system; and it is the parents and local educators who must have the vision and do most of the work to begin a preschool, finding the site and the funding themselves. Once all the local arrangements are made, the 'Aha Pūnana Leo, centered in Hilo, will train the teachers and provide the curriculum. The vision for this school started in 1990. It took five years of hard work and planning before it could open.

The teachers and parent volunteers here—as in all the schools I visited—are warmly enthusiastic about their work and deeply dedicated to the survival of Hawaiian language and culture. They admit to being what they tell me are called "university speakers," having learned their language in the college classroom. And it is here that I first hear of some of the inevitable conflict that comes with language revitalization: lots of the *kūpuna*—the Hawaiian word for elders—really don't like to hear the language spoken that way, the teachers tell me.

Later I will learn more about this conflict: there are two ways in which university speech differs most obviously from the speech of the kūpuna—one is in intonation, and the other is vocabulary. I see that dictionary of new words in a prominent place in every classroom I visit. There is a much larger dictionary in existence of traditional vocabulary, but it is the new words that the teachers need most in the classroom. If so much of the vocabulary learned by the children consists of new words made up in the last ten years, the kūpuna must sometimes feel that they are hearing a foreign language!

The teachers tell me about a few activities that take place in a typical day in the Pūnana Leo. They open and close the day with a traditional song and prayer, and the same before lunch. Singing, the teachers tell me, is the most important activity in the school; the children pick up more Hawaiian language through singing than through any other activity, and once you start singing you have their complete attention.

Many different things can happen at the Pūnana Leo—sometimes the kūpuna will come in to talk or show the kids how to make things. Sometimes special activities are planned. But always, in the morning after the prayer, there is work with the calendar and the weather. A child is asked each day to go look out the door and then come tell the class what the weather is like. Is it sunny? Raining? Foggy? (Weather changes so quickly in Hawai'i that it may have changed since the children got to school.) I can see around the walls the evidence of other activities the children engage in: there are pictures colored by the children, with Hawaiian labels printed laboriously by three- and four-year-old hands just learning to write; photographic posters with small colored circles and squares stuck to them (this looks like language practice, where children are told "put the orange circle on the milk"); Hawaiian-language books, including some old favorites such as *The Little Engine That Could*, with the Hawaiian version printed on labels and pasted over the English text; and of course a giant collection of musical instruments—sticks, rattles, gourd drums, and clapper sticks of all shapes and sizes.

The family base is the most important feature of the Pūnana Leo. Those books are made up by the parents, who receive the labels bearing the Hawaiian versions from Hilo and then paste them into the books. A very beautiful, large set of brightly colored building blocks is in one corner—one of the fathers made it. Parents must volunteer eight hours a month in the classroom; they clean and disinfect toys, help the teachers during classes, and make learning materials and toys. They also attend a once-a-week, two-hour evening class in Hawaiian, where they learn

things they can say to their kids, in school or at home. They have all been taught the meaning of the Hawaiian-language signs around the classroom. A teacher translated one of them for me:

> *E'olu'olu*
> *E wehe i nā kāma'a*
> *Mahalo!*

Please remove your shoes—thank you!

Finally it is time for the children to wake up. The teachers wander about the room among the mats that the children are sleeping on, calling out gently, *"E ala mai"* (wake up). While this is going on, one teacher puts on a tape of a group singing a Hawaiian song with *"E ala mai"* in the chorus. The children sleepily put away their bedding and then come to the rug and sit down, yawning. A story book is read to them as they wake up. Much as I wish I could stay longer, I must leave: two of the teachers are giving me a ride to Hilo.

Throughout my trip in Hawai'i I hear English and what the Hawaiians call Pidgin—an English-based creole—everywhere except in these special schools. Most of the time, teachers and the more dedicated parents who have sent their children to the Pūnana Leo speak to each other only in Hawaiian. This is important for people trying to save endangered languages: people who know the language have to make a commitment to speak it to each other, and not be tempted back to English by the presence of English speakers in the conversation. Thus, on the drive to Hilo, my hosts speak to me in English but to each other always in Hawaiian. Through such discipline, the language begins to make its way back into public again.

UNIVERSITY OF HAWAI'I AT HILO

Bill (Pila) Wilson, one of the leaders of the Hawaiian language program at the University of Hawai'i at Hilo, meets me in Hilo. He puts me under the charge of one of the students, Ola, who shows me the workroom for the Hawaiian language program. She shows me the program ClarisWorks, all in Hawaiian—they have an agreement with the company that if they buy a copy of the English version, they get the Hawaiian version with it for free. Ola runs the Hawaiian language newspaper on campus, named *Nā Maka O Kana*, The Eyes of Kana (Kana is a demigod who can stretch his body to reach all the islands). It was founded for the immersion schools, and goes to students, parents, and teachers from preschool to college level. Four thousand copies per month are printed, with one of the immersion schools featured each month. This month's issue also includes information on making Christmas decorations and a serialized portion of the story of Kana.

The workroom and nearby storerooms also house some important archives—Hawaiian-language newspapers from the 19th and early 20th century, used for developing materials for history classes; and fifteen years' worth of a weekly radio show ("Ka Leo Hawai'i," hosted by Larry Kimura, another leader of the Hawaiian language movement and a professor at Hilo) that aired from 1972 to 1989 and consisted of interviews of Hawaiian Native speakers. This is the largest collection of Native Hawaiian in existence, and is used a great deal in advanced Hawaiian classes. There is also a collection of videos on Hawaiian culture, all in the Hawaiian language, and copies of the books being produced or translated at a feverish rate for the schools. I see translated copies of *Charlotte's Web*, *Island of the Blue Dolphins*, and other popular children's books that are state-required reading in the public elementary schools. Other books are traditional Hawaiian literature collected and produced for Hawaiian language arts classes.

The University of Hawai'i (at Hilo and at Mānoa) trains all the teachers who teach in the immersion schools; most of them did not know the Hawaiian language until college age. At the University you can take beginners' through advanced Hawaiian language classes, Hawaiian linguistics, Hawaiian history, and Hawaiian cultural studies such as fish net making, hula, and chant (*oli*). Here you learn vocal styles (high, low, and vibrating), composition, different Hawaiian song types, and *kaona*—metaphor and indirectness—two of the most important literary devices in Hawaiian song. A new master's program in Hawaiian studies, due to begin in fall 1997, will be taught entirely in the Hawaiian language. Teacher certification, which used to be done only in English, will now be done in the Hawaiian language as well.

A HAWAIIAN-SPEAKING HOME

In the evening, Pila and his children Hulilau (tenth grader) and Keli'i (eighth grader) take me out to dinner. At my request we go to a cafe that serves poi (even though it is mainly a Chinese restaurant), so that I can try that traditional Hawaiian food. (I love it!) Hulilau and Keli'i are fine young people, responsible and articulate, with a strong social awareness. They both go to the Hawaiian-language high school

in Hilo, Nāwahīokalani'ōpu'u, named after a famous Hawaiian, Joseph K. Nawahī. After supper we go to their home, where I have been invited to spend the night. We arrive about the same time as Pila's wife, Kauanoe Kamanā, who is the senior teacher at the high school. This is one of the first families to decide to run an entirely Hawaiian-speaking household. In the same pattern I have found in the schools and on my car trips, they speak only Hawaiian to each other at all times. To me, they will speak English, but they do not accommodate to my presence when speaking to each other. Nevertheless, I never feel excluded. During family conversations, one of the children will turn to me from time to time to translate; and in the morning when the family sits in a circle to read from the Hawaiian-language Bible, I am invited to sit with them and try reading a paragraph myself.

This consistency in speaking only Hawaiian to each other is one of the most important habits to form for language revitalization. Endangered languages often lose out to English (or other dominant languages) when, because someone in the household does not speak the endangered language, the rest of the household switches to English. The threatened language loses its final stronghold, and the children growing up there will not learn to speak it.

NĀWAHĪOKALANI'Ō PU'U HIGH SCHOOL

The next morning we all head out to the high school after a breakfast of Hawaiian pancakes. The school has 48 teenagers attending, with fifteen teachers (seven full-time). My poor daughter is in a California high school with a much different teacher-student ratio, and I am jealous! A sizable number of the children went to the same Pūnana Leo preschool and have known each other throughout their education. The tenth-graders are the "lead class," the group from the very first year of the founding of the Pūnana Leo. Right now, of course, because the program is still young, the tenth-graders are the oldest children in the school. The school is preparing for them to become eleventh-graders, and then twelfth—the curriculum is being prepared right now at Hilo. And the school is growing—each year it will have more students.

At 7:40 A.M., one of the seventh graders blows the conch shell. The traditional Hawaiian instrument for the call to assembly is used at the school instead of a buzzer. The students enter the assembly room and sit on wooden benches, while Pila escorts me to a bench on the side. After the morning chant, Pila introduces me, and then a student sings for me, as a guest of the school, a welcoming chant and presents me with a lei. (This is the third time that I have been "lei-ed" this trip; I find myself completely charmed. At Pila and Kauanoe's home, I saw dried leis hanging over baby pictures of their children. I saved my leis too, and they hang now in a place of honor at home in Berkeley.) After that, the students go to their classes, and I am invited to wander about and watch. The most memorable period is spent observing Kauanoe herself give a lesson in traditional chant to the seventh graders. She tells me that chanting almost disappeared in Hawai'i under the hostility of missionaries and the government; but she learned it later in life as it was preserved by some teachers of hula, and now through her classes (as well as classes elsewhere), traditional chant is coming back alive. She teaches the students how to chant in a very strong, full voice. Today she is teaching a chant from the old traditional literature, the voice of a goddess singing, "I am standing here on the bank on one side. I've been waiting a long time, I want to cross over. I have great longing to cross. It's cold, it's cold here, it's cold and damp."

At the high school, some classes are taught in English—including, ironically, the Japanese foreign language class, whose teacher does not speak Hawaiian. 'Aha Pūnana Leo recognizes the need for having some education in English. Despite the new Hawaiian-language master's program in Hawaiian studies at the university, it is understood that most of these children will receive much or all of their university education in English. It is not the goal of the parents and teachers to see all their children major in Hawaiian studies. As Pila says, they want these children to become doctors, or lawyers, or storekeepers, or carpenters—they want the Hawaiian language to spread into all walks of life in Hawai'i, so that doctors, nurses, and their patients, storekeepers and their customers, will talk to each other in Hawaiian.

I also get to see the main office, located at the high school, where Hawaiian-language materials and books are produced. Books of all kinds are in boxes ready to ship out to the schools. This is also where the labels for converting books to Hawaiian are produced. In another room there is state-of-the-art computer and video equipment for the production of educational videos.

PŪNANA LEO O HILO

My last visit on the island of Hawai'i is to one more preschool, Pūnana Leo o Hilo, the first Pūnana Leo school on the island. Here I feel like I already know

many of the staff, for they are all on a video about the Hawaiian language program that I show regularly to my classes in Berkeley. I meet Nāmaka Rawlins, the director of the whole wonderful Pūnana Leo program, who first gave me permission to begin this odyssey. Nā'ilima Gaison, the head teacher, is telling a story to the children, full of songs and dance-like hand motions which the children do along with him. His expressiveness and the raptness of his students mark him as a master storyteller. Later he explains the curriculum to me. The daily routine goes like this:

7:15	Snack
8:30	Exercise
9:00	First circle
9:15	Class
10:00	Second circle
10:30	Playtime and structured activities
11:30	Lunch
12:30	Nap
2:30	Art
3:00	Story
3:15	Snack
3:30–5:00	Play and structured activities, while parents start coming to take the children home

Nā'ilima also explains the curriculum, which progresses from the self in ever-widening circles: self, family, school, community, the island, Hawai'i, the world.

I can't help but notice that "the United States" is not one of the levels mentioned. Hawai'i is culturally and ecologically distinct from the other states. More tourists visit Hawai'i from Asia than from the U.S. mainland. The Nāwahi High School kids have to take a foreign language, and the one that is taught at the high school is Japanese. And we must remember that it was just about a century ago that political power was wrested from the hands of the Hawaiian queen, and Hawaiians are justifiably bitter about the loss of their independence.

Nā'ilima explains some of the different circles: for the "self," the children learn body parts, hygiene, basic needs, and concepts of independence. "Family" includes the whole extended family, and cultural values such as helping, respect, and giving thanks. "Community" is about different places, safety, transportation, and community helpers. For "the island," they learn about the land and sea, plants, animals, and weather. For Hawai'i, they learn about famous people, the history of the state, multi-ethnic culture, and current events. For "the world," they learn about world history, culture and events, and about how Hawai'i fits into the world as a whole.

It is here at the Pūnana Leo o Hilo that the California connection comes into focus. First of all, I ask Nā'ilima if he knows Cody Pata, a young Nomlaki man who came to Hawai'i as a teenager and spent several years learning the language and teaching in the Pūnana Leo. "Oh, Pueo!" says Nā'ilima, revealing Cody's Hawaiian name. "Yes, he worked with us. How's he doing?" Also, here and at the high school, I meet again the wonderful ladies who came to California a few years ago for a language conference: Ululani Morales, 'Ekelela Aiona, Ō'pūlani Alkino, Leilani Camara, Wailana Purdy Ka'ai, Kaleihōkū Kala'i, and lastly, Lolena Nicholas, a Native speaker from Ni'ihau.

Hilo is not the only place on the islands where language action is going on; there are Pūnana Leo and elementary schools on several other islands as well. On O'ahu, there is even a Hawaiian immersion public school that goes from kindergarten through the twelfth grade (well, tenth grade right now, and heading to twelfth as the lead group matures). I fly from the island of Hawai'i back to O'ahu after visiting Pūnana Leo o Hilo, and have supper in Honolulu that night with several of the faculty of the University of Hawai'i at Mānoa, who are also key in the Hawaiian language movement—No'eau Warner, Laiana Wang and his family, and Kathy Davis, a colleague of theirs in the ESL department. Laiana tells me about a grant they have received recently from the Administration for Native Americans to bring the language beyond the schools into daily community life. They are planning recreational activities like cookouts and a volleyball series, where the Hawaiian language will be used while having fun.

ĀNUENUE PUBLIC SCHOOL

Through No'eau's help, I am able to go the next day to Ānuenue School, the K-12 public school where Hawaiian is spoken in all the classrooms. *Ānuenue* means rainbow, and appropriately, there is a beautiful rainbow over the school as I drive up. I am just in time for the morning chant, which the children sing in the schoolyard. After checking in at the office, I visit a first-grade class. Roll is called, and as their names are called the children come, one by one, to sit on the floor at the front of the room. One child seems to be the teacher of the moment: he points to the calendar and asks what day of the week it is, and then points to each day of the month and the children count the days all the way to today: November 27th. This kid is a good teacher. He asks all kinds of questions I can't follow, but the other children know exactly what is being asked and answer clearly in chorus. Then the grown-up teacher, who has been observing from the back of the room, comes to the front and starts asking more questions. She has the children count the number of boys and the number of girls in the room (six of each), and then has them add the two to find out how many students there are altogether. She has them count by fives. Once the math session is over, the class launches into a discussion of the *Mayflower*, the pilgrims, and the origin of Thanksgiving. And again, all of this, throughout the morning, is in Hawaiian. After a while the teacher sends the children off to get pencils and clipboards, and gives them pictures of the *Mayflower* and other Thanksgiving themes to color. She writes some sentences on the board for the children to copy under their pictures.

I wander off to the kindergarten room, where the children are in their circle, discussing different kinds of fruits. Then they go to their desks—each child has his own desk, but they are linked in groups of six. They get their crayons from their cubbyholes and start coloring pictures of fruits that their teacher has handed out. Some children finish their pictures, and the teacher gives them folders of another project they have already started—the familiar Thanksgiving turkey with cutouts of the children's own hands for tails. One child starts humming "Jingle Bells" (the spirit of Christmas season seems to be just as strong here as elsewhere), and pretty soon he starts singing it softly, using Hawaiian words. Other children join in as they color, and after a while there are at least six children singing "Jingle Bells" in Hawaiian. As they color, I look around to see what is on the walls. Two things catch my attention: one is a poster with the numbers written like this:

Numbers	Nāhelu
1	'ekahi
2	'elua
3	'ekolu
4	'ehā
5	'elima
6	'eono
7	'ehiku
8	'ewalu
9	'eiwa
10	'umi

Another is a "weather circle," a large cutout circle on the wall in four quadrants: rain, sun, clouds, and wind. Each day at circle time, they put a dot-sticker on the appropriate weather, and at the end of the month they can see how many days were rainy, how many were sunny, and so on.

Next I go to the seventh-grade room, where the children are studying Native Americans. There are world maps with pointers to the Aztec, Maya, and Inca taped on. Another map focuses on the Pacific and has arrows pointing from the South Pacific islands to Hawai'i along the path of migration.

I make quick stops at other rooms, and tarry longest in the science classroom, where Mahakoa Lujan teaches science. He is obviously a talented and charismatic teacher, and the students love him. He talks with me at some length about the science curriculum, and shows me a fine set of Hawaiian-language books showing general science centered around the Hawaiian Islands—meteorology, marine and terrestrial wildlife, oceanography. Once again the issue of new words comes up. Mahakoa tells me his ideas about how new words ought to be designed, citing "explanatory value" as the most important principle. He points out a poorly designed word: the word for carbon dioxide, which was merely given a Hawaiian zed pronunciation: *karabiner diokesaside*, or its even more Hawaiianized variant *kalapona kiokekakike*. The original word in English (based on Latin roots) clearly shows that there are two (di-) oxygen molecules to one carbon, and Mahakoa thinks the Hawaiian word ought to be similarly explanatory.

Mahakoa's viewpoint is part of an ongoing debate in the Lexicon Committee about scientific terminology in general. One school of thought is to invent individual Hawaiian terms based generally on Hawaiian morphemes, as is done with other words. The other school of thought asserts that this is a unique set of international terms that scientists use in all languages, with the speakers of each language modifying them slightly to meet their pronunciation and writing traditions. Proponents of the second school of thought also argue that there are so many of these terms, and they are being invented at such a rapid pace, that Hawai'i cannot keep up with inventing new words for them. It would also be a major problem for science teachers to have to commit all these new words to memory, whereas simply committing the international terms to Hawaiianized pronunciation can be done readily and even spontaneously.

At lunch I talk with a number of ninth and tenth graders, including 'Ānela Lopez, tenth grader and student council president. When I ask this outgoing, intelligent deep thinker about her college plans, she replies "University of Hawai'i" without hesitation. "Why would I ever want to leave my beautiful Hawai'i?"

I talk with her, as I have with other tenth graders, about their thoughts on the Hawaiian language. I have heard children, especially those of high-school age, talking a great deal of English (or sometimes Pidgin) to each other. There are at least two theories given to me about why the children do this—probably both of them correct. One is that the kids who went to public schools, even if they were in Hawaiian language classrooms, got into the habit of using English with their non-Hawaiian-speaking friends on the playground, and this habit then transferred over to the Hawaiian-speaking kids as well. The other theory is that the teens talk English to each other as a kind of teen rebellion, to point out their growing independence from the older generation of people who have been running their schools and lives. In either case the question is, what does this usage of English portend for the future of Hawaiian? Despite this practice of speaking English to each other frequently, everyone said "Hawaiian, of course" when I asked what language they thought they would speak when they married and had children.

One of my colleagues is fond of saying that the future of a language lies in whether the teenagers are using it with each other; whatever they speak to each other will become the language of their future homes. But I realized after talking with these teenagers that it is not that simple. One might wonder how many of these children will really end up speaking Hawaiian in the home—certainly many obstacles will be in the way. But in case of doubt, it is important to remember that some of these children have grown up in households where their parents committed to using Hawaiian as the language of the home, even when they didn't learn it until they were college age. Thus these children have a model of conscious decision making about the home language, and will probably use this model themselves. But the decision will be theirs: each generation will have to make its own decision, and each generation is sure to view the situation differently from the preceding one. Some of the high school students I spoke with fear that their knowledge of English is inadequate for good college-level writing. Perhaps they will find that it is not a problem after all when they attend college; but if it is, it may well be that they will want their children to have a better education in English. Perhaps, once Hawaiian is well established in the home, the next generation will experiment with a model that is closer to bilingual education, aimed at a thorough education in both languages. It is impossible to tell now what these children will decide, but I am looking forward to finding out!

FINAL REMARKS

The Hawaiian language immersion program is by far the most successful language revitalization program I have seen in the United States—indeed, it is one of the three or four major success stories in the world. Like anything else that involves a group of people, it has problems: in this case, factionalization, controversy over language modernization, and constant battles with state agencies.

Right now, one big problem is determining who gets to attend the Hawaiian-language classrooms in the public schools. Many families want their children in this program, not only because of the Hawaiian language and culture, but because of positive academic and social aspects of the program. The state wants a lottery system to decide who gets to attend the Hawaiian immersion classes. This would mean that children who attend the Pūnana Leo preschools could find themselves displaced by English-speaking children when they get to public school. Leaders in the Hawaiian language movement take the view that everyone is welcome, but that children who enter school already speaking Hawaiian and using it at home should have the first priority, with others included if there is room. They argue that Hawaiian-speaking children today are just as likely to lose the language when put into English-speaking classrooms as their elders were. They also note that families who have not already begun to support Hawaiian language use in the home before kindergarten are much less likely to support full use of the language in the home, community, and even the school.

The tough, brave people I met will fight this one through, and will then come up against other problems. But their persistence has created a great program, and it has created a fine future for their language. As Pila said to me, "If we hesitated every time something became controversial, we wouldn't get anywhere."

"Completing the Circle," by Leonard F. Chana, Tohono O'odham artist. © 1995 Leonard F. Chana.

CALL TO CONSCIOUSNESS ON THE FATE OF MOTHER EARTH
GLOBAL WARMING AND CLIMATE CHANGE

Jose Barreiro

For more than half a century, Native elders have called attention to humanity's impacts on Mother Earth. In the late 1940s, as the Seneca scholar John Mohawk liked to remind us, Hopi elders met with other traditional peoples to share prophecies about humanity's destructive impact on the ability of our planet to sustain life. The Hopi meeting with Haudenosaunee (Iroquois) traditionalists exchanged prophecies and observations warning about "civilized" society's assault on nature.

Since then, Native prophesies have been converging with scientific prediction and empirical observation. More than 50 years after the Hopi outreach and 30 years after American Indians first took their "call to consciousness" to the United Nations' 1977 Conference On Discrimination against the Indigenous peoples of the Americas, these warnings echoed from the garden of the National Museum of the American Indian (NMAI) on the National Mall in Washington, D.C. during the global event *Live Earth* 7/7/07. NMAI participated with its own program, *Mother Earth*, presenting voices from the American Indian world, luminaries, and musicians of international stature.

Tim Johnson (Mohawk), NMAI's acting director and programmer of the *Mother Earth* program, signaled 7/7/07 as "a day of education and cultural programming dedicated to increasing awareness about climate change." Johnson cited the many American Indian cultures "rich in precepts that

Jose Barreiro, in *American Indian* (National Museum of the American Indian, Smithsonian), Fall 2007, pages 34, 36, 37, 38, 40.

acknowledge the natural world and that contain powerful messages of gratitude for our Mother Earth. . . . Scientific assessment and determination are important. So too—and these are not mutually exclusive—are the lessons of living American Indian traditions."

Mother Earth, the Indigenous gathering at NMAI, issued a "call to consciousness about human impacts upon the Natural World." Simultaneously, former Vice President and former Smithsonian Regent Al Gore, scientists, and keepers of American Indian culture issued a call for increased attention to climate change.

NMAI shared its exclusively crafted program with the international *Live Earth* feed that would reach over two billion people. Al Gore spoke at the *Mother Earth* kickoff at the Museum, thanking Indians for reminding humanity how we're all connected to the natural world." County music giants Garth Brooks and Trisha Yearwood came out of retirement to help introduce Native groups for 12 hours of music, cultural, and scientific presentations.

Cheyenne Elder Henrietta Mann, grandmother, full professor, and advisor to the president of Montana State University, issued the American Indian "Call to Consciousness": "From the grounds of the National Museum of the American Indian in Washington, D.C.—we call upon all the peoples of the world to awaken and respond to our collective human responsibility to the seventh generation!"

Mohawk midwife Katsi Cook stood next to her. Cook added, "We have another ancient instruction. It teaches us that before every important gathering, we must express the words of gratitude—in our language the Ohen:ton karihwa tehkwen—our Thanksgiving Address. This teaching forms the essence and core of our value system. . . . We are instructed thus to remind ourselves that as human beings, we must gather our minds together and express Thanksgiving for the gifts of the natural world."

Mann and Cook emphasized that their message is non-partisan and focused on the long term and the future generations. All the Native speakers during the 12 hours emphasized the importance considering long-term impacts and of encouraging a more integrative science. They carried forward the message of Native traditional elders of the past half-century, that uncaring industrial development would in time fray the very fabric of natural systems. This message was always coupled with a call for science to see the whole and not just focus on specialties, and for culture to refocus on ecological values in society.

During a break from a concert that included Blues Nation, Garth Brooks and Trisha Yearwood, Native Roots, the Plateros, Yarina, and other bands, important scientists in the field joined their voice to the Native elders.

Dr. Anthony Socci spoke on the broad and increasingly integrated scientific consensus on the causes of climate change. Socci is senior fellow at the American Meteorological Society, a former senior climate science advisor with the Environmental Protection Agency's Office of Atmospheric Programs, and a designer of the U.S. government's extensive, multibillion-dollar scientific research programs on environment and climate-related changes.

Socci echoed the elders' call for a deeper change. "It would be naive in the case of climate change to suppose that we can technologized our way out of the problem without altering our lifestyles and reassessing our relationship with Mother Earth," he said.

Socci reviewed the work of the Intergovernmental Panel on Climate Change (IPCC), which today involves scientific experts from over 130 countries. The most recent assessment, in 2007, involved over 800 authors and over 1,000 expert reviewers. Socci emphasized that consensus on the causes of climate change is broadly shared by the world's major scientific organizations, including an international cadre of national academies of science. The scientific consensus achieved by the IPCC is "nothing less than historically unprecedented," he asserted.

Socci explained, "At the core of the scientific consensus on global warming are multiple, independent lines of evidence converging on a single coherent account." While no argument carries 100 percent certainty, "the fact remains that there are no identifiable 'alternative hypotheses' for which there is any substantial evidence that can explain the observed climate effects." In four IPCC reports spanning nearly 20 years, leading scientific experts from around the globe have affirmed the reality of a human-induced warming—no longer a prediction, but an observational reality.

He was joined by NASA scientist Dr. Nancy Maynard, who runs NASA's programs with tribal colleges and universities. She noted that "models of climate change—and, indeed, some current evidence point toward increased drought, more frequent severe storms, the drop of water levels in lakes and rivers, and a rise in sea level. The northward migration of warmer temperatures is bringing changes to vegetation, growing seasons, and animal behavior as well as diseases and pests that attack humans, plants, and animals."

Maynard has recognized the Native role in the understanding of specific habitats. She emphasized for the *Mother Earth* audience the importance of studying the impacts of climate change on Indian homelands because: "Tribal lands and Indian reservations are present in all of the major ecosystems across the U.S., including the unique environments in Alaska and the islands of the Pacific and Caribbean regions."

Maynard reminded the audience that tribal lands in the continental U.S. include 56 million acres (3 percent of U.S. lands), and Alaska Native lands amount to 44 million, acres. There also are important tribal rights and tribal knowledge about lands beyond reservation boundaries, including activities in fishing, hunting, and gathering. Native lands often are located in ecological peripheries and give early indication of troubling signs. Historical and cultural special areas are good places to observe changes over time.

The Arctic Region's climate is changing very rapidly, resulting in widespread melting of glaciers and sea ice and a shortened snow season. The reductions in sea ice drastically shrink marine habitat for polar bears, ice-inhabiting seals, and some seabirds, pushing some species toward extinction. For Native Alaskans this can turn into a serious loss of subsistence food and animals central to their culture.

Coastal communities such as Shishmaref, Alaska face severe coastal erosion as the rising sea level and reduction in sea ice allow higher waves and storm surges to reach the shore and destroy land and buildings.

Native peoples in other parts of the U.S. are also already experiencing impacts, with major economic and cultural implications.

Beyond the negative impacts, Maynard urged the audience to become aware of successful programs by Indigenous peoples working for ecological solutions. Among the many Native projects throughout the hemisphere stemming from traditional cultural knowledge systems, she pointed to the sustainable forest management of the Menominee Tribe, using traditional tree species and ways of logging. Maynard also reinforced the concept of listening to elders' wisdom and knowledge about historical solutions to changes over the years. Increasing partnerships between Native climate change response groups (like Yuchi Muscogee Professor Dan Wildcat's American Indian and Alaska Native Climate Change Working Group at Haskell Indian Nation University and other tribal colleges) with other universities and agencies like NASA have great potential for cooperative research and teaching programs.

Native elders have been speaking out with increasing urgency since the Hopi first met with the Haudenosaunee more than half a century back. Thirty-five years ago, Onondaga Clan Mother Alice Papineau and Hopi spokesman David Monongwe led a delegation of Native elders and activists to the Human Environment Forum in Stockholm, Sweden, to deliver a warning on the fate of Mother Earth. Five years later, at the seminal United Nations conference on Indigenous peoples in 1977, it fell to Onondaga faithkeeper Oren Lyons to issue the statement of purpose, as agreed to by dozens of American Indian elders. Faithkeeper Lyons: "I do not see a delegation for the Four Footed. I see no seat for the Eagles. We forget and we consider ourselves superior. But we

are after all a mere part of Creation. And we must consider to understand where we are. And we stand somewhere between the mountain and the Ant. Somewhere and only there as part and parcel of the Creation."

Always on behalf of the traditional chiefs council at Onondaga, Lyons has been one of the indefatigable Indian leaders to have addressed the world on this concern. In Geneva in 1977, in a room full of delegates carrying files on human rights violations, assassinations of Indian leaders, and massacres of whole villages, the Native elders requested that the main speakers, Faithkeeper Lyons included, deliver this primary message from the Indigenous delegates—their concern about the plight of Mother Earth. The troubles of Mother Earth come first, said the Native elders. Lyons' delegation delivered the message, titled *Basic Call to Consciousness*, at that 1977 seminal congress.

"In our ancient instructions," Cook told the assembled public on the Mall on July 7, 2007, ". . . the mothers of our clans are taught to continually remind the leaders of our nations that in all their deliberations, they must consider the effect of their decisions on the seventh generation yet to come. Do not think of one season, they said—do not think of a year or a decade—consider the effect of your decisions for seven generations to come."

Preserving the health of Mother Earth the gravest responsibility of our generation and the primary reason why the National Museum of the American Indian, as an institution of living cultures, is focusing on this initiative of human awareness and action. It is an issue of science, of culture and worldview, and of action. There is no more important matter before humankind than the question of how to live successfully and sustainably on Mother Earth.

ERODING ALASKA TOWN SUES 24 OIL AND ENERGY COMPANIES FOR DESTRUCTION CAUSED BY GLOBAL WARMING

NARF Legal Review

The Native American Rights Fund (NARF) and The Center on Race, Poverty & the Environment—plus six law firms—filed a lawsuit on behalf of a tiny and impoverished Alaskan village of Inupiat Eskimos located in the Arctic Circle against

industrial corporations that emit large quantities of greenhouse gases. The Native Village of Kivalina faces imminent destruction from global warming due to the melting of sea ice that formerly protected the village from coastal storms during the fall and winter. The diminished sea ice, due to global warming, has caused a massive erosion problem that threatens the village's existence and urgently requires the village be relocated. The Native Village of Kivalina, which is a federally recognized Indian Tribe, and the City of Kivalina, which is an Alaskan municipality, filed the lawsuit in the United States District Court for the Northern District of California, located in San Francisco. They filed the case on their own behalves and on behalf of all tribal members against defendants ExxonMobil Corp., Peabody Energy Corp., Southern Company, American Electric Power Co., Duke Energy Co, Chevron Corp., and Shell Oil Co., among others. In total there are nine oil company defendants, fourteen electric power company defendants and one coal company defendant. The suit claims damages due to the defendant companies' contributions to global warming and invokes the federal common law of public nuisance. The suit also alleges a conspiracy by some defendants to mislead the public regarding the causes and consequences of global warming. The residents of Kivalina are among the nation's poorest people.

Colleen Swan, Tribal Administrator of the Native Village of Kivalina, said "The campaign of deception and denial about global warming must stop." She added, "Global warming and its effects are a reality we have to deal with. Peoples' lives are in danger because of it." Swan noted that "official reports from the U.S. Army Corps of Engineers and the Government Accountability Office have found that Kivalina is directly harmed by global warming and must relocate at an expense that could cost $400 million or more."

"We need to relocate now before we lose lives," echoed Janet Mitchell, City Administrator for the City of Kivalina. "We are seeing accelerated erosion because of the loss of sea ice. We normally have ice starting in October, but now we have open water even into December so our island is not protected from the storms."

"In recent years it has become evident that another, perhaps more impending threat to Alaska Native lifeways looms," stated NARF Alaska attorney Heather Kendall-Miller. "Global climate changes are wreaking havoc on the Arctic causing loss of habitat and widespread erosion. Subsistence practices, too, are being threatened. Upon learning that many villages along Alaska's coastline were eroding into the ocean necessitating relocation, NARF's Alaska office took on the challenge of developing new litigation that would seek compensation from industry polluters for the cost of village relocation."

Kendall-Miller further added that, "Working with the environmental public interest firm, Center on Race, Poverty & the Environment, NARF reached out to the private bar to establish a team of top notch attorneys to develop the first climate change case that seeks damages from industry for the loss of property due to global warming. While the private firm attorneys bring the workforce and tort experience to the case, NARF brings the client and the relationship. Together this coalition of law firms hope to establish the climate change equivalent of the tobacco cases."

From *NARF Legal Review*, 33, no. 1 (Winter/Spring 2008): 1–4.

Alaska Natives are the canary in the coal mine regarding climate change

Climate change is wreaking havoc in Alaska. Scientists agree that Alaska has warmed more than any other place on Earth—over four times the global average. In recent years, scientists have documented melting ocean ice, rising ocean levels, rising river temperatures, thawing permafrost, increased insect infestations and threats to Arctic wildlife. As a result, Alaska Native peoples are those who are most dramatically experiencing the consequences.

Because of Alaska Natives' close relationship and reliance on the land, water, vegetation, animals and weather conditions for subsistence, virtually every aspect of their traditional culturally lifeways practiced for more than 4,000 years are severely impacted by climate change. In 2006, during the Alaska Forum on the Environment, Alaska Native participants described increased forest fires, more dangerous hunting, fishing and traveling conditions, visible changes in animals and plants, and infrastructure damage from melting permafrost and coastal erosion as well as from fiercer storms. A number of traditional Alaska Native villages are also literally being washed away as result of the dramatic changes in the environment and their very existence is now endangered.

According to Deborah Williams, Executive Director of the Alaska Conservation Foundation, "The polar ice cap's retreat due to global warming threatens a vast circumpolar ecosystem and its polar bears, walruses, seals and whales, while northern Alaska communities are left increasingly vulnerable to unprecedented storm-wave erosion."

Up to nine Alaska Native villages are in danger of being washed away and literally destroyed by the effects of global warming within the next few years. Several villages have already lost many buildings to the ocean due to melting permafrost and increased storms from global warming. Villagers are now faced with the imminent reality of relocation that could cost hundreds of millions of dollars.

Because of these and other dramatic changes, the cultural and traditional lifeways of Alaska Natives and their very basic nutritional needs are jeopardized. As a result, NARF attorney Heather Kendall-Miller is spearheading the NARF Climate Change Project to address these life-threatening issues in Alaska. The Project has already begun to make some headway on behalf of several Alaska Native villages.

NARF successfully gathered 162 Tribal and Corporate Resolutions calling on Congress and the Executive Office to adopt legislation reducing carbon emissions. The resolutions were carried to Washington, D.C. by tribal leaders and presented to the Alaska delegation on Climate Change Crisis Day last March, NARF also assisted the Alaska Native "Mothers" from throughout rural Alaska to travel to Anchorage to provide testimony before the Alaska Climate Impact Assessment Commission. Their testimony highlighted the devastating impacts that climate change is having on infrastructure, habitat, subsistence and culture.

To learn more about NARF's Climate Change Project, visit www. narf.org.

CLOSING ADDRESS

Phillip Deere

At this time I will bring a short message coming from my ancient ancestors that has never been mentioned because the message had remained with the traditional Indian people.

The prophecies of my people have come about. This is what we have witnessed. Many of the traditional people here understand this. That the Russell Tribunal here is a part of the prophecies within my own people; it was said that this could come about within these prophecies. It is hard to translate into the borrowed language; however, I would like to bring this to your attention that we too had prophets who told my people that there is a white room leaning up against the western skies. This will sweep across our country; and from the north the white bear would come to us. From the east we will see a man in a red coat that will come to us. From the south, there will be a feeling of warm air and we will hear the winds coming through the forest blowing against the reeds and bamboos. We'll be able to hear music in this wind. It is to be remembered that when these prophecies begin to fulfill, that the Indian people will go somewhere known to us, as King of Kings, leaders of leaders will assemble. The Indian people will sit somewhere as if they are criminals. Around this time when these prophecies are beginning to happen among the Indian Nations, there will be found a boy perhaps an orphan boy with raggedy clothes.

Phillip Deere, "Closing Address," *Native Peoples in Struggle.* Copyright © 1982 by the Anthropology Resource Center, Inc., and E.R.I.N. Reprinted with permission.

Note: This moving statement by Chief Deere (Creek) was delivered at the Fourth Russell Tribunal on the Rights of the Indians of the Americas, held in Rotterdam in November 1980. The tribunal provided a forum for Native representatives from North, Central, and South America to present evidence of Indigenous rights violations. The tribunal was one of several important international gatherings leading to the Declaration on the Rights of Indigenous Peoples, which was adopted by the United Nations on September 13, 2007.

Around his neck will be the identity of the Indian people—on his chest the identity of the Indian people will be there. The young boy will have eyes of an eagle. The eagle that can see direct into the sun. With the clear eyes he will lead the people.

Beyond the black smokes he will be able to see beyond the sun. He will be able to see and those that follow will find life there. These are the prophecies of our ancient ancestors. Here, in the Russell Tribunal we find many nations of people. It is now time that we search out who this leader is. That as Native people we must have a clear understanding of these prophecies. That our eyes be not glazed to the spiritual leaders and medicine people. These they have preserved in their minds from one generation to the other.

There are instructions that you fix your feathers. The birds of the night who do not sleep at night—certain people must pick up these feathers that they will be able to sit-up all night and to overcome. I thought of this last night when the jury sat—working continuously until 6:00 this morning. It is the fulfillment of these prophecies that their eyes must be strong at certain times. Therefore, I sat with them till this morning. This is no accident, no coincidence that we are here. The people of the red clay of Americas will always continue to go on. The religion, the prophecies, no government will ever stop it—no human being can prevent it that these prophecies will come about. And in time to come we will see from the Russell Tribunal, and time will tell us that these prophecies will be fulfilled. The spiritual connections that we have with our brothers from the south are also connected with the countries throughout the whole universe. And at this time, conclusion of this Russell Tribunal, we felt that warm air, we felt that wind from the south, perhaps all over the world we have felt that warm air. During this time, it is now time that we hear the winds blowing through the forest of Brazil, it is time that we hear the winds blowing against the reeds and bamboos, that is music, that has a sound that has a rhythm that has been handed down for thousands and thousands of years. We are people that are made and placed here for a purpose. Through many struggles, through many years of struggle and sufferings we refuse to die—Thank you.

Wilverna Reece, a Karuk basket weaver from the Klamath River region of northern California, participates in the annual gathering of the California Basket Weavers Association. Such events have contributed to the revitalization of basket weaving traditions. Reprinted by permission of the California Indian Basketweavers Association (CIBA).

PART REVIEW

DISCUSSION QUESTIONS

Tom LaBlanc, *Indianismo!*
1. What do you think the poet means by the term *Indianismo*?

John Mohawk, *Directions in People's Movements*
1. List and briefly explain some of the important policies and laws that have had an impact on U.S. Indian peoples in the past two centuries.
2. What were the developments that led up to the 1973 protest at Wounded Knee on the Pine Ridge Reservation in South Dakota?
3. What are some of the recent protests and political developments in the U.S. Indian struggle?

Declaration on the Rights of Indigenous Peoples
1. What is the significance of the declaration? How would you explain it to a friend or an associate? Why was it formally debated for over 20 years before its adoption by the United Nations?
2. There are 46 articles in the declaration. Name at least 4 of the rights it ensures to Indigenous peoples. What is meant by *self-determination*?

3. Although the vast majority of nation-states at the United Nations voted for the declaration, four opposed it. Which are the four nations? Why do you think they voted "no"?

National Congress of American Indians, *Resolution in Support of the UN Declaration on the Rights of Indigenous Peoples*
1. What is the National Congress of American Indians?
2. Which of the declaration's rights does the resolution specifically address?

Jose Barreiro, *Visions in Geneva: The Dream of the Earth*
1. What international gathering of Native people does the article feature, and what is its significance to the Declaration of the Rights of Indigenous Peoples?
2. Why did the Mapuche elders want "a deeper conversation" among the Indigenous delegates than what was being discussed in the conference's official sessions?
3. What values and traditions did they find in common?

Leanne Hinton, *Hawaiian Language Schools*
1. Why did a small group of Hawaiian educators establish the Pūnana Leo preschools in 1983.
2. The author concludes that the Hawaiian language immersion program is the most successful language revitalization program in the United States. Explain why it is so successful. Give some examples.

Jose Barreiro, *Call to Consciousness on the Fate of the Mother Earth: Global Warming and Climate Change*
1. What was the occasion of the Indigenous gathering at the National Museum of the American Indian in July 2007?
2. Why is the issue of global warming and climate change a critical concern to Indigenous people? What does the author mean by "a call to consciousness"?

NARF Legal Review, *Eroding Alaska Town Sues 24 Oil and Energy Companies for Destruction Caused by Global Warming*
1. Why are Alaska Natives "the canary in the coal mine" regarding climate change?
2. Why is the Native village of Kivalina suing oil and energy companies?

Phillip Deere, *Closing Address*
1. Describe Phillip Deere's vision of an Indigenous perspective on the relationship of all things.

KEY TERMS

aboriginal rights
Indianismo
International Year of the World's Indigenous People (1993)
James Bay
Johnson v. M'Intosh (1823)
language immersion
National Congress of American Indians (NCAI)
nongovernmental organizations (NGOs)
Nunavut

Pūnana Leo
revitalization
Rigoberta Menchú Tum
self-determination
sovereignty
treaty federalism
UN Declaration on the Rights of Indigenous Peoples
Working Group on Indigenous Populations

SUGGESTED READINGS

AKWESASNE NOTES. *A Basic Call to Consciousness: The Hau de no sau nee Address to the Western World.* Geneva, Switzerland, Autumn 2005. Published by Native Voices, Summertown, Tennessee.

BARINGER, SANDRA K. "Indian Activism and the American Indian Movement: A Bibliographical Essay." *American Indian Culture and Research Journal,* 21, no. 4 (1997): 217–250.

BARSH, RUSSEL, and JAMES YOUNGBLOOD HENDERSON. *The Road: Indian Tribes and Political Liberty.* Berkeley: University of California Press, 1980.

BURGOS-DUBRAY, ELISABETH, ed. *I, Rigoberta Menchú: An Indian Woman in Guatemala,* trans. Ann Wright. New York: Verso, 1984.

CHAMPAGNE, DUANE. "Self-determination and Activism Among American Indians in the United States 1972–1997." *Cultural Survival Quarterly* (Summer 1997): 32–35.

CORNELL, STEPHEN. *The Return of the Native: American Indian Political Resurgence.* New York: Oxford University Press, 1988.

DELORIA, VINE, JR. *Custer Died for Your Sins: An Indian Manifesto.* Norman: University of Oklahoma Press, 1969.

DELORIA, VINE, JR. *Behind the Trail of Broken Treaties: An Indian Declaration of Independence.* Austin: University of Texas Press, 1985.

DUDLEY, MICHAEL KIONI, and KEONI KEALOHA AGARD. *A Hawaiian Nation II: A Call for Hawaiian Sovereignty.* Honolulu: Naa Kaane O Ka Malo Press, 1990.

EWEN, ALEXANDER, ed. *Voice of Indigenous Peoples: Native People Address the United Nations.* Santa Fe: Clear Light Publishers, 1994.

HINTON, LEANNE. "Languages and Language Programs," *Handbook of North American Indians,* vol. 2 Washington, D.C.: Smithsonian Institution, 2008: 351–354.

ISMAELILLO and ROBIN WRIGHT, eds. *Native Peoples in Struggle: Cases from the Fourth Russell Tribunal & Other International Forums.* Bombay, N.Y.: Anthropology Resource Center and E.R.I.N. Publications, 1982.

JAIMES, M. ANNETTE, ed. *The State of Native America: Genocide, Colonization, and Resistance.* Boston: South End Press, 1992.

JOHNSON, TROY, JOANE NAGEL, and DUANE CHAMPAGNE. *American Indian Activism: Alcatraz to the Longest Walk.* Urbana: University of Illinois Press, 1997.

JORGENSEN, JOSEPH. "A Century of Political Effects on American Indian Society, 1880–1980." *Journal of Ethnic Studies,* 6, no. 3 (1978): 1–82.

KAME'ELEIIWA, LILIKALA. *Native Land and Foreign Desires. Pehea La E PonoAi?* Honolulu: Bishop Museum Press, 1992.

LYONS, OREN, and JOHN MOHAWK. *Exiled in the Land of the Free: Democracy, Indian Nations, and the U.S. Constitution.* Santa Fe: Clear Light Publishers, 1992.

MATTHIESSEN, PETER. *In the Spirit of Crazy Horse*, 2nd ed. New York: Viking Press, 1991.

NAGEL, JOANE. *American Indian Ethnic Renewal: Red Power and the Resurgence of Identity and Culture*. New York: Oxford University Press, 1995.

NAGEL, JOANE, and TROY JOHNSON, eds. "Special Edition: Alcatraz Revisited: The 25th Anniversary of the Occupation, 1969–1971." *American Indian Culture and Research Journal*, 18, no. 4 (1994).

"Native Rebellion and U.S. Intervention in Central America." *Cultural Survival Quarterly*, 10, no. 1 (1986): 59–65.

NIEZEN, RONALD. *Defending the Land: Sovereignty and Forest Life in James Bay Cree Society*. Needham Heights, Mass.: Allyn and Bacon, 1998.

ROSS, JOHN. *Rebellion from the Roots: Indian Uprising in Chiapas*. Monroe, Maine: Common Courage Press, 1995.

SELVERSTON, MELINA H. "Pachacutik." *Native Americas* (Summer 1998): 11–21.

SMITH, LINDA TUHIWAI. *Decolonizing Methodologies: Research and Indigenous Peoples*. New York: Zed Books, 2001.

STOLL, DAVID. *Rigoberta Menchú and the Story of All Poor Guatemalans*. Boulder, Colo.: Westview Press, 1999.

TALBOT, STEVE. "'Free Alcatraz': The Culture of Indian Liberation." *Journal of Ethnic Studies*, 6, no. 3 (1978): 83–96.

TALBOT, STEVE. "The Meaning of Wounded Knee, 1973: Indian Self-Government and the Role of Anthropology." Pages 227–258 in *The Politics of Anthropology*, ed. Gerrit Huizer and Bruce Mannheim (The Hague: Mouton, 1979).

TRASK, HUANANI-KAY. *From a Native Daughter*. Monroe, Me.: Common Courage Press, 1993.

WEARNE, PHILLIP. *Return of the Indian: Conquest and Revival in the Americas*. Philadelphia: Temple University Press, 1996.

WEINBERG, BILL. "La Miskitia Rears Up." *Native Americas* (Summer 1998): 22–33.

WEINBERG, BILL. "Mexico's Other Indian War: Fire in the Sierra Madre del Sur." *Native Americas* (Spring 1999): 48, 50–57.

WELLS, ROBERT N., Jr., ed. *Native American Resurgence and Renewal: A Reader and Bibliography*. Metuchen, N.J.: Scarecrow Press, 1993.

WEYLER, REX. *Blood of the Land: The U.S. Government and Corporate War Against the American Indian Movement*. New York: Everest House, 1983.

Homeland Security: Fighting Terrorism Since 1492.
© Colleen-Lloyd/*West Wind World*. From *www.nativeamericanproducts.com*. Reprinted by permission.

APPENDICES

APPENDIX A

NATIVE AMERICAN LINKS TO INTERNET RESOURCES

UNITED STATES

Indian Organizations and Businesses

http://www.hanksville.org/NAresources/ Index of Native American Resources on the net

http://www.jammed.com/%7emlb/nawbt.html Native American Web Sites

http://www.ncai.org/ National Congress of American Indians

http://www.atnitribes.org Affiliated Tribes of Northwest Indians

http://www.amerind-corp.org/ AMERIND

http://www.apachehousing.com/ Apache Housing of OK

http://www.itcn.org/ Inter-Tribal Council of Nevada

http://ncseonline.org/NAE/ Native Americans and the Environment

http://www.nwiha.org/ Northwest Indian Housing Association

http://www.rossanderson.org Ross Anderson Fastest Native American on Mother Earth

http://www.picenter.qwestoffice.net/ Phoenix Indian Center

http://www.heard.org/ Heard Museum

http://www.nmai.si.edu/ National Museum of the American Indian, Smithsonian Institution

http://www.itcaonline.com Inter Tribal Council of Arizona

http://www.cba.nau.edu/caied/ Center for American Indian Economic Development

http://personal.riverusers.com/%7eapaches4cultural Apaches For Cultural Preservation

http://www.cba.nau.edu/ice/ Indigenous Community Enterprises

http://www.nativeamericanfathers.org Native American Fatherhood

http://www.narf.org Native American Rights Fund

http://www.nascsports.org Native American Sports Council

http://www.nafws.org/ Native American Fish and Wildlife Society

http://www.nicwa.org National Indian Child Welfare Association

http://www.aicae.org/ American Indian Council of Architects and Engineers

http://www.indiangaming.org National Indian Gaming Association

U.S. Government Sites

http://www.hud.gov/offices/pih/ih/codetalk/ Codetalk—HUD's Office of Native American Programs

http://indian.senate.gov/public/ U.S. Senate Committee on Indian Affairs

http://www.frbsf.org/community/native/index.html Indian Country Lending Information

http://www.iacb.doi.gov Indian Arts and Crafts Board

Indian Health Sites

http://www.ihs.gov Indian Health Services

http://www.olderindians.org/ Older Indians Data

http://web.cast.uark.edu/other/nps/nacd/ Native American Consultation Database

http://natamcancer.org/ Native American Cancer Research

http://americanindianhealth.nlm.nih.gov/ National Library of Medicine American Indian Health

http://hsc.unm.edu/library/nhd/ Native Health History Database

Educational Sites

http://www.niea.org/ National Indian Education Association

http://www.indianeducation.org/ Indianed.org

http://www.u.arizona.edu/%7eecubbins/useful.html Links for American Indian Tribal Libraries

http://www.innovations.harvard.edu/ Government Innovators Network

http://www.hks.harvard.edu/hpaied/ Harvard Project on American Indian Economic Development

National Native Media

http://www.pechanga.net Pechanga.Net Native Internet News Resource

http://www.indiancountry.com Indian Country Today

http://www.falmouthinstitute.com Falmouth Institute

http://www.indianz.com Indianz.com

http://www.thenativepress.com/ The Native Press

http://www.nativepeoples.com Native Peoples Magazine

http://www.native-voic.com The Native Voice

CENTRAL AND SOUTH AMERICA

It is estimated that there are well over 40 million Native people in Central and South America. There are also many hundreds of Native organizations that can be accessed via the web. It is well worth taking the plunge and doing some research on the web to look at information coming directly from some of these indigenous organizations. Some have translations into English. To get started, the following links are recommended.

www.redindigena.net
(Indigenous Information Network. In English and Spanish)

www.prensaindigena.org
(scroll down to see "Sitios de interes" for links to various Native organizations)

www.nativeweb.org
www.servindi.org

www.amazonia.org.br
(Focus on Native Peoples in the greater Amazon Basin. In English and Portoguese.)

www.iidh.ed.cr
Instituto Interamericano de Derechos Humanos
(InterAmerican Institute on Human Rights)

CANADA

(There are many Canadian Native or Aboriginal organizations. These links are a good start.)

www.aboriginalcanada.gc.ca
(An excellent source with full listings)

www.aboriginalcanada.com/firstnation/

www.nativeculturelinks.com/organizations.html
(United States and Canada)

APPENDIX B

NATIVE AMERICAN STUDIES PROGRAMS
IN THE UNITED STATES AND CANADA

Website: *http://oncampus.richmond.edu/faculty/ASAIL/guide/guide.html*

The new guide at the website above is an attempt to update and expand the original guide published by the Association for the Study of American Literature in 1993. This guide is being published in both hard copy and electronic form. It is a comprehensive survey of U.S. and Canadian Native American Studies programs being offered as majors, minors, and certifications at the baccalaureate level or above. The following is a list, arranged by region, of the institutions that offer such programs. Robert M. Nelson, editor.

EASTERN U.S.

GA: U of Georgia

MA: Amherst C
U of Massachusetts
Hampshire College
Mount Holyoke C
Smith C

ME: Colby C
U of Maine

NH: Dartmouth C

NY: Colgate U
Cornell U
St. Lawrence U
SUNY at Buffalo
SUNY at Cortland
SUNY, C at Oswego
SUNY at Potsdam

NC: UNC-Chapel Hill
UNC at Pembroke
UNC, Wilmington
Western Carolina U

VA: Virginia Tech

WV: West Virginia U

NORTH CENTRAL U.S.

IL: U of Illinois Urbana, Champaign

IN: Ball S U
Valparaiso U

IA: U of Iowa
Iowa S U
KS: Haskell Indian Nations U

U of Kansas
KY: Northern Kentucky U

MI: U of Michigan
Michigan S U
Northern Michigan U

MN: Augsburg C
Bemidji S U
C of St. Scholastica
U of Minnesota, Twin Cities
St. Cloud State U
Southwest Minnesota S U

NE: Creighton U
U of Nebraska, Lincoln
U of Nebraska at Omaha

ND: Minot S U
U of North Dakota
OH: Ohio S U

SD: Black Hills S U
Dakota Wesleyan U
U of South Dakota
South Dakota S U

WI: Northland C
U of Wisconsin, Eau Claire
U of Wisconsin Green Bay
U of Wisconsin, Madison
U of Wisconsin, Milwaukee
U of Wisconsin, Stevens Point
U of Wisconsin, Superior

SOUTH CENTRAL U.S.

OK: Northeastern S U
U of Oklahoma
Oklahoma S U
Southeastern Oklahoma S U
U of Science. and Arts of Okla.

WESTERN U.S.

AK: U of Alaska, Fairbanks
AZ: U of Arizona
Arizona State U
Northern Arizona U

CA: U of California, Berkeley
U of California, Davis
U of California, Irvine
U of California, Los Angeles
U of California, Riverside

C S U, Chico
C S U, East Bay
C S U, Long Beach
C S U, Northridge
C S U, Sacramento
C S U, San Marcos
Humboldt S U
Mills C
San Diego S U
San Francisco S U
Stanford U

CO: U of Colorado, Boulder

HI: U of Hawai'i at Hilo
U of Hawai'i at Mänoa

ID: U of Idaho
Idaho State U

MT: Montana S U
Montana S U Billings
U of Montana

NM: U of New Mexico
New Mexico S U

OR: Portland S U
Southern Oregon U

UT: Brigham Young U
WA: Eastern Washington U
The Evergreen S C
U of Washington
Western Washington U

WY: U of Wyoming

Note: The following institutions also have Native Studies programs, but have not yet provided us with information on their programs. They are linked to their home pages rather than to Guide entries.

Brandon U
CSU Fresno
U of Illinois at Chicago
Indiana U-Purdue U Fort Wayne
Malaspina U-C
U of Minnesota-Duluth Montana State U-Northern
St. Thomas U
SUNY Fredonia
University College of the North
Utah U
Washington State U

CANADA

AB: U of Alberta
U of Lethbridge

BC: U of British Columbia
U of Northern British Columbia
Simon Fraser U
U of Victoria

MN: U Manitoba

NS: Cape Breton U

ON: Lakehead U
Laurentian U
McMaster U
U of Toronto
Trent U

SK: U of Saskatchewan
First Nations U of Canada (formerly SIFC)
QB: U Laval

APPENDIX C

AMERICAN INDIAN HIGHER EDUCATION

CONSORTIUM: TRIBAL COLLEGES

AIHEC – Headquarters
121 Oronoco Street Alexandria, Virginia 22314 (703) 838-0400
e-mail: aihec@aihec.org

Bay Mills Community College, Michael Parish,
12214 West Lakeshore Dr., Brimley, MI 49715,
(906) 248-3354, Fax: (906) 248-2011

Blackfeet Community College, John Salois,
P.O. Box 819,
Browning, MT 59417,
(406) 338-7755, Fax: (406) 338-3272

Cankdeska Cikana Community College, Cynthia Lindquist Mala,
P.O. Box 269,
Fort Totten, ND 58335,
(701) 766-4415, Fax: (701) 766-4077

Chief Dull Knife College, Richard Littlebear,
P.O. Box 98,
Lame Deer, MT 59043,
(406) 477-6215, Fax: (406) 477-6219

College of Menominee Nation, Verna Fowler,
P.O. Box 1179,
Keshena, WI 54135,
(715) 799-5600, (Toll Free) (800) 567-2344,
Fax: (715) 799-1308

Diné College, Ferlin Clark,
P.O. Box 126,
Tsaile, AZ 86556,
(928) 724-6669, Fax: (928) 724-3327

Fond du Lac Tribal and Community College,
Larry Anderson,
2101 14th St., Cloquet, MN 55720,
(218) 879-0800, Fax: (218) 879-0814

Fort Belknap College, Carole Falcon-Chandler,
P.O. Box 159,
Harlem, MT 59526,
(406) 353-2607, Fax: (406) 353-2898

Fort Berthold Community College,
Russell D. Mason, Jr.,
220 8th Avenue North,
P.O. Box 490,
New Town, ND 58763,
(701) 627-4738, Fax: (701) 627-3609

Fort Peck Community College,
James Shanley,
P.O. Box 398,
Poplar, MT 59255,
(406) 768-6300, Fax: (406) 768-5552

Haskell Indian Nations University, Linda Warner,
155 Indian Ave.,
P.O. Box 5030,
Lawrence, KS 66046-4800,
(785) 749-8404, Fax: (785) 749-8411

Ilisagvik College, Beverly Patkotak Grinage,
P.O. Box 749,
Barrow, AK 99723,
(907) 852-3333, Fax: (907) 852-1821

Institute of American Indian Arts,
Robert Martin,
83 Avan Nu Po Rd., Santa Fe, NM 87508,
(505) 424-2300, Fax: (505) 424-0050

Lac Courte Oreilles Ojibwa Community College, Danielle Hornett,
13466 West Trepania Rd., Hayward, WI 54843, (715) 634-4790, Fax: (715) 634-5049

Leech Lake Tribal College, Ginny Carney,
P.O. Box 180,
Cass Lake, MN 56633,
(218) 335-4200, Fax: (218) 335-4215

Little Big Horn College, David Yarlott, Jr.,
P.O. Box 370,
Crow Agency, MT 59022,
(406) 638-3100, Fax: (406) 638-3169

Little Priest Tribal College, Darla LaPointe,
P.O. Box 270,
Winnebago, NE 68071,
(402) 878-2380, Fax: (402) 878-2355

Navajo Technical College, Elmer Guy,
P.O. Box 849,
Crownpoint, NM 87313,
(505) 786-4100, Fax: (505) 786-5644

Nebraska Indian Community College,
Micheal Oltrogge,
College Hill,
P.O. Box 428,
Macy, NE 68039,
(402) 837-5078, Fax: (402) 837-4183

Northwest Indian College, Cheryl Crazy Bull,
2522 Kwina Rd., Bellingham, WA 98226,
(360) 676-2772, Fax: (360) 738-0136

Oglala Lakota College, Thomas Shortbull,
490 Piya Wiconi Rd., Kyle, SD 57752,
(605) 455-6000, Fax: (605) 455-6023

Saginaw Chippewa Tribal College, Carla Sineway,
2274 Enterprise Dr., Mount Pleasant, MI 48858,
(989) 775-4123, Fax: (989) 772-4528

Salish Kootenai College, Joseph McDonald,
P.O. Box 70, Pablo, MT 59855,
(406) 275-4800, Fax: (406) 275,4801

Sinte Gleska University, Lionel Bordeaux,
101 Antelope Lake Circle,
P.O. Box 105, Mission, SD 57555,
(605) 856-8100, Fax: (605) 856-5401

Sisseton Wahpeton College, Diana Canku,
Agency Village Box 689, Sisseton, SD 57262,
(605) 698-3966, Fax: (605) 698-3132

Sitting Bull College, Laurel Vermillion,
1341 92nd St., Fort Yates, ND 58538,
(701) 854-8000, Fax: (701) 854-3403

Southwestern Indian Polytechnic Institute, Jeffrey Hamley,
9169 Coors Rd., NW,
P.O. Box 10146,
Albuquerque, NM 87184,
(505) 346-2348, Fax: (505) 346-2343

Stone Child College, Melody Henry,
RR1, Box 1082,
Box Elder, MT 59521,
(406) 395-4875, Fax: (406) 395-4836

Tohono O'odham Community College, Olivia
Vanegas-Funcheon,
P.O. Box 3129,
Sells, AZ 85634,
(520) 383-8401, Fax: (520) 383-8403

Turtle Mountain Community College, James Davis,
P.O. Box 340,
Belcourt, ND 58316,
(701) 477-7862, Fax: (701) 477-7807

United Tribes Technical College, David Gipp,
3315 University Dr., Bismarck, ND 58504,
(701) 255-3285, Fax: (701) 530-0605

White Earth Tribal and Community College, Robert
"Sonny" Peacock,
210 Main St. South,
P.O. Box 478,
Mahnomen, MN 56557,
(218) 936-5610, Fax: (218) 935-0708

ASSOCIATE MEMBERS

College of the Muscogee Nation,
James King, Ed.D.,
600 N Mission, Okmulgee, OK 74447,
(918) 758-1480, Fax: (918) 293-5313

Comanche Nation College, Consuelo Lopez,
1608 SW 9th St., Lawton, OK 73501,
(580) 591-0203, Fax: (580) 353-7075

Keweenaw Bay Ojibwa Community College,
Debra J. Parrish,
111 Beartown Rd.,
P.O. Box 519,
Baraga, MI 49908,
(906) 353-4600, Fax: (906) 353-8107

Wind River Tribal College,
Marlin Spoonhunter,
P.O. Box 8300,
Ethete, WY 82520,
(307) 335-8243, Fax: (307) 335-8148

INTERNATIONAL MEMBER:

Red Crow Community College,
Marie Smallface Marule,
P.O. Box 1258,
Cardston, Alberta, Canada TOKOKO,
(403) 737-2400, Fax: (403) 737-2101

ILLUSTRATION CREDITS

INDEX

The Indigenous peoples—nations or tribes discussed in this book—and their subjects and page references are set boldface in this index.

© 1997 H.J. Tsinhnahjinnie.